Methods for Fish Biology

Methods for Fish Biology

is a special project of the

**Education Section
American Fisheries Society**

Major support for publication of this book
was provided by

Exxon Company, U.S.A.

Methods for Fish Biology

Edited by

Carl B. Schreck

Oregon Cooperative Fishery Research Unit
U.S. Fish and Wildlife Service
Oregon State University

and

Peter B. Moyle

Department of Wildlife and Fisheries Biology
University of California–Davis

American Fisheries Society
Bethesda, Maryland, USA
1990

Suggested Citation Formats

Entire Book

Schreck, C. B., and P. B. Moyle, editors. 1990. Methods for fish biology. American Fisheries Society, Bethesda, Maryland.

Chapter within the Book

Thorgaard, G. H., and J. E. Disney. 1990. Chromosome preparation and analysis. Pages 171–190 *in* C. B. Schreck and P. B. Moyle, editors. Methods for fish biology. American Fisheries Society, Bethesda, Maryland.

Library of Congress Catalog Card Number 90–83196

ISBN 0–913235–58-X

Address orders to

American Fisheries Society
5410 Grosvenor Lane, Suite 110
Bethesda, Maryland 20814–2199, USA
Telephone (301) 897–8616

Contents

Contributors x

List of Fish Species xiii

Preface xvii

1 Research Methods: Concept and Design
WILLIAM E. WATERS AND DON C. ERMAN

1.1 Introduction 1
1.2 Conceptual Framework and Basic Considerations 2
1.3 Observational Studies 14
1.4 Controlled Experience Studies 18
1.5 Controlled Experiments 23
1.6 Conclusion 32
1.7 References 32

2 Genetics
FRED W. ALLENDORF AND MOIRA M. FERGUSON

2.1 Introduction 35
2.2 Mechanisms of Inheritance 36
2.3 Mendelian Genetics 40
2.4 Polygenic Traits 47
2.5 Genetics of Natural Populations 51
2.6 Overview 58
2.7 References 59

3 Systematics
JOHN G. LUNDBERG AND LUCINDA A. MCDADE

3.1 Introduction 65
3.2 Principles of Phylogenetic Systematics 66
3.3 Practical Systematics at the Species Level 70
3.4 Systematics above the Species Level 74
3.5 Phenetics 88
3.6 Biological Classification 92
3.7 Nomenclature 96
3.8 Identification 97
3.9 Collections for Systematic and Faunistic Research 99
3.10 Museums and Research Collections 102
3.11 References 103

4 Taxonomic Methods: Morphology
RICHARD E. STRAUSS AND CARL E. BOND

4.1 Introduction 109
4.2 General External Features 109
4.3 Meristic and Other Enumerable Characters 117
4.4 General Internal Features 121

    4.5   Larval Fish Morphology 123
    4.6   Morphometric Characters 125
    4.7   Photographing Fishes 131
    4.8   References 133

5   **Starch Gel Electrophoresis and Species Distinctions**
    ROBB F. LEARY AND HENRY E. BOOKE
    5.1   Introduction 141
    5.2   Rationale of Electrophoresis 143
    5.3   Electrophoretic Methodology 143
    5.4   Collection and Analysis of Data 150
    5.5   Diagnostic Loci 164
    5.6   Concluding Remarks 166
    5.7   References 166

6   **Chromosome Preparation and Analysis**
    GARY H. THORGAARD AND JANE E. DISNEY
    6.1   Introduction 171
    6.2   Basic Principles of Chromosome Preparation 171
    6.3   Collecting Dividing Cells 172
    6.4   Preparing Chromosome Spreads on Slides 176
    6.5   Staining and Banding of Chromosomes 178
    6.6   Chromosome Analysis and Photography 184
    6.7   Future Developments 186
    6.8   References 187

7   **Histological Techniques**
    DAVID E. HINTON
    7.1   Introduction 191
    7.2   Important Aspects of Processing Methodology 191
    7.3   Staining 199
    7.4   Mounting Media for Stained Sections 206
    7.5   High-Resolution Light Microscopy 207
    7.6   Radioautography 207
    7.7   Quantitation of the Histological Image 208
    7.8   Conclusion 208
    7.9   References 209

8   **Anesthesia, Surgery, and Related Techniques**
    ROBERT C. SUMMERFELT AND LYNWOOD S. SMITH
    8.1   Introduction 213
    8.2   Anesthesia 213
    8.3   Surgery 245
    8.4   Related Techniques 259
    8.5   References 263

9   Blood and Circulation
ARTHUR H. HOUSTON
9.1   Introduction 273
9.2   Blood Sample Acquisition 273
9.3   Routine Hematological Methods 285
9.4   Circulation 312
9.5   References 322

10   Respirometry
JOSEPH J. CECH, JR.
10.1   Introduction 335
10.2   Types of Respiratory Measurements 335
10.3   Apparatus and Techniques 338
10.4   Considerations for the Future 356
10.5   References 356

11   Growth
GREG P. BUSACKER, IRA R. ADELMAN, AND
EDWARD M. GOOLISH
11.1   Perspectives of Growth 363
11.2   Numerical and Mathematical Expressions of Growth 363
11.3   Quantification of Changes in Size 364
11.4   Physiological and Biochemical Indices of Growth 370
11.5   Estimation of Growth in Natural Populations 372
11.6   Considerations for Laboratory Growth Studies 378
11.7   Conclusion 381
11.8   References 382

12   Bioenergetics
S. MARSHALL ADAMS AND JAMES E. BRECK
12.1   Introduction 389
12.2   Direct Measurements of Major Bioenergetic Components 391
12.3   Estimation of Bioenergetic Components with Equations 404
12.4   Criteria for Applying the Bioenergetics Approach 407
12.5   References 409

13   Nervous System
DAVID F. RUSSELL
13.1   Introduction 417
13.2   Types of Preparations 417
13.3   Electrophysiology 422
13.4   Sensory Systems 433
13.5   Neuroanatomy 435
13.6   Neurochemistry 439
13.7   Electrical Principles of Neurophysiological Research 442
13.8   References 445

14   Stress and Acclimation
GARY A. WEDEMEYER, BRUCE A. BARTON, AND
DONALD J. MCLEAY

14.1   Introduction 451
14.2   Evaluating Tolerance and Acclimation to Stress:
       Aspects of Physiological and Whole-Animal Responses 453
14.3   Effects of Stress on Performance Capacity: Challenge
       Tests as Indicators of Tolerance Limits 469
14.4   References 477

15   Aquatic Toxicology
JOHN B. SPRAGUE

15.1   Introduction 491
15.2   Terminology 492
15.3   Sources of Information 494
15.4   Tests of Acute Lethality 495
15.5   Sublethal Tests 510
15.6   Other Topics 519
15.7   References 522

16   Reproduction
LAURENCE W. CRIM AND BRIAN D. GLEBE

16.1   Introduction 529
16.2   Sex Determination 529
16.3   Determination of Maturity and Ripeness 530
16.4   Enumeration of Gametes 535
16.5   Gamete Viability, Preservation, and Fertilization 536
16.6   Control of Gonad Development and Spawning 539
16.7   Methods of Sex Control and Inhibition of Maturation 541
16.8   References 547

17   Behavior
DAVID L. G. NOAKES AND JEFFREY R. BAYLIS

17.1   Introduction 555
17.2   Observation and Recording 555
17.3   Experimental Design and Analysis 561
17.4   Preference Tests 563
17.5   Social Structure 568
17.6   Learning in the Life of Fishes 573
17.7   Conclusions 577
17.8   References 577

18   Autecology
DONALD M. BALTZ

18.1   Introduction 585
18.2   Basic Life History 587

18.3 Distribution and Abundance 590
18.4 Movements 593
18.5 Microhabitat Descriptions 593
18.6 Physicochemical Determinants of Niche 599
18.7 Overview 600
18.8 References 600

19 **Community Ecology**
LARRY B. CROWDER
19.1 Introduction 609
19.2 Methodological Approaches to Community Ecology 609
19.3 Studying Species Interactions 613
19.4 Analysis of Food Webs 620
19.5 Species Diversity 624
19.6 Conclusions 626
19.7 References 627

20 **Maintaining Fishes for Research and Teaching**
ROBERT R. STICKNEY AND CHRISTOPHER C. KOHLER
20.1 Introduction 633
20.2 Water Supply 633
20.3 Holding and Culture Systems 637
20.4 Water Quality 645
20.5 Carrying Capacity of Holding Facilities 649
20.6 Species, Sources of Fish, and Permitting Requirements 650
20.7 Disease and Parasite Control 650
20.8 Feeding Captive Fishes 655
20.9 Handling and Transportation 659
20.10 Disturbance 659
20.11 Pest Control 660
20.12 Effluent Treatment 660
20.13 References 661

Symbols and Abbreviations 664

Index 665

Contributors

S. Marshall Adams (Chapter 12): Environmental Sciences Division, Oak Ridge National Laboratory, Building 1505, Oak Ridge, Tennessee 37831–6036, USA.

Ira R. Adelman (Chapter 11): Department of Fisheries and Wildlife, University of Minnesota, 1980 Folwell Avenue, St. Paul, Minnesota 55108, USA.

Fred W. Allendorf (Chapter 2): Division of Biological Sciences, University of Montana, Missoula, Montana 59812, USA.

Donald M. Baltz (Chapter 18): Coastal Fisheries Institute, Department of Oceanography and Coastal Sciences, Center for Wetland Resources, Louisiana State University, Baton Rouge, Louisiana, 70803–7503, USA.

Bruce A. Barton (Chapter 14): Utah Division of Wildlife Resources, Fisheries Experiment Station, 1465 West North Street, Logan, Utah 84321, USA. *Present address:* Department of Biology, Box 8238, University of North Dakota, Grand Forks, North Dakota 58202, USA.

Jeffrey R. Baylis (Chapter 17): Department of Zoology, University of Wisconsin, Bridge Hall, Madison, Wisconsin 53706, USA.

Carl E. Bond (Chapter 4): Department of Fisheries and Wildlife, Oregon State University, Corvallis, Oregon 97331, USA.

Henry E. Booke (Chapter 5): Massachusetts Cooperative Fishery Research Unit, University of Massachusetts, Amherst, Massachusetts 01003, USA.

James E. Breck (Chapter 12): Environmental Sciences Division, Oak Ridge National Laboratory, Oak Ridge, Tennessee 37831, USA. *Present address:* Michigan Department of Natural Resources, Institute of Fisheries Resources, 1109 North University Avenue, Ann Arbor, Michigan 48109–1084, USA.

Greg P. Busacker (Chapter 11): Department of Fisheries and Wildlife Biology, University of Minnesota, St. Paul, Minnesota 55108, USA. *Present address:* Minnesota Department of Transportation, Transportation Building, Room 124, St. Paul, Minnesota 55155, USA.

Joseph J. Cech, Jr. (Chapter 10): Department of Wildlife and Fisheries Biology, University of California, Davis, California 95616, USA.

Laurence W. Crim (Chapter 16): Marine Sciences Research Laboratory, Memorial University of Newfoundland, St. Johns, Newfoundland A1C 5S7, Canada.

Larry B. Crowder (Chapter 19): Department of Zoology, North Carolina State University, Box 7617, Raleigh, North Carolina 27695, USA.

Jane E. Disney (Chapter 6): Department of Zoology, Washington State University, Pullman, Washington 99164, USA. Present address: The Jackson Laboratory, Bar Harbor, Maine 04609, USA.

Don C. Erman (Chapter 1): Department of Forestry and Resource Management, University of California, Berkeley, California 94720, USA.

Moira M. Ferguson (Chapter 2): Department of Zoology, University of Montana, Missoula, Montana 59812, USA. Present address: Department of Zoology, University of Guelph, Guelph, Ontario N1G 2W1, Canada.

Brian D. Glebe (Chapter 16): Huntsman Marine Laboratory, St. Andrews, New Brunswick E0G 2X0, Canada.

Edward M. Goolish (Chapter 11): Department of Fisheries and Wildlife, University of Minnesota, 1980 Folwell Avenue, St. Paul, Minnesota 55108, USA. *Present address:* University of Michigan, School of Natural Resources, Ann Arbor, Michigan 48109–1115, USA.

David E. Hinton (Chapter 7): Department of Medicine, School of Veterinary Medicine, University of California, Davis, California 95616, USA.

Arthur H. Houston (Chapter 9): Department of Biological Sciences, Brock University, St. Catharines, Ontario L2S 3A1, Canada.

Christopher C. Kohler (Chapter 20): Cooperative Fishery Research Laboratory, Southern Illinois University, Carbondale, Illinois 62901, USA.

Robb F. Leary (Chapter 5): Division of Biological Sciences, University of Montana, Missoula, Montana 59812, USA.

John G. Lundberg (Chapter 3): Department of Zoology, Duke University, Durham, North Carolina 27706, USA.

Lucinda A. McDade (Chapter 3): Department of Botany, Duke University, Durham, North Carolina 27706, USA.

Donald J. McLeay (Chapter 14): D. McLeay and Associates Limited, 502 Kapilano 100, West Vancouver, British Columbia V7T 1A2, Canada.

Peter B. Moyle (Coeditor): Department of Wildlife and Fisheries Biology, University of California, Davis, California 95616, USA.

David L. G. Noakes (Chapter 17): Department of Zoology, University of Guelph, Guelph, Ontario N1G 2W1, Canada.

David F. Russell (Chapter 13): Department of Anesthesiology, Research Unit, Box 8054, Washington University Medical School, 660 South Euclid Avenue, St. Louis, Missouri 63110, USA.

Carl B. Schreck (Coeditor): Oregon Cooperative Fishery Research Unit, U.S. Fish and Wildlife Service, Oregon State University, Corvallis, Oregon 97331, USA.

Lynwood S. Smith (Chapter 8): School of Fisheries, WH-10, University of Washington, Seattle, Washington 98195, USA.

John B. Sprague (Chapter 15): Department of Zoology, University of Guelph, Guelph, Ontario N1G 2W1, Canada. *Present address:* J. B. Sprague Associates Ltd., 166 Maple Street, Guelph, Ontario N1G 2G7, Canada.

Robert R. Stickney (Chapter 20): School of Fisheries WH-10, University of Washington, Seattle, Washington 98195, USA.

Richard E. Strauss (Chapter 4): Department of Ecology and Evolutionary Biology, University of Arizona, Tucson, Arizona 85721, USA.

Robert C. Summerfelt (Chapter 8): Department of Animal Ecology, 124 Sciences Hall II, Iowa State University, Ames, Iowa 50011, USA.

Gary H. Thorgaard (Chapter 6): Department of Zoology, Washington State University, Pullman, Washington 99164, USA.

William E. Waters (Chapter 1): Department of Forestry and Resource Management, University of California, Berkeley, California 94720, USA.

Gary Wedemeyer (Chapter 14): U.S. Fish and Wildlife Service, National Fishery Research Center, Building 204, Naval Station Puget Sound, Seattle, Washington 98115, USA.

List of Fish Species

The colloquial names of many fish species have been standardized in *Common and Scientific Names of Fish Species from the United States and Canada* (4th edition, 1980; 5th edition, 1990) and *World Fishes Important to North Americans* (1991), published by the American Fisheries Society. Throughout this book, species listed in those publications are cited only by common name except when a fuller identification is important. The respective scientific names of these species follow.

Alewife .... *Alosa pseudoharengus*
American eel .... *Anguilla rostrata*
American plaice .... *Hippoglossoides platessoides*
Arctic char .... *Salvelinus alpinus*
Arctic cod .... *Boreogadus saida*
Arctic grayling .... *Thymallus arcticus*
Atlantic cod .... *Gadus morhua*
Atlantic herring .... *Clupea harengus harengus*
Atlantic menhaden .... *Brevoortia tyrannus*
Atlantic salmon .... *Salmo salar*

Barramundi perch .... *Lates calcarifer*
Bicolor damselfish .... *Pomacentrus partitus*
Black crappie .... *Pomoxis nigromaculatus*
Bloater .... *Coregonus hoyi*
Blueback herring .... *Alosa aestivalis*
Bluefin tuna .... *Thunnus thynnus*
Bluefish .... *Pomatomus saltatrix*
Bluegill .... *Lepomis macrochirus*
Blue tilapia .... *Tilapia aurea*
Brook silverside .... *Labidesthes sicculus*
Brook trout .... *Salvelinus fontinalis*
Brown bullhead .... *Ictalurus nebulosus*
Brown trout .... *Salmo trutta*

Central mudminnow .... *Umbra limi*
Channel catfish .... *Ictalurus punctatus*
Char .... *Salvelinus* spp.
Cherry salmon .... *Oncorhynchus masou*
Chinook salmon .... *Oncorhynchus tshawytscha*
Chum salmon .... *Oncorhynchus keta*
Coelacanth .... *Latimeria chalumnae*
Coho salmon .... *Oncorhynchus kisutch*
Common carp .... *Cyprinus carpio*
Common shiner .... *Notropis cornutus*
Cunner .... *Tautogolabrus adspersus*

Cutthroat trout[1] .... *Oncorhynchus clarki*

Dace .... *Phoxinus* spp.
Damselfish .... *Pomacentrus* spp.

Eelpout .... *Zoarces viviparus*
Eels (freshwater) .... Anguillidae
Eurasian perch .... *Perca fluviatilis*
European eel .... *Anguilla anguilla*
European flounder .... *Platichthys flesus*

Fathead minnow .... *Pimephales promelas*
Flagfish .... *Jordanella floridae*
Fourhorn sculpin .... *Myoxocephalus quadricornis*

Gizzard shad .... *Dorosoma cepedianum*
Golden shiner .... *Notemigonus crysoleucas*
Goldfish .... *Carassius auratus*
Grass carp .... *Ctenopharyngodon idella*
Green sunfish .... *Lepomis cyanellus*
Guppy .... *Poecilia reticulata*

Inland silverside .... *Menidia beryllina*

Kokanee .... *Oncorhynchus nerka*

Lake trout .... *Salvelinus namaycush*
Lake whitefish .... *Coregonus clupeaformis*
Lampreys .... Petromyzontidae
Largemouth bass .... *Micropterus salmoides*
Lingcod .... *Ophiodon elongatus*

Marbled swamp eel .... *Synbranchus marmoratus*
Medaka .... *Oryzias latipes*
Milkfish .... *Chanos chanos*
Mosquitofish .... *Gambusia affinis*
Mountain whitefish .... *Prosopium williamsoni*
Mozambique tilapia .... *Tilapia mossambica*
Mummichog .... *Fundulus heteroclitus*
Muskellunge .... *Esox masquinongy*

Nile perch .... *Lates niloticus*
Northern anchovy .... *Engraulis mordax*
Northern pike .... *Esox lucius*
Northern searobin .... *Prionotus carolinus*
Nurse shark .... *Ginglymostoma cirratum*

Oriental weatherfish .... *Misgurnus anguillicaudatus*

Pacific herring .... *Clupea harengus pallasi*
Pacific salmon .... *Oncorhynchus* spp.
Pacific sardine .... *Sardinops sagax*

---

[1]Formerly *Salmo clarki*.

Peacock cichlid . . . . *Cichla ocellaris*
Pinfish . . . . *Lagodon rhomboides*
Pink salmon . . . . *Oncorhynchus gorbuscha*
Plaice . . . . *Pleuronectes platessa*
Port Jackson shark . . . . *Heterodontus portusjacksoni*
Pumpkinseed . . . . *Lepomis gibbosus*

Rainbow darter . . . . *Etheostoma caeruleum*
Rainbow trout[2] . . . . *Oncorhynchus mykiss*

Sacramento blackfish . . . . *Orthodon microlepidotus*
Sacramento sucker . . . . *Catostomus occidentalis*
Sargassumfish . . . . *Histrio histrio*
Sauger . . . . *Stizostedion canadense*
Sea lamprey . . . . *Petromyzon marinus*
Sea raven . . . . *Hemitripterus americanus*
Sharksucker . . . . *Echeneis naucrates*
Sheepshead minnow . . . . *Cyprinodon variegatus*
Shorthead sculpin . . . . *Cottus confusus*
Skipjack tuna . . . . *Euthynnus pelamis*
Slimy sculpin . . . . *Cottus cognatus*
Smallmouth bass . . . . *Micropterus dolomieui*
Sockeye salmon . . . . *Oncorhynchus nerka*
Southern platyfish . . . . *Xiphophorus maculatus*
Spanish mackerel . . . . *Scomberomorus maculatus*
Spiny dogfish . . . . *Squalus acanthias*
Spot . . . . *Leiostomus xanthurus*
Spotted tilapia . . . . *Tilapia mariae*
Steelhead[2] . . . . *Oncorhynchus mykiss*
Striped bass . . . . *Morone saxatilis*
Striped mullet . . . . *Mugil cephalus*
Striped shiner . . . . *Notropis chrysocephalus*
Sunfish . . . . *Lepomis* spp.

Tench . . . . *Tinca tinca*
Threadfin shad . . . . *Dorosoma petenense*
Threespine stickleback . . . . *Gasterosteus aculeatus*
Tidewater silverside . . . . *Menidia peninsulae*
Tilapia . . . . *Tilapia* spp.
Tilefish . . . . *Lopholatilius chamaeleonticeps*
Toadfish . . . . *Opsanus tau*
Tui chub . . . . *Gila bicolor*

Vendace . . . . *Coregonus albula*

Walleye . . . . *Stizostedion vitreum*
Walleye pollock . . . . *Theragra chalcogramma*
White bass . . . . *Morone chrysops*
White crappie . . . . *Pomoxis annularis*

---

[2]Formerly *Salmo gairdneri*.

White perch .... *Morone americana*
White sturgeon .... *Acipenser transmontanus*
White sucker .... *Catostomus commersoni*
Winter flounder .... *Pseudopleuronectes americanus*

Yellow bullhead .... *Ictalurus natalis*
Yellowfin tuna .... *Thunnus albacares*
Yellow perch .... *Perca flavescens*

Zander .... *Stizostedion lucioperca*

Preface

Methods for Fish Biology is designed as both a reference and a handbook for the study of fishes. It is a source of methods commonly used to research fish genetics, systematics, anatomy, physiology, developmental biology, toxicology, behavior, and ecology. Standard methods and their theoretical frameworks are presented for all these fields. Each of the book's 20 chapters also contains a background literature review which, though not exhaustive, allows readers to delve more deeply into subjects that particularly interest them. The main emphasis is on methodology, but the pros and cons of alternative procedures also are treated, as are the uses and misuses of data generated by the techniques.

We believe this book will be useful to students or professional biologists who need a quick introduction to an unfamiliar area, to biologists or technicians who use standard techniques irregularly and need recipes to follow, to administrators who must judge the validity of techniques proposed in research or management plans, to biologist-planners who need to know what techniques can be used to solve a management problem, and to students who take advanced laboratory and field courses. Even in a book of this size, it is impossible to cover every technique employed to study fish; ecological methods alone would fill a volume. In deciding what to include, we used the broad term "biology" as our primary criterion. Topics that might best be covered in manuals for more specific disciplines were displaced from this one. For example, methods for studying digestion and nutrition are not covered here because a better context would be a book on fish diets and feeding; immunological techniques logically belong in a work on disease. Further, this book complements *Fisheries Techniques*, edited by L. A. Nielsen and D. L. Johnson (American Fisheries Society, 1983), so it does not duplicate the many field-oriented techniques given there.

Teleostean fishes are the main focus of this book, though many methods are applicable to other types of fish as well. Whatever species is studied, investigators must recall the ethics of research on animals and treat their subjects humanely. Housing and care of experimental fish must be of high quality. Experiments should be designed so that no more animals are used than are necessary to provide valid, interpretable data.

Like *Fisheries Techniques, Methods for Fish Biology* is a product of the American Fisheries Society's Education Section. Many people identified the need for this book and contributed ideas for its contents. Each chapter received several external peer reviews, which were thorough and constructive. For the time and care they invested as peer reviewers, we thank F. W. H. Beamish, E. Birmingham, T. Brandt, L. J. Buckley, G. Carmichael, L. Curtis, J. S. Diana, E. M. Donaldson, A. A. Echelle, S. Flickinger, G. W. Fowler, J. Gold, G. Helfman, J. D. Hendricks, R. L. Herman, J. B. Hunn, S. H. Hurlbert, G. W. Klontz, H. Lane, H. W. Li, G. S. Losey, D. F. Markle, P. Mehrle, R. G. Northcutt, B. L. Olla, L. R. Parenti (two chapters), D. P. Philipp, R. B. Phillips, C. Pla, J. A. Rice, J. B. Shaklee, J. Smith, S. A. Sower, C. Stephan, F. M. Utter, L. J. Weber, and T. E. Wissing.

Several authors also wish to acknowledge the help they received as they created their respective chapters.

Fred Allendorf and Moira Ferguson thank Anthony Echelle and Fred Utter and his coworkers for helpful reviews of Chapter 2. When they prepared the manuscript, Allendorf was supported by National Science Foundation grants and Ferguson by a Natural Sciences and Engineering Research Council of Canada postgraduate fellowship.

John Lundberg and Lucinda McDade thank J. R. Bailey, A. Bornbusch, D. Buth, P. Mabee, B. Mishler, L. Parenti, L. Roth, and W. R. Taylor for comments on various drafts of Chapter 3, and P. Moyle and W. Starnes for editorial assistance.

Gary Thorgaard and Jane Disney received helpful suggestions about Chapter 6 from John Gold, Marilyn Lloyd, and Ruth Phillips; Marilyn Lloyd also provided the negatives for Figure 6.3. The authors were supported by U.S. Department of Agriculture grants CRSR-2–1058 and CRCR-1–1732 at the time.

Robert Summerfelt and Lynwood Smith benefited from comments on early versions of Chapter 8 by Edward J. Peters, John Grizzle, G. W. Klontz, Gary D. Marty, Fred P. Meyer, John Plumb, Rosalie Schnick, Richard Spall, Lavern Weber, and Gary A. Wedemeyer. The authors are grateful to Pitman-Moore, Inc., Washington Crossing, New Jersey, for permission to use information that is in Table 8.3. Although they mentioned particular commercial products in their chapter, they remind readers that alternative proprietary products of equal value often exist.

Arthur H. Houston expresses his very real appreciation to Ajmal Murad for discussion and comment on Chapter 9.

Joe Cech appreciates the comments from Bill Beamish and Peter Moyle on a draft of Chapter 10 and the guiding hand of Curly Wohlschlag during his student years.

Greg Busacker, Ira Adelman, and Edward Goolish are grateful to Raymond M. Newman and George Spangler for advice on parts of Chapter 11. Their work was supported in part by the University of Minnesota Agricultural Experiment Station, project 75, and the chapter is Scientific Journal Series 14982 of the Agricultural Experiment Station.

Marshall Adams and James Breck's Chapter 12 was sponsored by the Office of Health and Environmental Research, U.S. Department of Energy, under contract DE-AC05–74OR21400 with Martin Marietta Energy Systems, Inc. The chapter is publication 2762 of the Environmental Sciences Division, Oak Ridge National Laboratory.

David Russell thanks W. Brunken, S. Highstein, R. Miller, and C. Rovainen for consultation and comments on Chapter 13. His writing was supported by U.S. National Institutes of Health grant NS23028.

Gary Wedemeyer, Bruce Barton, and Donald McLeay appreciate the editorial assistance of Susanna Hornig, who greatly facilitated development of Chapter 14.

John Sprague acknowledges the good advice given by Charles E. Stephan on an early draft of Chapter 15.

Laurence Crim and Brian Glebe's Chapter 16 is Memorial University of Newfoundland Marine Sciences Research Laboratory contribution 690.

David Noakes and Jeffrey Baylis thank George Losey and Bori Olla for thorough reviews of the whole of Chapter 17; M. White for preparing the figures; and E. K. Balon, F. W. H. Beamish, J. W. A. Grant, J. M. Gunn, J. F. Leatherland, C. P. Nunan, W. Pot, S. Skulason, and C. G. Soto for comments on aspects of the manuscript. The authors' studies of fish behavior have been supported by the Natural Sciences and Engineering Research Council of Canada, the Ontario Ministry of Natural Resources, the Canadian National Sportsmen's Fund, and the University of Wisconsin Research Foundation.

Donald Baltz appreciates the critical reviews of Chapter 18 by Gene Helfman, Peter Moyle, Wayne Starnes, Fred Utter, Bruce Vondracek, and Gary Winans.

Larry Crowder appreciates the manuscript critiques of Chapter 19 provided by John Magnuson, James Kitchell, Peter Sale, Barry Johnson, Peter Moyle, Bruce Vondracek, and graduate students at North Carolina State University. His work on the chapter was supported in part by grants from the U.S. National Science Foundation (BSR-8615161 and BSR-8709108) and the University of North Carolina Sea Grant (R/ES-C39, R/MER-12, and R/ES-40).

Robert Stickney and Christopher Kohler acknowledge the important contributions to Chapter 20 made by William M. Lewis, who helped develop the initial outline and who made many valuable suggestions as the writing progressed.

We also appreciate the help provided by John and Mary Nickum, particularly regarding the publication process. Robert Kendall, Wayne Starnes, Sally Kendall, Robert Gabel, Bera Knipling, and Catherine Richardson of the Society's headquarters staff contributed editorial improvements in the final manuscripts and saw the book through production.

Many trade names and product vendors are mentioned in this book as a convenience for readers. Specific citations do not imply endorsements by the American Fisheries Society, the authors and editors, or the employers of the book's contributors.

CARL B. SCHRECK
PETER B. MOYLE

Chapter 1

Research Methods: Concept and Design

WILLIAM E. WATERS AND DON C. ERMAN

1.1 INTRODUCTION

The process of research has been variously defined to include chance discovery, pure reasoning, application of the scientific method, and the use of statistical concepts and methods. All of these elements may be included in a research investigation. For purposes of this book, we define research as *a systematic and orderly process by which new knowledge or information is obtained in accordance with specified objectives*. This definition implies a utilitarian purpose and, indeed, utility is a basic motivation for research in fish biology just as in other fields of natural resource science (utility does not necessarily mean direct or immediate application of the new information). The definition excludes *sole* reliance on casual observation and chance discovery, simple reasoning, random trial and error, and bibliographic searches. Our emphasis is on *process*.

The qualifier *new* may mean (1) a more complete description or explanation of a biological pattern, process, or relationship, (2) an extension of the time or space dimensions of existing information, (3) modification of current explanations or theories, (4) an entirely new explanation that provides a different base of knowledge with new vistas for future research, or (5) a new way of combining information for improved prediction and decision making. A research project may be conceived and designed to achieve one or any combination of these goals. The research process, then, can be depicted in a very general way as

$$\text{prior} \begin{cases} \text{knowledge} \\ \text{experience} \end{cases} \rightarrow \text{new information} \rightarrow \text{improved} \begin{cases} \text{description.} \\ \text{explanation.} \\ \text{prediction.} \\ \text{decision making.} \end{cases}$$

The intended use of the new information is a basic factor that determines the concept and design of every study or experiment. It also determines the approach to be taken in statistical analysis. Description and explanation draw on methods of *statistical inference*. Prediction (related to specific actions) and decision making utilize procedures of *statistical decision making*. For some situations, this dichotomy may not be entirely clear. It may be contended, for example, that a good description of a pattern of occurrence or an explanation for a change in population size is sufficient for a management decision. This frequently occurs because expediency and necessity override risk and uncertainty. However, if one understands at the start what kind of data and form of analysis are required for a predictive model or other decision tool, one should see the need for a different kind of study that extends research beyond the descriptive–explanatory stage. Barnett (1973) gave a historical perspective of the distinction between these dual

1

functions of statistics and some basic considerations on the requisites and techniques of each.

Another way of characterizing the purpose of research is by separating the kinds of questions or hypotheses that pertain to *what* is going on—and, perhaps, *where* and *when*—from those dealing with *why*. This distinction is applicable to all levels of research: molecular, cellular, organismic, population, community, ecosystem. It also is fundamental to the choice of approach and methods of analysis to be employed. For example, there may be a need to better determine what factors affect the distribution of a particular species of fish in a stream. General knowledge of this and similar species suggests that water depth, rate of flow, substrate characteristics, and cover are the major factors involved. An experiment is suggested (by an administratively minded supervisor, say) to determine why the fish are distributed as observed. In order to carry out this assignment, some basic questions first need to be answered. Is the evidence for the importance of the four factors sufficient to exclude all others? Does the information available cover a representative range of stream conditions? How should each of these factors be measured and manipulated? Are there possible interactions among the factors that should be assessed? How should the response variable of interest, instream distribution of the fish, be measured? Are there differences in diurnal and seasonal behavior that should be considered? Lack of knowledge or uncertainty regarding any of these questions (and others similarly important) should dictate that a detailed study first is needed of how the fish are distributed in the stream. That is, *what* is going on needs to be determined before any attempt is made to determine *why*. Arrays of questions like the foregoing, relating to the kind of information available and the intent of the research, arise at every step of the research process and lead to the many choices and decisions that must be made.

This chapter focuses on how research in fish biology should be conceived, planned, and organized. A general schema for this process (applicable to the life sciences generally) will be presented, and some basic considerations and techniques of design and data analysis will be discussed as they apply to three levels, or phases, of research as described by Wilm (1952): (1) observational studies, (2) controlled experience studies, and (3) controlled experiments. This spectrum, or sequence, of research was divided into "mensurative experiments" and "manipulative experiments" by Hurlbert (1984). The latter classification is helpful in many instances, and reference to it will be made where appropriate. Details of execution, including specialized techniques of preparation, description, measurement, and data gathering, are covered in other chapters for particular applications in fish biology.

1.2   CONCEPTUAL FRAMEWORK AND BASIC CONSIDERATIONS

Critical steps in the research process often are overlooked, or arbitrary decisions are made at different points, without explicit recognition of the constraints and assumptions involved. Interpretations of findings then may lack credibility, or the extent to which the findings can be extrapolated to practical situations may be questioned. Such basic shortcomings are probably the most

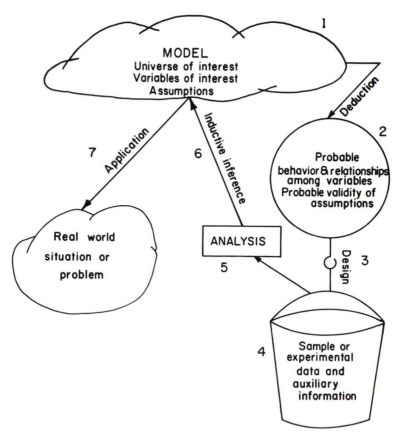

Figure 1.1 A general schema of the research process. (Adapted from Barnett 1973; reproduced with permission of John Wiley & Sons.)

common source of contention not only among researchers in a particular field, but between researchers and users as well.

Is there a general framework for guidance that applies to all types and levels of study and experimentation? What are the components, and how are they linked to provide a logical sequence of concept, design, analysis, and interpretation?

With slight modification, Barnett's (1973) general schema, developed to describe the role of statistical theory and applications in solving real problems and dealing with uncertainty, portrays the whole research process. We have found it a useful guideline for research planning and for consultation with colleagues, graduate students, and others in the development of research projects. This schema (Figure 1.1) has seven steps.

1.2.1 Step 1: Conceptualization

The process begins with a conceptual "model"—a perception of the situation to be investigated or the problem to be solved. Operationally, this leads to (a) a statement of the situation or problem and definition of its spatial and temporal bounds, (b) a review or consideration of prior knowledge and experience relating to (a), (c) a specification of the variables of interest, including the dependent or response variables that express or reflect the biological characteristics of concern and the "independent" variables that, in a relevant context, might affect, be associated with, or have some relationship to the dependent variable(s), and (d) a careful consideration of any assumptions and constraints implied in the conceptualization—the model—of the situation or problem. Holling (1978) called this "bounding the problem."

At this stage, the objective is conceived in general terms, and one or several possible approaches to it are identified.

1.2.2   Step 2: Formulation

Model formulation is simply the logical extension of the basic premises and specifications of step 1 into an analytical framework. Here, the probable behavior of and relationships among the specified variables of interest are deduced and the probable validity and relative importance of the basic assumptions are considered. This step results in a tightening of the conceptual model and clearer recognition of the constraints and limitations that will affect interpretation and extrapolation of the findings.

This leads to a statement of the objective in specific terms and selection of the approach to be taken. Both objective and approach should relate directly to the *structure* of the "model"; for example, several subobjectives may need to be specified, involving somewhat different approaches and procedures. Also, both the objectives as stated and the approaches should be compatible with the intellectual process to be followed, such as answering questions, testing hypotheses, estimating biological parameters, or developing predictive models. Limitations of the information to be obtained should be indicated as explicitly as possible at this point.

1.2.3   Step 3: Design

Study design encompasses all elements of sampling and experimental design necessary to achieve the purposes and mode of the research defined in steps 1 and 2. Techniques and procedures applicable to research in fish biology can be found throughout the literature of physics, chemistry, biology, and statistics. Here, we address the kinds and sequence of choices and decisions that must be made in the actual design phase. Step 3 includes the following six elements.

Specification of the Universe of Interest. The universe of interest should be defined. It might be, for example, a single- or multispecies population and its spatial structure and limits. The bounds of the subject universe define the levels of variation involved, such as

global,
regional,
major area (mountain range, physiographic zone, etc.),
specific area (geographic locality, watershed, etc.),
subarea (lake, stream, estuary, etc.),
major unit (lake zone or stratum, stream zone or segment, estuarine segment or
   habitat type, etc.), or
minor (ultimate) unit (individual organism).

Analogous hierarchies can be applied to cellular or molecular studies, in which the ultimate unit is simply a smaller entity. The largest spatial entity and its smaller components define both the limits and structure of the universe of interest for design purposes. They also define the degree to which the study or experiment can represent the range of conditions under which the organism, or other level of organization, operates.

Specification of the Time Frame. The time frame includes the absolute time limit (minutes, weeks, years) and the frequency of observations. The latter defines the temporal structure of the study or experiment. Representativeness with respect to time, as well as to space, must be decided upon in advance, and the consequent constraints on interpretation and extrapolation must be recognized.

Specification of the Sampling Universe. If less than a complete census of the universe of interest is to be made, what part of it is to be sampled or represented in an experiment? In a strict sense, the relationship between sampling and population universes must be known in order to obtain valid, unbiased estimates of population parameters. Further, a sampling "frame" must be explicitly defined in terms of the sampling or observational units used. This requirement applies to estimates of total abundance, average density, or average values of other biological variables. It also applies to estimates of variability in these values, which are necessary for testing hypotheses and calculating confidence limits. Moreover, the method of sampling that is used must assure that all components of the population universe are fully and equitably represented by an appropriate probability-sampling procedure.

Establishment of a sampling frame may be feasible when definition of the population universe is restricted to a particular lake or stream, or to a portion thereof (in which case the findings apply only to that entity). For example, one might conduct a study of zinc accumulation in fish based on samples of rainbow trout collected from a particular montane lake (the population universe). If an appropriate sampling design is implemented throughout the lake, the findings apply to this species in this lake, but they cannot be extrapolated to other species in the same lake or to rainbow trout in other lakes.

In many situations, however, the population bounds are very large or are undefined, and only the sampling universe is defined. When this is the case, there is no way to determine how well observations of the sample represent the whole population. Thus, the true accuracy and precision of any estimates of population parameters are unknown, and interpretations must be qualified accordingly. In the study of zinc accumulation in rainbow trout, for example, if the samples of fish are taken only from a particular portion of the lake—say, within 100 m of the shoreline (the sampling universe)—it is not known how well the fish caught and examined from this segment represent the whole population in the lake with respect to zinc accumulation. The findings apply at best only to rainbow trout in the specified zone. The same constraint applies to sampling universes defined by a time span or by particular fish species, age-classes, morphotypes, etc.

In still other situations, the sampling universe itself is undefined. This is the case generally when methods are used to obtain relational estimates such as catch per unit fishing effort or population size from recapture of marked fish. Here, the range of options for data analysis and interpretation are even more limited. Such estimates often can only be summarized in tables or graphs and evaluated subjectively. This manner of data gathering may be sufficient for survey or monitoring purposes, but it is useful in research only at an exploratory or preliminary stage.

These comments on the sampling universe apply to observational studies (Section 1.3) and controlled experience studies (Section 1.4), but basically the same question arises for field or laboratory experimentation: what are the experimental subjects and placement of experimental units intended to represent? Practical considerations often limit the scope of an experiment, and the constraints on interpretation of results should be recognized accordingly.

Definition of Sampling or Observational Units. The choice of sampling and observational unit depends on the purpose of the study or experiment and on how the variables of interest are to be measured and expressed. Examples of such units for field studies are specified areas or volumes of water or substrate. Certain field sampling devices, such as the Surber sampler, are constructed to provide these measures directly. Counts made with these devices represent absolute population estimates, which generally are expressed as number of organisms per unit area or per unit volume (i.e., as absolute density). The size and shape of this kind of sampling or observational unit is determined largely by the relative size and movement pattern of the organism involved. When two or more organisms are to be sampled simultaneously, different unit sizes and shapes may be needed to minimize bias in the respective counts or in other observations.

Alternatively, habitat units such as individual plants, stream pools, or littoral zones can be designated as the sampling or observational units. Counts made on this basis, expressed as number of organisms per habitat unit, represent estimates of population *intensity* as distinguished from population *density* (Southwood 1978). This distinction is important when abundances are to be compared for a species that may change habitats over time or between species that live in different habitats. In these cases, the numbers per habitat unit should be converted to absolute densities by determining the area or volume of the habitat unit or the number of plants (or other structural unit) per unit of area or volume.

The various passive and active sampling gears (Hayes 1983; Hubert 1983) used to estimate abundance and composition of fish populations are, in a sense, "sampling" units. However, many factors affect the kinds and numbers of fish caught, and the magnitude of variation due to catchability is such that these devices are best considered strictly as collection units. Moreover, the sampling universes usually are undefined and the devices do not represent defined spaces, so the catches per device per unit time are only relative population estimates, subject to many possible biases.

Electrofishing (Reynolds 1983), toxicant applications (Davies and Shelton 1983), and tagging and marking techniques (Wydoski and Emery 1983) do not have a sampling unit per se. Therefore, the factors involved in their choice do not include the matter of sampling unit size and shape. These methods provide only relative estimates, and the degree and direction of bias generally are unknown.

The foregoing considerations apply also to field experiments in which the basic data are obtained by sampling. In laboratory experiments, all treated subjects usually are examined, counted, and otherwise included in the data base, and thus no measure of chance variation or sampling error is involved. The "sampling" is accomplished in the process of selecting individuals or materials to be included in the experiment. In experiments to determine the effects of a treatment on organs, tissues, cells, and subcellular components, both the treated fish and the parts examined represent "samples," but no sampling error is ever invoked.

In both field and laboratory experiments, the treatment or experimental unit may be an individual subject or object, a group of same, or a specified area or volume of water (or other medium). However, when measures of response are obtained from a sample of individual fish in a treated medium, or from a sampling of subunits, the individual fish or subunits are not the experimental units for purposes of analysis. Consider a controlled experiment to determine the effect of zinc concentration on uptake of the metal by rainbow trout. Five zinc concentrations are used and there are four replicates of each concentration, giving 20 experimental units (separate tanks). Each tank contains 12 fish, selected at random from a given stock. The analysis of treatment effects is based on the variation in zinc uptake among and within the treatments as indicated by the mean values for each experimental unit (i.e., the mean amount of zinc found in the 12 fish in each tank). In this experiment, the individual fish is *not* the experimental unit, and any estimate of experimental error based on variation in zinc uptake among the individuals subjected to each treatment is invalid. Use of such data in an analysis constitutes pseudoreplication (Hurlbert 1984).

The kind, size, and shape of experimental unit chosen depend basically on the nature of the treatments applied or the environmental conditions that are manipulated. Other practical considerations may affect the choice, also.

Specification of Parameters. The parameters (population attributes) of interest must be specified. Then, appropriate measures of those attributes can be selected, and a data format can be chosen that will facilitate later analysis. Attributes may be expressed and recorded in *qualitative* terms as classes or categories, or in *quantitative* terms as measurements or counts. The choice of exactly how each parameter or variable of interest should be accounted for—of what attributes or expressions of them are most relevant and realistic—is not easy, nor should it be arbitrary. The decision is partly subjective, based on knowledge and experience, and even on the conventional wisdom of traditional practice (which may or may not be adequate for a particular situation). The choices here also should be based on considerations of the objectives and intended output of the study or experiment and the way in which the data will be analyzed; one should "look back" to steps 1 and 2 and "look ahead" to step 4.

With respect to controlled field experiments, a distinction should be made between *treatment factors* that are actually manipulated or imposed on the experimental area, and *site factors* that are intrinsic to the area in question (treatment versus classification factors sensu Cox 1958). An experimenter often wishes to determine how different levels of a treatment—food supply, say—affect a particular organism under different environmental conditions, and the experiment is designed so that a selected set of conditions is included in the experimental layout. The effects of both the treatment and the selected environmental factors on the response (however measured) of the target organism then can be assessed. The environmental or site factors may be *biological* (e.g., relative density of the target organism, relative abundance of competing species, algal biomass), *physical* (e.g., water temperature, flow rate), or *chemical* (e.g., pH, O_2 concentration). Further, these factors may be considered random or fixed effects for purposes of analysis, depending on the experimental conditions and procedure. In laboratory experiments, the same environmental factors may be imposed as treatments and, of course, analyzed as fixed effects.

In observational and controlled experience studies, these factors are simply site or environmental variables of interest. Their effects, in these instances, may be either random or fixed, depending on whether the measures of them are based on samples drawn at random or on samples drawn from selected, "representative," portions of the specified universe.

Selection of the Sampling or Experimental Design. Finally, the study design is chosen. This involves a series of decisions, all related to those preceding.

If sampling is involved, a variety of designs is available: simple random sampling, stratified random sampling, cluster sampling, systematic sampling, variable-probability sampling, subsampling (nested designs), double sampling (sampling with regression), sequential sampling, two- or three-stage sampling, and various combinations of these such as a stratified–nested design. These designs are applicable for both absolute and relative estimates. When successive observations over some time period are needed, sampling can be repeated at the same sampling stations (sampling without replacement, in a temporal sense) or at the same number of stations of which a certain proportion is replaced by new, randomly selected stations on each occasion (sampling with partial replacement). All of these designs involve certain basic assumptions, procedural requirements, statistical features, advantages and disadvantages, and practical limitations. They differ in efficiency under different conditions. These considerations will be discussed further in the sections of this chapter dealing with observational studies (1.3) and controlled experience studies (1.4). Every sampling design lends itself to, or requires, particular forms of statistical analysis. Bear in mind that different procedures may be used for hypothesis testing, estimation with confidence limits, and description of functional relationships or associations.

The most useful references on sampling concepts and design for research in fish biology probably are those that combine biological–ecological insights with statistical knowledge. Johnson and Nielsen (1983) gave practical sampling guidelines specifically oriented to fisheries investigations. The texts by Watt (1968), Elliott (1977), Southwood (1978), and Green (1979), though not focused on fish biology, provide much information relevant to this field and, importantly, give attention to biological factors and practical situations not generally covered in statistics tomes. Hurlbert (1984) illuminated some of the most thorny problems in the design and execution of ecological field studies, and gave particular emphasis to pseudoreplication and randomization. A simple but rigorous treatment of the fundamental elements of sampling is Stuart's (1976) delightful monograph *Basic Ideas of Scientific Sampling.*

For controlled experiments, a wide range of designs differing greatly in scope and complexity is available. These designs include simple paired and unpaired tests; completely randomized experiments; randomized-block designs; Latin-square, factorial, split-plot, and lattice designs; and others developed primarily for use in particular disciplines such as genetics, toxicology, and behavior. Variants of these designs have been devised to minimize the work involved with no loss of information. Familiarity with alternative experimental designs always is desirable. Some suggested general references are Cox (1958), Cochran and Cox (1964), John and Quenouille (1977), Little and Hills (1978), and Hicks (1982). The essay by Hurlbert (1984) is very relevant to field experiments with fish.

The question of sample size or number of replicates is important for even the simplest of investigations. The term replicate is frequently misunderstood and misapplied, which leads to invalid statistical tests and erroneous conclusions. The problem of definition is partly one of context: in sampling, *replicate* applies to a sample; in an experiment, the term applies to a treatment or experimental unit.

In the case of sampling, a set of observations, counts, or measurements at a single place and time constitutes a sample. Similar samples taken independently and at random are replicates. One set of observations (i.e., a single sample or replicate) allows calculation of a mean value, the variance of the observations, and a confidence interval within which additional observations similarly taken should fall with given odds. An increase in the number of observations increases the precision of estimates (within limits) and correspondingly reduces the size of the confidence interval. But what does a single sample represent? When single samples (regardless of the number of observations they comprise) are taken at two or more places or times, a statistical test of significance can be used to compare them, but the difference, if any, between them represents only a difference between those particular samples. Any inferences regarding the places or times will be purely subjective. Valid comparisons among places or times, and other inferences about them, require two or more replicates within each. How these replicates are distributed throughout the universe of interest is a matter of sampling design; they may be completely at random, randomly allocated within defined strata, clustered, or systematically dispersed.

The number of replications needed to obtain a desired precision, expressed either as a confidence interval or coefficient of variation, depends on (a) the degree of variability in counts or other observed values within the sampling universe, based on a specific sampling unit and procedure, and (b) the sampling design. If at all possible, preliminary sampling should be conducted to estimate variability and to discern any pattern in variability for the places and times of the study. Information from other sources may help, but it may not accurately represent the study situation. The proper formulas to calculate sample size are given in most statistical texts (e.g., Cochran 1977). Many of these texts, however, give only the formulas appropriate for normally distributed data, that is, data whose frequencies fit a statistically defined bell-shaped curve. Karandinos (1976) provided formulas for the Poisson, binomial, and negative binomial distributions, which data from natural biological populations most commonly fit.

In the case of experiments, replicate refers to the entire experimental unit that receives a particular treatment or manipulation, not the individuals or subunits therein. The choice of how many replicates to use in laboratory experiments often is based on prior personal experience or on standardized practice known to discern meaningful differences. Because the experimental process, including design, allows one to control experimental error, adjustments in numbers of replicates can be made quickly. With field experiments, the number of replicates per treatment usually is determined more by practical limitations than by enlightened judgment. Simulation and analysis of expected responses, based on different experimental designs and different numbers of replicates, should improve insight and lessen guesswork. The practical rule, however, is to include as many true replicates as possible. In all circumstances, it is wise to assess the trade-off between number and complexity of treatments and number of replications per treatment.

One more complication to face in the design of experiments is the selection of treatments or manipulations of environmental variables and the manner in which they will be spatially and temporally allocated to the experimental units. These choices, of course, depend on the objectives of the experiment—the questions being addressed or the hypotheses being tested. They depend also on one's own knowledge, imagination, and innovativeness with respect to the biological events, processes, or relationships under study and to the statistical aspects of experimental design.

1.2.4 Step 4: Execution

The execution phase of research requires additional critical decisions. Most decisions relate to logistics, procedure, acquisition and handling of equipment, materials, personnel, and other practical matters. These are important but are not pertinent here. Other decisions may be needed about possible shifts in location, timing, frequency of observations, number of replications, certain aspects of design, and acquisition of data on factors or conditions that were not specified in the original research plan. Such changes or additions, especially if they alter the sampling or experimental design, should be carefully considered and fully justified with respect to the original concept and objectives. The criterion for making a change or addition is whether or not it will truly improve the data base, the rigor of the analysis, and the validity of the findings.

1.2.5 Step 5: Analysis

The analysis of data is an integral part of the research process. It can be relatively straightforward if all of the preceding steps have been carefully thought out and followed. The form and method of analysis depend on the design and conduct of the study or experiment and on whether the intent is to (a) discern and characterize discrete patterns or groupings, (b) make statistical comparisons, (c) assess correlations, (d) quantitatively describe functional relationships, including rates of change, or (e) develop a predictive model for management planning and decision making. Hypothesis testing is embedded in nearly all statistical procedures. It is involved explicitly in (b) and (c). For (a), (d), and (e), however, we suggest that these purposes are better expressed by a relevant question—for example, What is the form and spatiotemporal configuration of the pattern? What is the form and degree of relationship involved?—than by a simple hypothesis that there is or is not a pattern or relationship. The most relevant question for (e) is What kind and form of model will most reliably predict the variable of interest? A hierarchical sequence of hypothesis testing, as described by Platt (1964) and recommended by Green (1979), has a logical appeal, but it may not satisfy one's needs with respect to the immediate situation or problem.

When a statistical analysis is performed with reference to a specific hypothesis, a statistical model must be formulated that explicitly fits the hypothesis. Moreover, the random and fixed effects or components must be identified. An arbitrarily chosen statistical method may not meet these requirements.

All statistical methods involve some assumptions about the data. The analysis of variance (ANOVA) and related classical methods, for example, require assumptions that the error components in any set of sampling or experimental data are independent and normally distributed, that the variation in errors is homogeneous throughout, and that the effects recorded are additive. In field experiments particularly, these assumptions generally are violated. Green (1979) discussed these violations in both statistical and practical contexts, and indicated various ways to evaluate them by graphical and numerical means. One approach is to simulate empirical data that satisfy the stipulated hypothesis model but have the undesirable features of one's particular data. Such post hoc evaluations are part of the learning process, and they provide an objective basis for more rigorous interpretation of the results of an analysis. Familiarity with the assumptions of common statistical methods and with ways to ameliorate departures from these assumptions can help one avoid some pitfalls in both execution and interpretation.

Transformations such as square roots, logarithms, and arcsine values, can be used to convert raw data into a form more amenable to analysis by parametric methods. These are often used for types of data known to violate basic assumptions of ANOVA, regression analysis, and like methods. Though serving the desired statistical purposes, transformations alter absolute values and relationships and make interpretation of the analytical output more difficult. This is most troublesome in the analysis of field data. Experience and judgment are needed to decide whether or not a transformation is necessary or advantageous in each situation. Statistics texts that deal with analytical methods applicable to biology provide useful guidelines.

When the data are not too complex, nonparametric (distribution-free) methods can be used. These are most efficient for single or multiple comparisons and simple correlation analyses involving uncomplicated hypotheses. They can be more reliable and powerful than ANOVA and conventional correlation analysis when sample sizes are small, sample data are not normally distributed, and ANOVA assumptions for experimental data are seriously violated. Different tests provide answers to the questions, "Is there a difference?" or "Is there a correlation or association?" with specified probabilities of rejecting the null hypothesis. They do not provide quantitative estimates of functional relationships. Thus, they are most applicable to exploratory and observational studies. Their use should be considered before any analysis is conducted; they should not be resorted to only when problems are encountered with ANOVA or other parametric methods. Some useful references on the rationale, methodology, and limitations of nonparametric techniques of analysis are Hollander and Wolfe (1973), Mosteller and Rourke (1973), and Conover (1980).

A basic decision in statistical hypothesis testing is to specify the acceptable risk of wrongly rejecting the null hypothesis; this is the type I error, generally designated α. In biological terms, α specifies the probability of concluding that there is a biological effect or relationship when there actually is none. It is the criterion used almost invariably in tests of significance. The maximum α commonly is set at 0.05, but the risk of a type I error may be justifiably set at $\alpha = 0.10$, or even higher, in field studies or experiments or in observational studies intended only to gain clues about pattern and process.

There is the risk also of accepting the null hypothesis when it is not true. This is the type II error, β, which, biologically speaking, is the probability of concluding that there is no biological effect or relationship when there actually is. In some instances, when management actions depend on one's findings and adverse effects, in particular, are concerned, the type II error may be very important. The expressed level of both type I and type II errors depends on variability in the natural population, variability in individual responses to treatment, and sample size or number of experimental replicates. For each sampling or experimental design and method of analysis, a reduction in the probability α of a type I error results in a higher probability β of a type II error. The trade-off between the two can be adjusted by improvements in design, and one or both can be reduced by increased sample size or number of replicates.

The probability α is used also to calculate confidence intervals for estimated parameters and confidence limits for regression equations. For either hypothesis testing or estimation purposes, the choice of an appropriate α or β should be dictated by the particular circumstances and objective of the study or experiment. In all cases, it should be specified in advance, and not rationalized after perusal of the initial output of analysis.

When overall environmental or treatment effects are found to be significant and detailed statistical comparisons among the individual mean effects are desired, an appropriate multiple-comparison test must be chosen. Among such tests commonly used in fish biology are orthogonal contrasts, multiple t-tests, the least-significant-difference procedure, the Student–Newman–Keuls test, Duncan's multiple-range test, Scheffé's S-procedure, Tukey's ω-procedure, Dunnett's test, multiple χ^2 tests, and several nonparametric tests (some of which involve one or more of the foregoing). Sometimes, as an alternative to such tests, conclusions are based on whether or not confidence intervals for individual means overlap. The choice of the most appropriate test or procedure for a given situation depends on (a) the kind of data involved and assumptions about their distribution, (b) whether the data represent a single sampling or experiment or several that were conducted simultaneously, (c) the degree to which multiple sampling or experimentation was conducted independently, and (d) how conservative one wishes the conclusions to be. The latter judgment requires an understanding of the reasoning behind each of the standard multiple-comparison procedures and of how the error rate of each is determined. Jones (1984) provided a thorough critique of the tests that are likely to be used in the analysis of fisheries data. Mize and Schultz (1985) described experimental situations for which different methods of comparing treatments are most appropriate. For example, when treatments are different amounts or intensities of something, a regression analysis of the treatment–response relationship is more informative than direct comparisons of mean responses to individual treatments. Similarly, planned (orthogonal) contrasts are more appropriate and informative than multiple-comparison procedures when responses to a combination of types and levels of treatment are analyzed or when quantitative treatments include a control or zero level.

Green (1979) suggested that the statistical analysis chosen should be the most efficient one for the particular hypothesis and statistical model stipulated. That is, the test should be as conservative, powerful, and robust as possible. Here, conservative refers to a low probability of making a type I error, powerful relates to a low probability of making a type II error, and robust refers to the degree to which the specified error levels, both α and β, are affected by the statistical properties of the data involved.

Fish and wildlife environments are three-dimensional, and sometimes can be conceptualized in even more dimensions. Multivariate statistical applications to ecological field data have become more popular because of this complexity. These techniques essentially classify and ordinate habitats with respect to characteristics known or assumed to have some functional relationship with the populations of interest. They are often used to infer the effects that changes in habitat quality may have on population abundance, distribution, composition, and structure. These techniques include factor analysis, cluster analysis, principal components analysis, discriminant function analysis, canonical correlation analysis, and multivariate analogs of certain univariate statistical methods. Each provides a way to reduce and summarize large bodies of data into useful form. Each rests on some basic assumptions, such as linearity and independence, and they all generally involve greater subjectivity in both application and interpretation than standard univariate techniques. However, new variants and applications of multivariate techniques are being developed rapidly, and they should be considered for studies of environmental and habitat characteristics and of the quality and productivity of fish populations. Some suggested references are Sneath and Sokal (1973), Green (1979), Capen (1981), Gauch (1982), Pielou (1984), and Romesburg (1984).

1.2.6 Step 6: Interpretation and Comparison with Initial Model

Before inferences drawn from the analysis of data are extended directly to the real world, the interpretations and conclusions from the study or experiment should be checked against the original "model." This is an important but often-ignored step (see Figure 1.1). The spatial and temporal bounds of the situation or problem, the variables of interest and their probable relationships, the specific objectives, the basic hypotheses to be tested or questions to be answered, and the constraints and limitations that were perceived at the beginning all should be reexamined. Were they realistic? Are the conclusions consistent with the original specifications? Did something unexpected show up? If the basic assumptions, constraints, and limitations of the study or experiment, *as it was designed and conducted,* are reevaluated objectively, overgeneralization and extrapolation beyond justifiable bounds can be avoided. Furthermore, this exercise may show that more or different kinds of data are needed before meaningful new insights or recommendations for action can be presented with assurance.

1.2.7 Step 7: Application

Once step 6 has been taken successfully, the findings can be applied to the real world *in the context originally stated and circumscribed.* Modifications to any aspect of the concept, design, analysis, and interpretation must be adequately justified.

1.3 OBSERVATIONAL STUDIES

Observational is the term applied to studies in which the population universe is undefined, the sampling universe is restricted or undefined, and the data base consists of sample observations in the form of counts, measurements, or some qualitative attribute such as present or absent. The observations may be taken randomly or systematically, often the latter. They may be restricted to a single place and time or they may cover a range of places and times. Often, observational studies are conducted in some kind of sequence, the times and places of additional samples depending primarily on what already has been observed. Such studies may be purely exploratory, but they can be used to obtain more definitive information about spatial or temporal patterns in fish biology (occurrence, abundance, etc.). Preliminary observational studies can yield information on sample variances, data distributions, and other statistical characteristics associated with a sampling device or sampling unit that will be used in a more intensive study or field experiment. The mensurative experiments described by Hurlbert (1984) are observational studies that involve more-or-less complex field procedures. To contrast such studies with controlled experimentation, Cochran (1983) characterized them in this way: "For one reason or another, . . . the investigator cannot impose on a subject, or withhold from the subject, a procedure or treatment whose effects he desires to discover, or cannot assign subjects at random to different procedures." This description applies to controlled experience studies as well.

Observational studies always involve a high degree of subjectivity in design, conduct, data analysis, and interpretation. Though preliminary or limited in scope, they still should be well planned, carefully conducted, and objectively evaluated. The validity and applicability of the findings depend greatly on how much attention was given to the basic considerations in steps 1 and 2 of the research process. McKinlay (1975) reviewed the role of observational studies, the biases that arise in design and analysis, and appropriate analysis and interpretation. The text by Cochran (1983) treats these aspects in greater detail, and provides specific guidelines on planning such studies. Different ways of analyzing the various kinds of data obtained in exploratory studies were described in an innovative way by Tukey (1977). Because nonparametric methods generally work well for observational studies, the book by Conover (1980) is a helpful reference.

Some examples of observational studies will help to demonstrate their purpose and limitations.

Case 1. Information is desired on the natural diet of a fish species. Sample collections of this fish are made at 10 locations in a stream where the species is reported to be relatively abundant. The procedure used is electrofishing. Examinations are made of the stomach contents of the specimens recovered, and the findings are recorded by taxon and other useful categories. The data are summarized by percentage of fish containing the various categories of food, and these data are ordinated to show relative preference.

This is useful information, but how well the stream sampled represents all streams inhabited by this species, even in the same area, is undetermined. The places selected for sampling may or may not be representative of feeding sites in that stream; the timing of the collections may or may not give an accurate picture of what this species feeds on daily and throughout the year; and the method of sampling itself may be biased with respect to the age- and size-classes of fish recovered, which also are indeterminate. Obviously, interpretations of data from restricted exploratory studies such as this must be very limited.

Increasing the spatial and temporal allocation of sampling effort will provide more representative data, but this still has limits. There always is uncertainty about representativeness. Moreover, the nature and degree of bias from the method used for sampling must be judged subjectively. Errors in interpretation from this cause may be reduced if two or more methods of sampling are used concurrently (Green 1979).

Despite these limitations, some design strategies, such as stratification of sample collections within and among places or selective timing of samples, can be used to provide more definitive information in observational studies. Further, when there is a large, structured data base that involves a series of samples of fish and a variable such as food consumed, principal components analysis or cluster analysis may be used advantageously to discern some pattern of preference, occurrence, or association (Green 1979; Pielou 1984). Plant ecologists often sample one or more areas by quadrats (a sample space) and record species by number present or simply as present or absent in each quadrat. In case 1, each fish examined is analogous to a "quadrat."

Case 2. The problem is to determine if the abundance of a fish species differs in the upper, middle, and lower reaches of a particular stream. The species prefers pools to other habitats, and it is to be sampled with a suitable device and an appropriate removal procedure. The species' abundance and its standard error are estimated (White et al. 1982; Platts et al. 1983) for one pool chosen at random (or selected to represent a "typical" pool) in each reach (Figure 1.2A). The bounds of the reaches are not explicitly defined, however. The sampling is conducted in the three pools at similar times of day over a 3-d period. The volume of each pool is measured and the abundance estimates are converted to densities (number of fish per unit volume) to make them comparable among pools.

Pairwise statistical tests are applied to the three density estimates to determine the significance of their differences.[1] Because the samples were taken from only one pool in each reach, any inference from the statistical tests applies only to

---

[1]The z-test is appropriate in this instance; z is calculated as the difference between a pair of estimated densities ($\hat{N}$) divided by the square root of the sum of their estimated variances:

$$z = \frac{\hat{N}_1 - \hat{N}_2}{\sqrt{\hat{v}ar(\hat{N}_1) + \hat{v}ar(\hat{N}_2)}} .$$

This calculated value then is compared with a critical value of z such as 1.96 (the 0.95 probability level). If the calculated z is equal to or greater than 1.96, the difference between the two estimated densities is said to be significant; that is, the probability of a type I error is 0.05 or less. Use of the z-statistic is reasonable because the maximum-likelihood estimator recommended for removal sampling estimates (White et al. 1982) has an approximately normal distribution for large sample sizes. Also, 1.96 is the appropriate value for calculating the 95% confidence intervals for two or more estimates of population size when overlap of those intervals is of interest.

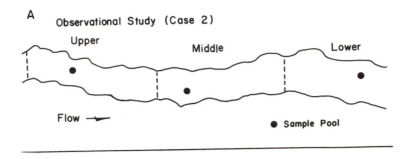

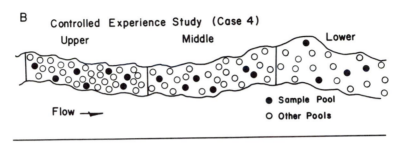

Figure 1.2 Study layouts for a comparison of abundance of a particular species of fish in the upper, middle, and lower reaches of a stream (cases 2 and 4).

these particular pools. There is no measure of the variability in fish density among the pools within each reach and thus no basis for determining if there is a significant difference in density among reaches. Moreover, the sampling was carried out only at one time, so no inference can be made about temporal variability in abundance or density.

Pools are the sampling units for the reaches, and sample estimates from two or more pools per reach are needed for a valid test of the significance of differences in fish abundance among reaches. A sample size greater than two pools per reach probably is needed for an adequate test of significance. Increasing the sample size will reduce the probabilities of type I and type II errors, but the true accuracy and precision of the abundance estimates remain uncertain because the bounds of the reaches are not defined explicitly and the number of pools in each reach is not known. Moreover, if the number of pools sampled in each reach is the same, the sampling of reaches will be disproportionate unless the total number of pools in each reach is the same. This unequal intensity of sampling will affect the precision of estimates of mean abundance per reach, and may introduce a serious but undetected bias into the statistical analysis.

As with case 1, this study could be expanded to other streams and times of the year to provide more information on spatial patterns and temporal changes in the species' abundance. Whatever the space and time dimensions, it is essential that the sampling design be consistent with the particular hypothesis or question posed. Randomization at the basic sampling level (individual pools, in this case) is desirable because it reduces potential bias. However, when the universe of interest is spatially limited and sample size is small, samples taken randomly may not be truly representative, and interspersion or systematic selection of samples may provide a more accurate estimate.

Studies of abundance, even of single species, do not always require quantitative data. Sample observations may be recorded as present–absent, rather than as actual counts. This will be particularly efficient when the cost in time and effort of making the counts is high relative to that of obtaining the samples, as it is with sampling fish food organisms. Because larger sample sizes almost always are needed, the time saved in recording simple presence and absence can be spent in taking more samples. When sample sizes are large, these data can be as sensitive a measure of abundance as actual counts, and they may be even more robust with respect to the errors and biases of sampling (Green 1979). The analysis of such binary data was described in detail by Cox (1970).

Case 3. Information is needed on the relative abundance and possible associations of seven species of fish in upper-elevation lakes of a national park in the Sierra Nevada of California. The elevation stratum is defined as 1,900 m and higher. Five "representative" lakes are chosen for study. Samples are taken by a device and procedure considered to have low capture biases for the seven species. All sampling is carried out in late July, when the species' movement patterns and habitat preferences are judged to have stabilized. Each lake is sampled in a single day; the sequence is random. Two sets of samples are taken on the given day, one in the early morning and the other in the evening, and the data from these are pooled. Spatially, the samples are taken in three horizontal surface zones measured from the shoreline (<30 m, 30–100 m, and >100 m) and three depths (<3 m, 3–10 m, and >10 m) at six randomly selected locations in each lake. At each location, four sample collections are taken in each surface zone–depth stratum allowable. Presence–absence data for each species are recorded for each sample catch.

These data are summarized for each lake by location, surface zone, and depth stratum. The time factor is fixed by the date and pooling of the data from the morning and evening sample catches. The data are summarized for each species as percentage presence in the respective zone–depth sample lots. Percentages must be used, rather than frequencies, because the number of depth strata sampled differs among and within the three surface zones of the different locations in the five lakes (nearshore areas lack deeper strata).

This is a structured observational study. Some representation in the specified universe, lakes at elevations 1,900 m and higher in a particular national park, is assured by the choice of five lakes in that physical location and, to a finer degree, by the spatial allocation of sampling in those lakes. Temporal differences or changes in abundance of the seven species are not addressed by the study design. Though the study is limited in scope and relatively simple in structure, the data set obtained is somewhat complex. Typically, the study concept and design contain many elements of subjectivity combined with some consideration of sampling principles. Analysis and interpretation of the data, therefore, are not simple.

With these kinds of data sets, it is always helpful to first display them graphically. In this case, the average percentage occurrence of each fish species can be plotted by surface zone and depth stratum for each lake in two- or three-dimensional diagrams. Some ingenuity usually is required for this, but reference to Lewis and Taylor (1967), Tukey (1977), and numerous computerized plotting programs that are available may help. For preliminary analysis, simple comparisons can be made by a nonparametric technique (e.g., the Kruskal–Wallis test) that ranks average percentage occurrences for the seven species of fish by lake, by surface zone, and by depth stratum.

A more comprehensive analysis can be made by ANOVA after percentage occurrences are transformed to arcsine values. The data of this study represent a mixed classification in that surface zones and depth strata are nested within lakes and are confounded (Watt 1968). The design is further complicated because the variation among the five lakes is a random effect (if the lakes were chosen at random from those available) and the variation due to location within these lakes is random, but the particular surface zones and depth strata specified must be considered to have fixed effects. The appropriate models and forms of ANOVA for this and similarly complex data sets are given in numerous texts (e.g., Huitson 1971; Sokal and Rohlf 1981). Watt (1968) described an analogous data set involving replicate samples of spruce budworm *Choristoneura fumiferana* taken from four quadrants at four crown levels in several trees, and gave the specific model and details of computation for the ANOVA.

Multivariate analyses by principal components or cluster analysis can also be applied to this and similar data sets to provide some insight into the natural groupings or association of species within the defined universe. Details of the applicable forms of analysis were given by Marriott (1974), Green (1979), Pielou (1984), and Romesburg (1984). Rahel (1984) described the application of ordination techniques to a study of factors determining the structure of fish assemblages along a successional gradient in a bog lake.

1.4 CONTROLLED EXPERIENCE STUDIES

In controlled experience studies, the universe of interest or population universe is defined in terms of specific spatial units, the sampling universe is similarly defined, and the relationship between them is known. The set of sample observations thus comprises a known fraction of the larger universe, and sample estimates can be expanded explicitly to population (or community) parameters. As with observational studies, the data may consist of counts, measurements, or one or more qualitative attributes, including presence or absence. The sample observations may be made in a random or systematic manner. However, because sampling principles are adhered to more rigorously in this type of study than in observational studies, and representativeness can be better assured through careful design, random selection of sampling units generally is the rule.

Controlled experience studies differ from observational studies basically in the degree to which variation in the primary variable of interest is controlled or accounted for. Statistically, there is better control of the sampling error. For this reason, and because the relationship between the sampling universe and the universe of interest (the "target population" of Cochran 1983) is known, the confidence limits calculated for the specified dependent variable are more reliable. That is, the nominal probability levels and specified odds are more likely to be realized than those derived from the data of observational studies. Controlled experience studies, therefore, are most applicable (essential, perhaps) when estimates of biomass or production are desired.

Because sampling design is especially critical in controlled experience studies, preliminary sampling of the universe of interest is strongly recommended to provide information on spatial and (if applicable) temporal patterns of abundance of the study species. This information is needed to properly evaluate the potential efficiency of different designs, to decide on a layout for the selected design (e.g., the number and boundaries of sampling strata), and to determine the number of replicates needed to attain the desired precision of estimates. Preliminary sampling also provides an opportunity to check out the performances of sampling devices, the practicalities of different sampling unit sizes, and other operational factors that will affect the accuracy and precision of the estimates.

Guidelines for the development of realistic and reliable sampling designs for fish and other aquatic organisms are spelled out in Green's (1979) "Ten Principles." Other pertinent references on sampling design and data analysis are Elliott (1977), Cochran (1983), and Johnson and Nielsen (1983). The use of multistage sampling designs for estimation of the total number of fish in small streams was described by Hankin (1984).

Watt (1968) made the important point for studies of this sort that the goal of sampling design (and execution) should be to keep the errors in estimates of different variables in balance with each other. As he indicated, there is no justification for spending time, effort, and money to reduce the estimation error to 10% for one variable if the error for another study variable is 50%. Chapman (1967) called such imbalances "the fallacy of misplaced concreteness." Usually, greatest cost is expended to obtain a desired precision in the estimate of the dependent, or primary, variable of interest, such as absolute abundance, food consumption, or a morphological characteristic. The associated or "independent" variables also have to be estimated with adequate precision, however, if their effects on the primary variable are to be detected and quantified.

Whether the intent of the study is to evaluate the effects of certain environmental variables on some property or process or to determine if there is a significant association or functional relationship between a species of fish and these environmental variables, there are five reasons why statistical tests may fail to show any significance (Watt 1968).

(1) The sampling errors for some of the input data may be too large because the design was faulty or the replication was inadequate.

(2) The model may have one or more major structural defects due to faulty assumptions about potential effects or relationships or to erroneous formulation of the model for statistical analysis.

(3) Some factors may not have been measured in the appropriate way; for example, flow rate in a stream may have been measured at a particular instant instead of over an hour or other biologically meaningful time.

(4) Some important factors may not have been measured at all.

(5) Nature is stochastic: a particular range of values for an independent variable does not produce a particular value for the dependent variable but rather a range of values, which results in a frequency distribution of responses.

The chances of accomplishing the objectives of a controlled experience study will be increased greatly if these points are considered carefully in advance and, to the extent possible, if they are tested before a fixed sampling design and a set of procedures are selected (refer to Watt 1968; Green 1979; Cochran 1983).

One major problem always is present in studies such as these: the confounding of variables in both space and time. Almost everyone who has conducted research on biological events, processes, or relationships recognizes that many environmental variables are intercorrelated in ways that cannot be separated by descriptive sampling studies. Apparent correlations in a time sequence are particularly tricky (Southwood 1978; Green 1979). For example, a correlation of fish growth or abundance with water temperature might be demonstrated, but other factors, such as the abundance of food organisms, might undergo concurrent changes, and the interrelations involved undoubtedly vary with the ecological circumstance. Sophisticated methods of time series analysis may help to separate the confounded effects out, but they do not eliminate the problem.

Every aquatic environment has its peculiar spectrum of spatially correlated variables. In streams, for example, width, depth, flow rate, and substrate particle size are mutually correlated. In lakes, distance from shore, depth, substrate characteristics, light, and concentrations of organic matter, dissolved oxygen and other elements are correlated, essentially in a gradient. In estuaries, depth, salinity, and substrate vary together. Under these circumstances, the dependent variable of interest may be associated or correlated with many combinations of environmental variables. This confounding can be alleviated in part by proper sampling design and procedure, and some measure of the joint effects of certain variables can be obtained through such statistical techniques as the analysis of determination described by Mott (1966). Some degree of confounding, and therefore of uncertainty, remains, however.

Some methods of sampling are confounded with environmental variables, and their efficiencies vary under different conditions. For example, the efficiency of seining devices varies with type of substrate, water depth and transparency, and currents or wave action.

Moreover, the spatial distribution, abundance, and age–size structure of a fish population may not be entirely due to the effects of physical and chemical attributes of the aquatic environment. Competition, predation, and other biotic interactions may have important influences (Moyle and Baltz 1985). These factors may have to be accounted for in any model intended to accurately describe or predict species occurrence and abundance.

The confounding problem obviously complicates analysis and interpretation of data from controlled experience studies, or of any data set based on sampling alone. Careful attention to sampling design, method of sampling, and statistical technique (e.g., covariance analysis) will reduce uncertainty, but the interpretation of findings and conclusions always involves much subjective judgment, and should be qualified accordingly.

Controlled manipulation of confounded environmental variables and control of biotic interactions are needed to isolate the effects of these factors on fish. Such manipulations or controls may alter natural interactions, however, and the results of a controlled experiment may not accurately reflect the real-world processes. The findings of a controlled experience study in the natural environment may have to be reconsidered to properly evaluate and interpret the results of the controlled experiment. Controlled experience studies thus are important in two ways: they provide basic information needed to conceive and design controlled experiments, and they provide background for evaluating the relevance of controlled experimental results.

Some examples will illustrate the features and role of controlled experience studies in fisheries research.

Case 4. Suppose, as in case 2, one wishes to determine if the abundance of a fish species differs in the upper, middle, and lower reaches of a stream. Again, this species is assumed to occupy only pools. This time, however, the bounds of the three reaches are first delineated and the number of pools is counted in each reach (it may be helpful also to locate them on a map). Suppose further that there are 35, 29, and 20 pools in the upper, middle, and lower reaches, respectively. From a preliminary snorkeling survey, a 20% sample (of pools) is deemed appropriate for estimates of average density (the direct counts are converted to density values) with a precision of ±10% or better (19:1 odds). Karandinos (1976) and Cochran (1977) provided guidelines and formulas for this calculation. To assure proportionate (equal intensity) sampling in all reaches (now considered strata), seven pools are randomly selected in the upper reach, six pools in the middle reach, and four pools in the lower reach (Figure 1.2B). In each of these pools, three separate counts, or sample estimates, are made by snorkeling. Again, these counts are converted to estimated densities. The sampling is carried out in all pools on three successive days.

This is a stratified random sampling design, with equal intensity of sampling but unequal sample sizes in each stratum. From the estimated density per pool (mean of three counts) as the basic sample statistic, the estimated mean density is calculated for each reach, and an appropriate statistical test of significance is conducted for the null hypothesis of no difference among the reaches. Pairwise comparisons can be made by means of the *t*-test, or a one-way ANOVA and *F*-test can be applied to determine the significance of differences among all three reaches. Analogous nonparametric ranking tests (e.g., the Mann–Whitney and Kruskal–Wallis tests) can be used with these data also. The level of significance (the probability of making a type I error) may be set at $\alpha = 0.05$. Or, in this case, perhaps a higher probability is acceptable. Also, as a learning experience at least, the probability β of making a type II error may be determined. Whatever significance level is involved, the inferences from the statistical tests now properly apply to the reaches, not just to the selected pools as in case 2.

Moreover, confidence bands (with a specified precision and odds) can be calculated for the estimates of each reach, and for the general mean abundance in that portion of the stream delineated by the three reaches.

If biomass estimates are desired, fish must be captured and weighed. Biomasses should be adjusted to weights per unit pool volume before they are compared among reaches.

Controlled experience studies such as this one can be designed to encompass more streams and more sampling times. If they are, the same design, methods, and allocation of sampling effort should be applied to each stream and time combination.

Case 5. The task is to determine the effects of an effluent on the abundance and biomass of rainbow trout in three branches of a particular stream. The effluent is

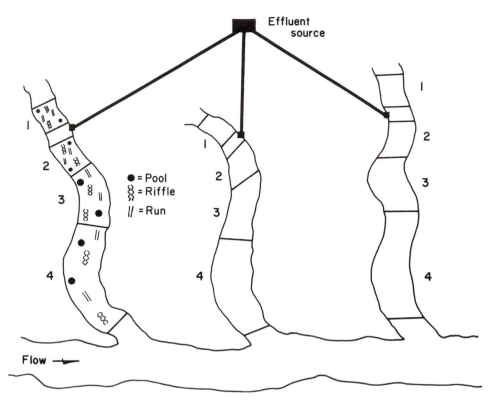

Figure 1.3   Layout of controlled experience study to determine the effects of an effluent on the abundance and biomass of rainbow trout (case 5). Sampling strata are numbered 1–4 in each stream tributary; two pools, two riffles, and two runs are sampled in each stratum.

discharged separately into each branch from pipelines originating at a common source. For this study, four stretches (or strata) are delineated in each branch: one extending from 15 to 150 m above the point of influx, and one each at 15–150 m, 150–300 m, and 300–600 m below the point of influx. Sampling is conducted twice, in mid-May when water levels are high and in mid-August when levels are low, in the evening hours on both occasions. At each time, in order to assure representativeness with respect to riffles, runs, and pools, two each of these habitats are sampled in each stratum of each branch (Figure 1.3). The habitats are selected at random from those present in each stratum of the three branches. Each sample consists of five seine catches, collected by the procedure most appropriate for each of the habitats. The number and total weight of fish caught in five seine hauls are recorded.

In this case, the universe of interest is that portion of each branch of the stream from 150 m above the input of effluent to 600 m below it. The sampling universe comprises the discrete riffles, runs, and pools within this restricted universe, and it is stratified by specified zones relative to the point of effluent influx. The basic sample observation is the individual seine catch but, in this particular situation, the sampling unit is the aggregate catch taken by the five seine hauls in each riffle, run, and pool. With this design, the individual stream segments are the sampling units for purpose of analysis.

From the standpoint of sampling design, the accounted-for sources of variation in the abundance and biomass of rainbow trout are the branches (3), strata (4), habitats (3), times (2), and chance (residual variation). There is another source of variation, of course, the effect of the effluent. In a sense, this is the "treatment." It is the primary interest, but it has not been manipulated or controlled in any way. Only sampling, not experimental, error is involved.

For statistical analysis, the total number and weight of rainbow trout per five-seine catch (the sampling unit) are tabulated for each selected riffle, run, and pool in each stratum of the three stream branches and the two sampling times. There are, then, $2 \times 3 \times 4 \times 3 \times 2 = 144$ values included in the analysis. Typically, this represents a rather complexly structured data base. It is a stratified, nested design with a mixture of fixed and random effects. The branches, strata, and times are fixed effects; the habitats are a random element. For ANOVA purposes, this constitutes a mixed model. Details of the ANOVA appropriate for this and similar cases cannot be spelled out here, but they are given in Watt (1968), Huitson (1971), and other appropriate texts.

Two separate ANOVAs are carried out for the data from this study, one for the abundance data (counts) and the other for the biomass data (weights). Each provides two sorts of information on the effects of the effluent: an assessment of the variation in effluent effect among the branches, strata, habitats, and times; and a comparison between rainbow trout abundance, or biomass, in the absence of the effluent and in its presence (i.e., above and below the points of influx). The appropriate F-tests will determine the overall significance of differences among the respective entities. If a significant difference exists among strata, an appropriate multiple-comparison test will determine if there are significant differences in average abundance and biomass of the fish in the successive strata below the effluent inputs relative to the average abundances and weights in the strata above the points of discharge.

Further information on the effects of the effluent can be obtained. For example, records can be kept of the different size-classes of fish caught above and below the points of influx, and statistical tests can be applied to these data to discern any differences. Water samples taken concurrently with the seine catches can be analyzed for effluent concentration, and the degree to which concentrations are related to fish abundance or biomass can be determined by regression analysis. Possible differences in such regressions between the two sampling times can be assessed also.

1.5 CONTROLLED EXPERIMENTS

The term "experiment" is used here to denote the purposeful manipulation of natural conditions, processes, or relationships, or the imposition of one or more extraneous factors (treatments) on a natural or selected group of subjects. The term is often loosely used, and sometimes abused, in biological research. For example, it often is used in laboratory and field situations when the technique or equipment used is relatively complicated. This is the case particularly when some kind of process is under study. But whether a study involves sampling of deep-sea fish or genotypic screening of hatchery animals, sophisticated or laborious methods do not in themselves justify the term experiment.

The distinctive feature of controlled experiments is, of course, that the experimenter determines where, when, and how treatments will be applied or other variables will be manipulated. Even under field conditions, environmental variables are better controlled or accounted for than in controlled experience studies. The intent of the latter is not to control or manipulate environmental factors, but to obtain accurate and precise estimates of their effects on specified biological features through the process of sampling, and reduction of sampling error is a goal. With controlled experiments, in contrast, attempts are made to simplify situations so that designated variables can be fixed at, or manipulated to, specific levels, and treatments can be applied at selected intensities and times. In this process, other variables are held constant, or their effects are mitigated through randomization or replication of experimental units, or their effects are removed by the design of the experiment or adjustments in the statistical analysis. Here, the goal is to reduce experimental error so that the probability of discerning real differences in environmental and treatment effects (and their interactions) is increased. The response variable involved may be genetic, biochemical, physiological, morphological, behavioral, or ecological in nature.

The precision of an experiment (e.g., the precision of the estimated response difference between two treatments) can be increased by good experimental design, by use of supplementary data, or both. Improved precision can be particularly important in field experiments. The effects that variation in major environmental conditions among experimental units may have on the estimate of treatment effects can be controlled or accounted for, in part, by the design of the experiment. For example, segments of an experimental area can be divided into strata or blocks differing in levels or quality of an environmental factor, and treatments can be allocated at random to experimental units within each subdivision. The effects of variation within experimental units can be accounted for (i.e., removed from the estimate of treatment effects) if additional data relevant to the response criterion are obtained for individuals within the experimental units. For example, the size or weight of fish might affect the response to a treatment, so the average size or weight of fish in the respective experimental units is used as a covariate, and this is included in the statistical procedure called analysis of covariance. This method of analysis is well described in most statistics texts, including those of Cochran and Cox (1964), Snedecor and Cochran (1981), and Hicks (1982). It is applicable, also, to controlled experience and observational studies, if the additional observations or measurements are feasible and warranted (Cochran 1983).

1.5.1   Field Experiments

In field situations, the "control" of environmental variables is only relative. Rarely, if ever, can the physical, chemical, and biotic variables in natural aquatic environments be controlled absolutely. Generally, there are just two options within the designated experimental area (stream, lake, estuary): either subareas might be delimited that have similar values of key environmental variables, or subareas might be manipulated or converted to achieve desired levels of the primary environmental variables.

In the first option (selection of similar subareas), several intensities of a treatment, or two or more different treatments, are applied to the subareas (experimental units) in accordance with some experimental design. The simplest layout is a completely randomized design, whereby the treatments are allocated wholly at random to the experimental units and each treatment has the same number of replicates. The randomization of treatments takes care of any possible selection bias. However, if the number of subareas available is limited (allowing only two replicates per treatment, say), the effects of differences in subarea characteristics on treatment response may not "average out," and a hidden bias may occur. The rule for completely randomized field experiments is to have as many replicates as possible—at least three, in any case. When a gradient in subarea character is evident or suspected, a systematic interspersion of the treatments is advisable. This will better assure representativeness of the experimental area for all treatments and reduce the chances of inadvertent bias. In this case, only the treatment starting the sequence is selected randomly (the random-start compromise). The advantages and disadvantages of random and systematic placement of experimental units in ecological field experiments were described by Hurlbert (1984).

Given the natural variation in environmental factors, a randomized block design generally reduces the experimental error, and thus provides a more precise measure of treatment effects than a completely randomized design. The experimental area is divided into "blocks," and the treatments are allocated independently and randomly to experimental units in each block. These blocks presumably represent true replicates. This rarely is the case, but the effects of variation in block characteristics can be accounted for and removed from experimental error during the statistical analysis of the data. If distinctive types of subarea occur in the experimental area, and one wishes to determine the effects of treatment under these different conditions, the subareas can be grouped and considered as strata. For example, shoreline zones of a lake may be defined by substrate types such as mud, sand, gravel, and rock, or a stream may be stratified by pool, riffle, and run. In such cases, the treatments are randomized and replicated in each stratum. The number of replicates per treatment should be the same within a stratum; it is desirable, but not required, that the number of treatment replicates in all strata be equal. This is a variant of the randomized block design used when the strata (blocks) are known to differ and thus are not true replicates. The interpretation of "block" effects and uses of "blocking" in experimental design are discussed in many statistics texts.

In the second option (manipulation of subareas), the alteration of environmental variables may be considered "treatments." Alternatively, a real treatment can be added and both it and the environmental manipulation can be evaluated with respect to some criterion of fish response. Both completely randomized and randomized block designs are applicable. Systematic interspersion of treatments usually is not needed because any gradient in environmental conditions has been altered or interrupted. A stratified block design may provide more information in this instance. For these designs, the same rules for randomization and replication apply.

Factorial and split-plot experiments sometimes are feasible in field situations. They are especially efficient when several levels of two or more treatments are to be tested. For a factorial experiment, an appropriate number of homogeneous subareas, or experimental units, must be established for the number of treatment combinations involved such that each experimental unit receives a different treatment combination. For example, one may wish to test the effects of two treatments, A and B, each at three intensities (or times). This would be a simple 2×3 factorial design requiring 6 experimental units, to which the following treatment combinations would be applied at random: A1, A2, A3, B1, B2, B3. A larger number of treatment combinations can be included in a factorial experiment, but this quickly becomes unwieldy for field conditions (3×3, 4×4, and $2 \times 3 \times 4$ factorial arrangements require 9, 16, and 24 experimental units, respectively). The "treatments" may be such things as selected species or age-classes of fish or environmental factors manipulated to specified levels as well as actual treatments, and any factorial setup can be replicated in space or time. Indeed, replication may be needed to assure a minimum of 10 degrees of freedom for a reliable estimate of the experimental error component of an ANOVA, as is generally recommended (Cochran and Cox 1964; Hicks 1982). An example of a replicated factorial field experiment is given later as case 6.

Split-plot experiments involve a type of factorial design in which two kinds of treatment are applied simultaneously but, for one reason or another, they do not require the same amount of space or are not of equal importance. Experimental units are of two sizes: the larger "major units," to which the treatment series of lesser importance is allocated; and, within each of these, a set of "minor units," to which the treatment of greater importance is allocated. For example, suppose, as described above, treatments A and B each are to be applied at three intensities, but this time they fit the conditions for a split-plot experiment. That is, treatment A can be applied most conveniently to a larger, major unit, and treatment B (in which there is more interest) can be better applied to the smaller, minor unit. For a single replicate, therefore, there are just three major experimental units, to which the three levels of treatment A are applied at random. Within each major unit are three minor units, to which the three levels of treatment B are applied. The "treatments" of a split-plot experiment also may be any combination of fish categories, environmental conditions, and actual treatments. Split-plot experiments require sufficient replication to assure at least 10 degrees of freedom for reliable estimation of the minor plot error component of an ANOVA (Cochran and Cox 1964; Hicks 1982). A split-plot alternative to a simple factorial design is described later as case 7.

If sampling is employed to obtain the basic data, the particular features of the foregoing experimental designs, and the forms of analysis applicable to them, are not altered by the method of sampling used. However, the magnitude of sampling error buried in the estimated experimental error will vary with the method used, and thus will affect the precision and efficiency of the experiment.

Because of their complexity and variability, aquatic environments do not lend themselves generally to complicated experimental designs. A good rule is to keep designs as simple as possible, with ample replication. But however simple the experimental design and however careful the execution, there will be problems in sifting out the effects of interrelated environmental factors, including biotic interactions, and in interpreting results. Hurlbert (1984) discussed the various kinds of problems that arise in ecological field experiments generally, and gave insightful suggestions on how to prevent or reduce these "sources of confusion" (Table 1.1).

Table 1.1 Potential sources of confusion in an experiment and means of minimizing their effects. (From Hurlbert 1984; reprinted with permission of the Ecological Society of America.)

Source of confusion	Features of an experimental design that reduce or eliminate confusion
Temporal change	Control treatments[a]
Procedure effects	Control treatments[a]
Experimenter bias	Randomized assignment of experimental units to treatments Randomization in conduct of other procedures "Blind" procedures[b]
Experimenter-generated variability (random error)	Replication of treatments
Initial or inherent variability among experimental units	Replication of treatments Interspersion of treatments Concomitant observations
Nondemonic intrusion[c]	Replication of treatments Interspersion of treatments
Demonic intrusion[d]	Eternal vigilance, exorcism, etc.

[a] Any treatment against which one or more other treatments is compared; usually, this is a "no treatment" condition or a procedural "standard" treatment.

[b] Usually employed only where measurement involves a large subjective element.

[c] The impingement of chance events on an experiment in progress.

[d] The occurrence of intentionally disruptive or malevolent changes in an experiment perpetrated by other persons or beings.

1.5.2 Laboratory Experiments

In the laboratory or laboratory-like settings, conditions are greatly simplified. Sometimes all variables can be fixed except the treatment. Such a procedure is appropriate for a bioassay designed to estimate or compare the potencies of contaminants or toxicants. It is very limiting to keep all things constant except the treatment, however, and other designs can be more informative. For example, the rate at which a presumably toxic chemical accumulates in a fish species can be determined by placing a specified number of fish in tanks of identical size and construction containing water drawn from a common source and held at a given temperature. A low concentration of the chemical is introduced into all tanks at the same time, and the fish are removed from randomly designated tanks after specified times of exposure and analyzed for uptake of the chemical. This may suit a particular purpose, but a more informative experiment could be conducted if the experimental design were altered to encompass different initial concentrations, two or more species of fish, several water temperatures, or other variables.

In all controlled experiments, the *accuracy* with which the response to a treatment can be estimated is determined largely by the exactness of the treatments applied, the type of equipment and procedure used, and the exactness and resolution of the method of measurement or analysis employed. These factors come under the heading of procedure effects (Table 1.1). Accuracy is also affected by experimenter bias (Table 1.1) such as a systematic difference in performance between two or more persons involved in the experiment. As indicated, random assignment of experimental units and procedural elements and use of "blind" procedures will ameliorate this source of bias. The *precision* of an experiment is affected by the consistency of application of procedures (experimenter-generated variability) and any initial or inherent variability among experimental units (Table 1.1). Replication reduces these effects. All of these factors operate, and are potentially important, in both field and laboratory experiments, but can be much better controlled in a laboratory setting. Moreover, laboratory situations generally allow more latitude to select experimental designs that enhance both precision and efficiency. The frequency and severity of disruptions by nondemonic and demonic intrusions (Table 1.1) also are diminished in laboratory experiments.

Examples of controlled experiments in field and laboratory settings are described below.

Case 6. Several small reservoirs, soon to be restocked with game fish for recreational management, have excessively high populations of competitive nongame species. A particular toxicant is being considered to eliminate or reduce the abundance of these "nuisance" fishes. It has been used successfully elsewhere, but dosage levels have varied and the aquatic environments involved have differed considerably. More definitive information is needed on the concentration required to eliminate the major species, at least, from the reservoirs (the universe of interest). It is decided to conduct a field experiment, one comprehensive enough to include several species and size-classes of the nongame fishes, a range of toxicant dosages, and replication.

For the experiment, the three most abundant species are chosen and two size-classes are specified for each. Three concentrations of the toxicant are selected. One approximates the median dosage reported as "successful" (not necessarily 100% effective), one is half that concentration, and the other is twice that concentration. These specifications indicate that a factorial experiment in a randomized block design will be most efficient. This will involve $3 \times 2 \times 3 = 18$ experimental units for one replicate of each combination of experimental variables. The aquatic conditions vary somewhat among the reservoirs, but it seems reasonable and more practical to conduct a replicated experiment in one "representative" reservoir, rather than in several reservoirs at the same time. This is a matter of judgment.

Further, because this is a management-oriented experiment, experience suggests that a satisfactory level of performance (of the toxicant) under these conditions should be specified in advance. This is set at 95% mortality. The experiment, then, has two objectives: (1) to determine the relative effectiveness of three concentrations of the toxicant in killing the designated species and size-classes of fish and (2) to determine what concentration equals or exceeds the specified level of satisfactory performance for each target species and size-class.

The experimental layout is as follows. In the chosen reservoir, three rectangular rafts are anchored at three locations where water depth approximates 3 m. Each raft is 30 m long. Nine polyethylene enclosures, extending from slightly above the water surface to the bottom, are attached to each side of the three rafts (Figure 1.4). Each enclosure is 3 m in diameter. The plastic permits exchange of gases and maintains the ambient water temperature. It is expected that each enclosure contains a normal complement of indigenous food organisms, sufficient for the short period of the experiment. There are, then, 18 enclosures (experimental units) for each of the three rafts (blocks).

One hundred fish of one species and size-class are placed in each enclosure. Each of the six combinations of three species and two size-classes are placed in

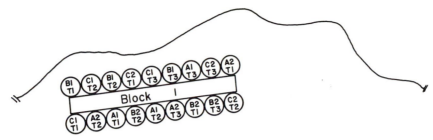

A, B, C = Fish Species
I, 2 = Size Classes
TI, T2, T3 = Toxicant Concentrations

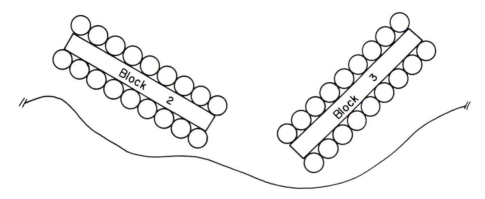

Figure 1.4 Layout of factorial field experiment to (a) determine the relative effectiveness of three concentrations of a toxicant in killing two size-classes of three species of fish and (b) compare the performance of these toxicant concentrations with a specified level of satisfactory performance for the respective species–size-class targets (case 6).

three of the 18 enclosures in each block. Enclosures are allocated independently and randomly to the combinations for each block. The toxicant is then introduced into the enclosures in appropriate amounts to obtain the specific concentrations. Each of the three concentrations is allocated randomly to each of the six combinations of species and size-class. For each block of treatments, then, there are 18 unique combinations of species, size-class, and toxicant concentration (Figure 1.4).

The time period of the experiment is 3 d. The number of fish that die in each enclosure during this time span is recorded.

Two analyses will be conducted to serve the two objectives of the experiment. The first will be an ANOVA. The form of analysis (four-way ANOVA) is well described in all texts on experimental design (e.g., Cochran and Cox 1964; Little and Hills 1978; Hicks 1982). For this analysis, transformation of the number of fish killed per experimental unit (enclosure) to arcsine values may be desirable. The raw counts actually constitute percentages (of the 100-fish lots), and the range of observed mortalities probably will exceed 30–70%, the range beyond which this transformation generally is considered necessary (Sokal and Rohlf 1981). Interest basically is in the average effectiveness of, and in the significance of differences in effectiveness between, the three toxicant concentrations applied to the target species and size-classes. However, possible inconsistencies in effectiveness with respect to the six groups of species and size-class should be examined as well. In ANOVA terms, such inconsistencies are assessed via the interactions of concentration × species and concentration × size-class. In this instance, there are sufficient degrees of freedom (df) available (total df = 54 − 1 = 53) to assess the significance of these interactions and still leave an adequate number to estimate the residual variation, or experimental error. Given the importance of this experiment and the investment of resources required to carry it out, a probability level (for the type I error) of $\alpha = 0.05$ is specified for all tests of significance.

For the second objective, one need only calculate confidence intervals for the mean mortality values of the six groups of species and size-classes and determine which of these equal or exceed the specified level of satisfactory performance, 95% mortality, with given odds. Odds of 19:1 (0.95 probability) are reasonable in this case. The comparison is in just one direction—mortality values less than the 95% standard are not being considered here—so the one-way value of t for $P = 0.05$ should be used to calculate the confidence intervals.

Case 7. Suppose some knowledge of zinc uptake in rainbow trout has been gained from field observations and a limited laboratory experiment involving several concentrations and a fixed time interval. More explicit information now is needed on the rate of zinc accumulation in this and another species, brown trout, particularly in relation to water temperature. It is decided that a controlled laboratory experiment is needed to achieve this objective. Three concentrations of zinc are selected within the range of concern. Three exposure durations are specified, 3, 9, and 27 d (a simple logarithmic increase in exposure time), and two water temperatures are chosen, perhaps to represent the "optimum" temperatures (which differ considerably) for the respective species of trout. These choices are, of course, a matter of individual judgment.

With these specifications, the complete set of experimental combinations is $2 \times 3 \times 3 \times 2 = 36$. A single, completely randomized setup (one replicate of each combination of experimental variables) thus requires 36 experimental units. Several factors now must be considered to determine if additional replication of the treatment combinations is needed. Because this is a laboratory experiment, realism depends on the choice of experimental conditions, and "replication" to account for natural variation in environmental conditions, as in the field, is not needed. Actually, replication is incorporated in every factorial experiment, the arrangement called for here, through the combinations of experimental variables. Here, each of the two trout species is subjected to 18 treatments, each concentration of zinc is applied 12 times, each exposure time is used 12 times, and each water temperature is maintained in 18 experimental units. Moreover, for ANOVA purposes, the total degrees of freedom available in the single complete setup is 36 − 1 = 35, and this allows 16 df for the estimate of experimental error after the direct effects of species, concentration, exposure time, and water temperature, as well as all first-order (two-way) interactions between these variables, have been accounted for. This should be adequate for the tests of significance. One complete factorial arrangement of 36 experimental units thus seems to be sufficient.

The experimental unit is a tank. All tanks are of the same size and construction, all are supplied with water from the same source, and all are maintained under the same laboratory conditions (light, etc.) except for water temperature.

Ten fish are placed in each tank; 18 tanks receive rainbow trout and 18 receive brown trout. The same size-class is used for both species. A standard diet is fed to each.

The zinc is introduced into the tanks in appropriate amounts at the start to obtain the specified concentrations. The two water temperatures are maintained throughout the experiment by proper equipment and procedure. Exposure times are controlled by removing the fish from designated tanks at specified times. Allocation of the 36 individual experimental combinations to tanks is made at random. After the treated fish are removed from the tanks at the successive times, zinc accumulation is determined by analysis of the appropriate tissues and recorded as milligrams of zinc per gram of tissue.

An ANOVA is conducted to determine the significance of differences in zinc accumulation between the two species of trout due to concentration, exposure time, and water temperature, and the significance of the first-order interactions. A significance level of $\alpha = 0.05$ seems reasonable for the associated F-tests. Again, reference is made to Cochran and Cox (1964), Hicks (1982), or other suitable text for details of the appropriate ANOVA and tests of significance.

The data from this experiment can be displayed graphically to show the trends in zinc accumulation over time of exposure for the two species of fish, the three concentrations, or two water temperatures. Three-dimensional graphs can be prepared with combinations of any two of these variables plotted against exposure time. Statistical analysis of these time trends can be attempted, but it is not likely to prove useful because of the wide variance in average values of the respective variables (due to differences in their experimentally fixed effects as well as to residual variation), difficulties in determining the appropriate model and form of analysis, and consequent constraints on interpretation.

For this experiment, an alternative to the factorial design might be considered. Rather than using 36 tanks for the individual experimental combinations, one could use just 12 (probably larger) tanks. These tanks, each containing 30 fish, would be allocated at random to the 12 combinations of species (2), zinc concentration (3), and water temperature (2). At each of the three specified times, 10 fish would be removed from each tank for analysis of zinc accumulation. This modified setup constitutes a split-plot design. The 12 tanks with the 12 combinations of species, concentration, and water temperature are the major units. The three time exposures effected by removal of a subset of fish from each tank at the specified times represent the minor units.

This design modification requires a somewhat different form of ANOVA, in which the sensitivity of the F-test for detecting differences and interactions among the experimental variables assigned to the major units is greatly reduced. This is due to the reduced number of experimental (major) units, which reduces the degrees of freedom available to estimate the residual variation or experimental error among these units. The sensitivity of significance tests for the minor unit variable, exposure time, and its interactions with the other variables remains about the same. This change in the sensitivity of the analysis with respect to species, concentration, and water temperature may or may not be acceptable.

However, it turns out that another replication of this split-plot setup (giving 24 tanks) adds enough degrees of freedom that experimental error at the major-unit level can be estimated about as well as with the factorial design involving 36 tanks. Moreover, this addition of a replicate more than doubles the degrees of freedom for the estimate of experimental error at the minor-unit level, and thus increases the sensitivity of the analysis with respect to exposure time.

In deciding which is the best design, practical considerations of space, equipment, procedural details, and so on must be balanced against the statistical factors involved. The choice should not be arbitrary. Every situation is more or less unique and the experimenter is best able to weigh the trade-offs among alternative designs.

1.6 CONCLUSION

Research is a complicated process. Flaws at any stage in the process result in flaws in the product. Of course, flawlessness in the sense of *certainty* in either process or product is unattainable. The subjective nature of the choices and decisions that must be made at every step guarantees this. There is no generally accepted standard for quality of research or for productivity or efficiency. What then is our guideline? Manuals on research methods assure us that adherence to principles of scientific method, principles of statistical inference and decision making, principles of sampling, principles of experimental design, principles of this or that will produce better (more credible?) results. This is good advice as far as it goes. Those of us doing research in fish biology certainly believe that such principles are the basic foundation of our work. But they fall short in the day-to-day process of carrying out a research mission in two regards: (1) it usually is not clear just how these principles translate into specific actions that must be taken to resolve the immediate problem; and (2) we all work from different bases of knowledge and experience, and we differ in our understanding of, and our ability to apply, these principles. Thus, the bridge to *our* reality is very tenuous.

Barnett (1973) referred in a humorous way to the *principle of minimum stupidity* in discussing the "mathematics of philosophy." He used it as an example of the need to define a concept (such as stupidity) explicitly in order to support a related principle. We think this is perhaps the best or most realistic principle that we can suggest. It can be applied to the research process if we define "stupidity" as ignorance of the basic principles of scientific research or as failure to follow the complete sequence of the research process as described in this chapter. In this regard, there is no substitute for experience.

1.7 REFERENCES

Barnett, V. 1973. Comparative statistical inference. Wiley, New York.
Capen, D. E., editor. 1981. The use of multivariate statistics in studies of wildlife habitat. U.S. Forest Service General Technical Report RM-87.
Chapman, D. W. 1967. Production in fish populations. Pages 3–29 in S. D. Gerking, editor. The biological basis of freshwater fish production. Blackwell Scientific Publications, Oxford, England.
Cochran, W. G. 1977. Sampling techniques, 3rd edition. Wiley, New York.
Cochran, W. G. 1983. Planning and analysis of observational studies. Wiley, New York.
Cochran, W. G., and G. M. Cox. 1964. Experimental designs. Wiley, New York.

Conover, W. J. 1980. Practical nonparametric statistics, 2nd edition. Wiley, New York.

Cox, D. R. 1958. Planning of experiments. Wiley, New York.

Cox, D. R. 1970. The analysis of binary data. Methuen, London.

Davies, W. D., and W. L. Shelton. 1983. Sampling with toxicants. Pages 199–213 in L. A. Nielsen and D. L. Johnson, editors. Fisheries techniques. American Fisheries Society, Bethesda, Maryland.

Elliott, J. M. 1977. Some methods for the statistical analysis of samples of benthic invertebrates. Freshwater Biological Association Scientific Publication 25, 2nd edition.

Gauch, H. G. 1982. Multivariate analysis in community ecology. Cambridge University Press, New York.

Green, R. H. 1979. Sampling design and statistical methods for environmental biologists. Wiley, New York.

Hankin, D. G. 1984. Multistage sampling designs in fisheries research: applications in small streams. Canadian Journal of Fisheries and Aquatic Sciences 41:1575–1591.

Hayes, M. L. 1983. Active fish capture methods. Pages 123–145 in L. A. Nielsen and D. L. Johnson, editors. Fisheries techniques. American Fisheries Society, Bethesda, Maryland.

Hicks, C. R. 1982. Fundamental concepts in the design of experiments. Holt, Rinehart, and Winston, New York.

Hollander, M., and D. A. Wolfe. 1973. Nonparametric statistical methods. Wiley, New York.

Holling, C. S., editor. 1978. Adaptive environmental assessment and management. Wiley, New York.

Hubert, W. A. 1983. Passive capture techniques. Pages 95–111 in L. A. Nielsen and D. L. Johnson, editors. Fisheries techniques. American Fisheries Society, Bethesda, Maryland.

Huitson, A. 1971. The analysis of variance—a basic course. Griffin, London.

Hurlbert, S. H. 1984. Pseudoreplication and the design of ecological field experiments. Ecological Monographs 54:187–211.

John, J. A., and M. H. Quenouille. 1977. Experiments: design and analysis, 2nd edition. Macmillan, New York.

Johnson, D. L., and L. A. Nielsen. 1983. Sampling considerations. Pages 1–21 in L. A. Nielsen and D. L. Johnson, editors. Fisheries techniques. American Fisheries Society, Bethesda, Maryland.

Jones, D. 1984. Use, misuse, and role of multiple-comparison procedures in ecological and agricultural entomology. Environmental Entomology 13:635–649.

Karandinos, M. G. 1976. Optimum sample size and comments on some published formulae. Bulletin of the Entomological Society of America 22:417–421.

Lewis, T., and L. R. Taylor. 1967. Introduction to experimental ecology. Academic Press, New York.

Little, T. M., and F. J. Hills. 1978. Agricultural experimentation: design and analysis. Wiley, New York.

Marriott, F. H. C. 1974. The interpretation of multiple observations. Academic Press, New York.

McKinlay, S. M. 1975. The design and analysis of the observational study—a review. Journal of the American Statistical Association 70:503–520.

Mize, C. W., and R. C. Schultz. 1985. Comparing treatment means correctly and appropriately. Canadian Journal of Forest Research 15:1142–1148.

Mosteller, F., and R. E. K. Rourke. 1973. Sturdy statistics: nonparametric and order statistics. Addison-Wesley, Reading, Massachusetts.

Mott, D. G. 1966. The analysis of determination in population systems. Pages 179–194 in K. E. F. Watt, editor. Systems analysis in ecology. Academic Press, New York.

Moyle, P. B., and D. M. Baltz. 1985. Microhabitat use by an assemblage of California stream fishes: developing criteria for instream flow determinations. Transactions of the American Fisheries Society 114:695–704.

Pielou, E. C. 1984. The interpretation of ecological data—a primer on classification and ordination. Wiley, New York.

Platt, J. R. 1964. Strong inference. Science (Washington, D.C.) 146:347–353.

Platts, W. S., W. F. Megahan, and G. W. Minshall. 1983. Methods for evaluating stream, riparian, and biotic conditions. U.S. Forest Service General Technical Report INT-138.

Rahel, F. J. 1984. Factors structuring fish assemblages along a bog lake successional gradient. Ecology 65:1276–1289.

Reynolds, J. B. 1983. Electrofishing. Pages 147–163 in L. A. Nielsen and D. L. Johnson, editors. Fisheries techniques. American Fisheries Society, Bethesda, Maryland.

Romesburg, H. C. 1984. Cluster analysis for researchers. Lifetime Learning Publications, Belmont, California.

Sneath, P. H. A., and R. R. Sokal. 1973. Numerical taxonomy: the principles and practice of numerical classification. Freeman, San Francisco.

Snedecor, G. W., and W. G. Cochran. 1981. Statistical methods, 7th edition. Iowa State University Press, Ames.

Sokal, R. R., and F. J. Rohlf. 1981. Biometry, 2nd edition. Freeman, San Francisco.

Southwood, T. R. E. 1978. Ecological methods, 2nd edition. Chapman and Hall, London.

Stuart, A. 1976. Basic ideas of scientific sampling, 2nd edition. Hafner, New York.

Tukey, J. W. 1977. Exploratory data analysis. Addison-Wesley, Reading, Massachusetts.

Watt, K. E. F. 1968. Ecology and resource management. McGraw-Hill, New York.

White, G. C., D. R. Anderson, K. P. Burnham, and D. L. Otis. 1982. Capture–recapture and removal methods for sampling closed populations. Los Alamos National Laboratory, LA-8787-NERP, Los Alamos, New Mexico.

Wilm, H. G. 1952. A pattern of scientific inquiry for applied research. Journal of Forestry 50:120–125.

Wydoski, R., and L. Emery. 1983. Tagging and marking. Pages 215–237 in L. A. Nielsen and D. L. Johnson, editors. Fisheries techniques. American Fisheries Society, Bethesda, Maryland.

Chapter 2

Genetics

FRED W. ALLENDORF AND MOIRA M. FERGUSON

2.1 INTRODUCTION

Children look like their parents, only different. This is the essence of genetics. How are morphological, behavioral, and physiological characteristics transmitted from generation to generation? The science of genetics began with the experiments of an Austrian monk who studied how seven morphological differences in the garden pea are inherited. The principles described by Gregor Mendel have proven to be universal in plants and animals and still stand as the foundation of modern genetics.

2.1.1 Genetic Variability

Genetics has been defined as the study of differences among individuals (Sturtevant and Beadle 1939). If all the individuals in a particular species were identical, we could still study their morphology, physiology, ecology, etc. However, geneticists would be out of work. The study of inheritance depends upon finding individual differences so that the similarity of parents and their offspring can be compared relative to the similarity among unrelated individuals.

Genetic variability can be thought of as existing at two levels: (1) genetic differences between individuals within local populations, and (2) genetic differences between local populations within the same species. The first level is investigated by traditional Mendelian genetics. However, the study of how individual variability becomes transformed into differences between populations is fundamental to the study of evolution. In this chapter, we are concerned with the study of both inheritance and evolutionary genetics as they relate to an understanding of the biology of fish populations.

2.1.2 Objectives of This Chapter

An understanding of the principles of genetics is important for many aspects of fisheries science. Genetics is, of course, fundamental to fish husbandry programs practiced in hatcheries. An understanding of the genetic bases of differences in morphology, physiology, and behavior is also essential to fisheries biology. Genetic analysis of population structure is critical for proper management of mixed-stock fisheries. In addition, the taxonomic classification and systematic investigation of fish species requires knowledge of the amount of genetic divergence among populations and species.

The central objective of this chapter is to introduce the reader to the essential principles of modern genetics that are important for fisheries biologists. We present a description of the molecular basis of heredity and the inheritance of traits controlled by single genes and multiple genes. Such a review is especially appropriate because of the recent tremendous advances in our understanding of the molecular basis of inheritance and because even the ''basic'' genetics of many fish species is complicated by a variety of factors such as polyploidy and unisexuality. We also consider the primary evolutionary forces affecting the frequencies of genes in populations.

2.2 MECHANISMS OF INHERITANCE

A ''minirevolution'' has radically changed our view of the organization of eukaryotic genes in the last 10 years. Many fisheries biologists educated prior to this period were not even introduced to the now established concepts of ''split genes'' or ''jumping genes'' (Gilbert 1985). Our treatment in this section of the molecular basis of genetics is necessarily brief, but it introduces the principles that underlie genetic applications to a variety of questions in fishery biology.

2.2.1 DNA

Deoxyribonucleic acid (DNA), the hereditary material, is a double-stranded molecule. Each strand is composed of a succession of four nitrogenous bases (adenine, guanine, cytosine, and thymine) attached to a deoxyribose sugar, which, in turn, is attached to a phosphate group. The bases of one strand are associated with those of the other by hydrogen bonds such that adenine always pairs with thymine and guanine with cytosine. The DNA molecule looks some-what like a ladder; the rungs are the pairs of nitrogenous bases and the supports are alternating sugar–phosphate molecules.

The DNA within the nucleus of each cell is replicated prior to cell division. The hydrogen bonds between the nitrogenous bases on the two strands are broken and the molecule ''unzips.'' Each parental strand of DNA is used as a template for the synthesis of a daughter strand. For example, a free guanine molecule bonded to sugar and phosphate molecules is matched with a cytosine molecule on the parental strand. The process continues linearly along the parental DNA until a new daughter DNA molecule has been formed. Each of the daughter DNA molecules is composed of a newly synthesized strand bonded to an original parental strand.

2.2.2 Protein Synthesis

Part of the DNA molecule codes for *proteins*. The linear order of nitrogenous bases on the DNA molecule determines the sequence of amino acids that will be joined together to produce the protein molecule (Figure 2.1).

The first step of protein synthesis is *transcription*. At this step, the section of the DNA molecule coding for a particular protein acts as a template for the production of a *messenger ribonucleic acid* (mRNA) molecule. Ribonucleic acid (RNA) is similar in structure to DNA except that it is single-stranded, has ribose instead of deoxyribose sugars, and contains uracil instead of thymine bases. The mRNA molecule is complementary to the original DNA strand: a DNA sequence of guanine–adenine–adenine–thymine results in an mRNA sequence of cytosine–uracil–uracil–adenine. The mRNA molecule is transported from the nucleus to the cytoplasm of the cell and then to an organelle known as a ribosome. Ribosomes are composed of *ribosomal RNA* (rRNA) and protein. Once the mRNA has reached the ribosome, the second stage of protein synthesis, *translation*, takes

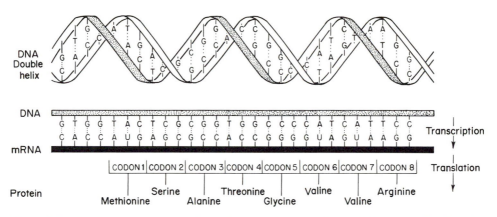

Figure 2.1 Synthesis of proteins through transcription and translation. The DNA molecule unwinds, exposing the section to be transcribed, and a complementary molecule of mRNA (messenger RNA) is synthesized. The mRNA then produces a protein molecule through translation that involves transfer RNA (not shown). Each amino acid (methionine, serine, etc.) is encoded by triplets (codons) of nucleic acid bases; the bases are adenine (A), cytosine (C), guanine (G), thymine (T), and uracil (U).

place. Each sequence of three bases on the mRNA is a *codon*. The linear order of these three bases within the codon determines which type of *transfer RNA* (tRNA) binds to the mRNA. Each type of tRNA molecule is bonded to a specific amino acid and also has an "anticodon" of three bases that is complementary to the order of bases within the codon. The anticodons of the tRNA molecules bind to the mRNA codons one at a time, and the amino acids carried by the tRNA molecules then are joined together to produce the protein molecule.

Differences in the amino acid sequence of specific proteins can be detected by a variety of biochemical methods. Gel *electrophoresis* of enzymes has revolutionized our understanding of genetic variation in natural populations of fish during the last 15 years (Allendorf and Utter 1979). Some of the changes in the DNA sequence coding for a protein are reflected in changes in the amino acid sequence of that protein. Many of these amino acid substitutions affect the mobility of a protein molecule in an electric field by altering the protein's charge, size, or shape. The application of this technique to the study of fish populations is discussed in detail in Chapter 5.

2.2.3 Gene Structure

Recent advances in molecular biology allow the sequence of genes along the DNA molecule to be determined. This research has produced some interesting surprises. Perhaps the biggest surprise is that the DNA code in many eukaryotic genes is broken up by lengths of DNA that appear to be "nonsense." The mRNA molecule is not used in its entirety as a template for translation at the ribosome. Specific sections of the mRNA molecule are systematically removed or excised prior to translation. The remaining sections are joined together to produce the mature mRNA molecule. The DNA sequences that code the excised portions of mRNA are known as intervening sequences or *introns*; the sections of DNA that code the translated protein are called *exons*. The function of introns is not completely understood. There is some evidence that different exons represent different functional domains of the protein molecule. It has been suggested,

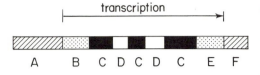

Figure 2.2 Hypothetical eukaryotic gene showing the six major regions: (A) the upstream flanking region, (B) the upstream untranslated region, (C) the protein-coding regions (exons), (D) the intervening regions (introns), (E) the downstream untranslated region, and (F) the downstream flanking region. The arrow shows the section of the gene that is transcribed.

therefore, that the shuffling of exons from two different genes sometimes may produce genes with new functions (Gilbert 1985).

The typical eukaryotic gene consists of six regions (Figure 2.2): (1) a flanking region "upstream" from the protein-coding region that helps to start transcription but is not itself transcribed; (2) an untranslated region upstream from the protein-coding region that is transcribed but is not translated and does not affect the structure of the coded protein; (3) exons; (4) introns (not all genes contain detectable introns); (5) a downstream region that is transcribed but not translated; and (6) a downstream region that is not transcribed. Data from a variety of species indicate that the protein-coding exons are the most evolutionarily conservative of these regions; that is, the exons show the least amount of intraspecific polymorphism and the slowest rate of evolutionary change between species (Li et al. 1985). Thus, the amount of genetic variation or interspecific divergence estimated via electrophoretic analysis of proteins represents only a small part of the actual genetic changes at the DNA level.

The recent development of restriction enzyme technology allows detection of genetic differences between individual organisms in these highly variable noncoding regions of DNA. *Restriction enzymes* are derived from various bacteria and are commercially available. These enzymes recognize specific DNA sequences that are four, five, or six base pairs long and cleave each strand of the DNA within or near the recognition sequence. The DNA fragments produced by restriction enzyme cleavage can be separated on the basis of size by electrophoresis and can be made visible by several staining or autoradiographic techniques. These "restriction fragment length polymorphisms" (RFLPs) currently are used extensively in human genetics to find variable markers that are closely linked to genes with known clinical effects (Marx 1985).

2.2.4 Organization of the Genome

Eukaryotic DNA is organized into chromosomes (see Chapter 6). Vertebrate chromosomes are composed of DNA bonded with protein. There are two types of chromosomes in most fishes: sex chromosomes and *autosomes*. As implied by their name, sex chromosomes carry the sex-determining genes and are morphologically distinct in some fishes. Most of the chromosomes are autosomes; these chromosomes do not differ morphologically between the sexes. In addition to the complement of chromosomes present in the nucleus, vertebrates have DNA in their mitochondria. We first discuss the organization of genetic elements in nuclear chromosomes and then describe the mitochondrial DNA genome.

Most genes can be placed into one of two conceptual categories: structural genes and regulatory genes. *Structural genes* code for a protein that is produced by the series of molecular events previously described. For example, rainbow trout have four loci that code the enzyme phosphoglucomutase. Phosphogluco-mutase (PGM)[1] is a glycolytic enzyme that catalyzes the reversible reaction between glucose-1-phosphate and glucose-6-phosphate. (Although the genome of a fish has perhaps 50,000 genes, we can only examine the protein products of about 100 of them with conventional biochemical techniques; see Chapter 5).

Regulatory genes control the timing and location of expression of structural genes. For example, most rainbow trout do not express one of the PGM loci (*PGM-1**) in liver tissue even though all somatic cells have the full complement of chromosomes and genes. However, some individuals have an allele at a regula-tory gene (*PGM-1r**) that allows the expression of *PGM-1** in liver (Allendorf et al. 1982). It has been difficult to identify and characterize regulatory genes in vertebrates with electrophoretic methods, and we still do not know the amount of variability in this class of genes.

Mobile Genetic Elements. There are mechanisms of chromosomal evolution that can cause genes to move from one chromosome to another (translocations). Such movements are infrequent relative to the life of the organism, but genes that can move relatively frequently have been described in many organisms. Mobile genetic elements, or *transposons*, were first described in maize *Zea mays* by Barbara McClintock in the early 1950s, but their importance was not appreciated until she was awarded the Nobel Prize for medicine in 1983. Even though no examples of transposons have been reported in fishes, their prevalence and potential evolutionary importance in organisms that are more often used in genetic studies (e.g., *Drosophila melanogaster*) make a short description of them worth-while.

We will illustrate our point with a short description of the "P-element" transposon family in *Drosophila*. The P-element is 2,900 bases long and has the same base sequence on both ends but in reverse direction (called an inverted repeat). When individuals with P-elements are crossed to those without them, the P-elements move from their original location on the chromosome to a new one. It is thought that the P-element contains a gene coding for an enzyme that excises the element from the chromosome and allows its insertion at a new site. The phenotypic consequences of P-element transposition are grouped under the term "hybrid dysgenesis" (Bregliano et al. 1980). The most common results are the inactivation or activation of genes at the locations where the P-elements were inserted and gonadal sterility. Some authors have suggested that the greatest evolutionary importance of P-elements is their potential to create reproductive isolation between different populations because hybrids may be sterile (Syvanen 1984).

---

[1]A uniform nomenclature for protein-coding loci in fish was published while this book was in press (Shaklee et al. 1990), and has been adopted as an editorial standard by the American Fisheries Society. Loci are named for the proteins they encode; enzyme names are those of the International Union of Biochemistry (IUBNC 1984). Abbreviations of protein and locus names are in uppercase letters; protein abbreviations are in normal (Roman) type and those of loci are italicized. A locus abbreviation is followed by an asterisk (*), an allele symbol (also italicized) is preceded by an asterisk, and locus and allele are separated by an asterisk. The notation in this chapter generally follows the recom-mended nomenclature, except asterisks are not used in generalized genotype codes.

Mitochondrial DNA. Mitochondria are threadlike, self-replicating organelles that function in oxidative phosphorylation and are found in every eukaryotic cell. Mitochondrial DNA (mtDNA) is much less complex than the nuclear genome. The vertebrate mtDNA molecule is a closed circular section of DNA about 15,000–18,000 bases long. Each mtDNA molecule codes for 2 ribosomal RNAs, 22 transfer RNAs, 13 polypeptides, and the D-loop region that is involved in replication (Borst and Grivell 1981).

The mtDNA genome is tightly packed, has no introns, and is transcribed as a single unit. Translation is directed by a genetic code different from that of the nucleus (Borst and Grivell 1981). Even though mtDNA contains genes coding for several RNA and protein molecules, it is not autonomous, and it depends upon proteins coded by the nuclear genome for complete functioning (i.e., replication). Almost all the enzymes that are located in the mitochondria (e.g., isocitrate dehydrogenase and malate dehydrogenase, see Chapter 5) are encoded in the nucleus. Thus, the inheritance of most mitochondrial enzymes follows Mendelian principles.

Mitochondrial DNA's small size and ease of separation from nuclear DNA make it susceptible to analysis with restriction enzymes. The thousands of mtDNA molecules within each cell of an individual are, with very few exceptions, identical in DNA sequence. Furthermore, mtDNA is not inherited in a Mendelian fashion. Individuals inherit their mother's mtDNA in clonal form through the egg (Gyllensten et al. 1985). A surprising amount of sequence differences have been found between individuals and between populations. Readers interested in these techniques are directed to the review of mtDNA polymorphisms in animal populations by Avise and Lansman (1983) and to two papers that review the use of mtDNA in studies with fish (Ferris and Berg 1987; Gyllensten and Wilson 1987).

2.3 MENDELIAN GENETICS

2.3.1 Inheritance of Single Genes

Each diploid individual has two copies of each gene, one that it inherited from its mother and one from its father. When both copies have the same observable phenotypic effect (e.g., brown eyes), the individual is *homozygous.* In contrast, *heterozygous* individuals have two different forms, or *alleles*, of the gene. Functional uses of the terms homozygous and heterozygous refer to the similarity or differences in the effects of the gene. The genetic code is "degenerate"—two or more differing codons often code the same amino acid—but although two gene copies may have different DNA sequences, they may be considered the same allele if they code the same sequence of amino acids. Most genes show much more variability in base sequence than had been expected (Ayala 1984).

The factorial basis of inheritance, or *segregation*, was discovered by Gregor Mendel. Each diploid individual has two sets of chromosomes, and therefore of genes, in its somatic cells. During the formation of gametes (eggs or sperm), however, the original chromosomal number of somatic cells is halved during meiosis so that gametes receive one set of chromosomes and genes. Fertilization results in a zygote with the same number of chromosomes as in the parental somatic cells. Mendel's law of segregation predicts that half of the gametes of a heterozygous individual of genotype *Aa* will receive the *A* allele and that the other

Table 2.1 Punnett square for an $Aa \times Aa$ mating of fish heterozygous for the A allele for normal skin color and the a allele for absence of skin pigment. Phenotypes are in parentheses.

Sperm	Eggs	
	½ A	½ a
½ A	¼ AA (normal)	¼ Aa (normal)
½ a	¼ Aa (normal)	¼ aa (albino)

half will receive the a allele. A homozygous (AA) individual will produce only gametes with the A allele.

In heterozygous individuals (Aa), the two alleles interact in one of several ways to produce the *phenotype*. One allele may be *dominant*, usually designated with a capital letter (e.g., A), and mask the expression of a *recessive* allele, designated with a lowercase letter (a). Therefore, Aa and AA individuals have different genotypes but identical phenotypes. For example, an allele designated A codes an enzyme associated with normal skin color in rainbow trout whereas the a allele results in no pigment production; an aa phenotype is an albino (Bridges and von Limbach 1972). Heterozygotes are expected to produce A and a gametes in equal numbers. A simple way of determining the expected genotypes and phenotypes is to construct a Punnett square. As shown in Table 2.1, a mating between Aa and Aa individuals will produce AA, Aa, and aa genotypes in a proportion of ¼ : ½ : ¼. Because A is dominant over a, the phenotypes for the same cross will be normal and albino in a proportion of ¾ : ¼.

Sometimes it is necessary to determine whether individuals with the dominant phenotype are homozygous (AA) or heterozygous (Aa). The type of mating used to determine this is called a "test cross." The AA or Aa individual is mated with the homozygous recessive genotype (aa), an albino in our example. If the unknown is AA (i.e., the cross is $AA \times aa$), all of the progeny will be of the dominant phenotype, because they will be genotypically Aa. However, if the unknown is Aa (the cross is $Aa \times aa$), then half of the progeny will be normal (Aa) and half will show the recessive phenotype.

Heterozygosity at some loci produces phenotypes that are intermediate between those of the two homozygotes because neither allele is dominant over the other. In these codominant systems, matings between heterozygotes produce three phenotypic classes rather than the two classes expected in dominant–recessive systems. A Punnett square can again be used to determine the expected ratios. One of the advantages of using starch gel electrophoresis of proteins to detect genetic variation is that each genotype usually produces a unique electrophoretic phenotype (see Chapter 5).

The first step in genetic analysis is to demonstrate the mode by which phenotypic variation is inherited (Fairbairn and Roff 1980). We now present the methodology and statistical testing used to determine the genetic bases of skin color in rainbow trout (Bridges and von Limbach 1972) and inheritance of an enzyme locus in brown trout (Ståhl and Ryman 1982).

Albinism in Rainbow Trout. Bridges and von Limbach (1972) produced two sets of matings (designated P, or parental, and F, or filial). A representative sample of

Table 2.2 Segregation of skin color among rainbow trout. Observed data (from Bridges and von Limbach 1972) are numbers of normally colored or albino progeny from various crosses. Numbers in parentheses are the progeny expected if the albino allele (*a*) is recessive. *G*-values smaller than 3.84 (for one degree of freedom) indicate that observed and expected numbers do not differ significantly ($P > 0.05$).

Parents		Type of data	Progeny		G (1 df)
Female	Male		Normal (*AA* or *Aa*)	Albino (*aa*)	
Parental generation					
Albino	Albino	Observed	0	19,834	
(*aa*)	(*aa*)	(Expected)	(0)	(19,834)	
Albino	Normal	Observed	3,552	0	
(*aa*)	(*AA*)	(Expected)	(3,552)	(0)	
Normal	Albino	Observed	11,365	0	
(*AA*)	(*aa*)	(Expected)	(11,365)	(0)	
Filial generation					
Normal	Normal	Observed	16,856	5,679	0.48
(*Aa*)	(*Aa*)	(Expected)	(16,901)	(5,634)	
Normal	Albino	Observed	4,879	4,922	0.19
(*Aa*)	(*aa*)	(Expected)	(4,900)	(4,900)	
Albino	Normal	Observed	3,253	3,145	1.82
(*aa*)	(*Aa*)	(Expected)	(3,199)	(3,199)	

these is given in Table 2.2. In the F matings, "full-sib" offspring (i.e., full brothers and sisters) of the P matings were mated. These data show that normal × normal and normal × albino matings resulted in normally colored fish, and albino × albino matings produced all albinos. Even though these data suggest that albinism in rainbow trout is a simple autosomal recessive character, it is necessary to statistically test the fit of these data to the expected ratios.

We calculated the expected number of progeny in each phenotypic class based on the total number of offspring and the expected ratio (Table 2.2). Traditionally, the fit of the observed-to-expected ratio would be tested by a chi-square goodness-of-fit test. The *G*-test (log-likelihood ratio test) has several theoretical and computational advantages over the chi-square test (Sokal and Rohlf 1981), and we have used the *G*-test throughout this chapter. The *G*-statistic is tested according to the chi-square distribution, with the same degrees of freedom as would be used in a chi-square test; the results of these two tests are generally concordant.

In the last cross in Table 2.2, 3,253 normal and 3,145 albino progeny were observed. The production of albino progeny and the correspondence to a 1:1 ratio suggest that the normal parent was heterozygous. If that parent had been homozygous, only normal progeny would have resulted. The expected number of progeny of each phenotype is 3,199. The *G*-value is 1.82; we conclude that these data are compatible with a 1:1 segregation ratio because 1.82 is smaller than the critical value of 3.84. These results support Bridges and von Limbach's conclusion that albinism is controlled by a recessive allele at a single Mendelian locus.

Table 2.3 Observed segregation of *G3PDH-2** alleles, and expected Mendelian segregation (in parentheses) following specified experimental matings of brown trout and electrophoretic examination of 54–200 offspring per cross (data from Ståhl and Ryman 1982). *G*-values smaller than 5.99 (for two degrees of freedom) indicate that observed and expected offspring ratios do not differ significantly from 1:1 (*P* > 0.05).

Parents		Offspring			
Female	Male	*100/100	*100/50	*50/50	G
*100/100	*100/150	101 (100)	99 (100)		0.50
*100/50	*100/50	48 (50)	94 (100)	58 (50)	1.67
*100/100	*100/100	172 (172)			
*50/50	*50/50			54 (54)	

G3PDH-2* *in Brown Trout.* Ståhl and Ryman (1982) showed that the inheritance of a glycerol-3-phosphate dehydrogenase[2] locus (*G3PDH-2**) in brown trout is compatible with a model in which an autosomal locus segregates as two codominant alleles. Heterozygous individuals (*100/50*)[3] express the protein products of both alleles. A mating between two heterozygous fishes (*100/50* × *100/50*) results in a progeny ratio of 1:2:1 (i.e., one-fourth *100/100*, one-half *100/50*, and one-fourth *50/50*). A *100/100* × *100/50* mating results in equal numbers of *100/100* and *100/50* individuals.

Table 2.3 summarizes Ståhl and Ryman's data. The phenotypic distributions of progeny from these crosses are in accordance with expected Mendelian ratios. The G-test of the 1:2:1 ratio with two degrees of freedom is based on two independent tests, each with one degree of freedom. The first test is for equal proportions (i.e., a 1:1 ratio) of the two alleles (*100* and *50*) and the second test is for an equal proportion of homozygotes (*100/100* + *50/50*) and heterozygotes (*100/50*).

Sex Linkage. The inheritance patterns just described apply to genes located on the autosomes. Genes also occur on the sex chromosomes of fishes. If the phenotypic ratios of a trait differ between males and females, the genes controlling that trait may be sex-linked. In some species, males are heterogametic (having two kinds of sex chromosomes); in others, females are heterogametic. If males are heterogametic (XY) and females are homogametic (XX), sons receive their father's Y chromosome and one of their mother's X chromosomes; daughters receive X chromosomes from both parents. Kallman (1984) reported that individuals of the southern platyfish have a third sex chromosome (W). Females may be either WY, WX, or XX and males can be XY or YY. Many of the codominant factors controlling pigment patterns in this species are sex-linked.

---

[2]This enzyme was abbreviated AGP by Ståhl and Ryman and some other authors.

[3]Alleles studied by electrophoresis often are denoted by the relative mobilities of their protein products in the electric field. Typically, the most common allele at a locus is designated *100*; an allele whose protein migrates half as far as the common one is called *50*, one whose protein moves 20% farther is *120*, and so on. Electrophoretic phenotypes are described in Chapter 5.

2.3.2 Single Genes with Major Effects

Single genes with simple inheritance patterns do not necessarily have a diminished role in phenotypic expression. We will discuss two genes in fishes that have major effects on development and life history: *P** in southern platyfish and *PGM-1r** in rainbow trout. Studies of both these genes showed that genetic differences at a single locus can have effects of potential adaptive significance.

P* Gene. The *P** gene is located on the sex chromosomes of southern platyfish and is associated with the onset of sexual maturity (Kallman and Schreibman 1973; Kallman and Borkoski 1978). Kallman and Borkoski (1978) identified five alleles at the *P* locus. Each allele is associated with a different timing of sexual maturity, which varies between 8 and 73 weeks under controlled conditions. Immature fish of all genotypes grow at the same rate. However, males grow more slowly once they mature, so males having alleles associated with earlier maturity are smaller than males having alleles associated with later maturity. The effect of this gene is correlated with the age or size of individuals at which the pituitary gland becomes physiologically active. The pituitary produces gonadotropins, which affect the growth of gonads, production of eggs and sperm, and development of secondary sexual characteristics in males.

PGM-1r*. Rainbow trout with the regulatory allele *PGM-1r*b* have an increase in activity of total phosphoglucomutase enzyme (PGM) in liver tissue (Allendorf et al. 1982). This is the expression of *PGM-1**, a locus that is not expressed in the liver of most rainbow trout. Differences in the expression of this locus are consistent with a model of a single gene with additive inheritance. Crosses between homozygous (**a/a*) individuals and heterozygous (**a/b*) individuals produce progeny with and without PGM-1 activity in a 1:1 ratio. Fish with liver PGM-1 develop faster, are larger, mature earlier (Allendorf et al. 1983), have lower meristic counts (Leary et al. 1984a), and show higher frequencies of agonistic behavior patterns (Ferguson and Danzmann 1985) than those without liver PGM-1.

2.3.3 Linkage

Genes that are physically connected on the same chromosome have a tendency to be inherited together; that is, they do not segregate independently to progeny. Crossing-over is a physical exchange between paired chromosomes during meiosis that results in recombination of genes on the two chromosomes. For example, consider two loci, each with a single dominant (*A*, *B*) and a single recessive allele (*a*, *b*). Assume that an individual received the *A* and *B* alleles on the chromosome inherited from its mother and the *a* and *b* alleles on the chromosome inherited from its father. Such an individual is heterozygous at both loci (*Aa* and *Bb*) and may pass on the parental types inherited (*A;B* and *a;b*) at a greater frequency than the recombinant types (*A;b* and *a;B*).

The amount of recombination between two loci is estimated by the proportion of all progeny that have recombinant chromosome types. The frequency of parental and recombinant types depends upon the physical distance between the two genes on the same chromosome because the probability of a crossover increases with the physical distance between two loci. Two loci that are on

Table 2.4 Joint segregation at enzyme loci resulting from the cross *EST-1** (*AA*);*IDH-2** (*BB*) × *EST-1** (*Aa*);*IDH-2** (*Bb*) between rainbow trout. $G(a)$ is the G-value associated with the expected 1:1 segregation of *EST-1** alleles among progeny, $G(b)$ is the G-value associated with the expected 1:1 segregation of *IDH-2** alleles, and $G(L)$ is the G-value associated with the expected 1:1 segregation of parental and recombinant types. R is the estimated proportion of progeny with recombinant genotypes. In family 114, the female parent was the double heterozygote; in the other two families, the male parent was the double heterozygote. G-values with asterisks indicate significant deviations from 1:1 segregation ($P < 0.05$* or $P < 0.001$***).

Family	Number of progeny with genotype				$G(a)$	$G(b)$	$G(L)$	$R(\%)$
	AABB	*AaBB*	*AABb*	*AaBb*				
114	20	5	4	27	1.1	0.6	28.3***	16.1
116	83	4	0	61	2.2	4.6*	168.4***	2.7
K60	21	1	0	16	1.0	0.4	49.3***	2.6

different chromosomes will show 50% recombination (equal frequency of parental and recombinant types). Two loci that are very far apart on the same chromosome may also show independent segregation (50% recombination).

Table 2.4 presents the phenotypes observed in the progeny of rainbow trout heterozygous at two enzyme loci (*EST-1** and *IDH-2**) mated with fish homozygous at both loci (Allendorf and Knudsen, unpublished data). In the nomenclature of the previous paragraph, *EST-1** is locus A and *IDH-2** is locus B. If these two loci are on separate chromosomes, all four progeny phenotypes are expected in equal proportions. Three statistical tests should be performed on joint segregation data from this type of mating: two tests of the expected 1:1 segregation at each locus individually, and one a test of 1:1 joint segregation of the parental and recombinant types should be performed.

Both loci segregated 1:1 when considered individually. (The difference at *IDH-2** in family 116 is not significant when we take into consideration that we have performed three independent tests for the segregation at this locus: Cooper 1968). However, these data show a significantly higher proportion of parental types (*AABB* and *AaBb*) than expected in all three families indicating linkage of the loci. Almost all of the known linkages in fish species are among protein-coding loci detected by electrophoresis. Morizot and Siciliano (1984) reviewed evidence of gene linkage in fishes.

Linkage among loci can have practical importance. Natural or artificial selection that favors a particular genotype at one locus also increases the frequency of alleles at other loci that are linked to the locus under selection. For example, different color phenotypes have been selected for in the culture of several fish species. Any alleles closely linked to the color allele being selected for also increase in frequency; this effect is called "hitchhiking." Many of these hitchhiking alleles may have harmful effects. For example, a hypothetical allele associated with shortened opercle may be linked to a gene resulting in faster growth rate that is being selected for in a fish culture program. After several generations, these fish may have a faster growth rate but they also will have an increased occurrence of shortened opercle.

2.3.4 Non-Mendelian Inheritance

Some fishes show types of inheritance that do not follow the rules of Mendelian inheritance just described. We will discuss two of these; one is primarily a consequence of chromosome duplication (*polyploidy*) and the other a result of reproductive mode (*unisexuality*).

Polyploidy. Some groups of fishes are polyploid and, therefore, have more than two copies of each gene. For example, it has been proposed that an ancestor of salmonid fishes underwent a genome duplication 25–100 million years ago (reviewed by Allendorf and Thorgaard 1984). The observation that these fishes have twice as much DNA than, and twice as many chromosome arms per cell as, closely related species supports this hypothesis. Similarly, catostomid fishes are believed to be tetraploid owing to a genome duplication (via hybridization) 50 million years ago (reviewed by Ferris 1984). Allendorf and Thorgaard (1984) listed other species reported to be polyploid. Schultz (1980) reviewed the role of polyploidy in the evolution of fishes.

The pattern of inheritance in polyploids is complex because all tetraploid individuals have four gene copies, each located on a different chromosome. At a locus with two alleles, the following genotypes are possible: *AAAA*, *AAAa*, *AAaa*, *Aaaa*, and *aaaa*. Gametes of tetraploids carry two copies of each gene. The situation is further complicated because some of the chromosomes in tetraploid fishes are evolving back to diploidy such that the original tetraploid locus eventually will become two distinct diploid loci. This process is thought to be complete at all loci in catostomids (Ferris 1984), but to be incomplete in salmonids (Allendorf and Thorgaard 1984). It is very important for any researcher studying inheritance in fishes to be aware of these processes. The mechanics of inheritance in tetraploids are beyond the scope of this chapter; interested readers may consult Allendorf and Thorgaard (1984) and the papers cited therein.

Unisexuality. Some groups of fishes are all female and reproduce by either gynogenesis or hybridogenesis (Schultz 1977). Both of these modes of reproduction produce genotypes that are similar to those of first-generation (F_1) hybrids, as shown in Figure 2.3 (Moore 1984). *Gynogenesis* is a strictly asexual form of reproduction. A female produces eggs with the same numbers of chromosomes as her somatic cells. Sperm from a coexisting sexual species is required to activate embryogenesis, but the male's chromosomes are not incorporated into the embryo. Therefore, the offspring have clonally inherited the entire complement of their mother's chromosomes. This mode of reproduction is common in triploid clones of the livebearers *Poeciliopsis monacha* and *Poeciliopsis lucida* (Figure 2.3; Vrijenhoek 1984), and is also found in both diploid and triploid clones of the Amazon molly *Poecilia formosa* (Monaco et al. 1984). Both triploid and tetraploid gynogenetic clones have been reported in the crucian carp *Carassius auratus gibelio* (Cherfas 1981).

Hybridogenesis is a semisexual form of reproduction that has been described in the genus *Poeciliopsis* (Figure 2.3; Schultz 1977). In hybridogenesis, mating occurs between two species, but there is no recombination of parental chromosomes. During meiosis, only the chromosomes of the maternal species are passed to the haploid egg (Moore 1984). The egg is fertilized by sperm from a second species, producing a diploid embryo that develops into a hybrid offspring. Hybridogenetic fishes are not true asexual clones because paternal genomes are

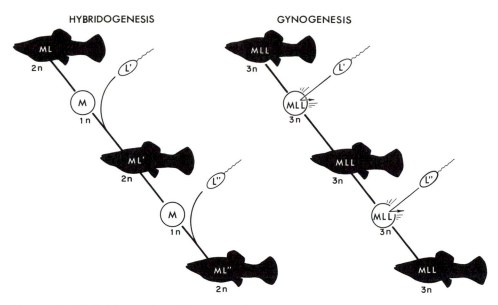

Figure 2.3 Hybridogenetic and gynogenetic modes of reproduction in *Poeciliopsis* spp. The letters M and L represent *P. monacha* and *P. lucida* genomes, respectively, the primes represent different allelic markers of the *lucida* genomes, and n is the number of chromosome sets (modified from Vrijenhoek 1984).

inserted into each generation. The maternal genome is perpetuated by selective meiosis.

Unisexuality may be a more pervasive and important factor in fish evolution than is commonly accepted. For example, all-female diploid gynogenetic clones of the atherinid fish *Menidia clarkhubbsi* have been detected (Echelle and Mosier 1981; Echelle et al. 1983). Unisexuality in fishes may not be the evolutionary dead end that it might appear to be. It is thought that a unisexual transitional stage may be a critical intermediate step in the production of evolutionarily successful sexual tetraploids such as salmonids and catostomids (Schultz 1977).

2.4 POLYGENIC TRAITS

2.4.1 Quantitative Traits

Quantitative (polygenic) traits are those controlled by many genes; they are covered thoroughly in the excellent text by Falconer (1981). There are two categories of polygenic traits: continuous and threshold. Continuous traits show a continuous phenotypic distribution (e.g., length and weight), and their numerical values follow a normal distribution. In contrast, the phenotypic distribution of threshold traits is divided into discrete categories (e.g., age at first sexual maturity). Some early geneticists thought that Mendel's principles did not apply to polygenic traits. Several classic studies soon showed that quantitative variation is due both to environmental influences and heritable differences at many genes. However, the continuous variation of polygenic traits combined with environmental effects makes it difficult to ascribe a genotype to a specific phenotype, as is possible for traits controlled by single genes. For instance, we could determine that albinos had two copies of a recessive allele and therefore had a genotype of (*aa*). With quantitative traits, however, there is no simple phenotype–genotype relationship; for example, many different genotypes may result in a phenotype of 354 grams. As a result, the genetic analysis of quantitative traits requires a different approach.

2.4.2 Heritability

The most fundamental question to ask in the genetic analysis of quantitative traits is "how much of the phenotypic variation is due to genetic differences between individuals?" To answer this, it is necessary to partitition the total phenotypic variation (V_p) into that fraction of the variation due to genetic differences (V_g) and that due to environmental differences (V_e) among individuals (Falconer 1981):

$$V_p = V_g + V_e.$$

The fraction of the total phenotypic variation that is due to genetic differences, V_g/V_p, is called the *heritability* in the broad sense (H^2). Genetic variation can be further partitioned into the following components:

$$V_g = V_a + V_d;$$

V_a is the additive genetic variation due to allelic substitution, and V_d is the dominance variation, which is the interaction between alleles at a locus (how much heterozygotes deviate from the mean value of homozygotes). Let us assume that body weight of rainbow trout is controlled by two unlinked loci (designated *A* and *B*) and, for the sake of simplicity, that the trait is not influenced by the environment. If the trait were determined by additive genetic effects only, such that each dominant allele would result in an increase of 5 g body weight above 100 g, we would expect to see the following type of distribution of weights:

	AA	*Aa*	*aa*
BB	120	115	110
Bb	115	110	105
bb	110	105	100

However, if most of the phenotypic variation for weight were dominance variation, we would expect a distribution such as the following:

	AA	*Aa*	*aa*
BB	110	115	110
Bb	115	120	115
bb	110	115	110

The fraction of the phenotypic variation that can be ascribed to additive genetic variation is the heritability in the narrow sense (h^2). Heritability in the narrow sense is of interest to plant and animal breeders because it allows one to predict the response to selection for a desirable trait; the larger the heritability, the larger the potential response. We now present methods to estimate heritability and then provide examples from rainbow trout.

Realized Heritability. There are many ways to estimate heritability. Realized heritability is defined as the response to selection (R) divided by the selection differential (S). For example, let us assume that the length of 3-year-old fish in a population of rainbow trout varies between 200 and 400 mm. The mean length (X) is 300 mm. We select all individuals over 350 mm to be used as parents for the next generation. The mean length of the selected parents (X_s) is 360 mm. The selection differential is, therefore, 60 mm. Assume we observed a mean of 352 mm for the 3-year-old offspring (X'). The realized heritability is

$$R/S = (X' - X)/(X_s - X) = (352 - 300)/(360 - 300) = 0.87.$$

Heritabilities of 0 and 1.0 would result in means of 300 and 360 mm, respectively, in 3-year-old fish of the next generation.

Resemblance between Relatives. Relatives have a certain proportion of their genes in common. We can estimate heritability from the relative genetic and phenotypic similarity of related individuals. Most of the methods calculating heritabilities in this way use either regression analysis or analysis of variance. In regression analysis, the phenotypic value of one relative is regressed on that of another. Heritability is then determined from the slope of the regression. The genetic resemblance between offspring and one parent is expected to be $\frac{1}{2}V_a$. Therefore, h^2 is equal to two times the slope (Falconer 1981).

The choice of relatives to estimate heritability often depends upon practical considerations. However, the closer the relationship between relatives, the more precise the estimate of heritability because the slope is multiplied by a smaller coefficient. Also, estimates may be inflated because of environmental influences (maternal effects). For example, offspring may resemble their maternal parent because of environmental effects such as quality of the egg. This potential bias can be estimated by doing two regressions, one of offspring on paternal parent and the other of offspring on maternal parent. Maternal effects can be estimated by the difference between the heritabilities calculated by the maternal parent regression and the paternal parent regression.

A second source of bias comes from the use of relatives with theoretical covariances that include nonadditive genetic sources of variation (i.e., dominance variation). For example, the covariance of full sibs includes $\frac{1}{4}V_d$. If we regressed the values for full sibs against each other, we could not determine what proportion of their similarity was due to dominance variation or additive genetic variation. In addition, full sibs may be similar because they share a common environment (V_e). For example, in fish studies, sibs are often raised together separate from other families until they are large enough to mark, and the shared tank environment may greatly exaggerate heritability estimates. Therefore, full-sib analyses set an upper limit to heritability estimates.

Analyses of variance can also be used to estimate heritability. These methods often are based on sib analysis and depend upon genetic covariances between relatives. A typical nested design is to mate several males each to several females. The offspring of a female are measured to provide the data. An analysis of variance is then used to determine the amount of variation in the progeny of different females attributable to having the same father (half sibs). Kirpicknikov (1981) and Becker (1984) provided a step-by-step outline of how to determine the

Table 2.5 Heritability estimates (h^2) of 17 traits of rainbow trout.

Trait	h^2	Source
Meristic characters		
Pyloric caeca	0.53	Chevassus et al. (1979)
Anal rays	0.93	Leary et al. (1985)
Dorsal rays	0.90	Leary et al. (1985)
Lower gillrakers	0.37	Leary et al. (1985)
Mandibular pores	0.18	Leary et al. (1985)
Pectoral rays	0.52	Leary et al. (1985)
Pelvic rays	0.84	Leary et al. (1985)
Upper gillrakers	0.67	Leary et al. (1985)
Vertebrae	0.84	Leary et al. (1985)
Weight		
Adult spawners, ♀	0.37–0.74	Gall and Gross (1978)
Adult spawners, ♂	0.14–0.63	Gall and Gross (1978)
Fingerlings	0.04–0.18	Chevassus (1976)
Length		
Fingerlings	0.03–0.37	Aulstad et al. (1972)
Reproduction		
Egg size	0.29–0.32	Gall and Gross (1978)
Egg number	0.30–0.67	Gall and Gross (1978)
Egg volume	0.32–0.76	Gall and Gross (1978)
Embryo viability	0.06–0.14	Kanis et al. (1976)

variance components from these types of data and other possible experimental designs, and we will not repeat these steps here.

Table 2.5 lists the heritabilities of 17 traits in rainbow trout. Traits with high heritabilities are expected to show a greater potential response to selection. Finally, and most importantly, heritability is a population-specific measurement. Estimates of heritability are only valid for a given population in a given environment. Therefore, it is incorrect to conclude that the difference between two populations, each showing a high heritability for the same trait, is mainly genetic. Heritability only tells us what proportion of the phenotypic variance within a population is due to genetic differences between individuals.

2.4.3 Genetic Correlations among Traits

Our discussion so far has ignored genetic correlations among traits. Two traits may be genetically correlated because of *pleiotropy*. Pleiotropy occurs when a gene affects two or more characters. For example, we have discussed in Section 2.3.2 that a single allelic substitution at the *PGM-1r** locus in rainbow trout affects developmental rate, size, meristic counts, behavior, and age at first sexual maturity.

Pleiotropy is especially important with regard to the possible effects of selective breeding programs. A selection program for any one characteristic is likely to affect a variety of other characteristics. For example, Donaldson rainbow trout were selected for increased egg number (Donaldson and Olson 1955). This selection was successful; it eventually produced females that yielded over 20,000 eggs at 2 years of age. Nevertheless, the ''success'' of the program was tempered by apparent pleiotropic effects of this selection. The eggs produced by these females were extremely small and had low survival (Hershberger et al. 1976).

2.5 GENETICS OF NATURAL POPULATIONS

2.5.1 Hardy–Weinberg Equilibrium

The fundamental model of population genetics is the *Hardy–Weinberg* equilibrium. The name is derived from the independent codiscoverers of this principle, G. H. Hardy, an English mathematician, and William Weinberg, a German physician. They showed, in 1908, that with random mating and Mendelian inheritance, genotype frequencies will remain unchanged from generation to generation. Furthermore, if two alleles, *A* and *a*, occur with frequencies of *p* and *q* ($p + q = 1$), the equilibrium genotypic frequencies are

$$p^2(AA), 2pq(Aa), \text{ and } q^2(aa).$$

If more than two alleles are present at a locus, the frequency of the homozygote for an allele is the square of the allele frequency of that allele. The frequency of the heterozygote for any two alleles is two times the product of their frequencies. This model requires the assumption that the locus under consideration is not affected by any evolutionary forces (e.g., natural selection, genetic drift, mutation, or migration).

The following genotypic frequencies were reported by Ryman (1981) at the *G3PDH-2** locus in a sample of brown trout from Lake Slengajaure in northern Sweden: 22 (**100/100*) fish, 30 (**50/100*) fish, and 17 (**50/50*) fish. The first step in the analysis of such genotypic data from natural populations is to estimate the allele frequencies, *p* and *q*. This is done by dividing the number of copies of an allele in the sample by the total number of alleles sampled ($2N$, *N* being the number of individuals sampled). Each homozygote for a particular allele carries two copies of that allele and each heterozygote carries one copy. Thus, the frequency of the **100* allele in the above sample is

$$p = \frac{(2 \times 22) + 30}{2 \times 69} = 0.536.$$

The frequency of the **50* allele, *q* can be calculated similarly or by $(1 - p) = 0.464$.

The expected genotypic proportions are estimated with the Hardy–Weinberg proportions, so the *expected* number of **100/100* homozygotes in a sample of 69 fish is

$$p^2N = 0.287 \times 69 = 19.8.$$

The other genotypic frequencies are calculated similarly, so the expected Hardy–Weinberg numbers of **100/100*, **50/100*, and **50/50* fish are 19.8, 34.3, and 14.9, respectively.

The fit of the observed fish numbers to Hardy–Weinberg expectations can be tested with a *G*-test with one degree of freedom. In this example, $G = 0.21$ ($P > 0.70$), so we accept the null hypothesis that genotypic frequencies at this locus are in Hardy–Weinberg proportions. This test can be expanded to more than two alleles by using the Hardy–Weinberg expectations, as discussed above, with degrees of freedom that are equal to the total number of genotypic classes minus the number of alleles.

Assumptions underlying the Hardy–Weinberg equilibrium are unrealistic, which suggests that this model may have little application to real populations.

However, the genotypic frequencies in any randomly mating population generally will be in expected Hardy–Weinberg proportions. This is because the effects of evolutionary forces on genotypic frequencies are so subtle that they cannot be detected even with fairly large sample sizes (e.g., >100). Furthermore, the term "equilibrium" refers to stability over time, from generation to generation. It is impossible to detect such changes by taking a sample from a population at one time. Thus, one can test for Hardy–Weinberg proportions (i.e., random mating) in a sample from a natural population, as we have described above, but it is incorrect to consider this a test for Hardy–Weinberg equilibrium.

2.5.2 Natural Selection

In the words of Charles Darwin (1859),

> Any being, if it vary however slightly in any manner profitable to itself, under the complex and sometimes varying conditions of life, will have a better chance of surviving, and thus be naturally selected. From the strong principle of inheritance, any selected variety will tend to propagate its new and modified form.

We can see that *natural selection* depends upon the two essential aspects of genetics: individual variability and the inheritance of such differences. Natural selection acts on differences between individuals in reproduction and survival (i.e., fitness) to bring about genotypic differences between generations.

The principle of natural selection remains as the only scientifically acceptable explanation for the adaptation of organisms to their environment. Nevertheless, it has been surprisingly difficult to demonstrate the action of natural selection and even more difficult to interpret the current phenotypic and genotypic characteristics of a population with regard to the past effects of natural selection. Natural selection often has been invoked without supporting evidence to explain patterns of variation among populations. We concentrate in this section on three possible manifestations of natural selection on fish populations: (1) morphological variation, (2) protein variation, and (3) evidence for local adaptation of fish populations.

Morphological Variation. Several investigators have used sticklebacks (Gasterosteidae) as model organisms to study the effects of natural selection on morphological variation. These studies have provided evidence for selective predation based on the numbers of lateral plates, dorsal spines, and gill rakers among survivors; Bell (1984) wrote an excellent review of these studies. Swain and Lindsey (1984) provided evidence of selective predation involving the number of vertebrae in the prey. They exposed young threespine sticklebacks to predation by pumpkinseeds in the laboratory. Survival was approximately 1.5 times greater for prey with 31 vertebrae than for those with 32. Fish with fewer vertebrae apparently were able to accelerate more rapidly and thus avoid predation.

Such selective morphological differences in survival in natural populations will only affect the distribution of the trait in future generations if the trait is under genetic control (that is, $h^2 > 0$). We are not aware of any published heritability studies of vertebral number in threespine sticklebacks. However, studies with a variety of other species indicate that vertebral number generally has high heritability (Kirpichnikov 1981). Indeed, most meristic characters that have been studied in fish populations have surprisingly high heritability (Leary et al. 1985). Thus, we expect that any differential survival related to meristic variation will affect the character distributions in future generations.

It is of historical interest that one of the first published studies of phenotypic similarity between parents and offspring in a nonhuman species was a study of the velvet belly shark *Etmopterus spinax* by R. C. Punnett (1904). This is the same Punnett who, in the early days following the rediscovery of Mendel's principles, introduced the checkerboard diagram, or Punnett square, that we used in Section 2.3.1 to predict offspring genotypes. He also was the first to report linkage between two genes in any organism (Bateson and Punnett 1906).

Protein Variation. The adaptive significance of protein variation has been a matter of debate for the last 15 years. A comprehensive review of this controversy is beyond the scope of this chapter. Nevertheless, this issue is of central importance for the application of protein markers to the description of the structure of fish populations. Allelic frequency differences among geographical samples are taken to reflect patterns of relative reproductive isolation. This approach requires the assumption that the proteins examined are unaffected by natural selection; that is, they are selectively neutral. Several authors have pointed out that this assumption, hence the approach, may not be valid (Mork et al. 1984; Williams and Koehn 1984).

Our view is that neither extreme is correct. There is good evidence for natural selection at individual loci in fish populations; the study of a lactate dehydrogenase locus in mummichogs by Powers et al. (1983) is now the classic example. Our own work has suggested that heterozygosity at many protein loci, or of chromosomal segments linked to those loci, does affect certain traits closely related to fitness (Leary et al. 1984b; Danzmann et al. 1986a, 1986b). Nevertheless, we believe that allele frequencies among natural populations provide insight into the pattern and amount of genetic exchange among populations. It is critical, however, that many polymorphic loci be examined. Two populations may be similar by chance at a single locus, but it is extremely unlikely that two isolated populations will remain or become genetically similar at many loci because of convergent natural selection. Thus, the similarity of allele frequencies at many polymorphic loci is a reliable indication of recent genetic exchange between two populations.

Nature has provided an elegant empirical test of the contrasting effects of genetic drift, migration, and natural selection of allele frequencies in natural populations (Aspinwall 1974). Pink salmon mature at 2 years of age and return to their native streams to spawn after spending the most of their lives at sea. The effect of this rigid timing is two genetically isolated populations within many streams, one that spawns in odd-numbered years and one that returns in even-numbered years. In the Southern part of the species' range, large numbers of pink salmon return in odd years but there are no even-year populations.

Several pink salmon populations from both even and odd years have been examined for two polymorphic enzyme systems. The allele frequencies of the two systems revealed near uniformity throughout the geographical range within even- or odd-year cycles. However, significant differences were found between some even- and odd-year populations that were sharing a single stream. These populations share the same environment but are genetically isolated. More recent studies have confirmed and extended the original findings of Aspinwall (Utter 1981; Gagal'chii 1984). These studies suggest that gene flow between populations within an odd- or an even-year cycle results in near uniformity of allele frequencies among populations inhabiting a wide range of environments. Populations using the same environment in different years, however, have very different allele frequencies. Selective neutrality combined with random genetic drift is the most plausible explanation of these results.

Local Adaptation. There is a well-documented tendency for salmonids to evolve genetically discrete, ecologically specialized populations by natural selection over many generations of adaptation to local environmental conditions (Behnke 1972; Ricker 1972; Ryman et al. 1979). The genetic basis of these adaptations has been demonstrated in several studies of Pacific salmon, in which fish in their native environment performed much better than fish derived from other populations (Bams 1976; Altukhov and Salmenkova 1987).

Bams's (1976) study of pink salmon is of special interest because protein studies of that species have indicated nearly uniform allele frequencies over a large geographical area and a wide range of environmental conditions. When Bams created pink salmon hybrids between a "donor" stock and a stock native to a particular stream, and then stocked both hybrids and donors of equal age back into that stream, the ratio of hybrids to donors that subsequently homed to the stream as adults was 10:1 instead of the expected 1:1. Thus, significant genetic adaptation to local conditions may be present even though there is no evidence of genetic variation at protein loci.

2.5.3 Genetic Drift

Genetic drift means chance fluctuations in allele frequencies from one generation to the next as a result of random sampling among gametes. The magnitude and importance of genetic drift varies inversely with population size. Genetic drift is relatively unimportant in large populations; in large breeding groups, gene frequencies in a new generation accurately reflect the gene frequencies in the parental generation. However, gene frequencies in small populations may fluctuate dramatically from generation to generation. The effects of genetic drift can best be demonstrated with computer simulations (see Figure 2.4).

The direction of gene-frequency changes due to genetic drift is completely random: the frequency of a particular allele is just as likely to increase as it is to decrease. Nevertheless, one change associated with genetic drift *is* predictable: genetic variation will be lost at a rate that is inversely proportional to population size. In the simulation shown in Figure 2.4, for example, all genetic variation is lost in the population with 25 individuals after only 32 generations. This effect can be very important in the founding and maintenance of hatchery populations, in extremely small natural populations, or in populations that experience "bottlenecks" (restriction of gene flow to a few breeding pairs) for one or several generations. *Heterozygosity* often is used to measure the amount of genetic variation in a population. Heterozygosity at an individual locus is defined as the proportion of individuals that are heterozygous at that locus. If a population is in random-mating (Hardy–Weinberg) proportions, the expected heterozygosity at a

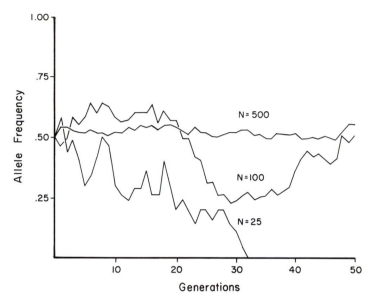

Figure 2.4 Computer simulation of allele frequencies, showing effects of genetic drift in populations of three sizes; N = number of individuals in the population. The fitnesses of all three genotypes were assumed to be equal in these simulations.

locus with two alleles is $2pq$. If there are more than two alleles, the expected heterozygosity is easier to estimate by subtraction of the expected proportion of homozygotes from one. For example, at a locus with three alleles at frequencies p, q, and r, the expected proportion of heterozygotes is $1 - p^2 - q^2 - r^2$.

Heterozygosity is lost in a population because of genetic drift at a rate of $1/2N_e$, N_e being the genetic population size or *effective population size*. Effective population size is not simply the number of animals in a population, because only reproductive animals can contribute to the next generation. A variety of factors can cause N_e to be considerably smaller than the census size of a population. An important one is the relative numbers of males and females; N_e will be reduced if one sex is underrepresented. Effective population size also will be reduced if some reproducing individuals have disproportionately more offspring than others. This effect may sometimes lead to counterintuitive recommendations. For example, assume we are founding a hatchery stock of trout and that we have a limited number of 2- and 3-year-old females. The older females may have up to five times as many eggs as the younger ones. The best strategy to maximize N_e, and thereby to reduce the harmful effects of genetic drift in the founding generation, would be to take approximately equal number of eggs from all females. Thus, N_e actually will be increased if the "excess" eggs from the 3-year-old females are not included in the future brood stock (Allendorf and Ryman 1987).

2.5.4 Inbreeding

Inbreeding is a word with several meanings (Jacquard 1975). A population is inbred if related individuals tend to mate together. An individual is inbred if its parents are related; that is, they have one or more ancestors in common. It is important to distinguish between these two concepts of inbreeding: population and individual.

Population inbreeding causes a deficit of heterozygotes relative to expected Hardy–Weinberg proportions. It does not affect allele frequencies, however, so the original heterozygosity in a population can be restored by random mating. Inbreeding is often confused with genetic drift. The confusion results because both are often associated with small populations. However, a local, randomly mating population is not inbred no matter how small the population size. Indeed, allele frequencies often differ between the sexes in small randomly mating populations, resulting in an excess of heterozygotes (Kirby 1975).

One way to clarify the difference between inbreeding and genetic drift is by example. Consider a population of trout living in a lake but spawning in four equal-sized tributaries. Assume that the trout home to their natal tributaries to spawn and that they mate at random there. Assume further that all four subpopulations initially have the same allele frequencies.

From these starting conditions, allele frequency differences will accumulate among the trout from different tributaries because of genetic drift. The smaller the size of the subpopulations, the more quickly they will accumulate allele-frequency differences due to genetic drift. However, as long as the trout within a subpopulation mate at random, the subpopulations themselves do not become inbred.

The total population of trout in this lake, however, is inbred because of the homing tendency: two related fish from the same tributary are more likely to mate with each other than with fish from other subpopulations. This type of inbreeding is usually measured by F, which is a type of inbreeding coefficient. This F is properly called a "fixation index" and measures the proportional deficit of heterozygotes relative to expected Hardy–Weinberg proportions:

$$F = \frac{H_e - H_o}{H_e};$$

H_e is the expected proportion and H_o the observed proportion of heterozygotes. The deviation from Hardy–Weinberg proportions is sometimes estimated by the complement of the fixation index, $1 - F$, which is called the panmictic index (P). A population is said to be *panmictic* if mating is completely random so that F is zero and P is 1.0.

The more genetically divergent the subpopulations become, the greater the deficit in observed proportion of heterozygotes. At the extreme, each subpopulation will become "fixed" for a single allele at one or more loci. If different subpopulations become fixed for different alleles, there still will be allelic variation in the population but there will be no heterozygotes in the lake; thus, F will be 1.0. However, if we took all the fish from the lake into a hatchery and mated them at random, the observed heterozygosity would return to that expected with Hardy–Weinberg proportions and F would be 0.0.

Individuals within a population may be inbred (i.e., their parents may share a common ancestor) even though the population is not. For example, a small randomly mating population will generally be in Hardy–Weinberg genotypic proportions and, thus, F will be zero. Nevertheless, the smaller the population, the greater the probability that two related individuals will mate. This form of inbreeding can be estimated from pedigrees and is measured by F_x, the inbreeding coefficient of individual X. For example, progeny produced by two full sibs have an inbreeding coefficient of 0.25. The text by Falconer (1981) explains the calculation of inbreeding coefficients.

The confusion of the term inbreeding is often greatest in reference to hatchery populations. When the statement is made that a hatchery strain is "inbred," it is usually meant that this population has been maintained by breeding a small number of parents and thus has lost genetic variation because of matings among related individuals. There is usually no implication that the strain is not panmictic.

2.5.5 Population Structure and Migration

In the previous section, we discussed a model in which a population of fish was divided into several genetic subpopulations. Such divisions occur in almost all species of fish. That is, a species rarely consists of a single, large randomly mating population; most are divided into subpopulations by space and time (i.e., geographical or temporal separation). Why, then, do the separate subpopulations not become fixed for alternative genetic types, as in our inbreeding example? The answer, of course, is that the subpopulations are not completely isolated. Rather, there is some amount of genetic exchange (migration) among subpopulations.

Genetic variation within a species can be conceptualized at two fundamental levels: genetic variation within subpopulations and genetic divergence among subpopulations. This is easiest to understand if we examine the two extremes. If there is a great deal of migration among subpopulations, the effect will be to integrate them into a single randomly mating population. Thus, there will be a large amount of genetic variation within every subpopulation and no genetic differences among subpopulations. The other extreme is complete isolation of the subpopulations. In this case, there will be less variation within each subpopulation but large divergences among subpopulations.

The distribution of genetic variation within a species depends upon the size of the local subpopulations, the length of time the subpopulations have been isolated, and the amount of migration that occurs. Genetic drift reduces genetic variation within small subpopulations; thus, the smaller the subpopulations, the less genetic variation they will maintain. The longer subpopulations have been isolated, the more time they have had to accumulate genetic differences. The less genetic exchange there is among subpopulations, the less genetically similar they will be. All of these factors interact to bring about the actual distribution of genetic variation within a species. The paper by Allendorf and Phelps (1981) provides an introduction to these dynamics.

Gyllensten (1985) compared the distribution of intraspecific genetic variation in 19 species of fish for which data were available in the literature. He concluded that there is more genetic variation in marine than in freshwater species. Furthermore, a much higher proportion of the intraspecific variation within freshwater species is due to genetic differences between geographic locations than it is within marine species (31.7 versus 4.2%, Table 2.6). Anadromous species were intermediate between marine and freshwater species for both of these measures. Gyllensten concluded that these differences result principally from larger population sizes and higher migration rates in marine species.

The rich potential for understanding genetic population structure through analysis of mtDNA has only begun to be realized. Polymorphism in mtDNA of

Table 2.6 Proportion of total intraspecific genetic variation resulting from genetic differences between local populations $(1 - G_S)$ in marine, anadromous, and freshwater species of fish (Gyllensten 1985).

Species	Number of Populations	Loci	$1 - G_S$ (%)
Marine species			
Atlantic herring	14	17	0.7
	7	5	1.4
Eelpout	34	3	1.4
Fourhorn sculpin	18	30	1.7
Milkfish	14	38	4.1
Pacific herring	21	40	18.1
Walleye pollock	14	28	2.1
Mean			4.2
Anadromous species			
Atlantic salmon	32	37	21.4
Chum salmon	13	12	2.2
Coho salmon	6	17	2.9
Sockeye salmon	13	26	7.5
Mean			8.5
Freshwater species			
Arctic char	10	37	24.4
	5	26	53.3
Bluegill	8	3	33.1
Brown trout	38	35	36.8
Lake trout	10	50	5.5
Lake whitefish	5	32	13.4
Rainbow trout	38	16	15.0
Shorthead sculpin	16	33	46.1
Slimy sculpin	6	33	76.2
Vendace	20	25	13.9
Mean			31.7

American and European eels provides an excellent example of the potential of this technique (Avise et al. 1986). Lack of geographical differentiation in mtDNA among American eel samples from 4,000 km of North American coastline is consistent with the hypothesis of random mating (panmixia) and random distribution of larvae. However, comparison of American and European eels revealed striking divergence that allows rejection of some previous suggestions that the two forms belong to a single panmictic population. These results of mtDNA studies support previous studies of genetic variation of proteins in populations of these fishes (Williams and Koehn 1984).

2.6 OVERVIEW

Genetics is a broad discipline that requires a detailed understanding of several different areas, ranging from the latest biochemical advances in molecular biology through the mathematics and statistics necessary to understand the mechanics of inheritance and population biology. Genetics has had a relatively low profile in fisheries biology. We believe this lack of emphasis on genetics resulted because, although they are extremely important in the long run, genetic considerations are not so important immediately. For example, disease can wipe out a hatchery's production in a week and must be guarded against constantly, but the continual loss of genetic variation because of improper breeding practices is likely to be detectable only after several generations.

Another problem in the maintenance of hatchery stocks is that selective changes through adaptation to hatchery conditions are unavoidable (Hynes et al. 1981). Perhaps more importantly, however, some of the selective mortality that would occur naturally in wild populations may not occur under hatchery conditions. Thus, physiologically, morphologically, or behaviorally inferior genotypes that would not survive in the wild may contribute to subsequent generations in the hatchery and, therefore, may be found at higher frequencies in hatchery stocks (e.g., Moyle 1969). This "release" from the selective pressures of the wild environment may contribute substantially to the deterioration of hatchery stocks. Again, however, these problems are not going to be of obvious immediate concern to a hatchery manager. Such selective changes are likely to affect the performance of the fish only after they are stocked into the wild; thus, expression of these genetic effects is likely to be delayed and even undetected without some evaluation of how different stocks perform after stocking.

Managers of natural fish populations traditionally have been concerned with the immediate resource of interest: the abundance and size of fish available for harvesting. Because of this short-term perspective, the biological perspective of fishery management has been dominated by ecology and population dynamics. Relatively little attention has been directed towards an understanding of the genetics of these populations. The elegant studies by Ricker (1981) of the possible genetic effects of harvesting on stocks of Pacific salmon have been an exception.

Interest in the genetics of fisheries resources has increased recently for three primary reasons. First is the concern about the selective effects of harvesting on fish populations and the potentially harmful genetic effects of such harvesting (e.g., Ricker 1981). Second is the recognition that genetically discrete races, stocks, or subpopulations of many fish species should be harvested as distinct units. Indiscriminate mixed harvesting of subpopulations can lead to the extirpation of local units through differential harvest rates. Third is the problem of species extinction caused by human alterations of aquatic habitats (Ono et al. 1983; Vrijenhoek et al. 1985). Genetics will play an increasingly important role in the future management of fisheries resources.

2.7 REFERENCES

Allendorf, F. W., K. L. Knudsen, and R. F. Leary. 1983. Adaptive significance of differences in the tissue-specific expression of a phosphoglucomutase gene in rainbow trout. Proceedings of the National Academy of Sciences of the USA 80:1397–1400.
Allendorf, F. W., K. L. Knudsen, and S. R. Phelps. 1982. Identification of a gene regulating the tissue expression of a phosphoglucomutase locus in rainbow trout. Genetics 102:259–268.
Allendorf, F. W., and S. R. Phelps. 1981. Use of allelic frequencies to describe population structure. Canadian Journal of Fisheries and Aquatic Sciences 38:1507–1514.
Allendorf, F. W., and N. Ryman. 1987. Genetic management of hatchery stocks. Pages 141–159 in N. Ryman and F. Utter, editors. Population genetics & fishery management. University of Washington Press, Seattle.

Allendorf, F. W., and G. H. Thorgaard. 1984. Tetraploidy and the evolution of salmonid fishes. Pages 1–53 *in* B. J. Turner, editor. Evolutionary genetics of fishes. Plenum, New York.

Allendorf, F. W., and F. M. Utter. 1979. Population genetics. Pages 407–454 *in* W. S. Hoar, D. J. Randall, and J. R. Brett, editors. Fish physiology, volume 8. Academic Press, New York.

Altukhov, Y. P., and E. A. Salmenkova. 1987. Stock transfer relative to natural organization, management, and conservation of fish populations. Pages 333–343 *in* N. Ryman and F. Utter, editors. Population genetics & fishery management. University of Washington Press, Seattle.

Aspinwall, N. 1974. Genetic analysis of North American populations of the pink salmon, *Oncorhynchus gorbuscha*, possible evidence for the neutral mutation–random drift hypothesis. Evolution 28:295–305.

Aulstad, D., T. Gjedrem, and H. Skjervold. 1972. Genetic and environmental sources of variation in length and weight of rainbow trout (*Salmo gairdneri*). Journal of the Fisheries Research Board of Canada 29:237–241.

Avise, J. C., G. S. Helfman, N. C. Saunders, and L. S. Hales. 1986. Mitochondrial DNA differentiation in North Atlantic eels: population genetic consequences of an unusual life history pattern. Proceedings of the National Academy of Sciences of the USA 83: 4350–4354.

Avise, J. C., and R. A. Lansman. 1983. Polymorphism of mitochondrial DNA in populations of higher animals. Pages 147–164 *in* M. Nei and R. K. Koehn, editors. Evolution of genes and proteins. Sinauer Associates, Sunderland, Massachusetts.

Ayala, F. J. 1984. Molecular polymorphism: how much is there and why is there so much? Developmental Genetics 4:379–391.

Bams, R. A. 1976. Survival and propensity for homing as affected by presence or absence of locally adapted paternal genes in two transplanted populations of pink salmon (*Oncorhynchus gorbuscha*). Journal of the Fisheries Research Board of Canada 33: 2716–2725.

Bateson, W., and R. C. Punnett. 1906. Experimental studies in the physiology of heredity. Reports to the Evolution Committee of the Royal Society, London.

Becker, W. A. 1984. Manual of quantitative genetics. Students Book Corporation, Pullman, Washington.

Behnke, R. J. 1972. The systematics of salmonid fishes of recently glaciated lakes. Journal of the Fisheries Research Board of Canada 29:639–671.

Bell, M. A. 1984. Evolutionary phenetics and genetics: the threespine stickleback, *Gasterosteus aculeatus*, and related species. Pages 431–528 *in* B. J. Turner, editor. Evolutionary genetics of fishes. Plenum, New York.

Borst, P., and L. A. Grivell. 1981. Small is beautiful—portrait of a mitochondrial genome. Nature (London) 290:443–444.

Bregliano, J. C., G. Picard, A. Bucheton, A. Pelisson, J. M. Lavige, and P. L'Heritier. 1980. Hybrid dysgenesis in *Drosophila melanogaster*. Science (Washington, D.C.) 207:606–611.

Bridges, W. R., and B. von Limbach. 1972. Inheritance of albinism in rainbow trout. Journal of Heredity 63:152–153.

Cherfas, N. B. 1981. Gynogenesis in fishes. Pages 255–273 *in* V. S. Kirpichnikov, editor. Genetic bases of fish selection. Springer-Verlag, New York.

Chevassus, B. 1976. Variabilite et heritabilite des performances de croissance chez la truite arc-en-ciel (*Salmo gairdneri* Rich). Annales de Genetique et de Selection Animale 8: 273–283.

Chevassus, B., J. M. Blanc, and J. M. Bergot. 1979. Genetic analysis of the number of pyloric caeca in brown trout (*Salmo trutta* L.) and rainbow trout (*Salmo gairdneri* Rich). II. Effet du genotype du milieu l'elevage et de l'alimentation sur la realization du caractere chex la truite arc-en-ciel. Annales de Genetique et de Selection Animale 11:79–92.

Cooper, D. W. 1968. The significance level in multiple tests made simultaneously. Heredity 23:614–617.

Danzmann, R. G., M. M. Ferguson, and F. W. Allendorf. 1986a. Does enzyme heterozygosity influence developmental rate in rainbow trout? Heredity 56:417–425.

Danzmann, R. G., M. M. Ferguson, F. W. Allendorf, and K. L. Knudsen. 1986b. Heterozygosity and developmental rate in a strain of rainbow trout (*Salmo gairdneri*). Evolution 40:86–93.

Darwin, C. 1859. The origin of species. John Murray, London.

Donaldson, L. R., and P. Olson. 1955. Development of rainbow trout brood stock by selective breeding. Transactions of the American Fisheries Society 85:93–101.

Echelle, A. A., A. F. Echelle, and C. D. Crozier. 1983. Evolution of an all-female fish, *Menidia clarkhubbsi* (Atherinidae). Evolution 37:772–784.

Echelle, A. A., and D. T. Mosier. 1981. All-female fish: a cryptic species of *Menidia* (Atherinidae). Science (Washington, D.C.) 212:1411–1413.

Fairbairn, D. J., and D. A. Roff. 1980. Testing genetic models of isozyme variability without breeding data: can we depend on the χ^2? Canadian Journal of Fisheries and Aquatic Sciences 37:1149–1159.

Falconer, D. S. 1981. Introduction to quantitative genetics, 2nd edition. Longman, New York.

Ferguson, M. M., and R. G. Danzmann. 1985. Pleiotropic effects of a regulatory gene (Pgm1-t) on the social behavior of juvenile rainbow trout (*Salmo gairdneri*). Canadian Journal of Zoology 63:2847–2851.

Ferris, S. D. 1984. Tetraploidy and the evolution of catostomid fishes. Pages 54–93 *in* B. J. Turner, editor. Evolutionary genetics of fishes. Plenum, New York.

Ferris, S. D., and W. J. Berg. 1987. The utility of mitochondrial DNA in fish genetics and fishery management. Pages 277–299 *in* N. Ryman and F. Utter, editors. Population genetics & fishery management. University of Washington Press, Seattle.

Gall, G. A. E., and S. J. Gross. 1978. A genetic analysis of the performance of three rainbow trout broodstocks. Aquaculture 15:113–127.

Gagal'chii, N. G. 1984. Biochemical polymorphism of Kamchatka pink salmon *Oncorhynchus gorbuscha* (Walb.). Part I. Frequencies of alleles of polymorphic loci in odd-year generation. Genetika 21:854–860.

Gilbert, W. 1985. Genes-in-pieces revisited. Science (Washington, D.C.) 228:823–834.

Gyllensten, U. 1985. The genetic structure of fish: differences in the intraspecific distribution of biochemical genetic variation between marine, anadromous, and freshwater species. Journal of Fish Biology 26:691–699.

Gyllensten, U., D. Wharton, and A. C. Wilson. 1985. Maternal inheritance of mitochondrial DNA during backcrossing of two species of mice. Journal of Heredity 76:321–324.

Gyllensten, U., and A. C. Wilson. 1987. Mitochondrial DNA of salmonids: inter- and intraspecific variability detected with restriction enzymes. Pages 301–317 *in* N. Ryman and F. Utter, editors. Population genetics & fishery management. University of Washington Press, Seattle.

Hershberger, W. K., E. L. Brannon, L. R. Donaldson, G. A. Yokoyama, and S. W. Roley. 1976. Salmonid aquaculture studies: selective breeding. Page 61 *in* Annual report of the College of Fisheries. University of Washington College of Fisheries, Contribution 444, Seattle.

Hynes, J. D., E. H. Brown, Jr., J. H. Helle, N. Ryman, and D. A. Webster. 1981. Guidelines for the culture of fish stocks for resource management. Canadian Journal of Fisheries and Aquatic Sciences 38:1867–1876.

IUBNC (International Union of Biochemistry, Nomenclature Committee). 1984. Enzyme nomenclature 1984. Academic Press, Orlando, Florida.

Jacquard, A. 1975. Inbreeding: one word, several meanings. Theoretical Population Biology 7:338–363.

Kallman, K. D. 1984. A new look at sex determination in poeciliid fishes. Pages 95–169 *in* B. J. Turner, editor. Evolutionary genetics of fishes. Plenum, New York.

Kallman, K. D., and V. Borkoski. 1978. A sex-linked gene controlling the onset of sexual maturity in female and male platyfish (*Xiphophorus maculatus*), fecundity in females and adult size in males. Genetics 89:79–119.

Kallman, K. D., and M. P. Schreibman. 1973. A sex-linked gene controlling gonadotrop species of poeciliid fish. Heredity 28:297–310.

Kanis, E., T. Reftie, and T. Gjedrem. 1976. A genetic analysis of egg, alevin and fry mortality in salmon (*Salmo salar*), sea trout (*S. trutta*) and rainbow trout (*S. gairdneri*). Aquaculture 8:259–268.

Kirby, G. C. 1975. Heterozygote frequencies in small subpopulations. Theoretical Population Biology 8:31–48.

Kirpichnikov, V. S. 1981. Genetic bases of fish selection. Springer-Verlag, New York.

Leary, R. F., F. W. Allendorf, and K. L. Knudsen. 1985. Inheritance of meristic variation and the evolution of developmental stability in rainbow trout. Evolution 39:308–314.

Leary, R. F., F. W. Allendorf, and K. L. Knudsen. 1984a. Major morphological effects of a regulatory gene: *Pgm1-t* in rainbow trout. Molecular Biology and Evolution 1:183–194.

Leary, R. F., F. W. Allendorf, and K. L. Knudsen. 1984b. Superior developmental stability of heterozygotes at enzyme loci in salmonid fishes. American Naturalist 124:540–551.

Li, W.-H., C. C. Cheng, and C. I. Wu. 1985. Evolution of DNA sequences. Pages 1–94 *in* R. J. MacIntyre, editor. Molecular evolutionary genetics. Plenum, New York.

Marx, J. L. 1985. Putting the human genome on the map. Science (Washington, D.C.) 229:150–151.

Monaco, P. J., E. M. Rasch, and J. S. Balsano. 1984. Apomictic reproduction in the Amazon Molly, *Poecilia formosa*, and its triploid hybrids. Pages 311–328 *in* B. J. Turner, editor. Evolutionary genetics of fishes. Plenum, New York.

Moore, W. S. 1984. Evolutionary ecology of unisexual fishes. Pages 329–398 *in* B. J. Turner, editor. Evolutionary genetics of fishes. Plenum, New York.

Morizot, D. C., and M. J. Siciliano. 1984. Gene mapping in fishes and other vertebrates. Pages 173–234 *in* B. J. Turner, editor. Evolutionary genetics of fishes. Plenum, New York.

Mork, J., R. Giskeodegard, and G. Sundnes. 1984. Population genetic studies in cod (*Gadus morhua* L.) by means of the haemoglobin polymorphism: observations in a Norwegian coastal population. Fiskeridirektoratets Skrifter Serie Havundersokelser 17:449–471.

Moyle, P. B. 1969. Comparative behavior of young brook trout of domestic and wild origin. Progressive Fish-Culturist 31:51–57.

Ono, R. D., J. D. Williams, and A. Wagner. 1983. Vanishing fishes of North America. Stone Wall Press, Washington, D.C.

Powers, D. A., L. DiMichele, and A. R. Place. 1983. The use of enzyme kinetics to predict differences in cellular metabolism, developmental rate, and swimming performance between LDH-B genotypes of the fish, *Fundulus heteroclitus*. Isozymes: Current Topics in Biological and Medical Research 10:147–170.

Punnett, R. C. 1904. Merism and sex in "*Spinax niger*." Biometrica 3:313–362.

Ricker, W. E. 1972. Hereditary and environmental factors affecting certain salmonid populations. Pages 27–160 *in* R. C. Simon and P. A. Larkin, editors. The stock concept in Pacific salmon. H. R. MacMillan. Lectures in Fisheries, University of British Columbia, Vancouver.

Ricker, W. E. 1981. Changes in the average size and average age of Pacific salmon. Canadian Journal of Fisheries and Aquatic Sciences 38:1636–1656.

Ryman, N. 1981. Conservation of genetic resources: experiences from the brown trout (*Salmo trutta*). Ecological Bulletin (Stockholm) 34:61–74.

Ryman, N., F. W. Allendorf, and G. Ståhl. 1979. Reproductive isolation with little genetic divergence in sympatric populations of brown trout (*Salmo trutta*). Genetics 92:247–262.

Schultz, R. J. 1977. Evolution and ecology of unisexual fishes. Evolutionary Biology 10:277–331.

Schultz, R. J. 1980. Role of polyploidy in the evolution of fishes. Pages 313–340 *in* W. W. Lewis, editor. Polyploidy: biological relevance. Plenum, New York.

Shaklee, J. B., F. W. Allendorf, D. C. Morizot, and G. S. Whitt. 1990. Gene nomenclature for protein-coding loci in fish. Transactions of the American Fisheries Society 119:2–15.

Sokal, R. R., and J. F. Rohlf. 1981. Biometry, 2nd edition. Freeman, San Francisco.

Ståhl, G., and N. Ryman. 1982. Simple Mendelian inheritance at a locus coding for α-glycerophosphate dehydrogenase in brown trout (*Salmo trutta*). Hereditas 96:313–315.

Sturtevant, A. H., and G. W. Beadle. 1939. An introduction to genetics. Dover, New York.

Swain, D. P., and C. C. Lindsey. 1984. Selective predation for vertebral number of young sticklebacks, *Gasterosteus aculeatus*. Canadian Journal of Fisheries and Aquatic Sciences 41:1231–1233.

Syvanen, M. 1984. The evolutionary implications of mobile genetic elements. Annual Review of Genetics 18:271–294.

Utter, F. M. 1981. Biological criteria for definition of species and distinct intraspecific populations of anadromous salmonids under the U.S. Endangered Species Act of 1973. Canadian Journal of Fisheries and Aquatic Sciences 38:1626–1635.

Vrijenhoek, R. C. 1984. The evolution of clonal diversity in *Poeciliopsis*. Pages 399–429 *in* B. J. Turner, editor. Evolutionary genetics of fishes. Plenum, New York.

Vrijenhoek, R. C., M. E. Douglas, and G. K. Meffe. 1985. Conservative genetics of endangered fish populations in Arizona. Science (Washington, D.C.) 229:400–402.

Williams, G. C., and R. K. Koehn. 1984. Population genetics of north Atlantic catadromous eels (*Anguilla*). Pages 529–560 *in* B. J. Turner, editor. Evolutionary genetics of fishes. Plenum, New York.

Chapter 3

Systematics

JOHN G. LUNDBERG AND LUCINDA A. McDADE[1]

3.1 INTRODUCTION

The waters of Earth support an enormous diversity of fishes. Recent compilations include 17,600 to 21,000 living species of fishes (Nelson 1984), or about half of all vertebrate species, and newly discovered species are described and named each year. Based on the fossil record, the number of extinct fishes is vast and our knowledge of them is expanding. Further, even superficial examination indicates that recognizable groups (taxa) of fishes exist above the species level. It is the task of systematics to discover taxonomic patterns of diversity and to relate these patterns to underlying evolutionary processes. Systematic ichthyology seeks to provide the ordered reference system of fish life and, therefore, is fundamental to both applied and pure aspects of fish biology. All disciplines that require knowledge of fish identification, relationships, and spatial and temporal distributions rely directly upon systematics. Its major goals are listed in Box 3.1 and are described further in the sections that follow.

There are three schools of modern systematic theory and practice: *phylogenetic systematics, evolutionary systematics,* and *phenetics.* Phylogenetic and evolutionary systematists share the premise that we can objectively infer the evolutionary history of life and that classification should be based on this history. These two schools differ in that phylogenetic systematists insist that all taxa be genealogical entities whereas evolutionary systematists argue that other aspects (e.g., morphological or ecological distinctiveness) should be considered in delimiting taxa (see Section 3.6.2). Many pheneticists argue that it is not possible to uncover evolutionary history with sufficient accuracy to provide the basis for classification (see Section 3.5). They maintain that it is best to classify organisms based on objective measures of their overall phenotypic similarity. In this chapter, we emphasize *phylogenetic systematics* or *cladistics.* This approach to systematics has won wide acceptance among ichthyologists (Nelson 1972). We will point to differences of opinion among systematists, but there is not space to exhaustively compare the schools. Additional journals and books on the theory and practice of systematics follow.

General. Journals: *Systematic Zoology, Systematic Botany, Evolution, Cladistics, Taxon;* books: Blackwelder (1967), Crowson (1970), Ross (1974).

Phylogenetic Systematics. Hennig (1966), Eldredge and Cracraft (1980), Nelson and Platnick (1981), Wiley (1981).

Evolutionary Systematics. Simpson (1961), Mayr (1969).

---

[1]This chapter reflects equal contributions by the coauthors.

Box 3.1   Goals of Systematic Ichthyology

1. Discover and describe taxonomic groups of fishes that are consistent with evolutionary principles. This goal includes discovery of phylogenetic groups at all levels, from intraspecific through specific to supraspecific.

2. Relate phylogenetic patterns to evolutionary processes.

3. Construct biological classifications of the taxonomic groups discovered.

4. Provide a uniform and, so far as possible, stable system of unique, internationally accepted names for taxa as well as a guide to their nomenclatural history (i.e., synonymy).

5. Carry out surveys of the fish faunas of the world.

6. Provide keys and field guides to facilitate identification of fishes.

7. Archive and curate fish specimens for study and reference.

8. Disseminate results of systematic research.

Phenetics. Sokal and Sneath (1963), Jardine and Sibson (1971), Sneath and Sokal (1973).

Although myriad questions remain, notable advances have been made in systematic ichthyology since the 1960s (e.g., Rosen 1985). Much progress has resulted from the development of a rigorous phylogenetic framework for handling systematic data and results, from new methods of data acquisition (e.g., molecular and morphometric), and from computerized data analysis. However, even more credit is due to leaders in this field for their pacesetting contributions and for their positive encouragement of colleagues. With this in mind, we dedicate this chapter to the late Donn E. Rosen, who was Curator of Ichthyology at the American Museum of Natural History from 1961 to 1986.

3.2   PRINCIPLES OF PHYLOGENETIC SYSTEMATICS

3.2.1   Phylogenetic Groups

Systematics involves the ordering of individuals into groups. The nature of these groups is a fundamental and controversial issue. Organisms could be grouped purely for human convenience (e.g., bait fish, sport fish, rough fish). Although such groupings serve some purposes, they are not based on any explanatory principle of diversity and will not necessarily reflect the order that has long been evident in the natural world. Groups that generally conform to species, as delimited by systematists, have been and continue to be recognized by humans who lack biological training (Gould 1979). The same is often true at higher taxonomic levels. Carr (1941) noted that "every damn fool knows a catfish," and the same can be said of lampreys, skates, pikes, anchovies, and so on. Further, a fundamental hierarchical or nested pattern of groups within larger groups was recognized by students of organic diversity long before Darwin.

Early systematists believed that this natural order was divinely imposed at the instant of creation (Futuyma 1979). This view has been virtually replaced by the theory that evolutionary processes (divinely guided or not) have produced the hierarchical pattern discernible in nature. A central principle of evolution is that all organisms share a common evolutionary history. There is one true genealogy for all life which, fully resolved, would depict the pattern of relationships that links all individuals, living and extinct. Evolutionarily minded systematists argue that groups should reflect this concept of the basis for order in the natural world. Two major objectives of phylogenetic systematics are, therefore, to reconstruct life's genealogy and to use that genealogy as the basis for classification.

3.2.1.1 Species

At a very fine level, life's genealogy includes all individuals that ever lived. One approach to phylogenetics would be to compile the genealogy of individuals. This approach is appealing because it merely extends the parent–offspring relationships with which we are all familiar. The unwieldiness of phylogenetic work at this level is, however, amply evidenced by problems encountered in tracking human genealogies for even a few generations.

Systematists usually proceed toward the goal of genealogical reconstruction by grouping organisms into species and using species as units for phylogenetic analysis. Approaching genealogical reconstruction with species rather than individuals increases the feasibility of the task, but at the same time, raises many difficult theoretical problems about species. Do species exist in nature or are they merely human constructs? Is there a universal species concept that is appropriate for vertebrates, plants, protozoa, bacteria, and so on (Doyen and Slobodchikoff 1974; Hull 1976; Mishler and Donoghue 1982)? Although species remain theoretically controversial, problems in delimiting species are, in practice, relatively rare. For example, considerable accord exists among ichthyologists as to the species of North American fishes (e.g., Lee et al. 1980; Robins et al. 1980), although this same group of scientists might find it difficult to agree on a precise definition of species.

We may proceed toward resolution of the species problem for ichthyological systematics from two perspectives. First, we might work from the kinship relations that we know exist among individuals and come to a strictly genealogical concept of species. Alternatively, we might begin with groups of organisms that are recognized as species by numerous independent observers and ask what biological characteristics these groups share that can provide criteria for a generally applicable concept of species.

A genealogical concept of sexually reproducing species includes temporally "horizontal" and "vertical" relationships among individuals. If horizontal mating relationships are emphasized, we view species as groups of individuals that interbreed; this is Mayr's (1963) *biological species concept.* If, instead, we stress vertical, ancestor–descendant relationships, the concept of species as lineages emerges (Simpson 1961; Wiley 1981). These two aspects of relationship are compatible: species include individuals from the same ancestor–descendant series, some of whom will compose the reproductive community that produces the next generation. However, this concept of species fails to distinguish species from *populations,* which are usually defined in much the same way: "a group of conspecific organisms that . . . exhibit reproductive continuity from generation to generation . . ." (Futuyma 1986). Unlike populations, many unanimously accepted species have ranges that are fragmented into isolated populations that cannot possibly form a single reproductive community. Because species are usually more inclusive units than populations, an adequate species concept must identify other criteria for uniting more than one population into a single species.

What properties do conspecific individuals share that allow biologists to agree on species delimitations with relative ease? In practice, the most important factor in species recognition is greater similarity of organisms within a species than among species. Two biological processes are identified most frequently as producing the observed similarity within species: natural selection and gene flow. The relative importances of natural selection and gene flow have been debated (Ehrlich and Raven 1969; Jackson and Pounds 1979), and it is clear that neither process alone can satisfactorily explain all of the groups recognized by systematists as species. Many studies have revealed significant, genetically based, ecotypic differentiation within species. Similarly, for species that are very wide-ranging or are made up of discrete populations, gene flow among isolated populations may be nonexistent. In these cases, species integrity must be ascribed to stabilizing selection or lack of divergence (whether due to selection or genetic drift) among genetically isolated subunits (Futuyma 1986). On the other hand, theoretical work has modeled the conditions under which divergent selection can cause genetic differentiation within an interbreeding group (Endler 1977). It appears to be an astonishing truth that no single biological principle can explain the existence of all species.

Clarification of the species problem might come from examining how systematists deal with "difficult" species. There are, for example, exceptions to the generalization that conspecific individuals look more like one another than like individuals of other species (e.g., poeciliids are sexually dimorphic such that females may be more similar to females of different species than to males of their own species). The evidence used to solve such problems is usually genealogical: we seek to demonstrate that offspring of a single female include dissimilar male and female morphs and that the two morphs interbreed. If such data are not available, the existence of unisexual phenotypes is usually accepted as evidence of sexual dimorphism within species (but see Box 3.2, example 5).

Another type of species problem involves populations that are phenotypically indistinguishable but cannot interbreed due to geographic, ecological, or temporal isolation. In such cases, systematists frequently join the isolated populations into a single species. In taking this step, they suggest that species are genealogical units that retain conspecific status until differentiation occurs. In other cases, systematists confront populations that are morphologically distinguishable but are mutually more similar than is typical of distinct species within the group. Such populations may be grouped into *subspecies,* which may be viewed as allopatric lineages in the process of genealogically dividing and differentiating. Subspecies may remain isolated and continue to differentiate, or may reunite following removal of the barriers that currently isolate them.

The strategy used by systematists to solve species "problems" suggests that the most useful concept of species combines genealogy with other biological factors to account for intraspecific coherence. We view species as *lineages of individuals belonging to one or more populations that owe their mutual similarities to common ancestry and lack of differentiation.* Differences may evolve among populations of a species through divergent selection and other mechanisms of change. Conspecificity persists, however, until populations become isolated as distinct lineages. For phylogenetic systematics, the concept of species as genealogical entities is critical: species must be distinct lineages in order for their relationships to provide an accurate depiction of the genealogy of life.

3.2.1.2 Speciation, Sister Groups, and Ancestors

The genealogy of life on Earth includes a multitude of extinct species, as well as millions of extant species. Clearly, an important aspect of life's history has been the multiplication of species, the division of ancestral species into genealogically separate descendant or daughter species. The evolutionary isolation of daughter lineages is *speciation* or *cladogenesis* and results in a hierarchical pattern of lineages.

Sister Groups.   Two lineages are sister groups if they share a more recent common ancestor than either shares with other known lineages. Sister-group pairs originate at the same time and are, therefore, of equivalent age. Subsequent cladogenesis may occur in one or both sister groups; there is no limit to their diversity. Later events do not alter the original sister-group relationship, but all descendant lineages of the original sister lineages must be included in the units called sister groups. For example, the hagfishes, which comprise about 33 known species, may have as their sister group the taxon composed of all other vertebrates, which number more than 43,000 living species (Maisey 1986).

Cladogenesis and speciation are not always considered synonymous. Imagine a single lineage that is well represented by fossils and has undergone evolutionary change (*anagenesis*) without splitting so that the oldest and youngest members of the lineage are markedly dissimilar. Some systematists would prefer to break the single lineage into separate species, arguing that conspecific individuals should be relatively homogeneous. However, no species remains static between even sequential generations and thus there can be no nonarbitrary criteria for determining how much change is necessary to justify segmenting unbranched lineages into distinct species.

Although the division of an ancestral lineage is usually depicted as a bifurcation, it is possible that a lineage may give rise to three or more daughter lineages essentially simultaneously and without the development of characters needed to resolve bifurcations that are closely spaced in time (McCune et al. 1984). Such multifurcations present some problems for classification and phylogenetic methodology, as discussed below, but they must be considered possible.

An added complication for depiction of genealogies as sequential bifurcations is the well-documented existence of hybrid species whose ancestors belonged to separate lineages. Such events are shown as reticulations between genealogical branches. The inclusion of hybrid species in genealogies does not pose serious problems in ichthyology because, although interspecific hybridization is common among fishes (Hubbs 1955), speciation by hybridization is apparently rare (but see Schultz 1969; Uyeno and Smith 1972; Menzel 1976; Buth 1979). Species of hybrid origin present greater problems for systematists working with other organisms (e.g., plants).

Ancestors and Descendants.   The actual ancestors of any two sister species were a subset of their most recent common ancestral species; that is, the ancestors were those individuals that were reproductively active at the time of speciation. The same is true of the ancestors of higher taxa. Statements identifying groups above the species level as ancestors, although frequently made, are imprecise. For examples, consider the expressions "agnathans are ancestral to gnathostomes" and "flatfishes are derived from perciforms." In each expression, the stated ancestral group is composed of numerous separate lineages (species and populations within species) that cannot possibly have served as direct ancestors of the stated descendant group. Perhaps what is intended by these statements is this: if we could identify the ancestral species with certainty, we would place it within the supraspecific taxonomic group identified as ancestral.

3.2.2 Phylogenetic Diagrams and Monophyly

At and above the species level, ancestor–descendant and sister-group relationships can be represented graphically in branching, tree-like diagrams.[2] Trees that depict relationships among several species can be partitioned to delimit groups or higher taxa. A group that is delimited to include *all* descendant branches from an ancestral node is, in the parlance of systematics, *monophyletic*. Because each monophyletic group has a unique origin and is complete (i.e., includes all descendant branches), such entities are genealogically real and have special significance in evolution and systematics (see Section 3.4.1). Trees can also be partitioned to form taxa that fail to meet the criteria of monophyly. Groups that do not include all descendants of their most recent common ancestor are non-monophyletic. *Paraphyletic* and *polyphyletic* are terms often applied to non-monophyletic groups, but systematists are not yet unanimous as to their precise meanings (Wiley 1981; Oosterbroek 1987).

3.3 PRACTICAL SYSTEMATICS AT THE SPECIES LEVEL

3.3.1 Species Delimitation

The same taxonomic boundaries for thousands of fish species are accepted by trained biologists and observant laypersons. Nevertheless, it is not possible to formulate universal criteria for delimiting fish species and there are numerous cases in which taxonomic decisions at this level are problematic. Such difficulties are expected because of the dynamics of evolution and the incomplete data base for many fish groups. Many problems are thought to represent examples of speciation in progress and may be handled by dividing a complex species into "semispecies" or subspecies (geographically isolated and morphologically distinct groups within a species: Mayr 1969). Other cases may represent *cryptic* or *sibling species* (related species that are genealogically isolated but scarcely distinguishable morphologically). Box 3.2 presents examples to illustrate the complexity of the issues, as well as the controversy that often remains when decisions are made. As these examples

---

[2]Different forms of tree-like diagrams are common in systematics and there is some consensus on their terminology. "Cladograms" represent the inferred sister-group relationships among a set of studied species or higher monophyletic taxa. "Phylogenetic trees" or "phylograms" represent genealogical relationships by branching pattern and degrees of evolutionary divergence by differences in branch lengths. "Phenograms" represent levels of observed character resemblance among taxa and need not imply anything historical.

suggest, systematists use direct and indirect evidence from a variety of sources to resolve problems in species delimitation. Direct evidence comes from observations of reproductive interactions (mate selection) among living fishes, and of times and sites of breeding. Indirect evidence comes from patterns of variation of genetic and phenotypic characters, and from geographic distribution of the samples. The sources of evidence used to make taxonomic decisions at the species level are outlined below.

Field Observations of Natural Populations. Where two putative species have syntopic populations (i.e., they are sympatric and occupy the same or adjacent habitats), it is possible to witness their life histories and ecologies. Repeated observation that interbreeding does not occur is taken as prima facie evidence that distinct species are present. Life history studies typically support recognized species boundaries (Breder and Rosen 1966; Barlow 1974; Thresher 1984). The detailed work of Holzberg (1978) and McKaye et al. (1984) on apparent reproductive isolation among closely spaced and similar cichlid fishes in Lake Malawi, Africa, exemplifies species determinations from direct observation of natural reproduction combined with traditional and biochemical analyses. Equally intriguing are discoveries of interbreeding among local polymorphic forms initially thought to represent separate species (Kornfield et al. 1982).

Reproductive Interactions of Transplanted Populations. Allopatric species or populations may come into contact via natural dispersal or introductions. This may allow application of reproductive criteria to assess species limits. Hybridization involving transplanted fishes is frequent, especially in disturbed habitats (Hubbs 1955). However, hybridization of transplanted fishes is difficult to interpret because fish may exhibit abnormal behavior when moved into strange environments and communities. In the case of transplanted stocks, Hubbs (1961) asserted that chances for hybridization are increased because transplants will often be less abundant than residents. Assessing the consequences of hybridization requires study of F_1 hybrids (e.g., Dowling and Moore 1984). Hybrids may have reduced viability, may be sterile, or may fail to backcross with the parental species. The extensive literature on such cases documents a diversity of outcomes, not all of which are easily interpreted. In some cases, hybridization does not result in breakdown of reproductive isolation, but in others, introgression or lineage fusion occurs (Svardson 1969; Behnke 1970; Dauble and Buschbom 1981; Whitmore 1983).

Experimental Crosses. The ability of fishes from problematic groups to interbreed can be tested in laboratories and experimental ponds. These tests may involve behavioral mate-preference experiments or artificial crosses by standard hatchery techniques. The results of such tests may be taken as evidence for conspecific status only with the caveat that there are many documented cases of species that do not interbreed in nature but readily do so in the laboratory. Failure to interbreed is also difficult to interpret because fish from different habitats or geographic regions may differ in the ecological conditions that induce reproduction. Nevertheless, numerous studies have revealed mate-choice behaviors that serve as reproductive isolating mechanisms among close relatives (Clark et al. 1954; Liley 1966; Fitzsimmons 1972). Artificial hybridization studies yield data on postmating isolating mechanisms (Hubbs and Strawn 1956; Hester 1970; Gold et al. 1979). However, because of the many documented cases of natural hybridization between species thought to be phyletically distant (e.g., intergeneric hybrids), development of viable F_1 hybrids is not unambiguous evidence of conspecificity.

Characters Functionally Related to Reproduction. The majority of fishes are difficult to observe directly and to breed experimentally. For these fishes, systematists must rely on genetically based, phenotypic characters of preserved

---

Box 3.2   Examples of Complex Problems in Species Delimitation

1. Threespine sticklebacks *Gasterosteus aculeatus* occur along the Pacific coast and adjacent inland waters in populations that are differentiated to varying degrees by morphology, reproductive isolation, or both (Hagen 1967; Hagen and McPhail 1970; Bell 1984). Apparent extensive parallel evolution confuses the relationship between similarity and genealogical proximity among the freshwater populations. Bell (1976) recommended that these be referred to by the single species name but that some of the more distinctive populations be named as subspecies, in recognition of their morphological distinctness and reproductive isolation.

2. Tui chubs *Gila bicolor* occur in isolated streams and lakes in the Great Basin area and have, like the threespine sticklebacks, variously differentiated morphologically, ecologically, and reproductively (reviewed by Moyle 1976). In some areas, distinctive stream forms enter lakes but maintain their identities when the lake form occurs with them (e.g., Lakes Tahoe and Pyramid), whereas in other areas, the forms do not remain distinct (e.g., Eagle Lake). The stream and lake forms were originally treated as species in different genera. They are now commonly referred to as subspecies (*G. b. obesus* and *G. b. pectinifer*), although this is contrary to the accepted definition of subspecies as allopatric or parapatric portions of single species.

3. Pink salmon *Oncorhynchus gorbuscha* have the usual drainage-basin isolation of breeding salmonid populations that results from strong homing tendencies; in addition, they have a strongly modal 2-year life cycle, although rare 3-year-old fish have been detected (Scott and Crossman 1973). The odd- and even-year breeding populations may be reproductively isolated and, therefore, genealogically distinct. Despite detectable morphological and genetic differences between the temporally isolated lineages (Aspinwall 1974), these continue to be treated as parts of a single species.

4. The common shiner *Notropis cornutus* and the striped shiner *N. chrysocephalus* occur sympatrically in a checkerboard pattern in the midwestern USA, where they hybridize extensively in some localities but not others (Dowling and Moore 1984). Their status as separate species has been hotly debated, but the weight of current opinion is that they are distinct because the F_1 hybrids, as identified by allozyme patterns ("genetic" markers), appear to be selectively inferior to the parental types. Selection against F_1 hybrids would emphasize the evolutionary distinctness of the parental species.

Box 3.2 Continued.

5. All-female, diploid populations of silversides of the genus *Menidia* occur along the Gulf of Mexico coast (Echelle and Mosier 1982; Echelle et al., in press). These arose from past, independent hybridizations between inland silverside *M. beryllina* and tidewater silverside *M. peninsulae*. Mitochondrial DNA and allozyme markers indicate that the unisexual forms are distinct lineages and do not form a bridge for gene flow between the parental species. In line with the position that species have unitary origins and are distinct evolutionary lineages, the unisexual forms derived from separate hybridization events are considered to be an undetermined number of separate species. One of these has been formally described by Echelle and Mosier (1982) as *Menidia clarkhubbsi*. In contrast, some well-known, all-female lineages of Mexican poeciliid fishes have not been designated as separate species (Schultz 1969).

specimens. Traits that function in mate selection or some other species-specific aspect of life history may have special significance. Such characters include (A) those used by fish to recognize suitable mates, (B) structure of genitalia, and (C) chromosome number and structure.

(A) Closely related species should best be distinguished by the same characteristics used by the fish in selecting mates. These characters are part of the reproductive isolating mechanisms (Mayr 1963). Often these are sexually dimorphic characters or characters that involve one or more sensory modalities. Many examples are found in the literature, but most remain inferential. To actually demonstrate that characters function as reproductive isolating mechanisms requires carefully controlled experimentation. Characters that researchers have suggested may be, or have shown to be, used by fishes to recognize compatible conspecifics are

• visual characters, including (i) courtship displays (Clark et al. 1954; Liley 1966; Fitzsimmons 1972; Kortmulder 1972), (ii) color patterns (Liley 1966; Holzberg 1978; Endler 1983), and (iii) bioluminescence patterns (Nicol 1969);

• chemical characters or pheromones (Pietsch 1976; Liley and Stacey 1983);

• tactile characters, such as nuptial tubercles (Wiley and Collette 1970);

• auditory cues or species-specific responses to sounds (Delco 1960; Gerald 1971);

• electric organ discharge signals (Hopkins 1983; Hagedorn 1988).

(B) Among internally fertilizing species, structural differences in male genitalia are frequently taken as evidence for species delimitation. In the Poeciliidae, marked divergence exists among otherwise similar species in the structure of the male intromissive organs (gonopodia). Such differences may function as mechanical barriers to cross-fertilization.

(C) Matched chromosome structure is generally essential for balanced distribution of chromosomes and genes to gametes, and marked differences in karyotype (see Chapter 6) are taken as evidence of species distinctness (Behnke 1970; LeGrande 1976). However, intraspecific variation in chromosome number is not uncommon in fishes (Behnke 1970; LeGrande and Cavender 1980; Thorgaard 1983; Turner et al. 1985). Therefore, chromosomal data cannot be used without supplemental data on crossability and the reproductive fate of F_1 fish.

Heritable Characters Not Functionally Related to Reproduction.   Most characters used in fish systematics at all taxonomic levels are part of the general,
nonreproductive anatomy. Genetic control of these characters must be known or
assumed and environmental effects on phenotypes must be considered; morphometric and meristic characters are subject to nongenetic, environmental influences (Barlow 1961; Svardson 1969; Lundberg and Stager 1985). Biochemical
characteristics, especially allozyme and mitochondrial DNA variations, are
increasingly used to supplement morphological data at and below the species level
(Avise 1974; Buth 1984; Avise et al. 1987). Unique molecular patterns can serve
as "genetic markers" for populations and species, and are especially useful for
detecting hybrids and gene flow between populations. Detailed treatments of
common morphological and biochemical characters in systematic ichthyology,
and methods for their analysis, are given in Chapters 4 and 5.

In using nonreproductive characters to delimit species, we assume that observed differences reflect postspeciation divergence rather than polymorphism.
The phenomena of polymorphism, polytypy, and sibling species point to the
frequent decoupling of the evolution of reproductive isolation from phenotypic
differentiation. There is no universal scale of morphological or biochemical
("genetic") difference that signals species-level distinctness. Character differences must be supplemented by data on geographic patterns and, whenever
available, on reproductive relations among the putative species.

3.4 SYSTEMATICS ABOVE THE SPECIES LEVEL

3.4.1 Units of Study

Phylogeny can be studied at many levels. A systematist may choose to study
the relationships of species of *Perca*, of the genera of the Percidae, or of the
families of Perciformes. It is essential that the lowest taxonomic units being
compared are monophyletic (Section 3.2.2). Box 3.3 demonstrates that, if study
units are not monophyletic, it may be impossible to discover their correct
genealogical relationships. Systematists working above the species level must
verify, as far as possible, that the lowest taxonomic units being compared in a
study are monophyletic. When monophyly of provisional study units is questionable, the systematist may select more restrictive subgroups as the units for study.
At the lower limit, these can be population samples or even individual specimens.

3.4.2 The Hennig Principle: Evidence of Relationship

Genealogy is real but intangible and relationships can only be inferred.
Sister-group and ancestor–descendant relationships cannot be seen directly. This
is true even for groups with a dense fossil record. Fossil fishes are, after all,
nothing more than preserved body parts that demand systematic interpretation.
The key to recognition of monophyletic groups and to phylogenetic reconstruction
was clearly stated by the German entomologist Willi Hennig (1966). The essence
of Hennig's principle lies in the heritable evolutionary changes that are passed
from ancestors to descendants. Every species is subject to unique evolutionary
events that change *ancestral* (i.e., primitive or *plesiomorphic*) features into
derived (i.e., advanced or *apomorphic*) features. Derived features permit recognition of monophyletic groups because they will be shared by the species in which

---

Box 3.3   The Monophyly Requirement

Unit taxa for a phylogenetic analysis must be monophyletic if the result is to accurately depict the genealogical relationships among the taxa.

Trees **A-D** below depict all possible results of a phylogenetic analysis of contemporaneous taxa X, Y, and Z. Provided the taxa are monophyletic, one of these diagrams correctly depicts phylogenetic relationships. However, if even one of the taxa is *not* monophyletic, such as taxon Y in trees **E** or **F**, the true genealogical relationships may not be among these possible outcomes, and the most thorough phylogenetic analysis will never yield the correct answer.

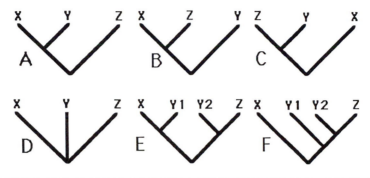

---

that feature evolved and all of that species' descendants as a unique marker of their common evolutionary history (Box 3.4). Such shared, uniquely derived features are called *synapomorphies* in Hennig's terminology.

In a phylogeny involving more than two groups, the groups share varying parts of their phylogenetic history: tarpons and flatfishes share only a relatively ancient portion of their phylogenetic histories, whereas flatfishes of the families Bothidae and Pleuronectidae share a more recent phylogenetic history. These levels of recency of common ancestry are reflected by a nested pattern of shared derived characters (synapomorphies, Box 3.4). Thus, tarpons and flatfishes share only synapomorphies that characterize all teleosts (e.g., expanded hypural and uroneural bones in the caudal skeleton), whereas the two flatfish families share an additional suite of synapomorphies (e.g., special asymmetry) that indicate their longer common evolutionary history (Lauder and Liem 1983).

Hennig's principle requires that each feature that organisms share be ascribed to one of three kinds of similarity: (1) shared uniquely derived similarity (synapomorphy), (2) shared primitive similarity (*symplesiomorphy*), and (3) shared independently derived similarity (*homoplasy*). Only synapomorphy is logically acceptable as evidence of relative recency of common ancestry. Taken together, the shared primitive features (symplesiomorphies) do not form a nested pattern and cannot be used as evidence for exclusive common ancestry (Box 3.4). Homoplasious similarity (parallelisms, convergences, secondary losses) does not reflect common evolutionary history of taxa.

Note that synapomorphy and symplesiomorphy are relative concepts. A feature that is a synapomorphy for a taxon will be a symplesiomorphy *within* that taxon. In Box 3.4, state 1 of character 5 is a synapomorphy for the taxon CDE. Within

Box 3.4 Character State Distribution

The use of ancestral character states (symplesiomorphies) and uniquely derived character states (synapomorphies) to recognize monophyletic groups is illustrated by the phylogeny of species A–E, here diagrammed with 12 numbered character changes from ancestral to derived states.

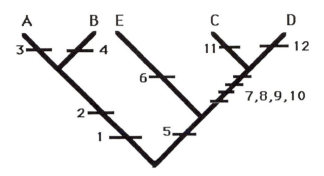

This pattern of character evolution results in the taxonomic distribution of states given in the following character-by-taxon matrix; character states are ancestral (0) or derived (1).

	Character											
Species	1	2	3	4	5	6	7	8	9	10	11	12
A	1	1	1	0	0	0	0	0	0	0	0	0
B	1	1	0	1	0	0	0	0	0	0	0	0
C	0	0	0	0	1	0	1	1	1	1	1	0
D	0	0	0	0	1	0	1	1	1	1	0	1
E	0	0	0	0	1	1	0	0	0	0	0	0

Together, the derived (1) states (synapomorphics) are hierarchically nested and characterize the nested monophyletic groups on the phylogenetic tree.

Characters	Groups sharing "1" state
1,2	A+B
3	A
4	B
5	C+D+E
6	E
7,8,9,10	C+D
11	C
12	D

In contrast, the ancestral (0) states (symplasiomorphies) are not hierarchically nested, and they characterize nonnested, mostly nonmonophyletic groups.

Box 3.4   Continued.

Characters	Groups sharing "0" state
1,2	C+D+E
3	B+C+D+E
4	A+C+D+E
5	A+B
6	A+B+C+D
7,8,9,10	A+B+E
11	A+B+D+E
12	A+B+C+E

Note that, although species E matches A and B in more character states than it does C and D, these are shared ancestral states that do not provide historical information about E's phylogenetic relationships. Only the synapomorphy in character 5 indicates species E's true relationship by common ancestry with C and D.

this taxon, however, state 1 is the ancestral, primitive condition. Similarly, the presence of the Weberian apparatus is a synapomorphy for Otophysi (minnows, catfishes, etc.) in relation to other groups of fishes, but within the subgroups of Otophysi, this feature is shared as a symplesiomorphy because it was already present before the evolution of their most recent common ancestor. Presence of the Weberian apparatus thus argues for monophyly of the Otophysi, but does not argue for monophyly of any taxa within Otophysi.

3.4.3   Sources of Characters and Synapomorphies

Features (or characters) with useful historical information must be heritable. Comparative morphology of adults, larvae, embryos, and fossils has provided most of the data used in phylogenetic inference in fish systematics. Increasingly, comparative data are coming from other fields: physiology (Foreman et al. 1985), behavior and ecology, parasitology (Brooks 1981), protein structure and composition (Avise 1974; Ferris and Whitt 1978; Buth 1984; also see Chapter 5), and karyology (see Chapter 6). Recent technological advances in nucleotide biochemistry have made comparative data available at the level of genetic material (e.g., DNA–DNA hybridization and nucleotide sequencing: Weirfield 1983; Sibley and Ahlquest 1984; Moritz et al. 1987).

It is of paramount importance for every biologist to understand that *all* sources of data are equally likely to yield historically valuable information (Hillis 1987). Before an analysis, there is simply no way to tell which kinds of characters will form the nested patterns of character states among taxa that reflect phylogenetic pattern. Examples of phylogenetically meaningless similarities are known from every type of character, from DNA sequences to osteology. What counts is that each datum be a synapomorphy and reflect a unique event in evolutionary history that is indicative of common ancestry.

3.4.4   Character Analysis

Once a study group has been selected, samples of unit taxa are surveyed comparatively for features that vary among them. In systematics, a character is any aspect of the phenotype or genotype that varies within the study group. A *character state* is the expression of a character found in a unit taxon or individual under study. Unit taxa may be monomorphic for a given character state (e.g., the Weberian complex is present in all otophysan species), or may be polymorphic (e.g., vertebral number varies within most otophysan species). Technical details for the elucidation and description of various types of characters are found in Chapters 4, 5, and 6. The following sections discuss the primary considerations of character analysis.

3.4.4.1   Homology

The different character states of a variable feature must be known sufficiently so that a convincing hypothesis of phylogenetic homology (direct evolutionary continuity) can be made for them. The first line of evidence for phylogenetic homology is similarity among the states in all tangible aspects (e.g., topographic position, material composition, embryonic derivation). The second line of evidence is a posteriori and results from mapping the putatively homologous states on the final phylogenetic hypothesis for the taxa based on all available evidence. The hypothesis of homology is substantiated if this mapping reveals no homoplasy. However, it is often the case that homology hypotheses for individual characters are rejected following analysis because the preferred overall genealogical hypothesis requires independent origins or losses of states previously thought to be homologous. An example is the rejection of the hypothesis of strict phylogenetic homology among fin spines in teleosts. Although spines appear to be the same sorts of things, our current concept of teleostean interrelationships indicates that fin spines evolved independently in different groups. At a higher taxonomic level of comparison, however, fin spines, as well as soft fin rays, are homologous as lepidotrichia. Note also that a posteriori rejections of hypotheses about homology may stimulate useful reexamination of the characters. For example, upon closer investigation, the fin spines of perciforms (perch-like fishes) and siluriforms (catfishes) are structurally and developmentally quite different.

3.4.4.2   Character Independence

When characters are selected, it is important to avoid redundancies due to obvious functional or logical correlations of characters. To include different expressions of a single evolutionary change in an analysis would differentially weight that event. Recall, however, that phylogenetic analysis depends upon the underlying hierarchical correlation of characters due to common history. It is difficult to determine whether two or more correlated features have the same taxonomic distribution because they arose together as parts of a single evolutionary event or because they arose by separate events in the same ancestral group. Most systematists attempt to avoid the problem of correlated characters by using numerous characters from diverse organ systems.

3.4.4.3   Evolutionary Polarity of Character States

An essential step in phylogenetic analysis by Hennig's principle is to distinguish between ancestral and derived character states, that is, to recognize synapomorphies. Is the absence of jaws a synapomorphy that provides evidence for a shared evolutionary history unique to agnathans or is it a primitive feature for all vertebrates? Criteria for addressing questions of polarity have been widely debated (reviewed by Eldredge and Cracraft 1980; Stevens 1980; Nelson and Platnick 1981; Wiley 1981). The major criteria are stated below along with critical comments and key references.

Paleontology. Features that appear earlier in the fossil record of a study group are plesiomorphic relative to features that appear in younger fossils or extant members. The obvious rationale is that just as ancestors necessarily precede descendants, so the ancestors and their ancestral features will be preserved as earlier fossils.

The paleontological criterion has several problems. (1) It requires unwarranted assumptions about the completeness of the sample. The fossil record is too incomplete with respect to time, space, preserved body parts, and relevant taxa to provide detailed information on character state precedence. (2) Application of the criterion requires an a priori assumption that the fossil is a direct ancestor of the groups in question. Temporal precedence alone does not prove direct ancestry. (3) Only rarely are fossils of direct ancestors uncovered, and it is impossible to recognize them as such by any independent method of analysis. (4) Fossils of extinct side lineages that had their own independent histories may be inadvertently used to polarize characters in extant taxa, leading to erroneous conclusions.

Although uncritical application of the paleontological criterion can cause serious difficulties, the fossil record should not be ignored. Paleontological research offers often dazzling glimpses of past fish life. Fossils provide the only direct evidence for the minimum ages of their clades (lineages) and of past distributions that differed from those of today. Fossils can add critically important data for character analysis (Gauthier et al. 1988), and especially at high taxonomic levels, polarity hypotheses derived by application of the paleontological criterion frequently are corroborated by the results of phylogenetic analyses that use other criteria for polarizing characters.

Simpson (1961) and Szalay (1977) have been proponents of the paleontological criterion. Schaeffer et al. (1972), Nelson (1978), Eldredge and Cracraft (1980), and Patterson (1982) have opposed it.

Outgroup Analysis. The plesiomorphic state of a character for the taxa under study (the *ingroup*) is the state that is also found in related taxa (*outgroups*), that is, in the sister group of the ingroup and also in the sister group of those two groups together (Box 3.5). The rationale here is the methodological approach of parsimony, which seeks to minimize assumptions. In this case, the "assumptions" are the evolutionary changes required to explain the observed distribution of character states among taxa.

The outgroup criterion has two principal problems. (1) Complete sampling of outgroups is required. Results may be biased if relevant groups have been omitted because of extinction, insufficient collection, or insufficient review of known materials. (2) Application of this criterion requires a higher-level hypothesis of sister-group relationships. More frequently than not, higher-level relationships are not fully resolved and this reduces the efficacy of the outgroup criterion. If incorrect groups are selected as outgroups, errors are likely. Watrous and

Box 3.5   Outgroup and Ingroup Criteria

Application of outgroup and ingroup criteria to systematics problems is illustrated by the following example.

Problem

Distinguish derived character states within the order Siluriformes from ancestral states in order to construct a phylogenetic hypothesis for selected catfish families within the order.

Working Hypotheses

(a) The ingroup as a whole, Siluriformes, is monophyletic.

(b) Taxa within the ingroup are monophyletic. The taxa considered are the catfish families Diplomystidae (DIP), Ictaluridae (ICT), Bagridae (BAG), Loricariidae (LOR), and Callichthyidae (CAL).

(c) Outgroups, the closest relatives of the ingroup, are monophyletic, and their relationships to the ingroup can be posited with considerable confidence. Outgroups are the orders Gonorhynchiformes (GON), Cypriniformes (CYP), Characiformes (CHA), and Gymnotiformes (GYM).

Application of the outgroup criterion requires hypotheses (a), (b), and (c). The ingroup criterion requires (a) and (b).

General Relationships

The hypothesized pattern of relationships of the ingroup (Siluriformes) to the outgroups is diagramed at right.

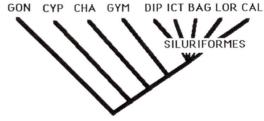

Character States

Four characters that vary within the ingroup are to be polarized with reference to the states of these characters in the outgroups.

Group and taxon	Character I: position of maxillary bone	Character II: maxillary condyle of palatine bone	Character III: nasal barbels	Character IV: external teeth on armor plates
Outgroups				
GON	In gape margin	Single	Absent	Absent
CYP	In gape margin	Single	Absent	Absent
CHA	In gape margin	Single	Absent	Absent
GYM	In gape margin	Single	Absent	Absent
Ingroup				
DIP	In gape margin	Double	Absent	Absent
ICT	Behind gape margin	Single	Present	Absent
BAG	Behind gape margin	Single	Present	Absent
LOR	Behind gape margin	Single	Absent	Present
CAL	Behind gape margin	Single	Absent	Present

Box 3.5   Continued.

Application of the Outgroup Criterion

The character states present in the outgroups are hypothesized to be ancestral among the ingroup taxa. Alternative character states are derived and thus indicate a more recent common ancestry within the ingroup. The following character polarities and ingroup relationships are inferred.

Character	Derived state	Phylogenetic hypothesis
I	Maxillary behind gape margin	
II	Double condyle	
III	Nasal barbels present	
IV	Armor plates with teeth	

Application of the Ingroup Criterion

The ingroup criterion stipulates that the most common character states among ingroup taxa (here, the catfish families) are ancestral. Rare states within the ingroup are derived. The following inferences result.

Character	Derived state	Phylogenetic hypothesis
I	Maxillary in gape margin	
II	Double condyle	
III	Nasal barbels present	
IV	Armor plates with teeth	

Evaluation

The ingroup criterion led to an incorrect conclusion about character I: the position of the maxillary bone in the gape margin of siluriforms was inferred to be derived. Thus, the character was recognized incorrectly as a synapomorphy for DIP. Actually, this alternative character state is a synapomorphy for nondiplomystid catfish families.

Wheeler (1981) and Maddison et al. (1984) examined these problems and made several suggestions to help systematists proceed in the face of incomplete data on outgroups.

Kluge and Farris (1969), Lundberg (1972), Watrous and Wheeler (1981), Wiley (1981), and Maddison et al. (1984) have favored the outgroup approach to character polarization. Nelson and Platnick (1981) and Patterson (1982) have faulted it.

Ingroup Analysis.   The character state that is most widespread among the unit taxa of the ingroup is the plesiomorphic state for the ingroup (Box 3.5). The rationale of ingroup analysis extends the parsimonious hypothesis that any character state universally present in a group under study was present in the common ancestor; thus, jaws are primitive for gnathostomes.

An inherent problem with the ingroup approach becomes evident when the basal-most sister groups of the ingroup differ markedly in diversity. Then, the truly derived states common to all members of the larger sister group will be treated erroneously as ancestral states. (See Box 3.5, Diplomystidae versus the rest of the catfishes for character I, as an example of this problem.) This problem supports a strong argument against use of the ingroup criterion except, perhaps, as a first crude approximation of character polarities.

Estabrook (1977) and Crisci and Stuessy (1980) have endorsed the use of ingroup analysis. Lundberg (1972), Stevens (1980), and Watrous and Wheeler (1981) have argued against it.

"Living Fossils" or Extant Primitive Taxa. Character states are plesiomorphic if they are present in taxa known or assumed to retain many other plesiomorphic features. Some extant taxa do retain more ancestral features than others, and it is not uncommon to encounter the suggestion that "living fossils" exist in which all ancestral conditions are retained. Eldredge and Stanley (1984) critically reviewed the most famous cases of putative arrested evolution from a phylogenetic perspective.

Although cases can be found in which descendant species appear to have changed little from their ancestors, this is not justification for a general criterion for primitiveness. There is no evolutionary principle that requires plesiomorphic conditions of genetically independent characters to remain associated in descendant groups. Rather, mosaic evolution appears to be the general rule.

Ontogeny.   Assume that we have observed the ontogenetic transformations of alternative character states in a pair of taxa. Then, "given an ontogenetic character transformation from a state observed to be more general to a state observed to be less general, the more general state is primitive and the less general derived" (Nelson 1978). In this statement, the phrase "more general" refers to a character state found in both members of a pair of taxa, and "less general" refers to a state found only in one member. The criterion appears to work for cases in which an evolutionary event changes a developmental program in one descendant lineage such that a recognizably different state is added to the series of ontogenetic transformations. This is especially convincing in cases of ontogenetically terminal additions of advanced states such as the metamorphosis of bilaterally symmetrical larval flatfish into an asymmetrical adult.

The ontogenetic criterion is not without problems, however. (1) If an evolutionary event in one descendant lineage changes a developmental program such that an ancestral terminal stage is lost, ontogenetic data are blind to the loss and suggest, incorrectly, that the ancestral ontogeny is derived by addition of the terminal stage. (2) It is often not possible to equate (exactly homologize) embryonic with adult states. (3) The ontogenetic criterion does not apply to certain characters, such as karyotype and nucleic acid and protein sequences, that have no ontogenies but that can have great historical information content (Kluge 1985).

Comparative data on development are of immense value in phylogenetic analysis, despite the serious questions about the use of the ontogenetic criterion for polarity decisions. Information on developmental sequences is an additional source of data for hypothesizing homology among adult features (Mabee 1988) and for ordering the states of multistate characters (Mabee 1989). Ontogenetic systems can themselves be a rich source of additional characters (e.g., diverse patterns of gastrulation: Ballard 1981; diverse larval forms: Moser 1984). Indeed, we may view alternative ontogenetic transformation series as unit characters instead of using each of the structural stages that make up the transformation series as characters (de Quieroz 1985).

Nelson (1978, 1985), Patterson (1982), and Rosen (1982) have favored the ontogenetic criterion to various degrees; de Beer (1958), Lundberg (1973), Brooks and Wiley (1985), de Quieroz (1985), and Kluge (1985) have found it problematic.

Overview.   In practice, the outgroup criterion is the most logically defensible and generally practical method for polarizing characters. Polarity hypotheses based on this criterion often may be compared with, and corroborated by, the paleontological and ontogenetic criteria. Critical application of the outgroup criterion, with careful attention to identification of outgroups, leads to well-supported and repeatable hypotheses about character polarities that will, in turn, allow reconstruction of genealogies.

3.4.5 Phylogenetic Analysis

When character information has been assembled, usually in the form of a character-by-taxon matrix (Box 3.4), phylogenetic hypotheses are generated by recognition of monophyletic groups based on Hennig's principle. If the data set involves few characters and taxa, and if there is little or no conflict in the genealogical relationships suggested by the data, phylogenetic relationships are readily inferred from the patterns of shared derived characters. The most closely related taxa will share the largest number of derived characters. Their sister groups will share some but not all of these characters, and so on, until the relationships of all taxa are resolved.

With a data set involving many characters and taxa, analysis is more difficult. Handling numerous pieces of information is cumbersome, and a large data set invariably includes characters that suggest conflicting patterns of relationships. Character conflict, or incongruence, indicates that at least some of the character states are not homologous due to parallelism, convergence, or errors in character analysis. If we had an a priori criterion for determining which characters are most likely to show homoplasy, we could simply remove them from the analysis or give them relatively low weight. There is no agreed-upon way to do this, however (Mayr 1969; Sneath and Sokal 1973; Wiley 1981). A variety of suggestions can be found for a priori recognition of the following unreliable (nonhomologous) characters: labile "adaptive" characters, characters with high variability within taxa, "loss" characters, characters of "simple" structure or genetic basis, or characters subject to environmental modification. There are logical flaws and exceptions to all of such recommendations.

We agree with Vooris (1971) and Patterson (1982) that characters "weight themselves" by their correlated distributions (or lack thereof) among taxa. This is a posteriori weighting, and it is conceptually equivalent to the a posteriori criterion for homology (see Section 3.4.4.1). For example, all ichthyologists agree that the absence of skin pigment and eyes does *not* indicate immediate common ancestry among all species of subterranean fishes (including several characids, cyprinids, catfishes, amblyopsids, and others) because there is a much larger suite of correlated characters that clearly aligns each subterranean species with a group of nonhypogean fishes. We conclude, therefore, that the pale and blind conditions are homoplasious (i.e., nonhomologous): they have evolved independently in the various hypogean forms.

Character correlation or congruence is the key to selection among conflicting phylogenetic hypotheses. Given a character set containing incongruences, the best phylogenetic hypothesis is that which implies the fewest character state changes. This best hypothesis simultaneously maximizes the number of inferred synapomorphies and minimizes the number of inferred homoplasies (incongruences). This "maximum parsimony" criterion is used to select among conflicting hypotheses in nearly all phylogenetic analyses.

3.4.5.1   Quantitative Methods

Several quantitative, computerized methods have been developed for phylogenetic analysis. These are essential when size and complexity of the data set make analysis by hand difficult. Each method is designed to generate phylogenetic hypotheses under certain specific assumptions about evolutionary patterns. It is essential that users understand the assumptions and limits of programs and not apply or interpret them blindly. Below, we describe some of the most widely used quantitative methods for phylogeny reconstruction (see also Felsenstein 1982).

Minimum-Length Tree or Parsimony Methods. Minimum-length tree methods for phylogeny reconstruction were introduced by Camin and Sokal (1965) and developed largely by J. S. Farris and D. L. Swofford. These methods are designed to find the phylogenetic hypothesis, depicted as a branching diagram, that minimizes the number of inferred evolutionary steps. Pairwise distances between study taxa are used to estimate the positions and relative distances of these taxa on the tree, which is constructed by sequential addition of taxa. Most of these methods involve reconstructions of likely character states of intermediate ancestors (hypothetical taxonomic units, HTUs, diagrammed as nodes on the tree).

(A)   *Directed tree* methods have been elucidated by Kluge and Farris (1969) and Farris (1970). Input consists of a matrix containing numerically coded character states for each taxon. Coding is set up to reflect inferred evolutionary transformations between states (Boxes 3.4, 3.6). Pairwise distances are computed among all taxa over all characters by the formula

$$d(J,K) = \sum_{i=1}^{n} \mid X(i, J) - X(i, K) \mid\ ;$$

$d(J,K)$ is the distance (in inferred character state changes or evolutionary steps) between taxa J and K; n is the number of characters; $X(i,J)$ is the state of character i in taxon J; and $X(i,K)$ is the state of character i in taxon K. This is a

---

Box 3.6 Construction of Hypothetical Taxonomic Units

In phylogenetic methods such as minimum-length trees that incorporate the parsimony criterion for selection among alternative hypotheses, hypothetical taxonomic units (HTUs) are computed to minimize the number of character state changes required to achieve the observed distribution of character states among real taxonomic units. As each real taxonomic unit is added to a tree, it is compared to existing pairs of adjacent taxa. Hypothetical taxonomic units are constructed from such three-way comparisons by a "median state rule": the HTU is assigned the most common state if two or three taxa share a state, or the intermediate state if the three taxa express different states of a character.

In the example below, the distribution of character states (0, 1, or 2) for four characters (I–IV) among three taxa (X, Y, Z) is used to infer the HTU. The HTU provides the "node" of the tree diagram at right, which represents a phylogenetic hypothesis.

| Taxon | Additively coded character | | | | Phylogenetic hypothesis |
	I	II	III	IV	
Ancestor X	0	1	1	0	
Descendant Y	0	0	0	1	
Unplaced Z	1	1	0	2	
Inferred HTU	0	1	0	1	

"lattice" distance that sums differences in character states between two taxa over all characters. In the phylogenetic context, this distance estimates the evolutionary steps separating taxa J and K. A hypothetical ancestor for the study group is taken as the collection of all ancestral character states. Tree construction begins with a branch connecting the most primitive real taxon to the hypothetical ancestor which, therefore, temporally "roots" the tree. Remaining taxa are added in sequence, on branches that connect to previously placed taxa or to HTUs, to minimize the implied number of character state changes (evolutionary steps). The basic method of HTU construction is exemplified in Box 3.6; for an advanced treatment, see Swofford and Maddison (1987).

The simplest approach to directed trees puts no constraints on character state reversals or parallelism if these kinds of changes shorten overall tree length (total evolutionary steps). Also, characters are usually weighted equally. Computerized versions are available to variously constrain reversals of character state and allow characters to be differentially weighted; some software programs are described below.

The directed-tree method is conceptually close to "manual" phylogenetic analysis within the framework of Hennig's principle. Thus, a taxon that branches separately from the inferred ancestor shares no synapomorphies with members of the study group other than those shared by all members. A taxon that stems directly from another real taxon shares all apomorphies of the latter and has additional apomorphies. A taxon that branches from an HTU shares with its sister group all apomorphies up to the HTU (which represents their hypothesized, most recent common ancestor).

(B) *Undirected trees (networks)* (Farris 1970; Lundberg 1972) involve inputs and computations like those for directed trees except that no a priori inferences are made about character state polarity. The initial branch of an undirected tree is formed by joining two real study taxa. Because these structures are not temporally directed, the phylogenetic status (synapomorphy versus symplesiomorphy) of similarities shared by adjacent taxa is not implied. Undirected trees, however, do show phylogenetic pattern. They can be "rooted" (transformed into directed trees) by application of criteria for inferring polarity of individual characters. This approach is recommended, and allows systematists to proceed, when polarization of some characters is difficult. Computer packages for phylogenetic analysis offer a variety of rooting options; see below.

Pairwise Distance and Statistical Methods. "Distance" methods (Farris 1972, 1986; Felsenstein 1982; Swofford 1981) take as input a matrix of pairwise taxon-by-taxon distances that are used as estimates of evolutionary distances (i.e., amount of character state changes) along the branch segments of a phylogenetic tree. Depending on the method, the tree preferred is the one that minimizes overall tree length (parsimony) or that maximizes some criterion of fit between the original (input) distances and the evolutionary distances implied by the tree. Original distance matrices might come directly from comparative methods such as immunological cross-reactivity or DNA–DNA hybridizability. For these, no character state information exists and, therefore, hypothetical taxonomic units are not inferred at branch points. Alternatively, original distances can be computed from a character-by-taxon matrix (e.g., genetic distances computed from allozyme frequency data: Avise et al. 1977). Reconstruction of HTUs is possible when a character-by-taxon matrix is available and each character can be fitted optimally to the tree by minimum-length methods.

Farris (1986 and references therein) argued against use of distance methods on several grounds. One concern is that computed lengths of tree branches cannot be interpreted logically as evolutionary distances because sometimes they are negative numbers. In contrast, Felsenstein (1981, 1982, 1986) argued that reconstruction of phylogeny can be viewed as a statistical problem in which original distances, as statistical estimates of true branch lengths, might be negative. Felsenstein (1981 and references therein) developed statistical maximum-likelihood estimation methods. These use such data as gene frequencies or DNA sequences with simplified probabilistic models of character evolution to assign probability values to various tree topologies. Computations are complex, and maximum-likelihood methods presently can handle only data sets with few taxa.

Character Compatibility Analysis. The character compatibility approach to phylogeny was developed by G. F. Estabrook and associates (Meacham and Estabrook 1985). It is based on the principle of character state association among the taxa under study (Wilson 1965): for two-state characters, polarized or not, if all four character state combinations (11, 01, 10, 00) are represented among taxa under study, all possible phylogenetic hypotheses will imply homoplasy in one or both characters. This means that the characters together cannot possibly support the same phylogenetic hypothesis; they are not compatible.

Input for character compatibility is a character-by-taxon matrix with two-state characters. If characters are initially multistate, they can be recoded as a set of two-state subcharacters; for example, a character with states 0, 1, 2 would be recoded as two two-state characters with $0 = 0,0$; $1 = 0,1$; and $2 = 1,1$. Character state distributions are surveyed in a pairwise manner over the study taxa, and characters found to be compatible are grouped together in sets or "cliques." The characters of the largest clique together describe the best-supported phylogenetic hypothesis. Characters in smaller cliques are not ordinarily considered, although Strauch (1984) suggested using them in secondary analyses when the original hypothesis is not fully resolved.

The hypothesis mandated by the largest clique is the minimum-length tree for just those characters; no homoplasy is present because the characters are fully compatible. It is not, however, necessarily the minimum-length tree over all characters. Character compatibility analysis has been criticized because it sets aside some of the original data, which, albeit not "perfect" (i.e., not fully compatible with the largest clique of characters), may still contain important historical information. Character compatibility is a useful method for determining the quality of character sets (the more compatibility the better) and the hypothesis implied by the "best" characters.

Phenograms as Phylogeny Estimates.   It has been suggested (e.g., Michener and Sokal 1957; Colless 1967) that phenograms based on overall similarity or distance (see Section 3.5) can be used as estimates of phylogenies. Levels of phenetic linkage are taken to indicate the recency of common ancestry. Viewed as a phylogenetic tree, the basal linkage level of a phenogram approximates the root or common ancestor, but no ancestral character states are reconstructed. This approach has been used commonly with genetic-distance data in biochemical systematics (e.g., Avise et al. 1977; but see Buth 1984). Because the positioning of taxa in phenograms depends on similarity due to homoplasy and shared primitive features, as well as on similarity due to shared derived characters, interpretation of phenograms as phylogenetic hypotheses is problematic. For phenograms to accurately depict phylogenetic relationships, evolutionary rates must have been roughly uniform among divergent lineages, extinction must not have left large phenetic gaps among study taxa, homoplasy must be relatively low, and character sampling must have been unbiased. Because we have no idea how frequently these conditions are met, this approach is not recommended for phylogeny reconstruction.

Computer Packages.   Several computer programs have been written for phylogenetic analysis. Brief descriptions of four packages that have proven helpful follow (also see Platnick 1987).

(A)   *PAUP* (*P*hylogenetic *A*nalysis *U*sing *P*arsimony) includes programs for finding minimum-length directed or undirected trees. It uses characters of two or more ordered or unordered states, or it can take nucleotide sequence data. It has numerous options for rooting undirected trees. Search algorithms can fit the data to all possible tree topologies for about 12 taxa, thus guaranteeing discovery of the shortest tree. For larger data sets, there are procedures for approximating exact solutions. A program written by C. Meacham for drawing labeled cladograms, phylograms, and phenograms on pen plotters and dot matrix printers is included. This package and an informative user's manual are available for most mainframe, IBM-compatible, and Apple MacIntosh computers. It can be obtained at modest cost from its developer: David L. Swofford, Illinois Natural History Survey, 607 East Peabody Drive, Champaign, Illinois 61820, USA.

(B) *PHYLIP* is an extensive package of 26 programs for many mainframe and microcomputers (source programs must be compiled in Pascal). It includes programs for discretely coded two- or multistate characters, gene-frequency data, distance matrix data, and protein and nucleic acid sequence data. For coded characters, there are Wagner parsimony and compatibility methods and a program to find all equally parsimonious trees. The program for gene frequencies uses Felsenstein's maximum-likelihood method. Programs for molecular sequences include parsimony, compatibility, and maximum likelihood. This free package also includes Meacham's tree-plotting program. For information, contact Joe Felsenstein, Department of Genetics, SK-50, University of Washington, Seattle, Washington 98195, USA.

(C) *Hennig '86* is a package of efficient programs for IBM-compatible microcomputers that emphasize parsimony methods. For information about this modestly priced package, contact J. S. Farris, Department of Ecology and Evolution, State University of New York, Stony Brook, New York 11794, USA.

(D) *McClade* is an interactive graphics program for the Apple MacIntosh computer. It analyses phylogenies and traces character evolution. The user inputs tree typologies (the program does not *find* trees), and the program parsimoniously fits characters to the trees. This is an excellent package for teaching methods and principles of phylogenetic systematics. Its price is trivial. For information, contact W. P. Maddison and D. R. Maddison, Museum of Comparative Zoology, Harvard University, Cambridge, Massachusetts 02138, USA.

3.5 PHENETICS

Phenetics, in its pure form, is a nonhistorical approach to systematics. Taxa are circumscribed and classified based on some *quantitative* measure of overall phenotypic similarity. The central idea is to base taxa on empirically determined correlations among character states regardless of the phylogenetic status of those states. Most pheneticists agree that, except for cases of convergence, the patterns of shared characteristics among organisms are due to common evolutionary history. They agree that speciation and evolutionary change have resulted in a common phylogenetic history for living organisms. They argue, however, that the development of sound phylogenetic hypotheses is frequently not possible due to problems in character analysis, such as in assessments of homology and evolutionary polarity. Sneath and Sokal's (1973) book "Numerical Taxonomy" is a review of this field. More recent developments may be found in the journal *Systematic Zoology,* both in regular articles and in reports on the annual numerical taxonomy conferences.

3.5.1 Phenetic Treatment of Species and Higher Taxa

Pheneticists argue that, although we are looking for evolutionary units in nature, we can find no operational biological criteria that will permit us to identify these units unambiguously. Definitions or concepts of species that rely on genealogy, selection, and gene flow are not operational. The best we can do is to objectively identify groups in nature that are morphologically similar to one another and distinct from individuals excluded from the group. The phenetic concept of species thus ignores the issue of *why* species are identifiable groups; rather, species are "the smallest (most homogeneous) cluster that can be recognized upon some given criterion as being distinct from other clusters. . . ." (Sneath and Sokal 1973).

Higher taxa are defined as clusters of similar species that are separated by phenetic gaps from other clusters. Successively higher taxa will include more phenetic diversity and will be separated by larger phenetic gaps from other taxa of the same rank. Pheneticists anticipate that, as phenetic methods are applied to more and more groups, it will be possible to set objective standards for the levels of phenetic diversity within, and for the gaps between, taxa for each taxonomic rank. Pheneticists argue that these taxa will, in most cases, approximate evolutionary entities and will have the distinct advantage of being nonarbitrary.

3.5.2 Numerical Phenetic Methods

Since its origin in the late 1950s, numerical phenetics has developed a battery of techniques for quantifying and displaying patterns of similarity among organisms (Sneath and Sokal 1973; Clifford and Stephenson 1975). Repeatedly, however, it has been shown that different techniques applied to the same data may produce different results (e.g., see Box 3.7). This makes a priori selection of methods difficult and arbitrary. There is no general agreement on which phenetic methods are best for producing classifications, although some techniques are used more frequently than others. The methodological flow of a typical numerical phenetic study is as follows.

First, character state information on study units (*operational taxonomic units*, OTUs) is assembled. The characters used in phenetics are the same as those used in phylogenetics. Genetic basis is known or assumed; logical and functional independence among characters is demonstrable or assumed. Homology is assessed only by a priori criteria (Section 3.4.4.1). Quantitative characters (measurements, counts, etc.) are used directly. States of "qualitative" characters are transformed to numerical codes. Characters that can be present or absent, or that have two alternative states, are coded 0 or 1. For example, the Weberian apparatus can be coded 0 if it is absent and 1 if it is present. Ordinated (graded) state series are coded additively to reflect relative similarity among character states. For example, if a sample includes organisms that are black, gray, or white, these states could be scored, respectively, 0, 1, and 2 (or 2, 1, and 0) to reflect the intermediacy of gray between the two extremes. Unordered states are coded nonadditively so that all nonidentical state comparisons are equally similar (or distant). If a systematist did not wish to assume that gray is intermediate between white and black, these states could be coded so that no state is intermediate and any difference would be counted as a distance of one.

Second, data sets containing characters measured on unequal scales (e.g., body depth measured in centimeters, eye diameter in millimeters) are rescaled or standardized; usually, either character states are recomputed as units of standard deviation from the mean value of each state or character ranges are equalized (Thorpe 1984). Standardization avoids differential character weighting when the overall similarity is calculated. Otherwise, for example, a nonstandardized difference of 10 cm in depth would swamp a difference of 2 mm in eye diameter, although the latter difference may have more taxonomic importance.

Third, a measure of overall similarity or distance is computed by comparison of each OTU pair. These pairwise resemblance measures are entered in a taxon-by-taxon matrix of original or "observed" similarities or distances. Several kinds of resemblance measures or coefficients are available.

• *Product-moment correlation coefficients* are calculated from the standardized data matrix. They measure the tendency of characters to vary in the same direction so that large positive values (maximum = 1) indicate greater overall similarity.

• *Matching or association coefficients* can be used with two-state (0, 1) data. These coefficients express similarity between two OTUs as a ratio of the sum of their character state matches to the total number of characters (or some other expression of the total set of characters). Many matching coefficients were described by Sneath and Sokal (1973).

• *Distance coefficients* sum differences in character states between two OTUs over all characters to provide a measure of distance. Frequently used coefficients are the Euclidean, or straight-line, distance computed by an *n*-dimensional extension of the pythagorean theorem (Sneath and Sokal 1973) and the lattice distance (Section 3.4.5.1).

Finally, the original resemblances are summarized and displayed by one or more of the following techniques.

• *Cluster analysis* creates groups or clusters of OTUs by one of several criteria based on their mutual resemblances. The most commonly used approach is the *"unweighted pair-group method with arithmetic averaging"* (UPGMA). In UPGMA, the most similar pairs of OTUs are "linked" at their observed level of resemblance to form the lowest-level clusters. Unplaced OTUs are added sequentially to the "closest" clusters. The resemblance of an unplaced OTU to a cluster is the average of its pairwise resemblances to each cluster member. The results of cluster analyses are usually displayed in phenograms (Box 3.7). Many clustering methods, including UPGMA, produce a hierarchy of nonoverlapping groups that can be translated into phenetic classifications. Some workers have treated phenograms as estimates of genealogies (see *Phenograms as Phylogeny Estimates* in section 3.4.5.1).

• *Graphical analysis* represents OTUs as points in two-dimensional space (or three-dimensional stereogram); the points are joined by lines (edges) based on resemblance values. When only the nearest-neighbor relations are graphed, the result is a "minimum spanning tree." Estabrook (1966) developed this approach further by adding second-neighbor connections, third-neighbor connections, and so on. The result was a graphical theoretic index of connectivity (tightness) for OTU clusters as a measure of taxonomic structure.

• *Ordination* involves multivariate statistical procedures, such as *principal components analysis* (PCA), that are applied to taxon-by-taxon resemblance

---

Box 3.7   Phenograms of Species of *Algansea* (Cyprinidae)

Jensen and Barbour (1981) constructed three phenograms representing morphological similarities among six species of the cyprinid genus *Algansea*. All were derived by the unweighted pair-group method with arithmetic averaging from the same character-by-taxon matrix, but they are based on different measures of resemblance. In their phenograms, reproduced here (with permission), the species are indicated by three-letter codes at right, and scales of resemblance are arrayed horizontally at the top of each. The cophenetic correlation coefficient (r_{cs}) is the product-moment correlation between the original pairwise similarities and the pairwise similarities implied by the phenogram; it is the measure of fit of the results to the original data. Phenogram B is the "best" of the three because it has the greatest r_{cs}.

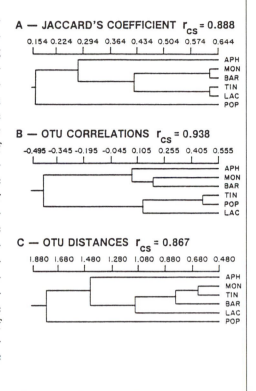

---

matrices and reduce the many pairwise phenetic relations to a few components or axes. In a sense, each component (or axis) represents the average member of a group of OTUs; the loading (correlation) of an OTU on a component measures the resemblance of other OTUs to the average member. Alternatively, PCA can be applied to character-by-character correlation or covariance matrices. The components are then linear combinations of characters. The loadings of characters on each component provide a set of weights. These are multiplied by the corresponding original character states of each OTU, and the products are summed to determine a score for OTUs on each component. The first two or three components are taken as axes defining a multivariate character space in which OTU positions are plotted by their scores. If the distribution of OTUs is clumped, taxonomic groups may be recognized.

Nonmetric, multidimensional scaling may be applied to an original distance matrix to achieve the best-fit geometric representation of the distances, usually in two or three dimensions. As with PCA, the distribution of OTUs may be clumped in the reduced space, suggesting taxonomic (phenetic) groups.

Computer Packages.   A package of computer programs for executing all major techniques in numerical phenetics, entitled NTSYS (for mainframes) and NTSYS-PC (for IBM-compatible personal computers), is available for about $100 from F. J. Rohlf, Exeter Publishing Ltd., 100 North Country Road, Building B, Setanket,

New York 11733. Some widely available statistical packages contain programs for multivariate ordination and cluster analysis, among them the Statistical Analysis System (SAS), the Statistical Package for the Social Sciences (SPSS), and the Biomedical Computer Programs (BMD).

3.5.3 Contributions of Phenetics

Phylogeneticists and evolutionary systematists reject much of the philosophy of phenetics, primarily because they are convinced that careful study can reveal phylogenetic patterns unambiguously. It would be foolish, however, to reject the notion that repeatable, objective, and nonarbitrary methods are desirable for systematics. Indeed, phenetics provided much of the challenge and impetus for the development of rigorous methods of phylogenetic analysis. Many methods developed by pheneticists are widely used in systematics and evolutionary biology. Phenetic techniques are used, for example, to detect natural fish hybrids (Neff and Smith 1979). The description of geographic and allometric patterns of phenotypic variation within taxa and the discrimination of species are increasingly treated as multivariate statistical problems. Ordination techniques are central in these areas, especially in ichthyology (Bookstein et al. 1985). Further, above the species level, quantitative phenetic techniques could be useful for comparative study of anagenesis (total evolutionary change) and cladogenesis, whereby overall phenotypic similarity (or distance) would be used to measure anagenesis. The relationship between anagenesis and cladogenesis has not been studied in enough groups to permit generalizations, but the implications of this comparison are numerous. If, for example, anagenesis and cladogenesis are not predictably related, phenograms cannot serve as estimates of phylogenetic relationships.

3.6 BIOLOGICAL CLASSIFICATION

Classification is a human affair with no *necessary* connection to any natural process. We design and construct classifications in order to facilitate communication about the diversity of organisms. Biological classifications help us remember or locate information about organisms by providing an ordered system of names to index that information. The kind of information to be indexed is a subject of continuing, spirited debate among systematists. Some argue that only information about observed diagnostic character states has to be considered, whereas other workers see value in using classifications to express hypotheses of interrelationships. These goals need not be mutually exclusive.

Because biological classifications have practical value and are used by many people, stability is a desirable, if not yet realized, characteristic. If a classification is well designed, it will be predictive of new information to be obtained from ongoing research. However, if important new information is obtained that conflicts with the present classification, it becomes necessary to modify the classification to reflect the new data. Further, if classifications are used to express hypothesized genealogies, conflicting hypotheses may demand different classifications.

The conventional form for biological classification is a hierarchy containing ranked, nonoverlapping categories. The familiar categories kingdom, phylum, class, order, family, genus, and species are used for all organisms. These categories are commonly supplemented by a variety of intermediate levels (divisions, tribes, cohorts, subfamilies, superorders, and so forth) to reflect growing knowledge of the details of organic diversity.

3.6.1 Phylogenetic Classification

The central objective of phylogenetic systematics is to construct a hypothesis of interrelationships that is well corroborated by independent characters. The format used to present a phylogenetic hypothesis may be a narrative, a tree-like diagram, or a hierarchical classification. Phylogenetic systematists argue that it should be possible to reconstruct the hypothesis of interrelationships among a group of taxa directly from the group's classification. Hierarchy is a major structural feature of phylogenetic pattern. Ancestors and their descendants are hierarchically ordered, as are sequentially younger sets of sister lineages within a larger lineage. Reflecting the genealogical hierarchy, sequentially more apomorphic sets of character states are hierarchically ordered (Box 3.4). A core principle of phylogenetic systematics is the identity between the genealogical hierarchy and the hierarchy of character-state transformations (i.e., Hennig's principle). A genealogical hypothesis for a group of organisms thus may be transcribed directly into a hierarchical classification. Provided that only strictly monophyletic taxa are recognized, the classification will be an exact index to genealogy and, therefore, to the synapomorphies that characterize its monophyletic groups, as illustrated in Box 3.8.

Several problems have been recognized for phylogenetic classification. In a fully resolved, strictly phylogenetic classification of a large group in which all monophyletic taxa are named, the number of categories would be large (compare the classifications of Fink and Fink with that of Wiley in Box 3.8). Further, if a new hypothesis of relationships is accepted, shock waves of change would spread up and down the ranks of the phylogenetic classification. However, both these concerns apply to classification in general. Any phenetic or evolutionary classification that is fully resolved will be as category-rich as a phylogenetic classification. Indeed, few phylogeneticists have seriously recommended that *all* monophyletic groups be formally named. Further, new information that changes our view of relationships among organisms will destabilize any classification.

Phylogenetic classification suffers inherent limitations in dealing with some natural phenomena. Although rare, reticulate phylogenetic patterns (hybridization) and multifurcations (synchronous multiple speciation) occur in nature but cannot be reflected in the traditional dichotomous format or easily depicted in classifications. It also is difficult to construct classifications that adequately portray cases of incompletely resolved phylogenies (these appear as multifurcations but are distinct from multiple speciation). Finally, putative ancestral species create problems if they are to be included in classifications. If, for example, a fossil species is the putative ancestor of two descendant sister lineages that are treated as genera, placement of the ancestor in either genus, or even in its own genus, would create a non-monophyletic taxon. Wiley (1979, 1981) provided a set of useful conventions for handling these issues and for converting even complex phylogenies into simply formatted, easily translated classifications. These involve "annotations" to the traditional Linnaean classification. The future of these conventions in classifications of fishes cannot be predicted. Their simplicity and informativeness are compelling, however.

Box 3.8   Phylogenetic and Evolutionary Classification

Fink and Fink (1981) discussed the relationships among orders (for which names end in -iformes) and suborders (-oidei) of the superorder Ostariophysi. They proposed the following hypothesis of phylogenetic relationships, for which GON = Gonorhynchiformes, CYP = Cypriniformes, CHA = Characiformes, SIL = Siluroidei, and GYM = Gymnotoidei.

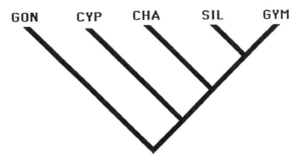

Fink and Fink provided a strictly phylogenetic classification for the Ostariophysi.

> Superorder Ostariophysi
> Series Anotophysi
>   Order Gonorhynchiformes
> Series Otophysi
>   Subseries Cypriniphysi
>   Order Cypriniformes
>   Subseries Characiphysi
>   Order Characiformes
>   Order Siluriformes
>   Suborder Siluroidei
>   Suborder Gymnotoidei

Wiley (1981) proposed an alternative, strictly phylogenetic, classification. He adopted the sequencing convention by which monophyletic groups forming a chain-like phylogenetic series are given the same categorical rank and are listed in the order of their branching sequence.

> Superorder Ostariophysi
>   Order Gonorhynchiformes
>   Order Cypriniformes
>   Order Characiformes
>   Order Siluriformes
>   Order Gymnotiformes

It is possible to directly reconstruct the phylogenetic hypothesis from both the above classifications, provided one knows that Wiley followed the sequencing convention for his.

Box 3.8 Continued.

An evolutionary classification of Ostariophysi can be designed to emphasize the similarity (based on primitive characteristics) of the cyprinoids and characoids (e.g., mostly silvery, scaled fishes), as well as the distinctiveness of the catfishes (siluriforms) and electric fishes (gymnotiforms).

Superorder Ostariophysi
Series Anotophysi
Order Gonorhynchiformes
Series Otophysi
Order Cypriniformes
Suborder Characoidei
Suborder Cyprinoidei
Order Gymnotiformes
Order Siluriformes

The hypothesis of phylogenetic relationships cannot be constructed from this classification, however, even if one knew that the classifier wished to emphasize the degrees of divergence described above.

3.6.2 Alternatives to Phylogenetic Classification

Strictly phylogenetic classification is widely, but not universally, accepted in ichthyology and in many other systematic disciplines. Here, we briefly discuss some alternatives and contrast these to the phylogenetic approach to classification.

Evolutionary Classification. "Evolutionary systematists" traditionally construct classifications using phylogenetic information as but one of several criteria for forming and ranking taxa. These systematists, for example, might assign relatively high taxonomic rank to groups separated by large phenetic gaps, arguing that this information should be included in the classification because gaps represent inferred evolutionary gaps created by extinction or large differences in evolutionary rates. When taxa are ranked, certain distinctive characteristics of the organisms may receive special weight even if these do not support monophyly (e.g., "jawlessness" of Agnatha). Taxon size is another nonphylogenetic consideration that has sometimes been used to help set group boundaries (e.g., genera should have no more than *n* species, etc.).

Phylogeneticists have been critical of this approach to classification largely because it destroys the relationship between genealogy and classification. As Box 3.8 demonstrates, when special (i.e., nonphylogenetic) information is "included" in classifications, it is not possible to reconstruct the hypothesis on genealogical relationships from those classifications. Neither is it possible to retrieve the "special" information underlying such a classification solely from the classification itself.

Phenetic Classification. In a strict sense, the "phenetic" approach to systematics does not involve genealogical hypotheses in the formation and ranking of taxa (Section 3.5). Taxa are recognized and ranked on the basis of a quantitative measure of overall similarity within and between groups. Two justifications are offered for preferring phenetic to phylogenetic classification. The first is based on the notion that character homology and polarity cannot be unambiguously determined and, therefore, phylogeny reconstruction is not reliable. Phenetic classifications, on the other hand, are empirical and repeatable, and they require fewer assumptions. Second, some have argued that phenetic classifications are preferable because they contain more information than phylogenetic classifications. That is, phenetic classifications contain information on patterns of all characters, whereas phylogenetic classifications mirror only the pattern of distribution of shared derived characters. Resolution of this point of contention has proved difficult because those involved cannot agree on the meaning of "information," do not agree that all kinds of information are equally desirable, and use different (and controversial) criteria and measures to determine information content. Currently, relatively few systematic ichthyologists take a purely phenetic approach to classification, although many use the numerical methods developed by pheneticists to examine patterns of character variation.

Numericlature, Indentation, and Tree Classifications. More radical alternatives to the traditional Linnaean system have been proposed. A numericlature system for ranking, similar to the numbering hierarchy used in this book for chapters and subsections, has been described by Hennig (1981). Ranking by indentation on the printed page was critically examined by Wiley (1981). Another possibility is to print the taxon names, one per lineage, directly on a phylogenetic tree diagram. The traditional categories would then be superfluous because level on the tree determines rank unequivocally. Alternatives such as these, even if less cumbersome than the traditional system, are unlikely to be adopted rapidly. The traditional system of biological classification has great inertia and it is familiar to a large group of users.

3.7 NOMENCLATURE

The objective of systematic nomenclature is to provide an internationally uniform and, so far as possible, stable system of unique "scientific" names for taxa. The need for such a system is obvious in light of the immense number of taxa that have been recognized. To achieve these ends, the world community of zoologists has created the International Code of Zoological Nomenclature (ICZN 1985), which is a set of legalistic conventions to guide in the selection and formation of scientific names for taxa. The International Commission on Zoological Nomenclature serves as a judicial body to deal with exceptional cases in which the rules might be suspended and to make recommendations for alterations of the Code.

Like many systematists, we view the international code as a necessary evil. Most of us chose biology over law as a career for reasons of personal interest and temperament and are frustrated by having to deal with a body of complex legalistic conventions. This frustration is acceptable, however, because a terrible confusion of names would prevail if we lacked such conventions. Here we provide an introduction to nomenclature that will suffice for biologists who need to interpret synonymies and understand why scientific names occasionally change.

Readers in need of detailed information on the rules of nomenclature should consult the most recent edition of the Code. Useful explanatory and critical reviews of the rules were given by Blackwelder (1967), Mayr (1969), and Wiley (1981).

Nomenclatural rules apply to taxa between the rank of superfamily and subspecies. By convention, ichthyologists give the names of certain taxa above the family level uniform endings; for example, ordinal names end in -iformes and subordinal names end in -oidei. Taxonomic names above the species level are uninominals (single words), species names are binomials, and subspecies names are trinomials. The names of taxa above the level of genus are plural nouns. Thus, the Osteichthyes *are* the most diverse vertebrates, and the Cyprinidae are freshwater fishes.

Part of the task of systematics is to provide *synonymies* or guides to the nomenclatural histories of genera and species. Boxes 3.9 and 3.10 give examples of synonymies, which illustrate some of the main goals of nomenclature and some of the guidelines provided by the rules.

3.8   IDENTIFICATION

Keys and other aids for fish identification are the most widely used practical products of systematic research in ichthyology. The original formal descriptions of taxa at all ranks are long and fairly technical; much of what is included has little relevance for identification. Original descriptions are necessary for continuing research, but are not efficient when field identifications are needed. Keys and field guides are designed to facilitate identification by nonscientists, researchers in nonsystematic disciplines, and systematists themselves.

Keys and other identification aids are not generally intended to be classifications or expressions of natural relationships. Hence they frequently are introduced by the phrase "artificial key to the . . . ." Identification aids vary tremendously in their quality. The efficacy of a key or field guide depends largely on the quantity and quality of knowledge of the fishes with which it deals. Users must be aware of the state of basic knowledge of the faunas or groups with which they are concerned in order to develop an appropriate degree of confidence in identifications. Keys to North American fishes, for example, though not perfect, are much more useful than those to South American or deep-sea fishes.

Taxonomic keys give contrasting diagnostic characters for alternative groups of taxa in a format that leads the user through successively smaller groups to the final identification. Keys are commonly included in regional faunistic works, taxonomic revisions, and monographs of genera or families. The strategy in key construction is to select characters that are constant for the group, exist in discrete (nonoverlapping) states, and are readily observed. Character constancy is sometimes impossible in groups that show marked sex dimorphism or age variation. In such cases, separate keys for different life stages are constructed (e.g., larval fish keys: Auer 1982). When possible, multiple characters should be used to contrast each group and the contrasts should be dichotomous. Computerized keys with interactive software have been developed in recent years (Pankhurst 1975).

Field guides, handbooks, and atlases are usually regional in scope and give information on ecology and distribution in addition to characters useful for

---

Box 3.9   Nomenclatural History of the Genus *Noturus*

An example of a nomenclatural history for a genus comes from Taylor's (1969) work on the ictalurid catfish genus *Noturus* reproduced here. Key points are numbered and explained below.

(1)   **Genus *Noturus* Rafinesque**   (2)

(3)   *Noturus* Rafinesque, 1818a, p. 41 (original description; type-   (4)
            species, *Noturus flavus* Rafinesque, by monotypy); 1820a,
            p. 48 (comparison).   (5)

(6)   *Pimelodon* Vaillant.—LeSueur, 1819, p. 155 (probably vernac-
            ular and used with the French *livrée*, thus nonbinomial).—
            Vaillant, 1896a, p. 28; 1896b, p. 14, pl. 24 (name first
            available, from LeSueur; type-species, *Pimelodon insig-
            narius* Vaillant [=*Noturus insignis* (Richardson)], by
            monotypy).
         Pimelode.—LeSueur, 1820, p. 44 (vernacular; used with the
            French *livrée*).
         Schilbeodes Bleeker, 1858, pp. 36, 249, 258 (original descrip-
            tion; type-species *Silurus gyrinus* Mitchill, by mono-
            typy).—Jordan and Gilbert, 1877b, p. 93 (misspelled as
            Schilbeoides).
         Rabida Jordan and Evermann, 1896a, pp. 144–146 (original
            description in key; *furiosus*, in parentheses, presumably
            intended as type-species).—Jordan, 1920, pp. 473, 566
            (misspelled as *Rabidus*; type species designated: *Noturus
            furiosus* Jordan and Meek); 1923, p. 147 (misspelled as
            Rabidus).

   (1) The names of genera are unique, singular nouns. "Unique" means that a generic name can be used only once among all groups of animals covered by the international rules of zoological nomenclature. If the name *Noturus* had been used previously for a group of flies, it could not be used for fish. Like all scientific names, generic names are Latin words or are constructed so they can be treated as Latin nouns. *Noturus* is formed from the Greek words for back and tail, in reference to the elongate adipose fins of these catfishes, and written as a Latin noun.
   (2) Rafinesque was the author of the genus *Noturus*; he described the genus and designated the first species to be placed in it.
   (3) The original description of the genus was published in 1818 and appears on page 41 of the referenced document.
   (4) A *type species* is designated for each genus as an objective reference point for the generic name. The phrase "by monotypy" means that *Noturus flavus* was the only species that Rafinesque placed in the genus when he described *Noturus*. If two or more species are described simultaneously in a new genus, one of them must be designated the type species for the genus. In an analogous manner, a *type specimen* is designated when a species is first described. Type species and specimens are designated for nomenclatural, legalistic reasons only. They do not

---

Box 3.9   Continued.

imply that the species or specimen is "typical" or "average," nor do they imply that systematists have a typological concept of taxa.

When an improved understanding of systematic relationships causes a change in classification, nomenclatural changes may be needed as well. If one or more species in genus *A* must be transferred to genus *B*, nomenclatural adjustments depend on whether or not the type species of *A* is involved.

• One or more species in *A*, but not the type species, correctly belongs in *B*. These species are simply transferred to *B* and take *B's* generic name. Their specific names usually remain intact, but spelling adjustments will be necessary if *B* has a different Latin gender from *A* (see Box 3.10, point 6).

• All species of *A*, including the type species, are transferred to *B*. The generic name of the combined group depends on which name, *A* or *B*, has *priority*, that is, the earliest date of valid publication. The older name is used, and the younger becomes a *junior synonym* (see point 6 below).

• The type species of *A* is transferred to *B*, either alone or with some other (but not all) species of *A*. The name of *A* moves with its type species, and the generic name of the new group again depends on whether *A* or *B* has priority; the other name becomes a junior synonym. The remnant species, once in *A*, require a new generic name (or "resurrection" of a junior synonym if one is available), and a new type species must be designated when the new name is established.

(5) In a later publication by Rafinesque, *Noturus* was compared to some other genera. This information may be very useful to systematists if problems arise over Rafinesque's concept of the genus *Noturus*.

(6) Between the time Rafinesque described *Noturus* and the time Taylor did his study, four other genera were named that now are considered synonymous with *Noturus*. Because these names are younger, *Noturus* retains priority and remains in use.

---

identification. Field guides to fishes are becoming more numerous, and some are fabricated of waterproof materials for underwater use. The "Atlas of North American Fishes" (Lee et al. 1980) is designed in a loose-leaf format to facilitate updating.

If, for some scientific or legal reason, identification of fish is particularly critical, permission to consult specimens archived in natural history museums or the advice of a specialist may be sought. Potential users of these "ultimate authorities" should be aware that consulting fees may be charged. This practice is still rare but is not inappropriate if one considers the meagre budgets of archival institutions and the limited time of systematists who maintain active research programs.

3.9   COLLECTIONS FOR SYSTEMATIC AND FAUNISTIC RESEARCH

Despite over 200 years of exploration and collection, the global inventory of fish life remains incomplete. Many extant fish species have yet to be collected,

Box 3.10   Synonymy of *Noturus eleutherus*

An example of a species synonymy is this partial listing for the ictalurid catfish *Noturus eleutherus*, which comes from the work of Taylor (1969). Numbers preceding the entries are keyed to explanations that follow.

(1)   ***Noturus eleutherus* Jordan**

(2)   Mountain madtom

(3)   *Noturus miurus* Jordan [misidentification].—Eigenmann and Fordice, 1886, p. 410 (Bean Blossom Cr., Monroe Co., Ind. [complex]).

(4)   *Noturus eleutherus* Jordan 1877, pp. 370–372 (original description; type from French Broad R., Tenn.).—Woolman, 1892, pp. 256, 287 (bayou of Green R., Ky.).—Lachner, 1956, p. 68 (ecology, upper Allegheny system).

(5)   *Schilbeodes eleutherus* (Jordan).—Smith, 1907, p. 70 (comparison; record compiled).

(6)   *Rabida eleuthera* (Jordan).—Jordan 1929, p. 93 (as *eleutherus*); description; range [in error]).

(7)   *Noturus latifrons*.—Jordan, 1885, p. 802 (nomen nudum; White R., Ind.; credited to Gilbert and Swain, Proc. U.S. Nat. Mus., 1885).

(8)   *Schilbeodes gallowayi* Fowler, 1945, pp. 2, 32, 122, figs. 155–157 (original description; type, * ANSP 54723, Holston R., above Bluff City, Tenn.).—Bailey and Taylor, 1950, pp. 31–38.

(1) Jordan's name, as author of the species, is given after the currently accepted species name. If the species now were in a genus other than the one in which it was originally described, Jordan's name would be in parentheses.

(2) Common names are optional. For North American fishes, common names normally follow recommendations of the American Fisheries Society's Committee on Names of Fishes. These names are updated every 10 years; the most recent list is that of Robins et al. (1980). The Committee also provides guidelines for forming vernacular names of new species.

(3) Eigenmann and Fordice misidentified specimens of *N. eleutherus* as *N. miurus*.

(4) Publications that refer to the species by its currently accepted binomen are listed in this entry, beginning with the original description. By convention, the starting point for zoological nomenclature is 1758, when the 10th edition of Linnaeus's "Systema Naturae" was published. Scientific names published before 1758 and not used by Linnaeus need not be considered available for use (i.e., no priority is associated with them).

(5) Smith placed the species in the genus *Schilbeodes*. When a species is assigned to a different genus, the name of the species' author is placed in parentheses. Smith actually followed a change that Jordan himself had made in 1894 to reflect a new concept of taxonomic affinities.

(6) Jordan moved the species yet again in 1929, this time to *Rabida*, a younger generic name than *Schilbeodes*. Generic names are Latin nouns that have either a masculine, feminine, or neuter form. Species names must agree in

---

Box 3.10 Continued.

gender with their generic names, so the spelling of *eleutherus* must change to *eleuthera* when the species is moved from *Noturus* (masculine) to *Rabida* (feminine). The phrases "as *eleutherus*" and "in error" mean that Jordan failed to correct the spelling when he moved the species to *Rabida*.

(7) In 1885, Jordan designated a new species, *Noturus latifrons*, but the specimens assigned to that species now are believed to be individuals of *N. eleutherus*, and *latifrons* thus is considered a junior (more recent) synonym of *eleutherus*. Further, *latifrons* was published "nude"—without a proper diagnosis and description of the specimens.

(8) Another name that is now considered a junior synonym was published by Fowler, though the "species" was properly diagnosed and described. The asterisk following the word "type" is Taylor's convention to indicate that he studied the type specimen, which has the catalog number 54723 and is stored at the Academy of Natural Sciences, Philadelphia (ANSP).

---

studied, and placed in the systematic framework. Studies of geographic variation within species, as well as ecological and historical zoogeographic investigations, utterly depend on thorough collecting efforts and accurate distributional data. Professional collecting activities are of fundamental importance in systematic ichthyology and fisheries biology. Collections provide the ultimate source of data on fish distributions and provide the raw materials for most systematic research.

Beyond the needs of "pure" systematic ichthyology, detailed knowledge of fish distributions is essential for stock assessments and environmental impact work in relation to all sorts of habitat modifications. The destruction and alteration of aquatic habitats is a major worldwide problem, and in ichthyology, as in most other systematic disciplines, the increasing pace of environmental alteration is far ahead of the accumulation of basic taxonomic and faunistic knowledge. Without baseline information on the composition of original fish faunas, followed by periodic monitoring, humankind will continue to face blindly the permanent loss of extraordinarily valuable and intriguing components of fish diversity.

It is no surprise that the state of knowledge of native fish faunas is very uneven. The fishes of north-temperate waters are best known, but even developed countries have many waters that have not been thoroughly surveyed. In North America, there are still many questions about the geographic limits of certain species, and new species are found occasionally (e.g., Jenkins 1976). The least-known ichthyofaunas are those of remote areas, areas of high diversity, and habitats that are vast or hard to sample. Of continental faunas, the riverine fishes of tropical southeastern Asia and tropical America are most poorly collected and understood. Recent collections from Borneo and the Amazon Basin have yielded many remarkable taxonomic finds (e.g., Bailey and Baskin 1976; Roberts, in press). Trawling operations in the deep river channels of the Orinoco River increased the known number of electric fish species in Venezuela by 30% (López-Rojas et al. 1984). In the unusually species-rich East African rift lakes, new taxa of cichlid fishes continue to be described at a high rate. Among marine faunas, those of the deep sea, especially the abyssal zone, and the Indo-Pacific coral reefs need much more sampling.

The selection of areas for collecting may be based on the taxonomic interests of an investigator, consideration of overall faunistic knowledge, or an impending environmental threat. Because all methods of collecting fishes are selective, a multigear approach is strongly recommended in survey work. Day and night as well as seasonal collecting is essential to insure capture of all faunal elements. Full use should be made of color photography to obtain the best possible records of life colors of fishes. Special preservatives for electron microscopy and histology, and rapid, ultracold freezing of representative specimens should also be used to maximize the potential benefits of field programs. Securing proper government and local clearances and permits to collect is an essential aspect of survey work in continental and coastal zones. It behooves investigators, especially those working abroad, to be keenly aware of all regulations and restrictions on collecting and to establish truly cooperative working relationships with the scientific community in the host country.

Collecting programs must have explicit provisions for follow-up work on samples. In systematic ichthyology, this generally includes transfer of samples from fixative (usually 10% buffered formalin) to alcohol preservative (usually 70% ethyl or 40% isopropyl); sorting, identifying and labeling individual lots of species from each sample; and deposition and cataloging of samples in appropriate museums, including those in the host country where appropriate. Because these are time-consuming activities, sorting and provisional identifications are expensive. When program or grant budgets permit, these tasks can be done by trained technical assistants, releasing the specialist to the analytical tasks of systematic research. At the unique Smithsonian Oceanographic Sorting Center in Washington, D.C., selected collections of marine and some freshwater fishes are prepared by a technical staff for worldwide distribution. This service has greatly enhanced the rate at which new material is made available to systematists in several disciplines, including ichthyology.

Collection of fishes on a large scale is expensive. Most major ichthyological surveys are sponsored and managed by government agencies. The U.S. National Marine Fisheries Service, Department of Interior, Bureau of Land Management, and various state government offices (e.g., Illinois Biological Survey) have supported surveys of continental, coastal, and marine fishes. The situaton is more or less comparable in other developed nations. In developing nations, however, governments may not have adequate finances or expertise available for large-scale survey programs. The United Nations Food and Agriculture Organization (FAO) has made noteworthy contributions towards faunistic surveys in Africa and southeastern Asia. The World Bank has also sponsored biotic surveys as parts of impoundment projects in little-known areas. Several governments have science agencies that grant support for pure research, including exploration in foreign lands. In the USA, the National Science Foundation's Systematic Biology Program offers such support. A relatively small fraction of exploratory activities in modern systematic ichthyology is supported by the private sector, including philanthropic individuals and foundations, or by the home institutions of investigators.

3.10 MUSEUMS AND RESEARCH COLLECTIONS

The importance of natural history museums to systematic ichthyology cannot be overemphasized. Whether public or private, natural history museums are the only reliable, widely accessible depositories for the primary study and care of voucher materials for systematics. These materials include preserved fish specimens (including type specimens; see Box 3.9) and skeletal and other special preparations. Museums must provide painstaking care of these materials if they are to remain useful for future generations of scientists. Museums maintain detailed records on specimens, including locality, habitat, and conditions of capture. Traditionally, such information is kept as "hard copy" in a handwritten catalog, but there is a trend toward computerization of catalog and collection data. In addition, museums and their curators almost always maintain ichthyological libraries, which are essential tools in systematic research.

Curators invite gifts of specimens of scientific value. Particularly important to archive are specimens collected from little-known areas and voucher specimens from important research projects for which identifications are critical.

Biologists wishing to study the fish collections at a museum should communicate in advance with the head curator about research goals. Permission is routinely granted, provided the work is part of a well-conceived scientific study. Procedures are also established for the loan of limited quantities of specimens to scientists working at other museums and laboratories.

In 1976, an advisory committee to the American Society of Ichthyologists and Herpetologists produced a report entitled "A National Plan for Ichthyology" (see Lachner et al. 1976). This document reviews the major collections of fishes in the USA and Canada. More than 100 collections exist in this region, of which 20 are recognized as major collections (Collette and Lachner 1976).

3.11 REFERENCES

Aspinwall, N. 1974. Genetic analysis of North American populations of the pink salmon, *Oncorhynchus gorbuscha,* possible evidence for the neutral mutation–random drift hypothesis. Evolution 28:295–305.

Auer, N. 1982. Identification of larval fishes of the Great Lakes basin with emphasis on the Lake Michigan drainage. Great Lakes Fishery Commission Special Publication 82-3, Ann Arbor, Michigan.

Avise, J. C. 1974. Systematic value of electrophoretic data. Systematic Zoology 23:465–481.

Avise, J. C., and seven coauthors. 1987. Intraspecific phylogeography: the mitochondrial DNA bridge between population genetics and systematics. Annual Review of Ecology and Systematics 18:489–522.

Avise, J. C., D. O. Straney, and M. H. Smith. 1977. Biochemical genetics of sunfish. IV. Relationships of centrarchid genera. Copeia 1977:250–258.

Bailey, R. M., and J. N. Baskin. 1976. *Scoloplax dicra,* a new armored catfish from the Bolivian Amazon. Occasional Papers of the Museum of Zoology, University of Michigan 674.

Ballard, W. W. 1981. Morphogenetic movements and fate maps of vertebrates. American Zoologist 21:391–399.

Barlow, G. W. 1961. Causes and significance of morphological variation in fishes. Systematic Zoology 10:105–117.

Barlow, G. W. 1974. Contrasts in social behavior between Central American cichlid fishes and coral-reef surgeon fishes. American Zoologist 14:9–34.

Behnke, R. J. 1970. The application of ontogenetic and biochemical systematics to phylogenetic problems in the family Salmonidae. Transactions of the American Fisheries Society 99:236–248.

Bell, M. A. 1976. Evolution of phenotypic diversity in *Gasterosteus aculeatus* superspecies on the Pacific coast of North America. Systematic Zoology 25:211–227.

Bell, M. A. 1984. Evolutionary phenetics and genetics: the threespine stickleback, *Gasterosteus aculeatus,* and related species. Pages 431–528 *in* B. J. Turner, editor. Evolutionary genetics of fishes. Plenum, New York.

Blackwelder, R. E. 1967. Taxonomy, a text and reference book. Wiley, New York.

Bookstein, F., B. Chernoff, R. Elder, J. Humphries, G. Smith, and R. Strauss. 1985. Morphometrics in evolutionary biology. Special Publication Academy of Natural Sciences Philadelphia 15.

Breder, C. M., and D. E. Rosen. 1966. Modes of reproduction in fishes. Natural History Press, Garden City, New York.

Brooks, D. R. 1981. Hennig's parasitological method: a proposed solution. Systematic Zoology 30:229–249.

Brooks, D. R., and E. O. Wiley. 1985. Theories and methods in different approaches to phylogenetic systematics Cladistics 1:1–13.

Buth, D. G. 1979. Biochemical systematics of the cyprinid genus *Notropis* I. The subgenus *Luxilis*. Biochemical Systematics and Ecology 7:69–79.

Buth, D. G. 1984. The application of electrophoretic data in systematic studies. Annual Review of Ecology and Systematics 15:501–522.

Camin, J. H., and R. R. Sokal. 1965. A method for deducing branching sequences in phylogeny. Evolution 19:311–326.

Carr, A. F., Jr. 1941. The fishes of Alachua County, Florida: a subject key. Dopeia. (Privately published.)

Clark, E., L. R. Aronson, and M. Gordon. 1954. Mating behavior patterns in two sympatric species of xiphophorin fishes. Bulletin of the American Museum of Natural History 103:135–226.

Clifford, H. T., and W. Stephenson. 1975. An introduction to numerical classification. Academic Press, New York.

Colless, D. H. 1967. The phylogenetic fallacy. Systematic Zoology 19:352–362.

Collette, B. B., and E. A. Lachner. 1976. Fish collections in the United States and Canada. Copeia 1976:625–642.

Crisci, J. V., and T. F. Stuessy. 1980. Determining primitive character states for phylogenetic reconstruction. Systematic Botany 5:112–135.

Crowson, R. A. 1970. Classification and biology. Neineman Education Books, London.

Dauble, D. D., and R. L. Buschbom. 1981. Estimates of hybridization between two species of catostomids in the Columbia River. Copeia 1981:802–810.

de Beer, G. R. 1958. Embryos and ancestors, 3rd edition. Oxford University Press, London.

Delco, E. A. Jr. 1960. Sound discrimination by males of two cyprinid fishes. Texas Journal of Science 12:48–54.

de Quieroz, K. 1985. The ontogenetic method for determining character polarity and its relevance to phylogenetic systematics. Systematic Zoology 34:280–299.

Dowling, T. E., and W. S. Moore. 1984. Level of reproductive isolation between two cyprinid fishes, *Notropis cornutus* and *N. chrysocephalus*. Copeia 1984:617–628.

Doyen, J. T., and C. N. Slobodchikoff. 1974. An operational approach to species classification. Systematic Zoology 23:239–247.

Echelle, A., A. S. Echelle, and D. T. Middaugh. In press. Evolutionary biology of the *Menidia clarkhubbsi* complex of unisexual fishes (Atherinidae): origins, clonal diversity and mode of reproduction. *In* R. M. Dally and J. P. Bogart, editors. Evolution and ecology of unisexual vertebrates. New York State Museum, Albany.

Echelle, A. A., and D. T. Mosier. 1982. *Menidia clarkhubbsi* n. sp. (Pisces: Atherinidae), an all-female species. Copeia 1982:533–540.

Ehrlich, P., and P. H. Raven. 1969. Differentiation of populations. Science (Washington, D.C.) 165:1228–1232.

Eldredge, N., and J. Cracraft. 1980. Phylogenetic patterns and the evolutionary process. Columbia University Press, New York.

Eldredge, N., and S. M. Stanley, editors. 1984. Living fossils. Springer-Verlag, New York.

Endler, J. A. 1977. Geographic variation, speciation, and clines. Princeton University Press, Princeton, New Jersey.

Endler, J. A. 1983. Natural selection and sexual selection of color patterns in poeciliid fishes. Environmental Biology of Fishes 9:173–190.

Estabrook, G. F. 1966. A mathematical model in graph theory for biological classification. Journal of Theoretical Biology 12:297–310.

Estabrook, G. F. 1977. Does common equal primitive? Systematic Botany 2:36–42.

Farris, J. S. 1970. Methods for computing Wagner trees. Systematic Zoology 19:83–92.

Farris, J. S. 1972. Estimating phylogenetic trees from distance matrices. American Naturalist 106:645–668.

Farris, J. S. 1986. Distances and statistics. Cladistics 2:144–157.

Felsenstein, J. 1981. Evolutionary trees from DNA sequences: a maximum likelihood approach. Journal of Molecular Evolution 17:368–376.

Felsenstein, J. 1982. Numerical methods for inferring evolutionary trees. Quarterly Review of Biology 57:379–404.

Felsenstein, J. 1986. Distance methods: a reply to Farris. Cladistics 2:130–143.

Ferris, S. D., and G. S. Whitt. 1978. Phylogeny of tetraploid catostomid fishes, based on the loss of duplicate gene expression. Systematic Zoology 27:189–206.

Fink, S. V., and W. L. Fink. 1981. Interrelationships of the ostariophysan fishes (Teleostei). Zoological Journal of the Linnean Society 72:297–353.

Fitzsimmons, J. M. 1972. A revision of two genera of goodeid fishes (Cyprinodontiformes, Osteichthyes) from the Mexican plateau. Copeia 1972:728–756.

Foreman, R. E., A. Gorbman, J. M. Dodd, and R. Olsson, editors. 1985. Evolutionary biology of primitive fishes. Plenum, New York.

Futuyma, D. J. 1979. Evolutionary biology, 1st edition. Sinauer Associates, Sunderland, Massachusetts.

Futuyma, D. J. 1986. Evolutionary biology, 2nd edition. Sinauer Associates, Sunderland, Massachusetts.

Gauthier, J., A. G. Kluge, and T. Rowe. 1988. Amniote phylogeny and the importance of fossils. Cladistics 4:105–210.

Gerald, J. W. 1971. Sound production during courtship in six species of sunfish (Centrarchidae). Evolution 25:75–87.

Gold, J. R., R. E. Pipkin, and G. A. E. Gall. 1979. Notes on a hybridization experiment between rainbow and golden trout. California Fish and Game 65:179–183.

Gould, S. J. 1979. A quahog is a quahog. Natural History 88:18–26.

Hagedorn, M. 1988. Ecology and behavior of a pulse-type electric fish, *Hypopomus occidentalis* (Gymnotiformes, Hypopomidae), in a fresh-water stream in Panama. Copeia 1988:324–335.

Hagen, D. W. 1967. Isolating mechanisms in threespine sticklebacks (*Gasterosteus aculeatus*). Journal of the Fisheries Research Board of Canada 24:1637–1692.

Hagen, D. W., and J. D. McPhail. 1970. The species problem within *Gasterosteus aculeatus* on the Pacific coast of North America. Journal of the Fisheries Research Board of Canada 27:147–155.

Hennig, W. 1966. Phylogenetic systematics. University of Illinois Press, Urbana.

Hennig, W. 1981. Insect phylogeny. Translated and edited by A. C. Pont. Wiley, New York.

Hester, F. E. 1970. Phylogenetic relationships of sunfishes as demonstrated by hybridization. Transactions of the American Fisheries Society 99:100–104.

Hillis, D. M. 1987. Molecular versus morphological approaches to systematics. Annual Review of Ecology and Systematics 18:23–42.

Holzberg, S. 1978. A field and laboratory study of the behaviour and ecology of *Pseudotropheus zebra* (Boulenger), an endemic cichlid of Lake Malawi (Pisces: Cichlidae). Zeitschrift für zoologische Systematik und Evolutionforschung 16:171–187.

Hopkins, C. D. 1983. Functions and mechanisms in electroperception. Pages 215–259 *in* R. G. Northcutt and R. E. Davis, editors. Fish neurobiology, volume 1. University of Michigan Press, Ann Arbor.

Hubbs, C., and K. Strawn. 1956. Infertility between two sympatric fishes, *Notropis lutrensis* and *Notropis venustus*. Evolution 10:341–344.

Hubbs, C. L. 1955. Hybridization between fish species in nature. Systematic Zoology 4:1–20.

Hubbs, C. L. 1961. Isolating mechanisms in the speciation of fishes. Pages 5-23 *in* W. F. Blair, editor. Vertebrate speciation. University of Texas Press, Austin.

Hull, D. L. 1976. Are species really individuals? Systematic Zoology 25:174–191.

ICZN (International Commission on Zoological Nomenclature). 1985. International code of zoological nomenclature, 3rd edition. International Trust for Zoological Nomenclature, London.

Jackson, J. F., and J. A. Pounds. 1979. Comments on assessing the dedifferentiating effect of gene flow. Systematic Zoology 28:78–85.

Jardine, N., and R. Sibson. 1971. Mathematical taxonomy. Wiley, London.

Jenkins, R. E. 1976. A list of undescribed freshwater fish species of continental United States and Canada, with additions to the 1970 checklist. Copeia 1976:642–644.

Jensen, R. J., and C. D. Barbour. 1981. A phylogenetic reconstruction of the Mexican cyprinid fish genus *Algansea*. Systematic Zoology 30:41–57.

Kluge, A. G. 1985. Ontogeny and phylogenetic systematics. Cladistics 1:13–27.

Kluge, A. G., and J. S. Farris. 1969. Quantitative phyletics and the evolution of anurans. Systematic Zoology 18:1–32.

Kornfield, I., D. C. Smith, P. S. Gagnon, and J. N. Taylor. 1982. The cichlid fish of Cuatro Cienegas, Mexico: direct evidence of conspecificity among distinct trophic morphs. Evolution 36:658–664.

Kortmulder, K. 1972. A comparative study of colour patterns and behavior in seven Asiatic *Barbus* species (Cyprinidae, Ostariophysi, Osteichthyes). Behaviour (Supplement 19).

Lachner, E. A., and six coauthors. 1976. A national plan for ichthyology. Copeia 1976:618–625.

Lauder, G. V., and K. F. Liem. 1983. The evolution and interrelationships of the actinopterygian fishes. Bulletin of the Museum of Comparative Zoology 150:95–197.

Lee, D. S., C. R. Gilbert, C. H. Hocutt, R. E. Jenkins, D. E. McAllister, and J. R. Stauffer, Jr. 1980. Atlas of North American freshwater fishes. North Carolina State Museum of Natural History, Raleigh.

LeGrande, W. H. 1976. Karyology of six species of Louisiana flatfishes (Pleuronectiformes: Osteichthyes). Copeia 1975:516–522.

LeGrande, W. H., and T. M. Cavender. 1980. The chromosome complement of the stonecat madtom, *Noturus flavus* (Siluriformes: Ictaluridae), with evidence for the existence of a possible chromosomal race. Copeia 1980:341–344.

Liley, N. R. 1966. Ethological isolating mechanisms in four sympatric species of poeciliid fishes. Behaviour (Supplement 13):1–197.

Liley, N. R., and N. E. Stacey. 1983. Hormones, pheromones, and reproductive behavior in fish. Pages 1–63 *in* W. S. Hoar and D. J. Randall, editors. Fish physiology, volume 9. Reproduction. Part B. Academic Press, New York.

López-Rojas, H., J. G. Lundberg, and E. Marsh. 1984. Design and operation of a small trawling apparatus for use with dugout canoes. North American Journal of Fisheries Management 4:331–334.

Lundberg, J. G. 1972. Wagner networks and ancestors. Systematic Zoology 21:398–413.

Lundberg, J. G. 1973. More on primitiveness, higher level phylogenies and ontogenetic transformations. Systematic Zoology 22:327–329.

Lundberg, J. G., and J. C. Stager. 1985. Microgeographic diversity in the neotropical knife-fish *Eigenmannia macrops* (Gymnotiformes, Sternopygidae). Environmental Biology of Fishes 13:173–181.

Mabee, P. M. 1988. Supraneural and predorsal bones in fishes: development and homologies. Copeia 1988:827–838.

Mabee, P. M. 1989. Assumptions underlying the use of ontogenetic sequences for determining character state order. Transactions of the American Fisheries Society 118:151–158.

Maddison, W. P., D. J. Donoghue, and D. R. Maddison. 1984. Outgroup analysis and parsimony. Systematic Zoology 33:83–103.

Maisey, J. G. 1986. Heads and tails: a chordate phylogeny. Cladistics 2:201–256.

Mayr, E. 1963. Animal species and evolution. Harvard University Press, Cambridge, Massachusetts.

Mayr, E. 1969. Principles of systematic zoology. McGraw-Hill, New York.

McCune, A. R., K. S. Thomson, P. E. Olsen. 1984. Semionotid fishes from the Mesozoic Great Lakes of North America. Pages 22–44 in A. A. Echelle and I. Kornfield, editors. Evolution of fish species flocks. University of Maine at Orono Press, Orono.

McKaye, K. R., T. Kocher, P. Reinthal, R. Harrison, and I. Kornfield. 1984. Genetic evidence for allopatric and sympatric differentiation among color morphs of a Lake Malawi cichlid fish. Evolution 38:215–219.

Meacham, C. A., and G. F. Estabrook. 1985. Compatibility methods in systematics. Annual Review of Ecology and Systematics 16:431–446.

Menzel, B. W. 1976. Biochemical systematics and evolutionary genetics of the common shiner species group. Biochemical Systematics and Ecology 4:281–293.

Michener, C. D., and R. R. Sokal. 1957. A quantitative approach to a problem in classification. Evolution 11:130–162.

Mishler, B. D., and M. J. Donoghue. 1982. Species concepts: a case for pluralism. Systematic Zoology 31:491–503.

Moritz, C., T. E. Dowling, and W. M. Brown. 1987. Evolution of animal mitochondrial DNA: relevance for population biology and systematics. Annual Review of Ecology and Systematics 18:269–292.

Moser, H. G., editor. 1984. Ontogeny and systematics of fishes. American Society of Ichthyologists and Herpetologists, Special Publication 1.

Moyle, P. B. 1976. Inland fishes of California. University of California Press, Berkeley.

Neff, N. A., and G. R. Smith. 1979. Multivariate analysis of hybrid fishes. Systematic Zoology 28:176–196.

Nelson, G. J. 1972. Comments on Hennig's "phylogenetic systematics" and its influence on ichthyology. Systematic Zoology 21:364–374.

Nelson, G. J. 1978. Ontogeny, phylogeny, paleontology and the biogenetic law. Systematic Zoology 27:324–345.

Nelson, G. J. 1985. Outgroups and ontogeny. Cladistics 1:29–45.

Nelson, G. J., and N. Platnick. 1981. Systematics and biogeography: cladistics and vicariance. Columbia University Press, New York.

Nelson, J. S. 1984. Fishes of the world, 2nd edition. Wiley, New York.

Nicol, J. A. C. 1969. Bioluminescence. Pages 355–400 in W. S. Hoar and D. J. Randall, editors. Fish physiology, volume 3. Academic Press, New York.

Oosterbroek, P. 1987. More appropriate definitions of paraphyly and polyphyly, with a comment on the Farris 1974 model. Systematic Zoology 36:103–108.

Pankhurst, R. J. 1975. Biological identification with computers. Systematics Association Special Volume 7.

Patterson, C. 1982. Morphological characters and homology. Pages 21–74 in K. A. Joysey and A. E. Friday, editors. Problems of phylogenetic reconstruction. Academic Press, London.

Pietsch, T. W. 1976. Dimorphism, parasitism, and sex: reproductive strategies among deepsea ceratiod anglerfishes. Copeia 1976:781–793.

Platnick, N. I. 1987. An empirical comparison of microcomputer parsimony programs. Cladistics 3:121–144.

Roberts, T. R. In press. The freshwater fishes of western Borneo (Kalimantan Barat, Indonesia). California Academy of Sciences Memoir 14.

Robins, C. R., and six coauthors. 1980. A list of common and scientific names of fishes from the United States and Canada, 4th edition. American Fisheries Society Special Publication 12.

Rosen, D. E. 1982. Do current theories of evolution satisfy the basic requirements of explanation? Systematic Zoology 31:76–85.

Rosen, D. E. 1985. An essay on Euteleostean classification. American Museum Novitates 2827:1–57.

Ross, H. H. 1974. Biological systematics. Addison-Wesley, Reading, Massachusetts.

Schaeffer, B., M. K. Hecht, and N. Eldredge. 1972. Paleontology and phylogeny. Pages 31-46 *in* T. Dobzhansky, M. K. Hecht, and W. C. Steere. Evolutionary biology, volume 6. Appleton-Century-Crofts, New York.

Schultz, R. J. 1969. Hybridization, unisexuality and polyploidy in the teleost *Poeciliopsis* (Poeciliidae) and other vertebrates. American Naturalist 103:605–619.

Scott, W. B., and E. J. Crossman. 1973. Freshwater fishes of Canada. Fisheries Research Board of Canada Bulletin 184.

Sibley, C. G., and J. E. Ahlquist, 1984. The phylogeny of hominoid primates, as indicated by DNA–DNA hybridization. Journal of Molecular Evolution 20:2–15.

Simpson, G. G. 1961. Principles of animal taxonomy. Columbia University Press, New York.

Sneath, P. H. A., and R. R. Sokal. 1973. Numerical taxonomy. Freeman, San Francisco.

Sokal, R. R., and P. H. A. Sneath. 1963. The principles of numerical taxonomy. Freeman, San Francisco.

Stevens, P. F. 1980. Evolutionary polarity of character states. Annual Review of Ecology and Systematics 11:333–358.

Strauch, J. G., Jr. 1984. Use of homoplastic characters in compatibility analysis. Systematic Zoology 33:167–177.

Svardson, G. 1969. Significance of introgression in coregonid evolution. Pages 33-59 *in* C. C. Lindsey and C. S. Woods. Biology of Coregonid fishes. University of Manitoba Press, Winnipeg, Canada.

Swofford, D. L. 1981. On the utility of the distance Wagner procedure. Pages 25–43 *in* V. A. Funk and D. R. Brooks, editors. Advances in cladistics. New York Botanical Garden, New York.

Swofford, D. L., and W. P. Maddison. 1987. Reconstructing ancestral character states under Wagner parsimony. Mathematical Biosciences 87:199–209.

Szalay, F. S. 1977. Ancestors, descendents, sister groups, and testing of phylogenetic hypotheses. Systematic Zoology 26:12–18.

Taylor, W. R. 1969. A revision of the catfish genus *Noturus* Rafinesque with an analysis of higher groups in the Ictaluridae. U.S. National Museum Bulletin 282.

Thorgaard, G. 1983. Chromosomal differences among rainbow trout populations. Copeia 1983:650–662.

Thorpe, R. S. 1984. Coding morphometric characters for constructing distance Wagner networks. Evolution 38:244–255.

Thresher, R. E. 1984. Reproduction in reef fishes. T. F. H. Publications, Neptune City, New Jersey.

Turner, B. J., T. A. Grudzian, K. P. Adkisson, and R. A. Worrell. 1985. Extensive chromosomal divergence within a single river basin in the goodeid fish, *Ilyodon furcidens*. Evolution 39:122–134.

Uyeno, T., and G. R. Smith. 1972. Tetraploid origin of the karyotype of catostomid fishes. Science (Washington, D.C.) 175:644–646.

Vooris, H. K. 1971. New approaches to character analysis applied to the sea snakes (Hydrophiidae). Systematic Zoology 20:442–458.

Watrous, L. E., and Q. D. Wheeler. 1981. The out-group comparison method of character analysis. Systematic Zoology 30:1–11.

Weir, B., editor. 1983. Statistical analysis of DNA sequence data. Dekker, New York.

Whitmore, D. H. 1983. Introgressive hybridization of smallmouth bass (*Micropterus dolomieui*) and Guadalupe bass (*M. treculi*). Copeia 1983:672–679.

Wiley, E. O. 1979. An annotated Linnean hierarchy, with comments on natural taxa and competing systems. Systematic Zoology 28:308–337.

Wiley, E. O. 1981. Phylogenetics: the theory and practice of phylogenetic systematics. Wiley, New York.

Wiley, M. L., and B. B. Collette. 1970. Breeding tubercles and contact organs in fishes: their occurrence, structure, and significance. Bulletin of the American Museum of Natural History 143:145–216.

Wilson, E. O. 1965. A consistency test for phylogenies based on contemporaneous species. Systematic Zoology 14:214–220.

Chapter 4

Taxonomic Methods: Morphology

RICHARD E. STRAUSS AND CARL E. BOND

4.1 INTRODUCTION

The morphology of fishes historically has been the primary source of information for taxonomic and evolutionary studies. Despite the value and availability of genetic, physiological, behavioral, and ecological data for such studies, systematic ichthyologists continue to depend heavily on morphology for taxonomic characters. Species have characteristic shapes, sizes, pigmentation patterns, disposition of fins, and other external features that aid in recognition, identification, and classification. In addition, there are important characters that can be examined by dissection or other means of internal examination. This chapter presents descriptions of important morphological characters and methods of studying them.

Our descriptions are representative of most fish groups. Hagfishes (Myxiniformes) and lampreys (Petromyzontiformes), however, lack such amenities as jaws and paired fins and are not considered to be true fishes. Thus most of the characters described in this chapter are not appropriate for their taxonomy. For a morphological review of lampreys, see Hubbs and Potter (1971); for hagfishes, see Hardisty (1979).

4.2 GENERAL EXTERNAL FEATURES

Information on the external morphology of fishes can be found in many standard references, including Hubbs and Lagler (1958), Miller and Lea (1972), Lagler et al. (1977), Bond (1979), Moyle and Cech (1981), and Trautman (1981). We present here a review of basic external features and kinds of variations observed, along with brief definitions of some of the more important morphological terms and conventional measurements.

4.2.1 Body Sections

A typical fish is a compact unit in which the head, trunk, and tail grade smoothly into one another, but these anatomical sections can be distinguished by reference to a combination of internal and external boundaries (Figure 4.1). The head is bounded dorsally by the *occiput* where the trunk muscles attach to the cranium. Although difficult to locate externally in some fishes, the occiput usually is evident as the position at which the dorsal scales begin (when present) or at which a hump at the *nape (nucha)* occurs. The head is bounded laterally by the posterior edge of the *operculum* and ventrally by the edge of the *branchiostegal membrane*. In traditional systematic work, head length is measured from the tip of the snout either to the most posterior edge of the operculum or to its dorsal articulation with

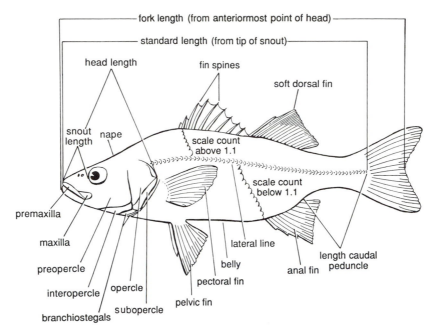

Figure 4.1   External features of a spiny-rayed fish.

the cranium. Other conventional measurements from the tip of the snout to a more posterior reference point include *predorsal length,* which extends to the anterior insertion of the first dorsal fin, and *standard length,* measured to the posterior end of the vertebral column.

In most fishes the trunk extends posteriorly from the head, where it articulates ventrally between the two halves of the lower jaw, to the anterior edge of the anal fin. Anal fin placement generally coincides with the position of the last abdominal vertebra, which marks the posterior end of the trunk internally. The tail consists of the flank above the anal fin, the *caudal peduncle* (between the anal fin and the caudal fin), and the caudal fin itself. Tail length and length of the caudal peduncle are not synonymous; the peduncle is measured from the posterior ray of the anal fin to the posterior edge of the vertebral column, an oblique measurement.

External recognition of head, trunk, and tail becomes difficult or impossible on fishes that have restricted or displaced opercular openings or unusual anal fins. Eels (Anguillidae) and elephant-nose fishes (Mormyridae) are examples. Even though the boundaries of the body sections in such fishes must be detected by dissection, by clearing and staining, or by radiographs (Section 4.4.1), descriptions of the relative sizes and shapes of these features may still be as important as for other, more typical fishes.

4.2.2   Features of the Head

On the head of a fish the *snout region* is between the eye and the anterior edge of the upper jaw, or the anteriormost part of the head if the jaw is subterminal. Snout length is measured from the anterior snout midline to the anterior edge of the eye *(orbit)* (Figure 4.1). The dorsal area between the eyes, usually overlying the supraorbital and frontal bones, is the *interorbital region,* and the area just

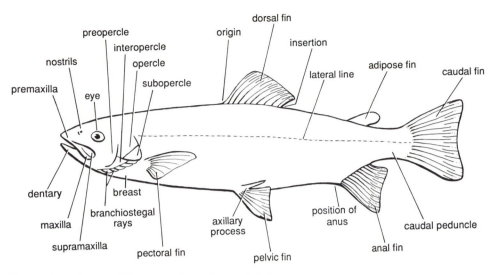

Figure 4.2 External features of a soft-rayed fish.

behind this is the *coronal region.* Interorbital width is usually measured as the width between the bones roofing the orbits or as the least width across the span, including soft tissues. The nape of the fish is usually demarcated by an elevation *(nuchal hump)* just behind the head at the point where the dorsal trunk musculature attaches to the cranium. Laterally, the region below and just behind the eye is the *cheek.* Behind this is the *operculum,* consisting of four bones: the *opercle,* the largest of the four in most fishes, which forms most of the upper and rear edges of the complex; the *preopercle,* usually forming an obtuse angle in front of the opercle; the the *subopercle,* below the opercle; and the *interopercle,* below the preopercle (Figures 4.1, 4.2) Conventionally, cheek height is the vertical distance from the near edge of the orbit to the ventral edge of the preopercle; cheek length is a more subjective measurement, usually taken from a point directly beneath the eye (often along a vertical line dropped from the anterior rim of the orbit) to the inner angle or posterior edge of the preopercle, including any spines. A related measurement is that from the orbit rim to the inner angle of the preopercle.

The upper jaw normally consists of the paired, lateral *premaxillary* and *maxillary* bones (Motta 1984). The premaxillae are small and anterior in most soft-rayed ("lower") fishes but extend more posteriorly in spiny-rayed ("higher") fishes, forming the inner border of the upper jaw. The maxillae form the major part of the mouth border in lower fishes but are excluded from the border by the premaxillae in higher groups. Length of the upper jaw is measured from the tip of the snout to the posterior edge of a maxilla. One or more *supramaxillae* may be attached to the upper edge of a maxilla. Most soft-rayed fishes and some specialized higher forms have nonprotractile premaxillae continuous with the snout. In others, the premaxillae are prevented from sliding forward during mouth protrusion by a narrow connection of skin *(frenum)* between the snout and upper jaw. A frenum can also be present on the lower jaw, binding the lower lip to the mentum. The large tooth-bearing bone on each side of the lower jaw or mandible is the *dentary.*

The mouth may be *terminal,* as in most fishes; *subterminal,* with the snout extending slightly above the premaxilla; *inferior,* placed well below the tip of the snout, as in suckers (Catostomidae); or *superior,* opening dorsally, as in the sandfishes (Trichodontidae) and killifishes (Cyprinodontidae).

At the tip of the lower jaw is the *mentum.* Behind this, between the rami of the jaw, is the *gular* region where, hidden by an external membrane, the body extends forward in a narrow structure called the *isthmus* and attaches to the head. The *branchial (branchiostegal) membrane,* below the operculum on each side, is supported by thin, rib-like *branchiostegal rays,* which may be diagnostic in number and relative lengths (McAllister 1968). The adult complement of branchiostegal bones usually forms very early in larval development.

Among the elasmobranchs, only the chimaeroids have an operculum-like structure covering the gills; sharks and rays have five to seven separate gill openings on each side. All elasmobranchs lack maxillae and premaxillae, and the mouth and nostrils of most species are positioned well behind the tip of the snout. A *spiracle* (remnant of the primitive mandibular gill slit) is usually present behind each eye.

Sensory Structures. The eye varies enormously in size and relative position among even closely related species. In many fishes, the orbit is one of the most allometrically changing structures of the body (Section 4.2.6), being relatively large in larvae (up to one-fifth the length of the body) and becoming progressively smaller in relative size in larger fishes. Thus, though orbit size and position are often important taxonomic characters, they must be carefully considered in relation to the size and age of the specimens at hand (Section 4.6.3).

Nostrils *(nares)* are located in front of each eye in bony fishes. On each side of the midline, nostrils may be either single, divided into anterior and posterior parts by a flap, or double, with the two apertures very close together or separated by up to half the length of the head. The posterior aperture is set well behind the head in some eels. The openings can be raised, tubular, or variously decorated. Nostril openings are usually larger than other porelike structures on the head. Because they are connected to the nasal sac, which in preserved specimens contains considerable fluid, they can often be located by pressing the skin with a blunt probe to extrude fluid.

Characteristics of *sensory canals* and *pits* are often used in species-level and genus-level descriptions, especially the positions of pores, the numbers of pores in the cephalic lateralis canals, and whether particular canals are complete or interrupted. Canals are named for their positions on the head. The medial *supratemporal* crosses the head dorsally, just anterior to the nape. The *lateral cephalic* canal courses anteriorly along the upper side of the head and splits to form the *supraorbital* and *infraorbital* canals, which may extend past the eye to the snout. The *preoperculomandibular* canal usually begins slightly below the lateral canal and runs along the jaw to the chin. Canal pores are often difficult to locate in wet preserved specimens; in such cases they can usually be located by applying a fine stream of air directed from a pipette or needle to dry localized areas of skin or scales.

Sensory barbels appear on the anterior part of the head in many groups, and are usually associated with the nares and mouth, especially the maxilla and mentum. They may be very elongated and protrusive, as are the "whiskers" of many catfishes (Siluriformes) or very small and hidden within the folds of skin between the jaw bones, as in some minnows (Cyprinidae). Placement, size, condition of branching, and number of barbels are taxonomically important.

Special Features of the Head.   Ridges and spines on the skull bones are prominent in many scorpaeniform and perciform fishes. Spines are characteristic of the opercular bones, especially the opercle and preopercle, but may appear on the roof bones of the cranium and on the suborbitals. In the scorpaeniforms, the second suborbital bone *(suborbital stay)* extends across the cheek toward the preopercle and, in some genera, bears spines. Some bones with free edges, such as the *lachrimal* (first suborbital or preorbital) and the preopercle, may be variously serrated. A feature used especially in the classification of the percoids is the extent to which the maxilla is hidden by the lachrimal when the mouth is closed.

Cirri are soft structures, present on the heads of many fishes, that may superficially resemble barbels but that are flattened, fringed, or branched and have no special sensory function. Cirri are usually associated with the nares or eyes but may also be located along the lower jaw or spread generally over the head.

4.2.3   Fins

Many characteristics of fins are important in systematics. Particularly useful are the number and relative positions of the fins and the numbers and types of rays composing them. The median fins include the dorsal, adipose (present in only a few groups), caudal, and anal fins; the paired fins are the pectoral and pelvic (ventral) fins. There are two basic types of fin rays: true spines and soft rays. *Spines* are single, median structures that are unbranched and lack joints. *Rays* comprise two longitudinal supports, jointed and typically branched. Spines normally occur in the anterior part of a single fin or in the anterior of two separate fins (Figure 4.1).

The *dorsal fin* is seldom absent and may show several distinctive variations. It is single in most soft-rayed fishes, although cods (Gadidae) may have multiple soft-rayed dorsal fins. The shape and size of the dorsal fin may distinguish species or sexes, as may its position in relation to other fins or body features. The extent of separation of the two (or more) dorsal fins may be taxonomically important because the gaps between fins are usually constant relative to the dimensions of the fins. The posterior edge of a dorsal fin may be either attached to (adnate) or free from the back. Other conditions to note are whether the dorsal fin is concealed in skin (as in some eelpouts, Zoarcidae) or is continuous with the caudal fin. A few groups, such as trouts and salmons (Salmonidae) and characins (Characidae), may have a dorsal *adipose fin* on the caudal peduncle; the tilefish has an adipose fin on the head.

The *caudal fin* is prominent in most fishes, but may be reduced or absent in eel-shaped species. Its size and shape often characterize genera or families of fishes. Common shapes include truncate (squared off), emarginate (having a slight indentation in the middle), forked, lunate (crescent-shaped), rounded, and pointed. Caudal fins may be continuous with one or both of the dorsal and anal fins.

The *anal fin* is generally single and short, positioned between the anus and the caudal fin. However, it may be exceptionally long in species that have the anus in an anterior position. Relatively few fishes have two anal fins; cods and jacks (Carangidae) are exceptions. In the "higher" bony fishes, spines are typically present in the anterior part of the fin. A few deep-sea fishes have adipose anal fins that are composed of fatty tissues and contain no rays. Tunas (Scombridae), carangids, and a few other groups may have *finlets*—small, detached, single-ray fins—following the dorsal or anal fin or both.

The *pectoral fins* are typically positioned just behind the opercular opening, but placement and form of the fins is highly variable among families and higher groups. In most soft-rayed fishes, the pectoral fins are placed low on the body, and the base of the fin is oblique so that the upper fin rays are more anterior than the lower. Typical spiny-rayed fishes have pectoral fins that are set higher on the body, just below or behind the outer curve of the operculum. Many perciform and scorpaeniform fishes may have a nearly vertical pectoral base. Silversides (Atherinidae), flying fishes (Exocoetidae), and a few other groups have pectorals set above the lateral midline. Pectorals may be modified as hydroplanes, tactile organs, or structures for walking on the substrate, or they may form part of a sucking disc in combination with the pelvic fins.

The *pelvic fins* are usually placed one on each side of the ventral midline, either just before the anus or just behind the pectorals. Presence or absence, size, and modifications of the paired fins are evaluated in taxonomic studies, as are their relative positions and the internal skeletal relationship between the pelvic and pectoral fin supports. Pelvic fins are completely absent in many families, especially those of eels and other elongate fish, and are lacking in many species of low-diversity groups such as swordfishes (Xiphiidae) and anglerfishes (Lophiiformes).

Most soft-rayed ("lower") fishes are distinguished by pelvic fins positioned in the *abdominal position;* typically, as in trouts (Figure 4.2) and minnows and carps (Cyprinidae), their placement is about midway between the pectorals and the anal fin. The pelvic girdle of such fishes is set into the muscular body wall and makes no bony or ligamentous connection with any other skeletal structures (Bond 1979; Moyle and Cech 1981). The abdominal position contrasts with the typically *thoracic* placement of the pelvic fins in the spiny-rayed fishes (Figure 4.1), in which they are positioned below the pectorals, with the pelvic girdle attached to the pectoral girdle. Between these extremes are groups of fishes with intermediate pelvic fin placement. *Subthoracic* pelvics are positioned behind the pectorals, and the fin girdles are connected by ligaments, as observed in trout-perches (Percopsidae). *Subabdominal* pelvics, as seen in some atheriniform fishes, are situated about midway between the typical abdominal position and the thoracic one and there is no connection between the girdles. Several kinds of fishes, including cods, blennioids, toadfishes (Batrachoididae), and anglerfishes have the pelvic fins placed in advance of the pectorals in a *jugular* position. In some of these, the pelvics are reduced in size or greatly elongated as tactile organs. Gobies (Gobiidae), clingfishes (Gobiesocidae), and some other groups have pelvic fins modified into adhesive structures.

Axillary appendages are elongate, triangular, scaly, or bony structures set in the axils of paired fins, usually the pelvics. They are absent in most fishes, but they are prominent in some herrings (Clupeidae) and salmonids.

4.2.4 Lateral Line

The *lateralis* sensory system (lateral line) is a prominent feature of the trunk and tail of most fishes; only a few groups, such as the herrings, lack the system on the body. The sensory pores of the system are usually associated with particular scale rows when scales are present. The lateral line generally courses from the top of the opercular opening to the caudal fin, but it may extend onto the caudal fin, as in the drums (Sciaenidae), or it may be incomplete. Incomplete lateral lines are described by noting the position of the terminal pore with respect to other prominent features of the body such as fins. Branched lateral lines are present in several groups. In some, such as the pricklebacks (Stichaeidae), the branching is multiple; in others, there may be a single branch. Interruption of the lateral line is encountered in some families, such as the Cichlidae, in which the line continues posteriorly a few scale rows below the interruption. Although such gross aspects of the lateralis system are important at higher taxonomic levels, finer variations are often diagnostic at the species and genus levels (DeLamater and Courtenay 1973). Like the cephalic canal pores, lateralis canal pores can be difficult to locate in wet preserved specimens but usually can be revealed by applying a fine stream of air to the skin or scales.

4.2.5 Scales and Other Dermal Structures

Scales. Typically, soft-rayed fishes have *cycloid* scales with smooth posterior margins, whereas the spiny-rayed fishes have *ctenoid* scales with one or more rows of spinules or ctenii on the posterior margin. However, a few characins, killifishes, and livebearers (Poeciliidae) have ctenoid-like structures on their exposed scale margins, whereas some spiny-rayed fishes (e.g., brook silverside) possess only cycloid scales. Other spiny-rayed species exhibit both ctenoid and cycloid scales. Scales may be of different sizes or types on the head or body, or may be lacking from specific areas. Even among closely related species, scales can vary enough to be useful as taxonomic characters (Hollander 1986). Scanning electron microscopy can aid the discovery of fine structural differences (Batts 1964; DeLamater and Courtenay 1974; Hughes 1981).

Scales may be modified into *bony plates* or *scutes,* as in sturgeons (Acipenseridae), sticklebacks (Gasterosteidae), jacks, armored catfishes (Callichthyidae, Loricariidae, etc.), and others. On jacks, the scutes may form a lateral *keel* on each side of the caudal peduncle. Lateral keels formed of soft tissue are found on the caudal peduncles of tunas and related species. A ventral keel is often formed by the scutes on the edge of the belly in the herrings. Many of the puffers (Tetraodontidae) and boxfishes (Ostraciidae) have scales modified into bony plates or stout spines. Others, such as the seahorses (Syngnathidae) and poachers (Agonidae), are enclosed in bony rings of specific shapes and numbers.

The *placoid* scales of some elasmobranchs, especially skates (Rajidae), are modified into hooks or spines in specific locations. These are usually sexually dimorphic and are useful in recognizing species.

Other Dermal Organs. Important sexually dimorphic features of the skin of some fishes are the *nuptial tubercles* ("pearl organs") that appear on males of minnows, suckers, and a few other groups during spawning season. Because they often have particular sizes and shapes and occur in distinctive locations on the head, fins, or body, they can be useful in classification (Collette 1965; Wiley and Collette 1970).

Photophores are light-producing organs usually situated in the skin of the head and body of certain fishes, but they may be internal. They are often sexually dimorphic in size and position and usually occur in diagnostic patterns (Marshall 1979; Moser et al. 1984a).

4.2.6 General Body Shape

As described above, most fishes possess a *fusiform* body form in which head, trunk, and tail merge smoothly into one another. However, the shapes of fishes are surprisingly diverse. Even closely related species may differ markedly in relative body length, depth, and width and in the relative size, shape, and placement of fins and other external structures. For this reason, body proportions are often used to describe taxa and discriminate closely related species.

Interspecific shape comparisons are best done after an analysis of within-species variation has been completed. Variation within species has two basic components (Barlow 1961): "geographic" variation among populations due to genetic divergence of phenotypic response to environmental factors, and within-population variation. This second component can be partitioned into body-size variation, sexual dimorphism, and functional effects correlated with age, seasonality, nutrition, etc. Body size is an important source of shape variation because most fishes have continuous, indeterminant growth and change shape allometrically as a function of size (Martin 1949; Bookstein et al. 1985). *Allometric* growth results in systematically changing proportions among morphological structures during ontogeny, and it can sometimes result in substantial differences in body form between juveniles and adults (Gould 1966; Strauss 1984).

The difficulty of describing body shapes in qualitative terms and the importance of understanding relative magnitudes of the basic components of morphological variation have together led to the widespread application of morphometric and statistical methods in fish biology (Section 4.6).

4.2.7 Pigmentation and Color Patterns

Coloration in fishes is due either to *schematochromes,* colors that result from the physical properties of tissues, or *biochromes,* true biological pigments such as carotenoids, melanins, purines, and pterins (Fujii 1969). Superficial biochromes, those that impart external color, are generally localized in special cells called *chromatophores,* which contain mostly colored pigments, and *iridophores,* which contain reflective crystals, primarily of guanine. Despite sometimes substantial variability among individuals, the placement and relative densities of chromatophores are under genetic control and thus often provide recognizable, consistent taxonomic characters useful for distinguishing species and subspecies.

Pigmentation patterns in fishes appear complex and difficult to describe objectively. However, the basic elements of most patterns can be readily identified and classified (Gregory 1951; Breder 1972). Breder (1972), for example, classified patterns as either primary, related to underlying scalation and myomere patterns, or secondary, unrelated to scalation. Longitudinal, transverse, and diagonal stripes are almost always aligned along scale rows. The darkness or width of such stripes is usually a function of the density and distribution of chromatophores on individual scales. Spots, vermiculations, and blotches also are usually aligned with scale rows, but less precisely than are stripes. Such elements form the bases of more complex patterns through a variety of combinations. Breder (1972) enumerated the many possible combinations of primary elements that have been observed in fishes; he also discussed assortments of primary elements that have not been observed. Secondary patterns include ocelli, concentric rings, and radial or polar arrangements. On most fishes, primary and secondary pigmentation patterns extend onto the fins and head; in the latter case, stripes or bars may be positioned so as to make the eyes inconspicuous to predators (Barlow 1972).

The most common taxonomic application of pigmentation patterns in fishes is to diagnose species and sexes. In such diagnoses, the pattern must be described as objectively as possible; stripes and bars should be enumerated when possible and the relative positions of pattern elements should be noted in relation to fins and other structures. Color-comparison charts can be used to precisely describe the observed hues, especially those of highly chromatic marine species. Specimens must be alive or freshly preserved for this purpose, and due consideration must be made for effects of ambient lighting conditions on color balance.

Pigmentation patterns have often been used as taxonomic characters to assess systematic relationships among species. General aspects of patterns, such as the presence or absence of particular stripes or ocelli in different species, can be coded as discrete characters under the assumption that the pattern elements are evolutionarily homologous among species (e.g., Wiley 1977; Rosen 1979). Patterns can also be treated quantitatively by counting stripes or spots in particular body regions and, when appropriate, by measuring elements and using their dimensions as morphometric characters (Section 4.6). As with other quantitative characters, however, relative numbers, sizes, and shapes of pigmentation elements may be influenced as much by environmental factors such as diet and predation intensity as by genetic history (Endler 1978, 1980).

4.3 MERISTIC AND OTHER ENUMERABLE CHARACTERS

Meristic characters are the body segments and other features, primarily fin rays and scales, that once, in evolutionary history, corresponded to the body segmentation. Other characters that can be counted (such as cephalic pores) are sometimes referred to as meristic even though they have no correspondence with the myomeres. Countable characters vary within and among species, so they are useful in describing or identifying fishes.

Meristic characters can be influenced substantially by environmental factors, especially by temperature during early development. Variation of this nature has been noted for many species (Hubbs 1922; Taning 1952; Weisel 1955; Lindsey 1958, 1962; Fowler 1970) and should be taken into account in studies involving meristic characters. Meristic features may also be size-dependent within or among species (Strauss 1985).

Because the evaluation of meristic and other countable characters can be subjective, published accounts should explicitly define the criteria used in making counts. Most North American ichthyologists use those of Hubbs and Lagler

(1958) as a standard. Unless otherwise referenced, the methods of counting described below are summarized from that work. For bilateral counts, it is standard practice to report the count first along the left side, then along the right, and to separate the two numbers by a hyphen (e.g., 12-13). By convention, the left side is used if only one side is counted; the right side may be used if the left is damaged.

4.3.1   Vertebrae

The vertebral column in fishes is composed of a series of segments, the *vertebrae*; each vertebra consists of a *centrum* and associated processes. There is usually a single vertebra per body segment, but two per segment may occur in some sharks. The rays of the caudal fin are usually supported by altered vertebral elements, including the *penultimate vertebra,* the *hypural* and *epural* elements, and the *urostyle* (Lundberg and Baskin 1969).

Conventional vertebral counts for salmonids (which have several sutures separating vertebrae within the hypural complex) and for fishes having heterocercal or abbreviated heterocercal tails are total counts of elements separated by sutures. In most fishes the hypural plate is fused to a ural centrum and is counted as a single vertebra. For fishes having variable ural centrum numbers, preural counts are used instead. If the vertebral count is to be separated into numbers of precaudal and caudal elements, the first vertebra bearing a hemal spine is designated as the first caudal vertebra.

4.3.2   Fin Rays

Conventional abbreviations for the various fins in the reporting of numbers of fin rays are: dorsal, D; anal, A; caudal, C; pectoral, P_1; and pelvic, P_2. All true spines (simple, unbranched, unsegmented fin rays) are designated by Roman numerals whether they are stiff or flexible. Hubbs and Lagler (1958) suggested using Roman numerals for the hardened, spinous soft rays in the pectoral fins of catfishes and in the dorsal and anal fins of common carp, although this is seldom done. Soft rays are designated by Arabic numerals (e.g., D 18).

In the dorsal and anal fins of soft-rayed fishes, the ray count is of "principal" rays. These are usually the branched rays plus the one unbranched ray that reaches more than one-half the height of the fin at the anterior edge. The short "rudimentary" rays at the anterior edge are not counted except in such species as pikes (Esocidae), catfishes, and graylings (Salmonidae) that have a graded series of separated rudiments and short rays supporting the anterior part of the fin. The last ray in the dorsal and anal fins of many species is branched at the base, each branch appearing as a separate ray. These are counted as a single ray, but care should be taken with some groups, such as sculpins (Cottidae), to insure that there are not actually two bases present and, therefore, two rays. All spines are counted regardless of size, and careful probing is required to disclose the first one or two spines of some species. If spines and rays occur in the same fin, the count of spines is separated from the count of rays by a comma (e.g., D IX,12). If there are two separate fins, the counts are separated by a hyphen (D IX-12).

For pectoral and pelvic fins, the count is of all rays regardless of size. Paired fins may have a tiny soft ray bound to the first well-developed ray; this is counted in the pectoral but not in the pelvic fin. In sculpins and other groups with reduced pelvic fins, the pelvic spine may be small and concealed beneath the skin, appearing upon dissection as a splint along the first soft ray.

Counts of caudal fin rays usually include the branched rays plus the unbranched rays at the dorsal and ventral edges.

4.3.3 Scales

Many reference points on a fish can serve as the beginnings and ends of scale counts. Because of this, the protocol used in a particular study must be explained clearly.

Some of the more taxonomically important counts deal with the number of lateral scales from the pectoral girdle to the caudal fin base. The most common count is that of the scales along the lateral line; this may be of the pored scales only or of all scales between the starting and ending points. Usually the first scale in a lateral count is the one that contacts the pectoral girdle and has immediately behind it one that is free from the girdle. The last scale counted is that directly in line with the posterior end of the hypural plate. The caudal peduncle tends to flex at this point, so dissection usually is not required to recognize the final scale in the count.

Other lateral scale counts are used occasionally. The number of diagonal scale rows along the side does not correspond to the number of lateral line scales on many fishes, and may actually display less variation among individuals (Dymond 1932; Neave 1943). The first row tallied is usually the one immediately behind the cleithrum of the pectoral girdle, and the last row is that crossing the lateral line at the posterior edge of the hypural plate. Another scale count, especially useful in salmonids, is of the longitudinal row immediately above the lateral line (Foerster and Pritchard 1935; Neave 1943).

Scales anterior to the dorsal fin are counted in a straight midsagittal line from the origin of that fin to the occiput. All scales intercepted by this line are counted. Scales above the lateral line are counted from the origin of the first dorsal fin obliquely backward and downward along one of the diagonal scale rows to the lateral line. The lateral line scale itself is not included. The count of scales below the lateral line is taken from the origin of the anal fin forward and obliquely upward to, but not including, the lateral line scale.

Circumferential scale counts around the trunk begin at the origin of the first dorsal fin. Circumferential counts around the caudal peduncle can be made in two ways. The usual count is made at the narrowest point of the peduncle, where the number of scales is lowest, but may be either a count of the scale rows around the peduncle or, alternatively, of all scales intercepted by a transverse line around the peduncle. The latter approximates a zigzag count and is higher than the count of rows.

4.3.4 Other Characters

When possible, gill rakers are counted on the first arch on the left side of the body. All rudiments are counted, so the arch must be carefully dissected for accuracy. If counts of rakers on the two limbs of the arch are reported separately, the upper count is given first, separated from the lower count by a plus sign (e.g., 6+12). A raker that lies directly on the angle of the arch is reported with those on the lower limb.

Pharyngeal teeth on the fifth gill arch of carps, minnows, and suckers are taxonomically very important (Eastman 1977). Their enumeration requires careful dissection of the pharyngeal region in order to remove the bony arch components *(ceratobranchials)* that bear the teeth. The edges of the pharyngeal arches are at the posterior edge of the gill opening just anterior to the cleithrum. These arches usually are removed by inserting the point of a fine, sharp scalpel between the cleithrum and the pharyngeal bone and carefully cutting the heavy muscles attached to the arches; care must be taken not to break the teeth. When the muscles are cut, the scalpel can be used with forceps to detach the arches above and below. Once the arches have been removed, they must be cleaned carefully to expose the teeth. The tooth count is recorded from left to right. For fishes with two rows of teeth on each arch, the teeth in the outer row on the left side are counted first, followed by those in the left inner row, right inner row, and right outer row. Typical formulas for fishes with one or two rows of pharyngeal teeth are 4-4 and 2,4-4,2, respectively. Some old-world minnows have three rows of teeth on each arch. The common carp, for example, has the count 1,1,3-3,1,1. A great deal of intraspecific variation exists among cyprinids (Eastman and Under-hill 1973), however, so that care must be taken if identifications of single specimens are based on tooth formulas. Counts are not always bilaterally symmetrical, and patterns of asymmetry themselves may be taxonomically useful.

The pores of the cephalic lateralis system (Section 4.2.2) are useful in identifying and describing species of several families, especially sculpins, pikes, and minnows. The most useful count is that of the preoperculomandibular canal; the number of pores along the mandibular section of the canal by itself is often diagnostic. In instances where there is a median chin pore, as on many sculpins, it can be separated from the remainder of the count by hyphens (e.g., 10-1-10; Bailey and Bond 1963).

Counts of branchiostegal supports include all elements regardless of size. Some dissection at the anterior part of the series might be necessary to obtain an accurate count.

Pyloric caeca are counted as tips, except in certain groups that commonly have branched caeca; in these, the caecal bases must be counted.

4.3.5 Recording and Analyzing Counts

The traditional method of recording is to use data ledger sheets with lines for each specimen and columns for counts. Alternatively, a voice-operated or foot-switch tape recorder or similar device may be employed to record the the values for later transfer to paper or computer disc. Counts also may be keyed directly into a portable computer.

As with body-shape comparisons (Section 4.2.6), interspecific meristic compar-isons must be carried out in relation to geographic and within-population variations. When differences are great or fine resolution is not sought, meristic data can be presented in frequency tables, accompanied by statistics such as means and standard deviations. Graphs are often used to present and analyze meristic data (Mayr et al. 1953; Simpson et al. 1960; Mayr 1969). A popular and useful graphical method is that of Hubbs and Hubbs (1953), in which ranges, means, standard errors, and standard deviations of sets of data are portrayed in one figure for comparison and assessment of statistical significance. "Box plots"

(Tukey 1977) are increasingly used to summarize nonparametric statistics such as medians and quartiles. If finer resolution is needed, meristic variation can be analyzed by multivariate statistics (Section 4.6.3).

4.4 GENERAL INTERNAL FEATURES

4.4.1 Skeletal Characteristics

The skeleton has traditionally been the primary basis of fish classification. Interrelationships among both recent and fossil fishes are assessed primarily through comparative study of the skeletal structure, including cartilage and certain ligaments. Important comparative information for study includes the presence or absence of features, the positions and relationships of structures to one another, configuration, size, and placement. The literature on skeletal morphology and variation among fishes is extensive; Greenwood et al. (1966, 1973) and Lauder and Liem (1983), among others, have discussed and illustrated the use of skeletons in fish classification.

The use of skeletal elements in species identification is usually restricted to features that are externally visible, such as fin rays, spines, suborbital bones, and mouth bones. However, internal skeletal features are important in the classification of lower taxa, and are as suitable for morphometric study (Section 4.6) as are external structures. Taxonomically important skeletal features include vertebrae (Section 4.3.1), pharyngeal teeth (Section 4.3.4), and the shapes and sizes of various cranial bones. The relationships of the fin rays to their supports *(pterygiophores)* and the relationships of the pteryiophore-like predorsal bones to the vertebral column are of importance in both the lower and higher taxa (Johnson 1984).

Otoliths, which are crystalline (calcium carbonate) structures within the inner ear, are useful for identification and classification as well as for age determination. They have distinctive shapes, sizes, and internal and surface features that can be studied by optical or electron microscopy (Fitch and Baker 1972; Casteel 1974; Brothers 1984). However, otoliths dissolve in formalin in a matter of days, so they must be carefully preserved in buffered formalin to remain useful (McMahon and Tash 1979).

Preparation of Skeletal Material.   Some skeletal structures can be conveniently studied by dissection, but less destructive methods must be used for others, especially those in very small individuals or in specimens that are not to be maimed or destroyed. Several methods are available for the preparation of dry articulated and disarticulated skeletons. These include the use of insect colonies (e.g., dermestid beetles), maceration in water, caustics, or enzymes and manual defleshing with hot water and hard work. An excellent method of preparing disarticulated skeletons of small fishes was described by Mayden and Wiley (1984). Dried bones can be lightly color-coded (e.g., a different color can be used for each species) by soaking them in a solution containing food coloring.

Tissue clearing and staining can provide specimens with the bones fully articulated and visible in their natural relationships to one another. Suitable techniques usually involve the staining of bone with alizarin red S and of cartilage with toluidine or Alcian Blue, followed by tissue clearing with caustics, enzymes, and glycerin (Taylor 1967; Dingerkus and Uhler 1977; Brubaker and Angus 1984).

The only nondestructive method of studying the internal skeleton is X-ray radiography. The use of radiography was first suggested by Gosline (1948) and is now common in systematic work. With proper equipment and technique (Miller and Tucker 1979), even very small specimens can be studied. Radiographs facilitate the counting of vertebrae, fin rays, and other skeletal elements, and they allow the presence or absence, size, and shapes of bones to be assessed. They can also be digitized for morphometric studies (Meyer 1987; and see Section 4.6.1).

4.4.2   Internal Organs

Occurrence.   Organs and structures typically present in most fishes may be lacking in others, so their simple presence or absence may be diagnostic for description or identification. Examples are teeth on various bones of the mouth or pharynx and special organs in the pharynx concerned either with respiration or feeding. The number of complete gill arches varies within some groups. The stomach may be lacking so that the gullet empties directly into the intestine, and pyloric caeca or the gall bladder may be missing. A discrete pancreas occurs in a few fish groups. Some species have only one ovary developed; others have two that are more or less consolidated. Oviducts are not present in some groups. In many species the urogenital sinus is absent and the gut, the genital duct, and the urinary duct empty separately to the exterior. In some species, a urogenital sinus is developed in one sex but not the other.

Size and Configuration.   Shape and relative size of internal organs can be important to systematists but may be difficult to quantify except in very simple terms. Relative length of the gut, for example, is used to identify many cyprinoid fishes (Kafuku 1958). Gas bladders vary in size among closely related deep-sea species (Marshall 1960), and sound-producing and sound detecting modifications are common in many groups. Stomach configuration (e.g., J-shaped, sigmoid, or linear) is helpful in identifying species in various groups, as is the degree to which the gut coils. Species of catfishes, drums, and other groups often differ in the shape of the gas bladder. In the tunas, the configuration of the liver is an aid to identification (Godsil and Byers 1944).

4.4.3   Muscles and Nerves

The musculature of fishes varies sufficiently that assessments of the relationships among higher taxa are aided by comparative myology (Greenwood et al. 1966, 1973; Wiley 1979; Lauder and Liem 1983). Even among genera and species in the same family there may be important differences in musculature (Winterbottom 1974b). Such differences may especially be associated with the trophic apparatus (Liem 1986), although allometric changes in muscle size and shape may also account for interspecific variation (Strauss 1984). Examples of muscles or muscle groups that have been used in classification are the retractor dorsalis and other branchial muscles (Liem 1986), the protractor pectoralis, the hyoid muscles, the adductor mandibulae and other jaw muscles (Gosline 1986), and the caudal fin musculature. Sources of information on musculature of fishes are the descriptive synonymy of Winterbottom (1974a) and various ichthyology texts and manuals such as Branson (1966) and Cailliet et al (1986).

There have been very few comparative studies of the peripheral nervous system of fishes (Herrick 1899, 1901; Freihofer 1963, 1970, 1978), primarily because sectioning and staining methods historically have been tedious, time consuming, and unreliable. Although histological techniques for studying the peripheral nerves of whole cleared specimens have been available since the last century, only recently have they been refined to the point that they may be used reliably in systematic studies (Freihofer et al. 1977; Filipski and Wilson 1984; Nishikawa 1987).

4.5 LARVAL FISH MORPHOLOGY

The study of morphological variation among fish species has conventionally been based on comparisons of adults. This is true in part because young stages are usually difficult to collect and identify. However, another important reason for emphasizing adults is that many fishes, particularly marine species, have distinctive larvae that are transitory forms (Balon 1984), often inhabiting entirely different microhabitats and niches from the reproductive stages and possessing very different body shapes and numerous, sometimes bizarre, temporary organs (*caenogenetic* adaptations; Moser 1981). In addition, the very simple, generalized forms of most larvae provide relatively few consistent taxonomically important characters with which to characterize and describe morphological relationships among species. Larvae possess a dynamic, continuously changing morphology. For example, the formation of fins and their complement of fin rays occurs gradually and almost continuously during the larval period, often beginning in the egg stage; the same is true for mouth parts and other cephalic elements. Taxonomically important characters therefore tend to be stage- and size-specific, making their use in taxonomic descriptions and comparisons more involved than corresponding characters of juveniles and adults.

4.5.1 Larval Stages

Many terminologies have been developed to describe the early life history stages of fishes; they differ according to which developmental events the investigator considered to be most fundamental (Hubbs 1943; Kendall et al. 1984; Balon 1985). The basic stages consist of (1) the egg or embryo, lasting from fertilization or activation to hatching; (2) the larva, from hatching to loss of larval characteristics and attainment of complete fin-ray counts; and (3) the juvenile or postlarva. The larval stage of teleosts can be conveniently divided into four substages delimited by yolk-sac absorption and the upward *flexion* of the posterior end of the notochord during development of the homocercal tail: the yolk-sac, preflexion, flexion, and postflexion substages. Transitional stages can also be recognized in some groups, such as the "transformation" stage between larva and juvenile during which a rapid and marked metamorphosis occurs in species having specialized larval forms.

There are two basic approaches to the study of fish eggs and larvae. One is to trace characters backward from the adult, through a series of collected material, to the early developmental stages. The other is to work forward from fertilized eggs obtained from known parents. Whenever fishes can be hatched and reared from eggs, the second method is preferred because the specimens being described are known with certainty. Berry and Richards (1973) recommended a dynamic approach to describing larvae, wherein first the smallest larva is described in detail, then the developmental sequences of individual characters and structures. This approach contrasts with the static, separate descriptions of larvae of various sizes and ages common in the older literature.

4.5.2 Uses and Limitations of Larval Characters

The primary limitation of larval characters in taxonomy is that they may be more variable and less discriminatory than corresponding features of adults. Characters with this problem include vertebral and myomere counts, fin-ray counts, relative body proportions, and pigmentation patterns (Berry and Richards 1973; Kendall et al. 1984). Their relative utility depends on when during development their numbers and patterns stabilize. Full complements of myomeres and caudal fin rays are usually complete by the time of caudal flexion; at that time they are typically uniform within orders and families, allowing identification to those taxonomic levels but, in many cases, not to lower levels (but see Moser et al. 1984b for important exceptions). Although many researchers have assumed that numbers of myomeres in larvae and numbers of vertebrae in adults are directly related, the correspondence is imperfect (Snyder 1979); vertebral numbers are often less variable than myomere counts (Fuiman 1982). Pigmentation patterns of larvae, particularly distributions of initial chromatophores, are sometimes important for discriminating closely related species (Fuiman et al. 1983).

Comparative morphometric studies of early free-swimming stages of fishes have been undertaken only recently (Martin 1949; Fuiman 1979, 1983, 1985; Strauss and Fuiman 1985). They should be more important in the future, both for taxonomic studies among closely related species (Berry and Richards 1973) and for studies of *heterochrony,* which treats mechanisms of evolutionary change that alter rates of development and the timing of developmental events (Alberch et al. 1979; Alberch 1980; Atchley 1987). A substantial amount of the morphological variation expressed by larvae is due to *allometry,* the systematic change in shape with growth. Morphometric methods (Section 4.6) can be used to describe and quantify allometric growth gradients, which then can be used to characterize the shape changes that take place during larval development (Strauss and Fuiman 1985). Allometries and relative growth rates are also useful as ontogenetic body-shape characters for taxonomic comparisons and phylogenetic inference (Kluge and Strauss 1985). The major problem is that larval and postlarval stages usually share few anatomical landmarks that can be compared directly. In addition, two variability problems confound sensitive quantitative studies of larval morphology. One is due to the extreme liability of larval fishes in response to environmental factors such as temperature, salinity, oxygen and carbon dioxide concentrations, food availability, and space (Blaxter 1969). The second is that larvae are very easily distorted when they are preserved—shrinkage is an especial problem (Heming and Preston 1981; Dabrowski and Bardega 1982)—and must be carefully fixed and preserved for study (Lavenberg et al. 1984; Markle 1984; Tucker and Chester 1984).

Although ontogenetic characters have been used to examine systematic relationships in several groups (Moser et al. 1984b), most information on gross morphology of larval fishes has been used to distinguish and identify species for purposes of fish biology and management (e.g., Lippson and Moran 1974; Boreman 1976). A great deal of excellent descriptive embryological work has been done on fishes during the past 100 years, but many more comparative studies are needed for this information to be of real taxonomic value (Fuiman et al. 1983; Kendall et al. 1984; Fuiman 1985).

4.6   MORPHOMETRIC CHARACTERS

Morphological differences among populations or species are usually described as contrasts in overall body form or in particular anatomical features. For example, one species might be relatively narrower and deeper bodied than another species or possess a relatively larger eye or shorter dorsal fin. Although such qualitative descriptions occasionally may be sufficient, it is often desirable to express differences quantitatively by taking various measurements of individual specimens and reporting statistics (such as means, ranges, variances, correlations) of the measurements. The same can be done with *meristic* (countable) features such as fin rays, lateral line pores, and vertebrae. However, meristic traits differ from measured (mensural) traits in a fundamental way: whereas counts usually become stable in number during growth after a threshold body size has been attained, mensural traits change continuously with size and age. This difference is particularly important for fishes because of their continuous growth. Thus we discuss meristic traits separately (Section 4.3) and restrict the term *morphometric* to those characteristics of form that can be measured in millimeters on the body. Body areas and volumes can be used as morphometric characters as well, but they usually must be transformed (e.g., by taking square and cube roots, respectively) to make them consistent in dimension with linear measurements.

Quantitative techniques have had three basic uses: (1) discrimination among sexes or species (Ouellette and Qadri 1968) and the categorization of uncertain specimens, such as putative hybrids (Neff and Smith 1979; Strauss 1986; Taylor et al. 1986); (2) description of patterns of morphological variation among populations or species (Poss and Miller 1983; Strauss 1985; Winans 1985); and (3) classification and the assessment of phylogenetic relationships.

4.6.1   Data Collection

Conventional morphometric measurements have been taken with dial or vernier calipers (for measures greater than 2–3 mm) or ocular micrometers (for those less than 5 mm), the data being manually recorded and subsequently tabulated by hand or keyed into a calculator or computer for analysis. With the advent of microprocessors, automated methods of data acquisition have become relatively inexpensive. Digital or analog calipers, for example, allow data to be entered directly into a computer file, which substantially speeds data collection and eliminates transcription and keying errors (McAllister and Planck 1981; Marcus 1982, 1983).

Morphometric measurements may also be derived indirectly from computed linear distances between "digitized" points (Bookstein et al. 1985). This procedure requires an electronic digitizer linked to a computer or microprocessor and a suitable projection of each specimen onto a flat surface. The projection might be a photograph, radiograph, camera lucida drawing, video-camera picture, or any other image. The only requirements are that the projection be perpendicular to the line of view (e.g., true lateral or true dorsal), to prevent artifactual variation among specimens due to inconsistent orientation, and that localized anatomical features *(landmarks)* to be digitized are clearly visible. Definition and choice of landmarks will be discussed below. Relative positions of landmarks may also be transferred to paper directly from preserved specimens with, for example, straight pins or a mechanical pantograph (Strauss and Fuiman 1985). The image is then placed on the digitizer; a cursor or pointer is used to signal the positions of landmarks in a predetermined sequence. Each point is translated by the digitizer into a pair of Cartesian *(X, Y)* coordinates, which are transmitted and stored on a computer file. A computer program is subsequently used to calculate Euclidean distances between selected pairs of points, distances that are proportional to the corresponding measurements on the projection. Typically the ends of a scale bar of specified length are digitized along with each specimen so that the distances between landmarks can be rescaled to millimeters by the program. In this way, many morphometric measurements may be generated from a relatively small collection of carefully placed, digitized points. The technology is rapidly becoming available to digitize three-dimensional positions of landmarks directly from a specimen by means of a pointer free to swivel in space. This procedure obviates the need for landmarks to lie within a single planar projection and allows a more comprehensive description of three-dimensional form.

Regardless of the method used to acquire morphometric measurements, care must be taken to ensure that specimens are not abnormal or otherwise deformed in shape or posture. Quantitative techniques are obviously much more sensitive to biological and artifactual distortion than are conventional morphological methods of study. A subtle but systematic source of artifactual variation is preservation distortion (Shetter 1936; Parker 1963; Jones and Geen 1977; Lee 1982). It has long been known, for example, that different tissues undergo different amounts and rates of shrinkage during fixation, and that such responses may be species-specific and may be cumulative over long periods of time. In addition, different preservation media (e.g., buffered versus unbuffered formalin; ethyl versus isopropyl alcohol) are likely to affect magnitudes and types of distortion. A second potential source of error is "researcher effect," due either to differences in technique between researchers when more than one person is involved in data collection, or to gradual but significant changes in the measurement technique of a single person over time. The former effect can be detected by performing statistical tests (e.g., analysis of variance) to check for differences between researchers or, preferably, by having a subset of specimens measured redundantly by different people. The latter effect can be checked by periodically remeasuring a standard set of specimens and checking for consistent deviations. Few investigators systematically screen their data for either preservation distortion or researcher effect, yet both sources of variation can lead to spurious results.

4.6.2 Character Sets

The complete set of measurements used to describe a form is a morphometric *character set*. A character in this sense is a feature that varies from one organism to another (Sneath and Sokal 1973). The character sets generally used by fish biologists are subsets or modifications of the measurements described by Hubbs and Lagler (1958). This conventional set has the advantages of characterizing the relative sizes of major morphological features and of providing standardization among different studies. As a means of describing differences in body form, however, it suffers from several disadvantages (Bookstein et al. 1985). For example, because the conventional characters are chiefly length, depth, and width measurements, with few diagonals, they tend to be repetitious and overlapping and to measure the form unevenly. In addition, many of the characters are "extremal," measured as minimum or maximum distances (e.g., greatest body depth, least peduncle depth), so their placement on the form might not be strictly comparable from one species to another. Because the measurements are selected independently without any strict relationship to one another, the character set generally has no collective or "emergent" geometric properties (Bookstein 1982). Other character sets proposed in the literature (Gregory 1928; Taliev 1955; McCune 1981; Fricke 1982) suffer from similar weaknesses, particularly those that are not based on anatomical landmarks.

Several procedures are possible for specifying sets of morphometric characters that circumvent these problems. One procedure recently applied in the ichthyology literature (e.g., Strauss and Fuiman 1985; Schaefer and Cavender 1986; Taylor et al. 1986) is the *truss* protocol (Figure 4.3) described in detail by Strauss and Bookstein (1982). The truss consists of a systematically arranged set of distances measured among a set of preselected anatomical *landmarks,* which are points identified on the basis of local morphological features and chosen to divide the body into functional units. Typical landmarks include bases of fin spines or rays, articulation points between bones, points where edges of bones cross the midsagittal plane of the body, etc. Landmarks are chosen to be evolutionarily or functionally comparable in position to corresponding landmarks on other species, and they often are explicitly assumed to be *homologous* among species (Bookstein et al. 1985; Strauss 1987). For each set of four landmarks forming a quadrilateral, the truss character set consists of the six possible pairwise measurements among them; when possible, landmarks are chosen to produce nonoverlapping quadrilaterals. The methodological advantages of the truss protocol over conventional character sets include the following. (1) The truss character set ensures regular coverage of the body in area and orientation, allowing detection of shape differences in oblique as well as longitudinal and vertical directions. (2) The method allows the configuration of landmarks to be reconstructed from the measured distances with no loss of information. The reconstruction procedure can be extended to three dimensions. (3) The method allows measurement error to be statistically removed from the data prior to analysis. (4) It allows entire forms to be averaged for populations and species, rather than individual measurements. (5) The procedure is based on explicit assumptions of homology, assuring a scientific basis of comparison. Such assumptions might often be weak or naive in the absence of detailed developmental information, and must be justified on a case-by-case basis. The important methodological distinction between this protocol and conventional ones is that the morphological landmarks are assumed to be homologous, rather than the measurements per se. Distance measures are merely the mechanism by which landmark configurations are "archived" and quantified for comparison.

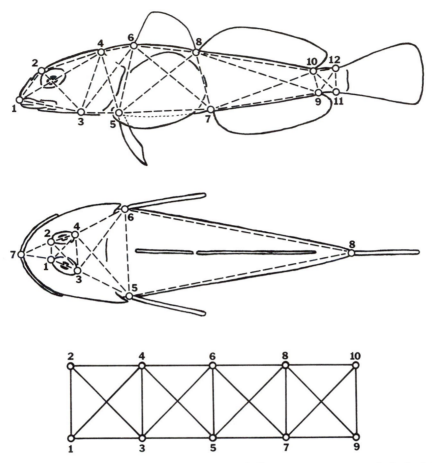

Figure 4.3 Sample truss networks of measured distances among morphological land-marks. Upper: truss measurements representing five truss cells (quadrilaterals) among a set of 12 well-defined midsagittal landmarks. Middle: two truss cells among six landmarks (three bilateral pairs) in dorsal projection; two medial terminal landmarks are triangulated to the truss network. Lower: an idealized square truss for 10 landmarks.

The systematic body coverage of the truss protocol is also its primary weakness, because it is primarily applicable to broad features of form rather than to localized features (e.g., Taylor et al. 1986). Thus, for most studies, a practical solution is a composite data set consisting both of truss measurements, covering the broad features of the body, and an auxiliary set of conventional measurements describing local anatomical features such as fin-ray lengths, eye diameter, dimensions of mouth parts, snout length, and so on.

Distance measurements have numerous advantages as morphometric charac-ters because they are easy to make and analyze, and they conform to allometric models of size and shape variation (Gould 1966). However, other kinds of data have been used to quantify morphological variation. These include radial func-tions and Fourier descriptors (Younker and Ehrlich 1977; Kincaid and Schneider 1983; Lohmann 1983; Rohlf and Archie 1984), medial axes (Blum 1973; Bookstein 1978), orthogonal mappings ("theta rho" analysis; Benson and Chapman 1982; Olshan et al. 1982; Siegel and Benson 1982), and biorthogonal grids (Bookstein

1977, 1984; Bookstein et al. 1985). Like ratios, the use of Fourier descriptors in morphometrics has been very controversial (Bookstein et al. 1982; Ehrlich et al. 1983; Read and Lestrel 1986). Medial axes, orthogonal mappings, and biorthogonal grids have been used too infrequently for an assessment of their ultimate utility in taxonomic and evolutionary studies.

4.6.3 Preparation and Analysis of Morphometric Data

Once morphometric data have been collected, the method of analysis depends on the nature of the data and the questions being asked (Oxnard 1978; Bookstein 1982; Reyment 1985). Distance measurements, the most common form of morphometric data, require special consideration because they vary continuously with body size. Unless the objective of a morphological study is to determine whether two samples of fishes differ in mean body size, one usually wishes to separate the effects of size differences from variation in body shape. A conventional technique for assessing shape differences is to use ratios (proportions or percentages) of measurements as characters. Ratios are generally assumed to remove the effects of body size by dividing out a "size variable" such as standard length. The ratio of head length to standard length, for example, is often assumed to reflect relative head size independent of body size. Despite their apparent simplicity, however, there are many biological and statistical problems associated with using ratios as "dimensionless" shape descriptors (Atchley et al. 1976; Albrecht 1978; Atchley and Anderson 1978; Bookstein et al. 1985). For example, ratios generally have larger sampling errors than the original measurements, and they also have nonnormal frequency distributions that violate the assumptions of standard statistical tests. The use of ratios can also introduce spurious character correlations that were not present in the original data, and it can introduce nonlinearities into previously linear relationships. Most important, however, ratios do not adequately compensate for differences in body size except in special circumstances (Strauss 1985). Size effects can be removed from a morphometric data set in several ways that rely on some type of regression analysis (Thorpe 1976; Bookstein et al. 1985).

Distance measurements are usually treated statistically; either one measurement is analyzed at a time by *univariate statistics,* or all characters are treated simultaneously by *multivariate statistics.* For example, if the purpose of the study is to determine whether two populations of fishes are more different from one another than we would expect from chance variation, tests of statistical difference could be performed to determine the significance or level of certainty of observed differences. This is a type of *confirmatory analysis* by which we either confirm or fail to confirm our research hypothesis (i.e., our prior expectations). Analysis of variance (ANOVA) is a univariate statistical method for carrying out such tests for any number of samples. The corresponding method for analyzing differences among many characters simultaneously via their pairwise correlations is called multivariate analysis of variance (MANOVA).

If the purpose of a study is to examine patterns of morphological variation among populations or species rather than to test for specific differences, then *exploratory analyses* serve the purpose better than confirmatory analyses. Although basic exploratory analyses are univariate in nature (Tukey 1977), the more useful and powerful methods are multivariate. *Principal components analysis*

(PCA), for example, is a widely used technique for assessing patterns of variation and covariation within and among a set of samples, such as populations or species, without having to predefine the groups of interest. When properly used, PCA permits the examination of size and shape differences independently, and does not rely on ratios of measurements (Jolicoeur and Mosimann 1960; Smith 1973; Humphries et al. 1981). It is, therefore, a valuable method for searching for morphological differences or groups that were previously unsuspected.

If one is interested in classifying individuals into known groups and determining which sets of characters best discriminate them, *discriminant function analysis* is a useful procedure (Fisher 1936; Ouellette and Qadri 1968; Albrecht 1980). Discriminant analysis is used to calculate the combination of original characters that maximally discriminates among known groups. Although the method is commonly used, it has two important problems when applied to morphometric data (Bookstein et al. 1985). First, the technique is not insensitive to size differences among groups; that is, if the groups differ in mean size, the resulting discriminant function discriminates at least in part on the basis of that size difference, however small. This can be critical with continuously growing organisms, in which case the size difference can be the result of artifactual sampling variation. Size effects can be removed from the characters one at a time by regression prior to discriminant analysis (Thorpe 1976; Strauss 1986), but several multivariate methods have been developed to circumvent this problem, such as Burnaby's (1966) size-invariant functions and the sheared principle components of Humphries et al. (1981). The second problem is that the character coefficients (weights) produced by a discriminant analysis are not always biologically interpretable with respect to shape differences. If two discriminatory characters are highly correlated, for example, one may be assigned a large weight and the other a near-zero weight (because it has no additional discriminatory value) even though both contain similar information about shape differences. Biological interpretations should be based instead on "vector" correlations of characters with the computer discriminant functions, which can be estimated from discriminant scores (Strauss 1985).

Morphometric data also can be used as taxonomic characters to examine evolutionary relationships among species. Structural measurements sometimes are used directly as characters if they are sufficiently discrete among taxa or if a tree-building procedure is used that allows the use of continuous characters (Farris 1970; Farris et al. 1970). However, measurements must usually be recorded into discrete character states for phylogenetic analysis, typically by employing a *gap-coding* procedure whereby clusters of measurements that are separated in value from other such clusters by "natural" gaps are given a common character-state designation for each cluster (Thorpe 1984; Archie 1985). Morphometric data have the advantage that size effects can be removed before the data are recoded so that inferred evolutionary relationships are based on body-form rather than body-size differences.

Good sources of information on univariate and multivariate methods for morphometric analyses include Sneath and Sokal (1973), Tukey (1977), Pimental (1979), Sokal and Rohlf (1981), and Bookstein et al. (1985).

4.7 PHOTOGRAPHING FISHES

Photography has become a necessary part of systematics because it gives the researcher a means of recording material that does not lend itself well to drawings, that is available for only a short time, or that cannot be preserved. Photographs may be taken of whole organisms, of important structures or organs, or of microscopic features. Photomicrography will not be covered here because of its specialized nature. The following is a brief outline of simple techniques that can be used with commonly available equipment to produce suitable photographs of fishes.

4.7.1 Techniques

Specimen Preparation.   Most fish specimens to be photographed for taxonomic purposes are dead or anesthetized (see Chapter 8 for details on anesthesia), so the photographer has a wide choice of lighting, exposure, and poses. Freshly killed specimens have several advantages over long-preserved specimens, including retention of color, normal reflectivity, and flexibility of body and fins.

Fresh specimens are usually "spread" for photography; their fins are extended and pinned out on styrofoam sheets, and a syringe or brush is used to inject or spread formalin into the fins and fin musculature (Randall 1961; Emery and Winterbottom 1980; Flescher 1983). Formalin must not be placed on the eye because it will cause an undesirable milky appearance. A polyethylene sheet can be placed under the fish to prevent it from adhering to the dry styrofoam. Blocks or small sheets of styrofoam are placed beneath the fins to hold them in line with the plane of the body. Small insect pins or larger stainless steel pins are used to spread the fins, depending on the size of the specimen. The pins can be removed after a few minutes and the specimens can be photographed with fins in extended positions. The pelvic fin on the off side can be hidden if desired.

Immersion Photography.   The method of photography can suit the purpose of the project, but the objective should be to show the fish and its salient features as clearly as possible without unlighted portions and distracting shadows. Photographing submerged specimens usually produces good results. Diffusion of light in the water aids in eliminating unlighted parts of the subject, and shadows do not appear if the background is placed far enough away from the subject.

One such procedure (Randall 1961) involves a glass-bottom aquarium positioned over a hole in the supporting table so that a desired background color can be placed beneath it on the floor. The subject is placed on a glass plate submerged in the aquarium and illuminated with photofloods. The main disadvantage of the technique is the placement of the subject flat on its side; if the subject is large and wide-angle lenses are not available, the apparatus must be placed very low or the camera high. Low placement of the subject invites shadows unless provision is made to illuminate the background. The water in the aquarium must be aged before use to prevent the accumulation of bubbles on the specimen and glass plate.

Pletcher (1966) provided an aquarium with a lighted background and circulating and filtered water for use aboard ship, though the system could have applications elsewhere. An inclined glass plate slightly higher than the aquarium holds the specimen upright against the front wall. The subject is placed in a vertical position with the head up, and inclined glass can be adjusted to the taper of the specimen. Flash units are positioned above and below the level of the aquarium.

Emery and Winterbottom (1980) described a simpler device for field use. Glass aquaria of three sizes ($45 \times 45 \times 15$ cm, $25 \times 20 \times 8$ cm, and $12 \times 8 \times 3$ cm) are used so that fish of several sizes can be photographed with a minimum adjustment of the apparatus. The bottom plate is cut a few centimeters oversize for stability. The glass for the aquaria can be taken into the field and assembled with silicon sealant. A glass plate, held in place by two small pieces of glass cemented to the bottom plate near the front wall, is used to hold the fish specimen against the front wall. The background used by Emery and Winterbottom was blue-gray cloth stretched on a collapsible frame. Illumination was by two strobes, supported on an aluminum frame that could be held in position by means of a tripod, placed about 75 cm from the front center of the tank at an angle of 65° from the glass. A black card with a hole through which the camera lens can project will keep the photographer's image from reflecting on the front glass.

Nonimmersion Photography. Photography of nonimmersed specimens for taxonomic purposes was discussed by Flescher (1983). The subject is placed upon a glass shelf held by a table frame that accepts a background board on a shelf 24 cm below the glass. Because the camera is held just outside the perpendicular from the edge of the glass plate (to prevent reflection of the camera or photographer) the subject must be placed on a slant, usually with the dorsal part slightly elevated with wooden wedges or plasticene. Flescher uses photofloods for illumination, placing them at each end of the table at distances and heights that prevent their reflections from showing in the photograph.

In field work where photographic tables or aquaria are not available, provision of suitable background material will improve the quality of the photographs. Flescher (1983) suggested carrying nonporous, matte-finish upholstery cloth rolled on a metal tube to prevent its creasing. Pale backgrounds (especially pale blue) are generally useful, but darker backgrounds, even black, can be used to good effect if the photographer is careful to set the exposure for the subject rather than for the background. Field photographs are best taken in open shade to avoid shadows. A photograph taken under poor conditions of lighting or background can later be made useful if the image is carefully cut out and affixed to a suitable background.

4.7.2 Record-Keeping

An accurate record should be kept of any photographs taken for research purposes. A written log can be kept, or printed data such as field number, size, scientific name, and location of capture can be photographed along with the subject. This ensures that the data cannot become lost or separated from their corresponding photographs.

Except in photographs intended for publication, a metric scale should always be used to indicate the length of the specimen. If no scale is available, an object of known size (e.g., a knife or coin) should be substituted.

4.7.3 Equipment

For field work and much laboratory work, 35-mm single-lens reflex cameras are preferred because of their portability and ease of operation. Lens combinations commonly used range from standard 50-mm lenses with close-up attachments, extension rings, or bellows, to macrolenses and close-focusing zoom lenses. In the laboratory, large-format cameras are often used, and excellent specimen photographs can be taken with cameras set up for copy work.

The type of film used is determined by lighting conditions, equipment, and intended use of the photographs. In general, slower films (ISO 25–100) produce sharper, more highly contrasted images than high-speed films.

4.7.4 Underwater Photography

Underwater photography requires specialized equipment and some training and experience, but allows the biologist to document characteristics of free-living fishes in natural situations. Waterproof cameras available range from fixed-lens, automatic-exposure models for less than US$200 to very expensive cameras for professional work in deep water. Most underwater photography involves close ranges and wide-angle lenses. Except in unusually clear, well-lighted water, a suitable light source, usually a strobe, is required.

Because of the specialized nature of underwater photography, the discussion here consists only of a short list of suggested references. Guides and handbooks were written by Hall (1982), Turner (1982), and Rowlands (1983). More serious and complete coverage of the subject can be found in books by Mertens (1970), Glover et al. (1977), Smith (1984), and George et al. (1985).

4.8 REFERENCES

Alberch, P. 1980. Ontogenesis and morphological diversification. American Zoologist 20:653–667.

Alberch, P., S. J. Gould, G. Oster, and D. Wake. 1979. Size and shape in ontogeny and phylogeny. Paleobiology 5:296–317.

Albrecht, G. H. 1978. Some comments on the use of ratios. Systematic Zoology 27:67–71.

Albrecht, G. H. 1980. Multivariate analysis and the study of form, with special reference to canonical variate analysis. American Zoologist 20:679–693.

Archie, J. W. 1985. Methods for coding variable morphological features for numerical taxonomic analysis. Systematic Zoology 34:326–345.

Atchley, W. R. 1987. Developmental quantitative genetics and the evolution of ontogenies. Evolution 41:316–330.

Atchley, W. R., and D. Anderson. 1978. Ratios and the statistical analysis of biological data. Systematic Zoology 27:71–78.

Atchley, W. R., C. T. Gaskins, and D. Anderson. 1976. Statistical properties of ratios. I. Empirical results. Systematic Zoology 25:137–148.

Bailey, R. M., and C. E. Bond. 1963. Four new species of freshwater sculpins, genus *Cottus,* from western North America. Occasional Papers of the Museum of Zoology, University of Michigan 634.

Balon, E. K. 1984. Reflections on some decisive events in the early life of fishes. Transactions of the American Fisheries Society 113:178–185.

Balon, E. K. 1985. The theory of saltatory ontogeny and life history models revisited. Pages 13–30 *in* E. K. Balon, editor. Early life histories of fishes. Dr. W. Junk, Dordrecht, The Netherlands.

Barlow, G. W. 1961. Causes and significance of morphological variation in fishes. Systematic Zoology 10:105–117.

Barlow, G. W. 1972. The attitude of fish eye-lines in relation to body shape and to stripes and bars. Copeia 1972:4–14.

Batts, B. S. 1964. Lepidology of the adult pleuronectiform fishes of Puget Sound, Washington. Copeia 1964:666–673.

Benson, R. H., and R. E. Chapman. 1982. On the measurement of morphology and its change. Paleobiology 8:328–339.

Berry, F. H., and W. J. Richards. 1973. Characters useful to the study of larval fishes. Pages 48–65 *in* A. L. Pacheco, editor. Proceedings of a workshop on egg, larval, and juvenile stages of fish in Atlantic Coast estuaries. U.S. National Marine Fisheries Service, Mid-Atlantic Coastal Fisheries Center, Technical Publication 1, Highlands, New Jersey.

Blaxter, J. H. S. 1969. Development: eggs and larvae. Pages 177–252 *in* W. S. Hoar and D. J. Randall, editors. Fish physiology, volume 2. Academic Press, New York.

Blum, H. 1973. Biological shape and visual science. Journal of Theoretical Biology 38:205–302.

Bond, C. E. 1979. Biology of fishes. Saunders, Philadelphia.

Bookstein, F. L. 1977. The study of shape transformation after D'Arcy Thompson. Mathematical Biosciences 34:177–219.

Bookstein, F. L. 1978. The measurement of biological shape and shape change. Lecture Notes in Biomathematics 24:1–191.

Bookstein, F. L. 1982. Foundations of morphometrics. Annual Review of Ecology and Systematics 13:451–470.

Bookstein, F. L. 1984. A statistical method for biological shape comparison. Journal of Theoretical Biology 107:475–520.

Bookstein, F. L., B. Chernoff, R. L. Elder, J. M. Humphries, G. R. Smith and R. E. Strauss. 1985. Morphometrics in evolutionary biology: the geometry of size and shape change, with examples from fishes. Special Publication Academy of Natural Sciences Philadelphia 15.

Bookstein, F. L., R. E. Strauss, J. M. Humphries, B. Chernoff, R. L. Elder, and G. R. Smith. 1982. A comment on the uses of Fourier methods in systematics. Systematic Zoology 31:85–92.

Boreman, J., editor. 1976. Great Lakes fish egg and larvae identification. U.S. Fish and Wildlife Service FWS-OBS 76/23.

Branson, B. A. 1966. Guide to the muscles of bony fishes, excluding some special fibers in siluroids and a few others. Turtox News 44:98.

Breder, C. M., Jr. 1972. On the relationship of teleost scales to pigment patterns. Contributions of the Mote Marine Laboratory 1:1–79. (Sarasota, Florida.)

Brothers, E. B. 1984. Otolith studies. American Society of Ichthyologists and Herpetologists Special Publication 1:50–57.

Brubaker, J. M., and R. A. Angus. 1984. A procedure for staining fishes with alizarin without causing exfoliation of scales. Copeia 1984:989–990.

Burnaby, T. P. 1966. Growth-invariant discriminant functions and generalized distances. Biometrics 22:96–110.

Cailliet, G. M., M. S. Love, and A. W. Ebeling. 1986. Fishes: a field and laboratory manual on their structure, identification, and natural history. Wadsworth, Belmont, California.

Casteel, R. W. 1974. Identification of the species of Pacific salmons (genus *Oncorhynchus*) native to North America based on otoliths. Copeia 1974:305–311.

Collette, B. B. 1965. Systematic significance of breeding tubercles in fishes of the family Percidae. Proceedings of the United States National Museum 117:567–614.

Dabrowski, K., and R. Bardega. 1982. The changes of fish larvae dimensions due to fixation in different preservatives. Zoologische Jahrbücher Abteilung für Anatomie 108:509–516.

DeLamater, E. D., and W. R. Courtenay, Jr., 1973. Variations in structure of the lateral-line canal on scales of teleostean fishes. Zeitschrift für Morphologie der Tiere 75:259–266.

DeLamater, E. D., and W. R. Courtenay, Jr., 1974. Fish scales as seen by scanning electron microscopy. Florida Scientist 37:141–149.

Dingerkus, G., and L. D. Uhler. 1977. Enzyme clearing of Alcian Blue stained whole small vertebrates for demonstration of cartilage. Stain Technology 52:229–232.

Dymond, J. R. 1932. The trout and other game fishes of British Columbia. Canadian Department of Fisheries, Ottawa.

Eastman, J. T. 1977. The pharyngeal bones and teeth of catostomid fishes. American Midland Naturalist 97:68–88.

Eastman, J. T., and J. C. Underhill. 1973. Intraspecific variation in the pharyngeal tooth formulae of some cyprinid fishes. Copeia 1973:45–53.

Ehrlich, R., R. B. Pharr, and N. Healy-Williams. 1983. Comments on the validity of Fourier descriptors in systematics: a reply to Bookstein et al. Systematic Zoology 32:302–306.

Emery, A. R., and R. Winterbottom. 1980. A technique for fish specimen photography in the field. Canadian Journal of Zoology 58:2158–2162.

Endler, J. A. 1978. A predator's view of animal color patterns. Evolutionary Biology 11:319–364.

Endler, J. A. 1980. Natural selection on color patterns in *Poecilia reticulata*. Evolution 34:76–91.

Farris, J. S. 1970. Methods for computing Wagner trees. Systematic Zoology 19:83–92.

Farris, J. S., A. G. Kluge, and M. H. Eckardt. 1970. A numerical approach to phylogenetic systematics. Systematic Zoology 19:172–189.

Filipski, G. T., and M. V. H. Wilson. 1984. Sudan black B as a nerve stain for whole cleared fishes. Copeia 1984:204–208.

Fisher, R. A. 1936. The use of multiple measurements in taxonomic problems. Annals of Eugenics 7:179–188.

Fitch, J. E., and L. W. Baker. 1972. The fish family Moridae in the eastern north Pacific with notes on morid otoliths, caudal skeletons, and the fossil record. U.S. National Marine Fisheries Service Fishery Bulletin 70:565–584.

Flescher, D. D. 1983. Fish photography. Fisheries 8(4):2–6.

Foerster, R. E., and A. L. Pritchard. 1935. The identification of the young of the five species of Pacific salmon. Pages 106–116 *in* Report of the British Columbia Fisheries Department 1934, Victoria, Canada.

Fowler, J. A. 1970. Control of vertebral number in teleosts—an embryological problem. Quarterly Review of Biology 45:148–167.

Freihofer, W. C. 1963. Patterns of the ramus lateralis accessorius and their systematic significance in teleostean fishes. Stanford Ichthyological Bulletin 8:79–189.

Freihofer, W. C. 1970. Some nerve patterns and their systematic significance in paracanthopterygian, salmoniform, gobioid, and apogonid fishes. Proceedings of the California Academy of Sciences, Series 4 38:215–264.

Freihofer, W. C. 1978. Cranial nerves of a percoid fish, *Polycentrus schomburgkii* (family Nandidae), a contribution to the morphology and classification of the order Perciformes. Occasional Papers California Academy of Sciences 128:1–78.

Freihofer, W. C., L. J. V. Compagno, and W. Rogers. 1977. Additional notes on the use of the Sihler technique of staining nerves of small, whole specimens of fishes and other vertebrates. Copeia 1977:587–588.

Fricke, R. 1982. Modification and use of McCune's shape measurement system for recent benthic fishes (Pisces). Braunschweiger Naturkundliche Schriften 1:533–559.

Fuiman, L. A. 1979. Descriptions and comparisons of catostomid fish larvae: northern Atlantic drainage species. Transactions of the American Fisheries Society 108:560–603.

Fuiman, L. A. 1982. Correspondence of myomeres and vertebrae and their natural variability during the first year of life in yellow perch. Pages 56–59 *in* C. F. Bryan, J. V. Conner, and F. M. Truesdale, editors. Proceedings of the fifth annual larval fish conference. Louisiana State University, Louisiana Cooperative Fishery Research Unit, Baton Rouge.

Fuiman, L. A. 1983. Growth gradients in fish larvae. Journal of Fish Biology 23:117–123.

Fuiman, L. A. 1985. Contributions of developmental characters to a phylogeny of catostomid fishes, with comments on heterochrony. Copeia 1985:833–846.

Fuiman, L. A., J. V. Conner, B. F. Lathrop, G. L. Buynak, D. E. Snyder, and J. J. Loos. 1983. State of the art of identification for cyprinid fish larvae from eastern North America. Transactions of the American Fisheries Society 112:319–332.

Fujii, R. 1969. Chromatophores and pigments. Pages 307–353 *in* W. S. and Hoar and D. S. Randall, editors. Fish physiology, volume 3. Academic Press, New York.

George, J. D., G. I. Lythgoe, and J. N. Lythgoe. 1985. Underwater photography and television for scientists. Oxford University Press, Oxford, England.

Glover, T., G. E. Harwood, and J. N. Lythgoe. 1977. A manual of underwater photography. Academic Press, New York.

Godsil, H. C., and R. D. Byers. 1944. A systematic study of the Pacific tunas. California Fish and Game, Fish Bulletin 60:1–131.

Gosline, W. A. 1948. Some possible uses of X-rays in ichthyology and fishery research. Copeia 1948:58–61.

Gosline, W. A. 1986. Jaw muscle configuration in some higher teleostean fishes. Copeia 1986:705–713.

Gould, S. J. 1966. Allometry and size and ontogeny and phylogeny. Biological Reviews of the Cambridge Philosophical Society 41:587–640.

Greenwood, P. H., M. S. Miles, and C. Patterson. 1973. Interrelationships of fishes. Academic Press, New York.

Greenwood, P. H., D. E. Rosen, S. H. Weitzman, and G. S. Myers. 1966. Phyletic studies of teleostean fishes, with a provisional classification of living forms. Bulletin of the American Museum of Natural History 131:339–456.

Gregory, W. K. 1928. The body-forms of fishes and their inscribed rectilinear lines. Paleobiologica 1:93–100.

Gregory, W. K. 1951. Evolution emerging. Macmillan, New York.

Hall, H. 1982. Guide to successful underwater photography. Marcor Publishers, Port Hueneme, California.

Hardisty, M. W. 1979. Biology of the cyclostomes. Chapman and Hall, London.

Heming, T. A., and R. P. Preston. 1981. Differential effect of formalin preservation on yolk and tissue of young chinook salmon (*Oncorhynchus tshawytscha* Walbaum). Canadian Journal of Zoology 59:1608–1611.

Herrick, C. J. 1899. The cranial and first spinal nerves of *Menidia:* a contribution upon the nerve components of the bony fishes. Journal of Comparative Neurology 9:153–455.

Herrick, C. J. 1901. The cranial nerves and cutaneous sense organs of the North American siluroid fishes. Journal of Comparative Neurology 11:177–249.

Hollander, R. R. 1986. Microanalysis of scales of poeciliid fishes. Copeia 1986:86–91.

Hubbs, C. L. 1922. Variations in the number of vertebrae and other meristic characters of fishes correlated with the temperature of water during development. American Naturalist 56:360–372.

Hubbs, C. L. 1943. Terminology of early stages of fishes. Copeia 1943:260.

Hubbs, C. L., and C. Hubbs. 1953. An improved graphical analysis and comparison of series of samples. Systematic Zoology 2:49–53.

Hubbs, C. L., and K. L. Lagler. 1958. Fishes of the Great Lakes region, 2nd edition. Cranbrook Institute of Science Bulletin 26:1–213.

Hubbs, C. L., and I. C. Potter. 1971. Distribution, phylogeny and taxonomy. Pages 1–65 *in* M. W. Hardisty, and I. C. Potter, editors. The biology of lampreys, volume 1. Academic Press, New York.

Hughes, D. R. 1981. Development and organization of the posterior field of ctenoid scales in the Platycephalidae. Copeia 1981:596–606.

Humphries, J. M., F. L. Bookstein, B. Chernoff, G. R. Smith, R. L. Elder, and S. G. Poss. 1981. Multivariate discrimination by shape in relation to size. Systematic Zoology 30:291–308.

Johnson, G. D. 1984. Percoidei: development and relationships. American Society of Ichthyologists and Herpetologists Special Publication 1:464–498.

Jolicoeur, P., and J. E. Mosimann. 1960. Size and shape variation in the painted turtle. A principal component analysis. Growth 24:339–354.

Jones, B. C., and G. H. Geen. 1977. Morphometric changes in elasmobranch *(Squalus acanthias)* after preservation. Canadian Journal of Zoology 55:1060–1062.

Kafuku, T. 1958. Speciation in cyprinid fishes on the basis of intestinal differentiation, with some reference to that among catostomids. Bulletin of the Freshwater Fisheries Research Laboratory (Tokyo) 8:45–78.

Kendall, A. W., Jr., E. H. Ahlstrom, and H. G. Moser. 1984. Early life history stages of fishes and their characters. American Society of Ichthyologists and Herpetologists Special Publication 1:11–22.

Kincaid, D. T., and R. B. Schneider. 1983. Quantification of leaf shape with a microcomputer and Fourier transform. Canadian Journal of Botany 61:2333–2342.

Kluge, A. G., and R. E. Strauss. 1985. Ontogeny and systematics. Annual Review of Ecology and Systematics 16:247–268.

Lagler, K. F., J. E. Bardach, R. R. Miller, and D. R. M. Passino. 1977. Ichthyology. Wiley, New York.

Lauder, G. V., and K. L. Liem. 1983. The evolution and interrelationships of the actinopterygian fishes. Bulletin of the Museum of Comparative Zoology 150:95–197.

Lavenberg, R. J., G. E. McGowen, and R. E. Woodsum. 1984. Preservation and curation. American Society of Ichthyologists and Herpetologists Special Publication 1:57–60.

Lee, J. C. 1982. Accuracy and precision in anuran morphometrics: artifacts of preservation. Systematic Zoology 31:266–281.

Liem, K. F. 1986. The pharyngeal jaw apparatus of the Embiotocidae (Teleostei): a functional and evolutionary perspective. Copeia 1986:311–326.

Lindsey, C. C. 1958. Modification of meristic characters by light duration in kokanee (Oncorhynchus nerka). Copeia 1958:134–136.

Lindsey, C. C. 1962. Experimental study of meristic variation in a population of threespine sticklebacks, Gasterosteus aculeatus. Canadian Journal of Zoology 40:271–312.

Lippson, A. J., and R. L. Moran. 1974. Manual for identification of early developmental stages of fishes of the Potomac River estuary. Maryland Department of Natural Resources, Power Plant Siting Program, PPSP-MP-13, Annapolis.

Lohmann, G. P. 1983. Eigenshape analysis of microfossils: a general morphometric procedure for describing changes in shape. Mathematical Geology 15:659–672.

Lundberg, J. G., and J. N. Baskin. 1969. The caudal skeleton of the catfishes, order Siluriformes. American Museum Novitates 2398:1–49.

Marcus, L. F. 1982. A portable, digital, printing caliper. Curator 25:223–226.

Marcus, L. F. 1983. Automated measurement with portable microcomputers. NATO ASI (Advanced Science Institute) Series, Series G, Ecological Sciences 1:620–624.

Markle, D. F. 1984. Phosphate buffered formalin for long term preservation of formalin fixed ichthyoplankton. Copeia 1984:525–528.

Marshall, N. B. 1960. Swimbladder structure of deep-sea fishes in relation to their systematics and biology. Discovery Reports 31:1–122.

Marshall, N. B. 1979. Developments in deep-sea biology. Blandford Press, London.

Martin, W. R. 1949. The mechanics of environmental control of body form in fishes. University of Toronto Studies, Biological Series 58:1–91.

Mayden, R. L., and E. O. Wiley. 1984. A method of preparing disarticulated skeletons of small fishes. Copeia 1984:230–232.

Mayr, E., 1969. Principles of systematic zoology. McGraw-Hill, New York.

Mayr, E., E. G. Linsley, and R. L. Usinger. 1953. Methods and principles of systematic zoology. McGraw-Hill, New York.

McAllister, D. E. 1968. Evolution of branchiostegals and classification of teleostome fishes. Bulletin of the National Museum of Canada 221.

McAllister, D. E., and R. J. Planck. 1981. Capturing fish measurements and counts with calipers and probe interfaced with a computer or pocket calculator. Canadian Journal of Fisheries and Aquatic Sciences 38:466–470.

McCune, A. R. 1981. Quantitative descriptions of body forms in fishes: implications for species level taxonomy and ecological inference. Copeia 1981:897–901.

McMahon, T. E., and J. C. Tash. 1979. Effects of formalin (buffered and unbuffered) and hydrochloric acid on fish otoliths. Copeia 1979:155–156.

Mertens, L. E. 1970. In-water photography: theory and practice. Wiley Interscience, New York.

Meyer, A. 1987. Morphological measurements from specimens and their X-rays: test of a method for the study of allometry and phenotypic plasticity in fishes. Netherlands Journal of Zoology 37:315–321.

Miller, D. J., and R. N. Lea. 1972. Guide to the costal marine fishes of California. California Department of Fish and Game, Fish Bulletin 157.

Miller, J. M., and J. W. Tucker. 1979. X-radiography of larval and juvenile fishes. Copeia 1979:535–538.

Moser, H. G. 1981. Morphological and functional aspects of marine fish larvae. Pages 89–131 in R. Lasker, editor. Marine fish larvae. Washington Sea Grant Program, Seattle.

Moser, H. G., E. H. Ahlstrom, and J. R. Paxton. 1984a. Myctophidae: development. American Society of Ichthyologists and Herpetologists Special Publication 1:218–239.

Moser, H. G., W. J. Richards, D. M. Cohen, M. P. Fahay, A. W. Kendall, Jr., and S. L. Richardson, editors. 1984b. Ontogeny and systematics of fishes. American Society of Ichthyologists and Herpetologists Special Publication 1.

Motta, P. J. 1984. Mechanics and functions of jaw protrusion in teleost fishes: a review. Copeia 1984:1–18.

Moyle, P. B., and J. J. Cech, Jr. 1981. Fishes: an introduction to ichthyology. Prentice-Hall, Englewood Cliffs, New Jersey.

Neave, F. 1943. Scale pattern and scale counting methods in relation to trout and other salmonids. Transactions of the Royal Society of Canada 1943:79–91.

Neff, N. A., and G. R. Smith. 1979. Multivariate analysis of hybrid fishes. Systematic Zoology 28:176–196.

Nishikawa, K. C. 1987. Staining amphibian peripheral nerves with sudan black B: progressive vs. regressive methods. Copeia 1987:489–491.

Olshan, A. F., A. F. Siegel, and D. R. Swindler. 1982. Robust and least-squares orthogonal mapping: methods for the study of cephalofacial form and growth. American Journal of Physical Anthropology 59:131–137.

Ouellette, R. P., and S. U. Qadri. 1968. The discriminatory power of taxonomic characteristics in separating salmonid fishes. Systematic Zoology 17:70–75.

Oxnard, C. E. 1978. One biologist's view of morphometrics. Annual Review of Ecology and Systematics 9:219–241.

Parker, R. R. 1963. Effects of formalin on length and weight of fishes. Journal of the Fisheries Research Board of Canada 20:1441–1455.

Pimental, R. A. 1979. Morphometrics: the multivariate analysis of biological data. Kendall/Hunt, Dubuque, Iowa.

Pletcher, T. F. 1966. A portable aquarium for use at sea to photograph fish and aquatic life. Journal of the Fisheries Research Board of Canada 23:1271–1275.

Poss, S. G., and R. R. Miller. 1983. Taxonomic status of the plains killifish, Fundulus zebrinus. Copeia 1983:55–67.

Randall, J. E. 1961. A technique for fish photography. Copeia 1961:241–242.

Read, D. W., and P. E. Lestrel. 1986. Comment on the uses of homologous-point measures in systematics: a reply to Bookstein et al. Systematic Zoology 35:241–253.

Reyment, R. A. 1985. Multivariate morphometrics and analysis of shape. Mathematical Geology 17:591–609.

Rohlf, F. J., and J. W. Archie. 1984. A comparison of Fourier methods for the description of wing shape in mosquitoes (Diptera: Culicidae). Systematic Zoology 33:302–317.

Rosen, D. E. 1979. Fishes from the uplands and intermontane basins of Guatemala: revisionary studies and comparative geography. Bulletin of the American Museum of Natural History 162:267–376.

Rowlands, P. 1983. The underwater photographer's handbook. Van Nostrand Reinhold, New York.

Schaefer, S. A., and T. M. Cavender. 1986. Geographic variation and subspecific status of Notropis spilopterus (Pisces: Cyprinidae). Copeia 1986:122–130.

Shetter, D. S. 1936. Shrinkage of trout at death and on preservation. Copeia 1936:60–61.

Siegel, A. F., and R. H. Benson. 1982. Robust comparison of biological shapes. Biometrics 38:341–350.

Simpson, G. G., A. Roe, and R. C. Lewontin. 1960. Quantitative zoology. McGraw-Hill, New York.

Smith, G. R. 1973. Analysis of several hybrid cyprinid fishes from western North America. Copeia 1973:395–410.

Smith, P. F. 1984. Underwater photography: scientific and engineering applications. Van Nostrand Reinhold, New York.

Sneath, P. H. A., and R. R. Sokal. 1973. Numerical taxonomy: the principles and practice of numerical classification. Freeman, San Francisco.

Snyder, D. E. 1979. Myomere and vertebra counts of the North American cyprinids and catostomids. Pages 53–69 *in* R.D. Hoyt, editor. Proceedings of the third symposium on larval fish. Western Kentucky University, Bowling Green, Kentucky.

Sokal, R .R., and F. J. Rohlf. 1981. Biometry, 2nd edition. Freeman, San Francisco.

Strauss, R. E. 1984. Allometry and functional feeding morphology in haplochromine cichlids. Pages 217–219 *in* A. A. Echelle and I. Kornfield, editors. Evolution of fish species flocks. University of Maine at Orono Press, Orono.

Strauss, R. E. 1985. Evolutionary allometry and variation in body form in the South American catfish genus *Corydoras* (Callichthyidae). Systematic Zoology 34:381–396.

Strauss, R. E. 1986. Natural hybrids of the freshwater sculpins *Cottus bairdi* and *Cottus cognatus* (Pisces: Cottidae): electrophoretic and morphometric evidence. American Midland Naturalist 115:87–105.

Strauss, R. E. 1987. The importance of phylogenetic constraints in comparisons of morphological structure among fish assemblages. Pages 136–143 *in* W. J. Matthews and D. C. Hines, editors. Community and evolutionary ecology of North American stream fishes. University of Oklahoma Press, Norman, Oklahoma.

Strauss, R. E., and F. L. Bookstein. 1982. The truss: body form reconstructions in morphometrics. Systematic Zoology 31:113–135.

Strauss, R. E., and L. A. Fuiman. 1985. Quantitative comparisons of body form and allometry in larval and adult Pacific sculpins (Teleostei: Cottidae). Canadian Journal of Zoology 63:1582–1589.

Taliev, D. N. 1955. Sculpins of Baikal (Cottoidei). Publication House of the Academy of Sciences, USSR, Moscow. (In Russian.)

Taning, A. V. 1952. Experimental study of meristic characters in fishes. Biological Reviews of the Cambridge Philosophical Society 27:169–193.

Taylor, J. N., D. B. Snyder, and W. R. Courtenay, Jr. 1986. Hybridization between two introduced, substrate-spawning tilapias (Pisces: Cichlidae) in Florida. Copeia 1986:903–909.

Taylor, W. R. 1967. An enzyme method of clearing and staining small vertebrates. Proceedings of the United States National Museum 122:1–17.

Thorpe, R. S. 1976. Biometric analysis of geographic variation and racial affinities. Biological Reviews of the Cambridge Philosophical Society 51:407–452.

Thorpe, R. S. 1984. Coding morphometric characters for constructing distance Wagner networks. Evolution 38:244–255.

Trautman, M. B. 1981. The fishes of Ohio. Ohio State University Press, Columbus.

Tucker, J. W., Jr., and A. J. Chester. 1984. Effects of salinity, formalin concentration and buffer on quality of preservation of southern flounder *(Paralichthys lethostigma)* larvae. Copeia 1984:981–988.

Tukey, J. W. 1977. Exploratory data analysis. Addison-Wesley, Reading, Massachusetts.

Turner, J. 1982. Underwater photography. Focal Press, New York.

Weisel, G. F. 1955. Variations in the number of fin rays of two cyprinid fishes correlated with natural water temperature. Ecology 36:1–6.

Wiley, E. O. 1977. The phylogeny and systematics of the *Fundulus nottii* species group (Teleostei: Cyprinodontidae). Occasional Papers of the Museum of Natural History, University of Kansas 66:1–31.

Wiley, E. O. 1979. Ventral gill-arch muscles and the interrelationships of gnathostomes, with a new classification of the Vertebrata. Zoological Journal of the Linnean Society 67:149–179.

Wiley, M. L., and B. B. Collette. 1970. Breeding tubercles and contact organs in fishes: their occurrence, structure and significance. Bulletin of American Museum of Natural History 143:147–216.

Winans, G. A. 1985. Geographic variation in the milkfish *(Chanos chanos)*. II. Multivariate morphological evidence. Copeia 1985:890–898.

Winterbottom, R. 1974a. A descriptive synonymy of the striated muscles of the Teleostei. Proceedings of the Academy of Natural Sciences of Philadelphia 125:225–317.

Winterbottom, R. 1974b. The familial phylogeny of the Tetraodontiformes (Acanthopterygii: Pisces) as evidenced by their comparative myology. Smithsonian Contributions to Zoology 155:1–201.

Younker, J. L., and R. Ehrlich. 1977. Fourier biometrics: harmonic amplitudes as multivariate shape descriptors. Systematic Zoology 26:336–342.

Chapter 5

Starch Gel Electrophoresis and
Species Distinctions

ROBB F. LEARY AND HENRY E. BOOKE

5.1 INTRODUCTION

Taxonomists and systematists attempt to distinguish species and hypothesize lineages by conducting studies of genetically based differences and similarities among populations. Historically, genetic differentiation has usually been inferred from a comparison of morphological characters. There is, however, an increasing trend in taxonomy to supplement morphological analyses with comparisons of physiological, ecological, ethological, biochemical, or karyotypic characters among populations as a means of detecting genetic divergence. In this chapter, we consider the electrophoretic analysis of proteins as a means of detecting genetic differences among populations and the application of these data to species problems. We hope to provide the reader with a basic understanding of the technical aspects of electrophoresis, the information content of the data, and the ways this information can be used to address certain issues that concern fish biologists.

5.1.1 Protein Chemistry

We do not believe that one can gain a basic understanding of the taxonomic usefulness of proteins without some knowledge of protein chemistry. Amino acids are the basic components from which proteins are constructed. Many amino acids exist in nature but only 20 are common. Each of the common amino acids is found in practically all proteins in all organisms. The general structure of these amino acids is

$$H_2N - \underset{\underset{R}{|}}{\overset{\overset{COOH}{|}}{C}} - H;$$

the differences among them stem from the chemical composition of the variable R-group or side chain.

Construction of a protein molecule begins with the binding of amino acids into a linear chain. The bonds link the carboxyl group (-COOH) of one amino acid to the amino group (-NH$_2$) of the adjacent amino acid. This bond is called a peptide bond and the resulting molecule is a polypeptide (Figure 5.1). The composition of a polypeptide (i.e., the type and position of each amino acid) is determined by the nucleotide sequence of a particular gene in the organism (see Chapter 2 for details).

The amino acid side chains can have a net electrical charge. The sign and magnitude of the charge depends on the side chain's chemical composition and the

141

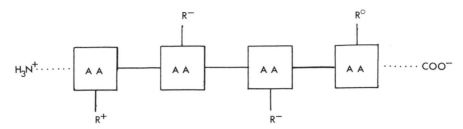

Figure 5.1. Generalized representation of a polypeptide chain: AA designates an amino acid; R^-, R^0, and R^+ designate side chains that have a negative, neutral, or positive charge. Solid horizontal lines represent peptide bonds that link amino acids. Dotted horizontal lines represent extensions of the polypeptide that terminate in an amino group (H_3N^+) and a carboxyl group (COO^-).

pH of its environment. At pH 7, most of the common amino acids have no charge, but others are either negatively or positively charged. If the liquid medium's pH changes, the side chains may take up or release hydrogen ions and their ionic charges will alter accordingly. Thus, a polypeptide often has a nonzero net charge, the sign and magnitude of which are determined largely by its amino acid composition at any given pH. Because the amino acid composition of a polypeptide is determined by the gene that codes its construction, the charge that a polypeptide has at a particular pH is genetically determined. It is their charges that mainly allow polypeptides, or the proteins they form, to be distinguished by the electrophoretic procedures discussed in this chapter.

Proteins may be composed of one or more polypeptides. The side chains of a polypeptide can interact with side chains of other polypeptides and create a weak bonding of polypeptides to each other. The number of polypeptides that compose a particular protein is referred to as its "quaternary structure." Proteins generally are composed of one, two, three, or four polypeptide chains and are classified as being monomeric, dimeric, trimeric, or tetrameric, respectively. The quaternary structure is an important attribute of proteins in electrophoretic studies because it affects the number of differently charged states a protein may have (Section 5.4.1).

Proteins perform several important biological functions. For example, they are used in formation of tissues, in defense against infectious diseases, and as catalysts of chemical reactions. It is this latter class of proteins, enzymes, that generally concern us in this chapter.

Enzymes as catalysts accelerate the rate at which chemical reactions occur. For example, the conversion of malic acid to oxaloacetic acid requires the removal of two hydrogen ions from malic acid. This process is greatly expedited when the enzyme malate dehydrogenase is present. In this reaction, malic acid is referred to as the substrate with which the enzyme reacts and oxaloacetic acid is termed the product of the reaction. Enzymes usually have a highly preferred substrate, catalyze only a highly specific reaction, and are extremely efficient catalysts. These attributes make it possible to use specific stains to identify the position of particular enzymes after electrophoresis.

Three principles thus underlie electrophoretic analysis of proteins, as elaborated in this chapter. (1) The amino acid composition and charge of a protein are genetically determined characteristics, and variation of these attributes can be used to obtain insights into the amount of genetic divergence that exists between populations. (2) Proteins may be composed of multiple polypeptide chains, and this structure influences the number of differently charged states that a protein may possess in an individual and thus the number of components into which it will be separated by electrophoresis. (3) It is possible to accurately determine the positions of particular enzymes after electrophoresis because they often catalyze highly specific chemical reactions and stains have been formulated to exploit these reactions.

5.2   RATIONALE OF ELECTROPHORESIS

Electrophoresis refers to the movement of charged particles in a medium through which an electrical current is passed. The rate at which a particle moves in the medium is directly related to its net charge and inversely related to its size. Negatively charged particles move toward the positive pole of the electrical field, and vice versa. Particles that differ in size, net charge, or both move at different rates and possibly in different directions through the medium. Electrophoresis is a method commonly used to separate or resolve the differently charged and sized constituents of a mixture into many of its individual components.

Protein molecules generally have a net charge (Section 5.1.1) and are amenable to separation by electrophoresis. In taxonomic studies, electrophoresis is used to detect genetic variation that mainly alters the charge of homologous proteins and thus the rate at which the proteins move through the medium. (Homologous proteins are those coded by a gene possessed by all individuals because it was acquired from a common ancestor.) Differences in protein migration are used to obtain insights into the amount of genetic variation that exists within populations and the amount of differentiation between populations. Degrees of differentiation among samples are then used to construct hierarchical groups of the populations from which the samples were drawn.

5.3   ELECTROPHORETIC METHODOLOGY

Electrophoretic methodology is exceptionally diverse and has numerous applications. There is no single correct or best way to conduct electrophoresis (e.g., Allendorf and Utter 1979; Aebersold et al. 1987). Most of the methodological differences among researchers and laboratories reflect personal preferences and nuances, often acquired from a previous mentor and subsequently modified. In this section, we present one method of electrophoresis to guide a general understanding of procedure. We do not imply that this method is superior to many others.

The variety of electrophoretic techniques can be classified into two general categories: moving boundary or zonal. In moving boundary electrophoresis, the particles are dissolved in and migrate through an ionic solution. This technique has little use in taxonomic studies. When a solution contains many constituents, such as crude protein extracts, many of the components migrate through the solution as broad, partially overlapping bands. In contrast, zonal electrophoresis involves migration of particles through a solid supportive medium. This technique can effectively resolve many components of a mixture because the medium retards the rate of migration and allows the constituents to move through it as discrete bands.

Several zonal electrophoretic media exist, but porous starch gels are often used in taxonomic studies. Starch gels often provide better resolution of proteins than do other media such as filter paper, cellulose acetate membranes, or agar gels. Starch gels have good resolving power because their pores are about the same size as many proteins. The gel sieves the proteins, and smaller molecules move through the gel faster than larger molecules. This enhances the separatory powers of the gel.

Starch gels are also amenable to large-scale studies. Samples from many individuals can be placed in the same gel and the gels can be sliced horizontally after electrophoresis so that several different proteins can be analyzed from each. Polyacrylamide gels often provide excellent resolution of proteins but do not lend themselves well to horizontal slicing. Because we are most familiar with starch gels and believe this medium is generally the best available for taxonomic studies, the remainder of this section will deal exclusively with starch gels. Books by Brewer (1970) and Harris and Hopkinson (1976) provide details for the use of other media.

We will further confine our discussion to horizontal electrophoresis, meaning the gels rest horizontally during electrophoresis. This is the technique we generally prefer, but electrophoresis can also be conducted with gels resting vertically. The major difference between these methods is that vertical gels are often run for longer periods of time than are horizontal gels and, therefore, generally produce better resolution. In our experience, however, horizontal gels reveal most of the variation detectable on vertical gels. Thus, the choice between horizontal or vertical electrophoresis is largely one of personal preference. For those interested in vertical electrophoresis, Brewer (1970) is an excellent reference.

5.3.1 Gel Preparation

Starch gels are prepared from hydrolyzed potato starch dissolved in "gel buffer." The solution is heated for an appropriate time, degassed, and poured into a mold; it then solidifies into a porous gel as it cools. Examples of gel buffers are given in Table 5.1.

We often use the following method to prepare a gel. For every 100 mL of gel buffer, 12 g of Connaught or Sigma starch are placed into a 1-L Erlenmeyer flask with approximately one-third (30–35 mL) of the buffer. The remaining gel buffer is heated to boiling in a volumetric flask and then added to the cold starch solution. The solution is swirled while the boiling buffer is added to ensure that the starch becomes completely dissolved in the gel buffer. This solution is heated until it is quite viscous and has numerous small bubbles suspended throughout it. The hot solution is degassed with an aspirator or vacuum line until only large air bubbles are formed (this takes 30–60 s), and then it is poured into a mold.

Several commercial molds are available, but it is easy to make them. A versatile mold for horizontal electrophoresis is composed of a porcelain pan, a glass plate (25.5 × 17.5 × 0.6 cm), four plexiglass strips (two of 21.5 × 1.5 × 0.6 cm, two of 17.0 × 1.5 × 0.6 cm), and four large paper clamps. The glass plate lies on the porcelain pan. A rectangular mold with internal dimensions of 9.5 × 21.5 × 0.6 cm is formed on the glass plate with the plexiglass strips, which are held in place by the paper clamps. Gels poured within such molds can easily accommodate 40

Table 5.1. Recipes for three gel and tray buffer systems, run times for the gels, and voltages required to generate 50 mA of current.

Buffer	Run time	Voltage	Reference
Amine–citric acid buffer			
Gel buffer	Thin gels: 3 h	125–150 V	Clayton and Tretiak
Citric acid, 0.42 g/L	Thick gels: 5 h	150–175 V	(1972)
Adjust pH to 6.1 with			
N-(3-aminopropyl)-morpholine			
Tray buffer			
Citric acid, 8.40 g/L			
Adjust pH to 6.1 with			
N-(3-aminopropyl)-morpholine			
Tris–boric acid–EDTA buffer			
Gel buffer			
Boric acid, 1.55 g/L	Thin gels: 3–4 h	200–250 V	Markert and Faulhaber
EDTA, 0.34 g/L	Thick gels: 5–6 h	250–300 V	(1965)
Tris, 5.45 g/L			
pH self-adjusts to 8.4			
Tray buffer			
Boric acid, 5.2 g/L			
EDTA, 1.1 g/L			
Tris, 18.2 g/L			
pH self-adjusts to 8.4			
Tris–citric acid buffer			
Gel buffer			
Citric acid, 10.5 g/L	Thin gels: 4 h	Begin at 150 V	Ridgway et al. (1970)
Tris, 36.3 g/L	Thick gels: 6 h	and, as current	
Add above to 900 mL distilled		drops, turn up	
water		to 200 V	
Add 100 mL of tray buffer			
pH self-adjusts to 8.5			
Tray buffer			
Boric acid, 18.54 g/L			
Lithium hydroxide, 2.5 g/L			
pH self-adjusts to 8.1			

specimens and thicker gels allowing analysis of more proteins can be made by stacking additional plexiglass strips on top of the first (see Table 5.2 for appropriate buffer volumes and weights of starch).

Gels are ready for electrophoresis after they have cooled to room temperature. The gels we have described give the best results if they are used the day after they are prepared. Gels should be covered with plastic wrap after the clamps have been removed to prevent them from drying out overnight.

5.3.2 Sample Storage and Tissue Preparation

The structure of proteins is labile. Excessive denaturation (structural change) of the proteins must be prevented after specimens have been collected or electrophoresis will give poor results. If the analysis will be done within 2 d of collection, the fish usually can be kept on ice or in a refrigerator. Specimens to be stored for longer periods of time, however, must be frozen. A temperature of −20°C is

Table 5.2. Volumes of gel buffer and weights of starch used to prepare gels 9.5 cm wide and 21.5 cm long. "Thin" and "thick" gels are 0.6 cm and 1.2 cm thick, respectively.

Volume of gel buffer (mL)	Weight of starch (g)	Number and type of gels produced
212	25.4	1 thin
425	51.0	2 thin or 1 thick
650	78.0	1 thin and 1 thick
750	90.0	3 thin or 2 thick

adequate for storage up to about 2 months. Fish that must be stored longer than this should be kept at $-40°C$ or colder; $-70°C$ to $-80°C$ is best. We prefer to store entire fish instead of tissues. Tissue samples lose water more readily than whole specimens, and dehydration causes proteins to denature. We thaw fish and dissect tissue samples the day before analysis.

A few grams of tissue generally suffice for electrophoresis. Just before electrophoresis, the tissue is ground in a liquid medium to liberate proteins from the cells. This can be done mechanically with a glass rod (for example) or ultrasonically by submerging the tip of a sonicator in the grinding solution. Distilled water is often an adequate grinding medium. If particular enzymes have weak or inconsistent staining activity after electrophoresis, a different grinding medium may greatly improve the results. One that we have found useful is a 0.25-g/L solution of pyridoxal-5-phosphate. Another contains 2.72 g imidazole, 0.61 g magnesium chloride, and 0.50 g ethylenediaminetetraacetic acid (EDTA) per liter of water, adjusted to pH 7.5 with 7 N hydrochloric acid.

Tissue fragments that remain when grinding is completed can be separated from the protein solution (homogenate) by centrifugation. This step often allows proteins to migrate more consistently during electrophoresis and, hence, to be better resolved.

5.3.3 "Running" the Gels

When gels are to be used, their plastic wraps are removed and a scalpel is run along their edges to free them from the plexiglass strips. Each gel is cut vertically along its length, 2.5–3.0 cm from one edge, and the narrow edge slice is pushed away. The sliced edge of the larger piece becomes the "origin," along which the protein homogenates will be applied.

Each homogenate is first absorbed into a 4 × 6-mm or a 4 × 12-mm wick (the larger size is used with thick gels) cut from number 470 filter paper (Schleicher and Schuell, Inc., Keene, New Hampshire). Excess fluid is blotted from the wicks to ensure good resolution, and the wicks are placed along the edge of the gel's origin. The first wick is placed about 5 mm from one corner, and at least 1 mm should separate adjacent wicks; the gels are easier to score (analyze) if larger spaces are left between groups of 10 wicks. Finally, a wick containing a dye marker (red food coloring diluted 1:1 with distilled water) is placed about 2 mm from each corner of the origin. The narrow gel section then is pushed back against the larger one; the contact must be continuous along the origin's entire length because the proteins will not migrate where there are gaps. The "loaded" gel is placed on the porcelain pan and covered with plastic wrap to insulate it and prevent it from drying during electrophoresis.

Two trays—the tops of plastic butter dishes work well—are filled with a tray buffer appropriate for the gel buffer (Table 5.1). One tray is placed next to the small gel section and the other is placed opposite it next to the large piece of gel. An absorbent cloth is submersed in each tray, then partially pulled out and placed in contact with the respective sides of the gel from end to end, after the plastic wrap has been folded back to expose 0.5–1.0 cm of the gel. Capillarity keeps the cloths wet and maintains an electricity-conducting medium between each tray and the gel. Electrodes from a direct current power source (e.g., Heathkit Regulated High-Voltage Power Supply, models IP-17 and IP-2717) are placed in the trays; the anode (positive electrode) goes in the tray adjacent to the large piece of gel and the cathode goes in the other tray. Electrodes must be made of platinum or a similar inert substance so they will not undergo electrolysis when they pass current.

Electrophoresis begins when the power is turned on for about 10 min to drive the proteins out of the wicks into the gel. The power is turned off while the wicks are removed (which generally enhances resolution of the proteins), then restarted. Electrophoresis continues until the dye markers reach or nearly reach the anodal edge of the gel. The time required for this migration depends on the thickness of the gel, the buffer system used, and the amount of power applied to the gel (Table 5.1; power = amperage × voltage = [amperage]^2 × resistance).

Gels must be kept cold during electrophoresis because the power generates heat, which can denature the proteins. The amount of heat produced depends more on the current than on the voltage, so the current is kept low—50–60 mA—by regulation of the voltage. Records should be kept of the voltage needed to produce the desired current for each buffer system used, because marked deviations in the required voltage can indicate a serious problem; the gel may have been prepared with the tray buffer, for example, or the gel and tray buffers may have been mismatched. Such mistakes usually produce useless results.

One way to cool the gels is to conduct electrophoresis in a cold room or refrigerator. The power sources must remain outside the cold chamber so they will not be subject to moisture condensation and corrosion. Alternatively, packs of synthetic "ice" or metal trays containing real ice may be placed above the gels, after the wicks have been removed. Such coolants must be separated from the gels by glass plates so the gels will not freeze.

More than one gel can be run off the same power source if they are connected in parallel and if they require the same voltage for the desired current. Although the same voltage is applied to each gel, the total current that must be produced increases with the number of gels. For example, if 150 V drives 50 mA of current across one gel, that 150 V must drive 150 mA altogether across three such gels connected in parallel. The number of gels that can be run simultaneously may be limited by the power source to be used.

5.3.4 Gel and Tray Buffers

The gel and tray buffers are very important because the pH and ingredients affect the net charge and activity of an enzyme. An enzyme may not have detectable activity in some buffers, or it may be so denatured that its resolution is poor. Variants of an enzyme may have the same charge in an acidic buffer system but different charges when the pH is basic, or vice versa. We recommend that an enzyme be analyzed in both an acidic and a basic buffer, if it can be resolved reliably in both, to increase the chances of detecting variation.

Buffers that work best for particular enzymes from particular species can only be determined by trial and error in the first instance. Many fish species have been analyzed electrophoretically, however, and buffers that work well for one species often do so for closely related species as well. Thus, much tedious screening of buffers already has been done; Nevo (1978) and Nevo et al. (1984) have summarized much of the relevant literature in this respect.

Nevertheless, experimentation with buffers will be needed for enzymes that have not been analyzed before or that gave unreliable results in systems used previously. Numerous buffer systems have been defined (Brewer 1970; Shaw and Prasad 1970; Selander et al. 1971; Harris and Hopkinson 1976; Siciliano and Shaw 1976). Those listed in Table 5.1 have been effective for many enzymes from a diverse array of fish species.

Gel and tray buffers usually are stable at room temperature for long periods of time. They can be prepared in large quantities and stored for future use.

5.3.5 Staining Gels for Particular Enzymes

After electrophoresis, gels must be stained to reveal the positions and identities of proteins. In preparation for this, each gel is sliced horizontally. Several commercial slicers are available, but 2-mm-thick plexiglass strips and monofilament nylon sewing thread or fishing line make a very effective slicer. A plexiglass strip is placed on opposite sides of the gel parallel to the origin, and the thread is pulled over the strips and through the gel. Additional strips are placed on top of the first, a second slice is made, and this process is repeated until no more slices can be made. The side of each slice that contains specimen 1 should be marked for future reference. The slices are placed in plastic trays with just enough staining solution to submerge the gel. A different stain can be used in each tray, allowing several enzymes to be analyzed concurrently. The top slice should be placed in the tray with the outside surface down because proteins migrate through, not over, the gel and will be exposed on the cut surface. A slice might break when it is put into its tray, but it still can be used. At first, both the anodal and cathodal portions of the gel should be stained for each enzyme. Staining often can be more localized once the migration behavior of proteins in the gel buffer is learned.

Trays with their gels often are placed in a dark incubator to expedite staining. Temperatures higher than 45°C should be avoided because they may denature many enzymes. Most enzymes produce scorable banding patterns within 0.5–3 h, but some may require more time.

General protein stains such as amido black show the positions of proteins, but they do not distinguish among the hundreds of kinds of proteins that may be in a homogenate. Further, the quantity of a protein type in a particular tissue, which is indicated by the intensity of staining, may vary with the physiological state of the organism when it is sampled. Thus, general protein stains have low value in taxonomic studies.

Histochemical protein stains are designed to reveal particular proteins in vivo or in vitro. Enzymes, which catalyze highly specific reactions, are especially amenable to histochemical techniques. Usually it is not the enzymes themselves that are stained but the chemical products of enzymatic reactions (of enzyme "activity"), the substrates for which are added with the stain. Because enzymes are very efficient catalysts, histochemical stains can reveal concentrations of enzymes much too small to be detected with general protein stains.

Histochemical stains generally are buffered to maintain a pH that allows good enzyme activity so the staining process can occur. Brewer (1970), Selander et al. (1971), Harris and Hopkinson (1976), and Allendorf et al. (1977) have described particular stain buffers. Two that allow reliable resolution of many enzymes are the tris–citric acid gel buffer (Table 5.1) and a tris–HCl buffer (24.2 g tris/L adjusted to pH 8.0 with 7 N HCl). The specific substrate upon which an enzyme acts, all coenzymes and cofactors required by the enzyme, and additional reagents required to form a colored or fluorescent product are dissolved in the buffer.

The staining of the enzyme malate dehydrogenase provides an example of the process. Malate dehydrogenase (MDH[1]) catalyzes the conversion of malic acid to oxaloacetic acid. In the process, two hydrogen ions are removed from the malic acid. Each is bound to the coenzyme beta-nicotinamide adenine dinucleotide (NAD), from which it is passed to other substances, one of which is a stain. The stain we use for MDH is nitro-blue tetrazolium (NBT). We dissolve it in the tris–citric acid buffer (Table 5.1) along with malic acid (the substrate), NAD (the coenzyme), and phenazine methosulfate (PMS, a transfer chemical). When a gel containing MDH is bathed in this buffer solution, hydrogen ions released from malic acid move successively to NAD, PMS, and NBT, causing NBT to precipitate as a blue dye at the points where MDH catalyzed the reaction. The intensity of the dye, which can be measured photometrically after a specified staining time, is an index of the amount of MDH activity in the gel.

The PMS–NBT system can stain other dehydrogenases if it is combined with the appropriate substrates, coenzymes, and cofactors. Its use can be extended even further to reveal enzymes whose product is a substrate for a dehydrogenase. In such cases, the dehydrogenase system is included in the staining buffer. For example, phosphoglucomutase (PGM) catalyzes the conversion of glucose-1-phosphate (G1P) to glucose-6-phosphate (G6P), which is a substrate for glucose-6-phosphate dehydrogenase (G6PDH). To assess the presence of PGM, we dissolve G6PDH, its coenzyme NAD-phosphate (NADP), and its cofactor magnesium chloride in the tris–HCl buffer along with PMS and NBT. The reaction can be diagrammed as

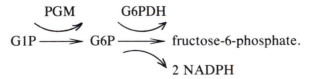

---

[1] A uniform nomenclature for protein-coding loci in fish was published while this book was in press (Shaklee et al. 1990), and has been adopted as an editorial standard by the American Fisheries Society. Loci are named for the proteins they encode; enzyme names are those of the International Union of Biochemistry (IUBNC 1984). Abbreviations of protein and locus names are in uppercase letters; protein abbreviations are in normal (Roman) type and those of loci are italicized. A locus abbreviation is followed by an asterisk (*), an allele symbol (also italicized) is preceded by an asterisk, and locus and allele are separated by an asterisk. The notation in this chapter generally follows the recommended nomenclature, except the figures were drawn according to a former system in which alleles were set off from loci by parentheses instead of by asterisks.

The hydrogen ions then cascade from NADP to PMS to NBT, and the blue dye shows the position of PGM activity.

Stain recipes are available for many enzymes, not just for dehydrogenases (Brewer 1970; Shaw and Prasad 1970; Selander et al. 1971; Harris and Hopkinson 1976; Allendorf et al. 1977). The recommended concentrations of ingredients in these recipes can be varied; when a stain produces only faint bands on a gel, for example, the intensity often can be enhanced if the concentration of ingredients is increased.

5.3.6   Gel Preservation

It is wise to preserve the gels as they are processed. Gels that have been stained with alcohol-insoluble dyes such as NBT can be soaked for 1–2 d in a solution of 5 parts distilled water, 4 parts methanol, and 1 part acetic acid. This fixes the banding pattern and dehydrates the gel, making it considerably tougher. These gels can be kept almost indefinitely if they are enclosed in plastic wrap and stored in a refrigerator or cold room. Another means of "preservation" is photography.

5.4   COLLECTION AND ANALYSIS OF DATA

5.4.1   Scoring Gels

Interpretation of the banding patterns on gels requires that the phenotypes expressed by the proteins be translated into genotypes at the loci[2] that encoded them. This requires an understanding of how a protein's quaternary structure—its number of polypeptide components—affects the banding pattern.

Recall from Chapter 2 that individuals homozygous at a locus are those in which both copies of the gene have the same allelic state; in heterozygotes, the copies have different allelic states. If a locus that codes for a polypeptide is homozygous, its identical alleles produce only one type of polypeptide. If the locus is heterozygous, each allele produces a unique polypeptide. For purposes of illustration, we denote the polypeptides A and a, representing the products of the two alleles, and molecular combinations of polypeptides by center dots: A·A, A·a, and so on.

First, consider monomeric enzymes, those consisting of only one polypeptide. At the hypothetical locus under consideration, homozygous individuals produce only one polypeptide, A or a, so all the enzyme molecules have the same structure and thus the same net charge. During electrophoresis, these molecules migrate through the gel at the same rate and appear as a single band after the gel is stained. In Figure 5.2, which introduces a genetic nomenclature based on relative protein mobilities (see also footnote 1 and Section 5.4.4), individuals 1, 3, 4, and 6–10 of the top panel are homozygous for one of the two possible monomeric enzymes (the other homozygous form is not shown). Heterozygotes, however, produce two different polypeptides. When these polypeptides have different charges, they migrate at different rates and produce two gel bands (individuals 2 and 5 in the top

---

[2] Technically, a locus is the *location* of a gene on a chromosome. In common usage, however, the locus is treated as though it were the gene. In this chapter, as elsewhere in the literature, "gene" and "locus" are used interchangeably.

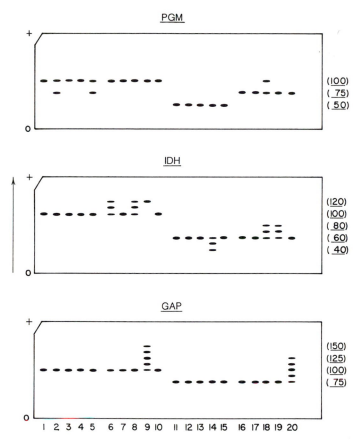

Figure 5.2. Hypothetical electropherograms that demonstrate banding patterns indicative of genetic variation within and between samples for a monomeric enzyme (top panel), a dimeric enzyme (middle), and a tetrameric enzyme (bottom). Individuals 1–5 constitute sample I, 6–10 sample II, 11–15 sample III, and 16–20 sample IV. Zero designates the gel origin, + designates the anodal edge of the gel, and the arrow indicates the direction of enzyme migration. Alleles associated with the enzyme bands are listed along the right margin. The enzyme form coded by the most common allele in sample I is denoted 100 in each panel; its allele is denoted *(100)*. Other enzyme forms are numerically designated according to their migration distances relative to that of the 100 form. For example, enzyme 75 migrated 75% as far as enzyme 100; enzyme 120 migrated 20% farther than 100. Genetic notation is underlined or italicized; phenotypic codes are in Roman type. Additional nomenclatural details are in Section 5.4.4.

Top. Electropherogram for the monomeric enzyme phosphoglucomutase (PGM); the locus that codes this enzyme is *PGM*. Individuals 1,3,4, and 6–10 are homozygous for the *(100)* allele; their genotype is denoted *(100/100)*. Individuals 2, 5, and 18 are heterozygous for the *(100)* and *(75)* alleles and have a *(100/75)* genotype. Individuals 11–15 are *(50/50)*, and 16, 17, 19, and 20 are *(75/75)*.

Middle. Electropherogram for the dimeric enzyme isocitrate dehydrogenase (IDH, locus *IDH*). Individuals 1–5, 7, and 10 have the genotype *(100/100)*, 6 and 8 are *(100/120)*, 9 is *(120/120)*, 11–13, 15–17, and 20 are *(60/60)*, 14 is *(60/40)*, and 18 and 19 are *(60/80)*.

Bottom. Electropherogram for the tetrameric enzyme glyceraldehyde-3-phosphate dehydrogenase (GAP, locus *GAP*). Individuals 1–8 and 10 have the genotype *(100/100)*, 9 is *(100/150)*, 11–19 are *(75/75)*, and 20 is *(75/125)*.

panel of Figure 5.2). Both polypeptides usually are produced in equal amounts, so their gel bands usually show equal staining intensity.

Dimeric enzymes are composed of two polypeptides. If the polypeptides are identical, A·A or a·a, the enzyme is homodimeric. If the polypeptides differ, A·a, the enzyme is heterodimeric. Homozygous individuals produce only the homodimers, A·A or a·a, which form a single band on gels (Figure 5.2, middle panel, individuals 1–5, 7, 9, and 10). Heterozygotes have both A and a polypeptides, and these generally pair at random to give three enzyme variants: the homodimers A·A and a·a, and the heterodimer A·a. The relative amounts of these variants usually follow approximately the binomial distribution: $(p + q)^2 = p^2 + 2pq + q^2 = 1$; p and q are the respective probabilities that a polypeptide will be A or a, and both probabilities are 0.5. Here, p^2 is the proportion of A·A variants (0.25), $2pq$ is the proportion of A·a variants (0.5), and q^2 is the proportion of a·a variants; twice as many heterodimers are produced as either homodimer. When the three enzyme variants have different charges and migrate at different rates, three bands appear on gels (Figure 5.2, middle panel, individuals 6 and 8). Thus, a three-banded pattern, the middle band staining more intensively than the others, is characteristic of individuals heterozygous at loci coding for dimeric enzymes.

Tetrameric enzymes contain four polypeptides. In heterozygotes, the polypeptides often combine at random to form two homotetrameric molecules, A·A·A·A and a·a·a·a, and three heterotetrameric molecules, A·A·A·a, A·A·a·a, and A·a·a·a. The relative quantities of these molecules usually conform approximately to the distribution $(p + q)^4 = p^4 + 4p^3q + 6p^2q^2 + 4pq^3 + q^4 = 1$. Thus, a five-banded gel pattern, the bands staining with relative intensities of 1:4:6:4:1, is characteristic of individuals heterozygous at loci coding for tetrameric enzymes.

5.4.2 Duplicate Loci

Many enzymes in fishes and higher vertebrates are encoded by more than one genetic locus—the result of gene duplication. Two of the major factors responsible for gene duplication are polyploidy (Ohno 1970; see also Chapter 2) and unequal crossing over when chromosomes mispair during meiosis. At first, the two pair of genes may encode the same polypeptides for a particular protein. In time, however, mutations at one or both locus pairs may cause the pairs to encode structurally different polypeptides. Moreover, mutations may occur in regulatory genes that control the time and place at which enzyme genes are expressed. Thus, not only may the structure of the polypeptides diverge through time, the tissues in which they are produced may change as well. Additional duplications can add genes and bring about even more tissue-specific expressions of loci. Gene duplication was discussed in greater depth by Ohno (1970), Whitt (1981), Allendorf and Thorgaard (1984), and Ferris (1984).

Lactate dehydrogenase (LDH) is a good example of an enzyme encoded by several genes. In many fishes, LDH is encoded by at least three pairs of genes that produce different polypeptides. The polypeptide produced from the *LDH-A** locus usually is present in skeletal muscle, that of the *B** locus usually predominates in the liver and heart, and that of the *C** locus usually is restricted to neural tissue.

Although the polypeptides of duplicate loci often are expressed in different tissues, they can occur together in some tissues. This is especially true for such

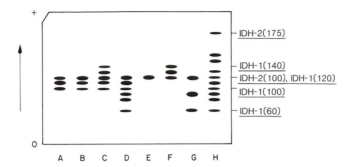

Figure 5.3. Hypothetical electropherogram showing banding patterns for the dimeric enzyme isocitrate dehydrogenase (IDH) that could appear when the products of two loci (*IDH-1* and *IDH-2*) encoding the enzyme appear in the same tissue of an individual. Zero denotes the gel origin, + denotes the anode (toward which the enzyme migrated, arrow), and A–H are the individuals sampled. Loci and alleles associated with the bands are listed at right; *(100)* represents the most common allele of each locus, and other allele numbers reflect the relative mobilities of their polypeptide products. The products are denoted in Roman type in this caption; the genetic terms are indicated by underlines (figure) or italics (caption). The relative size of the bands indicates the relative intensity of staining and hence the relative amount of protein in each band.

A. The genotype of individual A is *IDH-1(100/100)*, *IDH-2(100/100)*; i.e., A is homozygous at the two loci.

B. The banding intensity for individual B increases anodally, suggesting that an *IDH-1(100)* allele has been replaced by one whose protein product has the same mobility as IDH-2(100). The migration of IDH-2(100) was 20% farther than that of IDH-1(100), so the "new" protein is designated IDH-1(120). The inferred genotype is *IDH-1(100/120)*, *IDH-2(100/100)*.

C. The banding intensities for individual C are symmetrical, suggesting that C is heterozygous at *IDH-1*. Genotype: *IDH-1(100/140)*, *IDH-2(100/100)*.

D. The asymmetrical banding intensities for individual D also suggest that D is heterozygous at *IDH-1*. Genotype: *IDH-1(100/60)*, *IDH-2(100/100)*.

E. The single band implies that no *IDH-1(100)* alleles exist in individual E. Genotype: *IDH-1(120/120)*, *IDH-2(100/100)*.

F. The absence of the IDH-1(100) band also indicates that the corresponding allele is absent from individual F. Genotype: *IDH-1(140/140)*, *IDH-2(100/100)*.

G. Again, the *IDH-1(100)* allele is missing from individual G. Genotype: *IDH-1(60/60)*, *IDH-2(100/100)*.

H. Individual H is heterozygous at both loci: *IDH-1(100/60)*, *IDH-2(100/175)*. From the origin toward the anode, the bands correspond to the *IDH-1(60)* homodimer, the heterodimer between *IDH-1(60)* and *IDH-1(100)*, the *IDH-1(60)–IDH-2(100)* heterodimer, the *IDH-1(100)* homodimer, the *IDH-1(100)–IDH-2(100)* heterodimer, the *IDH-2(100)* homodimer, the *IDH-1(60)–IDH-2(175)* heterodimer, the *IDH-1(100)–IDH-2(175)* heterodimer, the *IDH-2(100)–IDH-2(175)* heterodimer, and the *IDH-2(175)* homodimer.

fishes as catostomids and salmonids whose duplicate loci are derived from ancient tetraploid events (Allendorf and Thorgaard 1984; Ferris 1984). The criteria for scoring gels that were outlined in Section 5.4.1 often are insufficient when the products of duplicated loci occur in the same tissue and cellular compartments. Consider a monomeric enzyme encoded by two homozygous loci, each of which produces a different polypeptide. Homogenates from tissues in which both polypeptides occur will produce two bands on electrophoretic gels—the pattern expected from an individual heterozygous at an unduplicated locus for a monomeric enzyme. The same relationship applies to enzymes of higher quaternary

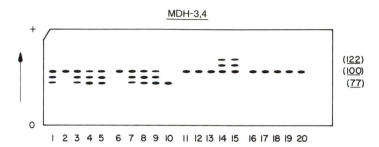

Figure 5.4. Gel-banding patterns that could appear when two polymorphic loci (loci with two or more distinct alleles) have one allele in common and encode variants of a dimeric enzyme that occur in the same tissue. The example is malate dehydrogenase (MDH), which is encoded by the loci *MDH-3* and *MDH-4*. Twenty patterns are depicted, representing four samples (I–IV) of five individuals each. Both loci are polymorphic for the same allele at least in samples I (individuals 1–5) and II (6–10), so genotypes at the two loci cannot be determined. Thus, the two loci are considered to be one locus (*MDH-3,4*) that is represented by four copies. Alleles are underlined at right. Allele *(100)* is the most common, based on the occurrence of its corresponding polypeptide, and other alleles are designated numerically according to the proportional electrophoretic mobilities of their polypeptides relative to that of the 100 polypeptide. Based on relative band densities, indicated by thicknesses of the drawn bands, the inferred "genotypes" of individuals are as follows:

    2, 6, 11–13, 16–20: *(100/100/100/100)*;
    1, 3, 7: *(100/100/100/77)*;
    5, 8: *(100/100/77/77)*;
    4, 9: *(100/77/77/77/)*;
    10: *(77/77/77/77)*;
    14 and 15: *(100/100/100/122)*.

structure: when duplicated loci are both homozygous, each of the loci encodes a different polypeptide and both polypeptides occur in the same tissue with about equal frequency, so the electrophoretic banding pattern usually mimics the pattern produced by an individual heterozygous at an unduplicated locus. Three examples are shown in Figure 5.3 (individuals A, F, and G).

Several banding patterns are possible when individuals are heterozygous at one or both loci. The dimeric enzyme isocitrate dehydrogenase (IDH), which is encoded by two loci (*IDH-1** and *IDH-2**), offers an example of intermediate complexity. Homogenates from individuals heterozygous at one locus and homozygous at the other could produce three, five, or six bands on a gel (Figure 5.3, individuals B–D). A three-band pattern results when the variant allele at the *IDH-1** locus (for example) produces a polypeptide with the same charge as the polypeptide encoded by the homozygous *IDH-2** locus. Although six dimeric molecules are produced—A·A, A·a, a·a, A·B, a·B, and B·B in the enzyme notation used before, B corresponding to a polypeptide coded by the second locus—only three charge states exist among them. One state corresponds to the A·A molecule, another to the A·a and A·B molecules, and the third to the a·a, a·B, and B·B molecules. Five- and six-band patterns result when the variant *IDH-1** allele produces a polypeptide with a unique charge. Individuals heterozygous at both loci can produce up to 10 bands when each allele encodes a uniquely charged polypeptide (Figure 5.3, individual H). A good way for the reader to learn how to translate banding patterns into genotypes is to diagram the banding patterns that can result from various genotypes at duplicate loci for monomeric and tetrameric enzymes.

Duplicate loci can preclude reliable inference of genotypes when they share the same common allele (Figure 5.4). In the case of a dimeric enzyme, individuals heterozygous at one such encoding locus but homozygous at the other will produce a banding pattern with asymmetric staining intensity such as those in Figures 5.3 and 5.4. However, if both loci are heterozygous or each is homozygous for a different allele, three bands of symmetric density will result (Figure 5.4, individuals 5 and 8). Although unambiguous genotypes cannot be determined in these circumstances, useful information can be obtained nonetheless. The number of times an allele occurs between the two loci can be inferred from the banding pattern. Thus, it is possible to estimate allele frequencies by treating the enzyme as one encoded by a single locus represented by four copies—that is, as a tetrasomic locus (see Chapter 2 and Section 5.4.5 for more detail).

5.4.3 Genetic and Nongenetic Variation

Nongenetic factors can cause proteins to develop multiple band patterns on electrophoretic gels. Heteropolymers might not form (Utter et al. 1979, 1987) or denaturation or posttranslational changes may cause polypeptides formed from the same allele to have different charges (Shami and Beardmore 1978; Utter et al. 1979). Phenotypic variation due to genetic variation becomes obscured because the banding patterns do not conform with expectations based on the protein's quaternary structure.

The only conclusive way to confirm that observed phenotypic variation reflects genetic variation is to demonstrate, through experimental matings, that the phenotypic ratios of progeny conform to Mendelian segregation ratios (Chapter 2). It frequently is impossible to do this, and the genetic basis of observed variation then must be inferred from other criteria. Three criteria can be used: (1) the banding pattern is consistent among the tissues of an individual in which the locus is expressed; (2) the banding pattern from individuals presumed to be heterozygous conforms with the quaternary structure of the enzyme; (3) the pattern is reproducible in subsamples taken from the same tissue of an individual. If at least one of these criteria is violated and no breeding data are available to explain the violation, it is best to attribute the observed variation to nongenetic factors and to eliminate the locus from further consideration.

5.4.4 Nomenclature of Loci and Alleles

It is very important to name loci and alleles informatively so other workers can reliably determine homologies among loci and identities among alleles. Several nomenclature systems satisfy these criteria and they generally share some essential features. Loci take their names from the proteins they encode. Alleles are distinguished by the absolute or relative electrophoretic distances moved by the polypeptides they encode. For polymeric enzymes, alleles are identified by the position of the homopolymers.

The nomenclature used in this chapter is based on the one recommended by Shaklee et al. (1990); the figures show an earlier but somewhat similar system devised by Allendorf and Utter (1979) and Allendorf et al. (1983). Loci are designated by a two- to four-letter uppercase, italic, asterisked abbreviation of the enzyme they encode (the abbreviation remains in normal Roman type when it refers to the enzyme). When two or more loci encode the same enzyme, they are distinguished by Arabic numerals that denote increasing anodal mobility of the most common enzyme form encoded by each locus. For example, *AAT-1** and *AAT-2** designate two loci that code for the dimeric enzyme aspartate aminotransferase, AAT. The homodimer formed from the polypeptide encoded by *AAT-2** migrates farther toward the gel anode than the homodimer formed from the polypeptide encoded by *AAT-1**.

Enzymes often have more than one common name. The International Union of Biochemistry Nomenclature Committee has recommended a standard list of common names and has assigned a classification number to each enzyme for more definitive identification (IUBNC 1984). We highly recommend the use of these names and numbers.

Alleles at a locus are numbered with reference to a "standard" allele, typically the most common allele at that locus in a population sample, and preceded by an asterisk. The distance that the standard allele's polypeptide migrates from the origin of a gel is denoted 100, and the allele takes that name: for example, *AAT-1*100*; note the italics (or underline) in the allele designation. The migration distances of other polypeptides for the locus are expressed as percentages of the standard migration distance. An allele at the *AAT-1** locus whose product moves half as far as the standard is labeled *AAT-1*50*; one whose product goes twice as far is *AAT-1*200*. If the polypeptide migrates toward the cathode instead of toward the anode, it and its allele are given a negative number, though the number still is a percentage of the standard distance.

Ideally, standard alleles should be those characteristic of a completely homozygous inbred line, which will ensure constancy over time. Few inbred lines of fish have been produced, however, so the choice of a reference population for the standards usually is subjective. The reference population should at least be one that can be resampled readily as needed.

5.4.5 Estimation of Allele Frequencies

The estimation of allele frequencies usually is straightforward. The frequency of an allele is simply the total number of times it was detected among individuals in a sample, divided by the sample size. Homozygous individuals contain two copies of an allele and heterozygotes one. The number of times an allele is detected, therefore, is twice the number of homozygotes plus the number of heterozygotes; the sample size is twice the number of all individuals analyzed. For example, the frequency p of the *PGM*100* allele among the five individuals in sample I, Figure 5.2, is $p = (2 \times 3$ homozygotes $+ 2$ heterozygotes$)/(2 \times 5$ individuals$) = 0.800$. The frequency q of the alternative allele *PGM*75* is $q = (2 \times 0 + 2)/(2 \times 5) = 0.200$. Half the 95% confidence interval around the frequency (0.800) of *PGM*100* is twice the standard deviation of the binomial distribution (i.e., twice the square root of $pq/2N$, N being the number of individuals analyzed). Thus, the full 95% confidence interval is $\pm 2(pq/2N)^{0.5} = \pm 0.253$, giving a range of 0.547–1.053 or, because a frequency cannot exceed 1.000, 0.547–1.000. Allele frequencies for the other loci shown in Figure 5.2 are given in Table 5.3; readers are encouraged to derive them.

This procedure cannot be used when genotypes cannot be assigned reliably to individual loci of a duplicate pair (Section 5.4.2). The several ways to estimate

Table 5.3. Allele frequencies and measures of genetic variation, in four hypothetical samples (I–IV) of five individuals each, at loci shown in the electropherograms of Figures 5.2 and 5.4.

Locus or measure	Allele	Sample and frequency			
		I	II	III	IV
PGM*	*100	0.800	1.000		0.100
	*75	0.200			0.900
	*50			1.000	
IDH*	*100	1.000	0.600		
	*120		0.400		
	*80				0.200
	*60			0.900	0.800
	*40			0.100	
GAP*	*100	1.000	0.900		
	*150		0.100		
	*125				0.100
	*75			1.000	0.900
MDH-3,4*	*100	0.650	0.500	0.900	1.000
	*122			0.100	
	*77	0.350	0.500		
Proportion of polymorphic loci (P)[a]		0.200	0.300	0.200	0.300
Average expected heterozygosity (h_e)[a]		0.112	0.151	0.049	0.062
Average observed heterozygosity (h_o)[a]		0.120	0.120	0.060	0.080

[a]For purposes of these calculations, it has been assumed that six other monomorphic loci have been analyzed in addition to those listed explicitly in this table. Thus, calculations are based on 10 loci, 2 or 3 of which (depending on the sample) are polymorphic.

allele frequencies in these situations fall into two broad categories: maximum-likelihood estimation and allele counting. It is not presently known, however, which of these alternative methods yields the most biologically realistic results.

As an example, we consider a simple allele-counting method that treats a duplicate locus pair as a single tetrasomic locus. The number of times a particular allele is observed in each individual is recorded. These numbers are summed over the N individuals in the sample and divided by $4N$ to estimate allele frequencies. Thus, the frequency of the MDH-3,4*100 allele in sample II of Figure 5.4 is $(4 + 3 + 2 + 1 + 0)/(4 \times 5) = 0.500$. The frequency of MDH-3,4*77 is $(1 + 2 + 3 + 4)/20 = 0.500$. It is often assumed that these frequencies pertain to the individual loci, but we prefer to treat the two loci as one in the data (Table 5.3) because the estimates then require no additional assumptions.

5.4.6 Quantifying Genetic Variation within Samples

The maintenance of genetic variation should be a principal goal of management programs designed to preserve a population or species. Loss of genetic variation has deleterious effects on the development, growth, fertility, and disease resistance of fishes, among other processes important to survival and reproduction (reviewed by Kirpichnikov 1981 and Kincaid 1983; see also Danzmann et al. 1985 and Leary et al. 1985b). Such losses also are expected to reduce a population's ability to adapt to future environmental changes (Ayala 1965, 1969; Frankham 1980). Preservation of genetic variation, therefore, should be part of any conservation program for fishes.

As Lewontin (1974) discussed, the amount of genetic variation in a population can be estimated only if one has information about the number of loci at which variation occurs (polymorphic loci) and does not occur (monomorphic loci). Electrophoretic data provide such information, and thus can be used to monitor levels of genetic variation in populations.

The proportion of polymorphic loci (*P*) is a commonly used measure of electrophoretically detectable variation in a population; *P* is the number of loci in a sample found to be polymorphic divided by the total number of loci examined. A locus usually is considered to be polymorphic if the frequency of its most common allele is estimated to be less than 0.990 or 0.950. The choice between these two criteria is arbitrary; both are intended to exclude from consideration loci whose variation may be maintained solely by recurrent mutation. With reference to Table 5.3, *PGM** and *MDH-3,4** are the only polymorphic loci in sample I. If, in addition to these two and the monomorphic *IDH** and *GAP** loci in Table 5.3, data were available for six other monomorphic loci, *P* in sample I would be 2/10 = 0.200. (We will carry this assumption—that a sample is analyzed for the four loci in Table 5.3 and for six loci monomorphic for the same allele in each sample—through the rest of this chapter to make the estimates of *P* and other parameters comparable to those normally observed in fish populations: Nevo 1984.)

Another commonly used measure of genetic variation is the average frequency of heterozygous loci per individual (*H*). This is either the observed or the expected proportion of heterozygous loci per individual averaged over all the loci examined. Recall from Chapter 2 that the expected heterozygosity at a locus (h_e) in a randomly mating population is one minus the sum of squared allele frequencies at the locus. Thus, h_e at the *PGM** locus in sample I (Table 5.3) is $1 - (0.8^2 + 0.2^2)$ = 0.320. The observed heterozygosity at a locus (h_o) is the proportion of individuals observed to be heterozygous; for *PGM** in sample I (Figure 5.2), h_o is 2/5 = 0.400. A composite value is obtained by averaging h_e or h_o over all the loci examined. In general, expected and observed heterozygosities at a locus are similar, so it usually makes little difference which parameter is used. Several factors can cause marked deviations between h_e and h_o; the two most common ones are selection and nonrandom mating (see Zouros and Foltz [1984] for an in-depth discussion of such deviations).

Duplicate loci such as *MDH-3,4** (Figure 5.4) are difficult to incorporate into an estimate of *H*. Alternative approaches are (1) to eliminate such loci from the estimate, (2) to estimate expected heterozygosity from allele frequencies obtained by allele counting (Section 5.4.5) or another procedure and to assume that these frequencies pertain to the individual loci, and (3) to estimate observed heterozygosity by considering individuals with two or more different alleles at the loci to be heterozygous. If option (2) is used, h_e at *MDH-3** and *MDH-4** in sample I (Table 5.3) is 0.455; if option (3) is used, h_o is 0.800. The heterozygosity in this sample is averaged over all the loci in Table 5.3 and the other six assumed monomorphic loci. Therefore, $h_e = (0.320 + 0.455 + 0.455)/11 = 0.112$, and $h_o = (0.400 + 0.800)/10 = 0.120$.

The parameters *H* and *P* are different, and the amount of genetic variation in a population is best measured by both. Because *H* is based on allele frequencies, loci that contain alleles at nearly equal frequencies make large contributions to *H*, whereas polymorphic loci with a common allele ($p > 0.900$) make only minor contributions. The loss of variant alleles at the latter loci may not appreciably alter H, but can profoundly affect P. Small changes in P, on the other hand, may have a large effect on H.

5.4.7 Migration and Species Distinctions

Populations develop genetic differences only if the exchange of genetic material (migration) between them is restricted (Chapter 2). If populations develop even partial reproductive isolation from each other, their allele frequencies begin to diverge, due largely to genetic drift and to local adaptive pressures that act on existing polymorphisms and new mutations. The amount of divergence typically increases with the time that the populations have been segregated.

In the absence of natural selection, populations without total reproductive isolation rarely become completely divergent such that they share no alleles at a locus. An average migration rate of only one individual per generation between two populations prevents those populations from becoming completely divergent for selectively neutral alleles at any locus (Wright 1978). A corollary of the nonselection model, therefore, is that complete divergence at one or more loci between populations implies a long period of essentially total reproductive isolation.

Whether or not electrophoretically detectable variation has adaptive value and is subject to selection remains controversial despite decades of theoretical and empirical study. Cases are known in which such variation at individual or groups of loci is associated with phenotypic characters likely to be of adaptive value, but failures to detect such associations also are numerous and may be less likely to be reported (reviewed by Mitton and Grant 1984; Allendorf and Leary 1986; Palmer and Strobeck 1986; Zouros and Foltz 1987). Although substantial selective differences between genotypes at protein-coding loci have been reported, such differences generally have been difficult to demonstrate (e.g., Frelinger 1972; DiMichele and Powers 1982a, 1982b; Watt et al. 1983, 1985). This does not prove that most variation detectable by electrophoresis is selectively neutral because fitness usually cannot be measured directly and all the components of fitness usually cannot be assessed. The data do suggest, however, that such variation generally is neutral or subjected to only weak selective forces. Electrophoretic differentiation among populations, therefore, probably reflects rates of migration and genetic drift more than it does local adaptation.

Electrophoretic data now are available from a wide diversity of organisms (Nevo et al. 1984). Complete divergences at loci seldom have been encountered between populations judged on other grounds to be of the same species, but they are common between populations of different species (Selander and Johnson 1973; Avise 1974; Ayala 1983). Thus, populations usually may be presumed to be from separate species if divergences between them are complete or nearly so at some loci, and to be conspecific if such divergences are absent. Exceptions to this ''rule'' occur, however: fish may be almost indistinguishable electrophoretically even though morphological or other criteria strongly indicate they are of different species (Turner 1974; Avise et al. 1976; Phelps and Allendorf 1983), and complete divergence at a few loci has been observed between populations otherwise considered conspecific (Allendorf et al. 1976). Such ambiguities mean that biochemical evolution and the evolution of other attributes have proceeded at different rates. For example, incomplete divergences at enzymatic loci of distinctively different fishes might imply recent speciation followed by rapid morphological evolution. Alternatively, the fish may be conspecific by strict genetic criteria and their distinct morphologies may be due to variation at only one or a few loci or to locally adaptive, nongenetic differences (e.g., Meyer 1987). There are several ways to distinguish among these possibilities, and final resolution of the problem may require nonelectrophoretic data (Grudzien and Turner 1984a, 1984b). In general, discrepancies between electrophoretic and other criteria should make one suspect a taxonomic error that might be corrected through analysis of more loci, other attributes, or more populations.

The species "rule" can be applied to the data in Table 5.3. Samples I and II share the same common allele at each locus examined, evidence that the samples came from conspecific populations. In contrast, complete divergence exists between these two samples and sample III at the *PGM**, *IDH**, and *GAP** loci, and between the first two samples and sample IV at the *IDH** and *GAP** loci. This is evidence that samples I and II are of a different species from samples III and IV. The latter two samples present a taxonomic problem, however. Complete divergence between them occurs only at the *PGM** locus. Perhaps the samples represent recently formed species that have not yet accumulated the amount of genetic divergence typical of species. Alternatively, the samples might represent conspecific populations with an unusual amount of genetic divergence. The populations represented by samples III and IV could reasonably be assigned to different species if (a) complete divergences were discovered at additional loci or (b) additional samples continued to show complete divergence at the *PGM** locus. If many samples have intermediate allele frequencies, however, the populations are best interpreted as falling near the extreme along a continuum of intraspecific genetic divergence—unless hybridization is the suspected cause of the intermediate frequencies (Section 5.5.3).

5.4.8 Phenetic Analysis, Phylogenetic Analysis, and Taxonomic Limitations

In biochemical taxonomy, one often arranges groups of samples into hierarchies based on the genetic similarities (or differences) among them. Allele-frequency similarities between populations at any locus may be given the same analytical weight as the similarities at any other locus. Classifications based on such similarities, and on the assumption that populations have evolved at equal rates, are called *phenetic* systems.

Electrophoretic data can be converted into phenetic estimates of genetic divergence. Observed similarities or differences between populations are combined, by an arithmetic procedure or algorithm, over all the loci examined. The algorithm yields a "coefficient," of which several have been developed (e.g., Cavalli-Sforza and Edwards 1967; Balakrishnan and Sanghvi 1968; Kurczynski 1970; Hedrick 1971; Nei 1972, 1975; Rogers 1972). Most of the available coefficients provide qualitatively similar results, and it makes little difference which one is used (Rogers 1972; Avise 1974). We present Nei's (1972, 1975) measure of standard genetic distance (*D*) as an example because, unlike other coefficients to which little evolutionary meaning can be attached, *D* was designed to estimate the number of mutations per gene that distinguish two populations.

Nei's D is reached through his normalized measure of genetic identity (I) between two populations, say populations X and Y. This measure is a ratio. For a particular locus, the numerator is the probability that one will draw at random the same allele from both populations. This is denoted j_{XY}. It is the frequency of the ith allele at locus j in population X (called x_i) multiplied by the frequency of the same allele in population Y (y_i), summed over all the alleles detected at locus j; thus, $j_{XY} = \Sigma x_i y_i$. The denominator is the probability that one will draw at random two copies of the same allele from within each population; in other words, it is the expected homozygosities at locus j in populations X and Y. The expected homozygosity in population X, for all alleles i at locus j, is $j_X = \Sigma x_i^2$; the corresponding value for population Y is $j_Y = \Sigma y_i^2$. The denominator of I is the square root of their product:

$$(j_X j_Y)^{0.5}.$$

Thus,

$$I_j = j_{XY}/(j_X j_Y)^{0.5}.$$

When allele frequencies at locus j are identical in populations X and Y, $j_X = j_Y = j_{XY}$, and $I_j = 1.000$. When the populations share no alleles at locus j, $j_{XY} = 0.000$, and thus $I_j = 0.000$. As discussed in the previous section, values of $I = 0.000$ generally are expected only when the samples come from different species.

As a numerical example, consider locus PGM^* for samples I and II in Table 5.3. The probability of drawing the same allele from the two samples is

$PGM_{I,II} = (0.800 \times 1.000$ for allele $*100$) + (0.200×0.000 for allele $*75$)
$= 0.800.$

The expected homozygosities are

$$PGM_I = (0.800)^2 + (0.200)^2 = 0.680$$

and

$$PGM_{II} = (1.000)^2 + (0.000)^2 = 1.000.$$

The normalized genetic identity between samples I and II at the PGM^* locus, therefore, is

$$I_{PGM} = 0.800/(0.680 \times 1.000)^{0.5} = 0.970.$$

The normalized genetic identity between populations X and Y with respect to all loci examined is denoted

$$I = J_{XY}/(J_X J_Y)^{0.5};$$

J_{XY}, J_X, and J_Y represent the arithmetic means of j_{XY}, j_X, and j_Y, respectively, over all loci. With respect to Table 5.3, recall that 10 loci were examined: the four loci shown plus six monomorphic loci. Then, for samples I and II,

$$J_I = [0.680 + 0.545 + 8(1.000)]/10 = 0.923,$$
$$J_{II} = [0.520 + 0.820 + 0.500 + 7(1.000)]/10 = 0.884,$$
$$J_{I,II} = [0.800 + 0.600 + 0.900 + 0.500 + 6(1.000)]/10 = 0.880,$$

and

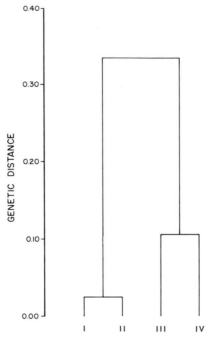

Figure 5.5. Dendrogram produced by hierarchical cluster analysis of genetic distances between samples I–IV computed from the data in Table 5.3.

$$I = 0.880/(0.923 \times 0.884)^{0.5} = 0.974.$$

From the normalized genetic identity, we return to standard genetic distance, to which it is related by the expression

$$D = -\log_e I.$$

For alleles judged to be selectively neutral, D is linearly related to the time since the populations first diverged, and it represents the average number of electrophoretically detectable mutations per locus that distinguishes the populations (Nei 1972). For our example, $D = 0.026$. Thus, if the assumption of neutrality holds for the loci in Table 5.3, only 0.026 electrophoretically detected mutations per locus exist between populations I and II. Genetic distances for the remaining pairs of samples in Table 5.3 are: I–III, 0.358; I–IV, 0.294; II–III, 0.358, II–IV, 0.319; III–IV, 0.107.

Estimates of genetic similarity or distance allow samples to be organized into hierarchical groups. A commonly used method for this is cluster analysis. Cluster analysis, which was described in depth by Sneath and Sokal (1973), groups or clusters samples along a scale of decreasing similarity or increasing distance. The result usually is depicted as a "tree" diagram, or dendrogram.

A dendrogram of genetic distances for the samples in Table 5.3 is depicted in Figure 5.5. Cluster analysis indicates little genetic distance between populations I and II, somewhat more distance between populations III and IV, and a large distance between group I–II and group III–IV. These results are consistent with the taxonomic conclusions we previously derived from the allele-frequency differences among these populations (Section 5.4.7), which were that I and II are the same species, that III and IV might be separate species, and that I and II are distinct from III and IV at the species level. We stress that taxonomic inferences from electrophoretic data should be based mainly on the degree of divergence at loci, not on the levels at which samples are grouped in dendrograms. Dendrograms and similar figures conveniently summarize the relative amounts of genetic differentiation among populations, and they may offer important clues about higher orders of taxonomic organization, but similarity or distance scales cannot be calibrated numerically for taxonomic decisions.

Electrophoretic data also can be organized by several cladistic techniques, as Buth (1984) has ably discussed (see also Chapter 3). Although cladistic and phenetic algorithms manipulate the data very differently, they generally group samples in qualitatively similar ways. The choice of approach depends mainly on one's taxonomic philosophy, that is, on whether one feels that classification should reflect mainly the purported genealogical relationships (cladistics) or the overall similarities (phenetics) among samples.

Both phenetic and cladistic analyses can order samples into groups that seem to represent taxa above the species level. In such cases, however, the data should be interpreted cautiously. An explicit assumption behind electrophoretic comparisons is that proteins with the same electrical charge (as indicated by their mobilities in an electric field) reflect genetic identity. This assumption usually is valid for populations that have been reproductively isolated for relatively short periods of time. Populations that are completely divergent at many of the loci examined are likely to have a long history of mutual isolation. For them, the assumption that electrophoretic identity reflects genetic identity is tenuous; there may be more genetic differences between the populations than the electrophoretic data imply.

5.4.9 Sample Sizes

The issue of sample size arises at two levels in electrophoretic studies: the number of individuals sampled, and the number of loci (specifically, the protein products of loci) examined per individual. A single locus is a minute portion of a genome, and it is very important to obtain electrophoretic data for many loci; otherwise, sampling error can produce seriously misleading information about the amount of genetic differentiation among populations. In general, inferences about genetic differentiation should be fairly reliable if they are based on at least 25 loci (Nei 1978). The products of many loci are expressed only in certain tissues, so it may be necessary to sample several tissues to survey the requisite number of loci.

We have stressed the importance of fixed allele-frequency differences between samples (that is, frequencies of 0.000 and 1.000) for species-level taxonomic decisions. Such differences can be detected reliably with sample sizes as small as one individual per population if the populations represent different species with normal amounts of electrophoretic divergence (Nei 1978; Gorman and Renzi 1979). Larger samples of individuals are needed when electrophoretic data are used to evaluate genetic differentiation between conspecific populations, species with little electrophoretic divergence, or genetic changes within a population through time (Chakraborty and Leimar 1987). In these instances, reliable estimates of divergence require more accurate estimates of allele frequencies at polymorphic loci. This usually requires analysis of 25 or more individuals.

We do not advocate the general use of small sample sizes but, if resources or opportunities are limited, it is better to curtail the number of individuals examined than the number of loci. Small samples of individuals should not seriously compromise electrophoretic data at the species level if the sample of loci remains adequately large.

5.5 DIAGNOSTIC LOCI

If two taxa rarely or never share electrophoretically detectable alleles at one or more loci, electrophoresis can be used to identify the taxa. Such loci often are called "diagnostic" (Ayala and Powell 1972). In this section, we briefly point out how diagnostic loci might be used to solve problems of interest to fish biologists. As examples, we discuss identifications of larvae and juveniles, discrepancies between morphological and protein evolution, and genetic consequences of species introductions for native fish.

5.5.1 Larvae and Juveniles

The adults of many fish species can be recognized easily by their morphological characteristics, but juveniles often look less distinctive, and larvae usually are difficult to tell apart by their external features. Problems in identification of early life stages have impeded our knowledge of such basic biological issues as the spatial and temporal distributions of young fishes and the forces that determine recruitment to fish populations. This knowledge has great practical importance when, for example, the potential effects of habitat alteration on fish species must be evaluated. The value of an effective means to identify young fishes cannot be overemphasized.

Electrophoretic studies have shown that fish species often are distinguishable at several diagnostic loci (Section 5.4.7). These genetic differences usually can be detected throughout most of a fish's life. Protein electrophoresis thus should be an effective means to identify larval and juvenile fishes accurately to species. Except for Comparini and Rodinò's (1980) work with American and European eel leptocephali, we are not aware of any published studies in which electrophoresis has been applied to such problems.

5.5.2 Sibling and Pseudo Species

Classifications based on morphological characters and on electrophoretic differences among populations generally are similar (Section 5.4.7), but exceptions occur. Disparate classifications apparently arise because morphological evolution and protein evolution have proceeded at different rates.

When external morphology evolves more slowly than proteins, "sibling species" may result. These are pairs or groups of species that look essentially the same but are genetically distinct. Sibling species seem to be rare among fishes, although this may simply reflect the difficulty in finding them. As far as we know, they have been described only in the bonefish genus *Albula* (Shaklee and Tamaru 1981), the silverside genus *Menidia* (Echelle and Mosier 1981; Echelle et al. 1983), the eel genus *Anguilla* (Comparini and Rodinò 1980), the sprat genus *Sprattus* (Smith and Robertson 1981), and the jack genus *Trachurus* (Stephenson and Robertson 1977; Altukhov and Salmenkova 1981). If the biological species concept is applied strictly, sympatric but reproductively isolated populations of brown trout also might qualify as sibling species (Ryman et al. 1979). Electrophoretic or similar biochemical data led to the discovery of these sibling forms. In each case, the presence of diagnostic loci segregated individuals from a single sample into two discrete groups. The only reasonable interpretation was that the sample contained two sympatric species.

When morphology evolves faster than proteins, the result can be morphs distinctive enough to be called species by classical taxonomic criteria but indistinguishable by electrophoretic criteria. The best known example of this situation is provided by the splitfin genus *Ilyodon* (family Goodeidae), the broad- and narrow-mouthed morphs of which have been treated as distinct species or genera (Hubbs and Turner 1939; Kingston 1979). Electrophoretic analyses, however, indicated no allele-frequency differences between the morphs within a locality, although there were differences between localities (Grudzien and Turner 1984b). Breeding studies confirmed that both morphs are members of the same polymorphic species (Grudzien and Turner 1984a). Some undescribed Mexican cichlids (Kornfield et al. 1982) and the shovelnose and pallid sturgeons (Phelps and Allendorf 1983) may provide other examples of this situation. The best explanation for such morphs is that they reflect genetic variation at only a few loci rather than to genetic differences at many loci (see Leary et al. 1984a for a specific example).

A lack of diagnostic loci in two groups of organisms does not automatically mean the groups are conspecific. In the *Ilyodon* example, if breeding experiments had not been done to resolve the issue, two alternative interpretations would be possible: conspecificity or recent reproductive isolation followed by rapid morphological divergence. Discrepancies between rates of morphological and biochemical evolution indicate that better understanding of fish lineages and relationships is apt to occur if these problems are studied by more than one technique.

5.5.3 Species Introductions

The deleterious effects that introduced fish can have on native species are of concern to biologists. Non-native fishes can distort energy flows within an ecosystem, compete with or prey upon native species, and import parasites and pathogens. Of particular concern to us in this section are the genetic implications of hybridization when introduced and native fishes are capable of interbreeding and their progeny are fertile. After the progeny have reproduced among themselves and backcrossed to the parental species for a few generations, "hybrid swarms" develop. In such introgressed populations—populations whose individuals carry genes from both introduced and native fishes in varying proportions—it is extremely unlikely that the "pure native genotype" will be preserved. If a native species is endangered and of limited distribution, its genotypes can be lost forever. Thus, it is important to have a reliable way to determine the presence and degree of introgression in populations.

Morphological comparisons have been the historical means to assess interbreeding between fish species. The presumption underlying such analyses is that hybrids have morphological characteristics that fall between parental extremes and thus can be distinguished from the parent species. This presumption often has proven invalid, however, when independent evidence has been obtained for hybrids and introgressed populations (Hubbs and Strawn 1957; Smitherman and

Hester 1962; West and Hester 1964; Simon and Noble 1968; Berry and Low 1970; Neff and Smith 1979; Ross and Cavender 1981; Joswiak et al. 1982; Leary et al. 1983, 1984b, 1985a). The situation is especially difficult when the parental species are very similar morphologically (Echelle and Mosier 1981). Thus, morphological analyses can seriously underestimate the extent and frequency of hybridization in a population (Joswiak et al. 1982; Leary et al. 1983, 1984b).

Diagnostic loci provide a very powerful means of identifying interspecific hybrids and introgressed populations. First-generation hybrids should be heterozygous at all the diagnostic loci for alleles characteristic of the parental species, and such "fixed heterozygosity" is indicative of hybrid status (Echelle et al. 1983). If the hybrids reproduce among themselves and backcross to the parental species, some diagnostic loci still will be heterozygous in individuals but others will have become homozygous again for one parental allele or the other; if such a pattern is found, it is evidence of true introgression (Allendorf and Phelps 1981; Busack and Gall 1981; Phelps and Allendorf 1982; Whitmore 1983; Leary et al. 1984b; Campton and Utter 1985; Gyllensten et al. 1985). More than one diagnostic locus must be examined if introgression is to be distinguished from hybridization. Broader surveys of loci diagnostic within a species group also can confirm the identities of presumed parental species, or allow the parents to be deduced if several candidates are possible.

Electrophoretic data can provide other information about introgressed populations. For example, the proportional contributions of the parental species to a population can be estimated by averaging each species' allele frequencies over all the diagnostic loci. The fashion in which parental genetic material is distributed among individuals in the population also can be determined. As described in detail by Campton (1987), this involves correlation analysis of alleles at diagnostic loci. Correlation of one parental species' alleles between loci implies that its genetic material is not randomly distributed among individuals in the population. Nonrandomness may have several causes; for example, introgression simply may be incomplete, some genotypes of hybrid ancestry may be selected against (Dowling and Moore 1985), or immigration by one or both parental species may be continuous. Electrophoretic data alone may not distinguish among these possibilities, and additional information may be needed to resolve the issue.

5.6 CONCLUDING REMARKS

We have focused our discussion of electrophoretic data on species-level problems because we believe the information content of the data is easiest to comprehend at this level. Protein electrophoresis also can be used, however, to address genetic differentiation below the species rank (Chakraborty and Leimar 1987). The basic principles are essentially the same as they are for species, except that allele-frequency differences usually are substantially smaller between conspecific populations than they are between species.

5.7 REFERENCES

Aebersold, P. B., G. A. Winans, D. J. Teel, G. B. Milner, and F. M. Utter. 1987. Manual for starch gel electrophoresis: a manual for the detection of genetic variation. NOAA

(National Oceanic and Atmospheric Administration) Technical Report NMFS (National Marine Fisheries Service) 61.

Allendorf, F. W., K. L. Knudsen, and R. F. Leary. 1983. Adaptive significance of differences in the tissue-specific expression of a phosphoglucomutase gene in rainbow trout. Proceedings of the National Academy of Sciences of the USA 80:1397–1400.

Allendorf, F. W., and R. F. Leary. 1986. Heterozygosity and fitness in natural populations of animals. Pages 57–76 in M. E. Soulé, editor. Conservation biology: the science of scarcity and diversity. Sinauer Associates, Sunderland, Massachusetts.

Allendorf, F. W., N. Mitchell, N. Ryman, and G. Ståhl. 1977. Isozyme loci in brown trout (*Salmo trutta* L.): detection and interpretation from population data. Hereditas 86:179–190.

Allendorf, F. W., and S. R. Phelps. 1981. Isozymes and the preservation of genetic variation in salmonid fishes. Ecological Bulletin (Stockholm) 34:37–52.

Allendorf, F. W., N. Ryman, A. Stennek, and G. Ståhl. 1976. Genetic variation in Scandinavian populations of brown trout (*Salmo trutta* L.): evidence of genetically distinct sympatric populations. Hereditas 83:73–82.

Allendorf, F. W., and G. H. Thorgaard. 1984. Tetraploidy and the evolution of salmonid fishes. Pages 1–53 in B. J. Turner, editor. Evolutionary genetics of fishes. Plenum, New York.

Allendorf, F. W., and F. M. Utter. 1979. Population genetics. Pages 407–454 in W. S. Hoar, D. J. Randall, and J. R. Brett, editors. Fish physiology, volume 8. Academic Press, New York.

Altukhov, Y. P., and E. A. Salmenkova. 1981. Application of the stock concept to fish populations in the USSR. Canadian Journal of Fisheries and Aquatic Sciences 38:1591–1600.

Avise, J. C. 1974. Systematic value of electrophoretic data. Systematic Zoology 23:465–481.

Avise, J. C., J. J. Smith, and F. J. Ayala. 1976. Adaptive differentiation with little genetic change between two native California minnows. Evolution 29:411–426.

Ayala, F. J. 1965. Evolution of fitness in experimental populations of *Drosophila serrata*. Science (Washington, D.C.) 150:903–905.

Ayala, F. J. 1969. Evolution of fitness. V. Rate of evolution in irradiated populations of *Drosophila*. Proceedings of the National Academy of Sciences of the USA 63:790–793.

Ayala, F. J. 1983. Enzymes as taxonomic characters. Systematics Association Special Volume 24:3–26.

Ayala, F. J., and J. R. Powell. 1972. Allozymes as diagnostic characters of sibling species of *Drosophila*. Proceedings of the National Academy of Sciences of the USA 69:1094–1096.

Balakrishnan, V., and L. D. Sanghvi. 1968. Distance between populations on the basis of attribute data. Biometrics 24:859–869.

Berry, P. Y., and M. P. Low. 1970. Comparative studies on some aspects of the morphology and histology of *Ctenopharyngodon idellus, Aristichthys nobilis* and their hybrid (Cyprinidae). Copeia 1970:708–726.

Brewer, G. J. 1970. An introduction to isozyme techniques. Academic Press, New York.

Busack, C. A., and G. A. E. Gall. 1981. Introgressive hybridization in populations of Paiute cutthroat trout (*Salmo clarki seleniris*). Canadian Journal of Fisheries and Aquatic Sciences 38:939–951.

Buth, D. G. 1984. The application of electrophoretic data in systematic studies. Annual Review of Ecology and Systematics 15:501–522.

Campton, D. E. 1987. Natural hybridization and introgression in fishes: methods of detection and genetic interpretations. Pages 161–192 in N. Ryman and F. Utter, editors. Population genetics & fishery management. University of Washington Press, Seattle.

Campton, D. E., and F. M. Utter. 1985. Natural hybridization between steelhead trout (*Salmo gairdneri*) and coastal cutthroat trout (*Salmo clarki*) in two Puget Sound streams. Canadian Journal of Fisheries and Aquatic Sciences 42:110–119.

Cavalli-Sforza, L. L., and A. W. F. Edwards. 1967. Phylogenetic analysis: models and estimation procedures. Evolution 21:550–570.

Chakraborty, R., and O. Leimar. 1987. Genetic variation within a subdivided population. Pages 89–120 *in* N. Ryman and F. Utter, editors. Population genetics & fishery management. University of Washington Press, Seattle.

Clayton, J. W., and D. N. Tretiak. 1972. Amine-citrate buffers for pH control in starch gel electrophoresis. Journal of the Fisheries Research Board of Canada 29:1169–1172.

Comparini, A., and E. Rodinò. 1980. Electrophoretic evidence for two species of *Anguilla* leptocephali in the Sargasso Sea. Nature (London) 287:435–437.

Danzmann, R. G., M. M. Ferguson, and F. W. Allendorf. 1985. Does enzyme heterozygosity influence developmental rate in rainbow trout? Heredity 56:417–425.

DiMichele, L., and D. A. Powers. 1982a. LDH-B genotype specific hatching times in *Fundulus heteroclitus* embryos. Nature (London) 296:563–565.

DiMichele, L., and D. A. Powers. 1982b. Physiological basis for swimming endurance differences between LDH-B genotypes of *Fundulus heteroclitus*. Science (Washington D.C.) 216:1014–1016.

Dowling, T. E., and W. S. Moore. 1985. Evidence for selection against hybrids in the family Cyprinidae (genus *Notropis*). Evolution 39:152–158.

Echelle, A. A., A. F. Echelle, and C. D. Crozier. 1983. Evolution of an all-female fish, *Menidia clarkhubbsi* (Atherinidae). Evolution 37:772–784.

Echelle, A. A., and D. T. Mosier. 1981. All-female fish: a cryptic species of *Menidia* (Atherinidae). Science (Washington, D.C.) 212:1411–1413.

Ferris, S. D. 1984. Tetraploidy and the evolution of catostomid fishes. Pages 55–93 *in* B. J. Turner, editor. Evolutionary genetics of fishes. Plenum, New York.

Frankham, R. 1980. The founder effect and response to artificial selection in *Drosophila*. Pages 87–90 *in* A. Roberston, editor. Selection experiments in laboratory and domestic animals. Commonwealth Agricultural Bureau, Farnham Royal, United Kingdom.

Frelinger, J. A. 1972. The maintenance of transferrin polymorphism in pigeons. Proceedings of the National Academy of Sciences of the USA 69:326–329.

Gorman, G. C., and J. Renzi, Jr. 1979. Genetic distance and heterozygosity estimates in electrophoretic studies: effects of sample size. Copeia 1979:242–249.

Grudzien, T. A., and B. J. Turner. 1984a. Direct evidence that the *Ilyodon* morphs are a single biological species. Evolution 38:402–407.

Grudzien, T. A., and B. J. Turner. 1984b. Genic identity and geographic differentiation in trophically dichotomous *Ilyodon* (Teleostei: Goodeidae). Copeia 1984:102–107.

Gyllensten, U., R. F. Leary, F. W. Allendorf, and A. C. Wilson. 1985. Introgression between two cutthroat trout subspecies with substantial karyotypic, nuclear, and mitochondrial genomic divergence. Genetics 111:905–915.

Harris, H., and D. A. Hopkinson. 1976. Handbook of enzyme electrophoresis in human genetics. North-Holland Publishing, Amsterdam.

Hedrick, P. W. 1971. A new approach to measuring genetic similarity. Evolution 25:276–280.

Hubbs, C., and K. Strawn. 1957. Relative variability of hybrids between the darters *Etheostoma spectabile* and *Percina caprodes*. Evolution 11:1–10.

Hubbs, C. L., and C. L. Turner. 1939. Studies of the fishes of the order Cyprinodontiformes. XVI. A revision of the Goodeidae. Miscellaneous Publications Museum of Zoology, University of Michigan 42.

IUBNC (International Union of Biochemistry, Nomenclature Committee). 1984. Enzyme nomenclature 1984. Academic Press, Orlando, Florida.

Joswiak, G. R., R. H. Stasiak, and W. S. Moore. 1982. Allozyme analysis of the hybrid *Phoxinus eos* × *Phoxinus neogaeus* (Pisces: Cyprinidae) in Nebraska. Canadian Journal of Zoology 60:968–973.

Kincaid, H. L. 1983. Inbreeding in fish populations used for aquaculture. Aquaculture 33:215–227.

Kingston, D. I. L. 1979. Behavioral and morphological studies of the fishes of the family Goodeidae. Doctoral dissertation. University of Michigan, Ann Arbor.

Kirpichnikov, V. S. 1981. Genetic bases of fish selection. Springer-Verlag, New York.

Kornfield, I., D. C. Smith, P. S. Gagnon, and J. N. Taylor. 1982. The cichlid fish of Cuatro Cienegas, Mexico: direct evidence for conspecificity among distinct trophic morphs. Evolution 36:658–664.

Kurczynski, T. W. 1970. Generalized distance and discrete variables. Biometrics 26:525–534.

Leary, R. F., F. W. Allendorf, and K. L. Knudsen. 1983. Consistently high meristic counts in natural hybrids between brook trout and bull trout. Systematic Zoology 32:369–376.

Leary, R. F., F. W. Allendorf, and K. L. Knudsen. 1984a. Major morphological effects of a regulatory gene: *Pgm1-t* in rainbow trout. Molecular Biology and Evolution 1:183–194.

Leary, R. F., F. W. Allendorf, and K. L. Knudsen. 1985a. Developmental instability and high meristic counts in interspecific hybrids of salmonid fishes. Evolution 39:1318–1326.

Leary, R. F., F. W. Allendorf, and K. L. Knudsen. 1985b. Developmental instability as an indicator of reduced genetic variation in hatchery trout. Transactions of the American Fisheries Society 114:230–235.

Leary, R. F., F. W. Allendorf, S. R. Phelps, and K. L. Knudsen. 1984b. Introgression between westslope cutthroat and rainbow trout in the Clark Fork River drainage, Montana. Proceedings of the Montana Academy of Sciences 43:1–18.

Lewontin, R. C. 1974. The genetic basis of evolutionary change. Columbia University Press, New York.

Markert, C. L., and I. Faulhaber. 1965. Lactate dehydrogenase isozyme patterns of fish. Journal of Experimental Zoology 159:319–332.

Meyer, A. 1987. Phenotypic plasticity and heterochrony in *Cichlasoma managuense* (Pisces, Cichlidae) and their implications for speciation in cichlid fishes. Evolution 41:1357–1369.

Mitton, J. B., and M. C. Grant. 1984. Associations among protein heterozygosity, growth rate, and developmental homeostasis. Annual Review of Ecology and Systematics 15:479–499.

Neff, N. A., and G. R. Smith. 1979. Multivariate analysis of hybrid fishes. Systematic Zoology 28:176–196.

Nei, M. 1972. Genetic distance between populations. American Naturalist 106:283–292.

Nei, M. 1975. Molecular population genetics and evolution. North-Holland Publishing, Amsterdam.

Nei, M. 1978. Estimation of average heterozygosity and genetic distance from a small number of individuals. Genetics 89:583–590.

Nevo, E. 1978. Genetic variation in natural populations: patterns and theory. Theoretical Population Biology 13:121–177.

Nevo, E., A. Veiles, and R. Ben-Shlomo. 1984. The evolutionary significance of genetic diversity: ecological, demographic, and life history correlates. Lecture Notes in Biomathematics 53:12–213.

Ohno, S. 1970. Evolution by gene duplication. Springer-Verlag, New York.

Palmer, A. R., and C. Strobeck. 1986. Fluctuating asymmetry: measurement, analysis, patterns. Annual Review of Ecology and Systematics 17:391–421.

Phelps, S. R. and F. W. Allendorf. 1982. Genetic comparison of upper Missouri cutthroat trout to other *Salmo clarki lewisi* populations. Proceedings of the Montana Academy of Sciences 41:14–22.

Phelps, S. R. and F. W. Allendorf. 1983. Genetic identity of pallid and shovelnose sturgeon (*Scaphirhynchus albus* and *S. platorynchus*). Copeia 1983:696–700.

Ridgway, G. J., S. W. Sherburne, and R. D. Lewis. 1970. Polymorphisms in the esterases of Atlantic herring. Transactions of the American Fisheries Society 99:147–151.

Rogers, J. S. 1972. Measures of genetic similarity and genetic distance. University of Texas Publication 7213:145–153.

Ross, M. R., and T. M. Cavender. 1981. Morphological analyses of four experimental intergeneric cyprinid hybrid crosses. Copeia 1981:377–387.

Ryman, N., F. W. Allendorf, and G. Ståhl. 1979. Reproductive isolation with little genetic divergence in sympatric populations of brown trout (*Salmo trutta*). Genetica 92:247–262.

Selander, R. K., and W. E. Johnson. 1973. Genetic variation among vertebrate species. Annual Review of Ecology and Systematics 4:75–91.

Selander, R. K., M. H. Smith, S. Y. Yang, W. E. Johnson, and J. B. Gentry. 1971. Biochemical polymorphism and systematics in the genus *Peromyscus*. I. Variation in the old field mouse (*Peromyscus polionotus*). Pages 49–90 *in* University of Texas Publication 7103, Austin.

Shaklee, J. B., F. W. Allendorf, D. C. Morizot, and G. S. Whitt. 1990. Gene nomenclature for protein-coding loci in fish. Transactions of the American Fisheries Society 119:2–15

Shaklee, J. B., and C. S. Tamaru. 1981. Biochemical and morphological evolution of Hawaiian bonefish (*Albula*). Systematic Zoology 30:125–146.

Shami, S. A., and J. A. Beardmore. 1978. Genetic studies of enzyme variation in the guppy, *Poecilia reticulata* (Peters). Genetica (The Hague) 48:67–73.

Shaw, C. R., and R. Prasad. 1970. Starch gel electrophoresis of enzymes: a compilation of recipes. Biochemical Genetics 4:297–320.

Siciliano, M. J., and C. R. Shaw. 1976. Separation and visualization of enzymes on gels. Pages 185–209 *in* H. Smith, editor. Chromatographic and electrophoretic techniques, volume 2. Zone electrophoresis. Heinemann, London.

Simon, R. C., and R. E. Noble. 1968. Hybridization in *Oncorhynchus* (Salmonidae). I. Viability and inheritance in artificial crosses of chum and pick salmon. Transactions of the American Fisheries Society 97:109–118.

Smith, P. J., and D. A. Robertson. 1981. Genetic evidence for two species of sprat (*Sprattus*) in New Zealand waters. Marine Biology 62:227–233.

Smitherman, R. O., and F. E. Hester. 1962. Artificial propagation of sunfishes with meristic comparisons of three species of *Lepomis* and five of their hybrids. Transactions of the American Fisheries Society 91:333–341.

Sneath, P. H. A., and R. R. Sokal. 1973. Numerical taxonomy. Freeman, San Francisco.

Stephenson, A. B., and D. A. Robertson. 1977. The New Zealand species of *Trachurus* (Pisces:Carangidae). Journal of the Royal Society of New Zealand 7:243–253.

Turner, B. J. 1974. Genetic divergence of Death Valley pupfish species: biochemical versus morphological evidence. Evolution 28:281–294.

Utter, F., P. Aebersold, and G. Winans. 1987. Interpreting genetic variation detected by electrophoresis. Pages 21–45 *in* N. Ryman and F. Utter, editors. Population genetics & fishery management. University of Washington Press, Seattle.

Utter, F. M., F. W. Allendorf, and B. May. 1979. Genetic basis of creatine kinase isozymes in skeletal muscle of salmonid fishes. Biochemical Genetics 17:1079–1091.

Watt, W. B., P. A. Carter, and S. M. Blower. 1985. Adaptation at specific loci. IV. Differential mating success among glycolytic allozyme genotypes of *Colias* butterflies. Genetics 109:157–175.

Watt, W. B., R. C. Cassin, and M. S. Swan. 1983. Adaptation at specific loci. III. Field behavior and survivorship differences among *Colias* PGI genotypes are predictable from in vitro biochemistry. Genetics 103:725–739.

West, J. L., and F. E. Hester. 1964. Intergeneric hybridization of centrarchids. Transactions of the American Fisheries Society 93:280–288.

Whitmore, D. H. 1983. Introgressive hybridization of smallmouth bass (*Micropterus dolomieui*) and Guadalupe bass (*M. treculi*). Copeia 1983:672–679.

Whitt, G. S. 1970. Developmental genetics of the lactate dehydrogenase isozymes of fish. Journal of Experimental Zoology 175:1–36.

Whitt, G. S. 1981. Evolution of isozyme loci and their differential regulation. Pages 271–289 *in* G. G. E. Scudder and J. L. Reveal, editors. Evolution today. University of British Columbia, Vancouver, Canada.

Wright, S. 1978. Evolution and the genetics of populations, volume 4. Variability within and among natural populations. University of Chicago Press, Chicago.

Zouros, E., and D. W. Foltz. 1984. Minimal selection requirements for the correlation between heterozygosity and growth, and for the deficiency of heterozygotes, in oyster populations. Developmental Genetics 4:393–405.

Zouros, E., and D. W. Foltz. 1987. The use of allelic isozyme variation for the study of heterosis. Isozymes: Current Topics in Biological and Medical Research 13:1–59.

Chapter 6

Chromosome Preparation and Analysis

GARY H. THORGAARD AND JANE E. DISNEY

6.1 INTRODUCTION

The study of fish chromosomes has become an active area of research in recent years. Chromosome analysis can be useful for addressing a variety of evolutionary and genetic questions about fishes. Because closely related species often differ in chromosome number and morphology, analysis of chromosomes can be useful in species identification. The degree of similarity in chromosome number and morphology can be used to estimate evolutionary relationships among species.

Chromosome number and morphology also can vary within fish species. Variations within and between populations can be used to estimate evolutionary relationships, to identify stocks for management, and for other purposes. Induced polyploidy has been investigated in several fish species recently, and chromosome counts can be used to identify polyploid fish with extra sets of chromosomes. Analysis of meiotic chromosomes from germ cells can enhance understanding about inheritance patterns within species and about chromosomal homologies among species and species hybrids.

Several useful reviews of work on fish chromosomes have been published. Gold et al. (1980), Vasil'yev (1980), Sola et al. (1981), and Yu et al. (1987) listed chromosome numbers and morphologies for diverse fish species. Denton (1973), Blaxhall (1975), and Ojima (1982) reviewed methods for making chromosome preparations from fish tissues. Ohno (1974) and Gold (1979) discussed the evolutionary and genetic significance of fish chromosome studies.

The objective of this chapter is to outline several basic methods for making chromosome preparations from fish. Techniques for counting, photographing, and analyzing chromosomes are discussed. Studies of fish chromosomes sometimes are frustrating because of technical difficulties, but they can be very rewarding. We hope that the information and references presented here will allow newcomers to the field to participate in and enjoy fish cytogenetics as much as we have.

6.2 BASIC PRINCIPLES OF CHROMOSOME PREPARATION

Fish chromosomes are most easily viewed with a light microscope at the metaphase stage of mitosis when they are most highly condensed and well defined. The basic approach in making chromosome preparations is to accumulate dividing cells at metaphase and to spread chromosomes from the metaphase cells on a microscope slide for observation. The same principles apply to studies with other animals (Macgregor and Varley 1983), including humans (Yunis 1974; Priest 1977).

Actively dividing tissues are used in chromosome preparations because they are a good source of metaphase cells. Embryonic tissues, gills, anterior kidneys, intestines, and scale epithelia often are good sources of dividing cells in fish. Cultures of lymphocytes and fibroblasts are also excellent sources of dividing cells.

Chemicals are used to block dividing cells at metaphase. Colchicine, Colcemid (demecolcine), and vinblastine sulfate all may be used to prevent spindle fiber formation. Duration of exposure to the chemical may range from 20 min to 6–8 h. Longer exposures result in more highly condensed chromosomes.

A hypotonic treatment then is used to separate the metaphase chromosomes from each other. This involves exposing the cells to a solution (e.g., 1% sodium citrate or 0.56% KCl) with a lower osmotic pressure than that of the cell itself. Water then enters the cell and causes it to swell, thus separating the chromosomes.

Next, cells are fixed to preserve the contents for staining. A fixative of three parts ethanol or methanol and one part glacial acetic acid (Carnoy's fixative) is most commonly used. The fixed cells are spread on a microscope slide and stained, and their metaphase chromosomes are observed with a compound microscope.

Procedures for collecting dividing cells at metaphase from a variety of fish tissues are described in Section 6.3. We describe two basic approaches for spreading the metaphase chromosomes on slides in Section 6.4.

6.3   COLLECTING DIVIDING CELLS

Good mitotic chromosome preparations can be made from a variety of tissues sampled at different life stages of fish. Because they are growing rapidly, embryos (Section 6.3.1) and fry (Section 6.3.2) are excellent sources of mitotic cells, though they will not survive the sampling procedure. Sources from adult fish include head kidney, gill, intestine, spleen, scale epithelium, and regenerating fin (Sections 6.3.3 and 6.3.4). Of these, scale epithelium and regenerating fin tissues typically are sampled without sacrifice of the fish, but biopsies of other tissues also may be possible. In general, tissues from healthy, rapidly growing individuals give the best results because such individuals have the highest proportion of actively dividing cells.

Leukocyte or primary cell cultures also provide an excellent source of dividing cells. Blood can be collected for leukocyte culture (Section 6.3.5) without killing the fish. Primary cell cultures can be established from whole embryos and from testes, spleen, kidney, swim bladder, ovary, and liver, typically with loss of the fish (Section 6.3.6). Good chromosome spreads with excellent chromosome definition can be obtained by either method.

6.3.1   Embryos

A simple procedure, adapted from Thorgaard et al. (1981), results in well-spread chromosomes and a high mitotic index (number of dividing cells/total number of cells on a slide). (1) Dissect early embryos (before the "eyed" stage, if possible) out of the chorion into 0.9% NaCl. The saline solution prevents proteins in the egg from precipitating. The embryo can be removed from the yolk sac at this point. (2) Incubate embryos in tissue culture medium or phosphate-buffered saline containing colchicine (25 μg/mL) for 3–5 h at the optimal physiological temperature. (3)

Box 6.1   Collecting Dividing Cells from Fish Fry

The following method, from Kligerman and Bloom (1977b), will lead to good chromosome preparations from fry.

(1) Place the fry in a well-aerated 0.005–0.01% colchicine solution and allow them to swim for 6–7 h.
(2) Decapitate the fry behind the gills.
(3) Cut the head and gills into 5-mm pieces.
(4) Expose the pieces to a hypotonic solution of cold 0.56% KCl or 1% sodium citrate for 30 min.
(5) Fix the tissues by washing the cut pieces several times in freshly made mixtures of 3:1 methanol:acetic acid for at least 30 min. Tissues may be stored in fixative for several months at 4°C.

Alternatively (Gold 1974), the head and gills may be macerated with forceps in cold hypotonic solution. After 30 min in hypotonic solution, the cell suspension is centrifuged at 450 × gravity for 5 min. The hypotonic solution is decanted and the cell preparation is washed three times in fixative.

Gill arches also can be fixed whole by the method of Rivlin et al. (1985). If tissues are collected in the field, they can be stored temporarily in an ice-cold isotonic solution such as fish Ringer's (Ginsburg 1963; see also Chapter 9, Section 9.2.4.6). As soon as possible, the tissues should be transferred to cold hypotonic solution and fixed.

Transfer embryos to cold 0.56% KCl or 1% sodium citrate for 30 min, then fix them in several washes of freshly prepared 3:1 methanol:acetic acid for 30 min. Embryos can be stored in fixative for up to several months at 4°C. Baksi and Means (1988) also described a procedure for preparing chromosomes from fish embryos.

6.3.2   Fry

The methods described by Kligerman and Bloom (1977b) and by Gold (1974) both result in good chromosome preparations from fry (Box 6.1).

6.3.3   Adult Head Kidneys, Gills, Intestines, Spleens, and Testes

The methods of collecting tissues from adults for chromosome preparation are the same as those described in Box 6.1 for fry, except colchicine or Colcemid is injected directly into the fish and specific tissues can be sampled rather than the whole head.

Intraperitoneal or intramuscular injection of colchicine or Colcemid is necessary to obtain an adequate number of metaphase figures from adult tissues. Kligerman and Bloom (1977b) suggested an intraperitoneal injection of 25 µg colchicine/g of fish. We have obtained good results with intramuscular injections of 0.5% colchicine in 0.8% NaCl (0.8 mL/100 g body weight).

6.3.4 Regenerating Fins or Scale Epithelia

Fish do not have to be killed to obtain mitotically dividing cells from regenerating fins or scale epithelia, making these tissues preferable in some cases. Prepare regenerating fins as follows. (1) Clip the caudal fin of an anesthetized fish two or more days before sampling (see Chapter 8 for methods of anesthetization). (2) When transparent regenerating tissue can be seen, anesthetize the fish, clip the regenerating tissue and transfer it to tissue culture medium containing colchicine (25 μg/mL), 10% fetal calf serum, and 0.03% glutamine, and incubate the tissue at the optimum physiological temperature for the fish species involved. (3) After 2–3 h of incubation, transfer the tissue to a hypotonic 0.4% KCl solution for 30 min. (4) Aspirate the hypotonic solution away, and fix the tissue in several washes of freshly made 3:1 methanol:acetic acid.

Scales can be handled in a similar manner. Remove 5–10 scales from an anesthetized fish and incubate them in tissue culture medium as described above. Denton and Howell (1969) and Ramirez (1980) described preparations of chromosomes from scale epithelia with and without the use of colchicine.

6.3.5 Leukocyte Cultures

Another method by which chromosomes can be obtained without sacrificing the fish is to collect blood and establish blood leukocyte cultures. Successful leukocyte culture requires that the normally nondividing leukocytes be stimulated to divide in tissue culture medium. When successful, leukocyte cultures are excellent sources of dividing cells. They are the best method for making chromosome preparations from adult fish when one wants to avoid sacrificing the animal.

Hartley and Horne (1983) varied some aspects of traditional leukocyte culture to develop a simple, inexpensive method of obtaining adequate numbers of mitoses for chromosome analysis of rainbow trout. The method described in Box 6.2 provides good results and serves as a general guide for leukocyte culture for other fish species.

6.3.6 Primary Fish Cell Cultures

Primary cell cultures are desirable sources of chromosome spreads for several reasons. Solid-tissue preparations from whole fish often give a low yield of well-spread metaphases, and chromosome condensation is often inconsistent from cell to cell. In contrast, good mitotic indices and more uniformly condensed chromosome spreads can be obtained from cultured cells. Cultured cells also lend themselves well to replication banding studies, which may help to characterize fish chromosomes (Section 6.5.2).

Primary cell cultures have some drawbacks. Anomalous chromosome counts often are obtained from fish cells maintained in culture over long periods of time. For this reason, Amemiya et al. (1984) suggested that fish cells not be subcultured more than three times.

Wolf and Ahne (1982) reported that the growth potential is greatest when cell cultures are started from embryonic tissue, less with juvenile tissue, and least with adult tissue. Wolf and Quimby (1976a, 1976b) described in exacting detail how to establish monolayer cultures of fish cells from minced or trypsinized tissues. Briefly, their techniques involve four steps. (1) The tissue is removed as

Box 6.2   Collecting Dividing Cells from Leukocyte Cultures

Hartley and Horne (1983) developed the following method of leukocyte culture to obtain dividing rainbow trout cells. This variant of traditional methods also works well with other fish species.

(1) Obtain 2 mL of blood from the caudal blood vessels of a 100–150-g fish and place the sample in a sodium-heparin tube. (See Chapter 9 for blood-sampling methods.)

(2) Centrifuge the heparinized blood at 7 × gravity for 5 min at room temperature (or allow the blood cells to settle by themselves) to obtain a crude separation of whole blood. Remove the plasma supernatant, which contains the white blood cells of interest.

(3) To further purify the leukocyte-rich plasma, centrifuge it several times at 100 × gravity and transfer the supernatant after each centrifugation.

(4) Incubate 0.25 mL of plasma in 5 mL of medium 199 (other media such as Eagle's minimum essential medium or RPMI 1640 can be used instead). Medium 199 contains an antibiotic–antimycotic mixture (100 international units penicillin, 100 μg streptomycin, and 0.25 μg fungizone), 10% fetal calf serum, and 5% PHA (phytohemagglutinin, a T cell mitogen). Hartley and Horne suggested that both a T cell mitogen and a B cell mitogen be used to increase the proportion of cell cultures that respond to this treatment, because these two types of white cell may vary in quantity among individual fish. Lipopolysac-charide from the bacterium *Escherichia coli* is a B cell mitogen used to stimulate fish leukocytes; pokeweed is another.

(5) After the culture has incubated for 5 d at 20°C, add colchicine to a final concentration of 5 μg/mL and incubate for an additional 4 h.

(6) Centrifuge the preparation at 450 × gravity for 5 min and discard the medium.

(7) Suspend the cell pellet in hypotonic solution (0.56% KCl) and leave for 10 min.

(8) Centrifuge the cells, discard the hypotonic solution, and wash the cells with three changes of a cold, freshly made 3:1 methanol:acetic acid mixture. Cells can be stored in this fixative at 4°C for several months.

The temperature and duration of incubation are the most important variables to consider for species other than rainbow trout. Leukocyte culture was described by Blaxhall (1983b) for common carp and by Wolters et al. (1981) for channel catfish.

aseptically as possible with sterile instruments. Although the methods described are for ovaries, they can be applied to embryonic and other tissues as well. (2) The tissue is transferred to cold Hanks' balanced salt solution or phosphate-buffered saline and thoroughly minced; alternatively, it is minced briefly and treated with trypsin. (3) The minced tissue or cell suspension is placed in a culture flask. (4) The cells are allowed to adhere to the flask and growth medium is added. The

---

Box 6.3 Chromosome Spreads from Cell Suspensions (Air-Dry Method)

Before air-dried chromosome preparations are made, cell suspensions that have been refrigerated more than 1 d should be centrifuged and resuspended in fresh 3:1 methanol:acetic acid fixative. Then, a drop of the cell suspension is released from a pipet to fall onto a clean microscope slide from a height of about 25 cm. Many investigators use slides that have been dipped in cold water to improve spreading of the chromosomes. We have obtained good results by holding the slide at a sharp angle under a heat lamp. Blowing on the slide helps to dry the drop rapidly, and better chromosome spreads result.

Chromosome spreading on the slide can be monitored by phase-contrast microscopy. In many cases, the chromosomes from a single cell may be underspread (clumped) or overspread (widely separated) on the slide. If either problem occurs, the height from which the cell suspension is dropped can be changed: a longer fall tends to increase chromosome spreading, a shorter fall to reduce it.

When the air-dry method does not produce good chromosome spreads, the flame-dry method can be used. The cell suspension is dropped onto a microscope slide as in the air-dry technique, but the slide is passed through a Bunsen burner flame, not held under a heat lamp or blown upon. The flame removes cytoplasm from chromosome preparations, which also can be accomplished by a 4-min treatment of the prepared slide with 4 N HCl.

---

growing (mitotically dividing) cells can then be harvested for chromosome preparation, or they can be subcultured.

6.3.7 Meiotic Chromosome Preparations from Ovaries and Testes

To obtain good meiotic preparations from testes of seasonal spawners, tissues must be collected 1–2 months prior to spawning. Ovaries of seasonal spawners can be collected even earlier, because primary oocytes are arrested at the pachytene stage. Testes can be treated with hypotonic solution and fixed as described in Box 6.1. Cell suspensions can be stored several months at 4°C or in the freezer. Testes can also be fixed whole when they are collected during early stages of spermatogenesis. Ovaries can be fixed whole in 3:1 methanol:acetic acid and can be stored up to a year at 4°C or −20°C.

6.4 PREPARING CHROMOSOME SPREADS ON SLIDES

In the past, chromosome preparations from all types of tissue were made by squashing the fixed and stained tissue between a coverslip and slide. In general, the squash technique is not preferred among fish cytologists because it often leaves the chromosomes in different focal planes, making analysis and photomicroscopy difficult. Today, the methods described in the following sections are more commonly used.

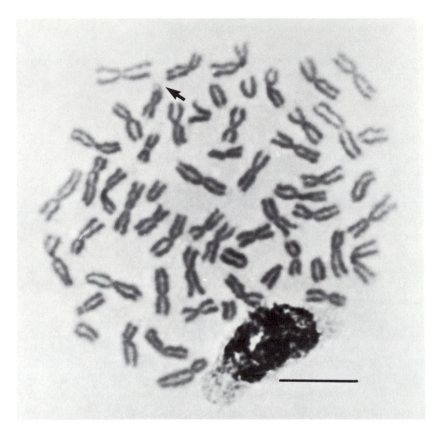

Figure 6.1 An air-dried chromosome preparation from a rainbow trout (2N = 58). The arrow indicates an association of chromosomes with secondary constrictions. Bar = 10 μm.

6.4.1 Air-Dried and Flame-Dried Preparations

Air- or flame-dried chromosome preparations are used whenever a cell suspension has been developed from macerated adult tissue (Gold 1974) or cultured cells. The procedure involves spreading chromosomes from a cell on a microscope slide by dropping cells in fixative onto the slide (Box 6.3; Figure 6.1).

6.4.2 Solid Tissue Preparations

The method of Kligerman and Bloom (1977b) is often used by fish cytologists to make chromosome preparations from embryos, fry, and actively dividing adult tissues (Box 6.4). This is the primary method by which ovarian meiotic preparations are made, and meiotic figures from testes can be prepared this way as well.

When whole gills (Rivlin et al. 1985) or scales (Denton and Howell 1969) have been fixed, (1) remove gill arches or scales from the fixative with curved forceps, (2) dab the tissue onto a clean slide to transfer swollen and fixed cells, and (3) air-dry the slide for 10 min.

6.4.3 In Situ Preparation from Cells in Culture

The in situ chromosome preparation technique involves growing cells directly on slides in petri dishes and fixing them at the middle of their logarithmic phase of

---

Box 6.4   Chromosome Spreads from Solid Tissues

Good chromosome spreads can be obtained from solid tissues by Kligerman and Bloom's (1977b) method.

(1) Remove the tissue or embryo from the fixative and blot it on a paper towel.
(2) Place the specimen in a well and add 2–3 drops of 45% glacial acetic acid.
(3) Gently mince the tissue with a spear-point needle or forceps for 1 min to form a cell suspension.
(4) Withdraw some of the suspension into a microhematocrit capillary tube and drop it onto a clean microscope slide heated to 40–50°C on a slide warmer.
(5) Withdraw some of the suspension back into the capillary tube, leaving a ring of cells on the slide.

Kligerman and Bloom (1977b) wrote a good discussion of the variables that affect chromosome spreading, such as heat, drop size, and length of time the drop remains on the warmed slide.

---

growth after a hypotonic treatment with diluted media. In situ chromosome preparations, like the one described by Schroy and Todd (1976), are fairly simple and straightforward to make, and they yield slides heavily populated with well-spread chromosome figures showing good chromosome definition. With this method of chromosome preparation, one can be sure that a single clone of cells did not take over a culture and that one anomalous cell is not responsible for what appears to be an individual polymorphism. Roberts (1968) made good in situ chromosome preparations from cultured cells of Atlantic salmon by seeding the cells on slides in Leighton tubes.

6.5   STAINING AND BANDING OF CHROMOSOMES

Unstained chromosomes on microscope slides can be observed by phase-contrast microscopy, which allows one to monitor the quality of chromosome preparations and the concentration of cells on a slide. It is desirable to stain the chromosomes for the best resolution of chromosome morphology, however.

Until about 1970, no techniques were available to differentially stain regions of individual chromosomes. The development of chromosome-banding techniques since then has led to major advances in human and mammalian cytogenetics (Hsu 1979) and to a better understanding of chromosome structure (Comings 1978; Sumner 1982). Chromosome banding, although difficult for many fish species, is becoming more widely used in fish cytogenetics.

6.5.1   Nonspecific Staining of Chromosomes

Giemsa stain is the standard stain used with the chromosome preparation techniques described in Section 6.4. It is also useful in many of the chromosome-

---

Box 6.5   Staining Chromosomes with Giemsa

It is more time-consuming to stain chromosomes with undiluted than with diluted Giemsa stain, but undiluted Giemsa stains the chromosomes more darkly and allows better resolution of detailed chromosome morphology.

Microscope sides bearing chromosome preparations are placed in undiluted Giemsa stain for 6 min; several slides can be mounted in a horizontal slide rack and stained simultaneously. The slides are transferred directly from the stain into 0.06 M NH_4OH for 2 min, then rinsed in tap water. Background staining can be removed by destaining the slides for 10 s each in acetone, a 1:1 acetone:xylene mixture, and xylene, in that order. *The destaining procedure should be done in a fume hood.*

When a diluted Giemsa stain is desired, the best is a 6% solution of Giemsa in 0.067 M Sorenson's buffer, pH 6.8. Sorenson's buffer contains 4.53 g KH_2PO_4 and 4.72 g Na_2HPO_4 per liter of distilled water. Slides are stained for 5–10 min, then rinsed in tap water.

---

banding methods discussed in Section 6.5.2. Giemsa stain is available as a powder, but it is easier to buy it as a ready-to-use liquid. A liquid Giemsa stock solution can be made from Giemsa powder by mixing 1.0 g of powder with 66 mL glycerin, heating the mixture in an oven at 60°C for 2 h, adding 66 mL methanol, and filtering the solution (Denton 1973).

Giemsa can be used to stain the chromosomes in undiluted form or after it is diluted in a sodium phosphate buffer (Box 6.5). Cover slips can be put on the stained slides with commercially available mounting media. We have found that cover slips are not necessary if care is taken to avoid scratching the slide. Immersion oil used during microscopy can be removed by rinsing slides in xylene or by carefully blotting them with lens paper.

6.5.2   Chromosome Banding

If detailed banding patterns are revealed along the arms of fish chromosomes, many advances in evolutionary and genetic research become possible. Without banding patterns, chromosome homologies can only be identified on the basis of chromosome size and the position of centromeres and secondary constrictions (Section 6.6.1). The ability to produce detailed banding patterns on the arms of mammalian chromosomes has made it possible to study chromosome rearrangements in mammalian evolution, to assign genes to individual mammalian chromosomes, and to identify specific chromosome abnormalities and understand their effects (Hsu 1979). Similar advances can be anticipated in fish cytogenetics as banding techniques become more widely applied.

To date, chromosome-banding techniques have been applied much less widely and successfully to fish than to mammals. This undoubtedly is partly because fewer researchers study fish than mammals. It also may be related to the smaller average size of fish chromosomes and to differences in chromosome structure between fish and mammals (Bernardi et al. 1985; Medrano et al. 1988). Hartley and Horne (1985) reviewed the methods that have been used to band fish chromosomes. Although the banding of fish chromosomes has not resulted in detailed analysis of banding patterns for many species as yet, the techniques for such studies now appear to be available.

6.5.2.1   C-banding

One chromosome-banding method that has been relatively successful with fish has been C-banding, a method that specifically stains constitutive heterochromatin, the genetically inactive chromosomal regions (Arrighi and Hsu 1971). Several authors have reported successful C-banding of fish chromosomes (e.g., Zenzes and Voiculescu 1975; Thorgaard 1976; Kligerman and Bloom 1977a; Gold et al. 1986). A method we have used to C-band fish chromosomes is that of Salamanca and Armendares (1974). (1) Treat the slides with 0.2 N HCl at room temperature for 30 min, then rinse them in distilled water. (2) Treat the slides with 37°C, 0.07 N Ba(OH)$_2$ for 7 min, and rinse in distilled water. Note that the Ba(OH)$_2$ solution is saturated at this concentration and temperature. (3) Incubate the slides for 2 h in 2XSSC (0.3 M NaCl, 0.03M trisodium citrate) at 60°C. This can be done in a Coplin jar. (4) Rinse the slides in distilled water and stain with 6% Giemsa in Sorenson's buffer for 10 min. A C-banded chromosome spread from rainbow trout is shown in Figure 6.2. Gold et al. (1986) substituted fluorochromes (acridine orange or DAPI) for Giemsa after the C-band treatments, and obtained excellent C-bands. Disney and Wright (1987) produced excellent C-bands and telomere staining by overtreating meiotic trout chromosomes with trypsin and raising the pH of the staining buffer.

C-banding can be useful for identifying homologous chromosomes and, in some cases, for identifying sex chromosomes (Haaf and Schmid 1984; Phillips and Ihssen 1985b). C-banding usually does not produce detailed patterns on the chromosome arms, which limits its value for many detailed studies.

6.5.2.2   Staining of Nucleolus Organizer Regions

Another banding method that has been successful with fish chromosomes has been "silver staining," a procedure that specifically stains the nucleolus organizer regions (NORs) that code for the 28 and 18S ribosomal RNAs in eukaryotes (Goodpasture and Bloom 1975). In many cases, NORs are located at the secondary constrictions (constrictions other than the centromere) on chromosomes. (S stands for Svedberg unit. A 1S molecule has a sedimentation coefficient of 1×10^{-13}s; a 28S molecule has a coefficient of 28×10^{-13}s.)

A silver-staining procedure we have used successfully (Howell and Black 1980) is as follows. (1) Two drops of a colloidal developer (2 g powdered gelatin USP [U.S. Pharmacopeia] in 100 mL distilled water and 1 mL pure formic acid) and four drops of a silver nitrate solution (4 g AgNO$_3$ in 8 mL distilled H$_2$O) are placed on a slide heated to 70°C. Gold and Ellison (1983) obtained good results using slides heated to 40–45°C. (2) A coverslip is placed over the mixed solutions. Within a few seconds, the mixture will turn yellow; a minute or two later (longer at 40–45°C) it will become golden brown. (3) The coverslip is rinsed with distilled water and the slide is allowed to air-dry. These slides should not be soaked in xylene at this point because xylene will remove the silver grains from the NOR sites. The NOR sites appear as darkly stained regions on yellow-stained chromosomes (best seen through a blue filter). A silver-stained chromosome spread from rainbow trout is shown in Figure 6.3.

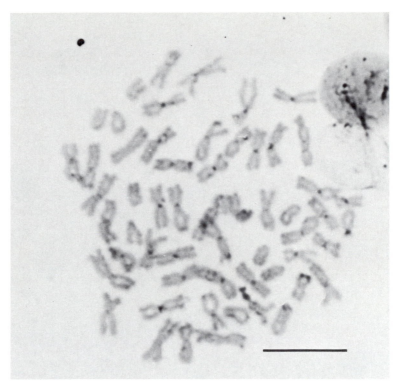

Figure 6.2   A preparation of Ba(OH)$_2$-treated, C-banded chromosomes from rainbow trout (2N = 58). Most centromere regions show dark staining, and some telomere regions also are stained. Bar = 10 μm.

Silver staining is valuable for identifying the site of the active NORs in the chromosome set. The fluorescent dye chromomycin A$_3$ appears to stain both the active and the genetically inactive (nontranscribed) NOR sites in fish chromosomes (Phillips and Ihssen 1985a; Amemiya and Gold 1986). This method thus may allow more detailed analysis of variations in NOR activity among individuals.

Variations in NOR location and activity occur both between and within species. There can be differences between species in the number of NOR sites, the type of chromosome on which they occur, and the position of the NOR on the chromosome. Comparative studies of NOR location and activity have been made among species of cyprinids (Gold 1984; Gold and Amemiya 1986; Amemiya and Gold 1988) and salmonids (Phillips and Ihssen 1985a). Within species, variations in NOR activity result in differences in the size of the silver-stained regions and differences in the number of active NOR sites (Foresti et al. 1981; Gold 1984). These NOR variations within species appear to be common, and might be useful genetic markers for evolutionary and fish-management studies.

6.5.2.3   Other Banding Methods

In addition to C-banding and NOR staining, several other banding methods have been applied to fish chromosomes. Although Q-, G-, and replication-banding methods have successfully produced bands along the arms of mammalian chromosomes, they have not been widely used to produce detailed bands on fish

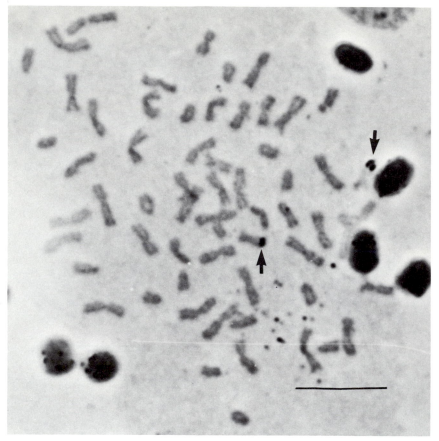

Figure 6.3   An AgNO₃-stained chromosome preparation from a rainbow trout (2N = 60), showing nucleolus organizer regions (arrows). Bar = 10 μm.

chromosomes. Both replication and G-banding show promise for this purpose, however. Below, we review the use of these banding techniques with fish—consult individual references for methodological details.

Q-banding involves use of the fluorescent dye quinacrine dihydrochloride to differentially stain regions of chromosomes. With mammals, Q-banding results in a detailed banding pattern along the chromosome arms. Fluorescent regions apparently correspond to regions rich in the nucleosides adenosine and thymidine and replicate late in the S phase of the cell cycle (Sumner 1982). Several people have applied Q-banding to fish chromosomes (e.g., Abe and Muramoto 1974; Kligerman and Bloom 1977a; Phillips and Zajicek 1982); in general, bright Q-bands appear in the same chromosomal locations as dark C-bands. Thus, Q-banding has not generated the detailed patterns on fish chromosomes that are evident on mammalian chromosomes. Q-banding, however, has proven useful in the study of intraspecific chromosome polymorphisms in lake trout and chinook salmon (Phillips and Zajicek 1982; Phillips et al. 1985) and in the identification of sex chromosomes in lake trout (Phillips and Ihssen 1985b).

G-banding involves exposure of chromosomes on the slides to one of a variety of treatments before the chromosomes are stained with Giemsa. Treatments include exposure to a hot saline solution ("ASG" method; Sumner et al. 1971) or to the proteolytic enzyme trypsin (Seabright 1971). On mammalian chromosomes, dark G-bands appear in the same locations as fluorescent Q-bands (Sumner 1982). Although several workers have been unable to induce detailed banding patterns on fish chromosomes with G-banding methods (e.g., Thorgaard 1976; Kligerman and Bloom 1977a), and although some other reports of G-banding on fish chromosomes are not convincing, several authors have reported encouragingly successful use of the technique with fish (Ojima 1982; Blaxhall 1983a; Wiberg 1983; Sola et al. 1984). It appears likely that short exposure to mitosis-arresting agents (e.g., Colcemid) and milder treatments than those used for mammals may be important for successful G-banding of fish chromosomes.

Replication banding is another promising way to produce differential banding on fish chromosomes (Ojima and Ueda 1982; Delany and Bloom 1984; Giles et al. 1988). The method involves incorporation of the base analog 5-bromodeoxyuridine in place of thymidine in DNA. The analog is added to cells during part of their last S phase before harvest for chromosome preparation. The chromosomes on the slides, after proper treatment, can be stained to reveal banding patterns that result because different chromosome regions replicate at different times during the S period. This method may prove particularly valuable for fish species that are difficult to G-band. One problem with replication banding is that a variety of banding patterns may be produced because cells from an animal or cell culture typically are not synchronized with respect to replication. Methods to synchronize cells are available, however (e.g., Yunis 1981), and might be used to produce more uniform and easily analyzed banding patterns.

Other methods are also being used to produce bands on fish chromosomes. Counterstain-enhanced fluorescent banding has made increased resolution of certain chromosome regions possible in humans (Schweizer 1981) and also appears promising for chromosome banding in fishes (Mayr et al. 1987). Restriction enzymes that clip specific four- or six-base sequences of nucleotides have provided valuable insights into chromosome structure in mammals by generating specific chromosome banding patterns (Miller et al. 1983). When applied to rainbow trout, this technique resulted in centromere or telomere banding, depending on the restriction enzyme used (Lloyd and Thorgaard 1988).

6.5.3   Sister Chromatid Exchange Analysis and Anaphase Aberrations

Sister chromatid exchanges are exchanges of chromosomal material at corresponding points between sister chromatids. They can be observed by allowing cells to grow for two generations in the presence of the base analog 5-bromodeoxyuridine and using special staining methods to differentially stain the sister chromatids. Procedures are similar to those used in replication banding. Chromosomes lacking a sister chromatid exchange have one light and one dark chromatid; those with exchanged material will have chromatids with both light and dark regions.

Sister chromatid exchange analysis is of interest because there appears to be a good correlation between frequency of sister chromatid exchange and exposure to chromosome-damaging agents (e.g., radiation and chemicals). Such analysis thus is a valuable way to study mutagenesis and environmental toxicology in fish.

Studies can be done on tissues in vivo, on cultured lymphocytes from experimental fish, or on cells exposed to agents in vitro. Consult Kligerman (1982), Park and Grimm (1982), and Vigfusson et al. (1983) for more information on sister chromatid exchange analysis.

Analysis of anaphase aberrations also should prove to be a useful way to study chromosome damage in fish (Kocan et al. 1982; Metcalfe and Sonstegard 1986). The frequency of chromosomes that lag at anaphase is correlated with exposure to damaging chemicals. This method may be especially useful with fish species that have many chromosomes, for which analysis of sister chromatid exchange is more difficult.

6.6 CHROMOSOME ANALYSIS AND PHOTOGRAPHY

6.6.1 Karyotypes and Terminology

A karyotype is a characterization of the chromosomes within a single nucleus. Images of chromosomes can be cut out of photographs and arranged in order of decreasing length and with regard to other regular features such as centromere location (Macgregor and Varley 1983). A karyotype of a male rainbow trout with the chromosomes arranged according to these conventions is shown in Figure 6.4.

Levan et al. (1964) described a classification system for chromosomes based on centromere position. Metacentric chromosomes have a centromere in the center of the chromosome. Submetacentric chromosomes have the centromere in a submedian location. If the centromere is terminal, the chromosome is termed acrocentric or telocentric. A subterminal location of the centromere defines a subtelocentric chromosome.

Macrochromosomes refer to the large subset of chromosomes in a complement that has chromosomes of two very different sizes. The small set is often dot-like, and its components are referred to as microchromosomes (Ohno 1974). Unlike microchromosomes, supernumerary or B chromosomes appear in some chromosome complements in addition to the normal diploid set and may be chromosome fragments (Pauls and Bertello 1983). Megachromosomes, often confused with macrochromosomes, are larger than other chromosomes in the karyotype (Denton 1973). Post (1973) reported megachromosomes in two fish species of the genus *Diretmus*, and Ojima and Takai (1981) reported such a chromosome in common carp.

When sex chromosomes can be identified they are set off as a pair in a karyotype (Figure 6.4). The identification is often based on size or morphological differences (see Gold 1979 for a review), or differences in banding patterns of a chromosome pair (Haaf and Schmid 1984; Phillips and Ihssen 1985b) between male and female karyotypes. When the male is the heterogametic sex, the sex chromosome pair is designated X-Y for males and X-X for females (e.g., Thorgaard 1977). When the female is the heterogametic sex, the sex chromosome pair is designated Z-W for females and Z-Z for males (e.g., Haaf and Schmid 1984). Some investigators have reported a complex sex chromosome system involving fusion between a Y chromosome and an autosome (a nonsex chromosome; Uyeno and Miller 1971; Thorgaard 1978; De Almeida Toledo et al. 1984; Carbone et al. 1987). Differences between sex chromosomes are not always

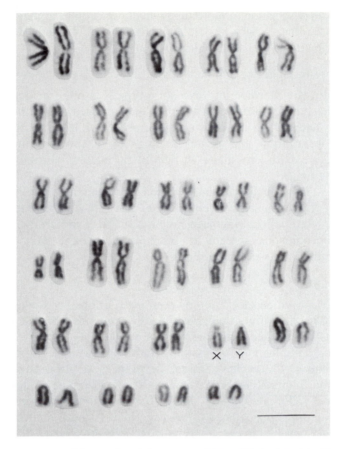

Figure 6.4 Karyotype of the male rainbow trout (2N = 58) depicted in Figure 6.1. X and Y denote the sex chromosomes. Bar = 10 μm.

apparent; in some fishes, the sex chromosomes are not morphologically differentiated from each other (Ohno 1974).

Chromosome arm number is usually reported in addition to chromosome number. Species with vastly different chromosome numbers can have similar arm numbers, suggesting that Robertsonian fusions (creation of one metacentric by the centric fusion of two acrocentric chromosomes) occurred in evolution (Ohno 1974). Centric fissions also may account for differences in chromosome number between species that have similar arm numbers. These types of rearrangements also occur within species. Thorgaard (1983) reported 2N counts of 58–64 chromosomes in rainbow trout, and all the fish studied had 104 arms.

Unlike mammals, fish with extra sets of chromosomes can be viable (Gold 1979; Thorgaard and Gall 1979). Normal individuals with two sets of chromosomes are termed *diploid* (2N); those with three sets are *triploid* (3N); and individuals with four sets are *tetraploid* (4N). Individuals with a single extra chromosome (2N+1) are termed *trisomic*, and those lacking one chromosome (2N−1) are *monosomic*.

Analysis of meiotic chromosomes involves descriptions of pairing arrangements at pachytene in females and at metaphase I in males. The term *univalent* designates an unpaired meiotic chromosome. Paired homologs are referred to as *bivalents*. *Multi-*

valent refers to an association of more than two chromosomes at meiosis I. Nygren et al. (1972), Lee and Wright (1981), and Disney and Wright (1987) described multivalent pairing in several salmonid species and species hybrids.

6.6.2 Chromosome Counting and Analysis

A freehand drawing, termed an "eye karyotype," is often made of mitotic or meiotic metaphase chromosomes as they are encountered under the microscope (Denton 1973). The camera lucida is a device used with a microscope to permit simultaneous observation and pencil tracings of a chromosome figure. An eyepiece objective with crosshairs is helpful in making chromosome counts without drawing figures.

Chromosomes may be lost from a spread because of excessive hypotonic treatment (e.g., too low a salt concentration or too long a treatment) or by rough handling of the fixed cells during slide preparation. It is important, therefore, to count enough chromosome spreads to obtain a modal count (we suggest at least 5–10 chromosome counts per individual).

6.6.3 Photography

Denton (1973) provided clear step-by-step instructions for developing photographic film and making prints. In general, he recommended Kodak products, but similar products from other companies can be used.

A suitable photographic film for photomicrography is Kodak technical pan 2415 ASA 100. Kodak D-11, a high-contrast developer, is often used to develop technical pan film. J. Gold (personal communication) recommended Diafine (made by Acufine) for developing this film. A high-contrast photograph is not desirable when subtle banding patterns need to be discerned. A more controlled development of technical pan film is permitted with HC 110 developer.

The paper on which the print is made also affects the degree of contrast. The use of "harder" papers (higher F value) results in higher-contrast prints. Kodabrome II glossy (RC) paper (F) is acceptable for publications and can be purchased in different weight grades. Kodabrome II glossy paper can be developed in Kodak Dektol (D-19) developer; the length of time the print is left in the developer also affects contrast.

The magnification of the objective, the tube factor of the microscope, and the enlargement from the negative to the print must be taken into consideration when the final enlargement factor is determined. A line of specified length (e.g., a line indicating a 10-μm span on the unmagnified preparation) is usually drawn on the photomicrograph to indicate the extent to which the image has been enlarged.

6.7 FUTURE DEVELOPMENTS

Developments in fish cytogenetics over the last 20 years typically have followed technical developments in human and mammalian cytogenetics. Activities in the latter fields make it certain that new methods for producing bands on fish chromosomes will be developed. New fluorescent dyes, treatment of elongated chromosomes, and wider use of replication and restriction-enzyme banding are likely to provide basic information about chromosome structure in fish and help generate banding patterns for evolutionary and genetic studies.

Human gene mapping has progressed rapidly as a result of advances in somatic cell genetics and in molecular biology. Genes have been assigned to individual human chromosomes through the use of human–rodent somatic cell hybrids (Hsu 1979). Restriction fragment length polymorphisms provide new genetic markers of considerable value for the generation of detailed genetic maps (Gusella et al. 1984). Up to now, gene mapping for fishes has relied on more classical methods (inheritance studies in individual families) and markers (protein polymorphisms), but these new approaches are likely to be possible and fruitful.

Exciting new techniques are being developed in mammalian cytogenetics. Fluorescence-activated chromosome sorting is making it possible to rapidly assign genes to individual chromosomes (Lebo et al. 1984). Computer analysis allows rapid and accurate construction of karyotypes of banded chromosomes (Bruschi et al. 1981); such methods are beginning to be applied in fish cytogenetics (e.g., Gold et al. 1986).

6.8   REFERENCES

Abe, S., and J.-I. Muramoto. 1974. Differential staining of chromosomes of two salmonoid species, *Salvelinus leucomaenis* (Pallas) and *Salvelinus malma* (Walbaum). Proceedings of the Japan Academy 50:507–511.

Amemiya, C. T., J. W. Bickham, and J. R. Gold. 1984. A cell culture technique for chromosome preparation in cyprinid fishes. Copeia 1984:230–235.

Amemiya, C. T., and J. R. Gold. 1986. Chromomycin A_3 stains nucleolus organizer regions of fish chromosomes. Copeia 1986:226–231.

Amemiya, C. T., and J. R. Gold. 1988 Chromosomal NORs as taxonomic and systematic characters in North American cyprinid fishes. Genetica 76:81–90.

Arrighi, F. E., and T. C. Hsu. 1971. Localization of heterochromatin in human chromosomes. Cytogenetics 10:81–86.

Baksi, S. M., and J. C. Means. 1988. Preparation of chromosomes from early stages of fish for cytogenetic analysis. Journal of Fish Biology 32:321–325.

Bernardi, G., and seven coauthors. 1985. The mosaic genome of warm-blooded vertebrates. Science (Washington, D.C.) 223:953–958.

Blaxhall, P. C. 1975. Fish chromosome techniques—a review of selected literature. Journal of Fish Biology 7:315–320.

Blaxhall, P. C. 1983a. Chromosome karyotyping of fish using conventional and G-banding methods. Journal of Fish Biology 22:417–424.

Blaxhall, P. C. 1983b. Lymphocyte culture for chromosome preparation. Journal of Fish Biology 22:279–282.

Bruschi, C., Tedeschi, P. P. Puglisi, and N. Marmiroli. 1981. Computer-assisted karyotyping system of banded chromosomes. Cytogenetics and Cell Genetics 29:1–8.

Carbone, P., R. Vitturi, E. Catalano, and M. Macaluso. 1987. Chromosome sex determination and Y-autosome fusion in *Blennius tentacularis* Brunnich, 1765 (Pisces, Blennidae). Journal of Fish Biology 31:597–602.

Comings, D. E. 1978. Mechanisms of chromosome banding and implications for chromosome structure. Annual Review of Genetics 12:25–46.

De Almeida Toledo, L. F., H. Foresti, and S. De Almeida Toledo Filho. 1984. Complex sex chromosome system in *Eigenmannia* sp. (Pisces, Gymnotiformes). Genetica 64:165–169.

Delaney, M. E., and S. E. Bloom. 1984. Replication banding patterns in chromosomes of the rainbow trout. Journal of Heredity 75:431–434.

Denton, T. E. 1973. Fish chromosome methodology. Thomas, Springfield, Illinois.

Denton, T. E., and W. M. Howell. 1969. A technique for obtaining chromosomes from the scale epithelium of teleost fishes. Copeia 1969:392–393.

Disney, J. E., and J. E. Wright, Jr. 1987. Cytogenetic analyses of a *Salvelinus* hybrid reveal an evolutionary relationship between parental species. Cytogenetics and Cell Genetics 45:196–205.

Foresti, F., L. F. Almeida Toledo, and S. A. Toledo. 1981. Polymorphic nature of nucleolus organizer regions in fishes. Cytogenetics and Cell Genetics 31:137–144.

Giles, V., G. Thode, and M. C. Alvarez. 1988. Early replication bands in two scorpion fishes, *Scorpaena porcus* and *S. notata* (order Scorpaeniformes). Cytogenetics and Cell Genetics 47:80–83.

Ginsburg, A. W. 1963. Sperm–egg association and its relationship to the activation of the egg in salmonid fishes. Journal of Embryology and Experimental Morphology 11:13–33.

Gold, J. R. 1974. A fast and easy method for chromosome karyotyping in adult teleosts. Progressive Fish-Culturist 36:169–171.

Gold, J. R. 1979. Cytogenetics. Pages 353–405 *in* W. S. Hoar, D. J. Randall, and J. R. Brett, editors. Fish physiology, volume 8. Academic Press, New York.

Gold, J. R. 1984. Silver-staining and heteromorphism of chromosomal nucleolus organizer regions in North American cyprinid fishes. Copeia 1984:133–139.

Gold, J. R., and C. T. Amemiya. 1986. Cytogenetic studies in North American minnows (Cyprinidae). XII. Patterns of chromosomal nucleolus organizer region variation among 14 species. Canadian Journal of Zoology 64:1869–1877.

Gold, J. R., C. T. Amemiya, and J. R. Ellison. 1986. Chromosomal heterochromatin differentiation in North American cyprinid fishes. Cytologia 51:557–566.

Gold, J. R., and J. R. Ellison. 1983. Silver staining for nucleolar organizing regions of vertebrate chromosomes. Stain Technology 58:51–55.

Gold, J. R., W. J. Karel, and M. R. Strand. 1980. Chromosome formulae of North American fishes. Progressive Fish-Culturist 42:10–23.

Goodpasture, C., and S. E. Bloom. 1975. Visualization of nucleolar organizer regions in mammalian chromosomes using silver staining. Chromosoma 53:37–50.

Gusella, J. F., and nine coauthors. 1984. DNA markers for nervous system diseases. Science (Washington, D.C.) 255:1320–1326.

Haaf, T., and M. Schmid. 1984. An early stage of ZW/ZZ sex chromosome differentiation in *Poecilia sphenops* var. *melanistica* (Poeciliidae, Cyprinodontiformes). Chromosoma 89:37–41.

Hartley, S. E., and M. T. Horne. 1983. A method for obtaining mitotic figures from blood leucocyte cultures of rainbow trout, *Salmo gairdneri*. Journal of Fish Biology 22:77–82.

Hartley, S. E., and M. T. Horne. 1985. Cytogenetic techniques in fish genetics. Journal of Fish Biology 26:575–582.

Howell, W. M., and D. A. Black. 1980. Controlled silver staining of nucleolus organizer regions with a protective colloidal developer: a one-step method. Experientia 36:1014–1015.

Hsu, T. C. 1979. Human and mammalian cytogenetics: an historical perspective. Springer-Verlag, New York.

Kligerman, A. D. 1982. Fishes as biological detectors of the effects of genotoxic agents. Pages 435–456 *in* J. A. Heddle, editor. Mutagenicity: new horizons in genetic toxicology. Academic Press, New York.

Kligerman, A. D., and S. E. Bloom. 1977a. Distribution of F-bodies, heterochromatin, and nucleolar organizers in the genome of the central mudminnow, *Umbra limi*. Cytogenetics and Cell Genetics 18:182–196.

Kligerman, A. D., and S. E. Bloom. 1977b. Rapid chromosome preparations from solid tissues of fishes. Journal of the Fisheries Research Board of Canada 34:266–269.

Kocan, R. M., M. L. Landholt, and K. M. Sabo. 1982. Anaphase aberrations: a measure of genotoxicity in mutagen-treated fish cells. Environmental Mutagenesis 4:181–189.

Lebo, R. V., and six coauthors. 1984. High resolution chromosome sorting and DNA spot-blot analysis assign McArdle's syndrome to chromosome 11. Science (Washington, D.C.) 225:57–59.

Lee, G. M., and J. E. Wright, Jr. 1981. Mitotic and meiotic analyses of brook trout, *Salvelinus fontinalis*. Journal of Heredity 72:321–327.

Levan, A., K. Fredga, and A. A. Sandberg. 1964. Nomenclature for centromeric position on chromosomes. Hereditas 52:201–220.

Lloyd, M. A., and G. H. Thorgaard. 1988. Restriction endonuclease banding of rainbow trout chromosomes. Chromosoma 96:171–177.

Macgregor, H., and J. Varley. 1983. Working with animal chromosomes. Wiley, New York.

Mayr, B., M. Kalat, P. Rab, and M. Lambrou. 1987. Band karyotypes and specific types of heterochromatins in several species of European percid fishes (Percidae, Pisces). Genetica 75:199–205.

Medrano, L., G. Bernardi, J. Couturier, B. Dutrillaux, and G. Bernardi. 1988. Chromosome banding and genome compartmentalization in fishes. Chromosoma 96:178–183.

Metcalfe, C. D., and R. A. Sonstegard. 1986. Relationship between anaphase aberrations and carcinogenicity in the trout embryo microinjection assay. Journal of the National Cancer Institute 77:1299–1302.

Miller, D. A., Y.-C. Choi, and O. J. Miller. 1983. Chromosome localization of highly repetitive human DNAs and amplified ribosomal DNA with restriction enzymes. Science (Washington, D.C.) 219:395–397.

Nygren, A., B. Nilsson, and M. Jahnke. 1972. Cytological studies in Atlantic salmon from Canada and Sweden and in hybrids between Atlantic salmon and sea trout. Hereditas 70:295–306.

Ohno, S. 1974. Animal cytogenetics, volume 4: Chordata 1. Protochordata, Cyclostomata and Pisces. Gebrüder Borntraeger, Berlin.

Ojima, Y. 1982. Methods in fish cytogenetics. Nucleus (Calcutta) 25:1–7.

Ojima, Y., and A. Takai. 1981. A karyotype study of colored-carp (Cyprinus carpio). Proceedings of the Japan Academy 57:7–12.

Ojima, Y., and H. Ueda. 1982. A karyotypical study of the conger eel (Conger myriaster) in vitro cells, with special regard to the identification of the sex chromosome. Proceedings of the Japan Academy 58:56–59.

Park, E.-H., and H. Grimm. 1982. Elevated sister chromatid exchange rate in lymphocytes of the Euorpean eel Anguilla anguilla with cauliflower tumor. Cancer Genetics and Cytogenetics 5:137–146.

Pauls, E., and L. A. C. Bertello. 1983. Evidence for a system of supernumerary chromosomes in Prochilodus scrofa Steindachner 1881 (Pisces, Prochilodontidae). Caryologia 36:307–314.

Phillips, R. B., and P. E. Ihssen. 1985a. Chromosome banding in salmonid fish: nucleolar organizer regions in Salmo and Salvelinus. Canadian Journal of Genetics and Cytology 27:433–440.

Phillips, R. B., and P. E. Ihssen. 1985b. Identification of sex chromosomes in lake trout (Salvelinus namaycush). Cytogenetics and Cell Genetics 39:14–18.

Phillips, R. B., and K. D. Zajicek. 1982. Q band chromosomal banding polymorphisms in lake trout (Salvelinus namaycush). Genetics 101:222–234.

Phillips, R. B., K. D. Zajicek, and F. M. Utter. 1985. Q band chromosomal polymorphisms in chinook salmon (Oncorhynchus tshawytscha). Copeia 1985:273–278.

Post, A. 1973. Chromosomes of two fish species of the genus Diretmus (Osteichthyes, Beryciformes: Diretmidae). Pages 103–111 in J. H. Schröder, editor. Genetics and mutagenesis of fish. Springer-Verlag, New York.

Priest, J. H. 1977. Medical cytogenetics and cell culture, 2nd edition. Lea and Febiger, Philadelphia.

Ramirez, S. A. 1980. A modified technique for fish karyotype analysis using scale epithelium. Copeia 1980:543–545.

Rivlin, K., J. W. Rachlin, and G. Dale. 1985. A simple method for the preparation of fish chromosomes applicable to field work, teaching and banding. Journal of Fish Biology 26:267–272.

Roberts, F. L. 1968. Chromosomal polymorphism in North American landlocked Salmo salar. Canadian Journal of Genetics and Cytology 10:865–875.

Salamanca, F., and S. Armendares. 1974. C bands in human metaphase chromosomes treated by barium hydroxide. Annales de Génétique 17:135–136.

Schroy, C. B., and P. Todd. 1976. Method for preparing chromosome spreads of glass-attached cultured animal cells. Tissue Culture Association Manual 2:287–289. (Rockville, Maryland)

Schweizer, D. 1981. Counterstain-enhanced chromosome banding. Human Genetics 57:1–14.

Seabright, M. 1971. A rapid banding technique for human chromosomes. Lancet 1971(2):971–972.

Sola, L., B. Camerini, and S. Cataudella. 1984. Cytogenetics of Atlantic eels: C- and G-banding, and DNA content. Cytogenetics and Cell Genetics 38:206–210.

Sola, L., S. Cataudella, and E. Capanna. 1981. New developments in vertebrate cytotaxonomy. III. Karyology of bony fishes: a review. Genetica 54:285–328.

Sumner, A. T. 1982. The nature and mechanisms of chromosome banding. Cancer Genetics and Cytogenetics 6:59–87.

Sumner, A. T., H. J. Evans, and P. A. Buckland. 1971. A new technique for distinguishing between human chromosomes. Nature New Biology 232:31–32.

Thorgaard, G. H. 1976. Robertsonian polymorphism and constitutive heterochromatin distribution in chromosomes of the rainbow trout (*Salmo gairdneri*). Cytogenetics and Cell Genetics 17:174–184.

Thorgaard, G. H. 1977. Heteromorphic sex chromosomes in male rainbow trout. Science (Washington, D.C.) 196:900–902.

Thorgaard, G. H. 1978. Sex chromosomes in the sockeye salmon: a Y-autosome fusion. Canadian Journal of Genetics and Cytology 20:349–354.

Thorgaard, G. H. 1983. Chromosomal differences among rainbow trout populations. Copeia 1983:650–662.

Thorgaard, G. H., and G. A. E. Gall. 1979. Adult triploids in a rainbow trout family. Genetics 93:961–973.

Thorgaard, G. H., M. E. Jazwin, and A. R. Stier. 1981. Polyploidy induced by heat shock in rainbow trout. Transactions of the American Fisheries Society 110:546–550.

Uyeno, T., and R. R. Miller. 1971. Multiple sex chromosomes in a Mexican cyprinodontid fish. Nature (London) 231:452–453.

Vasil'yev, V. P. 1980. Chromosome numbers in fish-like vertebrates and fish. Journal of Ichthyology 20(3):1–38.

Vigfusson, N. V., E. R. Vyse, C. A. Pernsteiner, and R. J. Dawson. 1983. In vivo induction of sister chromatid exchange in *Umbra limi* by the insecticides endrin, chlordane, diazinon and guthion. Mutation Research 118:61–68.

Wiberg, U. H. 1983. Sex determination in the European eel (*Anguilla anguilla*, L.). Cytogenetics and Cell Genetics 36:589–598.

Wolf, K., and W. Ahne. 1982. Fish cell culture. Pages 305–328 *in* K. Maramorosch, editor. Advances in cell culture, volume 2. Academic Press, New York.

Wolf, K., and M. C. Quimby. 1976a. Primary monolayer culture of fish cells initiated from minced tissues. Tissue Culture Association Manual 2:445–448. (Rockville, Maryland.)

Wolf, K., and M. C. Quimby. 1976b. Primary monolayer culture of fish cells initiated from trypsinized tissues. Tissue Culture Association Manual 2:453–456. (Rockville, Maryland.)

Wolters, W. R., C. L. Chrisman, and G. S. Libey. 1981. Lymphocyte culture for chromosomal analyses of channel catfish, *Ictalurus punctatus*. Copeia 1981:503–504.

Yu, X., T. Zhou, K. Li, and M. Zhou. 1987. On the karyosystematics of cyprinid fishes and a summary of fish chromosome studies in China. Genetica 72:225–236.

Yunis, J. Y. 1974. Human chromosome methodology. Academic Press, New York.

Yunis, J. Y. 1981. Mid-prophase human chromosomes: the attainment of 2000 bands. Human Genetics 56:293–298.

Zenzes, M. T., and I. Voiculescu. 1975. C-banding patterns in *Salmo trutta*, a species of tetraploid origin. Genetica 45:531–536.

Chapter 7

Histological Techniques

DAVID E. HINTON

7.1 INTRODUCTION

Strictly speaking, histology is the study of tissues, especially those minute parts beyond the reach of the naked eye. With a thorough prior knowledge of normal anatomy, the investigator uses histological analysis to detect alterations in tissues and organs (Hinton and Couch 1984). The scope of this chapter encompasses techniques necessary for the study of tissues and, to a lesser extent, cells.

Despite the inherent subjectivity of conventional morphologic findings, histology can be a powerful tool for biological assessment. For example, sections through entire adults of small fishes and through fry of larger species may be mounted on individual histological glass slides, from which general information may be obtained about a variety of tissues, organs, and organ systems (Couch et al. 1974; Couch 1984). Perhaps no other approach yields information simultaneously on so many different body sites. Histological analysis is commonly used in fisheries-related sciences to evaluate normal and pathological embryonated eggs and developing tissues (Hisaoka 1958; Rosenthal and Alderdice 1976; Daye and Garside 1980), normal (Ashley 1975; Ellis et al. 1978) and pathological anatomy related to diseases (Mawdesley-Thomas 1972; Ribelin and Migaki 1975; Roberts 1978), effects of toxicant exposures (Meyers and Hendricks 1985), nutrition (Halver 1972), carcinogenicity (Hoover 1984), and other aspects of the internal well-being of fishes.

Routine histological sections do not easily lend themselves to quantitation, although quantitative morphometric or stereological techniques are available that permit statistical analysis of histological data (Elias and Hyde 1983). Initial histological screening may steer the biologist to potentially instructive sites for subsequent, more quantitative, physiological or biochemical tests, ultimately providing a correlation of structure with function (Hinton and Couch 1984). The partial listing of major references for fish histology given in Table 7.1 indicates the types of information obtained by histological techniques.

7.2 IMPORTANT ASPECTS OF PROCESSING METHODOLOGY

Figure 7.1 illustrates steps in the preparation of histological material. Briefly, conventional processing begins with fixation of tissues or organs. Fixed tissues are trimmed and oriented, dehydrated, infiltrated with paraffin, and formed into blocks of tissue surrounded by supporting medium. These blocks are then sectioned and slices are mounted on glass slides and stained; once a coverslip is added, the section can be viewed microscopically. Alternatively, cryopreparation

191

Table 7.1 Partial listing of major fish histology references.

Reference	Description
Ashley (1975)	Comparative fish histology with emphasis on nervous and endocrine systems; references listed by organ system
Bucke (1972)	Basic methods and examples from normal and pathologic fish tissues
Ellis et al. (1978)	Concise, brief overview of histology in major teleost organs
Grizzle and Rogers (1976)	Systemic coverage of gross and microscopic anatomy of channel catfish; thorough bibliography
Groman (1982)	Histology of striped bass; well illustrated with extensive narrative and bibliography
Hinton et al. (1984)	Light and electron microscopic anatomy of selected fish tissues, with notes on fixation; extensive bibliography
Kubota et al. (1982)	Color atlas of gross and histopathology of fish tissues
Meyers and Hendricks (1985)	Histopathologic alterations associated with exposure to toxicants; thorough bibliography
Yasutake and Wales (1983)	Salmonid histology in systemic organization; extensive reference list and appendix with fixation and staining procedures

may be used. In the rapid version of cryopreparation, tissues are simply frozen, sectioned, stained, covered, and viewed. This approach may be used to localize enzymes whose activity is lost under conventional processing, but resultant preparations are not permanent and usually lack resolution of minute structural details. However, freeze-dried preparations that are embedded in suitable medium and taken through other conventional steps can provide both enzyme activity and resolution under certain conditions. Therefore, selection of a processing scheme depends on the time available, the expense that can be borne, and the level of resolution required, among other considerations.

In the rest of Section 7.2, the processing steps that lead to staining are treated in detail.

7.2.1 Fixation and Fixatives

With notable exceptions (smears of blood cells and isolated preparations of mesentery), tissues must be cut into sections thin enough to transmit light during microscopic observation. Therefore, histology is based on analysis of tissues whose cells have been killed. To prevent subsequent solubilization or breakdown of tissue components, it is first necessary to preserve or fix tissues. When an organ is removed from its blood supply, its cells die and undergo autolytic changes collectively termed necrosis (Trump et al. 1980). To minimize autolytic change and ensure optimal histological results, fixative must be applied in a timely fashion and by a route that insures rapid penetration.

Although poorly understood, fixation stops autolytic processes and, by physical and chemical means, allows tissues to withstand subsequent chemical treatment with various agents. Fixation minimizes tissue contraction and distortion, and

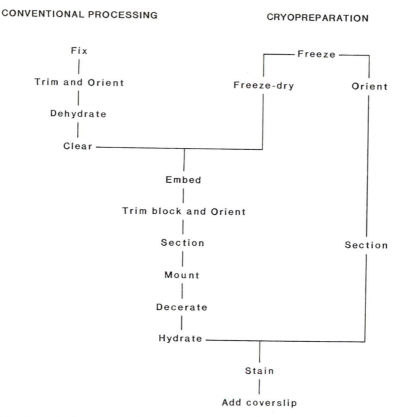

Figure 7.1 Steps in the preparation of histological sections.

maintains a state resembling that of living tissue. Fixatives have a variety of formulations. Some commonly used ones are

- 10% buffered neutral formalin: 100 mL formalin (formalin is a 37–40% solution of formaldehyde), 900 mL distilled water, 4 g monobasic sodium phosphate, and 6.5 g anhydrous dibasic sodium phosphate;
- Bouin's fixative: 750 mL saturated picric acid solution (aqueous), 250 mL formalin, and 50 mL glacial acetic acid;

and various mixtures of ethyl alcohol, acetic acid, and formalin (Luna 1968; Culling 1976; Hopwood 1977; Coolidge and Howard 1979; Humason 1979; Clark 1981). Electron microscopists frequently use mixtures of formalin and other aldehyde solutions as primary fixatives (i.e., before use of a secondary fixative, osmium tetroxide), which means that a single fixative can be used for both light and electron microscopy (McDowell and Trump 1976). Aldehyde fixatives act by cross-linking proteins, whereas alcohol and acetic acid mixtures (termed coagulant fixatives) denature or precipitate proteins, forming a sponge or meshwork that tends to hold other cell constituents (Hopwood 1977). No single fixative solution is optimal for all purposes (Hopwood 1969). For example, coagulant fixatives render subsequent electron microscopic analysis useless (Hopwood 1977). Therefore, the choice of fixative must be tailored to the desired form(s) of subsequent analysis.

When sections through small fish are desired, fixation of the entire body in certain solutions may save steps in tissue processing and, at the same time, permit sectioning through hard tissues such as bone. Acetic and formic acids decalcify structures, and various mixtures of acetic or formic acid, alcohol, and formaldehyde are commonly used by histologists studying fish tissues. Bouin's fixative is also used extensively. Fixation times of 4–24 h are recommended and the volume of fixative per container should be about 50 times that of the tissue pieces. If work schedules dictate prolonged storage, previously fixed tissues should be rinsed in 50% alcohol and then placed in 70% alcohol until subsequent workup.

Penetration of tissue occurs at a rate specific for each fixative. To insure uniform and rapid penetration, it is essential that pieces of tissue be trimmed just before they are immersed in fixative. When it can be done without destroying anatomical relationships, pieces should be reduced to less than 3 mm in one dimension (Gabe 1976). Alternatively, perfusion of fixative through the vascular bed of the fish (Hinton 1975; Hampton et al. 1985) will provide consistently excellent results.

In all phases of histological processing, care must be taken to avoid personal injury. Fixation and other preparatory procedures are best carried out inside a well-illuminated hood with an air flow of sufficient velocity to prevent exposure of the worker to fumes. The respiratory tract and particularly the eyes must be protected from fumes of fixatives such as osmium tetroxide (Pease 1960). Gloves should be worn to prevent skin contact with aldehyde mixtures. Picric acid, mainly used in Bouin's fixative, is highly explosive in a dry state and must be kept moist, preferably stored under distilled water (Brown 1969). Coolidge and Howard (1979) listed other hazards and provided safety precautions relevant to the histology laboratory. These include care in handling of sharp microtome knives; precautions with glassware, including proper disposal of broken glass; proper handling and storage of explosive and flammable materials; and prevention of chemical burns. The instrumentation of the modern histotechnique laboratory was well illustrated and described by Sheehan and Hrapchak (1980).

Several tissues from the same individual or different fish specimens are often processed as a group, so a system of labeling is essential for identification of each sample. To label glass vials, I have found that white athletic tape is satisfactory if strips are cut sufficiently long to completely encircle containers with some overlap. If applied in this way, labels will not be lost when alcohol or other processing fluids spill on them. Processing fluids dissolve many inks, so label codes should be written with a soft lead pencil. If individual tissue pieces require identification, a small strip of paper (from a white index card, for example) with penciled code may be used. This label accompanies each tissue piece through all processing steps. Alternatively, individually coded, perforated tissue holders of stainless steel or impervious plastic are available commercially.

7.2.2 Trimming and Orientation of Fixed Material

Fixed tissues are routinely trimmed before they are embedded. Much subsequent work can be eliminated if proper orientation of the specimen is maintained. Fixed tissues are firm, and pieces of individual organs or whole small fish specimens may be trimmed with a clean razor blade or scalpel to obtain desired dimensions and to cut away extraneous tissues not intended for subsequent examination. Intact specimens may be bisected transversely (yielding a cranial and a caudal piece), sagittally (yielding roughly equal right and left portions), or coronally (providing dorsal and ventral pieces). A sagittal section will bisect internal organs near the midline of the organism, such as heart, esophagus, or stomach. If the resultant pieces are positioned in paraffin molds (Section 7.2.4) with their cut or sliced surfaces down, the midline structures will be present in the first histological sections cut from the paraffin blocks. The general principle is that proper trimming and orientation of specimens will save time and effort, and emphasize structures of interest.

7.2.3 Dehydration, Clearing, and Infiltration

Paraffin wax, the most common medium for embedment (Section 7.2.4) does not penetrate tissues in the presence of water. Therefore, it is essential to remove both the water inherent to the tissue and any contributed by the aqueous fixative (Preece 1972; Gabe 1976). Dehydration is commonly achieved by passage of tissue pieces through a series of alcohol (ethanol) solutions, from 50% aqueous alcohol through 10% increments into 80% and then to several changes of 95 and 100% ethanol. However, progressive dehydration is questioned by some histologists who prefer to proceed from rinsing solutions straight to 95% and then to absolute ethanol (Gabe 1976).

Once dehydration is completed, alcohol must be removed because it is not miscible in paraffin (Drury and Wallington 1967; Gabe 1976; also see Chapter 2 of Humason 1979). If traces of alcohol are allowed to remain in tissue pieces, serious shrinkage will result and the consistency of the paraffin block will be unsuitable for sectioning.

Impregnation of tissues with an intermediate liquid, a solvent of paraffin, removes traces of alcohol and permits thorough infiltration of the mounting medium. Various solvents of paraffin have been used, including hydrocarbons, such as benzene, toluene, and xylene; cedar wood oil; and chloroform. The hydrocarbons, especially xylene, are the most commonly used and have the advantage of rapid penetration. They also "clear" tissue pieces, raising their refractive indices (Drury and Wallington 1967) and rendering them translucent. Actually a misnomer, the term "clearing" has been maintained to avoid complications in terminology with "infiltration," which is reserved for paraffin entry. Newer, commercially available, clearing agents are designed to decrease the potential for toxicity associated with the hydrocarbons.

In practice, dehydration of several tissue samples is done simultaneously. Perforated tissue holders (see Coolidge and Howard 1979) constructed of inert material (usually stainless steel wire mesh) are used to house tissue pieces and their appropriate labels. If an automated tissue processor is used, containers are placed in the first well and a mechanical program is selected and activated to carry tissue holders through progressive alcohol solutions, clearing agent, and melted paraffin (Culling 1976; Gordon and Bradbury 1977b; Coolidge and Howard 1979). Automated equipment is not essential; the entire process can be carried out by hand, and the tissue-processing steps can be integrated with other laboratory tasks.

Box 7.1 provides general steps and recommended times for tissue processing. Times vary within and between histological laboratories depending upon whether or not an automated processor is used, and on the type and dimensions of the tissue. Some authors use accelerated tissue-processing schedules, for which the fixative, alcohol solutions, and paraffin are heated to 60°C (Brown 1969).

Box 7.1   Recommended Tissue-Processing Schedules

From fixation to infiltration with an embedding medium, tissues may be processed either manually or in an automated vacuum tissue processor. In the following schedules, a repeated step means a change of medium. Room temperatures are implied unless otherwise stated.

1. Manual Processing (Brown 1969).

Step	Routine	Rapid
10% formalin	24 h	30 min at 60°C
70% ethanol	6 h	30 min at 60°C
90% ethanol	Overnight	30 min at 60°C
100% ethanol	2 h	30 min at 60°C
100% ethanol	1 h	
100% ethanol	1 h	
100% ethanol + acetone		15 min at 60°C
Acetone		15 min at 60°C
Xylene	1 h	15 min
Xylene	1 h	15 min
Paraffin	15 min at 60°C	15 min at 60°C
Paraffin	15 min at 60°C	15 min at 60°C
Paraffin	15 min at 60°C	15 min at 60°C
Paraffin	15 min at 60°C	15 min at 60°C
Paraffin	3 h at 60°C	1 h at 60°C

2. Automated Processing (times are minutes: Coolidge and Howard 1979).

Step	Tissue size			
	≥5 mm	<5 mm	<3 mm	<1 mm
80% ethanol	30 min	20 min	10 min	5 min
95% ethanol	60	20	10	5
95% ethanol	30	30	10	5
100% ethanol	60	40	20	5
100% ethanol	180	40	20	5
100% ethanol	180	40	20	5
100% ethanol	180	60	30	5
Xylene	30	20	20	5
Xylene	30	30	20	5
Xylene + paraffin (60°C)	60	60	20	5
Paraffin (60°C)	60	60	30	5
Paraffin (60°C)	60	60	30	5
Paraffin (60°C)	30	20	20	10

7.2.4   Embedment and Embedding Media

Tissues must be sectioned thinly to allow the resolution necessary for histological evaluation. Before they are sectioned, tissues must be embedded in a supporting medium of suitable hardness. Routinely, paraffin is used. Following dehydration, clearing, and infiltration by melted paraffin (57–60°C), tissues are placed in peel-away plastic or stainless steel molds (Culling 1976; Sheehan and Hrapchak 1980). Melted paraffin is added and care is given to insure orientation of tissue within the resultant block, which is allowed to cool within the mold. If stainless steel base molds are used, one of a variety of plastic adapters, shaped to fit within a rotary microtome, is attached to the cooling mold base and filled with additional paraffin. An identifying code for each tissue is transferred to each adapter and the paraffin block is allowed to harden.

In addition to paraffin, other media are available for embedment. The embedding medium most commonly employed in electron microscopy is epoxy resin. Techniques are available (Robinson 1977) for staining epoxy-embedded tissue. Stains play a very important role in the correlation of findings from light and electron microscopy, and they permit the investigator to determine specific areas of interest within the block face to facilitate thin sectioning for electron microscopy. Only a few staining procedures can be used with epoxy resins, however, and this has limited the use of epoxy as an embedding medium for light microscopy. In contrast, the water-soluble plastic resin glycol methacrylate has proved successful with a wide variety of light microscopic stains (Bennett et al. 1976; Dougherty 1981).

One major drawback to paraffin embedment is shrinkage (Bennett et al. 1976) caused by the temperature of the melted paraffin. When various processing steps were measured for their effect on tissue shrinkage, trout liver subjected to routine paraffin embedment underwent a shrinkage of approximately 25%, whereas tissue from the same liver processed for glycol methacrylate embedment and sectioning shrank only 1–2% (Hampton 1986).

Glycol methacrylate can be polymerized at temperatures low enough to preserve enzyme activity. Briefly fixed tissues to be embedded in methacrylate may be dehydrated through a graded series of aqueous to nonaqueous methacrylate monomer. This modification preserves enzyme activity normally destroyed by alcohol dehydration and gives superior resolution for localizing reaction products of the enzymes—gamma glutamyl transpeptidase, adenosine triphosphatase (Hinton et al. 1988), and carbonic anhydrase (Dobyan et al. 1982).

One problem with glycol methacrylate has been the exothermic nature of the polymerization reaction. Replacement of the catalyst, benzoyl peroxide, by one of several cyclic diketo carbon acids permits sufficient hardening of blocks without an exothermic reaction (Ruddell 1983). Thus, a unique advantage to methylacrylate embedment is the ability to dehydrate tissues in the monomer, or to freeze-dry and place them directly into the complete monomer, and then to let polymerization occur in the cold. Long-wavelength ultraviolet irradiation or storage in desiccated containers at very cold temperatures (−20 to −40°C) permits polymerization. These procedures preserve enzyme activity and allow comparison of serial sections alternatively obtained for routine light microscopy and for histo- and cytochemical tests. Recent evaluation has shown that freeze-drying and subsequently embedding tissues in low-temperature paraffin is superior to conventional paraffin processing for various immunohistochemical procedures (localization of a specific cell or tissue chemical by use of a labeled antibody; Stein et al. 1985). The improved resolution obtained from semithin sections (1–2 μm thick) of tissue embedded in glycol methylacrylate offers added precision for immuno-histochemistry.

When analysis of cell suspensions by light microscopy is needed, conventional processing techniques (Figure 7.1) usually are modified. For example, peripheral blood is commonly studied in smear preparations that are directly fixed and stained on a glass slide (Humason 1979). When suspensions of cells (for example, in tissue culture) are to be studied, they may be fixed by adding equal volumes of fixative. After each step in the dehydration process, suspensions are gently centrifuged, which concentrates the cells and allows processing fluids to be decanted. With this procedure, cellular suspensions may be dehydrated, cleared, and embedded in the appropriate medium. All subsequent steps are similar to those used in conventional processing (Figure 7.1).

In certain diagnostic procedures, frozen sections are commonly used. A 3–5-mm^2 piece of tissue is rapidly frozen on the quick-freezing block of a cryostat, or it is quenched in isopentane at $-170°C$ and subsequently transferred to a cryostat. The cryostat houses a microtome within a refrigerated box at a temperature of 0 to $-20°C$. Basic cryostat technique was described and illustrated in detail by Bancroft (1977). Tissues that have been frozen fresh, or briefly fixed and then frozen, may be sectioned and appropriately incubated to demonstrate locations of enzymes (Section 7.5). Cryostat sections usually lack the resolution provided by other methods, but they provide the most rapid means of obtaining histological information. Due to the importance and widespread use of frozen sections in human surgical pathology, histological technique manuals specify a variety of staining procedures and related techniques for them (Luna 1968; Bancroft 1977; Coolidge and Howard 1979; Humason 1979; Bancroft and Cook 1984).

7.2.5 Sectioning

Cells and tissues can be adequately viewed only in thin sections of biological materials, so the next step in the preparation of histological material involves microtomy. A variety of procedures and microtomes may be used to section embedded material; consult the histological technique manuals of Luna (1968), Bancroft (1977), Brown (1978), and Coolidge and Howard (1979) for details. Steel knives, or specially adapted razor blades with appropriate mounts, and a rotary microtome commonly are used. The paraffin block, in its holder, is clamped firmly inside the block carrier of the microtome. After it is in the microtome, but before it is sectioned, the paraffin block should be given a final trimming. Davenport (1960) provided detailed instructions for block trimming and effacement. This permits serial sectioning through an organ or tissue of interest without much space being committed to excess paraffin; less deformation and wrinkling of sections occur when paraffin margins are small.

The paraffin block with embedded tissue is sectioned as the microtome handle is revolved. Each revolution advances the tissue block a preset thickness and rotates the block face against the knife edge, forming a ribbon of sections. The first section of the ribbon should be gently grasped with fine forceps and guided away from the knife as succeeding sections are cut. When a ribbon of 10–15 cm is cut, it is detached from the knife by insertion of a dissection needle between it and the knife edge. Ribbons may be temporarily stored on black construction paper or floated onto a warm (40–44°C) water bath. For routine paraffin work, section thicknesses of 4–6 μm are common. Tissues from the nervous system, including the spinal cord, are sectioned 10–20 μm thick. Kidney biopsies are sectioned as thinly as possible, preferably in the range of 1–2 μm (Brown 1978).

If embedding media such as Epon or glycol methacrylate are used, sections as thin as 0.5–1.0 μm can be obtained. When adequately stained (Bancroft and Cook 1984), these provide better resolution than thicker sections cut through paraffin.

7.2.6 Attaching Sections to Slides

Various methods are available for attaching sections to slides. The most widely used adhesives are Mayer's albumen and gelatin (Luna 1968; Humason 1979; Coolidge and Howard 1979). A tiny drop of albumen adhesive is placed on the slide and spread with the tip of a finger over the surface, leaving a very thin film. The slide is then placed on a warming plate (37°C) and a drop or two of distilled water is placed on the slide. The section is spread on this drop. When flattened, the section may be positioned with a fine brush and the water may be drained from the slide. A simpler method is to add adhesive to the water in a flotation bath (Gordon and Bradbury 1977a); equal amounts of separate 1% stock solutions of gelatin and potassium dichromate are added to make the final concentration 0.002% (Drury and Wallington 1967). Sections are floated on the adhesive–water mixture (40–45°C). A slide is dipped under the section and lifted, whereupon the section adheres to the slide.

Care must be exercised to insure that glass slides are clean. For optimal results, even slides marked "precleaned" should be cleaned before use. To clean glass slides, place them in a glass-staining rack, immerse them in sulfuric acid–dichromate cleaning solution for a few minutes, wash them thoroughly in running water, and rinse them in distilled water.

Once paraffin sections have been mounted on cleaned and adhesive-coated slides, the slides may be placed in racks within an oven and heated overnight at 37°C. Controversy exists regarding the effect of melting paraffin during the drying process. If the tissues are well fixed and thoroughly infiltrated, drying the sections even at a temperature that just melts the paraffin (58–60°C) should not produce gross artifacts; indeed, this is widely practiced as a means of removing excess paraffin (Drury and Wallington 1980).

7.3 STAINING

Staining agents combine with tissues and improve the visibility of their components by imparting color to them. Perhaps the most commonly employed staining procedure involves hematoxylin and eosin (H&E). The H&E method illustrates the general principles of staining, which are introduced below.

7.3.1 Background Information, Staining

Hematoxylin, a naturally occurring dye derived from wood of *Haematoxylon campechianum,* is oxidized (or "ripened") to hematein (Gabe 1976). To increase the affinity of hematein for tissue components, aqueous "lakes" containing oxidized dye (organic pigment component: hematein, in the present case) plus a metal salt (inorganic carrier) are prepared. Combinations of hematein with aluminum (hemalum), iron, chromium, copper, or tungsten salts make particularly effective stains. Staining may be progressive or regressive. Nuclear staining with hemalum, for example, is progressive; the process is stopped when microscopic examination reveals that the structures stained have taken on the desired color (in this case, blue). By contrast, regressive staining initially is carried well beyond the desired point and the return process, during which the final tint is obtained, is called differentiation (Gabe 1976). When Weigert's iron–hematoxylin preparation is used to regressively stain nuclei, for example, differentiation is achieved in a few seconds by treatment with dilute (0.1–0.5%) hydrochloric acid in absolute ethanol.

Hematoxylin lakes are basic and therefore form salts with acids such as DNA and RNA. Because other tissue components are alkaline and will not form salts with a basic dye, a so-called counterstain may be used. Counterstains render the effects of another stain more discernible. Eosin is the counterstain for hematoxylin, but strictly speaking, eosin should be termed a secondary stain because it stains cytoplasmic inclusions specifically. Eosin stains cytoplasm pink.

Abundant, detailed, step-by-step procedures for staining are available (Luna 1968; Culling 1976; Gabe 1976; Bancroft and Stevens 1977; Coolidge and Howard 1979; Humason 1979; Drury and Wallington 1980; Sheehan and Hrapchak 1980; Clark 1981; Bancroft and Cook 1984). These reference books include procedures for general tissues, specific tissues (nerve processes and neuron cell bodies, bone, teeth, other connective tissue), cytoplasmic organelles and inclusions, hematologic and nuclear elements, fats and lipids, carbohydrates and mucoproteins, pigments and minerals, and microorganisms, as well as immunoenzyme methods for localizing specific antigens in tissues.

The procedures described in detail in the rest of this chapter were selected from numerous possibilities to illustrate common considerations for staining. Descriptions of histological staining techniques contain several important categories of information that should be considered before a particular technique is selected. These categories are outlined in Box 7.2.

Once a specific staining procedure is selected, several glass slides with sections attached are placed in a slide holder and subjected to each step of the procedure; this involves dipping the slides sequentially into solutions contained within glass staining dishes. The equipment needed for the laboratory staining area, the various types of staining glassware, and general preparatory considerations were illustrated and reviewed by Brown (1978).

7.3.2 H&E Stain for General Survey of Tissues

Box 7.3 describes Mayer's H&E stain as modified from Luna (1968). Some hematoxylins require up to 6 weeks for oxidation prior to their recommended use (Coolidge and Howard 1979), but Mayer's hematoxylin may be used immediately after preparation (Bancroft and Cook 1984). Other H&E procedures require additional solutions to tone the final color of hematoxylin-stained components (Culling 1976; Bancroft and Stevens 1977; Humason 1979).

7.3.3 Lipid Staining

Lipids usually are stained in frozen sections. Lipids may be lost from tissues if fat solvents such as alcohol are used, but they are insoluble or only partially soluble (as colloids) in water. They are normal constituents of cells in adipose tissue (where lipid is stored for energy production) and in special structures such as the myelin sheaths of nerves. Rarely found in a pure state, tissue lipids are

---

Box 7.2 Components of a Histological Staining Technique

Selection of an appropriate staining technique for a particular application involves several considerations. A full description of a method addresses these, and gives the following information (modified from Davenport 1960).

1. The tissues or tissue components to which the method can be applied are specified.

2. Suitable fixatives are listed.

3. The types of section that can be used (frozen, paraffin, other) are given.

4. Preparation of the section to receive the stain is described: whether the section should be mounted or unmounted; whether the section should be brought into water or into a certain percentage of alcohol before it is stained; which mordants should be used (substances that increase the affinity of tissue for a dye or stain); and other details.

5. The staining process is described clearly and completely; formulas for solutions are given or referenced, and reagents that should be kept in stock are listed.

6. Treatments that should follow staining are described, including those that may be needed to bring the final color of stained tissue components to the desired tone (differentiation or toning).

7. All subsequent steps are given, such as dehydration, clearing, and covering of stained sections.

8. The appearances of properly stained tissue components are described.

---

usually present with carbohydrates or proteins as glycolipids or glycoproteins, respectively (Bancroft and Cook 1984).

In routine laboratory procedures, fat stains are usually applied to verify the presence of lipid material. Lipids are normally revealed by Sudan dyes, which are lysochromes (Gabe 1976). These dyes are not stains in the strict sense but rather dissolve in the lipid, thus imparting color. This phenomenon is regulated by the partition coefficient between the stained lipid and the solvent for the lysochrome, formerly 70% ethanol but now more commonly 60% isopropyl alcohol or 60% triethyl phosphate (Bancroft and Cook 1984).

The oil red O technique is one of the most popular for staining lipids in present use. This technique was described by Bancroft and Cook (1984) and is related in detail in Box 7.4.

7.3.4 Carbohydrate Staining

Few types of carbohydrate occur in demonstrable amounts in tissues. Those that do are mostly complex polysaccharides such as mucins (mucosubstances, proteoglycans, glycoproteins, or glycoconjugates). One of the more commonly employed stains for complex carbohydrates is the periodic acid–Schiff's reagent technique (PAS). Substances containing vicinal glycol groups, or their amino or alkylamino derivatives, are oxidized by periodic acid to form dialdehydes, which combine with Schiff's reagent to form an insoluble magenta compound (Gabe 1976; Bancroft and Cook 1984). Because such substances are of the carbohydrate group, this method may be used to identify them. Bancroft and Cook (1984) showed that the PAS

Box 7.3   Mayer's Hematoxylin and Eosin Technique

The following description of Mayer's hematoxylin and eosin (H&E) technique parallels the categories of information outlined in Box 7.2.

1. Mayer's H&E is a survey stain for general use with most tissues.
2. The stain may be used on tissues treated with most general fixatives.
3. Use paraffin sections that have been partially deparaffinized (decerated) in
an oven at 56–60°C overnight.
4. Complete the deceration of mounted sections and hydrate them as follows.
   (a) Place slides in xylene for 2–3 min.
   (b) Transfer slides to fresh xylene for 1–2 min.
   (c) Transfer slides to absolute ethanol for 1–2 min.
   (d) Sequentially transfer slides to 95% ethanol, 70% ethanol, and 50%
       ethanol for 1 min each.
   (e) Place slides in distilled water.
5. Prepare (in advance as necessary) and apply stains.
   (a) Prepare Mayer's hematoxylin. Dissolve 1 g hematoxylin crystals in 1
       L distilled water. Then add 0.2 g sodium iodate, 1.0 g citric acid, and
       50 g chloral hydrate. Shake until all components are in complete
       solution.
   (b) Prepare a working eosin solution from a 1% alcoholic stock solution
       (The stock is 1.0 g water-soluble eosin Y, 20 mL distilled water, and
       80 mL 95% ethanol.) Add 1 part stock solution to 3 parts 80% ethanol.
       Just before use, add 0.5 mL glacial acetic acid for each 100 mL stain
       and stir.
   (c) Place slides in Mayer's hematoxylin for 15 min.
   (d) Wash slides in running tap water for 20 min.
   (e) Dip slides in the working eosin solution for 15 s to 2 min according to
       the depth of counterstain desired.
6. Differentiate slides by placing them in two 2-min changes of 95% ethanol
until excess eosin is removed. Verify the latter under a microscope; the
sections should have a clear background and the cytoplasm of cells should be
slightly pink to orange. If necessary, compare the sections to reference slides
to ascertain that they are properly differentiated.
7. Transfer slides at once to plain 95% ethanol to remove the excess
differentiating fluid. Then transfer slides to two 2-min changes of absolute
ethanol. Clear the slides (make them transparent) in two 2-min changes of
xylene. Apply mounting medium (Permount or Histoclad) and place a coverslip
on each.
8. In sections properly stained with Mayer's H&E, nuclei are blue. Regions
of cytoplasm with extensive rough endoplasmic reticulum (such as in hepatocytes and exocrine pancreatic cells) show a wispy blue to purple hue. The
remainder of the cytoplasm is various shades of pink.

Box 7.4   Oil Red O Technique for Staining Lipids

1. The oil red O technique may be used generally to stain tissues for lipids.

2. Use fresh unfixed sections or sections fixed with 10% formol calcium. Formol calcium is 10 mL formalin (40% formaldehyde solution) per 90 mL distilled water, to which calcium chloride (about 1.1 g) is added until the pH reaches 7.0.

3. Use frozen sections cut to thicknesses of 10–12 μm.

4. Mount frozen sections on glass slides with albumen adhesive (Section 7.2.6) and allow them to air-dry at room temperature. Gently rinse them first in distilled water and then in a 60% solution of isopropyl alcohol in distilled water.

5. Prepare a working oil red O solution from a stock solution. (The stock is 0.5 g oil red O dissolved in 200 mL of 100% isopropyl alcohol; this solution is warmed in a long-neck 2-L volumetric flask for 1 h in a 56°C water bath and then allowed to cool.) Add 6 parts stock solution to 4 parts distilled water. Let stand for 10 min and filter through number 42 Whatman paper.

Place the sections in the working dye solution and stain for 10 min.

6. Wash slides briefly in 60% aqueous isopropyl alcohol solution, and then wash them well in distilled water. Stain nuclei in Mayer's hematoxylin (Box 7.3) for 1–1.5 min.

7. Wash slides in distilled water, then add an aqueous mounting medium and a coverslip to each.

8. In properly stained sections, unsaturated hydrophobic lipids, triglycerides, and cholesterol esters are red, phospholipids are pink, and nuclei are blue.

---

technique is positive for glycogen, neutral mucin, some sialomucins, and strongly sulfated mucins associated with epithelial cells. The list of PAS-positive tissue components is long and includes basement membranes (basal lamina), certain microorganisms, most fungi, connective tissues (collagen and reticulin), some white blood cells, zymogen granules of the pancreas, mucous cells of the gastrointestinal tract, colloids of thyroid and pituitary, degenerated hyaline, and fibrin. Box 7.5 lists important steps in the McManus PAS technique for glycogen.

7.3.5   Connective Tissue Staining

The preceding staining methods are useful for detection of properties of cells or cellular components. Histological differentiation of the intercellular connective tissues—elastin, collagen, and reticulum—requires other techniques.

To reveal elastic fibers, which are components of the dermis, heart, and major blood vessel walls, special stains are needed. These include hydrochloric orcein–picrofuchsin, picro-indigocarmine, and Kornhauser's quad stain (Gabe 1976). In addition, elastase may be used as a control because sections treated with this enzyme should show loss of elastic fiber staining.

Collagen fibers are formed by fibroblasts and at least four types can be identified from variation in their protein contents. In pathological work, demonstration of collagen is done to show the extent of fibrosis in a given tissue or to identify specific tumors. The trichrome stains have been used extensively to demonstrate collagen. Of these, Masson's trichrome stain has been used with fish tissues. This procedure is described in detail in Box 7.6. Although more complicated than

---

Box 7.5   McManus Periodic Acid–Schiff Technique for Carbohydrates

1. The McManus periodic acid–Schiff (PAS) technique may be used generally to stain tissues for carbohydrates.
2. Freeze-dried material is best for demonstration of mucins. Formalin-fixed
tissues are satisfactory. Tissues fixed in Bouin's fluid are less satisfactory.
3. Paraffin sections are satisfactory.
4. Decerate paraffin sections on slides and hydrate them (Box 7.3).
5. Immerse slides in 1% aqueous periodic acid. Oxidation of vicinal glycol
groups takes place within 5 min at room temperature. Rinse well in distilled
water.
6. Prepare (in advance as necessary) and apply stains.
   (a) Prepare Schiff's reagent. Add 1 g basic fuchsin to 200 mL boiling
       distilled water, mix, and let cool to 50°C. Add 2 g potassium or sodium
       metabisulphite, mix, and let cool to room temperature. Add 2 mL
       Analar concentrated hydrochloric acid and 2 g decolorizing charcoal,
       mix gently, and leave overnight in the dark at room temperature.
       Filter and store in a dark container at 4°C.
   (b) Prepare Harris's hematoxylin solution. Dissolve 5 g hematoxylin in 50
       mL ethanol by heating gently at 56°C. Dissolve 100 g potassium or
       ammonium alum in 950 mL distilled water heated to 90°C; stir
       frequently. While the alum solution is still hot, add the alcoholic
       hematoxylin solution and bring the mix to a boil; stir frequently.
       Remove from heat. After the mix stops boiling, but while it is still hot,
       add 2.5 g mercuric oxide. Cool quickly and add 40 mL glacial acetic
       acid. Filter for use.
   (c) Place slides in Schiff's reagent for 15 min.
   (d) Wash slides in running tap water for 5–10 min.
   (e) Stain nuclei with Harris's hematoxylin solution.
   (f) Rinse in running tap water for 5 min.
7. Dehydrate (Box 7.3), clear (Box 7.3), and mount sections in Permount or
other suitable medium.
8. In properly stained sections, material positive for periodic acid–Schiff is
magenta; nuclei are blue or blue-black.

---

general survey stains, trichrome stains have the capacity to demonstrate features
not otherwise revealed.

Reticular fibers, actually collagen type III (Bancroft and Cook 1984), are
fine-diameter branching structures that are difficult to see in H&E preparations.
These fibers are normally best seen in liver and require special silver impregnation
methods of Gomori, of Del Rio Hortega, or of Oliveira (Gabe 1976).

7.3.6 Staining Procedures for Neural Tissues

Although H&E stains demonstrate general features of central and peripheral
nervous systems, staining procedures for neural tissues are highly specific and few
generally applicable methods exist. Clark (1981) reviewed staining techniques for
supporting elements, (i.e., astrocytes, oligodendrocytes and microglia), nerve cells,

---

Box 7.6   Masson's Trichrome Stain Technique

1. Masson's trichrome stain technique may be applied generally to tissues. It is used primarily to demonstrate fibrin or young collagen fibers, and to differentiate muscle from connective tissue.

2. Bouin's fluid is the preferred tissue fixative, but tissues fixed in 10% neutral buffered formalin may be used.

3. Use paraffin sections.

4. Prepare sections on slides for staining.

   (a) Decerate and hydrate sections (Box 7.3).

   (b) Prepare Bouin's fluid. To 1,500 mL saturated aqueous picric acid solution (21 g/L), add 500 mL formalin (37–40% formaldehyde solution) and 100 mL glacial acetic acid.

   (c) Place slides in Bouin's fluid, cover, and leave overnight at room temperature.

   (d) Wash slides in running tap water until sections are colorless.

5. Prepare (in advance as necessary) and apply stains.

   (a) Prepare an iron hematoxylin solution. Dissolve 1.0 g hematoxylin in 100 mL 95% ethanol. Dissolve 10 g aluminum chloride and 10 g ferrous sulfate in 100 mL distilled water. Mix the two solutions. To the mixture, add 2 mL concentrated hydrochloric acid and 2 mL of a saturated (9%) aqueous sodium iodate solution. Mix again, let stand 48 h, and filter for use.

   (b) Prepare a ponceau–acid fuchsin solution. Mix equal volumes of a 0.5% solution of Ponceau 2R in 1% acetic acid and a 0.5% solution of acid fuchsin in 1% acetic acid.

   (c) Stain nuclei by placing slides in iron hematoxylin for 10 min. Wash slides in running tap water for 10 min and rinse in distilled water for 1–2 min.

   (d) Place slides in ponceau–acid fuchsin solution for 2–3 min.

   (e) Wash slides in water and differentiate sections in a 1% aqueous phosphomolybdic acid solution for 5–15 min at room temperature.

   (f) Wash well in water.

6. Counterstain sections with a working light green solution for 1 min. The stock is a 2% solution of light green in acetic acid. The working solution, prepared just prior to use, is a 1:10 dilution of the stock with distilled water.

7. Wash slides in distilled water, then dehydrate, clear, and mount the sections (Box 7.3).

8. In well-stained slides, nuclei are blue-black. Muscle, fibrin, and red blood cells are red. Connective tissue is green.

Nissl granules, nerve fibers and endings, and neurofibrils. Methods that selectively stain degenerating axons are used to trace routes of axonal projections from various nuclei (collections of nerve cell bodies) within the brain and spinal cord. Applied after destruction of the neuron, these techniques may be used to trace degenerating axons through serial sections from individual nuclei to their central or peripheral destinations. Also, whole-animal injections of various tracer substances, such as horseradish peroxidase, that are taken up by axons form the basis for other techniques to determine neuronal routes within the central nervous system.

7.3.7 Enzyme Histochemical Techniques

Enzyme histochemistry (localization and identification of an enzyme in a tissue) has increased in importance as a subdiscipline of histology (Leblond 1981) and histopathology (Bancroft 1977). The number of enzymes demonstrable by histochemical techniques has increased dramatically during the past two to three decades. Enzymes are protein catalysts necessary for biochemical reactions, and their presence, absence, or relative amounts may be used to classify cells and tissues (Horobin 1982). Techniques exist for both hydrolytic and oxidative enzymes.

The basic strategy of most enzyme histochemical staining methods is to supply the appropriate substrate (plus cofactors and other essential chemical components) on which a specific enzyme acts within a tissue. An initial reaction product is thereby formed that may be trapped or subsequently reacted with a visualization reagent (also supplied) to yield a colored reaction product (see also Chapter 5, Section 5.3.5). Alternatively, the initial substrate–enzyme product may itself have a color different from that of the background tissue. Most of these techniques are not quantitative. However, when they include appropriate controls (e.g., sections incubated with improper or no substrate, or coincubation of fish and rat tissues), they permit precise localization of enzymes within regions and specific cells of tissues. Among other attributes, these techniques may provide a realistic approach to analysis of differentiation within developing cells and tissues. When the enzyme is localized within cells, the term cytochemistry rather than histochemistry is used. Papers by Bancroft (1977), Humason (1979), and Horobin (1982) and texts by Barka and Anderson (1963), Pearse (1980), and Troyer (1980) provide detailed procedures and strategies for localization of various enzymes.

7.4 MOUNTING MEDIA FOR STAINED SECTIONS

Final processing of paraffin sections on slides to make permanent preparations for storage and subsequent examination involves removal of all water and alcohol. In addition, a medium must be applied that will (1) maintain tissues in a clear and transparent condition, (2) not alter color or intensity of stains, and (3) hold the cover glass in place. Water is removed as sections are passed through successively increasing concentrations of ethanol until absolute ethanol is reached, just as was done when sections were prepared for paraffin infiltration (Box 7.1). The final reagent is xylene (or a similar solvent) that removes alcohol and renders the sections transparent (Humason 1979). Finally, a mounting medium is applied and coverslips are lowered into place, completely covering the sections. The solvent for most mounting media is xylene or toluene, but an aqueous mounting medium is used for cryostat sections.

For stained tissue sections to have maximum transparency, the refractive index of the mounting medium must be approximately that of dried protein (i.e., 1.53–1.54). The refractive index may change as a mounting medium dries, so it is important to know the final value. Of the resinous mounting media, synthetic resins are superior to natural resins in most respects. Their composition can be controlled, they are stable and inert, and they dissolve readily in xylene or toluene. The histological technique books by Bancroft and Stevens (1977) and Humason (1979) contain lists of appropriate mounting media and their refractive indices.

Various aqueous mounting media are also available for use with frozen sections; these also are treated in the texts just mentioned. If the mountant contains a volatile substance like water, and if slides are to be kept a long time, coverslips must be sealed with a ringing material. Cements such as Turtox Slide Ringing Cement are sold by supply houses. Other easily obtainable cements include Duco Cement, colorless nail polish, and asphaltum.

Consideration must also be given to the coverslip. Objective lenses of high-quality research-grade microscopes are calibrated for use with coverslips of controlled thickness. Coverslips are manufactured in a variety of flat dimensions, and a good supply of various sizes will allow diverse sections to be covered efficiently.

7.5 HIGH-RESOLUTION LIGHT MICROSCOPY

Plastic embedding media, by virtue of their hardness, may be sectioned to thicknesses of 0.5–1.0 μm, providing the microscopist with additonal resolving power to distinguish adjacent structures. In addition, solubility of the plastic monomer glycol methacrylate in water makes it possible to apply a wide variety of routine light microscopic stains. New microtomes and devices for preparing glass knives have recently been produced to facilitate sectioning of plastic material for light microscopy (Bennett et al. 1976). Initially, the only knife breakers available were designed for electron microscope ultramicrotomy, and knife width was limited. Newer glass knife breakers produce knives of 38 mm width, which is sufficient for most histological specimens. These knives can produce sections thinner than the conventional 6–8 μm, which reduces the vertical overlap of cells and thus enhances resolution. High-quality glycol methacrylate may be obtained from various suppliers.

Recent studies (Hinton et al. 1988) in my laboratory on livers from various fish species have shown that it is possible to obtain both cytochemical and routine morphologic data from serial sections. Fish liver, initially quenched in isopentane at liquid nitrogen temperature, was freeze-dried and vacuum-embedded in complete glycol methacrylate monomer. Two serial sections were incubated with substrates for respective demonstration of the enzymes gamma glutamyl transpeptidase and adenosine triphosphatase. After a third section was stained with H&E for orientation, the two enzymes were localized to specific regions of the liver in which alterations in staining properties were observed. Undoubtedly, the use of plastic-embedded material and high-resolution light microscopy will be more common in the future.

7.6 RADIOAUTOGRAPHY

The procedure used for the detection of radioactive elements in histological sections is termed "radioautography" (Leblond 1981). The investigator administers a radioactive precursor to the animal. The readily soluble precursor is transformed into a substance known as the product, which is rendered insoluble by histological fixation. Thymidine labeled with tritium (^{3}H) has been used as a precursor that is incorporated into DNA synthesized by cells preparing for mitosis. During histological fixation and processing, the unused thymidine is washed out of the tissue, but all DNA, including DNA labeled with tritiated thymidine, becomes insoluble and is retained in sections. After sections are coated with a commercially available silver grain emulsion, emissions from radioactive elements bombard the emulsion and reduce the silver. Following photographic development, black silver grains appear over sites in which the product is localized.

One major use of this technique has been to assess proliferative ability of cell populations (Leblond 1981). The technique can also be used to determine the incorporation sites of toxicants that bind covalently to tissue macromolecules. Kyono-Hamaguchi (1984) used these techniques to establish liver mitotic indices during chemical carcinogenesis in the medaka.

7.7 QUANTITATION OF THE HISTOLOGICAL IMAGE

Methods to extract numerical data from microscopic images are based on fundamental principles of geometric probability. Termed stereology (Elias and Hyde 1983), this approach coupled with computer-assisted technology (usually microcomputers are adequate) permits quantitative work to be performed in reasonable time (Rohr et al. 1976). This general approach was reviewed, with emphasis on its use in aquatic toxicology, by Hinton and Couch (1984) and Hinton et al. (1987).

Hughes and Perry (1979) used morphometry to study gill toxicity in rainbow trout exposed to heavy metals. The barrier over which gaseous diffusion must take place in the trout gill (water–blood barrier) was thicker after exposure. In addition, the ratio of outer to inner lamellar surface area on the gill filaments was altered. Both these variables returned to control levels once metals were removed from aquarium water. Zuchelkowski et al. (1986) studied the skin morphology of control and acid-stressed brown bullheads. Male and female control fish differed in their respective amounts of skin mucosubstance. Males responded to acid stress with both hyperplasia (increase in the number of mucous cells) and hypertrophy (increase in the size of individual mucous cells) of skin mucous; the female response involved the latter but not the former.

7.8 CONCLUSION

Although restricted to the analysis of "things dead," histological technique is a vital element of fisheries biology. The entry of the microcomputer into the morphology laboratory has facilitated the gathering of quantitative data amenable to statistical evaluation. This quantitative approach makes it easier for histologists to participate in multidisciplinary science. The recent developments of powerful and specific techniques of immunohistochemistry and cytochemistry are creating the tools to localize enzymes and isozymes within specific cells and organelles. The fisheries biologist will find continued need for conventional and novel approaches afforded by histological techniques.

7.9 REFERENCES

Ashley, L. M. 1975. Comparative fish histology. Pages 3–30 *in* W. E. Ribelin and G. Migaki, editors. Pathology of fishes. University of Wisconsin Press, Madison.

Bancroft, J. D. 1977. Enzyme histochemistry. Pages 287–304 *in* J. D. Bancroft and A. Stevens, editors. Theory and practice of histological techniques. Churchill Livingstone, New York.

Bancroft, J. D., and A. Stevens, editors. 1977. Theory and practice of histological techniques. Churchill Livingstone, New York.

Bancroft, J. D., and H. C. Cook. 1984. Manual of histological techniques. Churchill Livingstone, Edinburgh.

Barka, T., and P. J. Anderson. 1963. Histochemistry. Harper and Row, New York.

Bennett, H. S., A. D. Wyrick, S. W. Lee, and J. H. McNeil. 1976. Science and art in preparing tissues embedded in plastic for light microscopy, with special reference to glycol methacrylate, glass knives and simple stains. Stain Technology 51:71–97.

Brown, G. G. 1969. Primer of histopathologic technique. Appleton-Century-Crofts, New York.

Brown G. G. 1978. An introduction to histotechnology. Appleton-Century-Crofts, New York.

Bucke, D. 1972. Some histological techniques applicable to fish tissues. Symposia of the Zoological Society of London 30:153–189.

Clark, G. 1981. Staining procedures, 4th edition. Williams and Wilkins, Baltimore, Maryland.

Coolidge, B. J., and R. M. Howard. 1979. Animal histology procedures, 2nd edition. U.S. National Institutes of Health Publication 80-275.

Couch, J. A. 1984. Debate: mouse versus minnow: the future of fish in carcinogenicity testing. II. The fishy side. National Cancer Institute Monograph 65:229–235.

Couch, J. A., G. Gardner, J. C. Harshbarger, M. R. Tripp, and P. P. Yevich. 1974. Histological and physiological evaluations in some marine fauna. Pages 156–173 *in* G. La Roche, editor. Proceedings of a workshop on marine bioassays. American Petroleum Institute, U.S. Environmental Protection Agency, and Marine Technology Society, Washington, D.C.

Culling, C. F. A. 1976. Histology. Pages 1–1062 *in* S. Raphael, editor. Lynch's medical technology, volume 11, 3rd edition. Saunders, Philadelphia.

Davenport, H. A. 1960. Histological and histochemical technics. Saunders, Philadelphia.

Daye, P. G., and E. T. Garside. 1980. Structural alterations in embryos and alevins of the Atlantic salmon, *Salmo salar* L., induced by continuous or short-term exposure to acidic levels of pH. Canadian Journal of Zoology 58:27–43.

Dobyan, D. C., L. S. Magill, P. A. Friedman, S. C. Hebert, and R. E. Bulger. 1982. Carbonic anhydrase histochemistry in rabbit and mouse kidneys. Anatomical Record 204:185–197.

Dougherty, W. J. 1981. Preparation of semi-thin sections of tissues embedded in water-soluble methacrylate for light microscopy. Pages 1–26 *in* G. Clark, editor. Staining procedures, 4th edition. Williams and Wilkins, Baltimore, Maryland.

Drury, R. A. B., and E. A. Wallington. 1980. Carleton's histological technique, 5th edition. Oxford University Press, London.

Elias, H., and D. M. Hyde. 1983. A guide to practical stereology. Karger, Basel.

Ellis, A. E., R. J. Roberts, and P. Tytler. 1978. The anatomy and physiology of teleosts. Pages 13–54 *in* R. J. Roberts, editor. Fish pathology. Balliere Tindall, London.

Gabe, M. 1976. Histological techniques. Springer-Verlag, New York.

Gordon, K., and P. Bradbury. 1977a. Microtomy and paraffin sections. Pages 46–64 *in* J. Bancroft and A. Stevens, editors. Theory and practice of histological techniques. Churchill Livingstone, New York.

Gordon, K., and P. Bradbury. 1977b. Tissue processing. Pages 29–45 *in* J. Bancroft and A. Stevens, editors. Theory and practice of histological techniques. Churchill Livingstone, New York.

Grizzle, J. M., and W. A. Rogers. 1976. Anatomy and histology of the channel catfish. Auburn Printing, Auburn, Alabama.

Groman, D. B. 1982. Histology of the striped bass. American Fisheries Society Monograph 3.

Halver, J. E. 1972. The vitamins. Pages 29–103 *in* J. Halver, editor. Fish nutrition. Academic Press, New York.

Hampton, J. A. 1986. Structure of the rainbow trout, *Salmo gairdneri* Richardson, liver. Doctoral dissertation. West Virginia University, Morgantown. (Available from: University Microfilms International, Ann Arbor, Michigan.)

Hampton, J. A., P. A. McCuskey, R. S. McCuskey, and D. E. Hinton. 1985. Functional units in rainbow trout *(Salmo gairdneri)* liver. I. Arrangement and histochemical properties of hepatocytes. Anatomical Record 213:166–175.

Hinton, D. E. 1975. Perfusion fixation of whole fish for electron microscopy. Journal of the Fisheries Research Board of Canada 32:416–422.

Hinton, D. E., and J. A. Couch. 1984. Pathobiological measures of marine pollution effects. Pages 7–32 *in* H. White, editor. Concepts in marine pollution measurements. University of Maryland, College Park.

Hinton, D. E., J. A. Couch, S. J. Teh, and L. A. Courtney. 1988. Cytological changes during progression of neoplasia in selected fish species. Aquatic Toxicology 11:77–112.

Hinton, D. E., R. C. Lantz, J. A. Hampton, P. A. McCuskey, and R. S. McCuskey. 1987. Normal versus abnormal structure: considerations in morphologic responses of teleosts to pollutants. Environmental Health Perspectives 71:139–146.

Hinton, D. E., E. R. Walker, C. A. Pinkstaff, and E. M. Zuchelkowski. 1984. Morphological survey of teleost organs important in carcinogenesis with attention to fixation. National Cancer Institute Monograph 65:291–320.

Hisaoka, K. K. 1958. The effects of 2-acetylamino-fluorene on the embryonic development of the zebrafish. I. Morphological studies. Cancer Research 18:527–535.

Hoover, K., editor. 1984. Use of small fish species in carcinogenicity testing. National Cancer Institute Monograph 65.

Hopwood, D. 1969. Fixatives and fixation: a review. Histochemical Journal 1:323–360.

Hopwood, D. 1977. Fixation and fixatives. Pages 16–28 *in* J. Bancroft and A. Stevens, editors. Theory and practice of histological techniques. Churchill Livingstone, New York.

Horobin, R. W. 1982. Histochemistry. Butterworths, Boston.

Hughes, G. M., and S. F. Perry. 1979. A morphometric study of effects of nickel, chromium and cadmium on the secondary lamellae of rainbow trout gills. Water Research 13:665–679.

Humason, G. L. 1979. Animal tissue techniques, 4th edition. Freeman, San Francisco.

Kubota, S. S., T. Miyazaki, and S. Egusa. 1982. Color atlas of fish histopathology. Shin-Suisan Shingun-sha, Tokyo.

Kyono-Hamaguchi, Y. 1984. Effects of temperature and partial hepatectomy on the induction of liver tumors in *Oryzias latipes*. National Cancer Institute Monograph 65:337–344.

Leblond, C. P. 1981. The life history of cells in renewing systems. American Journal of Anatomy 160:113–158.

Luna, L. G., editor. 1968. Manual of histologic staining methods of the armed forces institute of pathology, 3rd edition. McGraw-Hill, New York.

Mawdesley-Thomas, L. E., editor. 1972. Diseases of fish. Academic Press, New York.

Meyers, T. R., and J. D. Hendricks. 1985. Histopathology. Pages 283–331 *in* G. M. Rand and S. R. Petrocelli, editors. Fundamentals of aquatic toxicology. Hemisphere, New York.

McDowell, E. M., and B. F. Trump. 1976. Histologic fixatives suitable for diagnostic light and electron microscopy. Archives of Pathology and Laboratory Medicine 100:405–414.

Pearse, A. G. E. 1980. Histochemistry. Theoretical and applied, volume 1, 4th edition. Churchill Livingstone, Edinburgh.

Pease, D. C. 1960. Histological techniques for electron microscopy. Academic Press, New York.

Preece, A. 1972. A manual for histologic technicians, 3rd edition. Little, Brown, Boston.

Ribelin, W. E., and G. Migaki, editors. 1975. The pathology of fishes. University of Wisconsin Press, Madison.

Roberts, R. J., editor. 1978. Fish pathology. Balliere Tindall, London.

Robinson, G. 1977. Electron microscopy. Pages 326–370 *in* J. Bancroft and A. Stevens, editors. Theory and practice of histological techniques. Churchill Livingstone, New York.

Rohr, H. P., M. Oberholzer, G. Bartsch, and M. Keller. 1976. Morphometry in experimental pathology: methods, baseline data and application. International Review of Experimental Pathology 15:233–325.

Rosenthal, H., and D. F. Alderdice. 1976. Sublethal effects of environmental stressors, natural and pollutional, on marine fish eggs and larvae. Journal of the Fisheries Research Board of Canada 33:2047–2065.

Ruddell, C. L. 1983. Initiating polymerization of glycol methacrylate with cyclic diketo carbon acids. Stain Technology 58:329–336.

Sheehan, D. C., and B. B. Hrapchak, editors. 1980. Theory and practice of histotechnology. 2nd edition. Mosby, St. Louis.

Stein, H., K. Gatter, H. Asbahr, and D. Y. Mason. 1985. Use of freeze-dried paraffin-embedded sections for immuno-histologic staining with monoclonal antibodies. Laboratory Investigation 52:676–683.

Troyer, H. 1980. Principles and techniques of histochemistry. Little, Brown, Boston.

Trump, B. F., E. M. McDowell, and A. U. Arstila. 1980. Cellular reaction to injury. Pages 20–111 *in* M. F. LaVia and R. B. Hill, editors. Principles of pathobiology, 3rd edition. Oxford University Press, New York.

Yasutake, W. T., and J. H. Wales. 1983. Microscopic anatomy of salmonids: an atlas. U.S. Fish and Wildlife Service Resource Publication 150.

Zuchelkowski, E. M., R. C. Lantz, and D. E. Hinton. 1986. Skin mucous cell response to acid stress in male and female brown bullhead catfish, *Ictalurus nebulosus* (LeSueur). Aquatic Toxicology 8:139–148.

Chapter 8

Anesthesia, Surgery, and Related Techniques

ROBERT C. SUMMERFELT AND LYNWOOD S. SMITH

8.1 INTRODUCTION

Anesthetics are chemical or physical agents that, with increasing exposure or concentration, first calm (sedate) an animal, then cause it successively to lose mobility, equilibrium, consciousness, and finally reflex action. In fisheries and aquaculture, the major use of anesthetics is to reduce the activity of fish during transportation and to immobilize fish so they can be handled more easily. Anesthetics, which eliminate the sensation of pain and relax the somatic muscles, also are widely used in various experimental studies to avoid suffering by the fish and to reduce the effect of trauma on the physiological variables under study. Fish surgery requires use of anesthesia, as well as aseptic techniques and antibiotics to prevent infection of the wound. Anesthesia and surgery are integral tools of many experimental studies in general physiology, endocrinology, and pharmacology.

We begin this chapter with a review of fish anesthesia, including definitions of terms, the nature of anesthesia, properties of many kinds of chemical and physical anesthetics, physiological effects of anesthetics, and some regulatory issues related to the use of chemicals on fish. We then outline the basic concepts of fish surgery, including use of anesthetics, instruments, and suture materials, and the procedures for pre- and postoperative care. Injection techniques and urinary cannulation are described because they are useful procedures that are not included elsewhere in this book.

8.2 ANESTHESIA

8.2.1 Historical Perspective

The first use of general anesthesia for human surgery in the USA was an application of ether, in about 1842 (Considine and Considine 1984) or 1846 (Davis 1968). Ether was also the first chemical anesthetic used on fish in the USA, in about 1939 (Griffiths et al. 1941). Ether was still used on fish in the 1960s by Russian scientists during surgery on digestive tracts (Krayukhin 1964).

In the early 1940s, urethane was used to anesthetize fish for physiological experiments (Hasler and Meyer 1942). Urethane was then recommended for weighing, measuring, and fin-clipping fish (Gerking 1949). By the late 1940s, urethane was used in Wisconsin fish hatcheries to facilitate handling of fish for spawning (Johnson 1954). However, use of urethane was discontinued when it was found to be carcinogenic (Wood 1956; Ball and Cowen 1959). Chloroform, an inhalation-type general anesthetic used in human medicine as early as 1847, also proved to be carcinogenic (Considine and Considine 1984) and it has been eliminated from biomedical usage.

Of the chemical anesthetics once used on fish, most have been discarded or are not widely used. Some, like urethane, ether, and chloroform, are carcinogenic; others are too slow-acting, cause undesirable physiological effects, or lack adequate efficacy. By 1986, only Finquel™ was registered by the Food and Drug Administration for use with food fish in the USA. Finquel is a formulation of tricaine (tricaine methanesulfonate); its registration label prohibits the immediate release or consumption of treated fish (Schnick et al. 1986a, 1986b). Carbon dioxide and sodium bicarbonate, although not registered as fish anesthetics, have been used as such. They are approved for use on food fish without a withdrawal period because they are "generally recognized as safe" (GRAS) as general purpose food additives (Schnick et al. 1986b).

Fish anesthesia and the nature of various anesthetics have been reviewed many times. McFarland (1959), Lumb (1963), Klontz (1964), Westhunes and Fritsch (1965), Smith and Bell (1967), Klontz and Smith (1968), McFarland and Klontz (1969), Randall and Hoar (1971), Jolly et al. (1972), Johansson (1978), Stuart (1981), Ross and Ross (1984), and Houston (see Chapter 9) updated information on kinds of anesthetics, dosages, toxicity, residues, and other information in various degrees of thoroughness to the date of their respective publication. In the USA, the U.S. Fish and Wildlife Service's National Fishery Research Laboratory, La Crosse, Wisconsin, publishes *Investigations in Fish Control,* a major source of information on anesthetics and other fishery chemicals. This laboratory is the leading U.S. facility involved with federal registration of such fishery chemicals as anesthetics, disinfectants, herbicides, lampricides, piscicides, and therapeutics. The laboratory should be contacted to obtain information on the current registration status of fishery chemicals.

8.2.2   Applications

Anesthesia has many experimental and other uses in fisheries, primarily to immobilize animals so they can be handled faster and less stressfully. Among its principal uses, anesthesia facilitates operations to weigh and measure fish, to mark and tag them, to study their physiology and behavior, to perform surgery on them, to collect them in tidepools and with scuba, to photograph them, to prepare them for live shipment and to transport them, to manually spawn them, to inject them with vaccines and antibiotics, and to collect blood and other tissues from them.

8.2.3   Terminology

Several terms are used to describe anesthesia and related phenomena. *Anesthesia* is loss of sensation over all or part of the body resulting from pharmacological depression of nerve function (Williams & Wilkins Company 1982). Anesthesia is assumed to be a reversible condition. *Anesthetics* are chemicals or physical agents (electroshock and cold) that produce anesthesia by preventing the initiation and conduction of nerve impulses; they may calm, or cause loss of mobility, sensation, or both, with or without the loss of consciousness.

Narcoanesthesia, narcotization, and narcosis imply a form of anesthesia produced by a narcotic such as scopolamine, pethidine, or morphine and other drugs of the morphine group (Horrobin 1968) that induce a stuporous condition or sleep (Butterworth and Company 1978). Morphine (an alkaloid of opium) and morphine sulfate are classified as narcotic analgesics whose abuse leads to habituation or addiction (Merck & Company 1983). Narcotics, muscle relaxants, or paralytic drugs (e.g., succinylcholine or other curariform drugs) are not true anesthetics and must not be used alone for surgical restraint (NIH 1985).

Anesthetics may be classified as general, local, and regional. General anesthesia affects the entire body; its manifestation varies from mild sedation to loss of equilibrium, consciousness, and reflex action. General anesthesia is the form usually applied to fish, which must be immobilized before a local or regionally active agent can be applied. Although the most common anesthetics used in human medicine are inhalants, which are administered through the respiratory system (cyclopropane and halothane—the chemical name for Fluothane™—are the major inhalants now used), carbon dioxide is the only gaseous anesthetic administered to fish. When administered in water, all fish anesthetics enter the circulatory system via the gills—that is, via the respiratory system.

The most common fish anesthetics, such as tricaine and quinaldine, depress the sensory centers of the central nervous system (Locke 1969). Quinaldine accumulates preferentially in the brain because it is lipid-soluble (Bradenburger Brown et al. 1972). General anesthesia may involve loss of swimming ability (immobilization) with or without loss of consciousness. Loss of consciousness for a fish is a stage of anesthesia synonymous with absence of response to stimuli, which usually means a loss of some specific reflex action as well.

Local anesthesia occurs when the loss of sensation (pain) is limited within a restricted segment of the body by action on sensory nerve endings; the animal is conscious. Local anesthetics such as benzocaine or lidocaine may be injected or applied topically to block nerve conduction from peripheral nerve endings. Benzocaine, used as a local anesthetic in veterinary practice, is used fairly widely as a general anesthetic on fish (Marking and Meyer 1985). A local anesthetic may be administered to produce a temporary block of the olfactory nerve or to immobilize a fin for study of swimming performance.

Regional anesthesia is accomplished by blocking the sensory innervation to an area with an anesthetic. Local anesthetics may be used to block nerve transmission to structures distal to the area of injection (Horrobin 1968). For example, a local anesthetic such as lidocaine hydrochloride injected near the spinal cord at midbody can sufficiently infiltrate the nerves of the spinal cord to block innervation of caudal trunk musculature without the loss of consciousness. In human medicine, an intravenous infusion of lidocaine hydrochloride is used to cause regional anesthesia by nerve blockage (Medical Economics Company 1987).

Sedation and *tranquilization* both imply calming or quieting by use of a drug (G. C. Merriam Company 1973; Williams & Wilkins Company 1982; Warren 1983). Pharmacologically, however, there are important differences between the sedative effects of early stages of anesthesia and the behavior produced by a tranquilizer. Tranquilizers form a large class of drugs, many of them derived from the compound phenothiazine, used in the treatment of anxiety, emotional stress, neuroses, and psychoneurotic states (Dorland 1981; Hampel and Hawley 1982; Warren 1983). Although psychotropic drugs such as tranquilizers may be regarded as sedative in nature, they do not provide any significant degree of analgesia.

"Animals tend to appear calm and asleep when tranquilized; however, if provoked or manipulated in such as way as to elicit pain, they are quite capable of responding. Tranquilizer drugs do not produce unconsciousness or anesthesia" (Warren 1983).

A concentration of anesthetic that produces a light sedation is desirable for transporting fish. When oxygen consumption and carbon dioxide and ammonia production are decreased, two to three times the normal weight of fish per volume of water can be accommodated (Piper et al. 1982). An ideal fish sedative should reduce oxygen consumption and stress during transportation (Marking and Meyer 1985). There is some difference of opinion about the concentration to be used to transport fish. Piper et al. (1982) recommended deep sedation (Section 8.2.4), but Dupree and Huner (1984) recommended light sedation. Opinion is unanimous, however, that a stage of anesthesia deep enough to cause loss of equilibrium and altered respiration is undesirable for transporting fish because the fish may sink to the bottom, pile up, and suffocate (Piper et al. 1982; Dupree and Huner 1984).

Analgesia means a state of insensitivity to pain. An *analgesic* is an agent for producing anesthesia, usually assumed to be an agent that provides symptomatic relief from mild pain in the conscious individual (Horrobin 1968). In human medicine, for example, aspirin (acetylsalicylic acid), other salicylates (nonsteroidal anti-inflammatory agents derived from salicylic acid), and acetaminophen are used to provide temporary analgesia for mild to moderate pain, particularly low-intensity pain of nonvisceral origin such as that associated with rheumatoid arthritis (ASHP 1985). Analgesics reduce or eliminate sensitivity to pain, but they do not have the properties needed to accomplish a full range of anesthesia.

Physical agents such as low temperature and electrical current can produce effects—hypothermia and electroanesthesia—similar to anesthesia. *Hypothermia* (Section 8.2.8.8) produces a state of torpor, a sluggishness or stagnation of function, and a lack of response to normal stimuli (Dorland 1981). It is also called *refrigerator* or *ice anesthesia* (Butterworth and Company 1978), or "cold" anesthesia (Chung 1980). *Cold narcosis* is a form of anesthesia produced in homeothermic animals by a deep lowering of the body temperature (Hoar 1975). It is said to be valuable in certain types of surgery, and usually is induced on a cutaneous surface to eliminate nerve function. In humans, nerve conduction ceases at body temperatures below 10–15°C (Schmidt-Nielsen 1975).

Electroanesthesia implies anesthetization of fish with electrical current (Section 8.2.8.9). It is important, however, to distinguish between electrical immobilization—stunning—caused by alternating current and the relaxation effect produced by direct current. Stunning is a state of involuntary muscle contraction (tetany) that renders a fish incapable of movement (Hartley 1977). The ability of alternating current to stun fish has been exploited for over 50 years to collect, measure, and mark specimens (Haskell 1940a, 1940b). The induced paralysis has been likened to anesthesia (Haskell 1940b; Madden and Houston 1976), but Hartley (1977) questioned this view because a fish stunned by alternating current is not in a relaxed state. Hartley (1967, 1977) advocated the use of direct current, which relaxes muscles and allows gill ventilation to continue freely.

8.2.4 Stages of Anesthesia

The neurological effects of general anesthesia are successive depressions of sensory centers in the brain cortex, the cerebellum, and the spinal cord; finally,

Table 8.1 Stages of anesthesia (modified from McFarland 1959 and Jolly et al. 1972).

Stage	Descriptor	Behavior, ventilation rate, and reflex action
0	Normal	Reactive to external stimuli; opercular rate and muscle tone normal
1	Light sedation	Slight loss of reactivity to external visual and tactile stimuli; opercular rate slightly decreased; equilibrium normal
2	Deep sedation	Total loss of reactivity to external stimuli except strong pressure; slight decrease in opercular rate; equilibrium normal
3	Partial loss of equilibrium	Partial loss of muscle tone; swimming erratic; increased opercular rate; reactive only to strong tactile and vibrational stimuli
4	Total loss of equilibrium	Total loss of muscle tone and equilibrium; slow but regular opercular rate; loss of spinal reflexes
5	Loss of reflex reactivity	Total loss of reactivity; opercular movements slow and irregular; heart rate very slow; loss of all reflexes
6	Medullary collapse (stage of asphyxia)	Opercular movements cease; cardiac arrest usually follows quickly

reflex actions are blocked, and the animal will not respond to a skin prick (Bell 1964). Physiological impairment develops in proportion to the length of exposure to an anesthetic.

McFarland (1959, 1960) recognized a sequence of physiological changes that indicate the depth of anesthesia. A progression of general anesthesia involves changes in reaction to visual and vibrational stimuli, equilibrium and muscle tone, and respiratory rate. McFarland (1959) used these changes to describe four stages (I–IV) of anesthesia and also a stage 0 for the normal condition, and he designated two "planes" of anesthesia for stages I and II. McFarland and Klontz (1969) later discarded the planes, and a simpler scheme of six stages (Table 8.1) has been followed by others (Jolly et al. 1972) or modified slightly (Schoettger and Julin 1967). Distinction between the stages of anesthesia varies by species; for example, the stages are less distinct in channel catfish than in salmonids exposed to tricaine (Schoettger et al. 1967).

Anesthesia begins with a slight loss of reactivity and locomotor activity (stage 1, light sedation) and progresses to almost complete loss of these functions (stage 2, deep sedation). As anesthesia further affects the spinal nerves, muscles relax, lose their tone, and cannot be voluntarily controlled (stages 3 and 4, partial and total loss of equilibrium); finally, all reflex activity disappears (stage 5).

The medullary center of respiration is affected in parallel. The respiration rate at first decreases slightly (stages 1–2) due to reduction in physical activity, but it rises as the fish loses equilibrium (stage 3). As anesthesia deepens (stages 4–5), ventilation becomes very slow, shallow, and irregular, and severe hypoxia may develop if the fish initially had a respiratory debt or if deep anesthesia is prolonged. At the extreme (stage 6), the respiratory center in the medulla ceases neurostimulation, gill ventilation stops, and the fish cannot meet a rapidly accumulating oxygen debt unless it is quickly removed to fresh water and resuscitated. During surgery, when fish are in stage-4 or -5 anesthesia, gill ventilation must be monitored or respiratory failure and cardiac arrest may occur; if anesthesia is prolonged the fish will succumb. To minimize the risk of an anesthetic overexposure, fish should be immediately transferred to fresh water if opercular activity ceases (Schoettger et al. 1967).

There is also a progressive reduction of blood pressure and heart rate by stage 5. At stages 5 or 6, the skin may conspicuously pale. The mechanism of control over melanophore contraction varies among fishes, however; it may involve nervous pathways through endocrine glands or efferent nervous pathways directly to the melanophores (Prosser and Brown 1961).

8.2.5 Exposure Conditions

Fish may be injected with an anesthetic, but usually they are subjected to general anesthesia in a dip or bath treatment with static or flowing water. Dip and bath treatments differ only in duration (Herwig 1979). The anesthetic must be water-soluble or capable of solution via carrier solvents such as acetone or alcohols. The amount of chemical in a given volume of water is the *concentration,* expressed as parts per million (ppm), milligrams per liter (mg/L), or grams per cubic meter (g/m^3). If concentrations are given as grams per gallon, they can be converted to the metric equivalent as follows: (g/gal) $\times$ 264 = mg/L. Injections are given as *dosages,* expressed as milligrams of chemical per kilogram live weight of the fish (mg/kg) or micrograms per gram ($\mu g/g$).

Toxicity of a chemical is expressed as the *lethal concentration-50* (LC50), the concentration that results in death of one-half the exposed population within a specified time, or as the lethal dose-50 (LD50), the amount administered by injection or feeding that results in death of one-half the treated population within a specified time. The *safety margin* for anesthetics is the difference between the concentration needed for effectiveness and that which is toxic to fish.

Induction time is the number of minutes required to reach a given stage of anesthesia. An induction time of 2 min to obtain a total loss of equilibrium was used by Schoettger and Julin (1969) to judge the anesthetic effect of quinaldine on fish. The *effective concentration* (EC50) of anesthetic is that which produces total loss of equilibrium in 50% of the fish in a specified time (Schoettger and Julin 1967). *Effective exposure time* is the product of anesthetic concentration and induction time. *Exposure time* refers to the total time the fish is in contact with the anesthetic solution or the time elapsed between induction of a particular level of anesthesia and removal from the anesthetic solution. Procedures that require long exposure may result in a prolonged recovery time, severe oxygen debt, anoxia, or subsequent death of the subject. *Recovery time* is the time required for the animal to return to full mobility after it is removed from the anesthetic solution; physiological variables altered by anesthesia, however, require more time to return to normal. *Efficacy,* as defined by Gilderhus and Marking (1987), is an anesthetic's ability to make fish handleable with an induction time of 3 min or less, to allow the fish to recover in 10 min or less, and to cause no mortality after a 15-min exposure.

Drug Interactions.   Anesthetics may be used to immobilize fish for injection of hormones, vaccines, antibiotics, and various pharmacological agents. When an anesthetic and two or more other drugs are used simultaneously, there is opportunity for chemical interaction; one drug may potentiate a second (synergism) or nullify its usual action. Sometimes an interaction can be exploited to enhance anesthesia. For example, the duration of effect of local or regional anesthetic drugs can be doubled if they are accompanied by 0.5–1.0 mL of a 1:100 solution of epinephrine or by a product containing epinephrine (Elmore 1981). Schoettger and Steucke (1972) proposed a synergistic combination of tricaine and quinaldine or quinaldine sulfonate: "the concentration of each required for effective anesthesia is substantially less than that required when either of the compounds is used alone." In other cases, however, drug interactions have undesirable effects. Houston notes in Chapter 9 (Section 9.2.2), for example, that use of tricaine in conjunction with EDTA (an anticoagulant) causes some hemolysis, which increases with storage. Researchers should be aware of, and alert for, drug interactions that may enhance or compromise a procedure.

Precautions. Until experience is attained with a given anesthetic for a given species, it is advisable to first test anesthetic concentrations on a few fish under conditions that simulate those anticipated for a larger or more sensitive experiment. One can place fish in a 20-L glass aquarium and observe behavioral changes while raising the concentration in increments of about 5–10 mg/L every 5–10 min until the desired stage of anesthesia is obtained. After the fish are returned to fresh water, the recovery time is determined, and the fish should be observed up to 96 h for delayed mortality. The concentration of anesthetic should not be stronger than that needed for an induction time of about 3 min; the risk of mortality increases as induction time decreases (i.e., risk is directly proportional to concentration and inversely proportional to induction time). When possible, a bioassay should be conducted to obtain more precise information. See Sprague (1973) and APHA et al. (1989) for standard bioassay procedures.

8.2.6 Characteristics of an Ideal Anesthetic

Selection of a general anesthetic for fish involves consideration of toxicity (or, conversely, safety to user and subject), efficacy, cost, restrictions on use, and intended use. Marking and Meyer (1985) listed several characteristics of an ideal anesthetic.

1. It has an induction time of less that 15 min and preferably less than 3 min.
2. Recovery time after its use is short, 5 min or less.
3. It is nontoxic to fish and has a large safety factor.
4. It is easy to handle and not harmful to humans during normal use.
5. It has no persistent effects on fish physiology and behavior.
6. It is rapidly excreted or metabolized, leaving no residues and requiring no withdrawal time.
7. It engenders no cumulative effects or problems from repeated exposures.
8. It is inexpensive.

In addition to these considerations, the choice of an anesthetic depends on the nature of the experiment, the species of fish, the expected duration of anesthesia, and whether or not the animal is to be used as human food.

8.2.7   Restrictions on Use of Fishery Chemicals

For environmental and human safety, the production, sale, and use of chemicals is regulated by government agencies. In the USA, the Environmental Protection Agency (EPA) is charged with control over the use of pesticides, and the use of chemicals on food fish is subject to requirements set forth by the Food and Drug Administration (FDA) to protect human health (Schnick et al. 1986b). When fish are exposed to an anesthetic, residues or metabolites of the anesthetic remain in the flesh for varying intervals until they are excreted or metabolized. Therefore, the FDA may require a specific withdrawal time for depuration (cleansing) before the animal can be used directly for food or released into the environment where it may be captured for food (Marking and Meyer 1985).

In 1979, 25 drugs and chemicals were registered for fishery uses in the USA (Schnick et al. 1979). By 1985, 26 drugs and chemicals (not all the same as in 1979) were registered: 13 algicides and herbicides, 6 therapeutants, 1 anesthetic (Finquel™), 2 disinfecting agents, and 4 piscicides and lampricides (Schnick 1985; Schnick et al. 1986b).

"A *registered compound* is an available commercial product bearing an Environmental Protection Agency (EPA) or Food and Drug Administration (FDA) label specifying its allowed uses" (Schnick et al. 1986a). Products with a registration label for fishery purposes must be used according to restrictions on that label and purchased from the approved label holder. Generic products are sold without a label and unlabeled chemicals cannot be used (Schnick 1985). Thus, except for experimental purposes, U.S. law does not authorize use of a generic form of tricaine in lieu of the registered product Finquel. If the sponsor of Finquel does not package, market, or sell the rights to it, legal use of this anesthetic may cease (Anonymous 1985). Carbon dioxide and sodium bicarbonate are *approved* for aquatic use, but do not have FDA registration labels because they are "generally recognized as safe" (GRAS) for use with food (Schnick et al. 1986b).

Warnings.   Use of chemicals that are not registered must be limited to situations in which the fish will be properly disposed of (incinerated or buried) after use. When a chemical is purchased from a supplier of fishery chemicals, the label may have a disclaimer such as:

> Solely for use or sale as a chemical; for laboratory and *in vitro* studies; for investigational purposes in laboratory research animals only. Not intended for drug or clinical use in humans or for food or food additive use.

"User beware" is an admonition to heed; the experimentalist using unregistered chemicals must evaluate the full scope of activity of the chemical or drug being used. Urethane, a potent carcinogen (Ball and Cowen 1959), is an example of the hazard an untested chemical may pose to the user. Regulatory restrictions and potential hazard to the user highlight a continuing need to identify anesthetics that produce the desired effect, are safe to the user, and have zero withdrawal times (Schnick et al. 1986a).

Alternatives.   The alternatives to Finquel as anesthetics for food fish have been mentioned above. Among chemicals listed as GRAS by the FDA, only carbon dioxide and sodium bicarbonate have known utility as anesthetics. The anesthetic properties of carbon dioxide have been known for a long time; although its use is currently minor, restrictions on Finquel have prompted renewed interest in it. However, carbon dioxide is more difficult to use and has a 5-min induction time at concentrations of 142–642 mg/L. Other alternatives are the use of electricity and low temperatures.

8.2.8 Characteristics of Major Anesthetics

In spite of restrictions for use on food fish, many compounds have been and continue to be used as anesthetics on nonfood fish and in research (Table 8.2). Piper et al. (1982) listed tricaine, ethyl aminobenzoate (benzocaine), and quinaldine as the most popular fish anesthetics currently used for spawning operations in U.S. fish hatcheries, and tricaine, secobarbital sodium, and Amytal Sodium™ as those most often used to transport live fishes. Dupree and Huner (1984) listed quinaldine, tricaine, tertiary amyl alcohol, methylpentynol, carbonic acid, and sodium bicarbonate for use in fish culture to sedate and immobilize fish. Among 183 fishery workers (60% of them hatchery personnel) who responded to a survey by Marking and Meyer (1985), 79% used tricaine, 22% used quinaldine, and 10% used carbon dioxide; other anesthetics cited were 2-phenoxyethanol, methylpentynol, sodium chloride, benzocaine, etomidate, Chloretone™, chlorobutanol, electricity, and tobacco juice (nicotine).

Some anesthetics may be more suitable for certain species than for others. For example, "quinaldine appears to be the most practical for warmwater fishes, although it may be damaging to trout and some other species"; tricaine "may be the chemical [anesthetic] of choice for trout" (Dupree and Huner 1984).

The concentration needed to obtain sedation or full anesthesia (loss of equilibrium and reflexes, stage 4) by a given anesthetic can be affected by many factors, but principally by the species of fish to be anesthetized. Fish differ greatly among species in the concentration of chemical required to bring them to a given level of anesthesia, their tolerance of a given chemical, and their recovery time. Intraspecific variables, including age, sex, diet, and individual health factors, are also important. In addition, the optimum anesthetic concentration varies with the biomass of fish per unit volume of water, water temperature and hardness, induction time, and duration of exposure. In general, higher temperatures reduce both induction and recovery times.

Many chemicals have been used as anesthetics for fish (Table 8.2), but some are not discussed here because they are carcinogens, narcotics, or barbiturates. Other chemicals are omitted because they have rarely been used or are of dubious value. Tricaine, quinaldine sulfate, benzocaine, and 2-phenoxyethanol were the most efficacious of 16 anesthetic chemicals tested on rainbow trout by Gilderhus and Marking (1987). The volume of available literature varies greatly among the chemicals treated in the following sections, and we cite only part of the literature for the well-documented ones. Tricaine has received more attention than any other chemical because it is the most commonly used fish anesthetic in North America (Marking and Meyer 1985); it was patented in Germany in 1927 and in the USA in 1928 (Merck & Company 1983). The original patent rights have expired, but only one formulation of tricaine, Finquel, has been registered as a fish anesthetic.

Table 8.2 Chemicals and drugs that have been used as fish anesthetics.[a] Compounds described in detail in Chapter 8 are preceded by an asterisk.

Amobarbital: 5-ethyl-5-(3-methylbutyl)-2,4,6(1H,3H,5H)-pyrimidinetrione; 2,4,6(1H,3H,5H)-pyrimidinetrione is an alternative name for barbituric acid
Amobarbital sodium: sodium salt of amobarbital
Amytal Sodium™: sodium salt of amobarbital
Amyl alcohol (tertiary): *see* *tert*-pentyl alcohol
Amylene hydrate: *see* *tert*-pentyl alcohol

Barbital sodium: any of several sodium salts of barbituric acid; *see* amobarbital
*Barbiturate: generic name for various salts and esters of barbituric acid; *see* amobarbital, Amytal Sodium™, secobarbital sodium, 2-thiouracil (Section 8.2.9.1)
*Benzocaine: *see* ethyl aminobenzoate
Brominated alcohols

*Carbonic acid[b]: reaction product of carbon dioxide and water
*Carbon dioxide[b] (Section 8.2.8.4)
Chloral hydrate: 2,2,2-trichloro-1,1-ethanediol
Chloretone™: *see* chlorobutanol
Chlorobutanol: 1,1,1-trichloro-2-methyl-2-propanol, Chloretone™
Cresol: cresylic acid; mixture of three isomeric cresols in which the *m*-isomer predominates
Cresylic acid: *see* cresol

Diethyl ether: *see* ethyl ether

Ether: *see* ethyl ether
Ethyl alcohol: ethanol
*Ethyl aminobenzoate: *p*-aminobenzoic acid ethyl ester, benzocaine (Section 8.2.8.5)
Ethyl ether: 1,1′-oxybisethane, ether, diethyl ether, ethoxyethane
*Etomidate: 1-(1-phenylethyl)-1H-imidazole-5-carboxylic acid ethyl ester; an analog of propoxate (Section 8.2.8.6)

*Finquel™: *see* tricaine[c]

*Lidocaine: 2-(diethylamino)-*N*-(2,6,-dimethylphenyl)acetamide, Xylocaine™; *also* lidocaine hydrochloride (Section 8.2.9.3)

Meparfynol: 3-methyl-1-pentyn-3-ol, methylpentynol
*Metacaine™: see tricaine[c]
Methylpentynol: *see* meparfynol
*2-Methylquinoline: *see* quinaldine
*MS-222™: *see* tricaine[c]

Nicotine: 3-(1-methyl-2-pyrrolidinyl)pyridine

Pentothal Sodium™: *see* thiopental sodium
tert-Pentyl alcohol: 2-methyl-2-butanol, *tert*-amyl alcohol, amylene hydrate
*Phenoxetol: *see* 2-phenoxyethanol
*2-Phenoxyethanol: 1-hydroxy-2-phenoxyethane, phenoxetol (Section 8.2.8.7)
*Piscaine: *see* thiazole
Procaine amide hydrochloride: *see* procainamide hydrochloride
Procainamide hydrochloride: 4-amino-*N*-[2-(diethylamino)ethyl]benzamide monohydrochloride, procaine amide hydrochloride
*Propanidid: 4-[2-(diethylamino)-2-oxoethoxy]-3-methoxybenzeneacetic acid propyl ester (Section 8.2.9.4)
*Propoxate: propyl-DL-1-(1-phenylethyl)imadazole-5-carboxylate hydrochloride (Section 8.2.9.5)

*Quinaldine: 2-methylquinoline (Section 8.2.8.2)
*Quinaldine sulfate: quinate[d] (Section 8.2.8.3)

Secobarbital sodium: 5-(1-methylbutyl)-5-(2-propenyl)2,4,6(1H,3H,5H)-pyrimidinetrione monosodium salt; there are many proprietary names for this barbiturate
Sodium amytal: *see* Amytal Sodium™

Table 8.2 Continued.

*Sodium bicarbonate[b]: sodium salt of carbonic acid
Sodium pentothal: *see* thiopental sodium
4-Stilbazole: 4-(2-phenylvinyl)pyridine, styrylpyridine, 4-styrylpyridide
Styrylpyridine: *see* 4-stilbazole

*"Thiazole"[e] 2-amino-4-phenylthiazole, piscaine, phenylthiazole (Section 8.2.9.2)
Thiopental sodium: 5-ethyldihydro-5-(1-methylbutyl)2-thioxo-4,6(1H,5H)-pyrimidinedione
            monosodium salt, Pentothal Sodium™
2-Thiouracil: 2,3-dihydro-2-thioxo-4(1H)pyrimidinone
Tribromoethanol
*Tricaine[c]: 3-aminobenzoic acid ethyl ester methanesulfonate, Finquel™, MS-222™, Metacaine™,
      tricaine methanesulfonate (Section 8.2.8.1)
*Tricaine methanesulfonate: *see* tricaine

Urethan: carbamic acid ethyl ester, urethane
Urethane: *see* urethan

*Xylocaine™: see lidocaine

[a]Chemical names follow Merck & Company (1983) to the extent possible. Proprietary trade marks are denoted ™. Not all proprietary names are given for each compound; the ones listed are those most commonly cited in the fisheries literature.
[b]Classified "generally recognized as safe" (GRAS) for use with food fish by the U.S. Food and Drug Administration (FDA).
[c]Finquel™ is the only anesthetic (and the only formulation of tricaine) registered for use with food fish by the FDA.
[d]Quinate™ also is used as a synonym for quinine sulfate.
[e]This is not the compound listed as thiazole in Merck & Company (1983).

8.2.8.1 Tricaine

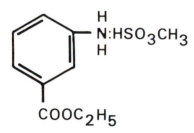

Tricaine
(Schoettger and Steucke 1972)

Alternative Names. Chemical names for tricaine are 3-aminobenzoic acid ethyl ester methanesulfonate, ethyl *m*-aminobenzoate methanesulfonate (Merck & Company 1983), methanesulfonate salt of alkyl aminobenzoate, and methanesulfonate salt of ethyl meta-aminobenzoate (Schoettger and Steucke 1972). Common and proprietary names include tricaine methanesulfonate, MS-222™, Finquel™, and Metacaine™. Although MS-222 is still widely used as the common name, that was the proprietary or trade name for the formulation produced by Sandoz Ltd., Pharmaceutical Chemicals Division, Basel, Switzerland (Bove 1962). Thus, tricaine should be used as the generic name. The term Finquel should be limited to the specific formulation registered by Fort Dodge Laboratories, Fort Dodge, Iowa, and sold by Argent Chemical Laboratories, Redmond, Washington.

Physicochemical Characteristics. Crystals of tricaine are readily soluble in water: 1 g/0.8 mL, also given as 1:9 (Merck & Company 1983). Molecular weight is 261.31. Tricaine is a lipid-soluble drug that moves across the gill by diffusion or by coupling to specific transport systems (Hunn and Allen 1974; Ohr 1976).

Research by Ohr (1976) and Smit et al. (1977) drew attention to the acidic nature of tricaine and the effect it has on the pH of weakly buffered fresh water. A stock solution of 100 mg/mL has a pH of about 2 in deionized water due to formation of methanesulphonic acid. A concentration of 100 mg/L for an anesthetic bath may have a pH as low as 5 in very soft water, less than 12 mg/L of $CaCO_3$ total hardness (Marking 1969b). Addition of NaOH produces a white precipitate in stock solutions, which thus cannot be neutralized without affecting the anesthetic properties. Buffering dilute solutions can avoid the acidity problem that causes so many of the physiological side effects often associated with use of tricaine.

Tricaine solutions are unstable in sunlight; color changes to yellow or brown. Although Bove (1962) stated that "this [color change] does not affect activity in any significant way," he noted that a 10-d-old solution with a brownish color had "an activity decrease of about 5%." Stock solutions probably should be replaced every month even when stored in brown or opaque bottles. Stock solutions may be stored frozen, and the crystals (powder) are stable when kept cool and dry (Bell 1967).

Concentration and Induction Time. Bove (1962) gave the "most effective" tricaine concentrations as 1:2,000–1:3,000 (500–333 mg/L), the concentration most generally "used to immobilize fish" as 1:10,000 (100 mg/L), and the "effective concentration" for producing anesthesia within 3–4 min in 99% of the fish (EC99) as 1:25,000 (40 mg/L).

For Finquel, Schnick et al. (1986b) recommended 15–66 mg/L for 6–48 h to induce sedation and 50–330 mg/L for 1–40 min to cause anesthesia. Schoettger and Julin (1967) and Schoettger et al. (1967) gave concentrations for tricaine that varied with species, induction time, and temperature.

A reasonable rule of thumb for sedating salmonids is 15–25 mg tricaine/L. Piper et al. (1982) gave a concentration of 26.4 mg/L for transport of salmonids in deep sedation (stage 2), but warned that anesthetized salmon have both a high oxygen consumption and a long recovery time. Loss of equilibrium (stage 3 and higher) and full anesthesia of adult salmonids requires 50–100 mg/L, the concentration depending on fish size, temperature, and the desired induction time.

Reflex action was lost (stages 4 and 5) in four species of trout and char in 3 min at a tricaine concentration of 100 mg/L; a 50–60-mg/L concentration produced anesthesia that was attained more slowly but could be maintained for approximately 30 min (Schoettger and Julin 1967). Rainbow trout required 60 mg/L to become handleable in 3 min or less (Gilderhus and Marking 1987). Coho and chinook salmon exposed to 100 mg/L for full anesthesia can be maintained in that state for 30–45 min (L. S. Smith, personal experience). However, a concentration of 20 mg/L is commonly used to anesthetize fingerling Pacific salmon; adults have been anesthetized with a mixture of 40 mg tricaine and 10 mg quinaldine per liter.

Channel catfish require 25–50 mg tricaine/L for sedation and 100–250 mg/L for full anesthesia with a 3-min induction time; dosage depends on their size and the water temperature. Schoettger et al. (1967) reported that 5–15-cm-long (total length) channel catfish reached full anesthesia in 2 min at concentrations of 100–120 mg/L, but 140–270 mg/L was needed for fish 18–30 cm long.

Striped bass weighing about 145 g lost equilibrium in 2.4–1.8 min when exposed to 120–140 mg tricaine/L at 20°C in water with 2% sodium chloride; their reflex action was lost in 8.1–5.4 min (Klar 1986). Survival was 100% after 24 h. Klar

(1986) recommended 100 mg Finquel/L for netting and moving striped bass of 15 cm or larger, and 120 mg/L for weighing, measuring, tagging, or bleeding them. Striped bass smaller than 3 cm may be more sensitive to Finquel.

The concentration of anesthetic needed to produce a given level of anesthesia is affected by the density (biomass) of fish in the container. Dupree and Huner (1984) reported tricaine concentrations for transporting fish that ranged from 26.4 to 264.2 mg/L. Ordinarily, as studies by Schoettger et al. (1967) showed, a concentration of 264 mg/L should render even channel catfish unconscious in 3 min. When fish are transported at high densities, however, the anesthetic is quickly absorbed, and the actual exposure concentration is reduced accordingly. Piper et al. (1982) reported that a 1% salt solution containing 264 mg tricaine/L reduced shipping mortality of threadfin shad. Generally, concentrations of tricaine in excess of 100 mg/L should not be used for salmonids, and ones higher than 250 mg/L should not be used for warmwater fish, unless the biomass of fish is very large relative to the container volume.

Temperature and Water Quality Effects. Schoettger and Julin (1967) found that tricaine anesthetized four species of salmonids more slowly, requiring longer exposure times, as temperature decreased between 17 and 7°C; however, anesthesia was more safely induced and maintained at lower temperatures. In contrast, the efficacy of tricaine for channel catfish was little influenced by temperature over the range of 7–27°C (Schoettger et al. 1967). Also, variation in pH between 5.0 and 8.5 did not affect tricaine's action against trout and char, but its efficacy decreased with water hardness (Schoettger and Julin 1967).

Recovery Time. Tricaine is rapidly excreted from fish by diffusion across the gills (Maren et al. 1968). After a bath treatment, recovery time varies according to tricaine concentration and exposure time, both of which affect the amount of anesthetic absorbed by the fish. Some functions take only minutes to return to normal, others may take days or weeks. The typical time for fish to return to upright swimming after a brief exposure to 110–220 mg/L is 3–5 min, but a somewhat longer exposure to a lower concentration (40–80 mg/L) increased the recovery time to 5–10 min (Bell 1967). Generally, a recovery time longer than 10 min suggests that too much anesthetic is being used or that the exposure times are too long. Both induction and recovery times decrease at higher temperatures.

Toxicity to Mammals. Reported LD50s for oral administrations of tricaine are 4.0 g/kg body weight for rabbits, 2.4 g/kg for mice, and 5.2 g/kg for rats (Bove 1962; Bell 1967 reported 5–10 g/kg for rats). Intravenous doses are more potent: LD50s are 78 mg/kg for rabbits and 170 mg/kg for mice (Bove 1962). Decomposition products of tricaine, which can result from sunlight or heat, may have different toxicities.

Toxicity to Fish. Bove (1962) reported a tricaine LC50 (bath exposure) of 82 mg/L for brown trout. Marking (1967) gave 33.8–63.0 mg/L as the range of LC50s for fish exposed 24 h in static toxicity tests[1]; variation was related to species, size, temperature, and water hardness. Ranges of LC50s for 14–96-h exposures are 66–51 mg/L for channel catfish, 52–31 mg/L for various salmonids, and 61–39 mg/L for northern pike, bluegill, largemouth bass, and walleye (Marking 1967). Toxicity may increase or decrease with temperature, but trout are slightly more resistant to the anesthetic at lower temperatures (Marking 1967). Exposure time also influences toxicity; for example, fingerling rainbow trout were immobilized by a short exposure to 50 mg tricaine/L (Barton and Peter 1982), but nearly all cutthroat trout died from a 5-h exposure to the same concentration (Thompson 1959). Subadult channel catfish can be safely exposed to 100 mg tricaine/L for 20 min (Plumb et al. 1983).

Tricaine is not mutagenic (Yoshimura et al. 1981).

Rapid induction of anesthesia (in less than 1 min) by tricaine concentrations of 200–400 mg/L can cause immediate changes in hematology and blood chemistry (C. B. Schreck, Oregon State University, personal communication). Tricaine may stress rainbow trout, causing elevation of plasma cortisol levels, due to its acidity in soft water (Barton and Peter 1982). Nevertheless, tricaine reduces handling stress in yearling chinook salmon, and its net benefit is positive (Strange and Schreck 1978).

Restrictions.   Residues of tricaine decline to less than the detection limit of 0.1 mg/L in fish flesh within 24 h after exposure. However, the FDA requires a 21-d withdrawal period for fish that will be used for food or released to public waters because mammalian safety data are lacking (Marking and Meyer 1985). Its registration label specifies that Finquel is approved only for fish of the families Ictaluridae, Salmonidae, Esocidae, and Percidae. For information on metabolism, degradation, and residues, see Schoettger et al. (1967), Walker and Schoettger (1967), Hunn et al. (1968), Maren et al. (1968), Hunn (1970), Luhning (1973), and Allen and Hunn (1986).

Suggestions for Use.   A stock tricaine solution of 100 mg/mL can be taken into the field. It should be kept in an opaque bottle so sunlight will not degrade it. The stock solution is diluted in a plastic bucket or other container in which the fish are to be anesthetized; it helps if the bucket has been marked with a standard volume to which a predetermined amount of stock will be diluted.

Seawater is sufficiently alkaline and buffered that tricaine has little effect on its pH. Concentrated freshwater solutions of tricaine, however, are very acidic, and even dilute solutions in soft water remain slightly or moderately so. Sodium bicarbonate ($NaHCO_3$) is the appropriate neutralizing chemical. Stock solutions of tricaine should not be neutralized because sodium bicarbonate causes the sulphonate group to separate from the aminobenzoate ethyl ester group when the tricaine is concentrated; this is evidenced by oil droplets at the water surface. After the solution is diluted, addition of 200–250 mg sodium bicarbonate per 100 mg tricaine generally turns the preparation neutral or slightly alkaline. The

---

[1]In "static" toxicity tests, the exposure water is not changed and the toxicant decreases in concentration as it is taken up by the test animals. In "flow-through" tests, a constant concentration of toxicant is flushed through the test chamber for the duration of the exposure.

solution may turn white when sodium bicarbonate is added, but vigorous stirring usually clears it.

Drawbacks. Although Finquel is registered for fishery use, the registration label requires a 21-d withdrawal. It is an expensive drug; 1990 prices were US$60/100 g for Finquel, versus $17.50 for quinaldine and $25 for quinaldine sulfate.

When used in fresh water with weak acid-neutralizing capacity, i.e., with total alkalinity of less than about 50 mg/L as $CaCO_3$, tricaine reduces the pH (Ohr 1976; Smit et al. 1977). The acidity of tricaine solutions may lower the pH of fish blood enough to produce respiratory stress from Bohr and Root effects (Smit et al. 1979a, 1979b, 1979c). These and other physiological changes from lowered pH or from anesthesia may persist for a considerable time (Houston 1971a, 1971b; Houston and Woods 1976; Soivio et al. 1977). Some of these changes, but not all, can be prevented by neutralizing tricaine solutions to the same pH as the water in which the fish have been held (Wedemeyer 1970; Ohr 1976; Smit et al. 1979a, 1979b, 1979c).

It has been reported that tricaine affects fish sperm motility (Allison 1961), but this might have been caused by low pH in unbuffered solutions rather than by a direct anesthetic effect on the sperm. Exposure to tricaine can destroy the cilia in the olfactory epithelium of channel catfish, however (Lewis et al. 1985). Anesthesia of adult chinook salmon with 100 mg tricaine/L did not affect their homing response (Quinn et al. 1988). Some fish cannot tolerate long exposure to tricaine (Schoettger and Steucke 1972), and the margin between effective and toxic concentrations is narrow for some species. In one study, for instance, the effective concentration of tricaine for rainbow trout fingerlings was 60 mg/L, but 80 mg/L killed 80% of the fish in a 15-min exposure (Gilderhus and Marking 1987). Deep anesthesia is lethal if fish are allowed to go into respiratory arrest without a means to artificially ventilate their gills (Thompson 1959), and recovery from tricaine anesthesia is too slow for some purposes (Marking and Meyer 1985).

Schoettger and Steucke (1972) patented a synergistic mixture of tricaine (20–60 mg/L) and quinaldine or quinaldine sulfate (20–60 mg/L) that is effective with smaller quantities of chemicals than when each component is used alone (Gilderhus et al. 1973b).

8.2.8.2 Quinaldine

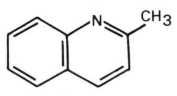

Quinaldine
(Merck & Company 1983)

Alternative Name. The chemical name for quinaldine is 2-methylquinoline.

Physicochemical Characteristics. Quinaldine is a colorless (Merck & Company 1968) or light yellow (Marking 1969a) oily liquid, but darkens to reddish brown after exposure to air (Merck & Company 1983) and should be protected from light. It has the distinctive odor of quinoline. Its molecular weight is 143.18.

Quinaldine is only slightly soluble in water but soluble in acetone and ethanol. Its low water solubility may prevent overdoses (Bell 1967). Its higher solubility in organic solvents makes it likely to accumulate in lipid-rich areas of the body, such as shark brains (Brandenburger Brown et al. 1972).

Concentration and Induction Time. Jodlbauer and Salvendi (1905) were the first to report use of quinaldine as an anesthetic for fish, according to Brandenburger Brown et al. (1972). Muench (1958) published the first report on the use of quinaldine as a fish anesthetic in the USA, and several other studies have followed. It is difficult to generalize from published reports, but salmonids require lower concentrations for anesthesia than warmwater fishes, and both groups usually become anesthetized faster and recover sooner at higher than at lower temperatures (Locke 1969; Schoettger and Julin 1969). Fish under full quinaldine anesthesia normally do not stop their gill ventilation, and they are not as susceptible to asphyxia due to respiratory arrest as they are with tricaine.

Salmonids are anesthetized in 1–6 min by quinaldine of 5–12 mg/L (Bell 1967; Locke 1969). A mixture of tricaine (40 mg/L) and quinaldine (10 mg/L) has been used to anesthetize adult Pacific salmon (Piper et al. 1982).

Effective quinaldine concentrations for warmwater fishes have varied among studies. Muench (1958) indicated that goldfish, golden shiners, yellow bullheads, green sunfish, and white crappies were anesthetized in 0.5–4 min by 2.5–20-mg/L exposures. Dupree and Huner (1984) gave 15–30 mg/L for use with warmwater fishes, but most other reports indicate higher concentrations are needed. Temperature and fish size are important variables for warmwater fishes. In studies with channel catfish, bluegills, and largemouth bass, anesthesia occurred at lower quinaldine concentrations, and recovery times were shorter, at higher than at lower temperatures (Schoettger and Julian 1969). At the same temperature, large fish usually require higher concentrations for anesthesia than smaller individuals.

Small (10–12-cm) grass carp lose equilibrium in 5 min at 13°C after exposure to 15 mg quinaldine/L (Jensen et al. 1978). Striped bass brood fish are sufficiently relaxed for egg stripping within 1 to 2 min after their gills are sprayed with a quinaldine solution of 1,000 mg/L (Piper et al. 1982). Tilapia seem to be extremely tolerant of quinaldine: concentrations of 25–50 mg/L were required to bring them to sedation or partial loss of equilibrium, and 50–1,000 mg/L were needed for complete anesthesia with induction times of 29 and 1.5 min, respectively (Sado 1985). Sharks absorb quinaldine rapidly, reach anesthesia quickly, and recover fast (Brandenburger Brown et al. 1972).

Recovery Time. Salmonids exposed to 5–12 mg quinaldine/L took 1–10 min to right themselves and maintain equilibrium (Bell 1967). After exposure to 5–25 mg/L, brook trout, lake trout, and Atlantic salmon recovered in 1–10 min, depending on species and temperature (Locke 1969). At temperatures above 7°C, warmwater species such as channel catfish, bluegill, and largemouth bass recovered in 1–30 min after exposure to 10–70 mg/L, but more than 60 min was necessary for bluegills and largemouth bass exposed at 7°C.

Toxicity to Mammals. The LD50 for oral administration of quinaldine to rats was 1.23 g/kg body weight (Merck & Company 1983), and the LD50 for cutaneous application of quinaldine to rabbits was 1.87 g/kg (Spector 1956). Brandenburger Brown et al. (1972) reported LD50 values ranging from 0.5 to 3.0 μmol/kg when quinaldine was administered intraperitoneally to various species. The chemical is highly irritating to the mucous membranes of the eyes or the nasopharyngeal region (Bell 1967; Merck & Company 1968). Ames tests of quinaldine mutagenicity have been negative, but reports from Japan indicate that some quinoline compounds related to quinaldine are potential carcinogens (NFRL 1986).

Toxicity to Fish. Fish first respond to quinaldine with coughing and avoidance behavior (Schoettger and Julin 1969). Ninety-six-hour LC50 values ranged from 2.0 to 25 mg/L for nine fish species in static toxicity tests at 12°C; channel catfish was the most resistant species (Marking 1969a). Increases in quinaldine toxicity with increasing temperature have been demonstrated for rainbow trout, bluegill, and grass carp (Marking 1969a; Schramm and Black 1984). Quinaldine is more toxic to some fish in hard than in soft water. It is harmless to fertilized rainbow trout eggs at concentrations and exposure times normally encountered in spawning operations (Schoettger and Julin 1969). Quinaldine is not transformed by the fish—it is excreted in its original form (Baldridge 1969). Muscle residues are essentially zero 24 h after exposure (Hunn and Allen 1974).

Restrictions. Quinaldine is not approved by the FDA for use on food fish. It and other quinolines occur in coal tar, a complex mixture of compounds derived from the destructive distillation of coal. Coal tar contains aromatic hydrocarbons, phenol, creosol, and other phenol bodies, as well as ammonia, pyridine, and organic bases such as aniline and triophene. Although some of these coal tar derivatives are carcinogenic, Schoettger and Julin (1969) reported that there is no evidence that quinaldine itself has carcinogenic properties.

Suggestions for Use. Quinaldine is generally dissolved in acetone or ethanol for use. Schoettger and Steucke (1972) recommended diluting liquid quinaldine with a 60:40 acetone:water solution. Stock solutions are relatively stable as anesthetics, but they should be stored in tightly capped brown bottles (Bell 1967). Liquid quinaldine has a pH of 4.4 (Sado 1985) and loses its effectiveness in final solutions having a pH less than 6 (Sills and Allen 1971). Water hardness, age of anesthetic solution, and repeated exposure of the same animal do not alter quinaldine's effectiveness (Schoettger and Julin 1969).

Because it is relatively inexpensive (US$17.50/100 g in 1990), quinaldine has been used to collect fish in tidepools and in more open water by scuba divers. It can be carried and dispensed in plastic squeeze bottles.

Drawbacks. Quinaldine's major drawback is its lack of registration; others include its poor solubility in water, its poor suppression of reflex actions by anesthetized animals, its irritability to mucous membranes, its strong odor, and its relatively long induction time (compared to tricaine). Quinaldine sulfate (Section 8.2.8.3) eliminates the water solubility and odor problems and reduces the induction time.

Fish that have totally lost their equilibrium from quinaldine exposure often retain a strong reflex response to being touched (Schoettger and Steucke 1972). This is undesirable for all procedures, particularly surgical procedures as noted by Schoettger and Julian (1969) for rainbow trout and by Schramm and Black (1984) for grass carp. Nevertheless, Bell (1967) found quinaldine useful for surgical operations on coho salmon, which were unreactive during blood sampling and scalpel cuts at quinaldine concentrations of 10–13 mg/L. Although a salmonid may twitch strongly when first touched, it will remain relaxed during further handling unless left undisturbed again for 20–30 s (Smith, personal experience). The reflex problem is variable and may be influenced by concentration of the anesthetic.

Schoettger and Steucke (1972) suggested that the induction time can be shortened, and the reflex twitch problem can be overcome, if a combination of tricaine and quinaldine is used. They gave 20–60 mg tricaine/L with 2.5–20 mg quinaldine or quinaldine sulfate per liter as a general range; for rainbow trout they gave 20–30 mg tricaine/L and 2.4–5.0 mg quinaldine or quinaldine sulfate per liter as the optimum combination. This mixture of anesthetics was said to have an induction time of 2.5 min and to allow recovery in 15 min after a 1-h exposure. Piper et al. (1982) gave a mixture of 40 mg tricaine/L and 10 mg quinaldine/L for anesthesia of adult Pacific salmon.

For surgery, an intramuscular injection of a skeletal muscle relaxant such as gallamine triethiodide, tubocurarine chloride, or pancuronium bromide after quinaldine anesthesia may eliminate the reflex problem. Gallamine triethiodide is used by veterinary surgeons to obtain muscular relaxation in anesthetized animals; doses for dogs and cats range from 0.1 to 2.0 mg/kg body weight. This and other muscle relaxants have been injected into fish (at doses of 1.0, 1.5, or 2.4 mg/kg body weight) to incapacitate them when general anesthesia would interfere with electrophysical measurements of sensory and central nervous systems (Echteler 1985; Kiyohara et al. 1985; Munz 1985).

8.2.8.3 Quinaldine Sulfate

Alternative Name. Quinaldine sulfate also is called quinate.

Quinaldine sulfate
(Allen and Sills 1973)

Physicochemical Characteristics. Quinaldine sulfate is a light-yellow crystalline powder. It lacks the strong odor of quinaldine, and it is freely soluble in water, but like quinaldine, it is highly irritating to mucous membranes (Merck & Company 1983). It should be neutralized in somewhat the same fashion as tricaine (Blasiola 1977).

Concentration and Induction and Recovery Times. Quinaldine sulfate induces anesthesia faster than quinaldine and fish recover faster from its effects (Blasiola 1977). Effective concentrations for warmwater species have ranged from 15 to 60 mg/L (Gilderhus et al. 1973a). Concentrations of about 25 mg/L anesthetize most salmonids in less than 4 min; the fish recover in 1–13 min. For example, 25–40 mg/L were effective for fingerling and adult rainbow trout, which recovered in 5–6 min (Gilderhus and Marking 1987).

Toxicity to Mammals. Quinaldine sulfate's toxicity to mammals presumably is the same as quinaldine's.

Toxicity to Fish. Acute toxicities (96-h LC50s) of quinaldine sulfate to fish range from 6.8 mg/L for largemouth bass to 72.5 mg/L for common carp. Toxicity is less in very soft water than in hard water because a decreased pH causes a decrease in the concentration of the active, un-ionized form (Marking and Dawson 1973).

Restrictions on Use. The restrictions for quinaldine apply to the sulfate.

Drawbacks. Many of the drawbacks for quinaldine do not apply to quinaldine sulfate. However, quinaldine sulfate produces an acid solution like tricaine, it is more expensive than quinaldine (US$25 versus $17.50 for 100 g), and it has not been registered.

8.2.8.4 Carbon Dioxide

Alternative Names. Other names for carbon dioxide are CO_2, carbonic acid, carbonic acid gas, and carbonic anhydride. When sodium bicarbonate is the source of CO_2, the resulting anesthesia is sometimes called sodium bicarbonate anesthesia.

Physicochemical Characteristics. Carbon dioxide, molecular weight 44.01, is a colorless, odorless, noncombustible gas at ordinary temperatures; it is a solid at about $-35°C$. It is commercially available as a gas over a liquid in steel cylinders under pressure or in solid form as dry ice ($-78.5°C$), but most commonly in the half-bound form as baking soda (sodium bicarbonate). The latter is a white powder that is very soluble in water. Post (1979) recommended mixing a 6.75% (weight per volume, w/v) sodium bicarbonate solution and a 3.95% (w/v) sulfuric acid solution to obtain the desired concentration of carbonic acid.

Concentration and Induction Time. Carbonic acid (H_2CO_3) is formed when carbon dioxide dissolves in and reacts with water. Regardless of whether carbon dioxide (free CO_2), bicarbonate (combined CO_2), or carbonic acid is used for anesthesia, the resulting solution should eventually equilibrate to a mixture of all three. The concentration of each member of the equation depends on the final pH

$$CO_2 + H_2O \Leftrightarrow H_2CO_3 \Leftrightarrow H^+ + HCO_3^-$$

| carbon dioxide | water | carbonic acid | hydrogen ion | bicarbonate ion |

of the solution. Between pH 7 and 9, bicarbonate dominates; below pH 6, free carbon dioxide dominates. (At higher pH, bicarbonate ions further dissociate to hydrogen and carbonate ions.) The occurrence of bicarbonate ions depends on the presence of a certain amount of free or equilibrium carbon dioxide. Surface waters of lakes normally contain less than 10 mg/L free carbon dioxide (APHA et al. 1989).

Free carbon dioxide can be measured by titration (potentiometrically or with phenolphthalein indicator) or with a selective ion electrode, or it can be determined from a nomograph (APHA et al. 1989). Compared with the titrametric procedures, the nomographic method is said to give a closer estimation of total free CO_2 when temperature, pH, alkalinity, and total dissolved solids are measured at the time of sampling. The nomographic and titrametric methods allow calculation of the free (CO_2), the half-bound (bicarbonate), and the bound (carbonate) forms of CO_2.

Carbon dioxide anesthesia is an old method, first described by Fish (1943). Fish (1943) produced CO_2 concentrations of 150–650 mg/L with sodium bicarbonate and sulfuric acid (soda–acid technique); he said that 200 mg/L was optimum for anesthetizing fingerling and adult salmon. Mishra et al. (1983), using Post's (1979) soda–acid technique, found that 500 mg/L was an optimum concentration of carbonic acid that allowed rohu fry *Labeo rohita* to be transported for up to 251 h with only 5% mortality. Takeda and Itzawa (1983) found that Post's method worked best at low densities of fish and they preferred to bubble a mixture of carbon dioxide and oxygen through their transport tanks. Booke et al. (1978) determined that a 642 mg/L solution of $NaHCO_3$ at a pH of 6.5 was the most effective medium for causing rainbow trout, brook trout, and common carp to cease swimming and to slow respiration within 5 min. They hypothesized that the mechanism was a pH-controlled release of carbon dioxide.

Toxicity to Mammals. Although generally recognized as safe (GRAS) when used with food items (i.e., there are no withdrawal restrictions on CO_2-treated fish), carbon dioxide poses some dangers. Air with more than 10% CO_2 causes humans to lose consciousness (Merck & Company 1983). Frostbite and skin blisters may occur from contact with dry ice. There are obvious hazards in the use of concentrated sulfuric acid to release CO_2 from $NaHCO_3$ (Post 1979).

Toxicity to Fish. High external concentrations of carbon dioxide may block excretion of hydrogen and bicarbonate ions (Post 1979). Borjeson and Hoglund (1976) documented several responses to hypercapnia (an excessive amount of CO_2 in the blood) that implicate osmoregulatory dysfunction in fish exposed to high CO_2. Nevertheless, Post (1979) discounted the possible dangers of carbon dioxide anesthesia to fish.

Restrictions on Use. Use of carbon dioxide is unrestricted (GRAS).

Suggestions for Use. The soda–acid technique described by Post (1979) can be used to produce H_2CO_3 concentrations of 150–600 mg/L. The procedure involves mixing equal volumes of 6.75% (w/v) $NaHCO_3$ and 3.95% (w/v) of concentrated (97–98%) H_2SO_4. Marking and Meyer (1985) said that bubbling carbon dioxide gas through Micro-Por™ tubing to attain CO_2 levels of 300–400 mg/L was superior to the soda–acid technique. Regardless of the method used to produce the high CO_2 levels needed for anesthesia, adequate dissolved oxygen (at least 5 mg/L) must be maintained (Britton 1983).

Drawbacks. Although Post (1979) described carbonic acid anesthesia as safe, inexpensive, effective, convenient, and easily attained, the user survey by Marking and Meyer (1985) suggested that it is only partly effective, slow-acting, stressful, and lethal after repeated exposures. According to the survey only a few people were using carbonic acid for anesthesia in 1984, and various techniques produced mixed results. Takeda and Itzawa (1983) said that the bubbling method worked but was impractical due to high cost and the difficulty in maintaining proper concentrations of oxygen and carbon dioxide.

Some criticisms of carbon dioxide anesthesia may be due in part to different expectations of users. It may be too slow for a user who expects an induction time of 2 min, but acceptable to one who can wait 5–10 min. Commercially available mixtures of CO_2 (up to 30%) and O_2 in pressurized cylinders may simplify the problem of balancing concentrations of these gases. Medical-grade mixtures are expensive, but cost depends on the local availability of high pressure gases. The soda–acid method may be less expensive, and reagents for the technique are available from local chemical supply houses; sodium bicarbonate is also available from grocery stores as baking soda.

8.2.8.5 Ethyl Aminobenzoate

Alternative Names. Ethyl aminobenzoate is also known as *p*-aminobenzoic acid ethyl ester, ethyl-*p*-aminobenzoate, and 4-aminobenzoic acid ethyl ester. There are several commercial trade names for ethyl aminobenzoate (Merck & Company 1983); benzocaine is the most commonly used generic name for this drug.

Ethyl aminobenzoate's therapeutic category is topical anesthetic (Merck & Company 1983), and it is used by humans to relieve pain and itch of insect bites and the discomfort of sunburn (e.g., Solarcaine™ contains 20% benzocaine) and hemorrhoids (Griffith 1987). It is also used in some throat lozenges.

Ethyl aminobenzoate and tricaine are ethyl esters of aminobenzoic acid (homologues of benzoic acid). The amine group is meta-substituted in tricaine and para-substituted in ethyl aminobenzoate.

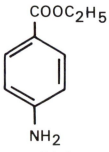

Ethyl
aminobenzoate
(Merck & Company
1983)

Physicochemical Characteristics. Ethyl aminobenzoate, molecular weight 165.2, is barely water soluble (Dawson and Gilderhus 1979). One gram of ethyl aminobenzoate dissolves in about 2,500 mL water, compared with 1 g in 9 mL for tricaine (Merck & Company 1983). Ethyl aminobenzoate may be dissolved in acetone (Dawson and Gilderhus 1979) or ethanol (Ross and Geddes 1979) and thence carried into water. Ferreira et al. (1979) synthesized a water-soluble form, benzocaine hydrochloride.

Concentration and Induction Time. McErlean and Kennedy (1968) reported that ethyl aminobenzoate is more effective at lower concentrations than tricaine, although more recent literature is ambivalent on this point. Ross and Geddes (1979) recommended a concentration of 100 mg/L at 25°C as a starting point for warmwater species whose sensitivity to ethyl aminobenzoate is unknown, but most other authors have found that lower concentrations produce anesthesia in both warmwater and coldwater species. Luhning (1973) induced deep anesthesia in striped bass, bluegills, and largemouth bass by 15-min exposures to 63.2 mg ethyl aminobenzoate/L buffered to pH 6.5 at 17.8°C. Ferreira et al. (1984a, 1984b) induced anesthesia in common carp, Mozambique tilapia, and rainbow trout with concentrations of 25–100 mg/L, though induction times were highly variable. Dawson and Gilderhus (1979) provoked total loss of equilibrium in rainbow and brown trouts, in less than 3 min, with an ethyl aminobenzoate concentration of 50 mg/L, but 100–200 mg/L were required to bring adult northern pike to the same state; rates of sedation (and recovery) were slower in cold than in warm water. Fingerling and small adult rainbow trout, maintained at 12°C in soft water (total alkalinity, 30–35 mg/L) could be made handleable in 3 min or less with a concentration of 35 mg/L (Gilderhus and Marking 1987). Gilderhus (1988) anesthetized rainbow trout and chinook salmon at concentrations of 25–45 mg/L; the efficacy of ethyl aminobenzoate was not affected by water hardness, alkalinity, or pH, but 10 mg/L less chemical was required to produce anesthesia at 17°C than at 7°C.

Recovery Time. The time needed by fish to recover from various stages of anesthesia induced by ethyl aminobenzoate varies with the chemical's concentration, temperature, species, and fish size (Dawson and Gilderhus 1979; Ross and Geddes 1979; Ferreira et al. 1984a). Ross and Geddes (1979) reported 120–150-min recovery times for tropical species (e.g., spotted tilapia) anesthetized in 100 mg ethyl aminobenzoate/L. Rainbow trout anesthetized to a handleable state recovered in 8.5 min (Gilderhus and Marking 1987; other rainbow trout recovered from a similar tricaine-induced state in 5.5 min). Recovery of brown trout, rainbow trout, and northern pike from ethyl aminobenzoate anesthesia was faster in warm than in cold water (Dawson and Gilderhus 1979).

Toxicity to Mammals. Mammals incur no measurable toxicity from topical applications of ethyl aminobenzoate. The chemical is approved by the FDA for use in human and veterinary medicine (Merck & Company 1983; Griffith 1987; Medical Economics Company 1987).

Toxicity to Fish. McErlean and Kennedy (1968) reported that ethyl aminobenzoate is more toxic than tricaine to white perch; immersion in a 0.20-mmol/L solution for 1 h killed all the test fish. Rainbow trout exposed 10 min to a 50-mg/L concentration incurred a 40% mortality, and 90% of brown trout died after exposure to 50 mg/L at 17°C (Dawson and Gilderhus 1979). The safety margin between effective and toxic concentrations was smaller at 17°C (30 and 35 mg/L, respectively) than at 7°C for chinook salmon and rainbow trout (Gilderhus 1988).

Suggestions for Use. Solutions of ethyl aminobenzoate diluted for use should be neutralized like those of tricaine (Ferreira et al. 1984b).

Drawbacks. Ethyl aminobenzoate is not registered by the FDA for fishery use. It is not more effective on fish or safer than tricaine. Concentrations that render fish handleable within 5 min generally are not safe for exposures longer than 15 min (Dawson and Gilderhus 1979). Allen (1988) found that residues of ethyl aminobenzoate in muscle were below control values for largemouth bass, and near control values for rainbow trout, after the fish were exposed for 15 min to the chemical and then held for 24 h in flowing, anesthetic-free water. However, fish meal prepared from Pacific salmon that had been anesthetized with benzocaine retained the chemical in substantial amounts (45.1 µg/g).

Wedemeyer (1970) and Soivio et al. (1977) compared the physiological effects of ethyl aminobenzoate and tricaine.

8.2.8.6   Etomidate

Alternative Names.   Etomidate is known as 1-(1-phenylethyl)-1H-imidazole-5-carboxylic acid ethyl ester, *R*-(+)-1-(alpha-methylbenzyl)imidazole-5-carboxylic acid ethyl ester, and ethyl-1-methylbenzyl-imidazole-5-carboxylate. Trade names are Amidate™ and Hypnomidate™ (Merck & Company 1983).

Etomidate
(Merck & Company 1983)

Physicochemical Characteristics.   Etomidate is a powder; its molecular weight is 244.29. It is highly soluble in water and has no color or odor (Plumb et al. 1983). It is an experimental hyponotic agent used intravenously to induce anesthesia in humans (Gooding and Corssen 1976).

Concentration and Induction Time.   The minimum effective concentrations of etomidate for several species of tropical aquarium fishes were 2–4 mg/L; the maximum safe concentrations were 7–20 mg/L. At 4 mg/L, induction took 90 s; lower doses gave slower induction and faster recovery (Amend et al. 1982). Plumb et al. (1983) stated that concentrations of 0.8–1.2 mg/L produced anesthesia in subadult channel catfish in 3–4 min. Mortality due to long-term exposure appeared to be less for etomidate than for tricaine (Limsuwan et al. 1983). Etomidate was reported to be more effective in alkaline than in acidic water and at higher than at lower temperature, but its effectiveness was not related to total hardness (Amend et al. 1982).

Recovery Time.   Following a 4-mg/L dose of etomidate, tropical fish took 40 min to recover (Amend et al. 1982). The time required for total recovery varies in direct proportion to effective exposure time. After 80 min in etomidate solutions, subadult channel catfish took 10–30 min to recover from a 2.0-mg/L exposure, but 180 min to recover from a 3.2- or 3.6-mg/L exposure (Plumb et al. 1983).

Toxicity to Mammals.   The LD50 for etomidate in mice and rats is 14.8–24.3 mg/kg body weight administered intravenously (Merck & Company 1983). Plumb et al. (1983) stated that etomidate has "no effect on man."

Toxicity to Fish.   Exposure to etomidate concentrations of 5 mg/L for 10 min, 4 mg/L for 20 min, and 90 mg/L for 10 min did not kill subadult channel catfish (Plumb et al. 1983). The 24-h LC50 is 0.61–0.68 mg/L for bluegills and 1.87–2.73 mg/L for golden shiners. Differences in pH and water hardness had little effect on toxicity (Limsuwan et al. 1983).

Restrictions on Use.   Etomidate is not approved by the FDA for use on food fish, but it is approved for selected applications in human and veterinary medicine (Marking and Meyer 1985). It is characterized as a hypnotic (Merck & Company 1983).

Suggestions for Use.   Plumb et al. (1983) prepared a 1% stock solution of etomidate in a 55% solution of propylene glycol and stored it at 5°C until used.

Drawbacks.   Concentrations strong enough to keep induction times within 2 min require long recovery times; conversely, lower concentrations require a long induction time. Thus, it does not meet certain criteria for a desirable fish anesthetic. Some hematological and plasma ion changes have been noted; such alterations peaked up to 3 h after recovery, but these might not be a problem for many uses of the anesthetic (Limsuwan et al. 1983; Gooding and Corssen 1977).

8.2.8.7 2-Phenoxyethanol

Alternative Names.   Other names of 2-phenoxyethanol are 1-hydroxy-2-phenoxyethane, ethylene glycol monophenyl ether, beta-hydroxyethyl phenyl ether, phenyl cellosolve, phenoxethol, and phenoxetol.

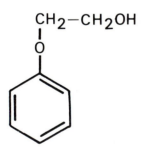

2-Phenoxyethanol

Physicochemical Characteristics.   2-Phenoxyethanol is a colorless, oily liquid slightly heavier than water (1.11 g/mL). It is moderately soluble in water (2.67 g/100 mL at 25°C) but freely soluble in ethanol. Its molecular weight is 138.16. It is used as a topical anesthetic (Merck & Company 1983).

Concentration and Induction Time.   2-Phenoxyethanol concentrations of 0.11–0.22 mg/L immobilized pink salmon fry in 2–4 min, and slightly higher concentrations (0.31–0.36 mg/L) gave similar results (Bell 1967).

Recovery Time.   Pink salmon fry took 3–6 min to right themselves after exposures to 2-phenoxyethanol concentrations of 0.11–0.22 mg/L, 5–10 min to recover from 0.31–0.36-mg/L concentrations, and required even longer recovery periods after longer exposure times.

Toxicity to Mammals.   Bell (1967) estimated that a fatal oral dose of 2-phenoxyethanol for humans was "10 grams," but did not give the dosage per unit body weight. The LD50 for rats is 1.26 g/kg body weight (Merck & Company 1983). A sublethal exposure may damage the kidney and liver. The chemical also is an irritant to sensitive tissues.

Toxicity to Fish. A lethal concentration of 2-phenoxyethanol for fish is 0.286 mL/L (Bell 1967).

Drawbacks. The margin of safety for 2-phenoxyethanol—the difference between effective and toxic concentrations—is narrow. Based on human toxicology, physiological effects are expected in fish, and possible liver and kidney damage might affect long-term survival. Induction times are long and hyperactivity sometimes occurs during recovery; exposed salmon have exhibited rapid and erratic swimming ("motorboating"). Given its inherent toxic effects, there seems no reason to continue using 2-phenoxyethanol as a fish anesthetic.

8.2.8.8 Hypothermia

Background. As the body temperature of ectothermic vertebrates—fish, amphibians, and reptiles—is depressed (hypothermia), they become immobile and impassive (torpid). All physiological processes, including sensitivity to stimuli, decline with temperature. A fish chilled from a higher temperature is passive or stuporous, may lose equilibrium, and cannot perform coordinated movements. Cold anesthesia is characterized by absence of motion, reduced power of exertion, and diminished nervous sensitivity. Before chemical anesthetics were widely used, low-temperature anesthesia was recommended for minor surgery of fish (Parker 1939). In human medicine, low temperature produced by the vaporization of ethyl chloride, diethyl ether, or solid carbon dioxide has been used to produce local anesthesia in restricted segments of the body; lowering the temperature of an extremity makes perception of pain in that area less apparent (Considine and Considine 1984). Cold anesthesia is reversible and leaves no residues in tissues. There are no FDA restrictions or hazards to the user, except for some danger in handling of solid carbon dioxide if that material is used to produce the low temperature.

Applications. Low temperature may be used alone (Mittal and Whitear 1978; Chung 1980) or in combination with an anesthetic drug (Williamson and Roberts 1981); both approaches have been used in fisheries work (Parker 1939; Meehan and Revet 1962; Mittal and Whitear 1978; Chung 1980; Williamson and Roberts 1981). Parker (1939) reported that it sufficed to immerse fish in crushed ice for 10–15 min for minor diagnostic procedures. Chung (1980) anesthetized tilapia and cyprinodontids by cooling them from acclimation temperatures of 24–33°C to 8.5–11.5°C (tilapia) or to 3.4–6.8°C (cyprinodontids). Recovery occurred in 0.1–2.0 min with 100% survival. Rodman (1963) successfully transported white sturgeons by cooling them to 4.4°C. Mittal and Whitear (1978) had equally good success in anesthetizing catfish, goldfish, and a marine blenny by cooling them from 23–25°C to 1°C in 2–20 min. However, fish adapted to 10°C were not entirely inactive at 1°C. All fish recovered with no apparent ill effects.

Meehan and Revet (1962) used reduced temperature alone and in combination with tricaine (25 mg/L) for transporting sockeye salmon fry. Williamson and

Roberts (1981) anesthetized sharks for 15 min in 20 mg tricaine/L, then put them on crushed ice (body temperature was approximately 5°C) without any gill perfusion. Smith (personal experience) anesthetized adult sockeye salmon in 100 mg tricaine/L, then transferred them to an operating table for cannulation surgery, where they were maintained on recirculating tricaine (20 mg/L) with ice floating in it (approximately 1°C). When the fish were rewarmed with untreated water at the acclimation temperature, they righted themselves and resumed breathing in only 1–2 min.

Drawbacks.   Major decreases in body temperature of fish that are sufficient to induce sedation or anesthesia also cause many changes in body fluids, ions, and hematology; these form a characteristic set of physiological changes called "cold shock" (see references in Chapter 9). Cold anesthesia is not now recommended for any purpose and is only rarely used.

8.2.8.9   Electroanesthesia

Background.   Electrical current can cause electrotaxis (forced swimming), electrotetanus (muscle contractions), and electronarcosis or galvanonarcosis (muscle relaxation) in fish. Generically, electroanesthesia includes electrotetanus and electronarcosis. However, electrotetanus, although immobilizing, is not the same as other forms of anesthesia, and the physiological reactions it induces may be quite distinct. Electricity is not widely used for anesthesia; only 2 of 183 respondents in Marking and Meyer's (1985) survey mentioned such use. Nevertheless, electroanesthesia may distort some physiological variables less than chemical anesthesia (Madden and Houston 1976; Curry and Kynard 1978; see also Chapter 9). Gunstrom and Bethers (1985) used electrical anesthesia for tagging studies of chinook salmon because FDA restrictions on withdrawal times prohibited use of chemical anesthetics.

Reynolds (1983) discussed basic considerations for the use of electricity to capture fish. Aspects of fish response to electroshock were treated in the several symposium papers edited by Vibert (1967). Electricity can produce electroanesthesia in three modes: alternating current (AC), direct current (DC), and pulsed DC with a square wave. Reynolds (1983) stated that unmodified AC is most damaging to fish; pulsed and rectified alternating currents elicit responses similar to those of unmodified AC, but are less harmful. A fish in a DC field turns toward the anode and exhibits forced swimming. Pulsed DC current has not been used for electroanesthesia.

Application.   Madden and Houston (1976) examined the use of an AC electric field—a 100-V AC discharge of 400 mA from an immersible bipolar electrode for 25–30 s—to immobilize common carp and rainbow trout. The field immobilized 200–500-g fish for 20–30 min. For smaller fish, they used shorter discharges. Gill ventilation ceased for 2–3 min and other physiological changes were noted. Gunstrom and Bethers (1985) designed a tagging basket for DC electroanesthesia of adult salmon. When they used a 12-V DC current from an automobile battery to immobilize fish for tagging, electroanesthesia occurred only while the fish were in the electrical field; recovery was "instantaneous" when the electricity was turned off. Fish held in on-board tanks showed no after effects, and tag recoveries from the fish subjected to electrical anesthesia were "satisfactory." They used the electrical basket over a month on fish weighing over 700 g without having to recharge the battery. Orsi and Short (1987) described a modification of Gunstrom and Bethers's (1985) electroanesthesia system involving six electrodes of alternating polarity and only 150 mA of current. They immobilized juvenile and adult chinook salmon in full-strength seawater. Fifty of the juvenile fish were held for 6 weeks after electroanesthesia with only 4% mortality.

Drawbacks. Alternating current stimulates contraction of skeletal, cardiac, and smooth muscle, and it induces tetany, not anesthesia—fish are stunned, not anesthetized (Hartley 1977). Electrotetany may cause fibrillation of the heart, respiratory musculature paralysis (respiratory arrest), and internal bleeding; a strong, sustained contraction of the somatic musculature may cause dislocated vertebrae (Hudy 1985). Yet, in spite of concern regarding immediate and delayed mortality from AC electrofishing, mortality from electrofishing is usually negligible (Hudy 1985). However rainbow trout were more vulnerable to predation after immobilization with direct current than untreated fish (Curry and Kynard 1978).

8.2.9 Miscellaneous Chemical Anesthetics

8.2.9.1 Barbiturates

Recognized by a name ending in "-al," barbiturates are chemically related to barbituric acid. They include amobarbital, barbital sodium, butabarbital, hexobarbital, mephobarbital, methohexital, phenobarbital, pentobarbital sodium, secobarbital, talbutal, thiamylal, thiopental sodium, and thioseconal (Merck & Company 1983; Griffith 1987). Barbiturate drugs are used for general anesthesia and anticonvulsant therapy and for their sedative, hypnotic, and sleep-inducing actions (Warren 1983). However, they may induce hypnosis (sleep) without analgesia (relief of pain). They are prescription drugs used as tranquilizers and to make people sleep. Some barbiturates such as thiopental sodium are used as the sole anesthetic agents for brief (16-min) procedures, for induction of anesthesia prior to administration of other anesthetic agents, for supplemental regional anesthesia, and other purposes (Medical Economics Company 1987).

The hypnotic (sleep-inducing) effects of barbiturates are anesthetic-like because they act as central nervous system depressants. At low concentrations they calm or tranquilize (sedate) because, with their high lipid solubility, they quickly penetrate brain tissue, dulling alertness and avoidance behavior. Higher concentrations that affect the brain stem and spinal cord impair coordination and balance, then immobilize an animal in a sleep-like stage. Walker (1972) used intravenous injections of sodium pentobarbital (10 mg/kg or less) for general surgical "anesthesia" of nurse sharks, but the drug also caused a loss of gill function requiring intubation and flow of seawater until the fish recovered. Overdoses of barbiturates in humans produce coma (narcosis), and can cause death because of respiratory and cardiovascular depression.

Their strong lipid solubility makes barbiturates useful as pre-anesthetics or as ultrashort-acting depressants of the central nervous system, but their subsequent slow release from fatty tissue, where they accumulate, causes prolonged effects (Medical Economics Company 1987). This effect often impairs motor skills for several hours after a sedative effect is lost (Considine and Considine 1984).

Prolonged recovery of fish from immobilizing doses of barbiturates is certainly problematic for most fishery applications.

Regular use of barbiturates by humans causes a physical dependence or addiction. Therefore, these drugs are regulated by the Controlled Substances Act of 1970 (Warren 1983). Purchase requires registration with the U.S. Drug Enforcement Administration (DEA), and DEA regulations prevent the general availability of barbiturates for field use. Security requirements, including storage of the substances in a locked cabinet with a solid door, make laboratory use excessively complicated.

8.2.9.2 Thiazole

Thiazole—2-amino-4-phenylthiazole, phenylthiazole, phenthiazamine, or piscaine—was used as a fish anesthetic in Japan during the 1970s (Ikeda et al. 1974; Kikuchi et al. 1974; Suzuki and Sekizawa 1979). Kikuchi et al. (1974) used thiazole concentrations of 30–40 mg/L to anesthetize common carp; induction time was 6–12 min, anesthesia was maintained for 20–40 min, and recovery took 10–35 min. Rainbow trout and Japanese yellowtails *Seriola quinqueradiata* required slightly lower doses. Concentrations of 8–12 mg/L produced sedation to stages 1 and 2 levels of anesthesia, which could be sustained for 3–72 h. Gilderhus and Marking (1987), however, found that 20-cm-long rainbow trout had a prolonged recovery time from thiazole. Suzuki and Sekizawa (1979) reported a 22-h half-life for thiazole residues; whole-body residues were 0.1 mg/kg after 24 h and 0.05 mg/kg after 48 h.

8.2.9.3 Lidocaine

Lidocaine
(Merck & Company 1983)

Lidocaine hydrochloride
(ASHP 1985)

The chemical name for lidocaine is 2-(diethylamino)-N-(2,6-dimethylphenyl) acetimide; Xylocaine™ is one of several proprietary formulations. Lidocaine hydrochloride is a closely related compound.

Lidocaine is insoluble in water, but soluble in organic solvents such as acetone or alcohol. Lidocaine Hydrochloride Injection™ (Abbott Laboratories) is a white powder freely soluble in water. Aqueous solutions of the hydrochloride are used in human medicine to control ventricular arrhythmias (antiarrhythmic properties) in acute myocardial infarction; it also is used as an anesthetic of the amide type for production of local or regional anesthesia, and as one of several ingredients in anesthetics for surface applications (Considine and Considine 1984). Lidocaine and Xylocaine are used in veterinary applications, applied topically (2–4% solution) or injected (1–2% solution) as a nerve block (Merck & Company 1968). Details of clinical pharmacology and toxicology and dosages for various anesthetic procedures (infiltration, periperal nerve blocks, sympathetic nerve blocks, and central neural blocks) are given in the "Physicians' Desk Reference" (Medical Economics Company 1987). Carrasco et al. (1984) used a combination of carbon dioxide and lidocaine to anesthetize common carp, tilapias, and catfish. Lidocaine is among the most promising of this miscellaneous group of chemicals for fishery applications because a substantial amount of efficacy and toxicological information is available for registration purposes.

8.2.9.4 Propanidid

Propanidid, 4-[2-(diethylamino)-2-oxoethoxy]-3-methoxybenzeneacetic acid propyl ester, has been used experimentally in human medicine as a short-duration, intravenously injectable anesthetic (Merck & Company 1968). It is practically insoluble in water but soluble in alcohol. Oral toxicity to rats is 10 g/kg body weight (Merck & Company 1983). Siwicki (1984) used propanidid as a bath and as an intraperitoneal injection to produce anesthesia in a variety of fishes. Induction times were 2–4 min and recovery times were 5–10 min for concentrations of 1.5–3.0 mg/L in water baths or for doses of 2.0 mg/kg as intraperitoneal injections. Siwicki (1984) reported little or no change in blood chemistry in fish exposed to propanidid.

8.2.9.5 Propoxate

Propoxate, propyl-DL-1-(1-phenylethyl)imidazole-5-carboxylate hydrochloride, resembles etomidate in structure, differing only by one side chain. Useful concentrations for anesthetizing fish range from 0.5 to 10.0 mg/L. These concentrations are similar to those used for etomidate, but they are about 10 times more potent than tricaine. Propoxate is freely soluble in both fresh and salt water. It produced respiratory arrest in fish after 15 min at 64 mg/L or after 1 h at 16 mg/L, but it was safe for 16 h at 0.25 mg/L (Thienpont and Niemegeers 1965).

8.2.10 Animal Experimentation

In the USA, the Animal Welfare Act (Public Law 89-544, as amended by Public Laws 91-579 and 94-279) and other federal, state, and local laws, regulations, and policies obligate an investigator to conduct animal experiments according to scientific and humane principles. According to NIH (1985) guidelines:

The proper use of anesthetics, analgesics, and tranquilizers in laboratory animals is necessary for humane and scientific reasons . . . . If a painful procedure must be conducted without the use of an anesthetic, analgesic, or tranquilizer—because such use would defeat the purpose of an experiment— the procedure must be approved by a committee (institutional) and supervised directly by the responsible investigator. Muscle relaxants or paralytic drugs (e.g., succinylcholine or other curariform drugs) are not anesthetics. They must not be used alone for surgical restraint, although they can be used in connection with drugs known to produce adequate analgesia.

8.2.11 Effects of Anesthesia on Physiology

A decision on whether or not to use an anesthetic must be considered in terms of the animal's welfare, the physiological effect of the anesthetic, and the consequences of not using an anesthetic. The physiological consequences of anesthesia are numerous and they may defeat the purpose of some experiments.

Chemical anesthetics depress neurosensory functions. Most of them affect the central nervous system, and many seem to concentrate in the brain preferentially. Anesthetics act first on the cerebral cortex; with increasing concentration or exposure time, their effects spread down through the brain stem to the medullary respiratory center and the spinal cord.

When fish are placed in a container with an anesthetic, they typically dart or thrash about, perhaps showing a response to netting and handling or to the irritating or acidic effects of the anesthetic. This initial activity leads to an increased rate and amplitude of respiration, but activity and respiration decline as the anesthetic action begins. To summarize many studies, it is known that exposure to an anesthetic may alter or impair stress response, metabolic rate, oxygen consumption, gill ventilation, cardiac rate, blood pressure, blood chemistry (blood sugar, glycogen, lactate, pH regulation, blood ions, and osmotic balance), excretion, olfactory acuity, and sperm motility. Physiological problems and anesthetic stress develop in proportion to the duration of physiological impairment. The physiological consequences of anesthesia can persist long after the chemical exposure has ceased (Bourne 1984).

In spite of these many problems, the stress from anesthesia may still be less than would result without anesthesia. For example, Strange and Shreck (1978) found tricaine effective for reducing handling stress in yearling chinook salmon. Anesthesia is professionally and humanely necessary to reduce pain during animal surgery. Without anesthesia, moreover, the survival of fish subjected to various manipulations (such as transportation) is often poor because of the trauma inflicted by handling, the increase in oxygen requirements caused by struggling, and the heightened disposition to invasion by bacteria (Jolly et al. 1972).

8.2.11.1 Stress Response

The physiological characteristics of stress were first explained for mammals by Selye (1950; 1973); the sequence of physiological and biochemical changes involved in a stress response by fish have been summarized by Wedemeyer et al. (1976; see also Chapter 14). Several physiological changes in blood and tissues are caused by exposure to tricaine (e.g., Forster and Berglund 1956; Garey and Rahn 1970; Hunn and Willford 1970; Wedemeyer 1970; Houston et al. 1971a, 1971b; Soivio et al. 1977). However, these studies were done with unneutralized tricaine, and they did not distinguish between the effects of lowered pH and those of anesthesia per se. However, Smit et al. (1979a, 1979b, 1979c) distinguished several hematological changes related to the pH effect as well as to handling, and found intra- and interspecific differences in response to anesthesia. Barton and Peter (1982) reported that elevated plasma cortisol levels in rainbow trout exposed to tricaine was due to the acidity produced by the tricaine in soft water. Houston et al. (1971a, 1971b) noted that handling alone led to significant alterations in plasma glucose and lacate and in the concentrations of major electrolytes.

It is unclear whether or not anesthetics act directly on stress hormone production. Strange and Schreck (1978) found no changes in plasma cortisol levels in rainbow trout after brief exposure to 50 mg tricaine/L, although cortisol increased after a longer exposure to 100 mg/L. European eels showed no changes in catecholamine levels after recovery from anesthesia (LeBras 1982), suggesting little or no depletion of hormone supplies. Most investigators, however have shown that large increases in cortisol result from anesthesia, although other stresses such as chases, capture, and confinement prior to anesthesia may have influenced the response.

Because catecholamines and cortisol are difficult to assay, blood sugar often has been used as a proxy for catecholamines and depletion of liver ascorbate (a precursor) for cortisol. A decrease in plasma chloride ions also has been used to indicate increased cortisol. Crowley and Berinati (1972) showed that blood sugar in rainbow trout increased from a normal level of 125 mg/100 mL to more than 300 mg/100 mL during 90-min exposures to tricaine.

8.2.11.2 Respiratory Effects

The gill ventilation system (buccal and opercular pumps) is normally stimulated by the respiratory center in the medulla. Anesthetics like tricaine depress activity of the brain; at high enough concentration or after a long exposure, the anesthetic accumulated in the brain stops impulse transmission from the medulla to the gills. An overdose of anesthetic or excessive exposure time causes ventilation to cease. An oxygen debt quickly accumulates, especially at high temperatures. When this happens, the fish should be immediately transferred to fresh water. Artificial resuscitation by manual gill ventilation is possible because the gills will allow passive diffusion of substances between blood and water. Gills can be partly exposed to air to allow rapid inward diffusion of oxygen, as long as the gills are kept moist and the heart continues to function. In salmonids, cardiac arrest typically occurs a few minutes after ventilation ceases (Smith, personal observation). However, channel catfish overdosed with quinaldine at 25°C maintained a heartbeat for at least 30 min after ventilation ceased (Summerfelt, personal observation).

The biochemical processes that require oxygen continue during anesthesia, at least at the basal level. To the extent that a fish's oxygen demand is not met, the fish accumulates lactate or other products that must be oxidized later—that is, the fish accumulates an oxygen debt, which is indicated by hyperventilation as the fish recovers from anesthesia. Because anesthesia reduces gill ventilation (Mann and Rajbanshi 1967) and oxygen consumption (Houston et al. 1973), deep anesthesia can be especially dangerous if the fish has a preexisting oxygen debt from excessive activity, a recent meal, or other causes. For example, if a fish is anesthetized after it has been exercised and stressed by hook-and-line capture, it may die during or after the treatment (Wydoski et al. 1976). Although lactate accumulation from hyperactivity can cause delayed mortality (Black 1958), such buildups can be reduced if fish are anesthetized before they are handled.

The oxygen concentration in the anesthetic solution affects oxygen debt, and becomes a serious problem when many fish are anesthetized in a small container without aeration or solution changes. Each fish removes part of the oxygen and anesthetic and adds mucous, carbon dioxide, and ammonia to the solution. Without aeration, diffusion of oxygen into the solution does not replace the oxygen removed by the fish. Because investigators usually do not measure the rates at which fish remove anesthetic and oxygen from solution, it is advisable to refresh the water and anesthetic at frequent intervals.

There are several ways to avoid cardiac–respiratory distress during procedures that require deep anesthesia. A surgical table and a respiratory cannula can be used to maintain a continuous flow of water and anesthetic over the gills (Figure 8.1). A supply of fresh, well-oxygenated water should be available to prevent anesthetic overdose. In the field, the depth of anesthesia can be adjusted by moving the fish back and forth between separate containers of anesthetic solution and untreated water.

8.2.11.3   Cardiovascular, Hematological, and Osmoregulatory Changes

The influence of tricaine on fish metabolism and various hematological and physiological variables has been thoroughly documented (e.g., Wedemeyer 1970). Both heart and ventilation rates tend to slow in salmonids during anesthesia (Randall and Smith 1967; Lochowitz et al. 1974), but they may increase in some other species such as tench *Tinca tinca* (Shelton and Randall 1962) and common carp (Serfaty et al. 1959). When Houston et al. (1971a) exposed brook trout to acidic tricaine for 30 s, however, blood pressure and ventilatory activity declined, but heart rate increased.

Changes during anesthesia include decreased blood flow through the gills (Fromm et al. 1971), decreased blood pH and increased blood carbon dioxide level (Hoglund and Persson 1971), decreased oxygen concentration in the dorsal aorta and erythrocyte swelling (Soivio et al. 1977), and vasodilation of the gill lamellae (Soivio and Hughes 1978). Documentation of hematological and plasma ion changes during anesthesia is extensive (Chapter 9). Pickering et al. (1982) found changes in the counts of lymphocytes but not of erythrocytes, neutrophils, or thrombocytes of brown trout. Smit et al. (1979a) listed many hematological effects of both neutralized and acid tricaine on rainbow trout, tilapia, and common carp. Houston et al. (1971a) reported rapid hemoconcentration (i.e., increase in hemoglobin, hematocrits, and total dissolved solids) and alterations in major electrolytes of the plasma and tissue following exposure of brook trout to 100 mg Finquel/L for 15 min. However, they also found that handling (physical trauma) alone produced departures from physiological norms, including changes in blood lactate, plasma glucose, plasma and cellular potassium, and plasma chloride and divalent cations. In some cases, electroanesthesia may be used to avoid, or to determine the effects of, chemical anesthetic (see Chapter 9).

Given the oft-cited changes in plasma ions that accompany anesthesia, it is surprising that few changes in urine composition have been noted. Koyama (1983) found that the urine output from common carp, and the chloride content of the urine, peaked 2 h after the fish were anesthetized with tricaine. However, Savitz (1969) found no change in the rate of nitrogen excretion from bluegills after anesthesia. Allen and Hunn (1977) believed that the changes they measured in renal output by channel catfish were related to experimental stress, not to anesthesia.

8.2.11.4 Neurosensory, Enzyme, and Reproductive Effects

Several investigators have shown direct effects of anesthetics on nerves and sensory organs. In squid axons, tricaine suppressed the peak current of sodium ions and the steady-state current of potassium ions, raised the excitation threshold, and blocked nerve conduction (Frazier and Narahashi 1975). It seems likely that fish axons would behave similarly. Hensel et al. (1975) showed that tricaine also stopped the activity of single nerve fibers in the lateral line in cod and in the ampullae of Lorenzini in sharks. Output from the lateral line nerves of tilapia decreased 70% during anesthesia, skin sensitivity decreased, and other changes occurred in the central nervous system (Spaeth and Schweickert 1977). Exposure to anesthetic had no subsequent effect on learning rate of rainbow trout (McNicholl and MacKay 1975).

Some enzymes are affected by anesthetics, others are not. The ubiquitous carbonic anhydrase showed a 50% decrease in activity during exposure of the catfish *Idus idus* to tricaine, but enzymes of the citric acid cycle were unaffected (Gronow 1974). In the liver, activity of many of the enzymes involved in processing hydrocarbon pollutants decreased from exposure to tricaine (Laitinen et al. 1981). The available information does not indicate that tricaine has a predictable pattern of effect on enzyme activities.

Lewis et al. (1985) found that a 10-min exposure of channel catfish to only 0.5 mg tricaine/L destroyed the cilia on olfactory sensory epithelia. Regeneration of the cilia required 28 d. Allison (1961) showed that brook trout sperm lost motility after about 10 s contact with tricaine. It is not clear whether this was due to the acidity or to a direct effect of the anesthesia; Duplinsky (1982) has shown that lowering the pH of water can affect the motility of esocid sperm. Crawford and Hulsey (1963) anesthetized channel catfish with 132 mg tricaine/L to spawn them and found no effect on the success of spawning or the viability of resulting fry.

8.3 SURGERY

8.3.1 Applications

Surgery on fishes has been especially useful for studies of endocrinology, pharmacology, and general physiology, but many other applications have been reported. Surgery is used, for example, to amputate fins for fish marking; to implant electrodes and telemetry devices for studies of physiology and behavior; to implant pharmacological and immunogenic substances; to repair wounds and treat injuries; to remove tumors, glands, and organs; and to obtain samples of tissues and body fluids.

Surgery is used to remove (ablate) or excise (ectomize) a gland or organ, often to assess the resulting physiological or behavioral changes. Examples are removal of the pituitary gland (hypophysectomy), gonads (gonadectomy or castration), and spleen (spleenectomy). Gonads have been the most frequently removed organs. Indirect evidence for gonadal regulation of gonadotropic function in sockeye salmon was detected from cytological changes in the pituitary after gonadectomy (McBride and Van Overbeeke 1969). Billard et al. (1971, 1976) provided direct evidence for gonadal regulation of gonadotropin secretion by measuring an increase in gonadotropin concentration in response to surgical castration of trout. Other examples are evaluations of steroid response to ovariectomy in elasmobranchs (Jenkins and Dodd 1982) and blue tilapia (Yaron et al. 1977) and measurement of cortisol levels in sockeye salmon following gonadectomy (Donaldson and Fagerlund 1970).

Hypophysectomy has been the focus of neurosurgery because of the "master gland's" tropic function in regulating other endocrine glands (Hoar 1957; Pickford and Atz 1957; Hoar and Randall 1969). Surgical removal of the digestive glands has received less attention, but Ince (1979) did a partial pancreatectomy of the northern pike and Kallner (1977) used a fistulated bile duct to study bile action on cholesterol in fourhorn sculpin.

Nerve function or sensitivity and behavioral response to impaired nerve transmission have been studied after nerve tracts were sectioned (axotomy; Hara 1975). In studies of fish migration and behavior, researchers have sectioned olfactory nerves to determine the involvement of olfaction in homing by salmon (Wisby and Hasler 1954; Hasler 1966). Some experimental studies of predator–prey relationships have involved sensory occlusion, amputation, and maiming. Herwig (1979) stated that "tumor removal [from fish] by surgical means is not now uncommon."

Telemetry devices extend the range to which humans can locate fish, and they permit the remote sensing of environmental and physiological variables (Winter 1983). Surgery is often used to implant a transmitter device into the abdominal cavity of a fish for long-term tracking studies (e.g., Hart and Summerfelt 1975; Bidgood 1980; Schramm and Black 1984). Lipid- and water-soluble substances can be incorporated in pellets or "pills," or enclosed in Silastic™ tubing (medical-grade dimethylpolysiloxane), then implanted for pharmacological purposes (Higgs et al. 1975; Jensen et al. 1978; Crim et al. 1983; Pickering and Duston 1983). A similar strategy has been used to vaccinate fish because of the advantages of slow, continuous release of a drug or antigen into the peritoneal cavity (Anderson 1974).

8.3.2 Implants

In addition to surgical procedures, the insertion of a device into the abdominal cavity of fish requires attention to the implant materials and their coatings. Implants must be chemically compatible with biological tissues, nonreactive, and certainly not irritating or toxic. Implant materials may be inert and smooth or inert with micropores; they may have a controlled-reactive surface or they may be resorbable (Hench and Ethridge 1982). Coatings, or encapsulants, are used to protect the electronics and to provide protection for the tissues. A coated implant should be suitable for sterilization and compatible with the host's tissues. Types of materials that have been used for coating implants include beeswax, paraffin, and Vistanex (a synthetic paraffin wax); elastomers (e.g., medical-grade silicone rubber such as Silastic™, a formulation of dimethylpolysiloxane); thermosetting plastics (epoxy); thermoplastic plastics (Teflon™, polyvinyl chloride, or nylon); urethane; and dental acrylic (Hench and Ethridge 1982; Winter 1983). The implant coating should not cause tissue irritation; serious incompatibility can cause adhesions and necrosis. However, even under optimum conditions, it is natural for implants to elicit a fibroblastic proliferation and encapsulation of the implant because of chronic inflammation (Marty and Summerfelt 1986).

8.3.3 Basic Techniques

Surgery is an art and a science, involving artful manipulation of surgical tools plus appropriate uses of anesthetics, antiseptics, and antibiotics. The extensive literature on experimental physiology of fish contains many surgical applications, yet fish surgery per se has not been the subject of substantive research. The text by Pavlovskii (1964) has several chapters on aspects of fish surgery. Malyukina (1964) described surgical methods for studies of brain and sensory functions. Krayukhin (1964) described surgical procedures for the digestive tract of fish, including installation of a gastric fistual (a passage from the body surface to the lumen of the digestive tract), and Pegel' (1964) described ligation procedures for closing off the bile duct with sutures.

The report by Smith and Bell (1967) seems to have been the first in North American literature to focus on experimental fish surgery. Klontz and Smith (1968) presented a synthesis of "surgical manipulations" and procedural details for laparotomy, the surgical opening of the abdomen. Goetz et al. (1977) described a surgical operating apparatus and procedures for doing cranial surgery (pinealectomy) on salmonids.

The prospective fish surgeon will benefit from works on fish anatomy (e.g., Smith and Bell 1975; Grizzle and Rogers 1976) and texts on surgery for human and veterinary medicine (e.g., Dougherty 1981; Sabiston 1981; Schwartz 1984). A useful illustrated reference on operative procedures is the Ethicon (1961) "Manual of Operative Procedure and Surgical Knots," and we also recommend Jochen's (1982) "Veterinary Surgical Sutures."

8.3.4 Materials

8.3.4.1 The Surgical "Table"

Fish and other vertebrates with gills require special consideration during surgery. The incision must be kept out of water, yet the skin must be kept moist and the gills must be continually perfused with oxygenated water and anesthetic solution. In most cases, the surgical table is a V-shaped trough, but Goetz et al. (1977) designed an apparatus that holds the body of the fish with clamps and the head with a "mouthpiece." Some surgical tables for fish have been designed with water-recirculation pumps and options to provide water flow over the gills from the mouth or from the operculum (reverse flow). Reverse flow provides only about 10% of the normal oxygen transfer and should be minimized or avoided to prevent oxygen debt (G. W. Klontz, personal communication).

The surgical trough or box should be large enough to accommodate the fish and also spacious enough to allow manipulation of surgical tools. A water-recirculating system, operated by a small submersible pump, can be used to move a stream of aerated water over the fish's gills and return the water to a small collecting reservoir. Foam rubber or a towel provides a cushion that conforms to the body of the fish, holding the fish with little or no tissue damage and no scale loss (Courtois 1981). Straps with a Velcro™ closure may be used as a restrainer in case of a violent reflex action and to hold the fish in proper position. Kaya et al. (1984) developed a restraining table for gonadal biopsies of live, unanesthetized tuna that has merits for other types of surgery as well.

For more complicated surgical procedures, A. H. Houston designed an operating assembly that features a tiltable table, jaw retractors, opercular supports, and an apparatus for branchial and buccal irrigation (Figure 8.1). In contrast, Reinecker and Ruddell (1974) described a simple operating table for fish surgery. In the field, transmitter implants are usually done in a shallow rectangular tank without recirculating water. However, Courtois (1981) designed a compact portable surgical table based on a Styrofoam ice chest for field use; the device included a self-contained water-recirculation pump to deliver the anesthetic solution to the gills.

When surgery is done out of water for more than a very brief interval, a cannula should be inserted to supply oxygenated water to the gills. Procedures that require less than 10–15 min may be done in a trough without recirculating water. Mulford (1984) noted that most investigators report taking 8–15 min to do a surgical implant and to suture the incisions with needle and thread. For simple procedures taking 2–4 min, the fish can be wrapped in a wet towel to prevent the skin from drying, and the surgical procedures can be conducted on a standard table top (Krayukhin 1964).

8.3.4.2 Aseptic Technique

In the early history of human surgery, patients often died because of infections. Joseph Lister, the English surgeon credited for developing aseptic surgery, emphasized cleanliness and use of antiseptic procedures to kill germs in the operating room. Since then, there has been a steady progression toward aseptic (completely sterile) surgical procedures, which include wearing of sterile surgical gloves, gowns, caps, and face masks; use of sterile instruments; and aseptic preparation of the surface area on the patient where the incision will take place. Aseptic procedures are not limited to human medicine; NIH (1985) requires aseptic techniques for "major survival surgery" on laboratory animals. This is defined as "any surgical intervention that penetrates a body cavity or has the potential for producing a permanent handicap in an animal that is expected to recover."

However, the NIH (1985) guide does not address any aspect of the care of aquatic vertebrates, and its recommendations for aseptic animal surgery do not address the problems peculiar to surgery on fish. Krayukhin (1964) performed fish surgery without anesthesia and stated, without elaboration, that "no sterilization of instruments, materials and hands of the surgeon is required." Pegel' (1964) used sterilized surgical instruments, but he stated that "Our experiences showed that strict aseptic or antiseptic measures were unnecessary in this operation"; However, the fish lived only 7–15 d after surgery.

Although it is possible to place a fish into sterile water, it is not possible to chemically disinfect the entire outer surface of a live fish. Moreover, the water of the surgical trough may quickly become contaminated if the fish should defecate or urinate. Thus, it is generally impractical to sterilize the surgical trough, nor is

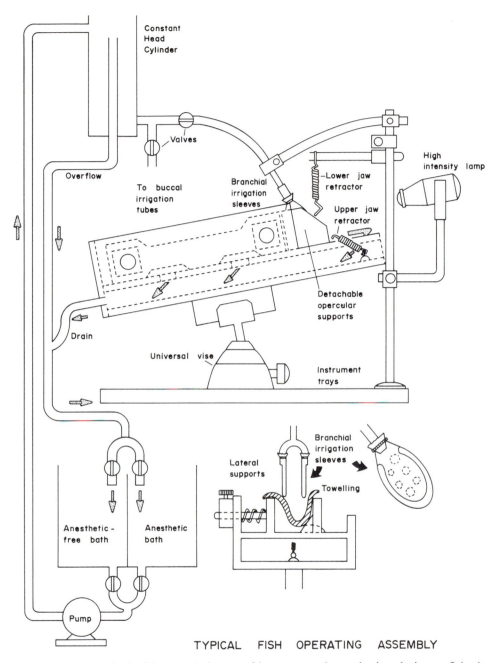

Figure 8.1 A surgical table (stage) that provides water and anesthetic solution to fish via buccal or branchial irrigation systems. A front view of a branchial irrigation system is shown at lower right. (Design and figure courtesy of A. H. Houston.)

it necessary to use sterile water in filling the trough. In the laboratory, dechlorinated tap water is as aseptic as practical for surgery on fish. Chlorine concentrations of tap water vary, but 5.0 mg/L is about maximum and the average may be about 2 mg/L. Brungs (1973) recommended that total residual chlorine not exceed

0.2 mg/L for a period of 2 h/d for the more resistant fish. Water may be dechlorinated by filtering it through activated charcoal or by adding 2 mg thiosulfate/L for each 1 mg chlorine/L (Cole and Lewis 1958).

Other aseptic procedures to be considered in surgery include use of sterile gloves, mask, and surgical tools. Although fish cannot be sterilized, aseptic procedures that prevent infections should be used. As a minimum, the surgical tools should be sterile and the surgeon should wear sterile gloves. A surgical mask looks professional, but its value for fish surgery is debatable; it is unlikely that the microbial flora of the human mouth or respiratory tract will cause diseases in fish.

The surgeon should use sterile surgical gloves because direct contact will be made with internal organs. The surgical assistant, who handles the fish and items that are not disinfected, and who also functions as the anesthesiologist, does not need to wear sterile gloves. To avoid contamination of an open incision from trough water or adjacent body surfaces, the incision area may be covered with a wetted sterile towel or sheet having an opening large enough to do the surgical procedure. The sheet screens the open wound from accidental contamination and provides a convenient sterile surface on which to temporarily place a needle or implant.

The surgical instruments may be sterilized with a germicide, such as 1:1,000 benzalkonium chloride or other quaternary ammonium compounds. Calcium hypochlorite, formulated to provide 200 mg available chlorine per liter for 1 h, may be used to sanitize utensils (Schnick et al. 1986b); however, it is quite corrosive on metals. Also, one can autoclave a surgical pack if convenient. Tools or implants exposed to a germicide should be rinsed in sterile water before use.

8.3.4.3   Instruments

The essential tools for surgery are simple and available in considerable variety. The basic surgical tools are scalpel, scissors, forceps, hemostat or clamps, needle holder and needles, and a blunt probe. A luminated speculum (such as a laparoscope or otoscope) is useful for examination of internal organs through a small incision, and may be helpful to illuminate and slightly magnify structures.

A scalpel with inexpensive disposable blades is needed mainly to start the incision (opening) through the skin. Scissors, less likely to cause accidental punctures, may be used to extend the opening to full length. Operating scissors are straight or curved, and the tips described as ''sharp/sharp'' (both blades sharp), ''sharp/blunt,'' or ''blunt/blunt.'' A 14-cm straight blunt/blunt type is a general purpose size useful for lengthening a surgical section of the body wall (laparotomy).

A hemostat, also called hemostatic forceps or clamp, is used for a temporary ligature of the severed ends of blood vessels. Unless used delicately, hemostats can crush tissue, and inappropriate use may cause necrosis and provide a locus of infection of the damaged tissue. A rat-toothed tissue forceps, which has a gripping tip, is more effective than a plain forceps to manipulate the body wall or peritoneum. A needle holder, also called a dissecting and ligature forceps, is similar to a hemostat but has a stronger closure pressure. The needle holder is essential to manipulate a suturing needle and to knot the sutures. Bone cutters and a high-speed drill with an assortment of blades may be needed for cranial surgery.

The type of needle selected is based on the size, shape, and depth of the wound (Jochen 1982). The variety of available needles may be confusing, but nearly any type of operation can be performed with one or two types. The needle should make a hole in the tissue only large enough to permit passage of the suture material, and thus should not be larger or stronger than necessary.

Needle types are designated by the point, eye, shape, and size. The points may be "spear," "triangular," "taper," "cutting," or "tracer" (Ethicon 1961). Needles have an eye or they are eyeless, or swaged. The eye may be closed or split. The swaged needle has the suture material attached to the shaft by mechanical pressure. It causes less trauma to tissue than the ordinary eyed and threaded needle, which pulls after it a double strand of suture that forms a hole through the tissue that is larger than necessary for the single strand of suture that follows.

Needle shape may be curved, straight, or a combination thereof with a straight shaft and a half-curved cutting edge. Straight needles are usually held with the fingers to suture thick skin. Curved needles are specified by degree of needle curvature and size. Curvature is designated as ¼-, ⅜-, ½-, or ⅝-circle. The choice of curvature is related to the depth, type, and dimensions of the wound. The ⅜- and ½-circle are the most common because they are the most versatile. The smaller ¼-circle needle is usually limited to surgery of the eye. The ½-circle needle is available in 13 sizes (8–20; the larger the number, the smaller the needle), and the ⅜-circle is available in 11 sizes (Henry Schein 1986). One should be aware that the designation of needle sizes may vary with the supply company.

The needle points are cutting or noncutting. The cutting edge can be on the inside of a needle curve or on the outside curve of a triangular needle such as the Atraloc™ (Ethicon Corporation) "reverse-cutting" needle (Ethicon 1961). The cutting needle is needed to penetrate such tough tissues as skin and tendon, though it can be used for other purposes as well. A noncutting or taper point needle is limited to use on soft tissues such as peritoneum, intestine, or muscle.

8.3.4.4   Suture Materials

The function of sutures is to close an incision and maintain tissue contact to aid healing. Many kinds of suture materials are available (Table 8.3), the synthetic ones often being proprietary. Sutures are classified as absorbable (reabsorbable) and nonabsorbable. Absorbable sutures are defined as materials that lose an appreciable amount of tensile strength within 60 d, whereas nonabsorbable sutures retain their original strength for more than 60 d (Jochen 1982). Absorbable sutures disintegrate rather quickly and should be used for internal closures; they may be used for external suturing when fish are to be released and the sutures cannot be removed. The suture material should not elicit more than a slight tissue reaction during absorption. Nonabsorbable sutures are used for external sutures when they can be removed or when wound healing would be too slow (as at low temperatures) to insure retention of the absorbable suture material.

The size of suture materials is designated in whole numbers (1, 2, 3, etc.), the larger numbers representing larger diameters, or in the aught series (0, 00, 000), in which more ciphers represent smaller diameters. For example, in designations of surgical chromic gut, the sequence 000, 00, 0, 1, 2 is a scale of increasing diameter. However, suture material in the combination number/aught series (2/0, 3/0, 4/0, etc., which is equivalent to 00, 000, 0000, etc.) decreases in size with increasing numerical value. General purpose suture material should be 3/0 and 4/0 for closure

Table 8.3 Characteristics and uses of selected absorbable and nonabsorbable suture materials commonly used in veterinary surgery. (From Jochen 1982, used with the permission of Pitman-Moore, Veterinary Division of Johnson & Johnson, Washington Crossing, New Jersey.)

Suture type	Raw material	Absorption	Frequent uses
Absorbable sutures			
Surgical gut, plain	Collagen from healthy mammals	Absorbed by body enzymes	Suturing subcutaneous and other tissues that heal rapidly; ligating blood vessels; may be used in presence of infection
Surgical gut, chromic	Collagen from healthy mammals, treated to resist digestion by body enzymes	Absorbed by body enzymes, but more slowly than plain gut due to chemical treatment	Most versatile of all materials for use in almost all tissues; any procedure in which sutures are buried or intended for absorption; may be used in presence of infection
Coated Vicryl[a] (polyglactin 900), braided	Copolymer of lactide and glycolide; polyglactin 370 with calcium stearate coating	Absorbed by slow hydrolysis in tissues, essentially complete in 60–90 d	Suturing or ligating tissues when an absorbable material is desired, except when strength under stress is required; subcuticular suturing
PDS[a] (polydiox-anone), monofila-ment	Poly(p-dioxanone)	Absorbed by slow hydrolysis within 6 months	Any use in which an absorbable suture and extended wound support are desirable
Nonabsorbable sutures			
Prolene[a] polypropy-lene, monofila-ment	Polypropylene polymer	None; remains encapsulated in body tissues	Any use in which tension is expected; inert; can be buried or used for skin closure
Ethilon[a] nylon, monofila-ment	Polyamide polymer	None; remains encapsulated in body tissues	Can be buried or used for skin closure; plastic surgery
Ethibond[a] polyester, braided	Polyester fiber coated with polybutilate	None; remains encapsulated in body tissues	Abdominal closure; cardiovascular and plastic surgery; cruciate ligament repair; can be used for skin closure
Surgical steel, mono- or multifilament	Iron alloy	None; remains encapsulated in body tissues	Used when strength is desirable; general and skin closures; tendon repair; orthopedic and neurosurgery
Surgical silk, braided	Natural protein fiber spun by silkworms	Absorbed very slowly; remains encapsulated in body tissues	Suturing and ligating most body tissues; ophthalmology and plastic surgery
Surgical cotton, twisted	Natural cotton fibers	None; remains encapsulated in body tissues	Suturing and ligating most body tissues

[a]Trademarks of Pitman-Moore.

of the skin, and 4/0 and 5/0 for closure of the peritoneum. For example, Yaron et al. (1977) sutured the body wall of tilapia with 4/0 silk.

Monel metal and stainless steel wire and pins have long been used for fish tags and to attach transmitter capsules to fish in the form of a saddle. Mulford (1984) used a surgical skin stapler to close the incision made for implanting ultrasonic transmitters in the abdominal cavities of striped bass.

8.3.5 Surgical Procedures

8.3.5.1 Preoperative Care and Preparation

Several preoperative variables require consideration. It is desirable to stop feeding fish 24–72 h before surgery to minimize regurgitation of food or defecation in the water. In the field, however, successful surgery often is done on wild-caught fish without control over this function. Because large wild fish such as striped bass may be stressed by transportation, handling, and laboratory environments, it is better to perform surgery on these fish in the field immediately after capture and return them to their natural environment as soon as possible. (Note, however, the restrictions on the registration label for the anesthetic.)

When wild fish are brought to the laboratory for surgery, or moved from one site to another, they should be acclimated to the new conditions to establish physiological homeostasis before they are subjected to the added stresses of anesthesia and surgical manipulation. It is inadvisable to deeply anesthetize a fish that is in an excited state or has just undergone strenuous exercise, because it has an unresolved oxygen debt that probably will become even larger during anesthesia and may cause postsurgical mortality from lactic acidosis.

8.3.5.2 Anesthetization

Some surgery has been done without any type of anesthesia (Pegel' 1964), but such procedures are not humane and should not be done unless the anesthesia "would defeat the purpose of the experiment" (NIH 1985). A central nervous system depressant, for example, would interfere with electrical measurement of intracranial neurophysiological functions. In such a case, surgery could be performed under general anesthesia; then, after it has recovered, the fish could be immobilized for electrophysiological measurements with a restraining device and injections of a skeletal muscle relaxant such as gallamine triethiodide (Echteler 1985; Kiyohara et al. 1985; Munz 1985).

When several fish are to be operated on successively over a short interval (3–4 h, say), such that fish in the holding tank must be disturbed as each new subject is captured, it is advisable to sedate the whole group with light concentrations of anesthetic before surgery begins (Summerfelt, personal experience). Group sedation makes fish easier to capture, and it reduces hyperactivity and accumulation of oxygen debts prior to surgery.

Each subject removed from the holding tank is placed in a smaller container for surgical anesthesia. The amount of anesthetic used should be derived from experience to avoid an overdose. During surgery, anesthesia is maintained in one of several ways. The fish's head may be immersed in anesthetic solution, the gills may be continuously irrigated with well-oxygenated water containing anesthetic (branchial irrigation), or the gills may be sprayed occasionally with anesthetic from a squeeze bottle.

8.3.5.3   Topical Disinfectants

For terrestrial animals, standard preoperative procedures include disinfection of the planned area of the incision. However, the skin of a fish is covered with living epithelium, not dead cells as in mammals. Alcohol or harsh disinfectants used for preoperative preparation of mammals may damage fish epithelial cells and should not be used on the incision site. Fish mucus has germicidal properties, and it is better to preserve mucus-producing cells than to create a large area of damaged epithelium. Klontz and Smith (1968) noted that many surface sterilants are protein coagulants. Tincture of iodine, 10% iodine solution in alcohol, and Betadine™ (Purdue Frederick Company), a complex of iodine and polyvinylpyr-rolidone that has 1% iodine (the synonym is provaline iodine, a viricide and bacteriocide used for egg disinfection and as a surgeon's handwash) have been used as topical disinfectants and painted on wounds with an artist's brush. These chemicals may "burn exposed tissue in marine fish or smooth-skinned fish" (Herwig 1979). However, information on this subject is limited and a critical evaluation of topical disinfectants for use in fish surgery is needed.

8.3.5.4   Procedures for Abdominal Surgery

The abdominal body wall of fish is thinner along the midventral axis than on the flank and no major blood vessels cross the median saggital plane. Schramm and Black (1984) found that midventral incisions were better than vertical incisions in the lateral body wall for implanting transmitters in grass carp because large scales did not have to be removed, suturing was easier, and abdominal tissues and organs were less likely to be damaged; however, 20% of fish implanted through midventral incisions expelled the implant due to ruptured sutures. On the other hand, lateral incisions in female grass carp often resulted in accidental puncture of the ovary, which lies close to the peritoneum. Schramm (personal communication) reported successful use of a lateral incision for transmitter implants in largemouth bass.

Incision length should only be as long as needed to adequately perform the desired procedure. On scaled fish, a row of scales the length of the planned incision should first be removed with forceps. An incision through the skin the length of the intended opening should be completed with a scalpel. The cut skin is held back with rat-toothed forceps, and a scalpel is used to incise the muscle and penetrate the parietal peritoneum. After a small aperture is made into the peritoneal cavity, a straight blunt/blunt scissors may be used to cut through the body wall and peritoneum, thus avoiding potential damage to the underlying viscera.

Care must be taken to avoid physical injury to internal organs during surgery because this can cause hemorrhage, necrosis of the affected tissue, and death of the fish if the damage is extensive. Internal bleeding may elicit organ-to-organ adhesions. Sterile gauze, folded into small pads, can be used to sponge blood. An electrosurgical unit or heat cautery, incorporating a small soldering iron with sharpened tips, is said to help limit bleeding of severed blood vessels (R. D. Spall, Idaho State University, personal communication).

8.3.5.5   Suturing

Suturing is achieved with absorbable or nonabsorbable sutures or stainless steel staples. Crim et al. (1983) reported surgery through the lateral body wall in trout

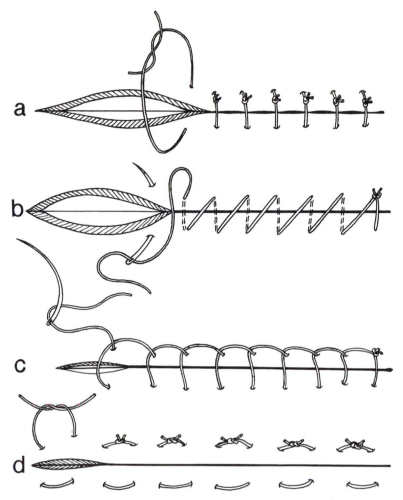

Figure 8.2 Types of sutures: **(a)** simple interrupted; **(b)** continuous; **(c)** locking (blanket); **(d)** interrupted horizontal mattress.

without use of sutures, but some form of suturing is generally preferred to enhance healing.

Common suture patterns are (a) simple interrupted, (b) continuous, (c) locking stitch, and (d) interrupted horizontal mattress (Figure 8.2). The simple interrupted suture and the interrupted horizontal mattress suture are the strongest and most suitable for closing the skin of fish. The continuous suture is the least traumatic; it is suitable for soft, internal tissues, but is less secure than the interrupted suture because it is knotted at only the beginning and the end of the suture. The knot is the weakest point, and if one knot comes out, the entire suture will pull apart. The locking stitch, also called a blanket stitch, is a modification of the continuous suture that allows one to apply more pressure perpendicular to the incision to tightly appose the two cut sides. This stitch has the same two-knot structural limitation as the continuous suture.

Suturing may be done with the one- or two-hand knot tie, or by use of the instrument tie (Ethicon 1961; Jochen 1982). Most surgeons prefer the instrument tie because it is easier to manipulate a small needle and thread with instruments than with fingers when surgical gloves are worn. The instrument tie can be done with one or two needle holders; the suturing process with one needle holder is illustrated in Figure 8.3.

The peritoneum and skin may be sutured separately for added strength (Figure 8.4). Alternatively, after an inner row of peritoneal sutures is applied, the skin may be held together with only tissue adhesives. Tissue adhesives, which are forms of cyanoacrylate esters similar to Super Glue™ (Loctite Corporation), can be used to bond tissue together without sutures. At least two commercial brands are available: Nexaband™ (BioNexus, Inc.), a "purified cyanoacrylate mono-mer"; and Vetbond™ (Animal Care Products–3M Company), an "*n*-butyl cy-anoacrylate." These compounds are used to close cuts on ears and pads of cats and dogs, and on declawed toes of cats. After abdominal incisions in river otters *Lutra canadensis* for transmitter implants, Nexaband adhesive was used to close the skin after an inner row of absorbable sutures was stitched into the peritoneum and subcutaneous tissues (Caroline Runyon, Iowa State University, personal communication). The incision must be blotted dry before the adhesive is applied, but the cyanoacrylate dries in 30–60 s. Tissue adhesive should be ideal for reassembling pieces of the cranial dermal skeleton. Houston (see Chapter 9) used Hitoacryl B, a "tissue cement," for sealing cannulas into blood vessels.

Waterproofing, not to be confused with adhesive tissue bonding, is used to seal a closed incision to prevent infection. Some investigators have smeared a sutured incision with petrolatum (petroleum jelly, e.g., Vaseline™) (Jenkins and Dodd 1982). If a petrolatum will adhere for at least a day or so, one of the several types of antibiotic-containing topical ointments may be considered. Some investigators have tried to seal cranial lesions of hypophysectomized fish with petrolatum or with beeswax or paraffin, which set up quickly (Malyukina 1964). Medical-grade silicone cannot be used for cranial seals because it does not set up fast enough, though it is preferred for encapsulating implants (Agnew et al. 1962; Braley 1970).

8.3.5.6 Postoperative Care

Complications of surgery may include osmotic shock (electrolyte losses), hemorrhage, localized inflammation and infection, peritonitis and systemic infec-tions, gut stasis (impaired peristalsis and retention of the feces), and adhesions. Preoperative as well as proper surgical procedures should be used to prevent occurrence of some of these problems. Treatment with antibiotics may prevent peritonitis and systemic infections.

For experimental purposes, when the fish will be euthanized, then incinerated or buried after the study, it may not matter whether the antibiotic is registered for use on fish, only that it be effective, not interfere with the study, and not be a hazard to the user. In such cases, chloramphenicol, kanamycin, and erythromycin may be considered.

Chloramphenicol (Chloromycetin™ is only one of many trade names), or the closely related chloramphenicol palmitate, injected at a rate of 55–165 mg/kg, presently is the drug of choice following experimental surgery (E. Shotts and J. Plumb, personal communications) because it is a broad-spectrum antibiotic effective against bacteria that cause bacterial hemorrhagic septicemia, bacterial fin rot, furunculosis, redmouth disease of trout, and other diseases (Herwig 1979;

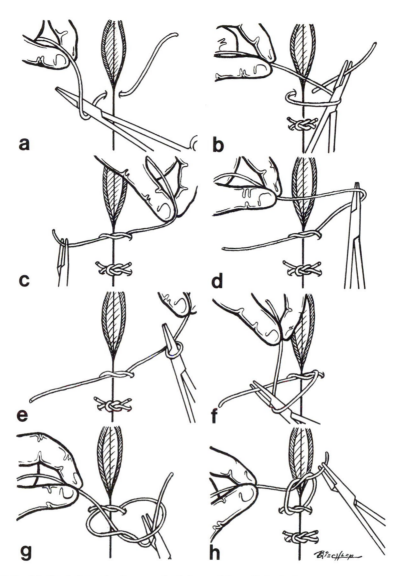

Figure 8.3 Method for closing an incision with a "single-instrument tie" of simple interrupted sutures in the form of square knots (modified from Merkley 1983). (**a**) A loop in the long end of the thread, held in the left hand, is made with a needle holder, held in the right hand. The needle, not shown, is at the end of the long thread portion. (**b**) The needle holder grasps the short end of the thread and pulls it through the loop. The needle holder should not grasp any part of the thread that will be included in the knot because crimping may weaken the thread. (**c**) The first loop is pulled tight. (**d**) and (**e**) The needle holder releases the short end of the thread and becomes a template for a new loop in the long end. (**f**) and (**g**) The needle holder, still within the new loop, grasps the short thread and pulls it through the loop. (**h**) The square knot is tightened, but not so snugly that the tissue puckers at the midline, and the thread is trimmed near the knot, as shown. The needle is still on the long piece of the thread and is used to start the next knot in the series.

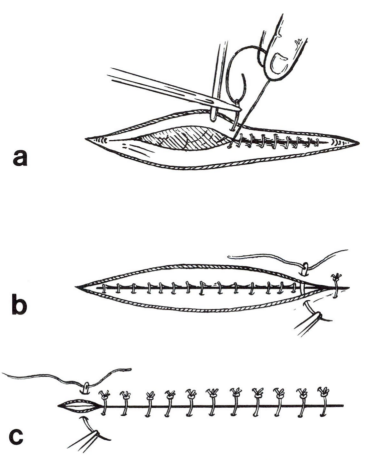

Figure 8.4 Closure of an incision with a double row of sutures, one each for the peritoneum and skin. This double-row procedure should be used with fish larger than about 5 kg. (**a**) The peritoneum is closed with a continuous suture. Note the use of forceps to hold back the skin. (**b**) and (**c**) Skin incision is closed with a series of simple interrupted sutures.

Bell 1986). Yaron et al. (1977) used chloramphenicol in a bath treatment (about 1 g/120 L) on the day blue tilapias were ovariectomized and for 3 d thereafter; they reported that the incisions healed in 6 d and only 1 of 27 fish died after the operation. However, chloramphenicol will not be registered for use with food fish because it is a possible carcinogen (Schnick 1985). It has been reported to cause blood dyscrasias, including leukemia, in humans receiving injections. (User Beware!)

Registered or approved therapeutants for use on food fish include Romet-30™ (sulfadimethoxine plus ormetoprim), sulfamerazine, and Terramycin™ (oxytetracycline) (Schnick et al. 1986a, 1986b). Terramycin has been a popular broad-spectrum antimicrobial agent administered by bath treatment (20 mg active ingredient per liter) or by intraperitoneal injection, or added to feed. Intramuscular injections of oxytetracycline sometimes cause tissue abscesses, so this route of administration should be avoided (Herwig 1979). Terramycin is registered for use in the feed of food fish (55–83 mg/kg of feed per day for 10 d), but a 21-d preslaughter withdrawal period is required (Schnick et al. 1986a, 1986b). Dosage for injections is highly variable: Inman and Hambric (1973) injected a 50-mg/mL "Terramycin Injectable Solution" intraperitoneally at the rate of 55 mg/kg of fish for internal control of bacterial diseases; Herwig (1979) gave 3 mg/100–400 g of fish weight, and Moore et al. (1984) gave 44 mg/kg.

Besides infection, trauma (shock) is another major problem resulting from surgery. Shock symptoms may be identical to those of stress (Pickering et al. 1982; Wedemeyer 1976). The transient posttraumatic physiological syndrome (TPPS) involves

oxygen debt;

negative nitrogen balance (i.e., increased nitrogen excretion);

tissue lysis, glucogenolysis, hydrolysis of depot fat, and release of amino acids from muscle;

inability to synthesize proteins (reduced growth rate);

loss of plasma and blood volume;

ion imbalance (loss of intracellular electrolytes such as potassium, phosphate, and sulfates, but conservation of sodium); and

elevation of plasma cortisol and glucose (indicators of stress).

After surgery, these variables may return to normal within a few hours or after several days. The time required for full recovery varies with species, physiological status before surgery, temperature, nature of the surgical procedure, skill with which the surgical procedure was completed, and details of postoperative care.

8.4 RELATED TECHNIQUES

Blood sampling, anticoagulants, and cannulations are described in Chapter 9. Here, we treat injection sites and urinary cannulations.

8.4.1 Injection Sites

The choice of an injection site depends on the purpose of the injection and on the substance and its quantity to be injected (Smith and Bell 1975). The most common reasons for injecting fish are to administer drugs, hormones, antibiotics, and vaccines.

Parenteral locations—all those other than oral—for injection into humans or mammals include intracardiac, intradermal, intramuscular, intraperitoneal, subcutaneous, intrathecal (into the subdural space of the lumbar region of the spinal cord), and intravenous sites. In fishery applications, subcutaneous, intramuscular, and intraperitoneal sites are the most common. Intracardiac or ventricular puncture, although potentially dangerous, is used successfully by several investigators. Other vascular sites are feasible: anterior dorsal aorta, caudal vein, efferent branchial artery, common cardinal vein, ventral aorta, and abdominal vein (Smith and Bell 1975).

Intradermal and subcutaneous injection sites are often ruled out for fishes because the medication leaks back out (Herwig 1979), it is poorly distributed, or it causes an adverse reaction. An intradermal or subcutaneous injection is much more likely to be sealed off by lymphocytes and form an abscess or necrotic lesion. Often, an abscess causes a sloughing of the superficial tissue from the underlying parts, leaving gaping lesions. Also, subcutaneous injections produce pockets of localized overdoses that kill cells by antibiotic toxicity, resulting in sterile abscesses, as happens with injections of oxytetracycline and some of the sulfanilamides. The intramuscular route provides slow distribution and adverse reactions. Compared with mammalian muscle, fish muscle has few blood vessels, and vascular distribution of any material injected there takes too long to be effective.

Intraperitoneal sites are preferred for antibiotic injections into fish. Vaccines also can be administered to fish intramuscularly and subcutaneously, but intraperitoneal injections are easiest to administer and lead to the most rapid development of protection (Anderson 1974). An intraperitoneal injection is done with a needle of sufficient strength and length to penetrate the body wall. Needle gauge refers to needle diameter, not length; gauge is inversely related to diameter. The needle size (usually 20–26 gauge) needed for a particular fish is related to the thickness of the body wall to be penetrated; small-gauge needles may plug with tissue. The site for an intraperitoneal injection of soft-rayed fishes (e.g., trout, catfish, carp), which have the pelvic girdle in an abdominal position, is just posterior to the pelvic girdle. With spiny-rayed species (e.g., largemouth bass, yellow perch, striped bass), which have the pelvic girdle in the jugular or thoracic position, the intraperitoneal injection must be given considerably posterior to the pelvic girdle (immediately anterior to the vent) to prevent accidental puncture of the liver or the pericardial cavity. In either group of fish, the injection is best given to an immobilized fish incumbent on its dorsum with the body inclined from the horizontal at a 30–45° angle. The needle should be inserted carefully through the body wall, at a shallow angle, only far enough that resistance suddenly ceases, to avoid puncture of abdominal organs; internal bleeding can cause adhesions among organs.

Some substances injected intraperitoneally are taken up slowly, but this is advantageous for treatments with antigens (i.e., vaccines) or other substances that need long-term action. Antigens, indeed, are often injected with a mineral oil solution (called an adjuvant) to provide reservoirs from which the active material is slowly but continuously released. Freund's adjuvant is a water-in-oil emulsion of antigens in paraffin oil; the oil retards absorption, destruction, and elimination of the antigen and permits continuous antigenic stimulation for long periods (Carpenter 1965).

Intraperitoneal implants of pellets (''pills'') containing lipid- or water-soluble substances are used to obtain release of the ingredients over an extended time. Intraperitoneal injections of hormones dissolved in cocoa butter have resulted in slow leaching of the hormone; hormone levels remained elevated for more than a week following the injection (Pickering and Duston 1983). The hormone is mixed into the cocoa butter as a liquid at 40°C, but it solidifies after injection into a fish at normal ambient temperature, less than 25°C. Crim et al. (1983) implanted a sustained dose of hormone in rainbow trout, and Higgs et al. (1975) used a similar technique with coho salmon. Silastic tubing, dimethylpolysiloxane, can be loaded with a chemical or drug, sealed, and then implanted to provide a release of substance (Jensen et al. 1978). It may be necessary to either poke holes in the tubing with a pin or leave the ends of the tubing open to facilitate release of the contents.

Intraperitoneal implants of large objects may not be secure within the abdominal cavity. Summerfelt and Mosier (1984) found that ultrasonic transmitters implanted in the peritoneal cavity of channel catfish could be expelled through the anus after being encapsulated by the intestinal wall and subsequently being taken completely into the intestine. Chisholm and Hubert (1985) had similar experiences with transmitters in rainbow trout. Jensen et al. (1978) recovered only 54% of the Silastic tubing implants (2.2 mm × 20 mm) in small (101–115-mm) grass carp; the disappearance of the implants was not explained.

Interspinal injections, placed in the midline space underlying the epaxial musculature of fish, provide moderately rapid uptake of chemicals—from one to a few hours (Smith, personal experience). The internal distribution of an interspinally injected chemical in salmonids depends on a lymphatic duct that runs lengthwise along the midline about halfway between the spinal cord and the dorsal body surface. The lymphatic duct drains fluid from the connective tissue spaces between the neural spines into the venous side of the heart and seems to take up anything liquid that is injected into the area. To make interspinal injections, a needle is inserted posterior to the dorsal fin, parallel to the neural spines, to a depth of about half of the distance to the spinal cord. Injected material should go easily into the fish; if it does not, the needle point probably has entered the epaxial muscle tissue instead of being in the midline space.

8.4.2 Cannulation

A cannula is a small tube that is inserted into a body cavity, duct, or vessel to remove a body fluid or to insert a substance. Cannulas are used in studies of organ function, toxicology (clearance rate determination), and blood gases, among various others. Cannulation of the vascular system (intravenous cannulation) is described in Chapter 9, Section 9.2.4. A branchial or respiratory cannula is used to deliver oxygenated water, anesthetic solution, or other substances to the gills. We have mentioned the use of a respiratory cannula in conjunction with surgical procedures. Cannulation of the urinary duct is relatively simple in salmonids and channel catfish once the relevant anatomy is learned and the techniques are practiced.

The material used for cannulation is soft polyethylene tubing (e.g., Intramedic™, Clay-Adams, New York). For cannulating urinary ducts and blood vessels in salmonids, PE 50 (0.58 mm inside and 0.965 mm outside diameters) and PE 60 (0.86 mm and 1.22 mm) are the best sizes. The smaller PE 50 provides minimum dead space for collection of urine and blood, but PE 60 may be needed for large fish.

The tubing can be shaped by melting an end of a tube close to a flame provided by a match or Bunsen burner. Exposed to a flame, an end of tubing forms an expanded rim or flare, not unlike that used for attaching brass fittings to metal tubing. Fittings for tubing are available from vendors of attachments for syringes or three-way valves, but hypodermic needles may be used instead: select a needle size that fits snugly inside the tubing. It is best to remove the sharp point from the needle; this may be done by bending the needle shaft back and forth with a hemostat or pair of pliers until it breaks. Usually there are no sharp edges at the break, but they can be smoothed with sandpaper or a sharpening stone. A short section of hypodermic needle tubing also can be used to join two pieces of

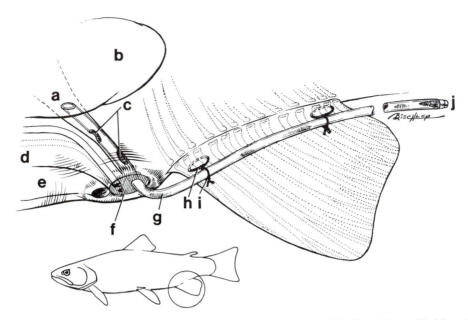

Figure 8.5 Urinary cannulation of a rainbow trout: (a) urinary bladder; (b) gas bladder; (c) openings in the wall of the cannular tubing; (d) spermatic ducts (vasa deferentia); (e) lower intestine; (f) urogenital papilla; (g) cannula; (h) loop of cannula suture around the bases of two fin rays; (i) suture around the cannula; (j) terminal plug.

polyethylene tubing. Passing a flame crosswise under a length of tubing causes the free end of the tubing to bend downward. This bend is helpful because it facilitates attachment of the tubing to the anal fin (see the procedure described below). Heatley and Weeks (1964) outlined additional methods for making more elaborate cannulas from medical polyethylene tubing.

When the urinary duct is cannulated, tubing inside the fish should not press against the swim bladder or kidney. If the end of the tubing is cut to a sharp point, it may penetrate the wall of the urinary duct, allowing the urine to be contaminated with peritoneal fluid. Experimentation with anesthetized or freshly killed fish may be needed to avoid mistaken cannulation of the gonadoduct. The tube is inserted by gently rotating it from side to side until it just passes the sphincter muscle. The sphincter muscle makes an adequate seal for at least a week and it prevents urine from leaking around the outside of the cannula.

After the cannula is properly inserted into the urinary duct, the external segment of tubing should be anchored in place along the base of the anal fin (Figure 8.5). By making a permanent bend in the tubing, one can take much of the strain off the urinary papilla. The tube is anchored to the anal fin with a loop of thread passed (with a straight needle) around the bases of two anal fin rays (as shown), or around one or two interhemal spines (bones supporting the fin rays), and then tied off with a square knot. Then the tubing is placed on top of the knot and a second knot tied tightly enough that it sinks into the tubing slightly. The tightness is tested by pulling on the tubing to see that the cannula does not slip through the knot. Two such anchor points are desirable, one near the anterior and the other near the posterior edge of the anal fin. This arrangement leaves a short length of tube trailing behind the fish; the trailing end is plugged or crimped shut.

For short-term sampling, the fish is anesthetized and the crimped end of the tubing is opened to drain the fluid. For collecting amounts of urine greater than the bladder capacity of the fish, the fish must be held in a chamber; the tubing from the fish is directed by the shortest way to the outside of the chamber and to a vessel in which the urine continuously accumulates. The major problem in this case is maintaining the fish in a stable position in the holding chamber, but various devices can be contrived for this purpose.

8.5 REFERENCES

Agnew, W. F., E. M. Todd, H. Richmond, and W. S. Chronister. 1962. Biological evaluation of silicone rubber for surgical prosthesis. Journal of Surgical Research 2:357–363.

Allen, J. L. 1988. Residues of benzocaine in rainbow trout, largemouth bass, and fish meal. Progressive Fish-Culturist 50:59–60.

Allen, J. L., and J. B. Hunn. 1977. Renal excretion in channel catfish following injection of quinaldine sulphate or 3-trifluoromethyl-4-nitrophenol. Journal of Fish Biology 10:473–479.

Allen, J. L., and J. B. Hunn. 1986. Fate and distribution studies of some drugs used in aquaculture. Veterinary and Human Toxicology 28 (Supplement 1):21–24.

Allen, J. L., and J. B. Sills. 1973. Preparation and properties of quinaldine sulfate, an improved fish anesthetic. U.S. Fish and Wildlife Service Investigations in Fish Control 47.

Allison, L. N. 1961. The effect of tricaine methanesulfonate (MS-222) on the motility of brook trout sperm. Progressive Fish-Culturist 23:46–47.

Amend, D. F., B. A. Goven, and D. G. Elliot. 1982. Etomidate: effective dosages for a new fish anesthetic. Transactions of the American Fisheries Society 111:337–341.

Anderson, D. P. 1974. Fish immunology. T.F.H. Publications, Neptune City, New Jersey.

Anonymous. 1985. Fish chemical and drug highlights: registration activities. Progressive Fish-Culturist 47:201.

APHA (American Public Health Association), American Water Works Association, and Water Pollution Control Federation 1989. Standard methods for the examination of water and waste water, 17th edition. APHA, Washington, D.C.

ASHP (American Society of Hospital Pharmacists). 1985. Drug information. ASHP, Bethesda, Maryland.

Baldridge, H. D. 1969. Kinetics of onset of responses by sharks to waterborne drugs. Bulletin of Marine Science 19:880–896.

Ball, J. N., and P. N. Cowen. 1959. Urethane as a carcinogen and as an anaesthetic for fishes. Nature (London) 184(Supplement 6):370.

Barton, B. A., and R. E. Peter. 1982. Plasma cortisol stress response in fingerling rainbow trout, *Salmo gairdneri* Richardson, to various transport conditions, anaesthesia, and cold shock. Journal of Fish Biology 20:39–51.

Bell, G. R. 1964. A guide to the properties, characteristics, and uses of some general anesthetics of fish. Fisheries Research Board of Canada Bulletin 148.

Bell, G. R. 1967. A guide to the properties, characteristics and uses of some general anaesthetics for fish. Fisheries Research Board of Canada Bulletin 148 (2nd edition, revised).

Bell, M. C. 1986. Fisheries handbook of engineering requirements and biological criteria. U.S. Army Corps of Engineers, North Pacific Division, Portland, Oregon.

Bidgood, B. F. 1980. Field surgical procedure for implantation of radio tags in fish. Alberta Department of Energy and Natural Resources, Fish and Wildlife Division, Fisheries Research Report 20, Edmonton, Canada.

Billard, R., M. Richard, and B. Breton. 1971. Stimulation of gonadotropin secretion after castration in rainbow trout. General and Comparative Endocrinology 33:163–165.

Billard, R., M. Richard, and B. Breton. 1976. Stimulation de la secretion gonadotrope hypophysaire apres castration chez a truite arc-en-ciel: variation de la response au cours du cycle reproducteur. Comptes Rendus Hebdomadaires des Seances de L'Academie des Sciences, Serie D, Sciences Naturelles. 283:171–174.

Black, E. C. 1958. Hyperactivity as a lethal factor in fish. Journal of the Fisheries Research Board of Canada 15:573–586.

Blasiola, G. C., Jr. 1977. Quinaldine sulfate, a new anaesthetic formulation for tropical marine fishes. Journal of Fish Biology 10:113–119.

Booke, H. E., B. Hollender, and G. Lutterbie. 1978. Sodium bicarbonate, an inexpensive fish anesthetic for field use. Progressive Fish-Culturist 40:11–13.

Borjeson, H., and L. B. Hoglund. 1976. Swimbladder gas and Root effect in salmon during hypercapnia. Comparative Biochemistry and Physiology A, Comparative Physiology 54:335–339.

Bourne, P. K. 1984. The use of MS-222 (tricaine methanesulphonate) as an anaesthetic for routine blood sampling in three species of marine teleosts. Aquaculture 36:313–321.

Bove, F. J. 1962. MS-222 Sandoz: the anaesthetic and tranquilizer of choice for fish and other cold-blooded organisms. Sandoz Pharmaceuticals, Report Ga3-1164, Hanover, New Jersey.

Braley, S. 1970. The chemistry and properties of medical grade silicon rubber. Journal of Macromolecular Science—Chemistry A 4:529–544.

Brandenburger Brown, E. A., J. E. Franklin, E. Pratt, and E. G. Trams. 1972. Contributions to the pharmacology of quinaldine (uptake and distribution in the shark and comparative studies). Comparative Biochemistry and Physiology A, Comparative Physiology 42:223–231.

Britton, E. 1983. Constant carbon dioxide (CO_2) and oxygen (O_2) aeration to anesthetize adult salmon. Fisheries and Oceans, Information Memo 49, Vancouver, Canada.

Brungs, W. A. 1973. Effects of residual chlorine on aquatic life. Journal of the Water Pollution Control Federation 45:2180–2193.

Butterworth and Company 1978. Butterworth's medical dictionary, 2nd edition. London.

Carpenter, P. L. 1965. Immunology and serology, 2nd edition. Saunders, Philadelphia.

Carrasco, S., H. Sumano, and R. Navahro-Fierro. 1984. The use of lidocaine–sodium bicarbonate as anaesthetic in fish. Aquaculture 41:395–398.

Chisholm, I. M., and W. A. Hubert. 1985. Expulsion of dummy transmitters by rainbow trout. Transactions of the American Fisheries Society 114:766–767.

Chung, K. S. 1980. Cold anaesthesia of tropical fish. Bulletin of the Japanese Society of Scientific Fisheries 46:391.

Cole, V. W., and W. M. Lewis. 1958. The removal of residual chlorine from tap water that is to be used in aquaria. Turtox News 36(8):204–206.

Considine, D. M., and G. D. Considine, editors. 1984. Van Nostrand Reinhold encyclopedia of chemistry, 4th edition. Van Nostrand Reinhold, New York.

Courtois, L. A. 1981. Light weight, adjustable, and portable surgical table for fisheries work in the field. Progressive Fish-Culturist 43:55–56.

Crawford, B., and A. Hulsey. 1963. Effects of MS-222 on the spawning of channel catfish. Progressive Fish-Culturist 25:214.

Crim, L. W., A. M. Sutterlin, D. M. Evans, and C. Weil. 1983. Accelerated ovulation by pelleted LHRH analogue treatment of spring-spawning rainbow trout (*Salmo gairdneri*) held at low temperature. Aquaculture 35:299–307.

Crowley, G. J., and D. J. Berinati. 1972. Effect of MS-222 (tricaine) on blood sugar and liver glycogen in rainbow trout. Transactions of the American Fisheries Society 101:125–128.

Curry, K. D., and B. Kynard. 1978. Effect of extended galvanonarcosis on behavior of rainbow trout, *Salmo gairdneri,* and channel catfish, *Ictalurus punctatus.* Journal of the Fisheries Research Board of Canada 35:1297–1302.

Davis, L. E., editor. 1968. Christopher's textbook of surgery, 9th edition. Saunders, Philadelphia.

Dawson, V. K., and P. A. Gilderhus. 1979. Ethyl-*p*-aminobenzoate (benzocaine): efficacy as an anesthetic for five species of freshwater fish. U.S. Fish and Wildlife Service Investigations in Fish Control 87.

Donaldson, E. M., and U. H. M. Fagerlund. 1970. Effect of sexual maturation and gonadectomy on cortisol secretion rate in sockeye salmon (*Oncorhynchus nerka*). Journal of the Fisheries Research Board of Canada 27:2287–2296.

Dorland, W. A. 1981. Dorland's medical dictionary, 26th edition. Saunders, Philadelphia.

Dougherty, R. W. 1981. Experimental surgery in farm animals. Iowa State University Press, Ames.

Duplinsky, P. D. 1982. Sperm motility of northern pike and chain pickerel at various pH values. Transactions of the American Fisheries Society 111:768–771.

Dupree, H. K., and J. V. Huner. 1984. Transportation of live fish. Pages 165–176 in H. K. Dupree and J. V. Huner, editors. Third report to the fish farmers. U.S. Fish and Wildlife Service, Washington, D.C.

Echteler, S. M. 1985. Organization of central auditory pathways in a teleost fish, *Cyprinus carpio*. Journal of Comparative Physiology A, Sensory Neural and Behavioral Physiology 156:267–280.

Elmore, R. G. 1981. Food-animal regional anesthesia. Veterinary Medicine Publishing Company, Bonner Springs, Kansas.

Ethicon (Incorporated). 1961. Manual of operative procedure and surgical knots, 12th edition. Somerville, New Jersey.

Ferreira, J. T., H. J. Schoonbee, and G. L. Smit. 1984a. The anaesthetic potency of benzocaine-hydrochloride in three freshwater fish species. South African Journal of Zoology 19:46–50.

Ferreira, J. T., H. J. Schoonbee, and G. L. Smit. 1984b. The uptake of the anaesthetic benzocaine hydrochloride by the gills and skin of three freshwater fish species. Journal of Fish Biology 25:35–41.

Ferreira, J. T., G. L. Smit, H. J. Schoonbee, and C. W. Holzapfel. 1979. Comparison of anesthetic potency of benzocaine hydrochloride and MS-222 in two freshwater fish species. Progressive Fish-Culturist 41:161–163.

Fish, F. F. 1943. Anaesthesia of fish by high carbon dioxide concentrations. Transactions of the American Fisheries Society 72:25–29.

Forster, R. P., and F. Berglund. 1956. Osmotic diuresis and its effect on total electrolyte distribution in plasma and urine of the aglomerular teleost, *Lophius americanus*. Journal of General Physiology 39:349–359.

Frazier, D. T., and T. Narahashi. 1975. Tricaine (MS-222): effects on ionic conductances of squid axon membranes. European Journal of Pharmacology 33:313–317.

Fromm, P. O., B. D. Richards, and R. C. Hunter. 1971. Effects of some insecticides and MS-222 on isolated perfused gills of trout. Progressive Fish-Culturist 33:138–140.

Garey, W. F., and H. Rahn. 1970. Normal arterial gas tensions and pH and breathing frequency in the electric eel. Respiration Physiology 9:141–150.

G. C. Merriam Company. 1973. Webster's collegiate thesaurus. Springfield, Massachusetts.

Gerking, S. D. 1949. Urethane (ethyl carbamate) in some fishery procedures. Progressive Fish-Culturist 11:73–74.

Gilderhus, P. A. 1988. Benzocaine is an effective anesthetic for salmonid fish. American Fisheries Society, Fish Health Section Newsletter 16(1):2. (Bethesda, Maryland.)

Gilderhus, P. A., B. L. Berger, J. B. Sills, and P. D. Harman. 1973a. The efficacy of quinaldine sulfate as an anesthetic for freshwater fish. U.S. Fish and Wildlife Service Investigations in Fish Control 49.

Gilderhus, P. A., B. L. Berger, J. B. Sills, and P. D. Harman. 1973b. The efficacy of quinaldine sulfate:MS-222 mixtures for the anesthetization of freshwater fish. U.S. Fish and Wildlife Service Investigations in Fish Control 54.

Gilderhus, P. A., and L. L. Marking. 1987. Comparative efficacy of 16 anesthetic chemicals on rainbow trout. North American Journal of Fisheries Management 7:288–292.

Goetz, F. W., Jr., R. A. Hoffman, and W. L. Pancoe. 1977. A surgical operating apparatus for fish and its use in the pinealectomy of salmonids. Journal of Fish Biology 10:287–290.

Gooding, J. M., and M. Corssen. 1976. Etomidate: an ultrashort-acting nonbarbiturate agent for anesthesia induction. Anesthesia and Analgesia 55:286–289.

Gooding, J. M., and M. Corssen. 1977. Effect of etomidate on the cardiovascular system. Anesthesia and Analgesia 56:717–719.

Griffith, H. W. 1987. Complete guide to prescription & non-prescription drugs. HPBooks, Tucson, Arizona.

Griffiths, F. P., G. Webb, and P. W. Schneider. 1941. Ether anesthesia of steelhead trout. Transactions of the American Fisheries Society 70:272–274.

Grizzle, J. M., and W. A. Rogers. 1976. Anatomy and histology of the channel catfish. Alabama Agricultural Experiment Station, Auburn University.

Gronow, G. 1974. Stress in *Idus idus* (Teleostei) due to capture, anesthesia, and experimental environment. Zoologischer Anzeiger 193:17–34.

Gunstrom, G. K., and M. Bethers. 1985. Electrical anesthesia for handling large salmonids. Progressive Fish-Culturist 47:67–69.

Hampel, C. A., and G. G. Hawley. 1982. Glossary of chemical terms, 2nd edition. Van Nostrand Reinhold, New York.

Hara, T. J. 1975. Olfaction in fish. Progress in Neurobiology (Oxford) 5:271–335.

Hart, L. G., and R. C. Summerfelt. 1975. Surgical procedures for implanting ultrasonic transmitters into flathead catfish (*Pylodictis olivaris*). Transactions of the American Fisheries Society 104:56–59.

Hartley, W. G. 1967. Electronarcosis of fish for handling. Pages 251–255 *in* R. Vibert, editor. Fishing with electricity: its application to biology and management. Fishing News Books, Surrey, England.

Hartley, W. G. 1977. The use of electricity for anaesthetizing fish. Journal of Fish Biology 11:377–378.

Haskell, D. C. 1940a. An electrical method of collecting fish. Transactions of the American Fisheries Society 69:210–215.

Haskell, D. C. 1940b. Stunning fish by electricity. Progressive Fish-Culturist 7(49):33–34.

Hasler, A. D. 1966. Underwater guideposts—homing of salmon. University of Wisconsin Press, Madison.

Hasler, A. D., and R. K. Meyer. 1942. Respiratory responses of normal and castrated goldfish to teleost and mammalian hormones. Journal of Experimental Zoology 91:391–404.

Heatley, N. G., and J. R. Weeks. 1964. Fashioning polyethylene tubing for use in physiological experiments. Journal of Applied Physiology 19:542–545.

Hench, L. L., and E. C. Ethridge. 1982. Biomaterials: an interfacial approach. Academic Press, New York.

Henry Schein (Incorporated). 1986. Pharmaceutical and surgical supply catalog, preview 1986. Port Washington, New York.

Hensel, H., B. Bromm, and K. Nier. 1975. Effect of ethyl-*m*-amino benzoate (MS-222) on ampullae of Lorenzini and lateral line organs. Experientia (Basel) 31:958–960.

Herwig, N. 1979. Handbook of drugs and chemicals used in the treatment of fish diseases: a manual of fish pharmacology and materia medica. Thomas, Springfield, Illinois.

Higgs, D. A., E. M. Donaldson, H. M. Dye, and J. R. McBride, Jr. 1975. A preliminary investigation of the effect of bovine growth hormone on growth and muscle composition of coho salmon (*Oncorhynchus kisutch*). General and Comparative Endocrinology 56:146–155.

Hoar, W. S. 1957. The endocrine organs. Pages 245–285 *in* M. E. Brown, editor. The physiology of fishes, volume 1. Academic Press, New York.

Hoar, W. S. 1975. General and comparative physiology, 2nd edition. Prentice-Hall, Englewood Cliffs, New Jersey.

Hoar, W. S., and D. J. Randall, editors. 1969. Fish physiology, volume 2. Academic Press, New York.

Hoglund, L. B., and A. Persson. 1971. Effect of locomotor restraint and of anesthesia with urethane or MS-222 on the reactions of young salmon, *Salmo salar,* to environmental fluctuations of pH and carbon dioxide tension. Institute of Freshwater Research Drottningholm Report 51:75–89.

Horrobin, D. F. 1968. Medical physiology and biochemistry. Williams and Wilkins, Baltimore, Maryland.

Houston, A. H., C. L. Czerwinski, and R. J. Woods. 1973. Cardiovascular–respiratory activity during recovery from anesthesia and surgery in brook trout (*Salvelinus fontinalis*) and carp (*Cyprinus carpio*). Journal of the Fisheries Research Board of Canada 30:1705–1712.

Houston, A. H., J. A. Madden, R. J. Woods, and H. M. Miles. 1971a. Some physiological effects of handling and tricaine methanesulfonate anesthetization upon the brook trout, *Salvelinus fontinalis*. Journal of the Fisheries Research Board of Canada 28:625–633.

Houston, A. H., J. A. Madden, R. J. Woods, and H. M. Miles. 1971b. Variations in the blood and tissue chemistry of brook trout, *Salvelinus fontinalis*, subsequent to handling, anesthesia, and surgery. Journal of the Fisheries Research Board of Canada 28:635–642.

Houston, A. H., and R. J. Woods. 1976. Influence of temperature upon tricaine methane sulphonate uptake and induction of anesthesia in rainbow trout (*Salmo gairdneri*). Comparative Biochemistry and Physiology C, Comparative Pharmacology 54:1–6.

Hudy, M. 1985. Rainbow trout and brook trout mortality from high voltage AC electrofishing in a controlled environment. North American Journal of Fisheries Management 5:475–479.

Hunn, J. B. 1970. Dynamics of MS-222 in the blood and brain of freshwater fishes during anesthesia. U.S. Fish and Wildlife Service Investigations in Fish Control 42.

Hunn, J. B., and J. L. Allen. 1974. Movements of drugs across the gills of fishes. Annual Review of Pharmacology 14:47–55.

Hunn, J. B., R. A. Schoettger, and W. A. Willford. 1968. Turnover and urinary excretion of free and acetylated MS-222 by rainbow trout, *Salmo gairdneri*. Journal of the Fisheries Research Board of Canada 25:25–31.

Hunn, J. B., and W. A. Willford. 1970. The effect of anaesthetization and urinary bladder catheterization on renal function in rainbow trout. Comparative Biochemistry and Physiology 33:805–812.

Ikeda, Y., H. Ozaki, and Y. Sekizawa. 1974. Absorption, distribution, and excretion of 3H·2-amino-4-phenylthiazole, a piscine anesthetic, in carp and crucian carp. Bulletin of the Japanese Society of Scientific Fisheries 40:339–350.

Ince, B. W. 1979. Metabolic effects of partial pancreatectomy in the northern pike, *Esox lucius* L. Journal of Fish Biology 14:193–198.

Inman, C. R., and R. N. Hambric. 1973. Diseases and parasites of warm-water fishes. Texas Parks and Widlife Department, Inland Fisheries Function, Technical Series 2, Austin.

Jenkins, N., and J. M. Dodd. 1982. Effects of ovariectomy of the dogfish *Scyliorhinus canicula* L. on circulating levels of androgen and oestradiol and on pituitary gonadotrophin content. Journal of Fish Biology 21:297–303.

Jensen, G. L., W. L. Shelton, and L. O. Wilken. 1978. Use of methyltestosterone silastic implants to control sex in grass carp. Pages 200–219 *in* R. O. Smitherman, W. L. Shelton, and J. H. Grover, editors. Culture of exotic fishes symposium proceedings. American Fisheries Society, Fish Culture Section, Auburn, Alabama.

Jochen, R. F. 1982. Veterinary surgical sutures. Pitman-Moore, Washington Crossing, New Jersey.

Jodlbauer, A., and H. Salvendi. 1905. Ueber die Wirkungen von Akridin. Archives Internationales de Pharmacodynamie et de Therapie 15:223–240 (Not seen; cited in Brandenburger Brown et al. 1972).

Johansson, N. 1978. Anesthetics for fish. Salmon Research Institute, Report 5, Sundsvall, Sweden.

Johnson, L. D. 1954. Use of urethane anesthesia in spawning eastern brook trout. Progressive Fish-Culturist 16:181–183.

Jolly, D. W., L. E. Mawdesley-Thomas, and D. Bucke. 1972. Anesthesia of fish. Veterinary Record 91(18):424–426.

Kallner, A. 1977. A study of the conversion of cholesterol to bile acids by the use of a fistulated bile duct. Journal of Fish Biology 11:343–347.

Kaya, C. M., M. K. K. Queenth, and A. E. Dizon. 1984. Capturing and restraining technique for experimental work on small tuna in large laboratory holding tanks. Progressive Fish-Culturist 46:288–290.

Kikuchi, T., Y. Sekizawa, Y. Ikeda, and H. Ozaki. 1974. Behavioral analyses of the central nervous system depressant activity of 2-amino-4-phenylthiazole upon fishes. Bulletin of the Japanese Society of Scientific Fisheries 40:325–337.

Kiyohara, S., I. Hidaka, J. Kitoh, and S. Yamashita. 1985. Mechanical sensitivity of the facial nerve fibers innervating the anterior palate of the puffer, *Fugu pardalis,* and their central projection to the primary taste center. Journal of Comparative Physiology A, Sensory Neural and Behavior Physiology 157:705–716.

Klar, G. T. 1986. Efficacy of Finquel[R] as an anesthetic for striped bass. U.S. Fish and Wildlife Service Research Information Bulletin 86-71.

Klontz, G. W. 1964. Anesthesia of fishes. Pages 350–374 *in* D. C. Sawyer, editor. Proceedings of the symposium on experimental animal anesthesiology. U.S. Air Force School of Aerospace Medicine, Aerospace Medical Division, Brooks Air Force Base, Texas.

Klontz, G. W., and L. S. Smith. 1968. Methods of using fish as biological research subjects. Methods of Animal Experimentation 3:383–385.

Koyama, J. 1983. Laboratory diuresis of carp. Bulletin of Japanese Society of Scientific Fisheries 49:883–887.

Krayukhin, B. V. 1964. Methods for installing chronic fistulas in the digestive tract of fish. Pages 125–137 *in* E. N. Pavlovskii, editor. Techniques for the investigation of fish physiology. Translated from Russian: Israel Program for Scientific Translations, Jerusalem. (Also: U.S. Department of Commerce, Office of Technical Services, OTS 64-11001, Washington, D.C.)

Laitinen, M., M. Nieminen, P. Pasanen, and E. Hietanen. 1981. Tricaine (MS-222) induced modification on the metabolism of foreign compounds in the liver and duodenal muscosa of the splake (*Salvelinus fontinalis* × *Salvelinus namaycush*) Acta Pharmacologia and Toxicologica 49:92–97.

LeBras, Y. M. 1982. Effects of anaesthesia and surgery on levels of adrenaline and noradrenaline in blood plasma of the eel (*Anguilla anguilla* L.). Comparative Biochemistry and Physiology C, Comparative Pharmacology 72:141–144.

Lewis, D. H., R. J. Tarpley, J. E. Marks, and R. F. Sis. 1985. Drug induced structural changes in olfactory organ of channel catfish *Ictalurus punctatus,* Rafinesque. Journal of Fish Biology 26:355–358.

Limsuwan, C., J. M. Grizzle, and J. A. Plumb. 1983. Etomidate as an anesthetic for fish: its toxicity and efficacy. Transactions of the American Fisheries Society 112:544–550.

Lochowitz, R. T., H. M. Miles, and D. R. Hafemann. 1974. Anesthetic-induced variations in the cardiac rate of the teleost, *Salmo gairdneri.* Comparative and General Pharmacology 5:217–224.

Locke, D. O. 1969. Quinaldine as an anesthetic for brook trout, lake trout, and Atlantic salmon. U.S. Fish and Wildlife Service Investigations in Fish Control 24.

Luhning, C. W. 1973. Residues of MS-222, benzocaine, and their metabolites in striped bass following anesthesia. U.S. Fish and Wildlife Service Investigations in Fish Control 52.

Lumb, W. V. 1963. Small animal anesthesia. Lea and Febiger, Philadelphia.

Madden, J. A., and A. H. Houston. 1976. Use of electroanesthesia with freshwater teleosts: some physiological consequences in the rainbow trout, *Salmo gairdneri* Richardson. Journal of Fish Biology 9:457–462.

Malyukina, G. A. 1964. Operations on [the] brain of fish. Pages 267–270 *in* E. N. Pavlovskii, editor. Techniques for the investigation of fish physiology. Translated from Russian: Israel Program for Scientific Translations, Jerusalem. (Also: U.S. Department of Commerce, Office of Technical Services, OTS 64-11001, Washington, D.C.)

Mann, H., and K. G. Rajbanshi. 1967. Die Einwirkung von Tricainmethansulfonate (MS-222) auf die Atmung von Fischem. Allgemeine Fishcherei-Zeitung 92:27.

Maren, T. H., L. E. Broder, and V. G. Stenger. 1968. Metabolism of ethyl-*m*-aminobenzoate (MS-222) in dogfish, *Squalis acanthias.* Bulletin of the Mount Desert Island Biological Laboratory 8:39–41.

Marking, L. L. 1967. Toxicity of MS-222 to selected fishes. U.S. Fish and Wildlife Service Investigations in Fish Control 12.

Marking, L. L. 1969a. Toxicity of quinaldine to selected fishes. U.S. Fish and Wildlife Service Investigations in Fish Control 23.

Marking, L. L. 1969b. Toxicological assays with fish. Bulletin of the Wildlife Disease Association 5:291–294.

Marking, L. L., and V. K. Dawson. 1973. Toxicity of quinaldine sulfate to fish. U.S. Fish and Wildlife Service Investigations in Fish Control 48.

Marking, L. L., and F. P. Meyer. 1985. Are better anesthetics needed in fisheries? Fisheries 10(6):2–5.

Marty, G. D., and R. C. Summerfelt. 1986. Pathways and mechanisms for expulsion of surgically implanted dummy transmitters from the peritoneal cavity of channel catfish. Transactions of the American Fisheries Society 115:577–589.

McBride, J. R., and A. P. Van Overbeeke. 1969. Cytological changes in the pituitary glands of the adult sockeye salmon (*Oncorhynchus nerka*) after gonadectomy. Journal of the Fisheries Research Board of Canada 26:1147–1156.

McErlean, A. J. 1967. Ethyl-*p*-aminobenzoate: an anesthetic for cold-blooded vertebrates. Copeia 1967:239–240.

McErlean, A. J., and V. S. Kennedy. 1968. Comparison of some anesthetic properties of benzocaine and MS-222. Transactions of the American Fisheries Society 97:496–498.

McFarland, W. N. 1959. A study of the effects of anesthetics on the behavior and physiology of fishes. Publication of the Institute of Marine Science, University of Texas 6:23–55.

McFarland, W. N. 1960. The use of anesthetics for the handling and transport of fishes. California Fish and Game 46:407–431.

McFarland, W. N., and G. W. Klontz. 1969. Anesthesia in fishes. Federation Proceedings 28:1535–1540.

McNicholl, R. G., and W. C. MacKay. 1975. Effect of DDT and MS-222 on learning a simple conditioned response in rainbow trout, *Salmo gairdneri*. Journal of the Fisheries Research Board of Canada 32:661–665.

Medical Economics Company. 1987. Physicians' desk reference, 41st edition. Oradell, New Jersey.

Meehan, W. R., and L. Revet. 1962. The effect of tricaine methanesulfonate (MS-222) and/or chilled water on oxygen consumption of sockeye salmon fry. Progressive Fish-Culturist 24:185–187.

Merck & Company. 1968. The Merck index, 8th edition. Rahway, New Jersey.

Merck & Company. 1983. The Merck index, 10th edition. Rahway, New Jersey.

Merkley, D. 1983. Knot tying techniques. Iowa State University, College of Veterinary Medicine, Ames.

Mishra, B. K., D. Kumar, and R. Mishra. 1983. Observations on the use of carbonic acid anaesthesia in fish fry transport. Aquaculture 32:405–408.

Mittal, A. K., and M. Whitear. 1978. A note on cold anesthesia of poikilotherms. Journal of Fish Biology 13:519–520.

Moore, B. R., A. J. Mitchell, B. R. Griffin, and G. L. Hoffman. 1984. Parasites and diseases of pond fishes. Pages 177–205 in H. K. Dupree and J. V. Huner, editors. Third report to the fish farmers. U. S. Fish and Wildlife Service, Washington, D.C.

Muench, B. 1958. Quinaldine, a new anesthetic for fish. Progressive Fish-Culturist 20:42–44.

Mulford, C. J. 1984. Use of a surgical skin stapler to quickly close incisions in striped bass. North American Journal of Fisheries Management 4:571–573.

Munz, H. 1985. Single unit activity in the peripheral lateral line system of the cichlid *Sarotherodon niloticus* L. Journal of Comparative Physiology A, Sensory Neural and Behavioral Physiology 157:555–568.

NFRL (National Fishery Research Laboratory). 1986. Fish culturists should use caution if using quinaldine. U.S. Fish and Wildlife Service Research Information Bulletin 23-86.

NIH (National Institutes of Health). 1985. Guide for the care and use of laboratory animals. NIH Publication 85-23, Bethesda, Maryland.

Ohr, E. A. 1976. Tricaine methanesulphonate—I. pH and its effect on anaesthetic potency. Comparative Biochemistry and Physiology C, Comparative Pharmacology 54:13–17.

Orsi, J., and J. W. Short. 1987. Modifications in electrical anesthesia for salmonids. Progressive Fish-Culturist 49:144–146.

Parker, G. H. 1939. General anesthesia by cooling. Proceedings of the Society for Experimental Biology and Medicine 42:186–187.

Pavlovskii, E. N., editor. 1964. Techniques for the investigation of fish physiology. Translated from Russian: Israel Program for Scientific Translations, Jerusalem. (Also: U.S. Department of Commerce, Office of Technical Services, OTS 64-11001, Washington, D.C.)

Pegel', V. A. 1964. Methods of study of the digestive properties of pancreatic juice and bile in fish in long-term experiments. Pages 141–142 in E. N. Pavlovskii, editor. Techniques for the investigation of fish physiology. Translated from Russian: Israel Program for Scientific Translations, Jerusalem. (Also: U.S. Department of Commerce, Office of Technical Services OTS 64-11001, Washington, D.C.)

Pickering, A. D., and J. Duston. 1983. Administration of cortisol to brown trout, *Salmo trutta* L., and its effects on the susceptibility of *Saprolegnia* infection and furnuculosis. Journal of Fish Biology 23:163–175.

Pickering, A. D., T. G. Pottinger, and P. Christie. 1982. Recovery of the brown trout, *Salmo trutta* L., from acute handling stress: a time-course study. Journal of Fish Biology 20:229–244.

Pickford, G., and J. W. Atz. 1957. The physiology of the pituitary gland of fishes. New York Zoological Society, New York.

Piper, R. G., I. B. McElwain, L. E. Orme, J. P. McCraren, L. G. Fowler, and J. Leonard. 1982. Fish hatchery management. U.S. Fish and Wildlife Service, Washington, D.C.

Plumb, J. A., T. E. Schwedler, and C. Limsuwan. 1983. Experimental anesthesia of three species of freshwater fish with etomidate. Progressive Fish-Culturist 45:30–31.

Post, G. 1979. Carbonic acid anesthesia for aquatic organisms. Progressive Fish-Culturist 41:142–143.

Prosser, C. L., and F. A. Brown, Jr. 1961. Comparative animal physiology. Saunders, Philadelphia.

Quinn, T. P., A. F. Olson, and J. T. Konecki. 1988. Effects of anesthesia on the chemosensory behavior of Pacific salmon. Journal of Fish Biology 33:637–641.

Randall, D. J., and W. S. Hoar. 1971. Special techniques. Pages 511–528 in W. S. Hoar and D. J. Randall, editors. Fish physiology, volume 6. Academic Press, New York.

Randall, D. J., and L. S. Smith. 1967. The effect of environmental factors on circulation and respiration in teleost fish. Hydrobiologia 29:113–124.

Reinecker, R. H., and M. O. Ruddell. 1974. An easily fabricated operating table for fish surgery. Progressive Fish-Culturist 36:111–112.

Reynolds, J. B. 1983. Electrofishing. Pages 147–163 in L. A. Nielsen and D. L. Johnson, editors. Fisheries techniques. American Fisheries Society, Bethesda, Maryland.

Rodman, D. T. 1963. Anesthetizing and air-transporting young white sturgeons. Progressive Fish-Culturist 25:71–78.

Ross, L. G., and J. A. Geddes. 1979. Sedation of warmwater fish species in aquaculture research. Aquaculture 16:183–186.

Ross, L. G., and B. Ross. 1984. Anaesthetic and sedative techniques for fish. University of Sterling, Institute of Aquaculture, Sterling, Scotland.

Sabiston, D. C., Jr., editor. 1981. David-Christopher textbook of surgery, 12th edition, volumes 1, 2. Saunders, Philadelphia.

Sado, E. K. 1985. Influence of the anesthetic quinaldine on some tilapia. Aquaculture 46:55–62.

Savitz, J. 1969. Effect of MS-222 (tricaine methane sulfonate) on nitrogen excretion of the bluegill, *Lepomis macrochirus*. Journal of the Elisha Mitchell Scientific Society 85:150–151.

Schmidt-Nielsen, K. 1975. Animal physiology: adaptation and environment. Cambridge University Press, New York.

Schnick, R. A. 1985. Use of unregistered fishery compounds poses problems. U.S. Fish and Wildlife Service, Research Information Bulletin 85-48:1–9.

Schnick, R. A., F. P. Meyer, and D. L. Gray. 1986a. A guide to approved chemicals in fish production and fishery resource management. University of Arkansas Cooperative Extension Service, Publication MP241-11M-1-86, Little Rock.

Schnick, R. A., F. P. Meyer, and H. D. Van Meter. 1979. Compounds registered for fishery uses. Fisheries 4(5):18–19.

Schnick, R. A., F. P. Meyer, and D. F. Walsh. 1986b. Status of fishery chemicals in 1985. Progressive Fish-Culturist 48:1–17.

Schoettger, R. A., and A. M. Julin. 1967. Efficacy of MS-222 as an anesthetic on four salmonids. U.S. Fish and Wildlife Service Investigations in Fish Control 13.

Schoettger, R. A., and A. M. Julin. 1969. Efficacy of quinaldine as an anesthetic for seven species of fish. U.S. Fish and Wildlife Service Investigations in Fish Control 22.

Schoettger, R. A., and E. W. Steucke. 1972. Anesthetization of fish. U.S. Patent 3,644,625 (February 22, 1972).

Schoettger, R. A., C. R. Walker, L. L. Marking, and A. M. Julin. 1967. MS-222 as an anesthetic for channel catfish: its toxicity, efficacy, and muscle residues. U.S. Fish and Wildlife Service Investigations in Fish Control 17.

Schramm, H. L., Jr., and D. J. Black. 1984. Anesthesia and surgical procedures for implanting radiotransmitters into grass carp. Progressive Fish-Culturist 46:185–190.

Schwartz, S. I., editor. 1984. Principles of surgery, 4th edition. McGraw-Hill, New York.

Selye, H. 1950. Stress and the general adaptation syndrome. British Medical Journal 1:1383–1392.

Selye, H. 1973. The evolution of the stress concept. American Scientist 61:692–699.

Serfaty, A., R. Labat, and R. Quiller. 1959. Cardiac reactions of carp (*Cyprinus carpio*) during the course of prolonged anesthesia. Hydrobiologia 13:144–151.

Shelton, G., and D. J. Randall. 1962. The relationship between heart beat and respiration in teleost fish. Comparative Biochemistry and Physiology 7:237–250.

Sills, J. B., and J. L. Allen. 1971. The influence of pH on the efficacy and residues of quinaldine. Transactions of the American Fisheries Society 100:544–545.

Siwicki, A. 1984. New anaesthetic for fish. Aquaculture 38:171–176.

Smit, G. L., J. Hattingh, and A. P. Burger. 1979a. Haematological assessment of the effects of the anaesthetic MS 222 in natural and neutralized form in three freshwater fish species: haemoglobin electrophoresis, ATP levels and corpuscular fragility curves. Journal of Fish Biology 15:655–663.

Smit, G. L., J. Hattingh, and A. P. Burger. 1979b. Haematological assessment of the effects of the anaesthetic MS 222 in natural and neutralized form in three freshwater fish species: interspecies differences. Journal of Fish Biology 15:633–643.

Smit, G. L., J. Hattingh, and A. P. Burger. 1979c. Haematological assessment of the effects of the anaesthetic MS 222 in natural and neutralized form in three freshwater species: intraspecies differences. Journal of Fish Biology 15:645–653.

Smit, G. L., H. J. Schoonbee, and W. T. Barham. 1977. Some effects of the anesthetic MS 222 on freshwater. South African Journal of Science 73:351–352.

Smith, L. S., and G. R. Bell. 1967. Anesthetic and surgical techniques for Pacific salmon. Journal of the Fisheries Research Board of Canada 24:1579–1588.

Smith, L. S., and G. R. Bell. 1975. A practical guide to the anatomy and physiology of Pacific salmon. Canada Fisheries and Marine Service Miscellaneous Special Publication 27.

Soivio, A., and G. M. Hughes. 1978. Circulatory changes in secondary lamellae of *Salmo gairdneri* gills in hypoxia and anaesthesia. Annales Zoologici Fennici 15:221–225.

Soivio, A., K. Nyholm, and M. Huhti. 1977. Effects of anaesthesia with MS-222, neutralized MS-222 and benzocaine on the blood constituents of rainbow trout, *Salmo gairdneri*. Journal of Fish Biology 10:91–101.

Spaeth, M., and W. Schweickert. 1977. The effect of metacaine (MS-222) on the activity of the efferent and afferent nerves in the teleost lateral-line system. Naunyn-Schmiedeberg's Archives of Pharmacology 297:9–16.

Spector, W. S. 1956. Handbook of toxicity, volume 1. Saunders, Philadelphia.

Sprague, J. B. 1973. The ABC's of pollutant bioassay using fish. Pages 6–30 *in* J. Cairns, Jr., and K. L. Dickson, editors. Biological methods for the assessment of water quality. American Society for Testing and Materials Special Technical Publication 528.

Strange, R. J., and C. B. Schreck. 1978. Anesthetic and handling stress on survival and cortisol concentration in yearling chinook salmon (*Oncorhynchus tshawytscha*). Journal of the Fisheries Research Board of Canada 35:345–349.

Stuart, N. C. 1981. Anaesthetics in fish. Journal of Small Animal Practice 22:377–384.

Summerfelt, R. C., and D. Mosier. 1984. Transintestinal expulsion of surgically implanted transmitters by channel catfish. Transactions of the American Fisheries Society 113:760–766.

Suzuki, A., and Y. Sekizawa. 1979. Residue analyses on 2-amino-4-phenyl-thiazole, a piscine anesthetic, in fishes: 4. GC/MS analysis in rainbow trout. Bulletin of the Japanese Society of Scientific Fisheries 45:167–172.

Takeda, T., and Y. Itzawa. 1983. Examination of possibility of applying anesthesia by carbon dioxide in the transportation of live fish. Bulletin of the Japanese Society of Scientific Fisheries 49:725–732.

Thienpont, D., and C. J. E. Niemegeers. 1965. Propoxate (R7464): a new potent anesthetic agent in cold-blooded vertebrates. Nature (London) 205:1018–1019.

Thompson, R. B. 1959. Tricaine methanesulfonate (M.S. 222) in transport of cutthroat trout. Progressive Fish-Culturist 21:96.

Vibert, R., editor. 1967. Fishing with electricity: its application to biology and management. Fishing News Books, Surrey, England.

Walker, C. R., and R. A. Schoettger. 1967. Residues of MS-222 in four salmonids following anesthesia. U.S. Fish and Wildlife Service Investigations in Fish Control 15.

Walker, M. D. 1972. Physiologic and pharmacologic aspects of barbituates in elasmobranchs. Comparative Biochemistry and Physiology A, Comparative Physiology 42:213–221.

Warren, R. G. 1983. Small animal anesthesia. Mosby, St. Louis, Missouri.

Wedemeyer, G. A. 1970. Stress of anesthesia with MS-222 and benzocaine in rainbow trout (*Salmo gairdneri*). Journal of the Fisheries Research Board of Canada 27:909–914.

Wedemeyer, G. A. 1976. Physiological response of juvenile coho salmon (*Oncorhynchus kisutch*) and rainbow trout (*Salmo gairdneri*) to handling and crowding stress in intensive fish culture. Journal of the Fisheries Research Board of Canada 33:2699–2702.

Wedemeyer, G. A., F. P. Meyer, and L. Smith. 1976. Environmental stress and fish diseases. T.F.H. Publications, Neptune City, New Jersey.

Westhunes, M., and R. Fritsch. 1965. Animal anesthesia. Translated from German by A. D. Weaver. Lippincott, Philadelphia.

Williams & Wilkins Company. 1982. Stedman's medical dictionary, 24th edition. Baltimore, Maryland.

Williamson, R. M., and B. L. Roberts. 1981. Body cooling as a supplement to anaesthesia of fishes. Journal of the Marine Biological Association of the United Kingdom 61:129–132.

Winter, J. D. 1983. Underwater biotelemetry. Pages 371–395 *in* L. A. Nielsen and D. L. Johnson, editors. Fisheries techniques. American Fisheries Society, Bethesda, Maryland.

Wisby, W. J., and A. D. Hasler. 1954. Effect of olfactory occlusion on migrating silver salmon (*O. kisutch*). Journal of the Fisheries Research Board of Canada 11:472–478.

Wood, E. M. 1956. Urethane as a carcinogen. Progressive Fish-Culturist 18:135–136.

Wydowski, R. S., G. A. Wedemeyer, and N. C. Nelson. 1976. Physiological response to hooking stress in hatchery and wild rainbow trout (*Salmon gairdneri*). Transactions of the American Fisheries Society 105:601–606.

Yaron, Z., A. Terkatin, Y. Shaham, and H. Salzer. 1977. Occurrence and biological activity of estradiol-17β in the intact and ovariectomized *Tilapia aurea* (Cichlidae, Teleostei). General and Comparative Endocrinology 33:45–52.

Yoshimura, H., M. Nakamura, and T. Koeda. 1981. Mutagenicity screen of anesthetics for fishes. Mutation Research 90:119–124.

Chapter 9

Blood and Circulation

ARTHUR H. HOUSTON

9.1 INTRODUCTION

In this chapter, consideration will be given to the variables most commonly used to characterize hematological status and circulatory flow, and to methods for their assessment. An enormous literature pertinent to these topics now exists. Mahajan and Dheer (1979) noted that some 900 articles had been published on the subject of fish hematology alone prior to 1970. At least 100 new papers concerned with blood and circulation have appeared each year since. Consequently, the choice of methods to be considered here has been limited primarily to those of general utility.

9.2 BLOOD SAMPLE ACQUISITION

9.2.1 Preparation of Vascular Casts

Most fishes have similar circulatory systems. Their systems are largely or wholly closed, and the heart, branchial and systemic microcirculatory beds, and macrocirculatory vessels are linked in linear array. The systems differ in detail, however, and prior examination of vascular anatomy is essential when blood-sampling procedures are developed, particularly for an unfamiliar species. Although radioautographic examinations are useful (Bell and Smart 1964), such preliminary studies of vascular anatomy are facilitated by simple casting methods. Both flexible or rigid vascular casts can be prepared readily, but the latter are more generally useful because they can be used for both dissection and permanent reference mounts. Smith and Bell (1976) and Bell (1978) adapted casting techniques outlined by Tompsett (1970) for application to fishes. Bell (1978) recommended use of the Batson Anatomical Corrosion Kit, available through Polysciences Inc. of Warrington, Pennsylvania. The only additional equipment needed is a specimen tray (40 × 15 × 0.5 cm, made of clear plastic with 45-cm-long stainless steel wires corner-mounted and linked to form a handle) and a standard caulking gun modified to hold a 20-mL disposable plastic syringe. The latter provides better control over injection than can usually be achieved with a hand-held syringe.

Specimens weighing at least 500 g are anesthetized (see Chapter 8) and suspended vertically by the head. The caudal peduncle is transected, and the severed end is immersed in warm isotonic NaCl. Bell (1978) recommended against prior injection of anticoagulants such as heparin or EDTA. When bleeding has ceased, the peduncle is cleaned and dried. Under low magnification, the caudal artery and vein can be located within the hemal arch. Short lengths of polyethylene tubing (PE-50 or PE-60) are then gently maneuvered 2–3 cm into each vessel. A tissue cement is used to seal these cannulae into the vessels.

Injection plastic is prepared according to the manufacturer's directions. Preliminary experimentation will be required to determine the polymerization time for each lot. A syringe is filled and placed in the caulking gun. A blunt-nosed adaptor is used to link the syringe to the arterial cannula. About 10 min before the plastic would be expected to harden, injection is begun, and continued slowly until plastic can be seen entering the gill filaments. Caution must be exercised to avoid rupturing the gill vessels. The syringe is then transferred to the venous cannula. Bell (1978) suggested that a wedge of tissue be removed from the back muscle of the specimen just anterior to the dorsal fin and that injection be continued until plastic appears on the cut surface.

After about an hour, the plastic should be hard enough for dissection. If a permanent mount is desired, the specimen on its tray should be immersed in about five times it own volume of 6N NaOH (340 g technical grade NaOH/L) at approximately 50°C in a fume hood. Most of the soft tissue will dissolve in 2 or 3 d. Remaining matter can be removed with forceps or washed away with the jet of a squeeze bottle or, if necessary, an additional bath can be used. The cast is then cleaned by agitation in warm water to which some detergent has been added. After it is rinsed and trimmed, the cast can be mounted as appropriate.

9.2.2 Optimization of Sampling Procedures

Blood indices are most commonly used as direct or inferential indicators of functional status. The validity of this practice depends on the critical assumptions that neither the sampling procedure used nor the subsequent sample treatment compromise information content. In many situations, the first of these assumptions is demonstrably invalid. As noted in Section 9.2.3 and Chapter 8, fish are stressed when they are handled for sampling or other purposes, and the effects of stress on blood indices are extensive and enduring. Consequently, many investigators now avoid serial blood sampling, which is the once-common practice of sampling blood from the same fish on several occasions.

Even with "once-only" sampling, several factors can influence the information obtained. These include, but are not limited to, the procedure used to immobilize specimens before sampling, the type of anticoagulant employed, and the duration and conditions of sample storage before use. Few studies have been done, however, to evaluate the effects of these and other influences on measured blood variables.

Fish blood usually coagulates rapidly, and this characteristic was exploited by earlier workers in sample preparation. Samples were allowed to clot, the clot was centrifuged down, and the supernatant serum was used for analysis. Although convenient, this practice has been abandoned. The procedure does not permit determinations of cellular composition, and these are increasingly of interest. More importantly, serum prepared in this way is not simply plasma from which clotting system elements have been removed. Coagulation is associated with transfer of ions and water between plasma and cells. Some cells inevitably break down and release their contents, altering composition. Anticoagulants are used, therefore, to permit separation of cells from plasma. Their use entails several problems and these should be borne in mind.

Two types of anticoagulants are usually employed. Oxalates, citrates, and chelating agents such as EDTA (ethylenediaminetetraacetate) retard clotting by complexing the calcium ions needed by thromboplastin to convert prothrombin to thrombin, the enzyme that promotes clotting. The alternative anticoagulant, heparin, found naturally in mast cells and other tissues, acts as an antithrombin.

Because of its effectiveness, and because it caused little distortion of cellular blood constituents, Klontz and Smith (1968) and Blaxhall (1972) regarded EDTA as the anticoagulant of choice. Lampasso (1965), who had earlier studied EDTA, reported that concentrations exceeding 2 mg/mL of sample led to unreliable hematocrit values, the ratios of packed (by centrifugation) red blood cell volume to the volume of whole blood. Subsequently Blaxhall (1973) found little change in hematocrit over 5-h periods of observation when EDTA concentrations of 4–5 mg/mL of sample were used. At lower concentrations, significant changes were apparent. Smit and Schoonbee (1976) confirmed Blaxhall's findings. In addition, they reported that sample pH decreased and the partial pressure of carbon dioxide (Pco_2) in the blood rose when higher EDTA concentrations were used. Evidence of an induced Root effect (a shift in the equilibrium between oxygen and blood) was sometimes also observed, and significant changes in Po_2 were common. Subsequent studies (Smit et al. 1977) substantiated and extended these findings. Such observations mediate against use of EDTA in sampling programs designed to obtain information on blood gas tensions or acid–base status. If EDTA is used, particular attention must be given to dosage. It is convenient to use sampling needles of measured volume containing enough EDTA to retard clotting during sampling. When the final sample volume is known, additional EDTA can be added to bring the concentration to 5 mg/mL of sample.

Heparin is a highly sulphated mucopolysaccharide of D-glucosamine and D-glucuronic acid and is commercially available as the ammonium, calcium, sodium, or lithium salt. Because biological levels of lithium are low, the latter is preferred by many investigators despite its somewhat higher cost. Most heparin preparations are rated at between 140 and 170 USP (U.S. Pharmacopeia) units/mg, and are effective at concentrations of 50–100 USP units/mL (i.e., from 0.30–0.75 mg/mL of sample). Heparin appears to have little effect on cell volume (Blaxhall 1973) or on blood pH, Pco_2, and Po_2 (Hattingh 1975; Smit et al. 1977).

Anesthesia is treated in detail in Chapter 8. It need be considered here only in relation to the effects of the anesthetization process on blood characteristics, which are numerous. Some effects (e.g., increases in blood or plasma titers of glucose, lactate, pyruvate, particular steroids, or catecholamines) seem to be generalized responses to handling, exposure to air, and other disturbances (Nakano and Tomlinson 1967; Chavin and Young 1970; Houston et al. 1971a; Wedemeyer 1972; Madden and Houston 1976). Others appear to be attributable to the anesthetic agent used (Houston et al. 1971a, 1971b; Reinitz and Rix 1977; Soivio et al. 1977; Smit et al. 1979; Ferreira et al. 1981a, 1981b).

When it is not important that a specimen recover, artifacts of chemical anesthesia can be eliminated by stunning the animal before its blood is sampled. A sharp blow with a steel wedge angled forward from the juncture of skull and vertebral column normally causes irreparable damage to the central nervous system and immediate immobilization of the fish. The blow must be placed precisely and without undue force to avoid rupture of the dorsal aorta.

Some laboratories routinely stockpile samples before they are analyzed or prepared for storage. There is, however, some evidence that storage time may be an important variable. For example, Lowe-Jinde and Niimi (1983) reported that hematocrit values of rainbow trout anesthetized in MS-222 (tricaine) increased significantly within minutes of sample withdrawal.

Korcock et al. (1988) studied the effects of immobilization method (stunning versus MS-222 anesthesia), anticoagulant type (heparin versus EDTA), sample storage time (0, 1, 3, 24 h), and storage temperature (0–2°C versus 22–25°C) on hematocrit, hemoglobin, concentrations of sodium, potassium, and chloride in plasma and packed cells, and concentrations of ATP in packed red cells. Their analysis led to one overriding conclusion: that samples must be prepared for analysis and storage without delay. Subsamples for determinations requiring whole blood should be taken quickly and the remaining sample should be centrifuged, preferably at low temperature. The supernatant plasma should be drawn off in a micropipette and transferred to a capped plastic tube. Plasma remaining on top of the packed cell column should be absorbed onto porous filter paper. If red cell samples are required, the overlying buffy layer of leucocytes should be removed. If white cell samples are needed, more elaborate separation and concentration procedures are required (Section 9.3.2.9).

Once separated, plasma and cellular components can be stored at least 6 months without significant changes in composition. For example, after the components are frozen in liquid nitrogen and stored at −75°C, there is little variation in plasma osmolarity or in packed-cell water content and ionic composition. Cellular hemoglobin contents, plasma protein concentrations, and the electrophoretic mobilities and relative abundances of hemoglobin isoforms and plasma protein fractions are little altered (Houston and Smeda 1979; Houston, Keen, and Gray, unpublished). On the other hand, enzymes decreased in activity during storage (see also Section 9.3.1.8). As a general precaution, plasma and red cell samples should not be refrozen. Because of this, decisions on sample subdivision must be made before storage.

When delays in processing cannot be avoided, refrigeration is essential. However, blood characteristics change even under refrigeration. Red cell volume and water content increase. Net transfers of sodium and chloride from plasma into cells and the opposite transfers of potassium occur. Concentrations of ATP drop precipitously; those of ADP exhibit transient increases. Under all circumstances, significant changes are evident within 1–3 h in refrigerated samples, and within 1 h or less at room temperature.

Some combinations of anesthetic and anticoagulant should be avoided. Use of EDTA in conjunction with MS-222 often leads to hemolysis, which increases with storage and is pronounced at room temperature. Samples obtained from mechanically stunned animals and treated with heparin rarely exhibit hemolysis or marked volume and compositional changes. The combination of stunning, heparin anticoagulation, cold storage, and rapid sample processing appear to yield the best results.

9.2.3 Once-Only Sampling Procedures

Although blood samples are taken primarily to obtain a realistic picture of conditions within the animal, the sampling process itself frequently compromises

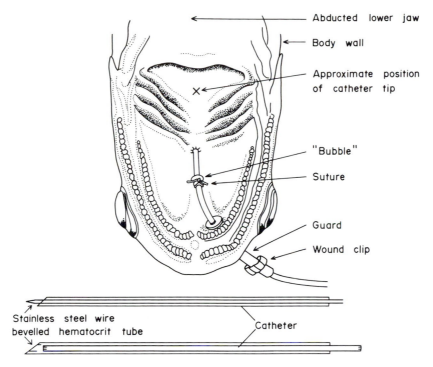

Figure 9.1 Interior of a fish's mouth viewed from the ventral side with the lower jaw pulled back, showing placement of a catheter for sampling blood from the dorsal aorta (modified from Schiffman 1959). The point at which the catheter enters the roof of the mouth is also the point of needle entry for direct aortic puncture. The microhematocrit or "external" trocar is modified from Houston (1971), and the wire-guided or "internal" system from Soivio et al. (1972).

attainment of this goal. As noted earlier, the effects of handling, anesthetization, blood withdrawal, and similar stresses on body fluid composition and distribution are widespread, severe, and persistent. In addition, they are well documented (e.g., Houston et al. 1969; Chavin and Young 1970; Houston et al. 1971a, 1971b; Wedemeyer 1972, 1976; Houston et al. 1973; Hattingh and van Pletzen 1974; Miles et al. 1974; Madden and Houston 1976; Swift 1983). When study goals permit, many investigators now employ once-only or terminal sampling regimes, simply stunning specimens before taking samples from them (Oikari and Soivio 1975; Strange and Schreck 1978; Wells et al. 1984).

When it is not essential that fish recover from the sampling procedure, many sampling sites can be used. With small specimens, for example, transection of the descaled, alcohol-cleansed caudal peduncle may provide the most convenient, or only, means by which an adequate volume of blood can be obtained. With larger animals and species of appropriate body configuration and cardiobranchial morphology (e.g., many salmonids, esocids, percids), dorsal aortic puncture (Schiffman 1959) will provide postbranchial or arterialized blood samples (Figure 9.1). Similarly, prebranchial (i.e., venous) samples can be drawn from some species via the ventral aorta, a procedure that can be facilitated by strong transillumination of the branchial isthmus to reveal the internal position of this vessel.

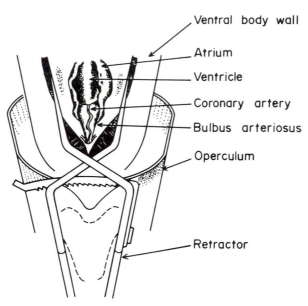

Ventral body wall
Atrium
Ventricle
Coronary artery
Bulbus arteriosus
Operculum
Retractor

Figure 9.2 Ventral exposure of the heart for withdrawal of blood from the bulbus arteriosus. The microretractor used to spread the incision also can support the syringe during sampling.

Prebranchial blood samples also can be obtained by direct cardiac puncture. However, the ventricular myocardium is trabeculated in many species, and the fibrous or membranous structures commonly block needles during sampling. Consequently, cardiac blood samples are most conveniently drawn from the bulbus after the heart is exposed by a midline incision, the pectoral girdle is retracted, and the restraining pericardium is partially removed (Figure 9.2). This approach is particularly useful with small and moderately sized species, and it is often convenient to collect samples directly into beveled and sharpened disposable microliter pipettes. This is an easy sampling method that can yield a larger sample than other techniques, but these advantages must be weighed against possible stress-related changes in blood composition during the extended sampling period. These may be negligible, as for some blood electrolytes, but they are marked for blood glucose, catecholamines, steroids, and other stress-sensitive variables. In such cases, a small, rapidly drawn sample is more valuable than a larger volume taken from a disturbed animal.

Blood samples from the heart can often be taken from the sinus venosus or ducts of Cuvier. Lied et al. (1975), Wingo and Muncy (1984), and Ikeda et al. (1985) described procedures for drawing samples from the ducts of Cuvier. Ames et al. (1966) proposed the efferent and afferent branchial vessels as sites for injection and sample withdrawal (Figure 9.3). Their method is well suited for injection purposes and, as noted in the succeeding section, offers some possibility for cannulation as well.

Blood also has been sampled from several other vessels. The most popular of these are the caudal vein and artery (Itazawa 1957). The caudal vessels usually are approached along the ventral midline posterior to the anal fin and between adjacent hemal arches (Figure 9.4), but they also can be reached by lateral

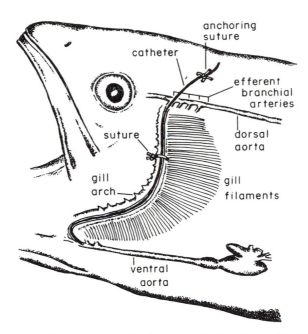

Figure 9.3 Blood sampling from vessels of the branchial arch (modified from Ames et al. 1966).

penetration from a position just ventral to the lateral line. The vein lies immediately ventral to the caudal extension of the dorsal aorta, and in many species, there is partial investment (i.e., the vein and aorta lie within the same sheath). Because of their close apposition, both vessels may be penetrated by a sampling needle, and a mixed arteriovenous sample will then be collected.

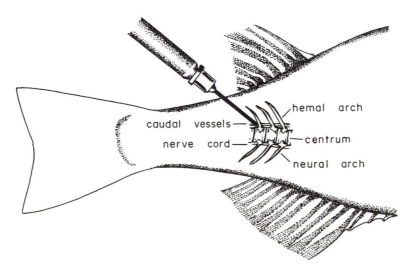

Figure 9.4 Blood sampling from the caudal vessels (modified from Itazawa 1957). The anal fin is up in this illustration.

Smith and Bell (1976) proposed the common cardinal vessel as a sampling site. This vessel is on the right side of the body; in salmonids it can be entered at an 80° angle to the lateral body wall behind the cleithrum and just above the lateral line. Relatively few investigators appear to have adopted this approach as yet. This is also true of the abdominal vein, a site advocated by Labat and Laffont (1964). Finally, small-volume samples can be obtained from many species by posterior orbital puncture, a method often used in small-mammal studies.

Much of the hematological information on fishes has resulted from studies of adult specimens, simply because common sampling techniques are unsuitable for larvae. Perry (1987), however, devised a procedure that allows morphological and similar studies on the blood cells of animals as small as 2 mm. In this procedure, heart and gills are removed by micromanipulator (2–14-mm specimens) or by free-hand dissection under a dissecting microscope (14–52-mm animals) and transferred to slides. A few drops of stain are then added, and the tissue is teased apart to release and spread the cells. Excess stain is then removed, and a permanent mount can be prepared.

Whatever sampling site is selected, some general precautions must be observed. Coagulation is less likely when plastic rather than glass syringes are used. In general, the largest usable needle should be combined with the smallest acceptable syringe. The barrel of the syringe is slowly withdrawn to make room for blood to enter, and not to create negative pressure. Because "bubbling" of blood as it enters the syringe promotes hemolysis, many investigators now routinely draw samples under oil.

9.2.4 Blood Vessel Cannulation

Experimental considerations may mediate against use of once-only sampling methods and in favor of the implantation of small tubes, or cannulae, from which blood samples can be drawn as required. A cannula is useful, for example, when hormone titers in minimally disturbed animals must be monitored or when experimental goals demand serial samples from the same specimen. Several methods have been developed for use with particular species or for particular sampling needs.

Prior to cannulation, specimens must be anesthetized, and a variety of chemical and physical techniques have been employed for this purpose (Chapter 8, Section 8.2). Whatever the method of anesthesia used, however, the goal is to bring the specimen to a surgical plane of anesthesia for a sufficient time without inducing major or persistent side effects, and the method of application is crucial. Animals excited from being netted and transferred to chemical anesthetic baths or electroanesthesia units invariably require much longer to return to normal status than animals anesthetized in tanks in which they have been quietly resting for several hours.

Cannulations are most conveniently carried out with operating assemblies such as those described by Smith and Bell (1967), Houston et al. (1969), and Reinecker and Ruddell (1974). All provide for adjustable restraint, branchial or buccal irrigation, and avoidance of dehydration.

9.2.4.1 Cannulation of the Dorsal Aorta

As originally described by Conte et al. (1963) and Smith and Bell (1964), aortic cannulation involved the emplacement of PE-50 or PE-60 tubing tipped with the shank of a 22- or 23-gauge Huber full-deflected-point hypodermic needle. Needle point and edges almost inevitably damaged the aortic wall. An extensively damaged vessel usually ruptured. In addition, foci for clot formation were established, and preparations of this kind had to be flushed at short intervals to maintain patency, or free flow (Smith and Bell 1967).

In an attempt to circumvent these problems, H. M. Miles introduced the cannulating syringe (Miles, personal communication). This allowed the use of a needleless catheter, the tip of which could be positioned well posterior to the point of aortic penetration. Preparations of this kind are both more durable and less prone to blockage through clot formation. Although the technique works well with large specimens, difficulties are encountered with smaller fish. The overall diameter of an 18-gauge needle (the size accommodating PE-50 tubing) and sheath is approximately 1.65 mm, close to the dimensions of the dorsal and ventral aortae of 200–300-g animals. Vessel rupture during cannulation is not uncommon. In addition, substantial blood losses are entailed. Up to 0.5 mL of blood can be accommodated between needle and sheath, and this represents a substantial fraction of total blood volume in small- to moderate-sized specimens.

The advantages of the cannulating-syringe method can be retained if a trocar, a sharp, separately removable instrument for introducing a cannula, is substituted for the bulkier syringe. Garey (1969), for example, used an 18T trocar with stylet on specimens of nine fish species in the 3–6-kg weight range. Subsequently, Houston (1971) used standard 75-mm hematocrit tubes for this purpose. A further refinement of the trocar system was developed by Soivio et al. (1972), who used PE-50 tubing with a beveled end fitted over a length of pointed stainless steel wire. An arrangement of this kind permits cannulation of relatively small animals. Both glass hematocrit tube and internal wire trocars offer several advantages over a fixed-needle catheter. Blood losses during emplacement are substantially reduced. There is relatively little vessel damage at the open end of the tube, although some necrosis at the point of aortic penetration appears to be almost inevitable. A small but important advantage that the internal trocar has over the hematocrit type is that small "bubbles" can be placed in the catheter wall (Figure 9.1). The bubbles can be used as anchoring points for suturing the cannula to the flesh. Bubbles are made by softening the catheter in the flame of an alcohol lamp and pushing the softened material together. Against this advantage must be balanced the awkwardness of manipulating a sometimes unwieldy length of wire.

Whichever catheter system is selected, the insertion procedure is basically the one originally described by Smith and Bell (1964). A short length of 12-gauge, stainless steel hypodermic tubing with a beveled end is first driven completely through the roof of the mouth just posterior to the premaxilla (Figure 9.1). Through this is passed a short length of PE tubing (of larger bore than the catheter), the end of which has been heat-flanged to support the catheter. The catheter is then marked at the length to be inserted into the aorta and filled with heparinized saline that has been sterilized by passage through a Sterivex-GS Millipore filter. The trocar is inserted into the roof of the mouth slightly anterior to the first gill bars (Figure 9.1), advanced posteriorly beneath the epithelium, and then angled down (dorsally) to the union of the anterior pairs of efferent branchial vessels with the aorta. When the hematocrit tube trocar is used, penetration of the aorta is quickly evident as blood moves up into the space between tube and catheter. The trocar is moved slowly into the aorta with a slight rotary motion. The cannula can now be gently maneuvered through it and into the vessel for the required distance. The hematocrit tube is then withdrawn, and light finger pressure is applied at the penetration site until clotting has occurred.

With the internal trocar, penetration of the aorta is evidenced in the same way, and can be confirmed by backing off slightly on the wire. The catheter is then gently rotated into the vessel, and the wire is withdrawn. The tubing is next plugged or clamped with a hemostat and positioned. It is then sutured to the roof of the mouth, anchored within the nasal supporting tube with clinch knots or wound clips, flushed with sterile saline containing 250 IU (international units) of lithium heparin per milliliter, and plugged. The procedure works well with specimens down to 200–500 g when the glass trocar is employed. With PE-90 tubing and matching wire, the internal trocar method can be used with specimens in the 100-g range. However, such preparations require a great deal of attention, for blood clots begin quickly and patency is difficult to maintain.

9.2.4.2   Dual Cannulation

Cannulation methods are commonly used in kinetic and volume studies. These usually involve infusion of isotope or dye labels followed by serial sampling. When a single catheter is employed, the absorption of tracer to the catheter wall may compromise samples subsequently taken from that catheter. This is referred to as "single catheter error." Nichols and Weisbart (1984) circumvented this problem by using trocars to place two small PE-50 catheters in the aortae of large (1–4-kg) specimens. Few deaths were reported, postsurgical trauma was relatively modest, and the catheters remained patent for a month or more. During development and testing of the procedure, the authors were also able to confirm the existence and magnitude of "single catheter error." In the case of plasma labeled with tritiated cortisol, this error ranged from 14 to 1,800%.

9.2.4.3   Cannulation of the Ventral Aorta

Holeton and Randall (1967a, 1967b) used needle-tipped catheters to cannulate the ventral aorta of rainbow trout. Subsequently, Garey (1969) and Saunders and Sutterlin (1971) employed needleless cannulae for this purpose. As applied to salmonids, Garey's method involved entry through the mouth. An 18T, 89-mm trocar and stylet unit was inserted medially at the base of the midline papilla on the floor of the mouth and advanced at a 45° angle directly into the aorta. The stylet was then withdrawn and the catheter was passed through the trocar into the vessel and sutured into position before being passed, via anchoring tubes, to the exterior.

Saunders and Sutterlin (1971) used a quite different approach with the sea raven. Animals weighing 1–3 kg were placed ventral side uppermost on an operating assembly and an incision was made in the midline of the branchial isthmus. The ventral aorta was then exposed by blunt dissection and a cannula was inserted. The skin was sewn tightly around the cannula and the wound was closed. These authors also developed a novel procedure for dorsal aortic cannulation, one suitable only for tolerant species. The gastric artery was exposed by means of a right lateral incision in the body wall near the pelvic fin insertion. The cannula was then passed through the artery to its junction with the aorta.

The ventral aorta of appropriately sized fish sometimes can be cannulated by either trocar method if the isthmus can be strongly transilluminated to reveal the vessel's position. Generally, however, direct cannulations of the ventral aorta are neither very successful nor very enduring. A less direct approach may be possible with large specimens. As noted earlier, Ames et al. (1966) described methods for sampling from, or injecting into, the afferent and efferent branchial vessels (Figure 9.3). Although satisfactory for injection, the method is not useful for sampling because the time required to draw samples of adequate volume usually compromises their integrity. Their experience suggested, however, that a catheter might be inserted into the bore of an afferent branchial artery near the base of a gill arch and worked back into the ventral aorta. Some success with this approach has been obtained in short-duration trials involving the use of flexible Silastic rather than polyethylene catheter tubing. The catheter is anchored by suturing it to the gill arch although this, of course, affects blood flow. It is also possible to enter the dorsal aorta via the efferent arteries at the top of the arches. This approach offers no obvious advantages over existing methods as far as salmonid and similar species are concerned. It could, however, provide a means for cannulating common carp and other species whose body configurations make the usual cannulation techniques difficult.

9.2.4.4   Cannulation of the Caudal Vessels

Cech and Rowell (1976) described a procedure for cannulating the caudal blood vessels. Although developed specifically for use with winter flounder, the method is of general applicability. An 18-gauge hypodermic needle fitted with PE-50 tubing is pushed into the hemal canal (Figure 9.4). From there it is forced into either the caudal artery (which lies next to the vertebral centrum) or into the caudal vein (which lies ventral to the caudal artery in the hemal canal). Cech and Rowell contended that the vessel penetrated could be identified on the basis of blood color and pressure, but recommended dissection to confirm the identification. They also successfully implanted a second cannula in the vessel not initially penetrated.

9.2.4.5   Recovery from Surgery

In common with other procedures, cannulation imposes stresses of varying types and intensities on the test animals. Either directly or indirectly, these lead to important deviations from normal status. Until compensation (i.e., "recovery") has occurred, blood sampling cannot be expected to yield data indicative of the normal state. For example, substances of the "local anesthetic" type such as tricaine (e.g., MS-222) appear to act at the cell membrane, prompting compositional changes that depress neuromuscular activity. During irrigation of the fish, anesthetic concentrations rise sharply (Houston and Woods 1972), substantially increasing the load that must be cleared. Although direct effects will persist until all anesthetic has been inactivated or removed, agents of this kind are usually cleared rapidly through the gills, kidneys, or both, or they are metabolically degraded within tissues. Houston and Woods (1972) noted that blood MS-222 levels in rainbow trout fell by 50% within 20 min after the fish were transferred to anesthetic-free water, and were indistinguishable from background values after 3–6 h. Similar observations were made by Walker and Schoettger (1967) and

Goldstein (1982). There are, however, well-documented effects in addition to those attributable to anesthetics per se. For example, no irrigation system is entirely effective. Because of this, Po_2 falls, Pco_2 rises, and acidosis is induced. Handling and similar stresses prompt sharp increases in plasma titres of some hormones. Fagerlund (1967), Nakano and Tomlinson (1967), and Mazeaud et al. (1977) reported significant changes in concentrations of corticosteroid, catecholamine, and other hormones after fish were disturbed. The osmotic fragility of erythrocytes is greater when blood is drawn shortly after cannulation than it is 24 h later, which may be related to these biochemical changes (Hughes and Martinez 1986).

Such complications suggest that as much consideration be given to stress minimization as to other aspects of the procedure. In general, anything that reduces the extent and duration of stress will also reduce the magnitude of changes from the normal state and the duration of the recovery process. Minimization of stress is consistent with the principle of least intervention and usually involves attention to small details. Is it worth neutralizing tricaine in soft water? Will one suture suffice, or are two absolutely essential? If the time required for anesthetic clearance depends on the acquired anesthetic load, is the use of mixtures of independently cleared synergistic anesthetics (e.g., tricaine plus quinaldine sulfate) preferable to single solutions at higher concentrations? Because osmo- and ionoregulatory changes are among the most persistent aftereffects of surgery on fishes, does irrigation with saline rather than water confer any advantage? Given the known effects of abrupt temperature changes, is it worth regulating anesthetic bath and irrigation system temperatures? In general, the answers to the foregoing and to similar questions are yes. Collectively, these individually small modifications usually reduce substantially the interval required before valid sampling can begin.

Finally, it should be appreciated that stress effects can be reduced but not wholly eliminated. Furthermore, different physiological processes recover at different rates. Many variables have been examined in this respect, among them hematological indices, several aspects of water–electrolyte status, blood gases, oxygen consumption, and a wide range of cardiovascular, ventilatory, renal, and other systemic functions (e.g., Hunn and Willford 1970; Houston et al. 1971a, 1971b, 1973; Soivio et al. 1977; Sleet and Weber 1983). Periods ranging from hours to days are usually needed for a process to return to preoperative levels or a steady state; some activities exhibit periods of deceptive pseudostability before finally stabilizing. Several indices and activities that have been examined required 4–8 d to "recover," and a few failed to stabilize or return to initial values within 10 d. Given the complexity of the recovery process, it obviously is important to ascertain when a specific variable can be validly measured.

Recovery and subsequent stability of specimens during experiments involving chronic sampling procedures sometimes can be improved through use of holding boxes or confining devices. Holding boxes have been described by Smith and Bell (1967), Lloyd and Orr (1969), and Swift (1981). Swift (1981) also provided data on hematocrit and compositional changes in fish confined in such boxes for periods of up to 7 d.

9.2.4.6   Saline Solutions

Saline solutions are required for all cannulation procedures, and many have been devised specifically for these and other purposes (Wolf and Quimby 1969). The modified Cortland saline formulation listed below is more complex than several now in use. However, as judged by several morphological and metabolic criteria, it provides a better functional match with plasma than do many alternative salines (Houston et al. 1985).

NaCl	7.250 g	NaHCO$_3$	2.500 g
CaCl$_2 \cdot$ 2H$_2$O	0.130 g	HEPES buffer	2.383 g
MgSO$_4 \cdot$ 7H$_2$O	0.230 g	Na pyruvate	0.440 g
KCl	0.250 g	Glucose	0.50 g
NaH$_2$PO$_4 \cdot$ 2H$_2$O	0.400 g	Glass-distilled H$_2$O to 1.00 L	

(HEPES is N'-2-hydroxyethylpiperazine-N'-ethanesulfonic acid.)

Saline pH is adjusted to 7.5 at 14°C, and the solution is pumped through a millipore 0.22-μm filter to sterilize it, and into a sterile, dark glass or plastic container for refrigeration. Immediately before it is used, lithium heparin (0.1 g/L) and bovine serum albumin (3.0 g/L) are added to the saline.

9.3   ROUTINE HEMATOLOGICAL METHODS

Almost all of the hematological and related analytical methods developed for use in human medicine have been, or can be, adapted for the examination of fish blood. This is particularly true of procedures already microscaled for pediatric application. As with human and veterinary medical practice, many investigators have attempted to define the "normal" hematological status for various fish species. The intent of such studies is clear. Departures from such values could be used to assess specimen condition or to diagnose pollutant- and pathogen-induced stress, among other applications. Whether or not a "normal" state can be defined remains open to question. As aquatic poikilotherms, fish respond readily to changes in their environments, and these changes can occur hourly and daily as well as seasonally. Aquatic animals probably are in an *adapting* state as frequently as they are in an *adapted* state. It is questionable if the term "normal" can be applied to aquatic ectotherms in the way it is used with mammals. "Normal" hematological status in fishes may represent a value range so broad as to be meaningless.

The foregoing notwithstanding, cautiously interpreted hematological data can provide useful information on a variety of functions. For this reason, much emphasis has been placed on the development and application of appropriate methodologies (e.g., Hesser 1960; Blaxhall and Daisley 1973; Casillas and Smith 1977; Christopher et al. 1978). These are conveniently considered in terms of erythrocytes (and thus of respiratory gas transport) and of leucocytes (and thus of blood coagulation and response to pathogens).

9.3.1   Erythrocytes

Erythrocyte status is usually described in terms of one or more of three primary and three derived indices. The primary indices are hemoglobin content (Hb), hematocrit (Hct), and red cell abundance (RBC). The derived indices are mean erythrocyte volume (MEV), mean erythrocytic hemoglobin (MEH), and mean erythrocytic hemoglobin content (MEHC). From the functional viewpoint, the primary indices are principally of value as indicators of blood oxygen-carrying capacity, and thus of an organism's ability to meet metabolic oxygen requirements. Hemoglobin, usually reported as g/100 mL of whole blood or, more usefully, as mM/L whole blood, is the most direct measure of capacity. Red cell counts would be of equivalent utility if, as is the case with many mammals and birds, all circulating red cells could be assumed to carry near-saturation loads of hemoglobin; however, this is not the case with fishes. Hematocrit is the most readily and, therefore, the most frequently measured of the primary indices, but it is the least useful in terms of respiratory and related functions because it depends on both cell numbers and volumes. Cell hemoglobin content is a function of cell maturity, and cell volume is governed by osmoregulatory factors involving more than simply the number of osmotically active hemoglobin molecules present. Thus, while statistically significant correlations between hematocrit and both hemoglobin and red cell numbers have been observed, these do not appear to have acceptable predictive value (Summerfelt et al. 1967; Houston and DeWilde 1968, 1972). Given these considerations, hematocrit values must be interpreted with caution.

Of the derived indices, MEH, the average hemoglobin content of individual red cells, is of obvious value from the viewpoint of respiratory function. The average cell volume, MEV, is frequently used in assessments of osmoregulatory status and, in addition, has important implications with respect to cardiac dynamics and blood flow. Less useful is MEHC, being simply hemoglobin content per 100 mL of packed red cells. These indices are estimated as follows.

$$MEV = \frac{Hct\ (\%) \cdot 10}{RBC,\ 10^6\ mm^3}, \qquad \text{reported in } nm^3.$$

$$MEH = \frac{Hb\ (g/L)}{RBC,\ 10^6\ mm^3}, \qquad \text{reported as } \mu g/cell.$$

$$MEHC = \frac{Hb\ (g/100\ mL)}{Hct\ (\%)}, \qquad \text{reported as } g/100\ mL.$$

9.3.1.1   Hemoglobin Determination

Although methods based on various hemoglobin derivatives have been employed, the determination of hemoglobin as the cyanomethemoglobin (Hb^+–CN^-) derivative is now regarded as the method of choice. Cyanomethemoglobin is the most stable of the known derivatives, and virtually all of the common hemoglobin derivatives can be readily and quantitatively converted to Hb^+–CN^-. The absorption spectrum displays a flat maximum around 540 nm, and this allows reasonably accurate determination with even a simple filter photometer. Cyanomethemoglobin solutions obey the Beer–Lambert law over a wide concentration range (i.e., absorption is directly proportional to concentration). The reagents required are stable for relatively long periods without refrigeration, and precisions of 2% or finer can be obtained. By comparison, determinations involving iron analysis by atomic absorption spectrophotometry have an average error of 13%, and the acid hematin method gives variations of up to 40%. Analyses involving the oxy- or deoxyhemoglobin derivatives exhibit errors of 2–10%. Indeed, only the methemoglobinazide ($Hb^+–N_3^-$) procedure provides equivalent precision. However, the $Hb^+–N_3^-$ absorption maximum at 542 nm is extremely narrow, unexpected deviations due to turbidity are sometimes encountered, and NaN_3 reagent cannot be stored at room temperature.

The reagent used in the cyanomethemoglobin procedure consists of 200 mg $K_3Fe(CN)_6$, 50 mg KCN, and 140 mg KH_2PO_4 (all analytical grade) and 1.0 mL NONIDET P40 or 0.5 mL Sterox SE detergent diluted with glass-distilled water to 1.0 L. This yields a clear, pale yellow solution of pH 7.0–7.4 and zero absorbance (A) at 540 nm when measured against a water blank. It must be stored in a closed, brown borosilicate glass bottle and will retain pH and absorbance characteristics for several months. It must not be frozen or allowed to contact acids.

Twenty-microliter samples of fresh whole blood and appropriate volumes of hemoglobin standard are diluted to 5.0 mL with cyanide reagent and agitated on a Vortex mixer. The reaction will proceed to completion within 10 min or less. Following centrifugation to remove suspended cellular debris, absorbance is read at 540 nm. Bracketing hemoglobin standards are used, and values are commonly reported as g/100 mL or mM/L whole blood. Stabilized human hemoglobin standards are available through Clinton Laboratories and Boehringer-Mannheim Diagnostics, Inc. These standards are manufactured in relation to the higher hemoglobin levels of humans.

9.3.1.2 Hematocrit Determination

Standard plain microhematocrit tubes, 75 mm long with 1.1–1.2-mm or 0.5-mm internal diameters, are commonly used for hematocrit measurements. Blood is drawn into the tube by capillary action, the end is closed with a commercial sealant (e.g., Critoseal™), and the sample is centrifuged, preferably at cold-room temperatures, in a standard microhematocrit centrifuge for 5 min at 7,000 revolutions/min. If sample volume is limiting, still smaller tubes can be used. The plain Drummond tube, 32 mm long with 0.8-mm outside diameter, is useful because it can be nested in a standard microhematocrit tube for centrifugation. The lengths of the columns containing packed red cells and packed red cells plus the buffy supernatant are measured; hematocrit is calculated as the ratio of values and expressed as a percentage. A micrometer and $3\times$ flat-field magnifier are useful for this purpose. Alternatively, a microhematocrit reader can be used. Precisions of ±2% are commonly attained.

9.3.1.3 Red Cell Counts

When available, electronic counting systems provide faster and more reliable red cell counts than can be obtained by visual methods. The instrumentation is costly in relation to data yield, however. Consequently, the time-consuming classical method, with its inherent imprecision (as much as ±10%), is frequently used. Freshly drawn blood is diluted 1:200 in a standard RBC diluting pipette (Figure 9.5) with Hendricks's diluting solution (Hendricks 1952), prepared as follows.

Na_2SO_4	10.0 g	Glacial acetic acid	50 mL
NaCl	2.5 g	Glass-distilled water	to 500 mL
Na citrate	1.5 g		

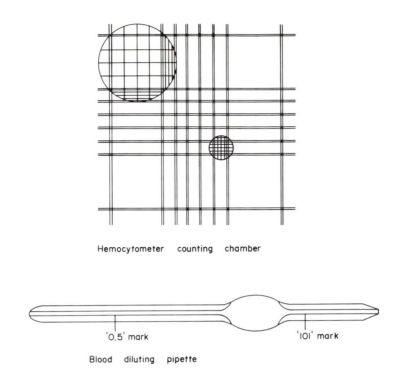

Hemocytometer   counting   chamber

'0.5' mark   'IOI' mark

Blood   diluting   pipette

Figure 9.5   Hemocytometer and blood-diluting pipette. The 0.5 mark on the pipette is the level to which blood is drawn, and the 101 mark is the level to which the blood is diluted with Hendricks's solution.

Blood is drawn into the pipette just beyond the 0.5 mark, the pipette is leveled and wiped, and blood is absorbed into tissue touched to the tip of the pipette until the meniscus is exactly on the mark. The pipette is then filled to the 101 mark with Hendricks's fluid, the ends are closed, and the pipette is placed on a shaker for 2 min. If a shaker is not available, the pipette can be shaken manually. This must be done carefully and thoroughly because non-uniform mixing of blood and diluting fluid is probably the single largest source of error in this method. A few drops of diluant are expelled from the tip to remove unmixed sample; the tip is again wiped and then touched to the edge (between the cover slip and counting chamber) of a Neubauer or a Spencer bright line hemocytometer. Capillarity draws the sample into the chamber. The hemocytometer is divided into 1-mm^2 areas (Figure 9.5). The center square is subdivided into 25 smaller squares and each of the latter into 16 squares. Typically, red cells lying in five of the secondary squares are counted; most commonly, these are the center and corner squares. By convention, cells touching the top and right boundary lines are counted, those touching the bottom and left boundary lines are not. Given the dilution used and the dimensions of the counting chamber, the total number of cells counted multiplied by 10^6 gives number of cells/mm^3 of whole blood.

Blaxhall and Daisley (1973) recommended Dacie's fluid as a diluting solution: 40% formaldehyde solution (i.e., full-strength formalin), 10 mL; trisodium citrate 31.3g; brilliant cresyl blue, 1 g; distilled water to 1.0 L. They made a 1:50 dilution by adding 20 μL of fresh whole blood to 0.98 mL of Dacie's fluid. This was then introduced into a hemocytometer, and cells were counted as previously.

Representative red cell counts for teleostean species were summarized by Houston (1980). Considerable variability is apparent, and it is not yet clear whether the differences observed are inherent or induced. A wide range of factors appear to influence hematological status in fishes. These are often superimposed upon seasonal variations whose initiating factors are themselves not well understood (Denton and Yousef 1975; Bridges et al. 1976; van Vuren and Hattingh 1978a, 1978b). Ambient temperature, oxygen availability, and photoperiod influence blood oxygen-carrying capacity, affecting both the amounts and kinds of hemoglobin formed (Houston 1980; Tun and Houston 1986). Considerable diversity of response to these factors is evident. For example, fishes exposed to normal dissolved oxygen concentrations and constant temperature frequently exhibit changes in both oxygen-carrying capacity and red cell levels of hemoglobin–oxygen affinity-altering modulators. Under the more ecologically realistic circumstances provided by diurnal sine-wave temperature cycles, hemoglobin rises to a level characteristic of specimens constantly exposed to the cycle's peak temperature, and there is little change in hemoglobin–oxygen affinity (Koss and Houston 1981). In yet other species, exposure to increased temperature leads to some increase in capacity, stabilization of affinity, and changes in ventilatory flow and cardiac output (Henry and Houston 1984). The expression of such responses often depends upon other factors. It has long been known, for example, that general nutritional state and specific dietary components have a profound effect upon hematological status (e.g., Kamra 1966; Smith 1968; Weinberg et al. 1973; Johansson-Sjöbeck et al. 1975). This is true of environmental pollutants as well (e.g., Johansson-Sjöbeck and Larsson 1978; Stromberg et al. 1983; Houston and Keen 1984).

Specimen size is also emerging as a factor of importance. Weight-specific oxygen demand ("metabolic intensity") in fishes, as in all organisms, is a negative power function of weight. A similar relationship between oxygen-carrying capacity and weight might reasonably be anticipated. This has been reported for only a few species, however (Guernsey and Poluhowich 1975; Green 1977; Burton and Murray 1979). No evidence of size-related variation was encountered in the African yellowfish *Barbus holubi,* common carp, the mudfishes *Labeo umbratus* and *L. capensis* (van Vuren and Hattingh 1978b), or in wild and captive cunners (Hickey 1982).

Most commonly, oxygen-carrying capacity varies directly with weight. Mean or significant increases in one or more of the primary indices have now been reported for black crappie and bluegill (Burke and Woolcott 1957) and mountain whitefish (McKnight 1966). Spanish mackerel exhibit increases in red cell numbers, hematocrit, and hemoglobin with increasing body length up to 25–50 cm (Pitombeira and Martins 1970). Lientz and Smith (1974) observed significant increases in hemoglobin and hematocrit with growth in cutthroat trout. This is true of rainbow and brook trout as well (Houston, Edwards, and Steele, unpublished observations). A similar relationship characterizes the air-breathing siluroid catfish *Heteropneustes fossilis* (Pandey et al. 1975). American plaice also exhibit well-defined positive correlations between all primary indices and weight, and this tends to become more pronounced with age (Smith 1977). Response to altered environmental circumstances may be conditioned by size. Smeda and Houston

(1979) found little change in the primary or secondary hematological indices of large common carp (200 g or more) exposed to increased temperatures. Smaller specimens (10–50 g), however, exhibited significant changes. Chudzik and Houston (1983) found no evidence of size-related variation in goldfish held at 7.5°C, but they found a highly significant correlation between hemoglobin and weight at 30°C. In short, the interpretation of this kind of information must be carried out with care in recognition of the multiple influencing agencies.

Peripheral Amitotic Erythrocyte Formation. The accepted view of erythropoiesis (red blood cell formation) in adult fishes is that it consists of mitotic proliferation largely or entirely confined to the spleen and head kidney (Catton 1951; Weinberg et al. 1976; Mahajan and Dheer 1979). After they are released to the circulating blood, the juvenile ovoidal cells become flattened ellipsoids, develop a variety of organelles, synthesize heme and globin, assemble hemoglobin, eliminate much of their organellar complement, and eventually become scenescent (Lane et al. 1982). Synthesis of DNA ceases (Mahajan and Dheer 1979) and, except for pre- and immediately posthatching salmon larvae (Catton 1951; Conroy 1972), evidence of mitosis in circulating erythrocytes has been wanting (Conroy 1972; Yamamoto and Iuchi 1975; Härdig 1978).

Nevertheless, reports consistent with peripheral red cell formation by amitotic processes are increasingly published. These have involved several species, including white sucker (Deutsch and Engelbert 1970), plaice *Pleuronectes platessa* (Ellis 1984), and Atlantic salmon (Benfey and Sutterlin 1984). Observations by Catton (1951) and Yasuzumi and Higashizawa (1955) also point to processes of this kind. Although such cells are usually characterized as "abnormal" or "bizarre," Engelbert (1979) has long contended that red cell formation in this fashion is common in vertebrates. Deutsch and Engelbert (1970) reported that such cells constitute up to 10% of the peripheral erythrocytes of the white sucker. In my laboratory they have been encountered, in smaller proportions, in virtually all specimens of rainbow trout, goldfish, and brook silverside examined, but they do not exhibit expected changes in DNA content.

9.3.1.4   Hemoglobin Electrophoresis

More than 90% of the teleosts examined possess polymorphic hemoglobin systems (Yamanaka et al. 1965; Sharp 1973; De Smet 1978; Fyhn et al. 1979). The hemoglobin variants—the isomorphs—may be useful qualitative and quantitative genetic markers in population studies. The isomorphs also frequently exhibit functional heterogeneity; i.e., they differ in their affinity for oxygen and in the extent to which this affinity can be influenced by affinity-modulating solutes. Just as the functional environment provided by the red cell can be adjusted during acclimation (Houston 1980; Powers 1980; Weber 1982), so also can the organization of the hemoglobin system. Consequently, it is often valuable to know the absolute and relative abundances of hemoglobin isomorphs.

The best technique to define the hemoglobin system is electrophoresis (Chapter 5). Differences in the electrophoretic mobilities of hemoglobin isomorphs are thought to reflect differences in the type and sequence, not in the number, of amino acids. It does not necessarily follow, however, that each mobility observed represents a unique hemoglobin. Discrimination by electrophoresis is based on the electrical charges and masses of molecules, and different kinds of molecules can have similar overall charge–mass relationships. In addition, mixtures of oxy- and deoxyhemoglobin and of free hemoglobin and hemoglobin–haptoglobin complexes exhibit differences in mobility. Because of these and similar considerations, care must be exercised in sample preparation, actual electrophoresis, and interpretation of results.

The essential elements of any electrophoretic system are the support medium, the buffer, and the electrical field. A wide range of media have been employed, among them papers of varying composition and porosity, starch gels, polyacrylamide gels, and cellulose acetate. Both uniform- and graded-porosity gels are available. Buffers of different kinds can be employed to exploit particular charge characteristics. For routine separations, however, cellulose acetate systems of the type available through Helena Laboratories are particularly useful. These are more convenient to use than either starch or acrylamide gels. Resolution is better than that ordinarily obtained with starch gels, and at least as good as that gained from many acrylamide gel systems. In addition, the transparency of cellulose acetate can be enhanced before densitometric evaluation, which improves precision. Systems of this type can also be used to separate plasma proteins. Finally, many of the reagents needed are available in prepackaged form and are convenient to store and use.

The electrophoretic procedure described in Box 9.1 is capable of high resolution and fractions comprising only a few tenths of 1% of the total proteins present can be separated. Positive identification of hemoglobins is, therefore, a matter of concern. Heretofore, a highly sensitive benzidine stain has been used for this purpose. This material is carcinogenic, however, and unsuitable for routine laboratory use. Kaiho and Mizuno (1985) tested 2,7-diaminofluorene as a hemoglobin detector. The procedure is based on the pseudoperoxidase activity of hemoglobin, and employs 2,7-diaminofluorene as a hydrogen donor. The method is said to be highly sensitive and suitable for blood hemoglobin analysis and histochemistry. Initial trials have been encouraging, but they suggest the need for modification if the method is to be used histochemically or for identification of hemoglobin separated by electrophoresis. Kuo and Fridovich (1988) described an alternative procedure said to be capable of detecting as little as 5 ng of protein-bound iron in polyacrylamide gel electropherograms. It is based on the catalysis by iron of the oxidation of diaminobenzoic acid by hydrogen peroxide to form an insoluble pigment.

The procedure for serum protein separation is much the same as that outlined for hemoglobin in Box 9.1. Titan III rather than III-H is used in conjunction with a tris-barbital–Na-barbital buffer (Helena Electra HK buffer, pH 8.8). Time and voltage settings are specified for each cellulose acetate lot. Ponceau S will stain all of the proteins present. Selective stains for glycoproteins, lipoproteins, and other constituents are also available.

Finally, when potentially adaptive changes in isomorph abundances are under investigation, several factors must be considered. As noted previously, red cell maturation involves organelle elimination. Presumably, synthetic capability is lost as well. This, and the longevity of mature red cells (Hevesy et al. 1964; Weinberg et al. 1976; Chudzik and Houston 1983), suggests that the hemoglobins present at any time reflect responses to earlier rather than to current conditions or to newly imposed experimental conditions. Associated with changes in isomorph abun-

Box 9.1   Electrophoretic Separation of Hemoglobin Isomorphs

A typical separation of hemoglobin isomorphs on the Helena Laboratories electrophoresis system is carried out as follows.

1. A small sample of whole blood is centrifuged at 3,000 revolutions/min (rpm) for 5 min at 4°C. The buffy layer and plasma are removed with a micropipette and the cells are resuspended in a saline washing solution. The cycle of centrifugation and resuspension is repeated at least three times to minimize the number of white cells and plasma proteins in the preparation or eliminate them altogether.

2. Two volumes of glass-distilled water are added to the volume of packed cells, and the suspension is agitated on a vortex mixer to induce hemolysis. After hemolysis, the sample is centrifuged at 5,000 rpm for 10 min at 4°C to remove cell fragments. The supernatant containing dissolved hemoglobin is drawn off.

3. Carbon monoxide is bubbled through the hemolysate for at least 5 min to convert hemoglobin to its stable carbon monoxide derivative. A small bottle of compressed CO feeding through a reduction valve to a 22- or 23-gauge hypodermic needle is a convenient gas-delivery system. For safety, this step must be carried out in a fume hood. If the sample is not to be used immediately, it can be capped, immersed in liquid nitrogen, and stored at very low temperature (e.g., −75°C).

4. Electrophoretic separation of the hemoglobin isomorphs follows the manufacturer's directions for the system to be used. Working with the Helena electrophoretic unit in my laboratory, we have found it advantageous to dilute one package of Supra Heme buffer to 1,090 mL with deionized, glass-distilled water, to pre-chill all solutions to 2–4°C, and to conduct separations at 400 V for 20 min at 2–4°C.

5. Cellulose acetate plates (Titan III-H) are marked for identification on one corner of the glossy mylar side. The plates must be uniformly soaked in buffer; the "bufferizer" developed for this purpose is a useful accessory.

6. Five-microliter samples of hemolysate and control (Helena AA$_2$ Hemocontrol) are transferred in a Hamilton syringe to the wells of the sample loader. One should work from one side of the loader to the other and draw a glass slide across each well as it is filled to retard evaporation. The AA$_2$ control will subsequently be used for determination of relative mobilities; it is the control ordinarily employed in human and comparative hematological studies.

7. The sample applicator is a multitipped device used to transfer samples from the loader wells to the acetate plates. The applicator tips are inserted into the sample wells to prime them. After they have been thoroughly wetted, the tips are blotted on blotting paper. Then the buffer-soaked cellulose acetate plate is quickly removed from the buffer bath, blotted once, and placed—acetate side up—on the aligning plate. The applicator is then reloaded with samples, aligned, pressed down on the acetate plate for 5 s, and removed.

8. The loaded plate is quickly transferred to the electrophoresis chamber. It is essential that the application line be perpendicular to current flow if band distortion is to be avoided. Only one plate should be run at a time. Do not delay the start of the run. Note also that even small differences in chamber buffer levels can lead to siphoning and distortion of the hemoglobin pattern.

Box 9.1   Continued.

9. Immediately clean the sample applicator.

10. After it is removed from the electrophoresis chamber, the plate is immersed in a stain for 5 min; the stain is 0.5% Ponceau S in an aqueous solution of trichloroacetic–sulfosalicylic acid. Three successive 2-min washes in 5% acetic acid are usually sufficient to remove background stain. The plate then is dehydrated in two successive 2-min methanol baths, and placed for 5 min in a clearing solution (30 volumes glacial acetic acid, 70 volumes methanol, 4 volumes Helena Clear Aid). It is air-dried for 1 min on a blotter—mylar side down—and placed with the blotter in an oven at 60°C for 3–5 min. The strip now is transparent and can be readily quantified by routine densitometric methods.

dances are potentially significant hemodynamic restrictions. Hematological responses are rarely accompanied by major changes in mean cellular hemoglobin content (Houston 1980). Thus, elevation of blood oxygen-carrying capacity can be achieved only through red cell proliferation. In the absence of some means to selectively eliminate mature and senescent erythrocytes, the organism must limit red cell proliferation or tolerate sharp increases in blood viscosity and cardiac work. Responsive changes in isomorph abundances, therefore, usually appear as only modest changes superimposed on an obscuring background of existing hemoglobins. These may be difficult to detect in species characterized by complex hemoglobin systems. Under such circumstances, the signal-to-noise ratio can be improved by reducing hemoglobin levels before imposition of new conditions. The hemolytic agent phenylhydrazine · HCl is frequently employed for this purpose. Animals can be treated by intraperitoneal injection (10–15 μg/g body weight) or immersion (1 mg/L for 24 h) at low temperatures (Byrne and Houston 1988; Houston et al. 1988). Depending on species and ambient conditions, maximum hemolytic effect is usually achieved within 10–14 d. Conditions then can be slowly adjusted to those of interest.

9.3.1.5   Blood Volume Determination

A knowledge of blood volume frequently is useful in assessing hematological status. Many attempts have been made to assess blood volume by exsanguination (drainage of blood from the body), none of them successful. Recent studies have, with few exceptions, been based on volume-of-dilution methods. These involve adding a known amount of a particular solute to a confining compartment. Solute concentration in the compartment is determined, and the volume in which the solute is diluted is calculated from

$$\text{concentration } (C) = \text{quantity } (Q)/\text{volume } (V), \text{ or } V = Q/C.$$

This principle underlies virtually all studies of body fluid compartmentalization, which have involved a variety of approaches. Conte et al. (1963), for example, devised a method for labeling trout red cells in vitro with ^{51}Cr. After the isotope's specific activity (disintegrations per unit time) was measured, the red cells were reinjected into the fish. Blood samples were then removed, isotope activity was remeasured, and the diminution of specific activity was used to estimate blood volume. This technique yields acceptable values, but it is time-consuming. Other markers have been used more recently, notably bovine serum albumin labeled with ^{131}I or with the vital dye Evan's blue (T-1824). The dye rapidly binds to circulating plasma proteins. Both these markers give measures of plasma rather than of blood volume. Consequently, red cell volume must be determined to obtain total blood volume. This is obtained from microhematocrit values following correction for plasma trapped in the interstices of the packed cell column. Catlett and Millich (1976) and Houston and Smeda (1979) obtained closely similar values (3%, 2.8%) for plasma trapped in the packed cell column of centrifuged whole blood. Thus,

$$\text{blood volume} = (\text{plasma volume})(100/10 - 0.97 \text{ Hct}).$$

There are obvious drawbacks associated with the administration of foreign proteins. Because of these, determinations of blood volume in fishes are increasingly based on the use of the T-1824 dye or similar labels (e.g., Houston and De Wilde 1969; Nikinmaa et al. 1981; Sleet and Weber 1983).

Marker-dilution estimates of blood volume rest on several important assumptions, and results are valid only to the extent that these assumptions are satisfied or discrepancies are corrected. Of particular importance are the assumptions that the label is confined to the plasma compartment and that it is uniformly distributed throughout that compartment. Smith (1966) noted major discrepancies between blood volume estimates based on T-1824 complexed with native plasma protein before injection and those based on direct injection of the dye; the directly injected dye was thought to have escaped from the blood before it bound to plasma elements. This is not surprising. The albumin fractions to which Evans blue binds most readily are relatively small components of the plasma protein complex of most teleosts (Houston 1973). These fractions presumably can be saturated at relatively low dye levels, so dye loads administered to fishes must be reduced relative to those normally used in mammals. Although there is little evidence to suggest that dye is lost by movement into blood cells, plasma proteins readily pass through capillary walls into the interstitial and connective tissue compartments. Consequently, plasma dye concentrations fall steadily with time. This factor, and the relatively slow rate of mixing in the peripheral circulation, makes sampling over an extended period of time essential. In the studies previously cited, for example, four or five samples were commonly taken over periods of 2–7 h.

Determinations of blood volume require emplacement of an aortic or other conveniently positioned cannula. The fish must be allowed at least 48 h to recover from this procedure. Evans blue dye is then injected in sterile saline via the cannula; 0.10 mL of a 2.0 mg/mL solution or approximately 0.2 mg dye/100 g body weight is adequate. Dye injection is followed by a slow flush with 0.5 mL sterile saline. Blood samples are taken after 1, 2, 3, and 5 h, and hematocrit and plasma dye concentration are estimated. The latter determinations are made spectrophotometrically against bracketing dye standards at 620 nm following 1:9 (volume: volume) dilution in saline. A least-squares regression is used to estimate the zero-time plasma dye concentration. This is the concentration that would be expected if all of the administered dye mixed, without loss, instantaneously and uniformly throughout the plasma compartment. The zero-time concentration and dye amount are used to estimate plasma volume. Hematocrit values are then used to determine total blood volume.

The largest single source of error in determinations of this kind is inadequate mixing. Many early studies, and even some of the more recent ones, involved mixing times of as little as 30 min (e.g., Conte et al. 1963; Datta Munshi et al. 1975). Incomplete mixing inevitably results in erroneously high zero-time estimates of dye concentration and correspondingly low calculated blood volumes.

Avtalion et al. (1974) attempted to estimate blood volume by direct red cell dilution. The method involved initial withdrawal of 20–50% of presumed blood volume, and was based on the assumption that hematocrit and blood volume bear the same relation to each other before and after blood withdrawal, provided that time is allowed for reequilibration. If this is true, and no other factors intervene, the following relationship should hold:

$$\frac{\text{initial hematocrit (Hct}_i\text{)}}{\text{blood volume (}V\text{)}} = \frac{\text{final hematocrit (Hct}_f\text{)}}{V - \text{volume of blood withdrawn (}V_w\text{)}};$$

$$V = \frac{\text{Hct}_i V_w}{\text{Hct}_i - \text{Hct}_f}.$$

The method is highly traumatic and involves several obvious assumptions, none of which appear to have been validated. Nevertheless, the volumes reported agree well with those derived from the use of the Evan's blue dye and ^{131}I markers.

9.3.1.6 Red Cell Size Distribution

Teleostean red cells are released to circulation at an early stage of development. Maturation involves changes in composition as well as morphology. Cellular hemoglobin, for example, rises sharply. There are changes in globin gene expression and, therefore, in the number of hemoglobin isomorphs (Lane et al. 1982; Keen and Houston, unpublished observations). Accompanying this are changes in cellular concentrations of ATP, Cl^-, and Mg^{2+}, which are important components of the system that regulates the affinity between hemoglobin and oxygen (Lane 1984; Houston and Gray, unpublished observations). In short, the peripheral erythrocyte population is both morphologically and functionally heterogeneous. Somewhat less than half of these cells appear to have the compositional properties needed for effective oxygen transport (Lane et al. 1982).

Some idea of red cell age distribution can be gained from microscopic examination of smear preparations. Leishmann and Giemsa stains allow reasonable distinctions between mature and immature erythrocytes. Air-dried smears are fixed in absolute methanol for 5 min, washed several times in distilled water, stained in Leishmann stain in acetone-free methanol for 20 min, and rinsed in absolute methanol. Stain intensity should be checked because additional staining may be necessary. Slides are then transferred to Giesma stain for 15 min then rinsed in distilled water. Again, stain intensity should be checked because increased exposure may be required. Finally, slides are rinsed several times in distilled water to remove all remaining traces of stain, and allowed to air-dry. Variations in cytoplasmic stain intensity indicate developmental differences in protein composition. Consequently, the ratio of immature to mature cells can be at least roughly calculated.

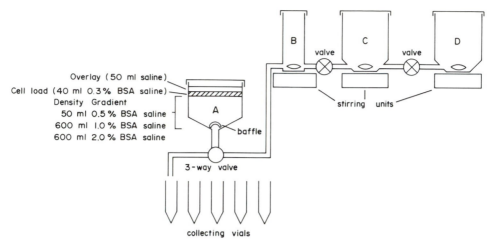

Figure 9.6 The STA-PUT velocity sedimentation system for assessment of size and density variations among peripheral erythrocytes. BSA is bovine serum albumin. (See Box 9.2.)

In addition, maturation is associated with changes in shape, size, and density of red cells. For example, the ratio of minor to major red cell axes in rainbow trout shifts from about 0.75 to roughly 0.53 (Iuchi 1973). Lane et al. (1982) reported width:length ratios of 0.74 for red cells in juvenile rainbow trout and 0.67 for those in adults and an increase in mean red cell volume from 280 to 475 μm^3. Some increase in mean erythrocytic hemoglobin was also observed. Cells can be separated on the basis of their size and density by velocity sedimentation at unit gravity (Miller and Phillips 1969). The technique offers several important advantages over alternative separation methods. The Johns–Miller STA-PUT apparatus (Johns Scientific, Toronto) used for this technique is simple, relatively inexpensive, and provides reasonably reproducible results. In addition, cells can be harvested more rapidly and in greater numbers for further study than is usually possible with density-gradient centrifugation.

The STA-PUT system (Figure 9.6) exploits differences in cell size, shape, and density to separate cells sedimenting at unit gravity. Such systems are sensitive to temperature-induced vertical convection currents and must be stabilized by introducing a density gradient with bovine serum albumin, fetal calf serum, Ficoll, or some similar material. The procedure is outlined in Box 9.2.

Velocity sedimentation at unit gravity is a relatively gentle way to separate cells without potentially damaging physical or chemical conditions. Reasonably homogeneous populations of mature erythrocytes can be obtained by this technique, but it is difficult to consistently obtain them for juvenile or senescent cells. Somewhat better results have been obtained in my laboratory with Percoll discontinuous-density-gradient centrifugation, a method widely used with fish leucocytes (Blaxhall 1981; Braun-Nesje et al. 1981; Blaxhall and Hood 1985; Blaxhall and Sheard 1985; Bayne 1986). No significant differences in mean erythrocytic hemoglobin or hemoglobin isomorph abundance are evident between cells of similar morphology separated by the two techniques. Further, Percoll does not seem to alter the cytochemical characteristics of lymphocytes (Blaxhall and Hood 1985).

Box 9.2. The STA-PUT Procedure for Size-Segregation of Red Blood Cells.

The following procedure is normally used to segregate red blood cells by the STA-PUT procedure.

1. All apparatus and solutions are precooled overnight at 4°C in a cold room, and the system is carefully leveled.

2. Approximately 2-mL samples of blood are placed in centrifuge tubes and washed three times (by inversion and mild agitation of the tubes) in small volumes of isotonic saline; after each wash, the samples are centrifuged at 1,000 revolutions/min for 5 min at 4°C. The packed cells are then resuspended in 25 mL of saline with bovine serum albumin (BSA).

3. Ten microliters of this suspension are diluted to 1.0 mL in 0.3% BSA saline to give a rough dilution of 1:100. The number of cells per milliliter of suspension is then determined.

4. A maximum of 1.5×10^9 cells can be loaded in the system. The number of milliliters of suspension providing this number is determined and this volume made up to 40.0 mL with 0.3% BSA saline.

5. The STA-PUT system then is prepared (Figure 9.6): 600 mL of 2% BSA saline are added to chamber D, 600 mL of 1% BSA saline to chamber C, and 50 mL of BSA-free saline to chamber B. The stirrers are turned on.

6. The three-way valve between chambers B and A is opened so that the 50 mL of saline in B can flow into A; this saline will overlay the density gradient that will be formed in A. During this loading, flow is adjusted so that the procedure is completed in roughly 2 min. It is essential that no air bubbles be trapped beneath the baffle or in the tubing connections.

7. The 40 mL of cell suspension is next added to chamber B and allowed to flow into chamber A, the separation chamber. The time (t_0) when the first cells arrive at the funnel in A is recorded.

8. After all cells have entered the tube leading from B, the valve between B and A is closed and the time is recorded. Chamber B is rinsed out with 100 mL of 0.5% BSA saline in aliquots. This rinse solution is pipetted out and chamber B is loaded with 50 mL of 0.5% BSA saline.

9. The valves between chambers D and C, then between C and B, and finally between B and A are opened. When the solution has reached the top of the funnel cone in chamber A and all cells have lifted off the bottom of the chamber, the flow rate can be increased. The result is a vertical density gradient in which successively denser solutions lie beneath the cell sample.

10. After loading is complete, cell sedimentation is allowed to proceed for 180 min after t_0. During this time, 30–32 graduated centrifuge vials are marked at the 40-mL level, numbered, and cooled.

11. The contents of chamber A are collected in successive 40-mL fractions.

12. Vials 1–3 are centrifuged and the cells are quantitatively transferred to a single vial, labeled A. In like manner, the original 30 vials are regrouped as 10 vials, A to J. These should account for roughly 80% of the cells originally loaded. Remaining vials are discarded. Roughly speaking, juvenile cells will be found in vials I and J, mature cells in vials D–H, and senescent cells in vials A–C. Separation must be checked, of course, and this is most readily done by measuring cell dimensions microscopically.

A stock Percoll solution is prepared by diluting 9 parts Percoll (Pharmacia Canada, Ltd.) with 1 part 1.5 M analytical grade NaCl and adjusting the pH to 7.5 with 1.0 N HCl. The stock solution is further diluted with 0.15 M NaCl to create solutions of differing densities (P), calculated from

$$P = (P_s V_s + P_d V_d)/(V_s + V_d);$$

P_s = density of stock Percoll solution (1.122 g/mL);
V_s = volume of stock Percoll solution (mL);
P_d = density of diluting medium (0.15 M NaCl, 1.0048 g/mL at 20°C);
V_d = volume of diluting medium (mL).

Ten-milliliter volumes of various densities can be prepared with the following combinations of stock and diluting solutions (the series can extend beyond the values shown).

Stock (mL)	10.0	9.5	9.0	8.5	8.0	7.5	7.0	6.5
Diluent (mL)	0.0	0.5	1.0	1.5	2.0	2.5	3.0	3.5
Density (g/mL)	1.122	1.116	1.110	1.104	1.099	1.093	1.087	1.081

One-milliliter aliquots of these solutions are layered into 12-mL graduated glass volumetric centrifuge tubes; a syringe pump or calibrated diluting pipette is used for this purpose. The density interfaces should be clearly visible. Densities can be checked with marker beads (Pharmacia).

Fresh blood samples should be used. The cells must be washed at least three times in modified Cortland saline (Houston et al. 1985). The buffy layer is discarded each time, and the cells are finally resuspended in an equal volume of saline. Fifty microliters of this suspension are carefully layered on the top of each density gradient and centrifuged at 400 × gravity for 45 min at 15°C. The cell layers can be harvested by a variety of methods (e.g., Brenner 1977).

In general, the density of red blood cells varies considerably among species, but is relatively consistent within species. After initial trials with a species, the range of gradient densities can be reduced.

9.3.1.7 Oxygen Equilibrium Curves

Hemoglobin and the other primary hematological indices reflect potential oxygen-carrying capacity and are of interest in relation to the ability of the animal to meet metabolic requirements. However, hemoglobin concentrations do not necessarily translate to the amount of oxygen carried. Furthermore, the critical variable is not carrying capacity, but rate of oxygen delivery, approximated as (oxygen-carrying capacity) times (cardiac output). However, the extent to which this potential is actually realized depends on hemoglobin–oxygen affinity. Affinity refers to the strength of the bonding between heme iron and oxygen. It is the factor that determines the readiness with which oxygen is taken up from, and released to, the plasma as the oxygen content of plasma changes.

Hemoglobin–oxygen affinity can be adjusted. The isomorphs making up the usually complex hemoglobin systems of fishes frequently have different intrinsic oxygen affinities and, more often, different sensitivities to affinity-modulating solutes. The latter solutes include H^+, ATP, GTP, Cl^-, and Mg^{2+}. All interact directly or indirectly with hemoglobin, influencing the equilibrium between the "tense" (deoxy-) and "relaxed" (oxy-) configurations of the molecule. The Bohr effect, the best known modulator influence, is basically a proton interaction that promotes the tense deoxyhemoglobin state and the release of oxygen. Chloride and the organophosphates, ATP and GTP, also favor the tense molecular state. Consequently, increases in red cell concentrations of these solutes facilitate oxygen release. By contrast, Mg^{2+} complexes nucleoside triphosphates (NTP) and precludes their modulatory interaction with hemoglobin. Increases in red cell Mg^{2+} reduce effective NTP concentrations and enhance oxygen loading. Fishes can alter both the relative and actual abundances of specific hemoglobin isomorphs and the intracellular modulatory environment in which these operate (Houston 1980; Powers 1980; Weber 1982). Consequently, a knowledge of blood oxygen content and affinity can be important. Affinity is usually defined as P_{50}, the oxygen partial pressure (tension) at which half of the total hemoglobin is oxyhemoglobin. This can be estimated from the oxygen equilibrium curve, the relationship describing the percentage of hemoglobin in the oxygenated state as a function of oxygen partial pressure.

Early procedures to measure hemoglobin–oxygen affinity (e.g., the Van Slyke and Natelson methods) involved forced release of oxygen from hemoglobin and measurement of resulting changes in pressure or volume. These methods, time-consuming and technically difficult to master, were largely abandoned with the advent of the Clark oxygen electrode. Micromodifications were quickly developed. Tucker (1967), for example, described a procedure involving whole blood samples of only 7 µL. Recent studies of hemoglobin–oxygen affinity in fishes have been based on four general methods. Edwards and Martin (1967) developed procedures for anaerobic mixing of fully oxygenated and completely deoxygenated blood samples in known proportions and subsequent determination of oxygen tension (Po_2) by electrode. Weber et al. (1979) applied this technique to studies on facultatively air-breathing fish, using the Radiometer BMS-2 Mk II system to equilibrate anaerobically mixed samples and a Radiometer BMS-3 electrode to measure Po_2. Following a methodological review (Hughes et al. 1975), Hughes et al. (1976) described an electrolytic method to determine oxygen equilibrium curves from 50–100-µL samples. Based on the Langmuir approach, in which deoxygenation is monitored in the presence of organelles metabolizing at constant rate, the procedure yields results comparable to those obtained with other methods.

Procedures originally described by Allen et al. (1950), Riggs and Wolbach (1956), and Nagel et al. (1965) are still used (e.g., Brunori et al. 1979; Galdames-Portus et al. 1979; Riggs et al. 1979). Methods falling into this category are based on the use of combined tonometer–optical cuvette systems.

Increasingly, however, emphasis has been given to spectrophotometric procedures. These are particularly valuable for the definition of oxygen equilibrium curves when thin films of whole blood are used in systems that allow progressive adjustment of oxygen partial pressures. They have been discussed by Gill (1981), Imai (1981), and Lapennas et al. (1981). Application of the Aminco Hem-O-Scan dissociation analyzer to the study of fish bloods was reported by Powers et al. (1979). These methods are the most sophisticated presently in use, but conven-

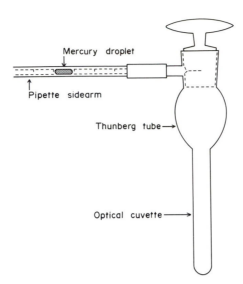

Mercury droplet

Pipette sidearm

Thunberg tube →

Optical cuvette →

Figure 9.7   A Thunberg tube adapted for determinations of oxygen–hemoglobin equilibrium curves (modified from Giardina and Amiconi 1981).

tional, relatively simple, and much less costly spectrophotometric techniques often can be used to advantage. One such is that described by Giardina and Amiconi (1981). Like all such procedures it depends on differences in the absorption spectra of oxy- and deoxyhemoglobin. The principal assumption underlying this method is that absorbance changes linearly between the spectral extremes of the fully oxygenated and fully deoxygenated states. The principal problems have to do with the tendency of hemoglobin to destabilize as a result of surface denaturation events and auto-oxidation reactions. The latter impose limitations with respect to time, temperature, mixing, and related factors.

The apparatus devised by Giardina and Amiconi (1981) consists of a Thunberg tube, the lower portion of which has been sealed to a Pyrex optical cuvette (Figure 9.7). A variety of cuvette sizes and optical cuvette spacers permits considerable flexibility in relation to sample volumes. The system is used with hemolysates rather than whole red cells. Red cells first are purified and stripped of adherent inorganic and organic ions; methods described by Martin et al. (1979) and Weber and Wood (1979) are convenient for this purpose. Then, the cells are washed three times in 1.5% NaCl with 10^{-2} M tris buffer at pH 7.4 and converted to the carboxy derivative. Next, they are lysed in two to three volumes of glass-distilled water. Following centrifugation (28,000 × gravity, 15 min, 4°C) to compact cell debris, the supernatant is drawn off, and its hemoglobin content is determined. If necessary, such solutions can be frozen in liquid nitrogen and stored at −75 to −80°C before use. Before analysis, salts, nucleoside triphosphates, and related solutes must be eliminated. This is most easily accomplished by passage through a 2.5 × 50 Sephadex G-25 column followed by treatment on a deionizing column. From top to bottom, the latter consists of 2 cm of Dowex-50 (w) ammonium form, 2 cm of Dowex-1 acetate form, and 20 cm of BioRad AG 501-X8 (D) mixed resin bed.

After it is stripped and deionized, the purified sample is reconstituted to provide the desired pH and appropriate relative concentrations of ATP (or GTP) and Hb,

Cl^- and Hb, Mg^{2+} and NTP, and other key chemical pairs. Hemoglobin concentration is adjusted so that the optical densities recorded at 560 and 580 nm do not exceed about 1.6. A known volume of hemolysate is then added to a Thunberg tube of known volume, the sidearm of the tube is linked to a vacuum line, and the system is deoxygenated. This should be done slowly, over 15 to 20 min, with gentle shaking in an ice bath. The extent of deoxygenation is checked by determining the absorption spectrum at about 10-nm intervals between 500 and 600 nm. When the hemoglobin has been wholly deoxygenated, the sidearm is closed. The tube is transferred to a thermostatically controlled bath and brought to the desired temperature. A graduated pipette containing a drop of mercury is attached to the sidearm and the position of the mercury meniscus is recorded. The sidearm is *cautiously* opened to admit air, the volume entering being indicated by movement of the mercury droplet. After each air addition, the system is re-equilibrated for at least 10 min and the spectrum is determined. Several air additions are made to establish several points on the curve. The last spectrum should be determined following addition of pure oxygen at 1 atmosphere pressure.

The degree of hemoglobin oxygenation (Y, % oxyhemoglobin) at any pressure is readily calculated from spectra for the fully deoxygenated (Hb) and fully oxygenated (HbO_2) conditions (OD is optical density; obs is observed):

$$Y = \frac{OD\ (obs) - OD\ (Hb)}{OD\ (HbO_2) - OD\ (Hb)}.$$

The best procedure is to average the Y values calculated for several wavelengths (e.g., 540, 560, 580 nm).

The oxygen partial pressure (P_i) in the Thunberg tube can be calculated from the volume of air introduced (V_i), the partial pressure of oxygen in air (P_o), and the volume of the gas phase in the vessel (V_t = vessel volume − sample volume): $P_i = (P_o V_i)/(V_t)$; Y is plotted against P_i to yield the oxygen equilibrium relationship and P_{50} can be interpolated from this.

Techniques of the foregoing type yield useful data on the capability for respiratory gas transport, but they allow only inferences abut actual tissue oxygen tensions. Accordingly, Lucchiari et al. (1984) devised a miniature system with an implantable platinum cathode and a silver–silver chloride reference electrode. This system seemed to give acceptable precision for estimates of tissue oxygen when it was tested on common carp.

9.3.1.8 Red Cell Enzyme Activity

Enzyme analyses have been used to investigate normal mammalian red cell functions and also to detect dysfunctional states (Miwa 1979). They have been applied profitably to fishes as well.

Diverse enzymatic methods have been used in medically oriented research, and the International Committee for Standardization in Haematology undertook a study of their accuracy, reliability, and convenience. The resulting report (Beutler et al. 1977) is a useful reference for newcomers in the field, as is Beutler's manual of some 30 enzyme assay procedures (Beutler 1984). These assays can be done on fish blood samples treated with heparin or EDTA. Leucocytes are removed from mammalian samples because these cells are metabolically much more active than are the anucleate red cells. This is not as critical for fishes; fish leucocytes are usually less abundant, and the erythrocytes remain metabolically active until they become senescent. Leucocyte elimination is, nevertheless, a prudent procedure.

Beutler et al. (1977) described a simple method that works well with rainbow trout blood samples, eliminating a large proportion of the leucocytes without major red cell losses. In this procedure, equal weights of α-cellulose and microcrystalline cellulose are combined with isotonic saline to form a slurry. A clean 5-mL glass syringe barrel is mounted vertically with a small piece of fine netting fitted into the barrel to cover the needle aperture. Two milliliters of the slurry are added to the syringe. Approximately 5 mL of saline are allowed to drain through and bed the column. About 1 mL of whole blood is then diluted 1:1 with ice-cold saline and loaded into the syringe barrel. This is allowed to enter the slurry and the red cells are then washed through by addition of 2–5 mL of saline. A smear should be taken and checked for leucocytes.

In addition to white cells, the plasma constituents should be removed prior to an assay. The foregoing procedure will remove many of these, but should be supplemented by at least two additional ice-cold saline washes. Washing procedures must be carried out gently to avoid premature hemolysis.

Once concentrated and washed, the sample can be hemolyzed for use or storage. A variety of techniques has been used for this purpose. The common practice of lysis by hypotonic shock is said to be unsatisfactory for wholly or partially membrane-bound enzymes. Ultrasonic lysis may inactivate some structurally unstable enzyme variants. Beutler et al. (1977) advocated mixing one volume of cell suspension with nine volumes of a solution made up of 2.7 mM EDTA (pH 7.0) and 0.7 mM 2-mercaptoethanol. This solution stabilizes sulfhydryl groups for several hours. Many red cell enzymes are heat sensitive and rapidly lose activity at room temperature. Assays should, therefore, be carried out as soon as possible. If this cannot be done, the samples should be quickly frozen and stored at −75° to −80°C before use; however, storage times should be minimal, and once thawed, samples should never be refrozen. After thawing, they should be well mixed, but not centrifuged if the assay involves membrane-bound enzymes.

Assays commonly are conducted under conditions that either maximize enzyme activity or mimic live cells; the latter approach probably is the better. Thus, many procedures involving mammalian tissues are conducted at or around 37°C and at pH values approximating those found in cells of such tissues. Assay conditions should, however, be matched to those normally experienced by the species in question. It may be reasonable to carry out enzyme assays for common carp or goldfish at the temperatures recommended for mammalian studies, but it would make little sense to do so with salmonid cells and tissues. In addition, when the system of interest functions as a lipoprotein, as many membrane-bound enzymes do (e.g., Hazel 1972), incubations should be carried out at acclimation temperature. Unless this is done, or activities are measured at both acclimation temperature and a standard temperature, errors of interpretation may be made (McCarty and Houston 1977).

Finally, a variety of units have been used to express red cell enzyme activities. The most common are (1) activity per cell or, more commonly, per 10^6 or 10^9 cells; (2) activity per unit volume of packed red cells or, less commonly, per unit volume of whole blood; (3) activity per gram of hemoglobin; (4) activity per milligram of dry cell solids; and (5) activity per milligram of nonhemoglobin protein. Of these, (2) is perhaps the least suitable. Individual cell volumes are almost certainly altered by osmosis during separation and washing procedures, and packed cell volumes reflect both this and centrifugation conditions. Expression of enzyme activity in terms of red cell numbers (1) is acceptable if a reliable automatic cell counter is available; manual dilution and counting methods take too long and involve too many errors. Hemoglobin (3) is an illogical standard. Its widespread use in mammalian studies may be justified for normal cells, which have relatively constant hemoglobin contents, but the practice is less defensible when anemias of various sorts are under investigation. The red cells of fishes are released to circulation at an early stage in development and only accumulate hemoglobin as they mature. Furthermore, mature cells vary in cellular hemoglobin content according to ambient temperature and oxygen availability. Activity should not be expressed in relation to hemoglobin units. Because hemoglobin is the major constituent of red cells, the foregoing arguments also apply to the use of dry solid content (4). Nonhemoglobin protein (5) probably represents the most meaningful reference point, even though it requires an additional determination.

9.3.2 Leucocytes

Leucocytes serve two principal functions. They participate in coagulation and thus curtail blood loss from injury sites. In addition, they are centrally involved in phagocytic and immune responses to parasitic, bacterial, viral, and similar challenges. Information on leucocyte types and numbers is of value in assessing general condition. Again, however, caution in interpretation is as critical as care in observation.

There has been a renewal of interest in the study of white blood cells in fishes, and a substantial body of morphological and ultrastructural information is now available. In some species, the origin, development, and function of these cells have been investigated as well. The field was reviewed by Ellis (1977, 1981).

The leucocytes described in higher vertebrates are also found in fishes. Consequently, brief consideration will be given to thrombocytes, lymphocytes, monocytes and macrophage cells, heterophils, basophils, and eosinophils.

9.3.2.1 Thrombocytes

Thrombocytes are the teleostean counterparts of the mammalian platelet cell, and are important elements in the blood clotting mechanism. Gardner and Yevich (1969) noted that the cytoplasm of thrombocytes spreads during clot formation, extending long threads that link with those of neighboring cells to form a meshwork. This structural framework traps other cells and debris in the forming clot (Ellis 1977).

Thrombocytes may also serve a phagocytic function (Fänge 1968). Support for this contention was provided by Ferguson (1976), who observed that injected carbon microparticles appeared within thrombocytes. Ellis (1977), however, felt that particle uptake might be due to passive entrapment. This seems reasonable because the peripheral cytoplasm of the thrombocyte has an extensive system of vesicles that communicate laterally with each other and to the exterior via large stomata.

The origin of such cells is not yet clear. It has been hypothesized that thrombocytes develop from small lymphocytes (e.g., Gardner and Yevich 1969), or that both thrombocytes and lymphocytes derive from small lymphoid hemo-blasts (Catton 1951; Klontz 1972). However, Ellis (1977) felt that there was little reason to anticipate a common origin for cells of such different functions: blood clotting in the case of the thrombocytes, immune and possibly phagocytic responses in the instance of lymphocytes.

In blood smears prepared without anticoagulant and visualized with Ro-manowsky-type stains (See Section 9.3.2.8 and Table 9.1) two principal throm-bocyte morphologies are usually seen (Williams and Warner 1976; Barber et al. 1981; Hightower et al. 1984). The smaller round to oval forms are thought to represent a relatively juvenile stage of development. Such cells usually have a deep purple-staining nucleus and a relatively scanty, pink-staining rim of cyto-plasm. Consequently, they are similar in many respects to small lymphocytes and easily confused with them. In the cyprinodont species examined by Gardner and Yevich (1969), a single nucleolus was evident, as were small numbers of intensely basophilic spheroidal cytoplasmic granules. Such granules were also observed in mummichogs (Hightower et al. 1984) and Oriental weatherfish (Ishizeki et al. 1984), but not in channel catfish (Williams and Warner 1976). The mature or definitive thrombocyte is more elongated (roughly 5×15 μm), and frequently is described as a spindle- or teardrop-shaped cell. The cytoplasm is light or pale blue. The cytoplasmic granules stain azurophilic. Hightower et al. (1984) reported that roughly 47% of the white cells of mummichogs fell into the first (juvenile) category, 30% into the second (mature) category. Thus, in this species, approx-imately three-quarters of all leucocytes were identified as thrombocytes. This conclusion is generally compatible with several recent reports.

Not all descriptions of the thrombocyte are consistent with the foregoing. Williams and Warner (1976) commented on the highly variable appearance of thrombocyte nuclei in channel catfish. These were round, oval, indented, bilobed, or U-shaped in profile. Ellis (1977) described four thrombocyte profiles: "spiked," "spindle," "oval," and "lone nucleus," but believed that the latter were mature cells stripped of cytoplasm during smear preparation. Saunders (1968) examined over 200 species and described differences in cell size, shape, and staining properties. Problems of identification, particularly in relation to small lymphocytes, have led to major discrepancies in reported relative leucocyte abundances.

Electron microscopic studies have revealed structural similarities between piscine thrombocytes and mammalian platelets. Cannon et al. (1980) observed deep indentations in the plasmalemma of the thrombocytes of channel catfish. If not actually communicating with the cell surface, these appeared as superficial vacuoles. Comparable structures have been observed in plaice (Ferguson 1976) and icefish *Chaenocephalus aceratus* (Barber et al. 1981), but not in goldfish (Weinreb 1963). This vesicular arrangement has been likened to the surface-connecting system of the platelet cell (Ferguson 1976). Thrombocytes of plaice, channel catfish, and Oriental weatherfish (Ferguson 1976; Cannon et al. 1980; Ishizeki et al. 1984), and possibly of icefish (Barber et al. 1981) but not of goldfish (Weinreb 1963), also resemble platelets in their possession of a cytoplasmic microtubular system. Such studies have also revealed lysosomes and electron-dense heterochromatin bands that completely traverse the nucleus in some species (e.g., Ishizeki et al. 1984).

9.3.2.2 Lymphocytes

Lymphocytes are typically found in the lymphatic circulation, the spleen with its extensive lymphoid areas (Fänge and Nilsson 1985), and the pronephric region of the kidney. The pronephros resembles the mammalian lymph node in some respects, particularly in the presence of a phagocytic reticulum and an immuno-competent lymphoid cell system (Chiller et al. 1969; Smith et al. 1970).

Because lymphocytes are commonly found throughout the vascular circulation, transfers between the lymphatic and vascular systems must occur. Consistent with this, Wardle (1971) found no unique cell types in lymph samples drawn from the neural lymphatic duct in plaice. This duct receives fluids from the lateral muscle masses and skin by way of lateral collecting tubules and enters the vascular system via the duct of Cuvier. No evidence of leucopoietic (white cell-producing) tissue was found in these collecting vessels; presumably these cells were formed elsewhere. However, lymphocyte origin remains obscure. Following review of then-available literature, Ellis (1977) postulated that lympho-cytes in lower vertebrates develop from a thymic stem cell population, and that these cells subsequently colonize other sites prior to or during thymic involution. During the latter process, the onset of which is often at least roughly correlated with sexual maturation, lymphoid cells are replaced by connective tissue. The spleen and head kidney then become increasingly important as leucopoietic sites.

Implicit in the foregoing is the suggestion that fish lymphocytes may consist of two or more distinct cell types. It has been suggested that the apparently similar lymphocytes of various vertebrates may actually represent populations of "small" (4–5-μm) and "large" (8–12-μm) cells (Ellis 1977). This distinction may be inapplicable. Barber et al. (1981) found a continuum of lymphocyte sizes in the icefish.

Studies on piscine lymphocytes include those of Ferguson (1976), Williams and Warner (1976), Cannon et al. (1980), Barber et al. (1981), Jeney and Jeney (1982), and Hightower et al. (1984). These and earlier reports indicate that, despite species differences, lymphocytes have several morphological features in common. Nuclei typically account for half or more of cell volume, are frequently positioned eccentrically, and are sometimes indented or lobed. Nuclear chromatin is elec-tron-dense, and usually peripherally located. Cytoplasm is scanty, mitochrondria are large and elongated, and small numbers of ribosomes are present. Golgi vesicles and both smooth and rough endoplasmic reticulum are present, but not abundant. Small lymphocytes are said to have fewer organelles than large ones. The surface membrane is frequently plicated, and small to large pseudopodia have been described in lymphocytes of several species. Cytoplasmic granules have been inconsistently reported.

Several investigators have commented upon the difficulty of distinguishing between small lymphocytes and thrombocytes and between large lymphocytes and monocytes. Confirming Ellis' findings (1976), Barber et al. (1981) felt that small lymphocytes could be distinguished from round thrombocytes on the basis of their sky-blue or dark blue, as opposed to pale blue, cytoplasm and the presence of pseudopodia. In electron micrographs, lymphocytes showed scattered patches of nuclear chromatin within a largely peripheral distribution, whereas thrombocytes had dense chromatin bands. Difficulties in cell identification have, as noted earlier, led to differences in reported values for absolute and relative leucocyte numbers. Early studies (e.g., Catton 1951; Weinreb 1963; Weinreb and Weinreb 1969; McCarthy et al. 1973) involving goldfish, yellow perch, and rainbow trout tended to support the view that lymphocytes constituted the single most abundant white cell type in fishes. Thrombocytes were frequently not identified, or were regarded as a minor element of the leucocyte population. This was also the case for sheatfish *Silurus glanis* (Jeney and Jeney 1982). Watson et al. (1963), Gardner and Yevich (1969), Cannon et al. (1980), and Hightower et al. (1984), on the other hand, found that thrombocytes accounted for 54–95% of all leucocytes identified in the species they studied. Ellis (1977) suggested that such discrepancies reflect the tendency of thrombocytes to begin cytoplasmic extension in response to the stresses associated with blood sample withdrawal. The extended cytoplasm is then torn away during smear preparation, leaving a stripped nucleus easily mistaken for a small lymphocyte. Accordingly, differential leucocyte counts should only be carried out with smears showing thrombocytes in good condition.

The relationships of fish lymphocytes to the T and B cell series of birds and mammals in terms of function ("helper" cells, immunocompetent cells), origin (thymus versus mammalian bone marrow or avian bursa of Fabricius), duration (long-lived, short-lived), and surface antigenic nature (immunoglobulin, theta antigen) is not yet clear. Ellis (1976) was able to demonstrate immunoglobulin surface sites by immunofluorescent methods in plaice blood and tissue lymphocytes. He noted, however, that thymic lymphocytes tended to be more weakly fluorescent than those of splenic or pronephric origin. Stolew and Mäkelä (1975) and Yocum et al. (1975) also provided evidence of separate antibody-producing and helper-cell immunocompetent cells in fishes, but they did not clearly identify the cell types involved.

There are probably sufficient grounds, however, to support Ellis' (1977) conclusion that the lymphocytes of fishes are ". . . the executive cells of specific immune mechanisms . . . ." Ellis (1977) did not accept that these cells were also phagocytic, as suggested by Weinreb and Weinreb (1969) and Klontz (1972). Consistent with the generalizing hypothesis advanced by Van Furth et al. (1972), Ellis (1977) contended that phagocytosis and immunoactivity are incompatible functions for cells and suggested that earlier reports of phagocytic activity may have involved misidentified monocytes.

9.3.2.3   Monocytes and Macrophages

The apparent absence of monocytes or macrophages from fish blood has been reported by Catton (1951), Jakowska (1956), Watson et al. (1956), Sabnis and Rangnekar (1962), McKnight (1966), Saunders (1968), Weinreb and Weinreb (1969), Conroy (1972), Klontz (1972), and Blaxhall and Daisley (1973). In some instances, the basis for this conclusion is not clear. For example, Weinreb and Weinreb (1969) described goldfish leucocytes comparable in morphology and phagocytic activity to the monocytes of mammals, yet agreed with Jakowska (1956) that such cells could not be identified as monocytes. However, it is frequently difficult to distinguish monocytes from large lymphocytes, and sometimes from heterophils, at certain stages of development.

Gluckman and Gordon (1953), Leib et al. (1953), Yuki (1957), Ferguson (1976), Williams and Warner (1976), Cannon et al. (1980), Barber et al. (1981), Jeney and Jeney (1982) and Hightower et al. (1984), on the other hand, described monocytes and macrophages in several species. Fish monocytes are relatively large (5–10 × 14–16 μm) but much less abundant than in mammals, where they make up about 0.10% of the total leucocyte population. Nuclei of monocytes are often eccentric, and range in profile from oval to indented to brain shaped. Electron microscope studies have revealed dense nuclear chromatin patchily distributed within a peripheral rim of chromatin in these cells, and a single nucleolus has been reported in those of some species. Under the light microscope, with the usual hematological stains, the cytoplasm appears flocculent and green to blue. The numerous cytoplasmic vacuoles present usually do not stain. Many mitochondria and lysosomes typically are present, and usually some endoplasmic reticulum as well. Multivesicular bodies and pinocytotic vesicles also have been reported.

Larger macrophages are seen infrequently in fish blood, although they are common in spleen and kidney. They are variable in shape and size and sometimes display accumulations of ingested materials. Although similar in many respects to monocytes, large macrophages can often be distinguished by their basophilic cytoplasm and the staining of their heterophagic vacuoles. Indeterminate or intermediate forms are common, however.

Cannon et al. (1980) suggested that monocytes could also be distinguished, at least on electron microscopic examination, from heterophils by several criteria, but most of these criteria are relative rather than absolute. For example, monocytes were said to have more rough endoplasmic reticulum and free ribosomes but fewer granules and less glycogen than heterophils. Other criteria, however, are more definite. The cytoplasmic tubular structures prominent in heterophil cytoplasm appear to be almost completely absent from monocytes. The cristae of monocyte mitochondria do not traverse the long axis of the organelle, whereas those of heterophils do. The latter characteristic is also a feature of the lymphocyte mitochondrion, however.

It seems probable that monocytes are formed in the kidney and are precursors of phagocytes (Ellis 1977). The scavenger functions of macrophages (and to a lesser extent of monocytes) have been well documented. Such cells increase rapidly, but transiently, in abundance following appropriate challenge, and are frequently found in necrotic tissues. Their participation in other forms of response is less clear but probable (Ellis 1977).

9.3.2.4 Heterophils

In mammals, neutrophils are mobile, chemotactic cells that play a major phagocytic role. Consistent with this, they are the most abundant white cell, constituting up to 65% of the leucocyte population. Heterophils, the counterparts of neutrophils in nonmammals, are relatively less abundant in fishes. With the exception of Ferguson (1976), who stated that heterophils were the predominant leucocyte type in plaice, and Gardner and Yevich (1969), who could identify no heterophils in the cyprinodont species they examined, most investigators have reported that heterophils make up 2–25% of the leucocyte population.

The typical heterophil is 10–15 μm in diameter and has a relatively low nucleus-to-cytoplasm ratio (approximately 1:3 to 1:2). The nucleus is often eccentrically positioned, and can vary in profile from spherical through ovoid to subequally or distinctly bilobed. Few or no nucleoli have been reported. The cytoplasm appears pinkish or blue-grey with Romanowsky staining under the light microscope. Granules are abundant and either do not stain or stain variably. Pseudopodia have been reported in heterophils of some species.

Electron microscope studies reveal that the abundant cytoplasmic granules in heterophils are usually oval to elongate, membrane-bound, and internally fibrillar, striated, or crystalline; they frequently incorporate glycogen granules. Numerous microtubules are typical, as are cytoplasmic glycogen granules. Moderate amounts of loosely stacked rough endoplasmic reticulum, small numbers of ribosomes, and occasional dictyosomes have been reported. As noted earlier, the elongate mitochondria have cristae traversing the long axes. Fish heterophils differ from mammalian neutrophils in some respects. Although the nucleus of the fish heterophil may be indented or bilobed, it does not fall into the polymorpho-nuclear category characteristic of mammals. Up to five cytoplasmic granule types may be found in the mammalian neutrophil. Light and electron microscopic studies have revealed only one or two in fishes. Mammalian neutrophils are myeloid in nature and derived from bone marrow. In teleosts, the kidney is the principal source of heterophils, the spleen playing a lesser role.

Numerous reports have described heterophil migration to injury sites such as those resulting from bacterial infection, parasite action, and mechanical injury (e.g., Thorpe and Roberts 1972; R. J. Roberts et al. 1973; Jay and Jones 1973; Lester and Daniels 1976). Heterophil chemotaxis was not regarded by Ellis (1977) as having been convincingly demonstrated, and reports on phagocytosis are contradictory. Klontz (1972), for example, found no evidence of phagocytosis by rainbow trout heterophils at sites of bacterial induced inflammation. Watson et al. (1963), Weinreb and Weinreb (1969), and Finn and Nielson (1971), however, observed both migration and phagocytic activity, the latter in rainbow trout.

9.3.2.5 Basophils

The characteristic feature of the basophil is an abundance of large, membrane-bound, cytoplasmic granules that stain intensely with base-active dyes. In mammals, where they make up about 0.5% of the leucocyte population, the precise function of basophils is not yet clear. They are believed to be a major source of histamine, however, and might play an important role in inflammatory responses.

Reports on their incidence in fishes have been inconsistent. Basophils were observed in common carp by Loewenthal (1930) and Haider (1968), but not by Hines and Yashouv (1970) or Hines and Spira (1973). Williams and Warner (1976) described basophils in channel catfish; Cannon et al. (1980) did not. Klontz (1972) and Blaxhall and Daisley (1973) were unable to identify basophils in brown and rainbow trout. Basophils were found, however, in pink, chum, and sockeye salmon (Watson et al. 1956; Lukina 1965). Basophils were not found in several species of anguillid eels, yellow perch, plaice, cunner, and other species (Michels 1923; Yokoyama 1960; Sherburne 1973; Ellis 1977; Hickey 1982). Weinreb (1963), Watson et al. (1963), and Murad and Houston (unpublished) observed them in goldfish blood samples and McKnight (1966) commented on their presence in mountain whitefish.

When present, basophils have a large, sometimes eccentric, round or oval nucleus with homogeneous chromatin. Cytoplasmic granules, unlike those of neutrophils, tend to be homogeneous. They are also relatively large, ranging from about 0.5 to 1.0 μm in diameter.

9.3.2.6 Eosinophils

In mammals, eosinophils usually make up less than 5% of the circulating leucocyte population, and they are relatively short-lived. Their function is not entirely clear (Ellis 1977), although they are phagocytic toward antibody–antigen complexes and accumulate in areas such as the lymph nodes following parasitic infection. The tissues of the lungs, gut, and skin, the most probable sites of antigenic stimulation, usually have high numbers of eosinophils.

Eosinophils are rounded cells, approximately 10–15 μm in diameter, with a bilobed nucleus and many large (0.5–1 μm), membrane-bound, round to oval granules. These granules stain red with Romanowsky-type (Table 9.1), Dominici tri-acid, and eosin stains. Their fine structure includes an outer homogeneous cortical region and an interior of axial crystalloid.

In fishes, eosinophils are identified primarily on the basis of granule staining properties, and in consequence, they almost certainly have been confused with heterophils and mast cells. Nonetheless, evidence of the typical eosinophil granular ultrastructure is accumulating (e.g., Ishizeki et al. 1984). Ellis (1977) reviewed earlier studies on eosinophil distribution; it is clear that both peripheral and tissue-sited eosinophils occur in fishes. More recent studies include those of Lester and Daniels (1976) on white sucker, Williams and Warner (1976) on channel catfish, Hickey (1982) on cunner, Jeney and Jeney (1982) on sheatfish, and Ishizeki et al. (1984) on Oriental weatherfish. To the extent that any function can be attributed to these cells, they appear to be phagocytic.

9.3.2.7 Total Leucocyte Counts

The methods previously outlined for red cell enumeration (Section 9.3.1.3) can be used for leucocytes as well. Such counts are accompanied by the same types of errors. Counts of mammalian white cells are facilitated by diluting solutions that cause red cell lysis, which allows the use of accurate and precise electronic counting systems. This procedure is not possible with fish blood because erythrocytes as well as the leucocytes are nucleated. Several staining–diluting solutions have been developed to assist in the counting process, however. Shaw's fluid (Hesser 1960) is particularly useful. This consists of two solutions that are mixed during sample dilution. Solution 1 (which must be made up *freshly* before use) consists of neutral red (25 mg) and NaCl (0.9 g) in 100 mL of glass-distilled water. Solution 2, which should be replaced weekly, includes crystal violet (12 mg), sodium citrate (3.8 g), and standard formaldehyde solution (0.4 mL) in 100 mL of glass-distilled water.

A 1:20 diluting pipette (Figure 9.5) is used. Blood is first drawn up to the "0.5" mark. Solution 1 is then drawn in until the pipette bulb is about one-half full, and the blood sample and diluting solution are gently mixed. The pipette is then filled to the "101" mark with solution 2 and gently but thoroughly mixed. After the mixing, a few drops are expelled to ensure that the unmixed fluids from the pipette stem are cleared, and the counting chamber is then filled by capillary. The leucocytes in the four large corner squares (16 small squares each) are counted according to the conventions noted previously. This count times 50 gives leucocytes per cubic millimeter.

9.3.2.8 Differential Leucocyte Counts

Differential leucocyte counts express the percentage contribution of each leucocyte type to the total white cell population. It will be apparent from the foregoing sections that several problems are associated with differential counting. The inherent fragility of thrombocytes provides an obvious source of error. If smear preparation causes their breakdown, proportionalities will be compromised both by their loss and by their misidentification (primarily as small lymphocytes). Another obvious problem lies in the categorization of cell types by differential staining techniques originally developed for mammalian blood cells. Three methods have been used quite widely in studies of fish leucocytology: the Romanowsky, Sudan black B, and periodic acid–Schiff (PAS) techniques.

Romanowsky Method. For the Romanowsky method, thin blood films are air-dried and fixed in methanol for 5 min. They are then exposed for 2 min to commercial Leishmann's stain, washed thoroughly in water, and counterstained for 10 min in commercial, buffered Giemsa's solution. After staining, the slides are washed in 0.1 M phosphate buffer (pH 6.4) and then in distilled water; finally, they are air-dried.

Table 9.1 summarizes salient morphological features and staining patterns reported in three recent and reasonably comprehensive studies involving brown trout (Blaxhall and Daisley 1973), channel catfish (Cannon et al. 1980), and goldfish (Murad and Houston, unpublished).

Sudan Black B. For Sudan black B staining, thin blood films are air-dried, fixed for 5 s in a fixative consisting of formalin (10 mL) and ethanol (90 mL), washed for 10 min in running water, and air-dried. They are then stained for 30–60 min in Sudan black B at room temperature, rinsed in 70% ethanol, and lightly counterstained (as in Romanowsky staining) with commercial, buffered Giemsa.

Phospholipids, neutral fats, sterols, and several other lipidic materials are stained by Sudan black B. Immature granulocytic cells frequently display faint, localized sudanophilia. In more mature cells, localized or overall heavy staining is seen. This may obscure other cytoplasmic detail. Lymphoid cells, particularly monocytes, occasionally exhibit small, weakly sudanophilic cytoplasmic or nuclear granules. They are, however, usually refractory to this stain.

Periodic Acid–Schiff. The periodic acid–Schiff (PAS) procedure is particularly sensitive for detection of glycerol-containing organelles and components. Freshly prepared, air-dried, thin films are fixed in formalin–ethanol (10 min), rinsed in running water (10 min), and stained (20 min) in commercial periodic acid solution. This is rinsed off with tap water, and the slides are immersed in commercial Schiff reagent for 20 min. Following washing, slides are *lightly* counterstained in commercial hematoxylin, washed, air-dried, and mounted.

Positive PAS staining manifests as a rich magenta. Granulocytic cells exhibit varied responses. Mature heterophils usually display high levels of both diffuse

Table 9.1 General morphology and staining properties of blood cells treated with Romanowsky-type stains. GF = goldfish (Murad and Houston, unpublished); BT = brown trout (Blaxhall and Daisley 1973); CC = channel catfish (Cannon et al. 1980).

Fish species	Cell size[a] (μm)	Cell shape[b]	Cytoplasm	Cytoplasmic granules	Nucleus
Erythrocyte					
GF	7–9×12–14 (m)	E	Light pink		2.8–3.7 × 3.7–4.7 μm
	7–9×7–10 (i)	R to O	Bluish cast		
BT	9×15.2 (m)	E	Buff		
	(i)	R to O	Greyish-blue		
Thrombocyte					
GF	4.7–5.6	R, O, or e	Faintly light pink		Large, round or elongate, deep purple
CC	6–13	R, O, or S	Light blue	Few, azurophilic	Round to ovoid, bilobed
BT		R, O, or S	Pale blue		Dark purple
Lymphocyte					
GF	7.4–8.4	R, P	Light pink or blue-grey		Large, round to oval, purple
CC	5	R	Sky-blue	Few, azurophilic	Round, occasionally indented
BT	7–9		Clear dark blue	Few, azurophilic	Dark purple with lighter interchromatin regions
Monocyte					
GF	N				
CC	7–17	R, P	Green to blue	Few, azurophilic	Brain-shaped or reniform
Heterophil					
GF	10.2–12.1	R	Weakly acidophilic, weakly basophilic strands	Abundant, neutrophilic	Eccentric, horseshoe-shaped or bilobed
CC	7–13	R to O	Blue-grey	Abundant, lilac to lavender, azurophilic	Eccentric, horseshoe-shaped or bilobed
BT	9.1		Pinkish		Up to five lobes, intense purple
Eosinophil					
GF	7.4–8.4	R	Pinkish	Abundant, pinkish-red	Eccentric
CC	N				
BT	N				
Basophil					
GF	11–15	R	Basophilic, vacuolated	Common, large basophilic	Large, round
CC	N				
BT	N				

[a]m = mature; i = immature; N = none identified.
[b]E = ellipsoidal; e = elongate; O = oval; P = occasional pseudopodia; R = round; S = spindle.

and localized staining; immature cells are less positive. Lymphocytes are sometimes characterized by small PAS-positive patches or granules. Thrombocytes
may exhibit weakly PAS-positive pinkish cytoplasm. By contrast, erythrocytes
and the early developmental stages of both agranular and granular cells are
negative.

9.3.2.9   Concentration of Leucocytes

Studies of fish white cells can often be facilitated by separation and concentration procedures. A density-centrifugation technique has been described by
Braun-Nesje et al. (1981). Although developed for enrichment of phagocytes from
the pronephric hemopoietic area, it can be used for isolation of other leucocyte
types as well. The procedure is relatively simple (Section 9.3.1.6). A discontinuous Percoll gradient is first established in a 25-mL tube. For rainbow trout, the
densities of bottom and over-layers should be 1.080 and 1.070 respectively; for
Atlantic salmon, they should be 1.068 and 1.060. These differences indicate that
preliminary studies must be carried out for each species to establish appropriate
density gradients. After samples are loaded, gradients are centrifuged for 40 min
at 15°C and 400 × gravity. Visible fractions are then collected by pipette. The
latter procedure is facilitated by use of a Brenner device (Brenner 1977), a simple
aspirating system that is easily constructed and can be adjusted, by using various
tip sizes, to collect even single cells.

9.3.2.10   Leucocyte Cytochemical Methods

The foregoing concentration methods can be usefully combined with a variety
of cytochemical methods. These provide a basis for leucocyte differentiation
which extends beyond that offered by Romanowsky-type staining procedures.
Furthermore, by analogy with mammalian immunological studies, methods of this
kind yield information on functional characteristics. The acid esterases and
phosphatases, for example, may provide a simple, relatively inexpensive means of
distinguishing between T- and B-type lymphocytes and their responses to pathogen challenge.

Blaxhall and Doggett (1987) applied esterases and phosphatases to the lymphocytes of rainbow trout, and outlined in detail the procedures for cell separation,
culture, staining, and electrophoresis. Hine et al. (1986) evaluated the combination of a wide range of cytochemical stains with light and electron microscope
methods for the differentiation of anguillid leucocytes.

9.4   CIRCULATION

Although the principal emphasis of this chapter is on blood and blood analyses,
some consideration of circulatory function is appropriate. Accordingly, following
a brief and general review of circulatory arrangements in fishes, this section will
focus on heart rate, blood pressure, cardiac output, and flow distribution and their
determinations.

9.4.1   Cardiac Structure and Function

The major structural features of the fish heart were reviewed by Satchell (1971),
Cameron (1975b), and Jones and Randall (1978). Farrell (1984) has recently
examined cardiac performance and its regulation in detail.

All piscine hearts have three similar chambers in linear array: sinus venosus, atrium, and ventricle. In bony fishes, the ventricle leads into the bulbus arteriosus. The walls of the bulbus arteriosus include smooth (as opposed to cardiac) muscle and elastic connective tissue investments, and the bulbus arteriosus does not contract in sequence with the chambers of the heart. By contrast, the corresponding structure in elasmobranchs, the conus arteriosus, includes cardiac muscle fibers, and it participates in the contraction cycle.

The sinus venosus receives the ducts of Cuvier laterally and the large hepatic veins posteriorly. In at least some cartilagenous fishes, the hepatic veins have smooth muscle valves (Johansen and Hanson 1967), but such structures have not been reported in teleosts. Although the walls of the sinus include cardiac muscle fibers, their sparsity, as well as the sinus's small volume, suggests that sinus contraction does not play a major or general role in atrial filling. Randall (1968), however, observed atrial pressure increases that preceded atrial contraction and coincided with sinus contraction in lingcod. Consequently, in some species, contraction of this chamber may be of some importance to atrial filling. Whatever role sinus contraction may have, there can be little doubt that this chamber provides a readily accessible supplementary blood volume. In addition, the bicuspid sinoatrial valve effectively blocks regurgitation during atrial contraction.

Atrial morphology varies (Satchell 1971). In most species, however, the walls are relatively well provided with cardiac muscle. Typically, two fans of muscle fibers, the musculi pectinati, originate at the atrioventricular junction and radiate out and over the roof of the chamber to form a tight meshwork. Upon contraction, the musculi pectinati pull the roof of the atrium down and cause ejection of blood into the ventricle. Atrioventricular volume ratios in fishes are often close to unity, and it is probable that atrial contraction makes a significant contribution to ventricular filling. Satchell (1971) reported that ventricular volume increased following atrial systole (contraction). The normally large atrioventricular ostium is doubly guarded. A membranous bicuspid valve extends into the ventricular lumen and is anchored by fibrous strands resembling chordae tendineae. The efficiency of this system presumably is like that of similar arrangements in higher vertebrates. In addition, this valvular action is supplemented by contraction of a circular muscle band surrounding the ostium.

As in other vertebrates, the principal propulsive chamber of the fish heart is the ventricle. The ventricle consists of two myocardial layers separated, in some species, by connective tissue. The inner layer typically makes up 70–80% of the cardiac mass, and it is highly trabeculated (Cameron 1975b). In most if not all species, this layer is essentially avascular; nutrients, oxygen, chemical regulators, carbon dioxide, and metabolic wastes can be brought to or removed from it only by the blood that passes through the lumen. Metabolic limitations on cardiac performance would therefore be anticipated. Jones (1971) and Kiceniuk and Jones (1977) examined this possibility by exercising rainbow trout and analyzing cardiac work costs, oxygen delivery to working tissues, and metabolic efficiencies. Reasonable (but unverified) assumptions regarding efficiency led to the conclusion that unless these tissues possess some means to extract oxygen from venous blood at very low oxygen tensions, anoxia must be accepted at maximum performance levels and a shift must be made to anaerobiosis. Such considerations have less application to cortical tissue. It constitutes a much smaller proportion of the heart and is normally well supplied by the coronary circulation.

The final chambers, the conus and bulbus, are structurally and functionally distinct. The former is well developed in cartilagenous fish, some holostean species, and lungfishes, animals that possess relatively rigid pericardia. The conus has complex valve arrangements and a myocardial element that normally contracts in sequence with those of the other heart chambers. The arrangement of the valves, however, is often such that they are incompetent (i.e., leaky) during at least the initial phases of ventricular contraction. Consequently, the cardiac cycle may not include a phase of true isovolumetric ventricular contraction.

The bulbus arteriosus in bony fishes has smooth muscle and may be irregularly contractile. In any event, it does not contract during the cardiac cycle. The single tier of valves remains competent until intraventricular pressure exceeds that in the ventral aorta. Therefore, the teleostean heart displays a period of isovolumetric contraction and intraventricular pressure increase. Consequently, like the hearts of higher vertebrates, those of teleosts can act as impulse generators, imparting momentum to the blood mass. Elastic connective tissues are a functionally important component of the bulbus. Their fibers store energy when they are stretched during ventricular systole (contraction). During ventricular diastole (relaxation), pressure in the bulbus does not fall to zero because energy stored in the fibers is released as elastic recall. Thus, the systole–diastole pressure pulse is truncated at both ends, or "depulsed." This is known as Wind–Kessel effect.

9.4.2 Electrocardiograms and Their Determination

Although the fish heart is myogenic, nodal tissues and pacemaker cells are less discretely localized than is the case with higher vertebrates. Laurent (1962), for example, reported that the teleostean species he examined lacked nodal tissues but possessed scattered cell masses exhibiting pacemaker characteristics. These observations also confirmed earlier studies (e.g., Jullien and Ripplinger 1957) and lead to the conclusion that the heart is paced from sinal, sinoatrial, or atrial sites.

There is some evidence that these pacemaker cells are stretch-sensitive and depolarize more rapidly after they are extended (Labat et al. 1961; Harris and Morton 1968; Jensen 1969; Sutterlin 1969). Thus, if venous pressures increase (e.g., during exercise), expanding chamber volumes should stretch the pacemaker cells and a compensatory positive chronotrophic response should then occur. However, relatively large pressure increases are needed to evoke such responses. Accordingly, it is not yet clear whether a mechanism of this kind plays an important role in heart function.

Action potentials and electrocardiograms (ECGs) have long been recorded from fish, and are much the same as those of other vertebrates. Studies by Labat (1966) and others (e.g., Oets 1950; Nanba et al. 1973; M. G. Roberts et al. 1973) clearly demonstrated the usual P, QRS, and T waves. In some species, an additional V wave, corresponding to sinus depolarization, can be identified prior to the P wave (Oets 1950). Labat (1966) also referred to a T_a wave associated with atrial repolarization. This wave, however, usually is obscured by the prominent QRS complex. Several useful time periods can be obtained from the ECG. The interval between the V and P waves indicates the duration of the sinal contraction phase. Atrial contraction is signaled by the P wave, ventricular contraction by the Q wave. The P–Q interval indicates the period between the two, and, approximately, the duration of atrial contraction. The duration of the QRS complex corresponds to the period of electromechanical activity at the beginning of ventricular contraction, and the Q–T interval suggests the overall duration of ventricular activity. The QRS amplitudes indicate something of the strength of contraction. All change during adaptation (Henry and Houston 1984), so useful information other than simple heart rate can be obtained from well-recorded electrocardiograms. The data desired dictate selection of recording technique. Records can be obtained from superficial monopolar electrodes (e.g., Yamamori et al. 1971a, 1971b; Nanba et al. 1973). Cardiac rates can then be estimated from superimpositions of the QRS complex on the slower rhythm generated by the ventilatory musculature (e.g., Figure 9.8). Selection of an appropriate time constant (e.g., 0.01 s) may exclude or reduce the magnitude of these large, low-frequency waves (Ueno et al. 1986). Bipolar superficial electrodes provide similar data (Itazawa 1970; Nanba et al. 1973).

The quality of ECG recordings can be improved through electrode implantation. This surgical procedure requires all of the precautions outlined previously (Section 9.2.4). A variety of recording assemblies can be employed. We have found the Grass model 7 or 7B polygraph with a 7P6B EKG-pulse preamplifier or TP4 tachograph preamplifier to be satisfactory (Houston et al. 1973). Grass E2B subdermal pin electrodes, bent through 90°, are lacquered to leave exposed tips some 2 mm long; the tips are dry-sterilized. The anesthetized specimen is transferred to an operating assembly and electrodes are positioned as indicated in Figure 9.8. A third electrode, although not essential, provides some flexibility in electrode selection for best definition. The shank of each electrode is anchored by a single epidermal suture, and additional sutures are made to support the assembly. Satisfactory records can be obtained for several days from preparations of this kind.

M. G. Roberts et al. (1973) described a procedure suitable for chronic recording. Electrodes are prepared from numbers 12 or 20 entomological pins to which 12-cm lengths of miniature 7/40 wire, insulated with polyvinyl chloride, are soldered. Electrode and solder joint are insulated with several coats of polyurethane varnish. The tips are then scraped for about 1.5 mm, and the leads are linked to a miniature watertight plug. Electrodes are inserted between cleithrum and scapula, or just anterior to the scapula (Figure 9.8), so that the electrode tips lie immediately adjacent to the pericardium. The area around the point of electrode insertion can be descaled and dried, and the electrode, solder joint, and descaled area can be liberally coated with Eastman 910 adhesive. A single dorsal suture is then used to anchor the leads. Records can be made from both tethered fish or, by radiotelemetry, from free-swimming animals. In the latter instance, leads are shortened and linked to a transmitter (e.g., Devices SNR 102F) supported by a small polystyrene float. A Devices SNR 102R receiver linked to a Devices M4 polygraph can be used for recording the transmitted ECG pattern. Such preparations yield useful records for periods of up to 2 weeks. The method was developed specifically for goldfish, but it can be employed with a variety of species. As with cannulation techniques, however, a knowledge of pertinent anatomy is critical.

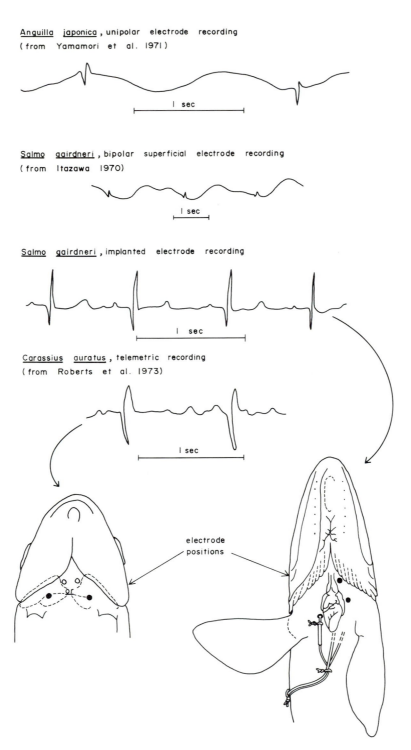

Figure 9.8 Typical electrocardiograms obtained with superficial and internal electrodes from Japanese eel, rainbow trout, and goldfish. The placements of internal electrodes in goldfish and rainbow trout are shown in the bottom drawings.

9.4.3 Blood Pressure Determinations

Ventricular contractile force, supplemented in some species by contraction of the conus arteriosus or, in teleosts, by the Wind–Kessel function of the bulbus, generates the pressure gradient driving circulation. Blood pressure measurements, therefore, can be used to assess several circulatory functions and adaptations. Various investigations have involved cannulations of virtually all cardiac chambers and their input and output vessels to define the driving forces between them. Resistances of various segments of the circulatory system are commonly approximated in terms of pressure–flow relationships. For example, gill resistance is estimated as (ventral aortic pressure − dorsal aortic pressure)/cardiac output. Overall systemic resistance can be approximated as dorsal aortic pressure/cardiac output (if venous pressure can be assumed to be zero) or, more properly, as (dorsal aortic pressure − sinal pressure)/cardiac output. Total body resistance is the sum of the two.

The most commonly measured pressure, however, is that in the dorsal aorta. This is the residual of the pressure initially developed by ventricular systole, and represents the force that drives systemic circulation. Pressure decreases of 50–75% are common, reflecting the very high gill resistance.

Virtually all recent blood pressure measurements have involved stiff-membrane transducers in which membrane movements produce changes in resistance, capacitance, or inductance. Stiff-membrane transducers react to relatively small fluid displacements with a high-frequency response that can be amplified without distortion to drive recording galvanometers of various kinds. As judged from the recent literature, unbonded resistance-wire strain gauges (Statham gauges) are the transducers of choice. These consist of a metal bellows that can be compressed by pressure increases. The downward displacement of the bellows is transmitted to a metal slide supported by four sets of strain-sensitive wires wound under tension and connected to form a Wheatstone bridge. Slide displacement stretches half of these while relaxing the remainder. These changes in resistance unbalance the bridge in proportion to the applied pressure. The consequent voltage output from the bridge can then be amplified and recorded.

No perfect pressure-recording system exists. In any situation, the operating characteristics of transducer, amplifier, and recorder must be matched. This inevitably involves compromises with respect to sensitivity, stability, frequency response, and convenience. This is particularly true of the system's frequency response, which should be fast enough to faithfully reproduce pressure changes. Individually, the frequency responses of transducer, amplifier, and recorder are readily determined. It is, however, the dynamic response of the entire system that is crucial. When the transducer is linked to a saline-filled catheter tube emplaced in a blood vessel or heart chamber, frequency response is greatly reduced. This is a consequence of the inertia imposed by the fluid mass, which must be moved to transmit pressure changes in the animal to the bellows of the transducer. Any small air bubbles inadvertently left in the tubing, valves, or transducer head will also reduce the system's frequency response to very low levels because air is much more elastic than the diaphragm. In a fully closed system of this kind, maximal sensitivity can be obtained only if the transducer diaphragm is at the same height as the point from which pressures are to be recorded. Long lengths of catheter tubing are required to link animal and transducer, particularly when respirometer systems with constant-pressure heads are used. Fluid mass can be reduced by using small-caliber tubing, but this increases frictional resistance to fluid movement, damping the system as a whole. Accordingly, considerable care must be exercised if valid measurements are to be made.

9.4.4 Cardiac Output and Flow Distribution

Several methods have been employed to estimate cardiac output in fishes. Among these are techniques based on the Fick and Stewart principles and the Faraday effect as well as those involving thermoelectric, electromagnetic, and ultrasonic flowmeter systems. Reynolds and Casterlin (1978) described an ingenious procedure by which cardiac output can be determined from measurements of thermal equilibrium and heart rates under regularly fluctuating ambient temperatures.

9.4.4.1 Fick Method

The Fick approach is simple in principle and reasonably easy to apply. Numerous estimates of cardiac output based on this method can be found (e.g., Holeton and Randall 1967b; Stevens and Randall 1967; Garey 1970; Itazawa 1970; Kiceniuk and Jones 1977; Itazawa and Takeda 1978; Wood et al. 1979; Neumann et al. 1983).

The method is based on a mass balance statement: the amount of a solute emerging from a compartment equals the amount that entered the compartment plus additions or less deletions within the compartment; i.e.,

$$V = \frac{\pm dx/dt}{[I_x] - [O_x]};$$

$V =$ flow per unit time through the compartment;
$[I_x] =$ inflow solute concentration;
$[O_x] =$ outflow solute concentration;
$\pm dx/dt =$ rate of addition or deletion of solute during flow through the compartment.

If the solute is oxygen, this relationship can be used to evaluate blood flow rate through the gills. In such cases, $V =$ flow rate, I_x is venous oxygen content, O_x is arterial oxygen content, and dx/dt is oxygen consumption. If it can be assumed that all of the blood ejected by the heart passes through the gills, that dx/dt is positive and equal to oxygen consumption, and that oxygen transfers take place only at the gills, the flow value obtained must equal cardiac output. Thus,

$$V(h) = V(O_2)/[C(O_2)_a - C(O_2)_v];$$

$V(h) =$ volume of flow through the heart, or cardiac output, in mL/(kg·min);
$V(O_2) =$ volume of oxygen consumed (standard temperature, pressure, and dryness), in mL O_2/(kg·min);
$C(O_2)_a - C(O_2)_v =$ difference in oxygen concentration between arterial and venous blood (standard conditions), in mL O_2/100 mL blood.

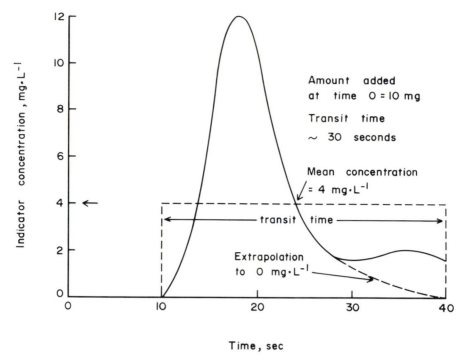

Figure 9.9 Idealized dye-dilution curve, such as might result when dye is injected into the bloodstream above the heart and monitored downstream of the heart to measure cardiac output.

Blood samples for the determination of $C(O_2)_a$ can be obtained by dorsal aortic cannulation. As was noted earlier, ventral aortic cannulations are more difficult to carry out and less enduring. Useful alternative procedures involve the ducts of Cuvier and the method of afferent branchial artery cannulation developed from the procedure of Ames et al. (1966). Several methods for determining oxygen consumption under resting conditions or during forced activity are described in Chapter 10.

Existing evidence suggests that few of the assumptions embodied in the Fick approach are actually satisfied. Oxygen uptake is not confined to the gills. Any reasonably well-vascularized epithelium can participate in the process, and in many species, substantial amounts of oxygen are transferred across the buccopharygngeal surfaces, diverticula and invaginations, unscaled or microscaled portions of the integument, gastrointestinal tract, and similar regions. Not all of cardiac output passes to the gills, and branchial blood flow does not place all blood in contact with lamellar surfaces. In addition, the gills consume substantial quantities of oxygen. Accordingly, estimates of cardiac output tend to be erroneously high (Wood et al. 1978; Davie et al. 1982).

9.4.4.2 Dye-Dilution Method

The dye-dilution method is a variant on procedures of the kind used for blood volume determinations. Blood volume can be estimated by administering a known amount of confined indicator (dye, isotope), allowing sufficient time for the indicator to become homogeneously distributed throughout the compartment of interest, and measuring its equilibrium concentration. Volume then equals amount/concentration. Volume flow through a compartment is determined in much the same way. In the case of cardiac output, the indicator is injected upstream of the heart and continuously monitored downstream of the heart until the indicator has completely passed. The data can be graphed as dye concentration versus time, an idealized example of which is depicted in Figure 9.9.

To calculate cardiac output from such a dye-dilution curve, one must know the amount of indicator administered, the transit time, and mean indicator concentration during transit. The first of these is operator-determined. Transit time begins with the first appearance of indicator at the monitoring point. Definition of transit time will be complicated if some of the indicator is recycled back through the heart (by normal blood circulation) before the indicator concentration falls to zero. It is usually assumed that decreases in concentration follow a negative exponential time course. A semilogarithmic plot of concentration against time should then yield a straight line that can be extrapolated to zero. Mean concentration can then be determined from the corrected curve by the usual summation procedures.

With reference to Figure 9.9, for example, if the initial indicator load had been 10 mg, and the transit time 30 s, the amount per minute passing the monitoring point would have been 20 mg. As estimated from the curve, mean dye concentration is 4 mg/L. For 20 mg to pass, the flow would have to be 20/4, or 5 L/min.

Murdaugh et al. (1965) successfully used the dye-dilution method to estimate cardiac output in the spiny dogfish. It is, however, a technically demanding procedure that embodies several limitations and has not gained great popularity with fish physiologists.

9.4.4.3 Thermal-Equilibration Method

The thermal-equilibration technique, outlined by Reynolds and Casterlin (1978) and applied to largemouth bass, is based on a procedure originally devised by Spaargaren (1976) for the estimation of stroke volume and cardiac output in crustaceans. Its basis is as follows. In fish, heat exchange with the environment depends, in part, on transfers through the general body surface and, in part, on transfers through the much larger surface provided by the gills. Heat flow through the surface depends largely on rate of water movement past the fish, which is affected by locomotor activity. Accordingly, the Reynolds–Casterlin technique is most conveniently applied to resting animals. Branchial heat transfers depend on cardiac rate and stroke volume plus other determinants, such as ventilatory rate, that are usually well correlated with circulatory activities.

Spaargaren (1976) related the principal variables as follows:

$$k \frac{V}{w} F + \frac{P}{w} \; ;$$

k = $1/\gamma$ (γ is the thermal time constant, the time required for temperature to go 63% of the way to a new applied temperature);

V/w = weight-specific stroke volume; V = stroke volume (mL/contraction);

w = weight in g;

F = cardiac rate (contractions/min);

P/w = weight-specific heat-transfer constant.

To solve the equation, values for cardiac rate and for core and ambient temperatures are required under circumstances of modest but abrupt and well-regulated temperature change. Because cardiac rate is the only circulatory variable to be measured, the less precise, noninvasive methods can be employed. A sensitive thermocouple (accuracy within $\pm 0.05°C$; time constant <0.5 s) inserted in the intestine is used to record core temperature. An identical thermocouple is used to monitor surrounding water temperature. If available, a transducer mixer can be employed to record temperature differential. All data are recorded on a suitable polygraph. The animal is then exposed to small ambient temperature changes (e.g., $\pm 2.0°C$), and cardiac rate and core temperature are monitored until the latter reaches the new value. The thermal time constant γ can be estimated from the rate at which core temperature changes. The reciprocal of γ is k. When an adequate sample of pairs of F and k values is available, these are related by least-squares regression. The regression's slope is V/w; P/w is given by the residual. With values for w, V/w, and F, weight-specific cardiac output is readily calculated.

This procedure offers interesting possibilities, but has not been widely tested. The values reported by Reynolds and Casterlin (1978) included some estimates comparable to those obtained by other methods but tended, on the whole, to be relatively high.

9.4.4.4   Flowmeters

Finally, several types of flowmeters have been used to monitor cardiac output (Johansen 1962; Satchell and Jones 1967; Stevens et al. 1972; Jones et al. 1974; Farrell 1979; Davie and Forster 1980; Farrell and Driedzic 1980; Petterson and Nilsson 1980; Wood and Shelton 1980). Satchell and Jones (1967) employed an electromagnetic flow probe in Port Jackson sharks. This technique uses the Faraday effect. When a conductor such as blood moves at right angles to the lines of force of a magnetic field, it produces an electrical potential, the magnitude of which is proportional to the flow velocity of the conductor. An electromagnetic flowmeter is basically a small electromagnet, which can be placed around a vessel, and a set of recording electrodes. The system provides a picture of flow velocity as a function of time. Integration of the velocity–time curve provides volume of flow per unit time. If the vessel employed is the ventral aorta, the resulting flow values represent cardiac output.

Thermoelectric flowmeters operate along somewhat similar lines. Because blood has measurable heat capacity, its flow velocity can be estimated by recording the rate at which an intravascular probe is cooled when it is held at some temperature higher than that of blood. Most commonly, cooling rates are measured in terms of the heating rate needed to maintain constant probe temperature. Again, the outcome is a velocity–time curve that can be integrated to yield flow rate.

These methods, and the Doppler ultrasonic flowmeter system used by Johansen (1962) to estimate cardiac output in Atlantic cod, offer both advantages and disadvantages. A prominent advantage is that all these methods provide direct estimates of flow. In addition, once a flowmeter is in place, continuous, prolonged, or intermittent recordings can be carried out without further disturbance of the subject. The surgical trauma attending probe emplacement is probably not greater than that associated with vascular cannulation. Some reduction in this trauma presumably will accompany increasing miniaturization of such probes. The advent of physiological adhesives, such as mecrylate (methyl 2-cyanoacrylate), has provided a way to seal the necessarily large incisions. Accordingly, there can be little question that such probes, and particularly those of the electromagnetic and ultrasonic types, currently represent the method of choice for cardiac output determinations.

9.4.4.5 Blood Flow Distribution

Information on blood flow distribution can aid assessments of cardiovascular responses to imposed stresses. Stevens (1968) appears to have been the first to investigate this in fishes when he measured the blood volumes of various tissues by using ^{131}I-labelled protein. More recently, Cameron (1975a) employed ^{85}Sr- or ^{51}Cr-impregnated polyester resin microspheres (15 ± 5 μm; density 1.3) obtained from 3M Corporation. These were suspended in dextran–saline and injected by way of previously implanted dorsal aortic catheters. Saline rinses were used to flush cannulae. After 2–5 min (i.e., one or more circulation times), the animals were killed and whole-body and individual-tissue isotope disintegrations were counted. Autopsies provided estimates of specific tissue contributions to overall body weight, permitting calculation of relative flow distribution. Values reported by Cameron (1975a) for the Arctic grayling can be taken as representative:

Gills	14.1 ± 7.85%	Liver	12.7 ± 0.98%
Ventricle	1.0 ± 0.57	Anterior white muscle	9.7 ± 3.30
Kidney	7.3 ± 1.31	Middle white muscle	12.7 ± 2.75
Spleen	2.5 ± 1.01	Posterior white muscle	11.6 ± 4.21

Cameron (1975a) also assessed several factors that influenced the distribution of injected microspheres, because these can affect estimates of flow. The first involved injection site. Cameron had injected by way of a dorsal aortic cannula at the junction of the efferent branchial arteries, and he felt that this caused estimates of flow to the head region to be too low. Capillary entrapment of microspheres provided another potential source of error. In earlier studies, Cameron (1974) had demonstrated microsphere entrapment in branchial lamellae. Cameron did not regard entrapment as a serious problem, but he found that microspheres tended to settle in the syringe, needle, and catheter. Total injected doses were overestimated; consequently, overall flow to tissues was underestimated. The foregoing problems notwithstanding, this approach is of considerable utility in studies on circulatory function, adaptation, and regulation.

9.5 REFERENCES

Allen, D. W., K. F. Guthe, and J. Wyman. 1950. Further studies on the oxygen equilibrium of hemoglobin. Journal of Biological Chemistry 187:393–410.

Ames, W. E., R. M. Condie, and B. Pollara. 1966. A method for intravascular injection and bleeding of fishes. Transactions of the American Fisheries Society 95:317–318.

Avtalion, R. R., A. Gorlin, E. Gutwirt, and A. Woodjani. 1974. Determination of blood volume in fish by a new method. Bulletin of Fish Culture in Israel 26:16–20.

Barber, D. L., J. E. M. Westermann, and M. G. White. 1981. The blood cells of the Antarctic icefish Chaenocephalus aceratus Lönnberg: light and electron microscope observations. Journal of Fish Biology 19:11–28.

Bayne, C. J. 1986. Pronephric leucocytes of *Cyprinus carpio:* isolation, separation and characterization. Veterinary Immunology and Immunopathology 12:141–151.

Bell, G. R. 1978. Preparation of rigid plastic casts of the blood vessels of fish. Progressive Fish-Culturist 40:103–104.

Bell, G. R., and M. J. Smart. 1964. *In vivo* angiography of the Pacific salmon (*Oncorhynchus*). Journal de l'Association Canadienne des Radiologistes 15:200–201.

Benfey, T. J., and A. M. Sutterlin. 1984. Binucleated red blood cells in the peripheral blood of an Atlantic salmon, *Salmo salar* L., alevin. Journal of Fish Diseases 7:415–420.

Beutler, E., K. G. Blume, J. C. Kaplan, G. W. Löhr, B. Ramot, and W. N. Valentine. 1977. International committee for standardization of haemotology: recommended methods for red-cell enzyme analysis. British Journal of Haematology 35:331–340. (ICSH reference EP12/1(TS):1976).

Beutler, M. D. 1984. Red cell metabolism: a manual of biochemical methods, 3rd edition. Grune & Stratton, Orlando, Florida.

Blaxhall, P. C. 1972. The haematological assessment of the health of freshwater fish. Journal of Fish Biology 4:593–604.

Blaxhall, P. C. 1973. Error in haematocrit value produced by inadequate concentration of ethylenediamine tetra-acetate. Journal of Fish Biology 5:767–769.

Blaxhall, P. C. 1981. A comparison of methods used for the separation of fish lymphocytes. Journal of Fish Biology 18:177–181.

Blaxhall, P. C., and K. W. Daisley. 1973. Routine haematological methods for use with fish blood. Journal of Fish Biology 5:771–781.

Blaxhall, P. C., and T. Doggett. 1987. Esterases and phosphatases in the leucocytes of rainbow trout, *Salmo gairdneri* Richardson. Journal of Fish Biology 30:35–40.

Blaxhall, P. C., and K. Hood. 1985. Cytochemical staining of fish lymphocytes separated on a Percoll gradient. Journal of Fish Biology 27:749–755.

Blaxhall, P. C., and P. R. Sheard. 1985. Preliminary investigation of the characteristics of fish lymphocytes separated on a Percoll discontinuous gradient. Journal of Fish Biology 26:209–216.

Braun-Nesje, R., K. Bertheussen, G. Kaplan, and R. Seljelid. 1981. Salmonid macrophages: separation, *in vitro* culture and characterization. Journal of Fish Diseases 4:141–151.

Brenner, M. 1977. A simple device for harvesting biological fluids at the microscopic level. Experimental Cell Research 105:281–284.

Bridges, D. W., J. J. Cech, and D. N. Pedro. 1976. Seasonal hematological changes in winter flounder, *Pseudopleuronectes americanus*. Transactions of the American Fisheries Society 105:596–600.

Brunori, M., J. Bonaventura, A. Focesi, M. I. Galdames-Portus, and M. T. Wilson. 1979. Separation and characterization of the hemoglobin components of *Pterygoplichthys pardalis,* the acaribodo. Comparative Biochemistry and Physiology A, Comparative Physiology 62:173–177.

Burke, J. D., and W. S. Woolcott. 1957. A comparison of the blood oxygen capacity in the black crappie (*Pomoxis nigromaculatus*) and the bluegill (*Lepomis macrochirus*). Virginia Journal of Science 8:113–120.

Burton, C. B., and S. A. Murray. 1979. Effects of density on goldfish blood—I. Hematology. Comparative Biochemistry and Physiology A, Comparative Physiology 62:555–558.

Byrne, A. P., and A. H. Houston. 1988. Use of phenylhydrazine in the detection of responsive changes in hemoglobin isomorph abundances. Canadian Journal of Zoology 66:758–762.

Cameron, J. N. 1974. Evidence for the lack of by-pass shunting in teleost gills. Journal of the Fisheries Research Board of Canada 31:211–213.

Cameron, J. N. 1975a. Blood flow distribution as indicated by tracer microspheres in resting and hypoxic Arctic grayling (*Thymallus arcticus*). Comparative Biochemistry and Physiology A, Comparative Physiology 52:441–444.

Cameron, J. N. 1975b. Morphometric and flow indicator studies of the teleost heart. Canadian Journal of Zoology 53:691–698.

Cannon, M. S., H. H. Mollenhauer, T. E. Eurell, D. H. Lewis, A. M. Cannon, and C. Tompkins. 1980. An ultrastructural study of the leukocytes of the channel catfish, *Ictalurus punctatus*. Journal of Morphology 164:1–23.

Casillas, E., and L. S. Smith. 1977. Effect of stress on blood coagulation and haematology in rainbow trout (*Salmo gairdneri*). Journal of Fish Biology 10:481–491.

Catlett, R. H., and D. R. Millich. 1976. Intracellular and extracellular osmoregulation of temperature acclimated goldfish, *Carassius auratus* L. Comparative Biochemistry and Physiology A, Comparative Physiology 55:261–269.

Catton, W. T. 1951. Blood cell formation in certain teleost fishes. Blood 6:39–60.

Cech, J. J., and D. M. Rowell. 1976. Vascular cannulation method for flatfishes. Progressive Fish-Culturist 38:74–75.

Chavin, W., and J. E. Young. 1970. Factors in the determination of normal serum glucose levels of goldfish. *Carassius auratus* L. Comparative Biochemistry and Physiology 33:629–653.

Chiller, J. M., H. O. Hodgins, V. C. Chambers, and R. S. Weiser. 1969. Antibody response in rainbow trout (*Salmo gairdneri*). I. Immunocompetent cells in the spleen and anterior kidney. Journal of Immunology 102:1193–1201.

Christopher, G. M., J. T. Fiandt, and B. A. Poeschl. 1978. Cells, proteins and certain physical-chemical properties of brook trout (*Salvelinus fontinalis*) blood. Journal of Fish Biology 12:51–60.

Chudzik, J., and A. H. Houston. 1983. Temperature and erythropoiesis in goldfish. Canadian Journal of Zoology 61:1322–1325.

Conroy, D. A. 1972. Studies on the haematology of the Atlantic salmon (*Salmon salar* L). Pages 101–127 *in* L. E. Mawdesley-Thomas, editor. Diseases of fish. Academic Press, London.

Conte, F. P., H. H. Wagner, and T. O. Harris. 1963. Measurement of blood volume in the fish (*Salmo gairdneri gairdneri*). American Journal of Physiology 205:533–540.

Datta Munshi, J. S., P. K. Pandey, and N. Mishra. 1975. Measurement of blood volume in the Indian mud eel *Amphipnous cuchia* (Ham.) (*Amphipoidae Pisces*). Folia Haematologica (Leipzig) 102:438–447.

Davie, P. S., C. Daxboeck, S. F. Perry, and D. J. Randall. 1982. Gas transfer in a spontaneously ventilating, blood-perfused trout preparation. Journal of Experimental Biology 101:17–34.

Davie, P. S., and M. E. Forster. 1980. Cardiovascular responses to swimming in eels. Comparative Biochemistry and Physiology A, Comparative Physiology 67:367–373.

Denton, J. C., and M. K. Yousef. 1975. Seasonal changes in the hematology of rainbow trout, *Salmo gairdneri*. Comparative Biochemistry and Physiology A, Comparative Physiology 51:151–153.

De Smet, W. H. O. 1978. A comparison of the electrophoretic haemoglobin patterns of the vertebrates. Zoologica et Pathologica Antverpiensia, 70:119–131.

Deutsch, M., and V. E. Engelbert. 1970. Erythropoiesis through clone cell formation in peripheral blood of the white sucker, *Catostomus commersoni,* studied after labelling with ^{3}H-thymidine for various exposure intervals. Canadian Journal of Zoology 48:1241–1250.

Edwards, M. J., and R. T. Martin. 1967. Mixing technique for the oxygen–hemoglobin equilibrium and Bohr effect. Journal of Applied Physiology 21:1898–1902.

Ellis, A. E. 1976. Leucocytes and related cells in the plaice, *Pleuronectes platessa*. Journal of Fish Biology 8:143–156.

Ellis, A. E. 1977. The leucocytes of fish: a review. Journal of Fish Biology 11:453–491.

Ellis, A. E. 1981. Stress and the modulation of defence mechanisms in fish. Pages 147–169 *in* A. D. Pickering, editor. Academic Press, London.

Ellis, A. E. 1984. Bizarre forms of erythrocytes in a specimen of plaice, *Pleuronectes platessa* L. Journal of Fish Diseases 7:411–414.

Engelbert, V. E. 1979. Alternatives to classical mitosis in hemopoietic tissues of vertebrates. International Review of Cytology 60:93–120.

Fagerlund, U. H. M. 1967. Plasma cortisol concentration in relation to stress in adult sockeye salmon during the freshwater stage of their life cycle. General and Comparative Endocrinology 8:197–207.

Fänge, R. 1968. The formation of eosinophilic granulocytes in the oesophageal lympho-myeloid tissue in the elasmobranchs. Acta Zoologica (Stockholm), 49:155–161.

Fänge, R., and S. Nilsson. 1985. The fish spleen: structure and function. Experientia 41:152–158.

Farrell, A. P. 1979. The Wind-Kessel effect of the bulbus arteriosus in trout. Journal of Experimental Zoology 208:169–174.

Farrell, A. P. 1984. A review of cardiac performance in the teleost heart: intrinsic and humoral regulation. Canadian Journal of Zoology 62:523–536.

Farrell, A. P., and W. R. Driedzic. 1980. A comparison of cardiovascular variables in resting eel pout and sea raven. Bulletin of the Mount Desert Island Biological Laboratory 20:28–30.

Ferguson, H. W. 1976. The ultrastructure of plaice leukocytes. Journal of Fish Biology 8:139–142.

Ferreira, J. T., G. L. Smit, and H. J. Schoonbee. 1981a. Haematological evaluation of the anaesthetic benzocaine hydrochloride in the freshwater fish Cyprinus carpio. Journal of Fish Biology 18:291–297.

Ferreira, J. T., G. L. Smit, and H. J. Schoonbee. 1981b. The effect of the anaesthetic benzocaine hydrochloride on red cell fragilities in Cyprinus carpio. Journal of Fish Biology 18:123–126.

Finn, J. P., and N. O. Nielson. 1971. Inflammatory response in rainbow trout. Journal of Fish Biology 3:463–478.

Fyhn, U. E. H., H. J. Fyhn, B. D. Davis, D. A. Power, W. L. Fink, and R. L. Garlick. 1979. Hemoglobin heterogeneity in Amazonian fishes. Comparative Biochemistry and Physiology A, Comparative Physiology 62:39–66.

Galdames-Portus, M. I., and seven coauthors. 1979. Studies of the functional properties of the hemoglobins of Osteoglossum bicirrhosum and Arapaima gigas. Comparative Biochemistry and Physiology A, Comparative Physiology 62:145–154.

Gardner, G. R., and P. P. Yevich. 1969. Studies on the blood morphology of three estuarine cyprinodontiform fishes. Journal of the Fisheries Research Board of Canada 26:433–447.

Garey, W. F. 1969. Sampling blood from freely swimming fish. Journal of Applied Physiology 27:756–757.

Garey, W. 1970. Cardiac output of the carp (Cyprinus carpio). Comparative Biochemistry and Physiology 33:181–189.

Giardina, B., and G. Amiconi. 1981. Measurement of gaseous and nongaseous ligands to hemoglobins by conventional spectrophotometric procedures. Methods in Enzymology 76:414–427.

Gill, S. J. 1981. Measurement of oxygen binding by means of a thin-layer optical cell. Methods in Enzymology 76:427–438.

Gluckman, M. A., and M. Gordon. 1953. Hematology of normal and melanomatous fishes: a preliminary report. Zoologica (New York) 38:151–154.

Goldstein, L. 1982. Gill nitrogen excretion. Society for Experimental Biology Seminar Series 16:193–206.

Green, J. 1977. Haematology and habits in catfish of the genus Synodontis. Journal of Zoology (London) 182:39–50.

Guernsey, D. L., and J. J. Poluhowich. 1975. Blood oxygen capacity of eels acclimated to fresh-, brackish- and salt water environments. Comparative Biochemistry and Physiology A, Comparative Physiology 52:313–316.

Haider, G. 1968. Vergleichende Untersuchungen zur Blutmorphologie und Hematopoese einiger Teleostier. III. Beobachtungen an Leukozyten und Plasmazellen. Zoologischer Anzeiger 182:110–129.

Härdig, J., 1978. Maturation of circulating red cells in young Baltic salmon (Salmo salar L.). Acta Physiologica Scandanavica 102:290–300.

Harris, W. S., and M. J. Morton. 1968. A cardiac intrinsic mechanism that relates heart rate to filling pressure. Circulation Supplement 6:95–106.

Hattingh, J. 1975. Heparin and ethylene diamine tetra-acetate as anticoagulants for fish blood. Pflugers Archives 355:347–352.

Hattingh, J., and A. J. J. van Pletzen. 1974. The influence of capture and transportation on some blood parameters of fresh water fish. Comparative Biochemistry and Physiology A, Comparative Physiology 49:607–609.

Hazel, J. R. 1972. The effect of temperature acclimation upon succinic dehydrogenase activity from the epaxial muscle of the common goldfish (*Carassius auratus* L.): lipid reactivation of the soluble enzyme. Comparative Biochemistry and Physiology B, Comparative Biochemistry 43:837–882.

Hendricks, L. J. 1952. Erythrocyte counts and hemoglobin determinations for two species of suckers, genus *Catostomus,* from Colorado. Copeia 1952:265–266.

Henry, J. A. C., and A. H. Houston. 1984. Absence of respiratory acclimation to diurnally cycling temperature conditions in rainbow trout. Comparative Biochemistry and Physiology A, Comparative Physiology 77:727–734.

Hesser, E. F. 1960. Methods for routine fish hematology. Progressive Fish-Culturist 22:164–171.

Hevesy, G. D. Lockner, and K. Sletten. 1964. Iron metabolism and erythrocyte formation in fish. Acta Physiologica Scandanavica 60:256–266.

Hickey, C. R. 1982. Comparative hematology of wild and captive cunners. Transactions of the American Fisheries Society 111:242–249.

Hightower, J. A., L. J. McCumber, M. G. Welsh, D. S. Whatley, R. E. Hartvigsen, and M. M. Sigel. 1984. Blood cells of *Fundulus heteroclitus* (L.). Journal of Fish Biology 24:587–598.

Hine, P. M., J. M. Wain, N. C. Boustead, and D. M. Dunlop. 1986. Light and electron microscope studies on the enzyme cytochemistry of leucocytes of eels, *Anguilla* species. Journal of Fish Biology 29:721–735.

Hines, R., and D. T. Spira. 1973. Ichthyophthiriasis in the mirror carp. III. Leukocyte response. Journal of Fish Biology 5:527–534.

Hines, R., and A. Yashouv. 1970. Differential leucocyte counts and total leucocyte and erythrocyte counts for some normal Israeli carp. Bamidgeh 22:106–113.

Holeton, G. F., and D. J. Randall. 1967a. Changes in blood pressure in rainbow trout during hypoxia. Journal of Experimental Biology 46:297–306.

Holeton, G. F., and D. J. Randall. 1967b. The effect of hypoxia upon the partial pressure of gases in the blood and water afferent and efferent to the gills of rainbow trout. Journal of Experimental Biology 46:317–327.

Houston, A. H. 1971. A simple improvement in the vascular catheterization procedure for salmonid and other teleost fishes. Journal of the Fisheries Research Board of Canada 28:781–783.

Houston, A. H. 1973. Environmental temperature and the body fluid system of the teleost. Pages 87–162 *in* W. Chavin, editor. Responses of fish to environmental changes. Thomas, Springfield, Illinois.

Houston, A. H. 1980. Components of the hematological response of fishes to environmental temperature change. Pages 241–298 *in* M. A. Ali, editor. Environmental physiology of fishes. Plenum, New York.

Houston, A. H., C. L. Czerwinski, and R. J. Woods. 1973. Cardiovascular–respiratory activity during recovery from anesthetization and surgery in brook trout (*Salvelinus fontinalis*) and carp (*Cyprinus carpio*). Journal of the Fisheries Research Board of Canada 30:1705–1712.

Houston, A. H., and M. A. De Wilde. 1968. Hematological correlations in the rainbow trout, *Salmo giardneri.* Journal of the Fisheries Research Board of Canada 25:173–176.

Houston, A. H., and M. A. De Wilde. 1969. Environmental temperature and the body fluid system of the freshwater teleost—III. Hematology and blood volume of thermally acclimated brook trout, *Salvelinus fontinalis.* Comparative Biochemistry and Physiology 28:877–885.

Houston, A. H., and M. A. De Wilde. 1972. Some observations upon the relationship of microhaematocrit values to haemoglobin concentrations and erythrocyte numbers in the carp, *Cyprinus carpio* L., and brook trout, *Salvelinus fontinalis* (Mitchill). Journal of Fish Biology 4:109–115.

Houston, A. M., M. A. De Wilde, and J. A. Madden, 1969. Some physiological consequences of aortic catheterization of brook trout, *Salvelinus fontinalis*. Journal of the
Fisheries Research Board of Canada 26:1847–1856.

Houston, A. H., and J. E. Keen. 1984. Cadmium inhibition of erythropoiesis in goldfish,
Carassius auratus. Canadian Journal of Fisheries and Aquatic Sciences 41:1829–1834.

Houston, A. H., J. A. Madden, R. J. Woods, and H. M. Miles. 1971a. Some physiological
effects of handling and tricaine methanesulphonate anesthetization upon the brook
trout, *Salvelinus fontinalis*. Journal of the Fisheries Research Board of Canada
28:625–633.

Houston, A. H., J. A. Madden, R. J. Woods, and H. L. Miles. 1971b. Variations in the
blood and tissue chemistry of the brook trout, *Salvelinus fontinalis*, subsequent to
handling, anesthetization, and surgery. Journal of the Fisheries Research Board of
Canada 28:635–642.

Houston, A. H., C. A. M. McCullough, J. Keen, C. Maddalena, and J. Edwards. 1985.
Rainbow trout red cells *in vitro*. Comparative Biochemistry and Physiology A,
Comparative Physiology 81:555–565.

Houston, A. H., A. Murad, and J. D. Gray. 1988. Induction of anemia in goldfish,
Carassius auratus L., by immersion in phenylhydrazine. Canadian Journal of Zoology
66:729–736.

Houston, A. H., and J. S. Smeda. 1979. Thermoacclimatory changes in the ionic microen-
vironment of haemoglobin in the stenothermal rainbow trout (*Salmo gairdneri*) and
eurythermal carp (*Cyprinus carpio*). Journal of Experimental Biology 80:317–340.

Houston, A. H., and R. J. Woods. 1972. Blood concentrations of tricaine methane
sulphonate in brook trout, *Salvelinus fontinalis,* during anesthetization, branchial
irrigation, and recovery. Journal of the Fisheries Research Board of Canada 29:1344–
1346.

Hughes, G. M., and I. Martinez. 1986. Comparison of the osmotic fragility of red blood
cells in samples from anaesthetized and unanaesthetized trout and eel and the effect of
varying oxygen levels. Experimental Biology 46:59–65.

Hughes, G. M., J. G. O'Neill, and W. J. van Aardt. 1976. An electrolytic method for
determining oxygen dissociation curves using small blood samples: the effect of
temperature on trout and human blood. Journal of Experimental Biology 65:21–28.

Hughes, G. M., L. Palacios, and J. Palomeque. 1975. A comparison of some methods for
determining oxygen dissociation curves of fish blood. Revista Espanola de Fisiologia
31:83–90.

Hunn, J. B., and W. A. Willford. 1970. The effect of anesthetization and urinary bladder
catheterization on renal function of rainbow trout. Comparative Biochemistry and
Physiology 33:805–812.

Ikeda, Y. H. Ota, A. Fujikata, A. Kakuno, and M. Maita. 1985. Effects of blood stirring
and the material of syringe on plasma constituent levels in carp. Bulletin of the
Japanese Society of Scientific Fisheries 51:13–20.

Imai, K. 1981. Measurement of accurate oxygen equilibrium curves by an automatic
oxygenation apparatus. Methods in Enzymology 76:438–449.

Ishizeki, K., T. Nawa, T. Tachibana, and S. Iida. 1984. Hemopoietic sites and development of eosinophil granulocytes in the loach, *Misgurnus anguillicaudatus*. Cell and
Tissue Research 235:419–426.

Itazawa, Y. 1957. Gas content of the blood in response to that of medium water in fish.
Bulletin of the Japanese Society of Scientific Fisheries. 23:71–80.

Itazawa, Y. 1970. Heart rate, cardiac output and circulation time of fish. Bulletin of the
Japanese Society of Scientific Fisheries. 36:926–931.

Itazawa, Y., and T. Takeda. 1978. Gas exchange in the carp gills in normoxic and hypoxic
conditions. Respiration Physiology 35:263–269.

Iuchi, I. 1973. The post-hatching transition of erythrocytes from larvae to adult type in the
rainbow trout, *Salmo gairdneri irideus*. Journal of Experimental Zoology 184:383–396.

Jakowska, S. 1956. Morphologie et nomenclature des cellules du sang des téléostéens.
Revue d'Hematologie 11:519–539.

Jay, J. E., and L. P. Jones. 1973. Observations on the inflammatory response within the dermis of a white bass, *Morone chrysops,* infected with *Lernea cruciata.* Journal of Fish Biology 5:21–23.

Jeney, G., and Z. Jeney. 1982. Morphological study of sheatfish (*Silurus glanis* L.) fingerling leukocytes. Aquacultura Hungarica (Szarvas) 3:77–84.

Jensen, D. 1969. Intrinsic cardiac rate regulation in the sea lamprey. *Petromyzon marinos,* and rainbow trout, *Salmo gairdneri.* Comparative Biochemistry and Physiology 30:685–690.

Johansen, K. 1962. Cardiac output and pulsatile aortic flow in the teleost *Gadus morhua.* Comparative Biochemistry and Physiology 7:169–174.

Johansen, K., and D. Hanson. 1967. Hepatic vein sphincters in elasmobranchs and their significance in controlling hepatic blood flow. Journal of Experimental Biology 46:195–203.

Johansson-Sjöbeck, M. L., G. Dave, Å. Larsson, K. Lewander, and U. Lidman. 1975. Metabolic and hematological effects of starvation in the European eel, *Anguilla anguilla* L. II. Hematology. Comparative Biochemistry and Physiology A, Comparative Physiology 52:431–434.

Johansson-Sjöbeck, M. L., and A. Larsson. 1978. The effect of cadmium on the hematology and on the activity of δ-aminolevulinic acid dehydratase (ALA-D) in blood and hematopoietic tissues of flounder, *Pleuronectes flesus* L. Environmental Research 17:191–204.

Jones, D. R. 1971. Theoretical analysis of factors which may limit the maximum oxygen uptake of fish. The oxygen cost of the cardiac and branchial pumps. Journal of Theoretical Biology 32:341–349.

Jones, D. R., W. Langille, D. J. Randall, and G. Shelton. 1974. Blood flow in dorsal and ventral aortae of the cod, *Gadus morhua.* American Journal of Physiology 266:90–95.

Jones, D. R., and D. J. Randall. 1978. The respiratory and circulatory systems during exercise. Pages 425–502 *in* W. S. Hoar and D. J. Randall, editors. Fish physiology, volume 7. Academic Press, New York.

Jullien, A., and J. Ripplinger. 1957. Physiologie du coeur des poissons et son innervation extrinsèque. Annales Scientifiques de l'Universite de Besancon Zoologie et Physiologie 9:35–192.

Kaiho, S.-I., and K. Mizuno. 1985. Sensitive assay systems for detection of hemoglobin with 2,7-diaminofluorene: histochemistry and colorimetry for erythrodifferentiation. Analytical Biochemistry 149:117–120.

Kamra, S. K. 1966. Effects of starvation and refeeding on some liver and blood constituents of Atlantic cod (*Gadus morhua*). Journal of the Fisheries Research Board of Canada 23:975–982.

Kiceniuk, J. W., and D. R. Jones. 1977. The oxygen transport system in trout (*Salmo gairdneri*) during sustained exercise. Journal of Experimental Biology 69:247–260.

Klontz, G. W. 1972. Haematological techniques and the immune response in rainbow trout. Pages 89–99 *in* L. E. Mawdesley-Thomas, editor. Diseases of fish. Academic Press, London.

Klontz, G. W., and L S. Smith. 1968. Methods of using fish as biological research subjects. Methods of Animal Experimentation 3:323–385.

Korcock, D. E., A. H. Houston, and J. D. Gray. 1988. Effects of sampling conditions on selected blood variables of rainbow trout, *Salmo gairdneri* Richardson. Journal of Fish Biology 33:319–330.

Koss, T. F., and A. H. Houston. 1981. Hemoglobin levels and red cell ionic composition in goldfish (*Carassius auratus*) exposed to constant and diurnally cycling temperatures. Canadian Journal of Fisheries and Aquatic Sciences 38:1182–1188.

Kuo, C.-F., and I. Fridovich. 1988. A stain for iron-containing proteins sensitive to nanogram levels of iron. Analytical Biochemistry 170:183–185.

Labat, R. 1966. Electrocardiologie chez les poisson téléostéens: influence de quelques facteurs ecologiques. E. Privat, Toulose, France.

Labat, R., and J. Laffont. 1964. Catheterisme des veines sus-hepatiques chez la carpe commune. Bulletin de la Societe d'Histoire Naturelle de Toulouse 99:459–462.

Labat, R., P. Raynaud, and A. Serfaty. 1961. Réactions cardiaques et variations de masse sanguine chez les téléostéens. Comparative Biochemistry and Physiology 4:75–80.

Lampasso, J. A. 1965. Error in haematocrit value produced by excessive ethylenediamine tetraacetate. American Journal of Clinical Pathology 44:109–110.

Lane, H. C. 1984. Nucleoside triphosphate changes during the peripheral lifespan of erythrocytes of adult rainbow trout (Salmo gairdneri). Journal of Experimental Zoology 231:57–62.

Lane, H. C., J. W. Weaver, J. A. Benson, and H. A. Nichols. 1982. Some age related changes of adult rainbow trout, Salmo gairdneri Rich., peripheral erythrocytes separated by velocity sedimentation at unit gravity. Journal of Fish Biology 21:1–13.

Lapennas, G. N., J. M. Colacino, and J. Bonaventura. 1981. Thin-layer methods for determination of oxygen binding curves of hemoglobin solutions and blood. Methods in Enzymology 76:449–478.

Laurent, P. 1962. Contribution á l'étude morphologique et physiologique de l'innervation de coeur des téléostéons. Archives d'Anatomie Microscopique et de Morphologie Experimentale 51:337–458.

Leib, J. R., G. M. Slane, and C. G. Wilber. 1953. Hematological studies on Alaskan fish. Transactions of the American Microscopical Society 72:37–47.

Lester, R. J. G., and B. A. Daniels. 1976. The eosinophilic cell of the white sucker, Catostomus commersoni. Journal of the Fisheries Research Board of Canada 33:139–144.

Lied, E., J. Gjerde, and O. Brackken. 1975. Simple and rapid technique for repeated blood sampling in rainbow trout (Salmo gairdneri). Journal of the Fisheries Research Board of Canada 32:699–701.

Lientz, J. C., and C. E. Smith. 1974. Some hematological parameters for hatchery-reared cutthroat trout. Progressive Fish-Culturist 36:49–50.

Lloyd, R., and L. Orr. 1969. The diuretic response by rainbow trout to sublethal concentrations of ammonia. Water Research 3:335–344.

Loewenthal, N. 1930. Nouvelles observations sur les globules blancs du sang chez animaux vertébrés. Archives d'Anatomie d'Histologie et d'Embryologie 11:245–332.

Lowe-Jinde, L., and A. J. Niimi. 1983. Influence of sampling on the interpretation of haematological measurements of rainbow trout, Salmo gairdneri. Canadian Journal of Zoology 61:396–402.

Lucchiari, P. H., E. F. Feofiloff, A. T. Bascardium, and M. Bacila. 1984. A technique for the determination of the available oxygen in living carp (Cyprinus carpio) muscle. Comparative Biochemistry and Physiology A, Comparative Physiology 78:675–679.

Lukina, O. V. 1965. Morphological features of the blood of Pacific salmon. Sbornik Nauchnykh Trudor Vladivostokskii Meditsinskii Institut 3:109–111.

Madden, J. A., and A. H. Houston. 1976. Use of electroanesthesia with freshwater teleosts: some physiological sequelae in rainbow trout, Salmo gairdneri. Journal of Fish Biology 9:457–462.

Mahajan, C. L., and J. M. S. Dheer. 1979. Autoradiography and differential hemoglobin staining as aids to the study of fish hematology. Experientia 35:834–835.

Martin, J. P., and seven coauthors. 1979. The isolation and characterization of the hemoglobin components of Mylossoma sp., an Amazonian teleost. Comparative Biochemistry and Physiology, A, Comparative Physiology 62:155–162.

Mazeaud, M., F. Mazeaud, and E. M. Donaldson. 1977. Primary and secondary effects of stress in fish: some new data with a general review. Transactions of the American Fisheries Society 106:201–212.

McCarthy, D. H., J. P. Stevenson, and M. S. Roberts. 1973. Some blood parameters of the rainbow trout (Salmo gairdneri Richardson). I. The Kamloops variety. Journal of Fish Biology 5:1–8.

McCarty, L. S., and A. H. Houston. 1977. Na^+/K^+- and HCO^-_3-stimulated ATPase activity in the gills and kidneys of thermally-acclimated rainbow trout, Salmo gairdneri. Canadian Journal of Zoology 55:704–712.

McKnight, I. M. 1966. A hematological study of the mountain whitefish, Prosopium williamsoni. Journal of the Fisheries Research Board of Canada 23:45–64.

Michels, N. A. 1923. The mast cells in the lower vertebrates. III. Fish. Cellule 33:339–451.

Miles, H. M., S. M. Loehner, D. R. Michaud, and S. L. Salivar. 1974. Physiological responses of hatchery reared muskellunge (*Esox masquinongy*) to handling. Transactions of the American Fisheries Society 103:336–342.

Miller, R. G., and R. A. Phillips. 1969. Separation of cells by velocity sedimentation. Journal of Cellular Physiology 73:131–202.

Miwa, S. 1979. Significance of the determination of red cell enzyme activities. American Journal of Hematology 6:163–179.

Murdaugh, H. V., E. D. Robin, J. E. Millen, and W. F. Drewry. 1965. Cardiac output determinations by the dye dilution method in *Squalus acanthias*. American Journal of Physiology 269:723–726.

Nagel, R. L., J. B. Wittenberg, and H. M. Ranney. 1965. Oxygen-equilibria of the hemoglobin–haptoglobin complex. Biochimica and Biophysica Acta 100:286–289.

Nakano, T., and N. Tomlinson. 1967. Catecholamine and carbohydrate concentrations in rainbow trout (*Salmo gairdneri*) in relation to physical disturbances. Journal of the Fisheries Research Board of Canada 24:1701–1715.

Nanba, K., S. Murachi, S. Kawamoto, and Y. Nakano. 1973. Studies on electrocardiograms of fishes. I—Test of method to detect the ECG from fish. Journal of the Faculty of Fisheries and Animal Husbandry Hiroshima University 12:150–154.

Neumann, P., G. F. Holeton, and N. Heisler. 1983. Cardiac output and regional blood flow in gills and muscles after strenuous exercise in rainbow trout (*Salmo gairdneri*). Journal of Experimental Biology 105:1–4.

Nichols, D. J., and M. Weisbart. 1984. Dual cannulation of free-swimming Atlantic salmon, *Salmo salar*. Canadian Journal of Fisheries and Aquatic Sciences 41:519–521.

Nikinmaa, M., A. Soivio, and E. Railo. 1981. Blood volume of *Salmo gairdneri:* influence of ambient temperature. Comparative Biochemistry and Physiology A, Comparative Physiology 69:767–769.

Oets, J. 1950. Electrocardiograms of fishes. Physiologia Comparata et Oecologia 2:181–186.

Oikari, A., and A. Soivio. 1975. Influence of sampling methods and anaesthetization on various haematological parameters of several teleosts. Aquaculture 6:171–180.

Pandey, P. K., B. N. Pandey, B. J. Choubey, and J. S. Datta Munshi. 1975. Total plasma and corpuscular volume in relation to body weight of an air-breathing siluroid fish, *Heteropneustes fossilis* (Bloch). Zoologischer Anzeiger (Jena) 194:387–392.

Perry, D. M. 1987. A procedure for obtaining erythrocytes from larval fish for cytological study and a description of larval blood of red hake, *Urophycis chuss* (Walbaum) and Atlantic mackerel, *Scomber scombrus* (Linnaeus). Journal of Fish Biology 30:743–748.

Petterson, K., and S. Nilsson. 1980. Drug induced changes in cardio-vascular parameters in the Atlantic cod, *Gadus morhua*. Journal of Comparative Physiology 137:131–138.

Pitombeira, M. da S., and J. M. Martins. 1970. Hematology of the Spanish mackerel, *Scomberomorus maculatus*. Copeia 1970:182–186.

Powers, D. A. 1980. Molecular ecology of teleost fish hemoglobins: strategies for adapting to changing environments. American Zoologist 20:139–162.

Powers, D. A., H. J. Fyhn, U. E. H. Fyhn, J. P. Martin, R. L. Garlick, and S. C. Wood. 1979. A comparative study of the oxygen equilibria of blood from 40 genera of Amazonian fishes. Comparative Biochemistry and Physiology A, Comparative Physiology 62:67–85.

Randall, D. J. 1968. Functional morphology of the heart in fishes. American Zoologist 8:179–189.

Reinecker, R. H., and M. O. Ruddell. 1974. An easily fabricated operating table for fish surgery. Progressive Fish-Culturist 36:111–112.

Reinitz, G. L., and R. Rix. 1977. Effects of tricaine methanesulfonate (MS-222) on hematocrit values in rainbow trout (*Salmo gairdneri*). Comparative Biochemistry and Physiology C, Comparative Pharmacology 56:115–116.

Reynolds, W. W., and M. E. Casterlin. 1978. Estimation of cardiac output and stroke volume from thermal equilibration and heartbeat rates in fish. Hydrobiologia 57:49–52.

Riggs, A., H. J. Fyhn, U. E. H. Fyhn, and R. W. Noble. 1979. Studies of the functional properties of hemoglobins of *Hoplias malabaricus* and *Hoplerythrinus unitaeniatus*. Comparative Biochemistry and Physiology A, Comparative Physiology 62:189–193.

Riggs, A. F., and R. A. Wolbach. 1956. Sulphydryl and the structure of hemoglobin. Journal of General Physiology 39:585–605.

Roberts, M. G., D. E. Wright, and G. E. Savage. 1973. A technique for obtaining the electrocardiogram of fish. Comparative Biochemistry and Physiology A, Comparative Physiology 44:665–668.

Roberts, R. J., A. McQueen, W. M. Shearer, and H. Young. 1973. The histopathology of salmon tagging. I. The tagging lesion of newly tagged parr. Journal of Fish Biology 5:497–504.

Sabnis, P. B., and P. V. Rangnekar. 1962. Blood cell formation in the freshwater teleost, *Ophiocephalus punctatus* (Block). Journal of Animal Morphology and Physiology 9:121–130.

Satchell, G. H. 1971. Circulation in fishes. Cambridge University Press, Cambridge, England.

Satchell, G. H., and M. P. Jones. 1967. The function of the conus arteriosus in the Port Jackson shark, *Heterodontus portusjacksoni*. Journal of Experimental Biology 46:373–382.

Saunders, D. C. 1968. Variations in thrombocytes and small lymphocytes found in circulating blood of marine fishes. Transactions of the American Microscopical Society 87:39–43.

Saunders, R. L., and A. M. Sutterlin. 1971. Cardiac and respiratory responses to hypoxia in the sea raven, *Hemitripterus americanus*, and an investigation of possible control mechanisms. Journal of the Fisheries Research Board of Canada 28:491–503.

Schiffman, R. H. 1959. Method for repeated sampling of trout blood. Progressive Fish-Culturist 21:151–153.

Sharp, G. D. 1973. An electrophoretic study of hemoglobins of some scombroid fishes and related forms. Comparative Biochemistry and Physiology B, Comparative Biochemistry 44:381–388.

Sherburne, S. W. 1973. Differential blood cell counts of Atlantic herring, *Clupea harengus harengus*. U.S. National Marine Fisheries Service Fishery Bulletin 71:1011–1017.

Sleet, R. B., and L. J. Weber. 1983. Blood volume of a marine teleost before and after arterial cannulation. Comparative Biochemistry and Physiology A, Comparative Physiology 76:791–794.

Smeda, J. S., and A. H. Houston. 1979. Evidence of weight-dependent differential hematological response to increased environmental temperature by carp, *Cyprinus carpio*. Environmental Biology of Fishes 4:89–92.

Smit, G. L., J. Hattingh, and A. P. Burger. 1979. Haematological assessment of the effects of the anaesthetic MS 222 in natural and neutralized form in three freshwater fish species: haemoglobin electrophoresis, ATP levels and corpuscular fragility curves. Journal of Fish Biology 15:655–665.

Smit, G. L., J. Hattingh, and H. J. Schoonbee. 1977. Observations on some effects of disodium ethylenediamine tetra-acetate and heparin on fish blood. Comparative Biochemistry and Physiology C, Comparative Pharmacology 57:35–38.

Smit, G. L., and H. J. Schoonbee. 1976. Problems encountered with EDTA as an anticoagulant for fish blood. South African Journal of Science 72:380–381.

Smith, A. M., N. A. Wivel, and M. Potter. 1970. Plasmacytopoiesis in the pronephros of the carp (*Cyprinus carpio*). Anatomical Record 167:351–370.

Smith, C. E. 1968. Hematological changes in coho salmon fed a folic acid deficient diet. Journal of the Fisheries Research Board of Canada 25:151–156.

Smith, J. C. 1977. Body weight and the haematology of the American plaice, *Hippoglossoides platessoides*. Journal of Experimental Biology 67:17–28.

Smith, L. S. 1966. Blood volume of three salmonids. Journal of the Fisheries Research Board of Canada 23:1439–1446.

Smith, L. S., and G. R. Bell. 1964. A technique for prolonged blood sampling in free-swimming salmon. Journal of the Fisheries Research Board of Canada 21:711–717.

Smith, L. S., and G. R. Bell. 1967. Anesthetic and surgical techniques for Pacific salmon. Journal of the Fisheries Research Board of Canada 24:1579–1588.

Smith, L. S., and G. R. Bell. 1976. A practical guide to the anatomy and physiology of Pacific salmon. Canada Fisheries and Marine Service Miscellaneous Special Publication 27R.

Soivio, A., K. Nyholm, and M. Huhti. 1977. Effects of anaesthesia with MS-222, neutralized MS-222 and benzocaine on the blood constituents of rainbow trout, *Salmo gairdneri*. Journal of Fish Biology 10:91–101.

Soivio, A., K. Westman, and K. Nyholm. 1972. Improved method of dorsal aorta catheterization: haematological effects followed for three weeks in rainbow trout (*Salmo gairdneri*). Finnish Fisheries Research 1:11–21.

Spaargaren, D. H. 1976. On stroke volume of the heart and cardiac output in aquatic animals. Netherlands Journal of Sea Research 10:131–139.

Stevens, D. E., and D. J. Randall. 1967. Changes in blood pressure, heart rate and breathing rate during moderate swimming activity in rainbow trout. Journal of Experimental Biology 46:307–316.

Stevens, E. D. 1968. The effect of exercise on the distribution of blood to various organs in rainbow trout. Comparative Biochemistry and Physiology 25:615–625.

Stevens, E. D., G. R. Bennion, D. J. Randall, and G. Shelton. 1972. Factors affecting arterial blood pressures and blood flow from the heart in intact, unrestrained lingcod, *Ophiodon elongatus*. Comparative Biochemistry and Physiology 43:681–695.

Stolew, J. S., and O. Mäkelä. 1975. Carrier preimmunisation in the antihapten response of a marine fish. Nature (London) 254:718–719.

Strange, R. J., and C. B. Schreck. 1978. Anesthetic and handling stress on survival and cortisol concentration in yearling chinook salmon (*Oncorhynchus tshawytscha*). Journal of the Fisheries Research Board of Canada 35:345–349.

Stromberg, P. C., J. G. Ferrante, and S. Carter. 1983. Pathology of lethal and sublethal exposure of fathead minnows, *Pimephales promelas,* to cadmium: a model for aquatic toxicity assessment. Journal of Toxicology and Environmental Health 11:247–259.

Summerfelt, R. C., W. M. Lewis, and M. G. Ulrich. 1967. Measurement of hematological characteristics of the goldfish. Progressive Fish-Culturist 29:13–20.

Sutterlin, A. M. 1969. Effects of exercise on cardiac and ventilation frequency in three species of freshwater teleosts. Physiological Zoology 42:36–42.

Swift, D. J. 1981. A holding box system for physiological experiments on rainbow trout (*Salmo gairdneri* Richardson) requiring rapid blood sampling. Journal of Fish Biology 18:309–319.

Swift, D. J. 1983. Blood component value changes in the Atlantic mackerel (*Scomber scombrus* L.) subjected to capture, handling and confinement. Comparative Biochemistry and Physiology A, Comparative Physiology 76:795–802.

Thorpe, J. E., and R. J. Roberts. 1972. An aeromonad epidemic in the brown trout (*Salmo trutta* L.). Journal of Fish Biology 4:441–452.

Tompsett, D. H. 1970. Anatomical techniques, 2nd edition. Livingstone, Edinburgh.

Tucker, V. A. 1967. Method for oxygen content and dissociation curves on microliter blood samples. Journal of Applied Physiology 23:410–414.

Tun, N., and A. H. Houston. 1986. Temperature, oxygen, photoperiod and the hemoglobin system of the rainbow trout, *Salmo gairdneri*. Canadian Journal of Zoology 64:1883–1888.

Ueno, S., H. Yoshikawa, Y. Ishida, and H. Mitsuda. 1986. Electrocardiograms recorded from the body surface of the carp, *Cyprinus carpio*. Comparative Biochemistry and Physiology A, Comparative Physiology 85:129–133.

Van Furth, R., Z. A. Cohn, J. G. Hirsch, J. H. Humphrey, W. G. Spector, and H. L. Langevoort. 1972. The mononuclear phagocytic system: a new classification of macrophages, monocytes and their precursor cells. Bulletin of the World Health Organization 46:845–852.

van Vuren, J. H. J., and J. Hattingh. 1978a. A seasonal study of the haematology of a wild freshwater fish. Journal of Fish Biology 13:305–313.

van Vuren, J. H. J., and J. Hattingh. 1978b. Seasonal changes in the haemoglobins of freshwater fish in their natural environment. Comparative Biochemistry and Physiology A, Comparative Physiology 60:265–268.

Walker, C. R., and R. A. Schoettger. 1967. Residues of MS-222 in four salmonids following anesthesia. Bureau of Sport Fisheries and Wildlife Investigations in Fish Control 5:1–11.

Wardle, C. S. 1971. New observations on the lymph system of the plaice *Pleuronectes platessa* and other teleosts. Journal of the Marine Biological Association of the United Kingdom 51:977–990.

Watson, L. J., K. W. Guenther, and R. D. Royce. 1956. Haematology of healthy and virus diseased sockeye salmon, *Oncorhynchus nerka*. Zoologica (New York) 41:27–37.

Watson, L. J., I. L. Schechmeister, and L. L. Jackson. 1963. The haematology of goldfish (*Carassius auratus*). Cytologia 28:118–130.

Weber, R. E. 1982. Intraspecific adaptation of hemoglobin function in fish to oxygen availability. Pages 87–102 *in* A. D. F. Addink and N. Spronk, editors. Exogenous and endogenous influences on metabolic and neural control. Pergamon, New York.

Weber, R. E., and S. C. Wood. 1979. Effects of erythrocytic nucleoside triphosphates on oxygen equilibria of composite and fractionated hemoglobins from the facultative air-breathing Amazonian catfish, *Hypostomus* and *Pterygoplichthys*. Comparative Biochemistry and Physiology A, Comparative Physiology 62:179–183.

Weber, R. E., S. C. Wood, and B. J. Davis. 1979. Acclimation to hypoxic water in facultative air-breathing fish: blood oxygen affinity and allosteric effectors. Comparative Biochemistry and Physiology A, Comparative Physiology 62:125–129.

Wedemeyer, G. 1972. Physiological consequences of handling stress in the juvenile coho salmon (*Oncorhynchus kisutch*) and steelhead trout (*Salmo gairdneri*). Journal of the Fisheries Board of Canada 29:1780–1783.

Wedemeyer, G. 1976. Physiological response of juvenile coho salmon (*Oncorhynchus kitsutch*) and rainbow trout (*Salmo gairdneri*) to handling and crowding stress in intensive fish culture. Journal of the Fisheries Research Board of Canada 33:2699–2702.

Weinberg, S. R., J. LoBue, C. D. Siegel, and A. S. Gordon. 1976. Hematopoiesis of the kissing gourami (*Helostoma temmincki*). Effects of starvation, bleeding and plasma-stimulating factors on its erythropoiesis. Canadian Journal of Zoology 54:1115–1127.

Weinberg, S. R., C. D. Siegel, and A. L. Gordon. 1973. Studies on the peripheral blood cell parameter and morphology of the red paradise fish, *Macropodus opercularis*. Effect of food deprivation on erythropoiesis. Anatomical Record 175:7–14.

Weinreb, E. L. 1963. Studies on the fine structure of teleost blood cells. Anatomical Record 147:219–238.

Weinreb, E. L., and S. Weinreb. 1969. A study of experimentally induced endocytosis in a teleost. I. Light microscopy of peripheral blood cell response. Zoologica (New York) 54:25–34.

Wells, R. M. G., V. Tetens, and A. L. Devries. 1984. Recovery from stress following capture and anaesthesia of Antarctic fish: hematology and blood chemistry. Journal of Fish Biology 25:567–576.

Williams, R. W., and M. C. Warner. 1976. Some observations on the stained blood cellular elements of channel catfish, *Ictalurus punctatus*. Journal of Fish Biology 9:491–497.

Wingo, W. M., and R. J. Muncy. 1984. Sampling walleye blood. Progressive Fish-Culturist 46:53–55.

Wolf, K., and M. C. Quimby. 1969. Fish cell and tissue culture. Pages 253–305 *in* W. S. Hoar and D. J. Randall, editors. Fish Physiology, volume 3. Academic Press, New York.

Wood, C. M., B. R. McMahon, and D. G. McDonald. 1978. Oxygen exchange and vascular resistance in the totally perfused rainbow trout. American Journal of Physiology 234:R201–208.

Wood, C. M., B. R. McMahon, and D. G. McDonald. 1979. Respiratory, ventilatory and cardiovascular responses to experimental anaemia in the starry flounder, *Platichthys stellatus*. Journal of Experimental Biology 82:139–162.

Wood, C. M., and G. Shelton. 1980. Cardiovascular dynamics and adrenergic response of the rainbow trout *in vivo*. Journal of Experimental Biology 87:247–270.

Yamamori, K., I. Hanyu, and T. Hibiya. 1971a. Electrocardiography of the eel by means of underwater electrodes. Bulletin of the Japanese Society of Scientific Fisheries 37:94–97.

Yamamori, K., I. Hanyu, and T. Hibiya. 1971b. Monopolar lead of electrocardiograms from the body surface of the eel. Bulletin of the Japanese Society of Scientific Fisheries 37:90–93.

Yamamoto, M., and I. Iuchi. 1975. Electron microscopic study of erythrocytes in developing rainbow trout, *Salmo gairdneri irideus*, with particular reference to changes in the cell line. Journal of Experimental Zoology 191:404–426.

Yamanaka, H., K. Yamaguchi, and F. Matsuura. 1965. Starch gel electrophoresis of fish hemoglobins—II. Electrophoretic patterns of various species. Bulletin of the Japanese Society of Scientific Fisheries 31:833–839.

Yasuzumi, G., and S. Higashizawa. 1955. Submicroscopic structure of the carp erythrocyte as revealed by electron microscopy. Cytologia 20:280–290.

Yocum, D., M. Cucheus, and L. W. Clem. 1975. The hapten-carrier effect in teleost fish. Journal of Immunology 114:925–927.

Yokoyama, H. O. 1960. Studies on the origin, development and seasonal variations in the blood cells of the perch, *Perca flavescens*. Wildlife Diseases 6:1–103.

Yuki, R. 1957. Blood cell constituents in fish. I. Peroxidase staining of leucocytes in rainbow trout. Bulletin of the Faculty of Fisheries Hokkaido University 8:36–44.

Chapter 10

Respirometry

JOSEPH J. CECH, JR.

10.1 INTRODUCTION

Respiration by fish includes the uptake of oxygen from the environment at sites of gas exchange (typically the gills), the use of oxygen at mitochondria within individual cells, and the excretion of waste gases to the environment. Respiration provides oxygen for aerobic conversion of the energy contained in food to high-energy chemical bonds, such as those formed when adenosine diphosphate (ADP) is changed to adenosine triphosphate (ATP). The energy thus stored is then used to keep fish alive (maintenance) and to allow fish to move, digest food, grow, reproduce, and carry out all other energy-requiring functions (see the review by Eckert and Randall 1983). In this chapter, the methods of measuring fish respiration are surveyed and evaluated.

10.1.1 Why Respirometry?

Measurements of respiration often can tell us how a fish is responding to environmental conditions and what its physiological state may be. Respirometry gives quantitative measures of how rapidly energy and oxygen are used. Respiratory data are important in the construction of bioenergetic models (Chapter 12) that can be used, for example, to calculate capacities for growth and reproduction (Ware 1982). Respiration rates and gill ventilatory rhythms can be sensitive indicators of altered environmental conditions or physiological states, and thus can reveal much about a fish's recent and current activity, acclimation, and stress.

10.2 TYPES OF RESPIRATORY MEASUREMENTS

The scope of this chapter is limited to measurements of respiratory (aerobic) metabolism and gill ventilation. Published techniques used with several species are reviewed, and some helpful details and expected advances are presented. Kaufmann et al. (1989) presented another interesting discussion on the subject.

10.2.1 Methods Used to Measure Respiratory Metabolism

Two basic methods are used to measure metabolic rates: direct and indirect calorimetry. Direct calorimetry, the measurement of heat production, is commonly used for birds and mammals. It is rarely used for fish because metabolic and heat production rates of fishes are generally low (Brett 1970b) and the heat capacity of water is great; consequently, the sensitivity of metabolic rate measurements by direct calorimetry is less than the sensitivity of an indirect measure such as oxygen consumption rate (Brett and Groves 1979). However, some direct calorimetry has been conducted on fish (see review by Van Waversveld et al. 1989c). For example, Smith (1976) determined the heat production of four species of salmonids using a modified adiabatic calorimeter, and Gnaiger (1979, 1983) described a flow-through microrespirometer that functioned simultaneously as an indirect (O_2 consumption) and a direct calorimeter for eggs of Arctic char. Gnaiger et al. (1989) provided a review of direct colorimetry methods.

Oxygen consumption rate has become the conventional metabolic measure for fishes because dissolved oxygen can be determined with relative ease and reliability. The iodometric or Winkler method (Winkler 1888) of measuring O_2 *concentrations* (mg or mL O_2/L H_2O) is highly accurate when fresh reagents are available to fix and titrate water samples (APHA et al. 1975). Clark-type polarographic electrodes (see below) measure O_2 *tension* or *partial pressure* (Po_2) and are easier and faster to use than the Winkler method. The wide availability of these electrodes has enhanced the rate at which fish metabolism data have been collected in the past 25 years.

Oxygen consumption rates, however, are accurate measures of overall metabolism only when anaerobic contributions are insignificant. During high-speed swimming (e.g., burst swimming) or exposure to extreme hypoxia, O_2 consumption does not keep pace with metabolic requirements and substantial anaerobiosis can be expected in fishes. Anaerobic metabolic measurements are beyond the scope of this chapter. In brief, anaerobic metabolism is often estimated from the accumulation of its end products (e.g., lactate) in the blood (Bartholomew 1977) or from O_2 consumption rates during recovery from hypoxic exposure as the O_2 debt is repaid (Heath and Pritchard 1965). Heath et al. (1980), Hochachka (1980), and Gäde and Grieshaber (1989) have reviewed anaerobic metabolism.

Besides oxygen consumption, carbon dioxide production is a focus of indirect calorimetry. The quantity of CO_2 produced per quantity of O_2 consumed is termed the *respiratory quotient* (RQ); this ratio varies from 0.7 to 1.0, depending on the organic substrate being catabolized (Schmidt-Nielsen 1979). However, the comparatively low rate at which fish produce CO_2 and the high solubility of this gas in water (Randall 1970) make it difficult to measure the partial pressure of CO_2 (Pco_2) accurately with an electrode. Problems include the electrode's stability and responsiveness, and the considerable amount of CO_2 bound as carbonates and bicarbonates, especially in hard water (Burggren 1979). Measurements of total CO_2 circumvent these problems. Van den Thillart et al. (1983) measured total CO_2 in seawater samples from a respirometer, using Cameron's (1971) method. Recently, Van Waversveld et al. (1989a, 1989b) used a flow-through microcalorimeter to simultaneously measure heat production (direct calorimetry) and O_2 and CO_2 production (indirect calorimetry) by goldfish. This approach allowed both aerobic and anaerobic metabolism to be quantified under normoxic, hypoxic, and anoxic conditions.

10.2.2 Levels of Respiratory Metabolism

Aerobic metabolism in fishes can be categorized as standard, resting routine, routine, swimming, and active. *Standard* metabolism is the minimum rate for intact fish (Fry 1971). *Resting routine* metabolism is the rate for quiescent fish, but not necessarily the lowest rate during the 24-h cycle. *Routine* metabolism is the rate including spontaneous movements. *Swimming* metabolism rates are measured at some voluntary or forced level of swimming. *Active* metabolism is the maximum aerobic rate associated with swimming at the greatest sustainable velocity.

The standard (basal, maintenance, or resting) metabolic rate is the minimum required to sustain life. It should be measured when fish are absolutely quiescent—that is, when they are expending no energy for activity (even random activity), food digestion, reproductive development, growth, or stress responses. Fish should be carefully shielded from changes in water temperature and chemistry and from all disturbances, and they should be given adequate time to habituate to the respirometer. Metabolic data should be taken throughout the diurnal cycle to determine the minimum rate. The innate restlessness of pelagic fishes such as salmon or tuna makes it much more difficult to determine standard metabolism for these species than for demersal or sedentary forms such as flatfishes.

Some workers have calculated standard metabolism from data on swimming fish. First, a relationship between swimming velocity and the logarithm of metabolic rate is established. Then, the relationship is extrapolated to zero velocity, which gives an estimate of standard rate (Brett 1964). It can be very difficult to induce a quiescent state in species that willingly swim in respirometers, and allowing these fish to swim over a range of moderate rates may eliminate much of the random activity that increases metabolic rate (Smit 1965). A drawback of such estimates is the statistical problem associated with extrapolation (Snedecor and Cochran 1967). Another drawback is the differing physiology of active and quiescent fish. Swimming rainbow trout, for example, secrete the hormone epinephrine into the blood (Nakano and Tomlinson 1967), where it dilates gill blood vessels, and constricts systemic blood vessels (Wood and Shelton 1980); it also binds to the membranes of red blood cells, thereby changing the affinity of hemoglobin for O_2 (Nikinmaa 1982). High swimming velocities (Hoar and Randall 1978) may cause fish to enter anaerobic metabolism and to release lactate from muscle tissue (Webb 1971). These and other dynamics of active fish make extrapolation of metabolic rate to a quiescent state problematic.

The resting routine metabolic level (Cech et al. 1979) falls between standard and routine metabolism. Measurements of resting routine metabolism require a quiescent fish without food in its gut, a respirometer with dimensions that constrain swimming but are not overly confining, and isolation of the fish from laboratory stimuli. However, these measurements do not account for the diel activity cycles that fish normally undergo (e.g., Forstner 1983).

Most metabolic values reported for fishes are routine rates, which represent generally quiescent (Fry 1971) to moderately active (Brett 1962) fish. Routine metabolic rates include spontaneous activity, possibly due to daily activity cycles, and they may include forced swimming at a velocity of up to 1 body length/s (Brett 1970a).

Swimming metabolic rates are measured during various voluntary or forced levels of swimming. Active metabolic rates are generally defined as those attained while a fish is swimming at the greatest sustainable velocity for a particular period of time, such as 1 h (Fry 1971).

"Scope for activity" (Fry 1957) is calculated by subtracting the standard metabolic rate from the active metabolic rate. The "metabolic expansibility index" (Brett 1965; Dabrowski 1986) is calculated by dividing active by standard metabolic rate. Both of these indices are measures of an animal's capacity for exercise.

10.2.3 Gill Ventilation

Oxygen uptake across the respiratory surfaces is a passive phenomenon in fishes, driven by diffusion. The rate of O_2 diffusion is directly proportional to the partial-pressure gradient (Randall 1970). The movement of ventilation water over the gills replaces the boundary layer of water next to the lamellar epithelium (where O_2 is diffusing inward), thereby maintaining the Po_2 gradient between water and blood. Thus, gill ventilation is an essential respiratory process in most fishes. Ventilation volume is the total volume of water pumped or rammed over the gills. Ventilatory frequency is the frequency of buccal or opercular movements—sometimes called "opercular rate." Ventilatory stroke volume is the volume of water pumped per buccal–opercular stroke or movement. Percentage utilization of oxygen is the percentage of available oxygen removed by respiration from the inspired water.

10.3 APPARATUS AND TECHNIQUES

10.3.1 General Considerations

For any type of respirometric measurement, regardless of the apparatus or species of fish used, high water quality should be maintained and stress on the fish should be minimized. In field studies, plankton, algae, or detrital particles may significantly affect the O_2 concentration in the respirometer. Even though a "blank" respirometer is used (see below), the amount of oxygen-consuming or -producing material in the water should be kept as small as possible. In the laboratory, an ultraviolet sterilizer helps minimize microbial populations on the walls of the respirometer, especially at high temperatures and during experiments lasting several days. The vinyl tubing that connects components of flow-through respirometry systems provides especially good bacteria-developing surfaces. Dalla Via (1983) advised against adding antibiotics to the water because they may have toxic or physiological effects on the fish, especially antibiotics that "interfere with nucleic acid or protein biosynthesis" and those "affecting the function of the cytoplasmatic membrane." Often, the best approach is to scrupulously clean the respirometry system between experiments and to use blank respirometers that can account for microbial and other extraneous influences.

After an experiment, when fish have been removed, respirometer systems can be cleaned with a chlorine solution. Household bleach can be used at a concentration (0.5–2 mL/L) that depends on the chlorine demand of the system. Chlorine demand is the difference between the amount of chlorine applied and the amount of free, combined, or total available chlorine remaining at the end of the contact period (APHA et al. 1975). The germicidal effect of chlorine depends on its concentration and contact time. Great care must be taken to ensure that *all* traces of chlorine are gone before fish are reintroduced into the system. Systems should be drained and flushed thoroughly at least once before they are refilled with new water for experiments. Chlorinated tap water must be dechlorinated by an acceptable method (see Seegert and Brooks 1978; Herwig 1982). Chlorine in water is lethal to fish at low levels (e.g., Heath 1977), and sublethal levels can induce a variety of histological, behavioral, and physiological responses in fishes (Grothe and Eaton 1975; Buckley 1977; Zeitoun 1977; Cherry et al. 1982; Hose et al. 1983; Mitchell and Cech 1983). Residual chlorine concentrations should be checked by a sensitive method such as amperometric titration (APHA et al. 1975; Brooks and Seegert 1979).

Another general consideration is that stress on the test fish should be avoided as much as possible. Careful attention to sequences of fish acclimation, to nutrition, and to health contributes to the best possible experimental results. Fry (1971) reviewed the acclimation of fish to various temperatures. In general, fish can be acclimated faster to warmer temperatures (e.g., at rates of 1–2°C/d) than to colder ones (for which temperature changes should be 0.5–1°C/d). For most fish, much less is known about acclimation to variables such as salinity, dissolved oxygen concentrations, and photoperiod. In many cases, one should either conduct preliminary experiments to determine acclimation schedules or use conservatively long acclimation times.

Fish held for long periods of time in the laboratory should be fed a nutritionally complete diet (Halver 1972; NRC 1983). Fish at colder temperatures will subsist longer without feeding than those at warmer temperatures. Fish also must be starved longer in cold water (2–3 d, for example) than in warm water (1–2 d) to ensure that food absorption is complete before respiratory metabolic measurements are made.

Adequate nutrition and minimal stress contribute to healthy experimental fish. If a continuous flow of high-quality water is available, stresses due to metabolites such as ammonia in holding tanks are minimized and tanks do not need biological filters. Bacterial populations and the disease problems associated with them are reduced by weekly or twice-weekly cleaning of holding tank surfaces with a brush or sponge. Nevertheless, fish disease treatments with antibiotics or other chemicals sometimes are necessary; Roberts (1978) and Spotte (1979) discussed such treatments. When chemicals are added to the tank water, the time needed to wash out 99% of the chemical from well-mixed flow-through systems may be calculated from

$$t = \log_e 100 \ (V/\dot{V}),\tag{1}$$

or

$$t = 4.6 \ V/\dot{V};\tag{2}$$

$t = 99\%$ washout time (min), $V =$ tank volume (mL), and $\dot{V} =$ flow rate (mL/min). (It is common in respiratory physiology to denote a rate by a dot over the symbol.)

10.3.2 Oxygen Measurements

Oxygen dissolved in water is usually measured electrometrically or titrimetrically. A common electrometric measurement system uses the Clark-type oxygen electrode. This electrode consists of an anode (e.g., silver–silver chloride) and a cathode (e.g., platinum), which are bathed in an electrolytic solution in the electrode body. An O_2-permeable membrane is stretched across the electrode tip. When a small polarizing voltage is applied across the anode and cathode, O_2 diffusing across the membrane is reduced at the cathode, producing a current through the electrode. This current is proportional to the partial pressure of oxygen in the water. The current is amplified and displayed on a meter or digital readout; the display equipment varies from battery-powered portable units to more elaborate units featuring interfaces for strip chart recorders and computers. Some meter and electrode systems for dissolved oxygen, such as YSI® units, automatically calculate O_2 concentrations from detected O_2 tensions if water temperature and salinity values are known. Other units (e.g., IL® and Radiometer®) produce measures of O_2 scaled in millimeters of mercury, tension torr, pascals, or kilopascals. These can be converted to O_2 concentration (usually mL O_2/L) with the aid of a nomogram or oxygen solubility tables (Green and Carritt 1967; Weiss 1970) and the formula

$$Co_2(\text{ws}) = \frac{Po_2(\text{ws}) \cdot Co_2(\text{as})}{Po_2(\text{as})}; \qquad (3)$$

$Co_2(\text{ws})$ = O_2 concentration (mL O_2/L) in the water sample,
$Po_2(\text{ws})$ = O_2 tension (mm Hg) in the water sample,
$Co_2(\text{ws})$ = O_2 concentration in water at air saturation (from nomogram or tables), and
$Po_2(\text{as})$ = O_2 tension at air saturation (from equation 4, below).

The oxygen tension at air saturation is

$$Po_2(\text{as}) = 0.2094 \, (P\text{B} - P\text{wv}); \qquad (4)$$

0.2094 = mole fraction or volumetric fraction of O_2 in the atmosphere,
    $P\text{B}$ = total barometric pressure (mm Hg), and
    $P\text{wv}$ = water vapor pressure at the experimental temperature (mm Hg).

Oxygen concentrations in mL O_2/L can be converted (Green and Carritt 1967) to mg O_2/L by the equivalency

$$\text{mg } O_2 = 1.428 \cdot \text{mL } O_2. \qquad (5)$$

Because of possible "drifting," calibration of O_2 electrodes should be checked frequently. Gnaiger and Forstner (1983) exhaustively reviewed polarographic oxygen electrodes, including their design, construction, calibration, and use. Helpful operational hints for using Po_2 electrodes were also provided by Gambino (1970), Severinghaus and Bradley (1971), and Cameron (1986).

The Winkler or iodometric method is the standard titrimetric measurement of dissolved oxygen. The various details and modifications of the Winkler method are reviewed elsewhere (APHA et al. 1975; Golterman 1983). It is imperative that water samples from the respirometer be taken with the minimum possible exposure to the atmosphere. This is usually accomplished with a siphon tube from a static respirometer or the outflow tube from a flow-through respirometer. The end of the tube is thrust to the bottom of an empty bottle, which usually has a capacity of 125 or 250 mL. The initial water, which is exposed to the air in the bottle, is displaced by the latter portion of the sample. Typically, two volumes of the sample bottle are displaced before the tube is carefully removed to ensure that the sample is minimally contaminated by air. Then, appropriate (excess) volumes of manganous chloride and an alkaline iodide solution are added before the sample bottle is carefully stoppered and shaken. A precipitate forms; when it settles, the bottle is carefully unstoppered and the correct volume of H_2SO_4 is added (displacing some water, but no precipitate). The acid liberates I_2, which makes a clear, yellow solution for subsequent titration.

Winkler titrations may be completed with very small samples (3–5 mL). Because of the small sample volumes, either more samples from a large respirometer may be taken or a smaller respirometer may be used. The water sample is drawn into a glass syringe that has been flushed with sample water at least once to minimize atmospheric contamination. The appropriate volumes of reagents are then drawn into the syringe (Fox and Wingfield 1938). However, because the reagent volumes are proportionately quite large compared with the standard Winkler, the reagents must be degassed to remove as much of the dissolved oxygen from them as possible. The degassing can be accomplished by placing the reagents in a strong, lubricated (with mineral oil) glass syringe with attached needle, and expelling the air bubble above the liquid. Then, the needle tip is inserted into a rubber stopper and the syringe plunger is withdrawn. The resulting partial vacuum in the syringe draws dissolved gases from the liquid into a bubble, which can be expelled. The process is repeated. Because of the risk of implosion, each degassing syringe should be tested with water, and safety glasses and protective clothing should be worn.

Gasometric methods of O_2 measurement usually involve volumetric or manometric measurements of gas spaces (e.g., bubbles in a calibrated capillary tube) as O_2 is consumed and CO_2 is chemically absorbed. These methods are especially convenient for measuring O_2 consumption rates of small air-breathing animals, but they also can be used with fish (and fish eggs) if there is adequate equilibration of the aqueous and atmospheric gas phases in the respirometer. Conventional gasometric methods were reviewed by Dixon (1951) and Umbreit et al. (1972). Coulometric microrespirometry is a variation of this method in which the manometric liquid (a $CuSO_4$ solution) moves through a capillary tube as O_2 is consumed and touches a platinum electrode connected to a capacitor. The capacitor is discharged through the $CuSO_4$ solution, releasing a set amount of O_2 into the system for further consumption. Oxygen consumption rates are quantified by the number of discharges during the experiment. Because the capacitor is automatically discharged and recharged as long as the liquid is in contact with the electrode, this system is well suited to long-term measurements, once properly calibrated (Heusner et al. 1982).

10.3.3   Body Mass Considerations

Large fish generally consume more O_2 than small fish. However, on a unit-weight or -mass basis, small fish consume more O_2 than large fish. This allometric relationship can be described as

$$Y = a X^b, \tag{6}$$

or

$$\log_{10} Y = \log_{10} a + b \log_{10} X; \tag{7}$$

$Y = O_2$ consumption rate (mg O_2/min), a = mass coefficient, X = body mass (g or kg), and b = mass exponent.

The log–log plot of X and Y (equation 7) is a linear one, but with a slope (b) that usually is less than 1.0. Therefore, it is inadvisable to divide O_2 consumption rate data by unit mass to compare rates of different-size fish (i.e., comparisons of mg $O_2 \cdot g^{-1} \cdot h^{-1}$ are ill-advised). Heusner (1982a, 1982b, 1984) presented the theoretical arguments for using 0.67 as the mass exponent (b) when only the mass of an individual changes (i.e., the animal remains biologically similar with respect to density, proximate composition, etc.). Empirical evidence from measurements of standard metabolism (Heusner et al. 1963) support this relationship. However, because some degree of activity is expected, (e.g., routine metabolism), and because activity is an intensive rather than an extensive property of metabolism, the mass exponent is likely to be greater than 0.67 (Heusner 1984). Winberg (1956) reviewed much of the early metabolic literature on fishes and found an average mass exponent value of 0.8 for routine metabolic rates. Subsequent researchers have calculated mass exponents between 0.65 and 0.86 for fishes variously resting or showing routine activity (e.g., Glass 1969; Caulton 1978; Innes and Wells 1985). Brett (1965) calculated a mass exponent of 0.97 for the active metabolism of sockeye salmon.

Intra- and interspecific comparisons of respiratory metabolic rates must be conducted carefully. To compare different groups of the same species of fish, it is best if the mean body masses of the two groups are statistically indistinguishable and the ranges around these means are small. If the two groups of fish have significantly different mean masses, one of two other analyses might be appropriate. The first is an analysis of covariance that relates metabolic rate to temperature, with mass as the covariate (e.g., Cech et al. 1985). The other is to either assume a mass exponent of 0.67 (standard metabolism) or to determine the actual mass exponent (e.g., $b = 0.81$) for the particular group of fish and divide the raw data by (mass^b) (Innes and Wells 1985). This last technique yields "mass-independent" metabolic rates that are most correctly analyzed in $\log_{10}$-transformed form. These two analyses are also appropriate when different species of fish are compared. Unless such species are coincidentally homomorphic (Heusner 1982b), their regression intercepts (mass coefficients, a, equations 6, 7) would be expected to be different even though their slopes (b) would be the same (e.g., 0.67). Naturally, all the assumptions inherent in any suggested statistical test should be assured prior to use of the test (see Chapter 1). Also, mass exponents should be determined over as wide a size range of homomorphic individuals as possible (one to two orders of magnitude).

10.3.4 Respiratory Metabolism

A respirometer incorporates a chamber for the fish and a surrounding respiratory medium (usually water, though air or access to air may be appropriate). There are essentially two types of respirometers: *closed respirometers,* in which the same volume of respiratory medium is continuously used with little replacement; and *open respirometers,* in which the medium is continuously replaced.

Closed respirometers are of two types. In *static* respirometers, the medium is not moved in directed currents, though it may be kept well mixed by stirrers, aerators, and the fish itself. In *swimming* respirometers, the medium flows within the vessel, forcing the fish to swim against a directed current. In contrast, fresh water continually flows into and out of *open* (or "*flow-through*") respirometers,

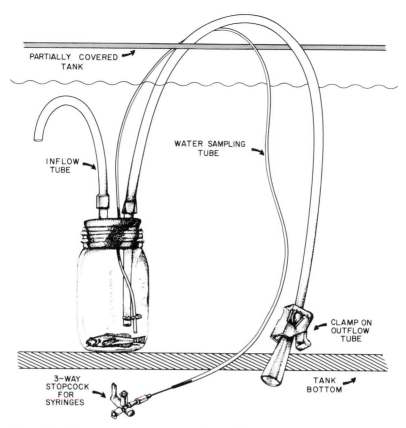

PARTIALLY COVERED TANK

INFLOW TUBE

WATER SAMPLING TUBE

CLAMP ON OUTFLOW TUBE

TANK BOTTOM

3-WAY STOPCOCK FOR SYRINGES

Figure 10.1 A basic static respirometer. Large-diameter tubes are used to flush the respirometer between experiments. The small-diameter tube is used to obtain water samples for O_2 analyses.

the object being to maintain water quality. In general, static and open respirometers are used to measure similar aspects of fish respiration, though the measurements are made differently. Swimming respirometers can be quite elaborate and expensive. Whatever system is chosen, the study will progress most efficiently if several replicate setups can be used simultaneously.

10.3.4.1 Static Respirometers

A static respirometer contains a noncirculating, fixed volume of water. It may be as simple as a glass jar or flask and a tight-fitting stopper to which water-sampling and -flushing tubes have been fitted (Figure 10.1). The jar or other container should be impermeable to gases and at least partially transparent. Transparency makes it easier to detect bubbles, which must be removed because the air they contain is rich in oxygen and thus a source of respirometry error. A transparent chamber also may help the enclosed fish to visually orient to the tank or stream in which the respirometer is placed, and thereby to habituate to the confines of the respirometer. Some species, however, habituate more readily if the vessel is nearly opaque; examples are gobies (Gobiidae) and toadfish (Batrachoididae), which have secretive habits.

Measurements of O_2 consumption are calculated from dissolved O_2 concentration, respirometer volume, and time data:

$$\dot{M}O_2 = \frac{(Co_2(A) - Co_2(B))V}{T}; \tag{8}$$

$\dot{M}O_2$ = O_2 consumption rate (mg O_2/h)

$Co_2(A)$ = O_2 concentration in water (mg O_2/L) at the start of the measurement period;

Co_2 (B) = O_2 concentration in water (mg O_2/L) at the end of the measurement period;

V = volume of respirometer (L); and

T = time elapsed during measurement period (h).

Corrections for microbial O_2 consumption or production are made by use of a blank (fishless) respirometer with dimensions and tubing lengths similar to those of respirometers containing fish. Some investigators measure microbial O_2 consumption rates in the fish's respirometer after the fish is removed (e.g., Graham and Baird 1984), a correction technique that is especially recommended for extended metabolic studies because microbial dynamics may differ between experimental and blank vessels.

The volume of the respirometer should generally be 30–50 times that of the fish. A respirometer that is too small may stress the test fish and elevate respiratory metabolic rates (Cech et al. 1985). In one that is too large, the fish's ventilatory and fin movements will not keep the water mixed well enough to assure the investigator of representative samples. Large static respirometers, such as sealed tanks (Gooding et al. 1981), must be used for long-term studies, however, or else pairs of water samples must be taken frequently for dissolved-oxygen analysis, and sampling must be alternated with flushing flows through the respirometer. Water in a large respirometer can be kept mixed by a small submersible pump or stirring device. Such devices may stimulate fish and so might be used in one of two modes: continuously at low, nonstressful levels, or vigorously just before the final sample is taken. Submersible pumps add heat energy to the system, which could affect metabolic rates.

Considerable effort should be made to minimize stress. When fish must be moved, they should be transferred quickly from one tank to another with a dip net. If possible, the water source and quality should be the same in the respirometers' water bath as it is in the fishes' holding tank. The tank containing the respirometers should be at least partially covered to shield test fish from the glare of lights and the movements of people. Fish should be guided carefully into the respirometer opening. Bubbles are quite easily removed from underwater respirometers and temperature conditions can be carefully controlled. The respirometers can be flushed with water from the respirometer tank while the fish is initially settling down and between experiments. One effective way to flush water through static respirometers is to siphon from an extension of the outflow tube (Figure 10.1) to a reservoir below the level of the respirometer tank. Centrifugal or peristaltic pumps are not recommended to directly flush respirometers because they may send vibrations or pulsations through the water and stimulate the fish.

When the measurement period begins, the outflow tubing normally is clamped off and the initial water sample is taken for O_2 analysis. The outflow tube may be used for this purpose, especially if large samples are needed for Winkler titrations (Moore 1970), but a small-diameter, heavy-walled sampling tube is recommended if only a few milliliters are needed. The dead-space water filling the sampling tube is easily removed with a syringe through a three-way stopcock (Figure 10.1); the stopcock is then turned and the sample is drawn into a second syringe. Small water samples insure that replacement water drawn into the respirometer from the water bath does not measurably contaminate the sampled water with oxygen.

Spontaneous activity from fish in "routine" metabolic states has been quantified with a variety of methods including deflected paddles, heater–thermometer combinations, electrical and magnetic contacts, light–photocell combinations, and field shifts in high-frequency sound (see review by Beamish 1978). All of these devices detect fin or body movements of the fish or the water currents associated with them. One of the best devices for measuring spontaneous activity is a heater–thermometer flowmeter described by Beamish and Mookherjii (1964).

Special static respirometers can be used to isolate the respiratory contributions from different gas exchange sites. Kirsch and Nonotte (1977) described a respirometer for eels that can be separated with a rubber sleeve into an anterior compartment for measuring branchial O_2 uptake and a posterior one for cutaneous respiration. In each compartment, the water is circulated past an oxygen electrode by a pump, allowing O_2 consumption rates from each gas exchange site to be measured separately. Special static respirometers that incorporate an air phase can be used to study respiration by fishes with air-breathing organs (e.g., lung, swim bladder). Graham and Baird (1984) placed marbled swamp eels *Synbranchus marmoratus* in an L-shaped respirometer that had a gas space at the top of its vertical arm; changes in volume and O_2 content in the gas space allowed calculation of instantaneous O_2 consumption rates. Bicudo and Johansen (1979) studied the partitioning of water and air breathing by the same species (Box 10.1).

Basic static respirometers are simple to construct and relatively easy to operate. They have been manipulated from manned submersibles to measure the respiration of deep-sea fish in situ (Smith and Baldwin 1983). Elaborate static respirometers have been designed, but their construction and operation require a great deal of technical skill.

Because fish eventually deplete the O_2 in the enclosed volume of water, the main limitations of the static respirometer concern long-term experiments, especially those in which fish are to be exposed to prolonged stable levels of hypoxia. Metabolic rates decrease, in fishes that display respiratory dependence, when oxygen partial pressures fall below the *critical* Po_2 (Cech et al. 1979). At very low Po_2, metabolic rates can temporarily increase due to excitement and activity. For metabolic studies under normoxic conditions, measurements must be made before chamber Po_2 declines to the critical level. Flushing the respirometer with hypoxic water permits measurements at predetermined hypoxic Po_2 ranges (Castleberry and Cech 1986).

Dissolved metabolic wastes (CO_2, ammonia) also increase during static experiments. High dissolved CO_2 levels in the water may increase blood CO_2 levels in fish (Cameron 1976) and lower the affinity of hemoglobin for oxygen (Riggs 1970). However, CO_2 is 25–35 times more soluble than O_2 in water, so low Po_2 will affect

Box 10.1   Simultaneous Measurement of Oxygen Consumption from Air and Water

Bicudo and Johansen (1979) studied breathing by marbled swamp eels in air and water. In their static respirometer (illustrated below), water filled the main chamber into a narrow neck, above which was a layer of air. The neck allowed the fish access to the air, but it was small enough that transfer of gases across the air–water interface was negligible (a necessary condition for this type of experiment). A magnetic stirrer kept the water well mixed. An air stone reaerated the water after an experiment, or equilibrated the water with other known gas mixtures if experiments called for them.

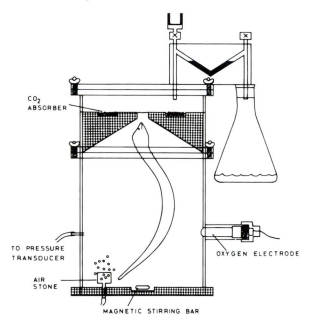

Consumption of dissolved O_2 by the fish was determined from the rate at which the partial pressure of oxygen (Po_2) in the water declined, as measured by a polarographic oxygen electrode connected to a recorder. Consumption of gaseous O_2 was measured manometrically as the amount of pure O_2 needed to keep the manometer balanced. Evolved CO_2 was continuously taken up by Carbosorb®- or Baralyme®-type absorbents.

The frequency of air breaths and the tidal volume (amount of air breathed in by the fish) were measured with a "strain-gauge" type of pressure transducer wired to a recorder. Inhalation increased the volume of the fish, raising the height of the water column in the respirometer neck and increasing the hydrostatic pressure at the transducer. The transducer was calibrated for tidal volume measurements by additions of known volumes of water to raise the fluid level in the narrow neck. Volume additions of this sort result in linear pressure increases.

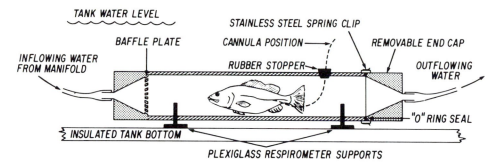

Figure 10.2 A basic flow-through respirometer. Fresh water continuously enters a cylindrical fish chamber through a baffle plate. Baffle holes are incrementally angled from horizontal in the center of the plate to the angle of the expansion cone at the margins. Dye studies show that this design minimizes eddies and dead spaces in the respirometer. Blood can be sampled through an optional vascular cannula that is led out of the respirometer via a hypodermic needle shaft inserted through a rubber stopper. (From Cech et al. 1979.)

fish in a sealed respirometer before high P_{CO_2}. Ammonia is the primary nitrogenous waste of bony fish and is especially toxic in the un-ionized (NH_3) form (Wuhrmann and Woker 1948). Automated systems that incorporate intermittent flows (e.g., Forstner 1983; Steffensen 1989) have solved some of the problems inherent in long experiments with static respirometers.

10.3.4.2 Open (Flow-Through) Respirometers

Open respirometers (Figure 10.2) solve many of the problems that arise during long-term studies with static systems. Continuous flows of water over the fish eliminate the need for periodic flushing flows; wastes do not accumulate, and desired characteristics such as oxygen concentration are maintained. A constant flow of water must be set to exceed the gill ventilation volume of the fish. Overly slow flows will force the fish to rebreathe water, causing hypoxia such as occurs in static systems. Excessively high flows will reduce the accuracy of metabolic rate determinations because there will be an insufficient difference in oxygen concentration between inflowing and outflowing water.

Under stable environmental conditions, oxygen consumption rates are calculated by the equation

$$\dot{M}_{O_2} = (C_{O_2}(I) - C_{O_2}(O))\ \dot{V}_W; \tag{9}$$

$\dot{M}_{O_2}$ = O_2 consumption rate (mg O_2/min),
$C_{O_2}(I)$ = O_2 concentration in inflowing water (mg O_2/L),
$C_{O_2}(O)$ = O_2 concentration in outflowing water (mg O_2/L), and
$\dot{V}_W$ = water flow rate through the respirometer (L/min).

When the relation between activity and metabolism is of concern or when water conditions are changing rather quickly in a flow-through respirometer, a time-lag correction factor must be appended to equation (9) (Fry 1971; Niimi 1978; Steffensen 1989):

$$\dot{M}_{O_2} = (C_{O_2}(I) - \overline{C}_{O_2}(O))\ \dot{V}_W + (C_{O_2}(O,1) - C_{O_2}(O,2))\ V_R; \tag{10}$$

$\overline{Co}_2(o)$ = mean O_2 concentration in outflowing water over the experimental
          period (mg O_2/L),

$Co_2(o,1)$ = O_2 concentration in outflowing water at the start of the experimental
          period (mg O_2/L),

$Co_2(o,2)$ = O_2 concentration in outflowing water at the end of the experimental
          period (mg O_2/L), and

V_R = volume of the respirometer.

For this time-lag correction it is assumed that a "slug" of water moves through the respirometer without mixing or creating major eddies and that $Co_2(I)$ is constant throughout the experimental period. Flow properties can be checked by injecting dye into the inflow water and observing its pattern throughout the chamber.

Samples of outflowing water for dissolved O_2 analysis can be collected from the outflowing-water tubes. Rigid positioning of these tube outlets helps ensure consistent water flows through the respirometers. When water samples are drawn, care must be taken to minimize occlusion of these outlets, or pressure changes in respirometers will stress the test fish. Samples of inflowing water are best drawn from an outflow tube of a fishless respirometer having identical dimensions, tubing lengths, and flow rate as the others. An automated design has been described by Ross and McKinney (1988).

Generally, water flow rates are set so that the difference in oxygen concentration between inflowing and outflowing water is 0.5–1.0 mg/L. It should be remembered that a fish's ventilation volume is likely to increase in hypoxic water, possibly without a consistent change in oxygen consumption rate. Thus, water flow through the respirometer may have to be adjusted when the dissolved oxygen condition changes. Water flows are typically measured as the weight (1 g = 1 mL) or volume of outflowing water collected per unit time. Water flowmeters also may be used, but they are usually not precise enough for metabolic calculations.

Flow-through respirometers are generally constructed of clear, thick-walled acrylic plastic such as Plexiglas®. Some inert, virtually gas-impermeable tubing (e.g., a heavy-walled transparent vinyl such as Tygon®) directs the inflowing water to this chamber. This tubing should be as short as possible to minimize the buildup of attached organisms, and should be of the same length on multiple respirometers if these are used. Rubber tubing is more permeable to gases and should not be used (Fry 1957). It is important to spread the flow from the small-diameter tubing across the larger diameter of the chamber without creating eddies or dead spaces. A smooth-walled cone connecting the two and a baffle plate usually serve this function (Figure 10.2). Sacca and Burggren (1982) used a special flow-through respirometer that incorporated a rubber sleeve and an air phase to partition the respiratory contributions of the skin, gills, and lungs of the reedfish *Calamoichthys calabaricus* (Figure 10.3).

10.3.4.3 Swimming Respirometers

Swimming respirometers usually contain a closed volume of water that is circulated past a fish, inducing the fish to swim. As in static systems, changes in dissolved oxygen concentration through time in the enclosed volume reflect the rate of respiratory metabolism, in this case at a particular swimming velocity. Four basic designs of swimming respirometers are in current use. The most

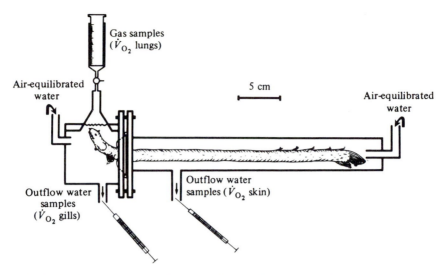

Figure 10.3 A flow-through respirometer designed for the simultaneous measurement of O_2 uptake by the lungs, gills, and skin of reedfish. The chamber is divided into anterior and posterior chambers by a rubber membrane (condom) through which the fish's body passes. Water in gaseous equilibrium with air flows through both chambers; gill respiration is measured in the anterior chamber, skin respiration in the posterior one. An overhead inverted funnel contains an air bubble from which the fish breathes. Changes in the partial pressure of oxygen in the funnel represent O_2 uptake by the lungs. (From Sacca and Burggren 1982.)

common is the water tunnel or "Brett-type" respirometer (Brett 1964), which consists of a closed loop of pipe containing a centrifugal pump (Box 10.2). A variable-speed drive connected to the pump changes the water velocity past the fish. The fish is restricted to its chamber by screens, flow-straightening tubes, or an electrifiable grid at the rear of the chamber. Gradual turns of custom-bent polyvinyl chloride pipe in the tunnel loop and gradual tapers ($<7°$) in sections connecting the swimming chamber with other pipes minimize turbulence and temperature increases. Priede and Holliday (1980) induced plaice *Pleuronectes platessa* to swim by mounting the entire tunnel respirometer on gimbals and tilting it to induce "lift-off" from the bottom of the chamber.

Water velocity through the swimming chamber is proportional to pump speed, measured in revolutions of the pump shaft per minute. Water velocity can be measured by the timed passage of visible particles, a flowmeter, or a Pitot tube in the swimming chamber and then compared with speed settings on the motor or pump shaft. After this calibration, water velocity can be determined by measuring pump speed with a tachometer. A large fish obstructs a greater cross-sectional area of the chamber than a small one, causing the water to flow at a greater velocity around it. If the test fish occupies more than 10% of the cross-sectional area of the swimming chamber, a correction factor for this solid blocking effect must be applied (Bell and Terhune 1970; Smit et al. 1971; Webb 1971). An automated version of the Brett-type respirometer incorporates a computer that automatically corrects for solid blocking effects when it calculates oxygen consumption rates (Box 10.2). This version also reoxygenates respirometer water via an artificial lung perfused with O_2 gas (Steffensen et al. 1984; Gehrke et al. 1990).

Box 10.2   Brett-Type Swimming Respirometer

The tunnel respirometer pictured below is a closed system in which water is propelled, forcing a fish to swim, but not replaced during a metabolic test. Its various devices, many of them computer-controlled, create and measure the current, restrict turbulence and temperature changes, monitor the oxygen concentration, and reaerate the water between tests.

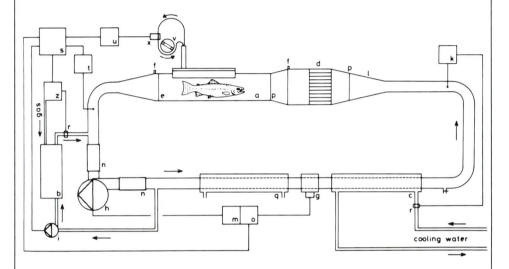

a swimming chamber	i lung circuit pump	q heating shell
b artificial lung	k temperature control	r magnet valve
c cooling shell	with thermister	s computer
d turbulence tubes	l expansion cone	t thermometer
e electrified screen	m motor control	u oxygen meter
f bubble trap	n rubber joints	v roller pump
g turbine flowmeter	o flow gauge	x oxygen electrode
h main pump	p turbulence screens	z oxygen regulator

The temperature control unit opens or closes a magnetic valve to regulate the flow of chilled water to the cooling shell, where heat generated by pumps, motors, and friction is removed from the main system. Some of the test water is diverted from the swimming chamber past the oxygen electrode, which continuously monitors the partial pressure of oxygen and relays measurements to the computer. The computer automatically calculates oxygen consumption values by a model similar to text equation (8). Between experiments, water is reoxygenated to a preset value as it is diverted by the lung circuit pump through the artificial lung. The lung works as a membrane oxygenator, whereby oxygen moves into the water through a gas-permeable membrane of large surface area without creating any bubbles. (From Steffensen et al. 1984.)

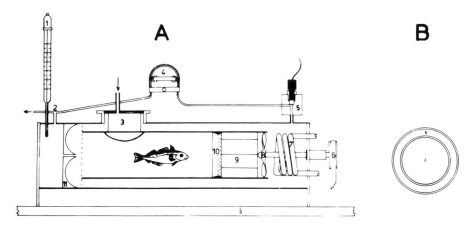

Figure 10.4   The Blazka respirometer, side (A) and end (B) views: (1) contact thermometer; (2) outlet; (3) hatch with outflow; (4) peristaltic pump; (5) oxygen electrode; (6) belt drive; (7) cooling coil; (8) propeller; (9) radial plates; (10) baffle screens; (11) flow former (domed cap); (a) inner tube; (b) outer tube. The water is pushed by the propeller through the radial plates and baffle screens (which remove the torque imparted to the water by the propeller) and past the fish. The domed end cap guides the water into the outer concentric shell, where it returns to the propeller. The partial pressure of dissolved oxygen can be monitored continuously with an electrode placed in the peristaltic pump circuit. (From Tytler 1978.)

The second basic swimming respirometer design is based on concentric (coaxial) tubes; the swimming chamber is in the inner tube and water returns between the inner and outer tubes (Figure 10.4; Blazka et al. 1960). A propeller, driven by a variable-speed electric motor, or a submersible water pump pulls or pushes water past the fish and returns it to the front of the swimming chamber via the outer tube after it is deflected by a domed end cap (Wohlschlag and Wakeman 1978). The spiralling movement imparted to the water by the rotating propeller can be minimized by replacing the conventional propeller with a jet outboard impeller (Smith and Newcomb 1970) and by incorporating flow-straightening vanes in the outer tube and small-diameter tubes at the ends of the inner tube. The small-diameter tubes also provide the function of confining the fish to the swimming chamber. These tubes vary in diameter from thin-walled 1.25-cm polyvinyl chloride pipe in larger Blazka respirometers to 3-mm plastic soda straws in small ones. This respirometer also may have an electrified wire grid (8–10 V AC) behind the fish to encourage it to swim if it is uncooperative (Dickson and Kramer 1971). The relatively small water volume of the Blazka design minimizes the time needed to measure oxygen consumption rates at a particular temperature and swimming velocity.

The third swimming respirometer design incorporates a transparent chamber, annular or toroidal in shape, that can be rotated at speeds to match, in the counter direction, the swimming velocity of the fish (Figure 10.5). Because of the continuous swimming path available to the fish, its activity is likely to be more volitional than forced and its progress around the ring can be matched in opposition by the chamber rotational speed. Consequently, the fish remains at a relatively constant position, relative to either the water bath or the natural habitat in which the respirometer is suspended, while it swims into the current induced by

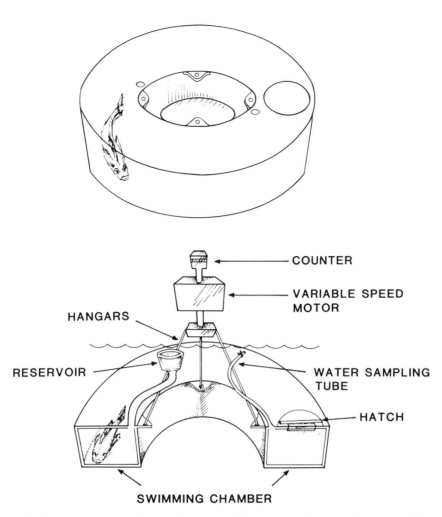

Figure 10.5 A rotating annular respirometer. The chamber is rotated by a variable-speed motor to match the volitional swimming velocity of the fish. Water drawn off for dissolved oxygen measurements is replaced by a known volume from a reservoir.

the internal boundary friction of the rotating chamber. Sometimes a dim light source or tape stripes on the walls of the external water bath help to orient the fish (Fry 1957). Chamber revolutions are usually counted mechanically. Swimming velocity and distance are calculated from chamber speed (revolutions per minute), the midline distance around the chamber, and time. Wohlschlag (1964) found that various Antarctic fishes tended to swim a constant distance per revolution—they swam along the midline—"within about 10%." The disadvantages of an annular respirometer include its curved swimming path and its inability to reach the highest sustainable swimming velocities for many species (Fry 1971). It is also likely that the velocity profile is uneven due to water slippage within the rotating chamber (Beamish 1978), placing the true swimming velocities and travel distances of the test fish in doubt.

Dabrowski (1986) described an annular flow-through swimming respirometer with small-diameter inflowing and outflowing water tubes and a constricted area in the ring. Except for the gradual flow-through of water, the test fish is not confronted with a current because this annular chamber does not rotate. The fish is induced to swim by its optimotor reaction to a drum, painted with alternating white and black stripes, that rotates outside the respirometer. (The Brett and Blazka designs described above also can be used in a flow-through mode if a *constant* flow of bubble-free water is circulated through the system, and the inflowing and outflowing oxygen partial pressures are accurately determined.)

The final swimming respirometer design described here is simply a static respirometer with a stirring bar on the bottom (MacLeod and Smith 1966). Innes and Wells (1985) stimulated 5–10-min bursts of activity by the benthic, intertidal triplefin blenny *Helcogramma medium* by magnetically rotating the stirring bar. They found it "impossible to monitor steady-state swimming by the methods employed for other more active teleosts which possess a swimbladder (cf., Brett 1964)." However, the stirrers excite and stress the fish, which limits the usefulness of this design in comparison with others for measurement of swimming metabolism.

Metabolic rates of swimming fish have also been estimated from heartbeat, ventilation, and swimming muscle contraction frequencies by telemetry. Heart rate was not a precise estimate of metabolism in rainbow trout, brown trout, or Atlantic cod (Priede and Tytler 1977). However, telemetered electromyographic signals from the epaxial (Weatherley et al. 1982) and opercular (Rogers and Weatherley 1983) muscles of swimming rainbow trout showed closer correlations. These telemetric techniques point the way to improved in situ metabolic measurements. However, activities that require different muscles may not yield accurate metabolic estimates (Weatherley et al. 1982).

10.3.5 Gill Ventilation

Gill ventilation is accomplished in two ways: water is *actively pumped* by the buccal–opercular apparatus (Hughes 1963), or it is *passively rammed* over the gills as fish swim (Roberts 1975). Ram ventilation requires only that a fish maintain a buccal–opercular gape while it swims at or above a threshold velocity (Roberts 1975). Freadman (1981) showed that swimming bluefish and striped bass conserve energy with ram ventilation.

Active pumping of gill ventilation water is commonly measured in a respirometer that directs ventilatory water flows into a container or past a flow probe. Respirometers designed for water collection usually incorporate a thin rubber membrane or mask fitted to the fish's head to separate inspired from expired water for measurements of ventilation volume (e.g., Van Dam 1938). The fish is situated in a two-chamber respirometer with the membrane sealing the barrier between the two chambers except for the fish's head (Figure 10.6). The water levels in both chambers are set to the same height by adjustment of surface drains so that hydrostatic pressure does not aid or inhibit gill ventilation. Water continuously flows into the anterior chamber (any excess flows out through the surface drain) and is moved from the anterior to the posterior chamber only by the fish's active ventilation. As the fish ventilates its gills, water equal to the ventilation volume is displaced from the posterior chamber via the posterior surface drain. This water is collected for a time as a measure of ventilation volume. Ventilatory movements of the buccal or opercular apparatus can be counted visually or detected with

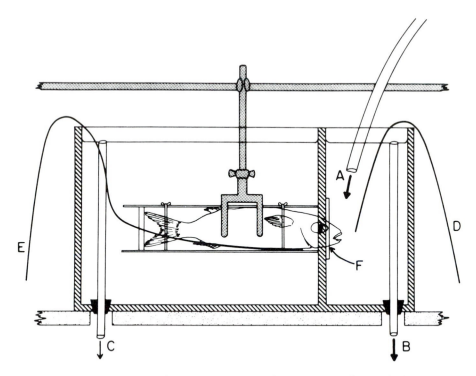

Figure 10.6   A Van Dam respirometer: (A) water inlet; (B) anterior drain from the water surface; (C) posterior drain from the surface; (D) cannula to draw samples of water that will be inspired; (E) cannula to draw samples of expired water; (F) latex membrane around the fish's head. Water is pumped from the anterior to the posterior chamber by the fish itself. (From Cech and Wohlschlag 1982.)

immersed electrodes wired to an appropriate amplifier and recorder (Spoor et al. 1971). Measured simultaneously over a specified time period, the frequency of ventilation (F_G, movements/min) and the volumetric rate of ventilation ($\dot{V}_G$, mL/min) allow calculation of ventilatory stroke volume (V_S, mL/movement: $V_S = \dot{V}_G/F_G$). Simultaneous measurements of oxygen concentrations in inspired and expired water, sampled near the mouth and gills (Figure 10.6), permit estimation of the oxygen consumption rate by the Fick equation:

$$\dot{M}o_2 = \dot{V}_G(Co_2(\text{I}) - Co_2(\text{E}));\tag{11}$$

$\dot{M}o_2 = O_2$ consumption rate (mg O_2/min);
$\dot{V}_G$ = volumetric ventilation rate (mL water/min);
$Co_2(\text{I}) = O_2$ concentration in inspired water (mg O_2/mL water); and
$Co_2(\text{E}) = O_2$ concentration in expired water (mg O_2/mL water).

Equation (3) can be used to calculate oxygen concentrations from partial pressures. Because these oxygen consumption rates are calculated from oxygen concentrations immediately adjacent to the mouth and gills, they may underestimate total respiration because cutaneous gas exchange can represent an important proportion of total oxygen uptake, even for scaled fishes (Kirsch and Nonnotte 1977).

Percentage utilization ($\%U$) of oxygen taken up at the gills can be calculated from the same data. Either oxygen tensions or concentrations can be used in this measure of the gills' oxygen extraction efficiency:

$$\%U = \frac{P_{O_2}(I) - P_{O_2}(E)}{P_{O_2}(I)} \times 100 = \frac{C_{O_2}(I) - C_{O_2}(E)}{C_{O_2}(I)} \times 100; \qquad (12)$$

$P_{O_2}(I)$ = O_2 tension of the inspired water (mm Hg), and
$P_{O_2}(E)$ = O_2 tension of the expired water (mm Hg).

Fish with smooth tapered heads and mouths fully anterior to the branchiostegal apparatus can usually be fitted to a two-chamber respirometer. Fish with a small terminal mouth, such as striped mullet (Cech and Wohlschlag 1982) and Sacramento blackfish (Campagna and Cech 1981), fit well through an oval opening in a flat rubber membrane such as a thin-gauge dental dam. In contrast, a fish whose mouth overlaps its branchiostegal apparatus, such as a rainbow trout, requires a more contoured membrane cut from the thumb and palm area of a surgical rubber glove. This membrane must be attached to the skin on the anesthetized fish's head with many sutures to provide a leak-proof seal (Davis and Cameron 1971). Other variations on the same theme are demanded by differences in fish anatomy. Hughes and Knights (1968) fitted ''rubber horns'' to the opercular apertures of the dragonet *Callionymus lyra* to collect and sample expired water. Burggren and Randall (1978) fitted a piece of condom to white sturgeons to measure gill ventilation. Lomholt and Johansen (1979) constructed custom-contoured masks to the heads of common carp, using molds cast from dead specimens of the same size, and measured $\dot{V}_G$ directly with electromagnetic flow probes fitted to openings in the mask.

An elegant determination of $\dot{V}_G$, F_G, $\%U$, and $\dot{M}_{O_2}$ for European flounder was described by Kerstens et al. (1979). The fish were allowed to bury themselves almost completely in a 5-cm-thick layer of sand within a seawater aquarium. Plastic funnels, one with a water sampling tube and the other with an electromagnetic flow probe, were placed over the upper operculum and mouth, respectively (Figure 10.7). Simultaneous measurements of P_{O_2} and $\dot{V}_G$ in inspired and expired water permitted calculation of $\dot{M}_{O_2}$ (equation 11) and $\%U$ (equation 12) for fish unencumbered by rubber masks or membrane.

The energetic cost of gill ventilation has been determined by a variety of respirometric methods. Steffensen and Lomholt (1983) summarized these and measured the cost of ventilation for sharksuckers attached to the inside of a tunnel respirometer by their dorsal cephalic suction disks. Oxygen consumption rates were determined at velocities below and above the transition from active ventilation to passive ram ventilation. Because the attached sharksucker did not consume O_2 for swimming, the relative costs of active and ram ventilation were measured directly. The use of anesthetics to prevent swimming for measurements of this sort (e.g., Schumann and Piiper 1966) is not recommended because anesthetics may depress overall metabolism.

Attempts also have been made to calculate gill water flows for fish in flow-through respirometers. This requires measurements of oxygen concentration in samples of inspired and expired water, and the Fick relationship (equation 11) shows the calculation to be theoretically possible. Because fish are free to move in the respirometer, the water-sampling cannulae must be attached to the fish.

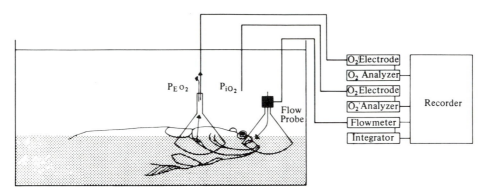

Figure 10.7   Schematic illustration of the experimental arrangement for measuring oxygen consumption by European flounder. The fish is mostly buried in sand. Ventilation flows are measured by a probe in the plastic funnel over the mouth. Oxygen tension in inspired water (P_iO_2 in the figure's notation) is measured in samples drawn from near the head. Oxygen tension in expired water (P_EO_2) is measured in samples drawn from the funnel over the gills. (From Kerstens et al. 1979.)

Opercular cannulation of rainbow trout, however, was ineffective in sampling true, "mixed" expired water (Davis and Watters 1970). Mitchell (1986) offered an explanation for this problem by showing (in work with channel catfish) that the dorsoventral position of the main exit flow from the gills changes at various ventilatory flows.

10.4   CONSIDERATIONS FOR THE FUTURE

Future respiratory measurements and bioenergetic determinations should significantly aid our understanding of fish function and, consequently, help us solve the challenges posed in managing wild and cultured fish populations. Recent advances in respirometer design (e.g., Steffensen et al. 1984) and Po_2 measurement (Hale 1983) point the way to improved laboratory measurements. Extrapolation of laboratory measurements to field or fish culture settings is always difficult, but advances in radiotelemetry (e.g., Rogers and Weatherley 1983) and the expected availability of smaller, lighter, less expensive, and more sophisticated electronic components allow us to anticipate better respiration data in the future. Less conventional metabolic measurements with techniques from biochemistry (e.g., high-performance liquid chromatography) and biophysics (e.g., nuclear magnetic resonance) are just starting to be developed. The resulting wide availability of techniques will improve our understanding of fish respiration and metabolism.

10.5   REFERENCES

APHA (American Public Health Association), American Water Works Association, and Water Pollution Control Federation. 1975. Standard methods for the examination of water and wastewater, 14th edition. APHA, Washington, D.C.

Bartholomew, G. A. 1977. Energy metabolism. Pages 57–110 *in* M. S. Gordon, editor. Animal physiology: principles and adaptations, 3rd edition. MacMillan, New York.

Beamish, F. W. H. 1978. Swimming capacity. Pages 101–187 *in* W. S. Hoar and D. J. Randall, editors. Fish physiology, volume 7. Academic Press, New York.

Beamish, F. W. H., and P. S. Mookherjii. 1964. Respiration of fishes with special emphasis on standard oxygen consumption. I. Influence of weight and temperature on respiration of goldfish, *Carassius auratus* L. Canadian Journal of Zoology 42:161–175.

Bell, W. H., and L. D. B. Terhune. 1970. Water tunnel design for fisheries research. Fisheries Research Board of Canada Technical Report 195.

Bicudo, J. E. P. W., and K. Johansen. 1979. Respiratory gas exchange in the airbreathing fish, *Synbranchus marmoratus*. Environmental Biology of Fishes 4:55–64

Blazka, P., M. Volf, and M. Cepela. 1960. A new type of respirometer for the determination of the metabolism of fish in an active state. Physiologia Bohemoslovenica 9:553–558.

Brett, J. R. 1962. Some considerations in the study of respiratory metabolism in fish, particularly salmon. Journal of the Fisheries Research Board of Canada 19:1025–1038.

Brett, J. R. 1964. The respiratory metabolism and swimming performance of young sockeye salmon. Journal of the Fisheries Research Board of Canada 21:1183–1226.

Brett, J. R. 1965. The relation of size to the rate of oxygen consumption and sustained swimming speeds of sockeye salmon (*Oncorhynchus nerka*). Journal of the Fisheries Research Board of Canada 22:1491–1501.

Brett, J. R. 1970a. Fish—the energy cost of living. Pages 37–52 *in* W. J. McNeill, editor. Marine aquiculture. Oregon State University Press, Corvallis.

Brett, J. R. 1970b. The metabolic demand for oxygen in fish, particularly salmonids, with a comparison with other vertebrates. Respiration Physiology 14:151–170.

Brett, J. R., and T. D. D. Groves. 1979. Physiological energetics. Pages 279–352 *in* W. S. Hoar, D. J. Randall, and J. R. Brett, editors Fish physiology, volume 8. Academic Press, New York.

Brooks, A. S., and G. L. Seegert. 1979. Low-level chlorine analysis by amperometric titration. Journal of the Water Pollution Control Federation 51:2636–2640.

Buckley, J. A. 1977. Heinz body hemolytic anemia in coho salmon (*Oncorhynchus kisutch*) exposed to chlorinated wastewater. Journal of the Fisheries Research Board of Canada 34:215–224.

Burggren, W. 1979. Bimodal gas exchange variation in environmental oxygen and carbon dioxide in air-breathing fish, *Trichogaster trichopterus*. Journal of Experimental Biology 82:197–213.

Burggren, W. W., and D. J. Randall. 1978. Oxygen uptake and transport during hypoxic exposure in the sturgeon *Acipenser transmontanus*. Respiration Physiology 34:171–183.

Cameron, J. N. 1971. A rapid method for determination of total carbon dioxide in small blood samples. Journal of Applied Physiology 31:632–634.

Cameron, J. N. 1976. Branchial ion uptake in Arctic grayling: resting values and effects of acid–base disturbance. Journal of Experimental Biology 64:711–725.

Cameron, J. N. 1986. Principles of physiological measurement. Academic Press, Orlando, Florida.

Campagna, C. G., and J. J. Cech, Jr. 1981. Gill ventilation and respiratory efficiency of Sacramento blackfish, *Orthodon microlepidotus* Ayres, in hypoxic environments. Journal of Fish Biology 19:581–591.

Castleberry, D. T., and J. J. Cech, Jr. 1986. Physiological responses of a native and an introduced desert fish to environmental stressors. Ecology 67:912–918.

Caulton, M. S. 1978. The effect of temperature and mass on routine metabolism in *Sarotherodon (Tilapia) mossambicus* (Peters). Journal of Fish Biology 13:195–201.

Cech, J. J., Jr., C. G. Campagna, and S. J. Mitchell. 1979. Respiratory responses of largemouth bass (*Micropterus salmoides*) to environmental changes in temperature and dissolved oxygen. Transactions of the American Fisheries Society 108:166–171.

Cech, J. J., Jr., M. J. Massingill, B. Vondracek, and A. L. Linden. 1985. Respiratory metabolism of mosquitofish, *Gambusia affinis:* effects of temperature, dissolved oxygen and sex difference. Environmental Biology of Fishes 13:297–307.

Cech, J. J., Jr., and D. E. Wohlschlag. 1982. Seasonal patterns of respiration, gill ventilation and hematological characteristics in the striped mullet, *Mugil cephalus* L. Bulletin of Marine Science 32:130–138.

Cherry, D. S., S. R. Larrick, J. D. Giattina, J. Cairns, Jr., and J. Van Hassel. 1982. Influence of temperature selection upon the chlorine avoidance of cold-water and warmwater fishes. Canadian Journal of Fisheries and Aquatic Sciences 39:162–173.

Dabrowski, K. R. 1986. A new type of metabolism chamber for the determination of active and postprandial metabolism of fish, and consideration of results for coregonid and salmon juveniles. Journal of Fish Biology 28:105–117.

Dalla Via, G. J. 1983. Bacterial growth and antibiotics in animal respirometry. Pages 202–218 in E. Gnaiger and H. Forstner, editors. Polarographic oxygen sensors. Springer-Verlag, Berlin.

Davis, J. C., and J. N. Cameron. 1971. Water flow and gas exchange at the gills of rainbow trout, Salmo gairdneri. Journal of Experimental Biology 54:1–18.

Davis, J. C., and K. Watters. 1970. Evaluation of opercular catheterization as a method for sampling water expired by fish. Journal of the Fisheries Research Board of Canada 27:1627–1635.

Dickson, I. W., and R. H. Kramer. 1971. Factors influencing scope for activity and active and standard metabolism of rainbow trout (Salmo gairdneri). Journal of the Fisheries Research Board of Canada 28:587–596.

Dixon, M. 1951. Manometric methods. Cambridge University Press, London.

Eckert, R., and D. Randall. 1983. Animal physiology, mechanisms and adaptations, 2nd edition. Freeman, San Francisco.

Forstner, H. 1983. An automated multiple-chamber intermittent-flow respirometer. Pages 111–126 in E. Gnaiger and H. Forstner, editors. Polarographic oxygen sensors, aquatic and physiological applications. Springer-Verlag, Berlin.

Fox, H. M., and C. A. Wingfield. 1938. A portable apparatus for the determination of oxygen dissolved in a small volume of water. Journal of Experimental Biology 15:437–445.

Freadman, M. A. 1981. Swimming energetics of striped bass (Morone saxatilis) and bluefish (Pomatomus saltatrix): hydrodynamic correlates of locomotion and gill ventilation. Journal of Experimental Biology 90:253–265.

Fry, F. E. J. 1957. The aquatic respiration of fish. Pages 1–63 in M. E. Brown, editor. The physiology of fishes, volume 1. Academic Press, New York.

Fry, F. E. J. 1971. The effect of environmental factors on the physiology of fish. Pages 1–98 in W. S. Hoar and D. J. Randall, editors. Fish physiology, volume 6. Academic Press, New York.

Gäde, F., and M. K. Grieshaber, 1989. Measurements of anaerobic metabolites. Pages 262–278 in G. R. Bridges and P. J. Butler, editors. Techniques in comparative respiratory physiology. Cambridge University Press, Cambridge, England.

Gambino, S. R. 1970. Oxygen, partial pressure (Po_2) electrode method. Pages 171–182 in R. P. MacDonald, editor. Standard methods of clinical chemistry, volume 6. Academic Press, New York.

Gehrke, P. C., L. E. Fidler, D. C. Mense, and D. J. Randall. 1990. A respirometer with controlled water quality and computerized data acquisition for experiments with swimming fish. Fish Physiology and Biochemistry 8:61–67.

Glass, N. R. 1969. Discussion of calculation of power function with special reference to respiratory metabolism in fish. Journal of the Fisheries Research Board of Canada 26:2643–2650.

Gnaiger, E. 1979. Direct calorimetry in ecological energetics: Long term monitoring of aquatic animals. Experientia Supplementum (Basel) 37:155–165.

Gnaiger, E. 1983. The twin-flow respirometer and simultaneous calorimetry. Pages 134–166 in E. Gnaiger and H. Forstner, editors. Polarographic oxygen sensors, aquatic and physiological applications. Springer-Verlag, Berlin.

Gnaiger, E., and H. Forstner. 1983. Polarographic oxygen sensors, aquatic and physiological applications. Springer-Verlag, Berlin.

Gnaiger, E., J. M. Schick, and J. Widdows. 1989. Metabolic microcalorimetry and respirometry of aquatic animals. Pages 113–135 in C. R. Bridges and P. J. Butler, editors. Techniques in comparative respiratory physiology. Cambridge University Press, Cambridge, England.

Golterman, H. L. 1983. The Winkler determination. Pages 346–351 *in* E. Gnaiger and H. Forstner, editors. Polarographic oxygen sensors, aquatic and physiological applications. Springer-Verlag, Berlin.

Gooding, R. M., W. H. Neill, and A. E. Dizon. 1981. Respiration rates and low-oxygen tolerance limits in skipjack tuna, *Katsuwonus pelamis*. U.S. National Marine Fisheries Service Fishery Bulletin 79:31–48.

Graham, J. B., and T. A. Baird. 1984. The transition to air breathing in fishes. III. Effects of body size and aquatic hypoxia on the aerial gas exchange of the swamp eel *Symbranchus marmoratus*. Journal of Experimental Biology 108:357–375.

Green, E. J., and D. E. Carritt. 1967. New tables for oxygen saturation of sea water. Journal of Marine Research 25:140–147.

Grothe, D. R., and J. W. Eaton. 1975. Chlorine-induced mortality in fish. Transactions of the American Fisheries Society 104:800–802.

Hale, J. M. 1983. Factors influencing the stability of polarographic oxygen sensors. Pages 3–17 *in* E. Gnaiger and H. Forstner, editors. Polarographic oxygen sensors, aquatic and physiological applications. Springer-Verlag, Berlin.

Halver, J. E. 1972. Fish nutrition. Academic Press, New York.

Heath, A. G. 1977. Toxicity of intermittent chlorination to freshwater fish: influence of temperature and chlorine form. Hydrobiologia 56:39–47.

Heath, A. G., D. T. Burton, and M. J. Smith. 1980. Anaerobic metabolism in fishes: environmental thresholds and time dependence. Revue Canadienne de Biologie 39:123–128.

Heath, A. G., and A. W. Pritchard. 1965. Effects of severe hypoxia on carbohydrate energy stores and metabolism in two species of freshwater fish. Physiological Zoology 38:325–334.

Herwig, N. 1982. Toxic chloramine induced intravascular hemolytic anemia in fish. Freshwater and Marine Aquarium 5(10):11–13.

Heusner, A. A. 1982a. Energy metabolism and body size. I. Is the 0.75 mass exponent of Kleiber's equation a statistical artifact? Respiration Physiology 48:1–12.

Heusner, A. A. 1982b. Energy metabolism and body size. II. Dimensional analysis and energetic non-similarity. Respiration Physiology 48:13–25.

Heusner, A. A. 1984. Biological similitude: statistical and functional relationships in comparative physiology. American Journal of Physiology 246(Regulatory Integrative Comparative Physiology 15):R839–845.

Heusner, A. A., J. P. Hurley, and R. Arbogast. 1982. Coulometric microrespirometry. American Journal of Physiology 243 (Regulatory Integrative Comparative Physiology 12):R185–192.

Heusner, A., C. Kayser, C. Marx, T. Stussi, and M. L. Harmelin. 1963. Relation entre le poids et la consommation d'oxygène. II. Etude intraspécifique chez le poisson. Compte Rendu des Séances de la Societe de Biologie Paris 157:654–657.

Hoar, W. S., and D. J. Randall. 1978. Fish physiology, volume 7. Academic Press, New York.

Hochachka, P. W. 1980. Living without oxygen: closed and open systems in hypoxia tolerance. Harvard University Press, Cambridge, Massachusetts.

Hose, J. E., R. J. Stoffel, and K. E. Zerba. 1983. Behavioural responses of selected marine fishes to chlorinated seawater. Marine Environmental Research 9:37–59.

Hughes, G. M. 1963. Comparative physiology of vertebrate respiration. Harvard University Press, Cambridge, Massachusetts.

Hughes, G. M., and B. Knights. 1968. The effect of loading the respiratory pumps on the oxygen consumption of *Callionymus lyra*. Journal of Experimental Biology 49:603–615.

Innes, A. J., and R. M. G. Wells. 1985. Respiration and oxygen transport functions of the blood from an intertidal fish, *Helcogramma medium* (Tripterygiidae) Environmental Biology of Fishes 14:213–226.

Kaufmann, R., H. Forstner, and W. Wieser. 1989. Respirometry—methods and approaches. Pages 51–76 *in* C. R. Bridges and P. J. Butler, editors. Techiques in comparative respiratory physiology. Cambridge University Press, Cambridge, England.

Kerstens, A., J. P. Lomholt, and K. Johansen. 1979. The ventilation, extraction and uptake of oxygen in undisturbed flounders *Platichthys flesus:* responses to hypoxia acclimation. Journal of Experimental Biology 83:169–179.

Kirsch, R., and G. Nonnotte. 1977. Cutaneous respiration in three freshwater teleosts. Respiration Physiology 29:339–354.

Lomholt, J. P., and K. Johansen. 1979. Hypoxia acclimation in carp—how it affects O_2-uptake, ventilation and O_2 extraction from water. Physiological Zoology 52:38–49.

MacLeod, J. C., and L. L. Smith, Jr. 1966. Effect of pulpwood fiber on oxygen consumption and swimming endurances of the fathead minnow, *Pimephales promelas*. Transactions of the American Fisheries Society 95:71–84.

Mitchell, S. J. 1986. Gas exchange and cardiovascular dynamics in channel catfish: effects of hypoxia and chronic ammonia exposure; with information on gill histological changes due to chloramine exposure. Master's thesis. University of California, Davis.

Mitchell, S. J., and J. J. Cech, Jr. 1983. Ammonia-caused gill damage in channel catfish *(Ictalurus punctatus):* confounding effects of residual chlorine. Canadian Journal of Fisheries and Aquatic Sciences 40:242–247.

Moore, R. H. 1970. Diurnal variations in the activity and metabolism of the Atlantic midshipman, *Porichthys porosissimus*. Contributions in Marine Science 15:33–43.

Nakano, T., and N. Tomlinson. 1967. Catecholamine and carbohydrate metabolism in rainbow trout *(Salmo gairdneri)* in relation to physical disturbance. Journal of the Fisheries Research Board of Canada 24:1701–1715.

Niimi, A. J. 1978. Lag adjustment between estimated and actual physiological responses conducted in flowthrough systems. Journal of the Fisheries Research Board of Canada 35:1265–1272.

Nikinmaa, M. 1982. Effects of adrenaline on red cell volume and concentration gradient of protons across the red cell membrane in the rainbow trout *Salmo gairdneri*. Molecular Physiology 2:287–297.

NRC (National Research Council). 1983. Nutrient requirements of warmwater fishes and shellfishes. National Academy Press, Washington, D.C.

Priede, I. G., and F. G. T. Holliday. 1980. The use of a new tilting tunnel respirometer to investigate some aspects of metabolism and swimming activity of the plaice *(Pleuronectes platessa* L.). Journal of Experimental Biology 85:295–309.

Priede, I. G., and P. Tytler. 1977. Heart rate as a measure of metabolic rate in teleost fishes; *Salmo gairdneri, Salmo trutta* and *Gadus morhua*. Journal of Fish Biology 10:231–242.

Randall, D. J. 1970. Gas exchange in fish. Pages 253–292 *in* W. S. Hoar and D. J. Randall, editors. Fish physiology, volume 4. Academic Press, New York.

Riggs, A. 1970. Properties of fish hemoglobins. Pages 209–252 *in* W. S. Hoar and D. J. Randall, editors. Fish physiology, volume 4. Academic Press, New York.

Roberts, J. L. 1975. Active branchial and ram gill ventilation in fishes. Biological Bulletin (Woods Hole) 148:85–105.

Roberts, R. J. 1978. Fish pathology. Bailliere Tindall, London.

Rogers, S. C., and A. H. Weatherley. 1983. The use of opercular muscle electromyograms as an indicator of the metabolic costs of fish activity in rainbow trout, *Salmo gairdneri* Richardson, as determined by radiotelemetry. Journal of Fish Biology 23:535–547.

Ross, L. G., and R. W. McKinney. 1988. Respiratory cycles in *Oreochromis niloticus* (L.), measured using a six-channel microcomputer-operated respirometer. Comparative Biochemistry and Physiology, A, Comparative Physiology 89:637–643.

Sacca, R., and W. Burggren. 1982. Oxygen uptake in air and water in the air-breathing reedfish *Calamoichthys calabaricus:* role of skin, gills and lungs. Journal of Experimental Biology 97:179–186.

Schmidt-Nielsen, K. 1979. Animal physiology: adaptation and environment. 2nd edition. Cambridge University Press, Cambridge, England.

Schumann, D., and J. Piiper. 1966. Der sauerstoffbedarf der atmung bei fischen nach messungen an der narkotisierten schleie *(Tinca tinca)*. Pfuegers Archiv fuer die Gesamte Physiologie des Menschen und der Tiere 288:15–26.

Seegert, G. L., and A. S. Brooks. 1978. Dechlorination of water for fish culture: comparison of activated carbon, sulfite reduction and photochemical methods. Journal of the Fisheries Research Board of Canada 35:88–92.

Severinghaus, J. W., and A. F. Bradley. 1971. Blood gas electrodes or what the instructions didn't say. Radiometer Company, Publication, ST59, Copenhagen.

Smit, H. 1965. Some experiments on the oxygen consumption of goldfish (*Carassius auratus* L.) in relation to swimming speed. Canadian Journal of Zoology 43:623–633.

Smit, H., J. M. Amelind-Koutstaal, J. Vijverberg, and J. J. C. Von Vaupel-Klein. 1971. Oxygen consumption and efficiency of swimming goldfish. Comparative Biochemistry and Physiology, A, Comparative Physiology 39:1–28.

Smith, K. L., Jr., and R. J. Baldwin. 1983. Deep-sea respirometry: in situ techniques. Pages 298–319 *in* E. Gnaiger and H. Forstner, editors. Polarographic oxygen sensors, aquatic and physiological applications. Springer-Verlag, Berlin.

Smith, L. S., and T. W. Newcomb. 1970. A modified version of the Blazka respirometer and exercise chamber for large fish. Journal of the Fisheries Research Board of Canada 27:1321–1324.

Smith, R. R. 1976. Studies on the energy metabolism of cultured fish. Doctoral dissertation. Cornell University, Ithaca, New York.

Snedecor, G. W., and W. G. Cochran. 1967. Statistical methods, 6th edition. Iowa State University Press, Ames.

Spoor, W. A., J. W. Neiheisel, and R. A. Drummond. 1971. An electrode chamber for recording respiratory and other movements of free-swimming animals. Transactions of the American Fisheries Society 100:22–28.

Spotte, S. 1979. Fish and invertebrate culture, water management in closed systems, 2nd edition. Wiley, New York.

Steffensen, J. F. 1989. Some errors in respirometry of aquatic breathers: how to avoid and correct for them. Fish Physiology and Biochemistry 6:49–59.

Steffensen, J. F., K. Johansen, and P. G. Bushnell. 1984. An automated swimming respirometer. Comparative Biochemistry and Physiology A, Comparative Physiology 79:437–440.

Steffensen, J. F., and J. P. Lomholt. 1983. Energetic cost of active branchial ventilation in the sharksucker, *Echeneis naucrates*. Journal of Experimental Biology 103:185–192.

Tytler, P. 1978. The influence of swimming performance on the metabolic rate of gadoid fish. Pages 83–92 *in* D. S. McLusky and A. J. Berry, editors. Physiology and behaviour of marine organisms. Pergamon, New York.

Umbriet, W. W., R. H. Burns, and J. F. Stauffer. 1972. Manometric and biochemical techniques. Burgess, Minneapolis, Minnesota.

Van Dam, L. 1938. On the utilization of oxygen and regulation of breathing in some aquatic animals. Doctoral dissertation. University of Groningen, Groningen, Netherlands.

Van den Thillart, G., D. Randall, and L. Hoa-Ren. 1983. CO_2 and H^+ excretion by swimming coho salmon, *Oncorhynchus kisutch*. Journal of Experimental Biology 107:169–180.

Van Waversveld, J., A. D. F. Addink, and G. Van den Thillart. 1989a. Simultaneous direct and indirect calorimetry on normoxic and anoxic goldfish. Journal of Experimental Biology 142:325–335.

Van Waversveld, J., A. D. F. Addink, and G. Van den Thillart. 1989b. The anaerobic energy metabolism of goldfish determined by simultaneous direct and indirect calorimetry during anoxia and hypoxia. Journal of Comparative Physiology, B, Biochemical, Systemic, and Environmental Physiology 159:263–268.

Van Waversveld, J., A. D. F. Addink, G. Van den Thillart, and H. Smit. 1989c. Heat production of fish: a literature review. Comparative Biochemistry and Physiology, A, Comparative Physiology 92:159–162.

Ware, D. M. 1982. Power and evolutionary fitness of teleosts. Canadian Journal of Fisheries and Aquatic Sciences 39:3–13.

Weatherley, A. H., S. C. Rogers, D. G. Pincook, and J. R. Patch. 1982. Oxygen consumption of active rainbow trout, *Salmo gairdneri* Richardson, derived from electromyograms obtained by telemetry. Journal of Fish Biology 20:479–489.

Webb, P. W. 1971. The swimming energetics of trout. II. Oxygen consumption and swimming efficiency. Journal of Experimental Biology 55:521–540.

Weiss, R. F. 1970. The solubility of nitrogen, oxygen and argon in water and seawater. Deep-Sea Research 17:721–735.

Winberg, G. G. 1956. Rate of metabolism and food requirements of fishes. Fisheries Research Board of Canada, Translation Series 194, Ottawa.

Winkler, L. W. 1888. The determination of dissolved oxygen in water. Berichte der Deutschen Chemischen Gesellschaft 21:2843.

Wohlschlag, D. E. 1964. Respiratory metabolism and ecological characteristics of some fishes in McMurdo Sound, Antarctica. Antarctic Research Series 1:33–62.

Wohlschlag, D. E., and J. M. Wakeman. 1978. Salinity stresses, metabolic responses and distribution of the coastal spotted seatrout, *Cynoscion nebulosus*. Contributions in Marine Science 21:171–185.

Wood, C. M., and G. Shelton, 1980. Cardiovascular dynamics and adrenergic responses of the rainbow trout *in vivo*. Journal of Experimental Biology 87:247–270.

Wuhrmann, K., and H. Woker. 1948. Experimentelle untersuchungen uber die ammoniak und blausaurevergiftung. Schweizerische Zeitschrift für Hydrologie 11:210–244.

Zeitoun, I. H. 1977. The effect of chlorine toxicity on certain blood parameters of adult rainbow trout *(Salmo gairdneri)*. Environmental Biology of Fishes 1:189–195.

Chapter 11

Growth

GREG P. BUSACKER, IRA R. ADELMAN, AND
EDWARD M. GOOLISH

11.1 PERSPECTIVES OF GROWTH

Growth may be viewed as an ongoing process or as something that has occurred in the past history of animals. The concept of growth implies many things and is too frequently presented in a misleading way. This imprecision can lead to misinterpretation of observations or experimental results.

Growth may be positive or negative, temporary or long-lasting. It may occur at all levels of biological organization: cells, tissues, organs, whole organisms, populations, communities. Depending on the level of organization, growth can be measured in terms of number, linear dimension, weight, volume, energy content, or the amount of a specific component such as protein. Furthermore, growth can be measured as an incremental change or as a rate of change. Finally, a variety of indices have been developed, such as glycine uptake by scales or RNA:DNA ratios, that are related to growth but in themselves are not direct measurements of growth. Thus, a precise universal definition of growth is precluded by the variety of processes that can be considered as growth and the variety of measurements that can be applied. However, it is imperative that growth be clearly defined within the context of specific investigations and that the method of measurement be appropriate for that definition.

For the purposes of this chapter, growth is defined as any change in size or amount of body material, regardless of whether that change is positive or negative, temporary or long-lasting. In the following sections, we examine techniques that are used in the study of growth and provide guidance to the appropriate uses of those methods.

11.2 NUMERICAL AND MATHEMATICAL EXPRESSIONS OF GROWTH

Numerical expressions of whole-body growth of fish may be based on absolute changes in length or weight (absolute growth) or changes in length or weight relative to the size of the fish being considered (relative growth). Measurements of growth expressed in terms of some interval of time (day, month, year) constitute a growth rate (Ricker 1979). For example, if t_1 is the time at the beginning of an interval and t_2 the time at the end, and if Y_1 and Y_2 are the respective fish sizes at those times,

$$\text{absolute growth} = Y_2 - Y_1;$$

$$\text{absolute growth rate} = (Y_2 - Y_1)/(t_2 - t_1);$$

relative growth $= (Y_2 - Y_1)/Y_1$; and

relative growth rate $= (Y_2 - Y_1)/[Y_1(t_2 - t_1)]$.

Relative growth and relative growth rate frequently are multiplied by 100 and expressed as percentages. These calculations imply a linear growth rate over the time interval of interest.

When growth rate is exponential, as it usually is over intervals of a year or less, growth should be expressed as an instantaneous rate. The instantaneous growth rate (G) is defined as the difference between the natural logarithms of successive sizes over a unit of time. This measurement has also been called the specific, intrinsic, exponential, or logarithmic growth rate. The working formula is

$$G = (\log_e Y_2 - \log_e Y_1)/(t_2 - t_1).$$

Instantaneous growth rate also is frequently multiplied by 100 and expressed as a percentage; then, it is more commonly called the specific growth rate.

Ricker (1975, 1979) provided detailed descriptions of these numerical expressions.

11.3   QUANTIFICATION OF CHANGES IN SIZE

11.3.1   Length

Measurements of body length give direct evidence for growth or lack of growth. Increases in length generally are retained, though a fish might shrink somewhat during starvation. Body length can be measured in many ways, although total length, fork length, and standard length are used most commonly for fish. Methods were described in depth by Ricker (1979), Anderson and Gutreuter (1983), and Weatherly and Gill (1986). Length can be easily and inexpensively measured in the field or laboratory, on live or preserved fish. Changes in length commonly occur with preservation but these changes are quantifiable and cease with time (Anderson and Gutreuter 1983).

11.3.2   Weight

Change in weight (mass) is probably the most commonly used assessment of whole-body growth of fish as well as of suborganismal growth. Weight also is the traditional measure for estimates of production—the elaboration of a group's or population's biomass—which are of interest to ecologists and resource managers.

Weight is relatively easy to measure and whole animals can be weighed without killing them. Scales and balances for weighing quantities in excess of 1 g generally are neither sophisticated nor expensive. Electronic balances that can weigh very small quantities or that can be used in an unsteady environment such as on a boat are costly by comparison.

Frequently, length and weight of a fish are both measured. One may be calculated from the other, though with statistical error, if the population's length–weight relationship is known. With small numbers of fish, it is more precise to measure weight as well as length to estimate growth rates. With large numbers of fish, it may be as accurate to measure only length and to convert it to weight. The length–weight relationship is generally expressed by the equation

$$W = aL^n;$$

W = weight, L = length, a is a constant, and n is an exponent. Values of n are often near 3.0 and generally fall between 2.5 and 3.5. Values outside of this range are generally erroneous (Lagler 1956; Carlander 1969, 1977; Weatherly 1972; Ricker 1975, 1979; Pauly 1984). Interspecific or interstock comparisons should not be based on values of a unless values of n are the same for the groups under consideration (Pauly 1984). Also, weights determined by calculation are generalized and cannot be used for determinations of condition factor or for intraspecific comparisons (Lagler 1956; Weatherly 1972; Ricker 1975; Pauly 1984).

As a fish grows, changes in weight are relatively greater than changes in length, due to the approximately cubic relationship between fish length and weight. Thus, measurement of change in weight may provide greater precision over short periods of time.

In contrast to a change in length, a change in weight may be a very transient indicator of growth, so weight may not be a suitable measure in some growth studies. This is particularly true if wet weight is measured. A change in water content generally is not considered to be growth, but if a fish gains water because its water balance mechanisms fail, its weight will increase even though it has not added new body tissue. Weight can also increase due to change in body lipids, which may or may not be considered as growth. Weight varies with development of the gonads and with fullness of the stomach. If the purpose of the study allows, these problems can be surmounted by measuring dry weight or changes in mass of specific body components such as protein, or by eliminating the weight of gonads or stomach contents from the measurement.

11.3.2.1 Wet Weight

The simplest way to assess changes in weight is to periodically weigh the animals of interest; the individuals may represent a sample from a large population. If variations in individual weights are not of interest, the sampled fish can be weighed en masse and an average individual weight can be computed. These values are compared with weights determined previously to calculate growth or growth rates. Obvious sources of error in measurements of wet weight include retention of excess water on the surface or in the buccal cavity of live fish and dehydration of dead fish. Balances of appropriate sensitivity should be used. Anesthesia can quiet agitated fish during weighing, but its use may not be desirable or practical (see Chapter 8). Live fish may be less stressed if they are weighed in water; the weight of the water and container (tare) are subtracted from the total. Wet weights of tissue and organ samples also may be determined, but dehydration may be a problem if samples are stored in areas of low relative humidity and if they are not weighed quickly.

11.3.2.2 Dry Weight

When a whole fish or tissue sample is dried under reasonably benign conditions, it reaches an asymptotic or "constant" weight: the dry weight. The procedure removes internal water, which is a transient material (Snell and Biffen 1964; Dowgiallo 1975), and eliminates the errors due to excess external water or dehydration that plague wet-weight determinations. In most cases, dry weights can be accepted if changes in weight between successive weighings are less than 0.1% (Snell and Biffen 1964). A temperature of 60°C for 24 h is usually adequate for samples of small size (0.5 g or less), but larger quantities may require higher temperatures or longer time periods. Bound water can be eliminated at 100–110°C, but volatile oils and lipids may also be lost. Oxidation reactions may either add weight to the sample or add to the apparent loss of volatile materials; these problems can be avoided if samples are dried to a constant weight at reduced pressure in a vacuum oven. At higher temperatures, large pieces of fresh material should be dried slowly at first, because rapid heating may burst steam pockets and cause loss of material. Freeze drying removes most of the water from tissue samples, but it is a slow process requiring special equipment, and up to 5% of the water is very difficult to remove (Crisp 1971). Dry weight is often expressed as a percentage of wet weight.

Tared weighing containers for dry weight determinations should be made of aluminum foil, platinum, ceramics, glass, or heat-resistant plastic that will not react with the samples (Snell and Biffen 1964). Most plastics will not tolerate 110°C without deforming.

11.3.2.3   Ash Weight

Ash weight, which may be the measurement least influenced by transient growth, is the weight of mineral residues left after organic materials have been burned away. Combustion temperatures are required for this measurement, and suitable sample containers are made of platinum, high-silica glass (Vycor, Pyrex, or equivalent), and some ceramics (Snell and Biffen 1964). Samples and containers are placed in a muffle furnace at 450–500°C for 30 min for samples of 0.1 g or less and up to 24 h or longer for larger quantities. Temperatures above 550°C may cause calcium carbonate to decompose and should be avoided (Dowgiallo 1975). Ash weight is determined by subtracting the tare weight. The difference between the dry weight and the ash weight is the amount of organic material lost to ignition, often called ash-free dry weight. Ash weight is often expressed as a percentage of dry weight or wet weight.

11.3.3   Proximate Analysis

Proximate analysis, the determination of categories of compounds in a mixture, is done when changes in absolute or relative amounts of body materials are of interest in defining the growth process. Information about the probable growth rate of an individual fish can be obtained from the composition of muscle or of the entire animal. Fish experiencing low energy intake have to use energy stored in the body tissue as lipid and protein, much of which is mobilized from the muscle tissue (Love 1980). After a time, the concentration of lipid and protein in the muscle tissue will decrease, as will the energy content (joules per gram, J/g). As these substances are removed from the tissues, much of their volume will be replaced by water. As a result, as shown by controlled laboratory studies, percent water content is inversely correlated with growth rate; conversely, the protein, lipid, and caloric contents of fish are strongly, and positively, correlated with growth rate (Brett et al. 1969; Elliot 1976). In natural populations of fish, tissue composition reflects the nutritional state of the individual (Parker and Vanstone 1966; Adams et al. 1982), and therefore is an indirect index of growth rate.

Materials most commonly measured under the heading of proximate analysis are (1) carbohydrates such as glucose, glycogen, and mucopolysaccharides; (2) proteins of molecular weights greater than 10,000; and (3) lipids. Often the material of interest must be physically separated from the others or broken down into its components to prevent analytical interferences (Snell and Biffen 1964; Dowgiallo 1975). For example, high levels of lipid interfere with the biuret protein reaction and usually must be extracted before the protein can be analyzed (Dowgiallo 1975).

Tissue for proximate analysis should, if possible, be removed from freshly killed animals and, if necessary, preserved for later analysis. However, preservation may present special problems. Samples should be processed for storage so they do not degrade and decompose. In the field situation, samples can be rapidly frozen in dry ice or liquid nitrogen, and stored for short periods therein. For long-term storage, samples should be kept in freezers capable of maintaining temperatures at $-80°C$. Freezers with automatic defrosting cycles are unsuitable for general long-term storage because their daily temperature variations cause water to translocate out of samples. At the normal temperature of common household freezers, $-20°C$, subcellular components may not freeze completely, allowing some localized biochemical reactions to continue. Cross-contamination can be prevented by wrapping samples individually. Even under proper storage conditions, tissues have limited shelf lives. Storage techniques can be examined by analyzing some samples at once, storing the rest by the chosen method, and removing some samples for analysis at regular intervals.

11.3.3.1 Protein Analysis

Change in protein content is considered a measure of sustainable growth, although body protein is readily used as a source of energy during starvation (Brett and Groves 1979). Tissue samples homogenized for protein analysis can be treated with trichloroacetic acid to quantitatively precipitate the protein and separate it from the soluble materials (Mendel and Hoogland 1950). The precipitates can then be subjected to short-term alkali digestion to denature the protein structure; this ensures that the amino acids important for colorimetric analysis are not masked by quaternary molecular structure (Peterson 1979).

There are three general colorimetric methods for protein analysis: Kjeldahl nitrogen method (Snell and Biffen 1964; Dowgiallo 1975), biuret reaction method (Gornall et al. 1949; Richterich 1969), and Lowry or Folin phenol method (Lowry et al. 1951; Richterich 1969; Peterson 1977, 1979). The Kjeldahl nitrogen method measures total protein nitrogen if protein has been isolated from other nitrogenous compounds, or total nitrogen if there has been no such separation. (Nitrogen is an integral part of the molecular structure of amino acids, and some amino acids have more than one nitrogen atom. Only amino acid nitrogen will be measured by the Kjeldahl process if proteins are isolated from other cellular and tissue constituents.) The biuret reaction attaches a color-developing substance to the free amino groups on polypeptide chains. The Lowry reaction depends upon the presence of the amino acids tyrosine and tryptophan for color development. None of these methods give results that are strictly proportional to the total quantity of amino acids because the proportion of amino acids that produce color varies from protein to protein. It is convenient to standardize the colorimetric method being used by doing a single Kjeldahl nitrogen determination on a tissue (Dowgiallo 1975) so that others using the biuret or Lowry reaction on the same tissue can make more accurate comparisons.

Macro- or microprocedures are available for conducting Kjeldahl nitrogen analyses (Snell and Biffen 1964; Jacobs 1965). Samples are digested in sulfuric acid to convert organic nitrogen to ammonia, which is then held as ammonium sulfate. The solution is refluxed or distilled, and the acid-neutralized concentrations of ammonia are measured. The micromethod allows samples with as little as 2 mg total nitrogen in a 200-mg sample to be analyzed (Snell and Biffen 1964). For the macromethod, samples should contain 30–40 mg of nitrogen.

The Lowry reaction is more sensitive to false positive color interferences from several substances than is the biuret reaction. Bensadoun and Weinstein (1976), Cookson (1978), and Peterson (1979) listed interfering materials as well as methods for coping with them. Lipid extraction is generally not required if tissues have low lipid content, although it may be required for the biuret reaction. The Lowry reaction is more sensitive than the biuret method, giving good results with protein concentrations as low as 5–25 μg/mL; the biuret reaction is typically effective for concentrations of 0.5–3 mg/mL. Both techniques have been adapted for automated chemical analysis (Huemer and Lee 1970; Honn and Chavin 1975).

11.3.3.2 Lipids

Lipids may be very transient body materials, but they are an important source of potential chemical energy, and their presence or absence reflects the physiological capacity of fish. Lipids are readily separated from proteins, carbohydrates, and other cellular compounds by their solubility in nonpolar solvents such as ethyl ether, chloroform, methanol, and methylene chloride (Entenman 1957a). Total lipid content may be determined gravimetrically following extraction and evaporation of the solvent (Dowgiallo 1975). "Total lipids" also have been estimated by colorimetric procedures (Holland and Gabbott 1971; Barnes and Blackstock 1973). Lipid classes such as triglycerides and long-chain fatty acids can be assayed by enzymatic or colorimetric methods (Entenman 1957b; Holman 1957) and kits for these types of analysis are commercially available (e.g., Sigma kits 336 and 405; Sigma Chemical Co., St. Louis, Missouri). Fatty acids may be determined specifically by chromatography or generally by oxidative and other chemical procedures (Snell and Biffen 1964). In addition, lipid class analysis can be accomplished relatively easily with a system involving thin-layer chromatography and a flame ionization detector (Ackman 1980; Fraser et al. 1985). Proper sample storage is important to avoid decomposition and oxidation. Samples should not be dried with heat and are better stored frozen without exposure to oxygen.

11.3.3.3 Carbohydrates

Quantities of carbohydrates in fish are generally low and not typically analyzed in growth studies. Carbohydrate stores, particularly as liver and muscle glycogen, are important sources of energy for intense activity by fish, and may be of interest in certain investigations.

Most reactions for determining carbohydrates are colorimetric (Dische 1955; Ashwell 1957). Typical analytical procedures for carbohydrates first require homogenization of tissues, then fractionation of the slurry to simple hexoses and pentoses, glycoproteins, glycogen, or total sugars. Hexoses and pentoses are soluble in alcohol and trichloroacetic acid. Glycogen can be precipitated with 80% alcohol, dried, and then reacted with phenol and concentrated H_2SO_4 (Montgomery 1957). Total sugars can be separated from protein by alkali digestion followed by acid hydrolysis and final testing for hexoses and pentoses (Dubois et al. 1956). Hexoses react with anthrone and H_2SO_4, pentoses react with orcinol–$FeCl_3$ (Dowgiallo 1975). Glucose may be determined by a simple enzyme-coupled colorimetric reaction (Blaedel and Uhl 1975) available in kits (e.g., Sigma kit 510). Glycogen can be estimated by the same procedure if the homogenate is first incubated with amyloglycosidase to convert glycogen to free glucose (Carr and Neff 1984; Gould et al. 1985). Glycoproteins alone are difficult to separate because of their diverse makeup and solubilities, which generally do not allow quantitative separation by precipitation techniques. They can be separated by column chromatography (Wold and Selset 1977; Uskova et al. 1981).

11.3.4 Calorimetric Analysis of Energy Content

Calorimetry measures the heat given off by various processes such as chemical reactions. It is a general analytical tool that may be used to determine energy contents of organic materials or the energy used for metabolism of living organisms. The heat given off by the combustion of samples is related to the total available energy in the sample. For biological samples, this heat is the theoretical energy available for work if the sample were to be completely metabolized and no losses occurred during the transformations. Calorimetry is important for bioenergetic determinations because it defines growth in terms of energy equivalents and allows partitioning of energy intake into anabolic and catabolic processes. Many bioenergetic models use energetic units of measurement because many dissimilar materials (protein, lipids, carbohydrates) and processes (ingestion, assimilation, growth, catabolism, etc.) can be described in terms of units of energy required or contained (Warren and Davis 1967). See Chapter 12 for more details on bioenergetics.

The energy contents of whole fish or their food, organs, and tissues can be measured by direct combustion in a calorimeter. In some cases, interference during combustion requires that sample components be separated before calorimetry. For example, large amounts of inorganic bone may prevent complete combustion of a sample in the short time necessary for accurate measurements. However, most of the problems of calorimetry are not in the actual measurements but making the appropriate decisions about what the resulting data actually mean (Brown 1969; Beezer 1980). In part this is because tissues are complex mixtures of carbohydrates, lipids, and proteins and the ratios of these constituents can vary dramatically according to the general physiological condition of the fish. Also, there is not necessarily a direct correspondence between energy content and physiological fitness. Therefore, caution must be exercised when judgments about an animal's physiological condition are based upon the results of calorimetry.

Metabolic energy of living organisms can be measured by direct calorimetry—whereby the heat produced by organisms is measured—or by indirect methods (Brown 1969; Prus 1975; Beezer 1980). Live fish are generally unsuitable for direct calorimetry because they produce heat at a low rate and the heat capacity of their aquatic medium is high (Brett and Groves 1979). Indirect calorimetry, which involves measurement of respiratory gas production, is typically used to determine fish metabolism (Chapter 10). Energetic equivalents for oxygen uptake and carbon dioxide production by fish are based on the heat of combustion of different energy substrates such as proteins, lipids, or carbohydrates. These equivalents have been measured by direct calorimetry and values are available in the literature (Brett and Groves 1979; Nestle 1981). Biological data from calorimeters traditionally have been expressed as total kilocalories (kcal) per unit wet weight, dry weight, or ash-free dry weight. The conversion factor for calories to joules (J), the current international standard unit of energy, is 1 cal = 4.2 J (1 kcal = 4.2 kJ). Kilocalories are also equivalent to Calories (Cal).

11.4 PHYSIOLOGICAL AND BIOCHEMICAL INDICES OF GROWTH

The previously discussed methods of measuring growth require changes in a fish's size, amount of material, or energy content over time. Several methods have been developed to estimate the growth rate of a fish at the time it is sampled. These methods are largely indirect measurements of growth rate because they do not measure a change in size. They measure either a rate at which body tissue is elaborated, as is the case with protein synthesis, or something that is correlated with the rate of growth of the fish, such as the RNA:DNA ratio, glycine uptake by scales, or nutritional status. The value of some of these methods is in their ability to measure changes in growth rate over very short periods of time, particularly growth in response to changing environmental conditions. Other indices reflect the growth rate of the fish during preceding weeks or months.

Aside from the influence of growth rate, all the indices can be affected by internal and environmental variables such as species, sex, age, season, acclimation temperature, and reproductive state. Their value is greatest in studies for which the experimental design and sampling regime provide some control over these extraneous sources of variability.

11.4.1 Protein Synthesis

Because protein synthesis plays a major role in the growth of fish (Haschemeyer and Smith 1979; Haschemeyer et al. 1979), the rate of protein synthesis should be correlated with whole-body growth rate. Typical procedures for measuring protein synthesis involve administering a radioactive amino acid to the fish and subsequently analyzing the amount of radioactivity incorporated into proteins. In vivo methods include injection or infusion of the amino acid into the fish and subsequent analysis of its incorporation into protein, usually in muscle tissue if the study concerns growth rate (Haschemeyer and Smith 1979; Fauconneau et al. 1981; Smith 1981; Pocrnjic et al 1983). In vitro determinations of protein synthesis have measured amino acid incorporation into mitochondria of isolated liver cells and slices (Kent and Prosser 1980), into isolated hepatocytes (Saez et al. 1982), and into ribosomes isolated from muscle tissue (Lied et al. 1982).

The theoretical and methodological pitfalls in measuring protein synthesis are numerous and failure to follow appropriate procedures easily produces erroneous results (Haschemeyer 1973, 1976). The methodology is complex, time consuming, and not easily applied to large numbers of animals or tissue samples.

11.4.2 Glycine Uptake by Fish Scales

Based on traditional practices of measuring distances between annuli on fish scales to determine annual growth rates and the fundamental assumption that growth rate of the scale is proportional to growth rate of the fish, Ottaway and Simkiss (1977) proposed that the rate at which a fish scale takes up glycine in vitro would provide a relative index of the rate at which protein is synthesized in the scale. An assumption upon which the method is based is that living cells associated with scale formation remain viable after they are detached with the scale from the fish; thus, the rate of uptake of the amino acid reflects the growth rate of the fish.

The methodology involves removing one or more scales from a fish, incubating the scales for 2 h in physiological saline containing ^{14}C-glycine (glycine containing an atom of radioactive carbon-14), rinsing the scales in saline, drying and weighing the scales, then counting the radioactivity taken up by the scales after the scale is digested in a tissue solubilizer. Busacker and Adelman (1987) provided detailed methods. Radioactivity is usually expressed in terms of scale surface area.

Highly significant correlation coefficients between glycine uptake by scales and growth rate of individual fish have been found for the sea bass *Dicentrarchus labrax* (Ottaway and Simkiss 1979), for white suckers, yellow perch, bluegills, and common carp (Adelman 1980; Goolish and Adelman 1983a), and for largemouth bass (Smagula and Adelman 1982).

As with the more direct analysis of protein synthetic rate, glycine uptake by scales responds in the expected manner to growth-influencing factors such as temperature, meal size, low dissolved oxygen, and handling stress (see review by Adelman 1987). The methodology is nonsacrificial and is relatively easy to perform, and large sample sizes can be handled quickly. Acclimation temperature of the fish and temperature of the scale incubation medium influence glycine uptake, and these factors must be considered during the analysis and interpretation of results (Goolish and Adelman 1983b).

11.4.3 Nucleic Acids

The ratio of RNA (ribonucleic acid) to DNA (deoxyribonucleic acid) content of various tissues has been used as a measure of growth rate. Because DNA content is relatively constant within a cell and RNA content varies with rate of protein synthesis, the ratio of RNA to DNA provides an index of protein synthetic activity and growth (Bulow 1987). In addition to the RNA:DNA ratio, RNA content and concentration have also been used in growth studies. Both DNA content and DNA concentration in tissue samples have been used to indicate cell number and thus may be used to indicate growth in terms of cell number. The protein:DNA ratio has been used as a relative index of cell mass and thus may be used to indicate growth in cell size (Bulow 1987).

Of the various tissues that might be used for determining RNA:DNA ratios, white muscle is the best indicator of somatic growth (Bulow 1987). Red muscle is more active metabolically (Mustafa 1977b) and liver metabolic activities often are not directly related to growth (Emmersen and Emmersen 1976; Buckley et al. 1985). In larval fish it is possible to use the whole-body RNA:DNA ratio (Barron and Adelman 1984; Buckley 1984). Size, stage of maturation, temperature acclimation of the fish, contaminants, and species all affect the RNA:DNA ratio

(Mustafa 1977a; Lone and Ince 1983; Rosenlund et al. 1983; Barron and Adelman 1984; Buckley 1984; Goolish et al. 1984).

At present there is no standard technique for extraction and quantification of fish nucleic acids. Buckley and Bulow (1987) briefly reviewed analytical techniques for nucleic acids and made recommendations for analysis of larval, juvenile, and adult fish tissues. Typically, two different assays must be run following nucleic acid extraction from the tissue sample. The RNA can be quantified by the orcinol method of Schneider (1957) and DNA by the diphenylamine method (Burton 1956). The Schmidt–Thannhauser (1945) technique, as modified by Munro and Fleck (1966), has been used for both RNA and DNA in fish tissue (Buckley 1979; Barron and Adelman 1984). Fluorometric methods can offer greater sensitivity and ease of use (Buckley 1980; Rosenlund et al. 1983), but fluorometric spectrophotometers presently are not common laboratory instruments. Other methods are based upon detection of nucleic acids by ultraviolet and visible light spectrophotometers (Schmidt and Thannhauser 1945; Burton 1956; Schneider 1957; Bulow 1971; Buckley 1979).

11.4.4 Liver–Somatic Index

Fish store energy in muscle tissue, but they also accumulate energy in the liver during periods of high energy intake; much of this stored energy is in the form of glycogen. Therefore, the relative size of the liver should be correlated with the nutritional state of the fish and with the growth rate. This indirect measure of growth rate is referred to as the liver–somatic index (LSI) and is expressed as

$$LSI = (liver\ weight/body\ weight) \times 100.$$

This index is often used in studies of the seasonal and yearly changes in growth of natural populations of fish (Bulow et al. 1978; Adams and McLean 1985).

11.4.5 Condition Factor

During periods when fish have high energy intake, the growth of tissues and the storage of energy in muscle and liver can cause an individual to have a greater-than-usual weight at a particular length. This excess is usually revealed by the coefficient of condition (K) or by Fulton's condition factor (Bagenal and Tesch 1978; also see the exponent n in the length–weight equation, Section 11.3.2) and is calculated as

$$K = weight/(length)^3.$$

The condition factor reflects the nutritional state or "well-being" of an individual fish, and, by the same reasoning as in Section 11.4.4, is sometimes interpreted as an index of growth rate.

11.5 ESTIMATION OF GROWTH IN NATURAL POPULATIONS

Methods for estimating growth of fish in natural populations fall into three general categories: length-frequency analysis of fish in identifiable cohorts (age-groups) that are followed through time; back-calculation of previous fish lengths

Table 11.1 Key for selection of options for methods of estimating growth of fish in natural populations.

1. Sample representative of the population... 2
   Not representative.. 5

2. Fish can be aged accurately 3
   Cannot be aged accurately... 4

3. Options
   A. Identify cohorts
      a. Determine numbers at age in sample
      b. Examine lengths at current age
      c. Growth rates
   B. Length-frequency analysis to confirm ages and to apportion length-classes to ages
   C. Back-calculations
      a. Identify cohorts at previous ages
      b. Estimate size at previous age
      c. Growth rates
   D. Mathematical models
      a. Growth rate
      b. Estimate of maximum size

4. Options
   A. Validate ages (may then be possible to go to choice 3)
      a. Mark and recapture
   B. Assign cohorts
      a. Length-frequency analysis to assign ages and to apportion length-classes to assigned ages
      b. Determine numbers at assigned ages in sample
      c. Examine lengths at assigned ages
      d. Calculate growth, assuming increments represent average growth
   C. Mathematical models
      a. Growth rate
      b. Estimate of maximum size

5. Sampling bias can be corrected 2
   Bias cannot be corrected 6

6. Recognize bias effect on final analysis 2
   Redesign study or abandon analysis

by reference to permanent growth records in hard body parts; and recapture of marked individuals whose size at a previous time is known. The success of all these methods depends strongly on proper sampling procedures.

11.5.1 Collection of Data

The method for estimating growth of wild fish in a natural population should be chosen after a consideration of possible biases in the sample. If the sample is not representative of the population, sampling biases could lead to erroneous conclusions about the true nature of the population. Technical problems, such as the ability to accurately identify cohorts, also must be considered. A decision key for considerations of this type is presented in Table 11.1.

Accurate and complete records of sampling procedures and data collection will help to eliminate subsequent uncertainties about the data base. Generalized archival requirements are given below; see Lagler (1956) for examples of data sheets. Items chosen from the list will vary with the intent of the study (Bagenal and Tesch 1978).

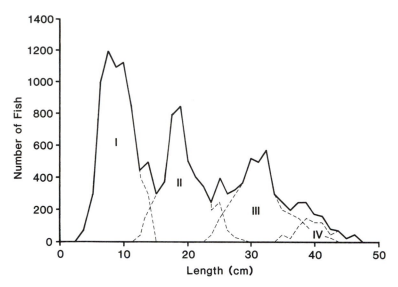

Figure 11.1 Frequency distribution of a hypothetical fish population showing numbers of fish versus fish length. The dashed lines indicate numbers at each age where there is overlap between age-classes. Age-classes are designated by Roman numerals.

(1) Record field conditions, date, place, and method of capture.
(2) Record—for each individual—length and weight, sex, gonadal maturity, and obvious deformities or pathological conditions.
(3) Collect scales or bony structures to be used for aging and store them in labeled coin envelopes.
(4) Complete laboratory measurements for each individual if fish are preserved.
(5) Begin numerical analysis using appropriate procedures.

11.5.2 Cohort Identification

Cohorts may be identified by grouping members of common length-classes, then using the modal lengths of these groupings to represent the lengths of those cohorts. Generally, these groupings will identify fish of common age-classes, but there will be some overlap (Figure 11.1). Cohorts can also be identified by mark-and-recapture methods—the marked group being the cohort—and by aging individual fish from annular marks on scales or other bony structures.

Cohorts identified in one sample may be followed over several years or over intervals shorter than 1 year. Growth or growth rates can be calculated with the equations in Section 11.2.

11.5.3 Growth Estimates

11.5.3.1 Length-Frequency Analysis

Lengths of fish are easily and quickly determined in field investigations and then are available for a preliminary examination of sample data. Because lengths of fish of a single age tend to form a normal frequency distribution, ages may be determined from a length-frequency distribution as in cohort analysis (Figure

11.1). However, cohort distributions increasingly overlap as fish become older, and the method generally is unreliable for assigning ages to older fish. If ages and median length can be determined for each cohort (age-group) in the population, a growth rate for that cohort from hatch till time of sampling can be calculated. Graphical and statistical approaches for separating polymodal size frequency distributions into cohorts are available (Bagenal and Tesch 1978; Jearld 1983). Even if age cannot be precisely determined, the growth rate of a distinct cohort within the population may be estimated by following that cohort in subsequent samples (Ebert 1973; Pauly 1984).

11.5.3.2 Back-Calculation

There are several methods available for back-calculation of size at a given age. Although we describe them in terms of scales, they apply equally to any body part (otolith, bone, spine, etc.) that carries a record of growth episodes.

(1) The Fraser–Lee method (covered in detail below).
(2) Regression methods. Simple regression equations can be used to relate scale radius (distance from the scale's focus to its edge) to fish length. Then, measurements along a scale radius from focus to annual marks can be applied to the equation to give a fish's length at past ages (Carlander 1981).
(3) The covariance method (Bartlett et al. 1984). A modification of the direct regression approach, covariance analysis can address some problems that invalidate simple regression, such as nonlinearity and different body–scale relations among age-groups or year-classes.
(4) The linear model approach (Weisberg and Frie 1987). Linear models accept growth increments directly from the scale measurements, and they allow age-group and year (environmental) effects to be distinguished. Comparisons of growth after good and bad years can be made and statistically tested to assess age effects. The method may be used to describe effects on growth from environmental manipulations that fishery managers might use (Weisberg and Frie 1987).

In general, back-calculation only allows growth to be resolved at yearly intervals. Growth rates over fractions of a year can be determined by sampling a single cohort on several occasions, by using back-calculation techniques on scale margin from the edge to the last annulus, or by measuring the daily growth increments that often are recorded in the hard parts of young fish.

If a population can only be sampled once, back-calculations can be used to determine previous growth rates for individual fish and provide an estimate of the actual growth rate of all fish in the population. The actual instantaneous growth rate for individuals can be determined by the equation for G (Section 11.2), and a method for determining the population instantaneous growth rate was given by Bagenal and Tesch (1978). As an alternative, the apparent population growth rate can be used if the fish are aged but back-calculation is not done. Using the identified age for each fish, one can determine the mean size at each age represented in the population sample. The growth interval is 1 year, and size differences between successive age-classes constitute an estimate of annual

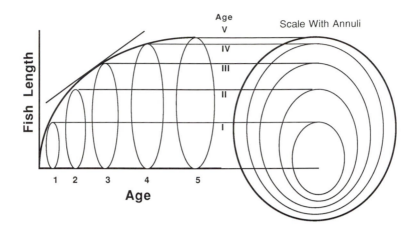

Figure 11.2 Proportionality between length of a fish and "radius" (distance from focus to edge) of its scale. The growth history of an individual fish can be back-calculated from scale annuli, or the growth rate for the population can be estimated from mean fish size at each age.

growth for that age interval. If it can be assumed that an age-class always has the same growth rate—that 3-year-olds always grow the same amount, for example—the apparent population rate can be determined from a single sample estimate. The use of apparent population growth rate can cause spurious results, however, particularly with short-lived fish species subject to size-selective mortality and large annual variation in growth rates due to climatic and other variables.

If fish age can be established from scales or other body structures, the proportionality between size of these structures and size of the whole fish permits the calculation of growth in previous years (Figure 11.2). The increments of growth for individuals in those years can be determined by back-calculation techniques, discussed in more detail below (also see Lagler 1956; Carlander 1981, 1982; Frie 1982; Jearld 1983; Newman and Weisberg 1987; Weisberg and Frie 1987). For the use of otoliths to determine growth over short time increments such as a day, see Panella (1971), Mayo et al. (1981), and Campana and Nielson (1985). Recently, there has been increased concern about the accuracy of aging methods applied to older fish, particularly when scales are used (Casselman 1983).

Back-calculated lengths are often based on the traditional Fraser–Lee method, which describes the body–scale relationship as the rectilinear regression

$$L = a + bS;$$

L = body length, S = scale length (radius) from the focus to the anterior edge, and a and b are constants (Lagler 1956; Hile 1970; Carlander 1981, 1982). This body–scale relationship is typically developed by measuring scales on a subsample of fish from all size-groups. The lengths at previous ages (L_i) are then calculated by a modification of the Fraser–Lee equation:

$$L_i = a + (L_c - a)(S_i/S_c);$$

L_c = length of fish at capture, L_i = calculated length at age i, S_c = distance from focus to edge of scale, S_i = distance from focus to annulus i, and a = intercept of the body–scale regression or a standard value from the literature (Carlander 1981, 1982; Frie 1982). These increments of growth over annual time periods can be used to calculate growth rates in different years for each individual represented by a scale sample. Average increments for all individuals in the sample will suggest actual population growth during these years. Microcomputers can markedly reduce the effort needed to calculate the body–scale relationship and to back-calculate previous lengths (Frie 1982). Various transformations of regression equations are sometimes used to linearize estimates of the body–scale relationship (Bagenal and Tesch 1978).

Various problems or considerations are associated with back-calculations of length.

(1) Special care must be taken to insure that annuli are valid indicators of age (Bagenal and Tesch 1978; Beamish and McFarlane 1983; Jearld 1983).

(2) Wide variations in a, the intercept of the body–scale relationship, occur between populations of the same species due to problems associated with fish collection, scale sampling, and measurement. Standard intercept values from the literature may reduce this variance for common species (Carlander 1982), although these values may also cause problems when they are grossly incorrect.

(3) Individuals in the sample must provide an adequate representation of the body–scale relationship in the different size-classes (Carlander 1981).

(4) Variability in back-calculated lengths is likely to be higher among younger fish due to the nature of the variance associated with a regression equation used to describe the body–scale relationship (Carlander 1981). For least-squares regressions of the type $Y = a + bX$, the variance associated with predicted body length (Y) increases as the measured scale length (X) departs from the mean of all scale lengths in the population (Snedecor and Cochran 1967).

(5) Back-calculated lengths are more accurate if a key scale or scales from the same region of each fish are chosen. Newman and Weisberg (1987) presented methods to determine the number of scales to collect per fish and the number of fish to sample in order to attain a given precision.

(6) Larger fish in a year-class often have a mortality rate different from that of the smaller members of the same age. This may induce an artifact known as Lee's phenomenon, which occurs when back-calculated lengths of a given age-group are smaller when calculated from older fish than they are when derived from younger fish (Ricker 1975, 1979; for a reverse effect, see Frie 1982). This difference may also be due to biased (nonrandom) sampling, size-selective mortality, or improper back-calculation methods (Bagenal and Tesch 1978). Newman and Weisberg (1987) suggested that scale growth increments be examined to determine if Lee's phenomenon occurs independently of back-calculation techniques.

11.5.3.3   Mathematical Models

Several mathematical models can be used to describe increases in fish size with age. Empirical data usually can be represented adequately by the von Bertalanffy growth equation, which has the formula

$$L_t = L_\infty \left[1 - e^{-K(t - t_0)}\right].$$

The time units, t, represent the age of the fish, usually (but not necessarily) measured in years from a starting time, t_0. The length of the fish at age t, L_t, is a function of maximum (asymptotic) length L_∞, the growth coefficient K, and age; e is the base of the natural logarithm. An analogous formula can be used with weight data. In theory, t_0 is the age at which the fish would have had zero size if it had always grown as described by the equation. In practice, however, t_0 is a time at which the fish already has attained a finite size.

When the von Bertalanffy equation is fitted to size-at-age data, values can be calculated for maximum size, size at t_0, and K (Ricker 1979; Pauly 1984). Maximum size cannot be estimated directly from body–scale data and back-calculations. If true ages are unknown but growth over known time intervals can be determined by, for example, recapture of tagged fish, the von Bertalanffy formula can still be used. In this case, the equation gives maximum size and K, but not t_0, so size at t_0 cannot be calculated (Fabens 1965; Pauly 1984). Other methods can be used to estimate maximum size and the growth coefficient when data on size increases with time are available but ages and sizes at age are unknown (see Pauly 1984; Schnute 1985).

11.6 CONSIDERATIONS FOR LABORATORY GROWTH STUDIES

The major influences on fish growth are temperature and food consumption rate, but there are many other characteristics of fish and experimental design that can affect the outcome of a growth study. These should be considered early in an experiment to assure that results will be easily analyzed and interpreted, as well as comparable with results of other studies. It is beyond the scope of this chapter to examine in detail the effects of environmental and trophic factors that affect growth (see Brett 1979; Brett and Groves 1979; Tytler and Calow 1985).

11.6.1 Characteristics of the Fish

It is important to choose the species and life stage that best suit the purposes of the study and the facilities available. Younger fish are more easily domesticated than older ones and usually feed more readily in new surroundings. Immature fish also present none of the complications (for growth studies) of gonad development. Piscivorous species are often best for quantitative studies of food consumption because exact ration sizes can be easily measured; pelleted food often dissolves or is not eaten once it settles to the bottom of the tank. A species may have many strains and races that can display different growth potentials (Reinitz et al. 1979).

As poikilotherms, fish adapt to decreased ambient temperature through a variety of mechanisms, most of them associated with increased enzyme activity (Hochachka and Somero 1984), and growth rate at a particular temperature depends on a fish's thermal history. For this reason, a fish should be acclimated to the chosen experimental temperature for at least 1 week before a growth study begins. Acclimation may not occur in 1 week if the difference between ambient and experimental temperatures is large, but probably will in 3–4 weeks. Gradual changes in temperature, as might occur seasonally, generally result in the same growth as would occur at the mean temperature over the interval, but exceptions have been noted. The effect of daily fluctuating temperature on growth is more complex, but there is some indication that fluctuations may stimulate growth if temperatures are below the optimum (Brett 1979; Spigarelli et al. 1982).

Growth rate also is affected by the fish's previous nutritional history (Weatherley and Gill 1981; Talbot et al. 1984). Prior starvation, even short-term deprivation, can result in changes in intestinal morphology and enzyme activity that influence subsequent food consumption and growth rates. Furthermore, if fish are obtained from the field, one may encounter populations that are "stunted" because of food shortages or a low genetic potential for growth (Murnyak et al. 1984).

Finally, fish in general (but wild fish in particular) have endogenous seasonal rhythms in growth potential (Baker and Wigham 1979). Thus, growth experiments conducted at different times of the year may result in different growth rates. The greatest growth can usually be expected in the spring and summer.

11.6.2 Experimental Conditions

Little attention is given to the feeding regime of growth studies, but the way in which a particular ration is presented can influence the response of the fish. For example, maximum ration size is often estimated as the maximum amount of food eaten in one or, at best, several feedings per day. However, the true maximum ration can only be presented when food is constantly available to the fish so they can feed ad libitum. Automatic feeders can be used to dispense feed at short, timed intervals. Demand feeders are useful for some fish, but many species cannot be trained easily to use them. Even when fish are fed the same ration size, the number of feedings per day can change the efficiency of food processing by the fish and therefore their growth rate (Yamada et al. 1981). In general, large rations are best presented as several smaller meals, usually 1% of body weight per meal. Regardless of the number of feedings, it is probably best to condition the fish by feeding them at the same times each day and, if possible, to match these times with the natural feeding times of the species. Finally, feeding should be stopped 1 or 2 d before fish are weighed so that gastric evacuation will be complete; the time necessary for intestines to empty depends on species and temperature.

The particle size of the food presented can be important in growth studies. In nature, fish actively choose prey of certain sizes such that food processing is energetically most efficient (Townsend and Hughes 1981; Mittelbach 1983). In the laboratory, food items that are too small or too large can result in less-than-maximum growth. In long-term studies during which fish grow appreciably, food particle sizes should be increased accordingly.

Fish density can influence growth by affecting social interactions and water quality. The rate of food consumption by a fish raised in isolation may be increased by "social facilitation" if the fish is placed with others. The number of fish present can determine the character of the interactions and change the feeding behavior of the fish. For example, if a hierarchy of fish dominance develops, a few fish will often feed more aggressively than others. The result will be high variability in the growth data (Koebele 1985) that will decrease the statistical resolution of growth trends or of differences between experimental treatments. Species of fish that form dominance hierarchies are not well suited for growth

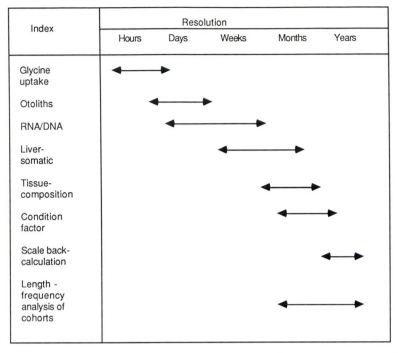

Figure 11.3 Time periods over which growth rate may be determined by various indices.

studies. In general, reducing the concentration of fish or increasing the frequency of feeding (Jobling 1985) reduces the effects of social interactions.

Photoperiod can act as a cue to fish and, by acting through hormonal mechanisms, influence their growth rates (Brett 1979). Responses to photoperiod are often very complex; the photoperiod effect interacts with those of temperature and endogenous rhythms. For most species, it seems that the greatest growth can be expected with long day lengths or with increasing day lengths (Brett 1979). For some species, longer day lengths may simply allow a longer feeding period. The intensity of light may also affect feeding behavior. Many fish species are less stressed and feed better under low-light conditions.

Water quality affects growth and optimum conditions should be maintained. If possible, dissolved oxygen concentrations should be maintained above 5 mg/L and preferably at saturation. Piper et al. (1982) provided suggestions for maintaining optimum water quality.

11.6.3 Statistical Considerations

To assure unbiased estimates of growth rate, fish should be randomly assigned to treatment groups. Proper methods for doing this were described by Snedecor and Cochran (1967). If fish are subsampled for weighing, efforts should be made to obtain representative fish. For example, chasing fish with a net should be minimized because this often leads to capture of the smaller or weaker individuals, which will bias the growth estimates. It is usually advantageous to mark each fish uniquely so individual growth rates can be obtained, allowing an estimate of variance. Methods for marking fish have been reviewed by Wydoski and Emery (1983).

Table 11.2 Logistic considerations for selection of indices of growth

Index	Complexity of analysis[a,b]	Cost[a,c]	Sample size[a,d]	Suitable location	Lethal	Individual or population measure	Special needs
Change in size							
Length	L	L	H	Lab, field	No	Ind, pop	Measuring board
Weight	L	L	H	Lab, field	No	Ind, pop	Balance
Proximate analysis							
Protein	M	M	L	Lab, field	Yes	Ind	Spectrophotometer
Lipid	M–H	M	L	Lab, field	Yes	Ind	Spectrophotometer
Carbohydrates	M	M	L	Lab, field	Yes	Ind	Spectrophotometer
Energy content	H	H	L	Lab, field	Yes	Ind	Calorimeter
Change in physiology or biochemistry							
Protein synthesis	H	H	L	Lab	Yes	Ind	Conclusions
Glycine uptake	H	H	M	Lab, field	No	ind	Liquid scintillation counter, sensitive balance (1 µg)
Nucleic acids	H	H	H	Lab, field	Yes	Ind	Centrifuge, spectrophotometer
Liver–somatic	L	L	H	Field	Yes	Ind	Balance
Condition factor	L	L	H	Field	No	Ind	Balance, measuring board
Growth in natural populations							
Cohort identification	L	L	M	Field	No	Pop	Graph paper
Growth estimates							
Length frequency	L	L	M	Field	No	Pop	Graph paper, computer
Back-calculation and daily increments	M	M	M	Field	No	Ind, pop	Scale projector, microscope, or scanning electron microscope
Mathematical models	H	L	H	Field	No	Pop	Calculator or computer

[a]L = low; M = medium; H = high.
[b]No previous experience assumed.
[c]Exclusive of specific equipment and capitalization costs.
[d]Number of fish required for estimates.

As fish become larger during a growth experiment, their physiological potential to grow decreases. Therefore, determination of maximum growth rate depends on the length of the experiment. Also for this reason, it is best to start an experiment with fish of similar size to minimize the variability in growth. Corrections have been proposed by Jobling (1983) for comparing the growth rates of fish of different sizes. These corrections may be of value in the analysis of experimental results.

11.7 CONCLUSION

The methods available for growth studies are numerous and the choice among them depends upon the focus of the study, the study's objectives, and the resources available. There is no single reference that gives all or even most of the decision points in the conduct of growth studies. Guidance for matching the appropriate methodology to the period of study is given in Figure 11.3. Other characteristics of growth indices that may influence the choice of methods are given in Table 11.2. Further aspects of growth investigations are available in the cited literature.

11.8 REFERENCES

Ackman, R. G. 1980. Flame ionization detection applied to thin-layer chromatography on coated quartz rods. Methods in Enzymology 72:205–252.

Adams, S. M., and R. B. McLean. 1985. Estimation of largemouth bass, *Micropterus salmoides* Lacépède, growth using the liver somatic index and physiological variables. Journal of Fish Biology 26:111–126.

Adams, S. M., R. B. McLean, and J. A. Parrotta. 1982. Energy partitioning in largemouth bass under conditions of seasonally fluctuating prey availability. Transactions of the American Fisheries Society 111:549–558.

Adelman, I. R. 1980. Uptake of ^{14}C-glycine by scales as an index of fish growth: effect of fish acclimation temperature. Transactions of the American Fisheries Society 109:187–194.

Adelman, I. R. 1987. Uptake of radioactive amino acids as indices of current growth rate of fish: a review. Pages 65–79 *in* R. C. Summerfelt and G. E. Hall, editors. Age and growth of fish. Iowa State University Press, Ames.

Anderson, R. O., and S. V. Gutreuter. 1983. Length, weight, and associated structural indices. Pages 283–300 *in* L. A. Nielsen and D. L. Johnson, editors. Fisheries techniques. American Fisheries Society, Bethesda, Maryland.

Ashwell, G. 1957. Colorimetric analysis of sugars. Methods in Enzymology 3:73–103.

Bagenal, T. B., and F. W. Tesch. 1978. Age and growth. Pages 101–136 *in* T. B. Bagenal, editor. Methods for assessment of fish production in fresh waters, 3rd edition. Blackwell Scientific Publications, Oxford, England.

Baker, B. I., and T. Wigham. 1979. Endocrine aspects of metabolic coordination in teleosts. Pages 89–103 *in* P. J. Miller, editor. Fish phenology: anabolic adaptiveness in teleosts. Academic Press, London.

Barnes, H., and J. Blackstock. 1973. Estimation of lipids in marine animals and tissues. Detailed investigation of the sulfophosphovanillin method for total lipids. Journal of Experimental Marine Biology and Ecology 12:103–118.

Barron, M. G., and I. R. Adelman. 1984. Nucleic acid, protein content, and growth of larval fish sublethally exposed to various toxicants. Canadian Journal of Fisheries and Aquatic Sciences 41:141–150.

Bartlett, J. R., P. F. Randerson, R. Williams, and D. M. Ellis. 1984. The use of analysis of covariance in the back-calculation of growth in fish. Journal of Fish Biology 24:201–213.

Beamish, R. J., and G. A. McFarlane. 1983. The forgotten requirement for age validation in fisheries biology. Transactions of the American Fisheries Society 112:735–743.

Beezer, A. E., editor. 1980. Biological microcalorimetry. Academic Press, London.

Bensadoun, A., and D. Weinstein. 1976. Assay of proteins in the presence of interfering materials. Analytical Biochemistry 70:241–250.

Blaedel, W. J., and J. M. Uhl. 1975. Nature of materials in serum that interfere in the glucose oxidase-peroxidase-*o*-dianisidine method for glucose, and their mode of action. Clinical Chemistry 22:119–124.

Brett, J. R. 1979. Environmental factors and growth. Pages 599–675 *in* W. S. Hoar, D. J. Randall, and J. R. Brett, editors. Fish physiology, volume 8. Academic Press, New York.

Brett, J. R., and T. D. D. Groves. 1979. Physiological energetics. Pages 279–352 *in* W. S. Hoar, D. J. Randall, and J. R. Brett, editors. Fish physiology, volume 8. Academic Press, New York.

Brett, J. R., J. E. Shelbourn, and C. T. Shoop. 1969. Growth rate and body composition of fingerling sockeye salmon, *Oncorhynchus nerka,* in relation to temperature and ration size. Journal of the Fisheries Research Board of Canada 26:2363–2394.

Brown, H. D., editor. 1969. Biochemical microcalorimetry. Academic Press, New York.

Buckley, L. J. 1979. Relationships between RNA–DNA ratio, prey density, and growth rate in Atlantic cod *(Gadus morhua)* larvae. Journal of the Fisheries Research Board of Canada 36:1497–1502.

Buckley, L. J. 1980. Changes in ribonucleic acid, deoxyribonucleic acid, and protein content during ontogenesis in winter flounder, *Pseudopleuronectes americanus*, and effect of starvation. U.S. National Marine Fisheries Service Fishery Bulletin 77:703–708.

Buckley, L. J. 1984. RNA–DNA ratio: an index of larval fish growth in the sea. Marine Biology 80:291–298.

Buckley, L. J., and F. J. Bulow. 1987. Techniques for the estimation of RNA, DNA, and protein in fish. Pages 345–354 *in* R. C. Summerfelt and G. E. Hall, editors. Age and growth of fish. Iowa State University Press, Ames.

Buckley, L. J., T. A. Halavik, G. C. Laurence, S. J. Hamilton, and P. Yivich. 1985. Comparative swimming stamina, biochemical composition, backbone mechanical properties, and histopathology of juvenile striped bass from rivers and hatcheries of the eastern United States. Transactions of the American Fisheries Society 114:114–124.

Bulow, F. J. 1971. Selection of suitable tissues for use in the RNA–DNA ratio technique of assessing recent growth rate of a fish. Iowa State Journal of Science 46:71–78.

Bulow, F. J. 1987. RNA-DNA ratios as indicators of growth in fish: a review. Pages 45–64 *in* R. C. Summerfelt and G. E. Hall, editors. Age and growth of fish. Iowa State University Press, Ames.

Bulow, F. J., C. B. Coburn, Jr., and C. S. Cobb. 1978. Comparison of two bluegill populations by means of the RNA–DNA ratio and liver–somatic index. Transactions of the American Fisheries Society 107:799–803.

Burton, K. 1956. A study of the conditions and mechanism of the diphenylamine reaction for the colorimetric estimation of deoxyribonucleic acid. Biochemical Journal 62:315–323.

Busacker, G. P., and I. R. Adelman. 1987. Uptake of ^{14}C-glycine by fish scales (in vitro) as an index of growth rate. Pages 355–357 *in* R. C. Summerfelt and G. E. Hall, editors. Age and growth of fish. Iowa State University Press, Ames.

Campana, S. E., and J. D. Nielson. 1985. Microstructure of fish otoliths. Canadian Journal of Fisheries and Aquatic Sciences 42:1014–1032.

Carlander, K. D. 1969. Handbook of freshwater fishery biology, volume 1. Iowa State University Press, Ames.

Carlander, K. D. 1977. Handbook of freshwater fishery biology, volume 2. Iowa State University Press, Ames.

Carlander, K. D. 1981. Caution on the use of the regression method of back-calculating lengths from scale measurements. Fisheries (Bethesda) 6(1):2–4.

Carlander, K. D. 1982. Standard intercepts for calculating lengths from scale measurements for some centrarchid and percid fishes. Transactions of the American Fisheries Society 111:332–336.

Carr, R. S., and J. M. Neff. 1984. Quantitative semi-automated enzymatic assay for tissue glycogen. Comparative Biochemistry and Physiology B, Comparative Biochemistry 77:447–449.

Casselman, J. M. 1983. Age and growth assessment of fish from their calcified structures— techniques and tools. NOAA (National Oceanic and Atmospheric Administration) Technical Report NMFS (National Marine Fisheries Service) 8:1–17.

Cookson, C. 1978. Interference of zwitterionic biological buffers with the Lowry method of protein determination. Analytical Biochemistry 88:340–343.

Crisp, D. J. 1971. Energy flow measurements. IBP (International Biological Programme) Handbook 16:197–279.

Dische, Z. 1955. New color reactions for determinations of sugars in polysaccharides. Methods of Biochemical Analysis 2:313–358.

Dowgiallo, A. 1975. Chemical composition of an animal's body and of its food. IBP (International Biological Programme) 24:160–199.

Dubois, M., K. A. Gilles, J. K. Hamilton, P. A. Rebers, and F. Smith. 1956. Colorimetric method for determination of sugars and related substances. Analytical Chemistry 28:350–356.

Ebert, T. A. 1973. Estimating growth and mortality rates from size data. Oecologia (Berlin) 11:281–298.

Elliot, B. J. M. 1976. Body composition of brown trout (*Salmo trutta* L.) in relation to temperature and ration size. Journal of Animal Ecology 45:273–289.

Emmersen, B. K., and J. Emmersen. 1976. Protein, RNA and DNA metabolism in relation to ovarian vitellogenic growth in the flounder, *Platichthys flesus* (L.). Comparative Biochemistry and Physiology B, Comparative Biochemistry 55:315–321.

Entenman, C. 1957a. General procedures for separating lipid components of tissue. Methods in Enzymology 3:299–317.

Entenman, C. 1957b. Preparation and determination of higher fatty acids. Methods in Enzymology 3:317–328.

Fabens, A. J. 1965. Properties and fitting of the von Bertalanffy growth curve. Growth 29:265–289.

Fauconneau, B., M. Arnal, and P. Luquet. 1981. Etude de la synthese proteique in vivo dans le muscle de la truite arc-en-ciel (*Salmo gairdneri* R.). Influence de la temperature. Reproduction, Nutrition, Développement 21:293–301.

Fraser, A. J., D. R. Tocher, and J. R. Sargent. 1985. Thin-layer chromatography–flame ionization detection and the quantitation of marine neutral lipids and phospholipids. Journal of Experimental Marine Biology and Ecology 88:91–99.

Frie, R. V. 1982. Measurement of fish scales and back-calculation of body lengths using a digitizing pad and microcomputer. Fisheries (Bethesda) 7(4):5–8.

Goolish, E. M., and I. R. Adelman. 1983a. ^{14}C-glycine uptake by fish scales: refinement of a growth index and effects of a protein-synthesis inhibitor. Transactions of the American Fisheries Society 112:647–652.

Goolish, E. M., and I. R. Adelman. 1983b. Effects of fish growth rate, acclimation temperature and incubation temperature on in vitro glycine uptake by fish scales. Comparative Biochemistry and Physiology A, Comparative Physiology 76:127–134.

Goolish, E. M., M. G. Barron, and I. R. Adelman. 1984. Thermoacclimatory response of nucleic acid and protein content of carp muscle tissue: influence of growth rate and relationship to glycine uptake by scales. Canadian Journal of Zoology 62:2164–2170.

Gornall, A. G., C. G. Bardawill, and M. M. David. 1949. Determination of serum proteins by means of the biuret reaction. Journal of Biological Chemistry 177:751–766.

Gould, E., R. A. Greig, D. Rusanowsky, and B. C. Marks. 1985. Metal-exposed sea scallops, *Placopecten magellanicus* (Gmelin): a comparison of the effect of cadmium and copper. Pages 157–186 in F. J. Vernberg, F. P. Thurberg, A. Calabrese, and W. B. Vernberg, editors. Marine pollution and physiology: recent advances. University of South Carolina Press, Columbia.

Haschemeyer, A. E. V. 1973. Control of protein synthesis in the acclimation of fish to environmental temperature changes. Pages 3–31 in W. Chavin, editor. Responses of fish to environmental changes. Thomas, Springfield, Illinois.

Haschemeyer, A. E. V. 1976. Kinetics of protein synthesis in higher organisms in vivo. Trends in Biochemical Sciences 1:133–136.

Haschemeyer, A. E. V., R. Persell, and M. A. K. Smith. 1979. Effect of temperature on protein synthesis in fish of the Galapagos and Perlas islands. Comparative Biochemistry and Physiology B, Comparative Biochemistry 65:91–95.

Haschemeyer, A. E. V., and M. A. K. Smith. 1979. Protein synthesis in liver, muscle and gill of mullet (*Mugil cephalus* L.) in vivo. Biological Bulletin (Woods Hole) 156:93–102.

Hile, R. 1970. Body–scale relation and calculation of growth in fishes. Transactions of the American Fisheries Society 99:468–474.

Hochachka, P. W., and G. N. Somero. 1984. Biochemical adaptation. Princeton University Press, Princeton, New Jersey.

Holland, D. L., and P. A. Gabbott. 1971. Micro analytical scheme for the determination of protein, carbohydrate, lipid, and RNA levels in marine invertebrate larvae. Journal of the Marine Biology Association of the United Kingdom 51:659–668.

Holman, R. T. 1957. Measurement of polyunsaturated fatty acids. Methods of Biochemical Analysis 9:99–138.

Honn, K. V., and W. Chavin. 1975. An improved automated biuret method for the determination of microgram protein concentrations. Analytical Biochemistry 68:230–235.

Huemer, R. P., and K. D. Lee. 1970. Automated Lowry method for microgram protein determination. Analytical Biochemistry 37:149–153.

Jacobs, S. 1965. The determination of nitrogen in biological materials. Methods of Biochemical Analysis 13:241–263.

Jearld, A., Jr. 1983. Age determination. Pages 301–324 in L. A. Nielsen and D. L. Johnson, editors. Fisheries techniques. American Fisheries Society, Bethesda, Maryland.

Jobling, M. 1983. Growth studies with fish—overcoming the problems of size variation. Journal of Fish Biology 22:153–157.

Jobling, M. 1985. Physiological and social constraints on growth of fish with special reference to Arctic charr, Salvelinus alpinus L. Aquaculture 44:83–90.

Kent, J., and C. L. Prosser. 1980. Effects of incubation and acclimation temperatures on incorporation of U-[^{14}C] glycine into mitochondrial protein of liver cells and slices from green sunfish, Lepomis cyanellus. Physiological Zoology 53:293–304.

Koebele, B. P. 1985. Growth and the size hierarchy effect: an experimental assessment of three proposed mechanisms: activity differences, disproportional food acquisition, physiological stress. Environmental Biology of Fishes 12:181–188.

Lagler, K. F. 1956. Freshwater fishery biology, 2nd edition. Brown, Dubuque, Iowa.

Lied, E., B. Lund, and B. von der Decken. 1982. Protein synthesis in vitro by epaxial muscle polyribosomes from cod, Gadus morhua. Comparative Biochemistry and Physiology B, Comparative Biochemistry 72:187–193.

Lone, K. P., and B. W. Ince. 1983. Cellular growth responses of rainbow trout (Salmo gairdneri) fed different levels of dietary protein and an anabolic steroid ethylestrenol. General and Comparative Endocrinology 49:32–49.

Love, R. M. 1980. The chemical biology of fishes, volume 2. Academic Press, New York.

Lowry, O. H., A. L. Farr, R. J. Randall, and N. J. Rosebrough. 1951. Protein measurement with the Folin phenol reagent. Journal of Biological Chemistry 193:265–275.

Mayo, R. K., V. M. Gifford, and A. Jerald, Jr. 1981. Age validation of redfish from Gulf of Maine–Georges Bank region. Journal of Northwest Atlantic Fishery Science 2:13–19.

Mendel, B., and P. L. Hoogland. 1950. Rapid determination of blood-sugar: simple methods. Lancet 2:16–17.

Mittelbach, G. G. 1983. Optimal foraging and growth in bluegills. Oecologia (Berlin) 59:157–162.

Montgomery, R. 1957. Determination of glycogen. Archives of Biochemistry and Biophysics 67:378–386.

Munro, H. N., and A. Fleck. 1966. The determination of nucleic acids. Methods of Biochemical Analysis 14:113–176.

Murnyak, D. F., M. O. Murnyak, and L. J. Wolgast. 1984. Growth of stunted and nonstunted bluegill sunfish in ponds. Progressive Fish-Culturist 46:133–138.

Mustafa, S. 1977a. Influence of maturation on the concentration of RNA and DNA in the flesh of the catfish Clarias batrachus. Transactions of the American Fisheries Society 106:449–451.

Mustafa, S. 1977b. Nucleic acid turnover in the dark and white muscles of some freshwater species of carps during growth in the prematurity phase. Copeia 1977:174–175.

Nestle, M. 1981. Nutrition. Pages 565–584 in D. W. Martin, P. A. Mayes, and V. W. Rodwell, editors. Harper's review of biochemistry, 18th edition. Lange Medical Publications, Los Altos, California.

Newman, R. M., and S. Weisberg. 1987. Among- and within-fish variation of scale growth increments in brown trout. Pages 159–166 in R. C. Summerfelt and G. E. Hall, editors. Age and growth of fish. Iowa State University Press, Ames.

Ottaway, E. M., and K. Simkiss. 1977. "Instantaneous" growth rates of fish scales and their use in studies of fish populations. Journal of Zoology (London) 181:407–419.

Ottaway, E. M., and K. Simkiss. 1979. A comparison of traditional and novel ways of estimating growth rates from scales of natural populations of young bass (Dicentrar-

chus labrax). Journal of the Marine Biological Association of the United Kingdom 59:49–59.

Panella, G. 1971. Fish otoliths: daily growth layers and periodical patterns. Science (Washington, D.C.) 173:1124–1126.

Parker, R., and W. E. Vanstone. 1966. Changes in chemical composition of central British Columbia pink salmon during early sea life. Journal of the Fisheries Research Board of Canada 23:1353–1384.

Pauly, D. 1984. Fish population dynamics in tropical waters: a manual for use with programmable calculators. International Center for Living Aquatic Resources Management, ICLARM Studies and Reviews 8, Manila.

Peterson, G. L. 1977. A simplification of the protein assay method of Lowry et al. which is more generally applicable. Analytical Biochemistry 83:346–356.

Peterson, G. L. 1979. Review of the Folin phenol protein quantitation method of Lowry, Rosebrough, Farr and Randall. Analytical Biochemistry 100:201–220.

Piper, R. G., I. B. McElwain, L. E. Orme, J. P. McCraren, L. G. Fowler, and J. R. Leonard. 1982. Fish hatchery management. U.S. Fish and Wildlife Service, Washington, D.C.

Pocrnjic, Z., R. W. Mathews, S. Rappaport, and A. E. V. Haschemeyer. 1983. Quantitative protein synthetic rates in various tissues of a temperate fish in vivo by the method of phenylalanine swamping. Comparative Biochemistry and Physiology B, Comparative Biochemistry 74:735–738.

Prus, T. 1975. Measurement of calorific value using Phillipson microbomb calorimeter. IBP (International Biological Programme) Handbook 24:149–160.

Reinitz, G. L., L. E. Orme, and F. N. Hitzel. 1979. Variations of body composition and growth among strains of rainbow trout. Transactions of the American Fisheries Society 108:204–207.

Richterich, R. 1969. Clinical chemistry. Translated from the 2nd German edition by S. Raymond and J. H. Wilkinson. Academic Press, New York.

Ricker, W. E. 1975. Computation and interpretation of biological statistics of fish populations. Fisheries Research Board of Canada Bulletin 191.

Ricker, W. E. 1979. Growth rates and models. Pages 677–743 *in* W. S. Hoar, D. J. Randall, and J. R. Brett, editors. Fish physiology, volume 8. Academic Press, New York.

Rosenlund, G., B. Lung, and A. von der Decken. 1983. Properties of white trunk muscle from saithe, *Pollachius virens,* rainbow trout, *Salmo gairdneri,* and herring, *Clupea harengus:* protein synthesis in vitro, electrophoretic study of proteins. Comparative Biochemistry and Physiology B, Comparative Biochemistry 74:389–397.

Saez, L., O. Goicoechea, R. Amthauer, and M. Krauskopf. 1982. Behavior of RNA and protein synthesis during the acclimatization of the carp. Studies with isolated hepatocytes. Comparative Biochemistry and Physiology B, Comparative Biochemistry 72:31–38.

Schmidt, G., and S. J. Thannhauser. 1945. A method for the determination of deoxyribonucleic acid, ribonucleic acid, and phosphoproteins in animal tissues. Journal of Biological Chemistry 161:83–89.

Schneider, W. C. 1957. Determination of nucleic acids in tissues by pentose analysis. Methods in Enzymology 3:680–684.

Schnute, J. 1985. A general theory for analysis of catch and effort data. Canadian Journal of Fisheries and Aquatic Sciences 42:414–429.

Smagula, C. M., and I. R. Adelman. 1982. Temperature and scale size errors in the use of [^{14}C]glycine uptake by scales as a growth index. Canadian Journal of Fisheries and Aquatic Sciences 39:1366–1372.

Smith, M. A. K. 1981. Estimation of growth potential by measurement of tissue protein synthetic rates in feeding and fasting rainbow trout, *Salmo gairdneri* Richardson. Journal of Fish Biology 19:213–220.

Snedecor, G. W., and W. G. Cochran. 1967. Statistical methods. Iowa State University Press, Ames.

Snell, F. D., and F. M. Biffen. 1964. Commercial methods of analysis. Chemical Publishing, New York.

Spigarelli, S. A., M. M. Thommes, and W. Prepejchal. 1982. Feeding, growth, and fat deposition by brown trout in constant and fluctuating temperatures. Transactions of the American Fisheries Society 111:199–209.

Talbot, C., P. J. Higgins, and A. M. Shanks. 1984. Effects of pre- and post-prandial starvation on meal size and evacuation rate of juvenile Atlantic salmon, *Salmo salar* L. Journal of Fish Biology 25:551–560.

Townsend, C. R., and R. N. Hughes. 1981. Maximizing net energy returns from foraging. Pages 86–108 *in* C. R. Townsend and P. Calow, editors. Physiological ecology: an evolutionary approach to resource use. Sinauer Associates, Sunderland, Massachusetts.

Tytler, P., and P. Calow. 1985. Fish energetics: new perspectives. Johns Hopkins University Press, Baltimore, Maryland.

Uskova, E. T., A. V. Chaykovskaya, S. I. Davidenko, and D. M. Gerasimova. 1981. Changes in mucilaginous substances covering fish skin under various conditions. Hydrobiological Journal 17(4):40–44.

Warren, C. E., and C. E. Davis. 1967. Laboratory studies on the feeding bioenergetics and growth of fishes. Pages 175–214 *in* S. D. Gerking, editor. The biological basis of freshwater fish production. Blackwell Scientific Publications, Oxford, England.

Weatherly, A. H. 1972. Growth and ecology of fish populations. Academic Press, London.

Weatherley, A. H., and H. S. Gill. 1981. Recovery growth following periods of restricted rations and starvation in rainbow trout *Salmo gairdneri* Richardson. Journal of Fish Biology 18:195–208.

Weatherley, A. H., and H. S. Gill. 1986. The biology of fish growth. Academic Press, London.

Weisberg, S., and R. V. Frie. 1987. Linear models for the growth of fish. Pages 127–143 *in* R. C. Summerfelt and G. E. Hall, editors. Age and growth of fish. Iowa State University Press, Ames.

Wold, J. K., and R. Selset. 1977. Glycoproteins in the skin mucus of the char (*Salmo alpinus* L.). Comparative Biochemistry and Physiology B, Comparative Biochemistry 56:215–218.

Wydoski, R., and L. Emery. 1983. Tagging and marking. Pages 215–237 *in* L. A. Nielsen and D. L. Johnson, editors. Fisheries techniques. American Fisheries Society, Bethesda, Maryland.

Yamada, S., Y. Tanaka, and T. Katayama. 1981. Feeding experiments with carp fry fed an amino acid diet by increasing the number of feedings per day. Bulletin of the Japanese Society of Scientific Fisheries 47:1247.

Chapter 12

Bioenergetics

S. MARSHALL ADAMS AND JAMES E. BRECK

12.1 INTRODUCTION

All energy acquired by an organism through ingestion must ultimately be used in metabolic processes, lost as wastes through excretion and egestion, or synthesized into new tissue (energy gain). Physiological energetics, or bioenergetics, is concerned with the rates of energy intake, transformations, losses, and uses as functions of the whole organism (Brett and Groves 1979). Bioenergetics provides a theoretical framework for relating growth rates and feeding rates of an organism to environmental conditions and provides some insight into causal relationships among these variables (Allen and Wootton 1982). The application of bioenergetics in fisheries involves partitioning ingested energy into the major physiological components of the basic energy budget equation of Winberg (1956):

$$p \cdot C = M + G; \tag{12.1}$$

p = proportion of consumed food that is assimilated,
C = food consumed,
M = metabolism (catabolism), and
G = growth (anabolism).

Equation (12.1) is usually expanded to yield the generalized form proposed by Warren and Davis (1967):

$$C = (M_r + M_a + \text{SDA}) + (F + U) + (G_s + G_r); \tag{12.2}$$
$$\quad\;\; \text{(metabolism)} \qquad \text{(waste)} \quad \text{(growth)}$$

C = rate of energy consumption,
M_r = standard metabolic rate,
M_a = metabolic rate increase (above the standard rate) due to activity,
SDA = metabolic rate increase due to specific dynamic action,
$F + U$ = waste losses due to egestion (feces) and excretion (urine) rates,
G_s = somatic growth rate due to protein synthesis and lipid deposition, and
G_r = growth rate due to gonad (reproductive) synthesis.

All components of the energy budget must be expressed in the same units. The units can be biomass (wet or dry weight), energy (joules or calories), carbon, or nitrogen, and can be expressed as rates (e.g., cal/d) or as amounts gained or lost in some reference time period. Biomass estimates can be used directly only when the energy value of consumed food and the energy density of the fish are similar; otherwise, large errors can result in the balancing of the energy budget equation.

389

For example, the caloric density of alewife, the primary prey of lake trout in Lake Michigan, varies from 1.03 to 2.3 kcal/g of body weight over the year (Flath and Diana 1985), whereas the caloric density of lake trout varies with fish size between 1.26 and 3.35 kcal/g (Stewart et al. 1983). These energy content differences between predator and prey could cause estimates of alewife consumption by lake trout to err by a factor of 2 or more if they are not taken into account. Both the food (prey) and growth (predator) must be converted from biomass to common energy units to balance the budget; then the results can be converted back to biomass units if desired.

The life history of a fish dictates, to a large degree, how consumed energy is partitioned into its major functional processes of growth, metabolism, and production. For example, the generally sedentary largemouth bass, which employs an "ambush" type of feeding behavior, partitions ingested energy differently from the actively swimming skipjack tuna, which forages continuously. Both species allocate similar proportions of consumed energy to standard metabolism, specific dynamic action (food assimilation), and waste losses, but tunas devote a much larger fraction of their energy intake to activity than do basses (Figure 12.1). As a consequence, a much smaller proportion of the total energy intake of tunas is available for growth. However, tunas still achieve higher growth rates than basses by maintaining higher feeding rates.

12.1.1   Uses of Bioenergetics in Fishery Biology

Bioenergetic budgets have been applied in fishery biology for a variety of purposes. Common applications of the balanced energy budget have been estimation of growth or production (Paloheimo and Dickie 1966; Kerr 1971; Healey 1972; Ware 1975) and prediction of food consumption rates to evaluate the impacts of predators on their prey (Kitchell and Breck 1980; Stewart et al. 1981, 1983; Rice and Cochran 1984). Energy budgets can also be an efficient means of evaluating the relative importance of environmental factors that control growth, such as temperature or prey availability (Kitchell et al. 1977; Rice et al. 1983). The effects of multiple stresses on growth can also be examined with the bioenergetic budget (Vaughan et al. 1984; Rice 1990).

An understanding of how fish partition consumed energy into metabolic pathways, reproductive demands, and growth is important for studying life history strategies of fish (Williams 1961); these strategies include diel migration (Caulton 1978), seasonal feeding patterns (Kitchell and Breck 1980), and reproduction (MacKinnon 1972). Bioenergetic models have been used to estimate the rate at which pollutants such as PCBs are taken up by salmonids in the Great Lakes (Weininger 1978; Thomann and Connolly 1984), to determine the uptake of PCBs and methylmercury by yellow perch (Norstrom et al. 1976), and to evaluate the consequences of stress in fish (Rice 1990). Bioenergetics also has been applied to studies of early life history stages of fish (Cooney 1973; Laurence 1977; Eldridge et al. 1982).

Bioenergetic budgets can be used to address a variety of fishery-related needs and objectives (Table 12.1). The purpose of this chapter, therefore, is to provide practical guidelines for applying bioenergetics in fish biology. For more detailed discussions of the theoretical aspects of fish bioenergetics, see reviews by Beamish et al. (1975), Webb (1978), Brett and Groves (1979), Elliott (1979), Kitchell (1983), From and Rasmussen (1984), and Tyler and Calow (1985).

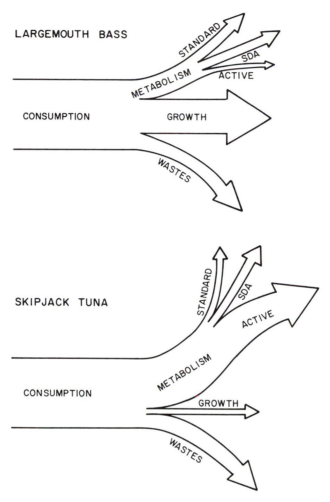

Figure 12.1 Allocation of consumed energy into the major components of the bioenergetics budget at maximum rations in the relatively sedentary largemouth bass and the actively foraging skipjack tuna. Widths of arrows are scaled to represent actual proportions of consumed energy allocated to each process. SDA is specific dynamic action. (Data from Kitchell 1983.)

12.2 DIRECT MEASUREMENTS OF MAJOR BIOENERGETIC COMPONENTS

In very few studies have all components of the bioenergetic budget for fish been measured independently. More typically, one or more of the major components is estimated from other studies or calculated by difference to balance the budget (Kitchell 1983). Because they form a balanced equation, determinations (or well-founded estimates) of any three of the main components—growth, metabolism, waste, consumption—allow the fourth to be calculated by difference. All errors associated with the three determinations, however, become a pooled error in the fourth component (Brett and Groves 1979; Solomon and Brafield 1972). Methods of estimating the four basic components of the balanced energy budget, as well as their limitations, are discussed in the following sections.

Table 12.1 Representative applications of bioenergetics to the study of fish biology.

Research use or objective	Species	Reference
Basic bioenergetic components		
Growth, consumption, metabolism	Northern pike	Diana (1983)
	Sauger	Minton and McLean (1982); Wahl and Nielsen (1985)
	Walleye	Swenson and Smith (1973)
	Largemouth bass	Adams et al. (1982b)
	Sockeye salmon	Brett (1976)
	Brown trout	Elliott (1976)
	Threespine stickleback	Allen and Wootton (1984)
	Eurasian perch	Thorpe (1977)
	Gizzard shad	Megrey (1978); Pierce (1977)
	Sand goby[a]	Healey (1972)
	Sargassumfish	Smith (1973)
	Rainbow trout	From and Rasmussen (1984)
	Six European species	Backiel (1971)
	Alewife	Stewart and Binkowski (1986)
Accumulation of contaminants		
Uptake of PCBs	Lake trout	Weininger (1978); Thomann and Connolly (1984)
Accumulation of PCBs and methylmercury	Yellow perch	Norstrom et al. (1976)
Effects of environmental variables		
Temperature effects on growth	Walleye, yellow perch	Kitchell et al. (1977)
Temperature effects on condition	Largemouth bass	Rice et al. (1983)
Prey availability on energy partitioning	Largemouth bass	Adams et al. (1982b)
Macrophyte harvesting on predator–prey relations	Bluegill	Breck and Kitchell (1979)
Prey availability and temperature on consumption	Walleye, sauger	Swenson (1977)
Food density	Atlantic menhaden	Durbin and Durbin (1983)
Food level, temperature	Largemouth bass	Rice (1990)
Life history strategies		
Diel migration	Tilapia[b]	Caulton (1978)
Feeding	Sea lamprey	Kitchell and Breck (1980)
Reproduction	American plaice	MacKinnon (1972)
	Threespine stickleback	Wootton et al. (1980)
	Northern anchovy	Hunter and Leong (1981)
Foraging	Skipjack tuna	Kitchell (1983)
Effects of predators on their prey		
	Lake trout	Stewart et al. (1981, 1983)
	Largemouth bass	Cochran and Adelman (1982)
	Sea lamprey	Kitchell and Breck (1980)
	Pacific sardine	Lasker (1970)
	Walleye	Lyons (1984)
Fish culture and management		
Manipulation of ponds	Channel catfish	Cuenco et al. (1985)
Optimal growth in hatcheries	Salmonids	Stauffer (1973)
Fishery management in Great Lakes	Salmonids and their prey	Stewart et al. (1981)
Stocking strategies	Esocids	Bevelhimer et al. (1985)
Population limitation processes	Yellowfin tuna	Sharp and Francis (1976)
Control of bluegill populations	Largemouth bass	Carline et al. (1984)
Closed-loop fish farming	Rainbow trout	Jorgensen (1976)

Table 12.1 Continued.

Research use or objective	Species	Reference
Energy balance of plant and animal food	Grass carp	Fisher (1972)
Energy balance of various foods	Salmonids	Cho et al. (1982)
Energy budgets for larval and young-of-year fish		
Growth, respiration	Blueback herring	Burbidge (1974)
Daily ration, growth, respiration	White bass	Wissing (1974)
Consumption, growth	Yellow perch	Mills and Forney (1981)
Growth, development	Striped bass	Eldridge et al. (1982)
Consumption, growth	Atlantic menhaden, spot, pinfish	Peters and Kjelson (1975)

[a] *Gobius minutus.*   [b] *Tilapia rendalli.*

12.2.1 Growth

Growth or production of fish populations is the total elaboration or synthesis of fish tissue during a specified time interval, including tissue produced by individuals that do not survive to the end of an interval (Ivlev 1966). Growth can be calculated as changes in biomass (weight), energy (calories), carbon, or nitrogen during an interval of measurement and includes somatic (protein and lipid) growth and the development of gonads. For the purpose of a basic bioenergetic budget, protein synthesis and lipid storage are usually considered together as somatic growth; gonadal development is not usually measured separately except for mature female fish. Detailed techniques and approaches for measuring growth, including their uses and limitations in both the laboratory and field, are addressed in Chapter 11; see also Bagenal and Tesch (1978), Weatherley (1978), and Jearld (1983).

Even though changes observed in growth over a time interval may include energy deposition in protein, lipid, and reproductive components, fishery biologists are usually interested in the sum of energy changes occurring in the interval of measurement. Protein elaboration may be the major concern of fish culturists or fishermen for economic reasons, whereas deposition of energy into lipid and gonad compartments may be critical for the species' survival and reproductive success. Protein growth is usually a positive energy change throughout the year (except possibly for starving fish), but quantities of lipids and gonad sizes can undergo relatively large temporal fluctuations, including net losses during certain periods of the year. Fish usually accumulate lipids during the summer and fall, then use them during the winter when food consumption is low and also during the spring for spawning. During spawning, female fish can lose up to 85% of their somatic energy (Glebe and Leggett 1981). Temporal changes in lipid storage levels usually can be accounted for by caloric analysis, whereas the energy value of spawned eggs can be calculated from sudden reductions in the gonadosomatic index, the ratio of gonad weight to total body weight (Scott 1979; Ursin 1979). Energy values of gonadal material should be accounted for calorimetrically because the energy content of eggs can be different from that of most somatic tissue.

Growth can be estimated from field data or in the laboratory by methods detailed in Chapter 11. It also can be derived indirectly from the balanced energy budget if metabolism, consumption, and assimilation are known. Direct measurement of growth has three principal advantages. (1) Growth data integrate feeding rate over time, and the effects of frequent variations in temperature and daily ration are minimized. (2) Growth rate is relatively easy to measure, and, of all the bioenergetic components, it is the one for which field data are most readily available. (3) The uncertainties of growth estimates in the energy budget are generally less than those of other components (Kitchell et al. 1977; Bartell et al. 1986). Growth estimates, obtained either directly or via the balanced budget, can be sensitive to proximate analysis of body constituents and, in particular, to caloric density; these measurements can have large effects on the energy budget's balance. Proximate analysis of the body constituents and calorimetry are addressed in Chapter 11.

12.2.2 Metabolism

Energy loses to metabolic demands are usually a large component of the bioenergetic budget of a fish (Figure 12.1). These energy costs can be partitioned into standard metabolism, metabolic costs of activity, and specific dynamic action (SDA).

12.2.2.1 Standard Metabolism

Standard metabolism (M_r in equation 12.2) is the rate of energy use by a fasting fish at rest. It is primarily a function of water temperature and body size. Because standard metabolism defines the baseline or lower bound for the scope for growth, it is an important variable in the bioenergetic budget. Energy use for metabolism is typically measured as the rate of oxygen consumption. Oxygen units can be converted to energy units with the oxycaloric average of 3.20–3.24 cal/mg O_2 (Brafield and Solomon 1972; Elliott and Davison 1975). Oxycaloric values can vary, however, according to the proportions of fat, carbohydrate, and protein catabolized (Elliott and Davison 1975). Detailed methods for measuring metabolic rates are discussed in Chapter 10. For many of the more common fish species, standard metabolic rates at various water temperatures and fish sizes can be obtained from the literature (some references are given in Table 12.1).

12.2.2.2 Activity-Dependent Metabolism

The activity metabolism component in the bioenergetic budget accounts for metabolism above that of the standard metabolic rate, such as occurs during foraging or spawning migrations. Fry (1957) defined "active metabolism" as the maximum metabolic rate at which an animal can sustain a high level of activity. Because fish typically operate at activity levels requiring more than standard metabolism but less than active metabolism, Rice et al. (1983) suggested the term "activity-dependent metabolism" to refer to energy costs associated with standard metabolism plus activity (i.e., $M_r + M_a$).

Activity-dependent metabolism may vary with species, sex, and time of year. If activity costs are high and are not properly accounted for, large errors can result when the metabolism term is used in the bioenergetic equation to calculate another major component such as energy consumption or growth. For some species with sedentary life styles such as largemouth bass, activity-dependent metabolism can be approximated by standard metabolism (Adams et al. 1982b;

Rice et al. 1983). In other species such as skipjack tuna, activity-dependent metabolism (M_a) can be a major fraction of total respiratory metabolism (Figure 12.1). Ware (1975) indicated that activity-dependent metabolism should be about 3 times standard metabolism for juvenile pelagic fish. Brett and Groves (1979) determined that the metabolic rate of migrating sockeye salmon was 8.5 times the standard. Minton and McLean (1982) reported that metabolic rates of sauger appear to be almost 4 times the standard during spring. Brett (1964) calculated that a 20-s burst of activity by a sockeye salmon cost as much energy as 179 min of standard metabolism.

Estimates of activity-dependent metabolism have been obtained by several methods. (1) Fish have been forced to swim against currents in laboratory respirometers (Brett 1964; Beamish 1970). (2) The Winberg multiplier (Winberg 1956) has been used, whereby the standard metabolic rate is doubled (Winberg II: Mann 1965; Gerking 1972) or tripled (Winberg III: Ware 1975) to estimate activity of fish in the wild. (3) Bioenergetic equations and models have been used to simulate activity-dependent metabolism as a function of fish size, swimming speed, and water temperature (Rice et al. 1983; Stewart et al. 1983). (4) The energy budget has been balanced by difference when there was little or no information about activity costs (Elliott 1976; Adams et al. 1982b).

12.2.2.3   Specific Dynamic Action (SDA)

Specific dynamic action comprises the energetic costs of processing and assimilating food, such as deamination of proteins and transport and deposition of lipids. It is usually calculated as a constant fraction of the energy consumed, and averages about 15% for carnivorous and omnivorous fish (Muir and Niimi 1972; Beamish 1974; Schalles and Wissing 1976).

12.2.3   Wastes: Egestion and Excretion

The energy lost with wastes can vary greatly among species, and depends on the nature of the diet. Winberg (1956) proposed that the assimilation efficiency of fish consuming a mixed diet was approximately 80%. Detritivores and herbivores, whose diets are high in fiber and ash, typically have efficiencies less than 80%; piscivores, whose diets are high in protein, commonly have efficiencies higher than 90% (Brett and Groves 1979). Even though Elliott (1976) found that egestion and excretion are functions of temperature and ration size, nonassimilated energy (egestion) and excretion can be estimated as a constant proportion of energy consumed (Beamish 1972, 1974; Niimi and Beamish 1974; Kitchell et al. 1977). Estimates of assimilation efficiency for many species are available in the literature. Direct measurements of assimilation efficiency can be made with the Conover (1966) method, the chromic oxide method (Windell and Bowen 1978), or fecal collection methods (Smith 1973).

12.2.4   Food Consumption

Ingestion represents the only route of energy input into a consumer; the remainder of the bioenergetic components depend on this input. We emphasize consumption over the other components in this chapter because it is not addressed elsewhere in the book, because the uses and limitations of several widely applied consumption methodologies developed since 1977 have not been summarized previously for practical use by fishery scientists, and because field estimates of consumption typically are infrequent and highly variable (Cochran and Adelman 1982; Diana 1983; Rice and Cochran 1984) and lack confidence limits (Diana 1979). The advantages and limitations of methods to estimate consumption rate must be recognized before the estimates are used in energy budget calculations.

Estimates of food consumed by fish in the field are influenced by many factors, including size of fish, amount of food eaten in a meal, number of meals in a day, rate of gastric clearing, water temperature, activity of the fish, type of food eaten, and prior feeding history (Windell 1978). Several of these variables are difficult to quantify outside the laboratory, so some investigators have used growth data coupled with metabolic estimates in the bioenergetic budget to predict consumption rates for fish in the wild (Kitchell and Breck 1980; Stewart et al. 1981; Kerr 1982; Rice and Cochran 1984).

The daily rations of fish have been estimated from field measurements (despite the problems mentioned), predicted from laboratory studies, and calculated from the balanced energy equation. Field estimates of daily ration are based primarily on measurements of gut contents and the rate at which the contents are evacuated from the stomach. Laboratory studies develop empirical relationships between food consumption and growth rates, which are applied to field measurements of growth to estimate consumption by wild fish (Warren and Davis 1967; Carline and Hall 1973; Wootton et al. 1980). The principal limitation of the laboratory approach is the expense in time and facilities necessary to study even a few of the many variables—temperature, day length, food density, fish activity, competition, etc.—that can affect growth and consumption in the field (Mann 1978). In this section, we discuss the methods used to directly estimate feeding rates in the field. For further discussions of methods for estimating consumption, see Mann (1978) and Windell (1978).

Field consumption rates have been estimated by three basic approaches. One is to assume that stomach contents decline exponentially with time for a given portion of food (as the remainder becomes increasingly refractory) and that feeding is continuous between sampling intervals. Another is to follow the chronology of feeding. The third is to assume that digestion is linear (i.e., a constant amount is digested per unit time) and that digestion times are long relative to periods of feeding.

12.2.4.1 Continuous Feeding Models

In the method originally proposed by Bajkov (1935) and modified by Thorpe (1977) and Eggers (1979), feeding is assumed to be continuous and constant over a feeding cycle:

$$C = 24 \cdot s \cdot k; \tag{12.3}$$

C = daily ration (percentage of body weight/d, or sometimes mg/[g $\cdot$ d]),
s = average amount of food in the stomach or gut over 24 h (percentage or mg/g), and
k = the instantaneous rate of gastric evacuation (h^{-1}).

This formula gives valid consumption estimates only if the sampled fish have the same average amount of food in their stomachs at the beginning and end of 24 h, and if the gastric evacuation rate is exponential (i.e., evacuation declines with the amount of material in the stomach).

Typically, s is estimated by sampling several fish at 2–6-h intervals during a 24-h period. The stomach contents of each interval are weighed, expressed as a proportion (percentage) of the fish's body weight to account for variations in body weight among individual fish, and averaged. Methods for calculating the amount of food present in the digestive tract of fish were described by Windell and Bowen (1978) and Bowen (1983). If nondestructive sampling is desired, the method of Seaburg and Moyle (1964) can be used to pump the stomach contents without killing the fish.

The stomach contents of many species vary substantially over the course of 24 h, violating a key assumption underlying equation (12.3). If this happens, the daily ration can be estimated from the stomach contents of fish sampled at various times of day. The amount of food ingested in the time between two sampling periods (C_t) is

$$C_t = S_t - S_0 + A; \qquad (12.4)$$

S_0 and S_t are the respective amounts of food in the stomach at the beginning and end of a sampling interval, and A is the amount of food evacuated from the stomach during the interval. Daily ration is calculated by summing the interval values for C_t.

The consumption model of Elliott and Persson (1978) is

$$C_t = \frac{(S_t - S_0 \, e^{-kt})kt}{1 - e^{-kt}}. \qquad (12.5)$$

As before, S_0 and S_t are amounts of food in the gut at the beginning and end of a sampling interval t hours long and k is the instantaneous rate of gastric evacuation. This model appears to be the most applicable one for estimating daily ration of fish collected in the field when (1) feeding is more or less continuous during daylight hours, (2) the amount of food in the gut at the start and at the end of a sampling interval is not necessarily the same, and (3) the digestion rate is exponential.

Equations (12.3) and (12.5) can be generally applied to species with a "fine-grained" diet (i.e., large numbers of small food particles) such as planktivores, detritivores, herbivores, and omnivores. It is less reliable with fish such as piscivores that typically consume and process a few large prey (Tyler 1970; Persson 1979; Cochran and Adelman 1982). The accuracy of consumption estimates obtained with these models increases with the frequency of sampling, because the assumption of constant feeding over a time interval is easier to meet when the interval is shorter (Elliott and Persson 1978).

Determination of Stomach Evacuation Rate. Stomach evacuation rate must be estimated accurately if calculations of daily rations are to be reliable (Darnell and Meierotto 1962; Jobling 1981; Allen and Wootton 1984). The form of the evacuation rate process (exponential or linear) is also important; compared to a linear digestion process, exponential digestion often gives lower estimates of consumption when digestion times are long. The coefficient *(k)* of the exponential evacuation rate can be calculated as

$$k = (1/t) \log_e (S_0/S_t); \qquad (12.6)$$

the terms are as defined for equation (12.5). As with most other physiological processes in fish, gastric evacuation rate increases with temperature; therefore, water temperature must be taken into account when k is estimated (Elliott 1972). Body size also influences stomach evacuation rate. Many workers have observed faster stomach evacuation rates in smaller fish (Flowerdew and Grove 1979; Mills et al. 1984). Failure to consider the effect of body size on evacuation rates can lead to underestimates of consumption for smaller fish and overestimates for larger fish.

To obtain k from field measurements, a time of day is selected during which fish are assumed not to feed. For fish that do not feed during darkness, for example, the decline in weight of stomach contents (relative to fish weight) during the night reflects evacuation of the stomach. Thus, the value of k over this nonfeeding period can be estimated from the slope of the regression of $\log_e$ (stomach contents) against time. The serial-slaughter method of Windell (1967) can also be used to estimate k from the decline in mean weight of gut contents. In this procedure, some fish in the sample are examined immediately after capture, and others are examined after they have been held in food-free environments such as cages for different time intervals. Another method is to feed groups of starved fish known amounts of food (or, less accurately, feed them to satiation) in the laboratory, examine subsamples of these fish at regular intervals to determine the percentage of food remaining in the guts, and regress these percentages against time (Elliott 1972; Peters and Hoss 1974). Other less-often applied but potentially accurate methods for measuring gastric evacuation rate, such as the X-ray and radioisotopic procedures, were discussed by Windell (1978). Exponential digestion rate models were discussed in detail by Jobling (1981). A sample calculation for determining exponential gastric evacuation rate and daily ration for continuous feeders is presented in Box 12.1.

12.2.4.2   Chronology-of-Feeding Methods

The chronology-of-feeding methods proposed by Keast and Welsh (1968) and Nakashima and Leggett (1978) to estimate consumption are based primarily on stomach content analyses for a large number of fish sampled over a 24-h period, and do not require information about stomach evacuation rate. Keast and Welsh (1968) summed the differences between successive maximum and minimum mean weights of stomach contents over a diel cycle to calculate consumption. Nakashima and Leggett (1978) summed mean food weights at feeding peaks over 24 h. Both methods assume noncontinuous or synchronous feeding of fish and no evacuation of food from the digestive tract during sampling. Fish with empty stomachs are included in the calculations.

A promising new method to estimate daily ration from a single collection of fish within a 24-h period was developed by Hayward and Margraf (1987). This procedure, which combines elements of both the Elliott–Persson model (equation 12.5) and the chronology-of-feeding method, was used to predict the daily ration of yellow perch in Lake Erie. First, 24-h feeding studies were done, trawl samples being taken every 3 h. These allowed daily consumption rates to be calculated, and established the times of peak feeding by yellow perch. Then, weight-specific food quantities were computed (dry weight of food divided by whole-body dry weight) for the time of maximum feeding. The median food quantity was

---

Box 12.1   Calculation of Exponential Stomach Evacuation Rate and Consumption Rate for an Omnivorous Fish that Feeds Continuously

Assume that samples of fish are collected in close proximity to each other in the same stream at 1000 hours (t_0), 1600 hours (t_1), 2200 hours (t_2), and 0400 hours (t_3). Average food contents in the stomachs of fish sampled on each occasion are $S_0 = 14$, $S_1 = 23$, $S_2 = 12$, and $S_3 = 4$ mg/g of fish.

For fish with "fine-grained" diets that feed more or less continuously during daylight hours but not at night, the exponential digestion rate coefficient (k) is calculated for a nighttime interval when there is no new food intake:

$$k = (1/t) \log_e (S_2/S_3).$$

In this example, $S_2 = 12$ and $S_3 = 4$ mg/g; the time interval between these measurements is $t = 6$ h:

$$k = (1/6) \log_e (12/4) = 0.18 \cdot h^{-1}.$$

The ration or consumption of this species for the first 6-h period can then be calculated from equation (12.5):

$$C_t = \frac{(S_1 - S_0 e^{-kt})kt}{1 - e^{-kt}};$$

$$C_{6h} = \frac{(23 - 14e^{-0.18(6)}) (0.18 \cdot 6)}{1 - e^{-0.18(6)}} = \frac{(23 - 4.75) (1.08)}{0.66};$$

$C_{6h} = 30$ mg/g in 6 h, or 3.0% of body weight.

---

multiplied by a temperature-dependent evacuation rate (k in equation 12.6) and regressed against calculated daily consumption. Thereafter, this calibration curve allowed daily consumption rate to be determined graphically from analysis of a single trawl sample taken during the peak feeding hours.

Most methods involving chronologies of feeding have two principal difficulties. First, they are likely to underestimate daily rations (Elliott and Persson 1978; Jobling 1981; Allen and Wootton 1984). Second, they generally require that large numbers of fish be collected at several intervals over a 24-h period, which may not be feasible for many species.

12.2.4.3   Carnivore Feeding Models

Fish with "fine-grained" diets composed of a large number of small food items are generally herbivores, detritivores, planktivores, and omnivores that feed at lower trophic levels of the biological community. These fish usually feed more or less continuously during daylight hours, and their digestion process can be described by an exponential digestion function. In contrast, the top carnivores are generally piscivores that consume a few relatively large prey over a feeding cycle. In these fish, digestion rate is typically a linear process (Swenson and Smith 1973; Forney 1977; Diana 1979; Adams et al. 1982a), digestion time is long relative to the length of the feeding period, and diurnal feeding patterns can be either synchro-nous (i.e., most or all of the fish feed at the same time) or asynchronous.

The methods for calculating daily ration of piscivores are of two types. The choice of method depends primarily on the length of digestion time relative to the length of time between meals, and on whether diurnal feeding patterns are synchronous or asynchronous. For coldwater fish such as northern pike, digestion time is considerably longer than the time between meals. For warmwater piscivores such as largemouth bass, digestion time can be less than the time between meals.

Coldwater Fish. For fish with digestion times considerably longer than 24 h, the model proposed by Diana (1979) can be used to calculate daily ration:

$$C = \frac{M \cdot n}{B' \cdot N};$$
(12.7)

C = daily ration (% body weight/d),
M = average size of ingested meal (percentage of body weight),
n = number of fish that contain food in the stomach,
B' = number of days for gastric evacuation, and
N = total number of fish, including those with empty stomachs.

This feeding model has the same form as equation (12.3) because the average meal size of the population is Mn/N, and the stomach evacuation rate per day $(24 \cdot k)$ has the same unit (d^{-1}) as $(1/B')$. In equation (12.7), daily ration is calculated by (meal size)/(meal frequency), frequency (f) being the ratio $f = B'N/n$. An important assumption inherent in consumption models based on meal size and frequency is that feeding by the population is asynchronous, and that a sample of predators taken at any time during the day would include prey representative of all levels of feeding.

The consumption model developed by Popova and Sytina (1977) is also applicable to coldwater piscivores whose digestion lasts several days:

$$C = \frac{n}{N} \sum_{i=1}^{V} \frac{(S_i/n_i)}{V};$$
(12.8)

C = daily ration (% body weight/d),
N = total number of fish in the sample,
n = number of fish in a sample that contained food,
V = number of days for digestion at a given temperature,
n_i = number of fish in the sample that contained food eaten on day i, and
S_i = original undigested weight of all prey items eaten by n_i predators on day i, expressed as a percentage of body weight.

This type of consumption model has also been applied to the energy budget of sauger (Minton and McLean 1982). The feeding model developed by Swenson and Smith (1973) for walleye, and also applied to sauger by Wahl and Nielsen (1985), is similar to the Diana (1979) model for northern pike but takes into account ingestion of a range of prey size-classes by a predator and calculates the daily ration for several periods during a feeding cycle.

Examples of food consumption calculations by both methods for coldwater species are presented in Box 12.2.

Warmwater Fish. Predators that have short digestion times relative to periods between meals generally have digestion times of less than 24 h. For these fish, rates are calculated in units of hours, compared to units of days for coldwater piscivores, and calculation of daily ration is very sensitive to estimated digestion rate. The feeding model of Adams et al. (1982a) can be used to calculate the daily consumption *(C)* of warmwater piscivores:

$$C = 100 \sum_{i=1}^{N} \frac{(Pw_i/Bw_i)}{N};$$

(12.9)

C = daily ration (% body weight/d),
Pw_i = estimated total weight at capture of prey when ingested by predator i over a defined 24-h period,
Bw_i = weight of predator i that consumed those prey, and
N = total number of predators in a sample, including those with empty stomachs.

In addition to the large variations in digestion rate times, the principal differences between this consumption model and the one for coldwater predators are that this method (equation 12.9) does not require calculation of meal frequency or consumption estimates at separate intervals over a feeding cycle—provided that the time to 90 or 95% digestion is less than 24 h. The feeding model for warmwater piscivores is particularly applicable to fish that display synchronous feeding, such as the largemouth bass (DeAngelis et al. 1984). Calculation of daily ration based on meal frequency (equation 12.7) seems to be justified for asynchronous feeders, such as some of the coldwater piscivores (northern pike, sauger), but does not appear to be the most straightforward methodology for nonrandom or synchronous feeders.

An example calculation of food consumption for a warmwater fish is presented in Box 12.3.

12.2.4.4 Determination of Feeding Model Components.

Calculation of daily ration for both cold- and warmwater piscivores requires estimates of the original weight of the ingested prey and the digestion rate of prey at various temperatures, and knowledge of whether the diurnal feeding pattern is synchronous or asynchronous.

Weight of Ingested Prey. Predators sampled from a population typically have stomach contents that range from freshly ingested prey to the hard remains (e.g., bones and chitin) of completely digested organisms. The original weights of consumed prey can be estimated in three ways. (1) Ingested prey can be compared to preserved specimens of prey that have been weighed, fed to predators, and digested for various periods before they were recovered (Darnell and Meierotto 1962; Popova 1978). (2) Prey lengths can be compared with preestablished length–weight regressions for the prey species; the regressions can be based on total length, standard length, backbone length, or some other appropriate measure

---

Box 12.2   Calculation of Food Consumption for Coldwater Predators

Example 1. Daily ration *(C)* calculation for northern pike (equation 12.7)

$$C = \frac{M \cdot n}{B' \cdot N};$$

M = 50 g/kg (average meal size),
n = 50 (fish containing food),
B' = 3 d (gastric evacuation time),
N = 100 (total fish in sample).

$$C = \frac{(50 \text{ g/kg}) (50 \text{ fish})}{(3 \text{ d}) (100 \text{ total fish})} = 8.3 \text{ g/(kg} \cdot \text{d)}.$$

Example 2. Daily ration calculation for zander (equation 12.8).

$$C = \frac{n}{N} \sum_{i=1}^{V} \frac{(S_i/n_i)}{V};$$

N = 50 (total number of fish),
n = 32 (fish containing food),
V = 3 d (gastric evacuation time),
n_1, n_2, n_3 = 10, 15, and 7, respectively (number of fish in a sample that contained food on days 1, 2, and 3).
S_1, S_2, S_3 = 15, 23.5, and 18, respectively (sum of percent body weights consumed by all predators on days 1, 2, and 3; for example, S_3 = 1.6% + 2.3% + 4.7% + 1.7% + 1.1% + 3.2% + 3.4% = 18%).

$$C = \left(\frac{32}{50}\right) \left(\frac{(15/10) + (23.5/15) + (18/7)}{3}\right) = 1.2 \text{ g/(kg} \cdot \text{d)}.$$

(Minton and McLean 1982). (3) The size or weight of relatively indigestible parts of prey (otoliths, bone fragments, gizzards, etc.) can be compared with standard regressions against whole body weight for the prey species to estimate the original weight of the ingested animal (Popova 1967; Minckley and Paulson 1976).

Digestion Rates. Methods used to determine digestion rates of carnivorous fish differ from those used with fish that have fine-grained diets, continuous feeding patterns, and exponential digestion rates. For piscivores, fish prey of known weights that were eaten voluntarily or force-fed are recovered at various intervals either by killing the predator or by pumping its stomach (Hunt 1960; Beamish 1972; Swenson and Smith 1973; Steigenberger and Larkin 1974; Diana 1979; McGee et al. 1979; Adams et al. 1982a; Minton and McLean 1982). For a particular experimental temperature, the fraction of original prey weight digested is graphed against hours since feeding, and the resulting regression is used to calculate digestion. In carnivorous fish, time to either 90 or 95% digestion is typically used as the endpoint of digestion time; digestion of the remaining 5–10% is slowed significantly because of hard parts such as skeletal remains and chitin.

Box 12.3 Calculation of Daily Food Consumption for a Warmwater Predator

For a warmwater piscivore such as largemouth bass, the daily ration of the population can be calculated, as percent of body weight, from equation (12.9):

$$C = 100 \sum_{i=1}^{N} \frac{(Pw_i/Bw_i)}{N}.$$

Example. The stomachs of six largemouth bass contained fish prey in various stages of digestion. Reconstruction of the original weights of these prey is explained in Adams et al. (1982a).

Fish	Estimated weight of ingested prey (g)	Fish weight (g)
1	50, 34, 30	1,160
2	40	650
3	30, 29	710
4	70, 57	1,000
5	0	700
6	45	615

$$C = 100 \left(\frac{(114/1,160) + (40/650) + (59/710) + (127/1,000) + (0/700) + (45/615)}{6} \right)$$

$$= 7.4\% \text{ of body weight or } 74 \text{ mg/(g} \cdot \text{d).}$$

Water temperature, body sizes of predator and prey, meal size, and meal frequency all may affect digestion rate, as discussed by Windell (1978), Flowerdew and Grove (1979), and Mills et al. (1984). In addition, force-feeding of fish may prolong digestion because of handling stress, leading to underestimates of consumption (Swenson and Smith 1973).

Diurnal Feeding Pattern. Fish may feed synchronously (at particular periods of the day) or asynchronously (randomly), and this affects the choice of a consumption model. Calculation of daily ration based on meal frequencies requires that feeding be asynchronous throughout the day. To determine the diel feeding pattern of a fish, the average amount of food in the digestive tract (expressed as a percentage of body weight or as mg/g) or the number of prey in the gut should be measured at each of several intervals over a feeding cycle. To determine if gut contents are uniform over all sampling intervals (i.e., if the feeding pattern is asynchronous), average digestive tract contents (as percent weight or numbers) can be analyzed statistically by chi-square procedures (Minton and McLean 1982), nonparametric tests such as Kruskal–Wallis or Mann–Whitney (Godin 1981), one-way analysis of covariance combined with inferential analysis (Jenkins and Green 1977), or negative bionomial distribution statistics (Sibert and Obrebski 1976).

12.3 ESTIMATION OF BIOENERGETIC COMPONENTS WITH EQUATIONS

In the previous section, guidelines were given for obtaining direct estimates of the major bioenergetic budget components from field or laboratory studies. These components can also be estimated indirectly with size- and temperature-dependent bioenergetic equations.

Fish size and water temperature are two of the most important variables that influence estimation of consumption and metabolism in bioenergetic equations. In the simple versions of the balanced energy budget (equations 12.1 and 12.2), none of the main components except respiration include adjustments for weight and temperature. Kitchell et al. (1974, 1977) and Elliott (1976) expanded the basic version of the energy budget to account for the influences of fish weight and water temperature on consumption, egestion, and excretion. The metabolism term, called "respiration" in their models (because metabolism is measured by respirometry) and denoted R, was also modified to explicitly include the costs of activity. The main components can be expressed as

$$C = R + F + U + \frac{dB}{B \cdot dt}. \tag{12.10}$$

As before, C, F, and U are consumption, egestion, and excretion rates, but total metabolism now is R and growth is dB/Bdt, B being biomass and t being time.

As always, C can be estimated by addition if the other terms are known. It also can be estimated independently as a fraction of maximum consumption:

$$C = C_{\max} \cdot P \cdot r_c;$$

$C_{\max} = a_1 B^{b_1}$, the weight-specific maximum consumption rate by fish fed ad libitum at their optimum temperature (g food/g fish); B is biomass in grams; and a_1 and b_1 are constants;

r_c = a temperature-dependent proportional adjustment (0.0–1.0) of $C_{\max}$ used when temperature is suboptimal ($r_c = 1.0$ at optimum temperature), not to be confused with the r that denotes standard metabolism in equation (12.2); see Parker (1974), Kitchell et al. (1977), Thornton and Lessem (1978), and Weininger (1978) for alternative expressions of this term; and

P = a scaling factor (0.0–1.0) that indicates the proportion of temperature-adjusted $C_{\max}$ (i.e., of $C_{\max} \cdot r_c$) that is actually consumed. The bioenergetic model of Hewett and Johnson (1987) uses an iterative technique to find the required P value.

The coefficient (a_1), exponent (b_1), and adjustment factors (r_c) in this expression are determined from prior laboratory experiments.

The total metabolic or respiration rate has two terms:

$$R = R_{r+a} + s \cdot C; \tag{12.11}$$

R_{r+a} is activity-dependent metabolism (standard plus activity metabolism, Section 12.2.2.2), and s is the coefficient for specific dynamic action (SDA = $s \cdot C$,

Section 12.2.2.3). The coefficient s, usually around 0.15, is determined in laboratory studies.

Activity-dependent metabolism is affected by temperature (T, °C) and swimming speed (S, cm/s):

$$R_{r+a} = a_2 B^{b_2} e^{mT} e^{gS};$$ (12.12)

again, the coefficients and exponents a_2, b_2, m, and g are determined empirically in the laboratory.

The function for R_{r+a} was first derived by Stewart et al. (1983) for lake trout, and Rice et al. (1983) applied it to largemouth bass. In the bioenergetic models developed for percids, the respiration equation is also a function of temperature and fish weight (Kitchell et al. 1977), but a different function is used for temperature dependence (a function similar to r_c), and a single constant is used to adjust for the effects of activity rather than the activity metabolism term based on swimming speed as in equation (12.12).

For the waste loss components ($F + U$) of equation (12.10), Elliott (1976) developed equations for the temperature dependence of egestion and excretion. However, such parameter resolution may not be necessary in all cases. Kitchell et al. (1977) showed that the sum of these two waste losses is essentially independent of temperature (the temperature effects nearly cancel out). For practical purposes, the waste term can be treated as an empirically determined, constant proportion of consumption (Section 12.2.3). Bartell et al. (1986) demonstrated that uncertainty in the waste loss parameters contributes only a relatively small amount to the uncertainty in predicted growth or consumption.

Use of the bioenergetics equation to calculate daily ration is demonstrated in Box 12.4.

Because temperature has a dominating influence on the metabolism, growth, digestion, and consumption rate of fish, the value of the temperature parameter used in bioenergetics models such as equation (12.11) is critical for accurate model predictions. When actual temperatures of the water occupied by fish living in a heterothermal environment (e.g., lakes or reservoirs that stratify in summer) are unknown, preferred temperature or optimal temperature for growth will provide a more realistic estimate for use in the bioenergetics equations than temperatures representing only one part of the environment. For example, bioenergetic simulations by Kitchell et al. (1977) showed that the predicted and observed growth of age-3 walleyes was similar only when the optimal temperature for growth (22°C) was used in the model instead of the observed surface water temperature of 27°C.

One of the most useful applications of the bioenergetics model is to estimate consumption from laboratory data on the physiological energetics of a species, field data on growth, and thermal history information (Hewett and Johnson 1987). Because growth is an integrator of food consumption over time, bioenergetics models generally have less error when they calculate consumption from growth data than when they predict growth from ration data (Bartell et al. 1986; Hewett and Johnson 1987).

Physiological data are unavailable for many fish species, but it still may be possible (and useful) to treat them in generalized bioenergetic models. Physiological parameters can be estimated from data on closely related species or

Box 12.4   Calculation of Daily Consumption Rate with the Bioenergetic Equation

Problem: calculate the daily ration of a 100-g largemouth bass that is growing at the average rate of 1 g/d at a temperature of 20°C as it swims at an average speed of 2 cm/s over a 24-h period. Use the empirically derived constants of Rice et al. (1983) with equations (12.10)–(12.12) of this chapter.

The governing bioenergetic equation is

$$C = R + F + U + (dB/Bdt);$$

C = daily consumption (to be calculated),
R = total metabolism (measured as respiration),
F = egestion,
U = excretion,
B = biomass = 100 g (given),
t = time = 1 d (given), and
dB/Bdt = growth = 1g/(100g · d) = $0.010 \cdot d^{-1}$ (given).

Note that all of the components of the equation are weight-specific rates, that is, g/(g · d).

Waste $(F + U)$ is assumed to be a constant proportion of consumption:

$$F + U = (f + u) \cdot C;$$

f = egestion coefficient = 0.104 (from Rice et al.), and
u = excretion coefficient = 0.079 (from Rice et al.).

Thus,

$$F + U = (0.104 + 0.079) \cdot C = 0.183C,$$

and the bioenergetic equation so far is

$$C = R + 0.183C + 0.010.$$

Total metabolism is

$$R = R_{r+a} + \text{SDA} = R_{r+a} + s \cdot c,$$

and activity-dependent metabolism (R_{r+a}) is

$$R_{r+a} = a_2 B^{b_2} e^{mT} e^{gS};$$

SDA = specific dynamic action, assumed to be a constant proportion of consumption,
s = SDA coefficient = 0.142 (from Rice et al.),
a_2 = 0.027 (expanded from hourly respiration in Rice et al. to account for caloric density: [0.348 mg O_2/(g · h)] × [24 h/d] × [3.24 cal/mg O_2] × [0.001 g/cal]),
b_2 = −0.355 (from Rice et al.),
m = 0.0313°C^{-1} (from Rice et al.),

Box 12.4 Continued.

T = temperature = 20°C (given),
g = 0.0196 s/cm (from Rice et al.), and
S = swimming speed = 2 cm/s (given).

Thus,

$$R_{r+a} = 0.027(100)^{-0.355}e^{0.0313(20)}e^{0.0196(2)} = 0.010 \text{ g/(g} \cdot \text{d)},$$

and

$$R = 0.010 + 0.142C.$$

The bioenergetic equation now is

$$C = 0.010 + 0.142C + 0.183C + 0.010;$$

$$C = 0.02/0.675 = 0.030 \text{ g/(g} \cdot \text{d)}.$$

Solution: the fish is consuming an average 3% of its body weight daily.

---

approximated from regressions based on data from many species (Robinson et al. 1983). Sensitivity analyses performed by Bartell et al. (1986) and Stewart and Binkowski (1986) on bioenergetics models indicate that, for some parameters, species-specific values impart little more precision to predicted growth or consumption than generalized values.

Bioenergetic models are now available for use on microcomputers (Hewett and Johnson 1987, 1989; Hewett 1989). To predict consumption, for example, the model of Hewett and Johnson (1987) requires input of the main physiological parameters, initial and final fish weights, and the thermal history of the fish. Documentation supplied with the models includes all the necessary physiological input parameters for lake trout, coho and chinook salmon, largemouth bass and bluegill, walleye and perch, lamprey, dace, and alewife.

Used with both species-specific parameters and parameters pooled from several species, bioenergetic models have been applied to more than 30 fish species to address a variety of research objectives and needs (Table 12.1). Most of these fish are important game and forage species representing primarily salmonids (Elliott 1976; Stewart et al. 1981, 1983), centrarchids (Breck and Kitchell 1979; Rice et al. 1983; Rice and Cochran 1984), percids (Kitchell et al. 1977), and esocids (Bevelhimer et al. 1985).

12.4 CRITERIA FOR APPLYING THE BIOENERGETICS APPROACH

A variety of factors should be considered when the bioenergetics (balanced energy budget) approach is applied in fishery biology. The importance of the research needs and objectives should be a large influence on the level of effort, cost, and time allocated for development and application of a bioenergetics budget. For example, if the principal objective of a research project were to develop a management strategy for salmonids and their prey in the Great Lakes, this could require a much larger allocation of research resources than would the estimation of sunfish growth in a small farm pond.

In addition to the importance of the research objectives, the information available on the principal components of the energy budget should be an important consideration in the development and application of an energy budget for a particular research need. For several species of percids, salmonids, and centrarchids, the important bioenergetic parameters are available from previous studies (Table 12.1). For species in these groups, a relatively smaller effort would be required to estimate the major components of the energy budget with the equations (12.10 and 12.11) in section 12.3 than to do so by direct measurements (Section 12.2).

The accuracy and reliability of results will be affected both by the methods by which the bioenergetic components will be estimated and by the precision of the input terms. If the penalty for incorrectly predicting production (growth) is high, such as economic failure in a fish culture system, then increased effort and resources should be channeled into obtaining more precise estimates of such critical input parameters as temperature and feed consumption.

Sensitivity analysis is a useful way to evaluate how uncertainty or variation in the input parameters affects the uncertainty in predicted consumption or growth. Sensitivity analyses have been applied to bioenergetics models by Kitchell et al. (1977), Weininger (1978), Majkowski and Bramall (1980), Stewart et al. (1981), and Rice et al. (1983) and have been further evaluated by Bartell et al. (1986). These analyses can be used to assess the relative importance of the various input parameters for growth predictions, and thus can be employed to identify those model parameters and components that require further research efforts (e.g., allocation of research money), refinement, or simplification. For example, sensitivity analyses of growth models have indicated that uncertainty in parameter estimates for egestion and excretion contributes only a small amount to uncertainty in predicted growth or consumption (Bartell et al. 1986). Typically, the highest sensitivities for model parameters tend to be in the allometric functions for routine metabolism and consumption (Rice et al. 1983; Stewart et al. 1983).

Tests of bioenergetic model predictions are rare because the necessary data are difficult to obtain (Hewett and Johnson 1987). Model predictions can be tested by comparing independently measured bioenergetic components with those estimated by balancing the energy budget. Validation procedures for bioenergetics models have been discussed and applied by Rice and Cochran (1984). In the few studies in which the predictions of energy budgets have been compared with observed field values (Healey 1972; Adams 1976; Mills and Forney 1981; Diana 1983; Rice and Cochran 1984), the values have agreed reasonably well.

In summary, the use of bioenergetic budgets is a powerful approach for addressing a variety of research and management questions that may not be easily answered otherwise. Bioenergetics can be used to estimate patterns and magnitudes of growth and consumption, to evaluate the effects of environmental variables on fish dynamics and the effects of predators on their prey, to assess the effectiveness of various fish culture and management techniques, to predict the uptake and accumulation of contaminants in fish, and to help interpretation of various life history strategies. This chapter has provided some practical methods and guidelines for obtaining estimates of the major energy budget components and has suggested ways to apply bioenergetics in fishery biology.

12.5 REFERENCES

Adams, S. M. 1976. The ecology of eelgrass, *Zostera marina* (L.), fish communities. II. Functional analysis. Journal of Experimental Marine Biology and Ecology 22:293–311.

Adams, S. M., R. B. McLean, and M. M. Huffman. 1982a. Structuring of a predator population through temperature-mediated effects on prey availability. Canadian Journal of Fisheries and Aquatic Sciences 39:1175–1184.

Adams, S. M., R. B. McLean, and J. A. Parrotta. 1982b. Energy partitioning in largemouth bass under conditions of seasonally fluctuating prey availability. Transactions of the American Fisheries Society 111:549–558.

Allen, J. R. M., and R. J. Wootton. 1982. The effect of ration and temperature on the growth of the three-spined stickleback, *Gasterosteus aculeatus* L. Journal of Fish Biology 20:409–422.

Allen, J. R. M., and R. J. Wootton. 1984. Temporal patterns in diet and rate of food consumption of the three-spined stickleback (*Gasterosteus aculeatus* L.) in Llyn Frongock, an upland Welsh Lake. Freshwater Biology 14:335–346.

Backiel, T. 1971. Production and food consumption of predatory fish in the Vistual River. Journal of Fish Biology 3:369–405.

Bagenal, T. B., and F. W. Tesch. 1978. Age and growth. Pages 101–136 *in* T. Bagenal, editor. Methods for assessment of fish production in fresh waters. Blackwell Scientific Publications, Oxford, England.

Bajkov, A. D. 1935. How to estimate the daily food consumption of fish under natural conditions. Transactions of the American Fisheries Society 65:288–289.

Bartell, S. M., J. E. Breck, R. H. Gardner, and A. L. Brenkert. 1986. Individual parameter perturbation and error analysis of bioenergetics models of fish growth. Canadian Journal of Fisheries and Aquatic Sciences 43:160–168.

Beamish, F. W. H. 1970. Oxygen consumption of largemouth bass, *Micropterus salmoides,* in relation to swimming speed and temperature. Canadian Journal of Zoology 48:1221–1228.

Beamish, F. W. H. 1972. Ration size and digestion in largemouth bass, *Micropterus salmoides* Lacépède. Canadian Journal of Zoology 50:153–164.

Beamish, F. W. H. 1974. Apparent specific dynamic action of largemouth bass, *Micropterus salmoides*. Journal of the Fisheries Research Board of Canada 31:1763–1769.

Beamish, F. W. H., A. J. Niimi, and P. F. K. P. Lett. 1975. Bioenergetics of teleost fishes: environmental influences. Pages 187–209 *in* L. Bolis, H. P. Maddrell, and K. Schmidt-Nielsen, editors. Comparative physiology—functional aspects of structural materials. North-Holland Publishing, Amsterdam.

Bevelhimer, M. S., R. A. Stein, and R. F. Carline. 1985. Assessing significance of physiological differences among three esocids with a bioenergetics model. Canadian Journal of Fisheries and Aquatic Sciences 42:57–69.

Bowen, S. H. 1983. Quantitative description of the diet. Pages 325–336 *in* L. A. Nielsen and D. L. Johnson, editors. Fisheries techniques. American Fisheries Society, Bethesda, Maryland.

Brafield, A. E., and D. J. Solomon. 1972. Oxy-calorific coefficients for animals respiring nitrogenous substrates. Comparative Biochemistry and Physiology A, Comparative Physiology 43:837–841.

Breck, J. E., and J. F. Kitchell. 1979. Effects of macrophyte harvesting on simulated predator–prey interactions. Pages 221–228 *in* J. E. Breck, R. T. Prentki, and O. L. Loucks, editors. Conference on aquatic plants, lake management and ecosystem consequences of lake harvesting. Institute of Environmental Studies, University of Wisconsin, Madison.

Brett, J. R. 1964. The respiratory metabolism and swimming performance of young sockeye salmon. Journal of the Fisheries Research Board of Canada 21:1183–1226.

Brett, J. R. 1976. Scope for metabolism and growth of sockeye salmon, *Oncorhynchus nerka,* and some related energetics. Journal of the Fisheries Research Board of Canada 33:307–313.

Brett, J. R., and T. D. D. Groves. 1979. Physiological energetics. Pages 279–352 *in* W. S. Hoar, D. J. Randall, and J. R. Brett, editors. Fish physiology, volume 8. Academic Press, New York.

Burbidge, R. G. 1974. Distribution, growth, selective feeding, and energy transformation of young-of-the-year blueback herring, *Alosa aestivalis* (Mitchill), in the James River, Virginia. Transactions of the American Fisheries Society 103:297–311.

Carline, R. F., and J. D. Hall. 1973. Evaluation of a method for estimating food consumption rates of fish. Journal of the Fisheries Research Board of Canada 30:623–629.

Carline, R. F., B. L. Johnson, and T. J. Hall. 1984. Estimation and interpretation of proportional stock density for fish populations in Ohio impoundments. North American Journal of Fisheries Management 4:139–154.

Caulton, M. S. 1978. The importance of habitat temperatures for growth in the tropical cichlid *Tilapia rendalli* Boulenger. Journal of Fish Biology 13:99–112.

Cho, C. Y., S. J. Slinger, and H. S. Bayley. 1982. Bioenergetics of salmonid fishes: energy intake, expenditure and productivity. Comparative Biochemistry and Physiology B, Comparative Biochemistry 73:25–41.

Cochran, P. A., and I. R. Adelman. 1982. Seasonal aspects of daily ration and diet of largemouth bass *Micropterus salmoides* with an evaluation of gastric evacuation rates. Environmental Biology of Fishes 7:265–275.

Conover, R. J. 1966. Assimilation of organic matter by zooplankton. Limnology and Oceanography 11:338–345.

Cooney, T. D. 1973. Yolk sac stage energetics of the larvae of three Hawaiian fishes. Master's thesis. University of Hawaii, Honolulu.

Cuenco, M. L., R. R. Stickney, and W. E. Grant. 1985. Fish bioenergetics and growth in aquaculture ponds: I. Individual fish model development. Ecological Modelling 27:169–190.

Darnell, R. M., and R. R. Meierotto. 1962. Determination of feeding chronology in fishes. Transactions of the American Fisheries Society 91:313–320.

DeAngelis, D. L., S. M. Adams, and J. E. Breck. 1984. A stochastic predation model: application to largemouth bass feeding. Ecological Modelling 24:25–41.

Diana, J. S. 1979. The feeding pattern and daily ration of a top carnivore, the northern pike *(Esox lucius).* Canadian Journal of Zoology 57:2121–2127.

Diana, J. S. 1983. An energy budget for northern pike. Canadian Journal of Zoology 61:1968–1975.

Durbin, E. G., and A. G. Durbin. 1983. Energy and nitrogen budgets for the Atlantic menhaden, *Brevoortia tyrannus* (Pisces:Clupeidae), a filter-feeding planktivore. U.S. National Marine Fisheries Service Fishery Bulletin 81:177–199.

Eggers, D. M. 1979. Comments on some recent methods of estimating food consumption by fish. Journal of the Fisheries Research Board of Canada 36:1018–1019.

Eldridge, M. B., J. A. Whipple, and M. J. Bowers. 1982. Bioenergetics and growth of striped bass, *Morone saxatilis,* embryos and larvae. U.S. National Marine Fisheries Service Fishery Bulletin 80:461–474.

Elliott, J. M. 1972. Rates of gastric evacuation in brown trout *Salmo trutta.* Freshwater Biology 2:1–18.

Elliott, J. M. 1976. The energetics of feeding, metabolism and growth of brown trout *(Salmo trutta* L.) in relation to body weight, water temperature and ration size. Journal of Animal Ecology 45:923–948.

Elliott, J. M. 1979. Energetics of freshwater teleosts. Symposia of the Zoological Society of London 44:29–61.

Elliott, J. M., and W. Davison. 1975. Energy equivalents of oxygen consumption in animal energetics. Oecologia (Berlin) 19:195–201.

Elliott, J. M., and L. Persson. 1978. The estimation of daily rates of food consumption by fish. Journal of Animal Ecology 47:977–991.

Fisher, Z. 1972. The elements of energy balance in grass carp (*Ctenopharyngodon idella* Val.). Part III. Assimilability of proteins, carbohydrates, and lipids by fish fed with plant and animal food. Polish Archives of Hydrobiology 19:83–95.

Flath, L. E., and J. S. Diana. 1985. Seasonal energy dynamics of the alewife in southeastern Lake Michigan. Transactions of the American Fisheries Society 114:328–337.

Flowerdew, M. W., and D. J. Grove. 1979. Some observations of the effects of body weight, temperature, meal size and quality on gastric time in turbot, *Scophthalmus maximus* (L.), using radiography. Journal of Fish Biology 14:229–238.

Forney, J. L. 1977. Reconstruction of yellow perch *(Perca flavescens)* cohorts from examination of walleye *(Stizostedion vitreum vitreum)* stomachs. Journal of the Fisheries Research Board of Canada 34:925–932.

From, J., and G. Rasmussen. 1984. A growth model, gastric evacuation, and body composition in rainbow trout, *Salmo gairdneri* Richardson, 1836. Dana 3:61–139.

Fry, F. E. J. 1957. The aquatic respiration of fish. Pages 1–63 *in* M. S. Brown, editor. The physiology of fish, volume 1. Academic Press, New York.

Gerking, S. D. 1972. Revised food consumption estimate of a bluegill sunfish population in Wyland Lake, Indiana, USA. Journal of Fish Biology 4:301–308.

Glebe, B. D., and W. C. Leggett. 1981. Latitudinal variations in energy allocation and use during the freshwater migrations of American shad *(Alosa sapidissima)* and their life history consequences. Canadian Journal of Fisheries and Aquatic Sciences 38:806–820.

Godin, J.-G. J. 1981. Daily patterns of feeding behavior, daily rations, and diets of juvenile pink salmon *(Oncorhynchus gorbuscha)* in two marine bays of British Columbia. Canadian Journal of Fisheries and Aquatic Sciences 38:10–15.

Hayward, R. S., and F. J. Margraf. 1987. Eutrophication effects on prey size and food availability to yellow perch in Lake Erie. Transactions of the American Fisheries Society 116:210–223.

Healey, M. C. 1972. Bioenergetics of the sand goby *(Gobius minutus)* population. Journal of the Fisheries Research Board of Canada 29:187–194.

Hewett, S. W. 1989. Ecological applications of bioenergetics models. American Fisheries Society Symposium 6:113–120.

Hewett, S. W., and B. L. Johnson. 1987. A generalized bioenergetics model of fish growth for micro-computers. University of Wisconsin, Sea Grant Technical Report WIS-SG-87-245, Madison.

Hewett, S. W., and B. L. Johnson. 1989. A general bioenergetics model for fishes. American Fisheries Society Symposium 6:206–208.

Hunt, B. P. 1960. Digestion rate and food consumption of Florida gar, warmouth, and largemouth bass. Transactions of the American Fisheries Society 89:206–210.

Hunter, J. R., and R. Leong. 1981. The spawning energetics of female northern anchovy, *Engraulis mordax*. U.S. National Marine Fisheries Society Fishery Bulletin 79:215–230.

Ivlev, V. S. 1966. The biological productivity of waters. Journal of the Fisheries Research Board of Canada 23:1727–1759.

Jearld, A. 1983. Age determination. Pages 301–324 *in* L. A. Nielsen and D. L. Johnson, editors. Fisheries techniques. American Fisheries Society, Bethesda, Maryland.

Jenkins, B. W., and J. M. Green. 1977. A critique of field methodology for determining fish feeding periodicity. Environmental Biology of Fishes 1:209–214.

Jobling, M. 1981. Mathematical models of gastric emptying and the estimation of daily rates of food consumption for fish. Journal of Fish Biology 19:245–257.

Jorgensen, S. E. 1976. A model of fish growth. Ecological Modelling 2:303–313.

Keast, A., and L. Welsh. 1968. Daily feeding periodicities, food uptake rates, and dietary changes with hour of day in some lake fishes. Journal of the Fisheries Research Board of Canada 25:1133–1144.

Kerr, S. R. 1971. Prediction of fish growth efficiency in nature. Journal of the Fisheries Research Board of Canada 28:809–814.

Kerr, S. R. 1982. Estimating the energy budgets of actively predatory fishes. Canadian Journal of Fisheries and Aquatic Sciences 39:371–379.

Kitchell, J. F. 1983. Energetics. Pages 312–338 *in* P. Webb and D. Weihs, editors. Fish biomechanics. Praeger, New York.

Kitchell, J. F., and J. E. Breck. 1980. Bioenergetics model and foraging hypothesis for sea lamprey *(Petromyzon marinus)*. Canadian Journal of Fisheries and Aquatic Sciences 37:2159–2168.

Kitchell, J. F., J. F. Koonce, R. V. O'Neill, H. H. Shugart, J. J. Magnuson, and R. S. Booth. 1974. Model of fish biomass dynamics. Transactions of the American Fisheries Society 103:786–798.

Kitchell, J. F., D. J. Stewart, and D. Weininger. 1977. Application of a bioenergetics model to yellow perch *(Perca flavescens)* and walleye *(Stizostedion vitreum vitreum)*. Journal of the Fisheries Research Board of Canada 34:1922–1935.

Lasker, R. 1970. Utilization of zooplankton energy by a Pacific sardine population in the California current. Pages 265–284 *in* J. H. Steele, editor. Marine food chains. University of California Press, Los Angeles.

Laurence, G. C. 1977. A bioenergetic model for the analysis of feeding and survival potential of winter flounder, *Pseudopleuronectes americanus,* larvae during the period from hatching to metamorphosis. U.S. National Marine Fisheries Service Fishery Bulletin 75:529–546.

Lyons, J. 1984. Walleye predation, yellow perch abundance, and the population dynamics of an assemblage of littoral-zone fishes in Sparkling Lake, Wisconsin. Doctoral dissertation. University of Wisconsin, Madison.

MacKinnon, J. C. 1972. Summer storage of energy and its use for winter metabolism and gonadal maturation in American plaice *(Hippoglossoides platessoides)*. Journal of the Fisheries Research Board of Canada 29:1749–1759.

Majkowski, J., and L. Bramall. 1980. Sensitivity of bioenergetic growth models of animals to changes in the energy balance parameters. Journal of Theoretical Biology 85:645–655.

Mann, K. H. 1965. Energy transformation by a population of fish in the River Thames. Journal of Animal Ecology 34:253–275.

Mann, K. M. 1978. Estimating the food consumption of fish in nature. Pages 250–273 *in* S. D. Gerking, editor. Ecology of freshwater fish production. Wiley, New York.

McGee, M. V., J. S. Griffith, and R. B. McLean. 1979. Prey selection by sauger in Watts Bar Reservoir, Tennessee, as affected by cold-induced mortality of threadfin shad. Proceedings of the Annual Conference Southeastern Association of Fish and Wildlife Agencies 31:404–411.

Megrey, B. A. 1978. Applications of a bioenergetics model to gizzard shad *(Dorosoma cepedianum):* a simulation of seasonal biomass dynamics in an Ohio reservoir. Master's thesis. Miami University, Oxford, Ohio.

Mills, E. L., and J. L. Forney. 1981. Energetics, food consumption, and growth of young yellow perch in Oneida Lake, New York. Transactions of the American Fisheries Society 110:479–488.

Mills, E. L., R. C. Ready, M. Jahneke, C. R. Hanger, and C. Trowbridge. 1984. A gastric evacuation model for young yellow perch, *Perca flavescens*. Canadian Journal of Fisheries and Aquatic Sciences 41:513–518.

Minckley, C. O., and L. J. Paulson. 1976. Use of gizzard weights to determine total length and weight of threadfin shad eaten by predators. Transactions of the American Fisheries Society 105:409–410.

Minton, J. W., and R. B. McLean. 1982. Measurements of growth and consumption of sauger *(Stizostedion canadense):* implication of fish energetic studies. Canadian Journal of Fisheries and Aquatic Sciences 39:1396–1403.

Muir, B. S., and A. J. Niimi. 1972. Oxygen consumption of the euryhaline fish aholehole *(Kuhlia sandvicensis)* with reference to salinity, swimming, and food consumption. Journal of the Fisheries Research Board of Canada 29:67–77.

Nakashima, B. S., and W. C. Leggett. 1978. Daily ration of yellow perch *(Perca flavescens)* from Lake Memphremagog, Quebec–Vermont, with a comparison of methods for in situ determinations. Journal of the Fisheries Research Board of Canada 35:1597–1603.

Niimi, A. J., and F. W. H. Beamish. 1974. Bioenergetics and growth of largemouth bass *(Micropterus salmoides)* in relation to body weight and temperature. Canadian Journal of Zoology 52:447–456.

Norstrom, R. J., A. E. McKinnon, and A. S. W. DeFreitas. 1976. A bioenergetics-based model for pollutant accumulation by fish. Simulation of PCB and methylmercury residue levels in Ottawa River yellow perch *(Perca flavescens)*. Journal of the Fisheries Research Board of Canada 33:248–267.

Paloheimo, J. E., and L. M. Dickie. 1966. Food and growth of fishes. III. Relations among food, body size, and growth efficiency. Journal of the Fisheries Research Board of Canada 23:1209–1248.

Parker, R. A. 1974. Empirical functions relating metabolic processes in aquatic systems to environmental variables. Journal of the Fisheries Research Board of Canada 31:1550–1552.

Persson, L. 1979. The effects of temperature and different food organisms on the rate of gastric evacuation in perch *(Perca fluviatilis)*. Freshwater Biology 9:99–104.

Peters, D. S., and D. E. Hoss. 1974. A radioisotopic method of measuring food evacuation time in fish. Transactions of the American Fisheries Society 103:626–629.

Peters, D. S., and M. A. Kjelson. 1975. Consumption and utilization of food by various postlarval and juvenile fishes of North Carolina estuaries. Estuarine Research 1:447–472.

Pierce, R. J. 1977. Life history and ecological energetics of the gizzard shad *(Dorosoma cepedianum)* in Acton Lake, Ohio. Doctoral dissertation. Miami University, Oxford, Ohio.

Popova, O. A. 1967. The 'predator-prey' relationship among fish. Pages 359–376 *in* S. D. Gerking, editor. The biological basis of freshwater fish production. Blackwell Scientific Publications, Oxford, England.

Popova, O. A. 1978. The role of predaceous fish in ecosystems. Pages 215–249 *in* S. D. Gerking, editor. Ecology of freshwater fish production. Wiley, New York.

Popova, O. A., and L. A. Sytina. 1977. Food and feeding relations of Eurasian perch *(Perca fluviatilis)* and pikeperch *(Stizostedion lucioperca)* in various waters of the USSR. Journal of the Fisheries Research Board of Canada 34:1559–1570.

Rice, J. A. 1990. Bioenergetics modeling approaches to evaluation of stress in fishes. American Fisheries Society Symposium 8:80–92.

Rice, J. A., J. E. Breck, S. M. Bartell, and J. F. Kitchell. 1983. Evaluating the constraints of temperature, activity and consumption on growth of largemouth bass. Environmental Biology of Fishes 9:263–275.

Rice, J. A., and P. A. Cochran. 1984. Independent evaluation of a bioenergetics model for largemouth bass. Ecology 65:732–739.

Robinson, W. R., R. H. Peters, and J. Zimmerman. 1983. The effects of body size and temperature on metabolic rate of organisms. Canadian Journal of Zoology 61:281–288.

Schalles, J. F., and T. E. Wissing. 1976. Effects of dry pellet diets on the metabolic rates of bluegill *(Lepomis macrochirus)*. Journal of the Fisheries Research Board of Canada 33:2443–2449.

Scott, D. B. C. 1979. Environmental timing and the control of reproduction in teleost fish. Symposia of the Zoological Society of London 44:105–132.

Seaburg, K. G., and J. B. Moyle. 1964. Feeding habits, digestion rates, and growth of some Minnesota warmwater fishes. Transactions of the American Fisheries Society 93:269–285.

Sharp, G. D., and R. C. Francis. 1976. An energetics model for the exploited yellowfin tuna, *Thunnus albacares,* population in the eastern Pacific Ocean. U.S. National Marine Fisheries Service Fishery Bulletin 74:36–51.

Sibert, J., and S. Obrebski. 1976. Frequency distributions of food item counts in individual fish stomachs. Pages 107–114 *in* C. A. Simenstad and S. J. Lipovsky, editors. Fish food habits. First Pacific Northwest technical workshop proceedings. University of Washington, Washington Sea Grant Program, Seattle.

Smith, K. L., Jr. 1973. Energy transformations by the sargassum fish *Histrio histrio* (L.). Journal of Experimental Marine Biology and Ecology 12:219–227.

Solomon, D. J., and A. E. Brafield. 1972. The energetics of feeding, metabolism and growth of perch (*Perca fluviatilis* L.). Journal of Animal Ecology 41:699–718.

Stauffer, G. D. 1973. A growth model for salmonids reared in hatchery environments. Doctoral dissertation. University of Washington, Seattle.

Steigenberger, L. W., and P. A. Larkin. 1974. Feeding activity and rates of digestion of northern squawfish *(Ptychocheilus oregonensis)*. Journal of the Fisheries Research Board of Canada 31:411–420.

Stewart, D. J., and F. P. Binkowski. 1986. Dynamics of consumption and food conversion by Lake Michigan alewives: an energetics-modeling synthesis. Transactions of the American Fisheries Society 115:643–661.

Stewart, D. J., J. F. Kitchell, and L. B. Crowder. 1981. Forage fishes and their salmonid predators in Lake Michigan. Transactions of the American Fisheries Society 110:751–763.

Stewart, D. J., D. Weininger, D. V. Rottiers, and T. A. Edsall. 1983. An energetics model for lake trout, *Salvelinus namaycush*: application to the Lake Michigan population. Canadian Journal of Fisheries and Aquatic Sciences 40:681–698.

Swenson, W. A. 1977. Food consumption of walleye *(Stizostedion vitreum)* and sauger *(S. canadense)* in relation to food availability and physical conditions in Lake of the Woods, Minnesota, Shagawa Lake, and western Lake Superior. Journal of the Fisheries Research Board of Canada 34:1643–1654.

Swenson, W. A., and L. L. Smith. 1973. Gastric digestion, food conversion, feeding periodicity, and food conversion efficiency in walleye *(Stizostedion vitreum vitreum)*. Journal of the Fisheries Research Board of Canada 30:1327–1336.

Thomann, R. V., and J. P. Connolly. 1984. Model of PCB in the Lake Michigan lake trout food chain. Environmental Science and Technology 18:65–71.

Thornton, K. W., and A. S. Lessem. 1978. A temperature algorithm for modifying biological rates. Transactions of the American Fisheries Society 107:284–287.

Thorpe, J. E. 1977. Daily ration of adult perch *Perca fluviatilis* L. during summer in Lock Leven, Scotland. Journal of Fish Biology 11:55–68.

Tyler, A. V. 1970. Rate of gastric emptying in young cod. Journal of the Fisheries Research Board of Canada 27:1177–1189.

Tyler, P., and P. Calow. 1985. Fish energetics: new perspectives. Johns Hopkins University Press, Baltimore, Maryland.

Ursin, E. 1979. Principles of growth in fishes. Symposia of the Zoological Society of London 44:63–87.

Vaughan, D. S., R. M. Yoshiyama, J. E. Breck, and D. L. DeAngelis. 1984. Modeling approaches for assessing the effects of stress on fish populations. Pages 259–278 *in* V. W. Cairns, P. V. Hodson, and J. O. Nriagu, editors. Contaminant effects on fisheries. Wiley, New York.

Wahl, D. H., and L. A. Nielsen. 1985. Feeding ecology of the sauger *(Stizostedion canadense)* in a large river. Canadian Journal of Fisheries and Aquatic Sciences 42:120–128.

Ware, D. M. 1975. Growth, metabolism, and optimal swimming speed of a pelagic fish. Journal of the Fisheries Research Board of Canada 32:33–41.

Warren, C. E., and G. E. Davis. 1967. Laboratory studies on the feeding, bioenergetics, and growth of fish. Pages 175–214 *in* S. D. Gerking, editor. The biological basis of freshwater fish production. Blackwell Scientific Publications, Oxford, England.

Weatherley, A. H. 1978. Some aspects of age and growth. Pages 52–74 *in* S. D. Gerking, editor. Ecology of freshwater fish production. Wiley, New York.

Webb, P. W. 1978. Partitioning of energy into metabolism and growth. Pages 184–214 *in* S. D. Gerking, editor. Ecology of freshwater fish production. Wiley, New York.

Weininger, D. 1978. Accumulation of PCBs by lake trout in Lake Michigan. Doctoral dissertation. University of Wisconsin, Madison.

Williams, G. C. 1961. Adaptation and natural selection: a critique of some current evolutionary thought. Princeton University Press, Princeton, New Jersey.

Winberg, G. G. 1956. Rate of metabolism and food requirements of fishes. Byelorussian State University, Minsk. Translated from Russian: Fisheries Research Board of Canada Translation Series 194, 1960, Ottawa.

Windell, J. T. 1967. Rates of digestion in fishes. Pages 151–153 *in* S. D. Gerking, editor. The biological basis of freshwater fish production. Blackwell Scientific Publications, Oxford, England.

Windell, J. T. 1978. Digestion and daily ration of fishes. Pages 159–183 *in* S. D. Gerking, editor. Ecology of freshwater fish production. Wiley, New York.

Windell, J. T., and S. H. Bowen. 1978. Methods for study of fish diets based on analysis of stomach contents. Pages 219–226 *in* T. Bagenal, editor. Methods for the assessment of fish production in fresh waters. Blackwell Scientific Publications, Oxford, England.

Wissing, T. E. 1974. Energy transformations by young-of-the-year white bass *Morone chrysops* (Rafinesque) in Lake Mendota, Wisconsin. Transactions of the American Fisheries Society 103:32–37.

Wootton, R. J., J. R. M. Allen, and S. J. Cole. 1980. Energetics of the annual reproductive cycle in female sticklebacks, *Gasterosteus aculeatus* L. Journal of Fish Biology 17:387–394.

Chapter 13

Nervous System

DAVID F. RUSSELL

13.1 INTRODUCTION

Why do we study the nervous systems of fish? While some investigators have a comparative perspective, others take advantage of special features of fish such as large neurons (e.g., the Mauthner cells), or homogeneous tissues (e.g., the electroplax organs), or unique sensory modalities (e.g., electroreception). This chapter reviews convenient methods of neurophysiology, neuroanatomy, and neurochemistry. The literature on the fish nervous system is reviewed in *Fish Neurobiology, Fish Physiology, Traité de Zoologie, The Biology of Lampreys,* and *The Biology of Myxine*, each a multivolume series.

13.2 TYPES OF PREPARATIONS

The nervous system of fish can be studied in several ways: (1) chronically, via electrodes implanted in alert, freely behaving animals; (2) in vivo, the animal remaining alive, but restrained, anesthetized, paralyzed, and dissected to expose the nervous system; (3) in vitro, after part of the nervous system is excised but sustained for several hours in a saline bath; or (4) in tissue slices or as cells enzymatically dissociated from excised nervous tissue.

Procedures for surgery and anesthesia are detailed in Chapter 8. The following notes are supplementary. When severed blood vessels are closed, a spark-type cauterizer or a battery-operated "cold cauterizer" [Fine Science Tools][1] reduces the possibility of heat damage to nerves. Blood pressure and hence bleeding are reduced under deep anesthesia. Incisions can be closed quickly with a surgical type of cyanoacrylate glue [Histoacryl Blue, Vel Tec, telephone 514-589-6757]. To paralyze fish, pancuronium bromide (0.05 mg/kg) is preferred to curare or Flaxedil™ (gallamine triethiodide) because the heart and circulation are less affected. The seventh cranial nerves may have to be cut to stop respiratory motions. Transection of the spinal cord at cervical levels may stop swimming and escape motions, although this releases continuous swimming by dogfish sharks (family Squalidae). The electrocardiogram (ECG) and heart rate can be monitored as a vital sign with an electromyographic electrode near the heart (the ECG may also show up as an artifact in central nervous system recordings). If the fish is

---

[1]Product names and vendors are indicated in square brackets throughout this chapter. If not given in the text, addresses for vendors can be found in the "Guide to Scientific Instruments," published annually in the journal *Science* by the American Association for the Advancement of Science, Washington, D.C., or in the "Thomas Register" guide to industrial suppliers, published annually by Ruth Hurd, New York.

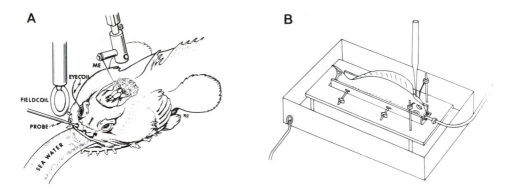

Figure 13.1 In vivo preparations for intracellular recordings from oculomotor neurons. (A) Toadfish with a glass intracellular electrode (ME); the probe allows the eye to be mechanically displaced, and the eye and field coils permit and record eye displacements (from Highstein and Baker 1985). (B) A winter flounder, turned on its side, with a micropipette that delivers horseradish peroxidase into brain neurons (from Graf and Baker 1985).

paralyzed, it must be artificially ventilated with a stream of water directed into the mouth (Chapter 10).

Ethical considerations are associated with surgical procedures. Anesthesia with tricaine (0.1–0.2 g/L for lampreys, buffered to pH 7) is routinely employed, and the central nervous system may be pithed under anesthesia if receptor or muscle preparations are to be isolated. If the brain stem or spinal cord is being studied, the more rostral parts of the brain can be removed under anesthesia. Pressure points can be infiltrated with a local anesthetic, which also has a practical aspect because pain can affect the central nervous system's function.

13.2.1 Preparations for Chronic Studies

Neural studies of freely behaving fish range from the strictly ethological to the use of implanted electrodes for stimulation (Guthrie 1981). Shuttle boxes and activity monitors for experimental psychology studies on fish are available [Columbus Instruments]. Learning of color discrimination and conditioning of autonomic responses have been studied with fish (Laudien et al. 1986; Morin et al. 1987). Alternatively, behavior such as feeding and courtship can simply be scored by visual observation (e.g., Kyle and Peter 1985). Behavior or conditioning provides a convenient assay for experimental manipulations such as drug injection or brain lesioning.

13.2.1.1 Motion Detection

The need often arises to monitor the position or motions of a fish with adequate time resolution. A coil of wire in a magnetic field has been used to track the eye motions of fish (Figure 13.1A). A simple approach is to connect a lever arm between the fish and the wiper of a potentiometer; the fixed taps of the potentiometer are connected to a battery and the center tap is connected to a recorder (Figure 13.2). Also, an image of a body region can be focused on a phototransistor (e.g., a Fairchild FPT 100) to detect motion (Prugh et al. 1982). The classic position monitor of Sandeman (1968) can be used even in seawater,

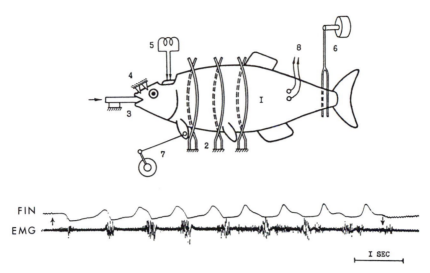

Figure 13.2 In vivo preparation of common carp to study neural control of swimming (from Kashin et al. 1974). The fish was restrained on the head and body by clamps (4, 2) and was supplied with water for respiration (3). Movements of a pectoral fin (7) and the tail (6) were recorded via linkages to potentiometer wipers. Electrodes (8) were inserted into myotomal muscle to record electromyographic (EMG) activity. The caudal tegmental area of the brain was stimulated at 50–100 Hz with a pair of insulated 0.1-mm nichrome wires (5). On the traces below, arrows indicate the onset and end of brain stimulation. The stimulation evoked swimming, as recorded by myotomal EMG bursts (lower trace) and rhythmic motions of the pectoral fin (upper trace).

although its effects on electroreceptors should be checked; a recent variant is to use the receiver lead to record both position and electromyographic activity of a muscle, and to separate these signals by electronic filtering. Ciné film and frame tracing are traditional approaches to studying fish swimming (Alexander 1977; Videler and Hess 1984) but are time-consuming. Such analyses can be aided by attaching reflective or fluorescent markers to the animal and by projecting the frame images on a digitizing pad for a computer. A video recorder having a stop-frame mode can also be used to trace the images from a television screen or from hard copy of the frames made on a Gould ES-1000 chart recorder. However, the frame rate on most videorecorders is limited to 60 Hz. A strobe light [Grass] synchronized to the frame advance can help freeze the motion. Wieland and Eaton (1983) described a 100 × 100 photodiode array used as an electronic camera to monitor rapid motions by fish. "Fishmills" have been devised in which the animal swims in a moving circuit of water and so remains stationary over a quadrille-lined background suitable for filming (Webb et al. 1984). Instead of photographing the animal, the motions of attached markers or lights can be directly abstracted with a computer and then converted into stick diagrams or plots of position or angle versus time. One approach is to digitize a television image and detect the markers by adjusting the gray tone scale (Rudell 1979; Godden and Graham 1983). Another system for large animals uses light-emitting diodes [SelSpot], although the diode leads may encumber the animal.

A synchronization signal is needed for correlating ciné film or videotape with electromyographic signals (EMG, Section 13.3.2.3) recorded simultaneously on a separate frequency-modulated tape recorder. If the camera has an electronic frame counter, the counter code can be led out to the EMG recorder (Eaton et al. 1981). Synchronization can also come from a tape-position counter (on the EMG recorder) in the field of view of the camera, or from a strobe light (i.e., recorders are started together and the strobes are counted). Alternatively, the inexpensive Vetter model 420 or 230 tape recorders allow two tracks of EMG data to be recorded with video, giving automatic synchronization.

13.2.2   In Vivo Preparations

In vivo preparation is perhaps the most widely used approach to studying the nervous systems of fish. Clamps and restraints for immobilizing fish are a major concern. Methods of restraint range from simply pinning a small fish through the fins to a layer of Sylgard™ (Section 13.2.3), to compressing the animal in Sylgard molds made from a preserved specimen of matching size, to applying metal fixtures with curved flanges conforming to the body shape. Adhesives, dental cements, and waxes ranging from tacky to hard are all part of the neurophysiologist's armamentarium and obtainable from surgical or dental suppliers. For intracellular recording, the cranium or spinal cord must be rigidly fixed (Furukawa and Ishii 1967; Leonard et al. 1978). The brain is usually approached from the dorsal aspect (Figure 13.1A); flatfish have to be supported on "edge" to accomplish this (Figure 13.1B; Graf and Baker 1985).

A Plexiglas™ box contains the animal. It is convenient to add a horizontal ledge around the lip, drilled to permit the bolting of posts and clamps. The water can be static for chronic studies of small fish, though air should be bubbled through it, but a flow of water into the mouth is needed to ventilate a paralyzed fish. For marine animals, such flows are best achieved on a running-seawater table at a marine station. Alternatively, the water can be recirculated through a canister-type filter [Magnum, Eheim]. The experimental room should have floor drains so equipment on the floor below will not be water-damaged.

13.2.3   In Vitro Preparations

In vitro preparations are better controlled than in vivo ones; for example, hormonal effects from circulating blood are avoided. They are ideal for intracellular recording because vascular pulsations and body motions are absent. They permit bath application of dissolved drugs or salines of altered ionic composition. They are also easier to work with; for example, lesions can be made in the brain without fear of bleeding, or Vaseline™ barriers can be made around a region of the central nervous system for local application of drugs (Russell and Wallén 1979). Drawbacks of in vitro preparations include limited survival time—typically 6–12 h (although the brain of a lamprey remains viable for 2–3 d)—and the state of shock from surgery, which may affect the excitability of reflexes. Isolated nerve–muscle or sensory receptor preparations are also popular.

To begin an in vitro preparation, a relatively large part of the body is removed from the deeply anesthetized fish and pinned to a layer of black wax [Fisher] or Sylgard in a large saline-filled dish. (Saline solutions are discussed in Box 13.1 and characterized in Table 13.1). Excess tissue is trimmed away to permit access of electrodes to the neurons of interest. A black surface or microscope stage provides contrast with the white tissue. The final preparation may be transferred

Box 13.1 Physiological Salines

Table 13.1 lists recipes for Ringer's solutions for representative species. In principle, the ionic composition, tonicity, and pH of the saline solution should match those of blood plasma or cerebrospinal fluid in the species under study. In practice, a formula may have a traditional and generalized character (e.g., "elasmobranch saline"), or may be a modification of amphibian Ringer (e.g., "lamprey saline"). Fish saline recipes may be found in Forster and Taggart (1950: marine teleost), Cavanaugh (1956: various species), Lockwood (1961: elasmobranch), Wolf (1963: freshwater teleosts), Potts and Parry (1964: various species), and Okitsu et al. (1978: marine catfish). Goldfish plasma has been analyzed by Houston and Koss (1982).

In general, the tonicity of plasma from freshwater fish may vary above or below that of human plasma (about 300 milliosmolar). Marine teleosts are hypertonic by 20–100% compared to humans. The plasma tonicity of marine elasmobranchs is extremely high and may be hypertonic with respect to sea water (Clark 1972) due to the presence of urea in the blood—the vitreum of the eyes of skates is 860 milliosmol. The tonicity of saline can be augmented by additions of NaCl, urea, or dextrose and reduced by dilution with H_2O. Plasma pH and levels of ion concentrations can depend on temperature and time of day (Cameron and Kormanik 1982; Houston and Koss 1982).

Blood pH tends to be slightly alkaline—for example, it is 7.4 in lampreys (Johansen et al. 1973) and 7.8 in freshwater catfish at room temperature (Cameron and Kormanik 1982)—and becomes more alkaline with lower temperature. As a pH buffer for salines, 2–10 mM HEPES (N'-2-hydroxyethylpiperazine-N'-2-ethanesulfonic acid, free acid form) is popular. Tris buffers are reputed to affect synaptic transmission. Bicarbonate buffer ($NaHCO_3$) is more physiological but requires continuous bubbling with accurate 5% CO_2 gas and tends to precipitate Ca^{++} (such precipitates can be removed from glassware with nitric acid). Phenol red (0.02 g/L) can be added as a pH indicator if a pH meter is not available; the reddish orange color at physiological pH can be compared to a set of standards. Test kits for aquarium water pH [pet shops] use phenol red or bromophenol blue as the indicator dye and give reliable results. Test papers for pH work poorly with such weakly buffered solutions (ditto for some pH electrodes). Finally, drugs added to the saline may affect the pH.

Preparations can be "static," in which the saline is not changed and oxygen diffuses from the air, or "superfused" continuously with saline if drugs are to be tested. The latter is more complicated, especially if the saline must be chilled before entering the dish. Glassware for saline should not be washed with detergent or used for other chemicals because traces linger; rinsing the glassware with distilled water suffices. Saline is typically chilled on ice for gross dissections to reduce enzymatic degradation of tissues, but the effect of chilling the preparation should be checked. The saline need not be sterile for acute preparations. If sterility is needed, the sterile techniques for fish described by Wolf (1979) can be used. Salines buffered with HEPES can be autoclaved. Alternatively, gentamicin antibiotic [Sigma], 10–100 µg/mL saline, can be added to kill the gram-negative bacteria usually found with fish.

Table 13.1 Formulas for saline solutions. Bubble salines with oxygen or air.

Constituent	Formula weight (g/mol)	Saline type (concentrations in mmol/L)				
		Tyrode[a]	Marine teleost[b,c]	Freshwater teleost[c]	Marine elasmobranch[c,d]	Lamprey[e]
NaCl	58.4	137	134	100	250	115
KCl	74.6	2.7	2.5	2.5	4	2.1
$CaCl_2 \cdot 2H_2O$	147	1.8	1.5	1.5	5	2.5
$MgCl_2 \cdot 6H_2O$	203	0.5	1	1	2	2
$NaH_2PO_4 \cdot H_2O$	138	0.32	0.5	0.5		
$NaHCO_3$	84	12	15	5		6
Urea	60				330	
Glucose	180	5.5				3.6

[a]Whitaker (1972). Mammalian saline; bubble with 5% CO_2 gas.
[b]Forster and Taggart (1950); bubble with 5% CO_2 gas.
[c]Cavanaugh (1956). Addition of a few millimoles of glucose is optional for in vitro preparations.
[d]Specifically for skates (Rajidae); add Na_2HPO_4 to pH 7.4.
[e]Rovainen (1982); 5 mmol HEPES (N'-2-hydroxyethlypiperazine-N'-ethanesulfonic acid) may be substituted for $NaHCO_3$, in which case the pH should be adjusted to 7.4 with NaOH.

to a smaller experimental chamber, such as a 60-mm-diameter petri dish, and pinned to a Sylgard layer with minutien pins [Fine Science Tools] or spines from cactus plants. The dish is then typically fixed (with modeling clay, for example) on a Plexiglas stage 8–15 cm high, and manipulators and electrodes are placed around it. When the preparation is rinsed or transferred, it must be kept covered with saline to avoid mechanical stress from contact with the air–water interface; pipettes, plastic spoons, or cover glasses can be used for transfers.

Transparent Sylgard resin, type-184 silicone elastomer, is available in 454-g kits [Dow Corning Corp.] A black surface can reportedly be obtained by treating the cured resin with aqueous 1% osmium tetroxide for 2 h (Mena and Frixione 1984).

13.2.4　Slices and Dissociated Cells

Studies of thin tissue slices and individual neurons aid in understanding the function of synapses, membrane properties, and pharmacological responses of single neurons, because feedback effects from neural networks are reduced or eliminated. Brain slices from fish have been little-used (Dingledine 1984; Shiells et al. 1986). The dendrites of the neurons of interest should have a restricted or planar morphology so as to be contained within the slice. Dissociation of neurons with low-calcium saline or proteases such as trypsin or papain have been applied to the retina of fish (Tachibana 1983; Dowling et al. 1985), as well as to vestibular receptors (Steinacker and Rojas 1988). The dissociated cells can be studied directly or cultured (Clark 1972; Wolf 1979).

13.3　ELECTROPHYSIOLOGY

The time-honored methods of neurophysiology continue to be powerful, flexible, and relatively direct means of studying the functional organization and pharmacology of the nervous system (Nastuk 1963; Barker and McKelvy 1983). Electrophysiology may be viewed as complementary to other modern powerful approaches such as immunocytochemistry and anatomical labeling with tracers. Although start-up costs for electrophysiology are high (chiefly for equipment), operation and supply costs may be modest.

13.3.1 Instrumentation

Commercial instruments for neurophysiology have been perfected over several decades. An electrophysiological "setup" comprises a table, a chamber for the preparation, life-support devices, optics and manipulators to position electrodes, and a relay rack to hold electronic instruments. Budget constraints notwithstanding, it is inefficient to use a single setup for different types of work because the equipment must be constantly rearranged. For example, it is convenient to have a separate dissecting microscope and work area reserved for preliminary dissections.

An experimental table is the basic workplace. This can be a wooden table for work with free-swimming or anesthetized fish, placed in the center of the room to allow access from all sides. For intracellular recording, an air-cushioned, vibration-damping table is justified [Technical Manufacturing Corp., Kinetic Systems, Newport]. A Faraday cage for electrical shielding is optional.

A stereo microscope on a swinging-arm stand placed on the table is needed for dissections and the placement of electrodes. The Reichert C and Olympus microscopes are cost-effective. The stand is almost as important as the optics; one that permits the microscope body to be swiveled about the optical axis is convenient [Reichert, Nikon, Olympus]. For chronic and in vivo work, a $0.5 \times$ auxiliary objective lens allows an increased working distance to the preparation, and an operating room type of universal floor stand is useful. Fiber-optic illuminators [Dolan-Jenner; Chiu] keep the preparation from being heated. Infrared-blocking filters are available in various sizes from Oriel or Fish-Schurman Corp. [Post Office Box 319, New Rochelle, New York, 10802-0319]. Near-horizontal incident illumination may increase contrast in the specimen, or light can be transmitted from below with a concave mirror to obtain bright-field or pseudodark-field illumination.

Differential amplifiers [Grass P15 or 7P511, A-M Systems] are used to record action potentials from nerves, or other signals, extracellularly. Extracellular signals are typically smaller than 200 μV. There should be high- and low-pass filters, which may be used to pass signals of 30–1,000 Hz when nerve action potentials are recorded. Such instruments are really three amplifiers in one; signals led to the noninverting (+) and the inverting (−) inputs are subtracted to reduce power line interference. A 60- or 50-Hz notch filter in some models will reduce residual noise.

Stimulators [Grass, WPI] evoke action potentials in a nerve or within the central nervous system by sending a brief electrical current through an electrode. Essential features include variable frequency, duration, and amplitude, and a prepulse to trigger an oscilloscope sweep before the stimulus. A stimulus isolation unit (SIU) is also needed; its function is to reduce the stimulus artifact (recorded with amplifiers) by creating a local flow of electrical current through the two leads of the stimulating electrode, separate from the rest of the electrical system. A constant-current SIU is advantageous for quantifying the stimulus current. With stimulus durations of 0.2–0.5 ms, currents less than 100 μA are considered "microstimulation."

Electrodes for nerves may be of the "hook" or "suction" varieties. There are always two leads for connection to a differential amplifier or SIU. Hook electrodes support the nerve on 0.02–0.2-mm silver or (stiffer) platinum–iridium wires [MedWire, A-M Systems, California Fine Wire] spaced 1–2 mm apart and soldered to flexible, shielded, double-lead cable like that used in phonograph arms [Cooner Wire]. The nerve–electrode contact must be insulated by immersion in oil, or by brief exposure to air. Mineral oil [pharmacies] may be stirred with saline and oxygenated; because it floats, the nerve is lifted into the oil. Fluorocarbon [3M type FC80] and certain silicon oils [Dow Corning type FS 1265] are denser than saline and hence can be used to fill cavities. Oxygen dissolves well in fluorocarbons (Dixon and Holland 1975).

Suction electrodes do not need oil insulation. The cut end of a nerve or a loop of a small intact nerve can be aspirated without harm into a tube. A silver wire inside the tube and another silver wire wrapped around the outside of the tip are the two leads. Tips that fit a nerve snugly can be made by scoring (with a diamond pencil) and breaking glass micropipettes and briefly fire polishing the tips over a small flame from a syringe needle connected to a gas line. Double-barrel tips for stimulation or recording can significantly reduce stimulus artifact; they are made from two capillaries held together by heat-shrink tubing [Radio Shack] and half-twisted as the heated glass is drawn manually. The "external" wire (to the inverting amplifier input) is inserted into the nonsuction barrel, which fills by capillarity. Alternatively, tips can be made from polyethylene tubing that is heated until it becomes transparent, let cool, then drawn out). Suction electrodes are available commercially [A-M Systems], or they can readily be fabricated from polyethylene tubing or from microelectrode holders that have a pressure port [WPI, E.W. Wright, A-M Systems].

Metal microelectrodes are used to stimulate within the central nervous system or to record the action potentials of single neurons ("single units") or the evoked potentials of ensembles of neurons. They are made from tungsten or stainless steel; it may be best to buy them commercially [A-M Systems, Haer, Bak, Micro Probe] because their fabrication is something of an art (Merrill and Ainsworth 1972). Stimulating electrodes have impedances of 50–100 kΩ, whereas those of recording electrodes for single units range to a few megohms. If pinholes are present in the lacquer insulation, artifactual stimulation of nontarget brain regions may result. Glass micropipettes filled with 4 M NaCl, with resistances of a few megohms, may also be used to record single units.

Micromanipulators for nerve electrodes need only permit coarse positioning. Available models include simple ball joints [Harvard, Stoelting, Palmer], several Narishige models [e.g., M-4N or M-3333; Biodyne, Medical Systems], and the Marzhauser MM33 [Fine Science Tools, WPI]. Micromanipulators should be compact so they can be placed next to the microscope, preferably with all knobs projecting away from the stage for easy access. They can be mounted on a framework of bars or on magnetic bases such as those available from optical or machine tool suppliers [Melles-Griot, Newport, Swiss Precision Instruments, Yuasa International, Narishige].

Intracellular electrodes allow more direct recording of synaptic and action potentials than extracellular ones, and they facilitate analysis of membrane properties. An amplifier, micropipette puller, and micromanipulator are needed. Traditionally, a cell's membrane is penetrated with a micropipette filled with electrolyte that forms an electrical connection with the interior. More recently, "seal" recording has been developed, for which a fine suction electrode adheres to a cell's membrane (Hamil et al. 1981). An amplifier having an "active bridge" permits both recording and stimulation with the same microelectrode [A-M Systems, Axon Instruments, Biodyne, Dagan, Getting, WPI]. Microelectrode pullers are available from Narishige, Kopf, Sutter Instruments, WPI, and Haer, among others. The Narishige vertical puller is versatile and robust. Gas-jet and moving-coil pullers [Sutter, Haer] aid in the fabrication of fine tips. Electrodes are pulled from glass tubing that contains a filament [WPI, A-M Systems, Haer]; capillary forces along the filament draw electrolyte solution into the tip after back-injection of the shank from a syringe and a number 30 needle [Popper, Hamilton]. Borosilicate glass tubing with an outside diameter of 1.2 mm and an inner:outer diameter ratio of 0.5 is widely available and easily injected. All amplifiers permit measurement of the electrode resistance, which reflects the tip size; values of 20–100 mΩ are usual. Electrodes may be filled with 3 M potassium chloride, although chloride ions that leak from the tip may affect inhibitory synapses. For this reason, 4 M potassium acetate (pH 7) or 2 M potassium methyl sulfate are used instead. After they are filled, electrodes are stored in a moist chamber (e.g., on a strip of modelling clay in a covered petri dish) for 1 h to allow air bubbles to migrate out of the tips. Penetrations may be either blind, in which the electrode is advanced into a region of the central nervous system on a "poke-and-hope" basis, or under visual control, in which the neuron to be impaled is viewed with a microscope and the electrode is micromanipulated to contact it. The micromanipulator must not undergo positional drift. The ability to advance the electrode axially is important for blind penetrations; the Kopf or Narishige hydraulic advances mounted on a coarse manipulator may be satisfactory. For visual control, the Narishige-style hydraulic manipulators [Nikon, Narishige USA] have recently been redesigned for reduced drift. Manipulators can also be assembled readily from optical translators and fixtures [Melles-Griot, Oriel, Newport, Stoelting]; a DC motor can be added to the axial advance for remote control of blind penetrations.

Some type of data recorder is needed, capable of registering signals in the DC to 2,000-Hz frequency range. "Instant" forms of hard copy are worth the extra expense. A storage oscilloscope [Tektronix 5111], Polaroid camera, FM tape recorder [Vetter, Hewlett-Packard, TEAC], and multichannel rectilinear chart recorder [Gould] are found in many laboratories. The limited bandwidth of the latter (DC–100 Hz) can be expanded by taping the signals and then playing back at reduced tape speed. Digital tape recorders can be adapted inexpensively from video cassette recorders [Dagan, Neuro Data] (Lamb 1985). Although expensive, the excellent Gould ES-2000 electrostatic chart recorder will handle both fast spikes and slow DC potentials and gives black-line-on-white-background records suitable for publication.

Although it is simplest to work at room temperature, fish preparations may need to be cooled to remain viable. One approach is to cool an aluminum stage (supporting the experimental chamber) with coolant that circulates through a chiller [Lauda]. For an aquarium, the coolant can be directed through 0.62-cm, type-316 stainless steel tubing (which is easily bent) lining one wall. Another approach is to have a chamber in contact with Peltier cells [Cambion] powered by a DC supply. A third approach is to direct a continuous flow of prechilled saline over the preparation. A heat exchanger–refrigerator for cooling large, specifically marine, systems is available from NesLab. Thermostats should be of the "proportional" type because thermostats that use a relay to switch on and off many generate electrical artifacts.

Many additional instruments such as signal averagers, pressure injection devices [General Valve, WPI], audio monitors [Grass], patch panels for interconnecting the instruments, fluorescence illuminators, oxygen meters [Diamond Electrotech, Instech], rate meters [Bak, Coulbourn], pumps, tension transducers [Harvard, Grass], and other transducers (Cobbold 1974) may be needed for particular studies. Inexpensive semiconductor pressure transducers [National LX0503A] (Delaunois 1974) perform well but should include a temperature compensation circuit for stability. Specialized electronic instruments can take the form of numerous "boxes," each with its own power supply; with more economy, they can be built on modules for cardcages [Vector, Bud, Newark]. Electrical connectors should be standardized to only a few types, such as banana and BNC connectors.

13.3.2 Specific Procedures

13.3.2.1 Grounding and Noise Reduction

Electrophysiological setups should have only one well-defined electrical ground to which all instruments and metal surfaces are connected. Most investigators simply use a grounded (three-connector) wall power outlet as ground; all the electronic instruments are plugged into one multiple outlet box (having a "wired" ground) connected to the wall outlet. Standard wall outlets for 110 V in the USA have a hot (black) wire, a neutral (white) wire, and a safety ground (green) wire. Most electronic noise comes from power lines, seen as a 60- or 50-Hz ripple on the signals. Hence, power cords should be routed away from the recording site; shielded power cords are helpful [Belden, Newark]. There may be less noise from a sensitive preamplifier if its ground connection at the power connector is defeated with a three-to-two-prong adapter [hardware stores]. The use of shielded (i.e., two-conductor) signal cables is recommended for connecting the instruments, mainly so the ground connections will be adequate. The experimental chamber, filled with water or saline, will contain a large chlorided silver electrode connected to the system ground; in the case of a freshwater aquarium, addition of a few millimoles of NaCl to the water may improve electrical contact. Sensitive preamplifiers are best placed close to the preparation.

13.3.2.2 Chloriding Electrodes

A reversible junction is desirable at the interface between metal and fluid in an electrode. This is readily achieved by chloriding silver wires and plates. The bright silver is immersed in 0.5–3 M NaCl and connected through a 1,000–10,000-Ω resistor to the positive pole of a 6-V battery. The negative pole is connected to another silver wire in the salt solution. A light tan color, developing over a few minutes, indicates that silver chloride has been deposited.

13.3.2.3 Electromyography

Electromyographs record motor patterns of swimming or respiration or other behavior. The intact animal is first lightly anesthetized or wrapped in cloth on ice to immobilize it. The electrodes consist of Teflon™-insulated silver wire [Med-

Wire, A-M Systems], 0.076–0.127 mm in diameter, which is flexible and durable. The insulation is scraped from the ends of two 1-m lengths to expose 1 mm of silver, and the two wires are threaded through a number 26 syringe needle and bent into a barb. The needle is then inserted into a muscle and withdrawn, leaving the wires in place. The wires are connected to a differential amplifier, and the fish is placed in a tank. What one records are the action potentials in pale muscle fibers and the excitatory junctional potentials in red muscle fibers (Roberts 1969; Kashin et al. 1974; Figure 13.2). The segregation of red and pale muscles in many fish may permit selective electrode placement. Eels present a special problem because they tend to rotate axially, coiling the electrode leads around themselves. Motion artifacts can be reduced by use of the 30- or 100-Hz high-pass filter in the amplifier. Stimulation through the wires, postmortem dissection, and electrodeposition of silver can confirm the electrode placement. To reveal silver deposition, a large current is passed through the electrode pair and then the anesthetized animal is perfused with photographic developer [Kodak D-19] to yield black silver granules at the electrode site. Semiquantitative measures of the EMG amplitude can be derived from "leaky integrators" (Section 13.7) or more advanced low-pass filters (Halbertsma and DeBoer 1981). Such low-pass filtering does not allow the firing rate of individual fibers to be picked out from the record for all active fibers. Raw electromyograph and motion records may be compared to correlate muscle activity with behavior.

13.3.2.4   Nerve Stimulation and Recording

Conventional terminology defines afferent impulses (e.g., from sensory receptors) and efferent impulses (e.g., to a muscle) as inputs or outputs, respectively. Antidromic impulses travel opposite to the normal (orthodromic) direction of impulse conduction in a neuron's axon. Recording such impulses requires certain preparations. Once a nerve has been exposed and freed from surrounding tissue, it can be lifted into oil on a hook electrode or drawn into a suction electrode. The stimulator is adjusted to give stimuli of 0.5-ms duration at a few hertz. The pole of the electrode towards the target organ is connected to the negative terminal (cathode) of the stimulus isolation unit and the other electrode pole to the positive terminal. The stimulus intensity is slowly increased until threshold for evoking action potentials is exceeded, typically at a few volts, and a result is obtained. In a neuromuscular preparation, contraction of the muscle signifies that the nerve is indeed being stimulated. Otherwise it may be necessary to place a recording electrode upstream on the same nerve to monitor the evoked compound action potential. This can be viewed with an oscilloscope, each sweep being triggered by the "prepulse" output of the stimulator; the oscilloscope display can be photographed. Given conduction velocities for action potentials of about 10 m/s and an electrode spacing of 2 cm, the evoked action potential can be viewed with a sweep speed of about 5 ms per horizontal division.

13.3.2.5   Intracellular Recording

Historically, intracellular recording was motivated by the presence of large neurons or axons in certain accessible fish preparations. These include the large Müller cells in the brain stem of lampreys, the Mauthner cells in teleost brains (Faber and Korn 1978), the magnocellular projection to the neurohypophysis

(Kandel 1964), auditory fibers in goldfish (Furukawa and Ishii 1967), and supramedullary neurons in puffers (family Tetraodontidae; Hagiwara and Saito 1959). Improvements in technique have extended the range of problems that can be addressed with intracellular recording from fish neurons (Bennett et al. 1967; Leonard et al. 1978; Graf and Baker 1985; Highstein and Baker 1985; Carr et al. 1986). For intracellular recording from dissociated cells by the gigohm seal method (Hamil et al. 1981), small cell size is not an obstacle.

The central nervous system of lamprey ammocoetes has been used for student laboratory exercises at Washington University (see Rovainen 1982). After a fish is anesthetized with tricaine (0.2 g/L) and eviscerated via a ventral-midline incision, it is transected at midbody and pinned dorsum upwards in a large dish filled with iced saline. The spinal cord is located at the cut end of either the caudal or rostral half of the body. From this point, the overlying skin, myotome, and fatty tissue are cut away with a scalpel blade held horizontally. The cut end of the spinal cord is then lifted and the spinal roots and (in rostral segments) cranial nerves are cut. The freed central nervous system is transferred to a saline-filled dish and pinned to Sylgard, dorsal side up, with minutien pins or cactus spines. The choroid plexus and meninges can be trimmed and stripped away from the brain. When transilluminated (from a mirror below the stage) and seen through a 40× dissection microscope, the Müller cells in the medulla and the large axons and sensory ''dorsal cell'' somata in the spinal cord present prominent targets at which to aim microelectrodes (20–40 MΩ resistance) under visual control. The electrode is advanced until the cell is seen to dimple. The output of the amplifier is coupled by direct current to an oscilloscope set at 20 mV per vertical division. The manipulator is lightly tapped (or the electrode can be made to vibrate by a brief increase in the capacitance compensation) until the recorded potential abruptly shifts negatively about 70 mV, signifying that the electrode has entered the cell. Oscilloscope photos can be used to record action or synaptic potentials evoked by stimulation of the spinal cord or dorsal or ventral roots.

13.3.2.6   Bath Application of Drugs

A simple way to apply drugs to nerves is to pipette a small aliquot of a concentrated (100×) drug solution to the preparation's bath; the final concentration can be calculated from the volume of the aliquot and the volume of saline in the chamber. Another method is to drain the saline and replace it with a drug solution of the final desired concentration. A third approach is to pour into the chamber a drug solution at the final concentration while the chamber fluid is aspirated. Due to dilution, 20–40 chamber volumes of drug solution must be exchanged before the target concentration is reached. A photometric dye dilution test with fast green or methylene blue will determine how much saline must be exchanged; the chamber volume should be small (<1 mL) to speed the experiment. Because of the skill required to sustain accurate intracellular recordings while solutions are being changed, the aliquot method is recommended. The pH of drug solutions may have to be adjusted. Perhaps the most extensive pharmacological analyses of fish neurons have involved the teleost Mauthner cell (see Faber and Korn 1978) and the lamprey central nervous system (Gold and Martin 1983; see Figure 13.3 for a lamprey example).

Basic pharmacological references include Goodman et al. (1985) and Budavari (1989). Drugs may be purchased at pharmacies under trade names listed in

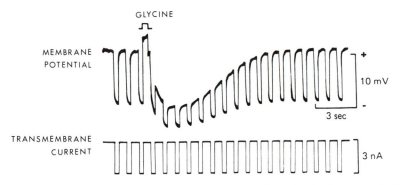

Figure 13.3 Pharmacological response of a Müller cell from the brain stem of a lamprey to glycine, a transmitter inhibitor. The negative shift in membrane potential occurred when glycine was briefly applied to the cell surface by iontophoresis (migration along a current path). For this intracellular recording, the cell was impaled with two micropipettes, one to apply constant-current pulses, the other to record membrane potentials; glycine was applied from a third micropipette. Inhibition was accompanied by a decline in the input resistance of the cell, calculated with Ohm's Law. (From Mathews and Wickelgren 1979.)

Physician's Desk Reference [Medical Economics Co.]. In some cases, prescriptions from a consulting physician may be needed.

13.3.2.7 Single-Unit Recording

To prepare for single-unit recording in the central nervous system (CNS), the fish is paralyzed and clamped and the CNS is exposed. A metal or glass microelectrode is fixed in a micromanipulator and connected to the noninverting input of an AC preamplifier. The other input terminal is connected to a chlorided electrode placed external to the brain (termed an "indifferent electrode"). The microelectrode tip is lowered axially until it touches the pia (vascular layer) of the CNS, at which point the depth indicated on the micromanipulator scale is noted. The electrode should not compress the brain as it is slowly advanced. Spikes of a consistent amplitude and waveform (i.e., single units) are relatively easy to record from many species of fish, but difficult from lampreys. A drawing of the penetration site should be made and the depth below the surface noted.

The recording site can be marked for later recovery in histological sections. With metal microelectrodes, this is done by passing a large sustained current to coagulate proteins in a small volume near the tip; the required amperage and time can be determined in tests on egg white. Glass micropipettes can be filled with 3% (weight/volume) Alcian Blue 8GX or 8GS in 3 M KCl, adjusted to pH 5.2 with 50 mM potassium acetate (Figure 13.4). The dye is ejected when the inside of the electrode is made positive and 0.5–1 μA is passed for 1–3 min; a blue spot of about 50 μm in diameter results (Harnischfeger 1979). Alternatively, the tip of a glass microelectrode can be broken off and left in place during histological processing (see Leonard et al. 1978). If stainless steel electrodes are used, the site can be marked by iron deposition (Section 13.3.2.10). Because the aim of such experiments is usually to correlate neuronal activity with behavior, raw records of spike discharges can be used, or the firing rate of a neuron can be abstracted with a rate meter and presented graphically in relation to the behavior.

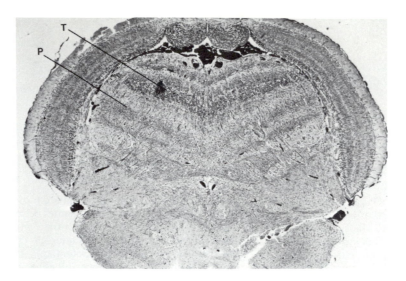

Figure 13.4 Transverse section through the midbrain of an electric fish *Eigenmannia* sp., showing a layered structure, the torus semicircularis, underneath the optic tectum. Neurons at sites P and T respond to different types of electroreceptors: "probability coders" and "phase coders," respectively. At site T, Alcian Blue dye had been ejected from a micropipette electrode to mark the site where neuronal activity had been recorded. The section also underwent Bodian staining for nerve fibers. (Cited in Bell 1979).

13.3.2.8   Evoked Potentials

An abrupt sensory stimulus or electrical stimulation of a peripheral nerve can simultaneously activate groups of neurons in the central nervous system. The summed activity of these neurons can be recorded extracellularly as an evoked potential (see Bullock et al. 1983). Standard terminology numbers the positive (P) or negative (N) peaks of an evoked response according to their delay in milliseconds after the stimulus. A response is recorded in monopolar fashion with one input of a differential amplifier connected to an electrode in the central nervous system and the other amplifier input connected to an "indifferent" electrode at some distance from the brain. The recording electrode can be a microelectrode in a nucleus, a silver ball on top of the spinal cord (under silicon oil, to record the arrival of impulses), or a suction electrode applied to the surface of the brain (Russell 1986). For example, evoked potentials might be used to help one guide microelectrodes to a bulbospinal nucleus. One would stimulate the neurons antidromically (at about 1 Hz) with an electrode on the spinal cord while tracking with a microelectrode in the brain region of interest in search of the maximal amplitude of the time-locked nuclear field potential. Evoked potentials can also be used to monitor the viability of a preparation (e.g., by monitoring the evoked response from a light flash) or to conveniently test the pharmacological sensitivity of different waves in the response that might suggest synaptic linkages. Evoked potentials may be slow, so the high-pass filter on the amplifier should be switched to near-DC coupling.

13.3.2.9   Chemoreception

The chemical senses in fish arise from olfactory and gustatory receptors as well as from free nerve endings (Lancet 1986). Silver and Finger (1984) described a

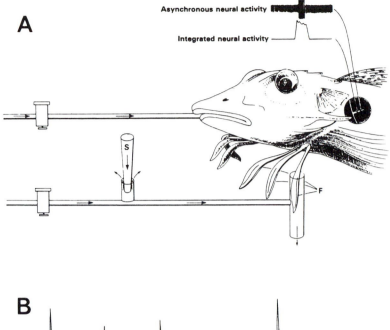

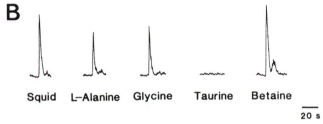

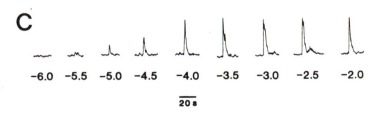

Figure 13.5   Measurement of chemoreceptor activity in the pelvic fin of a northern searobin. **(A)** A fish immobilized by a 2-mg injection of Flaxedil is ventilated through the mouth with seawater. Water also flows, at a rate of 20 mL/min, into a well surrounding a fin ray (F). One-milliliter aliquots of test solutions are introduced at S; dye tests indicate that test solutions are diluted by 78% when they reach the well. Impulses in the chemoreceptor axons are recorded with a hook electrode in oil, and then electronically integrated with a resistor and capacitor in parallel for display on a chart recorder. **(B)** Integrated neuronal responses to different substances, all at $10^{-2.7}$ mol/L. **(C)** Integrated neural responses to increasing concentrations (log-molar scale) of betaine. (From Silver and Finger 1984.).

particularly accessible chemoreceptor system on the pelvic fins of the northern searobin that illustrates the experimental paradigms (Figure 13.5). Test solutions are applied to a well surrounding the receptors; the impulses stimulated by the chemical are recorded from the receptor's afferent nerve with a hook electrode in

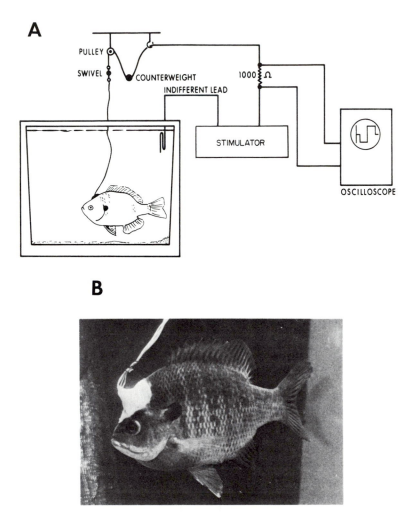

Figure 13.6   Stimulation of the brain with microelectrodes implanted in a freely behaving fish. (**A**) Experimental arrangement. The stimulus current is monitored as the voltage drop across a 1,000-Ω resistor. The oscilloscope trace illustrates a bipolar stimulus waveform. (**B**) Green sunfish with implanted microelectrodes; the cable is neutrally buoyant. Electrical stimulation of the brain near the oculomotor nucleus (1 ms, 20 μA, 50 Hz) evoked head-over-tail looping behavior. (From Demski 1983.)

mineral oil connected to a differential amplifier. A semiquantitative measure of the amount of firing can be obtained by low-pass filtering ("integrating") the nerve activity (Section 13.7). Homogenates of prey (squid in this example) can be used as a general test substance. Individual compounds such as amino acids are tested at concentrations over several log units (orders of magnitude) to determine a concentration–response curve for each. The results can be related to the structures and side groups of the stimulus molecules.

13.3.2.10   Brain Stimulation with Implanted Microelectrodes

The behavioral effects of stimulating a restricted region of the brain can be tested in freely behaving fish (Figure 13.6; Demski and Knigge 1971; Savage and

Roberts 1975; Demski 1983). After a fish is anesthetized, ventilated, and clamped, its cranium is exposed and a small hole is made with a dental drill. Three small wood screws are turned into the cranium near the hole until they just reach the inner cranial surface; their purpose will be to anchor the dental cement applied later. A microelectrode held in a micromanipulator is advanced into the desired region of the brain, either stereotaxically (Peter and Gill 1975) or under visual control with reference to brain landmarks. The cranial opening is covered with hemostatic gelfoam [Upjohn] and then with dental cement, thereby anchoring the microelectrode in relation to the cranium. The connecting cable requires strain relief, so it is soldered to the electrode (the junction is lacquered for insulation) and then covered with dental cement or threaded through dorsal musculature. A small float can be used to preserve the neutral buoyancy of the fish.

It is essential to mark and later identify the stimulation site. Most investigators use stainless steel microelectrodes made by lacquering insect pins with Insul-X lacquer. This permits iron to be electrodeposited at the stimulation site; the iron then can be revealed when histological sections of the brain are stained with Prussian blue (Akert and Welker 1961). Iron is deposited when the electrode is made positive and it passes 15 μA of direct current for 15–20 s.

Stimulation through a single electrode with respect to an indifferent electrode in the aquarium is termed "monopolar" stimulation. In principle, more localized stimulation can be obtained with two closely spaced ("bipolar") electrodes arranged either concentrically or as two parallel wires; such electrodes tend to be larger and to inflict more tissue damage, however. To ensure consistent stimulation, a constant-current stimulus isolation unit (SIU) is appropriate (a 100,000 -Ω resistor in series with the electrode is less satisfactory), and the stimulus current should be monitored with a 1,000-Ω resistor in the circuit (Figure 13.6A; Section 13.7). Stimulus intensities less than 100 μA generally keep the stimulation local, although the spread of current to adjacent brain regions is a potential problem. A bipolar stimulus waveform is typically used to counteract polarization of the stainless steel electrodes; a negative-going square wave of 0.5–1-ms duration is immediately followed by a similar positive-going square wave, such that the net current is zero. Bipolar waveforms are permitted by certain stimulators, or they can be generated with two stimulators and SIUs connected in series.

Data can be collected as chart records of motion and stimulus current, or as photographs. Stimulation is begun at 5–50 Hz and the intensity is slowly augmented from zero until a response is obtained. Rest periods are essential to allow dishabituation; the effect of a stimulus often wanes if it is given too frequently. The number and duration of stimulation epochs should be minimized to reduce damage to brain tissue. An example of these procedures is the study of Kashin et al. (1974), who showed that swimming can be evoked by stimulation in the caudal tegmentum.

Finally, the chronic stimulation of peripheral nerves can be achieved with implantable cuff electrodes available from Micro Probe Inc.

13.4 SENSORY SYSTEMS

The sensory systems of certain fish were extensively reviewed in volume 1 of *Fish Neurobiology*. In the following sections, I briefly survey published techniques used to study three of these: the auditory, retinal, and lateral line systems.

In any of these systems, the need can arise to generate small displacements of body or cell structures that indicate responses to stimuli. Displacements of tactile organs or hair cells can be accomplished with a probe attached to the cone of a small audio speaker or with bimorph piezoelectric elements (Corey and Hudspeth 1980). Highstein and Baker (1985) gave procedures for inducing and measuring displacements of an eye in studies of vestibulo-ocular reflexes (see Figure 13.1A).

13.4.1   Audition

The auditory system of fish was reviewed by Tavolga et al. (1981) and Popper and Fay (1984). Furukawa and Ishii (1967) described a goldfish preparation that allows intracellular recordings to be made from large auditory fibers near their synapses with the hair cells of the sacculus. It is also possible to record generator potentials from the somata of the smaller eighth cranial nerve fibers (Kyogoku et al. 1986).

13.4.2   Retina

The fish retina presents several experimental advantages. It can be studied at room temperature because fish are cold blooded. Goldfish have trichromatic color vision, which facilitates work on cone mechanisms, whereas ratfish (family Chimaeridae) have exclusively rod vision. Several species have large horizontal cells (good for intracellular recording), and certain sharks have giant ganglion cells.

The retina has been the subject of numerous electrophysiological, pharmacological, and immunohistochemical studies (Tachibana 1983; Dowling et al. 1985; Morgan 1985; Brunken et al. 1986; Tumosa and Stell 1986). As in other vertebrates, the cell types present in the retina may include rod and cone photoreceptors, interneurons (bipolar, horizontal, amacrine, interplexiform), and ganglion cells projecting to the optic tecta. Pharmacological agents can be applied in a bath or by perfusion of the retina, or by pressure ejection from micropipettes; spray applications (atomization) have been used (Wu and Dowling 1980), but do not allow the final concentration of agent to be known. It is relatively simple to record the electroretinogram with an extracellular electrode on the cornea; this is a gross potential recorded during a light flash, whose various waves can be interpreted in terms of the synaptic connectivity and changes in membrane potential of the retinal cell types (Tomita and Nanagida 1981). The retinotectal projection in goldfish has long been a favorite system for studying the regeneration of neuronal connections (Edwards and Grafstein 1983).

13.4.3   Lateral Line

The lateral line system in fish consists of a series of cutaneous receptors on the head and along the length of the body. It subserves mechanoreception as well as electroreception, and is part of the acousticolateralis sensory system. The mechanoreceptors are typical hair cells with cilia protruding into the gelatinous coating of the skin (Schwartz 1974). They respond to water waves and low-frequency acoustic stimuli, and they are under efferent control (Flöck and Russell 1976).

Electroreceptors are subcutaneous and connected with the exterior via a canal. They include ampullary organs for low-frequency electric signals and tuberous organs for high-frequency signals (Szabo 1974). Electroreception is widespread among fish species, as demonstrated by potentials in the brain evoked by weak external electric fields (Bullock et al. 1983). The sensitivity of electroreceptors is measured by applying an electric potential between two electrodes straddling the body, creating an electrical gradient measured in V/cm. The minimum stimulus to evoke a behavioral response or evoked firing in the lateral line nerve can be measured; threshold ranges from less than 1 μV/cm in elasmobranchs (e.g., *Raja* spp.) and lampreys (*Lampetra* spp.) to over 2 mV/cm in fish that generate their own electric fields.

Weakly electric fishes, including mormyrids and gymnotids, produce rhythmic electric discharges of 250–700 Hz in electric organs along the flanks of the body; the discharges are used to locate objects and to communicate in muddy waters. A discharge is driven by a pacemaker nucleus in the brain stem (Bennett et al. 1967; Elekes and Szabo 1985). If two fish with similar frequencies of electric organ discharge are placed in proximity, they shift their frequencies so they do not electronically jam one another. Many details of this behavior and of the central circuitry underlying it have been analyzed (Heiligenberg and Bastian 1984; Carr et al. 1986).

13.5 NEUROANATOMY

Lillie (1977), Humason (1979), and Clark (1981) reviewed general histological techniques, the Golgi, Bodian, and Nissl stains for neurons, and other stains (see Chapter 7). The survey of Golgi and tracer methods by Heimer and Robards (1981) is excellent. It is conventional to cut and stain nerve sections for light microscopy. Frozen sections are appropriate for histochemistry, but paraffin sections are more easily handled because they form a ribbon, and they are used for Nissl and Bodian staining (Fernald and Shelton 1985). If neurons are to be counted, one should be aware of the difficulties generally encountered, as discussed by Coggeshall et al. (1984). A convenient alternative to nerve sectioning is to make whole mounts of the brain, which is relatively small in many fish species (e.g., Peter and Fryer 1983; Filipski and Wilson 1984). For this purpose, objective lenses of 1.4–4× magnification are available for most microscopes; the large bottom lens of the condenser is used for illumination.

13.5.1 Tracers

A simple and elegant approach to revealing pathways in the central nervous system is to apply tracer substances that enter neurons, spread within them, and are then visualized. Tracers can enter neurons either by bulk diffusion into cut axons or by vesicular uptake at nerve terminals. It should be emphasized that tracers usually do not enter intact axons; the axons must be cut or damaged to allow the tracer to enter by bulk diffusion. Cut axons tend to reseal after about 1 h unless detergents (dimethyl sulfoxide, lysophosphatidal choline, Nonidet P-40, Triton) or cytotoxic agents (poly-L-lysine, poly-L-ornithine) are added to the tracer. Tracers injected into a muscle or the central nervous system may enter damaged axons as well as be taken up by nerve terminals. The tracer becomes packaged into membranous vesicles, which are then transported. Axonal transport towards the cell body is termed "retrograde" and is the usual mode of labeling; "anterograde" labeling away from the cell body may also occur but is usually fainter. In certain species (e.g., elasmobranchs) with blood of about 800-milliosmolar tonicity, care should be taken to adjust the tonicity of the tracer solution accordingly. For the first few days, the fish's postoperative care is a major consideration, particularly if the fish is to be kept anesthetized and artificially respirated.

Tracer substances may be revealed by autoradiography (if the tracer—an amino acid or a nucleotide base—carries a radioisotope), by histochemistry, or by fluorescence. Fluorescence is the simplest and quickest method. Fluorescent tracers include a variety of small molecules such as True blue, propidium iodide, nuclear yellow, Evans blue, and primulin (Kuypers 1981) [Sigma, Polysciences, Kodak, Aldrich]. Spectacular double-labeling experiments are possible in which different dyes are applied to different sites in the central nervous system and are then shown to localize together in neuronal somata. Tracers are dissolved in distilled water as 1–10% solutions (weight/volume), and then 0.1–1 µL is injected. The retrograde transport of tracers in cold-blooded species is fairly slow, and dyes such as Evans blue and propidium iodide tend to leak out of somata, so fish might have to be kept alive several days or weeks. After fixation with 4% paraformaldehyde (glutaraldehyde should not be used because it increases the background fluorescence), frozen sections are cut and directly examined with a fluorescence microscope.

Fluorescent microspheres containing rhodamine dye can similarly be injected for retrograde transport (Katz et al. 1984) [Tracer Technology, Post Office Box 7, Bardonia, New York 10954]. They have the advantage of diffusing only short distances, which improves the specificity of labeling.

The advantage of histochemical tracers such as horseradish peroxidase or alkaline phosphatase is that enzymatic reduction of many chromogen molecules amplifies the labeling. A drawback is that the procedures for processing the tissue are time-consuming.

Salt-free horseradish peroxidase is widely available. Other protein tracers such as lectins and fluorescent phycobiliproteins (Glazer and Stryer 1984) [Molecular Probes] may contain salts, buffers, and toxic preservatives such as azide. Dialysis and concentration of small volumes is easily done in Centricon tubes [Amicon Corp.]. The sample is centrifuged to force the solvent through a membrane that retains proteins larger than either 10,000 or 30,000 daltons. The sample is then resuspended in the desired buffer and concentrated again by centrifugation.

13.5.2 Horseradish Peroxidase

Horseradish peroxidase (HRP) is perhaps the most widely used tracer (Mesulam 1982; Figure 13.7). As typically employed, it gives granular staining of neuronal somata after retrograde transport of HRP-containing vesicles. However, HRP is known to travel anterogradely (towards the muscles) when injected into spinal motor nuclei of fish (Finger and Kalil 1985). Staining that is solid or "Golgi-like" or "cytoplasmic" is achieved when HRP can freely diffuse inside a neuron, either after it backfills cranial nerves cut close to the brain (Ekström 1985) or after it is injected intracellularly from a micropipette.

Many ingenious procedures have been devised to apply HRP in the form of liquids, pastes, pledgets, or crystals (Alheid et al. 1981). A simple procedure is to apply crystals of HRP to a target organ (e.g., a nerve or muscle) with sharp

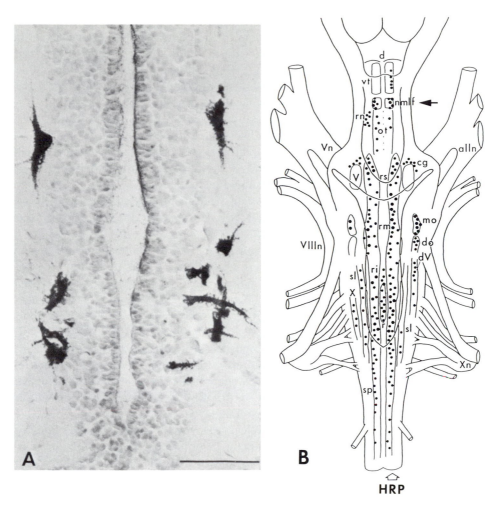

Figure 13.7 Use of horseradish peroxidase (HRP) to trace neural pathways. Bulbospinal neurons in an African lungfish *Protopterus* sp. were stained by retrograde transport of HRP applied to the cervical spinal cord. (Either a thick paste can be applied with the tip of a number 000 insect pin, or a gelfoam pledget soaked with 40–50% HRP can be inserted into a half-cut spinal cord.) (**A**) Transverse section of the brain at the level of the solid arrow in panel B. Dorsal (above) and ventral groups of neural cell bodies show darkly after histochemical processing with tetramethylbenzidine chromogen. The hypothalamus lies below the region shown. The vertical opening in the center is the third ventricle, lined by ependymal cells. Scale = 180 μm. (**B**) Plan diagram of the brain stem (forebrain at top, spinal cord at bottom) showing the bilateral distribution of bulbospinal neurons that were histochemically labeled after HRP was applied to one side of the spinal cord (open arrow). alln = anterior lateral line nerve; cg = granule cells of the cerebellar corpus; d = diencephalon; do = descending octaval nucleus; dV = descending trigeminal tract; mo = magnocellular octaval nucleus; nmlf = nucleus of the medial longitudinal fasciculus; ot = optic tectum; r = raphe; ri = inferior reticular nucleus; rm = middle reticular nucleus; rn = red nucleus; rs = superior reticular nucleus; sl = solitary nucleus and tract; sp = spinal gray matter; vt = ventral thalamus; V = trigeminal motor nucleus; Vn = trigeminal nerve; VIIIn = octaval nerve; X = vagal motor nucleus; Xn = vagal nerve. (From Ronan and Northcutt 1985.)

forceps, damaging axons in the procedure (Highstein and Baker 1985). Injections of 0.02–2 μL of liquid HRP into a muscle or the central nervous system can be made from a broken glass micropipette (5-μm-diameter tip) or a Hamilton syringe. About 30 μL of 20–40% (weight/volume) HRP solution in distilled water, saline, or 50 mM tris buffer (pH 7) can be conveniently made up in a conical-shaped vial; 5% Nonidet P-40 detergent [Sigma] can be added. Another popular technique is to dip the point of an insect pin or a glass micropipette into a concentrated tracer solution and to let the coating air-dry. The coated pin is inserted into a nerve, a spinal cord tract, or another site in the central system and left in place for 30 s–30 min (Ronan and Northcutt 1985). Whatever method is adopted, spillage of HRP must be avoided, and the target organ should be isolated with plastic, cyanoacrylate glues, cotton, Vaseline, etc. to prevent HRP from leaking. The problems of evaluating the effective uptake zone for HRP injected into the brain were reviewed by Mesulam (1982).

Intracellular injection of HRP into neurons can be accomplished with broken micropipettes filled with 4% (weight/volume) HRP in 50 mM tris buffer (pH 7.6) plus 0.5 M KCl. The HRP is ejected by making the inside of the electrode positive or by pressure (Kitai and Bishop 1981; Amaral and Price 1983). Only the tip need be filled with the costly HRP; 0.5 M KCl can be layered on to fill the remainder of the micropipette.

The survival time of experimental animals to allow retrograde transport of HRP is an important variable. It is typically about 1 week for cold-blooded animals such as fish, but longer survival times of 4–6 weeks may prove useful. Short survival does not permit complete transport. Anesthetics may reduce the amount of labeling that occurs. When labeling is judged to be complete, the animal is exsanguinated by perfusing from the heart, first with 10–100 mL (depending on fish size) of cold Ringer solution containing 10 units heparin per milliliter (e.g., from a bottle elevated 1 m), then with isotonic NaCl, then with 100–400 mL of fixative (e.g., 2% glutaraldehyde in 0.1 M sodium phosphate buffer, pH 7.4; paraformaldehyde inactivates HRP). The brain is then dissected out, cryoprotected (to prevent ice crystals from forming) by immersion in 30% sucrose in phosphate buffer until it sinks (indicating equilibration), and frozen on dry ice. Brain sections are cut to 20–100-μm thicknesses and placed in individual compartments such as those of ice cube trays. Because fish brains are relatively small, the unsectioned brain can also be treated with chromogen as a whole mount (Peter and Fryer 1983); a clearer background is obtained if the pia is stripped off, which may be aided by soaking the brain for 15 min in 0.1% (weight/volume) crude collagenase at room temperature.

The main variable in the procedure is the chromogen used to reveal the HRP. Popular chromogens include diaminobenzidine tetrahydrochloride (DAB), phenylene-diamine–pyrocatechol (Hanker et al. 1977), and tetramethylbenzidine (Mesulam 1982). The last is the most sensitive, complex, and artifact-prone chromogen. A convenient DAB procedure (Malmgren and Olsson 1978; Adams 1981) is to immerse the whole mount or unmounted tissue sections in a solution consisting of

20 mg diaminobenzidine tetrahydrochloride dissolved in 7 mL distilled H_2O,
3 mL of 0.3 M sodium cacodylate buffer, pH 5.1, and
0.1 mL of 1% hydrogen peroxide.

Optional addition:

0.25 mL of stock 1% (weight/volume) cobalt chloride.

The final pH is readjusted to 5.1 with NaOH (before adding peroxide) because this is the pH optimum of the enzyme. The reaction is allowed to run at room temperature for about 30 min with agitation while its progress is monitored through a microscope. The reaction product is reddish brown; it is black-purple if the cobalt is added. The reaction is stopped by rinsing the preparation in buffer. Because DAB is reported to be carcinogenic, it is best handled as a liquid from sealed containers [Sigma; Polysciences]; plastic gloves should be worn. All DAB solutions, glassware, and contaminated wipes should be inactivated by soaking them in laundry bleach (hypochlorite) before disposal.

Sections are then floated onto slides and air-dried at room temperature. The tissue is rapidly dehydrated in an alcohol series (50, 75, 95, 100, 100%, each for 15–30 s) and cleared in xylene or methyl salicylate. A whole mount can be viewed on a depression slide or an aluminum slide with a coverslipped opening. Counterstaining is optional; 1 min in 0.5% aqueous toluidine blue, or 2 min in 1% methyl green in 0.1 M sodium acetate buffer (pH 4.0) have been used with DAB. A blue filter (e.g., Wratten number 45, 46, or 47) may increase the contrast of the DAB-stained cells during photomicroscopy. Acidic solutions or alcohols tend to cause tissue shrinkage.

The sensitivity of labeling can be increased in several ways: (1) by using grades of HRP having a high specific activity (e.g., Type VI from Sigma or the Worthington HPOFF grade); (2) by using HRP conjugated to lectins [Vector Labs], including wheat germ agglutinin for enhancing retrograde labeling (Mesulam 1982); (3) by using PHA-L (*Phaseolus vulgaris* leucoagglutinin) for antero-grade labeling (Gerfen and Sawchenko 1984); (4) by adding detergents such as 2–25% dimethyl sulfoxide, Nonidet P-40, Triton, or lysophosphatidal choline to the tracer (Frank et al. 1980); (5) by using glucose oxidase to generate the hydrogen peroxide (Itoh et al. 1979); or (6) by using tetramethylbenzidine as the chromogen.

Appropriate controls can include unlabeled animals, unilateral labeling, and intraperitoneal or intravenous injection of HRP (to control for HRP leakage). Red blood cells, capillaries, or nervous tissues may possess endogenous peroxidase activity, yielding backgrounds that are not clear; pretreatment with 50–70% ethanol for 30–60 min can eliminate this. Improved washout of red blood cells is obtained by injecting 800 units of heparin and 0.1 mg propranolol in 0.2 mL of 0.6% NaCl 1 h prior to perfusion, and by adding 10 units heparin per milliliter to the initial perfusion fluid.

13.6 NEUROCHEMISTRY

13.6.1 Cholinergic Receptors of Electric Rays

Synaptic transmission in the electric organs of *Torpedo* rays continues to be intensively studied. The transmitter is acetylcholine, because electric organs are modified neuromuscular systems. The large mass of homogeneous tissue in the electric organ facilitates biochemical analysis, especially the chromatographic purification of proteins related to cholinergic synapses such as the nicotinic acetylcholine receptor (Wan and Lindstrom 1984). This has led to the cloning of the receptor genes (Noda et al. 1983). *Torpedo* electroplaxes (the modified muscle plates that make up the electric organ) have also been used as a source of antigens for generating monoclonal antibodies to cholinergic synapses (Kushner 1984).

13.6.2 Sodium Channels in Electric Eels

The well-known neurotoxin from the puffers (family Tetraodontidae), tetrodotoxin (TTX), selectively binds to Na^+ channels for the nerve action potential, which is blocked at 10^{-7} M TTX. This selective binding has been used to chromatographically purify and characterize voltage-dependent Na^+ channels from the electroplaxes of electric eels *Electrophorus electricus* again on account of their homogeneity (Levinson 1981). This in turn has permitted the structural genes for the electroplax Na^+ channel to be cloned (Noda et al. 1984), the first genes for an excitable membrane protein ever to be cloned.

13.6.3 Transmitter Immunocytochemistry

Immunochemical labeling is a powerful and flexible technique that may allow us to simultaneously define the location, morphology, and biochemical composition of neurons according to the transmitters and peptides they contain. The indirect antibody method amplifies the labeling: an antigen molecule leads to the deposition of tens or hundreds of chromogen molecules. A purified antigen (e.g., a neuropeptide) is first used to generate "primary" antibodies that may be either polyclonal (from immunization of a rabbit or goat) or monoclonal. The primary antibody is applied to sections of nervous tissue, where it (hopefully) binds selectively to the original antigen if it is present within neurons. The primary antibody is then revealed by a "secondary" antibody developed in a different species against the invariant regions of the primary immunoglobulin; thus several secondary antibodies bind to each primary antibody, amplifying the labeling. For visualization, a fluorescent dye can be conjugated to the secondary antibody, or HRP can be employed. With HRP, further amplification of the labeling is achieved when a complex is formed between the secondary antibody and HRP by either the PAP (peroxidase–antiperoxidase; Figure 13.8A) or biotin–avidin methods. Many different antibodies and their conjugates are available commercially [Vector, Boehringer, Miles, Polysciences, E-Y Labs] (Linscott 1990).

However, this labeling method has pitfalls (Landis 1985; Sternberger 1986). Nonspecific or artifactual labeling or failure of labeling can occur; in particular, peptides in fish tend to be somewhat different from their mammalian counterparts (W. Brunken, personal communication). Another problem is the limited penetration of antibodies and other proteins into sections of nervous tissue. Landis (1985) reviewed controls and companion biochemical studies for immunochemistry. A few of the recent studies on fish include those by Falcon et al. (1984), Finger (1984), Ritchie et al. (1984), Brunken et al. (1986), and Tumosa and Stell (1986); the series by Bullock and Petrusz (1989) is informative.

13.6.4 Fluorescence Histochemistry

A convenient method to detect epinephrine, norepinephrine, dopamine, and serotonin in nerve tissue slices or thin whole mounts is to convert these transmit-

A
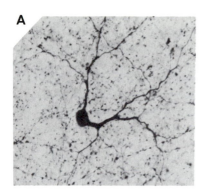

B
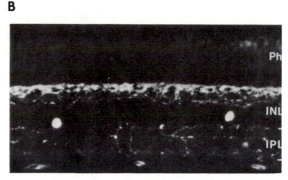

Figure 13.8 (A) Immunocytochemistry of the retina from a skate *Raja* sp. The neuron stained darkly when antibodies to tyrosine hydrolase were used with the peroxidase–antiperoxidase staining method. (From Brunken et al. 1986). (B) Fluorescence histochemistry of a goldfish retina (Falk–Hillarp method showing dopaminergic neurons in the inner layer (INL); Ph = photoreceptors; IPL = inner plexiform layer. Fluorescence was enhanced by injection of 1 μg of α-methylnoradrenaline into the vitreum of the eye 4 h before the fish was killed. (From Ehinger and Florén 1978.)

ters to a fluorescent analogue (Figure 13.8B). This can be done by exposure of tissue to formaldehyde gas (Falck–Hillarp method), glycoxylic acid (Lindvall and Björklund 1974), or aqueous aldehyde (Furness et al. 1978). The presence of protein is required to catalyze the reaction. The many technical variants were reviewed by Moore (1981). A simple 15-min method involving glycoxylic acid is presented here (de la Torre 1980). Only one solution is needed; it contains 10.2 g sucrose, 4.8 g monobasic KH_2PO_4, and 1.5 g glycoxylic acid monohydride [Sigma] dissolved in 100 mL H_2O. The solution is adjusted to pH 7.4 with 1 N NaOH and brought to a final volume of 150 mL. Glycoxylic acid monohydride is somewhat unstable and should be stored frozen and desiccated. Fresh (unfixed) tissue is rapidly dissected into 5–10-mm-thick slabs and immediately frozen onto precooled cryostat chucks with a film of water; the cryostat with the lid open should be at exactly −30°C. Frozen cryostat sections are cut to 6–32μm thicknesses and directly mounted on glass slides. A cut section is dipped immediately three times (one dip per second) in a beaker containing the above solution at room temperature. Excess solution is blotted, but the section is not touched. The section is then dried under hair dryers set at maximum cool air for several minutes; it must be completely dry (ground glass appearance). Next, one or two drops of light mineral oil (U.S. Pharmacopeia grade) are placed on the section to cover it. Slides are placed on copper metal blocks in a prewarmed oven at exactly 95°C for 2.5 min; longer times increase the background fluorescence. Slides are removed from the oven and drained by blotting the slide edges. A fresh covering of mineral oil is added (one or two drops) and cover slips are applied. A fluorescence microscope is needed. Yellow or greenish fluorescence is usually described for monoamines; the dopamine adduct of glycoxylic acid has a narrow excitation maximum at 350–400 nm (violet) and a broad emission maximum at 430–550 nm (blue–yellow–green). A cryostat is preferred to a freezing microtome because the section must be kept frozen to reduce the diffusion of monoamines that obscures localization. Tri-X or high-speed daylight Ektachrome films [Kodak] can be used. The data are usually presented as photographs of localized regions to document the presence of monoamine-containing cell bodies or synaptic terminals; negative results may, as usual, be due to deficient methodology. The glycoxylic acid method may not reveal serotonergic neurons, for which immunochemical approaches can be used. Improved sensitivity comes from pharmacological manipulations to load neurons with precursors. For example, dopamine or α-methylnoradrenaline has been injected into the eye for preferential uptake by dopaminergic neurons in the fish retina (Figure 13.8B), and serotonin or 5,6-dihydroxytryptamine has been injected for preferential uptake by indoleaminergic neurons (Ehinger and Florén 1978; Negishi et al. 1981). Inhibitors of monoamine oxidase (e.g., pargyline [Sigma], 75 mg/kg given intraperitoneally) increase the levels of monoamines by reducing breakdown (Cooper et al. 1986). It should also be mentioned that monoamine analogues such as 6-hydroxydopamine or 5,6-dihydroxytryptamine are toxic and can be used to selectively lesion monoaminergic neurons (Ehinger and Florén 1978; Cooper et al. 1986).

13.6.5 Receptor Binding

The binding of radioactive molecules (radioligands) to receptors on nerve cells can be studied either in homogenates of nervous tissue or (morphologically) in sections of the brain. Studies of opiate binding in goldfish retinas (Slaughter et al. 1985) and of benzodiazepine binding in rainbow trout brains (Wilkinson et al. 1983) illustrate how membrane fractions separated from tissue homogenates permit both demonstration of specific radioligand binding and study of its concentration dependence and pharmacology. For example, the specific binding of tritiated benzodiazepines in trout brain membranes has been demonstrated by showing that nonradioactive agonists displace the radioligand. The analysis becomes more complex if more than one type of ligand binding site exists (Peck and Kelner 1982).

Autoradiographic methods permit the localization of receptors in the brain, but are more demanding technically (see Herkenham 1985). One approach is to inject the radioligand in vivo; after a short period, the brain is removed, frozen, and sectioned, and emulsion is applied for autoradiography. This approach is limited to ligands that cross the blood–brain barrier and form high-affinity bonds to receptors (e.g., opiates). The alternative approach is in vitro binding, in which a radioligand is applied after the brain is sectioned. The problem that radioligands may diffuse or form low-affinity bonds with receptors has been overcome by "dry" autoradiographic procedures in which sections are dried and then overlaid with emulsion-coated coverslips or tritium-sensitive film. As with homogenates, the specificity of binding can be demonstrated by showing stereospecificity or displacement by nonradioactive agonists (Walmsley and Palacios 1982).

13.7 ELECTRICAL PRINCIPLES OF NEUROPHYSIOLOGICAL RESEARCH

Electrophysiological techniques record or apply a potential difference between two points, between which an electric current flows. In the case of intracellular recording, the two points are the electrode tip within a cell and a ground electrode in the bath or animal. In the case of differential extracellular recording, the two points are the two electrode tips. It is basic that current always flows in loops; the

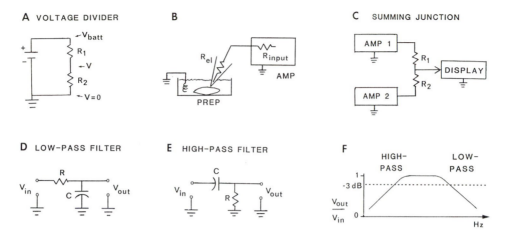

Figure 13.9 Basic electronic circuits; all voltages are measured with respect to ground ($\perp$). AMP = amplifier; C = capacitor; dB = decibel; PREP = preparation; R = resistor; R_{el} = electrode resistance; R_{input} = input resistance of the amplifier; V = voltage. For the filter circuits in panels D and E, the output goes to a display with a high input impedance (e.g., 1 MΩ). With respect to panel F, nerve preamplifiers typically are used as band-pass amplifiers that block both low and high frequencies, as shown by the graph.

flow of current in circuits can be idealized as the two poles of a battery connected by resistors. The relation between the potential difference (V), current flow (I), and resistance (R) is given by Ohm's law:

$$V \text{ (volts)} = I \text{ (amperes)} \times R \text{ (ohms)}.$$

For example, extracellular recording of the currents from nerve impulses depends on the resistance between the electrode tip and surrounding tissue that is provided by oil, air, etc.; it is the voltage drop of the current flowing across the resistance that one records. This is why more effective insulation of the electrode will give larger signals or oblige smaller stimulating currents.

The total resistance becomes larger for resistors (R_n) in series:

$$R = R_1 + R_2 + R_3;$$

resistors in parallel decrease the total resistance. A practical example of resistors in series is the voltage divider (Figure 13.9A), in which the voltage at the middle arrow is given by:

$$V = V_{batt} \times R_2/(R_1 + R_2).$$

Neurophysiological preamplifiers have input impedances of 10^{11} Ω or more so that signals from high-resistance electrodes (e.g., 1–100 MΩ) connected in series with the amplifier input are attenuated less than 1% (Figure 13.9B). By the same principle, a resistor of 100 MΩ can be interposed between a stimulator and a microelectrode—e.g., for iontophoresis of drugs—to ensure that the current passed will be largely independent of the electrode resistance (the latter will form only a small fraction of the total resistance). A related situation arises in the summing junction (Figure 13.9C), in which the outputs of two instruments are connected by resistors to a recorder. The resistors are needed to prevent shunting of the signal from one device into the output of the other device, because most instruments have an output impedance to ground of about 100 Ω. Of course, there will be attenuation of the signals; if $R_1 = R_2$, the signals from both devices will be attenuated by half.

Resistors introduce random noise, which increases with the resistance; a value of 10,000 Ω is especially useful. Commercial resistors are made of carbon or metal film. A power rating of 0.25 W for R > 1,000 Ω is typical. For values over 20 MΩ, special types are available from Eltec or Victoreen.

Capacitors do not pass DC voltages, but instead respond to transients according to the relation

$$I \text{ (amperes)} = C \text{ (farads)} \times dV/dt;$$

I = capacitive current, C = capacitance, and dV/dt = the rate of rise (or decline) of voltage in time (V/s). For example, a DC offset voltage from an amplifier can be eliminated by connecting a 1-μF capacitor in series with the output. Capacitors are often labeled in picofarads; the label "104" means $10 \times 10^4 \times 10^{-12}$ farads, or 0.1 μF. The physical size increases with the rated capacitance and breakdown voltage. Plastic film capacitors are inexpensive and perform well. Larger capacitors (>5 μF) are usually electrolytic types, in which case the lead polarity must be respected. The total capacitance is the sum of the capacitors that are added in parallel.

The combination of a resistor and a capacitor, either in parallel or series, has a time constant:

$$\tau \text{ (seconds)} = RC \text{ (ohms} \times \text{farads)}.$$

This relationship can be exploited to make low-pass filters that eliminate rapid transients (Figure 13.9D), or high-pass filters that eliminate DC offsets or slow potential shifts (Figure 13.9E). The "cut-off" frequency of a filter is usually stated as the frequency of a sinusoidal signal whose peak-to-peak amplitude (A) is attenuated by −3 dB. Because $dB = 20 \log_{10} A/A_0$, the attenuated signal retains about 70% of the peak-to-peak amplitude. The −3 dB point will occur at a frequency (f) of

$$f \text{ (Hz)} = 1/(6.28 \ RC).$$

If a graph of frequency versus amplitude is made (Figure 13.9F), the slope of the declining amplitude will be −6 dB per octave (doubling of frequency).

A low-pass filter with a τ of about 0.5 s acts as a "leaky integrator" that can be used to semiquantify the amount of activity in nerve or electromyographic recordings. It can also be used to convert fast spikes into a slower signal suitable for recording on pen recorders. More sophisticated integrators (Paynter filters) have been described (Halbertsma and DeBoer 1981) [Bak].

Intracellular stimulus currents can be measured with a 1,000-Ω resistor interposed in one lead of a hook electrode or between the bath and the system ground for microelectrode stimulation (Figure 13.6A). A differential amplifier (e.g., in an oscilloscope) is connected across the resistor, and the current is calculated from the voltage drop across the resistor by Ohm's Law. A better method for measuring intracellular stimulation is to use a current-to-voltage converter based on an operational amplifier [W-P Instruments].

A variety of simple analog circuits can be conveniently arranged by use of operational amplifiers, which are simply high-gain differential amplifiers. By addition of a few resistors and capacitors, many useful circuits can easily be made, including amplifiers, summing junctions, integrators, differentiators, filters, etc. (Horowitz and Hill 1980). The LF356 operational amplifier chip made by National Semiconductor is especially versatile and easy to use, and is pin-compatible with the common 741 operational amplifier chip. Impromptu circuits can be arranged on a breadboard [Jameco], or more permanent circuits can be built on standard-size perforated cards with edge connectors that fit modular cardcages [Vector, Bud]. The basic digital logic circuits are also easy to build (Lancaster 1974). It is necessary to choose one of the logic families (CMOS, low-power Schottky TTL, etc.) and then standardize the circuitry based on that families' particular requirements.

13.8 REFERENCES

Adams, J. C. 1981. Heavy metal intensification of DAB-based HRP reaction product. Journal of Histochemistry and Cytochemistry 29:775.

Akert, K., and W. I. Welker. 1961. Problems and methods of anatomical localization. Pages 251–260 in D. E. Sheer, editor. Electrical stimulation of the brain. University of Texas Press, Austin.

Alexander, R. M. 1977. Swimming. Pages 222–248 in R. M. Alexander and G. Goldspink, editors. Mechanics and energetics of animal locomotion. Chapman and Hall, London.

Alheid, G. F., S. B. Edwards, S. T. Katai, M. R. Park, and R. C. Switzer III. 1981. Methods for delivering tracers. Pages 91–116 in L. Heimer and M. J. Robards, editors. Neuroanatomical tract-tracing methods. Plenum, New York.

Amaral, D. G., and J. L. Price. 1983. An air pressure system for the injection of tracer substances into the brain. Journal of Neuroscience Methods 9:35–43.

Barker, J. L., and J. F. McKelvy. 1983. Current methods in cellular neurobiology, volumes 1–4. Wiley, New York.

Bell, C. C. 1979. Central nervous system physiology of electroreception, a review. Journal de Physiologie (Paris) 75:361–379.

Bennett, M. V. L., G. D. Pappas, G. Giminez, and Y. Nakajima. 1967. Physiology and ultrastructure of electronic junctions. IV. Medullary electromotor nuclei in gymnotoid fish. Journal of Neurophysiology 30:236–300.

Brunken, W. J., P. Witkovsky, and H. J. Karten, 1986. Retinal neurochemistry of three elasmobranch species: an immunohistochemical approach. Journal of Comparative Neurology 243:1–12.

Budavari, S., editor. 1989. The Merck index, 11th edition. Merck, Rahway, New Jersey.

Bullock, G. R., and P. Petrusz, editors. 1989. Techniques in immunocytochemistry, volume 4. Academic Press, San Diego.

Bullock, T. H., D. A. Bodznick, and R. G. Northcutt. 1983. The phylogenetic distribution of electroreception: evidence for convergent evolution of a primitive vertebrate sense modality. Brain Research Reviews 6:25–46.

Cameron, J. N., and G. A. Kormanik. 1982. Intracellular and extracellular acid–base status as a function of temperature in the freshwater channel catfish, *Ictalurus punctatus*. Journal of Experimental Biology 99:127–142.

Carr, C. E., W. Heiligenberg, and G. J. Rose. 1986. A time-comparison circuit in the electric fish midbrain. I. Behavior and physiology. Journal of Neuroscience 6:107–119.

Cavanaugh, G. M., editor. 1956. Formulae and methods VI of the marine biological laboratory chemical room. Marine Biological Laboratory, Woods Hole, Massachusetts.

Clark, G. 1981. Staining procedures, 4th edition. Williams and Wilkins, Baltimore, Maryland.

Clark, H. F. 1972. Cultivation of cells from poikilothermic vertebrates. Pages 287–325 *in* G. H. Rothblat and V. J. Cristofalo, editors. Growth, nutrition, and metabolism of cells in culture, volume 2. Academic Press, New York.

Cobbold, R. 1974. Transducers for biomedical measurements. Wiley, New York.

Coggeshall, R. E., K. Chung, D. Greenwood, and C. E. Hulsebosch. 1984. An empirical method for converting nucleolar counts to neuronal numbers. Journal of Neuroscience Methods 12:125–132.

Cooper, J. R., F. E. Bloom, and R. H. Roth. 1986. The biochemical basis of neuropharmacology, 5th edition. Oxford University Press, New York.

Corey, D. P., and A. J. Hudspeth. 1980. Mechanical stimulation and micromanipulation with piezoelectric bimorph elements. Journal of Neuroscience Methods 3:183–202.

de la Torre, J. C. 1980. An improved approach to histofluorescence using the SPC method for tissue monoamines. Journal of Neuroscience Methods 3:1–5.

Delaunois, A. L. 1974. Low-cost i.c. transducer for medical pressure measurements. Medical & Biological Engineering & Computing 12:364–365.

Demski, L. S. 1983. Behavioral effects of electrical stimulation of the brain. Pages 317–359 *in* R. E. Davis and R. G. Northcutt, editors. Fish neurobiology, volume 2. Higher brain areas and functions. University of Michigan, Ann Arbor.

Demski, L. S., and K. M. Knigge. 1971. The telencephalon and hypothalamus of the bluegill *(Lepomis macrochirus):* evoked feeding, aggressive and reproductive behavior with representative frontal sections. Journal of Comparative Neurology 143:1–16.

Dingledine, R., editor. 1984. Brain slices. Plenum, New York.

Dixon, D. D., and D. G. Holland. 1975. Fluorocarbons: properties and syntheses. Federation Proceedings 34:1444–1448.

Dowling, J., M. W. Pak, and E. M. Lasater. 1985. White perch horizontal cells in culture: methods, morphology and process growth. Brain Research 360:331–338.

Eaton, R. C., W. A. Lavender, and C. M. Wieland. 1981. Identification of Mauthner-initiated response patterns in goldfish: evidence from simultaneous cinematography and electrophysiology. Journal of Comparative Physiology 144:521–531.

Edwards, D. L., and B. Grafstein. 1983. Intraocular tetrodotoxin in goldfish hinders optic nerve regeneration. Brain Research 269:1–14.

Ehinger, B., and I. Florén. 1978. Chemical removal of indoleamine accumulating terminals in rabbit and goldfish retina. Experimental Eye Research 26:321–328.

Ekström, P. 1985. Anterograde and retrograde filling of central neuronal systems with horseradish peroxidase under in vitro conditions. Journal of Neuroscience Methods 15:21–35.

Elekes, K., and T. Szabo. 1985. The mormyrid brainstem. 3. Ultrastructure and synaptic organization of the medullary pacemaker nucleus. Neuroscience 15:431–444.

Faber, D. S., and H. Korn. 1978. Neurobiology of the Mauthner cell. Raven Press, New York.

Falcon, J., M. Geffard, M. T. Juillard, H. W. M. Steinbusch, P. Seguela, and J. P. Collin. 1984. Immunocytochemical localization and circadian variations of serotonin and N-acetylserotonin in photoreceptor cells. Light and electron microscopic study in the teleost pineal organ. Journal of Histochemistry and Cytochemistry 32:486–492.

Fernald, R. D., and L. C. Shelton. 1985. The organization of the diencephalon and the pretectum in the cichlid fish, *Haplochromis burtoni*. Journal of Comparative Neurology 238:202–217.

Filipski, G. T., and M. V. H. Wilson. 1984. Sudan black as a nerve stain for whole cleared fishes. Copeia 1984:204–208.

Finger, T. E. 1984. Vagotomy induced changes in acetylcholinesterase staining and substance P-like immunoreactivity in the gustatory lobes of goldfish *Carassius auratus*. Anatomy and Embryology 170:257–264.

Finger, T. E., and K. Kalil. 1985. Organization of motoneuronal pools in the rostral spinal cord of the sea robin, *Prionotus carolinus*. Journal of Comparative Neurology 239:384–390.

Flöck, A., and I. Russell. 1976. Inhibition by efferent nerve fibres: action on hair cells and afferent synaptic transmission in the lateral line canal organ of the burbot *Lota lota*. Journal of Physiology (London) 257:45–62.

Forster, R. P., and J. V. Taggart. 1950. Use of isolated renal tubules for the examination of metabolic processes associated with active cellular transport. Journal of Cellular and Comparative Physiology 36:251–270.

Frank, E., W. A. Harris, and M. B. Kennedy. 1980. Lysophosphatidyl choline facilitates labelling of CNS projections with horseradish peroxidase. Journal of Neuroscience Methods 2:183–189.

Furness, J. B., J. W. Health, and M. Costa. 1978. Aqueous aldehyde (Faglu) methods for the fluorescence histochemical localization of catecholamines and for ultrastructural studies of central nervous tissue. Histochemistry 57:285–295.

Furukawa, T., and Y. Ishii. 1967. Neurophysiological studies on hearing in goldfish. Journal of Neurophysiology 30:1377–1403.

Gerfen, C. R., and P. E. Sawchenko. 1984. An anterograde neuroanatomical tracing method that shows the detailed morphology of neurons, their axons and terminals: immunohistochemical localization of an axonally transported plant lectin, *Phaseolus vulgaris* leucoagglutinin (PHA-L). Brain Research 290:219–238.

Glazer, A. N., and L. Stryer. 1984. Phycofluor probes. Trends in Biochemical Sciences 4:423–427.

Godden, D. H., and D. Graham. 1983. 'Instant' analysis of movement. Journal of Experimental Biology 107:505–508.

Gold, M. R., and A. R. Martin. 1983. Analysis of glycine-activated inhibitory post-synaptic channels in brain-stem neurones of the lamprey. Journal of Physiology (London) 342:99–117.

Goodman, A. G., L. S. Goodman, T. W. Rall, and F. Murad. 1985. Goodman and Gilman's the pharmacological basis of therapeutics. MacMillan, New York.

Graf, W., and R. Baker, 1985. The vestibuloocular reflex of the adult flatfish. II. Vestibuloocular connectivity. Journal of Neurophysiology 54:900–916.

Guthrie, D. M. 1981. Neuroethology. An introduction. Wiley, New York.

Hagiwara, S., and N. Saito. 1959. Membrane potential changes and membrane currents in supramedullary nerve cell of puffer. Journal of Neurophysiology 22:204–221.

Halbertsma, J., and R. DeBoer. 1981. On the processing of electromyograms for computer analysis. Journal of Biomechanics 14:431–435.

Hamil, O. P., A. Marty, E. Neher, B. Sakmann, and F. J. Sigworth. 1981. Improved patch-clamp techniques for high-resolution current recording from cells and cell-free membrane patches. Pflügers Archiv 391:85–100.

Hanker, J. S., P. E. Yates, C. B. Metz, and A. Rustioni. 1977. A new specific, sensitive and non-carcinogenic reagent for the demonstration of horseradish peroxidase. Histochemical Journal 9:789–792.

Harnischfeger, G. 1979. An improved method for extracellular marking of electrode tip position in nervous tissue. Journal of Neuroscience Methods 1:195–200.

Heiligenberg, W., and J. Bastian. 1984. The electric sense of weakly electric fish. Annual Review of Physiology 46:561–584.

Heimer, L., and M. J. Robards, editors. 1981. Neuroanatomical tract-tracing methods. Plenum, New York.

Herkenham, M. A. 1985. Autoradiographic methods for receptor localization. Pages 44–60 *in* H. J. Karten, editor. Modern neuroanatomical methods. Society for Neuroscience, Washington, D.C.

Highstein, S. M., and R. Baker. 1985. Action of the efferent vestibular system on primary afferents in the toadfish, *Opsanus tau*. Journal of Neurophysiology 54:370–384.

Horowitz, P., and W. Hill. 1980. The art of electronics. Cambridge University Press, Cambridge, England.

Houston, A. H., and T. F. Koss. 1982. Water–electrolyte balance in goldfish, *Carassius auratus*, under constant and diurnally cycling temperature conditions. Journal of Experimental Biology 97:427–440.

Humason, G. 1979. Animal tissue techniques. Freeman, San Francisco.

Itoh, K., A. Konishi, S. Nomura, N. Mizuno, Y. Nakamura, and T. Sugimoto. 1979. Application of coupled oxidation reaction to electron microscopic demonstration of horseradish peroxidase: cobalt–glucose oxidase method. Brain Research 175:341–346.

Johansen, K., C. Lenfant, and D. Hanson. 1973. Gas exchange in the lamprey, *Entosphenus tridentatus*. Comparative Biochemistry and Physiology A, Comparative Physiology 44:107–119.

Kandel, E. R. 1964. Electrical properties of hypothalamic neuroendocrine cells. Journal of General Physiology 47:691–717.

Kashin, S. M., A. G. Feldman, and G. N. Orlovsky. 1974. Locomotion of fish evoked by electrical stimulation of the brain. Brain Research 82:41–47.

Katz, L. C., A. Burkhalter, and W. J. Dreyer. 1984. Fluorescent latex microspheres as a retrograde neuronal marker for *in vivo* and *in vitro* studies of visual cortex. Nature (London) 310:498–500.

Kitai, S. T., and G. A. Bishop. 1981. Horseradish peroxidase. Intracellular staining of neurons. Pages 263–277 *in* L. Heimer and M. J. Robards, editors. Neuroanatomical tract-tracing methods. Plenum, New York.

Kushner, P. D. 1984. A library of monoclonal antibodies to *Torpedo* cholinergic synaptosomes. Journal of Neurochemistry 43:775–786.

Kuypers, H. G. J. M. 1981. Procedure for retrograde double labeling with fluorescent substances. Pages 299–303 *in* L. Heimer and M. J. Robards, editors. Neuroanatomical tract-tracing methods. Plenum, New York.

Kyle, A. L., and R. E. Peter. 1985. Effects of forebrain lesions on spawning behaviour in the male goldfish. Physiology and Behavior 28:1103–1109.

Kyogoku, I., S. Matsuura, and M. Kuno. 1986. Generator potentials and spike initiation in auditory fibers of goldfish. Journal of Neurophysiology 55:244–255.

Lamb, T. D. 1985. An inexpensive digital tape recorder suitable for neurophysiological signals. Journal of Neuroscience Methods 15:1–13.

Lancaster, D. 1974. TTL cookbook. H. W. Sams, Indianapolis, Indiana.

Lancet, D. 1986. Vertebrate olfactory reception. Annual Review of Neuroscience 9:329–355.

Landis, D. M. D. 1985. Promise and pitfalls in immunocytochemistry. Trends in Neurosciences 8:312–317.

Laudien, H., J. Freyer, R. Erb, and D. Denzer. 1986. Influence of isolation stress and inhibited protein biosynthesis on learning and memory in goldfish. Physiology & Behavior 39:657–664.

Leonard, R. B., P. Rudomin, and W. D. Willis. 1978. Central effects of volleys in sensory and motor components of peripheral nerves in the stingray, *Dasyatis sabina*. Journal of Neurophysiology 41:108–125.

Levinson, S. R. 1981. The structure and function of the voltage-dependent sodium channel. Pages 315–331 *in* T. P. Singer and R. N. Ondarza, editors. Molecular basis of drug action. Elsevier, New York.

Lillie, R. D. 1977. H. J. Conn's biological stains, 9th edition. Williams and Wilkins, Baltimore, Maryland.

Lindvall, O., and A. Björklund. 1974. The glycoxylic acid fluorescence histochemical method: a detailed account of the methodology for the visualization of central catecholamine neurons. Histochemistry 39:97–127.

Linscott, W. D. 1990. Linscott's directory of immunological and biological reagents, 6th edition. (Available from W. D. Linscott, Mill Valley, California.)

Lockwood, A. P. M. 1961. "Ringer" solutions and some notes on the physiological basis of their ionic compositions. Comparative Biochemistry and Physiology 2:241–289.

Malmgren, L., and Y. Olsson. 1978. A sensitive method for histochemical demonstration of horseradish peroxidase in neurons following retrograde axonal transport. Brain Research 148:279–294.

Matthews, G., and W. O. Wickelgren. 1979. Glycine, GABA and synaptic inhibition of reticulospinal neurones of lamprey. Journal of Physiology (London) 293:393–415.

Mena, R., and E. Frixione. 1984. A black flexible support with excellent optic qualities for microdissection of nerve tissues. Journal of Neuroscience Methods 11:291–292.

Merrill, E. G., and A. Ainsworth. 1972. Glass-coated platinum-plated tungsten microelectrodes. Medical & Biological Engineering & Computing 10:662–672.

Mesulam, M.-M., editor. 1982. Tracing neural connections with horseradish peroxidase. Wiley, Chichester, England.

Moore, R. Y. 1981. Fluorescence histochemical methods: neurotransmitter histochemistry. Pages 441–482 *in* L. Heimer and M. J. Robards, editors. Neuroanatomical tract-tracing methods. Plenum, New York.

Morgan, W. W. 1985. Retinal transmitters and modulators: models for the brain, volumes 1 and 2. CRC Press, Boca Raton, Florida.

Morin, P.-P., J.-L. Verrette, J. J. Dodson, and F. Y. Doré. 1987. Computer-automated method to study cardiac conditioning to a chemical cue in young salmon. Physiology & Behavior 39:657–664.

Nastuk, W. L., editor. 1963. Physical techniques in biological research, volume 6. Parts A and B. Electrophysiological methods. Academic Press, New York.

Negishi, K., S. Kato, and T. Teranishi. 1981. Indoleamine-accumulating cells and dopaminergic cells are distributed similarly in carp retina. Neuroscience Letters 25:1–5.

Noda, M., and seventeen coauthors. 1984. Primary structure of *Electrophorus electricus* sodium channel deduced from cDNA sequence. Nature (London) 312:121–127.

Noda, M., and ten coauthors. 1983. Structural homology of *Torpedo californica* acetylcholine receptor subunits. Nature (London) 302:528–532.

Okitsu, S., S.-I. Umekita, and S. Obara. 1978. Ionic compositions of the media across the sensory epithelium in the ampullae of Lorenzini of the marine catfish, *Plotosus*. Journal of Comparative Physiology 126:115–121.

Peck, E. J., Jr., and K. L. Kelner. 1982. Receptor measurement. Pages 53–75 *in* A. Lajtha, editor. Handbook of neurochemistry, volume 2, 2nd edition. Plenum, New York.

Peter, R. E., and J. N. Fryer. 1983. Endocrine functions of the hypothalamus of actinopterygians. Pages 165–201 *in* R. E. Davis and R. G. Northcutt, editors. Fish neurobiology, volume 2. Higher brain areas and functions. University of Michigan, Ann Arbor.

Peter, R. E., and V. E. Gill. 1975. A stereotaxic atlas and technique for forebrain nuclei of the goldfish, *Carassius auratus*. Journal of Comparative Neurology 159:69–102.

Popper, A. N., and R. R. Fay. 1984. Sound detection and processing by teleost fish: a selective review. Pages 67–101 *in* L. M. Bolis, R. D. Keynes, and S. H. P. Maddrell, editors. Comparative physiology of sensory systems. Cambridge University Press, Cambridge, England.

Potts, W. T. W., and G. Parry. 1964. Osmotic and ionic regulation in animals. Pergamon Press, Oxford, England.

Prugh, J. I. P., C. B. Kinnel, and W. K. Metcalfe. 1982. Noninvasive recording of the Mauthner neurone action potential in larval zebrafish. Journal of Experimental Biology 101:83–93.

Ritchie, T. C., C. A. Livingston, M. G. Hughes, D. J. McAdoo, and R. B. Leonard. 1984. The distribution of serotonin in the central nervous system of an elasmobranch fish. Immunocytochemical and biochemical studies in the Atlantic sting ray *Dasyatis sabina*. Journal of Comparative Neurology 221:429–443.

Roberts, B. L. 1969. Spontaneous rhythms in the motoneurons of spiny dogfish *(Scyliorhinus canicula)*. Journal of the Marine Biological Association of the United Kingdom 49:33–49.

Ronan, M. C., and R. G. Northcutt. 1985. The origins of descending spinal projections in Lepidosirenid lungfishes. Journal of Comparative Neurology 241:435–444.

Rovainen, C. M. 1982. Neurophysiology. Pages 1–136 *in* M. W. Hardisty and I. C. Potter, editors. The biology of lampreys, volume 4. Part A. Academic Press, London.

Rudell, A. P. 1979. The television camera used to measure movement. Behavior Research Methods and Instrumentation 11:339–341.

Russell, D. F. 1986. Respiratory pattern generation in adult lampreys *(Lampetra fluviatilis)*: interneurons and burst resetting. Journal of Comparative Physiology A, Sensory, Neural and Behavioral Physiology 158:91–102.

Russell, D. F., and P. Wallén. 1979. On the pattern generator for fictive swimming in the lamprey, *Ichthyomyzon unicuspis*. Acta Physiologica Scandinavica 108:9A.

Sandeman, D. C. 1968. A sensitive position measuring device for biological systems. Comparative Biochemistry and Physiology 24:635–638.

Savage, G. E., and M. G. Roberts. 1975. Behavioral effects of electrical stimulation of the hypothalamus of the goldfish *(Carassius auratus)*. Brain Behavior and Evolution 12:42–56.

Schwartz, E. 1974. Lateral-line mechano-receptors in fishes and amphibians. Pages 257–278 *in* A. Fessard, editor. Handbook of sensory physiology, volume 3. Part 3. Electroreceptors and other specialized receptors in lower vertebrates. Springer-Verlag, New York.

Shiells, R. A., G. Falk, and S. Naghshineh. 1986. Iontophoretic study of the action of excitatory amino acids on rod horizontal cells of the dogfish retina. Proceedings of the Royal Society of London, Series B. Biological Sciences 227:121–135.

Silver, W. L., and T. E. Finger. 1984. Electrophysiological examination of a non-olfactory, non-gustatory chemosense in the searobin, *Prionotus carolinus*. Journal of Comparative Physiology A, Sensory, Neural and Behavioral Physiology 154:167–174.

Slaughter, M. M., J. A. Mattler, and D. I. Gottlieb. 1985. Opiate binding sites in the chick, rabbit and goldfish retina. Brain Research 339:39–48.

Steinacker, A., and L. Rojas. 1988. Acetylcholine modulated potassium channel in the hair cell of the toadfish saccule. Hearing Research 35:265–269.

Sternberger, L. A. 1986. Immunocytochemistry, 3rd edition. Wiley, New York.

Szabo, T. 1974. Anatomy of the specialized lateral line organs of electroreception. Pages 13–58 *in* A. Fessard, editor. Handbook of sensory physiology, volume 3. Part 3. Electroreceptors and other specialized receptors in lower vertebrates. Springer-Verlag, New York.

Tachibana, M. 1983. Ionic currents of solitary horizontal cells isolated from goldfish retina. Journal of Physiology (London) 345:329–351.

Tavolga, W. N., A. N. Popper, and R. R. Fay, editors. 1981. Hearing and sound communication in fishes. Springer-Verlag, New York.

Tomita, T., and T. Nanagida. 1981. Origin of the ERG waves. Vision Research 21:1703–1707.

Tumosa, N., and W. K. Stell. 1986. Choline acetyltransferase immunoreactivity suggests that ganglion cells in the goldfish retina are not cholinergic. Journal of Comparative Neurology 244:267–275.

Videler, J. J., and F. Hess. 1984. Fast continuous swimming of two pelagic predators, saithe *(Pollachius virens)* and mackerels *(Scomber scombrus)*: a kinematic analysis. Journal of Experimental Biology 109:209–228.

Wamsley, J. K., and J. M. Palacios. 1982. Receptor measurement by histochemistry. Pages 27–51 *in* A. Lajtha, editor. Handbook of neurochemistry, volume 2, 2nd edition. Plenum, New York.

Wan, K. K., and J. Lindstrom. 1984. Nicotinic acetylcholine receptor. Pages 377–430 *in* P. M. Conn, editor. The receptors, volume 1. Academic Press, Orlando, Florida.

Webb, P. W., P. T. Kostecki, and E. D. Stevens. 1984. The effect of size and swimming speed on locomotor kinematics of rainbow trout. Journal of Experimental Biology 109:77–95.

Whitaker, A. 1972. Tissue and cell culture. Williams and Wilkins, Baltimore, Maryland.

Wieland, C. M., and R. C. Eaton. 1983. An electronic cine camera system for the automatic collection and analysis of high-speed movement of unrestrained animals. Behavior Research Methods and Instrumentation 15:437–440.

Wilkinson, M., D. A. Wilkinson, I. Khan, and L. W. Crim. 1983. Benzodiazepine receptors in fish brain: [^{3}H]-flunitrazepam binding and modulatory effects of GABA in rainbow trout. Brain Research Bulletin 10:301–303.

Wolf, K. 1963. Physiological salines for fresh-water teleosts. Progressive Fish-Culturist 25:135–140.

Wolf, K. 1979. Cold-blooded vertebrate cell and tissue culture. Methods in Enzymology 58:466–477.

Wu, S. M., and J. E. Dowling. 1980. Effects of GABA and glycine on the distal cells of the cyprinid retina. Brain Research 199:401–414.

Chapter 14

Stress and Acclimation

GARY A. WEDEMEYER, BRUCE A. BARTON, AND
DONALD J. McLEAY

14.1 INTRODUCTION

The physiological systems of fishes can be severely challenged or "stressed" by a variety of biological, chemical, and physical factors. Knowledge of the tolerance limits for acclimation to the single or cumulative effects of such biotic and abiotic stress factors is an important part of the data base for species–habitat relationships needed for effective fishery resource management. The solution of problems ranging from prediction of the tolerance fish will have for proposed habitat alterations to evaluation of the effects on fish health exerted by modern intensive fish culture depends on such information.

It is well known that acute or chronic stress approaching or exceeding the physiological tolerance limits of individual fish will impair reproductive success, growth, resistance to infectious diseases, and survival. If the stress is severe or long-lasting, succeedingly higher levels of biological organization become affected. The cumulative effects of even sublethal stress factors may reduce recruitment to successive life stages and eventually cause populations to decline (Vaughn et al. 1984; Adams et al. 1985).

14.1.1 Concept of Stress

If terms are not used consistently, stress can be a confusing physiological concept. Stress was originally defined in general terms by Selye (1950) as "the sum of all the physiological responses by which an animal tries to maintain or reestablish a normal metabolism in the face of a physical or chemical force." More specifically, stress in fish results from biotic or abiotic challenges or forces that extend homeostatic or stabilizing processes beyond their ability to control routine physiological processes (Esch and Hazen 1978). The term "stressor" and "stress factor" should be used to mean the force or challenge that elicits a compensatory physiological response (Pickering 1981). Thus, an environmental or biological challenge (stressor) that is severe enough to cause stress is one that requires a compensating response by a fish, population, or ecosystem. Acclimation may be possible if the compensatory stress response can reestablish a satisfactory relationship between the changed environment and the fish or higher-order biological system. However, the cumulative effects of even sublethal stress factors may eventually lead to deaths even though the factors may not individually exceed physiological tolerance limits (Donaldson 1981; Carmichael 1984; Barton et al. 1986). Thus, the tolerance limits for acclimation to multiple stress factors are determined in part by the cumulative physiological effects of the prior stressors.

The success of fish and fish populations in acclimating to alterations in the aquatic environment depends to a large extent on the ability of individuals to effect and maintain successful compensatory responses. In turn, an understanding of the compensatory responses of fishes, and their physiological limits, is important to the development of defensible protective guidelines for the aquatic environment. In this chapter, we discuss concepts and methods for measuring the effects of single and multiple stress factors at the level of individual fish: physiological severities, recovery times needed, and tolerance limits for acclimation.

14.1.2 Physiological Adaptation: The Generalized Stress Response

Physiological adaptation in fishes is analogous to that of the higher vertebrates (Selye 1973; Peters 1979; Schreck 1981). It is characterized by changes in blood and tissue chemistry that are similar whether the stress results from fish cultural practices (handling, transport, disease treatments), habitat alterations (turbidity, pollution, water temperature changes), or behavioral factors (fright, dominance hierarchies, interspecific interactions). The various physiological changes that occur as fish respond to stressful challenges are compensatory (i.e., adaptive) in nature and are required to achieve acclimation. Collectively, they have been termed the General Adaptation Syndrome (GAS), a useful conceptual model first proposed by Selye (1936, 1950, 1973) in which the stress response is divided into three stages.

  (1) *Alarm.* The pituitary–interrenal axis is activated; catecholamine and corticosteroid "stress hormones" are released and initiate a series of physiological changes as homeostatic control systems begin to compensate.
  (2) *Resistance.* Compensatory processes successfully achieve acclimation; however, the bioenergetic costs involved may ultimately reduce performance capacity.
  (3) *Exhaustion.* Duration or severity of the stress factor(s) exceeds biological tolerance limits. The compensatory changes become maladaptive; adverse behavioral and physiological effects occur.

For fishes, a useful conceptual framework is to consider the stress response in terms of primary, secondary, and tertiary changes that involve succeedingly higher levels of biological organization. The following outline was developed from the work of Mazeaud et al. (1977), Donaldson (1981), Mazeaud and Mazeaud (1981), Schreck (1981), Wedemeyer and McLeay (1981), Hunn (1982), and Smith (1982b).

  (1) *Primary response* (the endocrine system). Following perception of a stressful stimulus by the central nervous system, hormones (e.g., cortisol and epinephrine) are synthesized and released into the blood stream. Cortisol is produced indirectly after corticotrophin releasing factor from the hypothalamus portion of the brain stimulates the pituitary gland to release adrenocorticotrophic hormone (ACTH). The ACTH is carried by the circulation to the interrenal cells located in the head kidney, which in turn secrete cortisol. Epinephrine (adrenaline) is released mainly from the chromaffin

tissue of the head kidney following direct stimulation by the sympathetic nervous system.

(2) *Secondary response* (blood and tissue alterations). Changes in blood and tissue chemistry and in hematology occur, such as elevated blood sugar levels (hyperglycemia) and reduced blood-clotting time. Diuresis begins, followed by blood electrolyte losses and osmoregulatory dysfunction. Tissue changes, including depletion of liver glycogen and interrenal vitamin C, hemorrhage of the thymus, and hypertrophy of the interrenal body, may eventually be noted.

(3) *Tertiary response* (individuals and populations). Reductions in growth, resistance to infectious diseases, reproductive success, and survival will occur. These may decrease recruitment to succeeding life stages sufficiently to result in population declines. At the community or ecosystem level, disruptions in energy flow through trophic levels may eventually alter species composition.

Several of the many changes that occur as physiological compensation begins can be used as measurable indices of the severity of stress on fish and the time needed for acclimation. The most practical of these methods are discussed in the following sections.

14.2 EVALUATING TOLERANCE AND ACCLIMATION TO STRESS: ASPECTS OF PHYSIOLOGICAL AND WHOLE-ANIMAL RESPONSES

14.2.1 Principles

In many cases, the documentation of fish kills or population declines has been the sole indication that the effects of environmental stress factors were exceeding acclimation tolerance limits. However, several physiological and whole-animal changes occur that can be used to provide a priori information on the point at which the effects of stress will exceed acclimation tolerance limits and lead to dysfunctions such as impaired fish health, growth, or survival. These changes are a direct or indirect result of the physiological response to environmental stress and can be quantified and used as predictive indices (Wedemeyer et al. 1984).

Before discussing specific physiological and whole-animal stress-assessment methodologies, we will review the functional significance of selected aspects of the compensatory responses to stress. Consistent with Schreck's (1981) conceptual model, these responses are considered to be initially adaptive, i.e., they help maintain homeostasis. However, they may ultimately become maladaptive in chronic situations and threaten the organism's well-being (Moberg 1985). The elevation of blood sugar as the stress response begins is due to the action of epinephrine and functions to provide caloric energy for the "fight-or-flight" reaction. The primary source of the elevated blood sugar is glycogen from liver and muscle, which is correspondingly depleted. Elevated blood sugar levels are sustained supposedly by the action of cortisol, which stimulates liver gluconeogenesis and may suppress peripheral sugar uptake or modify the action of other glycemic hormones. If the energy requirements for muscular activity are severe, respiratory metabolites such as lactic acid may appear in the circulation, reflecting the accumulation of an oxygen debt.

Although the stress response as conceptualized in the GAS model is a generalized one, biologists should be aware that not all physiological variables in fishes show the characteristic changes under all conditions. For example, anesthetization with tricaine (MS-222) at a concentration of 200 mg/L or more is acutely lethal but does not evoke a blood sugar or cortisol response; such high concentrations, therefore, can be used to anesthetize fish before blood sampling. Lower, immobilizing, doses are sublethal but elicit an acute stress response (Wedemeyer 1970; Strange and Schreck 1978; Barton and Peter 1982). Similarly, toxic materials such as endrin or cadmium may not elicit typical primary or secondary stress responses in fish even when they impair physiological functions critical to survival (Grant and Mehrle 1973; Schreck and Lorz 1978). The classical generalized stress response should be expected mainly in reactions to factors that cause fright or pain (Schreck 1981).

Finally, biologists should be aware that an energy cost is associated with the maintenance of homeostasis. The calories used to respond to stress and achieve compensation represent a portion of the fish's total energy budget (scope for activity: Fry 1947) that is thereby unavailable for other functions (Schreck 1982).

Because the physiological performance capacity of fish is genetically delimited (Schreck 1981), the ability of fish to acclimate to stress is also limited. If the severity or duration of the stress is excessive, primary physiological responses may ultimately become maladaptive and acclimation will not be achieved or will be lost. For example, the anti-inflammatory and immunosuppressive effects of corticosteroid hormones (e.g., cortisol), together with the hormones' catabolic gluconeogenic action, may be manifested as reduced growth, reduced white blood cell count, or suppressed disease resistance when stress persists (Wedemeyer and Goodyear 1984).

Many secondary physiological aspects of stress responses that are initially adaptive also may become maladaptive under chronic conditions. The most important of these are alterations in hematology and blood electrolytes. In addition to mobilizing liver glycogen to elevate blood sugar levels, stress-induced epinephrine also increases branchial blood flow and gill permeability, thus facilitating oxygen and carbon dioxide exchange. However, the accompanying osmotic influx of water and rapid diuresis can result in serious blood electrolyte imbalances that tax osmoregulatory capacity and rapidly become life-threatening. For example, a severe decline in blood chloride concentrations (hypochloremia) commonly occurs during stress. If the fish can acclimate, electrolyte concentrations return to initial levels. If they cannot acclimate, they may die.

Regardless of the exact biological significance (in many cases still unknown) of stress-induced changes in physiological condition, it is important to consider the fish holistically and to be aware that many of the physiological stress responses are related both among themselves and to whole-animal performance. A clear picture of the fish's overall health and degree of acclimation can best be obtained from physiological and performance capacity profiles rather than from single tests (Buckley et al. 1985).

14.2.2 Physiological Methods: Blood Chemistry, Hematology, and Histology

Several biochemical and physiological procedures have been developed to assess the severity of the physiological effects resulting from stress (Donaldson et al. 1984; Leatherland and Sonstegard 1984; Lockhart and Metner 1984; Passino 1984; Mehrle and Mayer 1985). Many of the blood chemistry tests that can be recommended are relatively inexpensive and can be automated if desired (Smith and Ramos 1980). These include measurements of epinephrine and cortisol or of the secondary blood chemistry changes that occur, such as blood sodium or chloride depletion (hyponatremia, hypochloremia), elevated blood sugar or lactic acid (hyperglycemia, hyperlacticemia), or diuresis (Mazeaud et al. 1977; Barton et al. 1980; Harman et al. 1980; Peters et al. 1981; Hunn 1982). The time course and persistence of these responses will differ among themselves and will also depend on the nature, severity, and duration of the stress factor(s) applied. It is critical that biologists carefully consider these characteristics before designing or interpreting their own research. When physiological data of this nature are analyzed statistically, standard analyses of variance followed by appropriate multiple-range tests of means to separate data points will usually be adequate. However, the variance of such parameters as blood glucose or cortisol often increases with mean values and logarithmic or other transformations will be required. In some instances the use of nonparametric methods will be the simplest approach.

14.2.2.1 Primary Stress Responses

A relatively direct assessment of the severity and duration of the primary stress response can be obtained by monitoring the rise and fall of plasma cortisol or catecholamine (epinephrine and norepinephrine) concentrations (Donaldson 1981; Mazeaud and Mazeaud 1981; Schreck 1981). Plasma levels of hormones such as thyroxine (Brown et al. 1978), prolactin (Spieler and Meier 1976), α-MSH (melanocyte-stimulating hormone; Gilham and Baker 1985), or endorphin (Sumpter et al. 1985) are also altered as a result of stress, but these substances are not considered "stress hormones" per se and have not been used as general stress indicators.

At present, binding assays involving radioactive tracers (e.g., radioimmunoassay or RIA) are the most widely used for hormone analyses. One popular prepackaged assay kit for measuring catecholamines incorporates a radioenzymatic procedure and requires plasma sample volumes of only 10–50 μL. The catecholamine hormones can be separated by thin-layer chromatography (TLC) if desired, so TLC equipment may be required as well as a liquid scintillation counter. Other analytical protocols are available for plasma catecholamine analysis that do not require radioactive isotopes, such as the spectrofluorometric methods of Diamant and Byers (1975) and Robinson (1977). The use of liquid chromatography (LC) for plasma catecholamine determination is as reproducible as the radioenzymatic method and much more rapid (Hjemdahl et al. 1979), but relatively large plasma sample volumes are required (1–3 mL). The initial high cost of the LC apparatus may be justified over a long term because isotopes and chemicals, or prepackaged kits, used in other catecholamine methods are also quite expensive.

Plasma cortisol measurements have been used more widely to index primary stress responses than epinephrine and norepinephrine analyses because it is difficult to assay the catecholamines and to measure their resting (control) values. In addition, more background literature on corticosteroids specific to fish is available, the assay is faster and less expensive, and, importantly, cortisol is more stable than catecholamines during normal freezer storage. Some assay protocols for plasma cortisol exploit immunological or other binding characteristics but most require the use of radioactive isotopes. Although several cortisol methods are available as prepackaged kits, the relatively simple and inexpensive radioimmunoassay of Foster and Dunn (1974) is suitable for salmonid plasma (Redding et al. 1984b; Barton et al. 1986). In this procedure, 10-μL samples of plasma, to which low-pH (about pH 3) buffer is added, are first heated to denature binding proteins and then incubated with [^{3}H]cortisol and cortisol-specific antiserum. After the excess tracer is washed out with charcoal, samples are prepared and counted with a liquid scintillation counter. Cortisol concentrations are determined from a standard curve prepared from log and logit transformations of known concentrations and their counts per minute, respectively; it is assumed that 100% of the cortisol-specific binding sites are bound with labeled cortisol in zero-value standards. About 100 samples plus standards and blanks can be assayed comfortably in 6–8 h. Major items of equipment required include a liquid scintillation counter and a refrigerated centrifuge.

Antiserum containing cortisol-specific antibodies is available from various suppliers and, regardless of manufacturers' claims, it should be tested for cross-reactivity with other steroids, especially cortisone (the other major corticosteroid in fish blood). Cross-reactivity is the concentration of competitor divided by the concentration of unlabeled cortisol (expressed as a percentage) when 50% of the bound [^{3}H]cortisol has been displaced (i.e., when the logit of the percent bound is zero). To further validate the assay, the following should also be checked: degree to which serial dilutions of an unknown parallel a standard curve, minimum level of detectability, level of nonspecific binding of both buffer and plasma blanks (without antiserum added), percent recovery, and intra- and interassay coefficients of variation (SD/mean). Researchers unfamiliar with the principles or limitations of RIA should consult a methodology text (e.g., Chard 1981) before using this technique.

It takes several minutes for hypercortisolemia to develop as a result of sampling stress, so two or three test fish at a time can be netted into a lethal dose of MS-222 (e.g., 200 mg/L); as soon as the fish have died, blood samples are taken serially from the caudal vessels with a syringe or directly from their severed caudal peduncles (Strange 1983). (Note: MS-222 can cause interference with a chromatography assay.) If each fish remains in the (aerated, cooled) anesthetic for only a few minutes, this technique effectively arrests the physiological response due to sampling and thus minimizes variability (Wedemeyer and Yasutake 1977). However, care must be taken to minimize disturbance of the remaining test fish as each sample is removed. As a precaution, personnel should avoid skin contact with MS-222 as much as possible. Various methods for obtaining blood samples are described in Chapter 9.

In cortisol analyses, as in the analysis of any physiological constituent, it is important to establish normal resting (control) values for the population being examined. Both the resting values and the magnitude of the corticosteroid stress response may be modified, within the innate genetic capacity to respond to stress, by developmental (Barton et al. 1985a) as well as external environmental factors (Specker and Schreck 1980; Strange 1980; Davis et al. 1984; Barton et al. 1985b, 1986; Pickering and Pottinger 1987).

14.2.2.2 Secondary Stress Responses

The secondary blood chemistry changes that occur with the primary (endocrine) responses also characterize the severity of stress in fishes and the time needed for recovery (Carmichael et al. 1984a, 1984b). The analytical methods tend to be simpler and less expensive than those for primary responses (McLeay and Brown 1975; Silbergeld 1975; Hattingh 1977; Wedemeyer and Yasutake 1977). A further advantage is that these analyses provide physiological information integrated at a higher level of biological organization.

Blood glucose and chloride levels are probably the two most frequently measured secondary changes that occur during the stress response. The methods are inexpensive and a hundred or more samples can easily be run in a day. Normally, test and control groups are sampled—10 fish per sample—at 0, 4, 8, 24, 48, and 96 h after the imposition of stress, resulting in 120 analyses per experiment. Hyperglycemia can be evaluated quickly and easily by any of several plasma glucose methods, but the ortho (o)-toluidine method (available as a prepackaged reagent kit) is recommended (Wedemeyer and Yasutake 1977). Normally, 20 µL of plasma is required, but manual or automated microprocedures can be used that require as little as 5 µL. The small blood volume required permits the severity of stress to be evaluated for fish weighing only a few grams and allows the repetitive blood sampling of individual larger fish. As a convenience in field sampling, plasma can be separated by centrifugation and stored frozen for later analysis.

The o-toluidine blood glucose assay consists of simply adding a fixed volume (5–20 µL) of plasma to a fixed volume (3–4 mL) of reagent (6% o-toluidine in glacial acetic acid) and then heating the sample tubes in a boiling-water bath for 10 min. A fume hood should be used and precautions should be taken to avoid breathing the vapor because commercial reagents may contain thiourea. The intensity of the blue-green color produced is proportional to the amount of blood glucose originally present. The optical absorbance of the samples is measured with a colorimeter or spectrophotometer at a wavelength of 635 nm. Absorbance values are converted to blood glucose concentrations against a standard absorbance–concentration curve for known glucose concentrations prepared before each assay. For stress assessment, a glucose concentration range of 25–300 mg/100 mL is suggested. As a quality control measure, preanalyzed clinical control serum should always be run. Detailed procedures can be found in Wedemeyer and Yasutake (1977) or most clinical chemistry textbooks. In field or hatchery situations where laboratory facilities are not available, one can use a portable electronic blood glucose analyzer similar to those used by diabetic patients. The procedure simply involves placing a drop of blood on a color-reactive strip and then reading the color change with the meter. Although results with these devices are fairly reproducible, the meters must be calibrated and data should be standardized against known glucose concentrations in plasma or blood to confirm the validity of the readings.

When blood glucose results are interpreted, extrinsic factors such as diet, life stage, time since last feeding, and season of the year must be considered because these can affect liver glycogen stores and thus the magnitude of the hyperglycemic response elicited by stress factors (Nakano and Tomlinson 1967; McLeay 1977; Gordon and McLeay 1978; Barton et al. 1988). Other environmental factors, notably acclimation temperature, also affect the magnitude of stress-induced hyperglycemia (Umminger and Gist 1973; Strange 1980; Carmichael et al. 1984b; Barton and Schreck 1987a). Thus, relatively wide variations in the magnitude of blood glucose responses may be expected and controls should always be included.

When blood chloride is monitored to evaluate the severity of stress, hypochloremia is the physiological effect of concern. The enhanced gill circulation and gas exchange that result from the action of epinephrine increases the osmotic influx of water, and blood chloride is lost via the copious urine that is produced. As a general rule, hypochloremia becomes life-threatening in salmonids after plasma chloride values decline to 90 milliequivalents (meq)/L or less.

The severity of any hypochloremia that has resulted from stress can be quickly and easily determined by collecting blood samples from the fish, separating the plasma by centrifugation, and measuring chloride levels by any of several clinical chemistry procedures. Of these, the recommended technique is an instrumental one involving a chloridometer (Wedemeyer and Yasutake 1977). Although an initial equipment purchase is required, samples can be processed rapidly at low unit cost. Small sample volumes (50 μL) and simple standard solutions for calibration (NaCl) are additional advantages. However, as with blood glucose determinations, preanalyzed clinical control serum should be run on a regular basis as a quality-control procedure. Details can be found in standard clinical chemistry manuals.

Interpretation of data is relatively straightforward because osmoregulatory processes tend to maintain plasma chloride concentrations within a normal range in the face of dietary or seasonal influences. However, control groups should always be run for comparison.

Both blood sugar and blood chloride determinations can be useful in the development of stress-mitigation procedures such as the addition of mineral salts to water used to transport fish (Carmichael et al. 1984a). Hyperglycemic and hypochloremic responses also can be helpful indicators in challenge tests to select genotypes physiologically best able to tolerate acute stress. By graphing blood glucose and blood chloride values as a function of time and measuring the area under the resulting stress-response curves with a planimeter (or other device), the relative magnitude of the stress response can be estimated (Wedemeyer et al. 1985); note, however, that this relationship is probably not linear. The variability of the resulting hyperglycemia or hypochloremia (judged by F tests of variance ratios) and the time needed to regulate disturbed blood glucose and chloride values back into the normal range (acclimation) are also important factors to be measured and compared.

Blood sugar can also be measured during challenge tests to assess a fish's ability to tolerate stress and acclimate to it within a given time period. In a standardized procedure, for example, the occurrence of hyperglycemia is a sensitive indicator of the exposure level at which contaminants begin to cause physiological disturbances (McLeay 1977; McLeay and Gordon 1978a, 1980). In this method, groups of fish are acclimated to test aquaria for 48 h, then exposed for 24 h to various dilutions of the contaminant. The hyperglycemia that results is usually dose-dependent.

One of the more traditional stress indicators has been blood lactic acid (Fraser and Beamish 1969; Soivio and Oikari 1976; Beggs et al. 1980; Pickering et al. 1982). The accumulation of lactic acid in muscle or blood (hyperlacticemia) is now well accepted as an indicator of anaerobic metabolism due to fright or severe exertion (Black et al. 1966; Driedzic and Kiceniuk 1976; Turner et al. 1983). However, the view that lactic acidosis is the ultimate cause of death that sometimes occurs after severe exercise (Black 1958; Caillouet 1968) has been challenged (Wood et al. 1983).

Lactic acid can be easily determined fluorimetrically or colorimetrically by an enzymatic procedure (involving lactate dehydrogenase) available commercially in prepackaged kit form. Unlike the ionic and enzymatic indicators, lactic acid can be measured in whole blood. Detailed procedures can be found in Wedemeyer and Yasutake (1977) or standard clinical chemistry texts.

Substantial diuresis commonly results from stress (Hunn 1982), but its measurement requires catheterization so it has not been used much as an indicator. However, the effects of sustained diuresis on ionoregulation (Eddy 1981) can be more easily evaluated. When fish are acutely or chronically stressed in fresh water, the resulting hemodilution and diuresis is manifested as a decline in total blood osmolality as well as in a loss of individual blood electrolytes such as sodium and chloride (Mazeaud et al. 1977). When fish are stressed in seawater, hemoconcentration occurs (see Section 14.3.2.6).

Effects on osmoregulation are normally determined by measuring either total plasma osmolality with a vapor-phase or freezing-point depression osmometer or individual blood electrolytes (e.g., Na^+, Cl^-, K^+) with a specific ion analyzer, chloridometer, flame photometer, or atomic absorption spectrophotometer. Analytical procedures can be found in Wedemeyer and Yasutake (1977) or in clinical chemistry texts. The interpretation of these relatively straightforward tests may be complicated, however, by the severity of the stress and whether or not it was accompanied by severe muscular activity. For example, Graham et al. (1982) found that both plasma sodium and plasma chloride levels rose after fish exercised strenuously in fresh water because the high intracellular lactate loading caused water to move into the cells, resulting in hemoconcentration (decreased blood volume). A rise in plasma potassium (hyperkalemia) following stress may be interpreted as an indication of the response to intracellular acidosis (Graham et al. 1982; Turner et al. 1983). Thus, changes in acid–base balance and osmotic balance may occur simultaneously and, as in the regulation of blood ions and pH, mechanisms and processes are interrelated (Spry et al. 1981). Less information on the responses of electrolytes and osmolality to stress is available for marine fishes, but some reverse responses should be anticipated because of the hypertonic environment.

Special attention should be paid to the effects on blood electrolytes of low pH in the aquatic environment because of the importance of acidic precipitation in fishery resource management. In general, total body sodium, chloride, and potassium decline in fish exposed to a low-pH environment, although an increase in plasma potassium may be evident. The resultant ionoregulatory dysfunction may be the potentiating factor in eventual death from circulatory failure (Wood and McDonald 1982). Details can be found in Fromm (1980), Spry et al. (1981), and Wood and McDonald (1982).

Hematological determinations can also provide useful information about an animal's tolerance of an applied stress factor (Peters and Schwarzer 1985). For example, acclimation to temperature-induced increases in oxygen demand by salmonids is commonly accompanied by erythropoiesis and increases in blood hemoglobin (Houston and Koss 1984; Chapter 9). Changes in the blood erythrocyte count (as approximated by the hematocrit) or in hemoglobin values following acute stress can also indicate that hemodilution or hemoconcentration has occurred. However, because anemias, stress polycythemia (increased red blood cell numbers), or erythrocyte swelling may occur in certain situations (Soivio and Nikinmaa 1981; Milligan and Wood 1982; Wells et al. 1984), direct measurement of plasma water is the preferred indicator of dehydration. Blood eosinophil counts may increase under certain conditions (eosinophilia), but few data yet attest their value in quantifying the stress response. Leucocyte increases (leucocytosis) are not normally associated with stress, but leucocyte decreases (leucopenia) commonly occur during the physiological response to acute stressors (McLeay and Gordon 1977; Wedemeyer et al. 1983).

Of all the hematological measurements, blood-clotting time and changes in the differential leucocyte count are among the most sensitive indicators of acute stress (McLeay 1975a; Casillas and Smith 1977). In general, stress, perhaps through the mediation of ACTH and corticosteroids, results in lymphopenia, monocytopenia, and neutrophilia (McLeay 1975b; Johansson-Sjöbeck et al. 1978; Agrawal et al. 1979; Peters et al. 1980). The mechanism in fishes is poorly understood but the effect of concern is suppression of the immune response and increased susceptibility to infectious diseases (Ellis 1981; Wedemeyer and McLeay 1981).

The most accurate and precise determination of leucopenia (or leucocytosis) is the classical differential white blood cell count obtained with a hemocytometer or from microscopic examination of fixed blood smears. Detailed methods for counting blood cells can be found in Wedemeyer and Yasutake (1977) or in Chapter 9. However, for many purposes the rapid, approximate leucocrit measurement will suffice (McLeay and Gordon 1977; Wedemeyer et al. 1983). To determine the leucocrit, blood is centrifuged as it is for a microhematocrit determination and the thickness of the white blood cell layer (buffy coat) above the packed erythrocytes is measured with an ocular micrometer in a low-power microscope. The leucocrit (packed cell volume of the leucocytes) is calculated as a percentage of the total volume in the tube in a manner exactly analogous to that of the hematocrit.

As one advantage, leucocrit values can be determined in (salmonid) fish as small as 1 g. However, young fish have characteristically low leucocrits and the use of fish 2 g or larger is recommended (McLeay and Gordon 1977). An additional advantage is that the small blood volume needed for the leucocrit determination usually makes it possible to take additional blood samples from the same fish for other analyses. In addition, the plasma within the hematocrit tubes can be removed for analysis following the determination of leucocrit values.

For salmonids and other fishes in which lymphocytes make up the majority of the circulating leucocytes (Yasutake and Wales 1983), the leucocrit can be used as a simple, rapid test for determining the point at which handling or other stress factors result in leucopenia. To calibrate the test, the leucopenic response to a standardized challenge should be used as the reference point. The interpretation of leucocrit test results may differ from that of other indices of the secondary stress response. For example, leucopenia appears not to be associated with elevated catecholamines, whereas hyperglycemia can result from both catechol-amine and glucocorticoid production (Srivastava and Agrawal 1977). Thus, the leucocrit and plasma glucose values can provide indices of two aspects of the stress response for each environmental factor examined.

The leucocrit test has also been used to determine the threshold concentrations at which contaminant exposure begins to adversely affect salmonid fishes (McLeay and Gordon 1977, 1979, 1980) and to estimate the toxic zone of waste discharges within receiving waters (McLeay and Gordon 1978b).

As with most other tests, conditions must be standardized and the fish's developmental stage and history of prior exposures to contaminants or other stressors are important. In addition, stress may sometimes result in leucocytosis rather than leucopenia and thus increase the leucocrit value (Pickford et al. 1971; McLeay 1973; McLeay and Brown 1974). Furthermore, in species in which lymphocytes do not constitute a preponderance of the total leucocyte volume, lymphopenia may occur while the leucocrit value remains unchanged (or is even elevated), due to a concomitant granulocytosis (Peters et al. 1980).

Because many of the biochemical changes that occur in response to stress are the end result of cellular pathology, histological examinations can frequently provide information on the effect of stress factors on fishes (Payne 1984). Pathological changes such as interrenal hypertrophy, atrophy of the gastric mucosa, and cellular changes in the spleen and kidney have been used as indices, especially of chronic stress (McLeay 1975b; Peters et al. 1981; Peters and Schwarzer 1985). In particular, interrenal hypertrophy is symptomatic of stress, and a semiquantitative histological method to detect this condition has been developed in which nuclear diameters or cell sizes are measured in stained sections of anterior kidney tissue (Scott and Rennie 1980; Fagerlund et al. 1981). Stress first causes depletion of interrenal vitamin C, corticosteroids, and other lipids. Under chronic stress, interrenal hypertrophy occurs, followed by eventual cellular degeneration and the irreversible loss of tissue function (Donaldson and McBride 1974; McLeay 1975b; Noakes and Leatherland 1977). Changes in the gastric mucosa, including decreased mucous cell diameter, have been used as indices of stress for European eels (Peters et al. 1981). Subordinate animals in the social hierarchies that develop among cultured eels show measurable degenera-tive changes in the gastric mucosa within 5–10 d. Other cellular and tissue chemistry changes that have been used as indicators of adverse environmental conditions include changes in skin mucus (Smith and Ramos 1976; Wechsler 1984), gill sialic acid content (Arillo et al. 1979), muscle or liver adenylate energy charge (Vetter and Hodson 1982; Heath 1984; Reinert and Hohreiter 1984), muscle and liver glycogen (Morata et al. 1982), interrenal vitamin C (Wedemeyer and Yasutake 1977), relative liver weight (Buckley et al. 1985), and mechanical properties of bone (Mehrle et al. 1982).

A listing of selected physiological indices that can be used to evaluate both the adverse effects of environmental stress and the tolerance limits for acclimation is given in Table 14.1. The information available for normal values is limited (Tables 14.2, 14.3) and controls should be used for comparison in most cases. It should be kept in mind that when stress is chronic, blood electrolytes, cortisol, glucose, hematological characters, and other variables may have been regulated back to normal or near-normal levels if acclimation (stage of resistance) has been achieved. However, this does not imply the absence of bioenergetic costs (McLeay et al. 1984).

14.2.2.3   Assessment of Clearance

Although not necessarily specific to the measurement of stress per se, clearance is an important consideration when any physiological perturbation is measured, particularly hormones or metabolites in blood. Individual measures of blood or tissue constituents represent only single points, or "snapshots," of dynamic physiological processes. One of these processes is clearance, the rate (per unit time) at which a compound is removed (cleared) from a unit of blood (O'Flaherty 1981). Clearance is often used to indirectly monitor the function of organs such as the kidney (Guyton 1981). When the term is applied to a tissue or organ other than blood (e.g., renal clearance), it refers to the rate at which that tissue or organ removes a substance from blood. In an organ that functions within its normal capacity, clearance "serves as an intrinsic homeostatic mechanism" (Shipley and Clark 1972). When a substance is lost from a tissue other than blood or from an organ, the appropriate term is "elimination." Elimination typically is measured in terms of the half-life of the compound in question; the half-life is the time needed to remove half the remaining amount of compound, whatever that amount may be. Elimination is a function of both metabolism and excretion. In toxicological studies, the compound of importance is normally a toxicant or its metabolites, and the elimination process is called depuration.

Metabolic clearance may occur at the liver, muscle, gut, gill, or other peripheral tissue, whereas excretion takes place primarily at the kidney or gill or from the liver by way of the bile. Total clearance is the sum of all these individual components. Elimination of a compound by metabolism and by excretion can take place simultaneously (O'Flaherty 1981). At the tissue level, clearance of simple compounds (e.g., ions) from plasma may involve forces of diffusion, electrostatic equilibrium, osmotic pressure, or active transport, whereas clearance of more complex compounds such as drugs, toxic chemicals, or steroid metabolites may require oxidation, conjugation, or hydrolysis (Allen et al. 1979). For example, one important clearance mechanism in fish is the hepatic microsomal cytochrome P-450 monooxygenase system (Lech et al. 1982).

The measurement of clearance, particularly clearance of physiological compounds, involves simply the infusion or injection of a tracer and the monitoring of tracer concentration over time. A radioactively labeled version of the compound under investigation is probably the most commonly used tracer. In practice, however, clearance is not easy to measure, and investigators should be aware of several problems. Simple kinetic models for single-compartment clearance rates are usually not appropriate for biological systems, most of which have multiple compartments—organs, tissues, or cell systems in which specialized physiological processes occur. The complexity of the model required—and therefore the difficulty in measuring clearance—increases with the number of pools (the

Table 14.1 Recommended physiological tests to assess the tolerance limits of fish for abiotic and biotic stress factors (compiled from Passino 1984; Reinert and Hohreiter 1984; Wedemeyer et al. 1984; Buckley et al. 1985). Normal range estimates for some tests are given in Tables 14.2 and 14.3, but data are limited and controls are usually needed for comparison. The interpretations of responses listed are general but not necessarily universal; investigators should be aware that there may be some stressful situations that do not evoke a change in one or more of these physiological conditions.

Physiological test	Interpretation if results are	
	Low	High
Blood variables		
Blood cell counts		
Erythrocytes	Anemias, hemodilution due to impaired osmoregulation	Stress polycythemia, dehydration, hemoconcentration due to gill damage
Leucocytes	Leucopenia due to acute stress	Leucocytosis due to bacterial infection
Thrombocytes	Abnormal blood-clotting time	Thrombocytosis due to acute or chronic stress
Chloride, plasma	Gill chloride cell damage, compromised osmoregulation	Hemoconcentration, compromised osmoregulation
Cholesterol, plasma	Impaired lipid metabolism	Chronic stress, dietary lipid imbalance
Clotting time, blood	Acute stress, thrombocytopenia	Sulfonamides or antibiotic disease treatments affecting the intestinal microflora
Cortisol, plasma	Normal conditions	Chronic or acute stress
Glucose, plasma	Inanition	Acute or chronic stress
Hematocrit, blood	Anemias, hemodilution	Hemoconcentration due to gill damage, dehydration, stress polycythemia
Hemoglobin, blood	Anemias, hemodilution, nutritional disease	Hemoconcentration due to gill damage, dehydration, stress polycythemia
Hemoglobin, mucus	Normal conditions	Acute stress
Lactic acid, blood	Normal conditions	Acute or chronic stress, swimming fatigue
Leucocrit	Acute stress	Leucocytosis, subclinical infections
Blood osmolality, plasma	External parasite infestation, contaminant exposure, hemodilution	Dehydration, salinity increases in excess of osmoregulatory capacity, diuresis, acidosis
Blood total protein, plasma	Infectious disease, kidney damage, nutritional imbalance, inanition	Hemoconcentration, impaired water balance
Tissue variables		
Adenylate energy charge, muscle and liver	Bioenergetic demands of chronic stress	No recognized significance
Gastric atrophy	Normal conditions	Chronic stress
Glycogen, liver and muscle	Chronic stress, inanition	Liver damage due to excessive vacuolation, diet too high in carbohydrates
Interrenal hypertrophy, cell size and nuclear diameter	No recognized significance	Chronic stress
RNA:DNA ratios, muscle	Impaired growth, chronic stress	Good growth

Table 14.2 Approximate normal limits for physiological variables expected in clinically healthy juvenile salmonids held in soft water (100 mg/L or less as $CaCO_3$) at 10°C and fed the Oregon moist pellet diet. Values are based on the experience of the present authors and are meant to be used as guidelines only.

Physiological variable[a]	Estimated normal range	
	Rainbow trout	Coho salmon
Blood cell count		
Erythrocytes (10^6/mm^3)	0.8–1.6	
Leucocytes (10^3/mm^3)	7.8–20.9	
Differential leucocyte count		
Lymphocytes (%)	89–98	
Neutrophils (%)	1–9	
Thrombocytes (%)	1–6	
Chloride, plasma (meq/L)	84–132	122–136
Cholesterol, plasma (mg/100 mL)	161–365	88–262
Clotting time, blood (second)		
Aortic cannula	150–250	
Cardiac or caudal vessel puncture	50–150	
Caudal peduncle severed	20–60	
Cortisol, plasma (ng/mL)	0–30	0–40
Glucose, plasma (mg/100 mL)	41–151	41–135
Glycogen, liver (mg/g)	20–30	20–30
Hemoglobin (g/100 mL)	5.4–9.3	6.5–9.9
Hematocrit, blood (%)	24–43	32–52
Lactic acid, plasma (mg/100 mL)	20–30	20–30
Leucocrit, blood (%)	0.8–1.8	0.8–1.8
Osmolality (milliosmolar)	288–339	
Potassium, plasma (meq/L)	4–5	4–6
RNA:DNA ratio, muscle		3.5–4.0
Sodium, plasma (meq/L)	150–155	150–155
Total plasma protein (g/100 mL)	1.4–4.3	2–6

[a]meq = milliequivalents.

compartmental contents). A single-compartment model may be used to investigate whole-animal clearance from multipool systems if the compound under study is eliminated only from the pool in question and all sources of the compound are associated directly with that primary, measured pool (DiStefano 1982). When a primary pool that is part of a system of interconnecting pools is treated as a single compartment for estimating clearance, the error may be large if there is much interchange between the primary pool and the secondary pools (Shipley and Clark 1972). Even in a single-pool system, multiple exits may exist for a compound. Further, a compound can be metabolized or otherwise converted to another chemical form, so measurements only of a tracer may inadequately represent the agent or process under study.

In fish, it is best to inject the tracer intravenously or intracardially to allow the tracer to completely mix in the blood, and then to sample from the arterial system. Initial samples (at least three) should be taken within minutes after injection. Additional samples may be spread out over a longer period. Intraperitoneal injections are the easiest to perform, but it cannot be assumed that all of the injected tracer will be absorbed into the circulation. Lipophilic substances such as steroids may be taken up readily by surrounding tissues when injected intraperitoneally, which could lead to erroneous results. A problem with a single injection of a tracer is that, as the concentration of the compound decreases with time in the

Table 14.3 Mean blood chemistry values (means ± SD) for selected cold-, cool-, and warmwater fishes of interest in environmental monitoring. Normal ranges are not available, but means ± 1.96 SD can be used as a guide. (Compiled from Hunn 1972 and J. B. Hunn, U.S. Fish and Wildlife Service, unpublished data.)

| Fish type and species | Hematological constitutent | | | |
	Cl^- (meq/L)[a]	Glucose (mg/100 mL)	pH	Hematocrit (%)
Coldwater				
Brown trout	108.6±6.9	52.0±6.5	7.51±0.08	33.0±4
Brook trout	108.6±1.6	59.2±4.3	7.71±0.06	31.0±5
Coolwater				
Northern pike	104.8±4.3	53.4±16.2	7.64±0.18	30.0±5
Walleye	62.0±10.5	152.5±78.3	7.85±0.08	46.0±4
Warmwater				
Channel catfish	114.0±5.0	29.1±17.7	7.55±0.05	32.1±4.1

[a]meq = milliequivalents.

sampled tissue (usually blood or plasma), the rate of removal from circulation may change, making it difficult to draw conclusions about clearance (a rate function). A constant infusion into the fish via a cannula is therefore preferred for clearance studies but requires that a steady state be reached before an assessment of constant rate can be made; this necessitates some prior manipulation of the system in order to achieve the desired results.

When radioactive tracers are used to determine clearance rates, samples frequently must be counted by liquid scintillation techniques. Before plasma, whole blood, or other tissues can be counted, they first must be solubilized with a strong base or appropriate commercially available solvent before the scintillation "cocktail" is added. Normally, plasma is used for clearance determinations because it is the plasma component that freely exchanges with the tissues. For scintillation counting, plasma has the advantage of having very little "quench," a term used to describe the degree to which sample color interferes with the counting efficiency of the apparatus. In solution, whole blood or tissue leaves a residual color in the sample from the heme or tissue pigments, for which quench curves must be established in order to quantitate the results.

This brief survey of problems associated with clearance estimates was written to encourage investigators planning such studies to be completely familiar with this subject and with the system in question. The quantitative calculation of clearance is relatively complex and beyond the scope of this chapter; readers may consult Shipley and Clark (1972), O'Flaherty (1981), and DiStefano (1982) for detailed descriptions of kinetic and dynamic models, and Tait and Burstein (1964) for clearance of steroids. For information on corticosteroid clearance in fishes, see Donaldson and Fagerlund (1972), Owen and Idler (1972), Henderson et al. (1974), Redding et al. (1984a), Nichols et al. (1985), and Patiño et al. (1985).

14.2.3 Determination of Whole-Animal Responses

Experience has shown that several tertiary stress responses, including changes in metabolic rate, health, behavior, growth, survival, and reproductive success,

can indicate that unfavorable environmental conditions have exceeded the tolerance limits of fish (Brett 1958; Wedemeyer et al. 1976; Esch and Hazen 1980;
Billard et al. 1981; Buckley et al. 1985; Little et al. 1985). Such holistic responses
result from adverse effects at lower levels of biological organization. Decreased
resistance to fish diseases is of particular importance in this regard (Snieszko
1974; Hodgins et al. 1977). Poor health, growth, reproduction, and survival, if
they affect enough fish, ultimately reduce the rates of recruitment to succeeding
life stages (Ryan and Harvey 1977; McFarlane and Franzin 1978; Esch and Hazen
1980). Thus, the determination of whole-animal responses is highly relevant to the
general problem of habitat-based predictive methodologies for environmental
impact assessments (Wedemeyer et al. 1984). The appropriate a posteriori
population-level measurements are discussed in Chapter 1.

Metabolic rate is a fundamental aspect of whole-animal performance capacity
that is affected by stress, but it is one of the least studied. A stress-induced
increase in metabolic rate consumes energy within the fish's metabolic scope for
activity (Fry 1947, 1971; Priede 1985) that could have been used for some other,
possibly necessary, function (Schreck 1982). As much as 25% of the scope for
activity may be required to cope with even mild and brief disturbances (Barton
and Schreck 1987b); the fraction is likely higher for more severe stress.

Metabolic activity can be determined by monitoring ventilatory frequency
(Heath 1973; Bass and Heath 1977) or from electronic measurements of opercular
muscle patterns (Rogers and Weatherley 1983) or heart rates (Priede and Tytler
1977). More usually, however, increases in metabolic rate are determined from
increases in oxygen consumption by fish held in a respirometer (Fry 1971;
Beamish 1978; Brett and Groves 1979; see Chapter 10 for respirometry methods).
Respirometry is a useful technique to assess changes in metabolism in fish
exposed to water-borne stimuli, such as pollutants or toxicants (MacLeod and
Smith 1966; Smith et al. 1966; Wohlschlag and Cameron 1967; Hargis 1976;
Skadsen et al. 1980). Respirometry is also quite sensitive in detecting metabolic
changes due to brief physical disturbances if the fish have had enough time to
acclimate to the apparatus and if they are not still absorbing their last meal. In a
protocol developed by Barton and Schreck (1987b), fish were held in a respirometer for 3 d to acclimate, given an 8-h "swimming up" period, and then stressed
within the apparatus. In order to compare respiration rates between stressed and
unstressed fish, Barton and Schreck (1987b) found it necessary to force the fish to
swim slowly (0.5 body length/s) to reduce the variance caused by spontaneous
activity.

Measurement of oxygen consumption is a direct way to evaluate the effects of
stress on the bioenergetic capacity of fish, and thus on scope for activity, and
provides a basis for understanding how other whole-animal performances may be
compromised by stress. However, closed-system, watertight respirometers in
which water velocity can be controlled are more difficult and expensive to
construct than the open systems used for swimming performance studies.
Furthermore, metabolic rates in fish are sensitive to other environmental and
behavioral conditions, including temperature, water chemistry, photoperiod,
nutritive state, and social interactions (Dickson and Kramer 1971; Brett and
Groves 1979).

Another way to assess whole-animal responses to stress is to determine the detrimental effects on reproduction as expressed by oocyte atresia, spawning inhibition, and decreased fecundity and hatching success (Gerking 1980; Munkittrick and Leatherland 1984). When gametogenesis is influenced by environmental factors such as photoperiod, water temperature, or salinity, fecundity can be adversely affected by changes in the normal fluctuations of these cues. In addition, some hormones that are components of the stress response are also normally involved in the reproductive cycle. Thus, altered reproductive success may indicate endocrine perturbations due to chronic stress as well as altered environmental cues due to habitat changes (Billard et al. 1981; Freeman et al. 1983). Assessment of circulating reproductive hormones, particularly the steroids, is now feasible and would complement whole-animal assessment of reproductive effects of stress and allow for more complete interpretation of any changes observed (Pickering et al. 1987; Thomas 1988, 1989).

The incidence of fish disease is an indicator of environmental stress that is receiving serious attention as a method of biological monitoring for environmental quality (Esch and Hazen 1980; Sindermann 1980, 1984; Walters and Plumb 1980; Ellis 1981). Fish diseases usually do not have single causes; they are outcomes of the many interactions among fish, their pathogens, and the aquatic environment. If the environment deteriorates, stressed fish may be unable to resist the pathogens that they normally can ward off or coexist with. Fish diseases in aquacultural facilities often indicate that environmental conditions are marginal or poor, particularly if facultative pathogens are involved (Sindermann 1984). In freshwater fishes, the stress-mediated diseases that best indicate that acclimation tolerance limits have been exceeded are those due to facultative bacterial pathogens such as the aeromonads, pseudomonads, and myxobacteria, which are normally present in surface waters. Myxobacterial gill disease in salmonid fishes usually indicates that population density is too high or that some physicochemical condition has exceeded tolerance limits. Other infectious fish diseases that indicate serious stress are bacterial hemorrhagic septicemia due to species of *Aeromonas* and *Pseudomonas* and fungal infestations such as *Saprolegnia* spp. (Neish 1977). Viral erythrocytic necrosis and vibriosis caused by *Vibrio anguillarum* are potentially useful indicator diseases of estuarine and marine fishes (MacMillan et al. 1980).

Certain diseases of marine fish in coastal and estuarine waters and at maricultural sites also are proving to be useful indicators that tolerances of adverse environmental conditions have been exceeded. The problems include chromosomal and morphological abnormalities of eggs and larvae, skeletal anomalies, liver neoplasms, fin erosion, and epidermal ulceration (Malins et al. 1980, 1982; Sindermann 1980). Tests of cytotoxicity and chromosomal damage to fish cell lines can help determine the specific conditions and contaminants involved (Landolt and Kocan 1984). A list of indicator diseases and their likely environmental causes is given in Table 14.4. Approved diagnostic methods for these and other fish diseases can be found in Department of Fisheries and Oceans (1984) or Amos (1985).

A test to detect the change in immune capacity of the fish may be incorporated into a disease-incidence monitoring program or may be used in conjunction with a disease challenge test (Section 14.3.2.4) as an additional indicator of fish

Table 14.4 Fish diseases that indicate that acclimation tolerance limits have been exceeded (Esch and Hazen 1980; Sindermann 1980; Wedemeyer and McLeay 1981; Malins et al. 1982).

Disease (causative agent)	Environmental factors involved
Furunculosis (*Aeromonas salmonicida*)	Low oxygen (4 mg/L for salmonids); crowding; handling in the presence of the pathogen
Bacterial gill disease (*Myxobacteria* spp.)	Crowding; unfavorable environmental conditions; chronic low oxygen (4 mg/L for salmonids); elevated ammonia (more than 0.02 mg/L for salmonids); excessive particulate matter in water
Columnaris (*Flexibacter columnaris*)	Crowding or handling during warmwater periods if carrier fish are present; temperature increase if the pathogen is present even if fish are not crowded or handled
Kidney disease (*Renibacterium salmoninarum*)	Water hardness less than about 100 mg/L (as $CaCO_3$); unfavorable diet composition
Hemorrhagic septicemias Red-sore disease (*Aeromonas* spp., *Pseudomonas* spp.)	External parasite infestations; inadequate pond cleaning; handling; crowding; elevated ammonia; low oxygen; chronic exposure to trace contaminants; elevated water temperatures; handling after fish have overwintered at low temperature
Vibriosis (*Vibrio anguillarum*)	Handling; dissolved oxygen lower than about 6 mg/L, especially at water temperatures of 10–15°C; brackish water, 10–15‰ salinity
Parasite infestations	Overcrowding of fry and fingerlings; low oxygen; excessive size variation among fish in ponds
Spring viremia of carp	Handling after overwintering at low temperatures
Fin erosion	Crowding; low dissolved oxygen; nutritional imbalances; chronic exposure to trace contaminants; high total suspended solids; secondary bacterial invasion
Epithelial tumors	Chronic, sublethal contaminant exposure
Epithelial ulceration	Chronic, sublethal contaminant exposure
Skeletal anomalies	Chronic adverse environmental quality; PCBs, heavy metals, kepone, toxaphene exposure; vitamin C deficiency

performance capacity. Relatively straightforward techniques are available for assessing change in the immunocompetence of fish. Two tests that are currently used are (1) evaluation of antibody titer in blood by a humoral agglutination response (Roberson 1990) and (2) measurement of the mitogenic and antibody-producing capacity of lymphocytes (Tripp et al. 1987; Maule et al. 1989). The latter method employs a modified plaque assay to quantify the amount of antibody generated by antigen-stimulated lymphocytes harvested from the hemopoietic tissue in fish and cultured *in vitro*.

For anadromous salmonids, a whole-animal indicator that tolerance limits have been exceeded is impairment of the parr–smolt transformation necessary for marine life. The physiological changes occurring during the smoltification of Atlantic and Pacific salmon and steelhead were extensively reviewed by Folmar and Dickhoff (1980). Stressful environmental alterations such as changes in water chemistry (contaminants), temperature, or photoperiod may inhibit one or more aspects of the parr–smolt transformation; impaired transformations, in turn, indicate serious stress (Wedemeyer et al. 1980). For example, otherwise sublethal exposures to copper, arsenic, and other heavy metals in fresh water partly or completely inactivate gill ATPase function, resulting in impaired migratory behavior, reduced seawater tolerance and preference, and thus reduced marine survival (Lorz and McPherson 1976; Nichols et al. 1984). Exposure to herbicides used in silviculture, agriculture, and range management may have the same effects (Lorz et al. 1978; Liguori et al. 1983). Acidification resulting from acid precipitation impairs the parr–smolt transformation of Atlantic salmon, as indicated by decreased salinity tolerance, gill ATPase development, and smolt growth rates (Saunders et al. 1983). These effects are sublethal while smolts remain in fresh water, but lead to high mortality after the fish enter seawater.

Smoltification also can be affected by temperature. The normal development of gill ATPase activity in steelhead is suppressed at temperatures above 13°C, resulting in "smolts" with impaired ability to osmoregulate in seawater (Adams et al. 1975). Similar water temperatures do not adversely affect the smoltification of coho salmon, however (Zaugg and McLain 1972).

14.3 EFFECTS OF STRESS ON PERFORMANCE CAPACITY: CHALLENGE TESTS AS INDICATORS OF TOLERANCE LIMITS

14.3.1 Principles

Challenge tests can be used to determine the limits of acclimation to stressful conditions. Their application is based on the presumptions that (1) a stress load that exceeds acclimation limits is debilitating and reduces performance capacity; (2) reduced performance capacity can be measured as reduced tolerance of subsequent stress; and (3) survival probability of the population as a whole will be reduced to the extent that reduced performance capacity impairs growth, survival, or reproduction of individual fish (Wedemeyer et al. 1984).

Selected performance tests are discussed here together with methodologies for conducting them under standardized conditions. The freshwater challenge test has been little used and we are proposing its development. The procedures given for conducting challenge tests may require modification to meet specific individual requirements. In addition, when reduced ability to tolerate a challenge is used to measure the effects of prior stress, the test must be carefully selected to best reveal the debilitation of most significance in a particular application.

The nominal end point of many challenge tests is death of the fish. True death is very difficult to pinpoint by observation, so a behavioral proxy typically is assessed. The most common of these are loss of equilibrium and cessation of opercular motion; failure to respond to the touch of a probe is an alternative criterion. Fish that reach any of these stages soon die unless they are transferred immediately to clean, flowing water. Even if they are so moved, their recovery is not certain. Consequently, any test criterion based on loss or impairment of reflex control is a reasonable indicator of lethality.

14.3.2   Methods and Protocols

14.3.2.1   Thermal Tolerance Tests

The effects of sublethal stress on the temperature tolerance of fishes can be of fundamental importance for both individuals and populations (Elliott 1981). In turn, subjecting fish to the stress of unfavorable water temperatures effects characteristic acclimation responses (Wedemeyer 1973; Strange et al. 1977). Thus, thermal challenge tests to determine whether prior stress has narrowed tolerance limits by reducing the ability of fish to achieve acclimation can provide ecologically significant physiological information.

One recommended method for assessing the effects of stress factors on thermal tolerance is the incipient lethal temperature (ILT) determination (Wedemeyer and McLeay 1981). Groups of test fish are acclimated to a particular temperature and then transferred directly into identical aquaria that, among them, contain water spanning the range of temperatures to be tested. The ILT is taken as the temperature (upper or lower) at which 50% of the test fish survive for a set period of time, usually 24 h. An alternative method is to determine the critical thermal maximum or minimum (CTM). In this test, groups of test fish are acclimated to a particular temperature and the water then is warmed or cooled at a constant rate until the fish lose equilibrium (Paladino et al. 1980; Bonin 1981). Conventionally, 1°C/min has been the rate of temperature change used; however, extensive evaluations by Becker and Genoway (1979) and Becker and Wolford (1980) showed that CTM determinations conducted at 0.3°C/min are to be preferred. Either the ILT or the CTM procedure can be used to determine if the zone of thermal tolerance has been adversely affected by cumulative prior stress.

As a specific application, thermal challenge can be used to determine whether acute or chronic exposure to contaminants has narrowed the normal temperature tolerance limits (Becker and Wolford 1980; McLeay and Gordon 1980). Such tests can be conducted both after contaminant exposure has occurred (to evaluate the effects of prior exposure and the recovery time needed) or during acute or chronic contaminant exposure. When the CTM is used to evaluate an ongoing acute exposure, the rate of temperature change should be much slower than 1°C/min in order to allow sufficient time during the test for the contaminant to exert its effect. Rates on the order of 1°C/h are usually used. Both mixed industrial waste discharges and effluents composed of single chemicals can lower the highest temperature normally tolerated when concentrations are substantially below the acutely lethal levels indicated by the LC50s, the concentrations lethal to 50% of the test animals (McLeay and Howard 1977).

In interpreting the results of such thermal challenge tests, the biological end point used, the thermal exposure, and the photoperiod must be standardized because these variables can appreciably alter these results (McLeay and Gordon 1978a; Becker and Genoway 1979). In addition, it should be expected that toxicant effects will vary. Some contaminants markedly reduce the upper temperature tolerance of fishes; others cause only a slight impairment (McLeay and Gordon 1980). For instance, acute or prolonged exposure of juvenile Arctic grayling to sediment from placer mining had no appreciable effect on the fishes' temperature tolerance (CTM), whereas acute, sublethal pentachlorophenol exposures caused a dose-dependent reduction in the CTM (McLeay et al. 1983, 1984). Similarly, sublethal nitrite exposure reduced the upper temperature tolerance of channel catfish by at least 2°C (Watenpaugh et al. 1985). Such differences presumably are due to physiological effects such as tissue anoxia that must occur during the process of thermal death if temperature tolerance has been affected (Heath and Hughes 1973). Thus, any effects of prior stress factors that have resulted in impaired gill oxygen exchange or tissue respiration rates, or that have increased metabolic rates, may reduce the ability of fishes to withstand subsequent increases in water temperature. Tests to detect suppressed thermal tolerance can be especially useful when stenothermal fishes are the species in question.

14.3.2.2 Tolerance of Hypoxia

The effect of prior stress on a fish's ability to withstand oxygen depletion can be measured rapidly and simply by the sealed-jar test originally proposed by Carter (1962). Hypoxia challenge tests have been used to identify pathological changes in contaminant-exposed marine and freshwater fish (Ballard and Oliff 1969; Giles and Klaprat 1979) and to determine the zone of influence of effluent discharges within receiving waters (McLeay and Gordon 1978b).

To conduct a test, individual fish are placed in separate 1- or 2-L containers filled with oxygen-saturated water at the desired temperature. The recommended loading density for salmonids is 4–5 g of fish per liter of solution. Ten replicates of each treatment should be used. The jars are sealed to exclude air and the dissolved oxygen remaining when each fish loses equilibrium or stops its opercular movements is determined. Normally, the fish-loading density (g/L) is adjusted so that death occurs within 5–8 h at a particular water temperature. Dead fish should not be allowed to remain overnight before dissolved oxygen is measured because decomposition of the body will further lower the oxygen concentration (Schreck and Brouha 1975). If stress has compromised the fishes' ability to exchange gases, test fish will die at higher residual oxygen concentrations than control fish. If stress has heightened the energy demands on fish (decreased their scope for activity), test fish may tolerate as much oxygen depletion as controls, but their greater respiration will depress oxygen concentrations faster and they will die sooner (McLeay et al. 1984).

Tests to detect adverse effects of contaminants have shown that residual dissolved oxygen (at "death") frequently is directly proportional to the contaminant concentration. Threshold-effect concentrations are usually approximately equal to the 96-h LC50 values (Vigers and Maynard 1977; Giles and Klaprat 1979).

Hypoxia challenge tests are useful if prior stress factors have damaged gills and impaired O_2 or CO_2 diffusion rates or if they have induced physiological changes that inhibit oxygen transport or associated metabolic pathways. For example, the ability of salmonids to withstand hypoxia is reduced by acute sublethal exposure to contaminants that impair respiration, but it is unaffected by acute or chronic exposure to contaminants that cause other deleterious effects (McLeay and Howard 1977; Vigers and Maynard 1977; McLeay and Gordon 1980; McLeay et al. 1984).

Hypoxia challenge tests also are merited for detecting the delayed effects of fish disease therapeutants such as formalin that cause gill pathology. Before hypoxia tests can be used defensibly to evaluate tolerances of many other stress factors, however, we must acquire better understanding of how those factors affect physiological processes in fish. For the present, the simplicity and rapidity of the procedure support its use as a screening method.

14.3.2.3   Swimming Performance

The impairment of overall swimming performance by prior stress can be evaluated in terms of stamina or swimming efficiency when fish are made to swim in (typically) oxygen-saturated water. The test chamber usually is a tunnel or a rotary-flow device that can also serve as a respirometer (Smith and Newcomb 1970; Beamish 1978; Wakeman and Wohlschlag 1979).

Swimming tests have been used to define the limits of acclimation to stresses associated with dissolved oxygen (Kutty and Saunders 1973), temperature (Berry and Pimentel 1985), salinity (Wakeman and Wohlschlag 1979), contaminants (Kovacs and Leduc 1982; Kumaraguru and Beamish 1983; Buckley et al. 1985), and physical stressors such as tagging (Clancy 1963) and capture methods (Horak and Klein 1967). In addition, such information can be used in the design of fish ladders, culverts, and water intake structures (Berry and Pimentel 1985). However, data showing a reduction in swimming stamina after exposure to a stress factor can be difficult to interpret biologically. For example, Horak (1972) showed that differences in swimming stamina probably do not have important effects on the survival of hatchery-reared rainbow trout released into lakes or streams. Anadromous salmonids naturally lose some swimming efficiency as they transform from parr to smolts (Smith and Margolis 1970; Glova and McInerney 1977; Flagg et al. 1983). Acute exposures to contaminants may impair swimming performance but stamina may return to normal during chronic exposures, and may even increase (Waiwood and Beamish 1978). Such a compensatory return to normal swimming performance may occur even when growth has been inhibited and pathological changes in the gills and other tissues have occurred (Webb and Brett 1973; McLeay and Brown 1979). Other adverse environmental conditions, particularly if hypoxia is involved, may also impair swimming performance temporarily but lead to compensatory development of a more efficient cardiorespiratory system and an ultimate swimming performance equal to or better than that of unstressed controls (Larmoyeux and Piper 1973). Determinations of swimming efficiency (tail-beat frequency versus swimming speed) and of swimming performance at low dissolved oxygen concentrations may prove to be useful tests of fish condition (Smith 1982a; Flagg et al. 1983).

A simple portable apparatus for measuring critical swimming speed or fatigue time can be made from a clear acrylic or polyvinyl chloride tube equipped with a capped port for introducing fish, a rotating screen for removing impinged fish near the outflow, and a flowmeter (calibrated to measure water velocity) near the inflow (Sigismondi 1985). The tube is connected to a variable-flow water supply that can produce water velocities up to five fish body lengths per second. Previously stressed fish are placed in the tubes and the water velocity is increased in steps until fish cannot continue swimming; this gives the critical swimming speed (Brett 1964). Alternatively, velocity is held constant and the mean time at which fish are unable to continue swimming is determined; this gives fatigue time. Placing the fish in the tube requires that they be handled, so otherwise unstressed (control) fish must also be tested for comparison. Ideally, fish should be allowed to adjust to the tube for at least 24 h, including a "swimming up" period, but this is not always feasible for field studies nor for the stress factor in question (e.g., acute handling). The apparatus is better for assessing stressful effects of altered water quality than for evaluating physical disturbances, because the affected water can be routed continuously through the tube—i.e., the stress factor can be continued—during the adjustment period and swimming trial (see Chapter 15 for more discussion of swimming performance in toxicology studies). For best results, fish should be tested one at a time, but testing three or four fish in the tube at once yields approximate and relative data more quickly. When this method is used to measure fatigue time, an occasional fish may continue to swim in spite of stress factors applied, thereby requiring the use of nonparametric statistical methods for data analysis (Sigismondi 1985). Investigators who wish to use swimming challenge tests should be aware of the many nonstress factors and constraints that affect swimming performance; these were reviewed by Beamish (1978).

14.3.2.4 Resistance to Fish Diseases

It is now well accepted that the occurrence of certain fish diseases indicates stress from environmental factors that has exceeded acclimation tolerance limits (Wedemeyer et al. 1976; Sindermann 1980; Ellis 1981). Thus, standardized disease challenge tests can be used to evaluate the effects of prior stress. Improved information on the point at which single and multiple environmental factors begin to reduce disease resistance is especially needed for biological monitoring and surveillance programs to assess environmental quality (Esch and Hazen 1978, 1980; Sindermann 1980).

The use of disease challenge tests requires standardization of methods for experimentally exposing fish to the pathogen and extensive knowledge about the virulence, dosage, and conditions required for clinical signs to develop. Several such challenge tests can be recommended. The bacterial kidney disease challenge developed by Iwama (1977) for juvenile chinook salmon reliably indicates when exposure to sodium pentachlorophenate begins to affect disease resistance. Similarly, a standardized challenge with infectious hematopoietic necrosis virus has been developed to assess disease susceptibility of rainbow trout exposed to dissolved copper (Hetrick et al. 1979). Standardized challenges with the bacteria *Aeromonas salmonicida* and *A. hydrophila,* devised by Groberg et al. (1978), can be used to determine the effects of water temperature on infectivity of anadromous salmonids. Walters and Plumb (1980) successfully used a challenge test with *A. hydrophila* to assess the degree to which environmental stressors (low dissolved oxygen, elevated CO_2, and ammonia) affected disease resistance and survival of channel catfish. The models for experimental furunculosis *(A. salmonicida)* in rainbow trout (Michel 1980) and for vibriosis *(Vibrio anguillarum)* in sockeye salmon (Gould et al. 1979) can also be recommended. Cipriano (1982) developed a contact challenge method for furunculosis in brook trout that gives consistent results, and Knittel (1981) reported a successful injection challenge for the bacterium *Yersinia ruckeri* in steelhead.

Standardized challenge tests are being developed to assess vulnerability to noninfectious disease vectors such as carcinogens (Sinnhuber et al. 1977; Grieco et al. 1978; Wales et al. 1978; Black 1986; Harshbarger 1986). These procedures may also allow us to characterize the influence of environmental factors on the mutagenicity or carcinogenicity of wastewater discharges, although specific challenge tests have not yet been developed for this purpose.

14.3.2.5   Tolerance of Chemicals

Challenge of fish with reference chemicals has been little used to indicate the cumulative effects of prior stress, but this approach has considerable potential as a practical test procedure (Wedemeyer and McLeay 1981; McLeay et al. 1983, 1984). Adelman and Smith (1976) used a sodium chloride challenge to reveal stresses imposed on goldfish by sublethal parasite infestations; infested fish tolerated the salt less well. Similarly, challenge with phenol differentiated unstressed rainbow trout from those stressed by food deprivation or chlorine (Alexander and Clarke 1978). However, phenol challenge did not reveal the effects of prior crowding stress, and the known stressful effects of hauling and handling were also not detected by challenge tests with sodium dodecyl sulfate (Pessah et al. 1976). Arctic grayling given a 6-week exposure to suspended placer-mining sediments were less able to withstand a subsequent pentachlorophenol challenge than unexposed controls (McLeay et al. 1984).

Several chemicals have been proposed and evaluated as reference toxicants, but few have all the characteristics considered necessary for this purpose. As originally conceived by Alderdice (1963), such chemicals should elicit a reproducible, nonspecific stress response in healthy fish; should reveal impaired health resulting from prior stress by effecting a deviant physiological response in such fish; and should be soluble and stable in water, easily measured, effective at low concentrations, and sufficiently novel that test fish will not have been exposed to them previously. Although no single chemical has yet met all these criteria, sodium pentachlorophenate, sodium chloride, and phenol challenges all have revealed otherwise nonapparent differences in fish condition. Thus, these three appear to be the best of the presently available candidates (Adelman and Smith 1976; Alexander and Clarke 1978).

During chemical challenge tests, fish are exposed to acutely lethal concentrations of the reference compound in question. Differences in either the 24- or 96-h LC50 are usually measured. Water quality characteristics, especially pH, hardness, temperature, and dissolved oxygen, must be carefully controlled in all such tests. The biological end point of such tests—death—does not reveal much specific information about the debilitation caused by the prior stress. Nevertheless, appropriate challenge tests with reference chemicals may help define the acclimation tolerance limits in selected instances. As a practical matter, standardization for each fish species will be required in order to establish a baseline from which comparisons can be made.

14.3.2.6   Salinity Tolerance

Tests to detect impaired ability to osmoregulate can be used to evaluate the effects of prior stress, but several extrinsic and intrinsic factors must be accounted for. These include species type (anadromous, euryhaline), stage of physiological development (parr, smolt, juvenile, adult), season, water chemistry and temperature, and test salinity (Eddy 1981). In the case of freshwater-acclimated fish, salinity challenge with seawater or an appropriate mixture of sea salts can be used to assess the effects of prior stress on osmoregulatory function (indicated by a fish's ability to maintain normal blood electrolyte levels) or on normal compensatory stress responses (indicated by, for example, plasma cortisol levels). Effects on either physiological function can be used as an indicator (Hirano 1969; Singley and Chavin 1975). Preliminary trials are required to establish the salt concentration that the controls will just tolerate. For salmonid smolts (Pacific and Atlantic salmon and steelhead), effects on ability to grow and develop normally in seawater are the biological end points of ultimate interest (Clarke 1982). The seawater challenge test can also be used to reveal adverse effects on the parr–smolt transformation that might be caused by suboptimal hatchery conditions or freshwater contaminants (Wedemeyer et al. 1980; Clarke 1982). Matthews et al. (1986) used salinity challenge tests to evaluate the stress on outmigrating Columbia River smolts caused by passage facilities at dams. The tolerance of juvenile salmonids for other stress factors could be tested similarly.

Clarke and Blackburn (1977, 1978) originally developed the seawater challenge–blood sodium test to assess the normal development of hypoosmoregulatory capability (smoltification) in juvenile anadromous salmonids and ultimately to predict the survival and growth of these fish in seawater (Clarke 1982). To conduct a test (Blackburn and Clarke 1987), fish are exposed to the stress factor(s) in question, and groups of 10 or more are transferred directly from fresh water into full-strength seawater (28–30‰) at the same temperature. Control groups should always be included for comparison. Blood sodium analyses are performed after 24 h. Functional coho salmon smolts with good long-term seawater growth potential are able to regulate their plasma sodium levels to 170 meq/L or less within 24 h following seawater challenge. Incompletely functional smolts suffer a substantial hypernatremia. Although such fish may eventually succeed in regulating their blood electrolytes back down into the normal range, their long-term survival and growth will be below normal (Clarke 1982).

The use of salinity challenge tests with other anadromous and catadromous species such as striped bass is merited. However, the optimum test conditions required to reveal the effects of prior environmental stress on hypoosmoregulatory ability are likely to be species specific, and little information is presently available for species other than salmonids.

There also is merit in developing variable-salinity challenge tests (0–30‰) for estuarine and marine fishes that are (or may be) required to osmoregulate under rapidly changing salinity conditions. Such conditions arise naturally during tidal cycles, wind-induced changes in water circulation, and rainwater runoff from land, but they also are consequences of human alterations of river flows and estuarine structure. A good data base on osmoregulatory tolerances is needed for both wild populations and species in mariculture if we are to correctly predict responses of fishes to perturbations of estuarine and marine environments. To assure ecological relevance, variable-salinity challenge tests should be designed with the marine survival, growth, and development of the relevant species in mind.

14.3.2.7 Crowding Tests

Crowding, whereby a species' biological requirement for space is exceeded (in terms of weight or number of fish per unit volume of water), is a physiological stress factor commonly encountered by fishes in intensive culture, and it provides the basis for an easily conducted challenge test. Crowding beyond acclimation tolerance limits elicits the characteristic stress-response syndrome in a variety of species (Strange et al. 1978; Burton and Murray 1979; Barton et al. 1980; Murray 1980), and it may adversely affect growth, development, disease resistance, and behavior, particularly if the crowding is chronic (Schreck 1982). Among anadromous salmonids, the aberrant effects on smoltification and seawater survival that occur (Fagerlund et al. 1981; Sandercock and Stone 1982; Schreck 1982) have population-level significance.

To conduct challenge tests, groups of fish are held under light loading conditions (for salmonids, density should be 0.04 kg/L or less) while they are subjected to the stress factor of interest. The density of fish is then increased to a preselected value (for salmonids, 0.2–0.6 kg/L for 6–8 h). After the desired time interval, the density is reduced to original conditions and the fish are allowed to recover. Blood samples are taken at regular intervals, usually at 0, 3, 6, 24, 48, and 96 h from the time crowding begins, and analyzed for plasma glucose, chloride, and cortisol. Both the magnitude of the hyperglycemia, hypochloremia, and hypercortisolemia that occur during the challenge test and the time fish need to regulate their blood chemistries back into the normal range provide information on the extent to which the stress adversely affected abilities to withstand a subsequent challenge. If the blood chemistry data are graphed as a function of time, the area under the resulting curves can be used to gauge the severity of the stress response relative to the controls. Water exchange rates, dissolved oxygen, carbon dioxide, and un-ionized ammonia concentrations must be held within the optimum range for the test species during the experiment.

14.3.2.8 Handling Tests

A handling challenge, in which fish are briefly suspended out of water in a net, elicits a typical stress response characterized by hyperglycemia, hypochloremia, and hypercortisolemia. Because the effects of multiple stress factors are cumulative (Carmichael et al. 1983, 1984b; Barton et al. 1986), the physiological response to a handling-stress test may be used to assess the effects of stress previously experienced by a fish. For example, Barton et al. (1985b) showed that rainbow trout exposed to acidity (pH 4.7) for 5 d and then challenged by handling suffered a hypercortisolemia that was twice as great as that exhibited by controls. This challenge test also has helped identify the stressful sections of fish-passage facilities in Columbia River dams (Maule et al. 1988).

To conduct the handling-stress test, the test group is simply suspended out of water for 30–60 s and replaced into a recovery tank. Periodic blood samples are then taken, usually at 0, 1, 3, 6, 12, 24, 48, and 96 h, and analyzed for cortisol, glucose, and chloride. Alternatively, the peak response time is first determined and then all treatment groups are sampled at that time.

The handling-stress challenge should be particularly useful when a chronic stress is not reflected by elevated plasma levels of corticosteroids because cortisol clearance or degradation also has increased or compensation has occured. Results should be interpreted cautiously, however, because the continuous negative feedback resulting from chronic stress (Fryer and Peter 1977) may suppress even the sudden cortisol output induced by handling (Barton et al. 1987).

14.3.2.9 Behavioral Tests

Several behavioral responses could be exploited to assess the effects of stress on individual fish and populations (Little et al. 1985; Rand 1985). In general, they have not been used as widely as other aspects of the stress response. Some responses have a qualitative component that makes them difficult to measure (e.g., anorexia, susceptibility to predation), but others can be used to quantify whole-animal performance. For example, avoidance of harsh stimuli such as a bright light (Sigismondi and Weber 1988) or a noxious odorant can be measured in a Y-trough selection apparatus (Rehnberg et al. 1985; Rehnberg and Schreck 1987). Behavioral tests should be selected that complement measurement of other stress-response indicators, and they should be designed to provide information that is ecologically relevant to the particular investigation. The use of behavioral responses to assess the effects of water-borne pollutants is discussed in greater detail in Chapter 15.

14.4 REFERENCES

Adams, B., W. Zaugg, and L. R. McLain. 1975. Inhibition of saltwater survival and Na^+K^+-ATPase elevation in steelhead trout *(Salmo gairdneri)* by moderate water temperatures. Transactions of the American Fisheries Society 104:766–769.

Adams, S. M., J. E. Breck, and R. B. McLean. 1985. Cumulative stress-induced mortality of gizzard shad in a southeastern U.S. reservoir. Environmental Biology of Fishes 13:103–112.

Adelman, I. R., and L. L. Smith, Jr. 1976. Fathead minnows *(Pimephales promelas)* and goldfish *(Carassius auratus)* as standard fish in bioassays and their reaction to potential reference toxicants. Journal of the Fisheries Research Board of Canada 33:209–214.

Agrawal, S. J., A. K. Srivastava, and H. S. Chaudhry. 1979. Haematological effects of nickel toxicity on a fresh water teleost *(Colisa fasciatus)*. Acta Pharmacologica et Toxicologica 45:215–217.

Alderdice, D. F. 1963. Some effects of simultaneous variation in salinity, temperature and dissolved oxygen on the resistance of juvenile coho salmon *(Oncorhynchus kisutch)* to a toxic substance. Journal of the Fisheries Research Board of Canada 20:525–550.

Alexander, D. G., and R. Clarke. 1978. The selection and limitations of phenol as a reference toxicant to detect differences in sensitivity among groups of rainbow trout *(Salmo gairdneri)*. Water Research 12:1085–1090.

Allen, J. L., V. K. Dawson, and J. B. Hunn. 1979. Biotransformation of selected chemicals by fish. Pages 121–129 *in* M. A. Q. Kahn, J. J. Lech, and J. J. Menn, editors. American Chemical Society Symposium Series 99, Washington, D.C.

Amos, K. H., editor. 1985. Procedures for the detection and identification of certain fish pathogens, 3rd edition. American Fisheries Society, Fish Health Section, Corvallis, Oregon. (Available from American Fisheries Society, Bethesda, Maryland.)

Arillo, A., C. Margiocco, and F. Melodia. 1979. The gill sialic acid content as an index of environmental stress in rainbow trout, *Salmo gairdneri* Richardson. Journal of Fish Biology 15:405–410.

Ballard, J. A., and W. D. Oliff. 1969. A rapid method for measuring the acute toxicity of dissolved materials to marine fishes. Water Research 3:313–333.

Barton, B. A., and R. E. Peter. 1982. Plasma cortisol stress response in fingerling rainbow trout, *Salmo gairdneri* Richardson, to various transport conditions, anaesthesia, and cold shock. Journal of Fish Biology 20:39–51.

Barton, B. A., R. E. Peter, and C. R. Paulencu. 1980. Plasma cortisol levels of fingerling rainbow trout *(Salmo gairdneri)* at rest, and subjected to handling, confinement, transport, and stocking. Canadian Journal of Fisheries and Aquatic Sciences 37:805–811.

Barton, B. A., and C. B. Schreck. 1987a. Influence of acclimation temperature on interrenal and carbohydrate stress responses in juvenile chinook salmon *(Oncorhynchus tshawytscha)*. Aquaculture 62:299–310.

Barton, B. A., and C. B. Schreck. 1987b. Metabolic cost of acute physical stress in juvenile steelhead. Transactions of the American Fisheries Society 116:257–263.

Barton, B. A., C. B. Schreck, and L. D. Barton. 1987. Effects of chronic cortisol administration and daily acute stress on growth, physiological conditions, and stress responses in juvenile rainbow trout. Diseases of Aquatic Organisms 2:173–185.

Barton, B. A., C. B. Schreck, R. C. Ewing, A. R. Hemmingsen, and R. Patiño. 1985a. Changes in plasma cortisol during stress and smoltification in coho salmon, *Oncorhynchus kisutch*. General and Comparative Endocrinology 59:468–471.

Barton, B. A., C. B. Schreck, and L. G. Fowler. 1988. Fasting and diet content affect stress-induced changes in plasma glucose and cortisol in juvenile chinook salmon. Progressive Fish-Culturist 50:16–22.

Barton, B. A., C. B. Schreck, and L. A. Sigismondi. 1986. Multiple acute disturbances evoke cumulative physiological stress responses in juvenile chinook salmon. Transactions of the American Fisheries Society 115:245–251.

Barton, B. A., G. S. Weiner, and C. B. Schreck. 1985b. Effect of prior acid exposure on physiological responses of juvenile rainbow trout *(Salmo gairdneri)* to acute handling stress. Canadian Journal of Fisheries and Aquatic Sciences 42:710–717.

Bass, M. L., and A. G. Heath. 1977. Cardiovascular and respiratory changes in rainbow trout, *Salmo gairdneri*, exposed intermittently to chlorine. Water Research 11:497–502.

Beamish, F. W. H. 1978. Swimming capacity. Pages 101–187 *in* W. S. Hoar and D. J. Randall, editors. Fish physiology, volume 7. Academic Press, New York.

Becker, C. D., and R. G. Genoway. 1979. Evaluation of the critical thermal maximum for determining thermal tolerance of freshwater fish. Environmental Biology of Fishes 4:245–256.

Becker, C. D., and M. G. Wolford. 1980. Thermal resistance of juvenile salmonids sublethally exposed to nickel, determined by the critical thermal maximum method. Environmental Pollution Series A, Ecological and Biological 21:181–189.

Beggs, G. L., G. F. Holeton, and E. J. Crossman. 1980. Some physiological consequences of angling stress in muskellunge, *Esox masquinongy* Mitchill. Journal of Fish Biology 17:649–659.

Berry, C. R., and R. Pimentel. 1985. Swimming performances of three rare Colorado River fishes. Transactions of the American Fisheries Society 114:397–402.

Billard, R., C. Bry, and C. Gillet. 1981. Stress, environment, and reproduction in teleost fish. Pages 185–208 *in* A. D. Pickering, editor. Stress and fish. Academic Press, London.

Black, E. C. 1958. Hyperactivity as a lethal factor in fish. Journal of the Fisheries Research Board of Canada 15:573–586.

Black, E. C., G. T. Manning, and K. Hayashi. 1966. Changes in levels of hemoglobin, oxygen, carbon dioxide, pyruvate, and lactate in venous blood of rainbow trout *(Salmo gairdneri)* during and following severe muscular activity. Journal of the Fisheries Research Board of Canada 23:783–795.

Black, J. J. 1986. The fish—the ultimate carcinogen assay. Canadian Technical Report of Fisheries and Aquatic Sciences 1480.

Blackburn, J., and W. C. Clarke. 1987. Revised procedures for the 24 hour seawater challenge test to measure seawater adaptability of juvenile salmonids. Canadian Technical Report of Fisheries and Aquatic Sciences 1515.

Bonin, J. D. 1981. Measuring thermal limits of fish. Transactions of the American Fisheries Society 110:662–664.

Brett, J. R. 1958. Implications and assessment of environmental stress. Pages 69–83 *in* P. A. Larkin, editor. The investigation of fish-power problems. H. R. MacMillan Lectures in Fisheries, University of British Columbia, Vancouver.

Brett, J. R. 1964. The respiratory metabolism and swimming performance of young sockeye salmon. Journal of the Fisheries Research Board of Canada 21:1183–1226.

Brett, J. R., and T. D. D. Groves. 1979. Physiological energetics. Pages 279–352 in W. S. Hoar, D. J. Randall, and J. R. Brett. Fish physiology, volume 8. Academic Press, New York.

Brown, S., K. Fedoruk, and J. G. Eales. 1978. Physical injury due to injection or blood removal causes transitory elevation of plasma thyroxine in rainbow trout, *Salmo gairdneri*. Canadian Journal of Zoology 56:1998–2003.

Buckley, L. J., T. A. Halavik, G. C. Laurence, S. J. Hamilton, and P. Yevich. 1985. Comparative swimming stamina, biochemical composition, backbone mechanical properties, and histopathology of juvenile striped bass from rivers and hatcheries of the eastern United States. Transactions of the American Fisheries Society 114:114–124.

Burton, C. B., and S. A. Murray. 1979. Effects of density on goldfish blood. I. Hematology. Comparative Biochemistry and Physiology A, Comparative Physiology 62:555–558.

Caillouet, C. W., Jr. 1968. Lactic acidosis in channel catfish. Journal of the Fisheries Research Board of Canada 25:15–24.

Carmichael, G. J. 1984. Long distance truck transport of intensively reared largemouth bass. Progressive Fish-Culturist 46:111–115.

Carmichael, G. J., J. R. Tomasso, B. A. Simco, and K. B. Davis. 1984a. Characterization and alleviation of stress associated with hauling largemouth bass. Transactions of the American Fisheries Society 113:778–785.

Carmichael, G. J., J. R. Tomasso, B. A. Simco, and K. B. Davis. 1984b. Confinement and water quality-induced stress in largemouth bass. Transactions of the American Fisheries Society 113:767–777.

Carmichael, G. J., G. A. Wedemeyer, J. P. McCraren, and J. L. Millard. 1983. Physiological effects of handling and hauling stress on smallmouth bass. Progressive Fish-Culturist 45:110–113.

Carter, L. 1962. Bioassay of trade wastes. Nature (London) 196:1304.

Casillas, E., and L. S. Smith. 1977. Effect of stress on blood coagulation and haematology in rainbow trout *(Salmo gairdneri)*. Journal of Fish Biology 10:481–491.

Chard, T. 1981. An introduction to radioimmunoassay and related techniques. Elsevier, Amsterdam.

Cipriano, R. 1982. Furunculosis in brook trout: infection by contact exposure. Progressive Fish-Culturist 44:12–14.

Clancy, D. W. 1963. The effect of tagging with Petersen disc tags on the swimming ability of fingerling steelhead trout *(Salmo gairdneri)*. Journal of the Fisheries Research Board of Canada 20:969–981.

Clarke, W. C. 1982. Evaluation of the seawater challenge test as an index of marine survival. Aquaculture 28:177–183.

Clarke, W. C., and J. Blackburn. 1977. A seawater challenge test to measure smolting of juvenile salmon. Canada Fisheries and Marine Service Technical Report 705.

Clarke, W. C., and J. Blackburn. 1978. Seawater challenge tests performed on hatchery stocks of chinook and coho salmon in 1977. Canada Fisheries and Marine Service Technical Report 761.

Davis, K. B., M. A. Suttle, and N. C. Parker. 1984. Biotic and abiotic influences on corticosteroid rhythms in channel catfish. Transactions of the American Fisheries Society 113:414–421.

Department of Fisheries and Oceans. 1984. Fish health protection regulations: manual of compliance. Canada Fisheries and Marine Service Miscellaneous Special Publication 31 (revised).

Diamant, J., and S. O. Byers. 1975. A precise catecholamine assay for small plasma samples. Journal of Laboratory and Chemical Medicine 85:678–693.

Dickson, I. W., and R. H. Kramer. 1971. Factors influencing scope for activity and active and standard metabolism of rainbow trout *(Salmo gairdneri)*. Journal of the Fisheries Research Board of Canada 28:587–596.

DiStefano, J. J., III. 1982. Noncompartmental vs. compartmental analysis: some bases for choice. American Journal of Physiology 243:R1–R6.

Donaldson, E. M. 1981. The pituitary–interrenal axis as an indicator of stress in fish. Pages 11–48 *in* A. D. Pickering, editor. Stress and fish. Academic Press, London.

Donaldson, E. M., and U. H. M. Fagerlund. 1972. Corticosteroid dynamics in Pacific salmon. General and Comparative Endocrinology 3(Supplement):254–265.

Donaldson, E. M., U. H. M. Fagerlund, and J. R. McBride. 1984. Aspects of the endocrine stress response to pollutants in salmonids. Pages 213–222 *in* V. W. Cairns, P. V. Hodson, and J. O. Nriagu, editors. Contaminant effects on fisheries. Wiley, Toronto.

Donaldson, E. M., and J. R. McBride. 1974. Effect of ACTH and salmon gonadotropin on interrenal and thyroid activity of gonadectomized adult sockeye salmon *(Oncorhynchus nerka)*. Journal of the Fisheries Research Board of Canada 31:1211–1214.

Driedzic, W. R., and J. W. Kiceniuk. 1976. Blood lactate levels in free-swimming rainbow trout *(Salmo gairdneri)* before and after strenuous exercise resulting in fatigue. Journal of the Fisheries Research Board of Canada 33:173–176.

Eddy, F. B. 1981. Effects of stress on osmotic and ionic regulation in fish. Pages 77–102 *in* A. D. Pickering, editor. Stress and fish. Academic Press, London.

Elliott, J. M. 1981. Some aspects of thermal stress on freshwater teleosts. Pages 209–245 *in* A. D. Pickering, editor. Stress and fish. Academic Press, London.

Ellis, A. E. 1981. Stress and the modulation of defence mechanisms in fish. Pages 147–170 *in* A. D. Pickering, editor. Stress and fish. Academic Press, London.

Esch, G. W., and T. C. Hazen. 1978. Thermal ecology and stress: a case history for red-sore disease in largemouth bass. Pages 331–363 *in* J. Thorp and J. Gibbons, editors. Energy and environmental stress in aquatic systems. DOE (U.S. Department of Energy) Symposium Series 48. (National Technical Information Service, CONF-7711111, Springfield, Virginia.)

Esch, G. W., and T. C. Hazen. 1980. Stress and body condition in a population of largemouth bass: implications for red-sore disease. Transactions of the American Fisheries Society 109:532–536.

Fagerlund, U. H. M., J. R. McBride, and E. T. Stone. 1981. Stress-related effects of hatchery rearing density on coho salmon. Transactions of the American Fisheries Society 110:644–649.

Flagg, T. A., E. F. Prentice, and L. S. Smith. 1983. Swimming stamina and survival following direct seawater entry during parr–smolt transformation of coho salmon *(Oncorhynchus kisutch)*. Aquaculture 32:383–396.

Folmar, L. C., and W. C. Dickhoff. 1980. The parr–smolt transformation (smoltification) and seawater adaptation in salmonids. Aquaculture 21:1–37.

Foster, L. B., and R. T. Dunn. 1974. Single-antibody technique for radioimmunoassay of cortisol in unextracted serum or plasma. Clinical Chemistry 20:365–368.

Fraser, J. M., and F. W. H. Beamish. 1969. Blood lactic acid concentrations in brook trout, *Salvelinus fontinalis,* planted by air drop. Transactions of the American Fisheries Society 98:263–267.

Freeman, H. C., G. B. Sangalang, G. Burns, and M. McMenemy. 1983. The blood sex hormone levels in sexually mature male Atlantic salmon (*Salmo salar*) in the Westfield River (pH 4.7) and the Medway River (pH 5.6), Nova Scotia. Science of the Total Environment 32:87–91.

Fromm, P. O. 1980. A review of some physiological and toxicological responses of freshwater fish to acid stress. Environmental Biology of Fishes 5:79–93.

Fry, F. E. J. 1947. Effects of the environment on animal activity. University of Toronto Studies, Biological Series 55:1–62.

Fry, F. E. J. 1971. The effect of environmental factors on the physiology of fish. Pages 1–98 *in* W. S. Hoar and D. J. Randall, editors. Fish physiology, volume 6. Academic Press, New York.

Fryer, J. N., and R. E. Peter. 1977. Hypothalamic control of ACTH secretion in goldfish. III. Hypothalamic cortisol implant studies. General and Comparative Endocrinology 33:215–225.

Gerking, S. D. 1980. Fish reproduction and stress. Pages 569–587 *in* M. A. Ali, editor. Environmental physiology of fishes. Plenum, New York.

Giles, M. A., and D. Klaprat. 1979. The residual oxygen test: a rapid method for estimating the acute lethal toxicity of aquatic contaminants. Canadian Special Publication of Fisheries and Aquatic Sciences 44:37–45.

Gilham, I. D., and B. I. Baker. 1985. A black background facilitates the response to stress in teleosts. Journal of Endocrinology 105:99–105.

Glova, G. J., and J. E. McInerney. 1977. Critical swimming speeds of coho salmon (Oncorhynchus kisutch) fry to smolt stages in relation to salinity and temperature. Journal of the Fisheries Research Board of Canada 34:151–154.

Gordon, M. R., and D. J. McLeay. 1978. Effect of photoperiod on seasonal variations in glycogen reserves of juvenile rainbow trout (Salmo gairdneri). Comparative Biochemistry and Physiology 60:349–351.

Gould, R. W., R. Antipa, and D. F. Amend. 1979. Immersion vaccination of sockeye salmon (Oncorhynchus nerka) with two pathogenic strains of Vibrio anguillarum. Journal of the Fisheries Research Board of Canada 36:222–225.

Graham, M. S., C. M. Wood, and J. D. Turner. 1982. The physiological responses of the rainbow trout to strenuous exercise: interactions of water hardness and environmental acidity. Canadian Journal of Zoology 60:3153–3164.

Grant, B. F., and P. M. Mehrle. 1973. Endrin toxicosis in rainbow trout (Salmo gairdneri). Journal of the Fisheries Research Board of Canada 30:31–40.

Grieco, M. P., J. D. Hendricks, R. A. Scanian, R. O. Sinnhuber, and D. A. Pierce. 1978. Carcinogenicity and acute toxicity of dimethyl nitrosamine in rainbow trout (Salmo gairdneri). Journal of the National Cancer Institute 60:1127–1130.

Groberg, W. J., Jr., R. H. McCoy, K. S. Pilcher, and J. L. Fryer. 1978. Relation of water temperature to infections of coho salmon (Oncorhynchus kisutch), chinook salmon (O. tshawytscha), and steelhead trout (Salmo gairdneri) with Aeromonas salmonicida and A. hydrophila. Journal of the Fisheries Research Board of Canada 35:1–7.

Guyton, A. C. 1981. Textbook of medical physiology, 6th edition. Saunders, Philadelphia.

Hargis, J. R. 1976. Ventilation and metabolic rate of young rainbow trout (Salmo gairdneri) exposed to sublethal environmental pH. Journal of Experimental Zoology 196:39–44.

Harman, B. J., D. L. Johnson, and L. Greenwald. 1980. Physiological responses of Lake Erie freshwater drum to capture by commercial shore seine. Transactions of the American Fisheries Society 109:544–551.

Harshbarger, J. C. 1986. Fish neoplasms: epizootiology, experimental carcinogenesis, risks and benefits. Canadian Technical Report of Fisheries and Aquatic Sciences 1480:81–82.

Hattingh, J. 1977. Blood sugar as an indicator of stress in the freshwater fish, Labeo capensis (Smith). Journal of Fish Biology 10:191–195.

Heath, A. G. 1973. Ventilatory responses of teleost fish to exercise and thermal stress. American Zoologist 13:491–503.

Heath, A. G. 1984. Changes in tissue adenylates and water content of bluegill (Lepomis macrochirus) exposed to copper. Journal of Fish Biology 24:299–309.

Heath, A. G., and G. M. Hughes. 1973. Cardiovascular and respiratory changes during heat stress in rainbow trout (Salmo gairdneri). Journal of Experimental Biology 59:323–338.

Henderson, I. W., M. N. Sa'di, and G. Hargreaves. 1974. Studies on the production and metabolic clearance rates of cortisol in the European eel, Anguilla anguilla (L.). Journal of Steroid Biochemistry 5:701–707.

Hetrick, F. M., M. D. Knittel, and J. L. Fryer. 1979. Increased susceptibility of rainbow trout to infectious hematopoietic necrosis virus after exposure to copper. Applied Environmental Microbiology 37:198–201.

Hirano, T. 1969. Effects of hypophysectomy and salinity change on plasma cortisol concentration in the Japanese eel, Anguilla japonica. Endocrinologia Japonica 16:557–560.

Hjemdahl, P., M. Daleskog, and T. Kahan. 1979. Determination of plasma catecholamines by high performance liquid chromatography with electrochemical detection: comparison with a radioenzymatic method. Life Sciences 25:131–138.

Hodgins, H. O., B. B. McCain, and J. Hawkes. 1977. Marine fish and invertebrate diseases, host disease resistance, and pathological effects of petroleum. Pages 95–148 *in* D. Malins, editor. Effects of petroleum on arctic and subarctic marine environments and organisms. II. Biological effects. Academic Press, New York.

Horak, D. L. 1972. Survival of hatchery-reared rainbow trout *(Salmo gairdneri)* in relation to stamina tunnel ratings. Journal of the Fisheries Research Board of Canada 29:1005–1009.

Horak, D. L., and W. D. Klein. 1967. Influence of capture methods on fishing success, stamina and mortality of rainbow trout *(Salmo gairdneri)* in Colorado. Transactions of the American Fisheries Society 96:220–222.

Houston, A. H., and T. F. Koss. 1984. Erythrocytic hemoglobin, magnesium and nucleoside triphosphate levels in rainbow trout exposed to progressive heat stress. Journal of Thermal Biology 9:159–164.

Hunn, J. B. 1972. Blood chemistry values for some fishes of the upper Mississippi River. Journal of the Minnesota Academy of Science 38:19–21.

Hunn, J. B. 1982. Urine flow rate in freshwater salmonids: a review. Progressive Fish-Culturist 44:119–125.

Iwama, G. 1977. Some aspects of the interrelationship of bacterial kidney disease infection and sodium pentachlorophenate exposure in juvenile chinook salmon *(Oncorhynchus tshawytscha)*. Master's thesis. University of British Columbia, Vancouver.

Johansson-Sjöbeck, M. L., D. Goran, A. Larsson, K. Lewander, and U. Lindman. 1978. Haematological effects of cortisol in the European eel, *Anguilla anguilla* L. Comparative Biochemistry and Physiology A, Comparative Physiology 60:165–168.

Knittel, M. D. 1981. Susceptibility of steelhead trout *Salmo gairdneri* Richardson to redmouth infection *Yersinia ruckeri* following exposure to copper. Journal of Fish Diseases 4:33–40.

Kovacs, T. G., and G. Leduc. 1982. Sublethal toxicity of cyanide to rainbow trout *(Salmo gairdneri)* at different temperatures. Canadian Journal of Fisheries and Aquatic Sciences 39:1389–1395.

Kumaragúru, A. K., and F. W. H. Beamish. 1983. Bioenergetics of acclimation to permethrin (NRDC-143) by rainbow trout. Comparative Biochemistry and Physiology C, Comparative Pharmacology 75:247–252.

Kutty, M. N., and R. L. Saunders. 1973. Swimming performance of young Atlantic salmon *(Salmo salar)* as affected by reduced ambient oxygen concentration. Journal of the Fisheries Research Board of Canada 30:223–227.

Landolt, M. L., and R. M. Kocan. 1984. Lethal and sublethal effects of marine sediment extracts on fish cells and chromosomes. Helgoländer Meeresuntersuchungen 37:99–112.

Larmoyeux, J. D., and R. G. Piper. 1973. Effects of water reuse on rainbow trout in hatcheries. Progressive Fish-Culturist 35:2–8.

Leatherland, J. F., and R. A. Sonstegard. 1984. Pathobiological responses to environmental stressors: interlake studies of the physiology of Great Lakes salmon. Pages 115–150 *in* V. W. Cairns, P. V. Hodson, and J. O. Nriagu, editors. Contaminant effects on fisheries. Wiley, Toronto.

Lech, J. J., M. J. Vodicnik, and C. R. Elcombe. 1982. Induction of monooxygenase activity in fish. Aquatic Toxicology (New York) 1:107–148.

Liguori, V., V. Zakour, M. Landolt, and S. Felton. 1983. Toxicity of the herbicide Endothall to juvenile chinook salmon *(Oncorhynchus kisutch)*. American Society for Testing and Materials, Special Technical Publication 802:530–544.

Little, E. E., B. A. Flerov, and N. N. Ruzhinskaya. 1985. Behavioral approaches in aquatic toxicity investigations: a review. Pages 72–96 *in* P. M. Mehrle, R. H. Gray, and R. L. Kendall, editors. Toxic substances in the aquatic environment: an international aspect. American Fisheries Society, Bethesda, Maryland.

Lockhart, W. L., and D. A. Metner. 1984. Fish serum chemistry as a pathology tool. Pages 73–86 *in* V. W. Cairns, P. V. Hodson, and J. O. Nriagu, editors. Contaminant effects on fisheries. Wiley, Toronto.

Lorz, H., S. Glenn, R. Williams, C. Kunkel, L. Norris, and B. Loper. 1978. Effects of selected herbicides on smolting of coho salmon. Oregon Department of Fish and Wildlife, U.S. Environmental Protection Agency Grant Report R-804283, Corvallis.

Lorz, H., and B. P. McPherson. 1976. Effects of copper or zinc in fresh water on the adaptation to sea water and ATPase activity, and the effects of copper on migratory disposition of coho salmon (Oncorhynchus kisutch). Journal of the Fisheries Research Board of Canada 33:2023–2030.

MacLeod, J. C., and L. L. Smith, Jr. 1966. Effect of pulpwood fiber on oxygen consumption and swimming endurance of the fathead minnow, Pimephales promelas. Transactions of the American Fisheries Society 95:71–84.

MacMillan, J. R., D. Mulcahy, and M. Landolt. 1980. Viral erythrocytic necrosis: some physiological consequences of infection in chum salmon (Oncorhynchus keta). Canadian Journal of Fisheries and Aquatic Sciences 37:799–804.

Malins, D. C., B. McCain, D. Brown, A. Sparks, and H. O. Hodgins. 1980. Chemical contaminants and biological abnormalities in central and southern Puget Sound. NOAA (National Oceanic and Atmospheric Administration) Technical Memorandum OMPA-2, Boulder, Colorado.

Malins, D. C., B. McCain, D. Brown, A. Sparks, H. Hodgins, and S. Chan. 1982. Chemical contaminants and abnormalities in fish and invertebrates from Puget Sound. NOAA (National Oceanic and Atmospheric Administration) Technical Memorandum OMPA-19, Boulder, Colorado.

Matthews, G. M., D. L. Park, S. Achord, and T. E. Ruehle. 1986. Static seawater challenge test to measure relative stress levels in spring chinook salmon smolts. Transactions of the American Fisheries Society 115:236–244.

Maule, A. G., C. B. Schreck, C. S. Bradford, and B. A. Barton. 1988. Physiological effects of collecting and transporting emigrating juvenile chinook salmon past dams on the Columbia River. Transactions of the American Fisheries Society 117:245–261.

Maule, A. G., R. A. Tripp, S. L. Kaattari, and C. B. Schreck. 1989. Stress alters immune function and disease resistance in chinook salmon (Oncorhynchus tshawytscha). Journal of Endocrinology 120:135–142.

Mazeaud, M. M., and F. Mazeaud. 1981. Adrenergic responses to stress in fish. Pages 49–76 in A. D. Pickering, editor. Stress and fish. Academic Press, London.

Mazeaud, M. M., F. Mazeaud, and E. M. Donaldson. 1977. Primary and secondary effects of stress in fish: some new data with a general review. Transactions of the American Fisheries Society 106:201–212.

McFarlane, G. A., and W. G. Franzin. 1978. Elevated heavy metals: a stress on a population of white suckers, Catostomus commersoni, in Hammel Lake, Saskatchewan. Journal of the Fisheries Research Board of Canada 35:963–970.

McLeay, D. J. 1973. Effects of a 12-hour and 25-day exposure to kraft pulp mill effluent on the blood and tissues of juvenile coho salmon (Oncorhynchus kisutch). Journal of the Fisheries Research Board of Canada 30:395–400.

McLeay, D. J. 1975a. Sensitivity of blood cell counts in juvenile coho salmon (Oncorhynchus kisutch) to stressors including sublethal concentrations of pulpmill effluent and zinc. Journal of the Fisheries Research Board of Canada 32:2357–2364.

McLeay, D. J. 1975b. Variations in the pituitary–interrenal axis and the abundance of circulating blood-cell types in juvenile coho salmon (Oncorhynchus kisutch), during stream residence. Canadian Journal of Zoology 53:1882–1891.

McLeay, D. J. 1977. Development of a blood sugar bioassay for rapidly measuring stressful levels of pulpmill effluent to salmonid fish. Journal of the Fisheries Research Board of Canada 34:477–485.

McLeay, D. J., and D. A. Brown. 1974. Growth stimulation and biochemical changes in juvenile coho salmon (Oncorhynchus kisutch) exposed to bleached kraft pulpmill effluent for 200 days. Journal of the Fisheries Research Board of Canada 31:1043–1049.

McLeay, D. J., and D. A. Brown. 1975. Effects of acute exposure to bleached kraft pulpmill effluent on carbohydrate metabolism of juvenile coho salmon (Oncorhynchus kisutch) during rest and exercise. Journal of the Fisheries Research Board of Canada 32:753–760.

McLeay, D. J., and D. A. Brown. 1979. Stress and chronic effects of untreated and treated bleached kraft pulpmill effluent on the biochemistry and stamina of juvenile coho salmon (Oncorhynchus kisutch). Journal of the Fisheries Research Board of Canada 36:1049–1059.

McLeay, D. J., G. L. Ennis, I. K. Birtwell, and G. F. Hartman. 1984. Effects on Arctic grayling *(Thymallus arcticus)* of prolonged exposure to Yukon placer mining sediment: a laboratory study. Canadian Technical Report of Fisheries and Aquatic Sciences 1241.

McLeay, D. J., and M. R. Gordon. 1977. Leucocrit: a simple hematological technique for measuring acute stress in salmonid fish, including stressful concentrations of pulpmill effluent. Journal of the Fisheries Research Board of Canada 34:2164–2175.

McLeay, D. J., and M. R. Gordon. 1978a. Effect of seasonal photoperiod on acute toxic responses of juvenile rainbow trout *(Salmo gairdneri)* to pulpmill effluent. Journal of the Fisheries Research Board of Canada 35:1388–1392.

McLeay, D. J., and M. R. Gordon. 1978b. Field study of the effects to fish of treated, partially treated and untreated kraft pulp mill effluent. Council of Forest Industries of British Columbia, B.C. Research Project Report 1-05-902, Vancouver.

McLeay, D. J., and M. R. Gordon. 1979. Concentrations of Krenite causing acute lethal, avoidance and stress responses with salmon. British Columbia Research, B.C. Research Project Report 1-04-156, Vancouver.

McLeay, D. J., and M. R. Gordon. 1980. Short-term sublethal toxicity tests to assess safe levels of environmental contaminants. Canada Department of Fisheries and Oceans, B.C. Research Project Report 1-11-299, Ottawa.

McLeay, D. J., and T. E. Howard. 1977. Comparison of rapid bioassay procedures for measuring toxic effects of bleached kraft mill effluent to fish. Pages 141–155 *in* W. R. Parker, editor. Proceedings of the third aquatic toxicology workshop. Environmental Protection Service, Technical Report EPS-5-AT-77-1, Halifax, Nova Scotia.

McLeay, D. J., A. J. Knox, J. G. Malick, I. K. Birtwell, G. Hartman, and G. L. Ennis. 1983. Effects on Arctic grayling *(Thymallus arcticus)* of short term exposure to Yukon placer mining sediments: laboratory and field studies. Canadian Technical Report of Fisheries and Aquatic Sciences 1171.

Mehrle, P. M., T. A. Haines, S. Hamilton, J. L. Ludke, F. A. Mayer, and M. A. Ribick. 1982. Relationship between body contaminants and bone development in east-coast striped bass. Transactions of the American Fisheries Society 111:231–241.

Mehrle, P. M., and F. L. Mayer. 1985. Biochemistry and physiology. Pages 264–282 *in* G. M. Rand and S. R. Petrocelli, editors. Fundamentals of aquatic toxicology. Hemisphere, Washington D.C.

Michel, C. 1980. A standardized model of experimental furunculosis in rainbow trout *(Salmo gairdneri)*. Canadian Journal of Fisheries and Aquatic Sciences 37:746–750.

Milligan, C. L., and C. M. Wood. 1982. Disturbances in haematology, fluid volume distribution, and circulatory function associated with low environmental pH in the rainbow trout, *Salmo gairdneri*. Journal of Experimental Biology 99:397–415.

Moberg, G. P. 1985. Biological response to stress: key to assessment of animal well-being? Pages 27–49 *in* G. P. Moberg, editor. Animal stress. American Physiological Society, Bethesda, Maryland.

Morata, P., M. J. Faus, M. Perez-Palomo, and F. Sanchez-Medina. 1982. Effect of stress on liver and muscle glycogen phosphorylase in rainbow trout *(Salmo gairdneri)*. Comparative Biochemistry and Physiology B, Comparative Biochemistry 72:421–425.

Munkittrick, K. R., and J. F. Leatherland. 1984. Abnormal pituitary–gonad function in two feral populations of goldfish, *Carassius auratus* (L.), suffering epizootics of an ulcerative disease. Journal of Fish Diseases 7:433–447.

Murray, S. A. 1980. Effects of loading density on catfish blood. Experientia (Basel) 36:205–206.

Nakano, T., and N. Tomlinson. 1967. Catecholamine and carbohydrate concentrations in rainbow trout *(Salmo gairdneri)* in relation to physical disturbance. Journal of the Fisheries Research Board of Canada 24:1701–1715.

Neish, G. A. 1977. Observations on saprolegniasis of adult sockeye salmon, *Oncorhynchus nerka* (Walbaum). Journal of Fish Biology 10:513–522.

Nichols, D. J., M. Weisbart, and J. Quinn. 1985. Cortisol kinetics and fluid distribution in brook trout *(Salvelinus fontinalis)*. Journal of Endocrinology 107:57–69.

Nichols, J. W., and six coauthors. 1984. Effects of freshwater exposure to arsenic trioxide on the parr–smolt transformation of coho salmon *(Oncorhynchus kisutch)*. Environmental Toxicology and Chemistry 3:143–149.

Noakes, D. L. G., and J. F. Leatherland. 1977. Social dominance and interrenal cell activity in rainbow trout, *Salmo gairdneri* (Pisces, Salmonidae). Environmental Biology of Fishes 2:121–136.

O'Flaherty, E. J. 1981. Toxicants and drugs: kinetics and dynamics. Wiley, New York.

Owen, W. H., and D. R. Idler. 1972. Identification and metabolic clearance of cortisol and cortisone in a marine teleost, the sea raven *Hemitripterus americanus* Gmelin (family Scorpaenidae). Journal of Endocrinology 53:101–112.

Paladino, F. V., J. P. Schubauer, and K. T. Kowalski. 1980. The critical thermal maximum: a technique used to elucidate physiological stress and adaptation in fishes. Revue Canadienne de Biologie 39:115–122.

Passino, D. M. 1984. Biochemical indicators of stress in fishes. Pages 37–50 *in* V. W. Cairns, P. V. Hodson, and J. O. Nriagu, editors. Contaminant effects on fisheries. Wiley, Toronto.

Patiño, R., C. B. Schreck, and J. M. Redding. 1985. Clearance of plasma corticosteroids during smoltification of coho salmon, *Oncorhynchus kisutch*. Comparative Biochemistry and Physiology A, Comparative Physiology 82:531–535.

Payne, J. F. 1984. Mixed function oxygenases in biological monitoring programs: review of potential usage in different phyla of aquatic animals. Pages 625–655 *in* G. Persoone, E. Jaspers, and C. Claus, editors. Ecological testing for the marine environment, volume 1. State University of Ghent and Institute of Marine Science Research, Bredene, Belgium.

Pessah, E., P. G. Wells, and J. R. Schneider. 1976. Dodecyl sodium sulphate (DSS) as an intralaboratory reference toxicant in fish bioassays. Pages 93–121 *in* G. Craig, editor. Proceedings of the second aquatic toxicity workshop. Ontario Ministry of the Environment, Toronto.

Peters, G. 1979. Zur interpretation des begriffs "Stress" beim Fisch. Fisch und Tierschutz, Fisch und Umwelt, Heft 7. Fischer-Verlag, New York.

Peters, G., H. Delventhal, and H. Klinger. 1980. Physiological and morphological effects of social stress in the eel (*Anguilla anguilla* L.). Archiv fuer Fischereiwissenschaft 30:157–180.

Peters, G., H. Delventhal, and H. Klinger. 1981. Stress diagnosis for fish in intensive culture systems. Pages 239–248 *in* K. Tiews, editor. Aquaculture in heated effluents and recirculation systems, volume 2. H. Heenemann, Berlin.

Peters, G., and R. Schwarzer. 1985. Changes in hemopoietic tissue of rainbow trout under influence of stress. Diseases of Aquatic Organisms 1:1–10.

Pickering, A. D. 1981. Introduction: the concept of biological stress. Pages 1–9 *in* A. D. Pickering, editor. Stress and fish. Academic Press, London.

Pickering, A. D., and T. G. Pottinger. 1987. Poor water quality suppresses the cortisol response of salmonid fish to handling and confinement. Journal of Fish Biology 30:363–374.

Pickering, A. D., T. G. Pottinger, and J. Carragher, and J. P. Sumpter. 1987. The effects of acute and chronic stress on the levels of reproductive hormones in the plasma of mature male brown trout, *Salmo trutta* L. General and Comparative Endocrinology 68:249–259.

Pickering, A. D., T. G. Pottinger, and P. Christie. 1982. Recovery of the brown trout, *Salmo trutta* L., from acute handling stress: a time-course study. Journal of Fish Biology 20:229–244.

Pickford, G. E., A. K. Srivastava, A. Slicher, and P. K. T. Pang. 1971. The stress response in the abundance of circulating leucocytes in the killifish *Fundulus heteroclitus*. Journal of Experimental Zoology 177:89–118.

Priede, I. G. 1985. Metabolic scope in fishes. Pages 33–64 *in* P. Tytler and P. Calow, editors. Fish energetics: new perspectives. Johns Hopkins University Press, Baltimore, Maryland.

Priede, I. G., and P. Tytler. 1977. Heart rate as a measure of metabolic rate in teleost fishes: *Salmo gairdneri* Richardson, *Salmo trutta* L. and *Gadus morhua* L. Journal of Fish Biology 10:231–242.

Rand, G. M. 1985. Behavior. Pages 221–263 *in* G. M. Rand and S. R. Petrocelli, editors. Fundamentals of aquatic toxicology. Hemisphere, Washington D.C.

Redding, J. M., R. Patiño, and C. B. Schreck. 1984a. Clearance of corticosteroids in yearling coho salmon, *Oncorhynchus kisutch,* in fresh water and seawater and after stress. General and Comparative Endocrinology 54:433–443.

Redding, J. M., C. B. Schreck, E. K. Birks, and R. D. Ewing. 1984b. Cortisol and its effects on plasma thyroid hormone and electrolyte concentrations in fresh water and during seawater acclimation in yearling coho salmon, *Oncorhynchus kisutch*. General and Comparative Endocrinology 56:146–155.

Rehnberg, B. G., B. Jonasson, and C. B. Schreck. 1985. Olfactory sensitivity during parr and smolt developmental stages of coho salmon. Transactions of the American Fisheries Society 114:732–736.

Rehnberg, B. G., and C. B. Schreck. 1987. Chemosensory detection of predators by coho salmon *(Oncorhynchus kisutch):* behavioral reaction and the physiological stress response. Canadian Journal of Zoology 65:481–485.

Reinert, R. E., and D. Hohreiter. 1984. Adenylate energy charge as a measure of stress in fish. Pages 151–162 *in* V. W. Cairns, P. V. Hodson, and J. O. Nriagu, editors. Contaminant effects on fisheries. Wiley, Toronto.

Roberson, B. S. 1990. Bacterial agglutination. Pages 81–86 *in* J. S. Stolen, T. C. Fletcher, D. P. Anderson, B. S. Roberson, and W. B. van Muiswinkel, editors. Techniques in fish immunology. SOS Publications, Fair Haven, New Jersey.

Robinson, R. L. 1977. The automated analysis of catecholamines: an improved procedure for the simultaneous differential analysis of epinephrine and norepinephrine in tissues, blood and gland perfusates. Microchemical Journal 22:514–527.

Rogers, S. C., and A. H. Weatherley. 1983. The use of opercular muscle electromyograms as an indicator of the metabolic costs of fish activity in rainbow trout, *Salmo gairdneri* Richardson, as determined by radiotelemetry. Journal of Fish Biology 23:535–547.

Ryan, P. M., and H. H. Harvey. 1977. Growth of rock bass, *Ambloplites rupestris,* in relation to the morphoedaphic index as an indicator of an environmental stress. Journal of the Fisheries Research Board of Canada 34:2079–2088.

Sandercock, F. K., and E. T. Stone. 1982. A progress report on the effect of rearing density on subsequent survival of Capilano coho. Pages 82–90 *in* R. Neve and B. Melteff, editors. Proceedings of the North American aquaculture symposium. University of Alaska, Sea Grant Report 82-2, Fairbanks.

Saunders, R. L., E. B. Henderson, P. R. Harmon, C. E. Johnston, and J. G. Eales. 1983. Effects of low environmental pH on smolting of Atlantic salmon *(Salmo salar)*. Canadian Journal of Fisheries and Aquatic Sciences 40:1203–1211.

Schreck, C. B. 1981. Stress and compensation in teleostean fishes: response to social and physical factors. Pages 295–321 *in* A. D. Pickering, editor. Stress and fish. Academic Press, London.

Schreck, C. B. 1982. Stress and rearing of salmonids. Aquaculture 28:241–249.

Schreck, C. B., and P. Brouha. 1975. Dissolved oxygen depletion in static bioassay systems. Bulletin of Environmental Contamination and Toxicology 14:149–152.

Schreck, C. B., and H. W. Lorz. 1978. Stress response of coho salmon *(Oncorhynchus kisutch)* elicited by cadmium and copper and potential use of cortisol as an indicator of stress. Journal of the Fisheries Research Board of Canada 35:1124–1129.

Scott, D. B., and S. E. Rennie. 1980. Nuclear diameter as a criterion of adrenocortical activity in a teleost fish *Coregonus lavaretus* (L.). Journal of Fish Biology 17:83–90.

Selye, H. 1936. A syndrome produced by divers nocuous agents. Nature (London) 138:32.

Selye, H. 1950. Stress and the general adaptation syndrome. British Medical Journal 1950(1):1383–1392.

Selye, H. 1973. The evolution of the stress concept. American Scientist 61:692–699.

Shipley, R. A., and R. E. Clark. 1972. Tracer methods for in vivo kinetics, theory and applications. Academic Press, New York.

Sigismondi, L. A., and L. J. Weber. 1988. Changes in avoidance response time of juvenile chinook salmon exposed to multiple acute handling stresses. Transactions of the American Fisheries Society 117:196–201.

Silbergeld, E. K. 1975. Blood glucose: a sensitive indicator of environmental stress in fish. Bulletin of Environmental Contamination and Toxicology 11:20–25.

Sindermann, C. J. 1980. The use of pathological effects of pollutants in marine environmental monitoring programs. Rapports et Procès-Verbaux des Réunions, Conseil International pour l'Exploration de la Mer 179:129–134.

Sindermann, C. J. 1984. Disease in marine aquaculture. Helgoländer Meeresuntersuchungen 37:505–532.

Singley, J. A., and W. Chavin. 1975. The adrenocortical-hypophyseal response to saline stress in the goldfish, *Carassius auratus* L. Comparative Biochemistry and Physiology A, Comparative Physiology 51:749–756.

Sinnhuber, R. O., J. D. Hendrix, J. H. Wales, and G. B. Putnam. 1977. Neoplasms in rainbow trout, a sensitive animal model for environmental carcinogenesis. Annals of the New York Academy of Sciences 298:389–408.

Skadsen, J. M., P. W. Webb, and P. T. Kostecki. 1980. Measurement of sublethal metabolic stress in rainbow trout (*Salmo gairdneri*) using automated respirometry. Journal of Environment Science and Health. Part B. Pesticides, Food Contaminants and Agricultural Wastes 12:193–206.

Smith, A. C., and F. Ramos. 1976. Occult hemoglobin in fish skin mucus as an indicator of early stress. Journal of Fish Biology 9:537–541.

Smith, A. C., and F. Ramos. 1980. Automated chemical analyses in fish health assessment. Journal of Fish Biology 17:445–450.

Smith, H. D., and L. Margolis. 1970. Some effects of *Eubothrium salvelini* on sockeye salmon, *Oncorhynchus nerka,* in Babine Lake, British Columbia. Journal of Parasitology 56:321–322.

Smith, L. L., Jr., R. H. Kramer, and D. M. Oseid. 1966. Long-term effects of conifer–groundwood paper fiber on walleyes. Transactions of the American Fisheries Society 95:60–70.

Smith, L. S. 1982a. Decreased swimming performance as a necessary component of the smolt migration in salmonids of the Columbia River. Aquaculture 28:153–161.

Smith, L. S. 1982b. Introduction to fish physiology. T.F.H. Publications, Neptune City, New Jersey.

Smith, L. S., and T. W. Newcomb. 1970. A modified version of the Blazka respirometer and exercise chamber for large fish. Journal of the Fisheries Research Board of Canada 27:1321–1324.

Snieszko, S. F. 1974. The effects of environmental stress on outbreaks of infectious diseases of fishes. Journal of Fish Biology 6:197–208.

Soivio, A., and M. Nikinmaa. 1981. The swelling of erythrocytes in relation to the oxygen affinity of the blood of the rainbow trout, *Salmo gairdneri* Richardson. Pages 103–120 *in* A. D. Pickering, editor. Stress and fish. Academic Press, London.

Soivio, A., and A. Oikari. 1976. Haematological effects of stress on a teleost, *Esox lucius* L. Journal of Fish Biology 8:397–411.

Specker, J. L., and C. B. Schreck. 1980. Stress responses to transportation and fitness for marine survival in coho salmon *(Oncorhynchus kisutch)* smolts. Canadian Journal of Fisheries and Aquatic Sciences 37:765–769.

Spieler, R. E., and A. H. Meier. 1976. Short-term serum prolactin concentrations in goldfish *(Carassius auratus)* subjected to serial sampling and restraint. Journal of the Fisheries Research Board of Canada 33:183–186.

Spry, D. J., C. M. Wood, and P. V. Hodson. 1981. The effects of environmental acid on freshwater fish with particular reference to the softwater lakes in Ontario and the modifying effects of heavy metals: a literature review. Canadian Technical Report of Fisheries and Aquatic Sciences 999.

Srivastava, A. K., and U. Agrawal. 1977. Involvement of pituitary–interrenal axis and cholinergic mechanisms during the cold-shock leucocyte sequence in a fresh water tropical teleost, *Colisa fasciatus*. Archives d'Anatomie Microscopique et de Morphologie Experimentale 66:97–108.

Strange, R. J. 1980. Acclimation temperature influences cortisol and glucose concentrations in stressed channel catfish. Transactions of the American Fisheries Society 109:298–303.

Strange, R. J. 1983. Field examination of fish.Pages 337–347 in L. A. Nielsen and D. L. Johnson, editors. Fisheries techniques. American Fisheries Society, Bethesda, Maryland.

Strange, R. J., and C. B. Schreck. 1978. Anesthetic and handling stress on survival and cortisol concentration in yearling chinook salmon *(Oncorhynchus tshawytscha)*. Journal of the Fisheries Research Board of Canada 35:345–349.

Strange, R. J., C. B. Schreck, and R. D. Ewing. 1978. Cortisol concentrations in confined juvenile chinook salmon *(Oncorhynchus tshawytscha)*. Transactions of the American Fisheries Society 107:812–819.

Strange, R. J., C. B. Schreck, and J. T. Golden. 1977. Corticoid stress responses to handling and temperature in salmonids. Transactions of the American Fisheries Society 106:213–218.

Sumpter, J. P., A. D. Pickering, and T. G. Pottinger. 1985. Stress-induced elevations of plasma α-MSH and endorphin in brown trout, *Salmo trutta* L. General and Comparative Endocrinology 59:257–265.

Tait, J. F., and S. Burstein. 1964. *In vivo* studies of steroid dynamics in man. Pages 441–557 in G. Pinchus, K. V. Thimann, and E. B. Astwood. The hormones, volume 5. Academic Press, New York.

Thomas, P. 1988. Reproductive endocrine function in female Atlantic croaker exposed to pollutants. Marine Environmental Research 24:179–183.

Thomas, P. 1989. Effects or Aroclor 1254 and cadmium on reproductive endocrine function and ovarian growth in Atlantic croaker. Marine Environmental Research 28:499–503.

Tripp, R. A., A. G. Maule, C. B. Schreck, and S. L. Kaattari. 1987. Cortisol mediated suppression of salmonid lymphocyte responses *in vitro*. Developmental and Comparative Immunology 11:565–576.

Turner, J. D., C. M. Wood, and D. Clark. 1983. Lactate and proton dynamics in the rainbow trout *(Salmo gairdneri)*. Journal of Experimental Biology 104:247–268.

Umminger, B. L., and D. H. Gist. 1973. Effects of thermal acclimation on physiological responses to handling stress, cortisol, and aldosterone injections in the goldfish, *Carassius auratus*. Comparative Biochemistry and Physiology A, Comparative Physiology 44:967–977.

Vaughn, D. S., R. M. Yoshiyama, J. E. Breck, and D. L. DeAngelis. 1984. Modeling approaches for assessing the effects of stress on fish populations. Pages 259–278 in V. W. Cairns, P. V. Hodson, and J. O. Nriagu, editors. Contaminant effects on fisheries. Wiley, Toronto.

Vetter, R. D., and R. E. Hodson. 1982. Use of adenylate concentrations and adenylate energy charge as indicators of hypoxic stress in estuarine fish. Canadian Journal of Fisheries and Aquatic Sciences 39:535–541.

Vigers, G. A., and A. W. Maynard. 1977. The residual oxygen bioassay: a rapid procedure to predict effluent toxicity to rainbow trout. Water Research 11:343–346.

Waiwood, K. G., and F. W. H. Beamish. 1978. Effects of copper, pH and hardness on the critical swimming performance of rainbow trout (*Salmo gairdneri* Richardson). Water Research 12:611–619.

Wakeman, J. M., and D. E. Wohlschlag. 1979. Salinity stress and swimming performance of spotted seatrout. Proceedings of the Annual Conference Southeastern Association of Fish and Wildlife Agencies 31:357–361.

Wales, J. H., R. O., Sinnhuber, J. D. Hendricks, J. E. Nixon, and T. A. Eisele. 1978. Aflatoxin B_1 induction of hepatocellular carcinoma in the embryos of rainbow trout *(Salmo gairdneri)*. Journal of the National Cancer Institute 60:1133–1139.

Walters, G. R., and J. A. Plumb. 1980. Environmental stress and bacterial infection in channel catfish, *Ictalurus punctatus* Rafinesque. Journal of Fish Biology 17:177–185.

Watenpaugh, D. E., T. L. Beitinger, and D. W. Huey. 1985. Temperature tolerance of nitrite-exposed channel catfish. Transactions of the American Fisheries Society 114:274–278.

Webb, P. W., and J. R. Brett. 1973. Effects of sublethal concentrations of sodium pentachlorophenate on growth rate, food conversion efficiency, and swimming performance in underyearling sockeye salmon *(Oncorhynchus nerka)*. Journal of the Fisheries Research Board of Canada 30:499–507.

Wechsler, S. J. 1984. Fish health assessment: a preliminary report on the use of impression smears of skin mucus. Journal of Fish Biology 25:365–370.

Wedemeyer, G. 1970. Stress of anesthesia with M.S. 222 and benzocaine in rainbow trout *(Salmo gairdneri)*. Journal of the Fisheries Research Board of Canada 27:909–914.

Wedemeyer, G. 1973. Some physiological aspects of sublethal heat stress in the juvenile steelhead trout *(Salmo gairdneri)* and coho salmon *(Oncorhynchus kisutch)*. Journal of the Fisheries Research Board of Canada 30:831–834.

Wedemeyer, G. A., and C. P. Goodyear. 1984. Diseases caused by environmental stressors. Pages 424–434 *in* O. Kinne, editor. Diseases of marine animals, volume 4. Part 1: Pisces. Biologische Anstalt Helgoland, Hamburg, West Germany.

Wedemeyer, G. A., R. W. Gould, and W. T. Yasutake. 1983. Some potentials and limits of the leucocrit test as a stress and fish health assessment method. Journal of Fish Biology 23:711–716.

Wedemeyer, G. A., and D. J. McLeay. 1981. Methods for determining the tolerance of fishes to environmental stressors. Pages 247–268 *in* A. D. Pickering, editor. Stress and fish. Academic Press, London.

Wedemeyer, G. A., D. J. McLeay, and C. P. Goodyear. 1984. Assessing the tolerance of fish and fish populations to environmental stress: the problems and methods of monitoring. Pages 163–195 *in* V. W. Cairns, P. V. Hodson, and J. O. Nriagu, editors. Contaminant effects on fisheries. Wiley, Toronto.

Wedemeyer, G. A., F. P. Meyer, and L. Smith. 1976. Environmental stress and fish diseases. T.F.H. Publications, Neptune City, New Jersey.

Wedemeyer, G. A., A. N. Palmisano, and L. E. Salsbury. 1985. Development and evaluation of transport media to mitigate stress and improve juvenile salmon survival in Columbia River barging and trucking operations. Final Report (Contract DE-A179-82BP-35460) to Bonneville Power Administration, Portland, Oregon.

Wedemeyer, G. A., R. L. Saunders, and W. C. Clarke. 1980. Environmental factors affecting smoltification and early marine survival of anadromous salmonids. U.S. National Marine Fisheries Service Marine Fisheries Review 42(6):1–14.

Wedemeyer, G. A., and W. T. Yasutake. 1977. Clinical methods for the assessment of the effects of environmental stress on fish health. U.S. Fish and Wildlife Service Technical Paper 89.

Wells, R. M. G., V. Tetens, and A. L. Devries. 1984. Recovery from stress following capture and anaesthesia of Antarctic fish: haematology and blood chemistry. Journal of Fish Biology 25:567–576.

Wohlschlag, D. E., and J. N. Cameron. 1967. Assessment of a low level stress on the respiratory metabolism of the pinfish *(Lagodon rhomboides)*. Contributions in Marine Science 12:160–171.

Wood, C. M., and D. G. McDonald. 1982. Physiological mechanisms of acid toxicity to fish. Pages 197–226 *in* R. E. Johnson, editor. Acid rain/fisheries. American Fisheries Society, Northeastern Division, Bethesda, Maryland.

Wood, C. M., J. D. Turner, and M. S. Graham. 1983. Why do fish die after severe exercise? Journal of Fish Biology 22:189–201.

Yasutake, W. T., and J. H. Wales. 1983. Microscopic anatomy of salmonids: an atlas. U.S. Fish and Wildlife Service Resource Publication 150.

Zaugg, W. S., and L. R. McLain. 1972. Changes in gill adenosine triphosphatase activity associated with parr–smolt transformation in steelhead trout, coho, and spring chinook salmon. Journal of the Fisheries Research Board of Canada 29:167–171.

Chapter 15

Aquatic Toxicology

JOHN B. SPRAGUE

15.1 INTRODUCTION

This chapter is intended primarily as a user's guide for interpreting and applying results in aquatic toxicology. Much of the chapter is guidance for evaluating procedures used in tests. There are thousands of results from aquatic toxicity tests in the published literature, and not all of them are based on good procedures. A person who actually wished to do a toxicity test would need further details, and appropriate references are given in Section 15.3 and elsewhere.

This chapter emphasizes toxicological studies on fish. However, there now is considerable emphasis on testing invertebrates (which often are more sensitive to toxicants than fish, and more variable in response) and to some extent algae and other plants (Stephan et al. 1985) because communities and ecosystems must be protected from toxicants, not just a single group such as fish. Many of the items covered for fish also apply to other organisms, but some reference will be made to particularly advantageous tests with invertebrates. This chapter also emphasizes applied toxicology and whole-organism effects. Sections 15.5.6 to 15.5.8 assess some within-organism effects without attempting to cover the myriad of specific biochemical and other techniques. There are important goals for such research (Section 15.5.6), but available data indicate that concentrations of toxicant causing meaningful within-organism changes are no lower than, and are often much higher than, those that cause sublethal whole-organism effects. Often there is a question as to whether a biochemical change is a deleterious one or merely an adaptation within the usual range of the organism; the importance of the change can be ascertained only within the context of the whole organism.

15.1.1 Purposes and Principles of Aquatic Toxicity Tests

The major reason for carrying out toxicity tests with fish and other aquatic organisms is to determine which concentrations of a substance are harmful to the organisms and which have no apparent effect. From the results, a toxicologist can recommend maximum concentrations for the well-being of aquatic organisms, engineers can design treatment systems to achieve desired levels, and fisheries managers can evaluate chemical measurements in local bodies of water. All the data provided by toxicity tests may be assembled to derive *water quality criteria*, which should be scientifically sound numbers relating concentration to effect. The criteria may be used to create water quality *standards* or *objectives* (see terminology in the next section).

A second major use of toxicity tests is to monitor the toxicity of effluents or evaluate the quality of surface waters. These tests offer an alternative to monitoring chemicals and trying to interpret the measurements. Using fish to assess the quality of an effluent is an economical and meaningful procedure, especially if many waste substances are present or if it is not known exactly what is present. Such tests could involve monitoring a cage of fish placed in a river below an industrial outfall or periodic standardized toxicity tests of an effluent. The latter has been a successful tool in Canada for over a decade, simple toxicity tests being specified in regulations for various industries (e.g., oil refineries: EPS 1974). A regulation might state that "full-strength effluent should not kill 50% of a sample of rainbow trout in 4 days" under specified test conditions. Although such a test ignores subsequent dilution of an effluent in the receiving water, results are easily understood by anyone, and can be beneficial in bringing about initial improvements in waste treatment.

One fundamental characteristic of aquatic toxicology governs many of the procedures: effects are seldom analyzed in terms of the *dose* of toxicant inside the animal, as would be the case when a drug is tested by injection into a mouse. Most aquatic tests evaluate toxicant concentrations in the water, and so duration of exposure is inextricably related to concentration. A second basic procedural feature is that each group of animals is exposed to a constant concentration, whereas levels of the pollutant in the real world change with time and might fluctuate widely. The main reasons for use of constant concentrations in the laboratory are the availability of standard and efficient techniques for analyzing results, and the reasonable hope of using those results to predict the effects of varying toxicant levels in the outside world. Conversely, there are no agreed-upon techniques for analyzing results of tests based on fluctuating concentrations of toxicants, although this important topic is being examined in some laboratories.

A third precept in aquatic toxicology is basic in any scientific research: all conditions are held constant except the condition of interest, i.e., the concentration of toxicant. In laboratory toxicity tests, the ancillary conditions are intended to be favorable for the fish: high levels of dissolved oxygen, clean water of acceptable composition, no physical disturbances, etc. This principle of providing favorable background conditions governs most of the procedures discussed below. Much of the chapter deals with methods for high-quality research in the laboratory. Some of the procedural rules can be relaxed for monitoring tests because the guiding principle is to imitate the local situation of interest. For instance, water used to dilute a test effluent probably would be local water before it received the effluent, even if it already contained waste substances from upstream or had reduced levels of oxygen. The test species might be one of local importance rather than a standard laboratory species.

15.2   TERMINOLOGY

The following terms are standard in aquatic toxicology and are used as defined throughout this chapter.

Lethal   Causing death, or sufficient to cause death.
Sublethal   Concentration or level that would not cause death; effect that is not directly lethal.
Acute   Coming speedily to a crisis or end point; happening quickly. An acute effect could be sublethal. For fish, the term customarily is used for effects

that occur within 4–7 d. It can also refer to the duration of exposure (e.g., an acute test).

Chronic Long-lasting or continued. The term can refer to the effect or the duration of exposure. In mammalian toxicology, it usually signifies exposures lasting one-tenth of a lifetime or longer. In aquatic toxicology, it has sometimes been used to mean a full life cycle test.

Life cycle test With aquatic organisms, a test in which exposure generally starts with newly hatched stages and continues at least until they reproduce.

LC50 Median lethal concentration (=TLm of older literature): the concentration of a substance that is estimated to kill half of a group of organisms. The duration of exposure must be specified.

EC50 Median effective concentration: the concentration of a substance estimated to have an effect—lethal or nonlethal—on half of a group of organisms. The effect as well as the exposure time must be specified. (Note that this statistic must be calculated on the basis that 50% of the *individuals* showed the specified effect, and hence it should not be used for such things as a 50% reduction in growth of an algal population, or 50% reduction in photosynthetic activity. The term IC50—inhibition concentration—is currently being used for such reductions in activity or other biological attributes.)

LD50 Median lethal dose; refers to the amount of toxicant inside the organism, such as by injection.

Incipient lethal level (incipient LC50, threshold LC50, asymptotic LC50) Concentration of a substance just sufficient to cause 50% mortality during an acute exposure. Additional mortality among the test organisms must have ceased by the end of the exposure for use of the term to be valid. Such a threshold indicates that the average fish can just tolerate the toxicant concentration on a basis of acute lethality. This level estimates the *tolerance* of the species.

Tolerance Highest concentration of a substance in which the median test organism could live for an indefinite time (i.e., the highest concentration that does not cause an acute LC50).

NOEC No-observed-effect concentration: the highest concentration in a sublethal test that does not cause a statistically significant adverse effect in comparison to the controls.

LOEC Lowest-observed-effect concentration: the lowest concentration that causes a statistically significant adverse effect in a sublethal test.

MATC Maximum acceptable toxicant concentration: a presumed threshold concentration for effects on survival, growth, and reproduction. For convenience of having a single number, it is sometimes estimated as the geometric mean of the NOEC and the LOEC for the three listed effects. This term is unique to aquatic toxicology.

Application factor Known ratio or assumed ratio of the threshold of sublethal toxicity for a substance to the LC50 for the same substance. The application factor may be used to predict the unknown sublethal threshold of a second substance from its LC50.

ACR Acute:chronic ratio. The inverse of the application factor: LC50 divided by MATC or, for some species, acute EC50 divided by MATC.

Water quality criterion   Number that may be used for judgment. A broad
definition (Thurston et al. 1979) reads in part: ". . . descriptions of certain
maximum or minimum physical, chemical, and biological characteristics of
water which reflect the tolerances and requirements of the aquatic
biota . . ." In aquatic toxicology, water quality criterion is commonly
restricted to mean the highest concentration (or maximum or minimum
level of a characteristic such as pH) that (on the basis of scientific data) is
not expected to cause an appreciable effect on an aquatic system or its
users. A water quality criterion is not necessarily synonymous with the
NOEC. There may be other sets of criteria for the same substance (e.g., for
drinking water, industrial use, etc.).

Water quality standard   Maximum concentration of a pollutant, or a maximum or
minimum level of some other characteristic, that is not to be transgressed
for a designated use of a body of water. These numbers are promulgated by
a government or its agency by means of laws or regulations. They may or
may not adhere closely to water quality criteria. Again there may be
different standards for different uses of water.

Water quality objective   Similar to water quality standard except that it is merely
an expression of a desirable goal and does not have the same force as a
regulation. It carries no penalty for transgression.

15.3   SOURCES OF INFORMATION

Specific details of many test procedures are provided in "Standard Methods . . ." (APHA et al. 1989), the 17th edition of this old standby for water
chemistry contains extensive sections on biological methods, and it is particularly
thorough for invertebrates. Documents describing particular tests have been
prepared by committees of the American Society for Testing and Materials
(ASTM), by the U.S. Environmental Protection Agency (USEPA), and by
Environment Canada (EC). These documents give excellent advice about methods for short-term lethality tests with fish (USEPA 1975, 1985a; ASTM 1980a;
Peltier and Weber 1985; EC 1990a; 1990b), daphnid crustaceans (USEPA 1982;
ASTM 1984b; Biesinger et al. 1987; EC 1990c), and other freshwater and marine
invertebrates (USEPA 1985b, 1985c); for reproductive tests with saltwater and
freshwater crustaceans (ASTM 1988, 1989a; Weber et al. 1989); for larval tests
with mollusks and fish (ASTM 1980b; Weber et al. 1989); for sublethal tests with
algae (Weber et al. 1989); and for the culture of food organisms to support the test
animals (ASTM 1989b). Publications of the ASTM and the USEPA may be
purchased at the addresses shown in Section 15.7.1. Training videos also are
available (Norberg-King 1989b; Norberg-King and Denny 1989).

The references listed above were produced by national organizations in North
America. States and provinces also have promulgated standard methods, as have
several countries in Europe and elsewhere. Among international bodies, the
International Organization for Standardization and the Organization for Economic
Cooperation and Development have published some toxicity test methods (e.g.,
ISO 1982; OECD 1984) and are developing others.

Rand and Petrocelli (1985) edited a complete textbook on aquatic toxicology; its
coverage is both broad and detailed. Buikema et al. (1982) wrote a compact review

that is particularly informative about general concepts. Certain other useful reviews are mentioned in appropriate places below.

One of the best overviews of the toxicity of some 50 substances and water quality characteristics is Thurston et al. (1979). Another source is a series of water quality documents compiled by the U.S. Environmental Protection Agency on specific toxic substances (e.g., USEPA 1980; other documents in the series were listed in the *Federal Register* of November 28, 1980, page 79318). These are available for a fee from the National Technical Information Service (Section 15.7.1). These documents give extensive listings of chemical toxicities to North American aquatic species, and presumably will be updated periodically. Monographs from the National Research Council of Canada provide critical evaluations of the literature for many water pollutants (e.g., NRCC 1981), and a list may be obtained from the Council (Section 15.7.1). Another excellent source for a limited number of more classical pollutants is Alabaster and Lloyd (1980). To proceed further, one must use a library to find recent review articles through abstract journals or on-line searches, or perhaps track down an expert.

15.4 TESTS OF ACUTE LETHALITY

Tests of acute lethality are relatively short; the tests last about a week or less for fish, and effects usually occur within 4 d. Mortality is the end point, and accordingly these are quantal tests: each organism either lives or dies. Lethal tests are useful

- as an initial benchmark of a substance's toxicity when no information is available and for an initial screening of new chemicals;
- for comparisons such as whether one effluent is more toxic than another, or one species more tolerant than another;
- for initial explorations of complex topics such as the relation between chemical structure and toxicity (Section 15.5.8), after which key relationships may be checked with more meaningful but time-consuming sublethal tests; and
- as a tool for monitoring effluents (Section 15.1).

Such tests do not assess "safe" concentrations, and they are occasionally dismissed as outdated or unuseful for decisions on protecting aquatic ecosystems. Nevertheless, their place in aquatic toxicology remains secure. For example, Slooff et al. (1986) concluded from a comprehensive analysis of data that sublethal effects in chronic tests were predicted with quite reasonable accuracy by acute tests, and even multispecies ("ecosystem") tests did not provide results that were dramatically more advantageous than those of single-species acute tests. The largest variation resulted from interspecies differences, and Slooff et al. pointed out that this could be explored much more quickly and economically by acute tests (further discussed in Section 15.6.2).

15.4.1 End Points and General Procedures

The desired end point is an accurate estimate of the concentration of toxicant that would kill the "typical" organism in a group, the LC50. The median effect is used because it is most precise. The ends of the concentration–effect relationship have greater variability; for example, a low-exposure situation might happen to include a particularly sensitive individual. The concentration that would just fail to kill any organism cannot be estimated meaningfully because it would depend on sample size (one out of a million fish?).

For invertebrates it may be difficult to determine whether an animal is dead, so immobilization may be used as the criterion of effect. The median is then an "effective concentration," say a 48-h EC50 for immobilization, which is ecologically meaningful and should be accepted. There are good arguments for using such a criterion for fish (Stephan 1982). The data used in estimating an EC50 for immobilization normally include dead individuals, so the EC50 usually is somewhat lower in numerical value than an LC50.

In simplest terms, equipment and procedures for acute toxicity tests consist of

- a series of test chambers, each of which will run for the duration of the experiment at a fixed concentration, as part of a series;
- a group of similar fish in each chamber;
- periodic observations of mortality during an exposure of at least 4 d for fish (2 d for some invertebrates); and
- estimates of the LC50 at 4 d, at any longer period used, and desirably, at shorter observation times.

Concentrations used in tests are in a geometric series (i.e., differing by a constant multiplier), not an arithmetic series, because effects on the organisms are almost always related to proportional increase. Most people have an intuitive understanding of this; for example, an increase from 10 to 20 mg/L is a doubling of the concentration, whereas the same arithmetic change from 100 to 110 mg/L is only a 10% increase. A typical series in a toxicity test might use a dilution factor of 0.6 to give, for example, 13, 22, 36, 60, and 100 mg/L in addition to a control of zero. (This may also be called a logarithmic series because there is a constant difference between logarithms of the concentrations.) Analysis of results must accordingly be carried out in terms of the logarithm of concentration, either base e or base 10 as long as there is consistency. In computer programs for estimating LC50, the input of concentration is automatically transformed to logarithms. Following the same rationale, mean concentration should be estimated as a geometric mean, not an arithmetic average. Exceptions are temperature and pH, which is already logarithmic. Exposure times should similarly be considered on a geometric basis.

The simplest type of exposure is a *static* test, in which batches of effluent or toxicant are made up to the desired concentration and simply allowed to stand in the test chambers for the duration of the test. This method can violate the principle of constant concentration if the toxic substance tends to volatilize or be sorbed to the tank during the exposure. Still, the ease and simplicity of a static test can make it the method of choice for initial exploration, for large screening programs, for on-site testing, or for work with effluents that are difficult to handle. Tanks might be immersed in a constant-temperature bath. It should not be necessary to aerate the test solution if enough is used (Section 15.4.6), and it is undesirable to do so unless it is known that the toxicant will not be volatilized. A *renewal* test is a variation of the static test in which test solution is replaced, or mostly replaced, by fresh solution each day, or the organisms are transferred to fresh solutions. In general, this is not desirable in tests with fish because disturbance causes physiological upset that may affect results.

Flow-through tests are the most desirable for research because all conditions can be kept more or less constant during the exposure. The initial building of apparatus may occupy several weeks or months. A simple but undesirable system has a regulated flow of dilution water for each test chamber and a small pump that delivers toxic solution. The problem is that the dilution and toxicant streams can vary independently in delivery rate, which has considerable effect on concentration. Most tests use some type of *proportional diluter* to deliver the desired five or six concentrations and a control. The important characteristic of such devices is that they are relatively fail-safe in producing the desired concentrations. Delivery of aliquots of toxicant stock solution is tied to the rate of flow of dilution water by means of a periodic siphon. If the flow of dilution water changes or ceases, the delivery of toxicant changes proportionally. The ingenious design of these devices may be appreciated from the illustrations in McKim (1985) and Parrish (1985), who provided references on methods of construction.

A typical diluter has a series of adjacent small chambers, one for each concentration in the test, and the chambers fill sequentially from a reservoir containing stock solution of the toxicant. A complementary series of chambers is filled sequentially by a flow of dilution water. When the last of the dilution chambers is full, it discharges by means of an automatic siphon, usually about every 10 min. This periodic siphoning action is used to activate the siphons of all chambers, by making use of the suction from the venturi effect of the automatic siphon. Discharges from each pair of chambers (toxicant and dilution water) combine and flow to a test container containing organisms. The relative sizes of the paired chambers (or the depths to which they siphon) are adjusted to deliver the correct volumes of the two fluids for the desired series of test concentrations. Once all chambers are emptied, the filling process starts over again in preparation for the next cycle. Ahead of the diluter, there could be a reservoir to precondition dilution water for temperature and oxygen, and there might be a device for controlling flow. The stock solution may overflow from a final chamber in the diluter, and the excess is collected and pumped back to the reservoir. There are usually valves to shut off flows to the diluter during the period of siphoning. Diluters of this kind are now found in most aquatic toxicology laboratories, and are particularly beneficial for chronic tests; once adjusted, they give reliable delivery of concentrations week after week.

Any test, whether static, renewal, or flow-through, might also be a *recirculation* test, in which a loop of tubing from each test chamber goes through a pump to create a current in the tank. This is desirable if an effluent being tested has some component that tends to settle, or if aggression between fish can be reduced by making them swim against a current.

15.4.2   Estimating the LC50

Many procedures are available for estimating the LC50, but most give similar answers for any reasonable set of data, and there is no single right answer (Stephan 1977). The relationship of concentration to effect may be visualized as a plot such as Figure 15.1, which represents one of the common methods. Concentrations are on a logarithmic scale to eliminate skew. Percentage effect is also transformed and plotted in terms of a *probit* scale; it may be seen in Figure 15.1 that the middle percentages are compressed whereas extreme ones are more

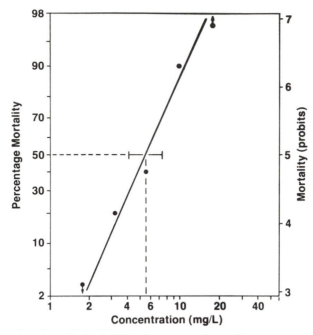

Figure 15.1   Estimation of the LC50 of a contaminant for any exposure time. In this hypothetical example, 10 fish were tested at each of five concentrations, and there was no mortality among the controls. The concentration expected to be lethal to half the tested fish can be read by following across from 50% mortality to the data line, then down to the concentration axis (broken lines). The concentration–mortality line could be fitted to the data by eye, but this one was fitted by probit analysis on a computer, which estimated the LC50 as 5.6 mg/L, the 95% confidence limits as 4.3 and 7.2 mg/L (end points on the solid horizontal line), the slope of the data line as 4.42 (in probits and log concentration), and chi-square as 0.87. Although probits are shown on the right axis, data normally would be plotted as mortality percentages on commercially available logarithmic-probability paper.

protracted. Because the percentage scale never reaches 0% or 100%, observed values of those magnitudes are customarily plotted at about 2 and 98% with arrows indicating an uncertain true position. The objective of the transformations is to obtain a straight line from what is really a cumulated log-normal curve (Buikema et al. 1982; Rand and Petrocelli 1985). In practice, it is convenient to purchase "logarithmic-probability" graph paper and simply plot the arithmetic values.

Some explanation of the log-probit transformations may be in order. If results of a lethal test were plotted on arithmetic paper, they would almost always be in the form of a sigmoid or "S" curve, skewed to the right. Plotting logarithms of concentration usually eliminates the skew. Probits are based on the usual distribution of frequencies in a normal curve: ±1 SD about the mean value includes about 68% of the observations; ±2 SD includes 95% of the observations; etc. If a cumulated normal curve is drawn (sigmoid), the theoretical relationship between cumulated percentages and standard deviations is still known. If the appropriate percentages on the vertical axis are relabeled in terms of standard deviations, and that scale of standard deviations is given regular or uniform spacing, the percentage scale becomes irregular, but the line is straightened. All that remains to be done is to add 5.0 to the standard deviations, and obtain a scale of "probits," as in Figure 15.1. It is possible to look up the probit for any particular percentage (Finney 1971; Hubert 1984), but more convenient to use log-probability paper.

Results should always be plotted as in Figure 15.1 and a line fitted by eye to check for reasonableness of the LC50 estimated by a mathematical procedure, no matter how sophisticated it is. Indeed the plot might reveal an irregular pattern of effects that should not be forced into a standard mathematical analysis. Figures showing probit lines are seldom published because of space and cost limitations, and it is usually difficult to ascertain whether an investigator has actually plotted data to check its form. If such graphs are mentioned in a report or paper, it is a sign that the analysis has been more than a mechanical one.

With some practice, eye-fitted lines will estimate the LC50 within a few percent of estimates from more formal procedures, so there is no reason to down-grade such graphical estimates. Mention of an estimate by "interpolation" should, however, arouse some doubts because this was an old method that merely used a straight line connecting the two points nearest to 50% mortality, one above and one below. All the points in the distribution should be used to fit the line, even though the value or "weight" of points decreases as they become more distant from 50% effect. (Values of 10% and 90% have about half the weight of those in the 40–60% range, and weight again drops by one-half for values of 3 and 97%.) Despite their low weight, one 0% and one 100% effect should be plotted if available, because they sometimes help to orient a line with scanty data. Once the line is fitted, it is a simple matter to note the intercept with 50% effect and then to read the LC50 on the concentration axis, as in Figure 15.1.

The 95% confidence limits of the LC50 should always be reported, and the slope of the fitted line and the chi-square estimate of goodness of fit are also desirable. Even these may be obtained from an eye-fitted line by the "short-cut" method of Litchfield and Wilcoxon (1949). That technique was frequently used into the 1960s, before the time of easy access to computers, and gave reasonable results that can be accepted.

An obvious mathematical method of fitting a line to data such as that in Figure 15.1 might seem to be a standard regression, but that procedure is not valid. The reason is the decline in value or weight of the points as variation increases towards the upper and lower ends of the line. Naive authors still attempt to use simple regression and sometimes manage to get such analyses published. It is not even possible to properly weight the points in a simple regression, because weights should be derived from the fitted line, not the observed effects.

The eye-fitted line described above is a form of *probit analysis*. The classical mathematical method of estimating the LC50 by probit analysis (Finney 1971; Hubert 1984) uses weighting to fit a line by maximum-likelihood techniques or iteration (successive approximations to the best line). Numbers of animals at each concentration are also used in the weighting process. This is considered the "most efficient" technique for good distributions of data that are lognormal (Gelber et al. 1985). Programs are widely available on mainframe computers at institutions and for personal computers. Among the latter, PROBIT2 is available from J. J. Hubert, Department of Mathematics and Statistics, University of Guelph, Guelph, Ontario N1G 2W1. The TOXDAT program for personal computers, described in Peltier and Weber (1985), calculates the LC50 by the probit method and also by binomial and moving-average methods. The availability of this program may be ascertained from its designer, C. E. Stephan, U.S. Environmental Protection Agency, 6201 Congdon Boulevard, Duluth, Minnesota 55804.

The trimmed Spearman–Kärber method is another widely used means to estimate the LC50. This method handles most sets of data as long as one concentration causes less than 50% mortality and a higher concentration causes more than 50% mortality (Hamilton et al. 1977). It provides estimates for unusual results such as zero mortality at one concentration and a complete or nearly complete mortality at the next highest concentration. Formal (mathematical) probit analysis cannot be used on such data because it requires partial mortalities of organisms at two different concentrations. Essentially, the Spearman–Kärber method does an arithmetic smoothing of percentage effects and interpolates to the LC50 by relatively simple calculations. A program for IBM personal computers is available (D. Disney, ADP Section, U.S. Environmental Protection Agency, College Station Road, Athens, Georgia 30613; a non-system-formatted, DS/DD diskette should be sent).

There are additional, less widely used methods for estimating the LC50 such as the logit method (Berkson 1953) and others discussed by Stephan (1977), Hubert (1984), APHA et al. (1989), and Gelber et al. (1985).

The estimate of a particular LC50 is quite precise because all of the above methods will give similar values. However, *estimates of LC50 differ considerably from time to time and place to place* for the same species and similar methods! In any compilation of data for a toxicant, one should expect to find a 5- or 10-fold range in estimates of LC50 from different laboratories for the same species (e.g., USEPA 1980; Buikema et al. 1982; Sprague 1985). Sometimes part of this variation can be explained by conditions such as pH of the dilution water or nutritional status of the fish. These modifying factors should be taken into account when results are used, and future research will no doubt improve our ability to allow for them. Sometimes procedural items may contribute—for example, insufficient test volume or erroneous chemical measurements of the toxicant—and those influences can be reduced or eliminated. Nevertheless, large portions of the variation may have no obvious explanation at present, and therefore the numerical values of LC50s cannot be interpreted too closely. If there is a list of LC50s for a species exposed under similar conditions, it would be quite unreasonable to pick the lowest value and use it as an estimate of toxicity. It might be an unusual outlier to the same extent as the highest value in the list. A geometric mean value for the species would usually be a better estimate, and such averaging is now standard in derivations of water quality criteria (Stephan et al. 1985). The variation in aquatic toxicity tests cannot be considered dissimilar to those for other kinds of toxicology. For example, Henig (1979) mentioned a sevenfold variation in results of drug testing, depending on how the subject rats were housed.

15.4.3 Confidence Limits, Differences, and Controls

Confidence limits from an individual toxicity test must not be mistaken for any sort of overall range for the LC50 of a substance. They are only internal estimates of variation for a particular test with a given group of fish under the conditions at that time. One should be prepared to encounter wide confidence limits occasionally. Hodson et al. (1977) estimated that a typical toxicity test with 10 fish per concentration and three concentrations causing partial mortalities would have an upper confidence limit that was almost 2.1 times the value of the LC50. For example, an LC50 of 10 mg/L would have lower and upper limits of 4.8 and 21 mg/L, asymmetric on an arithmetic scale but logarithmically symmetrical. The span of the limits could be cut in half by use of 30 fish per test chamber, and statisticians urge such greater numbers to increase precision. However, if 30 fish were to be used it would be preferable to divide them into replicates for a better assessment of variation.

The factor of 2.1 times the LC50 estimated for confidence limits by Hodson et al. (1979) seems unduly large. The upper confidence limit shown in Figure 15.1 is about 1.3 times the LC50; this represents good precision in an aquatic toxicity test and is commonly achieved in real tests. A ratio of 1.5 would be reasonable and represents an average from tests of many materials in my laboratory, usually with 10 fish per concentration. Even ratios in the vicinity of 1.8 would indicate acceptable precision for most purposes. The span of confidence limits is governed not only by the scatter of points about the line that relates effect to concentration (Figure 15.1) but also by the slope of that line. If the toxicant affected individual fish at quite different concentrations, the probit line would have a low slope, which would contribute to wide confidence limits. That happens with some toxicants, and does not necessarily indicate a procedural flaw such as incomplete acclimation of fish to the dilution water (Calamari et al. 1980). The customary use of 10 fish at each of five test concentrations usually yields results that are satisfactory in acute tests. Douglas et al. (1986) showed that the total number of test organisms could be reduced by 40%—to seven animals at each of four concentrations—with little loss in precision.

Significant difference between two LC50s may be estimated from confidence limits. If the limits do not overlap, the LC50s are of course different. Even with overlap, there would be a significant difference if the ratio (greater LC50) ÷ (lesser LC50) exceeded the statistic $f_{1,2}$. The value f_1 is simply the ratio (upper confidence limit) ÷ (LC50) for substance 1, f_2 is the same value for substance 2, and

$$f_{1,2} = \text{antilog } \sqrt{(\log f_1)^2 + (\log f_2)^2}. \qquad (15.1)$$

The method is derived from a recognized mathematical technique, standard error of the difference (Finney 1971, page 110; Zar 1974, page 105). The method is also a standard one in pharmacology; it was outlined by Litchfield and Wilcoxon (1949) but questioned by Hodson et al. (1977). If replicate LC50s were available, testing by conventional analysis of variance would be valid, but such replicates are seldom seen.

The primary use of formula (15.1) should probably be to detect which LC50s are *not* different, thus avoiding overinterpretation of variation that has not been shown to be real. Also, the variation in results from different laboratories or different times might lead to statistically significant differences, but the biological meaning of the difference might be in the realm of unexplained variation, and should be considered in that light. There does not seem to be a test available that uses confidence limits to simultaneously assess differences among several LC50s. Repeated tests with formula (15.1), between all possible pairs in a list of LC50s, can be expected to show a significant difference once in 20 comparisons because

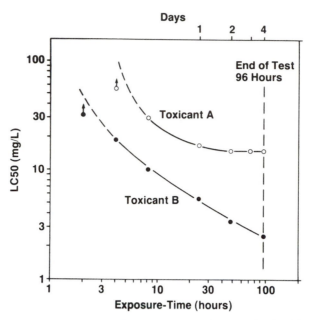

Figure 15.2 Toxicity curves for two hypothetical toxicants, obtained by fitting lines by eye to the LC50s associated with all the exposure times tested. Toxicant A apparently reached an incipient LC50 (i.e., acute mortality had ended) because the curve became asymptotic to the time axis after about 2 d. The incipient LC50 for A appears to be about 15 mg/L, but its actual value would be determined as in Figure 15.1 from data obtained at 96 h. Toxicant B did not reach an asymptotic LC50, and it would have been desirable to prolong the test to learn if one could be achieved. This shows the value of plotting a toxicity curve as an experiment proceeds. The axes of toxicity curves sometimes are reversed from those shown because the original and perhaps more revealing approach to fish lethality was to estimate the time to 50% mortality for each toxicant concentration.

of chance (if the statistical decision threshold is $P = 0.05$), as in repeated use of a t-test in situations when an analysis of variance would be the appropriate test.

Any mortality of control fish in acute tests should first be taken as an indication that something was wrong with the fish or the test conditions. An occasional 10% mortality may occur without invalidating tests and it is probably best not to apply a correction. However, some invertebrates are difficult to hold in the laboratory and there may be 20 or 30% mortality of controls. This casts considerable doubt on the accuracy of the LC50 or EC50 because there probably was interaction between the action of the toxicant and whatever factors caused the background mortality. Observations may be corrected for control mortality by Abbott's formula (Tattersfield and Morris 1924; APHA et al. 1989). I do not recommend that formula highly because it does not account for interactions due to stress, but it is the only statistically valid method of correction available.

15.4.4 Toxicity Curves and Incipient Lethal Levels

Periodic recording of mortalities during a test increases the information that the test provides. Approximate graphic estimates of LC50s can be made as the experiment proceeds, say at 4, 8, 24, 48, and 96 h of exposure, and these can be plotted as a toxicity curve (Figure 15.2). It may become evident that the curve has become asymptotic to the time axis, meaning that acute lethality has ceased (toxicant A in Figure 15.2). It is of considerable interest to know whether there is some concentration with which an average fish can cope during an acute exposure, perhaps by detoxifying or excreting the toxicant as quickly as it is taken in. The remaining fish would survive the acute exposure. There is no particular rule for determining whether such an incipient LC50 has been achieved, so the toxicity curve should be interpreted subjectively.

The investigator should take particular note if a curve develops that is similar to that for toxicant B in Figure 15.2. Even lower concentrations would apparently kill the fish with longer exposure because no incipient LC50 has been determined. The test might have to be prolonged to see whether an asymptote can eventually be attained. Some substances (e.g., chlorine) continue to cause mortality at lower and lower concentrations with longer exposure, and it is important to know of such a situation.

The incipient LC50 is estimated (by the probit, Spearman–Kärber, or another method) for an exposure time at which the toxicity curve parallels the time axis. The value of this asymptotic LC50 depends on the fish, and is thus quite meaningful for assessing acute toxicity. For most toxicants, the standard 96-h exposure of fish produces an incipient LC50 (Sprague 1969). If it does, this should be reported. If it does not, the investigator should report the 96-h LC50 as a standard value for comparison with other tests and either give the incipient LC50 as an additional meaningful number or note the absence of an observed asymptote in the toxicity curve. Most investigators do not publish toxicity curves or state whether an incipient LC50 was obtained; those who do show evidence of perceptive interpretation. Analysis of toxicity curves should not be made too formal, however. Proposals for fitting specific kinds of curves to predict effects during extended exposures are largely untested on broad sets of data; additional work to explore the proposals might be more usefully expended in other directions, such as testing additional species (Stephan 1982).

To summarize the advice offered so far, a well-conducted lethality test should allow the investigator to report

- acceptably low control mortality;
- an estimate of the LC50 or EC50 by an accepted method;
- a statement of confidence limits;
- a statement of the slope (with units) for the concentration–effect line, if the line was fitted by probit analysis, and the goodness of fit of the line; and
- a demonstration or statement of whether or not an incipient LC50 was achieved in the test.

15.4.5 Test Organisms

Reports on toxicity tests should clearly indicate the species and size of test organisms used. Two freshwater fish that are currently in wide use for tests of acute lethality in North America are the rainbow trout, which is somewhat of an international standard coolwater species, and the fathead minnow. Fathead minnows have gained prominence because they are good for life cycle tests (Section 15.5.1); they breed readily in aquaria and mature in about 6 months. There is less standardization among marine fish, but the sheepshead minnow is becoming the saltwater equivalent of the fathead minnow because it also breeds in the laboratory, and a life cycle test is possible in 5 or 6 months. The small size of the two minnow species is a distinct convenience for laboratory use.

Among invertebrates, the same characteristic of easy breeding in the laboratory is leading to frequent use of the freshwater cladocerans *Daphnia magna, D. pulex,* and *Ceriodaphnia dubia,* the marine mysid *Mysidopsis bahia,* and the marine daggerblade grass shrimp *Palaemonetes pugio.* Many other species have been used, especially among marine invertebrates such as annelid worms and the larval stages of bivalve molluscs and sea urchins. The ASTM (1980a) recommended only some commonly used species, but even that list includes 30 freshwater and 36 marine species.

For research purposes, an advantage of standardizing on a few species is fewer questions about interspecific variation when values are compared from the literature. A possible disadvantage is accidental escapement of a test species in a region where the species is not native (e.g., the fathead minnow is not native west of the Rocky Mountains). For evaluating a local problem, a sensitive species of regional prominence might be better than a standard species.

For many toxicants, especially those with generalized modes of action, tolerances often vary only within 5- or 10-fold among species of fish (reviewed by Sprague 1985). This is about the same as within- and between-lab differences for a single species (Section 15.4.2). Thurston et al. (1985) tested 10 organic chemicals, having at least four modes of action, on six species of fish. Nine of the chemicals had low ratios of 1.5 to 4.6 between the LC50s of the most tolerant and most sensitive species. For the tenth chemical (the insecticide permethrin) goldfish were 77 times more tolerant than the most sensitive species. There was no strong evidence of a "most sensitive" or "most tolerant" species. Goldfish were most tolerant in three of the 10 comparisons, mosquitofish and bluegill in two cases each, catfish and rainbow trout in one case each, and fathead minnows in none of the comparisons. There are, however, up to 900-fold differences in tolerance of organophosphate insecticides by fish (Pickering et al. 1962).

There is abundant evidence that invertebrates, algae, and other organisms show much greater variation in sensitivity than do fish (Klapow and Lewis 1979; Thurston et al. 1985; Slooff et al. 1986). Stephan (1982) compared acute toxicity results for 21 chemicals; 8–45 diverse organisms were tested for each in fresh or salt water or both. Altogether, he obtained 38 ratios of highest:lowest LC50s; 13 were greater than 1,000 and 15 more were greater than 100.

Adequate assessment of a chemical's toxicity should, therefore, include tests of a variety of organisms, rather than just different species of fish. The principle is recognized in recommendations for deriving water quality criteria (Stephan et al. 1985). From a massive comparison of data, Slooff et al. (1983) suggested that researchers screening chemicals for toxicity should use not only the often-suggested fish, daphnid, and green alga species, but also the bacterium *Microcystis aeruginosa.*

Test organisms must be in good condition, so holding conditions in the laboratory are important and should be described in ensuing research reports. The APHA et al. (1989) stated that mortality of more than 10% in a stock of laboratory fish means that the stock should be discarded. Fish must be acclimated to the water and all conditions that will be used in the test. Favorable holding conditions described in Chapter 20 should be used to evaluate procedures used in toxicological work.

The quality of a test should not be judged by the number of fish used. An inadequate number can be assessed from the width of confidence limits about the LC50 and the slope of the probit line (Section 15.4.3). Most toxicity tests involve the recommended minimum of 10 fish per concentration because of the very practical problems of supplying enough water or heating it. What must not be done is to increase the number of fish by lowering the ratio of test-solution volume to biomass (see next section); results might be precise but wrong. The obvious remedy is to use small fish (such as month-old minnows) and this is a recent trend.

15.4.6 Water

The overriding consideration about a test solution is that there must be enough of it. If there is too little for either static or flow-through tests the toxicant may decrease in concentration because a notable fraction of it is taken up by the fish, sorbed onto the chamber walls, or perhaps volatilized; further, waste products may accumulate, and dissolved oxygen may be depleted by fish respiration. All these shortcomings can affect the test results. The primary rule may be framed as volume of test solution per gram of fish per day. Various people, including me, have recommended at least 2 L/(g·d), on the premise that quantities of solution that satisfy respiratory demands also solve the other problems (Sprague 1969). That amount of solution would mean an oxygen depletion in the vicinity of 1–1.5 mg/L by juvenile fish of a few grams' weight, if there is no aeration of the water. (The depletion rate varies somewhat with feeding rate and other factors.) Some evidence supports this suggested requirement. Survival times of fish in pulp mill waste started to change if the test volume fell below 2.5 L/(g·d), and major changes occurred at less than 1 L/(g·d), in a study by Davis and Mason (1973). In other studies, however, 1 L/(g·d) has been satisfactory. For flow-through tests of acute lethality, ASTM (1980a) recommended 2 L/(g·d) at warmer temperatures and half of that for cooler temperatures, and APHA et al. (1989) appear to have recommended 2.4 L/(g·d) for warm tests and 1.2 for cool tests. Both organizations require less test solution for static tests, for reasons that are not clear.

The amount of test solution is one of the frequently neglected aspects of procedure in aquatic toxicology. The problem is worst in static tests in which toxicant concentrations are not measured after the solution is put in the test chamber. Investigators may put overly large fish into a normal-sized chamber of fluid and leave them for 4 d, apparently ignoring the likelihood of toxicant depletion and erroneous estimation of LC50. For example, if there were 10 fish per chamber, each fish weighing 10 g, the 2-L/(g·d) criterion would demand 800 L for a 4-d test and a chamber with the capacity of five oil barrels. Such a volume should not be dismissed as impractical; to use less runs the risk of a substandard test. Alternatives would be to use smaller fish or fewer fish per concentration, to divide the fish among several chambers, or, if necessary, to renew the solution.

In flow-through tests, a second consideration about test solutions is the desired turnover time of water in a chamber. That factor and the previously calculated inflow per day determine how much fluid is in the chamber at any time. The ASTM (1980a) recommended 5 or 10 tank volumes per day, and APHA et al. (1989) recommended at least 6 per day (i.e., the amount of water in the chamber should be set at one-fifth or one-sixth the required daily flow). That might lead to some very small chambers and crowding. A 95% molecular replacement of solution in the test chamber every 24 h seems satisfactory for nonvolatile toxicants, and would require the chamber volume to be set at one-third of the daily flow (there is a factor of about three between a flow of one tank volume and 95% molecular exchange: Sprague 1969). Volume in the chamber should not be greater than that, because replacement would not be fast enough to maintain steady conditions. For static tests, turnover time is not a consideration. In renewal tests, it is customary to replace all or most of the test solution each day.

In research tests, the water used for holding organisms and for dilution of toxicant should be clean, free of extraneous toxic substances, and suitable for the species. Uncontaminated groundwater is best. Surface water may contain organic matter, which binds and detoxifies the substance being tested. The worst choice is usually a municipal water supply because it is difficult to eliminate the last trace of chlorine, which is toxic to fish and to crustaceans. Carbon filters seldom remove all chlorine, and ASTM (1980a) suggested treatment with sodium bisulfite if such water must be used. Seawater should be drawn from an uncontaminated location. Reconstituted water is good for either freshwater or marine tests, and standard formulae were given by ASTM (1980a) and APHA et al. (1989).

Characteristics of water must be measured and reported. For fresh water, these must include at least calcium and magnesium or total hardness, alkalinity, conductivity, pH, and a measure of organic matter such as total organic carbon. Minimum seawater data include salinity, pH, and carbon. There also must be clear statements of average temperature, dissolved oxygen, and pH (and their variations) in holding and test tanks.

In summary, supporting information that should be given in reports of toxicity tests includes

- species and size of test organisms;
- a description of satisfactory holding conditions in the laboratory (Chapter 20), including details of diet;
- a statement of low mortality during holding;
- reassurance that the supply of test solution equaled at least 1.0 L per gram of fish per day in static, renewal, or flow-through tests, and preferably 2 $L/(g \cdot d)$;
- notice that the volume of solution in flow-through chambers was no greater than one-third of the daily flow; and
- clear statements about the source of dilution water, the absence of contaminants, and key physicochemical characteristics and their variation during holding and testing.

15.4.7 Chemical Measurements of the Toxicant

For a high-quality test, there should be enough measurements of the toxicant in test chambers to determine what concentrations the fish are actually exposed to and the degree to which the concentration varies. The frequency of measurement depends somewhat on stability of the toxicant and type of test and must be adequate for each test. At least, there should be a measurement in each chamber near the beginning of the exposure and near the end. Static tests in particular deserve careful measurements. If test volumes are low or the toxicant tends to degrade, concentrations at the end of the test can be as little as 40% of initial values. The meaning of such a test would be in doubt. Fluctuations during flow-through tests should be kept within ±20% of the mean. The minimum monitoring of flow-through tests is daily sampling of one chamber, usually the one with the concentration presumed to be nearest to the LC50.

The geometric mean of measured concentrations should be adopted as the measure of exposure and used in calculations. Individual measurements should be weighted for time if sampling was irregular. It is misleading to report an LC50 in terms of nominal concentrations (which the investigator thought were being added) if actual concentrations were, say, 70–80% of nominal values. Papers are still published with statements that concentrations were measured on such-and-such a schedule, but with calculations and conclusions based on the nominal values.

Sometimes it is not possible or necessary to measure the toxicant. Perhaps there is no suitable chemical procedure, or the toxicant is not known, or the test is intended solely to monitor an effluent. Such studies should clearly state that results are based on nominal concentrations.

General water quality must also be measured (Section 15.4.6). Suitable chemical procedures are given in the references cited in Section 15.3.

To summarize, investigators should report

- convincing measurements of the actual concentrations of toxicant in the exposure tanks;
- satisfactory limits for fluctuation and for decline of the toxicant during the test; and
- estimates of LC50s explicitly based on time-weighted geometric means of measured concentrations.

15.4.8   Variables that Modify Toxicity

Some modifying conditions have major effects on the toxicity of a substance, whereas others have much more modest effects than might be expected. Generalizations are made here; corroborating details and references were reviewed by Sprague (1985). Most of the information is on modification of LC50s or EC50s; it is presumed with some evidence that changes in chronic or sublethal effects parallel the acute changes.

Species differences were discussed in Section 15.4.5. In general, most fishes are affected similarly by most toxicants, although a few show much greater tolerance than others of particular classes of toxicants. Larger differences occur among invertebrates and other taxonomic groups, but it is not possible to specify the sensitive and tolerant groups because relative tolerance varies with the substance. For example, tubificid worms are extremely tolerant of sewage pollution with its low oxygen and high ammonia concentrations, but they are quite sensitive to metals. Many crustaceans are sensitive to a wide range of pollutants, but adult crayfish and lobsters are remarkably tolerant of acute exposures to some pollutants.

Life stage has a profound effect on the vulnerability of fishes to toxicants, and simple mortality of newly hatched individuals is among the most sensitive effects in life cycle tests (Section 15.5.1). Invertebrates usually are particularly sensitive when molting. Related to life stage is the *size* of an individual. Intuitively, it might be expected that tolerance would increase in larger fish, which have lower weight-specific metabolic rates than smaller fish. A two- or threefold increase in tolerance as fish grow from 1 g to 10 g has been found in some cases. In other investigations, however, there has been no apparent size effect, or there was an effect for one species but not for another with the same toxicant. The size effect on acute lethality among juvenile fish is largely an academic question, because protection should be based on the most sensitive of sublethal effects. Acute tests on juveniles are for initial exploration or comparison, and the usual practice of using fish of a gram or a few grams will minimize any size effect. Fish within any one test should be similar in size; the weight of the largest fish should not be more than 1.5 times that of the smallest.

I emphasized the *health* of fish as an important factor in acute tests (in Section 15.4.5), but that was more an article of faith than a documented consideration. Surprisingly, the few investigations comparing healthy organisms with parasitized or diseased ones have shown little or no difference in toxicant tolerance. *Nutritional status* has received little attention but appears to be important, and may account for much of the "unexplained" variation typical of many toxicity tests. In general, high-protein diets result in more tolerant fish, and the diet-related difference may be sixfold in tests with pesticides.

Acclimation of fish to a toxicant can affect tolerance, and sometimes increases the LC50 by two- or threefold. This factor may be built into some tests of acute lethality, because acclimation can occur in 5 d or less (Bradley et al. 1985). Acclimation can also be a normal component of life cycle tests, as shown by transfers of spawning and recently hatched fish between concentrations (Hutchinson and Sprague 1986). The influence on results seems to be a desirable imitation of the real world for cases of relatively steady pollution, although not for situations with pulses of pollution. The acclimation effect is appreciable, but not great compared to other sources of variation.

Temperature is one abiotic factor that might be expected to have major influences on toxicity of a substance to fish and other poikilotherms. From considerable research, the main conclusions appear to be (a) that temperature effects have no overall pattern and may run one way or the other or be absent; and (b) that the effects are not large, often twofold or less among test temperatures, as long as organisms are acclimated to the temperature they are tested at. Some perceptive sublethal research on invertebrates indicates little effect of temperature on sensitivity within the biokinetic range of the organisms. Temperature sometimes has a major chemical effect on toxicants, however; for example, a change from 0 to 30°C can increase the proportion of toxic un-ionized ammonia by a factor of 9.

Dissolved oxygen also has a modest effect on toxicity. Most investigations have shown increased lethality of a substance as oxygen declines below saturation, but only by factors of 1.5–2, even for dissolved oxygen as low as 30% of saturation. There is not yet a comprehensive picture for oxygen effects on sublethal toxicity, but some research indicates modifying effects as small as those at the lethal level.

Hydrogen-ion concentration has profound chemical influence on toxicants that ionize. For some substances, the un-ionized form accounts for most of the toxicity because it diffuses more easily across gill membranes. A well-known example is ammonia. The un-ionized form (NH_3) is only a fraction of 1% of total ammonia at pH 7 but makes up 35–45% of the total at pH 9, for higher temperatures. The relationship is chemically quite predictable and accounts for much of the variability in ammonia toxicity (Russo 1985). Hydrogen sulfide also shows a relationship to pH, except that the un-ionized form prevails at low pH and low temperature. For metals, the ionized form is usually the more toxic one. For example, total zinc at pH 9 has only one-thirtieth of its toxicity at pH 7 in soft water (Bradley and Sprague 1985b), because, at high pH, zinc and many other metals form a variety of carbonate and hydroxide complexes that have little or no toxicity (reviewed by Campbell and Stokes 1985). Changes in metal toxicity with pH are interwoven with modifying effects of water hardness (see below). For other categories of toxic substances, the effect of pH may be large, small, or absent, but it remains one of the major abiotic factors modifying toxicity.

Hardness of fresh water refers to the concentration of calcium and magnesium. In general, hardness, alkalinity (concentrations of carbonates and some other anions), and pH increase or decrease together. The majority of pollutants do not change their toxicity greatly between soft and hard waters. The notable exceptions are metals, most of which become much less toxic in hard water. Part of the effect is due to higher pH in hard water, but water hardness per se may have an order-of-magnitude effect, apparently because gills take up less metal from hard water (e.g., zinc: Bradley and Sprague 1985a, 1985b). Empirical relations of total metal toxicity to water hardness are useful for application to field situations, and the changes in sublethal toxicity apparently parallel those in lethality.

Salinity is an overwhelming factor in water composition but has surprisingly little influence on tolerance of toxicants. Marine and freshwater organisms are about equally tolerant when both are tested in their own waters (Klapow and Lewis 1979). Salinity has effects in special situations. Euryhaline species are usually most tolerant of a toxicant at their isotonic point (about one-third seawater for most fish), presumably because osmotic problems are lessened and the animal is physiologically more effective. Marine animals usually become more sensitive to pollutants at low salinities.

Organic matter may bind or sorb pollutants and detoxify them. In theory, this could be important for many substances, but most evidence is for metals, mainly copper. The organic matter may be dissolved or particulate, or living material such as algal cells. Standard measurements of metals by atomic absorption spectroscopy can be misleading because they represent total metals, whether free and toxic or bound and nontoxic. The usual remedy is microfiltration of samples to remove suspended matter.

These considerations of variables that modify toxicity can be summarized as follows.

- The pH of water can be very important in governing toxicity, particularly for substances that ionize.
- The hardness of fresh water is associated with major changes in toxicity of metals, but not of most other substances.
- Organic matter may bind metals and render them nontoxic.
- The nutritional status of fish may be a major factor in unexplained differences in susceptibility to pollutants; a diet that is high in protein appears to be protective.
- Larger juvenile fish are often more tolerant than very small ones. Invertebrates may be quite sensitive at the time of molt.

• Some items that are not usually of major importance in evaluating toxicity are dissolved oxygen content of the water, temperature (if fish are acclimated), and salinity (if fish are tested at their accustomed salinities).

15.5 SUBLETHAL TESTS

Tests for sublethal toxic effects can be divided roughly into whole-organism tests (Sections 15.5.1–5) and within-organism studies (Sections 15.5.6–8). In the first category, recent activity centers on life cycle, partial life cycle, and early life stage testing. In the second category, there is much biochemical research, mostly intended to discover mechanisms of toxic action.

15.5.1 Life Cycle Tests

Lifetime exposures of rats or mice to chemical substances have long been standard procedures in pharmacology, but these techniques came to aquatic toxicology relatively recently. The usual procedure is to start with recently hatched fish, to rear groups of them to maturity at different concentrations of the toxicant, and then to rear the second generation through early life at the same concentration as the parents. A researcher can assess many kinds of deleterious effects, and estimate the NOEC. In the first generation, the effects evaluated include long-term survival, growth, tumors or other evidence of ill health, abnormal behavior, time to maturity, and spawning success; in the second generation, hatching success and mortality of young stages, growth, and deformities are monitored.

The life cycle approach was pioneered for fish by Mount and Stephan (1967), who used fathead minnows in an experiment that lasted about 1 year. (Complete procedures for life cycle tests with fathead minnows were prepared by Benoit 1982.) A similar exposure of brook trout would require 2.5 years. The tedious exposures were soon shortened by using small tropical fish—for example, a 3- or 4-month experiment with flagfish—for which the estimates of NOEC were similar to those determined for more northerly species (McKim 1977, 1985). Almost as rapid were procedures for the estuarine sheepshead minnow, which can be tested at salinities of 15–30‰, essentially up to full-strength seawater (Hansen and Schimmel 1975; Hansen and Parrish 1977). Partial life cycle tests for longer-lived fishes such as brook trout start with older but immature fish, not recently hatched ones (McKim and Benoit 1974).

The early life stages were almost always the most sensitive during the life cycle tests, changes in development or simple mortality being evident among embryos, larvae, and very early juveniles. Exposures of only 1 month were sufficient to study those stages. Results of these short duration tests usually predicted the effects of full life cycle tests within a factor of two, and predicted them exactly in 83% of the cases (McKim 1985). Life cycle, partial life cycle, and early life stage tests are now extensively used to determine water quality criteria for aquatic organisms, almost to the exclusion of other sublethal tests. Procedures and references were given by McKim (1985). However, there are some problems; for example, the caveats about interpreting growth (next section) apply to life cycle tests.

Good results can be obtained from even faster techniques. Norberg and Mount (1985) used only 7-d exposures of newly hatched fathead minnows, and they evaluated only dry weight and mortality, but their results were generally predictive of those from longer tests because the early life stages are so sensitive (see reviews by McKim 1985; Norberg and Mount 1985; and Norberg-King 1989a). After 4-d exposures of newly hatched fish to various toxicants, measurements of nucleic acids (DNA, RNA) indicated effect thresholds close to those of 28-d tests (Barron and Adelman 1984; see also Chapter 11).

An intensive comparison among 10 U.S. laboratories demonstrated the reproducibility of 7-d tests with larval fish (API 1988). The 7-d test also has shown excellent agreement with ecological evaluations of polluted waters; for example, the mortality of larval fathead minnows in such tests was highly correlated with the number of resident fish species and the number and diversity of invertebrate species in sections of a Kentucky river affected by a wastewater effluent (Birge et al. 1989). Short-term tests with fish larvae make it possible to explore complicated topics, such as the toxicity of chemical mixtures, with meaningful sublethal responses instead of lethal ones. They also allow effluents or surface waters to be monitored with a test that is more sensitive than lethality.

Parallel developments with invertebrates often have involved crustaceans. An exposure of only 14 d is sufficient for *Daphnia pulex* to develop from newly released juvenile to reproducing adult (Westlake et al. 1983). With *Daphnia magna,* 21–28-d tests have been used and shorter ones have been proposed (Geiger et al. 1980). These animals are often more sensitive than fish, but there is more than a little art in rearing them, and Nebeker (1982) pointed out that some laboratories have not had success in testing daphnids. The mysid *Mysidopsis bahia* seems likely to become the common marine invertebrate for life cycle testing because it adapts well to laboratory conditions and releases young at about 17 d of age (Nimmo et al. 1977). Many other invertebrates, particularly marine larvae, have been suggested as suitable test organisms (McKim 1985).

The use of sensitive invertebrates in chronic or early life stage tests is highly desirable. Evaluating the quality of tests with invertebrates is difficult, however, because of the varied life histories and uncertainties about the suitability of laboratory conditions. A most important criterion is the success of control organisms. Newly hatched stages should be included in any test, either at the beginning or the end (second generation).

Statistical evaluation of these life cycle tests is fairly straightforward, and standard procedures are now available for personal computer (Gulley et al. 1989; also Section 15.7.1). Replicate test chambers are used at each concentration, so multiple-range tests can be used to distinguish the NOEC and the LOEC. The hypothetical threshold of effect is often estimated as the geometric mean of NOEC and LOEC, and called the "maximum acceptable toxicant concentration" or MATC. There are, however, both conceptual and practical problems with this statistical approach. The numerical values of LOEC and NOEC depend on the concentrations that an investigator happened to choose. The power of the experiment is very important (e.g., number of replicates). In an experiment that was under-designed or showed considerable variation among individual organisms, statistical testing might fail to confirm a real toxic effect and the estimated values would be too high for the LOEC, NOEC, or both. Alternatively, a random effect might happen to show statistical significance, and the estimate of LOEC or NOEC would be too low.

15.5.2   Growth and Bioenergetics

Growth might seem a simple and straightforward index of a chemical's effect on a fish because it should integrate all the effects within the fish. A prerequisite for its use, however, is a meaningful experiment with growth itself, which is not a simple thing. For example, if fish are fed ad libitum, they can compensate for toxicant-induced metabolic deficiencies by eating more, but fish exposed under conditions of restricted diet may fall further and further behind the controls in weight gain (Warren 1971, page 163). As another example, rainbow trout exposed to half the lethal concentration of copper showed an initial loss of appetite but compensated during a 39-d experiment so that their growth rate almost equalled that of controls. Furthermore, compensation was faster at a lower ration than at a higher one (Lett et al. 1976).

Thus a toxicologist gets into perplexing problems of interpretation, problems involving not only ration, but appetite, acclimation, and food conversion efficiency. If it is particularly desired to understand how a toxicant affects growth, the approaches outlined in Chapters 11 and 12 should be used. A specific hypothesis will be required, and an experiment must be designed to test it. No particular ration can be recommended as suitable for all toxicological tests, although ad libitum feeding is generally used. If an overall estimate of the NOEC for a given toxicant is desired, the early life stage procedures of Section 15.5.1 will be most cost efficient.

15.5.3   Locomotory Performance

Maximum swimming performance of fish should be another good indicator of toxicant effects because high levels of toxicants often damage the gills, and respiratory capacity is linked to swimming performance. As with growth, however, meaningful measurements of performance require carefully designed experiments, and interpretation of toxicant effects may be complicated by acclimation (Waiwood and Beamish 1978).

Swimming speed does not seem to be affected by toxicants as much as might be expected, and swimming tests are seldom used today as a primary method for toxicity testing. An appreciation of experimental method may be gained from Chapter 10 and from Beamish (1978). Brett (1967) recommended standard procedures, many of them strikingly similar to techniques for estimating LC50s and incipient LC50s.

15.5.4   Behavior

The contribution of behavioral research to aquatic toxicology remains at an unsatisfactory level. Behavioral reactions of fish and other organisms are among the least understood and understudied sublethal effects of toxicants. However, they are important because they may be affected by concentrations that do not cause apparent physiological damage, but may nevertheless affect populations in a given area.

The classic example of behavioral response to a toxicant is a field experiment in which an Ohio stream was dosed with copper to see whether laboratory estimates of "safe" levels were valid in a real community (Geckler et al. 1976). Physiologically speaking, the answer was yes. Fish held in chambers with creek water flowing through them showed successful reproduction only in zones where satisfactory copper concentrations were predicted. However, wild fish in the creek told an entirely different story. The same species did not spawn in zones where their caged cohorts reproduced, but fled downstream to lower concentrations until stopped by a barrier, then spawned in that location. The avoidance reaction was the most sensitive indicator of effects on fish.

The conclusion is clear—behavioral effects deserve a separate toxicological assessment that parallels physiological tests. Such work is being done to only a limited extent, perhaps because of the complexities and time-consuming nature of behavior studies (e.g., 3 months were needed for a single series of concentrations with one toxicant in a study by Westlake 1984).

A wide spectrum of behavioral responses might be assessed. These are reviewed in Chapter 17 and were surveyed, with special reference to toxicology, by Westlake (1984) and Rand (1985). Rand listed the following categories of response: undirected locomotor activity; feeding, predatory, and reproductive behavior; learning ability; social interactions such as territoriality, dominance, and schooling; and directed locomotion (preference or avoidance) in response to food, pheromones, physical differences in habitat, or the presence of a toxicant. Some of these would be assessed during life cycle tests inasmuch as they would affect growth or spawning, but two items would seem to deserve separate attention. Avoidance reactions could cause fish to leave an area where a pollutant was not physiologically damaging, as in the Ohio field test. Undirected locomotory activity (kinetic responses) might have the same result if fish increased their activity in a polluted zone, then decreased it when out of the zone. Assessments of both reactions have been made in the laboratory by giving fish a choice between clean and polluted water, but the complexities of interpretation are evident in most of the resulting publications and in the above-mentioned reviews.

Seemingly adequate laboratory research on behavior may not predict what would occur in the field. There is evidence of avoidance reactions by wild fish, but such studies are difficult and there are very few of them. The findings of Geckler et al. (1976) in an Ohio stream have been mentioned. Fish were scarce on the side of an Alberta river that received municipal effluent, although chemical measurements showed relatively mild pollution (Paterson and Nursall 1975). Fish appeared to actively avoid a Virginia power plant discharge in reaction to the concentration of chlorine (Cherry et al. 1977). Attempts have been made to use sonic tagging and acoustic echo analysis to track movements of fish in relation to pulp mill effluents (Elson et al. 1972; Kelso 1977). Saunders and Sprague (1967) documented severe interference with the spawning migration of salmon by mining pollution, but only at about 20 times the levels of metals that caused avoidance by young fish in the laboratory. Apparently, a fish's reaction in the real world may not be predicted by laboratory tests with a "clean side–polluted side" dichotomy; with territoriality included in a laboratory test, avoidance threshold may increase sixfold (Korver and Sprague 1989). Behavioral responses can be important, but they are poorly understood and much more perceptive research is warranted.

15.5.5 Field Validation and Artificial Ecosystems

It is always risky, and often foolish, to predict from knowledge gained at one level of biological integration what will happen at a higher or broader level of integration, as from the molecular to the cellular level or from tissues to whole organisms. Toxicological effects on spawning by individual fish in the laboratory do not necessarily foretell what will happen to populations in the wild, and effects on a species are not likely to predict changes in a community containing that species. Accordingly, it is highly desirable to validate single-species laboratory tests by studying effects in a functioning community.

One approach is to assess the biota of polluted water bodies ("field validation"). To some degree, the thousands of local biological surveys of pollution provide comparisons. The biggest problems in validation by survey results are that (a) field contamination usually involves more than one active pollutant, and (b) concentrations vary with time and may show extreme fluctuations. Nevertheless, field studies give general confirmation of laboratory estimates of harmful concentrations. This may be seen in documents used to develop water quality criteria by EIFAC, the European Inland Fisheries Advisory Commission (Alabaster and Lloyd 1980). For various water quality characteristics, EIFAC reviewed the literature on *both* laboratory and field work, and most comparisons were reasonably consistent. An ambitious approach to field validation by Mount et al. (1984) combined several techniques. Shortcut chronic tests with fish and daphnids were carried to the streamside to evaluate effluents and polluted waters, providing on-site "laboratory" tests. Simultaneously, there were standard field surveys of resident biota and water chemistry. These revealed some lower-than-expected toxicities of combined pollutants, but generally confirmed that results of single-species tests are in line with effects on real communities.

Some validation of laboratory results may involve cages of fish in polluted locations, but that approach usually assesses only mortality, which is of less interest than sublethal effects. Another approach is to use "artificial ecosystems," variously described as "multispecies toxicity tests," "laboratory streams," "mesocosms," or "microcosms," depending on design. The communities may or may not contain fish. There are many current attempts to develop standard microcosms for testing toxicants, with a few species in a flask, carboy, or aquarium. It is possible to use flow-through procedures to maintain constant concentrations (Hedtke 1984), although often that is not done. Most procedures are in developmental stages, and there are problems in deciding what degree and kind of change represents harmful effect.

Recirculating laboratory streams about 6 m long can be used to test small but complete communities of microorganisms, algae, invertebrates, and a few fish (Warren and Davis 1971). Simple effects in the laboratory streams (affecting biomass or diversity) are adequately predicted by single-species tests, but interactions between species are not (Hansen and Garton 1982). Interpretation may involve subjective assessment of complex ecosystem diagrams of energy flow and production (Warren 1971, page 315). At the mesocosm level, several investigators have studied large volumes of lake or seawater enclosed in plastic bags or in "limnocorrals" running to the bottom and added toxicant to some of the enclosures. Fish usually were excluded, and populations of other organisms were assessed by conventional sampling techniques. Enclosures are good research tools but do not compare well with laboratory tests because the toxicant is usually added only once, so constant concentrations are not maintained. One exception, with documented steady concentrations of cadmium in the enclosures, provided valuable estimates of metal concentrations affecting copepod populations (Kuiper

1981). Another problem is that these simplified or segregated communities tend to be unstable, and replicates may suddenly change composition for reasons that are not obvious. Chapter 19 gives advice on design and interpretation of community experiments. A book edited by Cairns (1985) covers testing with artificial ecosystems.

One of the most successful systems for validation of laboratory toxicity data is a series of parallel artificial streams constructed outdoors. In such a facility at Monticello, Minnesota, stream channels are of realistic size (1.4 m wide in riffle areas, wider in pools), replicates can be used, and steady flows of new water can be dosed to constant concentrations (Cairns 1985; Zischke et al. 1985). Small populations of fish live under seminatural conditions, and their survival, growth, and reproductive success can be measured during an experiment of a few months. Other components of the community can be evaluated by standard survey techniques or by sampling blocks of artificial substrate. An experiment involves at least six people for a summer, and thus is expensive, but it is a very meaningful approach to field validation. In at least one case, a previously accepted water quality criterion failed to protect the stream community (Zischke et al. 1985).

Manipulation of small lakes is possible, as in the Experimental Lakes Area of Ontario where some environmental toxicology has been done (Schindler et al. 1980). The ultimate validation experiment in a natural creek was the one in Ohio, mentioned above (Geckler et al. 1976). We may never see another test on that scale, because the instrumentation, the stream dosing to a constant concentration of copper for 2 years, and the assessments of wild and confined fish and other biota were enormously expensive. The Ohio test yielded good agreement with laboratory findings on the direct sublethal toxicity of copper. The major surprise of the study, that avoidance reactions were the most sensitive effect caused by the toxicant, emphasizes the need for field validation. Still, it is encouraging that, in general, "ecosystem testing does not lead to results that are dramatically different from those obtained with single-species tests" (Slooff et al. 1986).

In summary, when artificial ecosystems are used to validate single-species toxicity data obtained in the laboratory, the following questions should be raised.

- Were the observed effects of the toxicant clearly harmful ones, or were they changes of uncertain toxicological significance? In artificial communities, even the control replicates may diverge for reasons that are not apparent.
- Was the concentration of toxicant constant? A single addition of toxicant, which subsequently declines in concentration, makes comparisons with steady-state laboratory tests difficult.

15.5.6 Biochemical Physiology

There are many specific clinical tests for diagnosing human health, but relatively few for fish (see Chapter 14 for stress evaluation). Mehrle and Mayer (1985) pointed out that biochemical and physiological diagnoses in fish have seldom been related to performance of the whole organism, and they cited an example in which a group of experts rated such tests 10th of 11 alternative approaches in usefulness for aquatic toxicology. Gaps remain in our understanding of normal biochemical processes in fish, and extrapolations from mammals require demonstrations of relevance. Further, fish show considerable variation in levels of biochemical activity in relation to disease, nutritional status, and environmental stresses.

Biochemical tests should have at least three major uses in aquatic toxicology. First, they should provide standard tests of health. Various sets of tests have been proposed but have received little acceptance in aquatic toxicology. Second, biochemical and physiological research, along with histopathology, is the major means to learn a toxicant's mode of action. This is of great practical interest, notably for predicting toxicity on the basis of chemical structure (Section 15.5.8) and for predicting effects of two or more pollutants acting simultaneously (Section 15.6.3). Appreciable information is available on modes of action, and much of the knowledge gained from mammals is relevant to fishes.

Finally, biochemical tests could provide sensitive and rapid methods for detecting sublethal effects of toxicants on fish. Numerous reviews of individual toxicants indicate that most within-organism responses studied to date are no more sensitive than whole-organism ones, and some are much less sensitive. For any whole-organism effect, there must be biochemical assessments that would be very sensitive and fast, but the problem seems to be finding the right one. There are a few successful uses of biochemistry; for example, Hodson et al. (1979) demonstrated that malformation of fish skeletons by long exposure to lead can be predicted quickly by measuring activity of the enzyme D-aminolevulinic acid dehydratase (=porphobilinogen synthetase).

Anyone assessing information on aquatic toxicology should be aware that the predictive capacity of biochemical techniques still is rudimentary. Skepticism is warranted for numerous papers in journals that describe "a rapid new method for evaluating toxicity" by a biochemical procedure, unless the method is clearly related to whole-organism effect. Dixon et al. (1985) appraised biochemical indicators and their validation.

15.5.7 Histopathology and Epidemiology

Abnormal structures of tissues and cells are widely used to evaluate toxic effects on mammals and, to some extent, to diagnose what kind of chemical caused the effect. This approach has been only partly successful with fish and other aquatic organisms, for which histopathology is in an early developmental state. Part of the problem is the wide variety of species of interest. Another part is the surprising variety of histological abnormalities that are found in "normal" fish in the laboratory and in the wild. Various diseases and nutritional states leave their marks on the structure of the cells and tissues. Any toxicological assessment of tissue damage must include a strong effort to establish conditions in control fish. Another difficulty is that histological damage among fish appears to be largely nonspecific and the class of toxicant can seldom be identified from the observed damage (Mallatt 1985).

Chapter 7 shows that we know how to carry out histological assessments of fish and how to measure damage by quantifying the histological image. Meyers and Hendricks (1985) dealt specifically with the use of histopathology in aquatic toxicology and listed the terminology of abnormalities; some generalizations in this section are taken from their review.

Histopathology is not, at present, a primary working tool of aquatic toxicology. There have been some successful uses—for example, in judging the degree of gonad maturation and hence in explaining decreased reproductive ability (Lesniak and Ruby 1982).

One field that has developed rapidly over the last decade is epidemiology, particularly surveys of wild fish populations for the presence of tumors (Mix 1986). External neoplasms are easily recognized and quantified, and are particularly evident among bottom-dwelling fish such as brown bullheads in fresh water and winter flounder in marine environments. Tumors in the liver are also relatively easy to identify. Surveys have indicated apparent "hot spots" of tumors in certain polluted inshore areas of Puget Sound (Malins et al. 1984), along the Atlantic coast (Murchelano and Wolke 1985), and in industrialized rivers (Baumann and Harshbarger 1985). Gilbertson (1984) argued that epidemiological surveys should be a primary tool in aquatic toxicology. Discovery of anomalous conditions in fish populations would lead to laboratory study of potential causes, rather like the approach for identifying microorganisms responsible for human diseases. There are complications in epidemiological studies with fish; for example, large differences in tumor incidence can occur between species with similar habits, and high incidences can occur at locations that are not polluted (Stich et al. 1976).

The obverse of this procedure is to use fish for evaluating carcinogenic potential of chemicals. One type of test involves injection of a chemical into trout eggs; the eggs are hatched and the young are reared for 6 months, then examined for carcinomas. This is much faster and cheaper than using small mammals, and appears to give meaningful results (Hoover 1984; Black et al. 1985).

15.5.8   Residues in Fish and Chemical Prediction of Toxicity

Fish may take up chemicals selectively and store them in the body at elevated concentrations. *Bioaccumulation* is a general term for that phenomenon, and includes uptake from water or food. The *bioconcentration factor* (BCF) is the ratio of concentration of a substance in the fish to the concentration in the water where it has lived. The definition excludes dietary intake. Numerical values of the BCF will almost certainly have been derived from laboratory exposures. *Biomagnification* refers to accumulation through the food chain (i.e., higher trophic levels acquire more residues because of dietary intake). In field situations, the relative importance of uptake from water and food is often uncertain. The level of residue in an organism depends not only on the rate of uptake, but also on the mechanisms available for storing the chemical in tissues and on the rate at which the chemical is cleared from tissues (Chapter 14).

Because of concern for the health of humans who may eat contaminated fish, bioaccumulation has received a great deal of attention in the forms of monitoring, research, and technique development, as reviewed by Spacie and Hamelink (1985). Many of the dangerous bioaccumulative substances are organic, sparingly soluble in water but readily soluble in lipids. The classic example is DDT, but a more recent problem has been the dioxins, some of which are extremely toxic and occur in fish from Lake Ontario. The tendency of lipophilic chemicals to bioaccumulate can be predicted on the basis of their solubility in octanol compared to their solubility in water, the *octanol–water partition coefficient*, designated by the symbol P or K_{ow}. Mackay (1982) generalized that the BCF for a typical fish equals 5% of the value of P. In other words, a fish accumulates

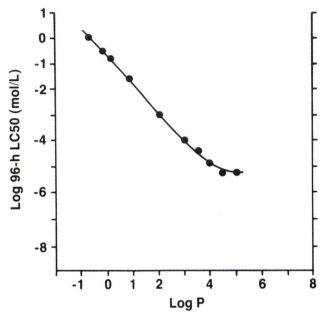

Figure 15.3 The 96-h LC50s, for fathead minnows, of a series of aliphatic alcohols, as related to the octanol–water partition coefficient (*P*). (Modified from Veith et al. [1983], with permission of Dr. Veith and the *Canadian Journal of Fisheries and Aquatic Sciences*.)

organic chemicals from the water as if the fish were composed of 5% octanol, but this can vary with ration and fat content of the fish (Shubat and Curtis 1986). A strongly bioaccumulative substance might show a value of 6 for $\log_{10}P$, its solubility in octanol being a million times greater than in water. The BCF of such a substance would be in the vicinity of 50,000. These relationships allow useful predictions of the bioaccumulative potential of organic chemicals.

Not all pollutants are organic chemicals, and fish have mechanisms to prevent accumulation of many substances. For example, fish exposed to high concentrations of cadmium accumulate the metal, but they readily excrete it at low concentrations and may have body levels that are among the lowest in a community. Fisheries scientists should thus exercise some caution on the topic of bioaccumulation. Newspapers may convey the impression that *all* toxic substances bioaccumulate, and this sometimes appears to influence scientists. Some monitoring studies have included costly analyses of substances, such as copper and zinc, that do not normally accumulate in fish and are not particularly toxic to human consumers.

A bioaccumulation study should be accompanied by an assessment of toxicity to determine if the accumulated chemical actually causes harm to the fish. Failure to make such a correlation is frequently seen in the scientific literature: the uptake of a chemical is monitored in detail and toxicity is implied, but no demonstration of toxicity is given. Such criticism would not apply if toxicity were known from other work.

There is a strong relationship between bioaccumulation and toxicity of numerous organic chemicals that have a very generalized toxic effect ("narcosis"). Both variables are related to the octanol–water partition coefficient. Figure 15.3 shows an example for aliphatic alcohols, for which $\log_{10}$ LC50 is linearly related to $\log_{10}P$ over most of the range of P values. Ketones, ethers, alkyl halides, and substituted benzenes fit the same relationship, whether test fish are fathead minnows or guppies (Veith et al. 1983). Furthermore, sublethal toxicity roughly parallels the lethal relationship (McCarty et al. 1985), adding even more usefulness to the prediction. Such correlations are described as "quantitative structure–activity relationships," or QSAR, and they give hope of sorting out dangerous organic substances from the flood of new chemicals that come into use every year.

Substances with specific toxic mechanisms (insecticides, pentachlorophenol, etc.) are much more toxic than indicated by the line in Figure 15.3. More varied and esoteric physicochemical characteristics must be considered in such cases, and predictive relationships are not well established. Some progress has been made by grouping metals according to their biological, as well as chemical, function (Nieboer and Richardson 1980).

15.6 OTHER TOPICS

15.6.1 Statistical Treatment

Much of the work in aquatic toxicology does not require particularly advanced methods of statistical analysis. Estimating LC50 and EC50 by the probit method involves moderately sophisticated procedures, but they are now standard and easily used through a computer program. The usual regression techniques can estimate growth rates. In sublethal testing, standard multiple-range tests are frequently used to distinguish the mean values of effects that differ from the control and, by implication, the concentrations that cause those effects.

Perhaps the most mathematically esoteric area is in the analysis of behavior experiments, which may require diverse considerations of design and response (Chapter 17). Westlake (1984) pointed out that a completely randomized design may be impossible in avoidance experiments, and he mentioned his use of split-plots analysis of variance—split on areas of the tank—with conservative degrees of freedom. He suggested that time-series analysis would be best, but that procedure remains at the outer boundaries of statistical knowledge. Heavy use of mathematics would also be involved in fitting three-dimensional response surfaces when, for example, two environmental variables modify toxic concentrations.

It is disturbing that rather few papers in aquatic toxicology first state a particular null hypothesis and then describe the findings necessary to accept or reject it. Perhaps that rigorous approach is out of place in routine tests to establish toxic concentrations, but it often is relevant in research to determine modes of action. At a much more rudimentary level, sets of LC50s are sometimes entered into a statistical program as arithmetic values. That not only distorts the logarithmic dose–effect relationship but may violate a statistical requirement for equal variances. Errors in such a simple thing indicate that the more profound aspects of experimental design and data analysis, set forth in Chapter 1, should also be examined when any toxicological work is evaluated.

15.6.2 Acute:Chronic Ratios and Application Factors

Subtle sublethal effects will obviously occur at lower concentrations than those that cause lethality. It is often useful to calculate the "acute:chronic ratio," or

ACR, as the LC50 divided by the MATC (or threshold concentration for sublethal effect). The value often is approximately 10, and usually is in the range 2–100 (Kenaga 1982). Classes of chemicals tend to have similar values for this ratio; for example, insecticides and metals generally have high values, meaning that sublethal effects occur at concentrations far below the LC50.

One practical use of such a ratio is to make rough predictions of sublethal thresholds in the absence of data. If the usual ACR for a class of insecticides is 100 and if the LC50 of a new insecticide has been determined as 300 µg/L, a sublethal threshold for the same species might be expected in the vicinity of 3 µg/L. This predictive approach found considerable use in the 1950s and 1960s when sublethal testing was poorly developed and relatively rare. Given an ACR for, say, one pulp mill, sublethal thresholds for other mills could be predicted from easily obtained LC50s at those mills. The concept is still used. One can generalize that certain classes of chemicals are dangerous if they have high ACRs. More particularly, use of ACRs is one option for developing water quality criteria in the USA (Stephan et al. 1985).

Until recently, it was customary to cite the inverse of the ACR, called an "application factor." Most people, however, find it easier to appreciate the magnitude of the ACR's whole numbers than the application factor's fractions.

15.6.3   Toxicity of Mixtures

Most published work in aquatic toxicology deals not only with a single species, but also with a single toxicant. This poorly represents the real world, where an effluent or location usually has a mixture of several toxicants. Models for practical evaluation of mixture toxicity remain in a relatively simplistic state, and results of testing are often complex and difficult to predict. Multiple-toxicant experiments are relatively rare in current research, though the topic is important. Criteria documents are written in terms of single toxicants (e.g., USEPA 1980). Compendia of criteria give no guidance on what to do when one must evaluate several simultaneous pollutants (Office of Water and Hazardous Materials 1977), although tentative suggestions were once given (NAS and NAE 1974).

If it is necessary to evaluate toxicity of mixtures, one could use the "toxic unit" method, which is naive but which has been used in practical situations. The concentration of each toxicant is expressed not in chemical units but as a fraction of its sublethal threshold or MATC (i.e., in sublethal toxic units, SLTU). If the concentration of a single chemical reached 1.0 SLTU, it would cause a sublethal effect. The same rationale is extended to mixtures by adding together the units for all toxicants; if the result is 1.0 or greater, a sublethal effect is predicted. The assumption that actions of different substances are exactly additive is certainly not true in all cases, but it is sometimes approximately so (see below). The method is likely to be overprotective. Other methods of assessing joint action were referenced by Hermens et al. (1984a, 1984b) and Marking (1985).

Rapid sublethal tests have been used to evaluate the combined action of toxicants, and some results are disconcerting. Mixtures of 5 to 25 organic substances having similar action were tested for their effect on reproduction by *Daphnia magna* (Hermens et al. 1984a). Toxicity was assessed by summing fractions of the effective concentrations for individual substances, as above. Mixtures were effective at 2 SLTU or less; that is, the individual substances appeared to retain about half of their potencies in the mixtures. Furthermore, the joint action in the mixture of 25 substances appeared to be stronger (1.5 SLTU) than in the mixture of 5 substances (2 SLTU), even though each substance was present at only about one-seventeenth of its individual effective concentration. This suggests that there may be no such thing as a sublethally "safe" level (NOEC) of an individual substance when it is part of a mixture of substances with similar action. Similar results were obtained for mixtures of chemicals with different modes of action. A mixture of 14 substances having several types of chemical structures and modes of action affected *Daphnia magna* reproduction at 1.9 SLTU (Hermens et al. 1984b). In other words, each of the dissimilar toxicants, present at about one-seventh of its individual effective concentration, apparently contributed about half of that toxicity to the action of the mixture. These are only two experiments, and others cited in the literature show a variety of results including lack of combined action. Still, they illustrate that the single-toxicant approach to water quality criteria may not protect ecosystems and that multiple sublethal toxicity deserves much more attention and exploration.

15.6.4 Hazard Assessment

All the testing in aquatic toxicology should have the ultimate objective of providing information that can be used to protect the environment. Results of individual tests on a substance can be assembled and used to establish a water quality criterion that is intended to be a safe concentration for most aquatic organisms. In current U.S. practice, two criteria are established, one for short-term peaks of pollution and one for long-term exposure (Stephan et al. 1985). These may be tailored for a particular region and its species. The criteria may be used as a basis for establishing regulations or water quality standards.

Beyond that, the toxicological information may be used as the first major component in a "hazard assessment" for a particular substance or effluent. The second major component that enters the assessment is prediction of concentrations expected in the environment. The process, which has been rather subjective in the past, is gradually becoming more formalized, and standard procedures are now available from ASTM (1984a). The objective of aquatic hazard assessment is to identify likely adverse effects on aquatic organisms or their users when a material is released to the environment.

The methods of estimating the first component, the "safe" concentration, have been outlined in this chapter. The second component (predicted concentration) involves estimates of anticipated production of the substance and the substance's use, wastage, and environmental fate, including degradation.

The initial stages of the assessment are tentative. Sequential decisions are made on the degree of hazard, at increasingly detailed levels of information, if required. It may be necessary to do additional toxicological testing, chemical and physical characterization of the substance to predict its behavior in the environment, or collection of more industrial and socioeconomic data. At any point in the sequence, a decision can emerge that (a) the hazard is so low that more detailed consideration is not necessary, or that (b) the hazard is so high that restrictions on use of the substance are necessary.

The value of the procedure clearly depends on the judgment of the individuals carrying it out. Hazard assessment is being used today, and despite its weaknesses, it should be welcomed as an attempt to forestall environmental degradation. Further details of the approach were given by ASTM (1984a) and by Maki and Bishop (1985).

15.7 REFERENCES

Alabaster, J. S., and R. Lloyd. 1980. Water quality criteria for freshwater fish. Butterworth, Woburn, Massachusetts.

APHA (American Public Health Association), American Water Works Association, and Water Pollution Control Federation. 1989. Standard methods for the examination of water and wastewater, 17th edition. APHA, Washington, D.C.

API (American Petroleum Institute). 1988. Fathead minnow 7-day test: round robin study. Intra- and interlaboratory study to determine the reproducibility of seven-day fathead minnow larval survival and growth test. API, API publication 4468, Washington, D.C.

ASTM (American Society for Testing and Materials). 1980a. Standard practice for conducting acute toxicity tests with fishes, macroinvertebrates, and amphibians. ASTM Standard E 729–80. ASTM, Philadelphia.

ASTM (American Society for Testing and Materials). 1980b. Standard practice for conducting static acute toxicity tests with larvae of four species of bivalve molluscs. ASTM Standard E 724–80. ASTM, Philadelphia.

ASTM (American Society for Testing and Materials). 1984a. Assessing the hazard of a material to aquatic organisms and their uses. ASTM Standard E 1023–84. ASTM, Philadelphia.

ASTM (American Society for Testing and Materials). 1984b. Standard practice for conducting static acute toxicity tests on wastewaters with *Daphnia*. ASTM Standard D 4229. ASTM, Philadelphia.

ASTM (American Society for Testing and Materials). 1988. Standard quide for conducting life-cycle toxicity tests with saltwater mysids. ASTM Standard E 1191-87. ASTM, Philadelphia.

ASTM (American Society for Testing and Materials). 1989a. Standard guide for conducting three-brood, renewal toxicity tests with *Ceriodaphnia dubia*. ASTM Standard E 1295-89. ASTM, Phildelphia.

ASTM (American Society for Testing and Materials). 1989b. Standard practice for using brine shrimp nauplii as food for test animals in aquatic toxicology. ASTM Standard E-1203. ASTM, Philadelphia.

Barron, M. G., and I. R. Adelman. 1984. Nucleic acid, protein content, and growth of larval fish sublethally exposed to various toxicants. Canadian Journal of Fisheries and Aquatic Sciences 41:141–150.

Baumann, P. C., and J. C. Harshbarger. 1985. Frequencies of liver neoplasia in a feral fish population and associated carcinogens. Marine Environmental Research 17:324–327.

Beamish, F. W. H. 1978. Swimming capacity. Pages 101–187 *in* W. S. Hoar and D. J. Randall, editors. Fish physiology, volume 7. Academic Press, New York.

Benoit, D. A. 1982. User's guide for conducting life-cycle chronic toxicity tests with fathead minnows (*Pimephales promelas*). U.S. Environmental Protection Agency, Environmental Research Laboratory, EPA-600/8-81-011, Duluth, Minnesota.

Berkson J. 1953. A statistically precise and relatively simple method of estimating the bioassay with quantal response based on the logistic function. Journal of the American Statistical Association 48:565–599.

Biesinger, K. E., L. R. Williams, and W. H. van der Schalie. 1987. Procedures for conducting *Daphnia magna* toxicity bioassays. U.S. Environment Protection Agency, Environmental Monitoring Systems Laboratory, EPA/600/8-87/011, Cincinnati, Ohio.

Birge, W. J., J. A. Black, T. M. Short, and A. G. Westerman. 1989. A comparative ecological and toxicological investigation of a secondary wastewater treatment plant effluent and its receiving stream. Environmental Toxicology and Chemisty 8:437–450.

Black, J. J., A. E. MacCubbin, and M. Schissert. 1985. A reliable efficient micro-injection apparatus and methodology for the *in vivo* exposure of rainbow trout and salmonid embryos to chemical carcinogens. Journal of the National Cancer Institute 75:1123–1128.

Bradley, R. W., C. DuQuesnay, and J. B. Sprague. 1985. Acclimation of rainbow trout (*Salmo gairdneri* Richardson) to zinc: kinetics and mechanism of enhanced tolerance induction. Journal of Fish Biology 27:367–379.

Bradley, R. W., and J. B. Sprague. 1985a. Accumulation of zinc by rainbow trout as influenced by pH, water hardness and fish size. Environmental Toxicology and Chemistry 4:685–694.

Bradley, R. W., and J. B. Sprague. 1985b. The influence of pH, water hardness, and alkalinity on the acute lethality of zinc to rainbow trout (*Salmo gairdneri*). Canadian Journal of Fisheries and Aquatic Sciences 42:731–736.

Brett, J. R. 1967. Swimming performance of sockeye salmon (*Oncorhynchus nerka*) in relation to fatigue time and temperature. Journal of the Fisheries Research Board of Canada 24:1731–1741.

Buikema, A. L., Jr., B. R. Niederlehner, and J. Cairns, Jr. 1982. Biological monitoring. Part IV—toxicity testing. Water Research 16:239–262.

Cairns, J., Jr., editor. 1985. Multispecies toxicity testing. Pergamon Press, Elmsford, New York.

Calamari, D., R. Marchetti, and G. Vailati. 1980. Influence of water hardness on cadmium toxicity to *Salmo gairdneri* Rich. Water Research 14:1421–1426.

Campbell, P. G. C., and P. M. Stokes. 1985. Acidification and toxicity of metals to aquatic biota. Canadian Journal of Fisheries and Aquatic Sciences 42:2034–2049.

Cherry, D. S., R. C. Hoehn, S. S. Waldo, D. H. Willis, J. Cairns, Jr., and K. L. Dickson. 1977. Field–laboratory determined avoidances of the spotfin shiner and the bluntnose minnow to chlorinated discharges. Water Resources Bulletin 13:1047–1055.

Davis, J. C., and B. J. Mason. 1973. Bioassay procedures to evaluate acute toxicity of neutralized bleached kraft pulp mill effluent to Pacific salmon. Journal of the Fisheries Research Board of Canada 30:1565–1573.

Dixon, D. G., P. V. Hodson, J. F. Klaverkamp, K. M. Lloyd, and J. R. Roberts. 1985. The role of biochemical indicators in the assessment of ecosystem health—their development and validation. National Research Council of Canada, Environmental Secretariat, Publication NRCC 24371, Ottawa.

Douglas, M. T., D. O. Chanter, I. B. Pell, and G. M. Burney. 1986. A proposal for the reduction of animal numbers required for the acute toxicity to fish test (LC_{50} determination). Aquatic Toxicology (Amsterdam) 8:243–249.

EC (Environment Canada). 1990a. Acute lethality test using rainbow trout. EC, Environmental Protection, Report EPS 1/RM/9, Ottawa.

EC (Environment Canada). 1990b. Acute lethality test using threespine stickleback (*Gasterosteus aculeatus*). EC, Environmental Protection, Report EPS 1/RM/10, Ottawa.

EC (Environment Canada). 1990c. Acute lethality test using *Daphnia* sp. EC, Environmental Protection, Report EPS 1/RM/11, Ottawa.

Elson, P. F., L. M. Lauzier, and V. Zitko. 1972. A preliminary study of salmon movements in a polluted estuary. Pages 325–330 *in* M. Ruivo, editor. Marine pollution and sea life. Fishing News Books, London.

EPS (Environmental Protection Service). 1974. Petroleum refinery effluent regulations and guidelines. Environment Canada, Report EPS 1-WP-74-1, Ottawa.

Finney, D. J. 1971. Probit analysis, 3rd edition. Cambridge University Press, London.

Geckler, J. R., W. B. Horning, T. M. Neiheisel, Q. H. Pickering, E. L. Robinson, and C. E. Stephan. 1976. Validity of laboratory tests for predicting copper toxicity in streams. U.S. Environmental Protection Agency, National Environmental Research Center Ecological Research Series EPA-600/3-76-116.

Geiger, J. G., A. L. Buikema, Jr., and J. Cairns, Jr. 1980. A tentative seven-day test for predicting effects of stress on populations of *Daphnia pulex*. American Society for Testing and Materials Special Technical Publication 707:13–26.

Gelber, R. D., P. T. Lavin, C. R. Mehta, and D. A. Schoenfeld. 1985. Statistical analysis. Pages 110–123 *in* Rand and Petrocelli (1985).

Gilbertson, M. 1984. Need for development of epidemiology for chemically induced diseases in fish in Canada. Canadian Journal of Fisheries and Aquatic Sciences 41:1534–1540.

Gulley, D. D., A. M. Boelter, and H. L. Bergman. 1989. TOXSTAT Release 3.2. University of Wyoming, Laramie.

Hamilton, M. A., R. C. Russo, and R. V. Thurston. 1977. Trimmed Spearman–Kärber method for estimating median lethal concentrations in toxicity bioassays. Environmental Science and Technology 11:714–719. (Correction: 1978. Environmental Science and Technology 12:417.)

Hansen, D. J., and P. R. Parrish. 1977. Suitability of sheepshead minnows (*Cyprinodon variegatus*) for life-cycle toxicity tests. American Society for Testing and Materials Special Technical Publication 634:117–126.

Hansen, D. J., and S. C. Schimmel. 1975. Entire life-cycle bioassay using sheepshead minnows (*Cyprinodon variegatus*). Federal Register 40:123(25 June 1975):26904–26905.

Hansen, S. R., and R. R. Garton. 1982. Ability of standard toxicity tests to predict the effects of the insecticide Diflubenzuron on laboratory stream communities. Canadian Journal of Fisheries and Aquatic Sciences 39:1273–1288.

Hedtke, S. F. 1984. Structure and function of copper-stressed aquatic microcosms. Aquatic Toxicology (Amsterdam) 5:227–244.

Henig, R. M. 1979. Animal experimentation: the battle lines soften. BioScience 29:145–148, 195–196.

Hermens, J., H. Canton, P. Janssen, and R. De Jong. 1984a. Quantitative structure–activity relationships and toxicity studies of mixtures of chemicals with anaesthetic potency: acute lethal and sublethal toxicity to *Daphnia magna*. Aquatic Toxicology (Amsterdam) 5:143–154.

Hermens, J., H. Canton, N. Steyger, and R. Wegman. 1984b. Joint effects of a mixture of 14 chemicals on mortality and inhibition of reproduction of *Daphnia magna*. Aquatic Toxicology (Amsterdam) 5:315–322.

Hodson, P. V., B. R. Blunt, D. Jensen, and S. Morgan. 1979. Effect of fish age on predicted and observed chronic toxicity of lead to rainbow trout in Lake Ontario water. Journal of Great Lakes Research 5:84–89.

Hodson, P. V., C. W. Ross, A. J. Niimi, and D. J. Spry. 1977. Statistical considerations in planning aquatic bioassays. Pages 15–31 in Proceedings of the 3rd aquatic toxicity workshop. Environment Canada, Environmental Protection Service, Technical Report EPS-5-AR-77-1, Halifax, Nova Scotia.

Hoover, K. L., editor. 1984. Use of small fish species in carcinogenicity testing. National Cancer Institute Monograph 65. (Also: National Institutes of Health, Publication 84-2653, Department of Health and Human Services, Washington, D.C.)

Hubert, J. J. 1984. Bioassay, 2nd edition. Kendall/Hunt, Dubuque, Iowa.

Hutchinson, N. J., and J. B. Sprague. 1986. Toxicity of trace metal mixtures to American flagfish (*Jordanella floridae*) in soft, acid water and implications for cultural acidification. Canadian Journal of Fisheries and Aquatic Sciences 43:647–655.

ISO (International Organization for Standardization). 1982. Water quality—determination of the inhibition of mobility of *Daphnia magna* Straus (Cladocera, Crustacea), 1st edition. ISO, Report ISO 6341-1982(E), Geneva, Switzerland.

Kelso, J. R. M. 1977. Density, distribution, and movement of Nipigon Bay fishes in relation to pulp and paper mill effluent. Journal of the Fisheries Research Board of Canada 34:879–885.

Kenaga, E. E. 1982. Predictability of chronic toxicity from acute toxicity of chemicals in fish and aquatic invertebrates. Environmental Toxicology and Chemistry 1:347–358.

Klapow, L. A., and R. H. Lewis. 1979. Analysis of toxicity data for California marine water quality standards. Journal of the Water Pollution Control Federation 51:2054–2070.

Korver, R. M., and J. B. Sprague. 1989. Zinc avoidance by fathead minnows (*Pimephales promelas*); computerized tracking and greater ecological relevance. Canadian Journal of Fisheries and Aquatic Sciences 46:494–502.

Kuiper, J. 1981. Fate and effects of cadmium in marine plankton communities in experimental enclosures. Marine Ecology Progress Series 6:161–174.

Lesniak, J. A., and S. M. Ruby. 1982. Histological and quantitative effects of sublethal cyanide exposure on oocyte development in rainbow trout. Archives of Environmental Contamination and Toxicology 11:343–352.

Lett, P. F., G. J. Farmer, and F. W. H. Beamish. 1976. Effect of copper on some aspects of the bioenergetics of rainbow trout (*Salmo gairdneri*). Journal of the Fisheries Research Board of Canada 33:1335–1342.

Litchfield, J. T., and F. Wilcoxon. 1949. A simplified method of evaluating dose–effect experiments. Journal of Pharmacology and Experimental Therapeutics 96:99–113.

Mackay, D. 1982. Correlation of bioconcentration factors. Environmental Science and Technology 16:274–278.

Maki, A. W., and W. E. Bishop. 1985. Chemical safety evaluation. Pages 619–635 *in* Rand and Petrocelli (1985).

Malins, D. C., and eleven coauthors. 1984. Chemical pollutants in sediments and diseases of bottom-dwelling fish in Puget Sound, Washington. Environmental Science and Technology 18:705–713.

Mallatt, J. 1985. Fish gill structural changes induced by toxicants and other irritants: a statistical review. Canadian Journal of Fisheries and Aquatic Sciences 42:630–648.

Marking, L. L. 1985. Toxicity of chemical mixtures. Pages 164–176 *in* Rand and Petrocelli (1985).

McCarty, L. S., P. V. Hodson, G. R. Craig, and K. L. E. Kaiser. 1985. The use of quantitative structure–activity relationships to predict the acute and chronic toxicities of organic chemicals to fish. Environmental Toxicology and Chemistry 4:595–606.

McKim, J. M. 1977. Evaluation of tests with early life stages of fish for predicting long-term toxicity. Journal of the Fisheries Research Board of Canada 34:1148–1154.

McKim, J. M. 1985. Early life stage toxicity tests. Pages 58–85 *in* Rand and Petrocelli (1985).

McKim, J. M., and D. A. Benoit. 1974. Duration of toxicity tests for establishing "no effect" concentrations for copper with brook trout (*Salvelinus fontinalis*). Journal of the Fisheries Research Board of Canada 31:449–452.

Mehrle, P. M., and F. L. Mayer. 1985. Biochemistry/physiology. Pages 264–282 *in* Rand and Petrocelli (1985).

Meyers, T. R., and J. D. Hendricks. 1985. Histopathology. Pages 283–331 *in* Rand and Petrocelli (1985).

Mix, M. C. 1986. Cancerous diseases in aquatic animals and their association with environmental pollutants: a critical literature review. Marine Environmental Research 20:1–141.

Mount, D. I., and C. E. Stephan. 1967. A method for establishing acceptable toxicant limits for fish—malathion and the butoxyethanol ester of 2,4-D. Transactions of the American Fisheries Society 96:185–193.

Mount, D. I., N. A. Thomas, T. J. Norberg, M. T. Barbour, T. H. Roush, and W. F. Brandes. 1984. Effluent and ambient toxicity testing and instream community response on the Ottawa River, Lima, Ohio. U.S. Environmental Protection Agency, National Environmental Research Center, Ecological Research Series EPA-600/3-84-080. (Also: National Technical Information Service, PB85-102333, Springfield, Virginia.)

Murchelano, R. A., and R. E. Wolke. 1985. Epizootic carcinoma in the winter flounder, *Pseudopleuronectes americanus*. Science (Washington, D.C.) 228:587–589.

NAS (National Academy of Sciences) and NAE (National Academy of Engineering). 1974. Water quality criteria 1972. U.S. Environmental Protection Agency, National Environmental Research Center Ecological Research Series EPA.R3.73.033.

Nebeker, A. V. 1982. Evaluation of *Daphnia magna* renewal life-cycle test method with silver and Endosulfan. Water Research 16:739–744.

Nieboer, E., and D. H. S. Richardson. 1980. The replacement of the nondescript term 'heavy metals' by a biologically and chemically significant classification of metal ions. Environmental Pollution Series B, Chemical and Physical 1:3–26.

Nimmo, D. R., L. H. Bahner, R. A. Rigby, J. M. Sheppard, and A. J. Wilson, Jr. 1977. *Mysidopsis bahia:* an estuarine species suitable for life-cycle toxicity tests to determine the effects of a pollutant. American Society for Testing and Materials, Special Technical Publication 634:109–116.

Norberg, T. J., and D. I. Mount. 1985. A new fathead minnow (*Pimephales promelas*) subchronic toxicity test. Environmental Toxicology and Chemistry 4:711–718.

Norberg-King, T. J. 1989a. An evaluation of the fathead minnow seven-day subchronic test for estimating chronic toxicity. Environment Toxicology and Chemistry 8:1075–1089.

Norberg-King, T. J. 1989b. Culturing of *Ceriodaphnia dubia*: supplemental report for video training tape. U.S. Environmental Protection Agency, Office of Water Enforcement and Permits, Report EPA/505/8-89/002a, Washington, D.C.

Norberg-King, T., and J. Denny 1989. Culturing of fathead minnows (*Pimephales promelas*): supplemental report for video training tape. U.S. Environmental Protection Agency, Office of Water Enforcement and Permits, Report EPA/505/8-89/002b, Washington, D.C.

NRCC (National Research Council of Canada). 1981. Acidification in the Canadian aquatic environment: scientific criteria for assessing the effects of acidic deposition on aquatic ecosystems. NRCC, publication 18475, Ottawa.

OECD (Organization for Economic Cooperation and Development). 1984. Guideline for testing of chemicals—fish, acute toxicity test. OECD, Document 203, Paris.

Office of Water and Hazardous Materials. 1977. Quality criteria for water. U.S. Environmental Protection Agency, Washington, D.C.

Parrish, P. R. 1985. Acute toxicity tests. Pages 31–57 *in* Rand and Petrocelli (1985).

Paterson, C. G., and J. R. Nursall. 1975. The effects of domestic and industrial effluents on a large turbulent river. Water Research 9:425–435.

Peltier, W. H., and C. I. Weber, editors. 1985. Methods for measuring the acute toxicity of effluents to freshwater and marine organisms. U.S. Environmental Protection Agency, Report EPA/600/4-85/013, Cincinnati, Ohio.

Pickering, Q. H., C. Henderson, and A. E. Lemke. 1962. The toxicity of organic phosphorus insecticides to different species of warmwater fishes. Transactions of the American Fisheries Society 91:175–184.

Rand, G. M. 1985. Behavior. Pages 221–263 *in* Rand and Petrocelli (1985).

Rand, G. M., and S. R. Petrocelli, editors. 1985. Fundamentals of aquatic toxicology. Methods and applications. Hemisphere, Washington, D.C.

Russo, R. C. 1985. Ammonia, nitrite, and nitrate. Pages 455–471 *in* Rand and Petrocelli (1985).

Saunders, R. L., and J. B. Sprague. 1967. Effects of copper–zinc mining pollution on a spawning migration of Atlantic salmon. Water Research 1:731–737.

Schindler, D. W., R. Wagemann, R. B. Cook, T. Ruszczynski, and J. Prokopowich. 1980. Experimental acidification of Lake 223, Experimental Lakes Area: background data and the first three years of acidification. Canadian Journal of Fisheries and Aquatic Sciences 37:342–354.

Shubat, P. J., and L. R. Curtis. 1986. Ration and toxicant pre-exposure influence on dieldrin accumulation by rainbow trout (*Salmo gairdneri*). Environmental Toxicology and Chemistry 5:69–77.

Slooff, W., J. H. Canton, and J. L. M. Hermens. 1983. Comparison of the susceptibility of 22 freshwater species to 15 chemical compounds. I. (Sub)acute toxicity tests. Aquatic Toxicology (Amsterdam) 4:113–128.

Slooff, W., J. A. M. van Oers, and D. de Zwart. 1986. Margins of uncertainty in ecotoxicological hazard assessment. Environmental Toxicology and Chemistry 5:841–852.

Spacie, A., and J. L. Hamelink. 1985. Bioaccumulation. Pages 495–525 *in* Rand and Petrocelli (1985).

Sprague, J. B. 1969. Measurement of pollutant toxicity to fish. I. Bioassay methods for acute toxicity. Water Research 3:793–821.

Sprague, J. B. 1985. Factors that modify toxicity. Pages 124–163 *in* Rand and Petrocelli (1985).

Stephan, C. E. 1977. Methods for calculating an LC_{50}. American Society for Testing and Materials, Special Technical Publication 634:65–84.

Stephan, C. E. 1982. Increasing the usefulness of acute toxicity tests. American Society for Testing and Materials, Special Technical Publication 766:69–81.

Stephan, C. E., D. I. Mount, D. J. Hansen, J. H. Gentile, G. A. Chapman, and W. A. Brungs. 1985. Guidelines for deriving numerical national water quality criteria for the protection of aquatic organisms and their uses. National Technical Information Service, PB 85-227049, Springfield, Virginia.

Stich, H. F., A. B. Acton, and C. R. Forrester. 1976. Fish tumors and sublethal effects of pollutants. Journal of the Fisheries Research Board of Canada 33:1993–2001.

Tattersfield, F., and H. M. Morris. 1924. An apparatus for testing the toxic values of contact insecticides under controlled conditions. Bulletin of Entomological Research 14:223–233.

Thurston, R. V., T. A. Gilfoil, E. L. Meyn, R. K. Zajdel, T. I. Aoki, and G. D. Veith. 1985. Comparative toxicity of ten organic chemicals to ten common aquatic species. Water Research 9:1145–1155.

Thurston, R. V., R. C. Russo, C. M. Fetterolf, Jr., T. A. Edsall, and Y. M. Barber, Jr., editors. 1979. A review of the EPA red book: quality criteria for water. American Fisheries Society, Water Quality Section, Bethesda, Maryland.

USEPA (U.S. Environmental Protection Agency). 1975. Methods for acute toxicity tests with fish, macroinvertebrates, and amphibians. USEPA, EPA-660/3-75-009. Committee on Methods for Toxicity Tests with Aquatic Organisms. April 1975. Corvallis, Oregon.

USEPA (U.S. Environmental Protection Agency). 1980. Ambient water quality criteria for cadmium. USEPA, EPA-440/5-80-025, Washington, D.C. (Available from: National Technical Information Service, Springfield, Virginia.)

USEPA (U.S. Environmental Protection Agency). 1982. Daphnid acute toxicity test. USEPA, Office of Toxic Substances, EG-1/ES-1, Washington, D.C.

USEPA (U.S. Environmental Protection Agency). 1985a. Acute toxicity test for freshwater fish. Standard evaluation procedure. USEPA, Hazard Evaluation Division, EPA-540/9-85-006, Washington, DC.

USEPA (U.S. Environmental Protection Agency). 1985b. Acute toxicity test for freshwater invertebrates. USEPA, Hazard Evaluation Division, Washington, D.C. (National Technical Information Service, PB86-129269).

USEPA (U.S. Environmental Protection Agency). 1985c. Acute toxicity test for estuarine and marine organisms (estuarine fish 96-hour acute toxicity test). Standard evaluation procedure. USEPA, Hazard Evaluation Division, EPA-540/9-85-009, Washington, D.C.

Veith, G. D., D. J. Call, and L. T. Brooke. 1983. Structure–toxicity relationships for the fathead minnow, *Pimephales promelas:* narcotic industrial chemicals. Canadian Journal of Fisheries and Aquatic Sciences 40:743–748.

Waiwood, K. G., and F. W. H. Beamish. 1978. Effects of copper, pH and hardness on the critical swimming performance of rainbow trout (*Salmo gairdneri* Richardson). Water Research 12:611–619.

Warren, C. E. 1971. Biology and water pollution control. Saunders, Philadelphia.

Warren, C. E., and G. E. Davis. 1971. Laboratory stream research: objectives, possibilities, and constraints. Annual Review of Ecology and Systematics 2:111–144.

Weber, C. I., and thirteen coauthors. 1989. Short-term methods for estimating the chronic toxicity of effluents and receiving waters to freshwater organisms. U.S. Environmental Protection Agency, EPA/600/4-89/001, Cincinnati, Ohio.

Westlake, G. F. 1984. Behavioral effects of industrial chemicals on aquatic animals. Pages 233–250 *in* J. Saxena, editor. Hazard assessment of chemicals: current developments, volume 3. Academic Press, New York.

Westlake, G. F., J. B. Sprague, and D. W. Rowe. 1983. Sublethal effects of treated liquid effluent from a petroleum refinery. V. Reproduction of *Daphnia pulex* and overall evaluation. Aquatic Toxicology (Amsterdam) 4:327–339.

Zar, J. H. 1974. Biostatistical analysis. Prentice-Hall, Englewood Cliffs, New Jersey.

Zischke, J. A., J. W. Arthur, R. O. Hermanutz, S. F. Hedtke, and J. C. Helgen. 1985. Effects of pentachlorophenol on invertebrates and fish in outdoor experimental channels. Aquatic Toxicology (Amsterdam) 7:37–58.

15.7.1 Sources of Key Documents

Important water quality documents and computer programs can be obtained from the following addresses.

American Society for Testing and Materials, 1916 Race Street, Philadelphia, Pennsylvania 19103.

National Research Council of Canada, Environmental Secretariat, R-88, Montreal Road, Ottawa, Ontario K1A 0M8.

National Technical Information Service, 5285 Port Royal Road, Springfield, Virginia 22161.

TOXSTAT Computer programs: Department of Zoology and Physiology, University of Wyoming, Laramie, Wyoming 82071.

Chapter 16

Reproduction

LAURENCE W. CRIM AND BRIAN D. GLEBE

16.1 INTRODUCTION

A vast and fast-growing body of literature documents our interest in fish reproduction. It also reveals a need to better understand the appropriate means of producing young fish of high quality. Methods to control and manage fish reproduction are diverse; they include storing gametes, changing fish gender, manipulating the timing of reproduction, and sterilizing fish. In this chapter, which deals with teleost fishes, we present ways to determine reproductive status and to manage or manipulate various aspects of reproduction; reproductive behavior is treated in Chapter 17. Our emphasis is on cultured species, for which the most reproductive information exists. We have been highly selective in our citations of published papers for this chapter, and we hope readers will consult the broader literature to gain a fuller understanding of reproductive physiology.

16.2 SEX DETERMINATION

Dead fish can be sexed easily by direct examination of the gonads; Guerrero and Shelton (1974) described a method for sexing juveniles from gonad squashes. There is strong interest, however, in developing rapid and practical methods of sexing live fish. Such methods would lead to improved estimates of stock reproductive potential, more efficient feeding and marketing of domesticated stocks, and more efficient sample sizes for sex-specific experiments, among other advantages.

Live juvenile fish are especially difficult to sex because they usually lack external features associated with sexual maturation, such as breeding tubercles or sexually dimorphic pigment patterns and urogenital pores. Even the adults of some species such as milkfish lack consistent, perceptible differences in external body characteristics. Reliable sex determinations for such fish presently must be based on direct examination of the gonads or by blood or mucus tests.

16.2.1 Visual Gonad Inspection

Noninvasive methods to sex live fish from gonads promise speed and convenience but they still are under development. For example, although Martin et al. (1983) used commercial ultrasonic instruments to sex mature coho salmon, imaging technology still cannot discriminate the gender of juveniles reliably.

The gonads of live fish can be directly examined by endoscopy, thanks to modern fine-needle fiber-optic instruments. Ovaries appear rough and pebbly, immature testes look like fine strings, and mature testes are smooth. Moccia et al. (1984) followed the seasonal development of rainbow trout ovaries by endoscopy.

Crim et al. (1986) obtained ovarian biopsies from ripening Atlantic salmon with the aid of endoscopic instrumentation. In ripening and spawned female salmon, the endoscope may be inserted directly through the urogenital pore and into the body cavity to view the ovaries or rapidly remove egg samples. The urogenital pore also can be cannulated and gametes can be removed by aspiration to estimate the stage of sexual maturity (Section 16.3.3).

16.2.2   Blood and Mucus Sex Tests

The sex of maturing fish can be determined by immunological or electrophoretic analysis of easily obtained blood or mucus samples. Sensitive radioimmunoassay (RIA) methods can detect the presence of vitellogenin, a female-specific egg-yolk protein (So et al. 1985). One can use RIA to detect elevated levels (>10 ng/mL) of steroid sex hormones in the blood of maturing fish, hormones such as estrogens in females (Lamba et al. 1983; de Vlaming et al. 1984) and 11-ketotestosterone in males (Simpson and Wright 1977). Rapid sex testing of fish in the field by this method was reported by Le Bail and Breton (1981). Small serum samples were mixed on a slide with a sheep red blood cell reagent sensitized with vitellogenin antibodies; clumping of the test cells in about 15 min positively identified females. Another convenient sexing procedure was developed by Gordon et al. (1984), who identified female fish by using an enzyme-linked immunosorbent assay (ELISA) to detect vitellogenin in mucus samples obtained simply by swabbing the skin of coho salmon. Sex-linked activities of the enzyme serum esterase in two species of maturing salmon were reported by Slyn'ko and Semenova (1978). Recently, E. Verraspore (Scotland Department of Agriculture and Fisheries, personal communication) distinguished male from female patterns of serum esterase activity by isoelectrofocusing electrophoresis of serum samples from both juvenile and adult Atlantic salmon and brook trout. Avtalion et al. (1984) reported a male-specific serum protein (MSP) in certain species of tilapia, but the precise relationship between amount of MSP and stage of sexual maturity of males requires further study.

The greatest drawback to blood or mucus tests of gender is the time required to obtain the laboratory results, which requires that all tested fish be tagged and held for extended periods. Also, these tests can fail when the circulating level of vitellogenin or sex hormones is very low, as they are in juvenile fish or early in the breeding season. However, Sumpter et al. (1984) showed that increases in blood vitellogenin are detectable in virgin rainbow trout as much as 12 months before ovulation. Thus, of the methods presently available, testing for presence or absence of vitellogenin provides the most reliable early indication of sex.

16.3   DETERMINATION OF MATURITY AND RIPENESS

Efficient management of brood stock depends upon an accurate prediction of ripening time to facilitate the collection of high-quality reproductive products. Whether spontaneous or induced spawning techniques are practiced, a precise knowledge of gonadal ripening may be critical; for example, the quality of striped bass eggs declines within 30 min of ovulation (Piper et al. 1982), and hatchery staff must have good predictions of ovulation so they can prepare ripe males or sperm samples for fertilization during a narrow time period.

16.3.1 Gonadosomatic Index and Gonad Histology

Accurate assessment of reproductive maturity is most easily accomplished with dead fish. The relative gonad weight or gonadosomatic index—GSI = 100 × gonad weight (g)/body weight (g)—is commonly used as a simple index of reproductive maturity. The GSI, however, does not reliably indicate specific maturation stages, especially for fish of widely differing sizes (de Vlaming et al. 1982). The nonlinear relationship between gonad weight and fish size is dealt with by the relative gonadal index of Erickson et al. (1985): $RGI_i = \alpha_i W/S^\beta$; W is gonad weight, S is body size (either length or body weight less gonadal weight), and α_i and β are parameters for gonad stage i.

For microscopic analysis, whole gonads from dead fish, or gonad biopsies from live fish, may be preserved in formalin or other suitable fixatives and further processed according to standard histological techniques (Humason 1967; Chapter 7). The dynamic processes involved with oocyte development have been fully discussed by Wallace and Selman (1981). From histological samples, ovarian tissues may be divided into seven (Van den Hurk and Peute 1979) or eight (Marte and Lacanilao 1986) stages of maturity based upon the dominant gametogenic cell types present (see Figure 16.1). *Previtellogenic (immature) oocytes* are small, spherical ovarian cells containing a central nucleus and increasing amounts of cytoplasm (stages 1–3). *Vitellogenic (maturing) oocytes* (stages 3–6) incorporate the yolky materials produced by the liver. Yolk granules aggregate first at the periphery and later towards the center of the egg. *Mature oocytes* (stage 7) are the largest and are filled with yolk, which hardens during fixation and makes their histological preparation in paraffin difficult (however, sections of vitellogenic and mature oocytes mounted in plastic are suitable for microscopic study: Selman and Wallace 1982; Sumpter et al. 1984). The *spent ovary* (stage 8), found in females that have spawned, contains empty follicles and postovulatory structures termed *corpora lutea*.

The developmental cycle of the fish testes can be divided into six stages based upon the appearance of the maturing germ cells (Henderson 1962). The cycle begins with spermatogonial (stem) cell proliferation (stage 1). Germ cell maturation proceeds with the appearance of spermatocytes (stage 2), spermatids (stage 3), and spermatozoa (stage 4). When males are ripe (stage 5), termed the period of functional maturity, the testicular lumina are packed with sperm masses and milt flows freely when the abdomen is compressed. Stage 6, after spawning ceases, comprises a period of testicular involution and phagocytic absorption of residual sperm. The histological pattern of testes maturation in the milkfish (see Figure 16.2) has been described by Marte and Lacanilao (1986).

16.3.2 External Signs of Maturity

In some species of fish, advancing sexual maturity is accompanied by obvious external changes in body shape or pigmentation, by alterations in jaw shape, or by development of gonopodia, tubercles, or other secondary sex characters. By close inspection of the brood stock, it may be possible to note such changes as softening of the belly wall or extrusion of the urogenital pore. Full reproductive maturity

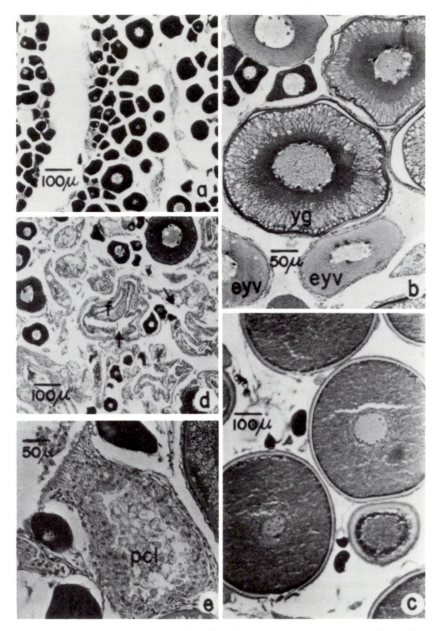

Figure 16.1　Ovarian development of milkfish. **(a)** Immature ovary with perinucleolar oocytes. **(b)** Maturing ovary with early yolk vesicle oocytes (eyv) and primary yolk granule oocytes (yg). **(c)** Mature ovary with tertiary yolk granule oocyte. **(d)** Spent ovary with empty follicles (f); arrows point to sites of follicle rupture. **(e)** Spent ovary with postovulatory corpus luteum (pcl) and developing oocyte. Scales are in micrometers. (Reproduced from Marte and Lacanilao 1986, with permission from *Aquaculture*.)

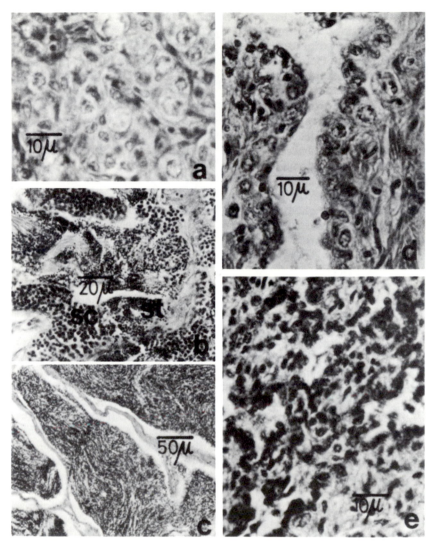

Figure 16.2 Testicular development of milkfish. **(a)** Immature testis with spermatogonia. **(b)** Maturing testis with spermatocytes (sc) and spermatids (st). **(c)** Mature testis with spermatozoa-filled lumina. **(d)** Spent testis with empty lumen. **(e)** Regressed testis. Scales are in micrometers. (Reproduced from Marte and Lacanilao 1986, with permission from *Aquaculture*.)

usually is detectable by the easy expulsion of eggs or sperm when the abdomen is pressed. However, reliable collection of high-quality gametes requires a precise knowledge of when eggs will mature, ovulation will occur, and sperm will fully ripen.

16.3.3 Staging the Maturity of Gametes

It may be necessary to sample gametes to properly stage the sexual condition of brood stock for species that typically do not show external signs of maturity. Egg samples have been obtained from the ovaries of the common carp by puncture of

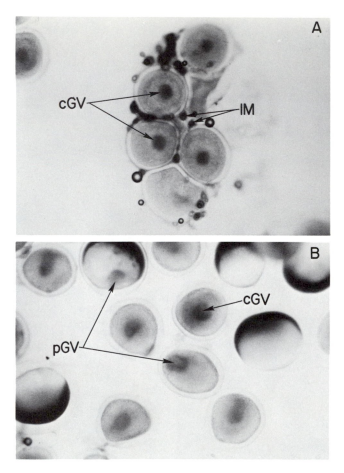

Figure 16.3 Cleared winter flounder oocytes with germinal vesicles in (**A**) the central position (cGV) and (**B**) the central and peripheral (pGV) positions; IM denotes immature oocytes.

the abdomen and gonad and aspiration of oocytes directly into a syringe fitted with a relatively large needle (Bieniarz and Epler 1976). Eggs collected by this method or by catheterization of the ovary may be examined and measured under a microscope (Kuo et al. 1974). Egg size corresponds to stage of reproductive maturity of striped mullet (Shehadeh et al. 1973) and channel catfish (Markmann and Doroshov 1983). Egg diameters also can indicate whether or not females are susceptible to hormonal induction of spawning (Section 16.6.2).

Reproductive maturity of females may also be estimated from the position of the nucleus or germinal vesicle within the oocyte. In immature eggs of winter flounder, for example, the germinal vesicle occupies a central position but migrates towards the egg periphery as development proceeds (Figure 16.3). When the germinal vesicle nears the animal pole, maturation and ovulation may be expected within a few days or weeks. The fish may be most sensitive to injected hormones at this time. Once the germinal vesicles break down, indicating eggs have matured, ovulation and spawning usually occur within hours. If the locations of the germinal vesicles are obscured by yolk material, the eggs can be exposed to a clearing solution for a short time in vitro. Crim et al. (1986) cleared eggs of Atlantic salmon with Davidson's fixative: 95% ethyl alcohol, formalin, glacial acetic acid, and distilled water in the ratio 3:2:1:3. Ng and Idler (1978) cleared eggs of winter flounder with buffered saline: 0.6% NaCl, glycerol, and glacial acetic acid in the ratio 90:6:4. In some fish species, yolk materials are very difficult to clear in vitro, and egg size remains the best index of reproductive maturity.

16.3.4 Hormone Profiles as an Indication of Maturity

Increases in plasma hormone concentrations, which can be monitored by sequential blood sampling, signal the onset of reproductive activity. The types and amounts of circulating hormones can be used to determine the sex and reproductive condition of live fish. For example, blood hormone profiles can be used to distinguish Atlantic salmon that will spawn in the current year from nonspawners as the fish approach their home rivers to breed; information of this type can improve management of the species (Idler et al. 1981). In goldfish, rising levels of the hormones estradiol-17β (sometimes called E_2) and testosterone signal ovarian development (Kagawa et al. 1983); plasma concentrations rise or remain elevated until spawning occurs. In rainbow trout, however, final oocyte maturation and impending ovulation are denoted by a drop in E_2 concentration in conjunction with rising plasma levels of gonadotropic hormone and progestogenic steroid hormones (Scott and Sumpter 1983). The growth and development of rainbow trout testes is marked by the appearance of androgenic steroid hormones in the plasma, particularly testosterone and 11-ketotestosterone (Scott et al. 1980; Fostier et al. 1982). The progestogenic steroid 17α, 20β-dihydroxyprogesterone also is present in the blood of fully ripe male rainbow trout (Scott and Baynes 1982).

16.4 ENUMERATION OF GAMETES

After their gonads ripen, brood-stock fishes may begin to spawn spontaneously or they may be artificially induced to spawn. Accurate estimates of fecundity will enhance the efficiency of brood-stock management and improve the predictions of offspring production.

16.4.1 Fecundity

A total count of ova in both ovaries yields an estimate of female reproductive potential, or fecundity. The fecundity of a milkfish was estimated by counting the yolky oocytes in a 1-g sample of a preserved mature ovary and multiplying that number by the total weight of both ovaries (Marte and Lacanilao 1986). Mason (1985) found three modes in the size distribution of ova in maturing walleye pollock. The smallest, immature oocytes were devoid of yolk and constituted a "reserve fund"; intermediate-size, yolked oocytes were in the developing class; and the largest, hydrating eggs were ripe and ready for imminent release.

Functional fecundity—the actual production of viable oocytes—may differ significantly from true reproductive potential because of incomplete spawning or atresia (degeneration) and resorption of oocytes. The extent to which fecundity understates reproductive potential can be estimated from examination of ovaries from recently spawned fish (Foucher and Beamish 1980). Vladykov (1956) demonstrated that the relative fecundity (eggs per unit fish weight) of brook trout declines throughout the summer and fall, suggesting that up to 40% of the eggs are lost to atresia prior to spawning. Fecundity may be affected by food availability; Springate et al. (1985) found that food deprivation reduced the rate of maturation and the total fecundity of rainbow trout.

When cultured species are spawned artificially, eggs may be counted as they are expressed by hand from females, but this is a tedious method of obtaining fecundity estimates. Several alternative methods of conveniently and accurately counting ovulated eggs were described by Leitritz and Lewis (1980). One usually estimates the volume of a subsample of eggs (e.g., number of eggs per 100 mL) and then determines total egg production simply by measuring the total volume of eggs collected or the total volume of fluid displaced by the eggs. Similarly, one can expand the number of eggs per unit weight of eggs to the total weight of ova collected.

Total sperm production is calculated by multiplying milt volume by the concentration of spermatozoa per unit volume of semen collected. Sperm concentrations may be determined from semen samples diluted 20 times with 0.9% NaCl by counting sperm heads per unit grid area of a hemacytometer under a microscope. A convenient index of sperm concentration is the spermatocrit, determined from the relative packed cell volume. Individual semen samples are drawn into microhematocrit tubes sealed at the bottom with clay; following centrifugation, the height of the white sediment (packed sperm volume) indicates the proportion of spermatozoa to total liquid semen volume. Bouck and Jacobson (1976) demonstrated the presence of a linear relationship between sperm concentration and packed cell volume of semen from trout and salmon. With the aid of a portable microhematocrit centrifuge, the spermatocrit determinations can be conducted in the field. Buyukhatipoglu and Holtz (1984) and Piironen (1985) demonstrated that the sperm output of male rainbow trout varies with age, season, frequency of stripping, and, to a lesser degree, the presence or absence of females.

16.5 GAMETE VIABILITY, PRESERVATION, AND FERTILIZATION

The quality of gametes is difficult to judge in the absence of fertilization tests. Gamete quality varies among individual fish and is further influenced by overripening, storage time, and other variables.

16.5.1 Sperm Viability

The difficulty in conveniently judging sperm quality is reflected by the traditional hatchery practice of using milt from more than one male to fertilize egg lots. An emerging trend, however, is to combine the gametes of one male and one female, which limits the detrimental effects of poor-quality gametes from a particular fish and restricts transmission of bacteria or viruses.

Gharrett and Shirley (1985) showed that the capacity of sperm to fertilize ova varies greatly among male salmon. Furthermore, fertilization success for individual sperm lots does not necessarily correspond directly with spermatocrit values, so additional estimates of sperm quality are advisable. These are ordinarily based upon a microscopic examination of spermatozoa; criteria include percent of sperm that are active, speed of movement, and duration of activity following activation by contact with water, collectively known as motility estimates. The rating of quality for mammalian sperm often includes a vitality test involving the supravital stain eosin Y (Eliasson and Treichl 1971; Mahadevan 1985), but this method appears not to have been tried on fish sperm to date. Daye and Glebe (1984) showed that sperm activity is affected by pH; the time to zero motility is reduced when pH falls below 4.5. Normally, fish milt and ovarian fluids have an alkaline pH.

16.5.2 Egg Quality

Egg quality is directly related to the timing of ovulation. For this reason, female rainbow trout brood stock are checked approximately every 10 d so eggs of equivalent states of ripeness can be obtained (Springate and Bromage 1985; see Section 16.6.2). Egg quality can vary greatly among females spawning for the first time, but the variability diminishes in subsequent breeding years (Craik and Harvey 1984). The histology of overripe eggs described by Nomura et al. (1974) aids the diagnosis of that condition. In fresh eggs, coagulation of oil droplets is thought to indicate poor quality. Nevertheless, rapid and reliable tests for predicting the quality of egg lots are lacking. Generally, the quality of an egg batch is assessed during incubation from the proportions of eggs that are fertilized, that reach the eyed and hatching stages, and that yield swim-up fry. One may determine the percentage of fertile ova 12 h after fertilization by fixing an egg sample in a solution of acetic acid, methanol, and water (1:1:1 by volume) and examining it microscopically for cell cleavages in the embryonic germinal discs.

Springate et al. (1984) noted that the rate of fertilization for particular batches of rainbow trout eggs may be used to predict mortalities at subsequent stages of development. However, when Hay (1986) held Pacific herring in captivity, which causes mature fish of this species to delay spawning, the viability of eggs and larvae declined rapidly as the holding period increased beyond 2 weeks—even though fertilization rates remained high. Presumably, the loss of quality was due to overripening of the eggs. If the biochemical changes that accompany the overripening of rainbow trout eggs (Craik and Harvey 1984) occur in herring eggs, the decline in egg viability was related to yolk decomposition, manifested (with trout) by a loss of dry matter, an increase in water content, and a decrease in precipitable protein.

Eggs of the red seabream *Chrysophrys major* change specific gravity according to their quality: viable eggs of this marine species are buoyant and abnormal eggs sink, according to Watanabe et al. (1985). These workers also showed that the quantity of dietary protein and pigments such as β-carotene and canthaxanthin influences both fecundity and egg quality. Torrissen (1984) and Tveranger (1986) found that carotenoid supplements in the diets of Atlantic salmon and rainbow trout had no effects upon fertilization rates and egg survival but enhanced the growth rate of first-feeding salmon fry.

16.5.3 Gamete Storage and Sperm Cryopreservation

Viability of both eggs and sperm can be prolonged for several days at temperatures maintained a little above freezing. Optimum short-term storage conditions for salmonid sperm include temperatures of 0–5°C, aeration, and the presence of antibiotics (Scott and Baynes 1980). Viable rainbow trout semen can be stored under oxygen in sealed jars for more than 3 weeks at $-2°C$ in the presence of 500 international units (IU) penicillin and 6,000 IU streptomycin per milliliter of semen to control bacterial and fungal growth; properly stored samples frequently retain their fertilizing ability despite the apparent loss of sperm motility (Stoss et al. 1978). Salmon eggs also can be stored for short periods at cool temperatures (3°C) under oxygen, but Jensen and Alderdice (1984) concluded that eggs suffer the deleterious effects of storage sooner than sperm.

Viability of sperm, but not of eggs, may be retained during storage at subzero temperatures. Cryopreservation at $-196°C$ in liquid nitrogen is the preferred method for long-term storage of spermatozoa for both freshwater and marine species (Scott and Baynes 1980; Harvey 1982; Stoss and Donaldson 1982). Sperm must be diluted before it is frozen to prevent cell injury that would otherwise result from the formation of ice crystals and from the increasing concentration of cellular solutes that occur as the supercooled sperm dehydrate. An extender composed of salts and organic substances is used to dilute sperm—usually 3 or 4 parts extender to 1 part semen—without activating it (without inducing motility). The extender also controls the tonicity of the preparation (thereby preventing cell rupture), buffers the pH, and offers membrane protection by adding phospholipid (e.g., lecithin). Cryoprotectants such as glycerol, dimethyl sulfoxide, ethylene glycol, and sucrose have been used to minimize the cell damage due to solute concentration during the freezing of diluted semen. It is thought that these protectants work by binding electrolytes (salts) after penetrating the cell membrane or by coating the membrane. It is important to control freezing and thawing rates to retain sperm viability. Lower rates of sperm fertility are commonly observed following periods of frozen storage. For example, the fertility of carp semen was 69% after 14 d of storage (versus 83% for fresh sperm) and about 30% after 342 d (Kurokura et al. 1984). Nevertheless, cryopreservation is a useful technique for special breeding purposes when high fertility rates are not required.

16.5.4   In Vitro Egg Fertilization

In vitro fertilization procedures may improve the percentage of eggs successfully fertilized. This may allow spermatozoa to be diluted to the minimum number necessary to obtain maximum fertilization (e.g., 10,000–300,000 sperm per egg), thereby reducing the number of male brood fish required. Ordinarily, the dry method of fertilization is used, whereby milt is added to eggs without additional water. Fertilization in the presence of ovarian fluid may prolong the activation of sperm beyond what could be obtained with a short activation period in water.

Billard (1985) discussed optimal conditions for in vitro fertilization of salmonid eggs. Briefly, sperm from all males is pooled and may be stored at a cool temperature under oxygen for a few hours. Egg batches are collected, and before they are pooled, each batch is examined separately to exclude those with high incidences of swollen or broken eggs or eggs with heterogeneous yolk. Batches judged to be of good quality are combined in a sodium chloride diluent buffered to pH 9 with tris and glycine; the ratio is 3 L of eggs to 1 L of diluent. This diluent improves fertilization rates over those obtained in plain water. Wilcox et al. (1984) noted that the presence of broken eggs reduced sperm motility and lowered egg fertility. The saline diluent helps correct this problem because it prevents the yolk of broken eggs from precipitating and trapping sperm; it also may keep the egg micropyle open for a longer time. Once the diluent has been added, 1–3 mL of sperm are decanted onto the eggs and the mixture is poured back and forth between containers. After 15 min, the eggs are rinsed in water and transferred into incubators.

16.6 CONTROL OF GONAD DEVELOPMENT AND SPAWNING

Predictable and cost-effective supplies of young fish often are needed for research or aquacultural purposes. Control of reproduction by captive brood stock is a distinct advantage in such circumstances.

16.6.1 Environmental and Genetic Influences

Annual spawning by temperate and subtropical fishes is closely linked to particular seasons of the year. Environmental variables such as temperature and photoperiod strongly influence the timing of reproduction (see reviews by Lam 1983 and Bye 1984). Reproductive development also is controlled by endogenous rhythms; seasonal spawning behavior continues even when fish are held in constant environmental conditions. Threespine sticklebacks exemplify the interactions between environmental and endogenous factors that affect reproduction by fishes (Baggerman 1980).

The propensity of fish to mature at a particular age and to spawn one or more times in a season is under genetic control. For example, strains of trout and salmon spawn in either spring or fall–winter, and there is little overlap in these breeding seasons. Such precise timing is a problem for researchers or culturists who need eggs at certain times of the year, but some practical methods have been devised—chiefly for trout—to extend or delay the breeding period and obtain out-of-season egg production (Bromage et al. 1984). For example, Bromage and Duston (1986) showed that spawning by rainbow trout could be advanced 6–8 weeks if the fish were subjected first to constant long days (17 h light:7 h darkness per 24-h photoperiod), then to constant short days (7 h light:17 h darkness); spawning could be delayed several weeks by a reversal of this sequence. Indeed, rainbow trout, which normally breed once per year, can be induced to spawn at 5–6-month intervals by exposure to constant long days or to continuous light (Scott et al. 1984; Bromage and Duston 1986), although there is a decline in spawning synchrony among individuals (Bromage and Duston 1986). In general, fish whose spawning season is advanced by photoperiod alterations produce greater numbers of eggs of smaller size, but survival to the fry stage seems unaffected by this (Bromage and Duston 1986).

16.6.2 Induced Spawning with Hormones and Drugs

Induction of spawning is of practical importance to fish culture because fish often resist breeding in captivity. The reasons for this resistance remain largely unknown, but they may be related to crowding stresses or the absence of natural breeding cues (appropriate substrate, water conditions, etc.). Growth and development of the gonads, or gonadal recrudescence, often takes place normally in captive fish, so reproductive inhibition results from a blockage of final maturation and ovulation or spermiation. It therefore becomes necessary to use hormones or other substances to overcome the block and induce spawning.

The practice of treating fish with crude extracts of donor fish pituitaries to induce spawning, a procedure termed hypophysation, began more than 60 years ago (Houssay 1931). Since then, the use of pituitary gonadotropic hormone for this purpose has become more refined (Harvey and Hoar 1979; Davy and Chouinard 1981; Lam 1982; Donaldson and Hunter 1983). Generally, brood stock receive intramuscular injections of donor pituitaries homogenized or macerated in a physiological saline solution (0.6% sodium chloride); the suspension is allowed to settle before the supernatant is taken off for injections. The pituitaries can be obtained fresh or stored dehydrated in acetone or absolute alcohol prior to use. The crude pituitary extract is administered in two injections, a smaller priming treatment and a later, larger resolving dose. For example, Bhowmick and Kowtal (1973, cited by Harvey and Hoar 1979) induced female carp to spawn by injecting each fish first with an extract of half a fresh carp pituitary and then with an extract of a full pituitary. Final oocyte maturation and ovulation normally occur within a few hours of the second injection, although the response time depends on the temperature at which the fish are held and the maturity of their gonads at the time of treatment.

Although the use of crude pituitary extracts to induce spawning is still widespread, the technique is unreliable at times because of the unknown potency of freshly collected pituitaries. Pituitary potency varies with the sex, age, and maturity of the donor fish. It also varies with species: pituitaries collected from the species being injected are more effective than pituitary gonadotropic hormone preparations from distantly related species.

The expense or limited and unpredictable supply of donor pituitaries has led to efforts to discover other, more reliable, sources of hormones for induction of spawning. Commercial preparations of partially purified salmon or carp pituitary containing gonadotropic hormone or the mammalian gonadotropins PMSG (pregnant mare serum gonadotropin) and HCG (human chorionic gonadotropin) have been successfully used to induce spawning (Lam 1985). These hormones are popular because their potencies are predictable by bioassay and the commercial supply is dependable. However, these partially refined biochemical reagents are expensive for practical fish culture.

In 1971, the structure of luteinizing hormone releasing hormone (LHRH) a synonym of gonadotropin releasing hormone (GnRH), was discovered during purification work on extracts of sheep and pig brains (see review by Vickery et al. 1984). This small peptide stimulates release of gonadotropic hormones from the mammalian pituitary. It is now well known that GnRH and especially GnRH analogs also prompt release of gonadotropic hormone from fish pituitary glands (Crim 1984; Peter 1986; Crim et al. 1987). Highly potent synthetic GnRH analogs, such as [D-Ala^6,Pro^9-NHEt]LHRH (the code indicates amino acid substitutions in the basic peptide) are effective agents for inducing spawning in brood-stock fishes. Optimal conditions for cost-effective use of GnRH analogs with fish are currently under study, but a successful procedure can be generally outlined as follows. Brood stock are injected twice, at an interval of 2–3 d, with 20 µg GnRH analog/kg body weight. The injection of many fish can be automated with a continuous-delivery syringe; the needle should be disinfected between injections. Single injections, even in large doses, appear to be less effective than repeated treatments. The GnRH analog treatment alone is effective in some types of fish (e.g., salmonids); however, other fish species (e.g., cyprinids) respond better when GnRH analog is injected with pimozide (10 mg/kg), a neurotransmitter antagonist (Sokolowska et al. 1985). Refinements in GnRH technology are currently under investigation. Greater economies might be obtained from single injections of long-lasting, sustained-release formulations of GnRH analogs, thereby reducing the stresses and costs connected with handling brood stock. For example, Lee et al. (1985) described a simple, inexpensive hormone pellet, made from cholesterol powder and melted cocoa butter (95:5 by weight), for long-term delivery of GnRH analog. Crim et al. (1988) and Sherwood et al. (1988) produced and tested GnRH pellets having short-term or relatively long-term release profiles. These simple hormone implantation devices have been successfully used to induce maturation and spawning by captive milkfish (Lee et al. 1986; Marte et al. 1987) and multiple spawning by barramundi perch (Almendras et al. 1988). The major advantage of GnRH analog technology is the ready commercial availability of certain potent synthetic hormones such as [D-Ala^6,Pro^9-NHEt]LHRH, Buserelin or [D-Ser(tBu)^6, Pro^9-NHEt]LHRH, and the salmon GnRH analog [D-Arg^6,Trp^7,Leu^8,Pro^9-NHEt]LHRH. These compounds will likely become less expensive compared to biologically active preparations of gonadotropic hormone. Furthermore, one may expect to avoid the problems with hormone insensitivity that brood stock develop after repeated treatments with gonadotropic hormone.

Once plasma gonadotropin levels are elevated in brood stock, from injections of either gonadotropic hormone itself or a GnRH analog that stimulates pituitaries to release it, final maturation of the gonads is activated and spawning is induced. Another way to achieve these responses is to lower the circulating levels of sex steroids. Sex steroids, particularly estrogen, inhibit release of gonadotropic hormone from the pituitary. Therefore, estrogen antagonists such as clomiphene and tamoxifen have been used effectively to induce spawning (Donaldson et al. 1981). Progesterone, which has been used to accelerate spawning in coho salmon (Jalabert et al. 1978), has a direct effect upon the gonads, inducing final maturation of oocytes. The most effective results with these latter methods are achieved with combinations of progesterone and gonadotropic hormone given to brood stock near the time gonadal recrudescence is complete.

16.7 METHODS OF SEX CONTROL AND INHIBITION OF MATURATION

The intensive culture of some fish species has created a demand for technological advances to improve productivity. The sexuality of fish has great importance in fish culture because the onset of maturation affects growth rate and market acceptability of fish. Similarly, sexual dimorphism and sex-specific life history variation are often counter productive in culture situations. Yamazaki (1983) has reviewed the diversity of sexual expression and maturation in fish. Control of reproduction has been achieved by manipulation of both physiological and chromosomal sex and by sterilization.

16.7.1 Manipulation of Physiological Sex

The administration of various steroids to incubating eggs and to the diet of juveniles has induced sex reversal in 15 gonochoristic fish species (these are nonhermaphrodite species, individuals of which have either testes or ovaries; Yamazaki 1983). Most cultured species are gonochoristic. Yamamoto (1969) and Hunter and Donaldson (1983) reviewed the manipulation of sex with exogenous steroid treatments and the potential benefits of unisexual populations. Essentially, androgens act as male inducers and estrogens as female inducers. The effectiveness of steroids for sex reversal depends on the timing of treatment, the dosage given, and the species being administered. The oral dose of the potent, commonly used androgen methyltestosterone ranges from 3 mg/kg of diet for Atlantic salmon (Johnstone et al. 1978) to levels approaching 25 mg/kg of diet for tilapia and goldfish (Yamamoto and Kajishima 1968; Guerrero 1975). Oral administration of the steroid usually is continued for 10–90 d, the duration depending on the species and whether or not steroid was applied to the eggs in aqueous solution. In salmonids, development of sex-specific gonadal tissue may vary according to age of the fry, which could explain why the success of sex reversal in these fishes depends on the timing of steroid administration. For instance, Goetz et al. (1979) failed to sex-reverse coho salmon by oral administration of methyltestosterone, but Johnstone et al. (1978) successfully administered this androgen to Atlantic salmon. For coho salmon, it was necessary to immerse eyed eggs and alevins in aqueous solutions of the steroid, as well as to dose the fry orally, before sex reversal was attained. This suggested that gonadal differentiation occurs earlier in coho than in Atlantic salmon.

To produce maximal numbers of sex-reversed fish, male steroids should be administered when young fish first accept prepared feeds. However, masculinization can still occur at high frequency if treatments are delayed 1–2 weeks after first feeding. The stage of gonadal differentiation most sensitive to exogenous steroid manipulation occurs during this time. If the parents are mouth-brooders, as they are in many tilapia and other cichlid species, eggs can be removed from the mouth and incubated artificially. After they hatch and absorb their yolk, the fry can be fed methyltestosterone-treated food (45 mg/kg feed) for 21 d to effect masculinization (Calhoun and Shelton 1983). The steroid, dissolved in alcohol, is sprayed onto dry feed and the alcohol is allowed to evaporate. Box 16.1 outlines one procedure for sex-reversing rainbow trout.

Estrogens such as estradiol-17β and estrone have been used to induce feminization in various fish species (reviewed by Yamazaki 1983). Estradiol is used most frequently to feminize salmonid fishes. Dietary doses (prepared like those for methyltestosterone, Box 16.1) at first feeding have ranged from 10 to 20 mg/kg administered for 30–70 d. Atlantic salmon could be feminized by dietary administration of the steroid alone, but coho salmon needed an immersion (0.5–5 mg estradiol-17β/L) at the alevin stage as well as dietary supplementation—a species difference that mirrors the masculinization of these fish with androgen. Dietary estrone, at levels of 100–200 mg/kg of food for the first 30 d of feeding, has been commonly used to feminize tilapia and goldfish (Guerrero 1975; Yamamoto 1975), but this steroid is less satisfactory because it often yields incomplete sex reversal.

Experimental use of steroids for sex control has almost reached commercial production levels in several countries. In several hatcheries in the United

---

Box 16.1 Sex-Reversing Rainbow Trout

The Ministry of Agriculture, Fisheries and Food in Scotland distributes to interested fish farmers the following recipe (here slightly modified) for producing all-male rainbow trout.

1. Weigh 1 kg of fry food into a plastic bucket.
2. Add 10 drops of benzyl alcohol to 3 mg methyltestosterone; stir to dissolve.
3. Add 200 mL ethyl alcohol (95%) to the benzyl alcohol–hormone solution.
4. Pour the alcohol-hormone mixture onto the food; stir the food as this is done to ensure even distribution of the hormone.
5. Spread the food in a thin layer on a polyethylene sheet to dry at room temperature for 24 h; stir the food occasionally so it dries evenly.
6. Store dried food in labeled bags in the freezer. Remove sufficient food for 1–2 d of feeding.
7. Feed treated food in the normal way for 750 degree-days (e.g., for 75 d at 10°C) from the time fry first accept food; then continue feeding with untreated food until fish mature.
8. Sex mature fish by pressing their abdomens; masculinized females cannot release milt.
9. Remove testes from males and cut criss-crossed incisions in them; leave the testes for 20 min while much of the sperm oozes out.
10. Dilute sperm in modified Cortland extender (physiological saline solution) and use them in the usual way to fertilize eggs.

Kingdom, sex-reversed rainbow trout are used to produce monosex progeny (Section 16.7.2). Similarly, in Japan, a state-run hatchery is supplying monosex trout to private aquaculturists. In Canada, the Department of Fisheries and Oceans has been providing experimental quantities of sperm from monosex female chinook salmon to commercial growers. Over 200,000 feminized salmon smolts were introduced to sea cages in 1986 for commercial grow-out.

The safety to consumers of steroids used for sex control of food fishes is without question. These substances are rapidly eliminated after treatment (Fagerlund and Dye 1979). Steroid levels drop to less than those found in naturally maturing fish within a matter of days, and steroid treatment ceases at least 1 year before the fish reach market size. In the UK, the sale of hormone-treated fish (which are intended for brood stock and not for food or sport) is not recommended because of the risk of adverse publicity. However, monosex progeny are one generation removed from hormone treatment and have no associated stigma.

Currently, use of steroids is allowed for research purposes only. In the UK, steroid applications to fish feed must be done under the supervision of a veterinarian. In Canada and the USA, certificates for experimental study are required from government regulatory agencies. However, it is expected that, after further trials, these compounds will be approved for use in North American aquaculture under specified conditions.

16.7.2 Manipulation of Genetic Sex

Sex control of fish can be accomplished by chromosomal manipulation. Sex is determined at fertilization by combination of chromosomes derived half from the ovum and half from the sperm. The absence of heteromorphic sex chromosomes in some fish species allows manipulation of sex ratios. Among Mozambique tilapias, for example, (Wohlfarth and Hulata 1981), either the female or male can be the homogametic sex (*XX*, as opposed to the heterogametic *XY*), depending on the geographic race being considered. When races having alternate sex heterogamety are crossbred, all-male hybrids result. Subsequent spawning, which could lead to overcrowding and stunting, does not occur.

Sex-reversal techniques have been applied to species having heterogametic sex genes (tilapia) and heteromorphic sex chromosomes (salmonids). Calhoun and Shelton (1983) produced functionally sex-reversed males of *Tilapia nilotica* (female homogamety) by adding methyltestosterone to the diet (45 mg/kg) for 21 d beginning at first feeding. Mass spawnings of these sex-reversed males with untreated females resulted in essentially all-female progeny. As in all-male populations, subsequent recruitment, overcrowding, and poor growth do not occur in all-female cultures (Anderson and Smitherman 1978). Similarly, heterogamety in salmonids has been used to control genetic sex. In rainbow trout and Pacific and Atlantic salmon, *XX* (sex-reversed) males sired all female progeny when crossed with normal *XX* females (Okada et al. 1979; Hunter et al. 1983; Johnstone and Youngson 1984). Presently, 100% female ova produced by breeding homogametic males and females are commercially available from several hatcheries in the UK. This indirect technique has several advantages over production of all-female populations by estrogen treatment: it is fully effective, the resultant fish are normal genotypic females (suitable as brood fish), and hormones are never applied to fish that may be destined for human consumption. However, the indirect process requires more lead time because two generations are required to produce monosex female groups. Donaldson and Hunter (1985) reviewed the potential benefits of all-female stocks for mariculture and the enhancement of capture fisheries.

Artificial gynogenesis (parthenogenic development of eggs after they are activated by genetically inert spermatozoa) and androgenesis (reverse of gynogenesis: the egg's genetic material is inactivated) have been used for sex control. Success with these techniques has been limited due to high egg mortalities, induced inbreeding, and abnormal embryogenesis. Heterogametic species can be used to gynogenetically produce all-male or all-female populations. The genetic material in the sperm of species such as grass carp (Stanley 1976b), rainbow trout, and Pacific salmon (Refstie et al. 1982) is inactivated by ultraviolet (UV) radiation. For example, UV light (6.5 mW/cm^2) from an ordinary germicidal lamp denatures sperm DNA in 5–10 min (Stanley 1976a), but the sperm retain their ability to induce completion of the second meiotic division in eggs. Extrusion of a polar body (one chromosome set) from eggs at this time is inhibited by temperature shock (as extreme as 28°C or more for salmonids) or hydrostatic pressure (up to 7×10^4 kPa), and egg development thus proceeds with two sets of maternal chromosomes. If the zygote is not so treated after gynogenetic fertilization, the yield of diploids is less than 1% of the eggs. Thermal shock of eggs interferes with normal meiotic cell divisions and can appreciably increase the yields of diploids (flatfish: Purdom and Lincoln 1973; common carp: Nagy et al. 1978). In heterogametic species whose females are homogametic (*XX* type), gynogenesis yields all-female eggs.

Sex control by androgenesis is in the developmental stage and has not been very successful to date. Arai et al. (1979) induced androgenetic haploid embryos of cherry salmon by irradiating eggs with gamma rays from a cobalt-60 source (5 × 10^3 röntgens) and inseminating them with normal sperm, but embryogenesis was abnormal. H. Onozato (Hokkaido University, unpublished) produced androgenetic diploid salmonid embryos with hydrostatic pressure, but the induction rate was only 1.5% at hatching.

Monosex fish populations resulting from gynogenesis could be more productive in aquaculture than normal populations, although one gynogenetic sex may be less useful than the other due to earlier maturation or poorer growth. Furthermore, if introduced exotic fish species are monosex, they will not reproduce and become pests should they escape. An example is the introduction of diploid gynogenetic grass carp to the USA for biological control of aquatic vegetation (Stanley et al. 1975). Breeding of gynogenetic females with sex-reversed gynogenetic males from the same family is a rapid method of producing highly inbred lines or clones of fishes (Streisinger et al. 1981). The utility of highly inbred lines for aquaculture purposes has yet to be fully evaluated.

The production of triploid fish by crossing tetraploids with diploids has, to date, been unsuccessful. Tetraploids, produced by blocking the first mitotic cleavage of fertilized eggs either with heat shock (Thorgaard et al. 1981) or with the cytokinesis inhibitor cytochalasin B (Refstie 1981), have not generally been reproductively viable. The problem seems to be the large size of diploid sperm from tetraploid males that makes the sperm unable to penetrate the egg micropyle. (Triploidy is addressed further in Section 16.7.3).

16.7.3 Sterilization

The methods currently under investigation for inducing sterility, primarily for cultured fish species, include autoimmunity, exogenous steroid treatment, hybridization, triploidy induction, surgical gonadectomy, and irradiation.

Immunorejection of gonadal tissue was achieved in Atlantic salmon by intraperitoneal injection of testicular extract combined with Freund's adjuvant, followed 4 weeks later by injection of spermatozoa in buffered saline (Laird et al. 1978). However, the permanence of sterility induced this way is uncertain, and licensing of a ''vaccine'' that contains Freund's complete adjuvant probably will be hard to obtain from governmental authorities. This method thus may have limited applicability to aquaculture and wild stock management.

Androgenic treatment during alevin and early feeding stages has been successfully used to sterilize coho salmon, chum salmon, and kokanee (Hunter and Donaldson 1985). After the anadromous fish were released to go to sea, their return migration was inhibited, and they were larger than normal when captured in the fishery. The performances of androgen-sterilized Atlantic salmon in net pens (Glebe, unpublished data) and coho salmon in sea cages (E. M. Donaldson, Canada Department of Fisheries and Oceans, personal communication) are being evaluated, the latter under commercial growing conditions. In these trials, methyltestosterone (10–40 mg/kg feed) appears to be the most effective androgen for sterilizing salmonids, confirming the work of Yamazaki (1976), who used 50 mg methyltestosterone/kg feed to achieve long-term sterility of rainbow trout. Treatment protocols for induction of sterility are similar to those used for sex reversal (Section 16.7.1), but much higher androgen doses are required.

Anabolism is a positive side effect often associated with androgen treatments used to induce sterility or sex reversal. Methyltestosterone doses of 1–50 mg/kg diet have been reported to accelerate growth of rainbow trout and coho salmon (Fagerlund and McBride 1975; Yamazaki 1976). The use of steroids to improve feed conversion efficiency and growth might enhance aquacultural production, and would be safer for consumers (Section 16.7.1).

Hybridization of fish can affect sexual maturation to varying degrees by causing zygotic, gametic, or gonadic sterility (Chevassus 1983). Of most potential benefit to intensive aquaculture is gonadic sterility (complete absence of reproductive tissue) because good carcass quality is associated with the absence of sexual development. Interspecific crosses involving Arctic char and Atlantic salmon, brown trout and char, and plaice and flounder have generated gonadic sterility in one or both sexes (Refstie and Gjedrem 1975).

Inductions of *triploidy* have completely disrupted normal reproductive function, particularly of females, in several trials. Temperature shocks and treatments with chemicals such as cytochalasin B (Refstie et al. 1977) to suppress meiotic metaphase II and produce triploids have met with variable success (Purdom 1972). Both heat and pressure shocks seem to effectively induce triploidy in salmonids. Shelton et al. (1986) induced triploidy in 90% of rainbow trout eggs by exposing the eggs to nitrous oxide (an anesthetic gas) at 11 atmospheres pressure for 30 or 60 min after fertilization. The numbers of fry that survived to their first feeding were similar to those of controls, suggesting the technique may be less harsh than the more conventional heat and pressure shock methods. The utility of nitrous oxide and other anesthetic gases for induction of triploidy has not been tested with other species.

Triploids are identified most reliably by flow cytometry (Allen 1983) and microdensitometry (Johnstone and Lincoln 1986). These techniques are based on measurements of the greater amount of nuclear DNA in the red blood cells of triploids than in those of diploids. In most species, gametogenesis in triploids is prevented only in females (Lincoln and Scott 1983; Benfey and Sutterlin 1984). A simple light microscope examination of the juvenile ovary is all that is required to confirm the absence of oocytes in triploid females. Partial or complete sexual maturation of males remains a general problem, but one that was avoided with the induction of triploidy in monosex female egg lots from rainbow trout (Lincoln and Scott 1983). Triploid male common carp, unlike their salmonid counterparts, appear to have retarded sexual development (Gervai et al. 1980). Benfey et al. (1986) showed that triploid rainbow trout produce inviable aneuploid sperm, which have DNA contents intermediate between those of haploid and diploid sperm. This suggests that the stocking of triploid rainbow trout and possibly other triploid salmonids will not result in self-sustaining populations.

A combination of hybridization with triploidy induction may offer new opportunities for the production of sterile crosses that have better viability. In this instance, improved zygotic survival associated with the extra maternal chromosome set may allow production of new hybrid combinations. Such work is in the developmental stage (see review by Chourrout 1982). Glebe (unpublished) produced triploid Arctic char × Atlantic salmon hybrids that retained the fast growth of the paternal char and had an improved salinity tolerance (relative to diploid hybrids) associated with the two chromosome sets from the maternal salmon. Manipulation of chromosome number in this example allowed variable doses of genetic traits to be transmitted from parental species to the hybrid offspring.

Surgical gonadectomy, involving the removal of immature gonads from anethesized salmonids, has resulted in fish that grew faster than maturing controls (Robertson and Wexler 1962; Brown and Richards 1979). However, regeneration of testicular tissue and the expense of performing this operation on large numbers of fish limit the practical use of castration in commercial aquaculture.

Cobalt-60 *gamma radiation* (600 röntgens) applied to eyed rainbow trout and Atlantic salmon eggs sterilized most individuals (Konno and Tashiro 1982; Villarreal and Thorpe 1985). Histological examination showed that undeveloped gonads lacked germ cells and thus were permanently sterile. The application of this relatively simple technique for preventing maturation of cultured fish requires additional study because irradiation inhibits gametogenesis but does not prevent secretion of steroid sex hormones and development of secondary sex characteristics (Thorpe et al. 1987).

16.8 REFERENCES

Allen, S. J., Jr. 1983. Flow cytometry: assaying experimental polyploid fish and shellfish. Aquaculture 33:317–328.

Almendras, J. M., C. Duenas, J. Nacario, N. M. Sherwood, and L. W. Crim. 1988. Sustained hormone release. III. Use of gonadotropin releasing hormone analogues to induce multiple spawnings in sea bass, *Lates calcarifer.* Aquaculture 74:97–111.

Anderson, C. E., and R. O. Smitherman. 1978. Production of normal male and androgen sex-reversed *Tilapia aurea* and *T. nilotica* fed a commercial catfish diet in ponds. Pages 34–42 *in* R. O. Smitherman, W. L. Shelton, and J. H. Grover, editors. Culture of exotic fishes symposium proceedings. American Fisheries Society, Fish Culture Section, Auburn, Alabama.

Arai, K., H. Onozato, and F. Yamazaki. 1979. Artificial androgenesis induced with gamma irradiation in masu salmon, *Oncorhynchus masou.* Bulletin of the Faculty of Fisheries Hokkaido University 30:181–186.

Avtalion, R. R., R. Shahrabani, R. Agassi, and L. Gringrass. 1984. Sex specific markers in tilapias. Pages 119–128 *in* H. Rosenthal and S. Sarig, editors. Research on Aquaculture. European Mariculture Society, Special Publication 8, Bredene, Belgium.

Baggerman, B. 1980. Photoperiodic and endogenous control of the annual reproductive cycle in teleost fishes. Pages 533–567 *in* M. A. Ali, editor. Environmental physiology of fishes. Plenum, New York.

Benfey, T. J., and A. M. Sutterlin. 1984. Triploidy induced by heat shock and hydrostatic pressure in landlocked Atlantic salmon (*Salmo salar* L.). Aquaculture 36:359–367.

Benfey, T. J., I. I. Solar, G. de Jong, and E. M. Donaldson. 1986. Flow-cytometric confirmation of aneuploidy in sperm from triploid rainbow trout. Transactions of the American Fisheries Society 115:838–840.

Bhowmick, R. H., and G. V. Kowtal. 1973. Simplified technique of hypophysation of major carps. Journal of the Inland Fisheries Society of India 5:218–222. (Not seen; cited in Harvey and Hoar 1979.)

Bieniarz, K., and P. Epler. 1976. Preliminary results of the *in vivo* studies on ovarian resorption in carp, *Cyprinus carpio* L. Journal of Fish Biology 8:449–451.

Billard, R. 1985. Artificial insemination in salmonids. Pages 116–128 *in* R. N. Iwamoto and S. Sower, editors. Salmonid reproduction: an international symposium. University of Washington Sea Grant Program, Seattle.

Bouck, G. R., and J. Jacobson. 1976. Estimation of salmonid sperm concentration by microhematocrit technique. Transactions of the American Fisheries Society 105:534–535.

Bromage, N. R., and J. Duston. 1986. The control of spawning in the rainbow trout (Salmo gairdneri) using photoperiod techniques. Institute of Freshwater Research Drottningholm Report 63:17–26.

Bromage, N. R., J. A. K. Elliott, J. R. C. Springate, and C. Whitehead. 1984. The effects of constant photoperiods on the timing of spawning in the rainbow trout. Aquaculture 43:213–223.

Brown, L. A., and R. H. Richards. 1979. Surgical gonadectomy of fish: a technique for veterinary surgeons. Veterinary Record 104:215.

Buyukhatipoglu, S., and W. Holtz. 1984. Sperm output in rainbow trout (Salmo gairdneri)—effect of age, timing and frequency of stripping and presence of females. Aquaculture 37:63–71.

Bye, V. J. 1984. The role of environmental factors in the timing of reproductive cycles. Pages 188–205 in G. W. Potts and R. J. Wootton, editors. Fish reproduction: strategies and tactics. Academic Press, London.

Calhoun, W. E., and W. L. Shelton. 1983. Sex ratios of progeny from mass spawnings of sex-reversed broodstock of Tilapia nilotica. Aquaculture 33:365–371.

Chevassus, B. 1983. Hybridization in fish. Aquaculture 33:245–262.

Chourrout, D. 1982. La gynogenese chez les vertebres. Reproduction, Nutrition, Development 22:713–734.

Craik, J. C. A., and S. M. Harvey. 1984. Biochemical changes associated with overripening of the eggs of rainbow trout Salmo gairdneri Richardson. Aquaculture 37:347–357.

Crim, L. W. 1984. Actions of LHRH and its analogs in lower vertebrates. Pages 377–385 in B. H. Vickery, J. J. Nestor, Jr. and E. S. E. Hafez, editors. LHRH and its analogs: contraceptive and therapeutic applications. MTP Press, Lancaster, England.

Crim, L. W., B. D. Glebe, and A. P. Scott. 1986. Influence of LHRH analog on oocyte development and spawning in female Atlantic salmon, Salmo salar. Aquaculture 56:139–149.

Crim, L. W., R. E. Peter, and G. van der Kraak. 1987. Use of LHRH analogs in aquaculture. Pages 489–498 in B. H. Vickery and J. J. Nestor, Jr., editors. LHRH and its analogs: contraceptive and therapeutic applications, part II. MTP Press, London.

Crim, L. W., N. M. Sherwood, and C. E. Wilson. 1988. Sustained hormone release. II. Effectiveness of LHRH analog (LHRHa) administration by either single time injection or cholesterol pellet implantation on plasma gonadotropin levels in a bioassay model fish, the juvenile rainbow trout. Aquaculture 74:87–95.

Davy, F. B., and A. Chouinard. 1981. Induced fish breeding in southeast Asia. International Development Research Centre, IDRC-178e, Ottawa.

Daye, P. G., and B. D. Glebe. 1984. Fertilization success and sperm motility of Atlantic salmon (Salmo salar L.) in acidified water. Aquaculture 43:307–312.

de Vlaming, V., R. Fitzgerald, G. Delahunty, J. J. Cech, K. Selman, and M. Barkley. 1984. Dynamics of oocyte development and related changes in serum estradiol-17β, yolk precursor, and lipid levels in the teleostean fish, Leptocothus armatus. Comparative Biochemistry and Physiology A, Comparative Physiology 77:599–610.

de Vlaming, V., G. Grossman, and F. Chapman. 1982. On the use of the gonadosomatic index. Comparative Biochemistry and Physiology A, Comparative Physiology 73:31–39.

Donaldson, E. M., and G. A. Hunter. 1983. Induced final maturation, ovulation, and spermiation in cultured fish. Pages 351–403 in W. S. Hoar, D. J. Randall, and E. M. Donaldson, editors. Fish physiology, volume 9. Part B. Academic Press, New York.

Donaldson, E. M., and G. A. Hunter. 1985. Sex control in Pacific salmon: implications for aquaculture and resource enhancement. Pages 26–32 in R. N. Iwamoto and S. Sower, editors. Salmonid reproduction: an international symposium. University of Washington, Washington Sea Grant Program, Seattle.

Donaldson, E. M., G. A. Hunter, and J. M. Dye. 1981. Induced ovulation in coho salmon (Oncorhynchus kisutch). III. Preliminary study on the use of the antiestrogen tamoxifen. Aquaculture 26:143–154.

Eliasson, R., and L. Treichl. 1971. Supravital staining of human spermatozoa. Fertility and Sterility 22:134–137.

Erickson, D. L., J. E. Hightower, and G. D. Grossman. 1985. The relative gonadal index: an alternative index for quantification of reproductive condition. Comparative Biochemistry and Physiology A, Comparative Physiology 81:117–120.

Fagerlund, U. H. M., and H. M. Dye. 1979. Depletion of radioactivity from yearling coho salmon *(Oncorhynchus kisutch)* after extended ingestion of anabolically effective doses of 17α-methyltestosterone 1,2,-^{3}H. Aquaculture 18:303–315.

Fagerlund, U. H. M., and J. R. McBride. 1975. Growth increments and some flesh and gonad characteristics of juvenile coho salmon receiving diets supplemented with 17α-methyltestosterone. Journal of Fish Biology 7:305–314.

Fostier, A., R. Billard, B. Breton, M. Legendre, and S. Marlot. 1982. Plasma 11-oxotestosterone and gonadotropin during the beginning of spermiation in rainbow trout *(Salmo gairdneri* R.). General and Comparative Endocrinology 46:428–434.

Foucher, R. P., and R. J. Beamish. 1980. Production of nonviable oocytes by Pacific hake *(Merluccius productus)*. Canadian Journal of Fisheries and Aquatic Sciences 37:41–48.

Gervai, J., S. Peter, A. Nagy, L. Horvath, and V. Csanyi. 1980. Induced triploidy in carp, *Cyprinus carpio* L. Journal of Fish Biology 17:667–671.

Gharrett, A. J., and S. M. Shirley. 1985. A genetic examination of spawning methodology in a salmon hatchery. Aquaculture 47:245–256.

Goetz, F. W., E. M. Donaldson, G. A. Hunter, and H. M. Dye. 1979. Effects of estradiol-17β and 17α-methyltestosterone on gonadal differentiation in the coho salmon, *Oncorhynchus kisutch*. Aquaculture 17:267–278.

Gordon, M. R., T. G. Owen, T. A. Ternan, and L. D. Hildebrand. 1984. Measurement of a sex-specific protein in mucus of premature coho salmon *(Oncorhynchus kisutch)*. Aquaculture 43:333–339.

Guerrero, R. D., III. 1975. Use of androgens for the production of all-male *Tilapia aurea* (Steindachner). Transactions of the American Fisheries Society 104:342–348.

Guerrero, R. D., III, and W. L. Shelton. 1974. An aceto-carmine squash method for sexing juvenile fishes. Progressive Fish-Culturist 36:56.

Harvey, B. J. 1982. Cryobiology and the storage of teleost gametes. Pages 123–127 *in* C. J. J. Richter and H. J. T. Goos, editors. Reproductive physiology of fish. Pudoc, Wageningen, Netherlands.

Harvey, B. J., and W. S. Hoar. 1979. The theory and practice of induced breeding in fish. International Development Research Centre, IDRC-TS21e, Ottawa.

Hay, D. E. 1986. Effects of delayed spawning on viability of eggs and larvae of Pacific herring. Transactions of the American Fisheries Society 115:155–161.

Henderson, N. E. 1962. The annual cycle in the testis of the eastern brook trout, *Salvelinus fontinalis* (Mitchill). Canadian Journal of Zoology 40:631–645.

Houssay, B. A. 1931. Action sexuelle de l'hypophyse sur les poissons et les reptiles. Comptes Rendus des Seances de la Societe de Biologie et de ses Filiales 106:377–378.

Humason, G. L. 1967. Animal tissue techniques. Freeman, San Francisco.

Hunter, G. A., and E. M. Donaldson. 1983. Hormonal sex control and its application to fish culture. Pages 223–303 *in* W. S. Hoar, D. J. Randall, and E. M. Donaldson, editors. Fish physiology, volume 9. Part B. Academic Press, New York.

Hunter, G. A., and E. M. Donaldson. 1985. Contribution of ocean released sterile coho to the commercial and sports fishery. Page 41 *in* R. N. Iwamoto and S. Sower, editors. Salmonid reproduction: an international symposium. University of Washington, Washington Sea Grant Program, Seattle.

Hunter, G. A., E. M. Donaldson, J. Stoss, and I. Baker. 1983. Production of monosex female groups of chinook salmon *(Oncorhynchus tshawytscha)* by the fertilization of normal ova with sperm from sex-reversed females. Aquaculture 33:355–364.

Idler, D. R., S. J. Hwang, L. W. Crim, and D. Reddin. 1981. Determination of sexual maturation stages of Atlantic salmon *(Salmo salar)* captured at sea. Canadian Journal of Fisheries and Aquatic Sciences 38:405–413.

Jalabert, B., F. W. Goetz, B. Breton, A. Fostier, and E. M. Donaldson. 1978. Precocious induction of oocyte maturation and ovulation in coho salmon *(Oncorhynchus kisutch)*. Journal of the Fisheries Research Board of Canada 35:1423–1429.

Jensen, J. O. T., and D. F. Alderdice. 1984. Effect of temperature on short-term storage of eggs and sperm of chum salmon (*Oncorhynchus keta*). Aquaculture 37:251–265.

Johnstone, R., and R. F. Lincoln. 1986. Ploidy estimation using erythrocytes from formalin-fixed salmonid fry. Aquaculture 55:144–148.

Johnstone R., T. H. Simpson, and A. F. Youngson. 1978. Sex reversal in salmonid culture. Aquaculture 13:115–134.

Johnstone, R., and A. F. Youngson. 1984. The progeny of sex-inverted female Atlantic salmon (*Salmo salar* L.). Aquaculture 37:179–182.

Kagawa, H., G. Young, and Y. Nagahama. 1983. Changes in plasma steroid hormone levels during gonadal maturation in female goldfish *Carassius auratus*. Bulletin of the Japanese Society of Scientific Fisheries 49:1783–1787.

Konno, K., and F. Tashiro. 1982. The sterility of rainbow trout, *Salmo gairdneri*, irradiated with cobalt-60 gamma rays. Journal of the Tokyo University of Fisheries 68:75–80.

Kuo, C., C. E. Nash, and Z. H. Shehadeh. 1974. A procedural guide to induce spawning in grey mullet (*Mugil cephalus* L.). Aquaculture 3:1–14.

Kurokura, H., R. Hirano, M. Tomita, and M. Iwahashi. 1984. Cryopreservation of carp sperm. Aquaculture 37:267–273.

Laird, L. M., A. E. Ellis, A. R. Wilson, and F. G. Holliday. 1978. The development of the gonadal and immune systems in the Atlantic salmon (*Salmo salar* L.) and a consideration of the possibility of inducing auto-immune destruction of the testis. Annales de Biologie Animale, Biochimie. Biophysique 18:1101–1106.

Lam, T. J. 1982. Applications of endocrinology to fish culture. Canadian Journal of Fisheries and Aquatic Sciences 39:111–137.

Lam, T. J. 1983. Environmental influences on gonadal activity in fish. Pages 65–116 *in* W. S. Hoar, D. J. Randall, and E. M. Donaldson, editors. Fish physiology, volume 9. Part B. Academic Press, New York.

Lam, T. J. 1985. Induced spawning in fish. Pages 14–56 *in* C. S. Lee and I.-C. Liao, editors. Reproduction and culture of milkfish. Oceanic Institute, Waimanalo, Hawaii. (Also: Tungkang Marine Laboratory, Pingtung, Taiwan.)

Lamba, V. J., S. V. Goswami, and B. I. Sundararaj. 1983. Circannual and circadian variations in plasma levels of steroids (cortisol, estradiol-17β, estrone, and testosterone) correlated with the annual gonadal cycle in the catfish, *Heteropneustes fossilis* (Bloch). General and Comparative Endocrinology 50:205–255.

Le Bail, P. Y., and B. Breton. 1981. Rapid determination of the sex of puberal salmonid fish by a technique of immunoagglutination. Aquaculture 22:367–375.

Lee, C. S., C. S. Tamaru, J. E. Banno, C. D. Kelley, A. Bocek, and J. A. Wyban. 1986. Induced maturation and spawning of milkfish, *Chanos chanos* Forsskal, by hormone implantation. Aquaculture 52:199–205.

Lee, C. S., C. S. Tamaru, and L. W. Crim. 1985. Preparation of a luteinizing hormone-releasing hormone cholesterol pellet and its implantation in the milkfish (*Chanos chanos* Forsskal). Pages 215–226 *in* C. S. Lee and I.-C. Liao, editors. Reproduction and culture of milkfish. Oceanic Institute, Waimanalo, Hawaii. (Also: Tungkang Marine Laboratory, Pingtung, Taiwan.)

Leitritz, E., and R. C. Lewis. 1980. Trout and salmon culture (hatchery methods). California Department of Fish and Game, Fish Bulletin 164.

Lincoln, R. F., and A. P. Scott. 1983. Production of all-female triploid rainbow trout. Aquaculture 30:375–380.

Mahadevan, M. M. 1985. Supravital staining of frozen human spermatozoa. Fertility and Sterility 44:842–843.

Markmann, C., and S. I. Doroshov. 1983. Ovarian catheterization of the channel catfish, *Ictalurus punctatus*. Aquaculture 35:163–169.

Marte, C. L., and F. Lacanilao. 1986. Spontaneous maturation and spawning of milkfish in floating net cages. Aquaculture 53:115–132.

Marte, C. L., N. M. Sherwood, L. W. Crim, and B. Harvey. 1987. Induced spawning of maturing milkfish (*Chanos chanos* Forsskal) with gonadotropin-releasing hormone (GnRH) analogues administered in various ways. Aquaculture 60:303–310.

Martin, R. W., J. Myers, S. A. Sower, D. J. Phillips, and C. McAuley. 1983. Ultrasonic imaging, a potential tool for sex determination of live fish. North American Journal of Fisheries Management 3:258–264.

Mason, J. C. 1985. The fecundity of the walleye pollock, *Theragra chalcogramma* (Pallas), spawning in Canadian waters. Journal of Fish Biology 27:335–346.

Moccia, R. D., E. J. Wilkie, K. R. Munkittrick, and W. D. Thompson. 1984. The use of fine needle fibre endoscopy in fish for *in vivo* examination of visceral organs, with special reference to ovarian evaluation. Aquaculture 40:255–259.

Nagy, A., K. Rajki, L. Horvath, and V. Csanyi. 1978. Investigation on carp, *Cyprinus carpio* L. gynogenesis. Journal of Fish Biology 13:215–224.

Ng, T. B., and D. R. Idler. 1978. Big and little forms of plaice vitellogenic and maturational hormones. General and Comparative Endocrinology 34:408–420.

Nomura, M., K. Sakai, and F. Takashima. 1974. The over-ripening phenomenon of rainbow trout. I. Temporal morphological changes of eggs retained in the body cavity after ovulation. Bulletin of the Japanese Society of Scientific Fisheries 40:977–984.

Okada, H., H. Matsumoto, and F. Yamazaki. 1979. Functional masculinization of genetic females in rainbow trout. Bulletin of the Japanese Society of Scientific Fisheries 45:413–419.

Peter, R. E. 1986. Structure–activity studies on gonadotropin-releasing hormone in teleosts, amphibians, reptiles and mammals. Pages 75–93 *in* C. L. Ralph, editor. Comparative endocrinology: developments and directions. A. R. Liss, New York.

Piironen, J. 1985. Variation in the properties of milt from the Finnish landlocked salmon (*Salmo salar* M. *sebago* girard) during a spawning season. Aquaculture 48:337–350.

Piper, R. G., I. B. McElwain, L. E. Orme, J. P. McCraren, L. G. Fowler, and J. R. Leonard. 1982. Fish hatchery management. U.S. Fish and Wildlife Service, Washington, D.C.

Purdom, C. E. 1972. Induced polyploidy in plaice *(Pleuronectes platessa)* and its hybrid with the flounder *(Platichthys flesus)*. Heredity 29:11–24.

Purdom, C. E., and R. F. Lincoln. 1973. Chromosome manipulation in fish. Pages 83–89 *in* H. Schroder, editor. Genetics and mutagenesis of fish. Springer-Verlag, New York.

Refstie, T. 1981. Tetraploid rainbow trout produced by cytochalasin B. Aquaculture 25:51–58.

Refstie, T., and T. Gjedrem. 1975. Hybrids between salmonidae species: hatchability and growth rate in the freshwater period. Aquaculture 6:333–342.

Refstie, T., J. Stoss, and E. M. Donaldson. 1982. Production of all female coho salmon *(Oncorhynchus kisutch)* by diploid gynogenesis using irradiated sperm and cold shock. Aquaculture 29:67–82.

Refstie, T., V. Vassuik, and T. Gjedrem. 1977. Induction of polyploidy in salmonids by cytochalasin B. Aquaculture 10:65–74.

Robertson, O. H., and B. C. Wexler. 1962. Histological changes in the organs and tissues of senile castrated kokanee salmon *(Oncorhynchus nerka kennerlyi)*. General and Comparative Endocrinology 2:458–472.

Scott, A. P., and S. M. Baynes. 1980. A review of the biology, handling and storage of salmonid spermatozoa. Journal of Fish Biology 17:707–739.

Scott, A. P., and S. M. Baynes. 1982. Plasma levels of sex steroids in relation to ovulation and spermiation in rainbow trout *(Salmo gairdneri)*. Pages 103–106 *in* C. J. J. Richter and H. J. T. Goos, editors. Reproductive physiology of fish. Pudoc, Wageningen, Netherlands.

Scott, A. P., S. M. Baynes, O. Skarphedinsson, and V. J. Bye. 1984. Control of spawning time in rainbow trout, *Salmo gairdneri,* using constant long daylengths. Aquaculture 43:225–233.

Scott, A. P., V. J. Bye, S. M. Baynes, and J. R. C. Springate. 1980. Seasonal variations in plasma concentrations of 11-ketotestosterone and testosterone in male rainbow trout, *Salmo gairdnerii* Richardson. Journal of Fish Biology 17:495–505.

Scott, A. P., and J. P. Sumpter. 1983. A comparison of the female reproductive cycles of autumn-spawning and winter-spawning strains of rainbow trout (*Salmo gairdneri* Richardson). General and Comparative Endocrinology 52:79–85.

Selman, K., and R. A. Wallace. 1982. Oocyte growth in the sheepshead minnow: uptake of exogenous proteins by vitellogenic oocytes. Cell Tissue Research 14:555–571.

Shehadeh, Z. H., C. M. Kuo, and K. K. Milisen. 1973. Validation of an in vivo method for monitoring ovarian development in the grey mullet *(Mugil cephalus)*. Journal of Fish Biology 5:489–496.

Shelton, C. J., A. G. MacDonald, and R. Johnstone. 1986. Induction of triploidy in rainbow trout using nitrous oxide. Aquaculture 58:155–159.

Sherwood, N. M., L. W. Crim, J. Carolsfeld, and S. M. Walters. 1988. Sustained hormone release. I. Characteristics of in vitro release of gonadotropin-releasing hormone analogue (GuRH-A) from pellets. Aquaculture 74:75–86.

Simpson, T. H., and R. S. Wright. 1977. A radioimmunoassay for 11-oxotestosterone: its application in the measurement of levels in blood serum of rainbow trout *(S. gairdneri)*. Steroids 29:383–398.

Slyn'ko, V. I., and S. K. Semenova. 1978. Esterase as a sex-linked characteristic in salmon. Doklady Akademii Nauk SSSR 243:224–225. (Translated from Russian.)

So, Y. P., D. R. Idler, and S. J. Hwang. 1985. Plasma vitellogenin in landlocked Atlantic salmon *(Salmo salar ouananiche)*: isolation, homologous radioimmunoassay and immunological cross-reactivity with vitellogenin from other teleosts. Comparative Biochemistry and Physiology B, Comparative Biochemistry 81:63–71.

Sokolowska, M., R. E. Peter, and C. S. Nahorniak. 1985. The effects of different doses of pimozide and [D-Ala^6, Pro^9-N ethylamide] LHRH (LHRH-A) on gonadotropin release and ovulation in female goldfish. Canadian Journal of Zoology 63:1252–1256.

Springate, J. R. C., and N. R. Bromage. 1985. Effects of egg size on early growth and survival in rainbow trout *(Salmo giardneri* Richardson). Aquaculture 47:163–172.

Springate, J. R. C., N. R. Bromage, and P. R. T. Cumaranatunga. 1985. The effects of different ration on fecundity and egg quality in the rainbow trout *(Salmo gairdneri)*. Pages 371–393 *in* C. Cowey, editor. Feeding and nutrition in fish. Academic Press, London.

Springate, J. R. C., N. R. Bromage, J. A. K. Elliott, and D. L. Hudson. 1984. The timing of ovulation and stripping and their effects on the rates of fertilization and survival to eying, hatch and swim-up in the rainbow trout *(Salmo gairdneri* R.). Aquaculture 43:313–322.

Stanley, J. G. 1976a. A review of the methods for obtaining monosex fish and progress report on the production of monosex white amur. Journal of Aquatic Plant Management 14:68–70.

Stanley, J. G. 1976b. Female homogamety in grass carp *(Ctenopharyngodon idella)* determined by gynogenesis. Journal of the Fisheries Research Board of Canada 33:1372–1374.

Stanley, J. G., J. M. Martin, and J. B. Jones. 1975. Gynogenesis as a possible method for producing monosex grass carp *(Ctenopharyngodon idella)*. Progressive Fish-Culturist 37:25–26.

Stoss, J., S. Buyukhatipoglu, and W. Holtz. 1978. Short-term and cryo-preservation of rainbow trout *(Salmo gairdneri* Richardson) sperm. Annales de Biologie Animale, Biochimie, Biophysique 18:1077–1082.

Stoss, J., and E. M. Donaldson. 1982. Preservation of fish gametes. Pages 114–122 *in* C. J. J. Richter and H. J. T. Goos, editors. Reproductive physiology of fish. Pudoc, Wageningen, Netherlands.

Streisinger, G., C. Walker, N. Dower, D. Knauber, and F. Singer. 1981. Production of clones of homozygous diploid zebra fish *(Brachydanio rerio)*. Nature (London) 291:293–296.

Sumpter, J. P., A. P. Scott, S. M. Baynes, and P. R. Witthames. 1984. Early stages of the reproductive cycle in virgin female rainbow trout *(Salmo gairdneri* Richardson). Aquaculture 43:235–242.

Thorgaard, G. H., M. E. Jazwin, and A. R. Stier. 1981. Polyploidy induced by heat shock in rainbow trout. Transactions of the American Fisheries Society 110:546–550.

Thorpe, J. E., R. S. Wright, C. Talbot, and M. S. Miles. 1987. Secondary sexual characteristics developed by 60–Co sterilized Atlantic salmon. Page 139 *in* D. R.

Idler, L. W. Crim, and J. M. Walsh, editors, Reproductive physiology of fish. Memorial University of New Foundland, St. John's.

Torrissen, O. J. 1984. Pigmentation of salmonids: effect of carotenoids in eggs and start-feeding diet on survival and growth rate. Aquaculture 43:185–193.

Tveranger, B. 1986. Effect of pigment content in broodstock diet on subsequent fertilization rate, survival and growth rate of rainbow trout *(Salmo gairdneri)* offspring. Aquaculture 53:85–93.

Van den Hurk, R., and J. Peute. 1979. Cyclic changes in the ovary of the rainbow trout, *Salmo gairdneri,* with special reference to sites of steroidogenesis. Cell and Tissue Research 199:289–306.

Vickery, B. H., J. J. Nestor, Jr., and E. S. E. Hafez, editors. 1984. NHRH and its analogs: contraceptive and therapeutic applications. MTP Press, Lancaster, England.

Villarreal, C. A., and J. E. Thorpe. 1985. Gonadal growth and bimodality of length frequency distribution in juvenile Atlantic salmon *(Salmo salar)*. Aquaculture 45:249–263.

Vladykov, V. D. 1956. Fecundity of wild speckled trout *(Salvelinus fontinalis* L.) in Quebec lakes. Journal of the Fisheries Research Board of Canada 13:799–841.

Wallace, R. A., and K. Selman. 1981. Cellular and dynamic aspects of oocyte growth in teleosts. American Zoologist 21:325–343.

Watanabe, T., A. Itoh, S. Satoh, C. Kitajima, and S. Fujita. 1985. Effect of dietary protein levels and feeding period before spawning on chemical components of eggs produced by Red Sea bream broodstock. Bulletin of the Japanese Society of Scientific Fisheries 51:1501–1509.

Wilcox, K. W., J. Stoss, and E. M. Donaldson. 1984. Broken eggs as a cause of infertility of coho salmon gametes. Aquaculture 40:77–87.

Wohlfarth, G. W., and G. Hulata. 1981. Applied genetics of tilapias. International Center for Living Aquatic Resources Management, ICLARM Studies and Reviews 6.

Yamamoto, T. 1969. Sex differentiation. Pages 117–175 *in* W. S. Hoar and D. J. Randall, editors. Fish physiology, volume 3. Academic Press, New York.

Yamamoto, T. 1975. A YY male goldfish from mating estrone-induced XY female and normal male. Journal of Heredity 66:2–4.

Yamamoto, T., and T. Kajishima. 1968. Sex hormone induction of sex reversal in the goldfish and evidence for male heterogamety. Journal of Experimental Zoology 168:215–222.

Yamazaki, F. 1976. Application of hormones in fish culture. Journal of the Fisheries Research Board of Canada 33:948–958.

Yamazaki, F. 1983. Sex control and manipulation in fish. Aquaculture 33:329–354.

Chapter 17

Behavior

DAVID L. G. NOAKES AND JEFFREY R. BAYLIS

17.1 INTRODUCTION

Behavior is one of the most conspicuous properties of animals. It is of considerable importance to ecologists in general and fishery biologists in particular. Feeding, spawning, migration, and reactions to collecting gear are obvious examples of fish behavior that have practical significance. Although behavior is readily observed, it is not necessarily easy to study. Careful planning of observation schedules and precise definitions of behavior units to be recorded are just the first elements to be addressed in a behavioral study.

In this chapter we provide a selective review of fish behavior likely to be of practical interest and application. We follow the approach of behavioral ecology, an active and rapidly progressing field (Krebs and Davies 1984) that incorporates studies in such major areas as foraging, predator–prey interactions, sex and mating behavior, and life history strategies.

A fish could engage in many different kinds of activities: searching for food, avoiding predators, searching for mates, schooling with other individuals, and responding to physical factors in the environment, for example. These activities may be mutually incompatible because the motor patterns involved cannot be performed simultaneously and the orientations of the responses differ. Consequently, the fish must have some means of determining which activity to carry out at a particular time, based upon the external and internal stimuli impinging upon it.

This process of selecting among activities is referred to as "decision making" (McFarland 1977, 1985). This is not meant to imply any cognitive awareness or consciousness on the part of the fish. Behavior, as any other phenotypic attribute, is the product of interacting forces of natural selection that produce an optimal compromise in the phenotype. We (and others) may discuss examples of behavior in terms that might imply that the fish are engaged in a particular behavioral activity in order to achieve some end or object. The words strategy and tactics are sometimes used in this context, but again not to imply consciousness or forethought. Strategy means a preprogrammed rule an animal follows; tactic means the methods (i.e., behavioral actions) used to implement the rule (the strategy) (Dawkins 1982).

17.2 OBSERVATION AND RECORDING

17.2.1 Objectives of Behavioral Studies

17.2.1.1 Processes and Consequences

Behavioral studies may have one of two goals. One is to understand the processes by which a fish interacts with the environment; that is, the behavior itself is the subject of study. The second is to learn the consequences of a behavior; a detailed knowledge of how the consequences come about may not be necessary (Noakes 1986b).

In the first case, the fish's behavior is observed and recorded in detail by one or more direct observational techniques (Altmann 1974; Altmann and Altmann 1977; Lehner 1979). Studies of this type are time consuming and labor intensive, but they yield a very detailed picture of the animal's behavior. They are especially useful for determining values for the parameters of models used in behavioral ecology and for potential management plans. In the second case, a detailed moment-by-moment picture of the behavior of the individual may not be necessary to answer the question(s) posed. It may be possible to design the study so that the animal is placed in a particular experimental situation for a standardized time, and the experiment is evaluated by the consequences at the end of that period.

For example, one may need to know either the relative feeding success of a larval fish preying on various zooplankters, if it has encountered the prey item, or the "handling time" given a successful predation encounter. Then it is necessary to actually observe instances of predation and record the appropriate data. However, if one wishes only to know the relative effectiveness of a larval fish as a predator on "large" versus "small" prey when both types of prey items are at the same density, it may be sufficient to set up a tank with equal numbers of prey items of each size, and then count the number remaining at the end of the experiment (Werner and Hall 1974; O'Brien 1979). Because some applied problems in animal behavior concern the consequences and others the mechanisms of the behavior, much time and effort can be spared if the problem is carefully formulated at the outset, as we discuss below. Ideally, both types of observations should be done, at least to some degree, in any study.

17.2.1.2 Behavioral Variability

A special caution is necessary when behavioral studies are undertaken. Most phenotypic characters do not change or vary within the same organism once they have differentiated. If a fish larva develops a malformed jaw, for example, it will continue to have a malformed jaw as a juvenile and adult. However, behavioral phenotypes are rarely so easily defined, and an individual fish may exhibit one phenotype one day and a different one the next. Behavior can change as a result of experience, ontogeny, or the particular circumstances in which the animal finds itself. Some of these changes may be permanent; others may be reversible. Laboratory confinement itself may be the cause of such changes in behavior. Because of the inherent variability of behavior, evaluations of behavioral studies must always depend greatly upon statistical inference. Balanced design and careful control of all possible variables are especially important elements in the execution of any behavioral study.

17.2.2 Observational Methods

17.2.2.1 Techniques

Both laboratory and field studies are important in fish ethology. Field studies have the obvious advantage that any findings may be directly applicable to practical problems or concerns. However, they also have major logistical problems for practical experimental design. On the other hand, laboratory studies allow careful measurement and control of experimental variables, but their findings may be entirely an artifact of the laboratory situation and without reliable field application.

Whatever the setting, observational studies of behavior can be conducted in several ways, reflecting different approaches to data collection and analysis (Altmann 1974). For example, observations might be taken as a detailed, continuous record of the activity of one individual or, alternatively, as brief, successive records of many individuals. The occurrence of behavioral activities might be summed over an observation period, or the sequence and time of occurrence of all behavioral acts might be recorded. The advantages, disadvantages, and limitations of these and other observational procedures are well known (Altmann 1974; Johnson and Nielsen 1983), and it is important to resolve the choice as part of the initial design of any study.

Many fishes offer a distinct advantage over most other kinds of vertebrates for behavioral studies in that they habituate easily to human observers and allow a patient human to approach them closely. For example, although a diver cannot hope to approach the mobility of most fish in water, fish do not appear to be as shy of divers as most terrestrial animals are of human observers.

In the field, underwater observations can be carried out and recorded by a variety of means (see the extensive review by Helfman 1983). The greatest difficulty in field situations is that water is a physically demanding environment for humans, which limits practical diving observations of fish behavior. Observations can be made from submersible vehicles or underwater habitat structures, but these are not available to most researchers. When fishes are inshore in clear, shallow water, they can be observed from the shoreline or above-ground observation platforms with the help of polarizing sunglasses (Keenleyside 1979; Blumer 1985).

Because of these limitations on direct observation, remote automated sampling techniques are especially valuable tools in field studies of fish behavior. One technique involves the monitoring of specific sites with a closed-circuit video recorder (Myrberg 1973). An alternative approach is to use movie cameras in underwater housings to record the data at regular intervals. Inexpensive super-8 format cine cameras are readily available that have automatic exposure control and build-in intervalometers that can be set to take single frames at preset times. Such cameras have proven especially useful for monitoring the behavior of territorial male smallmouth bass on nests, for example (Raffetto 1987). The disadvantage of both these techniques is that behavior can be monitored only at the physical site where the camera is placed. Thus these remote techniques are most effective when used to monitor territorial individuals.

Laboratory studies offer greater freedom to choose methods and schedule observations than do field studies, but lose some relevance to field problems and restrict the sizes and kinds of fishes that can be considered. Most laboratory studies are carried out in relatively small aquaria or raceways; this may impose severe restrictions on the movements of fish relative to field circumstances. The greatest value of laboratory studies is the power to tightly control all the variables that may influence the study, including the individual history of the experimental subjects. Laboratory studies also permit observations on species that would otherwise be impossible to investigate, such as planktonic larval forms.

Fish brought into the laboratory from the wild may show fright reactions to the observer, which can be eliminated by observing the fish through a small slit opening in an opaque partition or screen placed in front of the tank. Laboratory-reared fish are usually habituated to human observers and may not require such precautions. Some laboratory experiments may permit fully automated data collection, such as those involving conditioning procedures wherein fish are required to perform some operant task (e.g., Adron et al. 1973; Magnuson and Beitinger 1978). In the artificial setting of a laboratory, control is needed for variables that might be of little but routine monitoring concern in a field study.

17.2.2.2   Identification of Fish

Scars, parasite cysts, and other natural marks or individual variations in color patterns sometimes can be used to identify individual fish (Pot and Noakes 1985), but individual identification usually requires capturing a fish and marking it in some manner. Methods of tagging or marking fish in the field are powerful tools in the study of behavior (Olla et al. 1975). Wydoski and Emery (1983) provided an extensive review and discussion of tagging methodology. If fish populations are already tagged for other purposes such as population estimates, recaptures of marked fish in various nets and traps can also provide indirect information on fish behavior. Diel activity can be inferred from captures at different times of the day (Steiner et al. 1982), and captures at different depths in selective gear such as gill nets can suggest habitat preferences and movements. Perhaps the most serious conceptual problems are with tracking studies that lack specific predictions (or even hypotheses) to be tested. If fish are simply tagged "to see where they go," the results will likely be very difficult to interpret. There is almost always individual variation in orientation and movement, and investigators sometimes are forced to include or exclude particular data points on a largely subjective basis after the fact.

17.2.2.3   Data Recording

Behavioral data should be recorded within a strictly defined quantitative format, to the extent possible. At its simplest, this need involve only a stopwatch, clipboard, data sheets, and a pencil. Data collection is best done on a standardized form on which categories can be checked off or events tallied as they occur. This minimizes the opportunity for errors due to ambiguous categories or differences between observers. Any research design should assure that data are collected by consistent criteria within a consistent format throughout the study to maximize reliability. This is best done by scoring the behavior directly into clearly defined, nonoverlapping categories that exhaustively describe the responses of the animal in the experimental situation.

The greatest risk in behavioral studies is changing behavioral categories or data collection procedures in the course of the study. For example, with experience, an observer might come to recognize subtle variants within what was originally defined as a single, simple behavioral category. In other instances, one might decide that data collection has become too tedious and begin to sample only every 5 min, rather than continuously as originally planned. In such cases, any deviation from the initial procedures will very likely make it impossible to compare data collected in the different ways, so much time and effort will be wasted. Preliminary observations can minimize these problems by verifying that the initial procedures do indeed perform as expected.

The data collection procedure should both promote easy and accurate recording of the behavior while it is being observed and facilitate the eventual transcription and analysis of data. Some methods of recording—dictation into a tape recorder or continuous videotaping, for example—are easy and accurate, but they can cause problems later. It usually requires at least 10 min to transcribe each minute of real-time recording, and the tedium and operator fatigue from such transcriptions can create serious problems if data sets are extensive.

A computer-compatible recording technique minimizes transcription effort and error as data are converted into a format suitable for analysis. Many such devices are now available (Lehner 1979). Some types of behavior can be analyzed by the use of devices that interface directly between an incoming video signal and a microcomputer (Gunn and Noakes, unpublished). However, the recent availability of battery-powered portable microcomputers has probably rendered most alternative devices obsolete. These inexpensive computers make ideal data-logging devices and are easily programmed for any data collection format.

One such portable computer, the Radio Shack model 100, is the basis of a flexible, real-time, user-defined laboratory and field data acquisition system (KEYBORED) developed by one of us (J.R.B.). Individual keys on the computer are programmed to represent specific behavioral acts, states, patterns, movements, and so on. Once initiated, the data-logging program refers to the internal clock in the computer to sample the positions of all keys at specified time intervals. Any "activated" keys are logged into the computer's memory at each timed sample. At the end of the recording session, there is a complete record of these in one file in the computer's memory. The software also allows the user to add comments, identifying information, and other alphanumeric material to each file. These files can then be stored on tape or diskettes, printed out, edited, collated, and subjected to many summary and analytical statistical procedures.

When the actual behavior of the fish is to be recorded (rather than the consequences of the behavior), representative individuals of the species should first be observed and at least a partial ethogram should be constructed for them. An ethogram is a descriptive catalogue of the basic motor patterns that constitute the behavior of a species. Such ethograms already exist for several fish species, and often one need only refer to published accounts (e.g., Myrberg 1972; see Figure 17.1 and Table 17.1). However, it is important to use categories of behavior that are descriptive rather than functional so the study can be compared to others and replicated at a later date. The following is an example of a descriptive behavior pattern (in the sense of a modal action pattern: Barlow 1977, 1981a) written by Baylis (1974):

> Jolting. The median fins may or may not be fully erected; the pelvic fins are folded up against the body. The head is jerked sideways and a rapid locomotory wave passes along the body. The pelvic and median fins are snapped erect as the pectoral fins brake the forward motion. The pelvic fins are then slowly folded back against the body.

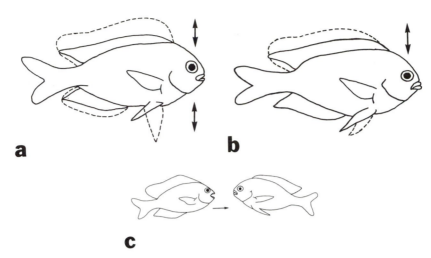

Figure 17.1 Selected illustrations of behavior patterns of bicolor damselfish: (a) fin-flick; (b) fin spread; (c) frontal-thrust (adapted from Myrberg 1972, with permission). The names of the behavior patterns are as given in Table 17.1. Positions and movement of fins or the entire body are indicated by dashed outlines and arrows.

A functional categorization of the same behavior pattern would be "calling the young away from danger." Clearly, if one wants to record behavioral data in a manner that can be compared from study to study and remains as consistent as possible within a single study, one must start with a good descriptive catalogue. Once the catalogue is constructed, the observer need only record the number of occurrences and the circumstances of occurrence of various behavior patterns under immediate study. Establishing an ethogram is equivalent to constructing a measurement scale for the behavior of the species. However, as noted above, if one is interested only in the consequences of the behavior, a detailed ethogram may not be necessary.

Table 17.1 Descriptive ethogram for the bicolor damselfish. Behavioral action patterns are listed according to the functional categorization of their occurrence (from Myrberg 1972).

A. Maintenance activities	D. Courtship activities	Head-up
Body-shake	Tilt	Head-down
Chafe	Dip	Duel-up
Fin-flick	Nudge	Parallel-swim
Defecate	Lead	Frontal-thrust
Tail-down	Quiver	Circle
Yawn	Close-swim	Half-circle
	Skim	Head-stand
B. Feeding activities	Flutter	Chase
Nip		Flee
Jerk-swim	E. Agonistic activities	
	Fin spread	F. Sounds produced
C. Nest activities	Close-down	Chirp
Fan-eggs	Veer-off	Long chirp
Nip-eggs	Tail-back	Grunt
	Lateral-display	Burr
	Frontal-display	Pop
		Strid

17.3 EXPERIMENTAL DESIGN AND ANALYSIS

17.3.1 Selection of Subject Animals

The previous history of animals observed in the field usually is unknown, but one often can control the history of the animals studied in the laboratory or released for field experiments. It is well known that prior experience is a major influence on the behavior of animals, fish included. Indeed, it was the manipulation of experience prior to release that provided a crucial experiment in the investigation of salmon homing behavior (Hasler and Scholz 1983). Unless experience itself is the variable under study, all test animals should be matched as closely as possible for prior experience.

When a study involves common species such as salmonids that are produced commercially or can be reared in the laboratory, researchers may be able to work with many individuals of uniform background, thus making it easier to control for prior experience. Prior experience means far more than just whether or not the animals have been previously exposed to the experimental stimulus. It includes the type and size of prior habitats (whether in the wild, in a hatchery, or in a laboratory), previous population densities, and many other variables.

Field studies have shown that many fish species occur as stocks or populations confined to particular ocean regions, lake basins, or stream drainage systems (Horrall 1981; Moyle and Cech 1982; Moyle and Vondracek 1985). Hence, behavioral differences between individuals from different populations within a species are regularly noted (Noakes 1986b). Again, unless such variation is itself a subject of study, all test animals for laboratory observations should come from a similar genetic background to the extent possible. Field studies cannot have such control over subjects, but identification of the fish and locality should be part of the protocol.

17.3.2 Preference Data

In any experimental design involving behavior, it is important to incorporate as many controls as possible. Perhaps the most important initial concerns are the experimental design to be used for the observations and the statistical tests to be applied to the data. There is often a strong temptation to begin observations quickly and to amass as many data as possible. This approach can produce large amounts of data, but it may be difficult or impossible to analyze the results. This caution is especially important in situations involving choice or preference tests.

Consider, for example, an examination of mate choice by female cichlid fish. A design could be used in which each female can choose freely to spawn with a large male at one side of an aquarium or a small male at the other. The females might seem to be choosing mates by size, but they could simply be choosing a particular side of the tank. they might also be mating randomly, without a consistent preference for size or any other attribute. (The possibility of "randomness"—lack of preference—should routinely be considered in all cases, at least as a null hypothesis.) Noonan (1983) controlled for these alternatives by switching the side of the tank at which the large and small male were placed after each run, and then testing for tank-side preferences by the females as well as for male-size preferences. Although this example involves mate choice (see also Barlow 1983), the control for position preference should be part of any preference study, particularly when the choice occurs along an axis. In choice studies involving gradients, it may be possible to avoid problems that can arise when the ends of a gradient coincide with the ends of a tank. For example, choice tests with a thermal gradient might be run in a circular tank (toroid) instead of a rectangular aquarium. Many fish (or other animals) in an enclosure show significant "end effects," spending significantly more time at the periphery than in any other equivalent area of the enclosure.

17.3.3 Statistical Analysis

Several textbooks discuss the broader questions of statistical procedures, but some specific comments are warranted here because of the nature of behavioral data. Sample sizes are often relatively small, there may be a good deal of individual variability, and some behavioral measures do not readily lend themselves to scoring on ordinal scales. One should not give too much weight to behavioral observations of a single individual because any one test animal might be aberrant. The outcome of behavioral studies is usually not clear-cut, and statistical tests are necessary to make a decision about the results. Virtually all statistical designs require independence and replication of observations. To truly meet the requirement of independence, each animal should be used only once in an experiment. Noonan's experiment with cichlid mate choice (Section 17.3.2), would have been interpreted very differently if she had run 20 trials with a single female instead of 1 trial with each of 20 females. Nonetheless, some experimental designs can allow for repeated observations on the same subjects without violating assumptions of the statistical procedures. An obvious example is the repeated observation of the same subjects to test for the effects of prior experience on behavior. Preliminary pilot studies are often very useful to determine sample sizes and to resolve the details of the experimental design.

However, given the variability among individuals often encountered in behavioral studies, it may be useful in some cases to expose each individual to all treatments, so that each individual becomes a "block" for purposes of analysis. It is important to decide between these alternative designs at the outset of a study because the design largely determines how the data can be analyzed. Sometimes one has to go beyond the level of the individual animal to analyze details of behavioral systems. For example, the behavioral strategy shown by one individual may depend on the strategy adopted by the rest of the population (Dawkins 1982). For social interactions such as schooling, it may be necessary to record the behavioral acts of two or more individuals simultaneously in order to make sense of the behavior of any one.

The sorts of data likely to be recorded vary with the type of experiment. For a preference test, one might record the time in seconds spent by a fish on each side of a tank and also some measure of intensity, latency, or persistence of response to the stimulus. If the test involves mating choice, the measure could be the number of females spawning on one side of the tank or the other. If time is the measure of preference, it would be wrong to treat the number of seconds one fish spent at each position as the "sample size" for a statistical test. (Otherwise, we could convert seconds to milliseconds, and increase the "sample size" by orders of magnitude.) The amount of time spent on each side of a tank can be compared statistically among several fish, but for one trial, for one fish, the sample size is one. Most experiments can be cast into a design with two, or at most four outcomes.

In general, nonparametric statistics are preferable to parametric tests for behavioral data because such data often cannot satisfy the assumptions required for parametric analyses. Some behavioral data are ratios, but most are gathered on ordinal or nominal scales (Hazlett 1977; Colgan 1978). If ordinal data are involved, a variety of useful rank-order statistical tests is available, including some that allow correlational or matched-pair comparisons. Such comparisons usually require that at least six items be ranked to have a reasonable chance of rejecting a null hypothesis. The Spearman rank-order correlation coefficient and the Wilcoxon matched-pairs signed-rank test are examples of these. A variety of tests is also available for nominal data. Experimental outcomes that can be cast into a 2 × 2 contingency table can be analyzed by a chi-square test of independence (if no expected value is less than 5) or a Fisher exact test. When the outcomes can be cast into two exclusive categories, the binomial test is a powerful nonparametric statistic (Siegel 1956; Lehner 1979). The G-test has also been recommended as an alternative to the chi-square test because it can be decomposed in an additive way like an analysis of variance (Sokal and Rohlf 1981). When nonparametric statistics are used, a sample size of 30 or larger is desirable.

When the social behavior of fishes is observed in the laboratory, it should be remembered that environmental circumstances can have a profound effect on social organization. For example, McNicol and Noakes (1984) found that population density, food supply, and water current velocity all affected territorial behavior by juvenile brook trout. Even when studied experimentally in ponds, fish may be at densities many times greater than they would be in the wild. Only careful field studies in conjunction with laboratory observations can indicate which laboratory results are artifacts and which can be reliably extended to the field.

17.4 PREFERENCE TESTS

17.4.1 Background

On a given day, a "typical" fish might search for food, escape from a predator, and undertake many more activities in an environment that itself varies in several physical factors. How and why the fish switches among activities, and how its movements and position are affected by external factors, are the subjects of much interest and experimentation. The interest in these preferences can stem from attempts to model decision-making processes in animals (Noakes 1986a), from efforts to understand the ecological relationships of a species, or from the need to establish tolerance limits for naturally occurring or anthropogenic stressors. Because the range of interests in these tests is so broad, and the theoretical and practical approaches so diverse, it is important to resolve both the fundamental principles and the practical procedures involved. What follows is not intended to be a comprehensive review of the extensive literature on preference tests for fishes (see, for example, Fry 1971; Sprague 1976; Coutant 1987). Rather, our objective is to resolve important conceptual and terminological issues, and to outline what we feel is a reasonable approach to empirical studies.

17.4.2   Interpreting Preference Measurements

The preference of an animal is the expression of its behavior when it is presented with a choice between two or more equally probable alternatives. An animal is said to show a preference when it consistently (at least under prescribed conditions) chooses one alternative from those available to it (Dawkins 1969; Dawkins 1980). Preference may be measured in terms of the time spent in one location or performing one activity, the activity chosen first or last, or combinations of these. In some situations, however, different measures of preference lead to contrary conclusions. For example, unless an animal has encountered, or at least is aware of, the alternatives available to it, any response it shows cannot be taken to truly indicate preference. Thus, if an animal moves into one side of a test tank and spends the entire observation period there, one can scarcely conclude that it prefers that side over the others. In this case, the measures of which side was selected first and where the animal spent the majority of its time could be misleading as indicators of preference.

A distinction has to be made between preferences measured when alternatives are presented simultaneously and response rates to alternatives that are presented singly. An animal might respond rapidly, or several animals might respond unambiguously, to a factor if it is the only one present, but this may not be indicative of behavior when two or more factors are present at the same time (Dawkins 1969). In another situation a fish might be prevented from expressing a preference known to exist under other circumstances. For example, a larger, dominant bluegill will occupy the preferred section of a temperature-choice tank and inhibit a smaller subordinate from entering that section, though the subordinate would do so in the dominant's absence (Beitinger and Magnuson 1975). In this example, it is obvious that the observed behavior of the subordinate does not indicate its temperature preference, but this discrepancy is not so obvious in many situations.

Preferences measured in the laboratory must always be treated with reservation unless and until their ecological relevance is known. For example, there is an extensive literature on temperature preference for many fish species in laboratory tests, no doubt because such data are relatively simple to collect. However, less is known about other factors that might influence these fish in nature, and it is difficult to conclude how meaningful univariate temperature tests really are. Animals are almost always subjected to conflicting motivational tendencies (McFarland 1985), and their priorities may shift over time depending on the decision-making processes involved. Motivation usually means the sum total of the internal causal factors responsible for the performance of any behavior (McFarland 1985). The physiological state of the animal is a consequence of its behavioral activities; in turn, the animal's behavior is a reflection of its need to maintain its physiological condition within nonlethal tolerance limits.

17.4.3   Physiological Correlates

17.4.3.1   Optima

A considerable body of physiological information indicates that animals can detect a wide range of physical and biological factors in the environment and respond to maintain their physiological functions at or near optimal values (e.g.,

Fry 1971; Beitinger and Fitzpatrick 1979; Magnuson and Crowder 1979; Hoar 1983; McFarland 1985). For example, a bluegill in a spatially or temporally heterogeneous thermal environment typically keeps itself at the environmental temperature closest to the optimum for its physiological functions (Magnuson and Beitinger 1978; Hoar 1983; Coutant 1987). Both the immediate physiological benefits and the long-term evolutionary benefits of this are obvious. However, one cannot necessarily infer a species' optimum temperature from the environmental temperature at which individuals are found. Preferences for temperature or any environmental feature often are overridden by other factors such as water currents, predators, or contaminants.

17.4.3.2 Compromises and Preferences

The ability of fish to behaviorally select an optimal habitat is the basis of experiments to establish an animal's preference for almost every conceivable environmental factor. In theory, such tests can indicate the priorities the animals themselves place on these conditions and the mechanisms whereby they resolve their choices. In practice, however, such tests may have important limitations. One stems from an underlying assumption that an animal perceives the world, or at least a particular test situation, in the same way the human investigator does. The sense organs and sensory capabilities of fishes can differ dramatically from our own. For example, some species have the ability to detect ultraviolet light (Hawryshyn and Beauchamp 1985) and others can detect weak electric fields, a sensory capability used variously for orientation, feeding, and social interactions (Hopkins 1980). Species like the brown bullhead rely almost entirely upon chemical senses (olfaction and taste) for orientation, foraging, and even recognizing individual conspecifics according to sex and dominance status. Freshwater eels and Pacific salmon are exquisitely sensitive to chemical cues for homing, and the chemically mediated fright responses of ostariophysan fishes are classical examples of chemical (pheromone) communication (Barnett 1977). Many species can detect minute differences in temperature, salinity, dissolved gases, or ions in the water (see Chapter 15). The sensitivity of both freshwater and marine fishes to sounds and low-frequency vibrations, detected by the acousticolateralis system, is well known (Myrberg 1980a, 1980b). The sensory world of any fish is quite different from a human's, and it is difficult to imagine how a fish might perceive its surroundings. Any simple assumption about a fish's perception of a particular test situation should be viewed skeptically. One must ensure that the animal really has been exposed to the alternatives available, that it is capable of detecting those alternatives, and that it truly perceives the choice situation as one designed it.

Suppose one tested the light intensity preference of fish by recording the side of a two-way, light–dark choice tank in which each of several individuals was found after 10-min trials (e.g., Nunan and Noakes 1985a). One would have to ensure either that each fish had visited each side of the tank at least once during the trial or that each was released into the tank so as not to produce any consistent directional bias. These concerns might seem obvious, but this is not always the case. A fish might have shown an immediate preference for the dark half of the tank, but only because it was responding to handling stress. If the trial did not last long enough for full recovery from stress, one might completely misinterpret the fish's true preference for light intensity. Then too, light and dark may not be particularly important alternatives for a species. Vertical movements, minor temperature differences, or water currents might override any response to light (Nunan and Noakes 1985b). These priorities might change according to the test animals' holding and pretreatment conditions and their age, genetic stock or strain, and state of sexual maturity (Olla et al. 1980b, 1985). McCauley et al. (1977), for example, demonstrated that adult sea lampreys respond to a thermal gradient and show temperature preferences comparable to those of teleost fishes, but only under appropriate light conditions. Under normal laboratory illumination, sea lampreys remained immobile regardless of the temperature to which they were exposed. When the light was turned off, however, the animals moved about the chamber and subsequently reattached to the walls of the chamber in the area of their preferred temperature.

17.4.3.3 Testing Apparatus

Perhaps the most basic concern with temperature preference tests is the physical design of the test apparatus. In principle, a fish is presented with a temperature gradient or a spatially heterogeneous series of temperatures within a test tank, and the places where it spends its time and eventually becomes localized are recorded; at least part of the temperature range must be within the tolerance limits of the fish. Of the two main tank designs used, one produces vertical and the other horizontal gradients. The advantages, limitations, and disadvantages of each are well known (Magnuson and Beitinger 1978). For most studies, the choice depends on the practical considerations of available space and equipment, financial resources, and the biology of the test species. To avoid the problems associated with earlier designs, some researchers have employed test tanks in which the fish itself controls the test temperatures (Figure 17.2). Such tanks vary somewhat in design and function, but they all require the test animal to push a lever, swim through a partition, move past photocells, or perform some other overt act to switch on heating or cooling units in the tank. The resulting water temperature in the tank is assumed to be that preferred by the animal. The appeal of this design is obvious (Magnuson and Beitinger 1978), and the possibilities it opens are intriguing (Colgan 1975), although it is clearly inappropriate for many species. Because it requires some action on the part of the animal to regulate the apparatus, either there must be an initial training period during which the animal learns to perform this task or enough experimental time must be allowed for the animal to trigger the control mechanism. This type of testing apparatus is more complex and expensive than simple gradient tanks and typically requires more time to complete one trial, which may restrict the number of trials or replications that can be done. (Learning is discussed in Section 17.6.)

17.4.4 Evolutionary Considerations

A general concern about preference tests is the question of proximate cues to which the animal responds, as distinct from the ultimate function of the choice. A wild fish will be naturally selected for the long-term (ultimate) consequences of its choices, even though it can only respond to immediate (proximate) cues. In nature, there are particular associations between proximate cues and ultimate consequences. When the animals are taken into captivity or tested under any but the conditions in which they have evolved, there is a risk of breaking down these

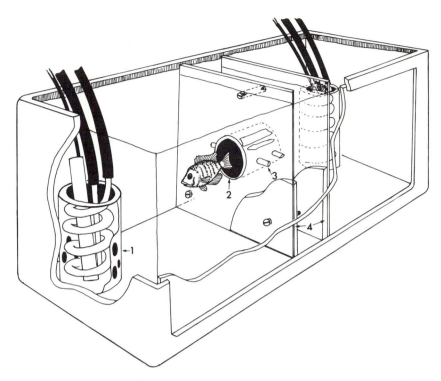

Figure 17.2 An operant design test apparatus for self-selection of temperature by bluegills (adapted from Magnuson and Beitinger 1978, with permission). When a fish swims through an opening in a central partition (2), it passes a set of photocells (3). The photocells are wired so they switch on a cooling unit if the fish passes in one direction and switch on a heating unit (1) if the fish passes in the opposite direction. The double central partition (4) insulates the two ends of the tank. Heating and cooling units change water temperatures at constant rates, once activated.

associations. An extreme example is the strong preference humans have for sugar in the diet. In nature, it is likely that the sensation of sweetness is associated with desirable food items (i.e., high in calories, safe to eat, etc.), but in the circumstances of modern civilization and highly processed foods, this response becomes maladaptive (Dawkins 1976). Similarly, in a laboratory testing apparatus a fish might respond to some cue that ordinarily would be associated with an important consequence in nature, but that is irrelevant or even inappropriate in captivity.

The only real safeguard against this type of problem is to constantly relate field and laboratory observations. The field situation must be the final standard, specifically the context within which the animal has evolved and in which it must survive. Not all "field" situations represent "true" standards, however, because habitats may have been altered, exotic species introduced, native flora and fauna lost, pollution imposed, and so on. One could (unknowingly or otherwise) present a fish with a laboratory test situation that extends some factor beyond the range the fish would ever encounter in the field, or present it with what could be described as a supernormal stimulus (Dawkins 1982). The response of a fish to a completely novel stimulus might be of interest, but it may not tell us much about that fish in nature. For example, the responses of territorial male threespine sticklebacks to artificial dummies during the breeding season have been studied in

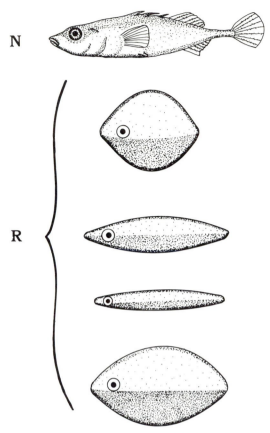

Figure 17.3 Artificial dummies of threespine stickleback (adapted from Tinbergen 1951, with permission). Dummies labeled R have the ventral surface painted bright red; dummy N is uniformly grey colored. Territorial males attack all dummies in the R series, and ignore the N dummy.

detail. These males respond to the ventral red coloration of other mature males and will challenge even a crude dummy that has this feature (Figure 17.3). A precise replica of a real male that lacks this red coloration is ignored (Tinbergen 1951). Females are recognized by the swollen, silvery abdomen, and dummies that accentuate these features are much more effective in eliciting courtship from males than are real females (Nelson 1965). Although it is correct to say that male threespine sticklebacks prefer to court these dummies, and although this may provide some useful insights into some aspects of the behavior, it does not necessarily indicate anything about the normal courtship behavior of this species in nature (see Rowland and Sevenster [1985] for further details of this example).

17.5   SOCIAL STRUCTURE

17.5.1   Dominance and Hierarchies

17.5.1.1   Definitions and Measurements

   Modern experimental studies of dominance relations among animals date from the pioneering work of Schjelderup-Ebbe (1922) on flocks of domestic chickens

Table 17.2 Dominance matrix for agonistic interactions within a group of rainbow trout (from Noakes and Leatherland 1977). Vertical columns are recipients of actions, horizontal rows are initiators. Colors refer to individual tags used to identify fish. Data are the numbers of agonistic actions directed by one fish (horizontal) to another (vertical).

Initiator	Recipient				Total wins
	White	Green	Yellow	Red	
White	—	56	23	26	105
Green	2	—	11	22	35
Yellow	1	8	—	0	9
Red	0	0	0	—	0
Total losses	3	64	34	48	149

Gallus domesticus. Because of the kind of agonistic interactions most common among chickens, the hierarchical social system exemplified by that species often is referred to as a peck order. In its simplest form, there is a linear social order from the most dominant or alpha individual to the least dominant or omega individual. The alpha animal dominates all other individuals in the group, the second-ranking (beta) animal dominates all but the alpha animal, and so on down to the omega animal, who is dominated by all others and dominates no individual. The apparent simplicity of this type of social organization and its consequences for the animals involved has led to numerous studies and reports of dominance and dominance-related behavior in animals, including many fishes (Gauthreaux 1978). Many species show agonistic interactions when confined in an experimental enclosure, and it is almost always possible to conceptually arrange the individuals in some kind of hierarchical order (Chase 1980a, 1980b). An animal may change its dominance status as it gains size, experience, sexual maturity, and so on without changing the hierarchical principle. It often happens that the idealized, strictly linear hierarchical arrangement of individuals is not observed, however; rather, several animals may have apparently equal rank within a hierarchy, and it may even happen that an otherwise lower-ranking animal dominates an animal above it in the general hierarchy (Brown 1975). Nevertheless, experimenters too often assume that a linear hierarchy is the fundamental social organization, and they merely fit their animals into such a system rather than testing whether that system really operates within the group.

The study of dominance hierarchies requires individual identification of all the animals involved and precise operational definitions of the behavioral actions that reliably indicate dominance. These actions typically include such events as chasing, biting, and attacking, as well as less obvious acts of displacing or supplanting other individuals. Observations can be recorded by watching groups of animals (either in captivity or in the field), or by staging encounters between pairs of individuals (a round-robin tournament) in captivity (Brown 1975). The data from these observations are then summarized in the form of a matrix (Table 17.2) so the relations among the individuals can be determined. Several criteria can be used to rank individuals—ratio of wins to losses, total number of wins, etc.—depending upon the relative importance attached to particular aspects of the data (Brown 1975; Chase 1982a, 1982b, 1985).

17.5.1.2 Consequences of Dominance

The consequences of dominance hierarchies are often assumed to be so obvious as not to require elaboration. If a hierarchical arrangement can be detected within a group of fish, the fish presumably respond to each other according to that arrangement and enjoy the benefits or suffer the consequences of their particular ranks. Higher-ranking individuals, virtually by definition, have first access to limited resources, whether food, mates, or nest sites. Such benefits of dominance are important in many cases (e.g., Krebs and Davies 1984), but dominance status carries costs as well as benefits. Presumably it is neither the total benefit nor the total cost so much as the net benefit (total benefit minus total cost) that is important to the individual.

Higher dominance status tends to be correlated with size, age, and experience. It takes time for an individual to gain enough of these qualities to improve its status, and the animal may have to defer reproductive opportunities so as to channel energy into somatic growth if it is to achieve greater dominance. The attainment and maintenance of dominance usually require individuals to threaten, chase, or attack others. These activities require energy, incur at least some risk of injury (or loss of dominance rank), and take time away from feeding, resting, and other activities necessary for bodily maintenance. There may also be less obvious physiological costs (Schreck 1982; Chapter 14). For example, Noakes and Leatherland (1977) found that the highest-ranking rainbow trout in dominance hierarchies had greater interrenal activity than those ranked second. It is important to distinguish between short- and long-term costs and benefits. In some species, small subordinates may employ alternative life history strategies and thereby gain a reproductive fitness comparable to that of large dominants (Dominey 1981; Gross 1984). Thus, although a lower-ranking individual derives fewer benefits than a higher-ranking one, it also incurs lower costs; the two individuals could have similar net benefits.

17.5.2 Home Ranges and Territories

17.5.2.1 Definitions

A *home range* is most simply defined as the area within which an individual typically spends its time when it is not dispersing or migrating. This definition says nothing about the use of this space by other individuals of the same or another species. Most if not all animals have a home range; possible exceptions are pelagic marine animals such as bluefin tunas that are in almost constant movement over very large areas. Most individual fishes, however, can regularly be found within the same, relatively circumscribed area (e.g., Sale 1971, 1975; Reese 1973, 1975; Moyle and Vondracek 1985).

A *territory* is a spatially fixed area from which one or a few individuals exclude others (usually, but not necessarily, of the same species: Losey 1981, 1982a, 1982b) by some combination of threat, attack, or advertisement (Brown 1975). The heart of this definition is the fixed area and its exclusive use by an individual, a pair of animals, or sometimes a small family or social group.

The particular home range of a fish may change with maturity, season, or habitat change (Olla et al. 1979, 1980a), but it is generally much more persistent than a territory. Many species defend territories only during their respective breeding seasons; North American sunfish are good examples (Keenleyside 1979). Some species defend territories only during particular intervals in their ontogeny; juvenile brook trout set up feeding territories, for instance (McNicol et al. 1985), and damselfish have territories only as adults (Sale et al. 1980).

17.5.2.2 Measurements

Several measures are needed to determine whether a fish has a home range or a territory and to estimate the location and extent of either. Fish must be individually identifiable from natural or artificial marks. The use of tags that transmit radio or ultrasonic pulses satisfies this requirement and also provides almost continuous data on position and movement. Conventional (nontransmitting) tags require that fish be recaptured or that they be relocated visually or by other means (encoded metal tags might trigger a sensor, for example). The data are then collated and plotted directly on a map of the study area or compiled for computer analysis. Several computational techniques and conceptual models can be used according to the nature of the data and the analysis to be performed (Noakes and McNicol 1982). The literature on territoriality in behavioral ecology is particularly extensive (e.g., Noakes and Grant 1986). Recent studies of territoriality have been less concerned with establishing the phenomenon than with testing hypotheses about its function. The analysis of territorial defense in terms of its costs and benefits has been a productive one (Davies and Houston 1984). In this approach, territoriality is treated as one strategy among several alternatives, and attempts are made to discover the functions of the behavior.

17.5.3   Schools and Shoals

Probably no type of social organization is so consistently associated with fishes as schooling. It is a striking phenomenon that has attracted many scientific studies (e.g., Hunter 1966; Keenleyside 1979), but only recently have investigators begun to define terms more carefully and precisely, and to ask whether schooling is such a simple or unitary behavior as it superficially seems (Pitcher 1983). Many of the earlier studies were concerned primarily with measurements of the spacing of individuals within schools and the proximate cues used by the fish to maintain their regular spacing. As with territoriality, the current trend is to strategic considerations (Hamilton 1971; Partridge et al. 1983; Pitcher 1985).

The critical aspect of any definition remains, however, that a school (or shoal) is essentially a social aggregation. Groups of fish may be found in close physical association, but they cannot be considered schools if the fish are responding to some common environmental feature such as temperature, food, or cover. An understanding of a species' preferences for physical factors often is necessary before an association of fishes can be labeled a true school or just an aggregation drawn together by a nonsocial stimulus.

Once the social definition has been satisfied (and it may not be simple in a field situation), further studies of schooling are straightforward. Measurement of social attraction is relatively simple in the laboratory but much more difficult with unconfined fish in the field (Keenleyside 1979).

Social attraction and interactions can be very important in schools. Individual foraging and feeding can be significantly enhanced (Olla and Samet 1974; see Section 17.6.2), and the individual's risk from predation can be reduced (Hamilton

1971). Some schools allow their members to successfully invade and feed in otherwise inaccessible territories of food competitors (Barlow 1974b). Migration and spawning can also be important functions of schooling. Schooling is typically thought of as intraspecific, but mixed-species schools do occur (Keenleyside 1979).

17.5.4 Reproductive Groupings

Most species of fish do not form any lasting social bonds based upon genetic (kin) relationships, but form only temporary pair bonds at the time of spawning and provide no parental care of their offspring (Baylis 1981). Hence there is no possibility for persistent or extended family groups in these species. Nevertheless, the timing of spawning and the organization of spawning groups by these species is of considerable theoretical and practical interest. For example, several authors searching for ultimate causes have suggested that dispersal of young from (or their retention in) the breeding area may have guided the evolution of spawning time and place for many species, particularly marine pelagic spawners (Johannes 1978; Barlow 1981b). The proximate factors that regulate spawning are of interest to those who manage fish production and harvest.

A few fish species form relatively prolonged pair bonds and some even have family groups (adults and young) that remain together for weeks or months (Myrberg 1975, 1980b). Some freshwater cichlid species and a variety of coral reef inhabitants are among the best known in this regard (Barlow 1974a).

Some species live for months or years in organized social groups with one mature female (or male), several mature males (or females), and some smaller, immature individuals; examples are anemonefish of the genus *Amphiprion* and the wrasse *Labroides dimidiatus* (see the review by Keenleyside 1979). In most cases, the animals probably are not genetically related. Indeed, individuals of some coral reef species change sex, a transformation influenced by age, size, or social status, and their young probably are dispersed widely in the plankton soon after spawning (Barlow 1981b). It is now realized that sex change is a widespread phenomenon, especially among some groups of marine fishes (Warner 1978). Research has demonstrated that sexual differentiation and maturation can be influenced by social interactions as well as by genetic and environmental factors.

The past three decades have brought major advances in the study of fish behavior. Scuba and remote sensing are but two of the many techniques that facilitate research on wild fish in situ; improved culture techniques and formulated diets allow more species to be sustained in the laboratory than ever before. Observational, recording, and analytical methods have improved apace. With the new tools available to them, behaviorists are learning that the reproductive and social repertoire of fishes is much richer and more complex than anyone had suspected. The literature now reflects some of this variety (Noakes et al. 1983), but this area of study will remain very productive for years to come. Much of the research on reproductive strategies has been and will be done with individual animals. Because these strategies are such a fundamental aspect of each species' existence, however, the knowledge gained from individual fish will be decidedly relevant to population biologists and fishery managers.

17.6 LEARNING IN THE LIFE OF FISHES

17.6.1 Definition

Learning can be generally defined as a process manifested by adaptive changes in individual behavior as a result of experience (Thorpe 1963). An unfortunate misconception has persisted that there is a fundamental dichotomy in the behavior of animals between elements that are learned and those that are innate or inborn. It has been clear for some time that not only is this dichotomy not correct, it is not even meaningful (Manning 1979). The behavior of any animal is the result of a complex interplay of the genetic constitution of that individual, the environment in which it develops, the interactions between those genetic and environmental factors, and the particular set of experimental factors to which it has been exposed. We will simply take as given that various kinds of learning can occur and have some importance in the lives of fishes (Fujiya et al. 1980; Hollis 1982).

17.6.2 Food, Feeding, and Feeding Preferences

There is an extensive descriptive literature on foods and feeding habits of many fish species, in part because such studies are simple and straightforward to carry out, and they can address several practical or theoretical questions (e.g., Bowen 1983; Simenstad and Cailliet 1986). However, attention seldom is given to the processes that generate the patterns observed—the prey items that are eaten, the sequence and times of consumption, and so on. Most studies are based upon analysis of stomach contents, in various stages of digestion, that have been preserved in the field. It is often difficult just to determine what prey items the fish were eating, and whether the prey were consumed in proportion to their availability in the environment. Any attempt to analyze the actual feeding behavior in finer detail probably would be unrealistic.

Laboratory studies of feeding behavior can provide these details, but they typically must be conducted under such controlled circumstances that it may be difficult to judge the relevance or application to the field situation. Nevertheless, several important studies have tested hypotheses stemming from work on foraging behavior, and these nicely link laboratory and field results (Milinski 1982; Marcotte and Browman 1986). Also, aquaculturists who intensively feed and rear fish are valuable sources of information on many aspects of feeding behavior (Bardach et al. 1980; Rosenthal and Oren 1981; Pullin and Lowe-McConnell 1982; Noeske and Spieler 1984). This diverse body of information and hypotheses leads to some useful generalizations and conclusions.

17.6.2.1 Learning

Evidence from most of the fish species studied indicates that feeding preferences exhibit at least some degree of plasticity, often expressed in terms of opportunism, that implies some type of learning. Past experiences and social influences from other individuals (typically conspecifics) are sources of learning in many cases. For example, rainbow trout raised in a hatchery can readily learn to push on a lever or paddle to obtain food pellets (Adron et al. 1973; Statler 1982). Demand feeders in aquaculture work because fish can learn to use them. Several investigators, most notably Bitterman (1975), have studied the details of learning and learning capabilities in fishes. Most experimental learning tasks have involved food or feeding responses (but see Hogan 1974; Coble et al. 1985; Hawryshyn and Beauchamp 1985).

17.6.2.2   Social Influences

In general, fish such as rainbow trout can develop a conditioned response to a feeding situation in about 10 trials; the extremes range from 1 trial (Hawryshyn and Beauchamp 1985) to many more than 10 (Bitterman 1975). A learned feeding response can be delayed by fear or fear-producing stimuli, a novel type of food, and social isolation. Conversely, the response can be facilitated if a fish has no fear, if its food is familiar, and if other fish are feeding around it.

Social facilitation can stimulate feeding in some improbable circumstances (Olla and Samet 1974). Anyone who keeps or rears fish in captivity very quickly discovers that if some of the fish can be induced to feed the others will almost invariably rush to join a "feeding frenzy." This reaction can be used to advantage. For example, North American darters of the genus *Etheostoma* typically feed only on small, live prey; in aquaria, they do not respond to inanimate food such as trout pellets or tropical fish flake food. Yet some rainbow darters held in a laboratory trough practically leaped out of the water to feed on dry trout pellets. These fish had originally been held in the trough with young rainbow trout, and they joined the trout in their usual feeding frenzies. The darters continued this response to the pellets even after the trout were removed (F. W. H. Beamish, University of Guelph, personal communication). This effect is even stronger among conspecifics, particularly in schooling species or those crowded together in captivity. The sight of even one or two fish rushing to the surface or otherwise starting a feeding response is almost certain to trigger a similar feeding response in most or all of the other fish in the group.

There is some indication that coho salmon injected with bovine growth hormone feed more often and in greater quantities, and consequently grow more quickly, than uninjected fish held under the same conditions (Markert et al. 1977). The extra feeding effort by a few injected fish in a much larger group of uninjected fish might stimulate all fish to eat more. If it does, this tactic might be used to increase aquacultural production or to induce fish to accept a novel or less palatable food.

17.6.2.3   Sensory Modalities

Because of the importance of feeding behavior to fish culture, the involvement of the various sensory modalities have frequently been studied (Atema 1980; Blaxter 1980; Iwai 1980). Food preferences appear to be greatly influenced by past experiences (Simenstad and Cailliet 1986). Physical texture, chemical and visual stimuli from the food, and particle size seem to be the most important immediate cues that affect feeding. Color and movement often enhance the attractiveness of food to visual feeders such as trout and increase the likelihood that fish will approach, attack, and attempt to ingest the food particles (Ringler 1983).

Species whose feeding behavior is directed more by gustatory or olfactory cues are more influenced through those sensory modalities. Catfish *Ictalurus* spp., for example, may not respond to the sight of food or food pellets, although auditory cues such as splashing and mechanical disturbances attract them once they have been conditioned to artificial feed and feeders. Chemicals diffusing from the food

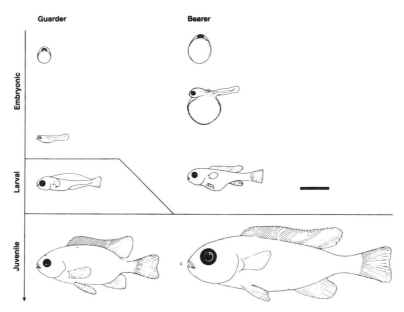

Figure 17.4 Comparison of early life history intervals of closely related tilapiine cichlid fishes. The guarder species, which protects its eggs and young on and near the substrate, has embryonic, larval, and juvenile periods before adulthood. The bearer species, which mouth-broods its eggs and young, does not have a larval interval. At the time of first exogenous feeding (when internal yolk reserves are depleted), the young bearer is significantly larger and more differentiated than the young guarder (adapted from Noakes and Balon 1982, with permission). Bar = 2 mm.

trigger the actual food-seeking and ingesting responses. Nocturnal and cave-dwelling species typically respond to chemical stimuli as well (Schemmel 1980).

17.6.2.4 Field Data

In nature, fish probably respond to food items in the same ways described above for artificial foods, for most of the same reasons. Most fish probably feed upon familiar food items as long as they are available (Ringler 1983). We still know little, however, about how fish first ''imprint'' on particular food items and when and why they subsequently change foods. There is a good deal of purely descriptive information on what fish eat, but little experimental evidence on why they eat it. Thus we know the prey items taken from the stomachs of many species (e.g., Hunter 1972), sometimes in relation to the abundance and distribution of the prey in the environment, but we do not understand the processes involved very well. At first feeding, young fish apparently take items that are relatively abundant and that are about as large as they can successfully capture and ingest. Whether this comes about purely by chance, by trial and error, or by some inborn preferences, perceptual cues, or some combination of these or other factors is not clear in most cases (e.g., Keenleyside 1979).

An important point, but one that is often not fully appreciated, is that the functional development of behavior varies markedly among species. Most importantly for the present discussion, species differ substantially in their state of development (in terms of anatomy, behavior, or physiology) at the time they begin feeding exogenously (Noakes 1978, 1981; Noakes and Balon 1982) (Figure 17.4).

The tremendous diversity of fish development, particularly as it relates to time of first feeding, is readily apparent (e.g., Lasker 1981). For example, the young of altricial species such as northern anchovy begin exogenous feeding after only a few days of development, when they are still very small (about 1% of adult size) and many of their organ systems are still incompletely formed or undifferentiated (Moser 1984). At the other extreme, young of precocial species such as the coelacanth begin exogenous feeding only after months of development, by which time they are fully formed juveniles about 30% of adult size (Balon 1985).

17.6.2.5   Optimal Foraging

Optimal-foraging theory (Green 1984; McFarland 1985) cannot necessarily help resolve questions of whether or not young fish have innate preferences for prey species, size, or shape at the time of first feeding, but it can be used to predict prey choices by fish when specified criteria are imposed on feeding behavior: energy maximization, handling time minimization, and so on. With information about potential prey—species, size, energy content, spatial and temporal distribution, etc.—one can formulate specific predictions to test in the field or laboratory (e.g., McNicol and Noakes 1984; McNicol et al. 1985; Noakes and Grant 1986).

We stress that the optimal-foraging approach does not test whether fish are feeding optimally; it assumes they are (see also Dawkins 1982; Krebs and McCleery 1984). What it does test are the assumptions that fish behave to maximize energy intake, minimize foraging and handling time, and so forth. Comparisons of observed and predicted results can illuminate some details of feeding behavior. For example, several optimal-foraging models have been proposed for exclusive feeding territories defended by fish (Dill 1978; Hixon 1980; Dunbrack and Dill 1983; Schoener 1983; Noakes and Grant 1986). Tests of predictions from these models have led to refinement of initial assumptions in some cases and at least partial validation of the models in others. It appears that individuals of some species behave to maximize food energy intake, whereas those of other species behave to minimize the time spent foraging. Experimental manipulation of a few variables often allows a choice to be made among alternative models.

17.6.3   Migration

The best known example of fish behavior involving learning undoubtedly is the migratory behavior of Pacific salmon as revealed by the studies of Hasler and his associates (Hasler and Scholz 1983). Adults migrate from the ocean to spawn in freshwater streams. Their progeny subsequently migrate downstream to the ocean to feed and grow, and themselves return to the area of their natal spawning bed to reproduce. Precise homing to the spawning ground depends largely on the specific chemical cues to which the progeny had been exposed as juveniles. This chemical imprinting not only forms the basis for natural spawning migrations, it also can be used by fishery managers to introduce stocks into new areas or to decoy mature adults on their spawning migrations (Horrall 1981). The response depends upon a relatively brief exposure early in the life of the fish, it is virtually irreversible, and it is expressed later in life, thus satisfying the criteria for classical imprinting (Immelmann 1980). It is a clear example of the role of learning in the ontogeny of fishes (Noakes 1981) in that it instructs us about both causal and functional aspects of behavior.

17.7 CONCLUSIONS

We hope that this chapter will encourage additional insightful studies of fish behavior. As we noted at the outset, behavior is readily observed, but careful planning and analysis are required if behavior is to be studied usefully. The first thing to resolve for a behavioral study is the specific question to be addressed; this will determine how observations are to be conducted, the kind of data that must be collected, and the conclusions that can be drawn from those data. The general categories of questions are "How?" and "Why?" The first category addresses immediate (proximate) causation, the second concerns the function or consequences (ultimate) of behavior. Although most questions are informally posed as "Why?" it is very important to define the question as precisely as possible.

Once the question has been specified, the actual behavioral measures to be taken must be resolved. If a description or catalogue (ethogram) of behavioral units already exists for the species, the behavioral units can probably be chosen directly. Otherwise, some preliminary observations will be required to identify and describe the major behavioral patterns relevant to the study. The choice of measures must also be influenced by the experimental design and statistical tests to be applied in the study.

However, the most fundamental concern is the theoretical framework of the study. This framework will influence broad considerations of the approach to be taken (physiological, ethological, etc.) and will narrow the definitions of the hypothesis and predictions to be tested. The advantages and limitations of laboratory and field studies, the complementarity of their results, and the primacy of the natural context for understanding behavior must always be kept in mind.

17.8 REFERENCES

Adron, J. W., P. T. Grant, and C. B. Cowey. 1973. A system for the qualitative study of the learning capacity of rainbow trout and its application to the study of food preferences and behavior. Journal of Fish Biology 5:625–636.

Altmann, J. 1974. Observational study of behavior: sampling methods. Behaviour 49:227–267.

Altmann, S. A., and J. Altmann. 1977. On the analysis of rates of behaviour. Animal Behaviour 25:364–372.

Atema, J. 1980. Chemical senses, chemical signals and feeding behavior in fishes. Pages 57–101 in J. E. Bardach, J. J. Magnuson, R. C. May, and J. M. Reinhart, editors. Fish behavior and its use in the capture and culture of fishes. International Center for Living Aquatic Resources Management, Manila.

Balon, E. K., editor. 1985. Early life histories of fishes. New developmental, ecological and evolutionary perspectives. Dr. W. Junk, The Hague, Netherlands.

Bardach, J. E., J. J. Magnuson, R. C. May, and J. M. Reinhart, editors. 1980. Fish behavior and its use in the capture and culture of fishes. International Center for Living Aquatic Resources Management, Manila.

Barlow, G. W. 1974a. Contrasts in social behavior between Central American cichlid fishes and coral reef surgeon fishes. American Zoologist 14:9–34.

Barlow, G. W. 1974b. Extraspecific imposition of social grouping among surgeonfishes (Pisces: Acanthuridae). Journal of Zoology 174:333–340.

Barlow, G. W. 1977. Modal action patterns. Pages 98–134 *in* T. A. Sebeok, editor. How animals communicate. Indiana University Press, Bloomington.

Barlow, G. W. 1981a. Genetics and development of behavior, with special reference to patterned motor output. Pages 191–251 *in* K. Immelmann, G. W. Barlow, L. Petrinovitch, and M. Main, editors. Behavioral development. Cambridge University Press, New York.

Barlow, G. W. 1981b. Patterns of parental investment, dispersal and egg size among coral-reef fishes. Environmental Biology of Fishes 6:65–85.

Barlow, G. W. 1983. The benefits of being gold: behavioral consequences of polychromatism in the midas cichlid, *Cichlasoma citrinellum*. Pages 73–85 *in* D. L. G. Noakes, D. G. Lindquist, G. S. Helfman, and J. A. Ward, editors. Predators and prey in fishes. Dr. W. Junk, The Hague, Netherlands.

Barnett, C. 1977. Aspects of chemical communication with special reference to fish. Biosciences Communications 3:331–392.

Baylis, J. R. 1974. The behavior and ecology of *Herotilapia multispinosa* (Teleostei, Cichlidae). Zeitschrift für Tierpsychologie 34:115–146.

Baylis, J. R. 1981. The evolution of parental care in fishes, with special reference to Darwin's rule of male sexual selection. Environmental Biology of Fishes 6:223–251.

Beitinger, T. L., and L. C. Fitzpatrick. 1979. Physiological and ecological correlates of preferred temperature in fish. American Zoologist 19:319–329.

Beitinger, T. L., and J. J. Magnuson. 1975. Influence of social rank and size on thermoselection behavior of bluegill (*Lepomis macrochirus*). Journal of the Fisheries Research Board of Canada 32:2133–2136.

Bitterman, M. E. 1975. The comparative analysis of learning. Science (Washington, D.C.) 188:699–709.

Blaxter, J. H. S. 1980. Vision and the feeding of fishes. Pages 32–56 *in* J. E. Bardach, J. J. Magnuson, R. C. May, and J. M. Reinhart, editors. Fish behavior and its use in the capture and culture of fishes. International Center for Living Aquatic Resources Management, Manila.

Blumer, L. S. 1985. The significance of biparental care in the brown bullhead, *Ictalurus nebulosus*. Environmental Biology of Fishes 12:231–236.

Bowen, S. H. 1983. Quantitative description of the diet. Pages 325–336 *in* L. A. Nielsen and D. L. Johnson, editors. Fisheries techniques. American Fisheries Society, Bethesda, Maryland.

Brown, J. L. 1975. The evolution of behavior. Norton, New York.

Chase, I. D. 1980a. Social process and hierarchy formation in small groups: a comparative perspective. American Sociological Review 45:905–924.

Chase, I. D. 1980b. Cooperative and noncooperative behaviour in animals. American Naturalist 115:827–857.

Chase, I. D. 1982a. Behavioral sequences during dominance hierarchy formation in chickens. Science (Washington, D.C.) 216:439–440.

Chase, I. D. 1982b. Models of hierarchy formation in animal societies. Behavioral Science 19:374–382.

Chase, I. D. 1985. The sequential analysis of aggressive acts during hierarchy formation: an application of the 'jigsaw puzzle' approach. Animal Behaviour 33:86–100.

Coble, D. W., G. B. Farabee, and R. O. Anderson. 1985. Comparative learning ability of selected fishes. Canadian Journal of Fisheries and Aquatic Sciences 42:791–796.

Colgan, P. 1975. Self-selection of photoperiod as a technique for studying endogenous rhythms in fish. Journal of Interdisciplinary Cycle Research 6:203–211.

Colgan, P., editor. 1978. Quantitative ethology. Wiley, New York.

Coutant, C. C. 1987. Thermal preferences: when does an asset become a liability? Environmental Biology of Fishes 18:161–172.

Davies, N. B., and A. I. Houston. 1984. Territory economics. Pages 148–169 *in* J. R. Krebs and N. B. Davies, editors. Behavioural ecology, 2nd edition. Sinauer, Sunderland, Massachusetts.

Dawkins, M. S. 1980. Animal suffering. The science of animal welfare. Chapman and Hall, London.

Dawkins, R. 1969. A threshold model of choice behaviour. Animal Behaviour 17:120–133.

Dawkins, R. 1976. The selfish gene. Oxford University Press, New York.

Dawkins, R. 1982. The extended phenotype. Freeman, San Francisco.

Dill, L. M. 1978. An energy-based model of optimal feeding-territory size. Theoretical Population Biology 14:396–429.

Dominey, W. J. 1981. Maintenance of female mimicry as a reproductive strategy in bluegill sunfish *(Lepomis macrochirus)*. Environmental Biology of Fishes 6:59–64.

Dunbrack, R., and L. M. Dill. 1983. A model of size dependent surface feeding in a stream dwelling salmonid. Pages 41–54 *in* D. L. G. Noakes, D. G. Lindquist, G. S. Helfman, and J. A. Ward, editors. Predators and prey in fishes. Dr. W. Junk, The Hague, Netherlands.

Fry, F. E. J. 1971. The effect of environmental factors on the physiology of fish. Pages 1–98 *in* W. S. Hoar and D. J. Randall, editors. Fish physiology, volume 6. Academic Press, New York.

Fujiya, M., S. Sakaguchi, and O. Fukuhara. 1980. Training of fishes applied to ranching of red sea bream in Japan. Pages 200–209 *in* J. E. Bardach, J. J. Magnuson, R. C. May, and J. M. Reinhart, editors. Fish behavior and its use in the capture and culture of fishes. International Center for Living Aquatic Resources Management, Manila.

Gauthreaux, S. A., Jr. 1978. The ecological significance of behavioral dominance. Pages 17–54 *in* P. P. G. Bateson and P. H. Klopfer, editors. Perspectives in ethology, volume 3. Plenum, New York.

Green, R. F. 1984. Stopping rules for optimal foragers. American Naturalist 123:30–43.

Gross, M. R. 1984. Sunfish, salmon, and the evolution of alternative reproductive strategies and tactics in fishes. Pages 55–75 *in* R. J. Wootton and G. Potts, editors. Fish reproduction: strategies and tactics. Academic Press, London.

Hamilton, W. D. 1971. Geometry for the selfish herd. Journal of Theoretical Biology 31:295–311.

Hasler, A. D., and A. T. Scholz. 1983. Olfactory imprinting and homing in salmon. Springer-Verlag, Berlin.

Hawryshyn, C. W., and R. Beauchamp. 1985. Ultraviolet photosensitivity in goldfish: an independent u.v. retinal mechanism. Vision Research 25:11–20.

Hazlett, B., editor. 1977. Quantitative methods in the study of animal behavior. Academic Press, New York.

Helfman, G. S. 1983. Underwater methods. Pages 249–369 *in* L. A. Nielsen and D. L. Johnson, editors. Fisheries techniques. American Fisheries Society, Bethesda, Maryland.

Hixon, M. 1980. Food production and competitor density as the determinants of feeding territory size. American Naturalist 115:510–530.

Hoar, W. S. 1983. General and comparative physiology, 3rd edition. Prentice-Hall, Englewood Cliffs, New Jersey.

Hogan, J. A. 1974. On the choice between eating and aggressive display in the Siamese fighting fish *(Betta splendens)*. Learning and Motivation 5:273–287.

Hollis, K. 1982. Pavlovian conditioning of signal-centered action patterns and autonomic behavior: a biological analysis of function. Pages 1–64 *in* J. S. Rosenblatt, R. A. Hinde, C. Beer, and M.-C. Busnel, editors. Advances in the study of behavior, volume 12. Academic Press, New York.

Hopkins, C. 1980. Evolution of electric communication channels of mormyrids. Behavioral Ecology and Sociobiology 7:1–13.

Horrall, R. M. 1981. Behavioral stock-isolating mechanisms in Great Lakes fishes with special reference to homing and site imprinting. Canadian Journal of Fisheries and Aquatic Sciences 38:1481–1496.

Hunter, J. 1966. Procedures for the analysis of schooling behavior. Journal of the Fisheries Research Board of Canada 23:547–562.

Hunter, J. 1972. Swimming and feeding behavior of larval anchovy, *Engraulis mordax*. U.S. National Marine Fisheries Service Fishery Bulletin 70:821–838.

Immelmann, K. 1980. Introduction to ethology. Plenum, New York.

Iwai, T. 1980. Sensory anatomy and feeding of fish larvae. Pages 124–145 *in* J. E. Bardach, J. J. Magnuson, R. C. May, and J. M. Reinhart, editors. Fish behavior and its use in the capture and culture of fishes. International Center for Living Aquatic Resources Management, Manila.

Johannes, P. 1978. Reproductive strategies of coastal marine fishes in the tropics. Environmental Biology of Fishes 3:63–84.

Johnson, D. L., and L. A. Nielsen. 1983. Sampling considerations. Pages 1–21 *in* L. A. Nielsen and D. L. Johnson, editors. Fisheries techniques. American Fisheries Society, Bethesda, Maryland.

Keenleyside, M. H. A. 1979. Diversity and adaptation in fish behaviour. Springer-Verlag, Berlin.

Krebs, J. R., and N. B. Davies, editors. 1984. Behavioural ecology. An evolutionary approach, 2nd edition. Sinauer, Sunderland, Massachusetts.

Krebs, J. R., and R. McCleery. 1984. Optimization in behavioural ecology. Pages 91–121 *in* J. R. Krebs and N. B. Davies, editors. Behavioural ecology. An evolutionary approach, 2nd edition. Sinauer, Sunderland, Massachusetts.

Lasker, R., editor. 1981. Marine fish larvae. Morphology, ecology, and relation to fisheries. University of Washington Press, Seattle, Washington.

Lehner, P. N. 1979. Handbook of ethological methods. Garland Press, New York.

Losey, G. 1981. Experience leads to attack of novel species by an interspecific territorial damselfish, *Eupomacentrus fasciolatus*. Animal Behaviour 29:129–143.

Losey, G. S. 1982a. Ecological cues and experience modify interspecific aggression by the damselfish, *Stegastes fasciolatus*. Behaviour 81:14–37.

Losey, G. S. 1982b. Intra- and interspecific aggression by the Central American midas cichlid, *Cichlasoma citrinellum*. Behaviour 79:39–80.

Magnuson, J. J., and T. L. Beitinger. 1978. Stability of temperatures preferred by centrarchid fishes and terrestrial reptiles. Pages 181–216 *in* E. S. Reese and F. J. Lighter, editors. Contrasts in behavior. Wiley, New York.

Magnuson, J. J., and L. B. Crowder. 1979. Temperature as an ecological resource. American Zoologist 19:331–343.

Manning, A. W. G. 1979. An introduction to animal behaviour, 3rd edition. Edward Arnold, London.

Marcotte, B. M., and H. I. Browman. 1986. Foraging behavior in fishes: perspectives on variance. Environmental Biology of Fishes 16:25–33.

Markert, J. R., D. A. Higgs, H. M. Dye, and D. W. MacQuarrie. 1977. Influence of bovine growth hormone on growth rate, appetite, and food conversion of yearling coho salmon *(Oncorhynchus kisutch)* fed two diets of different composition. Canadian Journal of Zoology 55:74–83.

McCauley, R. W., W. W. Reynolds, and N. H. Huggins. 1977. Photokinesis and behavioral thermoregulation in adult sea lampreys *(Petromyzon marinus)*. Journal of Experimental Zoology 202:431–437.

McFarland, D. 1985. Animal behaviour. Pitman, New York.

McFarland, D. J. 1977. Decision making in animals. Nature (London) 269:15–21.

McNicol, R. E., and D. L. G. Noakes. 1984. Environmental influences on territoriality of juvenile brook charr, *Salvelinus fontinalis,* in a stream environment. Environmental Biology of Fishes 10:29–42.

McNicol, R. E., E. Scherer, and E. J. Murkin. 1985. Quantitative field investigations of feeding and territorial behaviour of young-of-the-year brook charr, *Salvelinus fontinalis*. Environmental Biology of Fishes 12:219–229.

Milinski, M. 1982. Optimal foraging: the influence of intraspecific competition on diet selection. Behavioral Ecology and Sociobiology 11:109–115.

Moser, H. G., editor. 1984. Ontogeny and systematics of fishes. American Society of Ichthyologists and Herpetologists Special Publication 1.

Moyle, P. B., and J. J. Cech, Jr. 1982. Fishes. An introduction to ichthyology. Prentice-Hall, Englewood Cliffs, New Jersey.

Moyle, P. B., and B. Vondracek. 1985. Persistence and structure of the fish assemblage in a small California stream. Ecology 6:1–13.

Myrberg, A. A., Jr. 1972. Ethology of the bicolor damselfish *Eupomacentrus partitus* (Pisces: Pomacentridae): a comparative analysis of laboratory and field behaviour. Animal Behavior Monographs 5:197–283.

Myrberg, A. A., Jr. 1973. Underwater television—tool for the marine biologist. Bulletin of Marine Science 23:824–835.

Myrberg, A. A., Jr. 1975. The role of chemical and visual stimuli in the preferential discrimination of young by the cichlid fish Cichlasoma nigrofasciatum (Günther). Zeitschrift für Tierpsychologie 37:274–297.

Myrberg, A. A., Jr. 1980a. Fish bio-acoustics: its relevance to the 'not so silent world.' Environmental Biology of Fishes 5:297–304.

Myrberg, A. A., Jr. 1980b. Sensory mediation of social recognition processes in fishes. Pages 146–178 in J. E. Bardach, J. J. Magnuson, R. C. May, and J. M. Reinhart, editors. Fish behavior and its use in the capture and culture of fishes. International Center for Living Aquatic Resources Management, Manila.

Nelson, K. 1965. Aftereffects of courtship in the male three-spined stickleback. Zeitschrift für vergleichende Physiologie 50:569–597.

Noakes, D. L. G. 1978. Social behaviour as it influences fish production. Pages 360–386 in S. D. Gerking, editor. Ecology of freshwater fish production. Blackwell Scientific Publications, Oxford, England.

Noakes, D. L. G. 1981. Comparative aspects of behavioral ontogeny: a philosophy from fishes. Pages 491–508 in K. Immelmann, G. W. Barlow, L. Petrinovitch, and M. Main, editors. Behavioral development. Cambridge University Press, Cambridge, England.

Noakes, D. L. G. 1986a. When to feed: decision making in sticklebacks. Environmental Biology of Fishes 16:93–105.

Noakes, D. L. G. 1986b. Genetic basis of fish behaviour. Pages 3–22 in T. J. Pitcher, editor. The behaviour of teleost fishes. Croom Helm, London.

Noakes, D. L. G., and E. K. Balon. 1982. Life histories in tilapia. Pages 21–50 in R. S. V. Pullin and R. H. Lowe-McConnell, editors. The biology and culture of tilapias. International Center for Living Aquatic Resources Management, Manila.

Noakes, D. L. G., and J. W. A. Grant. 1986. Behavioral ecology and production of riverine fishes. Polish Archives of Hydrobiology 33:249–262.

Noakes, D. L. G., and J. F. Leatherland. 1977. Social dominance and interrenal cell activity in rainbow trout, Salmo gairdneri (Pisces: Salmonidae). Environmental Biology of Fishes 2:131–136.

Noakes, D. L. G., D. G. Lindquist, G. S. Helfman, and J. A. Ward, editors. 1983. Predators and prey in fishes. Dr. W. Junk, The Hague, Netherlands.

Noakes, D. L. G., and R. E. McNicol. 1982. Geometry for the eccentric territory. Canadian Journal of Zoology 60:1776–1779.

Noeske, T. A., and R. E. Spieler. 1984. Circadian feeding time affects growth of fish. Transactions of the American Fisheries Society 113:540–544.

Noonan, K. 1983. Female choice in the cichlid fish Cichlasoma nigrofasciatum. Animal Behaviour 31:1005–1010.

Nunan, C. P., and D. L. G. Noakes. 1985a. Light sensitivity and substrate penetration by eleutheroembryos of brook (Salvelinus fontinalis) and lake charr (S. namaycush) and their F₁ hybrid splake. Experimental Biology (Berlin) 44:221–228.

Nunan, C. P., and D. L. G. Noakes. 1985b. Response of rainbow trout (Salmo gairdneri) embryos to current flow in simulated substrates. Canadian Journal of Zoology 63:1813–1815.

O'Brien, W. J. 1979. The predator–prey interaction of planktivorous fish and zooplankton. American Scientist 67:572–581.

Olla, B. L., A. J. Bedja, and A. D. Martin. 1975. Activity, movements and feeding behavior of the cunner, Tautogolabrus adspersus, and comparisons of food habits with young tautog, Tautoga onitis, off Long Island, New York. U.S. National Marine Fisheries Service Fishery Bulletin 73:895–900.

Olla, B. L., A. J. Bedja, and A. D. Martin. 1979. Seasonal dispersal and habitat selection of cunner, Tautogolabrus adspersus, and young tautog, Tautoga onitis, in Fire Island Inlet, Long Island, New York. U.S. National Marine Fisheries Service Fishery Bulletin 77:255–261.

Olla, B. L., W. H. Pearson, and A. L. Studholme. 1980a. Applicability of behavioral measures in environmental stress assessment. Journal du Conseil, Conseil International pour l'Exploration de la Mer 179:162–173.

Olla, B. L., and C. Samet. 1974. Fish-to-fish attraction and the facilitation of feeding behavior as mediated by visual stimuli in striped mullet, *Mugil cephalus*. Journal of the Fisheries Research Board of Canada 23:1621–1630.

Olla, B. L., A. L. Studholme, and A. J. Bedja. 1985. Behavior of juvenile bluefish *Pomatomus saltatrix* in vertical thermal gradients: influence of season, temperature acclimation and food. Marine Ecology Progress Series 23:165–177.

Olla, B. L., A. L. Studholme, A. J. Bedja, and C. Samet. 1980b. Role of temperature in triggering migratory behavior of the adult tautog *Tautoga onitis* under laboratory conditions. Marine Biology 59:23–30.

Partridge, B., J. Johansson, and J. Kalish. 1983. The structure of schools of giant bluefin tuna in Cape Cod Bay. Environmental Biology of Fishes 9:253–262.

Pitcher, T. J. 1983. Heuristic definitions of fish shoaling behaviour. Animal Behaviour 31:611–613.

Pitcher, T. J., editor. 1985. The behaviour of teleost fishes. Croom Helm, London.

Pot, W., and D. L. G. Noakes. 1985. Individual identification of bluntnose minnows *(Pimephales notatus)* by means of naturally acquired marks. Canadian Journal of Zoology 63:363–365.

Pullin, R. S. V., and R. H. Lowe-McConnell, editors. 1982. The biology and culture of tilapias. International Center for Living Aquatic Resources Management, Manila.

Raffetto, N. S. 1987. The mating ecology and reproductive demography of smallmouth bass, *Micropterus dolomieui*. Doctoral dissertation. University of Wisconsin, Madison.

Reese, E. S. 1973. Duration of residence by coral reef fishes on "home" reefs. Copeia 1973:145–149.

Reese, E. S. 1975. A comparative study of the social behaviour and related ecology of reef fishes of the family Chaetodontidae. Zeitschrift für Tierpsychologie 37:37–61.

Ringler, N. H. 1983. Variation in foraging tactics of fishes. Pages 159–171 *in* D. L. G. Noakes, D. G. Lindquist, G. S. Helfman, and J. A. Ward, editors. Predators and prey in fishes. Dr. W. Junk, The Hague, Netherlands.

Rosenthal, H., and S. Oren, editors. 1981. Research on intensive aquaculture. European Mariculture Society, Bredene, Belgium.

Rowland, W. J., and P. Sevenster. 1985. Sign stimuli in the threespine stickleback *(Gasterosteus aculeatus)*: a re-examination and extension of some classic experiments. Behaviour 93:241–257.

Sale, P. F. 1971. Extremely limited home range in a coral reef fish, *Dascyllus aruanus* (Pisces: Pomacentridae). Copeia 1971:324–327.

Sale, P. F., 1975. Patterns of use of space in a guild of territorial reef fishes. Marine Biology 29:89–97.

Sale, P. F., P. J. Doherty, and W. A. Douglas. 1980. Juvenile recruitment strategies and the coexistence of territorial pomacentrid fishes. Bulletin of Marine Science 30:147–158.

Schemmel, C. 1980. Studies on the genetics of feeding behaviour in the cave fish *Astyanax mexicanus* F. *anoptichthys*. An example of apparent monofactorial inheritance by polygenes. Zeitschrift für Tierpsychologie 53:9–22.

Schjelderup-Ebbe, T. 1922. Beitrage zur Sozialpsychologie des Haushuhns. Zeitschrift für Psychologie 88:225–252.

Schoener, T. M. 1983. Simple models of optimal feeding-territory size: a reconsideration. American Naturalist 121:608–629.

Schreck, C. B. 1982. Stress and rearing salmonids. Aquaculture 28:241–249.

Siegel, S. 1956. Nonparametric statistics for the behavioral sciences. McGraw-Hill, New York.

Simenstad, C. A., and G. M. Cailliet, editors. 1986. Contemporary studies in fish feeding: the proceedings of GUTSHOP '84. Dr. W. Junk, Dordrecht, Netherlands.

Sokal, R. R., and F. J. Rohlf. 1981. Biometry, 2nd edition. Freeman, San Francisco.

Sprague, J. B. 1976. Current status of sublethal tests of pollutants on aquatic organisms. Journal of the Fisheries Research Board of Canada 33:1988–1992.

Statler, D. P. 1982. Use of self-feeders for rearing steelhead trout at Dworshak National Fish Hatchery. Progressive Fish-Culturist 44:195.

Steiner, W. W., J. L. Luczkovich, and B. L. Olla. 1982. Activity, shelter usage, growth and recruitment of juvenile red hake *Urophycis chuss*. Marine Ecology 7:125–135.

Thorpe, W. H. 1963. Learning and instinct in animals, 2nd edition. Methuen, London.

Tinbergen, N. 1951. The study of instinct. Clarendon Press, Oxford, England.

Warner, R. R. 1978. The evolution of hermaphroditism and unisexuality in aquatic and terrestrial vertebrates. Pages 77–101 *in* E. S. Reese and F. J. Lighter, editors. Contrasts in behavior: adaptations in the aquatic and terrestrial environments. Wiley, New York.

Werner, E. E., and D. J. Hall. 1974. Optimal foraging and the size selection of prey by the bluegill sunfish. *(Lepomis macrochirus)*. Ecology 55:1042–1052.

Wydoski, R., and L. Emery. 1983. Tagging and marking. Pages 215–237 *in* L. A. Nielsen and D. L. Johnson, editors. Fisheries techniques. American Fisheries Society, Bethesda, Maryland.

Chapter 18

Autecology

DONALD M. BALTZ

18.1 INTRODUCTION

Autecology is the study of single-species ecology. Many of the techniques used in autecology, such as methods to determine reproductive cycles, have been described elsewhere in this book (for other purposes) as well as in *Fisheries Techniques* (Nielsen and Johnson 1983). I draw them together in this chapter and describe in detail the ways to study microhabitat use by fishes. Box 18.1 contains a glossary of key ecological terms used in this chapter.

Interrelations of species are the focus of synecology, treated in Chapter 19. Synecologists use many autecological techniques because community dynamics cannot be understood unless the ecology of component species is known. Hixon (1980), Larson (1980), and Fausch and White (1981) are among those who have integrated aut- and synecology in their work.

18.1.1 Components of Autecology

Autecology comprises studies of a species' life history and environmental requirements.

A life history study primarily addresses the way in which a species lives. The usual characteristics of interest are age-specific growth rates, longevity, survivorship, reproduction, feeding habits, behavior, and general life history strategy.

A study of environmental requirements deals with a species' niche dimensions or axes (see *niche*, Box 18.1). Relevant physicochemical niche dimensions include temperature, light, water depth and velocity, dissolved oxygen concentration, salinity, and pH. Most descriptions of fish microhabitats emphasize the physical characteristics of sites or locations occupied by individual fish such as depth, substrate, and cover. Chemical variables often receive less attention because they normally do not vary much within an environment, but they should be described in detail when they do vary and especially when one or more of them determines the suitability of a habitat for spawning or some other important function (see, for example, Matthews and Hill 1977, 1979a, 1979b).

The goal of an environmental requirements study is to describe a species' niche—that is, how the species uses resources—in the fundamental sense without the presence of other species. However, niche dimensions measured in the field probably are restricted by competitors, predators, and symbionts (Hutchinson 1958; Colwell and Futuyama 1971; Hurlbert 1981). The influences of other species may not be immediately apparent, so inferences about fundamental niches should be made cautiously if field data are not supported by laboratory studies (Baltz et al. 1982).

Box 18.1   Terms in Autecology

Frequency-of-use distributions describe a population's response to a resource or environmental variable.

Habitat is the kind or range of environments in which a species can live. It is a general term that broadly defines where a species lives without specifying resource availability or use. A species has one habitat if it spends its entire life in the same environment. It has more than one habitat if individuals change environments during their lifetimes, as they do (for example) in anadromous species or in species whose young are pelagic but whose adults are demersal.

Microhabitat for an individual fish is the site where that fish is located at any point in time. Sites may be characterized by measuring physicochemical variables (e.g., depth, velocity, temperature, salinity) that describe resources or environmental constraints.

Microhabitat use describes the intensity of use of values on a site resource axis by a life stage or population. Frequency-of-use distributions indicate the relative intensity of use for value intervals (e.g., the velocity interval of 30–40 cm/s).

Microhabitat variables are abiotic variables to which individuals respond. They are intensive or local environmental variables to which individuals and populations are exposed.

Niche is best defined as the set of resources (i.e., energy, materials, and sites) used by an individual, life stage, population, species, or higher level of organization (Hurlbert 1981). Ever since Hutchinson (1958) characterized the niche as an "*n*-dimensional hyperspace," ecologists have thought of niches in terms of "dimensions," each dimension representing a physical, chemical, or biotic variable that influences the species in question.

Resource availability is a measure of the central tendency and dispersion of a resource variable. It is usually estimated by random sampling. Estimates of resource availability may require both temporal and spatial estimates of distributions. When the availability of a resource (e.g., prey availability) is assessed, intrinsic characteristics of the resource (e.g., prey size distribution) may also be important.

Resource characteristics include intrinsic and environmental characteristics. Substrate texture and prey size are examples of intrinsic properties. Environmental characteristics such as temperature, salinity, other physical factors, or other species may not be resources, but they may constrain the use of a resource if, for example, they exceed a species' physiological tolerance.

Resources used by fishes are energy (e.g., prey species), nonfood materials (e.g., oxygen, nest building materials), and sites (e.g., physical space occupied by an individual that may also provide shelter or permit access to food).

Site is a fine-scale spatial dimension that is considered a resource. Large-scale spatial dimensions (e.g., habitats) are generally not resources; however, territories and home ranges that are defended to protect nest sites, mates, food resources, or shelters may also be resources.

Suitability is a measure of the relative appropriateness of a site for an individual or life stage in the context of resources and constraining environmental characteristics. Suitability is calculated from estimates of microhabitat use and resource availability.

18.2 BASIC LIFE HISTORY

Current interest in life history strategies stems from the germinal work of Cole (1954), who examined the sensitivity of the intrinsic rate of population increase to changes in various life history variables. Cole compared the intrinsic rate of increase of semelparous species, which reproduce once in a lifetime, and iteroparous species, which reproduce several times. He pointed out that iteroparous reproduction is common, but he could discern no advantage of this over semelparous reproduction. Murphy (1968) provided an explanation for this apparent paradox by demonstrating the value of repeated reproduction in environments where mortality of adults is low but survival of juveniles is uncertain (see also Charnov and Schaffer 1973). Murphy and subsequent workers have documented some of the great diversity of life history strategies among and within semelparous and iteroparous species (Constantz 1974; Schaffer and Elson 1975; Roff 1981; Baltz and Moyle 1982; Baltz 1984). Stearns (1976, 1977, 1980) reviewed the theory of life history evolution; intraspecific variations in life history characteristics are thought to reflect species adaptations to distinct environments, each with its own set of selective forces. Nevertheless, one should be careful when describing differences as adaptive strategies (e.g., Gould and Lewontin 1979).

18.2.1 Age and Growth

Much fisheries research has focused on age and growth. Such studies are important because most fish species have indeterminate growth—they continue to grow throughout their lives—and many important aspects of their biology change with body size. Fishes show ontogenetic changes related to microhabitat selection (Baltz and Moyle 1982), reproduction (Roff 1981; Baltz 1984), feeding (Nikolsky 1963; Grossman 1980), and behavior (Bachman 1984; Helfman 1986). Accurate aging of fishes is a prerequisite for good fishery management and particularly for understanding a species' population dynamics. Aging techniques were reviewed by Bagenal and Tesch (1978) and Jearld (1983). Wilson et al. (1987) summarized the standard terminology used in age and growth studies.

Because fishes continue to grow throughout their lives, the fine structure of hard tissues such as opercular bones, otoliths, scales, vertebrae, and fin spines often show daily, seasonal, and annual patterns of growth that can be used to determine age. In many temperate-zone fishes, for example, the near cessation of growth during winter results in the formation of an annulus, a distinct pattern in the fine structure of hard tissues. If this pattern is formed once a year, it may be used to determine a fish's age in years.[1] Problems arise when variations in fine structure are incorrectly interpreted as annuli. Any process or event (e.g., disease or reproduction) that disrupts the allocation of resources to growth can cause a change in the fine structure of hard tissues that might be incorrectly interpreted as an annulus. Thus, if a fish forms an annulus during the winter and a "false annulus" during the reproductive season, its age could be greatly overestimated. Likewise, failure to recognize annuli on scales can lead to gross underestimates of

---

[1]"Annulus" means ring, and has no inherent connotation of time. In fisheries work, annulus traditionally (but not exclusively) means a ring laid down once a year at the periphery of a scale, otolith, or other hard body part. In this chapter, I use annulus to mean annual ring.

age (see papers in Summerfelt and Hall 1987). Age determinations are used in fisheries management to calculate acceptable levels of exploitation because populations of slow-growing fishes cannot withstand as much exploitation as populations of fast-growing fishes (e.g., Harris and Grossman 1985). Thus, inaccurate determinations may result in mismanagement of important fisheries. A variety of validation procedures can ensure the accuracy of aging estimations (Beamish and MacFarlane 1983). Validation is so important that all studies of age and growth should include an age validation, and ages not directly or indirectly validated should not be used to make management decisions.

18.2.2 Reproduction

Four questions relating to reproduction are of primary interest. (1) When does a species mature? (2) What is its spawning season? (3) Where does it spawn? (4) How many gametes does it produce? The age of first reproduction or maturity may differ between sexes and among populations or stocks of the same species. For a population, it may be useful to define the age at first reproduction as the lowest age at which at least half of a cohort reproduces (Roff 1981). However, when life tables are constructed, it is the proportion of each cohort actually reproducing that is of interest, and the fecundity (the number of eggs a female produces) is halved because only half of the progeny will be females.

The investigator may determine the seasonal timing of reproduction directly by documenting spawning activity in the field or indirectly by following gonadal cycles (Chapter 16). Spawning requirements may be described in terms of water depth, water velocity, substrate, and water quality; microhabitat description techniques are detailed later in this chapter. Snyder (1983) described methods for sampling eggs and larvae in the field and for estimating fecundity from individual fishes. Gonadal cycles may be documented with gonadosomatic indices or by histological staging of gonad maturation (Overstreet 1983; Snyder 1983; but see de Vlaming et al. 1982 for a discussion of the shortcomings of the gonadosomatic index).

Because the reproductive output of fishes is almost invariably related to body size as well as to age, it is generally useful to express fecundity on both a length-specific basis and an age-specific basis. This is true whether the species is semelparous or iteroparous. Fecundity can be measured directly for species that spawn once a year and produce only one batch of eggs. However, not all eggs in an ovary may actually mature (Nikolsky 1963), so the number of eggs actually spawned may be less than the maximum fecundity. Species having a short reproductive season are termed birth-pulse or total spawners (Caughley 1977). Other species may produce more than one batch of eggs per year and have an extended spawning season; they are termed birth-flow or fractional spawners. For them, fecundity is more difficult to estimate, especially if eggs are produced more or less continuously over several months (Nikolsky 1963; Parrish et al. 1986). Fertility, the number of viable offspring produced, is much more difficult to measure; however, it can be estimated for some of the species that provide parental care (Constantz 1979; Baltz 1984).

18.2.3 Life History Strategies

Life history strategies can be deduced by studying the same species in different locations or environments (McPhail 1977; Stearns 1978; Baltz and Moyle 1982) or by comparing similar species in the same or similar environments (Roff 1981; Baltz 1984). Life history characteristics of interest usually include age at first reproduction, reproductive life span, and age-specific and length-specific schedules of fecundity, longevity, mortality, and growth (Cole 1954). Intraspecific comparisons of life history characteristics of populations in different environments (e.g., still versus running waters) offer insights into how various selective pressures shape life histories. Ghiselin (1974) suggested that we can conduct natural experiments in which the species is held constant while the environment is varied. Such an approach is not straightforward because the populations of a species often vary considerably in many respects, their environments do not vary in a linear manner, and so-called "natural experiments" almost always lack experimental controls. Nevertheless, comparative field studies of populations are worthwhile because they can show which life history characteristics and environmental factors covary.

18.2.4 Stock Identification

The identification and discrimination of stocks are important to fisheries managers and to scientists trying to understand a species' life history strategy. Fish species often show geographic differences that may distinguish populations, stocks, or subspecies. Geographic differentiation is greatest in freshwater species, intermediate in anadromous species, and least in marine species (Gyllensten 1985; Utter 1987). Stock identification is simplified for some species—for example, Pacific salmon home with great accuracy to their natal streams (Hasler and Scholz 1978; Utter 1981)—but stocks of other species may be considerably harder to identify (see Shaklee 1983; Winans 1985; Avise et al. 1986; Kumpf et al. 1987). Chapters 2–5 offer information useful for stock-identification studies.

Two processes are sometimes included under the heading of stock identification: (1) the recognition of stocks, subspecies, or populations that have distinctive genomes or other biological features and that may benefit from individual management; and (2) the estimation of stock proportions within a mixture of stocks (Fournier et al. 1984). Researchers identify stocks by studying the variation of electrophoretic, morphometric, meristic, or other characteristics within a species. In a mixed-stock assemblage, individuals belonging to separate stocks are identified by character analysis involving, for example, genetic markers (Grant et al. 1980; Seeb et al. 1986), parasites (Helle 1987), or meristic features (Winans 1987); discriminant function analysis and principal component analysis are often used for this purpose.

Discriminant function analysis (DFA) is a very important statistical technique, but it is not necessarily appropriate for stock identification. An appropriate null hypothesis for stock identification is that no pattern in the data suggests that different stocks exist. The null hypothesis for DFA is that no differences exist among groups. This hypothesis is appropriate for stock discrimination, but may not be appropriate for stock identification. Because a DFA assigns individuals a priori to groups, it will almost always find statistical differences. A DFA applied to samples that do not adequately characterize populations in space and time is very likely to result in misleading or trivial conclusions; Gibson et al. (1984) presented a simple example of this problem. A better approach to stock identification, after steps are taken to adequately characterize variation in space and time, is to first use a principal components analysis (PCA) to discover patterns among samples (Neff and Smith 1979; Baltz and Moyle 1981; Chernoff 1982). If the PCA shows a pattern (i.e., if samples at some of the sampling sites are distinctive in spite of variations over time), some groups may be designated, and stock discrimination—perhaps by DFA—then can be based on justifiable groups.

18.2.5 Feeding Habits

Feeding habits are studied to learn how a species makes a living and who its competitors and its predators are likely to be. Bowen (1983) outlined the methods and considerations needed to plan and execute a meaningful feeding habit study. The "Gutshop" proceedings (Cailliet and Simenstad 1982; Simenstad and Cailliet 1986) contain useful evaluations of methods used to determine the feeding habits of fishes.

18.2.6 Behavior

Noakes and Baylis described methods for behavioral studies in Chapter 17. Analyses of microhabitat use by fishes (Section 18.5) also provide behavioral information, particularly when they address diel (Gordon et al. 1985) and seasonal variations in microhabitat use (Rimmer et al. 1983) or compare microhabitat use for different activities (Shirvell and Dungey 1983). Behavioral subjects of auteco-logical interest include reproduction (Lobel 1978; Dominey 1980; Gross and MacMillan 1981; Warner and Harlan 1982), schooling (Shaw 1978; Helfman 1984), and intraspecific aggression in defense of territories (Jenkins 1969), shelter (Shulman 1985), or food (Grossman 1979).

18.3   DISTRIBUTION AND ABUNDANCE

The distribution of a species in space and time may be assessed on a broad zoogeographic basis (Darlington 1957; Briggs 1974; Hocutt and Wiley 1986) or in narrow terms of habitat (Smith and Powell 1971). Zoogeographic studies are generally organized around drainage systems for freshwater species and around oceanographic or landmass barriers for marine species. Readers interested in zoogeographic studies should refer to papers by Ball (1975) and Rosen (1974, 1975a, 1975b). The focus of this section is on population surveys and habitat preferences.

Distributions of fish within and among habitats are often related to early life history requirements (Pearcy and Myers 1974), foraging efficiency (Werner et al. 1983b), predator avoidance (Werner et al. 1983a), or spawning requirements. Standard techniques for conducting population surveys, which include trapping, netting, electrofishing, and poisoning, were described in *Fisheries Techniques* (Nielsen and Johnson 1983). Underwater diving and photographic methods are becoming more common (Ebeling et al. 1980; Griffith 1981; Sale and Douglas 1981; Larson and DeMartini 1984), but have not been used to their full potential for survey work.

18.3.1 Diving Surveys

Diving surveys often can be used where other techniques are precluded by accessibility, depth, velocity, conductivity, or environmental considerations. Diving surveys may not be suitably quantitative for small or cryptic fishes, but the population estimates they generate usually compare favorably with those from electrofishing, seining, or poisoning surveys (Northcote and Wilkie 1963; Goldstein 1978; Griffith 1981; Sale and Douglas 1981). Snorkeling or scuba surveys can provide data on fish abundances, biomasses, and size distributions, as well as on habitat preferences if sampling is stratified.

Diving surveys of lakes and marine environments usually follow transect methods (Keast and Harker 1977; Werner et al. 1977; Ebeling et al. 1980; Helfman 1983; Larson and DeMartini 1984). In streams, a length of stream typically is surveyed; transects are rarely used. The snorkeler or snorkeling team normally should proceed upstream, but may move downstream where currents are strong (Griffith 1983). Scuba gear may be required where stream depth is greater than underwater visibility or when cryptic fishes must be located in cover. Fishes are counted as they pass downstream of the snorkeler or line of snorkelers. The number of snorkelers used in a survey should be small enough that fish are not herded upstream. Investigators can facilitate upstream surveys by selecting reaches with an obstacle at the upper end that fishes are reluctant to pass. The number of fish and their estimated lengths are recorded on an underwater slate (Helfman 1983) or called out to a recorder on the bank. Biomass is then estimated from length–weight relationships.

The quality of each stream survey should be recorded on the field data form. Survey quality depends primarily on maximum depth and underwater visibility. When the depth exceeds underwater visibility, many fishes may pass the observers undetected or (if detected) unidentified. Surveys conducted under conditions of poor visibility may be strongly biased and should be deleted from further analysis.

18.3.2 Habitat Stratification

The distribution of a species within an aquatic system may be better understood if the system is subdivided into strata such a riffles, runs, and pools in lotic systems (Griffith 1983) or littoral and pelagic zones in lentic systems. Platts et al. (1983) characterized such subdivisions as water column types. Although riffles, runs, and pools are not different habitats in an autecological sense, they may be considered such in a community context (Whittaker et al. 1973) because assemblages of species often differ along an environmental gradient (e.g., depth or velocity) within a system. A stratum represents a portion of the environment with a recognizable set of physical, chemical, or biological characteristics. The limits of a stratum are defined by biologists according to the scale of a particular study. In a large stream, for example, strata might be morphologic features like runs, riffles, and pools; in a smaller stream, they might be hydrologic zones differing in depth or water velocity. The important thing to recognize is that microhabitats and habitats are defined by observations of individual organisms, whereas strata are defined somewhat arbitrarily by biologists.

In streams, each study reach should be characterized in terms of stratum type, length, mean width, substrate composition, maximum depth, representative depths, surface velocities, and mean water column velocities (Box 18.2). Survey data may be analyzed in terms of numerical abundance or biomass per unit of length or area of each stratum type. A two-way analysis of variance (stratum by life stage) will be useful to decipher any differences within species if life stages or size-classes are identified. Survey data may be combined with habitat mapping data to compare population abundance and biomass between or among strata or

Box 18.2   Example of a Data Form for Stream Population Surveys

DATE _____   UNDERWATER VISIBILITY (m) _____
TIME _____   RECORDER _____
LOCATION _____   SURVEY QUALITY _____
HABITAT TYPE _____   OBSERVERS _____
LENGTH _____   WATER TEMP °C _____
FLOW METER NO. _____   FLOW MTR CALIB. EQ. _____

REPRESENTATIVE WIDTHS (m)
1. _____   2. _____   3. _____   4. _____   5. _____

SUBSTRATE COMPOSITION   MEAN WIDTH (m) _____   MAXIMUM DEPTH (m) _____
SUBSTRATE COMPOSITION (%): 1 ___ 2 ___ 3 ___ 4 ___ 5 ___ 6 ___ 7 ___ 8 ___

    TOTAL DEPTHS, SUBSTRATES, SURFACE VELOCITIES AND MEAN WATER COLUMN
    VELOCITIES AT FIVE POINTS ON ONE TO THREE REPRESENTATIVE TRANSECTS.

	LEFT BANK			RIGHT BANK	
DISTANCE	0	1/4	1/2	3/4	1/1
DEPTH (CM)	_____	_____	_____	_____	_____
SUBCODE	_____	_____	_____	_____	_____
VELOCITIES (CM/S)					
SURFACE	_____	_____	_____	_____	_____
0.8	_____	_____	_____	_____	_____
0.6	_____	_____	_____	_____	_____
0.2	_____	_____	_____	_____	_____

                        TOTAL LENGTH (mm)

SPP CODE													
1													
2													
N 3													
U 4													
M 5													
B 6													
E 7													
R 8													
9													
10													
11													
12													
13													
14													
15													
16													
17													
18													
19													
20													
21													
22													
23													
24													
25													

streams. When sampling sites are adequately characterized in terms of morphology and water quality, multiple-regression models can be developed to predict standing stocks of fish for future times and conditions (Binns and Eiserman 1979; Layher and Maughan 1985). Similar survey principles apply to lakes, estuaries, and other systems, but the ability to resolve fine details declines as the size of the system increases.

18.4 MOVEMENTS

The movements of fishes include diel, seasonal, and ontogenetic shifts among microhabitats. Diel movements may relate to food or predators, light or darkness, sex, or size (Wurtsbaugh and Li 1985; reviewed by Helfman 1986 and Wurtsbaugh and Neverman 1988). For example, brown trout make daily movements between feeding and sheltering microhabitats (Bachman 1984), and many nocturnal fishes forage only at night and spend daylight hours in dense cover (Helfman 1986). Schools of pelagic fishes break up at dusk, and individuals remain scattered in loose aggregations throughout the night until light levels allow schooling to resume (Hobson 1972; Emery 1973; Shaw 1978; Helfman 1981, 1984). Because the diel movement patterns of many species are poorly understood, it is difficult to determine the actual feeding locations of fishes that make vertical or horizontal migrations (O'Brien and Vinyard 1974; Ogden and Ehrlich 1977; Wurtsbaugh and Li 1985), and prey preferences or electivities (e.g., Strauss 1982) must be calculated cautiously. Seasonal movements may be associated with spawning (Cadwallader 1976) or with shifts of an important resource such as temperature (Neill et al. 1972; Neill and Magnuson 1974). Ontogenetic movements may be associated with size-related shifts in microhabitat use (Everest and Chapman 1972; Baltz and Moyle 1984) or with life history changes (e.g., Pacific salmon).

Several techniques often are used in combination to study fish movements. These include active and passive capture techniques (Hayes 1983; Hubert 1983), tagging and marking (Wydoski and Emery 1983), biotelemetry (Winter 1983; but see Mellas and Haynes 1985), hydroacoustics (Thorne 1983), and underwater observation (Helfman 1983, 1986). Captured fishes may be tagged or marked and then released for later recapture; however, recapture data may be biased if the recapture effort is limited to the initial capture locations. Vertical migrations in lakes and oceans can be studied with hydroacoustic (Thorne 1983; Vondracek et al. 1989) or gillnetting techniques (Wurtsbaugh and Li 1985). Biotelemetry can be used to follow the movements of individuals (Hubert and Lackey 1980; Helfman 1983) and also to gather correlated depth, velocity, and temperature data if duplex or multiplex transmitters are used (Spigarelli et al. 1983). Direct observations are useful for determining diel movements (Werner et al. 1977) and home ranges when individuals can be recognized by tags or unique body markings (Helfman 1983; Bachman 1984).

18.5 MICROHABITAT DESCRIPTIONS

18.5.1 Introduction

The microhabitat of a fish is the place where that fish is located at any point in time. Microhabitat use refers to the fine-scale use of space at sites occupied by individuals (Hurlbert 1981; Baltz et al. 1987). Sites can be characterized in terms of physicochemical variables to describe the microhabitat requirements of life stages and populations. Technically, "use" means the frequency of measured values of those variables at occupied sites. The measure of a life stage's or population's response to a variable is the relative frequency of use over the variable's range (e.g., the proportion or percentage of individuals found in each of several substrate categories, depth intervals, or velocity intervals). Odum (1959) was among the first to define microhabitat, by which he meant small differences in the location of individuals in the same habitat. Levins (1968) used the term "microhabitat niche" when comparing distributions of species in a community; later in the same book, he dropped "niche" and referred only to microhabitats. Microhabitat descriptions of the physical sites occupied by individuals help define the niche as the set of resources used (i.e., energy, materials, and sites) by populations or higher levels of organization (Hurlbert 1981).

Individuals of similar size and age are likely to choose similar microhabitats, so careful observations of several individuals can be used to characterize resource use by the population. The approach is to compile frequency-of-use distributions for each variable measured at microhabitats occupied by individuals. The mean or mode of a distribution is an estimate of the population's central tendency with respect to the variable. The range of the distribution, or other measure of dispersion, is an estimate of the population's tolerance for variation with respect to the variable. Microhabitat use may vary within species because of differences in the availability of resources or controlling environmental characteristics such as salinity, temperature, food supply, or the presence of other species. Until several populations have been studied, one should be cautious about extrapolating from one population to the entire species. For example, Baltz and Moyle (1984) and Moyle and Baltz (1985) found that Sacramento suckers and rainbow trout had different microhabitat use patterns in two substantially different California streams. Fausch (1984) showed that salmonids select microhabitats that maximize their ability to use local food supplies efficiently. Other studies have shown that temperature can strongly influence microhabitat use (Baltz et al. 1982; Smith and Li 1983). As always, ecological generalizations should be approached with circumspection.

18.5.2 Microhabitat Observation Techniques

Bovee and Cochnauer (1977) and Larimore and Garrels (1985) discussed the applications, advantages, and disadvantages of several techniques that can be used to collect microhabitat data. Methods include trapping (Mendelson 1975), seining (Baker and Ross 1981; Sheppard and Johnson 1985), spot electrofishing (Baltz et al. 1982), telemetry (Spigarelli et al. 1983), and direct observation (Ebeling and Laur 1982; Smith and Li 1983; Bachman 1984; Baltz and Moyle 1984; Sheppard and Johnson 1985). When conditions permit, direct observation of fish coupled with in situ measurement of variables generally yield the most accurate data.

Unbiased microhabitat data can be obtained only if the fish are undisturbed, though this can be difficult to determine. Fish are least likely to be disturbed by observers if they are watched from blinds on shore, a method Bachman (1984) used. Blinds limit the mobility of the observer, however, and water depth, obstructions, and ambient lighting may restrict the visibility of fish from above the water. Consequently, snorkeling and scuba techniques have gained in popularity for microhabitat work with freshwater (Werner et al. 1977; Baltz and Moyle 1984) and marine fishes (Hixon 1980; Ebeling and Laur 1982).

In streams, divers minimize disturbances to fish by moving upcurrent whenever possible. In this way, they approach fish from the rear (fish typically face into the current), where observers are least detectable and where disturbed sediments wash away from the fish. Once a fish is located and identified, its exact position is noted and its length and distance above the substrate (focal point elevation) are estimated with reference to some visual standard. The observer then moves to the fish's position and usually measures (1) the visual standards to which fish length and elevation had been compared, (2) water velocity where the fish's snout had been (i.e., focal point velocity), (3) water velocity at one or more additional points in the water column, (4) surface water velocity, (5) total depth of the water column, and (6) substrate composition below fish in an eighth- or quarter-meter-square quadrate. Later, mean water column velocity and relative depth of the fish—(total water depth − focal point elevation)/(total water depth)—are calculated. Similar methods can be used in lakes and marine environments (Werner et al. 1977; Ebeling and Laur 1982; Helfman 1983), though more patience may be needed to approach fish without disturbing them in areas without current.

In streams, depths and water velocities may be measured most efficiently with a top-setting wading rod, calibrated in length units, to which an electronic flowmeter is attached. Total water column depth and focal point elevation may be read directly from the wading rod. When water depth exceeds 0.75 m or the flow is obstructed by objects such as boulders or logs, the mean water column velocity should be calculated from measurements made at proportional depths of 0.2, 0.6, and 0.8 of the total depth and appropriately weighted. Otherwise, the velocity at the proportional depth of 0.6 usually is used as the standard single estimate of mean water column velocity (Bovee and Milhous 1978). If the flowmeter used does not average over time, several velocity readings taken at fixed time intervals and averaged will yield a better velocity estimate than a single reading, especially in turbulent flow conditions.

In streams and lakes, substrate composition can be estimated against the Wentworth particle-size scale (Bovee and Cochnauer 1977). This scale of 27 categories is usually reduced to 8–10 categories to fit the species of interest. The size range of spawning substrate should be defined by one or more categories.

Fish length can be estimated by comparisons with substrate elements; these elements, in turn, can be measured with the top-setting wading rod or a reference bar carried by the observer. A 300-mm length of reinforcing bar marked in 100-mm increments makes a handy reference and helps divers avoid error in length estimates caused by optical distortion. Knowing the length of one's hand, fingers, or feet can be useful.

Fishes may use banks, boulders, logs, roots, or aquatic vegetation as cover to avoid predators and high water velocities. Some stream fishes may use surface turbulence as cover from piscivorous birds. The cover used by fishes varies with species and life stage (Power and Matthews 1983). For example, young-of-year fishes may use shallow water as a refuge from fish predators, but as they grow and become less vulnerable to aquatic predators, they become vulnerable to piscivo-

Table 18.1   Cover codes and descriptions useful for small streams.

Code	Cover description
1	No cover
2	Objects less than 150 mm in diameter
3	Objects between 150 and 300 mm in diameter
4	Objects larger than 300 mm in diameter
5	Overhanging vegetation
6	Root wads or undercut banks
7	Surface turbulence

rous birds, so they shift their microhabitat to deeper water (Baltz and Moyle 1984). Cover use also may change daily or seasonally. A simple cover-coding scheme for use in streams might include 2–16 codes (Table 18.1); Bovee (1982) discussed several others.

18.5.3   Statistical Analyses

When an aquatic system has several habitats, population surveys and studies of microhabitat use and preference benefit from a stratified sampling design (Platts et al. 1983). This is particularly true if the entire aquatic system cannot be surveyed. When used in conjunction with habitat mapping, which describes the proportional contribution of each habitat or stratum (Section 18.5.5), stratification results in a more accurate description of abundance, preference, and microhabitat use. Because strata usually are not sampled in proportion to their actual importance, weighting factors based on the extent of each stratum sampled can be used to adjust for disproportionate sampling effort.

Microhabitat measurements should be independent observations of one or more fish. Repeated observations should not be made of the same individual because this would violate the assumption of independence needed for most statistical analyses. Transect techniques (Rinne 1985) that yield multiple measurements for individual fishes or groups of fishes may inflate sample size and lead to overestimates of the similarity in microhabitat use between species. Possible interactions between variables also should be considered (Baltz et al. 1987); for example, velocity preferences of stream fishes may depend upon temperature (e.g., Smith and Li 1983).

The microhabitats used by different size-classes or life stages can be compared, one variable at a time, by regression analysis (e.g., SAS general linear models: SAS 1985) combined with a posteriori testing. However, if sample sizes differ substantially among treatment groups, analysis-of-variance packages not suited for unbalanced designs should be avoided (Freund 1980). Some statistical packages that produce analyses that depend on model order may also yield misleading results (SAS 1985).

18.5.4   Characterization of Resource Availability

Resource availability data should be gathered with a randomization protocol in conjunction with microhabitat use surveys (Bovee 1982). All variables independent of fishes may be measured at randomly chosen points; among these variables are total depth, surface and mean water column velocities, substrate, cover, and temperature. Additional fish-specific measurements may also be made if assumptions about fish position can be easily made (e.g., focal point velocities for benthic species). The randomly collected data characterizing the resources available to a fish can then be compared to the microhabitat resources actually used to determine which values of resource variables are selected, avoided, or used in proportion to their abundances.

Resource availability data should be collected immediately after the microhabitat use survey, before the distributions of variables change. Several criteria should be used to determine the number and location of random sampling points. First, the number of random observations should equal or exceed the number of microhabitat use observations to adequately characterize the area or length of habitat surveyed. Second, in large streams, each survey reach should be stratified into sections (of, say, 20 m in length) and a random transect should be established within each section; this ensures that randomly chosen transects are not clustered (all at the head of a pool, for example). A fixed number of points, approximately 10, are surveyed at equal intervals along each transect, but the zero end of the measuring tape should be alternated between the right and left banks to sample both edges of the stream. Alternatively, for small streams, random three-digit numbers may be selected (if the length surveyed is less than 99 m), the first two representing intervals along the length of the stream surveyed and the third a proportion of the stream width at each interval. Thus, the random number 186 could indicate a sampling point 18 m from the start point of the survey and six-tenths of the width measured from the zero side of the stream. Finally, a unique set of random numbers should be selected for each survey, whether in small or large streams, to avoid repeated use of a potentially biased selection.

18.5.5 Habitat Mapping

Detailed habitat-mapping studies should be conducted in conjunction with microhabitat studies and population surveys, especially in large streams and lakes. This permits the microhabitat use and resource availability data set to be weighted to reflect the proportional composition of strata (e.g., pools versus riffles or littoral versus limnetic zones) of the system. In small streams, habitat mapping may not be necessary if strata are not clearly defined and the microhabitat use and resource availability data are collected over a large proportion of the stream. However, if the stream reaches differ in character (e.g., high versus moderate gradient), the stream strata should be mapped and the microhabitat data weighted accordingly.

Habitat mapping is accomplished by measuring the linear or areal extent of each stratum type. Measurements can be made directly in the field or sometimes indirectly from aerial photographs, topographic maps, and charts. Helfman (1983) outlined techniques suitable for mapping lentic and marine environments. For stream work, the lengths of riffles, runs, and pools in the study area usually describe the distribution of stratum types adequately. These strata are somewhat arbitrary, but can be defined (e.g., Platts et al. 1983). The number of relevant types depends on the aquatic system and the species of interest. A more detailed breakdown of stream strata might include pools, runs, riffles, glides, cascades, stair-step riffles, and high-gradient cascades; these could even be subdivided further by substrate type or some other relevant character.

18.5.6 Weighting Factors

When sampling to obtain microhabitat use and resource availability data is stratified by (for example) runs, riffles, and pools, weighting factors are needed to

Table 18.2 Weighting factors based on the total length of stratum types in a stream reach, and the length of strata surveyed during microhabitat data collection. Weighting factors are normalized by dividing all factors by the smallest factor.

Habitat stratum	Total length (m)	Length sampled (m)	Weighting factor	Normalized weighting factor
Pool	13,737.5	1,149.1	11.96	1.11
Run	12,908.2	591.0	23.53	2.18
Riffle	13,332.1	1,235.4	10.79	1.00

compensate for nonproportional sampling effort. Weighting factors (Table 18.2) for microhabitat descriptions are calculated from habitat-mapping and microhabitat-sampling data. They can also be used to improve estimates of population abundance. For streams, the length of each stratum type is summed over the entire reach (calculated from the stratum map) and over the portion of the reach actually sampled during the resource availability measurements. (For larger water bodies, areas probably would be summed instead of lengths.) Random observations of resource availability and observations of fish microhabitat use are treated similarly. The weighted frequency (f_j) in interval j of a frequency distribution is

$$f_j = \Sigma(L_i/l_i)n_{ij};$$

i = stratum type (e.g., 1 = run; 2 = riffle; 3 = pool); j = some interval in the distribution of a variable such as mean water column velocity (e.g., 0–5 cm/s); n_{ij} = number of observations in stratum type i at the jth interval; L_i = total length of stratum type i; and l_i = length of stratum type i sampled.

18.5.7 Microhabitat Electivities and Suitability Curves

Electivity indices are measures of an animal's preference, avoidance, or indifference with respect to resources. Electivities for microhabitat variables can be calculated from data on proportional use and availability with Jacobs's (1974) formula or similar formulae (e.g., Strauss 1982). For each interval of a variable's distribution, the electivity (D) is

$$D = \frac{r - p}{(r + p) - 2rp};$$

r is the proportion of the resource used by a species or size-class, and p is the proportion available in the environment. This index varies continuously between -1 (strong avoidance) and $+1$ (strong selection). This range may be arbitrarily subdivided to describe the magnitude of selection (e.g., Moyle and Baltz 1985):

-1.00 to -0.50 strong avoidance;
-0.49 to -0.26 moderate avoidance;
-0.25 to $+0.25$ neutral selection;
$+0.26$ to $+0.49$ moderate selection;
$+0.50$ to $+1.00$ strong selection.

The neutral range (-0.25 to $+0.25$) represents situations in which a species or life stage uses resources approximately in proportion to their availability. Electivities in the moderate or strong ranges indicate important behavioral selection for or avoidance of intervals on a resource axis.

Microhabitat suitability curves describe microhabitat selection by a species. They are important elements of the "instream flow incremental methodology" (IFIM) developed to model the effects of changed flow regimes on fish habitat in streams (Bovee 1982). Microhabitat suitability curves may be calculated from proportional frequency-of-use distributions by dividing the proportional use for an interval on a resource axis by the proportional availability for that interval. These proportions are independent estimates of the probability (P) that a particular value for an environmental variable will be encountered. Thus, Bovee (1982) defined suitability (S) as

$$S = \frac{P(E|F)}{P(E)} = \frac{\text{proportional use}}{\text{proportional availability}};$$

$P(E|F)$ is the probability (from frequency-of-use data for a species or life stage) of finding a particular value for a variable (E) given the presence of fish (F), and $P(E)$ is the probability (from random availability data) of finding that value whether fish are present or not.

For example, consider the suitability for age-0 brown trout of mean water column velocities in the interval 30–40 cm/s. From frequency-of-use data, it is known that 5% of the localities at which age-0 brown trout were found had mean velocities in this interval; thus, $P(E|F) = 0.05$. From random availability data, it is known that mean velocities in this interval occurred at 3% of all localities sampled; thus $P(E) = 0.03$. The suitability of these mean velocities for age-0 brown trout then is $S = 0.05/0.03 = 1.67$. After this calculation is made for all intervals across the total distribution of mean velocity, it is learned that the maximum value of S for any interval is 2.00. This interval is considered optimum and assigned a value of 1.00 (on a scale of 0.00 to 1.00). The values of S for all other intervals are standardized against the optimum; thus, the standardized suitability of the 30–40-cm/s velocity interval is $1.67/2.00 = 0.84$. A plot of S or standardized S against consecutive intervals of mean water column velocity yields the suitability curve.

Bovee (1982) also described joint suitability functions, which combine several variables to account for interactions among those variables. It should be remembered, however, that neither electivity indices nor suitability curves actually indicate a species' preferences. Innate preferences can be determined only under experimental conditions that make all relevant states of a resource equally available (e.g., Hill et al. 1981). Nevertheless, these tools, based as they are on field data, offer important insights into species' preferences in nature.

18.6 PHYSICOCHEMICAL DETERMINANTS OF NICHE

Factors other than depth, velocity, substrate, and cover may have important influences on the distribution and abundance of species, either because they exceed physiological tolerances (Norris 1963) or control movements related to reproduction (de Vlaming 1972). Water quality variables such as temperature, dissolved oxygen, pH, dissolved solids, and turbidity are important individually but often interact to determine habitat suitability (Hynes 1970). The zonation of fish assemblages in stream systems (Huet 1959; Moyle and Nichols 1973, 1974) and the restricted ranges of some marine species (Gunter 1961; Briggs 1974) are examples of distributions that can be determined by physiological limits. Within geographic ranges determined by their physiological limits, individuals typically select or avoid quantities along each niche dimension.

Temperature is a particularly important ecological resource for most fishes (Magnuson et al. 1979). Between a species' temperature limits, which may be measured as the critical thermal minimum and the critical thermal maximum (Matthews and Maness 1979), individuals exhibit temperature preferences that correlate well with conditions that allow optimal growth (Jobling 1981). Other physical factors may have even stronger influences on distribution. For example, although temperature strongly influences some marine fishes, which track narrow thermal preferences in their bathythermal distributions (Terry and Stephens 1976), other species are more eurythermal and subordinate temperature preferences to preferences for other microhabitat variables (Shrode et al. 1982). In temperate lakes and reservoirs, thermal stratification may also result in a chemocline (a rapid vertical change in chemical concentration), particularly of dissolved oxygen, which may be more important than temperature in determining the distribution of fishes (Matthews et al. 1985). The factors that determine species distributions can be unraveled by field and laboratory experiments to define physiological limits, test for preferences, and evaluate the relative importance of variables in double-gradient experiments (Matthews and Hill 1979a, 1979b; Hill et al. 1981; Shrode et al. 1982; Gordon et al. 1985).

18.7 OVERVIEW

Interactions between fishes and their environments make the study of individual species interesting from both ecological and evolutionary perspectives. Comparisons of populations that live in different environments and often have different gene pools offer insight into the selective pressures that shape the niches of populations, the life history strategies of species, and the structures of communities. Because the interactions between a population and its environment are complex, autecological studies should explore interpopulational variation to distinguish actual from virtual niches (Colwell and Futuyma 1971) and to place life history studies in an evolutionary context.

18.8 REFERENCES

Avise, J. C., G. S. Helfman, N. C. Saunders, and L. S. Hales. 1986. Mitochondrial DNA differentiation in North American eels: population genetic consequences of an unusual life history pattern. Proceedings of the National Academy of Sciences of the USA 83:4350–4353.

Bachman, R. A. 1984. Foraging behavior of free-ranging wild and hatchery brown trout in a stream. Transactions of the American Fisheries Society 113:1–32.

Bagenal, T. B., and F. W. Tesch. 1978. Age and growth. Pages 101–136 in T. Bagenal, editor. Methods for assessment of fish production in fresh waters. Blackwell Scientific Publications, Oxford, England.

Baker, J. A., and S. T. Ross. 1981. Spatial and temporal resource utilization by southeastern cyprinids. Copeia 1981:178–189.

Ball, I. R. 1975. Nature and formulation of biogeographical hypotheses. Systematic Zoology 24:407–430.

Baltz, D. M. 1984. Life history variation among female surfperches (Perciformes: Embiotocidae). Environmental Biology of Fishes 10:159–171.

Baltz, D. M., and P. B. Moyle. 1981. Morphometric analysis of tule perch (*Hysterocarpus traski*) populations in three isolated drainages. Copeia 1981:305–311.

Baltz, D. M., and P. B. Moyle. 1982. Life history characteristics of tule perch (*Hysterocarpus traski*) populations in contrasting environments. Environmental Biology of Fishes 7:229–242.

Baltz, D. M., and P. B. Moyle. 1984. Segregation by species and size class of rainbow trout (*Salmo gairdneri*) and the Sacramento sucker (*Catostomus occidentalis*) in three California streams. Environmental Biology of Fishes 10:101–110.

Baltz, D. M., P. B. Moyle, and N. J. Knight. 1982. Competitive interactions between benthic stream fishes, riffle sculpin, *Cottus gulosus*, and speckled dace, *Rhinichthys osculus*. Canadian Journal of Fisheries and Aquatic Sciences 39:1502–1511.

Baltz, D. M., B. Vondracek, L. R. Brown, and P. B. Moyle. 1987. Influence of temperature on microhabitat choice of fishes in a California stream. Transactions of the American Fisheries Society 116:12–20.

Beamish, R. J., and G. A. McFarlane. 1983. The forgotten requirement for age validation in fisheries biology. Transactions of the American Fisheries Society 112:735–743.

Binns, N. A., and F. M. Eiserman. 1979. Quantification of fluvial trout habitat in Wyoming. Transactions of the American Fisheries Society 108:215–228.

Bovee, K. D. 1982. A guide to stream habitat analysis using the instream flow incremental methodology. U.S. Fish and Wildlife Service Biological Services Program FWS/OBS-82/26.

Bovee, K. D., and T. Cochnauer. 1977. Development and evaluation of weighted criteria, probability-of-use curves for instream flow assessments: fisheries. U.S. Fish and Wildlife Service Biological Services Program FWS/OBS-77/63.

Bovee, K. D., and R. T. Milhous. 1978. Hydraulic simulation in instream flow studies: theory and techniques. U.S. Fish and Wildlife Service Biological Services Program FWS/OBS-78/33.

Bowen, S. H. 1983. Quantitative description of the diet. Pages 325–348 *in* L. A. Nielsen and D. L. Johnson, editors. Fisheries techniques. American Fisheries Society, Bethesda, Maryland.

Briggs, J. C. 1974. Marine zoogeography. McGraw-Hill, New York.

Cadwallader, P. L. 1976. Home range and movements of the common river galaxias, *Galaxias vulgaris* Stokell (Pisces: Salmoniformes), in the Glentui River, New Zealand. Australian Journal of Marine and Freshwater Research 27:23–33.

Cailliet, G. M., and C. A. Siemenstad, editors. 1982. Gutshop '81: fish food habit studies. Proceedings of the third Pacific workshop. Washington Sea Grant Publication, University of Washington, Seattle.

Caughley, G. 1977. Analysis of vertebrate populations. Wiley, New York.

Charnov, E. L., and W. M. Schaffer. 1973. The population consequences of natural selection: Cole's result revisited. American Naturalist 107:791–793.

Chernoff, B. 1982. Character variation among populations and the analysis of biogeography. American Zoologist 22:425–439.

Cole, L. C. 1954. The population consequence of life-history phenomena. Quarterly Review of Biology 29:103–137.

Colwell, R. K., and D. J. Futuyma. 1971. On the measurement of niche breadth and overlap. Ecology 52:567–576.

Constantz, G. D. 1974. Reproductive effort in *Poeciliopsis occidentalis* (Poeciliidae). Southwestern Naturalist 19:47–52.

Constantz, G. D. 1979. Life history patterns of a livebearing fish in contrasting environments. Oecologia (Berlin) 40:189–201.

Darlington, P. J. 1957. Zoogeography: the geographical distribution of animals. Wiley, New York.

de Vlaming, V. 1972. The effects of temperature and photoperiod on reproductive cycling in the estuarine gobiid fish, *Gillichthys mirabilis*. U.S. National Marine Fisheries Service Fishery Bulletin 70:1137–1152.

de Vlaming, V., G. Grossman, and F. Chapman. 1982. On the use of the gonosomatic index. Comparative Biochemistry and Physiology A, Comparative Physiology 73:31–39.

Dominey, W. J. 1980. Female mimicry in male bluegill sunfish—a genetic polymorphism? Nature (London) 284:546–548.

Ebeling, A. W., R. J. Larson, W. S. Alevizon, and R. N. Bray. 1980. Annual variability of reef-fish assemblages in kelp forests off Santa Barbara, California. U.S. National Marine Fisheries Service Fishery Bulletin 78:361–377.

Ebeling, A. W., and D. R. Laur. 1982. Does resource partitioning have a descriptive null hypothesis? Pages 158–177 *in* G. M. Cailliet and C. A. Simenstad, editors. Gutshop '81: fish food habit studies. Proceedings of the third Pacific workshop. Washington Sea Grant Publication, University of Washington, Seattle.

Emery, A. R. 1973. Preliminary comparisons of day and night habitats of freshwater fish in Ontario Lakes. Journal of the Fisheries Research Board of Canada 30:760–764.

Everest, F. H., and D. W. Chapman. 1972. Habitat selection and spatial interaction by juvenile chinook salmon and steelhead trout in two Idaho streams. Journal of the Fisheries Research Board of Canada 29:91–100.

Fausch, K. D. 1984. Profitable stream positions for salmonids relating specific growth rate to net energy gain. Canadian Journal of Zoology 62:441–451.

Fausch, K. D., and R. J. White. 1981. Competition between brook trout (*Salvelinus fontinalis*) and brown trout (*Salmo trutta*) for positions in a Michigan stream. Canadian Journal of Fisheries and Aquatic Sciences. 38:1220–1227.

Fournier, D. A., T. D. Beacham, B. E. Riddell, and C. A. Busack. 1984. Estimating stock composition in mixed stock fisheries using morphometric, meristic, and electrophoretic characteristics. Canadian Journal of Fisheries and Aquatic Sciences 41:400–408.

Freund, R. J. 1980. The case of the missing cell. American Statistician 34:94–98.

Ghiselin, M. T. 1974. The economy of nature and the evolution of sex. University of California Press, Berkeley.

Gibson, A. R., A. J. Baker, and A. Moeed. 1984. Morphometric variation in introduced populations of the common myna (*Acridotheres tristis*): an application of the jackknife to principal component analysis. Systematic Zoology 33:408–421.

Goldstein, R. M. 1978. Quantitative comparison of seining and underwater observation for stream fishery surveys. Progressive Fish-Culturist 40:108–111.

Gordon, M. S., D. J. Gabaldon, and A. Y.-W. Yip. 1985. Exploratory observations on microhabitat selection within the intertidal zone by the Chinese mudskipper fish *Periophthalmus cantonensis*. Marine Biology 85:209–215.

Gould, S. J., and R. C. Lewontin. 1979. The spandrels of San Marco and the Panglossia paradigm: a critique of the adaptionist programme. Proceedings of the Royal Society of London B, Biological Sciences 205:581–598.

Grant, W. S., G. B. Milner, P. Krasnowski, and F. M. Utter. 1980. Use of biochemical genetic variants for identification of sockeye salmon (*Oncorhynchus nerka*) stocks in Cook Inlet, Alaska. Canadian Journal of Fisheries and Aquatic Sciences 37:1236–1247.

Griffith, J. S. 1981. Estimation of the age-frequency distribution of stream-dwelling trout by underwater observation. Progressive Fish-Culturist 43:51–53.

Griffith, J. S. 1983. Snorkel and scuba. U.S. Forest Service General Technical Report INT-138:34–36.

Gross, M. R., and A. M. MacMillan. 1981. Predation and the evolution of colonial nesting in bluegill sunfish (*Lepomis macrochirus*). Behavioral Ecology and Sociobiology 8:163–174.

Grossman, G. D. 1979. Food, fights, and burrows: the adaptive significance of intraspecific aggression in the bay goby (Pisces: Gobiidae). Oecologia (Berlin) 45:261–266.

Grossman, G. D. 1980. Ecological aspects of ontogenetic shifts in prey size utilization in the bay goby (Pisces: Gobiidae). Oecologia (Berlin) 47:233–238.

Gunter, G. 1961. Some relations of estuarine organisms to salinity. Limnology and Oceanography 6:182–190.

Gyllensten, U. 1985. The genetic structure of fish: differences in the intraspecific distribution of biochemical genetic variation between marine, anadromous, and freshwater species. Journal of Fish Biology 26:691–700.

Harris, M. J., and G. D. Grossman. 1985. Growth, mortality, and age composition of a lightly exploited tilefish substock off Georgia. Transactions of the American Fisheries Society 114:837–846.

Hasler, A. D., and A. T. Scholz. 1978. Olfactory imprinting in coho salmon (*Oncorhynchus kisutch*). Pages 356–369 *in* K. Schmid-Koenig and W. T. Keeton, editors. Animal migration, navigation, and homing. Springer-Verlag, Berlin.

Hayes, M. L. 1983. Active fish capture methods. Pages 123–146 *in* L. A. Nielsen and D. L. Johnson, editors. Fisheries techniques. American Fisheries Society, Bethesda, Maryland.

Helfman, G. S. 1981. Twilight activities and temporal structure in a freshwater fish community. Canadian Journal of Fisheries and Aquatic Sciences 38:1405–1420.

Helfman, G. S. 1983. Underwater methods. Pages 349–370 *in* L. A. Nielsen and D. L. Johnson, editors. Fisheries techniques. American Fisheries Society, Bethesda, Maryland.

Helfman, G. S. 1984. School fidelity in fishes: the yellow perch pattern. Animal Behaviour 32:663–672.

Helfman, G. S. 1986. Diel distribution and activity of American eels (*Anguilla rostrata*) in a cave-spring. Canadian Journal of Fisheries and Aquatic Sciences 43:1595–1605.

Helle, J. H. 1987. Success of stock identification techniques used in the U.S./Canada salmon interception program in Alaska. NOAA (National Oceanic and Atmospheric Administration) Technical Memorandum NMFS (National Marine Fisheries Service) SEFC (Southeast Fisheries Center) 199:191–193, Miami.

Hill, L. G., G. D. Schnell, and W. J. Matthews. 1981. Locomotor responses of striped bass, *Morone saxatilis*, to environmental variables. American Midland Naturalist 105:139–148.

Hixon, M. A. 1980. Competitive interactions between California reef fishes of the genus *Embiotoca*. Ecology 61:918–931.

Hobson, E. S. 1972. Activities of Hawaiian reef fishes during evening and morning transitions between daylight and darkness. U.S. National Marine Fisheries Service Fishery Bulletin 70:715–740.

Hocutt, C. E., and E. O. Wiley. 1986. The zoogeography of North American freshwater fishes. Wiley, New York.

Hubert, W. A. 1983. Passive capture techniques. Pages 95–122 *in* L. A. Nielsen and D. L. Johnson, editors. Fisheries techniques. American Fisheries Society, Bethesda, Maryland.

Hubert, W. A., and R. T. Lackey. 1980. Habitat of adult smallmouth bass in a Tennessee River reservoir. Transactions of the American Fisheries Society 109:364–370.

Huet, M. 1959. Profiles and biology of western European streams as related to fish management. Transactions of the American Fisheries Society 88:155–163.

Hurlbert, S. H. 1981. A gentle depilation of the niche: Dicean resource sets in resource hyperspace. Evolutionary Theory 5:177–184.

Hutchinson, G. E. 1958. Concluding remarks. Cold Spring Harbor Symposia on Quantitative Biology 22:415–427.

Hynes, H. B. N. 1970. The ecology of running water. University of Toronto Press, Toronto.

Jacobs, J. 1974. Quantitative measurement of food selection: a modification of the forage ration and Ivlev's index. Oecologia (Berlin) 14:413–417.

Jerald, A., Jr. 1983. Age determination. Pages 301–324 *in* L. A. Nielsen and D. L. Johnson, editors. Fisheries techniques. American Fisheries Society, Bethesda, Maryland.

Jenkins, T. M. 1969. Social structure, position choice, and distribution of two trout species (*Salmo trutta* and *Salmo gairdneri*) resident in mountain streams. Animal Behavior Monographs 2:57–123.

Jobling, M. 1981. Temperature tolerance and the final preferendum—rapid methods for the assessment of optimum growth temperatures. Journal of Fish Biology 19:439–455.

Keast, A., and J. Harker. 1977. Strip counts as a means of determining densities and habitat utilization patterns in lake fishes. Environmental Biology of Fishes 1:181–188.

Kumpf, H. E., C. Grimes, A. Johnson, E. Nakamura, and R. Vaught, editors. 1987. Proceedings of the stock identification workshop—recent innovations and state of the art. NOAA (National Oceanic and Atmospheric Administration) Technical Memorandum NMFS (National Marine Fisheries Service) SEFC (Southeast Fisheries Center) 199, Miami.

Larimore, R. W., and D. D. Garrels. 1985. Assessing habitats used by warmwater stream fishes. Fisheries (Bethesda) 10(2):10–16.

Larson, R. J. 1980. Competition, habitat selection, and the bathymethric segregation of two rockfish (*Sebastes*) species. Ecological Monographs 50:221–239.

Larson, R. J., and E. E. DeMartini. 1984. Abundance and vertical distribution of fishes in a cobble-bottom kelp forest off San Onofre, California. U.S. National Marine Fisheries Service Fishery Bulletin 82:37–53.

Layher, W. G., and O. E. Maughan. 1985. Relations between habitat variables and channel catfish populations in prairie streams. Transactions of the American Fisheries Society 114:771–781.

Levins, R. 1968. Evolution in changing environments: some theoretical explorations. Princeton University Press, Princeton, New Jersey.

Lobel, P. S. 1978. Diel, lunar, and seasonal periodicity in the reproductive behavior of the pomacanthid fish, *Centropyge potteri*, and some other reef fishes in Hawaii. Pacific Science 32:193–207.

Magnuson, J. J., L. B. Crowder, and P. A. Medvick. 1979. Temperature as an ecological resource. American Zoologist 19:331–343.

Matthews, W. J., and L. G. Hill. 1977. Tolerance of the red shiner, *Notropis lutrensis* (Cyprinidae), to environmental parameters. Southwestern Naturalist 22:89–98.

Matthews, W. J., and L. G. Hill. 1979a. Age-specific differences in the distribution of red shiners, *Notropis lutrensis*, over physicochemical ranges. American Midland Naturalist 101:366–372.

Matthews, W. J., and L. G. Hill. 1979b. Influence of physico-chemical factors on habitat selection by red shiners, *Notropis lutrensis* (Pisces: Cyprinidae). Copeia 1979:70–81.

Matthews, W. J., L. G. Hill, and S. M. Schellhaass. 1985. Depth distribution of striped bass and other fish in Lake Texoma (Oklahoma–Texas) during summer stratification. Transactions of the American Fisheries Society 114:84–91.

Matthews, W. J., and J. D. Maness. 1979. Critical thermal maxima, oxygen tolerance and success of cyprinid fishes in a southwestern river. American Midland Naturalist 102:374–377.

McPhail, J. D. 1977. Inherited interpopulation differences in size at first reproduction in threespine stickleback, *Gasterosteus aculeatus* L. Heredity 38:53–60.

Mellas, E. J., and J. M. Haynes. 1985. Swimming performance and behavior of rainbow trout (*Salmo gairdneri*) and white perch (*Morone americana*): effects of attaching telemetry transmitters. Canadian Journal of Fisheries and Aquatic Sciences 42:488–493.

Mendelson, J. 1975. Feeding relationships among species of *Notropis* (Pisces: Cyprinidae) in a Wisconsin stream. Ecological Monographs 45:199–230.

Moyle, P. B., and D. M. Baltz. 1985. Microhabitat use by an assemblage of California stream fishes: developing criteria for instream flow determinations. Transactions of the American Fisheries Society 114:695–704.

Moyle, P. B., and R. D. Nichols. 1973. Ecology of some native and introduced fishes of the Sierra Nevada foothills in central California. Copeia 1973:478–490.

Moyle, P. B., and R. D. Nichols. 1974. Decline of the native fish fauna of the Sierra Nevada foothills, central California. American Midland Naturalist 92:72–83.

Murphy, G. I. 1968. Pattern in life history and the environment. American Naturalist 102:391–403.

Neff, N. A., and G. R. Smith. 1979. Multivariate analysis of hybrid fishes. Systematic Zoology 28:176–196.

Neill, W. H., and J. J. Magnuson. 1974. Distributional ecology and behavioral thermoregulation of fishes in relation to heated effluent from a power plant at Lake Monona, Wisconsin. Transactions of the American Fisheries Society 103:663–710.

Neill, W. H., J. J. Magnuson, and G. G. Chipman. 1972. Behavioral thermoregulation by fishes: a new experimental approach. Science (Washington, D.C.) 176:1443–1455.

Nielsen, L. A., and D. L. Johnson, editors. 1983. Fisheries techniques. American Fisheries Society, Bethesda, Maryland.

Nikolsky, G. V. 1963. The ecology of fishes. Academic Press, New York.

Norris, K. 1963. The function of temperature in the ecology of the percoid fish *Girella nigricans* (Ayres). Ecological Monographs 33:23–62.

Northcote, T. G., and D. W. Wilkie. 1963. Underwater census of stream fish populations. Transactions of the American Fisheries Society 92:146–151.

O'Brien, W. J., and G. L. Vinyard. 1974. Comments on the use of Ivlev's electivity index with planktivorous fish. Journal of the Fisheries Research Board of Canada 31:1427–1429.

Odum, E. P. 1959. Fundamentals of ecology, 2nd edition. Saunders, Philadelphia.

Ogden, J. C., and P. R. Ehrlich. 1977. The behavior of heterotypic resting schools of juvenile grunts (Pomadasyidae). Marine Biology 42:273–280.

Overstreet, R. M. 1983. Aspects of the biology of the spotted seatrout, *Cynoscion nebulosus*, in Mississippi. Gulf Research Reports 1(Supplement):1–43.

Parrish, R. H., D. L. Mallicoate, and R. A. Klingbeil. 1986. Age dependent fecundity, number of spawnings per year, sex ratio, and maturation stages in northern anchovy, *Engraulis mordax*. U.S. National Fisheries Service Fishery Bulletin 84:503–517.

Pearcy, W. G., and S. S. Myers. 1974. Larval fishes of Yaquina Bay, Oregon: a nursery ground for marine fishes. U.S. National Marine Fisheries Service Fishery Bulletin 72:201–213.

Platts, W. S., W. F. Megahan, and G. W. Minshall. 1983. Methods for evaluating stream, riparian, and biotic conditions. U.S. Forest Service General Technical Report INT-138.

Power, M., and W. J. Matthews. 1983. Algae grazing minnows (*Campostoma anomalum*), piscivorous bass (*Micropterus* spp.) and the distribution of attached algae in a small prairie-margin stream. Oecologia (Berlin) 60:328–332.

Rimmer, D. M., V. Pain, and R. L. Saunders. 1983. Autumnal shift of juvenile Atlantic salmon (*Salmo salar*) in a small river. Canadian Journal of Fisheries and Aquatic Sciences 40:671–680.

Rinne, J. N. 1985. Physical habitat evaluation of small stream fishes: point vs. transect, observation vs. capture methodologies. Journal of Freshwater Ecology 3:121–131.

Roff, D. A. 1981. Reproductive uncertainty and the evolution of iteroparity: why don't flatfish put all their eggs in one basket? Canadian Journal of Fisheries and Aquatic Sciences 38:968–977.

Rosen, D. E. 1974. Phylogeny and zoogeography of salmoniform fishes and relationships of *Lepidogalaxias salamandroides*. Bulletin of the American Museum of Natural History 127:217–268.

Rosen, D. E. 1975a. A vicariance model of Caribbean biogeography. Systematic Zoology 24:437–464.

Rosen, D. E. 1975b. Doctrinal biogeography, a review of *Marine Zoogeography* by J. C. Briggs. Quarterly Review of Biology 50:69–70.

Sale, P. F., and W. A. Douglas. 1981. Precision and accuracy of visual census technique for fish assemblages on coral patch reefs. Environmental Biology of Fishes 6:333–339.

SAS. 1985. SAS user's guide: statistics, version 5 edition. SAS Institute, Cary, North Carolina.

Schaffer, W. M., and P. F. Elson. 1975. The adaptive significance of variations in life history among local populations of Atlantic salmon in North America. Ecology 56:577–590.

Seeb, J. E., L. W. Seeb, and F. M. Utter. 1986. Use of genetic marks to assess stock dynamics and management programs of chum salmon. Transactions of the American Fisheries Society 115:448–454.

Shaklee, J. B. 1983. The utilization of isozymes as gene markers in fisheries management and conservation. Pages 213–247 *in* M. C. Rattazzi, J. G. Scandalios, and G. S. Whitt, editors. Isozymes: current topics in biological and medical research, volume 11. Medical and other applications. A. R. Liss, New York.

Shaw, E. 1978. Schooling in fishes. American Scientist 66:166–175.

Sheppard, J. D., and J. H. Johnson. 1985. Probability-of-use for depth, velocity, and substrate by subyearling coho salmon and steelhead in Lake Ontario tributary streams. North American Journal of Fisheries Management 5:277–282.

Shirvell, C. S., and R. G. Dungey. 1983. Microhabitats chosen by brown trout for feeding and spawning in rivers. Transactions of the American Fisheries Society 12:355–367.

Shrode, J. B., K. E. Zerba, and J. S. Stephens, Jr. 1982. Ecological significance of temperature tolerance and preference of some inshore California fishes. Transactions of the American Fisheries Society 111:45–51.

Shulman, M. J. 1985. Coral reef fish assemblages: intra- and interspecific competition for shelter sites. Environmental Biology of Fishes 13:81–92.

Simenstad, G. A., and G. M. Cailliet, editors. 1986. Contemporary studies on fish feeding: the proceedings of GUTSHOP '84. Environmental Biology of Fishes 16.

Smith, C. L., and C. R. Powell. 1971. The summer fish communities of Brier Creek, Marshall County, Oklahoma. American Museum Novitates 2458:1–30.

Smith, J. J., and H. W. Li. 1983. Energetic factors influencing foraging tactics of juvenile steelhead trout, *Salmo gairdneri*. Pages 173–180 *in* D. L. G. Noakes, D. G. Lindquist, G. S. Helfman, and J. A. Ward, editors. Predators and prey in fishes. Dr. W. Junk, The Hague, Netherlands.

Snyder, D. E. 1983. Fish eggs and larvae. Pages 165–198 *in* L. A. Nielsen and D. L. Johnson, editors. Fisheries techniques. American Fisheries Society, Bethesda, Maryland.

Spigarelli, S. A., M. M. Thommes, W. Prepejchal, and R. M. Goldstein. 1983. Selected temperatures and thermal experience of brown trout, *Salmo trutta*, in a steep thermal gradient in nature. Environmental Biology of Fishes 8:137–149.

Stearns, S. C. 1976. Life history tactics: a review of the ideas. Quarterly Review of Biology 51:3–47.

Stearns, S. C. 1977. The evolution of life history traits: a critique of the theory and a review of the data. Annual Review of Ecology and Systematics 8:145–171.

Stearns, S. C. 1978. Interpopulational differences in reproductive traits of *Neoheterandia tridentiger* (Pisces: Poeciliidae) in Panama. Copeia 1978:188–190.

Stearns, S. C. 1980. A new view of life-history evolution. Oikos 35:266–281.

Strauss, R. E. 1982. Influence of replicated subsamples and subsample heterogeneity on the linear index of food selection. Transactions of the American Fisheries Society 111:517–522.

Summerfelt, R. C., and G. E. Hall, editors. 1987. Age and growth of fish. Iowa State University Press, Ames.

Terry, C. B., and J. S. Stephens, Jr. 1976. A study of the orientation of selected embiotocid fishes to depth and shifting seasonal vertical temperature gradients. Bulletin Southern California Academy of Sciences 75:170–183.

Thorne, R. E. 1983. Hydroacoustics. Pages 239–260 *in* L. A. Nielsen and D. L. Johnson, editors. Fisheries techniques. American Fisheries Society, Bethesda, Maryland.

Utter, F. M. 1981. Biological criteria for identification of species and distinct intraspecific populations of anadromous salmonids under the U.S. Endangered Species Act of 1973. Canadian Journal of Fisheries and Aquatic Sciences 38:1626–1635.

Utter, F. 1987. Protein electrophoresis and stock identification in fishes. NOAA (National Oceanic and Atmospheric Administration) Technical Memorandum NMFS (National Marine Fisheries Service) SEFC (Southeast Fisheries Center) 199:63–104, Miami.

Vondracek, B., D. M. Baltz, L. R. Brown, and P. B. Moyle. 1989. Spatial, seasonal and diel distribution of fishes in a California reservoir dominated by native fishes. Fisheries Research 7:31–53.

Warner, R. R., and R. K. Harlan. 1982. Sperm competition and sperm storage as determinants of sexual dimorphism in the dwarf surfperch, *Micrometrus minimus*. Evolution 36:44–55.

Werner, E. E., J. F. Gilliam, D. J. Hall, and G. G. Mittelbach. 1983a. An experimental test of the effects of predation risk on habitat use in fish. Ecology 64:1540–1548.

Werner, E. E., D. J. Hall, D. R. Laughlin, D. J. Wagner, L. A. Wilsmann, and F. C. Funk. 1977. Habitat partitioning in a freshwater fish community. Journal of the Fisheries Research Board of Canada 34:360–370.

Werner, E. E., G. G. Mittelbach, D. J. Hall, and J. F. Gilliam. 1983b. Experimental tests of optimal habitat use in fish: the role of relative habitat profitability. Ecology 64:1525–1539.

Whittaker, R. H., S. A. Levin, and R. B. Root. 1973. Niche, habitat, and ecotope. American Naturalist 107:321–338.

Wilson, C. A., and eight coauthors. 1987. Glossary. Pages 527–530 in R. C. Summerfelt and G. S. Hall, editors. Age and growth of fish. Iowa State University Press, Ames.

Winans, G. A. 1985. Geographic variation in the milkfish, *Chanos chanos* II. Multivariate morphological evidence. Copeia 1985:890–898.

Winans, G. A. 1987. Using morphometric and meristic characters for identifying stocks of fish. NOAA (National Oceanic and Atmospheric Administration) Technical Memorandum NMFS (National Marine Fisheries Service) SEFC (Southeast Fisheries Center) 199:25–62, Miami.

Winter, J. D. 1983. Underwater biotelemetry. Pages 371–396 in L. A. Nielsen and D. L. Johnson, editors. Fisheries techniques. American Fisheries Society, Bethesda, Maryland.

Wurtsbaugh, W., and H. Li. 1985. Diel migrations of a zooplanktivorous fish (*Menidia beryllina*) in relation to the distribution of its prey in a large eutrophic lake. Limnology and Oceanography 30:565–576.

Wurtsbaugh, W., and D. Neverman. 1988. Post-feeding thermotaxis and daily vertical migration in a larval fish. Nature (London) 333:846–848.

Wydoski, R., and L. Emery. 1983. Tagging and marking. Pages 215–238 in L. A. Nielsen and D. L. Johnson, editors. Fisheries techniques. American Fisheries Society, Bethesda, Maryland.

Chapter 19

Community Ecology

LARRY B. CROWDER

19.1 INTRODUCTION

A "community" is often defined as a group of populations that occur in a common area and that interact with one another. Many ecologists prefer the term "assemblage" to define a group of co-occurring populations, a term that does not imply significant interactions among populations. In this paper, I often use the more common term "community" but do not intend it to mean that all communities must be highly interactive. Community ecology is a young science and its applications to fisheries are even more recent. As a result, there are few "standard methods" in fish community ecology. However, a community-oriented approach to fisheries biology is becoming increasingly necessary (Steele et al. 1980; May 1984b). Practical experience has shown that a particular fish population often cannot be studied and understood, much less managed, in isolation from other populations with which it interacts.

Many of the ideas and theories elaborated by community ecologists apply directly to fishes, but others do not. Most of the theory in community ecology derives from work with birds and mammals, which tend to have fairly predictable growth rates and for which the juveniles are similar in size to the adults. In strong contrast, fish growth rates can be highly variable, and fish can increase several orders of magnitude in size during their lifetimes. This often results in complex interactions among populations that are difficult to characterize. But we need to understand how ecological roles of fishes shift during ontogeny in order to manage multispecies fisheries (May 1984b).

In this chapter, I outline the major philosophical approaches to fish community ecology and give examples of how each can help us understand the structure and dynamics of fish communities. Competition, predation, and symbiotic interactions are important factors that structure fish communities, as are historical and stochastic factors. For each interaction, I review cases illustrating different approaches. Ultimately, the diversity of species occupying a particular system may be related to species interactions, although biogeographic factors will also be important.

19.2 METHODOLOGICAL APPROACHES TO COMMUNITY ECOLOGY

19.2.1 Descriptive Approaches

Initial approaches to a new system usually involve descriptive work or basic natural history. In community ecology, for example, early work on resource

Box 19.1   Definitions of Some Common Ecological Terms

Allopatry is the isolation of two species from each other; allopatric species do not co-occur in the same water body or other habitat. Compare *sympatry*.

Cascading trophic interaction hypothesis suggests that an increase in piscivore biomass leads to a decrease in planktivore biomass, an increase in herbivore biomass, and a decrease in phytoplankton biomass.

Character displacement is an increase in differences (often morphological) between two species where the species occur together, compared to the differences between them when they are separate.

Coevolution is the joint evolution of two or more taxa that have close ecological relationships such that each taxon exerts selective pressure on the others and the evolution of each partly depends on the evolution of the others.

Commensalism is a relationship between two kinds of organisms in which one obtains food or other benefits from the other without damaging or benefiting it in return.

Density compensation is an increase in the abundances of some species in a feeding guild (species that feed in similar ways on similar organisms or nutrient sources) when other species of the guild are absent, compared to abundances when the guild assemblage is species-rich.

Deterministic processes and patterns are the predictable outcome of antecedent causes. Compare *stochastic*.

Electivity index is a measure of prey selection by a fish in relation to prey availability in its foraging habitat.

Mutualism is a mutually beneficial association between different kinds of organisms.

Niche is the ecological "place" or "role" of an organism after the organism has adapted to all the biotic and abiotic factors (dimensions) of its environment.

Niche breadth is the range of resources used by a species in its local situation.

Niche overlap is the joint use of resources or other environmental variables by two species. Overlap is not directly related to competition.

Niche shift is a change in resource use patterns by one species when another species (usually assumed to be a competitor) is added to or removed from an ecological system.

Null models postulate that there will be no change in community-level patterns when one (or more) biotic interactions are suspended. Analagous to null hypotheses of statistics, null models are very difficult to formulate.

Resource partitioning is the subdivision of a resource between or among coexisting organisms, often assumed to be related to competition.

Stochastic processes and patterns result from the influence of one or more random variables; they appear to be random and probabilistic. Compare *deterministic*.

Sympatry is the coexistence of two species in the same water body or other habitat. Compare *allopatry*.

partitioning (see Box 19.1 for a brief glossary of ecological terms) was used to infer that competition is or has been an important force shaping a fish community. But such studies cannot provide conclusive evidence for competition or other particular ecological processes, and such inferences have been subject to severe criticism (Wiens 1977; Connell 1980).

Studies of fish diets, which account for a large and varied literature, provide similar descriptive evidence for predation. But it is impossible from diet studies alone to infer much about the importance of a particular predator–prey interaction. The appearance of prey X in the stomach of predator Y documents a single predation event, but additional information on prey availability, digestion rates, and so on, is necessary to convert descriptive diet data into a more thorough understanding of predator–prey interactions. Estimates of prey availability can be compared to diet data to establish preliminary estimates of prey selectivity.

The descriptive approach cannot go far to clarify mechanisms that underlie the dynamics of communities. Nevertheless, description is an essential precursor to the framing of useful mechanistic hypotheses and the design of observations or experiments to test those hypotheses (Chapter 1).

19.2.2 Comparative Approaches

Descriptive data from several sites or from the same site over time can be compared to infer mechanisms underlying patterns of community structure or function. For example, by comparing the species or size composition of forage fish in lakes with and without predators, one can infer effects of predators on prey communities. If the same patterns are observed repeatedly, they lend support to the idea that a particular interaction is important. But one must be careful: differences in species composition, growth rate, or any other response variable may be due to site differences other than the factor of interest (absence of a predator, say). Thus, comparative studies must involve many sites or a long time at one site. Comparing one "experimental" site (e.g., below a thermal outfall) with one "control" site (above the outfall) provides no firm evidence for the hypothesis being explored. All that can be concluded is that the sites differ; no causal mechanisms can be addressed. Despite such limitations, the comparative approach has made substantial contributions in limnology. It has particular advantages when system size or complexity preclude an experimental analysis (Diamond 1986).

As experience with a variety of similar systems increases, generalizations about system function are likely to arise. These may be treated as hypotheses, but the hypotheses must be tested with an independent data set. "Hypotheses" that derive from a descriptive or comparative study are really "explanations" of the patterns seen, not hypotheses—which must, by definition, be stated a priori. They only become hypotheses when they can be tested in controlled field experiments or against independently collected comparative data (Tonn et al. 1983).

So-called "natural experiments" amenable to comparative analysis often occur on large spatial scales that seem relevant ecologically. The invasion of sea lampreys into the Laurentian Great Lakes and the subsequent changes in the fish communities there revealed much about the ecology of that system (Smith 1972; Kitchell and Crowder 1986). Such an "experiment" would not (and perhaps could not) have been done on purpose. Using natural experiments to increase our understanding of how fish communities work is an opportunistic enterprise because it usually involves a catastrophe: a flood, a drought, a new estuarine inlet. When catastrophes do occur, they can be exploited only if previous data on the system exist or if the altered system can be monitored until it reverts to a previous state. Fisheries biologists sometimes have a time series of data against which recent system changes can be compared. Natural experiments usually lack the replication and controls necessary for a bona fide, statistically valid experiment.

19.2.3 Experimental Approaches

Community ecology is becoming more strongly experimental as the discipline strives to move beyond description and correlation to a mechanistic understanding of how fish communities work. Because many fishery management practices are manipulative (e.g., predator stocking, habitat alteration), fishery scientists are constantly experimenting when management actions are taken. Unlike more basic ecological research, fishery experiments occur on a larger, more realistic scale, but often lack the replication and controls necessary to infer causal linkages.

In ecology, experiments are based (in theory at least) upon a priori, testable hypotheses. Experiments designed to test a hypothesis should have appropriate replication and statistical rigor. Even within experimental ecology, however, experiments are often weakened by poor design or lack of replication (Hurlburt 1984). Given the high cost of field experiments in fisheries ecology, the benefits of each experiment must be maximized (Chapter 1). Many scientists feel that progress is most rapid when alternative hypotheses can be tested in the same experimental design (Platt 1964). Because a hypothesis cannot be "proven," the goal is to eliminate competing hypotheses.

The recent emphasis in ecology on field experimentation has focused on reasonably small systems that can be manipulated and controlled (Diamond 1986). Appropriate designs for field tests—of competition, for example—can be quite rigorous (Connell 1980, 1983) and require extensive effort even for short-term experiments conducted on a small spatial scale (<1 hectare). Although controlled experiments provide the most powerful approach to community ecology, some systems are just not amenable to direct field experimentation. Many of these difficult systems—large lakes and rivers; estuaries and coastal oceans—are important with respect to resource management or environmental degradation. One approach to these systems is adaptive management (Holling 1978): simulation models are used to project system responses to perturbation or manipulation, and the predictions are critically examined in light of actual system responses to subsequent management actions. In this way, managers can test hypotheses and iteratively adapt their practices according to what they learn about system behavior.

19.2.4 Null Models and the Reliability of Inferences

Ecologists are concerned about the quality of evidence that has been cited to show that species interactions are important features of communities (Strong et al. 1984). Are communities tightly integrated and highly interactive? Or are they merely assemblages of species more influenced by environmental factors and their own autecology? What role does stochastic environmental variation play in creating the patterns observed in animal communities? Until the late 1970s, many community ecologists focused on the effects that species interactions, especially competition, have on patterns of species distribution and abundance. Niche theory, in particular, was elaborated, primarily in the context of competition. Many field observations seemed consistent with theoretical expectations, but this consistency did not provide a hard test for the importance of competition in structuring ecological communities (Strong et al. 1984).

Beginning in the mid-1970s, several ecologists began constructing "neutral models" or "null hypotheses" to characterize the community patterns one might expect if species did not interact (May 1984a). If an appropriate null hypothesis could be generated, it would be possible to contrast patterns in natural communities with those expected in the absence of species interactions. Deviations from the null model could be more reliably attributed to the species interaction(s) specifically excluded from the model. Not surprisingly, it has proven difficult to develop adequate null hypotheses for the complex interactions typical of ecological communities (see Colwell and Winkler 1984 for an insightful review). A major result of this period of introspection among ecologists has been an increasing emphasis on experimental approaches to resolving the mechanisms underlying the structure of animal communities.

19.3 STUDYING SPECIES INTERACTIONS

19.3.1 Competition

Darwin (1859) defined competition as "the demand of more than one organism for the same resource of the environment in excess of the immediate supply." Simple elements of this definition suggest that, for competition to occur, (1) two organisms must share the resource, (2) the resource must be in short supply, and (3) there must be evidence of mutual negative effects on resource use, growth, or some other measure correlated with fitness (Larkin 1956; Moermond 1979). Various types of evidence have been proposed to document or support the competition hypothesis. As understanding of communities has increased, standards for the sort of data acceptable as evidence for competition have risen. Classes of evidence, listed in approximate order of increasing rigor, are

(1) complementary dynamics in descriptive data (when species A increases in abundance, species B declines);
(2) descriptive evidence for resource partitioning or niche segregation;
(3) documentation of resource limitation;
(4) ecological character displacement;
(5) niche shifts in allopatry or sympatry;
(6) repeatable changes in growth or abundance when resource levels or competitors are manipulated experimentally.

One of the common approaches to competition has been to describe patterns of resource use among species coexisting in a community. Certain patterns of niche segregation or resource partitioning are consistent with the competition hypothesis (Nilsson 1967; Schoener 1974, 1986). Such patterns have often been used to infer that competition is or has been an important force in determining community structure (Connell 1980). Based on a review of 230 studies, Ross (1986) concluded that fishes exhibit substantial resource partitioning. But species may differ in resource use for several reasons other than competition, including historical and

---

Box 19.2   Sample Calculation of Niche Overlap

One of the simplest measures of niche overlap is Schoener's (1970) index C_{xy}:

$$C_{xy} = 1 - 0.5\left(\sum |p_{xi} - p_{yi}|\right);$$

p_{xi} is the proportion of resource i used by species x and p_{yi} is the proportion of resource i used by species y. Both Hurlbert (1978) and Wallace (1981) agreed that this index provides a reasonable estimate of niche overlap while requiring few assumptions. Measures of niche overlap or breadth that take resource availability into account would be better (Petraitis 1979), but good availability data are uncommon.

In the following example of niche overlap calculations, the resources are invertebrate prey species that are eaten by both sunfish and bass in a lake. The numbers are the proportions that each prey constitutes in the total diet of each predator.

Prey species (i)	Sunfish (species x)	Bass (species y)	Absolute difference
1	0.21	0.06	0.15
2	0.07	0.35	0.28
3	0.46	0.17	0.29
4	0.26	0.42	0.16
Total	1.00	1.00	0.88

Thus, $C_{xy} = 1 - 0.5(0.88) = 0.56$. This simple measure of niche overlap is symmetrical. More complicated indices allow overlaps to be asymmetrical; they could accommodate a situation (for example) in which bass overlap a large part of the sunfish niche, but sunfish overlap only a small part of the bass niche. The Schoener index, however, probably is the least problematical, and it can be used to screen for potentially important interactions. The index should not be computed to more than two decimal places because confidence intervals can be quite large (Ricklefs and Lau 1980).

---

phylogenetic constraints, so resource partitioning provides only circumstantial evidence for competition. Further, it is almost always possible to detect differences in habitat use, diet, or time of activity among coexisting species if one looks closely enough; whether or not these imply competition or any other mechanism of community structure may be difficult to decide from observational data alone.

Overlap in the use of resources is a necessary (but insufficient) condition for competition. Many techniques have been suggested for estimating niche metrics such as overlap (Hurlbert 1978; Linton et al. 1981; Wallace 1981). Although these calculations are sometimes useful, all are based on assumptions that constrain their interpretation. Examples of overlap index calculations are given in Box 19.2. Few overlap indices have been calculated with confidence intervals, but simulations suggest that typical confidence intervals for a calculated niche overlap of

0.50 could be ±0.20 (Ricklefs and Lau 1980), suggesting that, for most purposes, overlap values should not be calculated beyond one or two decimal places. Further, niche overlap implies little about competition per se (Colwell and Futuyma 1971), although it can indicate where more rigorous studies of competition might be worthwhile. One promising technique is to relate niche metrics to resource availability (Petraitis 1979). In this approach, niche breadth and overlap formulas are based on the resources available; tests are available for detecting differences in resource use patterns that are independent of differences in resource availability among sites.

Resource use patterns alone cannot be used to infer competition because competition depends on resource limitation. However, growth rates of fishes are highly sensitive to per capita resource availability (Backiel and Le Cren 1978) and so may be useful indicators of competition. Fish populations subjected to fishing or experimental reductions in population size often show density-dependent increases in growth rate (Beckman 1941; Alm 1946; Johnson 1977; Healey 1980). Growth and recruitment also can be affected by the density and abundance of major prey species (Forney 1977).

Selection pressure related to competition between similar species may cause the species' niches to diverge from each other through behavioral, physiological, or morphological changes in the organisms (ecological character displacement). Several studies of ecological character displacement have been conducted since Brown and Wilson (1956) suggested the term, but only two involved fish. In both cases, one species changed the number of its gill rakers in the presence of a potential competitor. Crowder (1984, 1986) documented significant reduction in the number and lengths of gill rakers in bloaters, which are native ciscoes in Lake Michigan. This reduction was apparently in response to the invasion of alewives, which have extremely fine, long gill rakers. Dunham et al. (1979) used stepwise multiple linear regression to conclude that competition, not geographic and environmental variables, was the dominant cause of gill raker changes in catostomid fishes in different drainages.

Yet another approach to the study of competition is to compare resource use patterns of coexisting species with the resources used when each species is alone (i.e., when the species are sympatric and allopatric). Shifts in resource use patterns in such comparative studies provide reasonably strong evidence for competition (Andrusak and Northcote 1971; Svärdson 1976; Nilsson and Northcote 1981). One general pattern noted in these studies is that the more pelagic of a pair of ostensible competitors (generally the one with the finest gill rakers) often ''wins.'' When alewives invaded the Great Lakes, several species declined, perhaps in response to competition; most of these have fewer gill rakers than the alewife.

Tonn (1985) used a comparative approach to test the hypothesis that, if competition is important within an assemblage of fishes, a species should increase in numbers or biomass—should express density compensation—when some of its competitors are absent. Tonn compared five similar lakes in northern Wisconsin that contained one to three species in a nested pattern: central mudminnows alone, with yellow perch, or with both yellow perch and golden shiners. When central mudminnows were alone, they showed strong density compensation, reaching nearly 10 times the biomass they achieved where yellow perch were present. Comparative approaches can lend strong support to competition hypotheses, but are not as powerful as more experimental approaches.

Few experimental studies of competition have been performed with fishes. The primary examples of the approach involved fish of temperate marine reefs (Hixon 1980), streams (Fausch and White 1981), and small ponds (Werner and Hall 1976, 1979). In all cases, the experiments involved removal or addition of a potential competitor and assessments of shifts in resource use. With both the temperate marine reef fish and the stream salmonids, behavioral interference appeared to be a source of competitive stress. Werner and his colleagues performed a series of feeding trials and pond experiments that allowed them to compare the competitive abilities of several sunfish species in different habitats. In pond experiments, all three test species preferred a vegetated habitat over open water when held alone, but two species were apparently displaced from that habitat when the three species were held together (Werner and Hall 1976). Using foraging theory, Werner was also able to predict the temporal order of habitat switching by these three species (Werner and Hall 1979).

Competition was often, until recently, invoked as *the* major structuring force in animal communities. Attacks on this view have emphasized the importance of predation, environmental variability, and the lack of good experimental evidence for competition (Connell 1975, 1980; Wiens 1977; Hurlbert 1984; Strong et al. 1984). Schoener (1983) and Connell (1983), who reviewed the field competition experiments published through the early 1980s, both concluded that most such tests documented substantial competition. This literature may be biased, however, if (as seems likely) people are more likely to publish if evidence for competition is found than if it is not. Further, it seems unlikely that one would perform experiments to evaluate competition among particular organisms if competition were not expected.

19.3.2 Predation

In some ways, predation is easier to document than competition. Each item in the stomach of a fish documents a predation event that has occurred. But assessing how predators make their foraging decisions and determining the influence of predation on the abundance of prey species or the structure of the prey community is much more difficult. As with competition, information about the complementary abundance dynamics of predator and putative prey and a few diet data can be used to infer predator–prey interactions, but quantifying these interactions is difficult.

Because many fish are highly opportunistic feeders, diet studies should extend, with adequate samples, over appropriate diel periods and across habitats. Using an arbitrary number of fishes in diet analyses may be an inefficient way to determine diet diversity. Hurtubia (1973) provided a method for estimating the sample size necessary to characterize diet diversity of a population or a particular collection. Fish size also should be treated as a covariate in diet analyses because prey size and diet composition shift with changes in fish size (Werner and Gilliam 1984).

Although diet data from fishes are abundant, concurrent data on prey availability in the environment are much more rare, making it difficult to infer prey selectivity. Electivity indices, such as those developed by Ivlev (1961), Jacobs

(1974), Chesson (1978), Strauss (1979), and Vanderploeg and Scavia (1979), estimate relative prey selectivity by fishes (Box 19.3). As with the overlap measures cited above, few people have attempted to estimate confidence intervals for electivity indices (Strauss 1982). Given the strong differences between prey availability and stomach contents of fish predators that often are apparent, any index that depends upon ratios of prey available to prey eaten can be problematic. For example, prey common in the diets of planktivores (e.g., large zooplankters) may be so rare that it is difficult to estimate their true proportional representation in the zooplankton. Items common in the zooplankton samples may be so rare in fish stomachs that it is difficult to closely estimate the proportion of those prey in the diets. Further, prey "selection" may depend as much on the prey's escape behavior or propensity for refuges as on the predator's choices (Stein 1979; Drenner and McComas 1980).

Adult planktivorous fish tend to be size selective, taking larger than average zooplankton. But prey selectivity can shift as the abundances of prey in various size-classes change. Foraging theory has been extended to examine the profitability of various prey and to forecast diet selection, habitat choice, and feeding modes (Werner and Hall 1974; Mittelbach 1981; Crowder 1985). Experimental tests of diet and habitat choice models with bluegills have been promising (Werner et al. 1983b); however, some authors have questioned the utility of foraging theory for predictions of diet or habitat choice, particularly for juvenile fishes (Mills et al. 1984). Foraging models may prove very useful if they can be extended and improved so that one can reliably predict habitat choice by fishes, but they need much additional work.

Predator–prey interactions, of course, do not depend solely on the behavioral "choices" of predators. Many prey have behavioral responses that reduce their risk of being eaten. Behaviors that have been linked to predator avoidance include diel vertical migration by zooplankton, occupation of structural refuges during periods of vulnerability, schooling, reduction in foraging activity in the presence of a predator, and specialized escape movements during an attack (Stein 1979; Kerfoot and Sih 1987). Behavioral responses of prey may be modified by learning and concurrent motivations such as hunger. It may be necessary to study behavior explicitly to understand some predator–prey interactions (Sih 1987).

Among 139 experiments on predation and prey community structure reviewed by Sih et al. (1985), 23 involved fish. Most of these experiments involved removals of fish from or additions of fish to whole systems, fish exclosures (areas fenced to keep fish out), or enclosures (with and without fish). Predation had an important effect on the structure of prey communities in 22 of the 23 studies, and was more influential in lakes than in streams.

19.3.3 Symbiosis

Symbiosis simply means "living together"; the term embraces mutualism, commensalism, and parasitism. Little research has been done on the community-wide implications of symbiosis. Symbiotic interactions—including multispecies schooling (Barlow 1974), cleaning (Losey 1978), and burrow sharing with various invertebrates—are probably more common than generally supposed and deserve additional research. Intricate patterns of interspecific parental care documented for African cichlids suggest how complex these relationships can be (McKaye

Box 19.3   Electivity Indices.

Ivlev's (1961) index of electivity, E, has been widely used to characterize the degree to which a particular prey species is selected by the predator being studied. The relationship is

$$E = (r_i - p_i)/(r_i + p_i);$$

r_i is the relative abundance of prey item i in the gut (as a proportion of the total gut contents) and p_i is the proportion of prey type i in the environment. The index ranges from -1 to $+1$; negative values indicate avoidance of the prey or the prey's inaccessibility, zero indicates random selection, and positive values indicate active selection.

Another commonly used measure is the forage ratio, FR, which is the ratio of the proportional representation of the prey item in the gut to that in the environment:

$$FR = r_i/p_i.$$

The forage ratio ranges from 0 to 1 for negative selection and from 1 to infinity for positive selection.

Strauss (1979) developed confidence interval estimates of both these indices and noted several sources of bias. Both Ivlev's index and the forage ratio present problems when sample sizes for prey proportions differ between predator stomachs and the environment. The widths of confidence intervals depend on both the absolute and relative sample sizes as well as on the relative rarity of prey in the environment. This is an important problem because highly selected prey are often so rare in the environment that extremely large sample sizes (thousands) are required for reliable electivity measures.

To solve some of these problems, Strauss (1979) proposed a linear food selection index, L:

$$L = r_i - p_i;$$

r_i and p_i are defined as before. This index ranges between -1 and $+1$, positive values indicating preference and negative values indicating avoidance or inaccessibility. The sampling variance can be readily defined for this index and both confidence intervals and simple tests of hypotheses can be easily calculated. Large sample sizes may still be required when prey are rare.

As Strauss (1979) pointed out, sampling causes the major problems with electivity indices. It is difficult to get good estimates of the proportions of prey types actually available to fish in the environment. Prey can have elaborate predator-avoidance or escape behaviors that may not be reflected in net or grab samples. Establishing prey proportions in diets is somewhat easier, but still difficult for rare prey. Investigators probably have given too much emphasis to point estimates of electivity, especially given the small sample sizes often employed.

1977). Parasites of fishes have been well studied from the perspective of fish health, but not for their community implications.

19.3.4 Stochastic Effects

Increasing numbers of ecologists are challenging the notion that communities are tightly integrated by interactions among the component species. Droughts, floods, and other environmental variation may reduce the local abundances of many populations, thereby reducing the opportunity for competition and other interactions between species (Wiens 1977). Local assemblages of species may be more influenced by environmental factors or their own autecology than by species interactions. One characteristic of assemblages that are strongly influenced by stochastic factors is lack of persistence; that is, the relative abundances of assemblage members are not stable over time (Grossman et al. 1982). Assemblages more influenced by deterministic interactions have more persistent patterns of relative abundance.

Stream fish assemblages can be destabilized by floods and droughts, particularly if these occur during the spawning season. Streams in the Mississippi drainage provide the best evidence for stochastic effects (Grossman et al. 1982; Schlosser 1982). In contrast, Moyle and Vondracek (1985) concluded that a fish assemblage in a small California stream was more deterministic than stochastic. Matthews (1986) found that an Arkansas stream fish community was deterministic, despite a catastrophic flood. The concordance analysis presented by Grossman et al. (1982) has been criticized (Herbold 1984; Rahel et al. 1984; Yant et al. 1984), but the questions about the relative importance of biotic and abiotic factors raised by Grossman et al. remain valid. Experimental manipulations will ultimately be the most powerful technique for addressing the relative influences of species interactions and environmental variation on fish communities (Power 1987).

Sale (1977, 1984) also discussed the importance of stochastic factors for coral reef fish communities on small patch reefs. When a new small patch becomes available, the species that will first occupy it is unpredictable. Sale referred to this phenomenon as "lottery competition." Other researchers, most of whom worked on larger reefs, viewed reef fish communities as more deterministic (Smith and Tyler 1973; Goldman and Talbot 1976). Whether reef patches are small or large, they are only visited intermittently by investigators, so direct observations of patch colonization are rare. Sale (1984) was careful to point out that reef fish communities may appear to be deterministic during short studies because the life spans of the fish may exceed the study duration. Over a long-term study, however, the community appears to be more stochastic.

The controversy over stochastic and deterministic bases for community structure could be partly a matter of scale. What appears to be highly stochastic on a local scale such as a particular patch reef may well appear more deterministic on a larger spatial scale such as an archipelago of patch reefs (cf. Levin 1974). Differences in spatial and temporal scales also may contribute to the analogous controversy over community structure in streams.

19.3.5 Evolution and Species Interactions

Over evolutionary time, species can coevolve with respect to their interactions. Planktivores and their zooplankton prey exhibit a variety of adaptations that seem to both improve the efficiency of the predators and minimize the vulnerability of prey (O'Brien 1987). The effects of predators on their prey seem most obvious where the two have not coevolved. When the peacock cichlid was accidentally introduced into Gatun Lake, Panama, seven species of native fishes nearly disappeared, and effects of the introduction could be detected as far along the food web as the zooplankton (Zaret and Paine 1973). Sea lampreys had similar devastating effects on the larger fishes of the Great Lakes (Smith 1972; Kitchell and Crowder 1986). Introduced Nile perch may be drastically reducing the diversity of native haplochromine cichlids of Lake Victoria (Barel et al. 1985). Exotic planktivores have changed the species composition and size structure of zooplankton communities in small lakes (Brooks and Dodson 1965) and in Lake Michigan (Wells 1970; Evans and Jude 1986; Kitchell et al. 1988).

Coevolution of competitors is a more difficult problem to discern. Coevolution is often assumed to have shaped resource use patterns among competitors in communities. But, as Connell (1980) noted, two species must live together consistently to coevolve. Because predators and parasites depend upon their prey or hosts, they consistently co-occur with them and so should coevolve with them. Competing species, however, do not depend on each other; behavioral niche shifts displace them from each other and minimize the need for evolutionary divergence. Increased species diversity also reduces the co-occurrence of a particular species pair, reducing the chances for coevolution. Crowder (1986) documented rapid shifts in gill raker morphology and habitat use by Lake Michigan bloaters that were apparent responses to the increased abundance of exotic alewives. He suggested that one might profitably look for incipient coevolution of competitors among non-coevolved species that have come into contact recently. Connell (1980) proposed a rigorous set of criteria for demonstrating coevolution of competitors (Box 19.4), but noted that there are few convincing examples.

Regardless of their interest in evolutionary biology per se, it is useful for fishery biologists to consider evolution in fishery management contexts, particularly when management involves species introductions. The outcomes of stocking exotic predators have not been predictable and the effects on the native faunas have often been undesirable. However, when a new community is "assembled"— in a new reservoir, for example—it is often helpful to establish a coevolved assemblage or at least to consider the community in which each new component species evolved. Another reason for considering fish evolution is to take advantage of the theory and data on feeding strategies, life history strategies, and so on that have resulted from basic research in evolutionary ecology.

19.4   ANALYSIS OF FOOD WEBS

19.4.1   Ontogenetic Shifts in the Roles of Fishes

The substantial increase in body size that fish achieve during ontogeny has implications for species interactions (Werner and Gilliam 1984). Two species may compete as juveniles and not as adults or vice versa. Because almost all fishes start feeding in the plankton, important interactions are likely during that life stage. Older life stages may prey upon or compete with younger cohorts of their own or other species; indeed, cannibalism may be a selective force behind

Box 19.4   Coevolution of Competitors

Connell (1980) presented an experimental design for testing whether or not two species have coevolved as competitors. The experiment involves manipulation of allopatric and sympatric populations. Two propositions must be demonstrated:

I, competition is the underlying cause for the divergence of niches between competitors;

II, niche divergence has a genetic basis.

The field experiment outlined below (modifed from Connell 1980) can test these propositions. Only if the questions posed under treatments 1, 2, 5, and 6 are answered affirmatively can the propositions be accepted. In the notation of this matrix, allopatric populations of species X are X_a and sympatric populations are X_s. Species Y is the presumed competitor.

Test of competitive situation	Proposition I: competition exists	Proposition II: genetic basis
Test of proposition: observe change in niche breadth of	X_a	X_s[a]
Sympatric locality: species Y present naturally		
Species Y not removed	Treatment 1: X_a added, X_s removed. Does X_a niche become significantly more narrow than in treatment 2?	Treatment 4: X_a absent, X_s remains. (Control.)
Species Y removed	Treatment 2: X_a added, X_s removed. Does X_a niche remain broader than in treatments 1 and 5?	Treatment 5: X_a absent, X_s remains. If X_s niche expands, is it always narrower than the X_a niche in treatment 2?
Allopatric locality: species Y absent naturally		
Species Y absent	Treatment 3: X_a remains, X_s absent. (Control.)	Treatment 6: X_a removed, X_s added. If X_s niche expands, is it always narrower than the X_a niche in treatment 3?

[a]The niche breadth of X_s need not change for proposition II to be accepted.

intraspecific habitat segregation. Adults of a prey species (e.g., alewife) may feed on the young of its predator (e.g., largemouth bass): the hunted become the hunters.

Predators can have negative effects on prey without actually consuming them (Kerfoot and Sih 1987). Indirect effects associated with predation risk have been documented for several fishes. Small fishes appear to be confined to refuges (vegetation or rocks) even though the nearby open-water habitat would be a more profitable habitat in which to forage (Mittelbach 1981; Werner et al. 1983a). These individuals grow more slowly as a result. If several species are confined to limited refuges, competition between them may be intensified and growth rates reduced further (Mittelbach 1984, 1988).

Competition that leads to reduced size-specific growth rates can interact strongly with size-specific predation rates (Werner and Gilliam 1984); i.e., fish remain vulnerable longer to predators that take prey of a certain size or smaller. In general, mortality rates of fishes seem to be inversely related to size (Werner and Gilliam 1984); this could be due to predation or differential vulnerability to environmental change (Toneys and Coble 1979), among other factors. The principle can be expressed in terms of survivorship, L, which takes values from 0.0 to 1.0. If the growth rate of a size-group of fish changes by a factor of c, the new survivorship, L', is a power of the old (Werner and Gilliam 1984):

$$L' = L^{(1/c)}.$$

Suppose the normal survivorship is 0.4 during the first month after juvenile fish have absorbed their yolk sacs; that is, $L = 0.4$. Suppose further that unusually cool water or a poor food supply one year reduces the normal growth rate of such fish by half; that is, $c = 0.5$. The survivorship that year would be

$$L' = 0.4^{(1/0.5)} = (0.4)^2 = 0.16.$$

Thus, even modest reductions in growth can have strong effects on survivorship.

Werner and Gilliam (1984) developed a theoretical framework that may allow ontogenetic shifts in predation-related behavior by juvenile fishes to be predicted. The fishes' optimal behavior is that which minimizes the ratio of mortality to growth at each size. Such behavior should differ among sites that present different risks of predation and support different rates of growth. An experiment conducted by Werner et al. (1983a) with largemouth bass as predators and bluegills as prey showed the kind of trade-off small fish seem to make between predation avoidance and growth. This theoretical work stimulated much experimentation (Gilliam and Frazer 1987; Holbrook and Schmidt 1988; McIvor and Odum 1988; Werner and Hall 1988).

19.4.2 Predator Effects on Prey Communities

Size-selective predation by planktivores and its effects on zooplankton community composition are widely documented both descriptively and experimentally (Brooks and Dodson 1965; Wells 1970; Hall et al. 1976). The data from more complex habitats (sediments, littoral vegetation) are less clear. Some studies have shown significant effects of fish on their prey communities (Ball and Hayne 1952; Crowder and Cooper 1982; Gilliam et al. 1989), but others have not (Thorp and Bergey 1981; Allan 1982).

One major problem with assessing the effects of free-ranging predators on their prey is that a predator's stomach contents give no information about prey mortality rates. Predators, particularly top carnivores like the peacock cichlid or Nile perch, can have remarkable effects on community structure, but it has been difficult to quantify predator effects (Edwards et al. 1982; Menge 1982).

Bioenergetics models are proving to be helpful quantification tools for predation assessments (Rice and Cochran 1984). Stewart et al. (1981) used such a model to estimate total consumption of Lake Michigan alewives by stocked salmonids relative to the population of alewives available. They forecast a potential decline in the alewife population and associated changes in the aquatic ecosystem, most of which have subsequently occurred (Kitchell and Crowder 1986).

Bioenergetics models can also be used to examine temporal patterns of predation. Predation over time may be driven by seasonal differences in temperature, prey availability, caloric density of prey, and so on. The concept of predatory inertia (Stewart et al. 1981) is based on the notion that predators do not have their maximal effects on prey until some years after they are stocked or form a strong year-class. In Lake Michigan, lake trout have relatively high inertia; they do not have their major impact on forage fishes until they have been in the lake 4–5 years. Coho salmon are in the lake about 18 months before they have their peak effect. Bioenergetics models produce quantitative estimates of the total effect a predator population has on its prey as well as estimates of the time course of that effect.

19.4.3   Predatory Control of Food Web Dynamics

Fish species of interest to sport or commercial fishermen often occupy the role of apex predator in aquatic food webs. Fishery biologists often attempt to manage fish populations more or less independently from the aquatic ecosystems they occupy (Rigler 1982). Limnologists often attempt to manage lake ecosystems as if the only thing that mattered was the input of nutrients. But nutrient supply does not explain all the variation in the primary productivity of lake ecosystems. Nutrient inputs might control the average productivity at each trophic level, but the actual productivity at any time and level may depend on food web structure and on consumption and predation rates. From a nutrient–productivity point of view, fishes, and top piscivores in particular, are relatively unimportant. Do fishes have important effects on the structure and function of aquatic ecosystems (c.f., Carpenter 1988)?

The concept of cascading trophic interactions (Carpenter et al. 1985) suggests that fishes can play key roles in lake ecosystems. For example, an increase in piscivore biomass (through the production of a strong year-class or through stocking) produces increased predation pressure on forage fishes, resulting in a series of effects that cascade down the trophic structure of the aquatic community. Increased predation reduces planktivore biomass; this allows herbivore biomass (primarily zooplankton) to increase, leading to decreased phytoplankton biomass and clearer water.

Examples of predation effects on species composition, size structure, biomass, and productivity are available for each trophic level (Carpenter et al. 1985, 1988). One of the examples most familiar to fishery biologists is size-selective predation on zooplankton by planktivorous fishes and its effects on the size structure and species composition of the zooplankton (Brooks and Dodson 1965; Galbraith 1967; Hall et al. 1976). Shifts in zooplankton size structure can have profound effects on grazing upon edible phytoplankton as well as on nutrient recycling. The concept of cascading trophic interactions suggests that manipulations at the top of the food chain (the business of fishery managers) may be used to influence chlorophyll concentrations and thus to reduce eutrophication in lakes (the business of many lake managers). Fish also contribute to phosphorous cycling (Kitchell et al. 1979) so a fishery manipulation can directly affect both community structure and nutrient dynamics.

Efforts to extend and validate the idea of cascading trophic interactions by searching the literature for correlations between system components have not succeeded because of data inadequacies and time lags in the expression of effects (Carpenter et al. 1985; McQueen et al. 1986). An alternative validation approach is to experimentally manipulate fishes and measure theoretical expectations against the actual effects on other food web components. Several fish-removal experiments have been conducted with reasonably consistent results: planktivore removal resulted in higher densities of large zooplankton, which imposed higher grazing pressure on the phytoplankton; although grazing-resistant phytoplankters increased, total phytoplankton and chlorophyll *a* decreased, water became clearer, and epilimnetic nutrient concentrations declined (Henrikson et al. 1980; Benndorf et al. 1984; Shapiro and Wright 1984; others in Carpenter 1988). Primary productivity examined in one early study (Henrikson et al. 1980) declined to 10–20% of levels typical of the same lake before the fish were removed.

Current changes in the food web of Lake Michigan suggest that these interactions might extend to the largest aquatic ecosystems (Scavia et al. 1986; Kitchell 1988). Alewives, the major planktivore species, have declined recently to 10–20% of their peak abundance in the lake, perhaps in response to salmonid stocking (Stewart et al. 1981). Alewife reductions have allowed large *Daphnia* species to increase in abundance (Evans and Jude 1986). These cladocerans, with their large filtering capacity, have reduced chlorophyll levels and caused dramatic increases in water clarity.

In early experimental manipulations, all fish were removed, an extreme not of interest to most fishery biologists. However, if fishery managers can manipulate the biomass of piscivores via stocking and fishery regulations, they might be able to exploit linkages in the food web to enhance water quality, as the recent dynamics in Lake Michigan suggest. Shapiro and Wright (1984) called this management approach "biomanipulation." Nutrient loading obviously generates strong "bottom-up" effects that can also influence food web structure, so additional basic research will be necessary before biomanipulation becomes a standard lake management practice. Nonetheless, the concept of cascading trophic interactions links limnology and fishery biology directly and suggests that fishes should no longer be managed independently of the aquatic ecosystems in which they reside. This potentially powerful management tool was derived from basic research on the structure and function of lake ecosystems. It incorporates both modeling to elaborate hypotheses and experimental approaches to test them (Carpenter 1988).

19.5   SPECIES DIVERSITY

19.5.1   Determinants of Diversity in Aquatic Ecosystems

The diversity of species in a particular region is determined by biogeography (colonization and extinction rates), competition, predation, physical disturbance, and other factors. Diversity is usually characterized by two components: the number (richness) and relative abundances (evenness) of species. Many explanations for diversity patterns have been proposed; Pielou (1975), Grassle et al. (1979), and Huston (1979) have reviewed them. Stated hypotheses include the following. Competition may lead to increased diversity if niche breadths narrow (MacArthur and Wilson 1967) or to decreased diversity if species are excluded. Predation may increase diversity by reducing the abundance of the dominant competitor (the "keystone predator hypothesis": Paine 1966) or reduce diversity if it is excessive. Diversity tends to increase with environmental heterogeneity (MacArthur et al. 1966; Levin 1974), and physical disturbance can enhance diversity—at least in space-limited systems—particularly when diversity already is at intermediate levels (Connell 1978).

Huston (1979) noted that many of these hypotheses converge to a general principle: diversity tends to increase if biotic or abiotic processes drive a community away from equilibrium. If disequilibrium factors act at shorter intervals than the typical recovery time of organisms in the community, diversity should increase.

19.5.2 Diversity Indices

Diversity has been measured a variety of ways and several indices have been developed to characterize species richness and evenness (Pielou 1975; Grassle et al. 1979). Diversity indices are calculated to provide some quantitative measure of potential interactions or linkages among community components. They often integrate numbers of species, relative abundances of species, and other factors in one number. In the 1960s, it became popular to calculate diversity indices, particularly in environmental studies, but their ecological meaning has been difficult to interpret (Hurlbert 1971). Use of a particular diversity index depends upon the assumptions required by the index relative to a particular ecological community, so it is not possible to recommend any one index. It seems preferable, though, to use an index for which confidence intervals can be calculated and on which inferential statistical tests can be performed (Pielou 1975). As Pielou (1977) noted, the purpose for calculating indices of diversity is to solve problems, not to create them.

Diversity indices often are useful general indicators of an environmental effect—for example, when similar sites are exposed to different environmental conditions or before and after a single site is subjected to an environmental manipulation. If there seem to be big differences in species diversity, additional studies to explore causal relationships may be justified. In the past, too much effort has been put into calculating indices and trying to explain them as though the indices themselves were worthy of study. Certain indices might be more useful in the context of designed experiments when expected changes in diversity have been hypothesized a priori.

19.5.3 Biogeography and Species Diversity

One determinant of diversity worthy of additional discussion is historical or biogeographic constraint. A species cannot occupy an ecosystem that it has been unable to reach. The geographic separation of many lake and river systems is a barrier to natural colonization. A high degree of faunal endemism, such as occurs in Lakes Baikal and Tanganyika, attests to a system's isolation, as well as to its age (Barbour and Brown 1974).

Magnuson (1976) applied the equilibrium theory of island biogeography (MacArthur and Wilson 1967) to the diversity of fishes in lakes. In theory, the number of terrestrial species on an island, and by analogy the number of fish species in a lake, reaches a stable value that represents an equilibrium between immigration and extinction rates. Based on this theory, small, isolated lakes with simple habitats should have fewer species than larger or more complex lakes or lakes exposed to a source of new species. The effect of humans on all these systems is to accelerate immigration and extinction rates (Barel et al. 1985). The use of exotic species in fishery management contributes to this acceleration, and thereby may increase the uncertainty in future systems management.

19.6 CONCLUSIONS

Contemporary community ecologists need to examine multiple hypotheses and consider interactions among processes that influence community structure and function. Their emphasis recently has been on experimental approaches to these questions (Chapter 1). But ecologists as well as fishery biologists do not have a good record with respect to experimental design (Hurlbert 1984). An experimental approach can be claimed only if the hypotheses are stated a priori and the design allows for appropriately replicated treatments and controls.

Limited resources often prevent fishery ecologists from conducting experiments. The sheer size of many systems that must be managed often precludes controlled experimentation, but multiple alternate hypotheses still must be framed before the systems are manipulated (managed), and the risk of being wrong must be accepted. Too often, major management manipulations are funded, but no resources are allocated to test the basic premise underlying the management objectives. Improved use of comparative approaches and opportunistic natural experiments should increase understanding of aquatic systems. If similar patterns in response to system manipulations occur in several systems, working hypotheses can be created and then compared against the patterns observed in other systems. Finally, managers may have to take a more experimental approach.

Much of the ecological theory available is based on evolutionary biology. Most fisheries scientists study and manage fisheries in ecological time—measured in terms of life cycles and short-term recurrences of natural phenomena—and thus minimize evolutionary factors (Kerr 1980); nevertheless the importance of the evolutionary perspective should not be underestimated (Werner 1980). Theory and experiment in evolutionary ecology have allowed ecologists to ask questions in a different way or to use kinds of analyses (e.g., optimality theory) different from those typically used by fishery biologists. The ecologists' approach is based on their desire to understand the mechanisms underlying community structure and function, and it has already allowed some useful predictions of community dynamics in ecological time. This increased understanding should allow fishery biologists to make better use of the limited resources available to manage fish communities.

19.7 REFERENCES

Allan, J. D. 1982. The effects of reduction in trout density on the invertebrate community of a mountain stream. Ecology 63:1444–1455.

Alm, G. 1946. Reasons for the occurrence of stunted fish populations. Institute of Freshwater Research Drottningholm Reports 25:1–146.

Andrusak, H., and T. G. Northcote. 1971. Segregation between adult cutthroat trout (*Salmo clarki*) and Dolly Varden (*Salvelinus malma*) in small coastal British Columbia lakes. Journal of the Fisheries Research Board of Canada 28:1259–1268.

Backiel, T., and E. D. Le Cren. 1978. Some density relationships for fish population parameters. Pages 279–302 *in* S. D. Gerking, editor. Ecology of freshwater fish production. Blackwell Scientific Publications, London.

Ball, R. C., and D. W. Hayne. 1952. Effects of the removal of the fish population on the fish-food organisms of a lake. Ecology 33:41-48.

Barbour, C. D., and J. H. Brown. 1974. Fish species diversity in lakes. American Naturalist 108:473–488.

Barel, C. D. N., and twelve coauthors. 1985. Destruction of fisheries in Africa's lakes. Nature (London) 315:19–20.

Barlow, G. W. 1974. Contrasts in social behavior between Central American cichlid fishes and coral-reef surgeon fishes. American Zoologist 14:9–34.

Beckman, W. C. 1941. Increased growth of rock bass, *Ambloplites rupestris* (Rafinesque), following reduction in the density of the population. Transactions of the American Fisheries Society 70:143–148.

Benndorf, J., H. Kneschke, N. Kossatz, and E. Penz. 1984. Manipulation of the pelagic food web by stocking with predacious fishes. Internationale Revue der gesamten Hydrobiologie 609:407–428.

Brooks, J. L., and S. Dodson. 1965. Predation, body size, and composition of plankton. Science (Washington, D.C.) 150:28–35.

Brown, W. L., Jr., and E. O. Wilson. 1956. Character displacement. Systematic Zoology 5:49–64.

Carpenter, S. R., editor. 1988. Complex interactions in lake communities. Springer-Verlag, Berlin.

Carpenter, S. R., J. F. Kitchell, and J. R. Hodgson. 1985. Cascading trophic interactions and lake productivity. BioScience 35:634–639.

Chesson, J. 1978. Measuring preference in selective predation. Ecology 59:211–215.

Colwell, R. K., and D. J. Futuyma. 1971. On the measurement of niche breadth and overlap. Ecology 52:567–576.

Colwell, R. K., and D. W. Winkler. 1984. A null model for null models in biogeogrpahy. Pages 344–358 *in* D. R. Strong, Jr., D. Simberloff, L. G. Abele, and A. B. Thistle, editors. Ecological communities: conceptual issues and the evidence. Princeton University Press, Princeton, New Jersey.

Connell, J. H. 1975. Some mechanisms producing structure in natural communities: a model and evidence from field experiments. Pages 460–490 *in* M. L. Cody and J. M. Diamond, editors. Ecology and evolution of communities. Harvard University Press, Cambridge, Massachusetts.

Connell, J. H. 1978. Diversity in tropical rain forests and coral reefs. Science (Washington, D.C.) 199:1302–1310.

Connell, J. H. 1980. Diversity and the coevolution of competitors, or the ghost of competition past. Oikos 35:131–138.

Connell, J. H. 1983. On the prevalence and relative importance of interspecific competition: evidence from field experiments. American Naturalist 122:661–696.

Crowder, L. B. 1984. Character displacement and habitat shift in a native cisco in southeastern Lake Michigan: evidence for competition? Copeia 1984:878–883.

Crowder, L. B. 1985. Optimal foraging and feeding mode shifts in fishes. Environmental Biology of Fishes 12:57–62.

Crowder, L. B. 1986. Ecological and morphological shifts in Lake Michigan fishes: glimpses of the ghost of competition past. Environmental Biology of Fishes 15:147–157.

Crowder, L. B., and W. E. Cooper. 1982. Habitat structural complexity and the interaction between bluegills and their prey. Ecology 63:1802–1813.

Darwin, C. 1859. On the origin of species. John Murray, London.

Diamond, J. 1986. Overview: laboratory experiments, field experiments, and natural experiments. Pages 3–22 in J. Diamond and T. J. Case, editors. Community ecology. Harper and Row, New York.

Drenner, R. W., and S. R. McComas. 1980. The roles of zooplankter escape ability and fish size selectivity in the selective feeding and impact of planktivorous fish. Pages 587–593 in W. C. Kerfoot, editor. Evolution and ecology of zooplankton communities. University Press of New England, Hanover, New Hampshire.

Dunham, A. E., G. R. Smith, and J. N. Taylor. 1979. Evidence for ecological character displacement in western American catastomid fishes. Evolution 33:877–896.

Edwards, D. C., D. O. Conover, and F. Sutter, III. 1982. Mobile predators and the structure of marine intertidal communities. Ecology 63:1175–1180.

Evans, M. S., and D. J. Jude. 1986. Recent shifts in *Daphnia* community structure in southeastern Lake Michigan: a comparison of inshore and offshore regions. Limnology and Oceanography 31:56–67.

Fausch, K. D., and R. J. White. 1981. Competition between brook trout (*Salvelinus fontinalis*) and brown trout (*Salmo trutta*) for positions in a Michigan stream. Canadian Journal of Fisheries and Aquatic Sciences 38:1220–1227.

Forney, J. L. 1977. Reconstruction of yellow perch (*Perca flavescens*) cohorts from the examination of walleye (*Stizostedion vitreum vitreum*) stomachs. Journal of the Fisheries Research Board of Canada 34:925–932.

Galbraith, M. G. 1967. Size-selective predation on *Daphnia* by rainbow trout and yellow perch. Transactions of the American Fisheries Society 96:1–10.

Gilliam, J. F., and D. F. Frazer. 1987. Habitat selection under predation hazard: test of a model with foraging minnows. Ecology 68:1856–1862.

Gilliam, J. F., D. F. Frazer, and A. M. Sabat. 1989. Strong effects of foraging minnows on a stream benthic invertebrate community. Ecology 70:445–452.

Goldman, B., and F. H. Talbot. 1976. Aspects of the ecology of coral reef fishes. Pages 125–154 in O. A. Jones and R. Endean, editors. Biology and geology of coral reefs. Academic Press, New York.

Grassle, J. F., G. P. Patil, W. Smith, and C. Taillie, editors. 1979. Ecological diversity in theory and practice. International Cooperative Publishing House, Fairland, Maryland.

Grossman, G. D., P. B. Moyle, and J. O. Whitaker, Jr. 1982. Stochasticity in structural and functional characteristics of an Indiana stream fish assemblage: a test of community theory. American Naturalist 120:423–454.

Hall, D. J., S. T. Threlkeld, C. W. Burns, and P. H. Crowley. 1976. The size-efficiency hypothesis and the size structure of zooplankton communities. Annual Review of Ecology and Systematics 7:177–208.

Healey, M. C. 1980. Growth and recruitment in experimentally exploited lake whitefish (*Coregonus clupeaformis*) populations. Canadian Journal of Fisheries and Aquatic Sciences 37:255–267.

Henrikson, L., H. G. Nyman, H. G. Oscarson, and J. A. E. Stenson. 1980. Trophic changes, without changes in external nutrient loading. Hydrobiologia 68:257–263.

Herbold, B. 1984. Structure of an Indiana stream fish association: choosing an appropriate model. American Naturalist 124:561–572.

Hixon, M. A. 1980. Competitive interactions between California reef fishes of the genus *Embiotoca*. Ecology 61:918–931.

Holbrook, S. J., and R. J. Schmidt. 1988. The combined effects of predation risk and food reward on patch selection. Ecology 69:125–134.

Holling, C. S. 1978. Adaptive environmental assessment and management. Wiley, New York.

Hurlbert, S. H. 1971. The nonconcept of species diversity: a critique and alternative parameters. Ecology 52:577–586.

Hurlbert, S. H. 1978. The measurement of niche overlap and some relatives. Ecology 59:67–77.

Hurlbert, S. H. 1984. Pseudoreplication and the design of ecological field experiments. Ecological Monographs 54:187–211.

Hurtubia, J. 1973. Trophic diversity measurement in sympatric predatory species. Ecology 54:885–890.

Huston, M. 1979. A general hypothesis of species diversity. American Naturalist 113:81–101.

Ivlev, V. S. 1961. Experimental ecology of the feeding of fishes. Yale University Press, New Haven, Connecticut.

Jacobs, J. 1974. Quantitative measurement of food selection: a modification of the forage ratio and Ivlev's electivity index. Oecologia (Berlin) 14:413–417.

Johnson, F. H. 1977. Responses of walleye (*Stizostedion vitreum vitreum*) and yellow perch (*Perca flavescens*) populations to removal of white sucker (*Catostomus commersoni*) from a Minnesota Lake, 1966. Journal of the Fisheries Research Board of Canada 34:1633–1642.

Kerfoot, W. C., and A. Sih. 1987. Predation: direct and indirect impacts on aquatic communities. University Press of New England, Hanover, New Hampshire.

Kerr, S. R. 1980. Niche theory and fisheries ecology. Transactions of the American Fisheries Society 109:254–257.

Kitchell, J. F., and L. B. Crowder. 1986. Predator–prey interactions in Lake Michigan: model predictions and recent dynamics. Environmental Biology of Fishes 16:205–211.

Kitchell, J. F., M. S. Evans, D. Scavia, and L. B. Crowder. 1988. Regulation of water quality in Lake Michigan: report of the food web workshop. Journal of Great Lakes Research 13:109–114.

Kitchell, J. F., and six coauthors. 1979. Consumer regulation of nutrient cycling. BioScience 29:28–34.

Larkin, P. A. 1956. Interspecific competition and population control in freshwater fish. Journal of the Fisheries Research Board of Canada 13:327–342.

Levin, S. 1974. Dispersion and population interactions. American Naturalist 108:207–228.

Linton, L. R., R. W. Davis, and F. J. Wrona. 1981. Resource utilization indices: an assessment. Journal of Animal Ecology 50:283–292.

Losey, G. S., Jr. 1978. The symbiotic behavior of fishes. Pages 1–31 *in* D. I. Mostofsky, editor. The behavior of fish and other aquatic animals. Academic Press, New York.

MacArthur, R. H., H. Recher, and M. Cody. 1966. On the relation between habitat selection and species diversity. American Naturalist 100:319–332.

MacArthur, R. H., and E. O. Wilson. 1967. The theory of island biogeography. Princeton University Press, Princeton, New Jersey.

Magnuson, J. J. 1976. Managing with exotics—a game of chance. Transactions of the American Fisheries Society 105:1–9.

Matthews, W. J. 1986. Fish faunal structure in an Ozark stream: stability, persistence and a catastrophic flood. Copeia 1986;388–397.

May, R. M. 1984a. An overview: real and apparent patterns in community structure. Pages 3–18 *in* D. R. Strong, Jr., D. Simberloff, L. G. Abele, and A. B. Thistle, editors. Ecological communities: conceptual issues and the evidence. Princeton University Press, Princeton, New Jersey.

May, R. M., editor. 1984b. Exploitation of marine communities. Springer-Verlag, Berlin.

McIvor, C. C., and W. E. Odum. 1988. Food, predation risk, and microhabitat selection in a marsh fish assemblage. Ecology 69:1341–1351.

McKaye, K. R. 1977. Defense of a predator's young by an herbivorous fish: an unusual strategy. American Naturalist 111:301–315.

McQueen, D. J., J. R. Post, and E. L. Mills. 1986. Trophic relationships in freshwater pelagic ecosystems. Canadian Journal of Fisheries and Aquatic Sciences 43:1571–1581.

Menge, B. A. 1982. Reply to a comment by Edwards, Conover and Sutter. Ecology 63:1180–1184.

Mills, E. L., J. L. Confer, and R. C. Ready. 1984. Prey selection by young yellow perch: the influence of capture success, visual acuity, and prey choice. Transactions of the American Fisheries Society 113:579–587.

Mittelbach, G. G. 1981. Foraging efficiency and body size: a study of optimal diet and habitat use by bluegills. Ecology 62:1370–1386.

Mittelbach, G. G. 1984. Predation and resource partitioning in two sunfishes (Centrarchidae). Ecology 65:499–513.

Mittelbach, G. G. 1988. Competition among refuging sunfishes and effects of fish density on littoral zone invertebrates. Ecology 69:614–623.

Moermond, T. C. 1979. Resource partitioning: a dynamic competitive balance. Pages 303–310 in H. Clepper, editor. Predator–prey systems in fisheries management. Sport Fishing Institute, Washington, D.C.

Moyle, P. B., and B. Vondracek. 1985. Persistence and structure of the fish assemblage in a small California stream. Ecology 66:1–13.

Nilsson, N.-A. 1967. Interactive segregation between fish species. Pages 295–314 in S. D. Gerking, editor. The biological basis of freshwater fish production. Wiley, New York.

Nilsson, N.-A., and T. G. Northcote. 1981. Rainbow trout (Salmo gairdneri) and cutthroat trout (S. clarki) interactions in coastal British Columbia lakes. Canadian Journal of Fisheries and Aquatic Sciences 38:1228–1246.

O'Brien, W. J. 1987. Planktivory by freshwater fish: thrust and parry in the pelagia. Pages 13–16 in W. C. Kerfoot and A. Sih. Predation: direct and indirect impacts on aquatic communities. University Press of New England, Hanover, New Hampshire.

Paine, R. T. 1966. Food web complexity and species diversity. American Naturalist 100:65–76.

Petraitis, P. 1979. Likelihood measures of niche breadth and overlap. Ecology 60:703–710.

Pielou, E. C. 1975. Ecological diversity. Wiley-Interscience, New York.

Pielou, E. C. 1977. Mathematical ecology. Wiley-Interscience, New York.

Platt, J. R. 1964. Strong inference. Science (Washington, D.C.) 146:346–353.

Power, M. E. 1987. Predator avoidance by grazing fishes in temperate and tropical streams: importance of stream depth and prey size. Pages 333–352 in W. C. Kerfoot and A. Sih, editors. Predation: direct and indirect impacts on aquatic communities. University Press of New England, Hanover, New Hampshire.

Rahel, F. J., J. D. Lyons, and P. A. Cochran. 1984. Stochastic or deterministic regulation of assemblage structure? It may depend on how the assemblage is defined. American Naturalist 124:583–589.

Rice J. A., and P. A. Cochran. 1984. Independent evaluation of a bioenergetics model for largemouth bass. Ecology 65:732–739.

Ricklefs, R. E., and M. Lau. 1980. Bias and dispersion of overlap indices: results of some Monte Carlo simulations. Ecology 61:1019–1024.

Rigler, F. H. 1982. The relation between fisheries mangement and limnology. Transactions of the American Fisheries Society 111:121–132.

Ross, S. T. 1986. Resource partitioning in fish assemblages: a review of field studies. Copeia 1986:352–387.

Sale, P. F. 1977. Maintenance of high diversity in coral reef fish communities. American Naturalist 111:337–359.

Sale, P. F. 1984. The structure of communities of fish on coral reefs and the merit of a hypothesis-testing, manipulative approach to ecology. Pages 478–490 in D. R. Strong, Jr., D. Simberloff, L. G. Abele, and A. B. Thistle, editors. Ecological communities: conceptual issues and the evidence. Princeton University Press, Princeton, New Jersey.

Scavia, D., G. L. Fahnenstiel, M. S. Evans, D. J. Jude, and J. T. Lehman. 1986. Influence of salmonid predation and weather on long-term water quality trends in Lake Michigan. Canadian Journal of Fisheries and Aquatic Sciences 43:435–443.

Schlosser, I. J. 1982. Fish community structure and function along the habitat gradients in a headwater stream. Ecological Monographs 52:395–414.

Schoener, T. W. 1970. Non-synchronous spatial overlap of lizards in patchy habitats. Ecology 51:408–418.

Schoener, T. W. 1974. Resource partitioning in ecological communities. Science (Washington, D.C.) 185:27–39.

Schoener, T. W. 1983. Field experiments on interspecific competition. American Naturalist 122:240–285.

Schoener, T. W. 1986. Resource partitioning. Pages 91–126 *in* J. Kikkawa and D. J. Anderson, editors. Community ecology: pattern and process. Blackwell Scientific Publications, London.

Shapiro, J. and D. I. Wright. 1984. Lake restoration by biomanipulation. Freshwater Biology 14:371–383.

Sih, A. 1987. Predators and prey lifestyles: an evolutionary and ecological overview. Pages 203–224 *in* W. C. Kerfoot and A. Sih, editors. Predation: direct and indirect impacts on aquatic communities. University Press of New England, Hanover, New Hampshire.

Sih, A., P. Crowley, M. McPeek, J. Petranka, and K. Strohmeier. 1985. Predation, competition, and prey communities: a review of field experiments. Annual Review of Ecology and Systematics 16:269–312.

Smith, C. L., and J. C. Tyler. 1973. Population ecology of a Bahamian suprabenthic shorefish assemblage. American Museum Novitates 2528:1–38.

Smith, S. H. 1972. Factors in the ecologic succession of oligotrophic fish communities in the Laurentian Great Lakes. Journal of the Fisheries Research Board of Canada 29:717–730.

Steele, J., and eight coauthors. 1980. Fisheries ecology: some constraints that impede our understanding. National Academy of Sciences, Ocean Science Board, Washington, D.C.

Stein, R. A. 1979. Behavioral response of prey to fish predators. Pages 343–354 *in* H. Clepper, editor. Predator–prey systems in fisheries management. Sport Fishing Institute, Washington, D.C.

Stewart, D. J., J. F. Kitchell, and L. B. Crowder. 1981. Forage fishes and their salmonid predators in Lake Michigan. Transactions of the American Fisheries Society 110:751–763.

Strauss, R. E. 1979. Reliability estimates for Ivlev's electivity index, the forage ratio, and a proposed linear index of food selection. Transactions of the American Fisheries Society 108:344–352.

Strauss, R. E. 1982. Influence of replicated subsamples and subsample heterogeneity on the linear index of food selection. Transactions of the American Fisheries Society 111:517–522.

Strong, D. R., D. Simberloff, L. G. Abele, and A. B. Thistle. 1984. Ecological communities: conceptual issues and the evidence. Princeton University Press, Princeton, New Jersey.

Svärdson, G. 1976. Interspecific population dominance in fish communities of Scandinavian lakes. Institute of Freshwater Research Drottningholm Report 55:144–171.

Thorp, J. H., and E. A. Bergey. 1981. Field experiments on responses of a freshwater, benthic macroinvertebrate community to vertebrate predators. Ecology 62:365–375.

Toneys, M. L., and D. W. Coble. 1979. Size-related, first winter mortality of freshwater fishes. Transactions of the American Fisheries Society 108:415–419.

Tonn, W. M. 1985. Density compensation in *Umbra–Perca* fish assemblages in northern Wisconsin lakes. Ecology 66:415–429.

Tonn, W. M., J. J. Magnuson, and A. M. Forbes. 1983. Community analysis in fishery management: an application with northern Wisconsin lakes. Transactions of the American Fisheries Society 112:368–377.

Vanderploeg, H. A., and D. Scavia. 1979. Two electivity indices for feeding with special reference to zooplankton grazing. Journal of the Fisheries Research Board of Canada 36:362–365.

Wallace, R. K. 1981. An assessment of diet-overlap indexes. Transactions of the American Fisheries Society 110:72–76.

Wells, L. 1970. Effects of alewife predation on zooplankton populations in Lake Michigan. Limnology and Oceanography 14:556–565.

Werner, E. E. 1980. Niche theory in fisheries ecology. Transactions of the American Fisheries Society 109;257–260.

Werner, E. E., and J. F. Gilliam. 1984. The ontogenetic niche and species interactions in size-structured populations. Annual Review of Ecology and Systematics 15:393–425.

Werner, E. E., J. F. Gilliam, D. J. Hall, and G. G. Mittelbach. 1983a. An experimental test of the effects of predation risk on habitat use in fish. Ecology 64:1540–1548.

Werner, E. E., and D. J. Hall. 1974. Optimal foraging and the size selection of prey by the bluegill sunfish. (*Lepomis macrochirus*). Ecology 55:1042–1052.

Werner, E. E., and D. J. Hall. 1976. Niche shifts in sunfishes: experimental evidnce and significance. Science (Washington, D.C.) 191:404–406.

Werner, E. E., and D. J. Hall. 1979. Foraging efficiency and habitat switching in competing sunfishes. Ecology 60:256–264

Werner, E. E., and D. J. Hall. 1988. Ontogenetic habitat shifts in bluegill: the foraging rate–predation risk trade-off. Ecology 69:1352–1366.

Werner, E. E., G. G. Mittelbach, D. J. Hall, and J. F. Gilliam. 1983b. Experimental tests of optimal habitat use in fish: the role of relative habitat profitability. Ecology 64:1525–1539.

Wiens, J. A. 1977. On competition and variable environments. American Scientist 65:590–597.

Yant, P. R., J. R. Karr, and P. L. Angermeier. 1984. Stochasticity in stream fish communities: an alternative interpretation. American Naturalist 124:573–582.

Zaret, T. M., and R. T. Paine. 1973. Species introduction in a tropical lake. Science (Washington, D.C.) 182:449–455.

Chapter 20

Maintaining Fishes for Research and Teaching

ROBERT R. STICKNEY AND CHRISTOPHER C. KOHLER

20.1 INTRODUCTION

Laboratory research and controlled field experiments with live fishes necessitate the use of culture systems to maintain the animals before, during, and between experimental trials. Experiments often require specialized apparatus and we have not attempted to describe in detail the array of experimental fish-holding chambers that have been used. Instead, our purpose is to provide information about the general types of water systems that have been successfully employed and about other factors that must be taken into account when fish are maintained in captivity.

It is very important in fish culture to minimize stress on the animals. Stressed fish may behave abnormally and are much more susceptible to diseases and parasites than fish which are held under optimum conditions. Any behavioral, disease-related, or physiological manifestation of stress can render a group of fish useless for controlled experiments. Maintenance of fish under optimum conditions helps ensure that the responses seen during an experiment reflect the treatments and are not artifacts of holding stress. Some of the principal causes of stress in fish are handling, mechanical damage, poor water quality, dietary imbalances, diseases, parasitism, and extremes of or abnormal changes in light and temperature (see Chapter 14 and Simco et al. 1986). Culture systems should be designed and managed for the particular species being held.

Regulations governing the maintenance of laboratory animals have been promulgated in some nations, including the USA. The main purpose of such regulations is to provide humane treatment of laboratory animals. At least some U.S. government agencies apply the same doctrine to fishes that they do to higher vertebrates, requiring that certain standards be met in the care and handling of laboratory animals. Regardless of the circumstances and applicable governmental regulations, ethics dictate that fishes maintained for research or teaching purposes should be treated humanely.

20.2 WATER SUPPLY

Before a fish culture system is designed, the source, volume, and cost of water supplies must be considered. The type of culture system employed will depend, at least in part, on the characteristics of the water that will fill the system. Once the water system has been selected, the needs and methods for control of water quality can be determined. The volume that can be delivered to a system depends not only on total available supply, but also on pump performance, pipe size, water pressure, and other factors. In the case of wells, there may be limits on what a well can continuously draw from a given water table, and test pumping is required to determine the sustained capacity of a given well.

Fresh and salt water can be obtained from surface sources (e.g., lakes, reservoirs, streams, bays, oceans) or from appropriately placed wells. Municipal water—water treated to make it safe for human consumption—can also be used. No matter what the source, ample water for the needs of the culture facility is a basic requirement. For pond facilities, unless seepage is abnormally high, at least 100 L/min per surface hectare should be available to fill the ponds and replace losses to evaporation and seepage. The basic requirement for single-pass, flow-through systems is sufficient water for two turnovers (replacements) each hour. A completely closed recirculation system requires little additional water once the system is filled. Partial recirculation, which is common with such systems, requires sufficient new water for at least two turnovers per hour, less the amount of recirculated flow.

20.2.1 Surface Water

Surface water supplies may be abundant, but are less desirable than well water for fish maintenance. Surface waters of otherwise suitable quality are almost invariably inhabited by fish, predaceous insects and their larvae, fouling organisms, disease organisms, and parasites. Before it is introduced into culture chambers, surface water should be passed through a fine-mesh net or screen, then filtered. Rotating screens, rapid sand filters, or gravel filters can be used to remove large particles. When necessary, pressure sand filters or cartridge filters may be used to extract fine particulates. Following filtration, the water may be exposed to ultraviolet (UV) radiation or ozone, or both, to control pathogens (Section 20.3.4).

Supply pipes can be fouled by various types of organisms, sediments, and chemical precipitates when surface supplies of either fresh or saline water are used. Bryozoans, sponges, and mollusks are only a few of the fouling organisms. When sediment-laden water flows slowly or intermittently through supply lines, the sediment may settle within the pipes and restrict their diameters. Calcium deposits are common when fresh waters are hard and alkaline, and iron often precipitates from waters with high concentrations of that element.

Dual plumbing from the water source to at least the first screening or filtration device is recommended for removal of fouling organisms. Water to the culture system can be flowed through one set of pipes and left dormant in the other; oxygen will become depleted in the nonflowing water, killing the fouling organisms. In seawater systems, the introduction of fresh (nonsaline) water into the dormant line will hasten mortality of fouling organisms. Chlorine solutions can also be flushed through affected supply lines to kill the offending organisms. In any case, dead and decaying organic matter should be completely flushed from the pipes and properly disposed of before that part of the system is allowed to supply the culture system. Chlorine and other chemicals used to destroy fouling organisms should not be allowed to come in contact with the species being cultured.

Sediments can be removed from pipes by high-pressure pumping. Chemical deposits are a more serious problem. If it is not possible or feasible to redissolve

Figure 20.1 Paddlewheel aerators, operated electrically, hydraulically, or (as here) from the power takeoff of a tractor, are a popular means to replenish dissolved oxygen in ponds. (Photograph by Bruce L. Tetzlaff.)

precipitates with an acid flush, periodic replacement of the affected plumbing may be necessary.

20.2.2 Well Water

Well water is generally free of living organisms, but it still may have to be treated before it can be used in a fish culture system. Many wells produce water devoid of dissolved oxygen. Others contain high concentrations of carbon dioxide (CO_2), hydrogen sulfide (H_2S), or iron in the form of ferrous bicarbonate [$Fe(HCO_3)_2$]. Aeration can provide oxygen and will drive off CO_2 and H_2S.

Aeration causes reduced iron dissolved in the water to oxidize and precipitate as ferric hydroxide [$Fe(OH)_3$]. In ponds, ferric hydroxide is usually allowed to settle; total iron concentrations are generally on the order of 0.05 to 0.2 mg/L in natural waters (Boyd 1979). For aquaria, tanks, and raceways, it is sometimes necessary to remove the ferric hydroxide before the water is used. If maintenance of groundwater temperature is not a major consideration, well water can be flowed over the ground prior to use; the precipitated iron will adhere to soil particles and vegetation if the flow is sufficiently slow. When the temperature in the culture system must be similar to that of the well water, the water can be run through an aeration chamber with no more than a 30-min residence time, then through a rapid sand filter; this technique is most commonly used with aquarium, tank, and linear raceway culture systems. If allowed to remain in open or recirculated-water systems, ferric hydroxide precipitate will cloud the water and settle on tank surfaces and the inside of pipes. Pipes may become blocked as the iron accumulates.

Water can be aerated by mechanically agitating it, spraying it into the air, running it over splashboards, or passing it through a simple aeration tower. Paddlewheel aerators (Figure 20.1) are among the devices that can be used for emergency aeration in ponds.

20.2.3 Municipal Water

Municipal water supplies are often chlorinated and cannot be used directly because most fishes are highly sensitive to both chlorine and chloramines.

Chlorine is carried off when water is left standing with aeration for 24 h, but this procedure is not often practical. Chlorine can also be removed by activated charcoal. Charcoal filters require reactivation, usually by replacement of the activated charcoal. The rate at which adsorption sites fill depends on the chlorine level in the water and the rate at which water flows through the filter. The life of a charcoal filter increases as filter size increases and water flow decreases. Many systems have been designed to operate for several months or even a year between charcoal replacements. Whatever the design life of filters, the charcoal should be replaced whenever chlorine appears in water samples, which should be taken frequently. Simple colorimetric tests for chlorine are available for such purposes (Boyd 1979).

Neither aeration nor charcoal filtration completely removes chloramines; however, sodium thiosulfate and ferrous salts remove both chlorine and chloramines from water (Coventry et al. 1935). Commercial systems have been developed that monitor the water and continually add the appropriate amounts of chemical to remove the chlorine or chloramines.

Municipal water is commonly used for fish maintenance when modest amounts of water are needed continuously or when recirculating-water systems are in use. The cost of municipal water is often prohibitive for large raceway and pond systems.

20.2.4 Salt water

Salt water, even if it contains only a few parts per thousand salinity, is highly corrosive to metals. Polyvinyl chloride (PVC) plumbing is widely recommended for all types of culture systems, because it contains no toxic trace metals, but it is particularly important to use PVC or similar plastic materials in culture systems which use saline water. Polyvinyl chloride is strong, light weight, easy to work with, and readily reconfigured when modifications in a water system are desired. The pipe can be simply cut with a hand saw and the new configuration constructed with standard fittings that are glued into place.

Pumps supplying salt water should be run continuously if the impeller and pump head are constructed of metal or those parts will quickly deteriorate and malfunction. Nonmetallic impellers and pump heads are available and are recommended for use in saltwater systems.

Fouling problems in salt water can be reduced or eliminated if the water is taken from a well. Saline wells can be drilled in the sediments below or adjacent to surface saltwater bodies as well as in areas having saltwater aquifers.

Various synthetic sea salts are available commercially. When mixed with fresh water, they form solutions with proportions of major ions like those of natural seawater. Synthetic seawater is widely used to maintain marine fishes and can also be used to maintain and produce invertebrates and marine macrophytes and algae. Because synthetic sea salts are expensive, their use is largely restricted to static and recirculating-water systems. Some investigators have formulated their own sea-salt mixtures, which permits them to buy chemicals in bulk. A general-purpose seawater medium for the culture of marine plants and animals was described by Spotte (1979). Such solutions can be diluted to any desired salinity; the relative proportions of ingredients remain fixed.

20.3   HOLDING AND CULTURE SYSTEMS

Fish culturists think in terms of systems that are more or less "intensive," intensity increasing with the level of management and the production per unit area or volume. The least intensive (most extensive) systems are ponds in which the fish are stocked at low density and management is limited or absent. The most intensive are closely controlled tank or raceway systems that support annual productions of several hundred kilograms per square meter. Fish-holding facilities for teaching and research typically lie between these extremes. Glass aquaria or circular fiberglass tanks are commonly used for laboratory studies. When it is necessary to hold large numbers of fish, ponds or raceways may be the culture system of choice.

Water in systems may be static or flowing. Static-water systems, in general, support much lower biomasses of fish than flowing systems. Fish use oxygen and produce wastes, and water quality impairment occurs at much lower fish densities in static than in flowing water. Any system in which fish can be confined and concentrated—this includes flowing-water raceways and tanks and static-water aquaria and cages—makes it easier to feed fish, to train fish to take prepared feeds, and to harvest and sort fish. Systems in which fish can be readily seen—raceways, tanks, aquaria—facilitate recognition of disease outbreaks, which usually are first manifested by changes in behavior and body coloration. Recirculating-water systems and static-water aquaria have the additional advantage over flow-through systems in that optimum temperature can be maintained without excessive energy input (Lewis et al. 1981).

Various types of holding and culture systems are described in this section. Space does not allow complete treatment of any of these systems, so the reader is directed to such sources as Spotte (1970, 1979), Wheaton (1977), Stickney (1979), and Piper et al. (1982).

20.3.1   Static Aquaria

Perhaps the simplest fish-holding system, at least in terms of establishment, is the static aquarium: an aquarium in which water is not continuously added from an external source. Most modern aquaria are of all-glass construction with decorative rims around the top and bottom that add strength and protect the user from sharp glass edges. The pieces of glass, five for each rectangular aquarium, are held together with silicon cement. Such tanks are functional, nontoxic, and relatively inexpensive.

Static aquaria are normally fitted with some type of filter system to remove particulate matter and detoxify metabolites. This may be (1) a glass wool and activated charcoal filter within or outside the aquarium, (2) a subgravel filter at the bottom of the aquarium, or (3) a combination of the two. Both glass wool filters and subgravel filters commonly operate with airlifts, which pull water through the filter, maintain circulation in the aquarium, and aerate the water (Figure 20.2). Glass wool filters mechanically remove particulate matter; undergravel filters draw it into a space at the bottom of the aquarium. In either case, bacterial activity within the filters decomposes the organic particulates. In addition, ammonia is bacteriologically detoxified, as explained in Section 20.3.4. Glass wool and charcoal filters should be used when no substrate such as sand or gravel is present in the aquarium. If a substrate is used, the subgravel type of filter may be

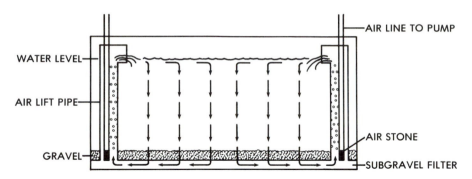

Figure 20.2 Airlifts pull water through the gravel in an aquarium fitted with a subgravel filter (arrows) and return oxygenated water to the main body of the aquarium.

preferable because it sequesters particulates more efficiently than glass wool filters. However, undergravel filters are prone to clogging and may have to be backflushed frequently.

Static aquaria are not generally recommended for replicated studies because water quality can vary considerably among them, particularly when fish numbers or biomasses are high. Such units have somewhat limited carrying capacities and may require water exchanges every few days or weeks and complete draining and cleaning after several weeks or months. The standard display or home aquarium, which typically contains low biomass, may be maintained in satisfactory condition for months or even years with only the addition of water to replace evaporative losses and food to maintain the fish. If such a system has a glass wool and charcoal filtration system, the filter medium should be changed every few weeks. Gross discoloration of the medium and high concentrations of particulate matter indicate when a change is required.

20.3.2 Flow-Through Aquaria

Aquaria can be provided with inflow plumbing and drains, thereby allowing water to flow through them intermittently or continuously. The incoming water may be discarded, or it may be recycled (Section 20.3.4). Supplemental aeration is usually provided.

Inflowing water can be passed through faucets fitted with inexpensive constant-flow regulators; various sizes of regulators allow flows of a few milliliters to several liters per minute. Flows to individual tanks can be shut off at the faucets when tanks are cleaned, fish are handled, or aquariums stand idle. Water pipes and fittings should be schedule-40 or schedule-80 PVC; the latter withstands higher temperatures and pressures. Drains may be thin-walled PVC unless they are subject to freezing, when such pipe tends to crack. Valves may be of PVC or brass, except as previously noted for seawater systems.

20.3.3 Raceways

A raceway is any culture chamber through which water flows. By that definition, a flow-through aquarium is a small raceway. Raceways may be linear, water entering one end and exiting the other, or they may be circular. Circular raceways have been constructed of concrete, metal, fiberglass, and various types

Figure 20.3 In this circular fiberglass tank, a box frame with fine-mesh screening has been placed around the standpipe. The large area of screening allows water to be exchanged rapidly in the tank without creating currents that might trap larval fish. The aeration system was turned off during photography. (Photograph by Bruce L. Tetzlaff.)

of plastic. Diameters of effective circular raceways have ranged from less than 1 m to at least 10 m.

Turnover time in raceways (time required to exchange one volume of water) may vary from a few minutes to a few hours according to the species and biomass of fish in the system. As a general rule, water flow should be sufficient to provide acceptable water quality. As fish grow, biomass increases, and the carrying capacity of the system may eventually be exceeded. Various techniques for determining optimum or maximum densities in raceway systems have been developed; these take into consideration flow rate, feeding rate, oxygen requirements, and other factors. For detailed descriptions of the approaches presently in use, see Piper et al. (1982) and Westers (1986).

When early life stages of fish are maintained, currents that would sweep the fish into screens surrounding the drain must be avoided. Specialized drains with screens of large surface area are required (Figure 20.3). Screen meshes must be small enough to prevent loss of the fish, some of which hatch at lengths of only a few millimeters and diameters much less than a millimeter. Small-mesh screens are subject to clogging by food particles and other debris, leading to eventual overflow of the tank and loss of fish. The advantage of a large screen area is that, for any rate of water exchange, the flow per unit area of screen decreases as the screen area increases. Flow through the screen must not be stronger than the fish can withstand, or they may become trapped against the screen and die.

Large numbers of larval fish can be safely held in properly designed tank systems. Their biomass is low, but their metabolic rates, and those of the live prey typically used to support them, are high, so water must be turned over constantly if its quality is to remain acceptable. As the fish grow and swim more strongly, the screen size around the drain and flow rates through it may be increased. In most systems, carrying capacity will eventually be reached, and fish density will have to be reduced if water quality is to be maintained.

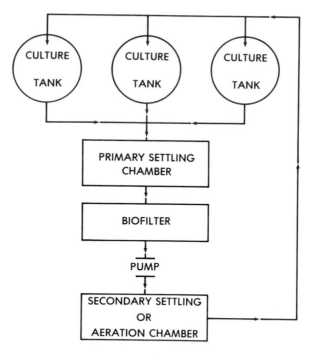

Figure 20.4 Diagrammatic arrangement of the basic components in a water recirculation system.

20.3.4 Recirculating-Water Systems

Holding facilities supplied with recirculated water and incorporating biofiltration are often the best option for maintaining fishes. Such systems can, when properly managed, provide an excellent environment for relatively large numbers of fish when water or space are restricted. Their limitations include cost, in terms of both initial investment and operation, and the dangers inherent in mechanical failure. Because of the potential for mechanical failure, emergency power sources, as well as backup pumps and other redundancies, are integral components of recirculating-water systems.

A generalized recirculating-water system is presented in Figure 20.4. The basic features have been described by Burrows and Combs (1968), Liao and Mayo (1974), Meade (1974), Spotte (1979), Stickney (1979), and Lewis et al. (1981), among others. Water carries dissolved metabolites and particulate matter from each culture chamber out through the standpipe drain (which also serves to regulate water depth) and drains by gravity to a primary settling basin, where much of the particulate matter is removed. The water then passes through a biofilter, where dissolved nitrogenous wastes (primarily ammonia) are converted to less toxic chemicals by bacteria growing on the biofilter medium. The clarified water is then pumped to a head tank, wherein secondary settling may occur and the water may be aerated before it flows by gravity back to the culture tanks. This basic scheme can be modified in various ways: chambers can be added or combined, for example, or the pump can be placed at locations other than that shown in Figure 20.4. Constant replacement of some of the water within such a

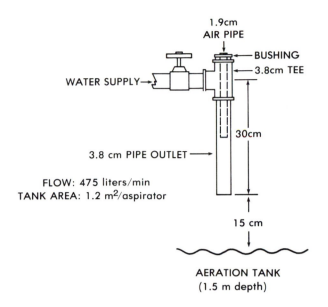

1.9cm
AIR PIPE

BUSHING

3.8cm TEE

WATER SUPPLY→

30cm

3.8 cm PIPE OUTLET →

FLOW: 475 liters/min
TANK AREA: 1.2 m²/aspirator

15 cm

AERATION TANK
(1.5 m depth)

Figure 20.5 Diagram of an aspirator used to efficiently aerate water in intensive culture systems (after Burrows and Combs 1968).

system (which then is called a partial-recirculation system) can help maintain good water quality, if necessary.

In general, the water must be oxygenated before it enters the biofilter and again before it returns to the fish-holding chambers (Lewis 1981). Aeration can be provided by several mechanical means (Section 20.4.2); the aspirator system developed by Burrows and Combs (1968) is particularly well suited for recirculating-water systems. In this aspirator, water flows through the outer of two concentric pipes (Figure 20.5). Venturi suction developed by the water flow draws atmospheric air into the inner pipe. The air–water mixture then plunges into a reservoir, with the result that 90–100% oxygen saturation occurs.

Settling chambers and a biofilter are essential features of a recirculating-water system when large numbers of fish are maintained. In the settling chambers, solids are removed from suspension either by gravity or mechanically. The major task performed by the biofilter is nitrification of the ammonia excreted by the kidneys and gills of fishes to nitrate (see Section 20.4.3). Species of the ubiquitous genera of aerobic, autotrophic bacteria *Nitrosomonas* and *Nitrobacter* carry out biological nitrification. *Nitrosomonas* spp. oxidize ammonia to nitrite; and *Nitrobacter* spp. carry the reaction from nitrite to nitrate. The species of these bacteria may differ among environments, but it can be generally assumed that the genera indicated perform the requisite functions. Meade (1974) calculated that between 4.0 and 4.6 g of oxygen are required for complete oxidation of 1.0 g of ammonia-nitrogen. Thus, biological nitrification only occurs in an oxygen-rich environment.

Several nontoxic materials have been successfully employed as biofilter media. Sand and gravel have been the most frequently used media, but both are subject to clogging and channelization and must be backflushed frequently to avoid anaerobic conditions. Inert materials such as styrofoam beads and cut-up pieces of PVC pipe are good substrates, as are several products specifically made for use in waste treatment plants.

Because nitrate and nitrite are released by bacteria as nitrous and nitric acids, the water must be well buffered to prevent major reductions in pH. Crushed limestone or oyster shell in the biofilter generally keeps pH near the desirable levels of 7.0 in freshwater and 8.0 in marine systems (Stickney 1979).

Although biofilter designs vary considerably, each can be basically placed into one of three groups: trickling, submerged, and revolving plate. In a trickling biofilter, water enters from the top and is allowed to pass by gravity through the filter at a rate that keeps the filter continuously moist. In a submerged biofilter, the filter medium is immersed in water. Revolving-plate or biodisc filters move the medium through the water. Rotating biofilter media are made up of numerous circular discs placed on an axle and set in a trough; half of each disc is submerged and the other half is exposed to the atmosphere. The discs, which support bacterial growth, are slowly rotated by mechanical means. Because the discs are out of the water half the time, aeration is ensured. Biofilters have been described in more detail by Wheaton (1977) and Stickney (1979).

The time that the culture water is exposed to nitrifying bacteria is determined by the surface area of the medium, the amount of void space in the medium, retention time, flow rate, and filter depth (Lewis et al. 1981).

The biofilter should be activated before fish are introduced into a recirculation-water system. Activation ensures that sufficient nitrifying bacteria will be present to handle the wastes later produced by the fish (Meade 1974). Activation can be achieved by inoculating the biofilter with garden soil. Commercial bacterial mixtures are also available for both freshwater and saltwater systems.

Ammonia can be removed from freshwater recirculation systems by passing the water through an ion exchange column or a column of natural zeolite, usually clinoptilolite. Clinoptilolite has a particularly good affinity for ammonia—90–97% reductions have been reported (Piper et al. 1982)—and it is less expensive than ion exchange resins. It may be advisable to use clinoptilolite as a support or backup system to standard biofiltration in some instances.

Ozone (O_3) generators have been used in aquaculture to oxidize organic matter and kill bacteria in the circulating water (Stickney 1979). However, ozone is also highly toxic to fish (Paller and Heidinger 1979) and to nitrifying bacteria, so ozonated water must be held long enough for the ozone to convert back to molecular oxygen before the water proceeds through the system. The half-life of ozone is about 15 min (Layton 1972). Sander and Rosenthal (1975) recommended that ozonated water be passed through an activated charcoal filter to remove the ozone.

Ultraviolet light is an effective bactericidal treatment that can be readily incorporated into a water reuse system. The UV lamps can be suspended over culture system components (except the biofilter) or submerged in the water, or water can be passed through pipes surrounded by UV lamps. Both commercial and home-made UV sterilization systems are widely employed by fish culturists. Details on UV and ozone treatment can be found in Wheaton (1977), Spotte (1979), and Dupree (1981). Both ozone and UV light treatments have been used in flow-through systems as well as in recirculation systems.

20.3.5 Ponds

Research with fish can be carried out in ponds, though raceways and aquaria are more commonly used for controlled, replicated experiments. Ponds are useful for breeding and holding various species used in research and teaching.

Before ponds are constructed, all vegetation should be removed from the area. If organic matter is incorporated in the overturned soils used to build the pond levees, its decay will weaken the levees and cause them to fail later.

Aquacultural ponds typically are rectangular. They should be constructed in soil that contains at least 25% clay. If soil of that quality is not available, it may be necessary to haul in clay to line the ponds; bentonite is a clay mineral often used for this purpose. Alternatively, sheets of polybutylene, polypropylene, or some other impervious plastic may be placed on the pond bottom. Sealing leaky ponds can be expensive and is not always foolproof.

The inflow plumbing to each pond should allow the pond to be filled with water within a few days. Drain lines should be large enough to allow large ponds to be drained within 48–72 h and ponds of 0.2 hectares or less to be emptied within a few hours.

Inflow lines may enter a pond almost anywhere. Some culturists prefer to have water enter the end opposite the drain so the pond can be turned into a slow raceway if water quality deteriorates. Others like to flow water in at the drain end so high water quality can be maintained when fish are concentrated near the drain for harvest. Perhaps the best arrangement is to have inflow water available at both ends of the pond.

Figure 20.6 Concrete drain structure of a pond, with access stairway, catch basin, standpipe for control of water level, and inflow line mounted to allow new water to flow directly onto fish in the catch basin. (Photograph by Robert R. Stickney.)

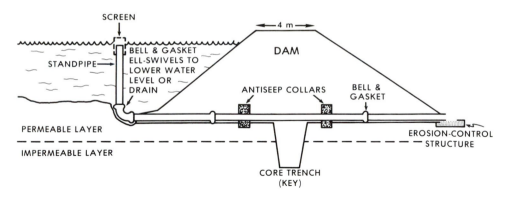

Figure 20.7 Cross section of a typical pond levee. Broad levees allow access by trucks and tractors. The steeper the levee, the more susceptible it is to erosion and the more difficult to mow.

Drains and the structures associated with them range in sophistication from simple standpipes that can be tilted to control water level to concrete structures containing catch basins and even stairways to help personnel reach the pond (Figure 20.6). Effluent from ponds may discharge into open ditches or be piped to a receiving water body or sanitary sewage system. Concrete, tile, PVC, and metal drain lines are equally effective.

As pond size increases, so does the complexity associated with management. For most research and teaching purposes, ponds of 0.05–0.10 hectares are adequate. A typical pond is 1.5–2.0 m in maximum depth. In regions where thick winter ice cover inhibits diffusion of atmospheric oxygen into the water, pond depth may have to reach 3.0 m so the water volume will be great enough to sustain fish through an extended period of no oxygen transfer. Pond bottoms should have about a 1% slope toward the drain. Research results from such ponds can be extrapolated to larger ponds and small lakes. The use of relatively small ponds reduces the expense of buying and maintaining fish.

Levees should be constructed with side slopes of 1:2 or 1:3; that is, for every 2 or 3 m of levee width, there is a 1-m increase in height (Figure 20.7). Steeper slopes are easily eroded and difficult to mow, and they make access to the pond by personnel treacherous. More gradual slopes leave large areas of shallow water that may become choked with aquatic vegetation. At least one levee of each pond should allow access by truck, and all levees should be wide enough to mow with a tractor.

20.3.6 Cages

Cages can be used to replicate treatments within a water body. They are useful when too few ponds or raceways are available for an experiment or when the water body (lake, river, estuary) is too large to permit easy recapture of experimental fish. Details of cage design and application were provided by Stickney (1979) and Brown (1983); the basic concepts are outlined below.

The typical research cage is rectangular or circular. Cages are generally constructed of welded wire (usually vinyl-coated), plastic, or seine netting stretched over a frame. Frames may be constructed of PVC pipe or other types of plastic, metal, bamboo, or wood. The netting covering the frame should be smooth (e.g., knotless seine material) so fish will not be abraded when they contact the walls of the cage. Mesh size should be as large as possible to both retain the fish and allow water to circulate freely through the cage. Very young fish may be retained in cages constructed of nylon plankton netting or window screen. The smaller the meshes, the more readily they become clogged, but even large meshes become occluded when fouling organisms are abundant.

Flotation should be provided to keep the tops of the cages slightly above the water surface. A collar of small-mesh netting around the upper few centimeters of cages will retain floating feed until fish consume the ration.

As with any aquacultural system, the density of fish that can be stocked into cages depends strongly on the frequency of water exchanges. Thus, cages placed in streams, rivers, or other sites of strong currents typically can have higher fish densities than cages in ponds or lakes. In any environment, mesh clogging reduces the water exchange rate in cages and thereby reduces the sustainable fish density.

20.4 WATER QUALITY

Virtually all fish-holding facilities differ with respect to water quality, and the amount of effort and expense required to maintain water quality varies from one aquatic laboratory to the next. Thousands of variables contribute to water quality, but only a few are routinely measured by fish culturists. If the fish have not been exposed to contaminants such as heavy metals, biocides, or toxic wastes, they usually can survive as long as certain water quality variables are maintained within acceptable ranges. Some of the more important water quality variables are discussed below. For a more complete treatment of the subject that emphasizes fish production ponds, see Boyd (1979). Seawater analysis has been addressed by Strickland and Parsons (1968).

20.4.1 Temperature

Depending upon the type of culture system, temperature control may or may not be practical or even feasible. Temperature control is not normally attempted in ponds unless geothermal water or heated effluent from a power plant is readily available at little or no cost. Temperature control is more frequently used in indoor culture systems, where it is achieved by adjustments of room temperature or by placement of heaters or chillers in the culture system (Huguenin 1976; Stickney and Person 1985).

Cultured fish generally survive a relatively wide range of environmental temperatures, though optimum growth and, to a degree, reduced susceptibility to diseases and parasites occur over a somewhat narrower range. Coldwater fishes such as trout and salmon can be found at temperatures ranging from just above freezing to somewhat above 20°C (Piper et al. 1982). Some warmwater fishes like channel catfish survive the same lower limit as trout and salmon (Piper et al. 1982), but occur in water up to about 35°C. Tropical fishes cannot survive cold temperatures; for example, most species of tilapia succumb in water below about 10°C. Coolwater fishes such as walleye, northern pike, and muskellunge have upper tolerances between those of coldwater and warmwater species.

For many experiments, maintenance of temperature within the optimum range is desirable. Optima vary with species, fish age, season of the year, and other factors. Rearing should be satisfactory at temperatures of 25–30°C for most warmwater fishes, 20–25°C for coolwater fishes, and 15–20°C for coldwater fishes. Metabolic rates, food intake, food conversion, and growth are altered when fishes are exposed to temperatures outside their optimum ranges.

When fish are moved directly from one temperature to another, the change should not exceed about 2°C. When a more drastic temperature change is necessary, as often occurs when fish are hauled from one environment to another, the fish should be tempered at a rate no greater than about 5°C/h until the final desired temperature is reached. This can be done by slowly adding water of the final temperature to that in which the fish are being held. When fish are in plastic bags, the bags can be floated in water of the final temperature until equilibrium is reached. Neither technique should be used when the change is more than about 10°C, however, or tempering will be too rapid and mortality could result. Tempering over a range of more than 10°C will require several hours for each 5°C increment (Johnson 1979). Our experience has shown that fish adapt more rapidly when the temperature change is toward their thermal optimum than they do when the change is away from that temperature.

Temperature is sometimes monitored continuously for intensive (high-density) culture systems, though daily or less-frequent measurements are more typical. Water temperatures should be recorded routinely to provide a thermal history of any experiment. Large fluctuations in temperature should be avoided to the extent possible. When such fluctuations occur, the fish should be carefully monitored for changes in behavior and for the onset of disease and parasitism that may follow the stress of thermal shock (Section 20.7).

20.4.2 Dissolved Oxygen

One of the most important water quality concerns of fish culturists is dissolved oxygen (DO). Oxygen is added to water by photosynthesis and diffusion from the atmosphere. To augment the slow process of diffusion, a variety of techniques can be applied: the water can be agitated, liquid or bottled oxygen can be added, and air compressors and blowers can be used to produce small bubbles through diffusers, U-tubes, air stones, and airlifts. Venturi systems of the plunge type (Section 20.3.4; Figure 20.5) are efficient means of aerating water. One of the more popular pieces of equipment for aeration in ponds is a paddlewheel aerator (Figure 20.1) operated from the power take-off of a tractor. It is employed when oxygen depletion has been detected or appears to be imminent. The system and technique were fully described by Armstrong and Boyd (1982).

As a general rule, DO concentrations should be maintained at 5.0 mg/L or higher. Additional aeration should be provided when the level falls to 3.0 mg/L or below, even though some fish species are able to tolerate lower DO levels without apparent stress.

Indoor static, flow-through, and recirculating-water systems may show only minor daily fluctuations in DO if proper aeration is provided. Some reduction in DO typically occurs after the fish feed, but critically low DO normally does not occur unless the carrying capacity of the system is exceeded or there is some type of mechanical failure. Severe diel fluctuations in DO concentration are commonly reported for ponds and cages, however. In most aquatic environments, photosynthesis during the daylight hours adds oxygen to the water more rapidly than it is removed by respiration. The reverse is true at night. Under an equilibrium state, there would be no net change in DO at the end of any 24-h period. However, when there are marked changes—die-offs as well as increases—in population densities of bacteria, algae, macrophytes, or animals, or if there is a change in the extent and duration of cloud cover that affects photosynthesis, there can be a net decrease or increase in DO within the diel cycle.

The DO level is lowest early in the morning because photosynthesis ceases at dusk and respiration (by bacteria, plants, and animals) gradually consumes the available oxygen throughout the night. As fish grow and organic matter such as fish wastes and uneaten feed accumulates in a culture pond, the early-morning DO level may become progressively lower on successive days. The problem can be compounded when there is a period of cloudy weather. Checks on DO should be made as near to dawn as possible in water systems that are subject to large diel oxygen fluctuations. Indoor culture systems should be routinely checked for DO, though the time of day when this is done is not critical. Daily determinations are recommended, though a lower frequency may be suitable for stable water systems. When it is desirable to continuously monitor DO, automated data acquisition systems can be employed.

20.4.3 Nitrogen

Nitrogen may occur in water as a gas (N_2) and as nitrite (NO_2^-), nitrate (NO_3^-), and ammonia in the un-ionized (NH_3) and ionized (NH_4^+) forms. Gaseous nitrogen originates in the atmosphere and also through bacterial denitrification of other nitrogenous compounds. Nitrite and nitrate are formed from ammonia by nitrifying bacteria. Ammonia is an intermediate breakdown product in the decay of most organic materials and is also an excretory product from fishes.

Nitrogen gas becomes a problem when it supersaturates the water. Fish exposed to N_2 levels much above 100% of saturation contract gas bubble disease like a human diver who experiences the bends. Among the causes of nitrogen supersaturation are rapid heating of water under pressure (as occurs when water passes through a power plant, particularly in winter) and pressurization of gas aspirated into a pump (Wheaton 1977; Stickney 1979). Dissolved gas concentrations vary with temperature, salinity, and pressure; Colt (1984) detailed the computations necessary to determine the levels of dissolved gases under various conditions.

Un-ionized ammonia (NH_3) is more toxic than ionized ammonia (NH_4^+). The relative proportions of the two are controlled chiefly by pH and to a lesser extent by temperature (Trussel 1972). Downing and Merkins (1955) determined that there is 10 times more NH_3 in the water at pH 8.0 than at pH 7.0. As either temperature or pH increases, so does the percentage of NH_3. Tables that show the percentage of NH_3 as a function of temperature and pH were provided by Emerson et al. (1975). Given a pH range of approximately 6.5–8.5 and temperatures within the optimum range, total ammonia values of 0.5 mg/L are generally considered to be safe for coldwater species such as salmonids. Total ammonia levels of up to 1.0 mg/L are considered safe for many warmwater species (Robinette 1983). Meade (1985) presented an excellent review of allowable ammonia levels for fish culture.

Ammonia can be removed from water with ion exchange columns (Wheaton 1977), but dilution and denitrification are the most economically effective control methods. In recirculating-water systems, biological filters provide the proper conditions for nitrifying bacteria (Section 20.3.4). In flow-through systems, water exchange rates can be kept high enough to prevent ammonia from reaching toxic levels. In ponds, ammonia toxicity can occur if biomasses become too high, but nitrification usually keeps ammonia within safe levels when normal biomasses (a few thousand kilograms per hectare) are cultured. Under the prevailing temperature and pH ranges maintained in culture ponds, ammonia should not become a problem.

Nitrite is most commonly found at toxic concentrations in recirculating-water systems when bacteria of the genus *Nitrosomonas* have become well established, but *Nitrobacter* spp. are not present in sufficient concentrations to quickly detoxify the NO_2^- to NO_3^-. The latter ion can be present at high levels (up to several hundred milligrams per liter) without interfering with fish performance. Nitrite toxicity, which occurs in ponds as well as in more intensive culture systems, is indicated by chocolate-colored blood in fish. Nitrite ions compete with oxygen for binding sites on hemoglobin; when the oxygen-binding capacity of the blood declines too far, the fish die of asphyxiation. Calcium chloride and sodium chloride have been used to enhance survival of channel catfish exposed to toxic levels of nitrite (Tomasso et al. 1980). Toxic levels vary among fish species. Levels below about 0.5 mg/L appear to be generally safe, and some warmwater species appear to tolerate nitrite concentrations of several milligrams per liter, at least for short periods.

20.4.4 Salinity

Many marine and strictly freshwater fish species have relatively narrow tolerances of salinity. Estuarine species and those that are transient in estuaries, on the other hand, can often tolerate wide salinity ranges. When fishes from the open ocean are cultured, salinities of 35‰ should be maintained. Estuarine species typically perform well at salinities of 10–30‰. Many freshwater fishes do not survive salinities above 15‰ and some are much less tolerant than that. Failure to maintain fishes within appropriate ranges of salinity can cause osmoregulatory stress (itself a cause of poor growth), altered behavior, reduced disease resistance, and death.

Fisheries scientists who maintain fish in salt water should be aware that salinity increases as evaporation occurs, because only water is lost. Therefore, in closed systems such as static aquaria, recirculating-water systems, and static ponds, only fresh water should be used to replace evaporative losses.

Rain and freshwater runoff into saltwater ponds can form a low-salinity lens of water at the pond surface because fresh water is less dense than salt water. Freshwater lenses eventually mix with the rest of the water column as the water is agitated by wind or mechanical aeration. The result is a reduction in salinity, the magnitude of which depends on the amount of new fresh water and the persistence of which depends on the rate of evaporation.

20.4.5 Acidity, Alkalinity, and Hardness

The pH of most natural waters is conducive to the survival and growth of fish. The desired range in pH is from about 6.5 to 9.0 in fresh water (Swingle 1961). Marine and estuarine fish should be maintained in water of pH 7.0–9.0. Drastic changes in pH can occur when the buffering capacity of a water system is disrupted. Waters of low alkalinity (low concentration of H^+-binding anions) may have their buffering capacity exceeded when high levels of photosynthesis or respiration deplete the carbonate–bicarbonate ion pool. Alkalinity affects the toxicity of heavy metals and such chemicals as fish toxicants. Extremely soft water bodies (i.e., waters with low cation concentrations, or hardness) often have low primary and secondary productivity, so fish that depend on natural food in such waters may grow slowly. Water with an alkalinity in excess of 40 mg/L (Boyd 1979) and a hardness of 20–200 mg/L (both measured in terms of calcium carbonate) is generally recommended.

Control of pH can be achieved by stabilization of the buffer system. The addition of calcium carbonate (usually in the form of crushed limestone) to ponds at the rate of a few thousand kilograms per hectare has been widely used. Incorporation of crushed limestone or oyster shell in recirculation systems is important because accumulation of acidic metabolites reduce pH if the systems are not well buffered. Gypsum ($CaSO_4 \cdot 2H_2O$) has been used to increase hardness while not affecting alkalinity. When pH is too high, alum $[Al_2(SO_4)_3]$ can be applied (Boyd 1979).

20.5 CARRYING CAPACITY OF HOLDING FACILITIES

Aquaculturists traditionally report carrying capacity, standing crop, and production in terms of weight of cultured organisms per surface area of culture unit. This can be misleading when such figures are compared among different types of culture systems. For example, annual production per surface hectare can be tens of thousands of kilograms of fish in a flow-through raceway but only a few thousand kilograms in a static pond (Mihursky 1969). However, the difference in production would be reduced, and might even shift in favor of the pond, if production were calculated on the basis of total water volume used during the culture period (Wheaton 1977). The point is that carrying capacity within the confined space of a holding facility can be increased in most instances by adding new water (flushing) or by recirculating existing water that has undergone biofiltration (Section 20.3.4). It is also important to realize that the carrying capacity of holding facilities depends upon a host of environmental variables, many of which can be manipulated to increase carrying capacity well above that which would occur in nature. In a fish hatchery, for example, carrying capacity depends upon water flow, volume, exchange rate, temperature, oxygen content, pH, size and species of fish being reared, and the accumulation of metabolic products (Piper et al. 1982). If it is necessary to determine carrying capacity fairly precisely for a system, the reader is referred to the pioneering work of Haskell (1955) and to several later studies (Buterbaugh and Willoughby 1967; Willoughby 1968; Speece 1973; Kincaid et al. 1976; Westers and Pratt 1977) that incorporated the basic tenets of Haskell for determinations of carrying capacity.

In most cases, food availability is a primary factor that limits the biomass within a water system. Under natural conditions, for example, the annual production of channel catfish in earthen ponds is about 100 kg/hectare (Carlander 1969). When such ponds are treated with inorganic or organic fertilizers, which stimulate production of natural foods, fish production increases to at least 370 kg/hectare. If the fish are given prepared feeds, production can reach 3,000 kg/hectare before water quality problems become limiting (Huner and Dupree 1984). Aeration and other management techniques can lead to annual production levels of 4,000 kg/hectare and higher (Boyd 1983).

Careful management can greatly increase production in all types of water systems. However, agonistic behavior, which may range from simple territorial disputes to predation (cannibalism), also affects carrying capacity. Such behavior sometimes can be circumvented by increasing rather than decreasing population density. For example, territoriality may break down when certain species of fishes are held at high density, whereas repeated altercations often occur when only a few individuals are held in close quarters (Stickney 1979). Cannibalism can often be minimized by stocking fish of uniform size and keeping them well fed. When inter- or intraspecific predation becomes a problem, the largest (fastest-growing) individuals should be culled, because they are the most likely culprits (Piper et al. 1982).

20.6   SPECIES, SOURCES OF FISH, AND PERMITTING REQUIREMENTS

Depending upon the species in question, fish may be obtained from the wild, from governmental hatcheries, through barter with colleagues, from commercial fish hatcheries, and through retail outlets. Collection of wild fish may require a permit from a federal, state, or provincial natural resource agency. Such permits can usually be obtained with little difficulty if the purpose of collecting the fish is research or teaching. The researcher should be careful to follow all collecting, holding, disposition, and reporting regulations specified by the agency granting the permit.

An additional layer of regulations may be imposed with respect to species that are exotic, endangered, have a history of massive epizootics, or are prohibited for one reason or another under local law. In the USA, for example, federal law prohibits the importation of any member of the catfish family Clariidae (Clugston 1986). Also prohibited are any live or dead fish or eggs of the family Salmonidae, unless they are certified to be free of whirling disease and Egtved disease, also known as viral hemorrhagic septicemia (Kohler and Stanley 1984). Health certificates are not required for other species, including aquarium fishes. Many states have prohibited the introduction of certain exotic species such as grass carp within their boundaries. In Canada, the Federal Fisheries Act prohibits the transport or introduction of live fish or fish eggs without specific written permission of the Minister of Fisheries (Crossman 1984).

It is advisable to check with personnel of the local natural resource agency to determine specific regulations covering transport of any fish species. Regulations concerning transportation of fish are in place for good reason and should always be closely followed.

20.7   DISEASE AND PARASITE CONTROL

Disease and parasite problems may be encountered with any fish species and within any of the types of culture systems described in this chapter. Problems often arise as a result of stress, nutritional deficiencies, gas bubble embolisms, epizootics of viruses and bacteria, and parasitic protozoans, nematodes, trematodes, cestodes, and crustaceans. Recognition of disease and parasite problems may be difficult in the early stages of infection. Accordingly, the researcher should be familiar with preventative measures that can be taken to reduce the probability of disease and parasite outbreaks. However, should a disease or parasite epizootic occur in a captive fish population, quick diagnosis and treatment are paramount if the problem is to be contained. The Fish Health Section of the American Fisheries Society publishes periodic updates of its *Procedures for the Detection and Identification of Certain Fish Pathogens*. It is recommended that fish researchers have a copy of the latest edition (currently the third: Amos 1985) readily accessible.

20.7.1 Preventative Measures

Virtually all populations of fish maintained for research or teaching purposes harbor low levels of disease and parasitic organisms. In most instances, severe problems (epizootics) do not occur if the water system is well managed and the fish are not stressed. Therefore, the first and generally best preventative measure for controlling disease and parasite infestations is to minimize stress. This can be achieved by maintaining favorable water quality (Section 20.4), providing proper nutrition (Section 20.8), handling and transporting fish with care (Section 20.9), and limiting exogenous disturbances (Section 20.10).

Whether in a highly controlled laboratory setting or in an outdoor pond facility, situations will occur that place cultured fish under stress. A certain amount of handling is inherent in any research or teaching endeavor. Mechanical failure or electrical outages occur without warning, and usually at the least opportune times. Outdoor facilities are subject to the whims of nature. Dissolved oxygen depletions, sudden temperature changes, and other stress-causing events may not always result in immediate losses of fish, but severe epizootics are often observed following such stresses. Depending upon the agents involved, the lag time between onset of stress and an epizootic can range from 1 to 14 d (discussed by Stickney 1979). Accordingly, many researchers provide prophylactic treatments to reduce the chances of an epizootic before an experiment is begun, after fish are handled or transported, and following periods of water quality deterioration.

20.7.2 Diagnosis of Disease and Parasite Problems

Symptoms of nutritional deficiency are often similar to those that may occur as a result of epizootics. For example, symptoms of vitamin deficiency in channel catfish include internal hemorrhage, skin lesions, scoliosis, and mortality, depending upon the vitamin involved (Robinson 1984). Nutritional diseases are most likely to occur in intensive culture systems when little or no natural food is available. Thus, complete diets are required when fish are held in such systems (Section 20.8.2). In addition to demonstrating some of the same signs as epizootics, nutritional deficiencies are a form of stress and, as such, increase the likelihood that a secondary disease or parasite problem will develop.

Gas bubble embolisms result from supersaturation of nitrogen or (sometimes) other gases in the water. They can be diagnosed in fish by the presence of small, clear bubbles under the surface of the skin and in the interstices of fin rays and

Table 20.1 Therapeutants registered or approved for aquatic or fishery uses in the USA (from Schnick et al. 1989).

Fishery use	Tolerance[a]	Comments[b]
Acetic acid, commercial grade (vinegar)		
Parasiticide: 1–2 g/L for 1–10 min	Exempted from tolerance	Food fish use; GRAS as general purpose food additive
Paracide-F (formalin) Sponsor: Argent Chemical Laboratory, Redmond, Washington		
Parasiticide for use on trout, salmon, catfish, largemouth bass, and bluegill: 25 mg/L in ponds; up to 250 mg/L for 1 h in tanks and raceways	None required	Food fish use
Fungicide for use on eggs of trout, salmon, and esocids: 1–2 g/L for 15 min in egg treatment tanks		
Furanace capsules (nifurpirinol, furpirinol, P-7138) Sponsor: Amdal Co., Division of Abbot Laboratories, North Chicago, Illinois		
Antibacterial drug against columnaris in aquarium fish: 3.8-mg capsule in 37.8 L for 1 h	None established	Nonfood fish use only; do not use in saltwater aquariums or while egg- or live-bearing fish are reproducing; currently not available
Masoten (trichlorfon) Sponsor: Mobay Chemical Corp., Kansas City, Missouri		
Parasiticide against anchorworms, lice, and gill flukes on goldfish or bait fish: 0.25 mg/L, active ingredient, for indefinite period	None established	Nonfood fish only; not for use in streams; do not apply to ponds used as a source of drinking water for humans or animals; currently not available
Romet-30, Romet-B (sulfadimethoxine + ormetoprim) Sponsor: Hoffmann-La Roche, Inc., Nutley, New Jersey		
Antibacterial drug against furunculosis on salmonids and against enteric septicemia on catfish: 50 mg/kg of fish per day for 5 d	0.1 mg/L for catfish and salmonids	Food fish use; do not treat salmonids within 6 weeks of marketing or stocking them; do not treat catfish within 3 d of marketing or stocking
Salt (sodium chloride) Sponsor: none		
Osmoregulatory enhancer: 5–10 g/L for indefinite period; 30 g/L for 10–30 min	Exempted from tolerance	Food fish use; GRAS
Sulfamerazine in Fish Grade (sulfamerazine) Sponsor: American Cyanamid Co., Princeton, New Jersey		
Antibacterial drug against furunculosis on salmonids: 10 g/45.4 kg of fish per day for 14 d in feed; discontinue after 14 d	Zero tolerance in edible tissues of trout	Food fish use; do not treat fish within 3 weeks of marketing them or stocking them in streams open to fishing; no longer available for food fish use
Terramycin for Fish (oxytetracycline) Sponsor: Pfizer, Inc., New York, New York		
Antibacterial drug against species of *Aeromonas*, *Hemophilus*, and *Pseudomonas*: 2.5–3.75 g/45.4 kg of fish per day for 10 d in feed	0.1 mg/L for salmonids and catfish	Food fish use; 21-d preslaughter withdrawal period[c]

spines. The etiology and control of the problem were fully discussed in a collection of papers edited by Fickeisen et al. (1980). The use of a stripping tower and packed columns to remove nitrogen gas was described by Owsley (1981).

Diagnosis of viral diseases in fish is based largely on symptoms (Piper et al. 1982). Although the presence and identity of viruses can sometimes be ascertained through laboratory testing and electron microscopy (Wolf 1970), time and money usually are not available for extensive diagnostic work. A confounding problem is that many of the signs of viral infections are the same as for other types of disease. Because few effective treatments for fish viral diseases have been developed, infected animals are commonly destroyed, as are fish expected to be nonsymptomatic carriers of the virus. Because destruction of a population is a drastic solution to the problem, all other possibilities should be ruled out before the diseased fish are firmly diagnosed as having a viral infection.

Bacterial and parasitic problems in fish are more easily recognized than viral diseases. Before fish are killed, bacterial or parasite loads must be heavy, so cures can be effected if the problem is identified early in its course. The probability of diagnosing an epizootic accurately increases if moribund animals are examined rather than those that appear healthy or which have already died. Apparently healthy fish may not be sufficiently infected to allow easy observation of the pathogen, whereas dead fish carry bacteria and other organisms associated with decomposition, making detection of the original pathogenic agent more difficult.

Infected fish should be examined fresh if possible, because freezing and thawing disrupt some pathogenic organisms. Fish preserved in formalin or alcohol can be examined for the presence of parasites, but bacteria will have been killed and cannot, therefore, be cultured—a requirement for positive bacterial identification. Protocols for examining fish for the presence of bacteria and parasites are in Amos (1985). Hoffman (1967) wrote a key to the primary groups of fish parasites.

Fungi generally occur as secondary infections after injury or some type of disease has led to integumentary lesions. The presence of fungi, which in freshwater fish are usually species of the genus *Saprolegnia*, can be readily detected as white, cottony growths that appear at the sites of lesions.

20.7.3 Treatment of Diseases and Parasites

Once an epizootic has been detected, every attempt should be made to prevent its spread by transfer of fish, water, or equipment among culture units. Nets and other equipment can be disinfected in a chlorine, formalin, or thimerosal (Merthiolate) solution, or separate pieces of equipment may be assigned to each culture chamber.

←

Table 20.1 Continued.

[a] Residue concentrations of drug or chemical that are permitted by regulatory agencies in food eaten by humans.

[b] Abbreviations: EPA = U.S. Environmental Protection Agency; FDA = U.S. Food and Drug Administration; GRAS = generally recognized as safe by the FDA; NADA = new animal drug application, a petition from a sponsor to the FDA requesting approval to use the drug for a special purpose; USFWS = U.S. Fish and Wildlife Service.

[c] Period of time that must pass after treatment with or exposure to a drug, chemical, or pesticide before an animal can be consumed by humans.

Table 20.2 Chemicals used for treatment of fish epizootics.

Pathogen	Treatment[a]
Virus	None
Bacteria	Acriflavin, erythromycin, Furacin, Furanace, Romet-30, sulfamerazine, Terramycin
Protozoa	Acetic acid, formalin, malachite green, potassium permanganate, sodium chloride
Fungus	Copper sulfate, formalin, malachite green, potassium permanganate
Gill worms	Dylox, formalin, Masoten, potassium permanganate
Alimentary worms	None generally required
Copepods	Dylox

[a] See Table 20.1 for therapeutic agents approved for use with food fish in the USA.

Although aquaculturists have used a variety of drugs and chemicals to treat disease and parasite problems, all are not considered safe if the fish are to be consumed by humans or if the treatment is applied in water bodies used as municipal water supplies. In the USA, the Food and Drug Administration (FDA) and the Environmental Protection Agency (EPA) regulate the use of drugs and chemicals that can be used as therapeutic agents to treat aquatic animals (Schnick et al. 1986, 1989). Regulations for ''food fish'' such as channel catfish and trout are more stringent than for ''nonfood fish'' such as baitfish and ornamental fishes. Information on products that have been registered or approved for use in U.S. aquaculture is presented in Table 20.1.

Table 20.3 English and metric conversion units for measurements commonly employed in fish culture.[a]

Unit	Conversion
Acre-foot (acre-ft)	1 acre of surface area covered by 1 ft water 43,560 ft^3 2,718,144 lb
Cubic foot (ft^3)	7.5 gal 28,354.6 g of water
Gallon (gal)	8.34 lb of water 3,800 cm^3 (mL, g)
Quart (qt)	950 cm^3 (mL, g)
Pound (lb)	453.6 (454) g 16 oz
Ounce (oz)	28.35 g

[a] A concentration of 1 part per million (1 mg/L) requires 2.7 lb/acre-ft, 0.0038 g/gal, 0.0283 g/ft^3, or 0.0000623 lb/ft^3.

When an epizootic has been diagnosed, or when the onset of an epizootic is anticipated following a stress episode, the appropriate chemical should be selected and properly applied. Depending upon the specific drug, the chemical may be mixed with the feed, added to the water, injected into the fish, or dissolved in a concentrated bath or dip solution in which fish are immersed. Externally administered chemicals may be applied as dip treatments, whereby fish are placed in a concentrated chemical bath for a short period (seconds or minutes); as prolonged baths in moderate concentrations of the chemical for periods of hours; or as indefinite prolonged treatments in which the chemical is added at a relatively low concentration to the culture system and allowed to degrade over an indefinite period (Piper et al. 1982). Generalized treatments for aquaculture diseases are presented in Table 20.2, and conversion units are provided in Table 20.3.

20.7.4 Sanitation and Quarantine

The spread of disease can be reduced or eliminated if certain precautions are taken. It is important to maintain sanitary conditions in fish-rearing facilities. In addition, nets and other supplies or equipment should be carefully cleaned after use. If the same net is used to handle fish from different tanks or ponds, it should be dipped in a disinfectant solution between uses. A good sanitizing solution is 1 L of household bleach in a 115-L plastic garbage can filled with water. Nets can be dipped in the solution between uses. Bleach solution can also be used to rinse buckets, pails, aquaria, and tanks between use. Any item placed in bleach must be thoroughly rinsed in unadulterated water because the oxidizing agents (chlorine compounds) are toxic to fish.

Ponds can be sanitized by spreading quicklime over the pond bottom after the ponds are drained (Hickling 1971). The lime kills lingering disease organisms and should be allowed to remain on the dry pond bottom for several days. Fish can be safely added once the pond has been refilled.

When fish are brought into a culture facility, it may be wise to subject them to a quarantine period before placing them in contact with fish already on hand (Piper et al. 1982). Generally, epizootics develop—if they develop at all—within 21 d after fish have been handled and transported. During that period, the quarantined fish should be maintained in isolation from other fish at the facility. There should be no comingling of the water between the two groups of fish and no use of nets or other supplies in common. Chlorination of effluent from fish culture systems, particularly when fish are in quarantine or an epizootic is present, will prevent the spread of diseases to other cultured or wild fish populations in receiving waters.

20.8 FEEDING CAPTIVE FISHES

The effort invested in feeding captive fishes varies from none to substantial. In the simplest case, fish are stocked at low density in ponds and allowed to browse on natural food organisms. (This method, when used with cannibalistic species can lead to the production of one or two rather large individuals.) Fertilization of the ponds with organic or inorganic materials to enhance natural food production represents the first level of feeding management. Information on fertilization is available in Stickney (1979), Brown and Gratzek (1980), Hepher and Pruginin (1981), Piper et al. (1982), and Brown (1983).

Most captive and cultured fishes (in North America, at least) are fed live or prepared foods, either as a supplement to natural food in ponds or as the entire diet. Historically, such nonliving items as fresh chopped organ meats, mollusks, and fish, along with boiled eggs or egg yolks, were offered to captive fishes, but these are little used at present.

20.8.1 Live Foods

Some fishes refuse prepared (manufactured) food and must be offered live organisms. When the number of such fish is small and the maintenance period short, it is often most efficient to purchase live foods. Minnows, crickets, and earthworms are readily available from bait stores in most areas. In some regions, live bait shrimp, killifish, and crayfish are also available. Because such foods are brought to the holding facility from outside, they might transmit diseases and parasites to the experimental fish. Their relatively high cost and, in some cases, their seasonal availability may limit the extent to which such natural foods can be employed.

Many scientists and culturists elect to produce their own live foods, particularly for larval fishes which may refuse or be unable to accept prepared feeds. Copepods and other invertebrates have been cultured as food for captive fish larvae, but the most popular food items are brine shrimp nauplii (*Artemia* sp.) and rotifers (in particular, *Brachionus* sp.). Brine shrimp cysts (a resting stage often mistakenly referred to as eggs) can be purchased in vacuum-packed cans. When the cysts are placed in a salt solution for about 24 h, the nauplii emerge. The nauplii can be fed directly to various species of marine and freshwater fish, though the culturist should determine the size at which their fish can first accept them. If fish larvae are too small to eat brine shrimp nauplii, they may accept rotifers (Stickney 1979). Because first-feeding fish of many species are difficult to feed in captivity and nutritionally complete diets have not been developed for them, it may be best to let them forage on natural foods for 1–2 weeks in ponds. Thereafter, they should be sufficiently large to accept live or formulated feeds in the laboratory.

It is possible to rear brine shrimp through their life cycle in the laboratory, but most people prefer the simplicity of purchasing cysts and hatching the nauplii (see Sorgeloos et al. 1978; Prescott 1980). Maintenance of all stages in the life cycles of brine shrimp and rotifers requires continuous production of algae upon which these planktonic forms feed. Thus, in order to maintain a population of fish, it may be necessary to culture at least two additional organisms: algae and zooplankton. For some carnivorous fishes, it may also be necessary to culture a forage fish, adding another trophic level to the system.

20.8.2 Prepared Foods

Prepared fish foods are formulated from the same types of feedstuffs used to manufacture foods for poultry, swine, other livestock, and pets. Included are such things as fish meal, meat and bone meal, corn, soybean meal, cottonseed meal, peanut meal, whey, distillers' grains, and wheat. In complete diets—those meeting all the nutritional requirements of the target fish species—vitamin and mineral packages are added. Nutritional requirements have been determined for only a few fish species (NRC 1981, 1983), but in general, trout or salmon formulations seem to support survival and promote growth of most species, and they can be used until sufficient information is obtained to allow development of species-specific diets.

Some fish feeds contain large amounts of water, the popular Oregon moist pellet (OMP) among them. It used to be necessary to freeze OMP to prevent its deterioration, but a shelf-stable, semisoft form of OMP now is available. Dry diets (usually with moisture contents of only a few percent) are supplied as flakes (commonly sold in tropical fish stores), crumbles, and pellets. Some fishes adapt better to a particular type of food, but many species can be trained to accept a variety of feed types. Moist foods such as the original OMP must be kept frozen or they will rapidly deteriorate. Because OMP contains fresh fish scraps, its manufacture is restricted to areas where fish are processed; because it was developed as a salmon ration, it is primarily available in the Pacific Northwest. The cost of transporting frozen OMP generally precludes its use in areas remote from the site of manufacture. The stabilized, semisoft form of OMP does not require special storage, but it is inherently expensive and not commonly used when hard pellets are an acceptable alternative.

Crumbles of various sizes are made by crushing pellets and grading them through sieves. Crumbled diets are used as starter feeds for fish such as trout and channel catfish that accept a prepared diet from the time of first feeding.

Typically, the largest diameter pellet for fish feeds is 6.4 mm. Smaller sizes are given to fish at first. As the fish grow, pellet size is increased. Once the fish accept 6.4-mm pellets, no further increase in pellet size is necessary.

Pellets can be manufactured by pressure pelleting or extrusion. Pressure pelleting involves passage of the mixed feed ingredients through a die and cutting the resulting particles to the desired length. Some natural heating occurs during the process, and supplemental steam may also be used. The residence time of the feed ingredients in the die is short and actual cooking does not take place. Pressure-pelleted diets have a specific gravity greater than 1.0 and sink when they are placed in water.

Extruded feeds are exposed to much higher temperatures and pressures than pressure-pelleted feeds. Extruded products pass through a long, externally heated die with a relatively long residence time. The ingredients are at least partially cooked in the process. When the material leaves the die, it expands and air is trapped as the starches present in the feedstuffs gelatinize. The trapped air may give the pellets a low specific gravity. Floating pellets are manufactured through the extrusion process.

Because of the heating that occurs during extrusion, vitamins such as ascorbic acid (vitamin C) may be at least partially destroyed. To offset the problem, the feeds must be overfortified, or one of the recently developed heat-stable forms of the vitamin may be used. This and the extra energy required for manufacture make extruded feeds somewhat more expensive than pressure-pelleted feeds.

There is no nutritional difference between floating and sinking pellets, and the two forms support equivalent fish production under similar culture conditions (Mgbenka and Lovell 1984). The feeding habits of a particular fish may dictate which feed type to use. Even some benthic species can be trained to accept floating rations, however, and many fish culturists prefer to use floating feeds, particularly in ponds, so feeding activity can be observed. When feeding can be seen, fish can be fed ad libitum; otherwise, the population biomass must be estimated so the fish can be fed a percentage of their body weight. In cages and certain types of raceways, substantial amounts of sinking feed are lost before they can be ingested, so floating feeds are preferred for these situations.

Properly manufactured sinking feed pellets should remain intact for at least 10 min after they are submerged in water. Floating pellets may maintain their integrity for several hours in water.

All prepared feeds should be stored in a cool, dry place out of direct sunlight. Proper storage helps protect the vitamins and retards the oxidation of lipids and the development of molds. Unless stored under refrigeration, feed should be used within 90 d of purchase. Moldy feed should be discarded because it may contain toxins.

20.8.3 Feeding Rates and Frequencies

Except for very young fish that require frequent feeding to survive, the primary rule is that fish should not be overfed. Most advanced juvenile and adult fishes can survive extended periods without food, but overfeeding can impair water quality, which can stress and then kill the fish. At first feeding, young fish are commonly offered considerably more than they will consume. The feed should be evenly distributed over the surface of the culture chamber so it will be readily available to all individuals. In raceways and aquaria, excess feed often must be siphoned off daily, before it decays. Fish in ponds often learn to enter a specific area to feed, so pellets do not have to be spread over the whole pond surface. Indoor culture chambers used to maintain fingerling or adult fish are generally small enough that even feed distribution is not a consideration.

Small fingerlings may require multiple feedings. For example, muskellunge fingerlings at the Jake Wolf Hatchery of the Illinois Department of Conservation are fed every few minutes to prevent cannibalism (T. Trudeau, personal communication). Similarly, Lewis et al. (1981) indicated that striped bass larvae should be fed brine shrimp at hourly intervals, 24 h a day. Channel catfish of less than 1.5 g should be fed every 3 h around the clock. The frequency can be reduced to four times daily for larger fish (Murai and Andrews 1976) and may be further reduced once the fish are a few grams in weight.

Feeding rates may be as high as 50% of body weight daily for first-feeding channel catfish, but they can be reduced to 10% daily when the fish reach 0.25 g and to 5% daily at 4 g (Murai and Andrews 1976). Feeding schedules for trout of various sizes are available (Piper et al. 1982).

Healthy, rapidly growing fingerlings usually eat 3–4% of their body weight daily in dry feed when the ambient water temperature is within their optimum range. Reduced feeding rates are recommended when temperature is above or below the optimum. Adults grow more slowly and may consume only 1% of their body weight or less daily. Feed should be offered once or twice a day, morning or afternoon, or both. In ponds, feed should not be provided in the morning until dissolved oxygen is well above 3.0 mg/L. If an oxygen depletion has occurred during the night, the fish, which are already stressed, should not be fed at all the following morning. When ad libitum feeding is practiced, fish should not be offered more than they will consume in approximately 30 min. Feeding practices for coldwater and warmwater fishes were reviewed by NRC (1981, 1983).

20.8.4 Feeding Methods

Depending upon the type and size of the culture system employed, fish may be fed by hand or with mechanical feeding devices. Demand feeders have been widely used for fish in raceways and ponds. These feeders release a few pellets each time a triggering mechanism is bumped by a fish. Species such as trout and channel catfish quickly learn to activate such an apparatus. Demand feeders may hold sufficient feed for several days. Frequent checks should be made to determine that feed is being taken, however, because changes in feeding activity are a common first sign that fish have been stressed and may be developing a disease or parasite problem.

Automatic feeders can be set to release controlled amounts of feed when activated. Timers associated with such feeders can be set to feed at nearly any desired interval. Automatic feeders may deliver dry diets or liquids and are particularly useful for feeding brine shrimp in suspension to larval fishes (Lewis et al. 1981). Automatic feeders are also widely used to feed salmon and various other species that consume pelleted feeds.

20.9 HANDLING AND TRANSPORTATION

Fish should always be handled with extreme care. If close attention is paid to the procedures used, most species can be handled safely, though fish of some species die readily if they are removed from the water even for a few seconds.

Fish usually have to be handled when they are counted, weighed, measured, and moved from place to place; they also are handled when tissue samples are taken from them or when they are tagged, cannulated, and so forth. The most important handling principles are to treat fish gently, to prevent their injury from scraping against rough nets or jumping from confinement, and to return them to the water as quickly as possible. Anesthetics are often used to keep fish from becoming excited and injured (See Chapter 8). Rehandling should be avoided for at least 24 h, and it is preferable not to handle any individual more often than once a week.

Handling is a source of stress, so fish should be observed periodically after each handling episode for signs of disease and parasitism. Posthandling prophylactic treatments sometimes are used, but most species recover readily from careful handling. For additional information on handling and transporting fish, see Stickney (1983).

20.10 DISTURBANCE

Fish used in experiments should be protected, insofar as possible, from disturbances that might affect their behavior or physiological state. It is difficult to completely prevent disturbances, but common sense suggests ways to minimize them. Loud noises should be avoided, as should abrupt changes in light quality or quantity.

Captive fishes seem to adjust fairly rapidly to the presence of people. For example, catfish and other species in ponds often approach the shore when someone nears the pond, particularly around feeding times. Yet, if several people appear when the fish are normally fed by only one or two individuals, feeding activity may be severely limited or even cease for a period. Similar reactions may occur in tanks and raceways.

When physiological or behavioral responses are monitored, fish frequently must be isolated from the researcher. It may be necessary to restrict nonessential personnel from an area, to block off culture chambers with opaque material, and to observe the fish remotely (on video monitors, for example). Some ways to isolate fish from detrimental external stimuli are discussed in Chapter 17.

20.11   PEST CONTROL

Various animals other than fish are frequently found in culture systems, particularly (though not exclusively) outdoors. Problems have been reported with crayfish, insects, frogs, turtles, snakes, alligators, birds, muskrats, nutria, otters, sea lions, and skunks, Some of these animals prey on fish; others dig holes in levees, rend holes in cage walls, or terrorize personnel.

Predaceous insects are a common problem in fish culture. Dragonflies and certain other insects and their larvae prey heavily on larval and early fingerling stages of fish and should be controlled. An application of 2.3 L of motor oil and 18–37 L of diesel fuel per hectare of water surface controls air-breathing insects. Insects that do not surface can be controlled with 0.25 mg Masoten/L (Piper et al. 1982).

Crayfish can be eliminated with the chemical Baytex at concentrations of 0.1–0.25 mg/L (Piper et al. 1982). Turtles, snakes, and mammals can often be trapped and removed from the site of fish culture. Some pests can also be shot, but only when required permits and licenses have been obtained in advance. Fences have been used to keep certain types of pests away from culture ponds.

Many of the birds that prey upon cultured fish are protected by law, so their control is often difficult. Devices such as noise cannons are not very effective. Some culturists have installed mist nets over ponds to prevent bird predation. Nets are effective, but costly if the area to be protected is extensive. Mist nets are economically feasible over outdoor tanks and raceways in many instances. We have observed such nets in use at various laboratories. For details of effective and legal pest controls within a given region of the USA, contact the state agricultural extension service office. Many other countries have parallel agencies.

One of the worst pests, and most difficult to control, is *Homo sapiens*. In most states, poaching fish is only a misdemeanor, even when valuable research fish are involved. Fish are easy to catch when they are present at high densities in ponds, raceways, tanks, or cages. Warning signs are sometimes effective, but some type of security system is advised to prevent losses to human predators.

20.12   EFFLUENT TREATMENT

Effluent water from fish holding facilities may have to be treated (Liao 1970; Page and Andrews 1974). Some laboratories are linked to sanitary sewers, so all their effluent water receives treatment. Many facilities expel water into surface waters and may be subject to governmental regulations that vary with the location and type of receiving water and the quality of the effluent. Permits may be required, and limitations may be placed on the amount of effluent that can be dumped. Toxic chemicals and radioisotopes used in research create special disposal problems. Laboratories in which these substances are to be used should be properly designed to accommodate them, and all regulations that apply to their use and disposal should be judiciously followed. Appropriate governmental agencies should be approached and permits should be obtained before research with controlled substances is conducted.

20.13 REFERENCES

Amos, K. H., editor. 1985. Procedures for the detection and identification of certain fish pathogens, 3rd edition. American Fisheries Society, Fish Health Section, Corvallis, Oregon. (Available from AFS, Bethesda, Maryland.)

Armstrong, M. S., and C. E. Boyd. 1982. Oxygen transfer calculations for a tractor-powered paddlewheel. Transactions of the American Fisheries Society 111:361–366.

Boyd, C. E. 1979. Water quality in warmwater fish ponds. Alabama Agricultural Experiment Station, Auburn University, Auburn.

Boyd, C. E. 1983. Theory of aeration. Pages 13–20 in C. S. Tucker, editor. Water quality in channel catfish ponds. Agriculture and Forestry Experiment Station, Southern Cooperative Series Bulletin 290, Mississippi State, Mississippi.

Brown, E. E. 1983. World fish farming: cultivation and economics. AVI, Westport, Connecticut.

Brown, E. E., and J. B. Gratzek. 1980. Fish farming handbook. AVI, Westport, Connecticut.

Burrows, R. E., and B. B. Combs. 1968. Controlled environments for salmon propagation. Progressive Fish-Culturist 30:123–126.

Buterbaugh, G. L., and H. Willoughby. 1967. A feeding guide for brook, brown, and rainbow trout. Progressive Fish-Culturist 29:210–215.

Carlander, K. D. 1969. Handbook of freshwater fishery biology, volume 1. Iowa State University Press, Ames.

Clugston, J. P. 1986. Strategies for reducing risks from introductions of aquatic organisms: the federal perspective. Fisheries (Bethesda) 11(2):26–29.

Colt, J. 1984. Computation of dissolved gas concentrations in water as functions of temperature, salinity, and pressure. American Fisheries Society Special Publication 14.

Coventry, F. L., V. E. Shelford, and L. F. Miller. 1935. The conditioning of a chloramine treated water supply for biological purposes. Ecology 16:60–66.

Crossman, E. J. 1984. Introduction of exotic fishes into Canada. Pages 78–101 in W. R. Courtenay, Jr., and J. R. Stauffer, Jr., editors. Distribution, biology, and management of exotic fishes. Johns Hopkins University Press, Baltimore, Maryland.

Downing, K. M., and J. C. Merkins. 1955. The influence of dissolved oxygen concentrations on the toxicity of unionized ammonia to rainbow trout (*Salmo gairdneri* Richardson). Annals of Applied Biology 43:243–246.

Dupree, H. K. 1981. An overview of the various techniques to control infectious diseases in water supplies and in water reuse aquacultural systems. Pages 83–89 in L. J. Allen and E. C. Kinney, editors. Proceedings of the bio-engineering symposium for fish culture. American Fisheries Society, Fish Culture Section, Bethesda, Maryland.

Emerson, K., R. C. Russo, R. E. Lund, and R. V. Thurston. 1975. Aqueous ammonia equilibrium calculations: effect of pH and temperature. Journal of the Fisheries Research Board of Canada 32:2379–2383.

Fickeisen, D. H., M. J. Schneider, and G. A. Wedemeyer, editors. 1980. Special section: Gas bubble disease. Transactions of the American Fisheries Society 109:657–771.

Haskell, D. C. 1955. Weight of fish per cubic foot of water in hatchery troughs and ponds. Progressive Fish-Culturist 17:8–10.

Hepher, B., and Y. Pruginin. 1981. Commercial fish farming with special reference to fish culture in Israel. Wiley-Interscience, New York.

Hickling, C. F. 1971. Fish culture. Faber and Faber, London.

Hoffman, G. L. 1967. Parasites of North American freshwater fishes. University of California Press, Berkeley.

Huguenin, J. E. 1976. Heat exchangers for use in the culturing of marine organisms. Chesapeake Science 17:61–64.

Huner, J. V., and H. K. Dupree. 1984. Warmwater fish farming: a thriving industry. Pages 1–5 in H. K. Dupree and J. V. Huner, editors. Third report to the fish farmers. U.S. Fish and Wildlife Service, Washington, D.C.

Johnson, S. K. 1979. Transport of live fish. Texas A&M University, Cooperative Extension Service Report FDDL-F14, College Station.

Kincaid, H. L., W. R. Bridges, A. E. Thomas, and M. J. Donahoo. 1976. Rearing capacity of circular containers of different sizes for fry and fingerling rainbow trout. Progressive Fish-Culturist 38:11–17.

Kohler, C. C., and J. G. Stanley. 1984. A suggested protocol for evaluating proposed exotic fish introductions in the United States. Pages 387–406 in W. R. Courtenay, Jr., and J. R. Stauffer, Jr., editors. Distribution, biology, and management of exotic fishes. Johns Hopkins University Press, Baltimore, Maryland.

Layton, R. F. 1972. Analytical methods for ozone in water and wastewater applications. Pages 15–18 in F. L. Evans, editor. Ozone in water and wastewater treatment. Ann Arbor Science, Ann Arbor, Michigan.

Lewis, W. M. 1981. Some applications of water reuse systems in aquaculture. Pages 29–35 in Second British freshwater fish conference. Liverpool, England.

Lewis, W. M., R. C. Heidinger, and B. L. Tetzlaff. 1981. Tank culture of striped bass production manual. Southern Illinois University, Fisheries Research Laboratory, Carbondale.

Liao, P. B. 1970. Pollution potential of salmonid fish hatcheries. Water and Sewage Works 117(9):291–297.

Liao, P. B., and R. D. Mayo. 1974. Intensified fish culture combining water reconditioning with pollution abatement. Aquaculture 3:61–85.

Meade, J. W. 1985. Allowable ammonia for fish culture. Progressive Fish-Culturist 47:135–145.

Meade, T. L. 1974. The technology of closed system culture of salmonids. University of Rhode Island, Sea Grant Publication, Marine Technology Report 30, Narragansett.

Mgbenka, B. O., and R. T. Lovell. 1984. Feeding combinations of extruded and pelleted diets to channel catfish in ponds. Progressive Fish-Culturist 46:245–248.

Mihursky, J. A. 1969. On using industrial and domestic waste in aquaculture. Agricultural Engineering 50:667–669.

Murai, T., and J. W. Andrews. 1976. Effects of frequency of feeding on growth and food conversion of channel catfish fry. Bulletin of the Japanese Society of Scientific Fisheries 42:159–161.

NRC (National Research Council). 1981. Nutrient requirements of coldwater fishes. National Academy Press, Washington, D.C.

NRC (National Research Council). 1983. Nutrient requirements of warmwater fishes and shellfishes. National Academy Press, Washington, D.C.

Owsley, D. C. 1981. Nitrogen gas removal using packed columns. Pages 71–82 in L. J. Allen and E. C. Kinney, editors. Proceedings of the bio-engineering symposium for fish culture. American Fisheries Society, Fish Culture Section, Bethesda, Maryland.

Page, J. W., and J. W. Andrews. 1974. Chemical composition of effluent from high density culture of channel catfish. Water, Air, and Soil Pollution 3:365–369.

Paller, M. H., and R. C. Heidinger. 1979. The toxicity of ozone to the bluegill. Journal of Environmental Science and Health Part A, Environmental Science and Engineering 14:169–193.

Piper, R. G., I. B. McElwain, L. E. Orme, J. P. McCraren, L. G. Fowler, and J. R. Leonard. 1982. Fish hatchery management. U.S. Fish and Wildlife Service, Washington, D.C.

Prescott, S. R. 1980. Economics of Artemia nauplii use in aquaculture. Proceedings of the World Mariculture Society 11:175–180.

Robinette, H. R. 1983. Ammonia, nitrite and nitrate. Pages 28–34 in C. S. Tucker, editor. Water quality in channel catfish ponds. Agriculture and Forestry Experiment Station, Southern Cooperative Series Bulletin 290, Mississippi State, Mississippi.

Robinson, E. H. 1984. Vitamin requirements. Pages 21–25 *in* E. H. Robinson and R. T. Lovell, editors. Nutrition and feeding of channel catfish (revised). Texas A&M University, Southern Regional Cooperative Series Bulletin 296, College Station.

Sander, E., and H. Rosenthal. 1975. Application of ozone in water treatment for home aquaria, public aquaria and for aquaculture purposes. Pages 103–114 *in* W. J. Blogoslawski and R. G. Rice, editors. Aquatic applications of ozone. International Ozone Institute, Syracuse, New York.

Schnick, R. A., F. P. Meyer, and D. L. Gray. 1989. A guide to approved chemicals in fish production and fishery resource management. University of Arkansas Cooperative Extension Service and U.S. Fish and Wildlife Service, MP241, Little Rock, Arkansas.

Schnick, R. A., F. P. Meyer, and D. F. Walsh. 1986. Status of fishery chemicals in 1985. Progressive Fish-Culturist 48:1–17.

Simco, B. A., J. H. Williamson, G. J. Carmichael, and J. R. Tomasso. 1986. Centrarchids. Pages 73–89 *in* R. R. Stickney, editor. Culture of nonsalmonid freshwater fishes. CRC Press, Boca Raton, Florida.

Soorgeloos, P., G. Persoone, M. Baeza-Mesa, E. Bossuyt, and E. Bruggeman. 1978. The use of *Artemia* cysts in aquaculture: the concept of "hatching efficiency" and description of a new method for cyst processing. Proceedings of the World Mariculture Society 9:715–721.

Speece, R. E. 1973. Trout metabolism characteristics and the rational design of nitrification facilities for water reuse in hatcheries. Transactions of the American Fisheries Society 102:323–334.

Spotte, S. 1970. Fish and invertebrate culture. Wiley-Interscience, New York.

Spotte, S. 1979. Seawater aquariums. Wiley-Interscience, New York.

Stickney, R. R. 1979. Principles of warmwater aquaculture. Wiley-Interscience, New York.

Stickney, R. R. 1983. Care and handling of live fish. Pages 84–94 *in* L. A. Nielsen and D. L. Johnson, editors. Fisheries techniques. American Fisheries Society, Bethesda, Maryland.

Stickney, R. R., and N. K. Person. 1985. An efficient heating method for recirculating water systems. Progressive Fish-Culturist 47:71–73.

Strickland, J. D. H., and T. R. Parsons. 1968. A practical handbook of seawater analysis. Fisheries Research Board of Canada Bulletin 167.

Swingle, H. S. 1961. Relationship of pH of pond waters to their suitability for fish culture. Pacific Science Congress Proceedings 10:72–75.

Tomasso, J. R., M. I. Wright, B. A. Simco, and K. B. Davis. 1980. Inhibition of nitrite-induced toxicity in channel catfish by calcium chloride and sodium chloride. Progressive Fish-Culturist 42:144–146.

Trussel, R. P. 1972. The percent unionized ammonia in aqueous ammonia solutions at different pH levels and temperatures. Journal of the Fisheries Research Board of Canada 29:1506–1507.

Westers, H. 1986. Northern pike and muskellunge. Pages 91–101 *in* R. R. Stickney, editor. Culture of nonsalmonid freshwater fishes. CRC Press, Boca Raton, Florida.

Westers, H., and K. M. Pratt. 1977. Rational design of hatcheries for intensive salmonid culture, based on metabolic characteristics. Progressive Fish-Culturist 39:157–165.

Wheaton, F. W. 1977. Aquacultural engineering. Wiley-Interscience, New York.

Willoughby, H. 1968. A method for calculating carrying capacities of hatchery troughs and ponds. Progressive Fish-Culturist 30:173–174.

Wolf, K. 1970. Guidelines for virological examination of fishes. American Fisheries Society Special Publication 5:327–340.

Symbols and Abbreviations

The Systeme International d'Unites (SI) is the universal system of metric notation. The following SI symbols and other abbreviations are used without definition in this book. Also undefined are standard mathematical and statistical tests, and symbols of elements in the Periodic Table.

A	ampere	N	sample size
AC	alternating current	NS	not significant
°C	degrees Celsius	n	ploidy
cm	centimeter	o	ortho (as a chemical prefix)
Co.	Company	P	probability
Corp.	Corporation	p	para (as a chemical prefix)
DC	direct current	pH	negative log of hydrogen ion activity
D	dextro (as a prefix)		
d	day	n	nanno (10^{-9}, as a prefix)
df	degrees of freedom	R	multiple correlation or regression coefficient
E	east		
e	base of natural logarithm (2.71828. . .)	r	simple correlation or regression coefficient
e.g.	(exempli gratia) for example	S	siemens (for electrical conductance)
et al.	(et aliae) and others		
etc.	et cetera		south (for geography)
F	filial generation	SD	standard deviation
g	gram	SE	standard error
Hz	hertz	s	second
h	hour	tris	trishydroxymethlyaminomethane (a buffer)
IU	international unit		
Inc.	Incorporated	UK	United Kingdom
i.e.	(id est) that is	U.S.	United States (adjective)
J	joule	USA	United States of America
K	Kelvin (degrees above absolute zero)	USSR	Union of Soviet Socialist Republics
k	kilo (10^3, as a prefix)	V	volt
kg	kilogram	V	variance
km	kilometer	W	watt (for power)
L	levo (as a prefix)		west (for geography)
log	logarithm		
M	mega (10^6, as a prefix)	Ω	ohm
	molar (as a suffix or by itself)	μ	micro (10^{-6}, as a prefix)
m	meter (as a suffix or by itself)		
	milli (10^{-3}, as a prefix)	°	degree (temperature as a prefix, anglular as a suffix)
min	minute		
mol	mole		
N	normal (for chemistry)	%	per cent (per hundred)
	north (for geography)	‰	per mille (per thousand)

Index

Abbott's formula, control mortality   502
abdominal surgery, procedures   254
absolute growth   363
absorbable sutures   251
abundance studies, observational studies   17
acclimation, stress   451–477
acclimation temperature, hyperglycemia   458
accuracy
   bioenergetics approach   408
   controlled experiments   27
   experimenter-generated variability   27
   laboratory experiments   27
   procedure effects   27
acid esterases, lymphocyte discrimination   312
acidity, fish culture systems   648
acidosis, recovery from surgery   284
acridine orange, chromosome stain   180
acrocentric chromosomes   184
action potentials   314
active metabolism   336, 394
activity-dependent metabolism   394, 404
acute lethality, toxicology   495–510
acute:chronic toxicity ratio   519
adhesives
   cover slips   207
   electrode attachment   315
   histological sections   199
   surgical closure   256, 322, 417
adipose fins, taxonomic characters   113
adjuvants   260
adult tissue, chromosome preparation   173
aeration
   fish culture systems   635, 646
   recirculating-water systems   641
affinity-modulating solutes, hemoglobin   298
affinity, hemoglobin–oxygen   298
age, fish growth   587
air-dry method, chromosome spreads   176, 177
airlifts   637
alarm, stage of stress   452
Alcian Blue, cartilage stain   122
aldehyde fixatives   193
alizarin red S, bone stain   121
alkalinity, fish culture systems   648
allele frequencies
   allele counting   157
   estimation   156
   protein variation   53
   starch gel electrophoresis   155
alleles   40
   nomenclature   155
allometric growth, body shape   116
allometry, larval characters   124
allopatric populations   621
allozyme variations, taxonomic decisions   74

Amidate, see etomidate
amido black, protein stain   148
amino acids
   incorporation into proteins   370
   structure and charge   141–142
amitotic erythrocytes, peripheral
     formation   290
ammonia, fish culture systems   642, 647
amperometric titration, chlorine   339
amplifiers
   evoked potentials   430
   intracellular electrodes   425
amyloglycosidase, glycogen analysis   369
Amytal Sodium, fish transport anesthetic   221
anabolism, androgens   546
anaerobic metabolism, measurements   336
anagenesis, evolution   69
anal fins, taxonomic characters   113
analgesia   216
analysis, choice of approach   2
analysis of variance
   confirmatory analysis   129
   multivariate   129
   statistical methods   11
anaphase aberrations, chromosome
     damage   183
ancestors
   ancestor–descendent relationships   67
   species   69
androgenesis, artificial   544
androgens
   sex reversal   542
   sterilization   545
anesthesia and anesthetics   213–245
   anesthetics, fish, list of   222
   applications   214
   bath, blood sampling   280
   effects on blood characteristics   275
   exposure conditions   218
   historical perspective   213
   ideal and choice   219
   stages   216
   surgical procedures   253, 418
animal experimentation   241
animal welfare xxi, 241–242, 633
animals, pest control   660
annular respirometer   351–353
annulus
   fish growth   587
   growth estimates   376
antibiotics
   injection sites   260
   surgery   213, 256
antibody titers, environmental stress   468
anticoagulants

blood sampling 274
 EDTA 219
anticodon, transfer RNA 37
antithrombin, heparin 275
aortic puncture, blood sampling 277
apomorphy, defined, systematics 74
aquaria
 flow-through 638
 immersion photography 131
 static 637
aquatic toxicology 491–522
artifactual variation, taxonomy 126
artificial ecosystems, toxicity tests 513
aseptic techniques, surgery 213, 248
ASG method, G-banding 183
ash-free dry weight 366
ash weight, growth 366
association coefficients, phenetics 90
asynchronous feeding, feeding models 401,
 403
atrioventricular volume ratios 313
atrium, cardiac structure 313
auditory systems, neural studies 434
autecology 585–600
autosomes 38
axillary appendages, taxonomic characters 114

B cell mitogens 175
B chromosomes 184
B lymphocytes, identification 312
back-calculations, growth estimates 375–377
bacteria, biological nitrification 641
bactericidal treatment, fish culture
 systems 642
banding methods, chromosomes 181
banding patterns, starch gel
 electrophoresis 150
barbiturates, anesthetics 239
base-active dyes, basophils 308
basophils 308
bath application of drugs, neural studies 428
bath treatments, anesthetic 218
Beer–Lambert law 286
behavior 555–577
 anesthesia 217
 autecology studies 590
 feeding 573–576
 stimulation by implanted electrodes 432–433
 stress challenge test 477
 toxicant effects 512
benzalkonium chloride, germicide 250
benzidine stain, hemoglobin 291
benzocaine, see ethyl aminobenzoate
bioassay, anesthesia 219
biochemical indices of growth 370
biochemical methods, gel electrophoresis 37
biochemical physiology, aquatic
 toxicology 515
biochemical taxonomic characteristics 74
biochromes, fish coloration 116

bioconcentration factor, toxicity 517
bioenergetics 389–409
 applications 390, 392
 criteria 407
 determinations 369
 estimating equations 404
 food web models 623
 models and tests 408
 toxicity tests 512
biofilters, recirculating-water systems 640
biogeography, species diversity 626
biological classification 92
biological species concept 67
biomanipulation, lake management 624
biomass, bioenergetics 390
biotin–avidin method, neuron labeling 440
birds, pest control 660
biuret reaction method, protein analysis 367
blank respirometers 338, 344
Blazka respirometer 351
blood 273–322
 cell stains 295, 310–312
 circulation 312–322
 clotting time in stress 460
 compartmentalization 293
 flow distributions 322
 hematological methods 285–312
 lactic acid in stress 459
 mean erythrocyte volume 286
 pH 421
 pressure determinations 317
 sampling 273–285
 sex determination 529
 volume determinations 293, 319
blood chemistry
 stress responses 453, 455, 457
 values 465
blood vessel cannulation 280
body–scale relation, growth estimates 376
body sections, morphology 109
body shape, taxonomic characters 116
Bohr effect 299
bone stain 121
bony plates, taxonomic characters 115
Bouin's fixative 193
brain stimulation, microelectrodes 432
branchial arch, blood sampling 279
branchial irrigation, surgery 253
branchial membrane, taxonomic
 characters 112
branchiostegal membrane 109, 112
branchiostegal supports, taxonomic
 characters 120
Brenner device, cell collection 312
Brett-type swimming respirometers 349, 350
brine shrimp, food for fish 656
bromodeoxyuridine, chromatid exchanges 183
buffers
 chromosome staining 179
 electrophoresis 145, 147, 291, 292
 fish culture systems 649

saline 421
bulbus, cardiac structure 314
bulbus arteriosus, blood sampling 277

caenogenetic adaptations 123
cages, fish culture systems 644
caloric analysis, bioenergetics 393
calories, stress responses 454
calorimetry 335
  energy content 369
camera lucida, chromosome analysis 186
canals, sensory 112
cannulation 261–263, 280–285
  caudal blood vessels 283
  dorsal aorta 280
  dual 282
  urinary duct 262
  ventral aorta 282
capacitors, electrophysiological techniques 444
captive fish, disturbances 659
capturing fish 238
carbohydrate analysis 368
carbohydrate stains 201
carbohydrates
  growth 368
  proximate analysis 367
carbon dioxide
  absorbents, respirometry 346
  anesthetic 214, 221, 231–233
  indirect calorimetry 336
carbonic acid, anesthetic 221, 231–233
carbonic anhydride, anesthetic 231–233
carcinogenic potentials, toxicology 517
carcinogens, challenge tests 473
cardiac output 318
cardiac puncture, blood sampling 278
cardiac structure and function 312
cardiovascular changes, anesthetics 244
carnivore feeding models 399
carnivorous fish, digestion rates 402
Carnoy's fixative 172
carrying capacity, fish culture systems 649
cartilage stains 121–122
cascading trophic interactions, food webs 623
catheter placement, blood sampling 277
catheter systems, blood sampling 281
caudal fin, taxonomic characters 113
caudal peduncle, taxonomic characters 110
caudal vessels
  blood sampling 278
  cannulation 283
cauterizers, severed blood vessels 417
C-banding, chromosomes 180
cell suspensions, histological techniques 198
cellulose acetate systems, electrophoresis 291
cements, see adhesives
central nervous system
  depressants: barbiturates 239
  single unit recordings 429
centric fissions, chromosome number 185

centrum, vertebrae 118
^{14}C-glycine uptake, scale growth 371
challenge tests, stress 458, 469–477
  behavior 477
  chemical tolerance 474
  crowding 475–476
  disease resistance 473
  handling 476
  hypoxia 471
  salinity tolerance 474–475
  swimming performance 472
  thermal tolerance 470
character analysis, systematics 78
character compatibility analysis,
    systematics 86
character conflict, systematics 83
character correlation, systematics 84
character independence, systematics 78
character sets, morphometry 126
character state 78
charcoal filters, fish culture systems 636
cheek, taxonomic characters 111
chelating agents, anticoagulants 275
chemical challenge tests, stress 474
chemical imprinting, migration 576
chemicals
  fishery 220
  site factors 8
  toxicity test measurements 506
  treatment of epizootics 654
chemoclines, species distribution 600
chemoreception, neural studies 430
chloramines, fish culture systems 635
chloramphenicol, surgical antibiotic 256
chloramphenicol palmate, antibiotic 256
Chloretone, anesthetic 221
chloride, plasma, secondary stress
    response 457
chloriding electrodes, neural studies 426
chloridometer, blood chloride 458
chlorine
  demand 338
  fish culture systems 636
  respirometric measurement 338
  toxicity tests 506
chlorobutanol, anesthetic 221
chloroform, anesthetic 213
Chloromycetin, surgical antibiotic 256
cholinergic receptors, electric rays 439
chromatophores, fish coloration 116
chromogen, horseradish peroxidase 438
chromomycin A3, chromosome stain 181
chromosomes 171–187
  analysis 171
  arm number 185
  autosomes 38
  banding techniques 179–183
  classification system 184
  damaging agents, analysis 183–184
  karyotypes 184–186
  manipulation, sex control 544

nuclear 38
number 185
organization 38
preparation, basic principles 171
sex 38, 184
sources 172–176
species delimitation 73
spreads, cell suspensions 176
vertebrate 38
chronic recording, electrocardiogram 315
chronic studies, nervous system 418
chronic toxicity
definition 493
tests and assays 510–519
chronology-of-feeding method,
bioenergetics 398
circulation, blood 273, 312–322
cirri, taxonomic characters 113
citrates, anticoagulants 275
cladistic analysis, electrophoresis 163
cladistics, systematics 65
cladogenesis 69
cladograms 70
Clark oxygen electrodes 299, 336, 339
classification
biological 92
evolutionary 95
indentation 96
numericlature 96
phenetic 95
phylogenetic 93
phylogenetic systematics 66
tree 96
clearance, metabolic 462, 464–465
clearing, histological sections 195
clinoptilolite, ammonia removal 642
clomiphene, estrogen antagonist 541
cluster analysis 162
phenetics 90
coagulant fixatives 193
codon, messenger RNA 37
coefficient of condition 372
coevolution, species interactions 619, 621
cohort identification, estimates of growth 374
Colcemid, metaphase block 172
colchicine, metaphase block 172
cold narcosis 216
cold shock 238
collagen, trichrome stains 203
collections
museums and research 102
systematic and faunistic research 99
color coding, dried bones 121
color patterns in fish, taxonomic
characters 116
colorimetric methods, protein analysis 367
community ecology 609–626
competition
coevolution 619, 621
community ecology 613–616
computer methods

genetic drift 55
karyotype 187
morphometric characters 125
numerical phenetics 91
phylogenetic analysis 84, 87–88
taxonomic keys 97
technology 208
conceptual framework, research 2
condition factor 372
confidence limits, toxicity tests 500
confining devices, recovery from surgery 284
confirmatory analysis 129
connective tissue stains 203
conspecific individuals, species 68
consumed energy, allocation 391
consumption rates
bioenergetics 391
bioenergetics models 405
calculation 399
contaminants in fish, bioenergetics 409
continuous feeding models, bioenergetics 396
controlled experience studies 18–23
controlled experiments 23–32
environmental variables 20
field experiments 24
field parameters 7
laboratory experiments 27
types of designs 9
controls
behavioral studies 561
lethality tests 502
neural pathway tracer 439
conus, cardiac structure 314
coolants, starch gel electrophoresis 147
coronal region, taxonomic characters 111
cortisol assays, plasma 456
Cortland saline formulation 285, 298
coulometric microrespirometry 341
countable characters, taxonomy 117
counterstains
enhanced fluorescent banding 183
histological techniques 200
neural pathway definition 439
covariance methods, growth estimates 375
cover use, microhabitats 595
coverslips, histological techniques 207
^{51}Cr-impregnated microspheres 322
critical partial oxygen 345
critical steps, research process 3
critical thermal maximum or minimum 470
crossing-over, genetics 44
cross-reactivity, radioimmunoassays 456
crowding challenge tests, stress 475
cryopreparation, histology 191, 193
cryopreservation, gametes 537
cryoprotectants, gamete storage 538
cryostat sections 198, 206
cryptic species 70
ctenoid scales, taxonomic characters 115
culture systems, fish, see fish maintenance
cyanomethemoglobin 286

cycloid scales, taxonomic characters 115
cytochemistry
   enzymes 206
   leukocytes 312
cytogenetics, future developments 186
cytotoxic agents, tracers 435

Dacie's fluid, blood diluent 288
daily ration, bioenergetics 396–407
   carnivore models 399–401
   chronology-of-feeding models 398–399
   coldwater predator 400, 402
   continuous feeding models 396–398
   warmwater predator 401, 403
DAPI, chromosome stain 180
data analysis
   model form 10
   research process 10
   statistical methods 11
data collection
   behavioral studies 558
   electrophoretic data 150
   estimating growth of wild fish 373
   morphometric characters 125
data presentations, graphic 17
data recorders, intracellular electrodes 425
decision making, behavior 555
definitions
   aquatic toxicology 492
   autecology 586
   ecology 610
defleshing, skeleton preparation 121
dehydration, histology 195
dehydrogenase system, staining buffer 149
deionizing columns, elimination of solutes 300
dendrograms 163
density-gradient centrifugation 296
dentary, taxonomic characters 111
depuration, measurement 462, 463–464
dermal structures, taxonomic characters 115
descriptive approaches, community
          ecology 610
destaining procedures, Giemsa stain 178
detergents, tracers 435
deterministic ecological interactions 619
diagnostic loci 164–166
diagrams, phylogenetic 70
diaminobenzidine tetrahydrochloride 438
diaminofluorene, hemoglobin stain 291
diel feeding 403
diel movements 593
differential leukocyte counts 310
   stress 460
differentiation, histological techniques 200
digestion rate
   carnivorous fish 402
   coefficient 397–398, 399
digitizer, morphometric measurements 125
diluters, toxicity tests 497
dilution water, toxicity tests 505

dimeric enzymes, electrophoresis 152
dimethylpolysiloxane, implants 260
dip treatments, anesthetic 218
diphenylamine method, DNA
          measurement 372
direct calorimetry 335
directed tree methods, phylogenetic
          analysis 84
discriminant function analysis 589
   morphometric data 130
disease
   challenge tests for 471, 473
   chemical treatments, list 654
   control of 650–655
   stress-related 467, 468
   therapeutants, list 652
disinfectants, topical 254
dissociated cells, neural studies 422
dissolved oxygen
   fish culture systems 635, 646
   toxicity tests 508
distance coefficients, phenetics 90
distance measurements, morphometric
          data 129
disturbances, fish culture 659
diuresis, stress 459
diurnal feeding patterns 403
diversity, species 625–626
diving surveys, fish populations 590
DNA
   indices of growth 371–372
   mitochondrial 40, 57, 74
   quantitation in tissues 372
   radioautography 208
   replication 36
   structure 36
DNA–DNA hybridization, synapomorphy 77
dominance
   behavioral studies 568
   hierarchy consequences 570
   laboratory growth studies 379
dopamine, fluorescent histochemistry 440
dorsal aorta
   blood pressure 317
   cannulation 280
dorsal fins, taxonomic characters 113
dosage, anesthetic, defined 218
drug interactions, anesthesia 218
drugs
   application to retina 434
   bath application 428
   disease treatments 652–655
dry weight, growth 365
dual cannulation, blood sampling 282
duplicate loci
   estimation of allele frequencies 156
   genetic variation 158
   starch gel electrophoresis 152
dye-dilution curve, cardiac output 319
dye markers, starch gel electrophoresis 146

EC50, see effective concentration-50
ECG, see electrocardiogram
ecology
    autecology   585–600
    community   609–628
EDTA
    anesthetic interactions   219, 276
    blood anticoagulant   273, 275
effective concentration-50 (EC50)   218, 496
effective exposure time   218
effective population size, genetics   55
efficacy, anesthesia   218
effluent treatment, fish culture   660
egestion, bioenergetics   395
eggs
    counting   536
    development   531
    fecundity   535
    in vitro fertilization   538
    quality   537
    sampling   533
electivity, microhabitat variables   598
electivity indices
    predation   616, 618
    resources   598
electric fish, neural studies   435
electrical charge, proteins   141
electricity
    anesthetics   221
    principles in neurophysiological
        research   442
    electroanesthesia   216, 238
    blood sampling   280
electrocardiogram   314–316
electrodes
    brain stimulation   432
    electrocardiogram implantation   315
    intracellular   424
    neurophysiological setups   423
    oxygen (Clark)   299, 336, 339
    starch gel electrophoresis   147
electrofishing   6
electromagnetic flowmeters   321
electromyography   419, 426
electron microscopy, thrombocytes   304
electronarcosis   238
electronic counting systems, erythrocytes   287
electronic noise reduction,
        electrophysiology   426
electropherograms, starch gel
        electrophoresis   151
electrophoresis   141–166
    buffers, 145, 147–148
    gel operation   146–147
    gel preparation   144–145, 146
    genetic analysis   150–164
    hemoglobin isomorphs   290–293
    protein analysis   148–150
    rationale   143
    stains   148–150
    tissue preparation   145–146

electrophysiology   422–433
electroreceptors, lateral line   434
electroretinograms, neural studies   434
electrotaxis   238
electrotetanus   238
elimination, metabolites   462
Elliott–Persson bioenergetics model   397
embedding media, histology   196–198, 199, 207
embryos, source of chromosome spreads   172
endocrine system, stress responses   452
endoscopy, sex determination   529
energy budget, bioenergetics
    balanced   389
    components   391, 393–403
energy content, calorimetric analysis   369
energy partitioning   390
environmental requirements, autecology   585
environmental variables
    community disruptions   619
    intercorrelation   20
    microhabitat measurements   595
    niche determinants   599
enzymes
    buffers   147
    chemical catalysts   142
    effects on, anesthetics   245
    erythrocytes   301
    histochemical techniques   206
    histological techniques   197
    stains for, electrophoresis   148
eosin, cytoplasm stain   200
eosinophils   309
epidemiology, aquatic toxicology   517
epinephrine
    anesthesia enhancer   219
    detection, histochemistry   440
epithelia, sources of chromosome spreads   174
epizootics
    chemicals used for treatment   654
    fish culture   651
    treatment   653
epural elements, taxonomic characters   118
erythrocytes (red blood cells)   285–303
    counts   287–289
    enzyme activity   301–303
    formation   290
    recovery from surgery   284
    size distribution   295–298
    size segregation   296–298
erythromycin, surgical antibiotic   256
erythropoiesis   290
estrogens
    sex reversal   542
    spawning   541
ether, anesthetic   213
ethogram, behavioral studies   559
ethyl aminobenzoate, anesthetic   233–235
    spawning operations   221
etomidate, anesthetic   221, 235–236
eukaryotic gene, structure   38
evacuation rate, stomach   397–398, 399

Evan's blue dye, blood tracer 294
evoked potentials, neural studies 430
evolution
  anagenesis 69
  classification 95
  phylogenetic groups 66
  polarity, character analysis 78
  preference tests 566
  relationships, chromosome analysis 171
  relationships, morphometric data 130
  speciation or cladogenesis 69
  species interactions 619
  systematics 65
excretion, bioenergetics 395
exhaustion, stage of stress 452
exons, gene structure 38
experimental crosses, taxonomic decisions 71
experimental designs
  behavioral studies 561
  community ecology 612
  competition 616
  laboratory growth studies 379
  optimum choice 32
  selection 8
experimental error, controlled experiments 24
experimental units 7
experimenter bias, accuracy 27
exploratory analysis 129
exponential growth rate 364
exposure conditions, anesthesia 218
exposure times
  anesthesia 218
  toxicity tests 496
external morphology, taxonomic
    characters 109
eye motions, in vivo preparations 418

factorial experiments, field experiments 25
facultative bacterial pathogens, stress 467
Faraday effect 321
fatigue time, swimming performance 472
fatty acids, chromatography 368
fecundity 535–536, 588
feeding
  behavior 573–576
  diurnal patterns 403
  habits: autecology 590
  mechanical feeding devices 659
  rates, cultured fish 658
  regime in laboratory growth studies 379
feeding models 399–403
ferric hydroxide in culture water 635
fertilization
  egg quality 537
  in vitro fertilization 538
Fick equation, oxygen consumption rate 354
Fick method, cardiac output 318
field experiments
  autecology 589
  community ecology 612

preference tests 567
randomized 25
replication 9
selection of similar subareas 24
sources of confusion 27
field validation, toxicity tests 513
filming, see photography
films
  fish photography 133
  fluorescent histochemistry 441
filters
  biofilters 640
  charcoal 636–637
  electronic 443, 444
  static aquaria 637
filtration, fish culture systems 634
finlets, taxonomic characters 114
Finquel, registered anesthetic 214, 223
fins, fin rays
  sources of chromosome spreads 174
  taxonomic characters 113–114, 118
fish culture
  bioenergetics 408
  holding systems 637–645
  measurement conversion units 654
  systems 633–661
  water supply 633–636
fish holding facilities 637–645
fish maintenance 633–661
  aquaria and raceways 637–642
  carrying capacity 649
  feeding practices 655–659
  fish health 650–655, 659
  permits and regulations 650
  ponds and cages 643–645
  water management 633–636, 645–649, 660
fish production, holding facilities 649
fish size
  bioenergetics equations 404
  dietary shifts 616
  measures of, growth 364–370
  mortality rates 622
fish sources, fish culture 650
fishery chemicals, restrictions on use 220
fixation, histological samples 192–194
fixation index, genetics 56
fixation times, histology 194
fixatives
  Bouin's, tissues 193
  Carnoy's, metaphase cells 172, 173, 175,
    176
  formalin 102 (whole animals), 193 (tissues)
fixed heterozygosity 166
fixed tissues
  dehydration, clearing 195–196
  embedment 196–198
  mounting 199, 206
  sectioning 198
  staining 199–206
  trimming, orientation 194
flame-dry chromosome spreads 176, 177

flowmeters, cardiac output 321
flow-through respirometers 347–348, 349
  gill ventilation 355
flow-through systems, fish culture 634, 638–639
flow-through toxicity tests 226, 497
fluorescence techniques
  chromosome sorting 187
  microsphere tracers, neurons 436
  neural histochemistry 440–442
  nucleic acid quantities 372
Folin phenol method, protein analysis 367
food
  behavioral studies 573
  consumption 389, 395–403
  feeding captive and cultured fish 655
  feeding methods 659
  feeding rates and frequencies 658
  mechanical feeding devices 659
  particle size 379
  specific dynamic action 395
  webs 620–624
forage ratios, predation 618
foraging theory
  feeding behavior 576
  predation 617
force-feeding of fish, digestion rates 403
formalin, fixatives 102, 193
Fraser–Lee method, growth estimates 375–377
freeze-drying
  dry weight 366
  histological techniques 197
frenum, taxonomic characters 111
Freund's adjuvant 260
frozen sections, histological techniques 198
fry, source of chromosome spreads 173
Fulton's condition factor 372
fungi, fish diseases 651

gallamine triethiodide, relaxant 230
galvanonarcosis 238
gametes
  counts 535–536
  development 531, 532, 533
  fertilization in vitro 538–539
  maturation stages 533–535
  quality 536–537
  sampling from ovaries 533–534
  storage 537–538
gap-coding of morphometric data 130
gas bubble embolisms, fish culture 651
gas exchange sites, static respirometers 345
gasometric methods, oxygen measurement 341
gastric evacuation rate 396–398
gastric mucosa, stress 461
G-banding, chromosomes 181–183
gels, see electrophoresis
gene duplication, electrophoretic analysis 152
gene flow, species 68
genealogical reconstruction, systematics 67

general adaptation syndrome 452–453
generally recognized as safe (GRAS) 220
genes
  duplicated 152–155
  eukaryotic 38
  regulatory 38
  structural 38
  structure 37–38
  transposons 39
genetic drift 54–55, 57, 159–160
genetic markers
  hemoglobin isomorphs 290
  taxonomic decisions 74
genetics 35–59, see also chromosomes, electrophoresis
  correlations among traits 50
  definition 35
  DNA 36
  drift 54, 57, 159–160
  evolutionary 35
  gene linkage 44–45
  gene structure 37–38
  genome organization 38–40
  Hardy–Weinberg equilibrium 51
  heritability 48–50
  inbreeding 55–57
  inheritance of single genes 40–44
  manipulation of sex 544
  Mendelian 35, 40–44
  natural populations 51
  natural selection 52–54
  niche divergence 621
  non-Mendelian inheritance 45–47
  panmictic index 56
  polygenic traits 47–50
  population structure and migration 57
  protein synthesis 36
  selective neutrality 159
  sex linkage 43
  single genes with major effects 44
germicides 250
germinal vesicle, reproductive maturity 534
Giemsa stain
  blood 295, 310
  chromosomes 178–179
gill, source of chromosome spreads 173
gill rakers, taxonomic characters 119
gill ventilation 338, 353–356
  anesthetization of 243
  energetic cost of 355
glucose determinations 369
glycerol detection, leukocytes 310
glycine uptake by fish scales, growth 371
glycogen determinations 369
glycol methacrylate, embedment 197, 199, 207
glycoxylic acid, fluorescent histochemistry 441
GnRH (gonadotropin releasing hormone) 540
gonadectomy, sterilization 547
gonadosomatic index 531
  bioenergetics 393
gonadotropin releasing hormone (GnRH) 540

gonads
  chromosome spreads from 173, 176
  development control 538
  histology 531
  ripening 530
  sex determination 529
graphical analysis
  daily consumption rate 399
  lethal concentration-50 498
  systematics 88, 90
GRAS (generally recognized as safe) 220
grinding medium, starch gel
     electrophoresis 146
grounding, electrophysiological setups 426
growth 363–382
  absolute 363
  back-calculation of 375–377
  bioenergetics 391, 393
  calorimetric measures 369
  competition 615
  estimates 374–378
  fish age 587
  indices 370–372
  instantaneous rate 364
  laboratory studies 378–381
  natural populations 372
  quantification of 364–366
  previous years
  relative 363, 364
  toxicity tests 512
gular region, taxonomic characters 112
gynogenesis
  artificial 544
  genetics 46

habitats 591–599
  mapping studies 597
  stratification 591
  suitability 599
handling challenge tests, stress 476
hardness
  fish culture systems 648
  toxicity tests 509
Hardy–Weinberg equilibrium 51
hazard assessment, toxicology 521
H&E (hematoxylin and eosin) stain 199, 200
head, taxonomic characters 110, 113
head kidney, chromosome spreads 173
hemalum, nuclear stain 199
hematocrit 275, 286, 287
hematological analyses 285–312
  blood volume 293–295
  erythrocytes 285–286, 287–290, 295–298,
    301–303
  hemoglobin 286–287, 290–293
  leukocytes 303–312
  oxygen equilibria 298–301
hematological changes
  anesthesia 244
  stress 460

hematoxylin stain 199, 200
hematoxylin and eosin (H&E) stain 199, 200
hemocytometer 288
hemoglobin
  isomorph electrophoresis 290–293
  measurement 285–286
  oxygen affinity 289, 298–301
hemostat, surgery 250
Hendricks's fluid, blood diluent 287–288
Hennig's principle, genealogy 74
heparin, blood anticoagulant 275, 276
heritability, 48–50
heterochromatin staining, chromosomes 180
heterochrony, evolutionary change 124
heterogametic sex chromosomes, linkage 43
heterogametic sex genes, sex control 544
heteromorphic chromosomes, sex control 544
heterophils 307
heterozygosity
  defined 40
  loss, genetic drift 54–55
  measurement of 158
hierarchies, behavioral studies 568
high-resolution light microscopy 207
histochemical tracers, neuroanatomy 436
histochemistry, fluorescence 440
histological techniques 191–208
  exams for stress 461
  fixation 192–194
  image quantitation 208
  section preparation 193, 194–199
  staining and mounting 199–207
histopathology, aquatic toxicology 516
holding boxes, recovery from surgery 284
holding conditions, toxicity test organisms 504
holding facilities, carrying capacity 649
home range, behavioral studies 570
homogenate, gel electrophoresis 146
homologous chromosomes, C-banding 180
homology, character analysis 78
homoplasy, defined, systematics 75
homozygosity, defined 40
horizontal electrophoresis 144
hormones
  primary stress responses 455
  profiles, sex and reproductive maturity 535
  recovery from surgery 284
  sex reversal 542–544
  spawning induction 539–541
  sterilization 545–546
horseradish peroxidase, neuroanatomical
    tracer 436–439, 440
human chorionic gonadotropin, spawning 540
hybridization
  production of sterile fish 546
  species 69
  species introductions 165
  taxonomic decisions 71
hydrochloric orcein–picrofuchsin stain 203
hyperglycemic response, stress 458
hyperlacticemia, stress 459

Hypnomidate, see etomidate   235
hypochloremia, stress   458
hypophysation, spawning   540
hypothermia, anesthesia   216, 237
hypotonic chromosome preparation   172
hypotonic shock, cell lysis   302
hypoxia challenge tests, stress   471
hypural elements, taxonomic characters   118

^{131}I markers   294
ice anesthesia   216
identification of fish
    individuals   558
    species   97, 99
    stocks   589
^{131}I-labeled protein, blood distributions   322
immobilization
    anesthesia   215, 221
    methods, blood samples   276
immune capacity, stress   467
immune mechanisms, lymphocytes   306
immunochemistry, neural transmitters   440
immunohistochemical procedures   197
immunorejection, sterilization   545
implants, see also cannulation, electrodes
    abdominal   246
in situ preparation, chromosome spreads   177
in vitro fertilization   538
inbreeding   55–57
incisions, surgery   254
indentation classification   96
indirect antibody labeling, neurons   440
indirect calorimetry   335, 369
induction time
    anesthesia, defined   218
    carbon dioxide   231
    ethyl aminobenzoate   233
    etomidate   235
    quinaldine   228
    quinaldine sulfate   230
    phenoxyethanol   236
    tricaine   224
infections, surgery   256
inferior mouth, taxonomic characters   111
infiltration, histological preparations   195
ingested prey, weight   401
ingroup analysis, character analysis   82
inheritance   36–40
injection plastic, vascular casts   274
injections
    needle gauge and size   260
    sites   259
insects
    cleaning of skeletal preparations   121
    control of, fish culture systems   660
instantaneous growth rate   364, 375
instream flow incremental methodology   599
instrument tie, suturing   255
instrumentation, neurophysiology   423
instruments, surgery   250

integrated neural responses,
        chemoreception   431
intergeneric hybrids   72
internal morphology, taxonomic
        characters   121
internal organs, taxonomic characters   122
internal wire trocars, blood sampling   281
interopercle, taxonomic characters   111
interorbital region, taxonomic characters   110
interrenal hypertrophy, stress   461
interspecific hybrids   166
interspinal injections   261
intestine, source of chromosome spreads   173
intracellular recording, neural studies   427
intracellular stimulus currents   444
intraperitoneal implants   260
intrinsic growth rate   364
introgressed populations, diagnosis   166
introns, gene structure   37
invertebrates, life cycle tests   511
iodometric oxygen measurement   336–340
iridophores, fish coloration   116
iron, fish culture systems   635
irrigation systems, recovery from surgery   284
isomorphs, hemoglobin variants   290
isthmus, taxonomic characters   112

junior synonyms   99
juvenile identification, electrophoresis   164

kanamycin, surgical antibiotic   256
karyology, synapomorphy   77
karyotypes, 184–186
kinetic studies, dual cannulation   282
Kjeldahl nitrogen method, protein analysis   367
knives, histological   207
Kornhauser's quad stain, connective
        tissue   203

labeling, histological specimens   194
laboratory experiments
    principles   27–28, 30–32
    replication   8–10
lactic acid, blood   459
lake management, biomanipulation   624
larval fish
    blood sampling   280
    identification, electrophoresis   164
    morphology   123
    stages   123
    taxonomic characters   124
lateral line
    sensory functions   434–435
    taxonomic characters   115
LC50, see lethal concentration-50
LD50, see lethal dose-50
learning   573–577
Lee's phenomenon, back-calculations   377

Leishmann stain, blood cells 295, 310
length-frequency analysis, growth
    estimates 374
length–weight relationship, equation 364
length
  growth 364
  taxonomic characters 110
lethal concentration-50 (LC50) 495–503
lethal dose-50 (LD50) 218
lethal temperature determination 470
lethality tests, toxicology 495
leucocytes, see leukocytes
leukocrit determinations, stress 460
leukocytes (white blood cells) 303
  concentration 312
  culture, mitotic cell source 172, 174, 175
  cytochemical methods 312
  differential leukocyte count 310
  properties of, table 311
  removal from erythrocyte assays 301–302
  total leukocyte counts 309
leukopenia, stress 460
lidocaine, anesthetic 240–241
lidocaine hydrochloride, anesthetic 215,
    240–241
life cycle toxicity tests 510–512
life history studies, autecology 587
life stages, toxicity tests 507
light conditions, laboratory growth studies 380
linear food selection index, predation 618
linear model approach, growth estimates 375
linkage, genetic 44–45
lipids
  analysis 368
  growth 368
  proximate analysis 367
  staining 200, 310
live food, fish culture 655
liver–somatic index, growth 372
living fossils, character analysis 82
loci
  duplicated 152–155
  nomenclature 155
logarithmic growth rate 364
log-probit transformations, toxicity 498
logic circuits 445
Lowery method, protein analysis 367
lymphatic circulation 305
lymphocytes 305
  stress 468
lysis 302
lysochromes 201

macrochromosomes 184
macrophages 306
maintenance, see fish maintenance
mapping, habitat 597
marker beads, blood densities 298
marker-dilution estimates, blood volume 294
marking and tagging

electrified tagging basket 238
  home range studies 571
  movement studies 593
  surgical marks and implants 245
mass, growth 364
mass exponents, oxygen consumption
    rates 342
mass-independent metabolic rates 342
Masson's trichrome stain, collagen 203, 205
matching coefficients, phenetics 90
maturation, erythrocytes 295
maturity, determination 530
maxillae, taxonomic characters 111
Mayer's H&E technique, stains 202
McManus periodic acid–Schiff technique 204
mean erythrocyte hemoglobin 286, 296
mechanoreceptors, lateral line 434
megachromosomes 184
meiotic chromosomes, terminology 185
melanophore concentration 218
Mendelian genetics 40–47
mentum, taxonomic characters 112
meristic taxonomic characters 117–121
messenger RNA (mRNA) 36
metabolic clearance, stress 462
metabolic expansibility index 337
metabolic intensity 289
metabolic rate
  measurement 335
  stress 466
metabolism, bioenergetics 391, 394–395
Metacaine, see tricaine
metacentric chromosomes 184
metaphase cells
  chromosome preparation 171
  sources 172–176
  spindle fiber formation 172
methemoglobinazide, hemoglobin measure 287
methylpentynol, anesthetic 221
methylquinoline, see quinaldine
microchromosomes 184
microcomputers, bioenergetics models 407
microelectrode pullers 425
microelectrodes, brain stimulation 432
microhabitats 593–599
microhematocrit reader 287
micromanipulators, nerve electrodes 424
microscopy
  high-resolution light 207
  neurophysiological setups 423
microtomy, histological techniques 198
migration
  fish behavior 576
  proteins, electrophoresis 143
minimum-length tree methods,
    systematics 84–86
mist nets, bird control 660
mitochondrial DNA (mtDNA)
  analysis for genetic population structure 57
  characterization 40
  taxonomic decisions 74

mitogens, lymphocyte culture   175
mitotic cells, sources   172–176
mitotic index   172
mixtures, toxicity   520–521
molds, horizontal electrophoresis   144
monoamines, fluorescent histochemistry   441
monocytes   306–307
monomeric enzymes, electrophoresis   150
monomorphic loci, genetic variation   158
monophyletic groups   70
monophyletic requirements, systematics   74, 75
monopolar brain stimulation   433
morphology, blood cells   311
morphology, fish bodies   109–133
    character sets   126–128
    data analysis   129–130
    larvae   123–125
    skeletal characters   121
    taxonomic characters   109–120, 122
    truss analysis   127–129
    X-ray radiography   122
morphometry   125–130
mortality, anesthesia   219
mosaic evolution   82
motion detection, neural studies   418
motivation, preference studies   563
mounting, histological sections
    procedures   199
    media   206
mouth, taxonomic characters   111
movement patterns, fish   593
moving boundary electrophoresis   143
mRNA   36
MS-222, see tricaine
mtDNA, see mitochondrial DNA
mucus, sex determination   530
muffle furnace, ash weight   366
Müller cells
    intracellular recording   427
    neural studies   429
multiple-comparison tests   12
municipal water, fish culture systems   635
muscles
    relaxants   230
    taxonomic characters   122
mutagenesis, sister chromatid exchanges   183

nape, body sections   109
narcoanesthesia   214
nares, taxonomic characters   112
natural experiments, community ecology   611
natural populations, estimations of growth   372
natural selection
    fish population genetics   52
    local adaptations   52, 54
    morphological variation   52
    protein variation   52, 53
    species   68
needle size and gauge, injections   260
needle types, surgery   251

Nei's measure of standard genetic
        distance   160
nerve blocks, lidocaine and Xylocaine   241
nerve–electrode contact   424
nerve stimulation and recording   427
nerves, taxonomic characters   122
nervous system   417–445
Neubauer hemocytometer   288
neural tissue stains   204
neurophysiology
    electrical principles   442–445
    instrumentation   423–426
neurosensory effects, anesthetics   242, 245
neutral models, community ecology   613
niche
    divergence, coevolution   620, 621
    overlap   614–615
    physicochemical determinants   599–600
nicotine, anesthetic   221
nitrates, fish culture systems   647
nitrification   641, 647
nitrites, fish culture systems   648
nitro-blue tetrazolium, enzyme stain   149
nitrogen, fish culture systems   647
no-observed-effect concentration   493, 511
nodal tissues, cardiac structure   314
nomenclature, systematics   96–97
nonabsorbable sutures   251
nongenetic variation, electrophoresis   155
nonparametric statistical methods   11
nonsense codons   37
nonspecific staining, chromosomes   178
norepinephrine, fluorescent histochemistry   440
nostrils, taxonomic characters   112
nucha, body sections   109
nuchal hump, taxonomic characters   111
nucleic acids, see also DNA, RNA
    indices of growth   371–372
    sequences: ontogenic criterion   82
nucleolus organizer region   180–181
nucleotide sequencing, synapomorphy   77
null models, community ecology   612–613
numerical expressions of whole-body
        growth   363
numerical methods, phenetics   89
numericlature, classification   96
nuptial tubercles, taxonomic characters   115
nutritional diseases, fish culture   651
nutritional history, growth studies   379

observation techniques
    behavioral studies   557
    frequency   4
    microhabitats   594
    units   6
occiput, body sections   109
octanol–water partition coefficient   517
oculomotor neurons, in vivo preparations   418
Ohm's law, electrophysiological
        techniques   443

oil red O stain, lipids 201, 203
ontogenetic shifts, food webs 620
ontogeny, character analysis 82
open respirometers 347
operational taxonomic units, phenetics 89
opercle, taxonomic characters 111
opercular rate, gill ventilation 338
operculum, taxonomic characters 109, 111
optimal habitat, preference studies 565
orcinol method, RNA measurement 372
ordination, phenetics 90
Oregon moist pellet, fish food 657
organic matter, toxicity tests 509
osmium tetroxide, fixative 194
osmoregulatory status
 anesthetic effect on 244
 erythrocyte volume measure of 286
 plasma measures of 459
 salinity challenge test of 474–475
otoliths, taxonomic characters 121
outgroup analysis, character analysis 79
ovaries, source of meiotic chromosomes 176
oxalates, anticoagulants 275
oxycaloric values 394
oxygen, see also respirometers
 blood equilibrium curves 298–301
 concentration, tension 299, 336, 339–341
 electrodes 299, 336, 339
 fish culture systems 635, 641, 646–647
 toxicity tests 508
oxygen consumption, see also respiration
 changes with fish size 341–342
 measure of metabolism 394–395
 measure of stress 466
 reduced by anesthesia 216–218
 uptake by gills 338, 353–356
oxytetracycline, surgery 258
ozone sterilizers, fish culture systems 642

P waves, electrocardiogram 314
P–Q interval, electrocardiogram 315
pacemaker cells, cardiac structure 314
paddle wheel aerators, fish ponds 635
pair bonds, behavioral studies 572
pairwise distance methods, systematics 86
paleontology, character analysis 79
pancuronium bromide, relaxant 230
panmictic index, genetics 56
paraffin wax, histology 195, 196–197, 198–199
paralyzation, neural studies 417
parameter specification 7
paraphyletic groups 70
parasites
 chemical treatments, list 654
 control of 650–655
 therapeutics, list 652
parr–smolt transformation, stress 468–469
parsimony methods, systematics 84–86, 87–88
pectoral fins, taxonomic characters 114
pelvic fins, taxonomic characters 114

Percoll density gradients 296, 298, 312
performance capacity, stress 469–477
periodic acid–Schiff stain 201, 203, 204, 310, 312
 carbohydrate stains 201
 tissue components 203
peripheral eosinophils 309
permitting requirements, collecting fish 650
peroxidase–antiperoxidase staining 440
pest control, fish culture 660
petroleum jelly, waterproofing 256
pH
 fish culture systems 648
 toxicity tests 508
pharmacology, fluorescent histochemistry 442
pharyngeal teeth, taxonomic characters 120
phenetic analysis, electrophoresis 160
phenetics 65, 88–92, 160
phenograms 70, 87
phenothiazine, tranquilizers 215
phenoxyethanol, anesthetic 221, 236–237
phenylhydrazine, hemolytic agent 293
phosphatases, lymphocyte discrimination 312
photography
 chromosomes 186
 developing and enlarging 186
 fish 131–133
 gel preservation 150
 swimming fish 419
photomicrography, photographic film 186
photoperiod
 growth rates 380
 spawning 538
photophores, taxonomic characters 116
phylogenetic systematics 65, 66–70, 74–88, 93–95
 analytical methods 83–88
 classification 93–95
 electrophoretic analysis 160–163
 phenogram estimates 87
 principles 66–70
phylograms 70
physical site factors 8
physicochemical niche determinants 599–600
physiological adaptation to stress 452
physiological condition, calorimetry 369
physiological correlates of behavior 564–566
physiological data, bioenergetics models 405
physiological indices of growth 370–372
physiological responses
 anesthetics 242–243
 stress 242–243, 453–466
physiological salines 285, 421, 422
physiological tests of stress, table 463
physiological variables, normal limits 464, 465
phytohemagglutinin, T cell mitogen 175
picro-indigocarmine stain, elastic fibers 203
pigmentation, taxonomic characters 116
pimozide, spawning 541
pipettes, blood-diluting 288
piscivorous species, food consumption 378

pituitary extracts, spawning 540
placoid scales, taxonomic characters 115
plasma tonicity 421
plasma water, dehydration 460
pleiotropy 50
plesiomorphy, defined, systematics 74
plumbing
    aquacultural ponds 643
    fish culture systems 634, 636
    flow-through aquaria 638
    raceways 638
pokeweed lipopolysaccharide, B cell
        mitogen 175
polyacrylamide gels, electrophoresis 144
polygenic traits, genetics 47
polymorphic loci, genetic variation 158
polypeptides, general structure 141–142
polyphyletic groups 70
polyploids
    chromosome analysis 171
    genetics 46
    reproduction 545
    triploidy 546
Ponceau S, protein stain 291
pond construction for research 643
populations
    density 6
    genetics 51
    growth estimates 375
    parameters 7
    stress responses 453
pore size, starch gels 144
portable computers, behavioral studies 559
postoperative care, surgery 256, 258–259
power, starch gel electrophoresis 145, 147
pre-anesthetics, barbiturates 239
prebranchial blood samples 277
precautions, anesthesia 219
precision
    controlled experiments 24
    laboratory experiments 27
    replicate number 9
predation
    effects on prey communities 622–623
    fish culture 650, 660
    food web dynamics 623–624
    inertia 623
    prey selection 616–617
predorsal length, taxonomic characters 110
preference studies, behavior 561, 563
pregnant mare serum gonadotropin 540
premaxillae, taxonomic characters 111
preoperative care, surgery 253
preopercle, taxonomic characters 111
preparation, surgery 253
prepared food, fish culture 656
preservation distortion of specimens 126
preservatives
    field collecting programs 102
    otoliths 121
    preservation distortion 126

pressure–flow relationships, blood 317
prey communities, predator effects 622
prey selectivity, predation 617
primary cell cultures, chromosomes 174–176
primary hematological indices 285
primitive taxa, character analysis 82
principal components analysis
    morphometric data 129–130
    phenetics 90–91
    stock identification 590
probit analysis, lethal concentration-50 499
product-moment correlation, phenetics 90
production estimates, studies 18
progesterone, spawning 541
progressive staining 199
pronephros, lymphocyte concentration 305
propanidid, anesthetic 241
prophylactic treatments, disease 651
propoxate, anesthetic 241
protein analysis, growth 367–368
protein-coding loci, nomenclature 149
protein synthesis 36–37
    index of growth 370
protein:DNA ratio, index of growth 371
proteins
    chemistry 141–143
    electrophoretic analysis 148–150
    homologous 143
    proximate analysis 367
proximate analysis, growth 366–369
pseudo species 164
Punnet square, Mendelian genetics 41
pyloric caeca, taxonomic characters 120

Q-banding methods, chromosomes 181–183
QRS waves, electrocardiogram 314
Q–T interval, electrocardiogram 315
quantitative (polygenic) traits, genetics 47
quarantine, aquaculture diseases 655
quaternary structure, proteins 142
quinacrine dihydrochloride, chromosomes 182
quinaldine, anesthetic 215, 219, 221, 227–230
quinaldine sulfate, anesthetic 230–231
quinate, see quinaldine sulfate

raceways, fish culture systems 638
radiation, sterilization 547
radioactive tracers, clearance rates 465
radioautography, histological techniques 207
radioimmunoassays 454
radioisotopes, effluent treatment 660
radioligand binding, receptor studies 442
radiotelemetry, electrocardiogram 315
ram ventilation, gills 353
random start compromise, field
        experiments 25
randomized block design, field experiments 25
ratios, morphometric data analysis 129
rays, fins 113

realized heritability 49
receptor binding, neural studies 442
recirculating-water systems, fish culture 640
recirculation toxicity tests 497
record keeping, fish photography 132
recording units, central nervous system 429
recovery time
  anesthesia, defined 218
  ethyl aminobenzoate 234
  etomidate 235
  phenoxyethanol 236
  quinaldine 228
  quinaldine sulfate 230
  tricaine 225
red blood cells, see erythrocytes
reflex action, anesthesia 217
refractive index, mounting media 206
refrigeration, blood samples 276
refrigerator anesthesia 216
registered compounds 220
regression methods, growth estimates 375
regressive staining 199
relative growth 363, 364
reliability of inferences, community
    ecology 612
reliability of results, bioenergetics
    approach 408
removal experiments, food webs 624
renewal tests, toxicology 496
replication
  banding, chromosomes 183
  experimental 8–10
reproduction 529–547
  anesthetics, effects 245
  autecology 588
  behavioral studies 572
  isolating mechanisms 73
  maturity signs 531
  sex determination 529
  stress 467
  taxonomic decisions 71, 72, 74
research
  application of findings 13
  bioenergetics approach 408
  checking study conclusions 13
  execution 10
  fish culture systems 633
  general 1
  study design 4
researcher effect 126
residues in fish, toxicity 517
resinous mounting media 206
resistance, stage of stress 452
resource availability data, microhabitats 596
resource partitioning, competition 613
respiration, see also oxygen consumption,
    respirometers
  anesthesia 216–218, 243–244
  blood hemoglobin content 286
  effect of fish size 341–342
  gill ventilation 338, 353–356

oxygen transport, blood 301
respiratory metabolism 335–338, 342–353
respiratory quotient 336
respirometers 338–339, 342–356
  annular 351–353
  blank 338, 344
  Blazka 351
  cleaning 338
  static 343–347
  swimming 348–353
  types 342
  volumes 343
respirometry 335–356
  stress 466
resting routine metabolism 336
restraints, neural studies 420
restriction enzymes 38
  banding techniques 183
  mitochondrial DNA analysis 40
restriction fragment length polymorphisms 38
retina, neural studies 434
Reynolds–Casterlin technique, cardiac
    output 320
ribosomal RNA (rRNA) 36
Ringer solutions
  chromosome preparation 173
  formulas 422
RNA
  quantitation in tissues 372
  types, protein synthesis 36–37
RNA:DNA ratio, indices of growth 371
Romanowsky staining, leukocytes 310, 311
Root effect 275
routine metabolism 336
rRNA 36

safety
  histological laboratory 194
  margin in anesthetics 218
saline solutions 285, 421, 422
salinity
  challenge tests, stress 474–475
  fish culture systems 636, 648
  toxicity tests 509
salt water, fish culture systems 636
sample collection, stratification 15
sample size 9
  electrophoretic studies 163
  observational studies 16
  predation 616
sample storage, electrophoresis 145
sampling
  design 4–10, 14, 19
  error 14, 15, 18, 19
  sites, blood 274
  units, study design 6–7
  universe, study design 5
  weighting factors 597–598
sanitation, fish culture 655
scale annuli, growth estimates 376

scales
  glycine uptake, growth index 371
  growth estimates 375–377
    source of chromosome spreads 174
    taxonomic characters 115, 119
schematochromes, fish coloration 116
schools, behavioral studies 571
scope for activity 337
scoring gels, electrophoresis 150
scutes, taxonomic characters 115
sea salts, synthetic 636
sealed-jar hypoxia challenge test, stress 471
seawater challenge test, stress 475
secobarbital sodium, fish transport 221
secondary hematological indices 285
sectioning, histological specimens 198
sedation 215, 221
selective ion electrode, carbon dioxide 232
sensitivity analysis, bioenergetics 408
sensory barbels, taxonomic characters 112
sensory canals and pits, taxonomy 112, 120
sensory modalities, feeding behavior 574
sensory structures, taxonomic characters 112
sensory systems, neurology 433–435
serial blood sampling 274
serial-slaughter method, bioenergetics 398
serotonin, fluorescence histochemistry 440
serum protein separation, electrophoresis 291
settling chambers, fish culture systems 641
sex change, behavioral studies 572
sex chromosomes 38, 184
    C-banding 180
    heterogametic, linkage 42
    manipulation of sex 544
sex control
    monosex populations 544–545
    sex reversal, steroids 542–545
sex determination 529
sex diagnosis, color patterns 117
Shaw's fluid, leukocyte staining 309
shock symptoms, surgery 259
sibling species 70, 164
silver grain emulsion, radioautography 208
silver impregnation methods, histologic 204
silver staining, nucleolus organizer region 180
single catheter error 282
sinus venosus, cardiac structure 313
sister chromatid exchange analysis 183
sister groups, lineages 69
site factors, parameters 7
size, see fish size
skeleton, taxonomic characters 121
skeletons, preparation 121
slides, microscope
    attaching histological sections 199
    cleaning 199
smoltification, stress 468
snout region, taxonomic characters 110
social facilitation, food consumption 379
social influences, feeding behavior 574
social structure, behavior 568–570, 571–572

sodium bicarbonate, anesthetic 214, 221, 231
sodium channels, electric eels 440
sodium chloride, anesthetic 221
sodium pentobarbital, anesthetic 239
solid tissue preparations, chromosomes 177, 178
somatic growth
    bioenergetics 393
    white muscle 371
spatially correlated variables 20
spawning
    behavioral studies 572
    control 539–540
Spearman–Karber toxicity estimates 500
speciation 69
species
    anesthetics 221
    autecology 585–600
    chromosome analysis 171
    community ecology 609–626
    concepts 67–69
    delimitation 70–74
    diagnostic coloration 117
    distinctions, genetic 159–160
    distribution and abundance 590–593
    diversity 624–626
    genealogical entity 69
    introductions, hybridization 165–166
    phenetics 89–92
    pseudo 164
    sibling 164
specific dynamic action 391, 395
specific growth rate 364
specimen preparation, fish photography 131
specimen size, hematological status 289
spectrophotometry, oxygen equilibrium 299
sperm
    concentrations 536
    cryopreservation 537
    development 531
    viability 536
spermatocrit 536
spines, fins 113
spiracle, taxonomic characters 112
split block experiments, field experiments 26
spontaneous fish activity, measurement 345
squash technique, chromosome analysis 176
[85]Sr-impregnated microspheres 322
stain buffers
    dehydrogenase system 149
    starch gel electrophoresis 149
staining 199–207
    mounting media 206
    technique selection 201
stains
    acridine orange 180
    Alcian Blue 122
    alizarin red S 121
    amido black 148
    benzidine 291
    bone 121

carbohydrate 201, 203, 204
cartilage 121–122
chromomycin A3 181
chromosomes 178–183
collagen 203, 204, 205
connective tissue 203, 204, 205
DAPI 180
diaminofluorene 291
electrophoresis 142
eosin 200
epoxy-embedded tissue 197
Giemsa 178–179, 295, 310
hematoxylin 199, 200
hematoxylin and eosin (H&E) 199, 200
hemalum 199
hemoglobin 291
histological techniques 199
hydrochloric orcein–picrofuchsin 203
Kornhauser's quad stain 203
Leishmann's stain 295, 310
lipid 200, 201, 203
Masson's trichrome stain 203, 205
Mayer's H&E technique 202
Mayer's hematoxylin 200
McManus periodic acid–Schiff 204
neural tissues 204
nitro-blue tetrazolium 149
nucleolus organizer region 180–181
oil red O technique 201, 203
periodic acid–Schiff 201, 203, 204, 310
peroxidase–antiperoxidase 440
picro-indigocarmine 203
Ponceau S 291
quinacrine dihydrochloride 182
silver impregnation methods 204
silver staining procedure 180
starch gel electrophoresis 148
substituted fluorochrome 180
Sudan black B 310
Sudan dyes 201
toluidine 122
trichrome 203
Weigert's iron–hematoxylin 200
standard length, taxonomic characters 110
standard metabolism 336
STA-PUT erythrocyte segregation 296, 297
starch gel electrophoresis 141–166
starch gels, use in electrophoresis 144
Statham gauges, blood pressure 317
static aquaria 637
static respirometers 343
 with stirring bar 353
static toxicity tests 496
statistical hypothesis testing 11
statistical inference 1
statistical methods
 analysis of variance 11, 23, 49, 129
 aquatic toxicology 519
 assumptions about data 11
 autecology 589
 behavioral studies 562

cluster analysis 15
controlled experience studies 19
decision making 1
failure to show significance 19
genetics 43
hypothesis testing 10
laboratory growth studies 380
large bodies of data 13
life cycle tests 511
microhabitats 596
morphometric data analysis 129
multiple-comparison tests 12
multivariate applications 13, 129
nonparametric techniques 11
observational studies 17
phylogenetic analysis 86
population genetics 51
researcher effect 126
sampling designs 8
toxicity tests 500–502, 519
stereology 208
sterilization
 aseptic surgery 248–250
 production of sterile fish 545–547
 saline solutions 281
 water, fish culture systems 634, 642
steroids, sex reversal 542
stiff-membrane transducers 317
stimulators, neurophysiological setups 423
stimulus isolation unit 433
stochastic ecological processes 619
stock identification, autecology 589
stomach evacuation rate, bioenergetics 397
storage temperature, blood samples 276
storage time, blood samples 276
strata, species distribution 591
stratified block design, field experiments 25
stream population surveys, data forms 592
stress 451–477
 anesthetic-induced 242–243
 challenge tests for 469–477
 chronic 476
 fish culture systems 633
 handling fish 659
 primary 452
 respirometric measurement 339
 secondary 457
 surgical 283–284
stress effects, recovery from surgery 284
stress responses 452
 anesthetics 242
 primary 452
 secondary 457
stressors 451
study design 5
subjectivity, observational studies 14
sublethal toxicity tests 510–519
submetacentric chromosomes 184
subopercle, taxonomic characters 111
suborganismal growth, weight 364
subspecies 68, 70

substituted fluorochrome stains 180
substrate composition, microhabitats 595
subtelocentric chromosomes 184
subterminal mouth, taxonomic characters 111
Sudan stains, lipids 201, 310
suitability, microhabitats 599
sulfamerazine, surgery 258
superficial electrodes, electrocardiogram 315
superior mouth, taxonomic characters 112
supernumerary chromosomes 184
supramaxillae, taxonomic characters 111
Surber sampler 6
surface water, fish culture systems 634
surgery 245–259
    abdominal 254
    applications 245
    basic techniques 247
    electrode implantation 315
    gonadectomy 547
    implants 246
    materials 247
    nervous system 417
    procedures 253
    quinaldine 230
    recovery 283
surgical tables 247, 249
survivorship, food webs 622
sutures
    materials 251–253
    techniques 254–256, 257, 258
swimming
    metabolism 336
    neural control 419
    toxicant effects 512
swimming performance, stress 472
swimming respirometers 348–353
symbiosis, community ecology 617
sympatric populations 621
symplesiomorphy, defined, systematics 75
synapomorphy, systematics
    defined 75
    sources 77
synaptic transmission, electric rays 439
synchronous feeding
    consumption models 403
    feeding models 401
synergism, drug interactions 219
synonymies 97
syntopic populations 71
systematic ichthyology
    goals 66
    museum collections 102
systematic nomenclature 96
systematics 65–103
systemic resistance, blood pressure 317
systole–diastole pressure pulse 314

T-1824 dye 294
T cell mitogens 175
T lymphocytes 312

T waves, electrocardiogram 314
tagging, see marking and tagging
tamoxifen, estrogen antagonist 541
taxonomic decisions 71
    species level 163
taxonomic error 160
taxonomic keys 97
taxonomic methods, morphology 109–133
telemetry
    electrocardiogram 315
    metabolic rates 353
    surgical implants 245
telocentric chromosomes 184
temperature
    bioenergetics models 405
    fish culture systems 645
    laboratory growth studies 378
    preference tests 566
    species distribution 600
    toxicity tests 508
    tricaine 225
terminal blood sampling procedures 277
terminal mouth, taxonomic characters 111
terminology
    anesthesia 214–216
    aquatic toxicology 492–494
    autecology 586
    ecology 610
    loci and alleles 155
    protein-coding loci 39, 149
Terramycin, surgical antibiotic 258–259
territory, behavioral studies 570
tertiary amyl alcohol, sedative 221
test cross, Mendelian genetics 41
test solutions, toxicity tests 505
testes, meiotic chromosomes 176
tetrameric enzymes, electrophoresis 152
tetraploids, reproduction 545
therapeutants, aquaculture 652–655
thermal equilibration technique,
        cardiology 320
thermal tolerance tests, stress 470
thermoelectric flowmeters 321
thiazole, anesthetic 240
thin-layer chromatography, hormones 455
thrombocytes 303
time frame, study design 5
time periods, growth rate determinations 380
tissue
    adhesives, surgery 256
    chemistry, stress responses 453
    oxygen tensions 301
    preparation, electrophoresis 145–146
    processing schedules, histology 196
    shrinkage, histology 197
    slices, neural studies 422
titration, carbon dioxide 232
tobacco juice, anesthetic 221
tolerance limits, stress 469–477
tolerances, toxicants 504
toluene, histological techniques 206

toluidine
  blood glucose assay 457
  cartilage stain 122
tonometer–optical cuvette systems 299
topical anesthetics 233
topical disinfectants, surgery 254
total body resistance, blood pressure 317
total leukocyte counts 309
total lipids, growth 368
toxic applications 6
toxic unit method, toxicity of mixtures 520
toxicant concentrations, toxicity tests 506
toxicity
  application factors 520
  carbon dioxide 232
  ethyl aminobenzoate 234
  etomidate 236
  phenoxyethanol 236
  quinaldine 229
  quinaldine sulfate 231
  tests 495–519
  tricaine 225
toxicology, aquatic 491–522
tracer substances, neuroanatomy 435
tracers, clearance 462
tranquilization 215
tranquilizers, barbiturates 239
transcription, protein synthesis 36
transducers, blood pressure
      determinations 317
transfer RNA (tRNA) 37
transient posttraumatic physiological
      syndrome 259
translation, protein synthesis 36
transmitter capsules 253
transporting fish 237
  anesthetics 221
  fish culture 659
  sedation 216
transposons 39
tray buffers, starch gel electrophoresis 147
treatment factors, parameters 7
tree classification 96
tricaine, anesthetic
  blood sampling 456
  hematological effects 219, 276, 283
  popularity 221
  properties and usage 223–227
tricaine methanesulfonate, see tricaine 214
trichloroacetic acid, protein analysis 367
trichrome stains, histological techniques 203
trimming, histological specimens 194–195
triploidy, sterilization 546
tritiated thymidine, radioautography 207
tRNA 37
trocar system, blood sampling 281
truss protocol 127
tubocurarine chloride, relaxant 230
tumors, aquatic toxicology 517
type species 98
type specimens 98

ultrasonic lysis 302
ultraviolet light, fish culture systems 642
ultraviolet sterilizers, respirometry 338
underwater photography 133
undirected trees (networks), systematics 86
unisexuality, genetics 46
units, red cell enzyme activities 302
units of study, systematics 74
universe of interest, study design 4
unweighted pair-group method with arithmetic
      averaging (UPGMA) 90
urethane, anesthetic 213, 220
urinary cannulation 262
urostyle, taxonomic characters 118

V waves, electrocardiogram 314
vaccines, injection sites 260
validation, toxicity tests 513
Van Dam respirometers 354
Van Slyke method, blood–oxygen affinity 299
variability, behavioral studies 556
vascular casts, preparation 273
velocity sedimentation, erythrocytes 296
venous blood sampling 277
ventilation rate, anesthesia 217
ventilatory frequency, gills 338
ventilatory stroke volume, gills 338
ventral aorta, cannulation 282
ventricle, cardiac structure 313
vertebrae, taxonomic characters 118
vertical electrophoresis 144
video recording, see photography
vinblastine sulfate, metaphase block 172
viral diseases, fish culture 653
vitellogenin, sex determination 530
voltage, starch gel electrophoresis 146
volume-of-dilution methods, blood 293
volume studies, dual cannulation 282
von Bertalanffy growth equation 377

wading rods, water velocity measurements 595
warnings, fishery chemicals 220
washout time, calculations 339
waste, bioenergetics 391, 395, 405
water flow rates, respirometers 348
water hardness, tricaine 225
water quality
  criteria, life cycle tests 510
  fish culture systems 645–649
  laboratory growth studies 380
  respirometric measurement 338
  toxicity tests 505, 507
water recirculation systems, fish culture 640
water samples, respirometers 340
water supply, fish culture systems 633–636
water temperature
  anesthetics 221
  bioenergetics equations 404
water treatment 634–636, 660

water tunnel respirometers   349
water velocity, measurements   595
waterproofing, surgery   256
waveforms, brain stimulation   433
Weigert's iron–hematoxylin stain   200
weight, growth   364
weighting factors, sampling   597
well water, fish culture systems   635
Wentworth particle-size scale   595
wet weight, growth   365
Wheatstone bridge, blood pressure   317
white blood cells, see leukocytes
white muscle, somatic growth   371
whole-animal responses, stress   465
whole-body growth   363, 364

wicks, starch gel electrophoresis   146
Wind-Kessel effect   314
Winkler method, dissolved oxygen   336, 340

X-ray radiography, internal skeleton
        studies   122
xylene, histological techniques   206
Xylocaine, see lidocaine

zonal electrophoresis   143
zygotic survival, triploidy   546